MW00803888

ARAMAIC PESHITTA NEW TESTAMENT

Parallel Translations

Janet M. Magiera
Light of the Word Ministry

Published by LWM Publications
A Division of Light of the Word Ministry
www.lightofword.org

ISBN 978-8200851-5

Acknowledgments

Throughout the years of preparation for this publishing, there have been many people who have contributed to the final product. I would like to gratefully acknowledge some of these contributors.

My thanks goes primarily to my first teacher of Aramaic, Mrs. Bernita Jess, and to her help in beginning study of Dr. George Lamsa's works.

Thanks for help with specific areas of expertise goes to Dr. James DeFrancisco of Miltha Ministries, Daniel J. Mahar, and Michael Bushell of BibleWorks. Jeffrey Moore has been invaluable in helping with the computer programming for the database. Many others have contributed time and effort in data entry and faithful financial contributions.

The greatest acknowledgment that I can give goes to my wonderful husband, Glen, not only for his tireless proofreading, but also for all the encouragement to complete the project through these past years. I could not have finished any of it without his steadfast support.

Introduction

Parallel Edition

The *Parallel Translations* of the Aramaic Peshitta New Testament text combines new and old translations to bring an unprecedented tool of study to the Bible student. It combines the standard King James Version and the new translation by Janet Magiera of the Peshitta with the most popular out of print translation of the New Testament by James Murdock.

This combination of translations gives an immediate method of comparison and enables the student of the Bible desiring to study the Biblical text from a variety of angles all in one place. The methods of translation vary from scholar to scholar, but with the ability to compare the verses, the student can check the variations in the choices of words, and then get an overall understanding of the passage. This volume is designed to be used with the Aramaic Peshitta New Testament *Vertical Interlinear, Dictionary Number Lexicon* and *Word Study Concordance*.

The Peshitta Text

The base text of the Aramaic Peshitta is taken from *The Syriac New Testament and Psalms*, published by United Bible Societies, specifically the Bible Society in Turkey. In 1905 the British and Foreign Bible Society published an edition of the Gospels in Syriac, reprinted by permission from a revised text of the Peshitta Version which had been prepared by the late Rev. G.H. Gwilliam, B.D., with a Latin translation and critical apparatus, and issued by the Clarendon Press in 1901. This is a critical text of the Peshitta that was completed from a collation of manuscripts at the British Museum Library. It is known as a "western" text of the Peshitta and therefore varies to a small degree from other eastern versions of the Peshitta.

Murdock Translation

James Murdock published *The New Testament, A Literal Translation from the Syriac Peshito Version*, in 1851. The publishers were Robert Carter & Brothers, New York. The preface of his volume contains a brief account regarding his reasons for producing an Aramaic translation. He began the translation in 1845 in order to extend his own knowledge of the Syriac language. He comments, "such exquisite pleasure the writer longed to have others share with him; but as few persons, even among the clergy, have either leisure or facilities for acquiring the Syriac language, he soon came to the conclusion, that he could do nothing better than first read the book carefully through, and then give a literal and exact translation of it." The style of the translation uses the solemn "thee's and thou's" as in the King James and translates Meshikha as the Messiah and not Christ. He endeavors to translate the idioms as fully as possible without sacrificing English grammar.

Light of the Word Ministry Translation (Magiera)

Janet Magiera has been working on a database of the Aramaic text of the New Testament for the last 20 years and it is now published and available in several formats. The translation is published by LWM Publications under the title, *Aramaic Peshitta New Testament Translation,* ISBN #.0-9679613-5-1. The purpose of this translation is to present a modern English translation in readable format. It uses the accepted English proper names for people and locations. It endeavors to bring a very literal style together with an idiomatic translation of the Syriac. The whole database is available as a module from BibleWorks software: www.bibleworks.com. In addition, a set of 4 books and CD Rom is now published as the *Aramaic Peshitta New Testament Library,* which includes this parallel edition, a 2 volume *Vertical Interlinear* and *Dictionary Number Lexicon.*

Use of Parallel Translations

When studying a particular verse or passage, the Bible student can compare the different translations and see the variations. On narrowing down his focus, he can then go to the *Vertical Interlinear* and find the Dictionary number of any word that he would like to study further. The CD Rom has the *Word Study Concordance* and searching for this word, the student can then print out the word study for that particular Dictionary Number. The *Dictionary Lexicon* has further meanings and notes regarding the word. Use of all these tools in conjunction with each other will provide the student with the most complete study of words in a verse.

Parallel Translations

	KJV	Murdock	Magiera

MATTHEW *Chapter 1*

	KJV	Murdock	Magiera
1	The book of the generation of Jesus Christ, the son of David, the son of Abraham.	The book of the nativity of Jesus the Messiah, the son of David, son of Abraham.	The book of the genealogy of Jesus Christ, the son of David, the son of Abraham;
2	Abraham begat Isaac; and Isaac begat Jacob; and Jacob begat Judas and his brethren;	Abraham begat Isaac: Isaac begat Jacob: Jacob begat Judah and his brothers:	Abraham fathered Isaac, Isaac fathered Jacob, Jacob fathered Judah and his brothers,
3	And Judas begat Phares and Zara of Thamar; and Phares begat Esrom; and Esrom begat Aram;	Judah begat Pharez and Zara of Tamar: Pharez begat Hezron: Hezron begat Ram:	Judah fathered Perez and Zerah by Tamar. Perez fathered Hezron, Hezron fathered Aram,
4	And Aram begat Aminadab; and Aminadab begat Naasson; and Naasson begat Salmon;	Ram begat Aminadab: Aminadab begat Nahshon: Nahshon begat Salmon:	Aram fathered Aminadab, Aminadab fathered Nahshon, Nahshon fathered Salmon,
5	And Salmon begat Booz of Rachab; and Booz begat Obed of Ruth; and Obed begat Jesse;	Salmon begat Boaz of Rahab: Boaz begat Obed of Ruth: Obed begat Jesse:	Salmon fathered Boaz by Rahab, Boaz fathered Obed by Ruth, Obed fathered Jesse, [and]
6	And Jesse begat David the king; and David the king begat Solomon of her that had been the wife of Urias;	Jesse begat David the king: David begat Solomon of the wife of Uriah:	Jesse fathered David the king. David fathered Solomon by the wife of Uriah,
7	And Solomon begat Roboam; and Roboam begat Abia; and Abia begat Asa;	Solomon begat Rehoboam: Rehoboam begat Abia: Abia begat Asa:	Solomon fathered Rehoboam, Rehoboam fathered Abijah, Abijah fathered Asa,
8	And Asa begat Josaphat; and Josaphat begat Joram; and Joram begat Ozias;	Asa begat Jehoshaphat: Jehoshaphat begat Joram: Joram begat Uzziah:	Asa fathered Jehoshaphat, Jehoshaphat fathered Joram, Joram fathered Uzziah,
9	And Ozias begat Joatham; and Joatham begat Achaz; and Achaz begat Ezekias;	Uzziah begat Jotham: Jotham begat Ahaz: Ahaz begat Hezekiah:	Uzziah fathered Jotham, Jotham fathered Ahaz, Ahaz fathered Hezekiah,
10	And Ezekias begat Manasses; and Manasses begat Amon; and Amon begat Josias;	Hezekiah begat Manasseh: Manasseh begat Amon: Amon begat Josiah:	Hezekiah fathered Manasseh, Manasseh fathered Amon, Amon fathered Josiah,
11	And Josias begat Jechonias and his brethren, about the time they were carried away to Babylon:	Josiah begat Jeconiah and his brothers, in the captivity of Babylon.	Josiah fathered Jechoniah and his brothers in the captivity of Babylon.
12	And after they were brought to Babylon, Jechonias begat Salathiel; and Salathiel begat Zorobabel;	And after the captivity of Babylon, Jeconiah begat Salathiel: Salathiel begat Zerubbabel:	And after the captivity of Babylon, Jechoniah fathered Shealtiel, Shealtiel fathered Zerubbabel,
13	And Zorobabel begat Abiud; and Abiud begat Eliakim; and Eliakim begat Azor;	Zerubbabel begat Abiud: Abiud begat Eliakim: Eliakim begat Azor:	Zerubbabel fathered Abiud, Abiud fathered Eliakim, Eliakim fathered Azor,
14	And Azor begat Sadoc; and Sadoc begat Achim; and Achim begat Eliud;	Azor begat Zadok: Zadok begat Achim: Achim begat Eliud:	Azor fathered Sadoc, Sadoc fathered Achim, Achim fathered Eliud,
15	And Eliud begat Eleazar; and Eleazar begat Matthan; and Matthan begat Jacob;	Eliud begat Eleazar: Eleazar begat Matthan: Matthan begat Jacob:	Eliud fathered Eleazer, Eleazer fathered Matthan, Matthan fathered Jacob,

MATTHEW *Chapter 1*

	KJV	*Murdock*	*Magiera*
16	And Jacob begat Joseph the husband of Mary, of whom was born Jesus, who is called Christ.	Jacob begat Joseph, the husband of Mary, of whom was born Jesus who is called the Messiah.	Jacob fathered Joseph, the husband of Mary, from whom Jesus, who was called the Messiah, was born.
17	So all the generations from Abraham to David are fourteen generations; and from David until the carrying away into Babylon are fourteen generations; and from the carrying away into Babylon unto Christ are fourteen generations.	All the generations, therefore, are, from Abraham to David fourteen generations, and from David to the captivity of Babylon fourteen generations, and from the captivity of Babylon to the Messiah fourteen generations.	Therefore, all the generations from Abraham until David [were] fourteen generations, and from David until the captivity of Babylon, fourteen generations, and from the captivity of Babylon until the Messiah, fourteen generations.
18	Now the birth of Jesus Christ was on this wise: When as his mother Mary was espoused to Joseph, before they came together, she was found with child of the Holy Ghost.	And the birth of Jesus the Messiah was thus. While his mother Mary was betrothed to Joseph, before they had cohabited, she was found to be with child by the Holy Spirit.	Now the birth of Jesus Christ was like this: when Mary his mother was engaged to Joseph, before they were joined in marriage, she was found [to be] pregnant from the Holy Spirit.
19	Then Joseph her husband, being a just man, and not willing to make her a publick example, was minded to put her away privily.	And Joseph her husband was a righteous man, and unwilling to expose her: and he thought of putting her away privately.	But Joseph her husband was upright and was not willing to disgrace her and he was thinking that he would dismiss her privately.
20	But while he thought on these things, behold, the angel of the Lord appeared unto him in a dream, saying, Joseph, thou son of David, fear not to take unto thee Mary thy wife: for that which is conceived in her is of the Holy Ghost.	And while he contemplated these things, an angel of the Lord appeared to him in a dream, and said to him: Joseph, son of David, fear not to take Mary thy wife; for that which is conceived in her, is from the Holy Spirit:	But while he was considering these [things], an angel of the LORD appeared to him in a dream and said to him, "Joseph, son of David, do not be afraid to take Mary your wife, for he that is fathered in her [is] from the Holy Spirit.
21	And she shall bring forth a son, and thou shalt call his name JESUS: for he shall save his people from their sins.	and she will bear a son; and thou shalt call his name Jesus, for he will resuscitate his people from their sins.	And she will give birth to a son and she will call his name Jesus, for he will give life to his people from their sins."
22	Now all this was done, that it might be fulfilled which was spoken of the Lord by the prophet, saying,	Now all this that occurred, was to fulfill what was spoken of the Lord by the prophet:	Now all this that happened [was] that it would be fulfilled what was spoken from the LORD by way of the prophet:
23	Behold, a virgin shall be with child, and shall bring forth a son, and they shall call his name Emmanuel, which being interpreted is, God with us.	Behold, a virgin will conceive, and will bear a son, and thou shalt call his name Emmanuel, which is interpreted, Our God with us.	BEHOLD, A VIRGIN WILL CONCEIVE AND WILL GIVE BIRTH TO A SON AND THEY WILL CALL HIS NAME EMMANUEL, WHICH IS INTERPRETED, OUR GOD [IS] WITH US.
24	Then Joseph being raised from sleep did as the angel of the Lord had bidden him, and took unto him his wife:	And when Joseph rose from his sleep, he did as the angel of the Lord commanded him, and took his wife.	And when Joseph rose up from his sleep, he did as the angel of the LORD had commanded him and he took his wife.
25	And knew her not till she had brought forth her firstborn son: and he called his name JESUS.	And he knew her not, until she had borne her firstborn son, and called is name Jesus.	And he did not know her until she had given birth to her firstborn son. And she called his name Jesus.

Parallel Translations

	KJV	*Murdock*	*Magiera*

MATTHEW *Chapter 2*

	KJV	Murdock	Magiera
1	Now when Jesus was born in Bethlehem of Judaea in the days of Herod the king, behold, there came wise men from the east to Jerusalem,	Now when Jesus was born in Bethlehem of Judaea, in the days of Herod the king, there came Magi from the east unto Jerusalem,	Now when Jesus was born in Bethlehem of Judea in the days of Herod the king, Magi came from the east to Jerusalem
2	Saying, Where is he that is born King of the Jews? for we have seen his star in the east, and are come to worship him.	saying: Where is the king of the Jews that is born? For we have seen his star in the east, and have come to worship him.	and said, "Where is the king of the Judeans who was born? For we have seen his star in the east and we have come to worship him."
3	When Herod the king had heard these things, he was troubled, and all Jerusalem with him.	And Herod the king heard, and he was disturbed; and all Jerusalem with him.	And Herod the king heard and was troubled and all Jerusalem with him.
4	And when he had gathered all the chief priests and scribes of the people together, he demanded of them where Christ should be born.	And he assembled all the chiefs of the priests and the scribes of the people, and inquired of them, Where is the birthplace of the Messiah?	And he gathered all of the chief priests and scribes of the people and was asking them where the Messiah was [to be] born.
5	And they said unto him, In Bethlehem of Judaea: for thus it is written by the prophet,	And they said: In Bethlehem of Judaea; for thus it is written in the prophet:	And they said, "In Bethlehem of Judea," for so it is written in the prophet:
6	And thou Bethlehem, in the land of Juda, art not the least among the princes of Juda: for out of thee shall come a Governor, that shall rule my people Israel.	Thou also, Bethlehem of Judaea, art not the little among the kings of Judaea, for a king shall come from thee who shall rule my people Israel.	YOU ALSO, BETHLEHEM OF JUDEA, YOU WILL NOT BE THE LEAST AMONG THE KINGS OF JUDEA, FOR FROM YOU WILL GO OUT A KING WHO WILL SHEPHERD MY PEOPLE ISRAEL.
7	Then Herod, when he had privily called the wise men, enquired of them diligently what time the star appeared.	Then Herod privately called the Magi, and learned from them at what time the star appeared to them.	Then Herod secretly called the Magi and learned from them at what time the star appeared to them.
8	And he sent them to Bethlehem, and said, Go and search diligently for the young child; and when ye have found him, bring me word again, that I may come and worship him also.	And he sent them to Bethlehem, and said to them, Go, search diligently for the child; and when ye have found him, come and tell me, that I also may go and worship him.	And he sent them to Bethlehem and said to them, "Go, search for the boy diligently and when you have found him, come, inform me that I may also go [and] worship him."
9	When they had heard the king, they departed; and, lo, the star, which they saw in the east, went before them, till it came and stood over where the young child was.	And they, when they had heard from the king, went forward: and lo, the star they had seen in the east went before them, until it came and stood over where the child was.	And when they had heard from the king, they went away and behold, the star that they had seen in the east went before them, until it came [and] stood over where the boy was.
10	When they saw the star, they rejoiced with exceeding great joy.	And when they saw the star, they rejoiced much, with great joy.	And when they saw the star, they rejoiced [with] very great joy.

Parallel Translations

	KJV	*Murdock*	*Magiera*
	MATTHEW *Chapter 2*		
11	And when they were come into the house, they saw the young child with Mary his mother, and fell down, and worshipped him: and when they had opened their treasures, they presented unto him gifts; gold, and frankincense, and myrrh.	And they entered the house; and they saw the child, with Mary his mother; and they fell down and worshipped him: and they opened their treasures, and presented to him gifts, gold, and myrrh, and frankincense.	And they entered the house and they saw the boy with Mary his mother and they fell down [and] worshipped him and they opened their treasures and offered him gifts, gold and myrrh and incense.
12	And being warned of God in a dream that they should not return to Herod, they departed into their own country another way.	And it was shown them in a dream, that they should not return to Herod. And by another way, they returned to their country.	And it was shown to them in a dream that they should not return to Herod and by another way, they went to their country.
13	And when they were departed, behold, the angel of the Lord appeareth to Joseph in a dream, saying, Arise, and take the young child and his mother, and flee into Egypt, and be thou there until I bring thee word: for Herod will seek the young child to destroy him.	And when they were gone, an angel of the Lord appeared to Joseph in a dream, and said to him, Arise, take the child and his mother, and flee into Egypt; and be thou there, until I tell thee: for Herod will seek for the child, to destroy it.	And when they had gone, an angel of the LORD appeared in a dream to Joseph and said to him, "Get up. Lead the child and his mother and flee to Egypt and stay there until I tell you, for Herod is going to seek for the child in order to destroy him."
14	When he arose, he took the young child and his mother by night, and departed into Egypt:	Then Joseph arose, took the child and his mother, by night, and fled to Egypt.	Now Joseph rose up, took up the child and his mother in the night, and fled to Egypt.
15	And was there until the death of Herod: that it might be fulfilled which was spoken of the Lord by the prophet, saying, Out of Egypt have I called my son.	And he was there, until the death of Herod; that so might be fulfilled that which was spoken of the Lord by the prophet, saying, From Egypt have I called my son.	And he remained there until the death of Herod, so that it would be fulfilled what was spoken from the LORD by the prophet who said: FROM EGYPT I HAVE CALLED MY SON.
16	Then Herod, when he saw that he was mocked of the wise men, was exceeding wroth, and sent forth, and slew all the children that were in Bethlehem, and in all the coasts thereof, from two years old and under, according to the time which he had diligently enquired of the wise men.	Then Herod, when he saw that he had been deluded by the Magi, was very angry. And he sent and slew all the children in Bethlehem, and in all its confines, from a child of two years and under, according to the time that he had carefully learned from the Magi.	Then Herod, when he saw that he was mocked by the Magi, was very angry and sent [and] killed all the boys of Bethlehem and of all its borders from two years old and under, according to the time that he had investigated from the Magi.
17	Then was fulfilled that which was spoken by Jeremy the prophet, saying,	Then was that fulfilled, which was spoken by Jeremiah the prophet, saying:	Then was fulfilled what was spoken by way of Jeremiah the prophet, who said:
18	In Rama was there a voice heard, lamentation, and weeping, and great mourning, Rachel weeping for her children, and would not be comforted, because they are not.	A voice was heard in Rama, weeping and great lamentation; Rachel bemoaning her children, and unwilling to be comforted, because they are no more.	A VOICE WAS HEARD IN RAMA, CRYING AND GREAT MOURNING, RACHEL CRYING FOR HER SONS AND NOT WANTING TO BE COMFORTED, BECAUSE THEY WERE NOT.
19	But when Herod was dead, behold, an angel of the Lord appeareth in a dream to Joseph in Egypt,	But when king Herod was dead, an angel of the Lord appeared in a dream to Joseph in Egypt,	Now when Herod the king died, an angel of the LORD appeared in a dream to Joseph in Egypt.

Parallel Translations

	KJV	*Murdock*	*Magiera*
	MATTHEW *Chapter 2*		
20	Saying, Arise, and take the young child and his mother, and go into the land of Israel: for they are dead which sought the young child's life.	and said to him: Arise, take the child and his mother, and go into the land of Israel; for they are dead who sought the life of the child.	And he said to him, "Get up. Lead the child and his mother and go to the land of Israel, for those who were seeking the life of the child have died."
21	And he arose, and took the young child and his mother, and came into the land of Israel.	And Joseph arose, and took the child and his mother, and went to the land of Israel.	And Joseph rose up [and] led the child and his mother and came to the land of Israel.
22	But when he heard that Archelaus did reign in Judaea in the room of his father Herod, he was afraid to go thither: notwithstanding, being warned of God in a dream, he turned aside into the parts of Galilee:	But when he heard that Archelaus was king in Judaea, instead of his father Herod, he feared to go thither. And it was revealed to him in a dream, that he should go into the land of Galilee.	But when he heard that Archelaus was king in Judah in place of Herod his father, he was afraid to go there and it was shown to him in a dream that he should go to the land of Galilee.
23	And he came and dwelt in a city called Nazareth: that it might be fulfilled which was spoken by the prophets, He shall be called a Nazarene.	And he came and dwelt in a city that is called Nazareth: that so might be fulfilled that which was said by the prophet, that he should be called a Nazarene.	And he came [and] lived in the city that is called Nazareth, so that it would be fulfilled what was spoken by the prophet: "He will be called a Nazarene."
	Chapter 3		
1	In those days came John the Baptist, preaching in the wilderness of Judaea,	And in those days came John the Baptizer. And he proclaimed in the desert of Judaea,	Now in those days John the baptizer came and was preaching in the desert of Judea.
2	And saying, Repent ye: for the kingdom of heaven is at hand.	and said: Repent; the kingdom of heaven hath approached.	And he said, "Repent. The kingdom of heaven is near."
3	For this is he that was spoken of by the prophet Esaias, saying, The voice of one crying in the wilderness, Prepare ye the way of the Lord, make his paths straight.	For this is he of whom it was said, by Isaiah the prophet: The voice of one crying in the wilderness, Prepare ye the way of the Lord, make smooth his paths.	For this is he about whom it was said by way of Isaiah the prophet: THE VOICE OF ONE CRYING IN THE DESERT: PREPARE THE WAY OF THE LORD AND MAKE STRAIGHT HIS PATHS.
4	And the same John had his raiment of camel's hair, and a leathern girdle about his loins; and his meat was locusts and wild honey.	And as to this John, his raiment was of camel's hair, and a girdle of skin was upon his loins; and his food was locusts and wild honey.	Now [this] John, his clothes were of the hair of camels and a girdle of skin [was] on his loins and his food [was] locusts and honey of the desert.
5	Then went out to him Jerusalem, and all Judaea, and all the region round about Jordan,	Then went out to him Jerusalem, and all Judaea, and all the country about the Jordan.	Then Jerusalem went out to him and all Judea and all the region that was around the Jordan.
6	And were baptized of him in Jordan, confessing their sins.	And they were baptized by him in the river Jordan, while they confessed their sins.	And they were baptized by him in the Jordan River when they confessed their sins.
7	But when he saw many of the Pharisees and Sadducees come to his baptism, he said unto them, O generation of vipers, who hath warned you to flee from the wrath to come?	But when he saw many of the Pharisees and of the Sadducees, who came to be baptized, he said to them: Generation of vipers, who hath taught you to flee from the wrath that cometh?	And when he saw many from the Pharisees and from the Sadducees who came to be baptized, he said to them, "Generation of vipers! Who has informed you to flee from the wrath that will come?
8	Bring forth therefore fruits meet for repentance:	Bring forth the fruits therefore, that accord with repentance.	Produce, therefore, the fruits that are proper for repentance.

MATTHEW Chapter 3

	KJV	Murdock	Magiera
9	And think not to say within yourselves, We have Abraham to our father: for I say unto you, that God is able of these stones to raise up children unto Abraham.	And do not think, and say within yourselves, that Abraham is our father: for I say to you, that God is able of these stones to raise up children to Abraham.	And do not think or say within yourselves that we have Abraham [as a] father, for I say to you, God is able from these stones to raise up sons to Abraham.
10	And now also the axe is laid unto the root of the trees: therefore every tree which bringeth not forth good fruit is hewn down, and cast into the fire.	And lo, the ax is put to the root of trees. Every tree, therefore, which beareth not good fruit, is felled, and falleth into the fire.	Now behold, the ax is placed on the root of the trees. Therefore, every tree that does not bear good fruit will be cut down and thrown into the fire.
11	I indeed baptize you with water unto repentance: but he that cometh after me is mightier than I, whose shoes I am not worthy to bear: he shall baptize you with the Holy Ghost, and with fire:	I indeed baptize you with water unto repentance; but he that cometh after me is more powerful than I; whose sandals I am not worthy to carry. He will baptize you with the Holy Spirit and with fire.	I baptize you with water for repentance, but he who comes after me is stronger than I [am], whose sandals I am not worthy to carry. He will baptize you with the Holy Spirit and with fire,
12	Whose fan is in his hand, and he will throughly purge his floor, and gather his wheat into the garner; but he will burn up the chaff with unquenchable fire.	His winnowing shovel is in his hand; and he will make clean his threshing-floor. The wheat he will gather into his storehouse; and the chaff he will burn with fire not extinguished.	he whose winnowing fan [is] in his hand and he will cleanse his threshing floors. And he will gather the wheat to his granaries, and he will burn the chaff in a fire that does not go out."
13	Then cometh Jesus from Galilee to Jordan unto John, to be baptized of him.	Then came Jesus from Galilee to the Jordan unto John, to be baptized by him.	Then Jesus came from Galilee to the Jordan to John to be baptized by him.
14	But John forbad him, saying, I have need to be baptized of thee, and comest thou to me?	But John refused him; and said, I need to be baptized by thee, and hast thou come to me?	But John restrained him and said, "I need to be baptized by you and are you coming to me?"
15	And Jesus answering said unto him, Suffer it to be so now: for thus it becometh us to fulfil all righteousness. Then he suffered him.	And Jesus answered, and said to him: Allow it now, for thus it becometh us to fulfill all righteousness. Then he permitted him.	But Jesus answered and said to him, "Allow [it] now, for so it is proper for us to fulfill all uprightness." And then he allowed him [to baptize him].
16	And Jesus, when he was baptized, went up straightway out of the water: and, lo, the heavens were opened unto him, and he saw the Spirit of God descending like a dove, and lighting upon him:	And when Jesus was baptized, he went up immediately from the water. And heaven was opened to him; and he saw the Holy Spirit descending like a dove, and it came upon him.	And when Jesus was baptized, immediately he came out of the water and heaven was opened to him and he saw the Spirit of God that was descending as a dove and it came on him.
17	And lo a voice from heaven, saying, This is my beloved Son, in whom I am well pleased.	And lo, a voice from heaven, which said: This is my beloved Son, in whom I have delight.	And behold, [there was] a voice from heaven that said, "This is my beloved Son in whom I am pleased."

Chapter 4

	KJV	Murdock	Magiera
1	Then was Jesus led up of the Spirit into the wilderness to be tempted of the devil.	Then was Jesus led by the Holy Spirit into the desert, to be tempted by the Calumniator	Then Jesus was led by the Holy Spirit to the wilderness to be tempted by the Accuser.
2	And when he had fasted forty days and forty nights, he was afterward an hungred.	And he fasted forty days and forty nights, and afterward he hungered.	And he fasted forty days and forty nights and afterwards he was hungry.

Parallel Translations

	KJV	*Murdock*	*Magiera*
	MATTHEW	***Chapter 4***	
3	And when the tempter came to him, he said, If thou be the Son of God, command that these stones be made bread.	And the Tempter came, and said to him: If thou art the Son of God, command that these stones to become bread.	And he who was tempting came near and said to him, "If you are the Son of God, say that these stones should become bread."
4	But he answered and said, It is written, Man shall not live by bread alone, but by every word that proceedeth out of the mouth of God.	But he replied, and said: It is written, that not by bread only, doth man live; but by every word proceeding from the mouth of God.	But he answered and said, "It is written: MAN DOES NOT LIVE BY BREAD ALONE, BUT BY EVERY WORD THAT COMES OUT OF THE MOUTH OF GOD."
5	Then the devil taketh him up into the holy city, and setteth him on a pinnacle of the temple,	Then the Calumniator took him to the holy city, and set him on a pinnacle of the temple,	Then the Accuser led him to the holy city and placed him on the outer edge of the temple.
6	And saith unto him, If thou be the Son of God, cast thyself down: for it is written, He shall give his angels charge concerning thee: and in their hands they shall bear thee up, lest at any time thou dash thy foot against a stone.	and said to him: If thou art the Son of God, cast thyself down: for it is written, that he will give his angels charge of thee, and in their hands will they sustain thee, lest thou strike thy foot against a stone.	And he said to him, "If you are the Son of God, throw yourself down, for it is written: HE WILL COMMAND HIS ANGELS CONCERNING YOU, and ON THEIR HANDS THEY WILL BEAR YOU UP, SO THAT YOU SHOULD NOT STRIKE YOUR FOOT ON A STONE."
7	Jesus said unto him, It is written again, Thou shalt not tempt the Lord thy God.	Jesus said to him: It is moreover written, that thou shalt not tempt the Lord thy God.	Jesus said to him, "Again it is written: YOU SHOULD NOT TEMPT THE LORD YOUR GOD."
8	Again, the devil taketh him up into an exceeding high mountain, and sheweth him all the kingdoms of the world, and the glory of them;	Again the Calumniator took him to a mountain that was very high, and showed him all the kingdoms of the world, and their glory;	Again, the Accuser took him to a mountain that was very high. And he showed him all the kingdoms of the world and their glory.
9	And saith unto him, All these things will I give thee, if thou wilt fall down and worship me.	and said to him: All these will I give thee, if thou wilt fall down and worship me.	And he said to him, "All these [kingdoms] I will give to you if you will fall down [and] worship me."
10	Then saith Jesus unto him, Get thee hence, Satan: for it is written, Thou shalt worship the Lord thy God, and him only shalt thou serve.	Then Jesus said to him: Begone, Satan; for it is written, that thou shalt worship the Lord, thy God; and him only shalt thou serve.	Then Jesus said to him, "Go, Satan! For it is written: YOU SHOULD WORSHIP THE LORD YOUR GOD AND FOR HIM ALONE YOU SHOULD WORK."
11	Then the devil leaveth him, and, behold, angels came and ministered unto him.	Then the Calumniator left him: and lo, angels came, and ministered to him.	Then the Accuser left him and behold, angels came near and ministered to him.
12	Now when Jesus had heard that John was cast into prison, he departed into Galilee;	And when Jesus had heard that John was delivered up, he retired to Galilee.	Now when Jesus heard that John had been delivered up, he went away to Galilee.
13	And leaving Nazareth, he came and dwelt in Capernaum, which is upon the sea coast, in the borders of Zabulon and Nephthalim:	And he left Nazareth, and came and dwelt in Capernaum, by the side of the sea, on the confines of Zebulon and Naphthali.	And he left Nazareth and came [and] lived in Capernaum by the shore of the sea in the territory of Zebulun and of Naphtali,
14	That it might be fulfilled which was spoken by Esaias the prophet, saying,	That so might be fulfilled that which was spoken by Isaiah the prophet, who said:	that it would be fulfilled what was spoken by way of Isaiah the prophet who said:

Parallel Translations

	KJV	*Murdock*	*Magiera*

MATTHEW *Chapter 4*

	KJV	Murdock	Magiera
15	The land of Zabulon, and the land of Nephthalim, by the way of the sea, beyond Jordan, Galilee of the Gentiles;	The land of Zebulon, the land of Naphthali, the way of the sea, the ford of Jordan, Galilee of the Gentiles;	THE LAND OF ZEBULUN, THE LAND OF NAPHTALI, THE WAY OF THE SEA, THE CROSSINGS OF THE JORDAN, GALILEE OF THE GENTILES,
16	The people which sat in darkness saw great light; and to them which sat in the region and shadow of death light is sprung up.	the people that sat in darkness, have seen great light; and to them who sat in the region and shadow of death, light is arisen.	THE PEOPLE WHO SIT IN DARKNESS HAVE SEEN A GREAT LIGHT AND A LIGHT HAS DAWNED TO THEM WHO SIT IN THE LAND AND THE SHADOWS OF DEATH.
17	From that time Jesus began to preach, and to say, Repent: for the kingdom of heaven is at hand.	From that time began Jesus to proclaim and say: Repent; for the kingdom of heaven hath approached.	From then [on], Jesus began to preach and to say, "Repent, for the kingdom of heaven is near."
18	And Jesus, walking by the sea of Galilee, saw two brethren, Simon called Peter, and Andrew his brother, casting a net into the sea: for they were fishers.	And as he walked on the shore of the sea of Galilee, he saw two brothers, Simon called Cephas, and Andrew his brother, who were casting nets into the sea; for they were fishermen.	And while he was walking along the shore of the Sea of Galilee, he saw two brothers, Simon who was called Peter and Andrew his brother, who were casting nets into the sea, for they were fishermen.
19	And he saith unto them, Follow me, and I will make you fishers of men.	And Jesus said to them: Follow me; and I will cause you to become fishers of men.	And Jesus said to them, "Follow me and I will make you to be fishermen of men."
20	And they straightway left their nets, and followed him.	And immediately, they left their nets, and went after him.	And they immediately left their nets and went after him.
21	And going on from thence, he saw other two brethren, James the son of Zebedee, and John his brother, in a ship with Zebedee their father, mending their nets; and he called them.	And as he passed on from there, he saw two other brothers, James the son of Zebedee, and John his brother, in a ship with Zebedee their father, who were mending their nets. And Jesus called them.	And when he crossed over from there he saw two other brothers, James, the son of Zebedee, and John, his brother, in a ship with Zebedee, their father, who were mending their nets and he called them.
22	And they immediately left the ship and their father, and followed him.	And they immediately left the ship and their father, and went after him.	And immediately they left the ship and their father and they went after him.
23	And Jesus went about all Galilee, teaching in their synagogues, and preaching the gospel of the kingdom, and healing all manner of sickness and all manner of disease among the people.	And Jesus traveled over all Galilee. and he taught in their synagogues and proclaimed the tidings of the kingdom; and he cured every disease and malady among the people.	And Jesus traveled around in all Galilee and taught in their synagogues and preached the gospel of the kingdom and cured every disease and sickness among the people.
24	And his fame went throughout all Syria: and they brought unto him all sick people that were taken with divers diseases and torments, and those which were possessed with devils, and those which were lunatick, and those that had the palsy; and he healed them.	And his fame spread through all Syria. And they brought to him all them that were very sick with diverse diseases, and them that were afflicted with pains, and demoniacs, and lunatics and paralytics; and he healed them.	And his fame was heard in all Syria and they brought to him all those who were very sick with various diseases and those who were oppressed with severe pains and possessed [ones] and [those] who were insane and paralyzed [ones] and he healed them.

Parallel Translations

	KJV	*Murdock*	*Magiera*

MATTHEW *Chapter 4*

	KJV	Murdock	Magiera
25	And there followed him great multitudes of people from Galilee, and from Decapolis, and from Jerusalem, and from Judaea, and from beyond Jordan.	And there followed him great multitudes from Galilee, and from the Ten Cities, and from Jerusalem, and from Judaea, and from beyond the Jordan.	And large crowds followed him from Galilee and from the Decapolis and from Jerusalem and from Judea and from beyond the Jordan.

Chapter 5

	KJV	Murdock	Magiera
1	And seeing the multitudes, he went up into a mountain: and when he was set, his disciples came unto him:	And when Jesus saw the multitudes, he ascended a hill; and when he was seated, his disciples drew near him:	And when Jesus saw the crowd, he climbed a mountain and when he sat down, his disciples came near to him.
2	And he opened his mouth, and taught them, saying,	and he opened his mouth, and taught them, and said:	And he opened his mouth and was teaching them and said,
3	Blessed are the poor in spirit: for theirs is the kingdom of heaven.	Blessed are the poor in spirit for the kingdom of heaven is theirs!	"Blessed [are] the poor in spirit, because theirs is the kingdom of heaven.
4	Blessed are they that mourn: for they shall be comforted.	Blessed are the mourners: for they shall be comforted!	Blessed [are] the mourners, because they will be comforted.
5	Blessed are the meek: for they shall inherit the earth.	Blessed are the meek: for they shall inherit the earth!	Blessed [are] the meek, because they will inherit the earth.
6	Blessed are they which do hunger and thirst after righteousness: for they shall be filled.	Blessed are they that hunger and thirst for righteousness: for they shall be satiated!	Blessed [are] those who hunger and thirst for uprightness, because they will be satisfied.
7	Blessed are the merciful: for they shall obtain mercy.	Blessed are the merciful: for on them shall be mercies!	Blessed [are] the merciful, because on them will be mercies.
8	Blessed are the pure in heart: for they shall see God.	Blessed are the clean in heart: for they shall behold God!	Blessed [are] those who are pure in their heart[s], because they will see God.
9	Blessed are the peacemakers: for they shall be called the children of God.	Blessed are the cultivators of peace: for they shall be called sons of God!	Blessed [are] the peacemakers, because they will be called the sons of God.
10	Blessed are they which are persecuted for righteousness' sake: for theirs is the kingdom of heaven.	Blessed are they that are persecuted on account of righteousness: for the kingdom of heaven is theirs!	Blessed [are] those who are persecuted because of uprightness, because theirs is the kingdom of heaven.
11	Blessed are ye, when men shall revile you, and persecute you, and shall say all manner of evil against you falsely, for my sake.	Blessed are ye, when they revile you and persecute you, and speak every evil thing against you, falsely, on my account.	You are blessed when they curse you and persecute you and say every evil word against you falsely because of me.
12	Rejoice, and be exceeding glad: for great is your reward in heaven: for so persecuted they the prophets which were before you.	At that time, rejoice and be glad: for your reward in heaven is great. For so they persecuted the prophets that were before you.	Then rejoice and be glad, because your reward is great in heaven, for so they persecuted the prophets who [were] before you.
13	Ye are the salt of the earth: but if the salt have lost his savour, wherewith shall it be salted? it is thenceforth good for nothing, but to be cast out, and to be trodden under foot of men.	Ye are the salt of the earth! But if the salt become insipid, with what shall it be seasoned? It is fit for nothing; but to be thrown out, and be trodden under foot by men.	You are the salt of the earth, but if the salt should go flat, with what will it be salted? It is not fit for anything, but to be thrown outside and to be trampled on by man.

Parallel Translations

	KJV	*Murdock*	*Magiera*
	MATTHEW	*Chapter 5*	
14	Ye are the light of the world. A city that is set on an hill cannot be hid.	Ye are the light of the world! A city built upon a hill, cannot be concealed.	You are the light of the world. It is not possible to hide a city that is built on a mountain.
15	Neither do men light a candle, and put it under a bushel, but on a candlestick; and it giveth light unto all that are in the house.	And they do not light a lamp and place it under a bushel; but upon a lightstand, and it giveth light to all that are in the house.	And they do not light a lamp and place it under a basket, but on a lampstand and it lights all those who are in the house.
16	Let your light so shine before men, that they may see your good works, and glorify your Father which is in heaven.	Let your light so shine before men, that they may see your good works, and may glorify your Father who is in heaven.	Likewise, your light should shine before men, so that they will see your good works and will glorify your Father who is in heaven.
17	Think not that I am come to destroy the law, or the prophets: I am not come to destroy, but to fulfil.	Do not suppose that I have come to subvert the law or the prophets: [I have come] not to subvert, but to fulfill.	Do not think that I have come to change the law or the prophets. I have not come to change, but to fulfill [them].
18	For verily I say unto you, Till heaven and earth pass, one jot or one tittle shall in no wise pass from the law, till all be fulfilled.	For verily I say to you, that until heaven and earth shall pass away, one iota or one letter shall not pass from the law, until all shall be fulfilled.	For truly I say to you, until heaven and earth pass away, not one jot or one stroke will pass from the law until everything happens.
19	Whosoever therefore shall break one of these least commandments, and shall teach men so, he shall be called the least in the kingdom of heaven: but whosoever shall do and teach them, the same shall be called great in the kingdom of heaven.	Therefore whoever shall break one of these small commands and shall so inculcate on the children of men, shall be called little in the kingdom of heaven: but every one that shall do and teach [them], shall be called great in the kingdom of heaven.	Therefore, whoever changes one [jot] of these small commandments (and will teach so to men) will be called little in the kingdom of heaven. But all who will do and teach this [law] will be called great in the kingdom of heaven.
20	For I say unto you, That except your righteousness shall exceed the righteousness of the scribes and Pharisees, ye shall in no case enter into the kingdom of heaven.	For I say to you, that unless your righteousness shall abound more than that of the Scribes and Pharisees, ye shall not enter into the kingdom of heaven.	For I say to you, unless your uprightness exceeds [that] of the scribes and Pharisees, you will not enter the kingdom of heaven.
21	Ye have heard that it was said by them of old time, Thou shalt not kill; and whosoever shall kill shall be in danger of the judgment:	Ye have heard that it was said to the ancients, Thou shalt not kill: and every one that killeth, is obnoxious to judgment.	You have heard that it was said to the ancient [ones]: YOU SHOULD NOT KILL. And ANYONE WHO KILLS IS CONDEMNED TO JUDGMENT.
22	But I say unto you, That whosoever is angry with his brother without a cause shall be in danger of the judgment: and whosoever shall say to his brother, Raca, shall be in danger of the council: but whosoever shall say, Thou fool, shall be in danger of hell fire.	But I say to you, That every one who is angry with his brother rashly, is obnoxious to judgment: and every one that saith to his brother, Raka! is obnoxious to the council: and every one that shall say, Fool is obnoxious to hell-fire.	But I say to you, whoever provokes his brother to anger without cause is condemned to judgment. And anyone who says to his brother, '[I] spit [on you]!' is condemned to the assembly. And he, who says, 'Fool,' is condemned to the Gehenna of fire.
23	Therefore if thou bring thy gift to the altar, and there rememberest that thy brother hath ought against thee;	If therefore thou shalt bring thy oblation to the altar, and shalt there remember that thy brother hath any offence against thee,	If, therefore, you offer your offering on the altar and there you remember that your brother holds a certain grudge against you,

Parallel Translations

MATTHEW Chapter 5

	KJV	Murdock	Magiera
24	Leave there thy gift before the altar, and go thy way; first be reconciled to thy brother, and then come and offer thy gift.	leave there thy oblation before the altar, and go first and be reconciled with thy brother; and then come and present thy oblation.	leave your offering there before the altar and first go, be reconciled with your brother and then come, offer your offering.
25	Agree with thine adversary quickly, whiles thou art in the way with him; lest at any time the adversary deliver thee to the judge, and the judge deliver thee to the officer, and thou be cast into prison.	Be at agreement with thy prosecutor, forthwith, and while on the way with him; lest the prosecutor deliver thee up to the judge, and the Judge deliver thee over to the sheriff, and thou fall into the house of prisoners.	Reconcile with your opponent at law quickly while you [are] with him on the journey, so that your opponent at law will not deliver you to the judge and the judge deliver you to the officer and you fall [into] prison.
26	Verily I say unto thee, Thou shalt by no means come out thence, till thou hast paid the uttermost farthing.	Verily I say to thee, Thou wilt not come out from there until thou hast paid the last farthing.	And truly I say to you, you will not come out from there until you give back the last coin.
27	Ye have heard that it was said by them of old time, Thou shalt not commit adultery:	Ye have heard that it hath been said, Thou shalt not commit adultery.	You have heard that it was said: YOU SHOULD NOT COMMIT ADULTERY.
28	But I say unto you, That whosoever looketh on a woman to lust after her hath committed adultery with her already in his heart.	But I say to you, That whoever gazeth on a woman with concupiscence, at once committeth adultery with her in his heart.	But I say to you, anyone who looks at a woman as desiring her immediately commits adultery with her in his heart.
29	And if thy right eye offend thee, pluck it out, and cast it from thee: for it is profitable for thee that one of thy members should perish, and not that thy whole body should be cast into hell.	If therefore thy right eye make thee offend, pluck it out, and cast it from thee; because it is better for thee that thy one member perish, than that thy whole body fall into hell.	Now if your right eye causes you to offend, tear it out and throw it from you. For it is better for you that one of your members should be lost and not [that] your whole body should fall into Gehenna.
30	And if thy right hand offend thee, cut it off, and cast it from thee: for it is profitable for thee that one of thy members should perish, and not that thy whole body should be cast into hell.	And if thy right hand make thee offend, cut it off, and cast it from thee; because it is better for thee that one of thy members perish, than that thy whole body fall into hell.	And if your right hand causes you to offend, cut [it] off [and] throw it from you. For it is better for you that one of your members should be lost and not [that] your whole body should fall into Gehenna.
31	It hath been said, Whosoever shall put away his wife, let him give her a writing of divorcement:	It hath been said, That if a man will put away his wife, he must give her a writing of divorcement.	It was said: HE WHO DISMISSES HIS WIFE MUST GIVE HER A WRITING OF DIVORCE.
32	But I say unto you, That whosoever shall put away his wife, saving for the cause of fornication, causeth her to commit adultery: and whosoever shall marry her that is divorced committeth adultery.	But I say to you, That whoever putteth away his wife, except for the offence of whoredom, causeth her to commit adultery: and he that taketh the divorced woman, committeth adultery.	But I say to you, anyone who dismisses his wife outside of the case of fornication makes her commit adultery and he who marries a dismissed woman commits adultery.
33	Again, ye have heard that it hath been said by them of old time, Thou shalt not forswear thyself, but shalt perform unto the Lord thine oaths:	Again, ye have heard that it hath been said to the ancients, Thou shalt not be false in thy oaths; but thou shalt perform thine oaths to the Lord.	Again, you have heard that it was said of the ancient [ones]: DO NOT BE FALSE IN YOUR OATH, BUT COMPLETE YOUR OATH TO THE LORD.

Parallel Translations

	KJV	*Murdock*	*Magiera*

MATTHEW *Chapter 5*

	KJV	Murdock	Magiera
34	But I say unto you, Swear not at all; neither by heaven; for it is God's throne:	But I say to you, Swear not at all: not by heaven, for it is the throne of God:	But I say to you, you should not swear at all, neither by heaven, which is the throne of God,
35	Nor by the earth; for it is his footstool: neither by Jerusalem; for it is the city of the great King.	and not by the earth, for it is the footstool under his feet: and likewise not by Jerusalem, for it is the city of the great king.	nor by earth, which is the footstool that is under his feet, not even by Jerusalem, which is the city of the great king.
36	Neither shalt thou swear by thy head, because thou canst not make one hair white or black.	Moreover, thou shalt not swear by thy head, for thou canst not make one hair in it either black or white.	You should not even swear by your head, because you are not able to make one separate hair [either] black or white.
37	But let your communication be, Yea, yea; Nay, nay: for whatsoever is more than these cometh of evil.	But let your language be, Yes, yes; or No, no; for whatever is beyond these proceedeth from evil.	But your word should be yes, yes, and no, no. Anything that is apart from these [things] abounds from evil.
38	Ye have heard that it hath been said, An eye for an eye, and a tooth for a tooth:	Ye have heard that it hath been said: An eye for an eye, and a tooth for a tooth.	You have heard that it was said: EYE FOR EYE AND TOOTH FOR TOOTH.
39	But I say unto you, That ye resist not evil: but whosoever shall smite thee on thy right cheek, turn to him the other also.	But I say to you: Resist not evil; but if a person smite thee on thy right cheek, turn to him the other also.	But I say to you, you should not oppose an evil [one], but he who strikes you on your right cheek, turn to him the other also.
40	And if any man will sue thee at the law, and take away thy coat, let him have thy cloke also.	And if one is disposed to sue thee and get away thy coat, relinquish to him also thy cloak.	And he who wants to go to court with you and to take your coat, give him your cloak also.
41	And whosoever shall compel thee to go a mile, go with him twain.	Whoever compelleth thee to go one mile, go with him two.	He who compels you [to go] one mile, go with him two.
42	Give to him that asketh thee, and from him that would borrow of thee turn not thou away.	Whoever demandeth of thee, give to him: and whoever wisheth to borrow of thee, deny him not.	Whoever asks you, give to him. And he who wants to borrow from you, you should not refuse him.
43	Ye have heard that it hath been said, Thou shalt love thy neighbour, and hate thine enemy.	Ye have heard that it hath been said: Thou shalt love thy neighbor, and hate thy enemy.	You have heard that it was said: LOVE YOUR NEIGHBOR AND HATE YOUR ENEMY.
44	But I say unto you, Love your enemies, bless them that curse you, do good to them that hate you, and pray for them which despitefully use you, and persecute you;	But I say to you: Love your enemies; and bless him that curseth you; and do good to him that hateth you; and pray for them that lead you in bonds, and that persecute you:	But I say to you, love your enemies and bless those who curse you and do that which is pleasing to him who hates you and pray for those who take you by force and persecute you,
45	That ye may be the children of your Father which is in heaven: for he maketh his sun to rise on the evil and on the good, and sendeth rain on the just and on the unjust.	that ye may be the children of your Father that is in heaven, who causeth his sun to rise upon the good and upon the bad, and sendeth his rain upon the righteous and upon the unrighteous.	so that you may be the sons of your Father who is in heaven, who causes his sun to rise on the good and on the bad and causes his rain to come down on the upright and on the wicked.
46	For if ye love them which love you, what reward have ye? do not even the publicans the same?	For, if ye love them that love you, what reward have ye? Do not even the publicans do this?	For if you love those who love you, what is the reward for you? Behold, [do] not even the tax collectors do the same?

MATTHEW *Chapter 5*

	KJV	*Murdock*	*Magiera*
47	And if ye salute your brethren only, what do ye more than others? do not even the publicans so?	And if ye salute your brethren only, what do ye that is not common? Do not even publicans do this?	And if you greet only your brothers, what extraordinary [thing] are you doing? Behold, [do] not even the tax collectors do this?
48	Be ye therefore perfect, even as your Father which is in heaven is perfect.	Be ye therefore perfect; even as your Father who is in heaven is perfect.	Therefore, be made perfect, as your Father who is in heaven is perfect.'

Chapter 6

	KJV	*Murdock*	*Magiera*
1	Take heed that ye do not your alms before men, to be seen of them: otherwise ye have no reward of your Father which is in heaven.	Be cautious in your alms-giving, not to perform it before men, so that ye may be seen of them: otherwise, ye have no reward from your Father who is in heaven.	And take heed with regard to your almsgiving that you should not do it before men, so that you may be seen by them, otherwise you [will] not have a reward from your Father who is in heaven.
2	Therefore when thou doest thine alms, do not sound a trumpet before thee, as the hypocrites do in the synagogues and in the streets, that they may have glory of men. Verily I say unto you, They have their reward.	Therefore, when thou doest alms thou shalt not sound a trumpet before thee, as the hypocrites do in the synagogues and in the streets, that they may get praise from men. Verily I say to you, They have gotten their reward.	Therefore, whenever you do almsgiving, do not sound a trumpet before you as the hypocrites do in the synagogues and in the marketplaces, so that they may be praised by men. And truly I say to you, they have received their reward.
3	But when thou doest alms, let not thy left hand know what thy right hand doeth:	But thou, when doing alms, let not thy left hand know what thy right hand doeth:	But when you do almsgiving, you should not let your left hand know what your right hand does,
4	That thine alms may be in secret: and thy Father which seeth in secret himself shall reward thee openly.	that thy alms may be in secret. And thy Father, who seeth in secret, will reward thee openly.	so that your almsgiving may be in secret and your Father, who sees in secret, shall repay you openly.
5	And when thou prayest, thou shalt not be as the hypocrites are: for they love to pray standing in the synagogues and in the corners of the streets, that they may be seen of men. Verily I say unto you, They have their reward.	And when thou prayest. thou shalt not be like the hypocrites, who are fond of standing up in the synagogues and at the corners of streets to pray, so that they may be seen by people. Verily I say to you, they have gotten their reward.	And when you pray, you should not be as the hypocrites, who love to stand in the synagogues and on the corners of the marketplaces to pray, to be seen by men. And truly I say to you, they have received their reward.
6	But thou, when thou prayest, enter into thy closet, and when thou hast shut thy door, pray to thy Father which is in secret; and thy Father which seeth in secret shall reward thee openly.	But thou, when thou prayest enter into thy closet and close the door, and pray to thy Father who is in secret; and thy Father, who seeth in secret, will reward thee openly.	But when you pray, enter your room and close your door and pray to your Father, who is in secret, and your Father, who sees in secret, will repay you openly.
7	But when ye pray, use not vain repetitions, as the heathen do: for they think that they shall be heard for their much speaking.	And when ye pray, be not garrulous like the heathen; for they expect to be heard for their abundance of words.	And when you are praying, you should not talk idly as the heathens [do], for they think that they are heard by much speaking.
8	Be not ye therefore like unto them: for your Father knoweth what things ye have need of, before ye ask him.	Therefore, be not like them; for your Father knoweth what is needful for you, before ye ask him.	Therefore, do not imitate them, for your Father knows what is needed by you before you ask him.

Parallel Translations

	KJV	*Murdock*	*Magiera*
	MATTHEW *Chapter 6*		
9	After this manner therefore pray ye: Our Father which art in heaven, Hallowed be thy name.	In this manner, therefore, pray ye: Our Father who art in heaven, hallowed be thy name:	Therefore pray like this: 'Our Father, who is in heaven, may your name be holy.
10	Thy kingdom come. Thy will be done in earth, as it is in heaven.	Thy kingdom come: Thy will be done; as in heaven, so on earth:	May your kingdom come. May your will occur, as in heaven, also on earth.
11	Give us this day our daily bread.	Give us our needful bread, this day:	Give us the bread of our need today
12	And forgive us our debts, as we forgive our debtors.	And forgive us our debts, as we forgive our debtors:	and forgive us our debts, as also we have forgiven our debtors.
13	And lead us not into temptation, but deliver us from evil: For thine is the kingdom, and the power, and the glory, for ever. Amen.	And bring us not into temptation, but deliver us from evil: For thine is the kingdom, and the power, and the glory, for ever and ever: Amen.	And do not let us enter into trial, but deliver us from the Evil [one], because the kingdom and the power and the glory are yours, forever and ever.'
14	For if ye forgive men their trespasses, your heavenly Father will also forgive you:	For if ye forgive men their faults, your Father who is in heaven will also forgive you.	For if you forgive men their offenses, your Father who is in heaven will also forgive you,
15	But if ye forgive not men their trespasses, neither will your Father forgive your trespasses.	But if ye shall not forgive men, your Father also forgiveth not you your faults.	but if you do not forgive men, your Father will also not forgive you your offenses.
16	Moreover when ye fast, be not, as the hypocrites, of a sad countenance: for they disfigure their faces, that they may appear unto men to fast. Verily I say unto you, They have their reward.	And when ye fast, be not sad like the hypocrites. For they distort their faces, that they may be seen of men to fast. Verily I say to you, they have gotten their reward.	Now when you fast, you should not be sad as the hypocrites, for they distort their faces so that they may be seen by men that they are fasting. And truly I say to you, they have received their reward.
17	But thou, when thou fastest, anoint thine head, and wash thy face;	But, when thou fastest, wash thou thy face, and anoint thy head:	But when you fast, wash your face and anoint your head,
18	That thou appear not unto men to fast, but unto thy Father which is in secret: and thy Father, which seeth in secret, shall reward thee openly.	that thou mayest not be seen by men as a faster, but by thy Father who is in secret: and thy Father who seeth in secret, will recompense thee.	so that [the fact that] you are fasting may not be seen by men, but by your Father who is in secret. And your Father, who sees in secret, will reward you.
19	Lay not up for yourselves treasures upon earth, where moth and rust doth corrupt, and where thieves break through and steal:	Lay not up for yourselves treasures on the earth, where moth and rust spoil, and where thieves dig through and steal.	You should not place for yourself treasures on earth, where moth and rust corrupt and where thieves break in and steal.
20	But lay up for yourselves treasures in heaven, where neither moth nor rust doth corrupt, and where thieves do not break through nor steal:	But lay up for yourselves treasures in heaven, where no moth and no rust can spoil, and no thieves dig through nor steal.	But place for yourself treasures in heaven, where neither moth nor rust corrupt and where thieves do not break in and do not steal.
21	For where your treasure is, there will your heart be also.	For where your treasure is, there will your heart also be.	For where your treasure is, there is also your heart.
22	The light of the body is the eye: if therefore thine eye be single, thy whole body shall be full of light.	The lamp of the body is the eye. If therefore thy eye shall be sound, thy whole body will be luminous.	The lamp of the body is the eye. Therefore, if your eye will be simple, your whole body also is enlightened.

Parallel Translations

MATTHEW *Chapter 6*

	KJV	*Murdock*	*Magiera*
23	But if thine eye be evil, thy whole body shall be full of darkness. If therefore the light that is in thee be darkness, how great is that darkness!	But if thy eye shall be diseased, thy whole body will be dark. If then the light that is in thee be darkness, how great will be thy darkness!	But if your eye will be evil, your whole body will be dark. If then the light that is in you is darkness, how great will be your darkness.
24	No man can serve two masters: for either he will hate the one, and love the other; or else he will hold to the one, and despise the other. Ye cannot serve God and mammon.	No man can serve two masters: for either he will hate the one and love the other, or he will honor the one and neglect the other. Ye cannot serve God and mammon.	No man is able to serve two lords. For either he will hate the one and will love the other or he will honor the one and will treat the other with contempt. You are not able to serve God and wealth.
25	Therefore I say unto you, Take no thought for your life, what ye shall eat, or what ye shall drink; nor yet for your body, what ye shall put on. Is not the life more than meat, and the body than raiment?	Therefore I say to you: Be not anxious about your life, what ye shall eat, and what ye shall drink; nor about your body, how ye shall clothe yourselves. Is not the life more important than food, and the body than raiment?	Because of this, I say to you, you should not be worried about your life, what you will eat and what you will drink and not about your body, what you will wear. Behold, is not life more than food and the body [more] than clothing?
26	Behold the fowls of the air: for they sow not, neither do they reap, nor gather into barns; yet your heavenly Father feedeth them. Are ye not much better than they?	Look at the birds of heaven; which sow not, and reap not, and gather not into storehouses, but your Father who is in heaven feedeth them. Are not ye more important than they?	Look at the birds in the sky that do not sow nor reap nor gather into storehouses, yet your Father who is in heaven feeds them. Behold, are not you more important than they?
27	Which of you by taking thought can add one cubit unto his stature?	And who of you that shall be anxious, can add to his stature a cubit?	And who among you, while worrying, is able to add one cubit to his height?
28	And why take ye thought for raiment? Consider the lilies of the field, how they grow; they toil not, neither do they spin:	And about raiment, why are ye anxious? Consider the lilies of the desert, in what manner they grow. They toil not; and they spin not.	And why are you worried about clothes? Consider the lilies of the field, how they grow without toil and without spinning.
29	And yet I say unto you, That even Solomon in all his glory was not arrayed like one of these.	Yet I say to you, that not even Solomon in all his glory, was arrayed like one of them.	But I say to you, not even Solomon in all his glory was clothed like one of these.
30	Wherefore, if God so clothe the grass of the field, which to day is, and to morrow is cast into the oven, shall he not much more clothe you, O ye of little faith?	And if God so clothe the grass of the field, which exists to-day, and tomorrow falls into the oven, will he not much more [clothe] you, ye small in faith?	Now if God so clothes the grass of the field that today is and tomorrow falls into the oven, [will he] not much more [clothe] you, oh little of faith?
31	Therefore take no thought, saying, What shall we eat? or, What shall we drink? or, Wherewithal shall we be clothed?	Therefore be not anxious; nor say, What shall we eat, or what shall we drink; or wherewith be clothed?	Therefore, do not be worried or say, 'What will we eat?' or, 'What will we drink?' or, 'What will we wear?'
32	(For after all these things do the Gentiles seek:) for your heavenly Father knoweth that ye have need of all these things.	For, all these things the people of the world seek after. And your Father, who is in heaven, knoweth that all these things are needful to you.	For the nations of the world seek all these [things]. And your Father who is in heaven knows that even all these [things] are needed by you.
33	But seek ye first the kingdom of God, and his righteousness; and all these things shall be added unto you.	But seek ye first the kingdom of God, and his righteousness: and all these things shall be added to you.	But seek first the kingdom of God and his justification and all these [things] will be added to you.

MATTHEW *Chapter 6*

	KJV	Murdock	Magiera
34	Take therefore no thought for the morrow: for the morrow shall take thought for the things of itself. Sufficient unto the day is the evil thereof.	Therefore be not anxious about the morrow: for the morrow hath its own anxieties. Sufficient for the day, is its own evil.	Therefore, do not be worried about tomorrow, for tomorrow will care for itself. Sufficient for the day is its [own] evil.

Chapter 7

	KJV	Murdock	Magiera
1	Judge not, that ye be not judged.	Judge not, that ye be not judged.	You should not judge, so that you will not be judged.
2	For with what judgment ye judge, ye shall be judged: and with what measure ye mete, it shall be measured to you again.	For with the judgment that ye judge, ye shall be judged; and by the measure that ye measure, shall it be measured to you.	For with the judgment that you judge, you will be judged and by the measure that you measure, it will be measured to you.
3	And why beholdest thou the mote that is in thy brother's eye, but considerest not the beam that is in thine own eye?	And why observest thou the straw in thy brother's eye, and regardest not the beam that is in thine own eye?	And why do you see the straw that is in the eye of your brother and you do not observe the beam that is in your eye?
4	Or how wilt thou say to thy brother, Let me pull out the mote out of thine eye; and, behold, a beam is in thine own eye?	Or how canst thou say to thy brother, Allow me to pluck the straw from thy eye; and lo! a beam is in thy own eye.	Or how do you say to your brother, 'Allow [me] to take out the straw from your eye,' and behold, a beam [is] in your eye?
5	Thou hypocrite, first cast out the beam out of thine own eye; and then shalt thou see clearly to cast out the mote out of thy brother's eye.	Thou hypocrite; pluck first the beam from thy own eye; and then thou wilt see clearly, to pluck the straw out of thy brother's eye.	Hypocrite! First take out the beam from your eye and then you will be proved capable to take out the straw from the eye of your brother.
6	Give not that which is holy unto the dogs, neither cast ye your pearls before swine, lest they trample them under their feet, and turn again and rend you.	Give not a holy thing to dogs: and cast not your pearls before swine; lest they tread them under their feet, and turn and lacerate you.	You should not give a holy [thing] to dogs and you should not throw your pearls before pigs, so that they will not trample them with their feet and turn [and] attack you.
7	Ask, and it shall be given you; seek, and ye shall find; knock, and it shall be opened unto you:	Ask, and it shall be given to you: seek, and ye shall find: knock, and it shall be opened to you.	Ask and it will be given to you. Seek and you will find. Knock and it will be opened to you.
8	For every one that asketh receiveth; and he that seeketh findeth; and to him that knocketh it shall be opened.	For, every one that asketh, receiveth: and he that seeketh, findeth: and to him that knocketh, it shall be opened.	For everyone who asks will receive and he who seeks will find and to him who knocks, it will be opened to him.
9	Or what man is there of you, whom if his son ask bread, will he give him a stone?	For what man is there among you, of whom if his son ask bread, will he reach him a stone?	Or what man among you, whose son asks him for bread, will hold out a stone to him?
10	Or if he ask a fish, will he give him a serpent?	Or if he ask of him a fish, will he reach him a serpent?	And if he asks for a fish, will he hold out a snake to him?
11	If ye then, being evil, know how to give good gifts unto your children, how much more shall your Father which is in heaven give good things to them that ask him?	If ye then, who are evil, know how to give good gifts to your children, how much more will your Father who is in heaven give good things to them that ask him?	And if therefore you who are evil know to give good gifts to your sons, how much more will your Father who is in heaven give good [gifts] to those who ask him?

Parallel Translations

MATTHEW *Chapter 7*

	KJV	*Murdock*	*Magiera*
12	Therefore all things whatsoever ye would that men should do to you, do ye even so to them: for this is the law and the prophets.	Whatsoever ye would that men should do to you; so also do ye to them: for this is the law and the prophets.	All that you desire that men should do to you, so also do to them, for this is the law and the prophets.
13	Enter ye in at the strait gate: for wide is the gate, and broad is the way, that leadeth to destruction, and many there be which go in thereat:	Enter ye in by the strait gate; for wide is the gate and broad the way which leadeth to destruction; and many are they that walk in it.	Enter by the straight door because wide is the door and broad [is] the road that leads to loss and many are those who go in it.
14	Because strait is the gate, and narrow is the way, which leadeth unto life, and few there be that find it.	How small the gate and straitened the way that leadeth to life, and few they who find it!	How narrow the door and straight the road that leads to life and few are those who find it.
15	Beware of false prophets, which come to you in sheep's clothing, but inwardly they are ravening wolves.	Beware of false prophets; who come to you in the garb of sheep, but internally they are rapacious wolves.	Beware of false prophets, who come to you in the clothing of lambs, but within are savage wolves.
16	Ye shall know them by their fruits. Do men gather grapes of thorns, or figs of thistles?	And from their fruits ye shall know them. Do men gather grapes from thorn bushes; or figs from thistles?	Now by their fruit you will know them. Do they pick grapes from thorns or figs from thistles?
17	Even so every good tree bringeth forth good fruit; but a corrupt tree bringeth forth evil fruit.	So every good tree beareth good fruits; but a bad tree beareth bad fruits.	So every healthy tree bears beautiful fruit, but a diseased tree bears diseased fruit.
18	A good tree cannot bring forth evil fruit, neither can a corrupt tree bring forth good fruit.	A good tree cannot bear bad fruits; nor can a bad tree bear good fruits.	A healthy tree is not able to bear diseased fruit and a diseased tree [is not able] to bear healthy fruit.
19	Every tree that bringeth not forth good fruit is hewn down, and cast into the fire.	Every tree that beareth not good fruits, is cut down and consigned to the fire.	Every tree that does not bear healthy fruit is cut down and thrown into the fire.
20	Wherefore by their fruits ye shall know them.	Wherefore, by their fruits ye shall know them.	So then, by their fruit you will know them.
21	Not every one that saith unto me, Lord, Lord, shall enter into the kingdom of heaven; but he that doeth the will of my Father which is in heaven.	Not whoever may say to me, My Lord, my Lord, will enter into the kingdom of heaven: but he that doeth the will of my Father who is in heaven.	Not all who say to me, 'My Lord, my Lord,' will enter the kingdom of heaven, but he who does the will of my Father who is in heaven.
22	Many will say to me in that day, Lord, Lord, have we not prophesied in thy name? and in thy name have cast out devils? and in thy name done many wonderful works?	Many will say to me in that day, My Lord, my Lord, have we not prophesied in thy name? and in thy name cast out demons? and in thy name wrought many works of power?	Many will say to me in that day, 'My Lord, my Lord, in your name have we not prophesied and in your name cast out demons and in your name done many miracles?'
23	And then will I profess unto them, I never knew you: depart from me, ye that work iniquity.	And then will I declare to them; I never knew you. Depart from me, ye doers of evil.	And then I will confess to them, 'I have never known you. Go away from me, workers of wickedness.'
24	Therefore whosoever heareth these sayings of mine, and doeth them, I will liken him unto a wise man, which built his house upon a rock:	Every one therefore that heareth these my discourses, and doeth them, will be like to a wise man, one that built his house upon a rock.	Therefore, everyone, who hears these words of mine and does them, will be compared to a wise man who built his house on a rock.

Parallel Translations

	KJV	*Murdock*	*Magiera*
	MATTHEW *Chapter 7*		
25	And the rain descended, and the floods came, and the winds blew, and beat upon that house; and it fell not: for it was founded upon a rock.	And the rain descended, and the floods came, and the winds blew; and they rushed upon that house; and it fell not, for its foundations were laid upon a rock.	And the rain fell and the floods came and the winds blew and they beat against the house but it did not fail, for its foundations were set on a rock.
26	And every one that heareth these sayings of mine, and doeth them not, shall be likened unto a foolish man, which built his house upon the sand:	And every one that heareth these my discourses, and doeth them not, will be like a foolish man that built his house upon sand.	And everyone, who hears these words of mine and does not do them, will be compared to a foolish man who built his house on the sand.
27	And the rain descended, and the floods came, and the winds blew, and beat upon that house; and it fell: and great was the fall of it.	And the rain descended, and the floods came, and the winds blew; and they rushed upon that house, and it fell; and great was the ruin of it.	And the rain fell and the floods came and the winds blew and they beat against the house and it fell and its fall was great."
28	And it came to pass, when Jesus had ended these sayings, the people were astonished at his doctrine:	And so it was, that when Jesus had ended these discourses, the multitudes were astonished at his teaching:	And it happened that when Jesus finished these words, the crowds were amazed at his teaching.
29	For he taught them as one having authority, and not as the scribes.	for he taught them as one having authority; and not as their Scribes and Pharisees.	For he was teaching them as [one having] authority and not as their scribes and the Pharisees.
	Chapter 8		
1	When he was come down from the mountain, great multitudes followed him.	And as he descended from the mountain, great multitudes gathered around him.	Now when he came down from the mountain, large crowds followed him.
2	And, behold, there came a leper and worshipped him, saying, Lord, if thou wilt, thou canst make me clean.	And behold, a leper came and worshipped him, and said: My Lord, if thou wilt, thou canst make me clean.	And behold, a certain leper came [and] worshipped him and said, "My Lord, if you desire, you are able to cleanse me."
3	And Jesus put forth his hand, and touched him, saying, I will; be thou clean. And immediately his leprosy was cleansed.	And Jesus stretched forth his hand, touched him, and said: I will: be thou clean. And immediately his leprosy was cleansed.	And Jesus stretched out his hand [and] touched him, and said, "I desire. Be cleansed." And immediately his leprosy was cleansed.
4	And Jesus saith unto him, See thou tell no man; but go thy way, shew thyself to the priest, and offer the gift that Moses commanded, for a testimony unto them.	And Jesus said to him, See, thou tell no man: but go, show thyself to the priests, and present an oblation as Moses enjoined, for a testimony to them.	And Jesus said to him, "See [that] you tell no one, but go, show yourself to the priests and offer an offering, as Moses commanded for their witness."
5	And when Jesus was entered into Capernaum, there came unto him a centurion, beseeching him,	And when Jesus had entered into Capernaum, a centurion came to him, and besought him,	Now when Jesus entered Capernaum, a certain centurion approached him and was entreating him.
6	And saying, Lord, my servant lieth at home sick of the palsy, grievously tormented.	and said: My Lord, my child lieth at home and is paralytic, and badly afflicted.	And he said, "My Lord, my child is lying at home and is paralyzed and seriously tortured with pain."
7	And Jesus saith unto him, I will come and heal him.	Jesus said to him, I will come and heal him.	Jesus said to him, "I will come and heal him."

Parallel Translations

	KJV	*Murdock*	*Magiera*
	MATTHEW *Chapter 8*		
8	The centurion answered and said, Lord, I am not worthy that thou shouldest come under my roof: but speak the word only, and my servant shall be healed.	The centurion replied, and said: My Lord, I am not worthy that thou shouldst come under my roof: but speak the word only, and my child will be healed.	The centurion answered and he said, "My Lord, I am not worthy that you should enter under my roof, but only speak a word and my child will be healed.
9	For I am a man under authority, having soldiers under me: and I say to this man, Go, and he goeth; and to another, Come, and he cometh; and to my servant, Do this, and he doeth it.	For I also am a man under authority, and there are soldiers under my hands, and I say to this one, Go, and he goeth; and to another, Come, and he cometh; and to my servant, Do this thing, and he doeth [it].	For I also am a man who is under authority and there are soldiers under my hand. And I say to this one, 'Go,' and he goes, and to another, 'Come,' and he comes and to my servant, 'Do this,' and he does [it]."
10	When Jesus heard it, he marvelled, and said to them that followed, Verily I say unto you, I have not found so great faith, no, not in Israel.	And when Jesus heard [this], he admired [it]; and he said to those walking with him, Verily I say to you, I have not found faith like this even in Israel.	And when Jesus heard [this], he marveled and said to those who had come with him, "Truly I say to you, not even in Israel have I found faith like this.
11	And I say unto you, That many shall come from the east and west, and shall sit down with Abraham, and Isaac, and Jacob, in the kingdom of heaven.	And I say to you, that many shall come from the east, and from the west, and shall recline with Abraham and Isaac and Jacob, in the kingdom of heaven;	And I say to you, many will come from the east and from the west and will lie down to eat with Abraham and Isaac and Jacob in the kingdom of heaven,
12	But the children of the kingdom shall be cast out into outer darkness: there shall be weeping and gnashing of teeth.	but the children of the kingdom shall go forth into the outer darkness. There will be weeping and gnashing of teeth.	but the sons of the kingdom will go out to outer darkness. There will be crying and gnashing of teeth."
13	And Jesus said unto the centurion, Go thy way; and as thou hast believed, so be it done unto thee. And his servant was healed in the selfsame hour.	And Jesus said to the centurion. Go; be it to thee as thou hast believed. And his child was cured in that same hour.	And Jesus said to the centurion, "Go! As you have believed, it will be to you." And his child was healed immediately.
14	And when Jesus was come into Peter's house, he saw his wife's mother laid, and sick of a fever.	And Jesus came to the house of Simon and saw his wife's mother prostrate, confined by a fever.	And Jesus came to the house of Simon and saw his mother-in-law who was lying down, and a fever had taken hold on her.
15	And he touched her hand, and the fever left her: and she arose, and ministered unto them.	And he touched her hand, and the fever left her: and she arose and ministered to them.	And he touched her hand and the fever left her and she got up and was serving him.
16	When the even was come, they brought unto him many that were possessed with devils: and he cast out the spirits with his word, and healed all that were sick:	And when it was evening, they brought many demoniacs before him; and he expelled their demons by a word, and healed all them that were diseased:	And when it became evening, they brought to him many possessed of devils and he cast out their devils by a word and he healed all those who were very diseased,
17	That it might be fulfilled which was spoken by Esaias the prophet, saying, Himself took our infirmities, and bare our sicknesses.	that so might be fulfilled that which was spoken by Isaiah the prophet, who said: He will bear our sorrows, and our infirmities he will take upon him.	so that it would be fulfilled what was spoken by way of Isaiah the prophet who said: HE WILL TAKE OUR SORROWS AND HE WILL BEAR OUR SICKNESSES.

Parallel Translations

	KJV	*Murdock*	*Magiera*

MATTHEW *Chapter 8*

	KJV	Murdock	Magiera
18	Now when Jesus saw great multitudes about him, he gave commandment to depart unto the other side.	And when Jesus saw great multitudes, around him, he ordered that they should go to the opposite shore.	And when Jesus saw the many crowds that were surrounding him, he commanded that they should go to the opposite shore.
19	And a certain scribe came, and said unto him, Master, I will follow thee whithersoever thou goest.	And a Scribe came and said to him: Rabbi, I will follow thee to the place whither thou goest.	And a certain scribe approached and said to him, "My Master, I will follow you to the place where you are going."
20	And Jesus saith unto him, The foxes have holes, and the birds of the air have nests; but the Son of man hath not where to lay his head.	Jesus said to him, For foxes there are holes, and for the birds of heaven there are nests; but for the Son of man, there is not where he may recline his head.	Jesus said to him, "Foxes have holes and the bird of heaven [has] a nest, but the Son of Man has no [home] where he may lay his head."
21	And another of his disciples said unto him, Lord, suffer me first to go and bury my father.	And another of his disciples said to him: My Lord, suffer me first to go and bury my father.	And another of his disciples said to him, "My Lord, allow me first to go [and] bury my father."
22	But Jesus said unto him, Follow me; and let the dead bury their dead.	But Jesus said to him: Follow thou me, and leave the dead to bury their dead.	But Jesus said to him, "Follow me and leave the dead to bury their dead."
23	And when he was entered into a ship, his disciples followed him.	And when Jesus entered the ship, his disciples embarked with him.	And when Jesus boarded a boat, his disciples boarded with him.
24	And, behold, there arose a great tempest in the sea, insomuch that the ship was covered with the waves: but he was asleep.	And lo, a great commotion arose in the sea, so that the vessel was covered by the waves. But Jesus was asleep:	And behold, a great earthquake occurred in the sea, so that the boat was covered by the waves. Now Jesus was asleep.
25	And his disciples came to him, and awoke him, saying, Lord, save us: we perish.	and his disciples came to awake him, and said to him: Our Lord, deliver us; we are perishing!	And his disciples came near [and] they woke him and said to him, "Our Lord, save us. We are being destroyed."
26	And he saith unto them, Why are ye fearful, O ye of little faith? Then he arose, and rebuked the winds and the sea; and there was a great calm.	Jesus said to them, Why are ye afraid, ye small in faith! Then he arose, and rebuked the wind and the sea; and there was great tranquillity.	Jesus said to them, "Why are you afraid, oh little of faith?" Then he stood and rebuked the wind and the sea and there was a great calm.
27	But the men marvelled, saying, What manner of man is this, that even the winds and the sea obey him!	And the men were amazed; and they said, What a man is this, to whom the winds and the sea are obedient!	And the men were amazed and said, "Who is this whom the winds and the sea obey?"
28	And when he was come to the other side into the country of the Gergesenes, there met him two possessed with devils, coming out of the tombs, exceeding fierce, so that no man might pass by that way.	And when Jesus arrived at the farther shore, in the country of the Gadarenes, there met him two demoniacs, who came out from the sepulchres, very furious, so that no one could pass that way.	And when Jesus had come to the opposite shore to the place of the Gadarenes, two [men] possessed of devils met him, who were coming out from the tombs, very evil, so that no one was able to pass by that road.
29	And, behold, they cried out, saying, What have we to do with thee, Jesus, thou Son of God? art thou come hither to torment us before the time?	And they cried out, and said: What have we to do with thee? Jesus, thou Son of God. Hast thou come hither before the time to torment us?	And they cried out and said, "What have we to do with you, Jesus, Son of God? Have you come here before the time to torment us?"

MATTHEW *Chapter 8*

	KJV	*Murdock*	*Magiera*
30	And there was a good way off from them an herd of many swine feeding.	And at a distance from them there was a herd of many swine feeding	Now there was a herd of many pigs a distance from them that was feeding.
31	So the devils besought him, saying, If thou cast us out, suffer us to go away into the herd of swine.	And the demons entreated of him, and said: If thou cast us out, suffer us to go into the herd of swine.	And those demons were begging him and said, "If you cast us out, allow us to go to the herd of pigs."
32	And he said unto them, Go. And when they were come out, they went into the herd of swine: and, behold, the whole herd of swine ran violently down a steep place into the sea, and perished in the waters.	And Jesus said to them, Go ye. And immediately they came out, and entered into the swine; and that whole herd ran straight to a precipice and plunged into the sea, and perished in the waters.	Jesus said to them, "Go!" And immediately they went out and attacked the pigs and that whole herd went straight over a steep rock and they fell into the sea and died in the water.
33	And they that kept them fled, and went their ways into the city, and told every thing, and what was befallen to the possessed of the devils.	And the herdsmen fled, and entered the city, and related all that had occurred, and concerning the demoniacs.	Now those who were tending [the herd] fled and went to the city and made known everything that had occurred and about those possessed of devils.
34	And, behold, the whole city came out to meet Jesus: and when they saw him, they besought him that he would depart out of their coasts.	And all the city came out to meet Jesus: and when they saw him, they besought him to retire from their coasts.	And the whole city went out for a meeting with Jesus. And when they saw him, they begged him to leave their borders.

Chapter 9

	KJV	*Murdock*	*Magiera*
1	And he entered into a ship, and passed over, and came into his own city.	And he entered the ship, and passed over and came to his own city.	And he boarded the ship and crossed [and] came to his city.
2	And, behold, they brought to him a man sick of the palsy, lying on a bed: and Jesus seeing their faith said unto the sick of the palsy; Son, be of good cheer; thy sins be forgiven thee.	And they brought to him a paralytic, lying on a bed. And Jesus saw their faith, and said to the paralytic: Take courage, my son; thy sins are forgiven thee.	And they brought to him a paralytic lying on a pallet. And Jesus saw their faith and said to the paralytic, "Take courage, my son, your sins are forgiven."
3	And, behold, certain of the scribes said within themselves, This man blasphemeth.	And some of the Scribes said in their minds, This man blasphemeth.	But some of the scribes said among themselves, "This one blasphemes."
4	And Jesus knowing their thoughts said, Wherefore think ye evil in your hearts?	But Jesus knew their thoughts: and he said to them, Why do ye think evil [things] in your heart?	But Jesus knew their thoughts and said to them, "Why do you think evil in your heart[s]?
5	For whether is easier, to say, Thy sins be forgiven thee; or to say, Arise, and walk?	For, which is the easier, to say, Thy sins are forgiven thee; or to say, Arise and walk?	For what is easier to say, 'Your sins are forgiven,' or to say, 'Get up [and] walk?'
6	But that ye may know that the Son of man hath power on earth to forgive sins, (then saith he to the sick of the palsy,) Arise, take up thy bed, and go unto thine house.	But that ye may know that the Son of man hath authority on earth to forgive sins, he said to the paralytic: Arise, take up thy bed, and go to thy home.	But that you will know that the Son of Man has authority to forgive sins on earth," he said to that paralytic, "Get up, take up your pallet and go to your house."
7	And he arose, and departed to his house.	And he arose and went to his home.	And he got up [and] went to his house.

Parallel Translations

	KJV	*Murdock*	*Magiera*
	MATTHEW *Chapter 9*		
8	But when the multitudes saw it, they marvelled, and glorified God, which had given such power unto men.	And when the multitudes saw [it], they were struck with awe; and they praised God, who had given authority like this to men.	Now when the crowds saw [this], they were frightened and glorified God, who gave authority such as this to men.
9	And as Jesus passed forth from thence, he saw a man, named Matthew, sitting at the receipt of custom: and he saith unto him, Follow me. And he arose, and followed him.	And as Jesus passed on from there, he saw a man sitting at the custom-house, whose name was Matthew. And he said to him, Follow me: and he arose and followed him.	And when Jesus passed over from there, he saw a man who was sitting [at] the customs-house, whose name [was] Matthew. And he said to him, "Follow me." And he rose up [and] went after him.
10	And it came to pass, as Jesus sat at meat in the house, behold, many publicans and sinners came and sat down with him and his disciples.	And as they were reclining in a house, many publicans an sinners came and reclined with Jesus and his disciples.	And as they were sitting to eat in the house, many tax collectors and sinners came and sat to eat with Jesus and with his disciples.
11	And when the Pharisees saw it, they said unto his disciples, Why eateth your Master with publicans and sinners?	And when the Pharisees saw [it] they said to his disciples, Why doth your Rabbi eat with publicans and sinners?	And when the Pharisees saw, they said to his disciples, "Why does your master eat with tax collectors and sinners?"
12	But when Jesus heard that, he said unto them, They that be whole need not a physician, but they that are sick.	And as Jesus heard [it], he said to them: They who are in health have no need of a physician, but they that are very sick.	But Jesus when he heard said to them, "The healthy have no need for a doctor, but those who are very diseased.
13	But go ye and learn what that meaneth, I will have mercy, and not sacrifice: for I am not come to call the righteous, but sinners to repentance.	Go and learn what that is: I require compassion, and not a sacrifice! For I did not come to call the righteous, but the sinful.	Go, learn what this is: I REQUIRE COMPASSION AND NOT SACRIFICE, for I did not come to call the just [ones], but sinners."
14	Then came to him the disciples of John, saying, Why do we and the Pharisees fast oft, but thy disciples fast not?	Then came to him the disciples of John, and said: Why do we and the Pharisees fast much and thy disciples fast not?	Then the disciples of John approached him and said, "Why do we and the Pharisees fast much and your disciples do not fast?"
15	And Jesus said unto them, Can the children of the bridechamber mourn, as long as the bridegroom is with them? but the days will come, when the bridegroom shall be taken from them, and then shall they fast.	Jesus said to them: Can the children of the nuptial chamber fast, so long as the bridegroom is with them? But the days will come when the bridegroom will be taken from them, and then they will fast.	Jesus said to them, "Are the guests of the wedding feast able to fast as long as the bridegroom [is] with them? But the days are coming when the bridegroom will be taken from them and then they will fast.
16	No man putteth a piece of new cloth unto an old garment, for that which is put in to fill it up taketh from the garment, and the rent is made worse.	No one inserteth a piece of new cloth on an old garment; lest that which filleth up, tear from that garment, and the rent become greater.	No one places a new patch on a worn-out garment, lest the patch should tear away from the garment and the hole become greater.
17	Neither do men put new wine into old bottles: else the bottles break, and the wine runneth out, and the bottles perish: but they put new wine into new bottles, and both are preserved.	And they do not put new wine into old sacks; lest the sacks burst, and the wine run out, and the sacks perish. But they put new wine into new sacks and they are both preserved.	And they do not place new wine in worn-out wineskins, lest the wineskins should rip and the wine would be poured out and the wineskins be ruined. But they place new wine in new wineskins and both of them are preserved."

Parallel Translations

MATTHEW Chapter 9

	KJV	Murdock	Magiera
18	While he spake these things unto them, behold, there came a certain ruler, and worshipped him, saying, My daughter is even now dead: but come and lay thy hand upon her, and she shall live.	And while he was thus discoursing with them a certain ruler came, drew near, worshipped him and said: My daughter is already dead, but come lay thy hand upon her, and she will live.	Now while he was speaking these [things] to them, a certain ruler came near [and] worshipped him and said, "My daughter is now dead. But come, place your hand on her and she will live."
19	And Jesus arose, and followed him, and so did his disciples.	And Jesus rose up, and his disciples; and they followed him.	And Jesus got up and his disciples followed him.
20	And, behold, a woman, which was diseased with an issue of blood twelve years, came behind him, and touched the hem of his garment:	And behold, a woman whose blood had flowed fourteen years, came up behind him, and touched the extremity of his robe:	And behold, a woman, whose blood had flowed [for] twelve years, came from behind him and touched the edge of his clothes,
21	For she said within herself, If I may but touch his garment, I shall be whole.	for she had said in her mind, If I but touch his garment I shall be cured.	for she was saying within herself, 'If I only touch his clothing, I will be healed.'
22	But Jesus turned him about, and when he saw her, he said, Daughter, be of good comfort; thy faith hath made thee whole. And the woman was made whole from that hour.	And Jesus turned himself, looked at her, and said to her: Take courage, my daughter; thy faith hath given thee life. And the woman was cured from that very hour.	Now Jesus turned [and] saw her and said to her, "Be comforted, my daughter, your faith has given you life." And that woman was healed immediately.
23	And when Jesus came into the ruler's house, and saw the minstrels and the people making a noise,	And Jesus came to the house of the ruler: and he saw there pipers, and multitudes making outcry.	And Jesus came to the house of the ruler and saw the musicians and the crowds, who were troubled.
24	He said unto them, Give place: for the maid is not dead, but sleepeth. And they laughed him to scorn.	And he said to them: Retire; for the maid is not dead, but sleepeth. And they scoffed at him.	And he said to them, "Go away, for the girl is not dead, but is asleep." And they were laughing at him.
25	But when the people were put forth, he went in, and took her by the hand, and the maid arose.	And when he had ejected the throngs, he entered in, and took her by the hand, and the maid rose up.	And when he dismissed the crowds, he entered in, took her by the hand and the girl got up.
26	And the fame hereof went abroad into all that land.	And the fame of this [thing] spread in all that land.	And this news went out into all this land.
27	And when Jesus departed thence, two blind men followed him, crying, and saying, Thou Son of David, have mercy on us.	And when Jesus had passed from there, two blind men followed after him, and said: Have mercy on us, Thou Son of David!	And when Jesus passed over from there, two blind men followed him, who were crying out and saying, "Have compassion on us, Son of David."
28	And when he was come into the house, the blind men came to him: and Jesus saith unto them, Believe ye that I am able to do this? They said unto him, Yea, Lord.	And when he had entered a house, those blind men approached him, and Jesus said to them: Believe ye that I am able to do this? They said to him, Yes, our Lord.	And when he came to the house, those blind men approached him. Jesus said to them, "Do you believe that I am able to do this?" They said to him, "Yes, our Lord."
29	Then touched he their eyes, saying, According to your faith be it unto you.	Then he touched their eyes, and said: As ye have believed, so shall it be to you.	Then he touched their eyes and said, "As you have believed will it be to you."

MATTHEW *Chapter 9*

	KJV	Murdock	Magiera
30	And their eyes were opened; and Jesus straitly charged them, saying, See that no man know it.	And forthwith their eyes were opened. And Jesus charged them and said: See, that no man know [of it].	And immediately their eyes were opened and Jesus rebuked them and said, "See [that] no man should know [about this]."
31	But they, when they were departed, spread abroad his fame in all that country.	But they went out and spread the fame of it in all that land.	But they went out [and] spread his fame in all that land.
32	As they went out, behold, they brought to him a dumb man possessed with a devil.	And as Jesus went out, they brought to him a dumb man in whom was a demon.	And when Jesus went out, they brought to him a mute in whom was a devil.
33	And when the devil was cast out, the dumb spake: and the multitudes marvelled, saying, It was never so seen in Israel.	And when the demon had gone out, the dumb man conversed. And the multitudes admired, and said: Never was it so seen in Israel!	And after the devil went out, that mute spoke and the crowds were amazed and said, "Never was it seen so in Israel."
34	But the Pharisees said, He casteth out devils through the prince of the devils.	But the Pharisees said: It is by the Prince of demons, he casteth out demons.	But the Pharisees were saying, "By the chief of devils, he casts out devils."
35	And Jesus went about all the cities and villages, teaching in their synagogues, and preaching the gospel of the kingdom, and healing every sickness and every disease among the people.	And Jesus traveled over all the cities and the villages: and he taught in their synagogues, and proclaimed the tidings of the kingdom, and healed all diseases and all pains.	And Jesus journeyed into all the cities and into the villages and was teaching in their synagogues and preaching the gospel of the kingdom and healing all their diseases and all their pains.
36	But when he saw the multitudes, he was moved with compassion on them, because they fainted, and were scattered abroad, as sheep having no shepherd.	And when Jesus looked on the multitudes, he pitied them; because they were wearied and dispersed, like sheep that have no shepherd.	And when Jesus saw the crowds, he had compassion on them, because they were weary and scattered as sheep that do not have a shepherd.
37	Then saith he unto his disciples, The harvest truly is plenteous, but the labourers are few;	And he said to his disciples, The harvest is great, and the laborers few.	And he said to his disciples, "The harvest is great, and the workers, few.
38	Pray ye therefore the Lord of the harvest, that he will send forth labourers into his harvest.	Entreat, therefore, of the Lord of the harvest, that he would send laborers into his harvest.	Entreat, therefore, the Lord of the harvest that he would send workers for his harvest."

Chapter 10

	KJV	Murdock	Magiera
1	And when he had called unto him his twelve disciples, he gave them power against unclean spirits, to cast them out, and to heal all manner of sickness and all manner of disease.	And he called his twelve disciples [to him], and gave them authority over unclean spirits to cast them out, and to heal every pain and disease.	And he called his twelve disciples and gave them authority over unclean spirits to cast [them] out and to heal every pain and disease.
2	Now the names of the twelve apostles are these; The first, Simon, who is called Peter, and Andrew his brother; James the son of Zebedee, and John his brother;	And the names of those twelve Legates are these: The first of them, Simon who is called Cephas, and Andrew his brother; and James the son of Zebedee, and John his brother;	Now the names of the twelve apostles are these: first, Simon, who was called Peter, and Andrew, his brother, and James, the son of Zebedee, and John, his brother,

Parallel Translations

	KJV	*Murdock*	*Magiera*
	MATTHEW *Chapter 10*		
3	Philip, and Bartholomew; Thomas, and Matthew the publican; James the son of Alphaeus, and Lebbaeus, whose surname was Thaddaeus;	and Philip, and Bartholomew, and Thomas, and Matthew the publican; and James the son of Alpheus, and Lebbeus who was called Thaddeus;	and Philip and Bartholomew and Thomas and Matthew, the tax collector, and James, the son of Alphaeus, and Lebbaeus, who was called Thaddaeus,
4	Simon the Canaanite, and Judas Iscariot, who also betrayed him.	and Simon the Canaanite, and Judas Iscariot, he who betrayed him.	and Simon, the Canaanite, and Judas Iscariot, who betrayed him.
5	These twelve Jesus sent forth, and commanded them, saying, Go not into the way of the Gentiles, and into any city of the Samaritans enter ye not:	These twelve Jesus sent forth: and he commanded them and said: Go not in the way of the Gentiles: and enter not the cities of the Samaritans.	Jesus sent these twelve and commanded them and said, "Do not go on the road of the heathens and do not enter the city of the Samaritans.
6	But go rather to the lost sheep of the house of Israel.	But, go ye rather to the lost sheep of the house of Israel.	But go rather to the sheep that are lost from the house of Israel.
7	And as ye go, preach, saying, The kingdom of heaven is at hand.	And as ye go, proclaim and say: The kingdom of heaven hath approached.	And as you are going, preach and say, 'The kingdom of heaven is near.'
8	Heal the sick, cleanse the lepers, raise the dead, cast out devils: freely ye have received, freely give.	Heal ye the sick; cleanse the leprous; [raise the dead;] and cast out demons. Freely ye have received; freely give.	Heal the sick and cleanse the lepers and cast out devils. Freely you have received, freely give.
9	Provide neither gold, nor silver, nor brass in your purses,	Provide not gold, nor silver, nor brass in your purses;	Do not have gold or silver or brass in your purses
10	Nor scrip for your journey, neither two coats, neither shoes, nor yet staves: for the workman is worthy of his meat.	nor a wallet for the journey: neither two coats, nor shoes, nor a staff. For the laborer is worthy of his food.	or a wallet for the journey or two coats or shoes or staff, for a worker is worthy of his food.
11	And into whatsoever city or town ye shall enter, enquire who in it is worthy; and there abide till ye go thence.	And into whatever city or town ye enter, inquire, who in it is worthy; and there stay until ye depart.	And into whatever city or village you enter, ask who in it is worthy and there stay until you leave.
12	And when ye come into an house, salute it.	And when ye enter a house, salute the household.	And when you enter a house, greet the household
13	And if the house be worthy, let your peace come upon it: but if it be not worthy, let your peace return to you.	And if the house be worthy, your peace will come upon it; but if it be not worthy, your peace will return upon yourselves.	and if the house is worthy, your peace will come on it. But if it is not worthy, your peace will return on you.
14	And whosoever shall not receive you, nor hear your words, when ye depart out of that house or city, shake off the dust of your feet.	And whoever will not receive you, nor hear your discourses, when ye depart from that house or that town, shake off the dust from your feet.	And whoever does not receive you and does not hear your words, when you leave the house or that village, shake off the dust from your feet.
15	Verily I say unto you, It shall be more tolerable for the land of Sodom and Gomorrha in the day of judgment, than for that city.	Verily I say to you, that it will be comfortable for the land of Sodom and Gomorrah in the day of judgment, rather than for that city.	And truly I say to you, it will be [more] pleasant for the land of Sodom and Gomorrah in the day of judgment than for that city.
16	Behold, I send you forth as sheep in the midst of wolves: be ye therefore wise as serpents, and harmless as doves.	Behold, I send you forth as sheep among wolves. Therefore be ye sagacious as serpents, and guileless as doves.	Behold, I send you as a lamb into the middle of wolves. Be therefore wise as snakes and harmless as doves.

Parallel Translations

	KJV	Murdock	Magiera
MATTHEW	*Chapter 10*		
17	But beware of men: for they will deliver you up to the councils, and they will scourge you in their synagogues;	And beware of men; for they will deliver you over to the tribunals, and will scourge you in their synagogues.	And beware of men, for they will deliver you to the courts and they will beat you in their synagogues.
18	And ye shall be brought before governors and kings for my sake, for a testimony against them and the Gentiles.	And they will bring you before governors and kings, on my account, for a testimony to them and to the Gentiles.	And they will bring you before governors and kings for my sake, for a witness to them and to the Gentiles.
19	But when they deliver you up, take no thought how or what ye shall speak: for it shall be given you in that same hour what ye shall speak.	And when they deliver you up, be not anxious how or what ye shall speak; for it shall be given you in that hour what to say.	Now when they deliver you up, do not be concerned how or what you should speak, for it will be given to you immediately what you should speak.
20	For it is not ye that speak, but the Spirit of your Father which speaketh in you.	For it is not ye that speak, but the spirit of your Father speaking in you.	For it will not be you speaking, but the Spirit of your Father speaking in you.
21	And the brother shall deliver up the brother to death, and the father the child: and the children shall rise up against their parents, and cause them to be put to death.	And brother shall deliver up his brother to death, and a father his son; and children shall rise up against parents, and cause them to die.	But brother will deliver his brother to death and father his son. And children will rise up against their parents and they will kill them.
22	And ye shall be hated of all men for my name's sake: but he that endureth to the end shall be saved.	And ye shall be hated by every one, on account of my name. But he that shall endure to the end, shall have life.	And you will be hated by all men, because of my name. But he who endures until the end will live.
23	But when they persecute you in this city, flee ye into another: for verily I say unto you, Ye shall not have gone over the cities of Israel, till the Son of man be come.	And when they persecute you in one city, flee to another: for verily I say to you, Ye shall not have completed all the cities of the house of Israel, till the Son of man shall come.	Now when they persecute you in this city, flee to another, for truly I say to you, you will not complete all the cities of the house of Israel before the Son of Man will come.
24	The disciple is not above his master, nor the servant above his lord.	No disciple is better than his rabbi; nor a servant, than his lord.	There is no disciple who is greater than his master, nor a servant [who is greater] than his lord.
25	It is enough for the disciple that he be as his master, and the servant as his lord. If they have called the master of the house Beelzebub, how much more shall they call them of his household?	It is sufficient for the disciple, that he be as his rabbi; and the servant, as his lord. If they call the lord of the house Beelzebub, how much more the children of his family?	It is sufficient for a disciple to be as his master and for a servant [to be] as his lord. If they call the lord of the house Beelzebub, how much more the sons of his house?
26	Fear them not therefore: for there is nothing covered, that shall not be revealed; and hid, that shall not be known.	Therefore be not afraid of them; for there is nothing covered up, that shall not be exposed; nor concealed, that shall not become known.	Therefore do not be afraid of them, for there is not anything that is covered that will not be revealed, or that is hidden that will not be made known.
27	What I tell you in darkness, that speak ye in light: and what ye hear in the ear, that preach ye upon the housetops.	Whatever I say to you in the dark, that speak ye in the light; and what ye have heard in your ears, proclaim ye on the housetops.	What I say to you in darkness, you speak in the light. And what you hear in your ears, preach on the roofs.

Parallel Translations

	KJV	*Murdock*	*Magiera*
	MATTHEW *Chapter 10*		
28	And fear not them which kill the body, but are not able to kill the soul: but rather fear him which is able to destroy both soul and body in hell.	And be not afraid of them that kill the body, but cannot kill the soul; but be afraid rather of Him who can destroy both soul and body in hell.	And do not be afraid of those who kill the body, but are not able to kill the soul. But be afraid rather of him who is able to destroy the soul and body in Gehenna.
29	Are not two sparrows sold for a farthing? and one of them shall not fall on the ground without your Father.	Are not two sparrows sold for a farthing? Yet one of them doth not fall to the ground without your Father.	Are not two sparrows sold for a copper coin? And one of them does not fall on the earth without your Father.
30	But the very hairs of your head are all numbered.	As for you, even the hairs of your head are all numbered.	Now yours, even all the hairs of your head are numbered.
31	Fear ye not therefore, ye are of more value than many sparrows.	Therefore be not afraid: ye are more important than many sparrows.	Therefore do not be afraid. You are more important than many sparrows.
32	Whosoever therefore shall confess me before men, him will I confess also before my Father which is in heaven.	Wherefore, whoever shall confess me before men, him will I also confess before my Father who is in heaven.	Everyone therefore who confesses me before men, I will confess him also before my Father who is in heaven.
33	But whosoever shall deny me before men, him will I also deny before my Father which is in heaven.	But whoever shall deny me before men, him will I also deny before my Father who is in heaven.	But he who denies me before men, I will deny him also before my Father who is in heaven.
34	Think not that I am come to send peace on earth: I came not to send peace, but a sword.	Think not that I have come to sow quietness on the earth: I have not come to sow quietness, but conflict.	Do not think that I have come to bring harmony on earth. I have not come to bring harmony, but a sword.
35	For I am come to set a man at variance against his father, and the daughter against her mother, and the daughter in law against her mother in law.	For I have come to set a man against his father, and a daughter against her mother, and a daughter-in-law against her mother-in-law.	For I have come to separate a man from his father and a daughter from her mother and a daughter-in-law from her mother-in-law.
36	And a man's foes shall be they of his own household.	And a man's foes will be the members of his household.	And the enemies of a man [will be] his household.
37	He that loveth father or mother more than me is not worthy of me: and he that loveth son or daughter more than me is not worthy of me.	He that loveth father or mother more than me, is not worthy of me: and he that loveth son or daughter more than me, is not worthy of me:	He who loves father or mother more than me is not worthy of me and he who loves son or daughter more than me is not worthy of me.
38	And he that taketh not his cross, and followeth after me, is not worthy of me.	and he that doth not bear his cross and follow after me, is not worthy of me.	And everyone who does not take up his cross and follow me is not worthy of me.
39	He that findeth his life shall lose it: and he that loseth his life for my sake shall find it.	He that preserveth his life, shall lose it: and he that loseth his life for my sake, shall preserve it.	He who finds his life will lose it, and he who will lose his life because of me will find it.
40	He that receiveth you receiveth me, and he that receiveth me receiveth him that sent me.	He that entertaineth you, entertaineth me: and he that entertaineth me, entertaineth him that sent me.	He who receives you receives me, and he who receives me receives him who sent me.

Parallel Translations

	KJV	*Murdock*	*Magiera*
	MATTHEW *Chapter 10*		
41	He that receiveth a prophet in the name of a prophet shall receive a prophet's reward; and he that receiveth a righteous man in the name of a righteous man shall receive a righteous man's reward.	He that entertaineth a prophet in the name of a prophet, shall receive a prophet's reward: and he that entertaineth a righteous man in the name of a righteous man, shall receive a righteous man's reward.	He who receives a prophet in the name of a prophet will receive the reward of a prophet, and he who receives a just [man] in the name of a just [man] will receive the reward of a just [man].
42	And whosoever shall give to drink unto one of these little ones a cup of cold water only in the name of a disciple, verily I say unto you, he shall in no wise lose his reward.	And whoever shall give one of these little ones to drink a cup of cold [water] only, in the name of a disciple, verily I say to you, he shall not lose his reward.	And everyone who gives one of these little ones only a cup of cold [water] to drink in the name of a disciple, "Truly I say to you, he will not lose his reward."
	Chapter 11		
1	And it came to pass, when Jesus had made an end of commanding his twelve disciples, he departed thence to teach and to preach in their cities.	And when Jesus had ended the instructions to his twelve disciples, he went from there, to teach and to proclaim in their cities.	And it happened that when Jesus completed directing the twelve disciples, he went away from there to teach and to preach in their cities.
2	Now when John had heard in the prison the works of Christ, he sent two of his disciples,	Now when John, in the house of prisoners, heard of the works of Messiah, he sent by the hand of his disciples,	Now when John, [being in] prison, heard of the deeds of the Messiah, he sent [word] by way of his disciples
3	And said unto him, Art thou he that should come, or do we look for another?	and said to him: Art thou he that cometh, or are we to expect another?	and said to him, "Are you he who will come or should we expect another?"
4	Jesus answered and said unto them, Go and shew John again those things which ye do hear and see:	Jesus answered, and said to them: Go, tell John the things that ye hear and see:	Jesus answered and said to them, "Go. Relate to John those [things] that you have heard and seen.
5	The blind receive their sight, and the lame walk, the lepers are cleansed, and the deaf hear, the dead are raised up, and the poor have the gospel preached to them.	the blind see, and the lame walk, and the leprous are cleansed, and the deaf hear, and the dead rise up, and the needy hear good tidings:	The blind see and the lame walk and the lepers are cleansed and the deaf hear and the dead are raised and the poor are given good news.
6	And blessed is he, whosoever shall not be offended in me.	and happy is he, who shall not be stumbled at me.	And he who is not offended by me is blessed."
7	And as they departed, Jesus began to say unto the multitudes concerning John, What went ye out into the wilderness to see? A reed shaken with the wind?	And when they were gone, Jesus began to say to the multitudes, concerning John: What went ye into the wilderness to see? A reed that waved in the wind?	Now when they had gone, Jesus began to speak to the crowds about John, "What did you go out to the wilderness to see? A reed that is shaken by the wind?
8	But what went ye out for to see? A man clothed in soft raiment? behold, they that wear soft clothing are in kings' houses.	And if not; what went ye out to see? A man clothed in delicate robes? Lo, they that are clothed in delicate [robes], are in the dwelling of kings.	And if not, what did you go out to see? A man who is clothed in soft robes? Behold, those who are clothed in soft [robes] are [in] the house of kings.
9	But what went ye out for to see? A prophet? yea, I say unto you, and more than a prophet.	And if not; what went ye out to see? A prophet? Yes, say I to you, and more than a prophet.	And if not, what did you go out to see? A prophet? Yes, I say to you, even [one] greater than the prophets.

Parallel Translations

MATTHEW Chapter 11

	KJV	Murdock	Magiera
10	For this is he, of whom it is written, Behold, I send my messenger before thy face, which shall prepare thy way before thee.	For this is he of whom it is written: Behold, I send my messenger before thy face, that he may prepare the way before thee.	For this is he about whom it was written: BEHOLD, I WILL SEND MY MESSENGER BEFORE YOUR FACE THAT HE WOULD ESTABLISH THE WAY BEFORE YOU.
11	Verily I say unto you, Among them that are born of women there hath not risen a greater than John the Baptist: notwithstanding he that is least in the kingdom of heaven is greater than he.	Verily I say to you, Among those born of women, there hath not arisen a greater than John the Baptizer: yet the small one in the kingdom of heaven, is greater than he.	Truly I say to you, among those born of women has not stood one who is greater than John the baptizer, but the least in the kingdom of heaven is greater than him.
12	And from the days of John the Baptist until now the kingdom of heaven suffereth violence, and the violent take it by force.	And from the days of John the Baptizer, until now, the kingdom of heaven is assailed by force, and the violent seize it.	Now from the days of John the baptizer and until now, the kingdom of heaven was being guided with restraint and the restrainers were robbing it.
13	For all the prophets and the law prophesied until John.	For all the prophets and the law prophesied, until the time of John.	For all the prophets and the law have prophesied until John.
14	And if ye will receive it, this is Elias, which was for to come.	And, if ye are willing, receive ye, that this is he who was to come.	And if you desire, accept that this is Elijah who was to come.
15	He that hath ears to hear, let him hear.	He that hath ears to hear, let him hear!	He who has ears to hear should hear.
16	But whereunto shall I liken this generation? It is like unto children sitting in the markets, and calling unto their fellows,	But to what shall I compare this generation? It is like to children, that sit in the marketplace and call to their associates,	But to what should I liken this generation? It is like children who sit in the marketplace and call out to their friends
17	And saying, We have piped unto you, and ye have not danced; we have mourned unto you, and ye have not lamented.	and say: We have sung to you, and ye did not dance: we have wailed to you, and ye did not lament.	and say, 'We sang for you and you did not dance, and we mourned for you and you did not lament.'
18	For John came neither eating nor drinking, and they say, He hath a devil.	For John came, not eating and not drinking; and they said, He hath a demon.	For John came not eating and not drinking, and they said, 'There is a devil in him.'
19	The Son of man came eating and drinking, and they say, Behold a man gluttonous, and a winebibber, a friend of publicans and sinners. But wisdom is justified of her children.	The Son of man came, eating and drinking; and they say: Behold, a gluttonous man, and a wine drinker, and a friend of publicans and sinners. But wisdom is justified by her works.	The Son of Man came eating and drinking and they said, 'Behold, a gluttonous man and [one who] drinks wine and a friend of tax collectors and of sinners.' Yet wisdom is justified by its works."
20	Then began he to upbraid the cities wherein most of his mighty works were done, because they repented not:	Then began Jesus to reproach the cities, in which his many deeds of power were wrought, yet they repented not.	Then Jesus began to berate the cities, those in which his many miracles occurred and yet they did not repent.
21	Woe unto thee, Chorazin! woe unto thee, Bethsaida! for if the mighty works, which were done in you, had been done in Tyre and Sidon, they would have repented long ago in sackcloth and ashes.	And he said: Woe to thee, Chorazin! Woe to thee, Bethsaida! For if the deeds of power done in you, had been done in Tyre and Sidon, doubtless, they would long ago have repented in sackcloth and ashes.	And he was saying, "Woe to you, Chorazin! Woe to you, Bethsaida! Because if the miracles that were done in you had been done in Tyre and Sidon, doubtless they [would have] repented in sackclothes and in ashes.

MATTHEW *Chapter 11*

	KJV	*Murdock*	*Magiera*
22	But I say unto you, It shall be more tolerable for Tyre and Sidon at the day of judgment, than for you.	But I say to you, It will be comfortable for Tyre and Sidon, in the day of judgment, rather than for you.	But I say to you, it will be [more] pleasant for Tyre and Sidon in the day of judgment than for you.
23	And thou, Capernaum, which art exalted unto heaven, shalt be brought down to hell: for if the mighty works, which have been done in thee, had been done in Sodom, it would have remained until this day.	And thou, Capernaum, which hast been lifted up to heaven, shalt be brought down to the grave. For if those deeds of power which were done in thee, had been done in Sodom, it would have stood to this day.	And you Capernaum, who has been raised up to heaven, will be brought down to Sheol. Because if the miracles had been done in Sodom that were done in you, she would stand to [this] day.
24	But I say unto you, That it shall be more tolerable for the land of Sodom in the day of judgment, than for thee.	But I say to thee, It will be comfortable for the land of Sodom, in the day of judgment, rather than for thee.	But I say to you, it will be [more] pleasant for the land of Sodom in the day of judgment than for you."
25	At that time Jesus answered and said, I thank thee, O Father, Lord of heaven and earth, because thou hast hid these things from the wise and prudent, and hast revealed them unto babes.	At that time Jesus answered and said: I praise thee, O my Father, Lord of heaven and earth, that thou hast hid these things from the wise and knowing, and hast revealed them to little children.	At that time, Jesus answered and said, "I give thanks to you my Father, Lord of heaven and of earth, that you have hidden these [things] from the wise and intelligent and you have revealed them to babies.
26	Even so, Father: for so it seemed good in thy sight.	Yes, my Father; for so it seemed good before thee.	Yes, my Father, because such was the desire before you.
27	All things are delivered unto me of my Father: and no man knoweth the Son, but the Father; neither knoweth any man the Father, save the Son, and he to whomsoever the Son will reveal him.	Every thing is given up by my Father to me. And no one knoweth the Son, except the Father. Also, no one knoweth the Father, except the Son, and he to whom the Son is pleased to reveal [him].	Everything has been delivered to me from my Father and no man knows the Son, except the Father. Also, no man knows the Father, except the Son and he whom the Son desires to reveal [him].
28	Come unto me, all ye that labour and are heavy laden, and I will give you rest.	Come unto me, all ye wearied and heavily burdened, and I will ease you.	Come to me, all of you [who] labor and bear burdens and I will refresh you.
29	Take my yoke upon you, and learn of me; for I am meek and lowly in heart: and ye shall find rest unto your souls.	Take my yoke upon you; and learn from me, that I am gentle and subdued in my heart: and ye will find rest for your souls:	Bear my yoke on you and learn from me that I am restful and I am meek in my heart, and you will find rest for your souls.
30	For my yoke is easy, and my burden is light.	for my yoke is pleasant, and my burden is light.	For my yoke is pleasant and my burden is light."

Chapter 12

	KJV	*Murdock*	*Magiera*
1	At that time Jesus went on the sabbath day through the corn; and his disciples were an hungred, and began to pluck the ears of corn, and to eat.	At that time Jesus, on the sabbath, walked in the tillage grounds: and his disciples were hungry, and began to pluck the ears and to eat.	At that time Jesus was walking on the Sabbath [in] the sown fields and his disciples were hungry and began picking grain and eating [it].
2	But when the Pharisees saw it, they said unto him, Behold, thy disciples do that which is not lawful to do upon the sabbath day.	And when the Pharisees saw them, they said to him: See; thy disciples are doing that which it is not lawful to do on the sabbath.	Now the Pharisees, when they saw them, said to him, "Behold, your disciples are doing what is unlawful to do on the Sabbath."
3	But he said unto them, Have ye not read what David did, when he was an hungred, and they that were with him;	But he said to them, Have ye not read what David did when he was hungry, and they that were with him?	But he said to them, "Have you not read what David did when he was hungry and those who were with him,

Parallel Translations

MATTHEW *Chapter 12*

	KJV	*Murdock*	*Magiera*
4	How he entered into the house of God, and did eat the shewbread, which was not lawful for him to eat, neither for them which were with him, but only for the priests?	How he went to the house of God, and ate the bread of the Lord's table; which it was not lawful for him to eat, nor for them that were with him, but solely for the priests?	how he entered the house of God and ate the bread of the table of the LORD, that which was not lawful for him, nor for those who were with him to eat, but only for the priests?
5	Or have ye not read in the law, how that on the sabbath days the priests in the temple profane the sabbath, and are blameless?	Or have ye not read in the law, how that in the temple the priests profane the sabbath, and are without fault?	Or have you not read in the law that the priests in the temple break the Sabbath and are without blame?
6	But I say unto you, That in this place is one greater than the temple.	But I say to you, that a greater than the temple is here.	But I say to you, a greater [one] than [a priest of] the temple is here.
7	But if ye had known what this meaneth, I will have mercy, and not sacrifice, ye would not have condemned the guiltless.	And if ye had known what that is, I desire mercy, and not sacrifice; ye would not have criminated them who are without fault.	Now if you would have known what [was meant by], I DESIRE MERCY AND NOT SACRIFICE, you would not have condemned those who are without blame,
8	For the Son of man is Lord even of the sabbath day.	For the Son of man, is lord of the sabbath.	for the Lord of the Sabbath is the Son of Man."
9	And when he was departed thence, he went into their synagogue:	And Jesus went from there, and came to their synagogue.	And Jesus went away from there and came to their synagogue.
10	And, behold, there was a man which had his hand withered. And they asked him, saying, Is it lawful to heal on the sabbath days? that they might accuse him.	And a man was there, whose hand was withered. And they questioned him and said, Is it lawful to heal on the sabbath? that they might defame him.	And a certain man was there whose hand was withered, and they were asking him and said, "Is it lawful to heal on the Sabbath?" so that they could accuse him.
11	And he said unto them, What man shall there be among you, that shall have one sheep, and if it fall into a pit on the sabbath day, will he not lay hold on it, and lift it out?	And he said to them, What man among you is there, who, if he have a sheep, and it fall into a pit on the day of the sabbath, doth not lay hold of it and lift it out?	Now he said to them, "What man among you who has a certain sheep, and if it falls into a pit on the Sabbath day, would not grab [it] and lift it out?
12	How much then is a man better than a sheep? Wherefore it is lawful to do well on the sabbath days.	Now, how much better is a human being than a sheep! Wherefore it is lawful to do what is good, on the sabbath.	Now how much more important [is] a man than a sheep? So then is it lawful on the Sabbath to do that which is good?"
13	Then saith he to the man, Stretch forth thine hand. And he stretched it forth; and it was restored whole, like as the other.	Then said he to the man, Stretch forth thy hand. And he stretched out his hand; and it was restored, and like the other.	Then he said to that man, "Stretch out your hand." And he stretched out his hand and it was restored like the other.
14	Then the Pharisees went out, and held a council against him, how they might destroy him.	And the Pharisees went out and held a consultation against him, that they might destroy him.	And the Pharisees left and took counsel about him, so that they could destroy him.
15	But when Jesus knew it, he withdrew himself from thence: and great multitudes followed him, and he healed them all;	But Jesus knew [it]; and he retired from there. And great multitudes followed him: and he cured them all.	But Jesus knew [of it] and he went away from there. And large crowds followed him and he healed all of them.
16	And charged them that they should not make him known:	And he charged them not to make him known:	And he charged them that they should not reveal him,
17	That it might be fulfilled which was spoken by Esaias the prophet, saying,	that what was spoken by the prophet Isaiah might be fulfilled, saying:	that it would be fulfilled what was spoken by way of Isaiah the prophet, who said:

	KJV	Murdock	Magiera
	MATTHEW *Chapter 12*		
18	Behold my servant, whom I have chosen; my beloved, in whom my soul is well pleased: I will put my spirit upon him, and he shall shew judgment to the Gentiles.	Behold my servant, in whom I have complacency; my beloved, in whom my soul delighteth. I will put my spirit upon him; and he shall proclaim judgment to the Gentiles.	BEHOLD, MY SERVANT WITH WHOM I AM WELL PLEASED, MY BELOVED, FOR WHOM MY SOUL LONGS. I WILL PLACE MY SPIRIT ON HIM AND HE WILL DECLARE JUDGMENT TO THE NATIONS.
19	He shall not strive, nor cry; neither shall any man hear his voice in the streets.	He shall not contend, nor be clamorous, nor shall any one hear his voice in the market-place.	HE WILL NOT DISPUTE AND HE WILL NOT CRY OUT AND NO MAN WILL HEAR HIS VOICE IN THE MARKETPLACE.
20	A bruised reed shall he not break, and smoking flax shall he not quench, till he send forth judgment unto victory.	The crushed reed he will not break; and the flickering lamp he will not extinguish; until he bring judgment to be victorious.	THE BROKEN REED, HE WILL NOT BREAK DOWN, AND THE LAMP THAT IS DYING OUT, HE WILL NOT EXTINGUISH, UNTIL JUDGMENT COMES TO PASS FOR VICTORY
21	And in his name shall the Gentiles trust.	And in his name shall the Gentiles trust.	AND THE NATIONS WILL TRUST IN HIS NAME.
22	Then was brought unto him one possessed with a devil, blind, and dumb: and he healed him, insomuch that the blind and dumb both spake and saw.	Then they brought to him a demoniac that was dumb and blind; and he healed him, so that the dumb and blind man both talked and saw.	Then they brought to him a certain [one] possessed of a devil that was mute and blind and he healed him so that the mute and blind man could talk and could see.
23	And all the people were amazed, and said, Is not this the son of David?	And all the multitude were amazed, and said: Is not this the son of David?	And all the crowds were marveling and said, "Is this not the Son of David?"
24	But when the Pharisees heard it, they said, This fellow doth not cast out devils, but by Beelzebub the prince of the devils.	But when the Pharisees heard [it], they said: This man doth not cast out demons, except by Beelzebub the prince of demons.	But the Pharisees, when they heard [this], were saying, "This [man] does not cast out demons, but by Beelzebub, the chief of devils."
25	And Jesus knew their thoughts, and said unto them, Every kingdom divided against itself is brought to desolation; and every city or house divided against itself shall not stand:	And Jesus knew their thoughts, and said to them: Every kingdom that is divided against itself, will become desolate; and every house or city which is divided against itself, will not stand.	Now Jesus knew their thoughts and said to them, "Every kingdom that is divided against itself will be destroyed. And every house and city that is divided against itself will not stand.
26	And if Satan cast out Satan, he is divided against himself; how shall then his kingdom stand?	Now if Satan cast out Satan, he is divided against himself; how then doth his kingdom stand?	And if Satan casts out Satan, he is divided against himself. How then does his kingdom stand?
27	And if I by Beelzebub cast out devils, by whom do your children cast them out? therefore they shall be your judges.	And if I by Beelzebub cast out demons, by whom do your children cast them out? Wherefore they will be your judges.	And if by Beelzebub I cast out devils, in what way do your sons cast them out? Because of this, they will be judges of you.
28	But if I cast out devils by the Spirit of God, then the kingdom of God is come unto you.	But if I by the Spirit of God cast out demons, the kingdom of God hath come near to you.	And if by the Spirit of God I cast out devils, the kingdom of God has come near to you.

Parallel Translations

MATTHEW *Chapter 12*

	KJV	Murdock	Magiera
29	Or else how can one enter into a strong man's house, and spoil his goods, except he first bind the strong man? and then he will spoil his house.	Or how can one enter the house of a strong man, and plunder his goods, unless he first bind the strong man? and then he may plunder his house.	Or how is a man able to enter into the house of a strong man and to rob his possessions, except first he will bind the strong man and then rob his house?
30	He that is not with me is against me; and he that gathereth not with me scattereth abroad.	He that is not with me, is against me; and he that gathereth not with me actually scattereth.	He who is not with me is against me. And he who does not gather with me indeed scatters.
31	Wherefore I say unto you, All manner of sin and blasphemy shall be forgiven unto men: but the blasphemy against the Holy Ghost shall not be forgiven unto men.	Therefore I say to you, that all sins and contumelies shall be forgiven to men; but the contumely which is against the Spirit, shall not be forgiven to men.	Because of this, I say to you, all sins and blasphemies will be forgiven to men, but blasphemy that is against the Spirit will not be forgiven to men.
32	And whosoever speaketh a word against the Son of man, it shall be forgiven him: but whosoever speaketh against the Holy Ghost, it shall not be forgiven him, neither in this world, neither in the world to come.	And whoever shall speak a word against the Son of man, it will be forgiven him: but whoever shall speak against the Holy Spirit, it will not be forgiven him;---not in this world, and not in the world to come.	And anyone who will say a word against the Son of Man will be forgiven. But anyone who will speak against the Holy Spirit will not be forgiven, neither in this age nor in the age that is to come.
33	Either make the tree good, and his fruit good; or else make the tree corrupt, and his fruit corrupt: for the tree is known by his fruit.	Either make the tree good, and its fruits good; or make the tree bad, and its fruits bad: for a tree is known by its fruits.	Either make the tree fine and its fruit fine or make the tree bad and its fruit bad, for a tree is known by its fruit.
34	O generation of vipers, how can ye, being evil, speak good things? for out of the abundance of the heart the mouth speaketh.	Offspring of vipers, how can ye who are evil, speak good things? For out of the fullnesses of the heart the mouth speaketh.	Generation of vipers! How are you who are bad able to speak good [things]? For from the fullness of the heart the mouth speaks.
35	A good man out of the good treasure of the heart bringeth forth good things: and an evil man out of the evil treasure bringeth forth evil things.	A good man out of good treasures bringeth forth good things, and a bad man out of bad treasures bringeth forth bad things.	A good man from good treasures produces good [things] and a bad man from bad treasures produces bad [things].
36	But I say unto you, That every idle word that men shall speak, they shall give account thereof in the day of judgment.	For I say to you, That for every idle word that men shall speak, they shall give account of it in the day of judgment.	For I say to you, [for] every idle word that men speak, they will give an account of it in the day of judgment.
37	For by thy words thou shalt be justified, and by thy words thou shalt be condemned.	For by thy words thou shalt be justified; and by thy words thou shalt be condemned.	For by your words you will be justified and by your words you will be condemned."
38	Then certain of the scribes and of the Pharisees answered, saying, Master, we would see a sign from thee.	Then answered some of the Scribes and of the Pharisees, and said to him: Teacher, we wish to see from thee a sign.	Then answered some of the scribes and of the Pharisees and said to him, "Teacher, we desire to see a sign from you."
39	But he answered and said unto them, An evil and adulterous generation seeketh after a sign; and there shall no sign be given to it, but the sign of the prophet Jonas:	But he replied and said to them: A wicked and adulterous generation demandeth a sign: but a sign will not be given to it, unless it be the sign of Jonah the prophet.	But he answered and said to them, "An evil and adulterous generation seeks a sign, yet a sign will not be given to it, except the sign of Jonah the prophet.

Parallel Translations

MATTHEW *Chapter 12*

	KJV	*Murdock*	*Magiera*
40	For as Jonas was three days and three nights in the whale's belly; so shall the Son of man be three days and three nights in the heart of the earth.	For as Jonah was in the belly of the fish three days and three nights; so will the Son of man be in the heart of the earth three days and three nights.	For as Jonah was in the belly of the fish three days and three nights, so will the Son of Man be in the heart of the earth three days and three nights.
41	The men of Nineveh shall rise in judgment with this generation, and shall condemn it: because they repented at the preaching of Jonas; and, behold, a greater than Jonas is here.	The people of Nineveh will stand up in the judgment against this generation, and will condemn it: for they repented at the preaching of Jonah; and lo, a greater than Jonah is here.	The Ninevite men will stand in judgment with this generation and will condemn it, because they repented at the preaching of Jonah. And behold, one who is greater than Jonah is present.
42	The queen of the south shall rise up in the judgment with this generation, and shall condemn it: for she came from the uttermost parts of the earth to hear the wisdom of Solomon; and, behold, a greater than Solomon is here.	The queen of the south will stand up in the judgment against this generation, and will condemn it: for she came from the extremities of the earth to hear the wisdom of Solomon; and lo, a superior to Solomon is here.	The queen of the south will stand in judgment with this generation and she will condemn it, because she came from the ends of the earth to hear the wisdom of Solomon. And behold, one who is more than Solomon is here.
43	When the unclean spirit is gone out of a man, he walketh through dry places, seeking rest, and findeth none.	And when an unclean spirit goeth out of a man, it wandereth in places where is no water, and seeketh comfort and findeth [it] not.	Now when an unclean spirit goes out from a man, it wanders in places in which there is no water and it seeks rest, yet does not find [it].
44	Then he saith, I will return into my house from whence I came out; and when he is come, he findeth it empty, swept, and garnished.	Then it saith: I will return to my house, from which I came out. And it cometh, and findeth it vacated, and swept clean, and set in order.	Then it says, 'I will return to my house from where I came out.' And it comes [and] finds that it is empty and swept and set in order.
45	Then goeth he, and taketh with himself seven other spirits more wicked than himself, and they enter in and dwell there: and the last state of that man is worse than the first. Even so shall it be also unto this wicked generation.	So it goeth and taketh with it seven other spirits, worse than itself, and they enter and dwell in it; and the end of that man is worse than his beginning. So will it be to this evil generation.	Then it will go [and] lead with it seven other spirits who are more evil than it and they will enter and dwell in it. And the end of that man will be more evil than his beginning. So it will be to this evil generation."
46	While he yet talked to the people, behold, his mother and his brethren stood without, desiring to speak with him.	And while he was discoursing to the multitudes, his mother and his brothers came and stood without, and sought to speak with him.	Now while he was speaking to the crowds, his mother and his brothers came [and] they were standing outside and requesting to speak with him.
47	Then one said unto him, Behold, thy mother and thy brethren stand without, desiring to speak with thee.	And a person said to him: Lo, thy mother and thy brothers stand without, and seek to speak with thee.	Now someone said to him, "Behold, your mother and your brothers are standing outside and requesting to speak with you."
48	But he answered and said unto him that told him, Who is my mother? and who are my brethren?	But he replied, and said to him that informed him: Who is my mother? and who are my brothers?	But he answered and said to the one who had spoken to him, "Who is my mother and who are my brothers?"
49	And he stretched forth his hand toward his disciples, and said, Behold my mother and my brethren!	And he stretched forth his hand towards his disciples, and said: Behold my mother, and behold my brothers!	And he stretched out his hand toward his disciples and said, "Behold, my mother and behold, my brothers.

Parallel Translations

MATTHEW *Chapter 12*

	KJV	*Murdock*	*Magiera*
50	For whosoever shall do the will of my Father which is in heaven, the same is my brother, and sister, and mother.	For every one that doeth the good pleasure of my Father who is in heaven, that person is my brother, and my sister, and my mother.	For everyone who does the will of my Father who is in heaven is my brother and my sister and my mother."

Chapter 13

	KJV	*Murdock*	*Magiera*
1	The same day went Jesus out of the house, and sat by the sea side.	And on that day Jesus went out of the house, and sat by the side of the sea.	Now on that day, Jesus went out from the house and sat by the shore of the sea.
2	And great multitudes were gathered together unto him, so that he went into a ship, and sat; and the whole multitude stood on the shore.	And great multitudes assembled around him; so that he embarked and seated himself in a ship, and all the multitude stood on the shore of the sea.	And large crowds were gathered around him so that he boarded a ship to sit down and the whole crowd was standing on the shore of the sea.
3	And he spake many things unto them in parables, saying, Behold, a sower went forth to sow;	An he discoursed with them much, by similitudes. And he said, Behold, a sower went forth to sow.	And he was speaking many [things] with them in parables and said, "Behold, a sower went out to sow.
4	And when he sowed, some seeds fell by the way side, and the fowls came and devoured them up:	And as he sowed, some [seed] fell upon the side of a path: and a bird came and devoured it.	And while he was sowing, it happened that [some seed] fell by the side of the road. And a bird came and ate it.
5	Some fell upon stony places, where they had not much earth: and forthwith they sprung up, because they had no deepness of earth:	And other [seed] fell upon a rock, so that it had not much soil: and it sprung up forthwith, because there was no depth of earth.	And other [seed] fell on rocky ground where there was not much soil and immediately it sprouted, because there was no depth of earth.
6	And when the sun was up, they were scorched; and because they had no root, they withered away.	But when the sun was up it wilted. And, because it lacked root, it dried up.	But when the sun came up, it became hot and because it had no root, it dried up.
7	And some fell among thorns; and the thorns sprung up, and choked them:	And other [seed] fell among thorns: and the thorns shot up, and choked it.	And other [seed] fell among thorns and the thorns grew up and choked it.
8	But other fell into good ground, and brought forth fruit, some an hundredfold, some sixtyfold, some thirtyfold.	And other [seed] fell on good ground; and bore fruits, some a hundredfold, some sixtyfold, and some thirtyfold.	And other [seed] fell on good earth and bore fruit, some a hundred and some sixty and some thirty[fold].
9	Who hath ears to hear, let him hear.	He that hath ears to hear, let him hear.	He who has ears to hear should hear."
10	And the disciples came, and said unto him, Why speakest thou unto them in parables?	And his disciples came and said to him, Why discoursest thou to them in similitudes?	And his disciples came near and said to him, "Why do you speak in parables with them?"
11	He answered and said unto them, Because it is given unto you to know the mysteries of the kingdom of heaven, but to them it is not given.	And he answered, and said to them: Because, to you it is given to know the mysteries of the kingdom of heaven, but to them it is not given.	Now he answered and said to them, "To you it is given to know the mystery of the kingdom of heaven, but it is not given to them.
12	For whosoever hath, to him shall be given, and he shall have more abundance: but whosoever hath not, from him shall be taken away even that he hath.	For to him that hath, shall be given; and he shall abound: but from him that hath not, even what he hath shall be taken from him.	For to him who has, it will be given to him and he will have abundance,

	KJV	Murdock	Magiera
	MATTHEW *Chapter 13*		
13	Therefore speak I to them in parables: because they seeing see not; and hearing they hear not, neither do they understand.	For this cause I discourse to them in similitudes, because they see and do not see, and they hear and do not hear, nor understand.	and to him who has not, even that which he has will be taken from him. Because of this, I speak with them in parables, because they see and do not see, and they hear and do not hear and they do not understand.
14	And in them is fulfilled the prophecy of Esaias, which saith, By hearing ye shall hear, and shall not understand; and seeing ye shall see, and shall not perceive:	And in them is fulfilled the prophecy of Isaiah, who said: By hearing ye shall hear, and shall not understand; and by seeing ye see, and shall not know:	And the prophecy of Isaiah is fulfilled in them, who said: HEARING YOU WILL HEAR AND YOU WILL NOT UNDERSTAND AND SEEING YOU WILL SEE AND YOU WILL NOT KNOW.
15	For this people's heart is waxed gross, and their ears are dull of hearing, and their eyes they have closed; lest at any time they should see with their eyes, and hear with their ears, and should understand with their heart, and should be converted, and I should heal them.	For the heart of this people hath grown fat, and with their ears they have heard heavily, and their eyes they have closed; lest they should see with their eyes, and should hear with their ears, and should understand with their heart, and should turn; and I should heal them.	FOR THE HEART OF THIS PEOPLE IS HARDENED AND WITH THEIR EARS THEY ARE HARD OF HEARING AND THEIR EYES ARE CLOSED, LEST THEY WOULD SEE WITH THEIR EYES AND WOULD HEAR WITH THEIR EARS AND WOULD UNDERSTAND WITH THEIR HEART. AND WOULD REPENT AND I [WOULD] HEAL THEM.
16	But blessed are your eyes, for they see: and your ears, for they hear.	But happy are your eyes, for they see; and your ears, for they hear.	But blessed are your eyes, because they see and your ears, because they hear.
17	For verily I say unto you, That many prophets and righteous men have desired to see those things which ye see, and have not seen them; and to hear those things which ye hear, and have not heard them.	For verily I say to you, That many prophets and righteous [men] longed to see what ye see, and did not see [it]; and to hear what ye hear, and did not hear [it].	For truly I say to you, many prophets and just [men] have longed to see what you see and they did not see [them], and to hear what you hear and they did not hear [them].
18	Hear ye therefore the parable of the sower.	But hear ye the similitude of the seed.	But hear the parable of the seed.
19	When any one heareth the word of the kingdom, and understandeth it not, then cometh the wicked one, and catcheth away that which was sown in his heart. This is he which received seed by the way side.	Every one that heareth the word of the kingdom, and understandeth it not, the evil one cometh and snatcheth away the seed sowed in his heart: this is what was sowed by the side of the path.	[From] everyone who hears the message of the kingdom and does not understand, the Evil [one] comes and grabs the word that was sown in his heart. This is that which was sown by the side of the road.
20	But he that received the seed into stony places, the same is he that heareth the word, and anon with joy receiveth it;	And that which was sowed on the rock, is he that heareth the word, and at once receiveth it with joy.	And that which was sown on rocky ground is he who hears the message and immediately receives it with joy.
21	Yet hath he not root in himself, but dureth for a while: for when tribulation or persecution ariseth because of the word, by and by he is offended.	Yet hath he no root in him, but is of short duration; and when there is trouble or persecution on account of the word, he soon stumbleth.	Yet he has no root in him, but is transient. And when trouble or persecution comes because of the word, he is offended quickly.

Parallel Translations

MATTHEW *Chapter 13*

	KJV	Murdock	Magiera
22	He also that received seed among the thorns is he that heareth the word; and the care of this world, and the deceitfulness of riches, choke the word, and he becometh unfruitful.	And that which was sowed among thorns, is he that heareth the word; and care for this world and the deceptiveness of riches, choke the word; and he is without fruits.	Now that which was sown among thorns is he who hears the word and the care of this world and the deception of riches choke the word and it becomes without fruit.
23	But he that received seed into the good ground is he that heareth the word, and understandeth it; which also beareth fruit, and bringeth forth, some an hundredfold, some sixty, some thirty.	But that which was sowed on good ground, is he that heareth my word, and understandeth. and beareth fruits, and yieldeth, some a hundredfold, some sixtyfold, and some thirtyfold.	But that which was sown on good earth is he who hears my word and understands [it] and produces fruit and yields some a hundred and some sixty and some thirty[fold]."
24	Another parable put he forth unto them, saying, The kingdom of heaven is likened unto a man which sowed good seed in his field:	Another similitude he proposed to them, and said: The kingdom of heaven is like to a man who sowed good seed in his field.	He spoke another parable to them and he said, "The kingdom of heaven is compared to a man who sowed good seed in his field.
25	But while men slept, his enemy came and sowed tares among the wheat, and went his way.	And while people were asleep, his enemy came and sowed tares among the wheat, and went away.	And when the people were asleep, his enemy came and sowed weeds in the middle of the wheat and [then] left.
26	But when the blade was sprung up, and brought forth fruit, then appeared the tares also.	And when the plant shot up and bore fruits, then appeared also the tares.	And when the plant sprouted and bore fruit, then the weeds also were seen.
27	So the servants of the householder came and said unto him, Sir, didst not thou sow good seed in thy field? from whence then hath it tares?	And the servants of the householder came, and said to him, Our lord, didst thou not sow good seed in thy field? From whence are the tares in it.	And the servants of the master [of] the house came near and said to him, 'Our lord, behold, did you not sow good seed in your field? From where are the weeds in it?'
28	He said unto them, An enemy hath done this. The servants said unto him, Wilt thou then that we go and gather them up?	And he said to them, An enemy hath done this. The servants said to him, Is it thy pleasure that we go and gather them out?	But he said to them, 'A man [who is] an enemy did this.' His servants said to him, 'Do you want us to go to pick them out?'
29	But he said, Nay; lest while ye gather up the tares, ye root up also the wheat with them.	And he said to them, [No,] lest, while ye gather out the tares, ye also eradicate the wheat with them.	But he said to them, '[No], lest while you are picking out the weeds, you will uproot the wheat with them also.'
30	Let both grow together until the harvest: and in the time of harvest I will say to the reapers, Gather ye together first the tares, and bind them in bundles to burn them: but gather the wheat into my barn.	Let them both grow together until the harvest; and at the time of harvest, I will say to the reapers, Gather out first the tares, and bind them in bundles to be burned; but the wheat gather ye into my granary.	Allow both to grow together until the harvest. And in the time of harvest, I will say to the reapers, 'Pick out the weeds first and bind them [into] bundles to be burned.' But gather the wheat into my granaries.'"
31	Another parable put he forth unto them, saying, The kingdom of heaven is like to a grain of mustard seed, which a man took, and sowed in his field:	Another similitude proposed he to them, and said: The kingdom of heaven is like to a kernel of mustard seed, which a man took and sowed in his field.	He spoke another parable to them. And he said, "The kingdom of heaven is compared to a grain of mustard seed that a man took [and] sowed in his field.

MATTHEW *Chapter 13*

	KJV	*Murdock*	*Magiera*
32	Which indeed is the least of all seeds: but when it is grown, it is the greatest among herbs, and becometh a tree, so that the birds of the air come and lodge in the branches thereof.	And this is the least of all seeds; but when it is grown, it is greater than all the herbs, and becometh a tree, so that a bird of heaven may come and nestle in its branches.	And this [seed] is smaller than all the small seeds, but when it grows, it is greater than all the small herbs and it becomes a tree, so that a bird of heaven will come [and] nest in its branches."
33	Another parable spake he unto them; The kingdom of heaven is like unto leaven, which a woman took, and hid in three measures of meal, till the whole was leavened.	Another similitude spake he to them, The kingdom of heaven is like the leaven, which a woman took and buried in three measures of meal, until the whole fermented.	He spoke another parable to them. "The kingdom of heaven is compared to leaven that a woman took [and] hid in three measures of flour, until all of it was leavened."
34	All these things spake Jesus unto the multitude in parables; and without a parable spake he not unto them:	All these things Jesus discoursed to the multitude in similitudes; and without similitudes he did not discourse with them.	All these [things] Jesus spoke in illustrations to the crowds. And without illustrations he did not speak with them,
35	That it might be fulfilled which was spoken by the prophet, saying, I will open my mouth in parables; I will utter things which have been kept secret from the foundation of the world.	That so might be fulfilled that which was spoken by the prophet, who said: I will open my mouth in similitudes; I will utter things concealed from before the foundation of the world.	so that it would be fulfilled what was spoken by way of the prophet, who said: I WILL OPEN MY MOUTH WITH PARABLES AND I WILL BRING FORTH HIDDEN [THINGS] THAT WERE FROM BEFORE THE FOUNDATIONS OF THE WORLD.
36	Then Jesus sent the multitude away, and went into the house: and his disciples came unto him, saying, Declare unto us the parable of the tares of the field.	Then Jesus sent away the multitudes, and went into the house. And his disciples came to him, and said: Explain to us the similitude of the tares and the field.	Then Jesus left the crowds and came to the house and his disciples came near to him and said to him, "Explain to us that parable of the weeds and of the field."
37	He answered and said unto them, He that soweth the good seed is the Son of man;	And he answered, and said to them: He that soweth the good seed, is the Son of God.	And he answered and said to them, "He who sowed the good seed is the Son of Man.
38	The field is the world; the good seed are the children of the kingdom; but the tares are the children of the wicked one;	And the field is the world. And the good seed are the children of the kingdom; but the tares are the children of the wicked One.	And the field is the age and the good seed are the sons of the kingdom. And the weeds are the sons of the Evil [one].
39	The enemy that sowed them is the devil; the harvest is the end of the world; and the reapers are the angels.	The enemy that sowed them, is Satan. The harvest is the end of the world: and the reapers are the angels.	And the enemy who sowed them is Satan. And the harvest is the culmination of the age and the reapers [are] the angels.
40	As therefore the tares are gathered and burned in the fire; so shall it be in the end of this world.	As therefore the tares are gathered and burned in the fire; so will it be in the end of the world.	As therefore the weeds are picked out and burned in the fire, so it will be in the culmination of this age.
41	The Son of man shall send forth his angels, and they shall gather out of his kingdom all things that offend, and them which do iniquity;	The Son of man will send forth his angels, and they will gather out of his kingdom all the stumbling blocks, and all the doers of evil;	The Son of Man will send his angels and they will pick out from his kingdom all the stumbling blocks and all the servants of wickedness

Parallel Translations

	KJV	*Murdock*	*Magiera*
	MATTHEW	*Chapter 13*	
42	And shall cast them into a furnace of fire: there shall be wailing and gnashing of teeth.	and will cast them into a furnace of fire. There will be wailing and gnashing of teeth.	and they will throw them into the furnace of fire. In that place will be crying and gnashing of teeth.
43	Then shall the righteous shine forth as the sun in the kingdom of their Father. Who hath ears to hear, let him hear.	Then will the righteous shine as the sun, in the kingdom of their Father. He that hath ears to hear, let him hear.	Then the just [ones] will shine as the sun in the kingdom of their Father. He who has ears to hear should hear.
44	Again, the kingdom of heaven is like unto treasure hid in a field; the which when a man hath found, he hideth, and for joy thereof goeth and selleth all that he hath, and buyeth that field.	Again, the kingdom of heaven is like a treasure that is hid in a field; which when a man findeth, he concealeth it, and, from his joy, he goeth and selleth all that he hath, and buyeth that field.	Again, the kingdom of heaven is compared to a treasure that is hidden in a field that a man found and hid. And from his joy, he went [and] sold everything he had and bought that field.
45	Again, the kingdom of heaven is like unto a merchant man, seeking goodly pearls:	Again, the kingdom of heaven is like a merchantman, who sought after rich pearls:	Again, the kingdom of heaven is compared to a merchant who was seeking expensive pearls.
46	Who, when he had found one pearl of great price, went and sold all that he had, and bought it.	and when he found one pearl of great price, he went and sold all that he had, and bought it.	And when he found a certain precious pearl, he went [and] sold everything that he had and bought it.
47	Again, the kingdom of heaven is like unto a net, that was cast into the sea, and gathered of every kind:	Again, the kingdom of heaven is like a sweep net, which was cast into the sea, and collected [fishes] of every kind.	Again, the kingdom of heaven is compared to a net that was thrown into the sea and gathered together [fish] of every kind.
48	Which, when it was full, they drew to shore, and sat down, and gathered the good into vessels, but cast the bad away.	And when it was full, they drew it to the shores of the sea; and they sat down and culled over: and the good they put into vessels, and the bad they cast away.	And when it was full, they pulled it out to the shore of the sea and sat down [and] sorted [it]. And the good [fish] they placed in containers and the bad they threw away.
49	So shall it be at the end of the world: the angels shall come forth, and sever the wicked from among the just,	So will it be in the end of the world. The angels will go forth, and will sever the wicked from among the just;	So it will be in the culmination of the age. The angels will go out and separate the evil [ones] from among the just [ones]
50	And shall cast them into the furnace of fire: there shall be wailing and gnashing of teeth.	and will cast them into a furnace of fire. There will be wailing and gnashing of teeth.	and they will throw them into the furnace of fire. In that place will be crying and gnashing of teeth.
51	Jesus saith unto them, Have ye understood all these things? They say unto him, Yea, Lord.	Jesus said to them: Have ye understood all these things? They say to him: Yes, our Lord.	Jesus said to them, "Do you understand all these [things]?" They said to him, "Yes, our Lord."
52	Then said he unto them, Therefore every scribe which is instructed unto the kingdom of heaven is like unto a man that is an householder, which bringeth forth out of his treasure things new and old.	He said to them: Therefore every Scribe who is instructed for the kingdom of heaven, is like a man who is master of a house, who bringeth forth from his treasures things new and old.	He said to them, "Because of this, every scribe who is instructed for the kingdom of heaven is compared to a man [who is] a master [of] a house, who brings out from his treasures the new and old."

Parallel Translations

	KJV	*Murdock*	*Magiera*

MATTHEW *Chapter 13*

	KJV	Murdock	Magiera
53	And it came to pass, that when Jesus had finished these parables, he departed thence.	And it was so, that when Jesus had ended these similitudes, he departed thence.	And it happened that when Jesus completed these parables, he went away from there.
54	And when he was come into his own country, he taught them in their synagogue, insomuch that they were astonished, and said, Whence hath this man this wisdom, and these mighty works?	And he entered into his own city. And he taught them in their synagogues, in such manner that they wondered, and said: Whence hath he this wisdom and [these] works of power?	And he came to his [own] city and was teaching them in their synagogues, so that they marveled and were saying, "From where [does] this wisdom and [these] miracles [come] to this [man]?
55	Is not this the carpenter's son? is not his mother called Mary? and his brethren, James, and Joses, and Simon, and Judas?	Is not this man the carpenter's son? Is not his mother called Mary, and his brothers James and Joses and Simon and Judas?	Is not this the son of the carpenter? Is not his mother called Mary and his brothers, James and Joses and Simon and Judas?
56	And his sisters, are they not all with us? Whence then hath this man all these things?	And all his sisters, are they not with us? Whence then hath this man all these things?	And all his sisters, behold, are they not with us? So from where [do] all these [things] [come] to this [man]?"
57	And they were offended in him. But Jesus said unto them, A prophet is not without honour, save in his own country, and in his own house.	And they were stumbled at him. But Jesus said to them: There is no prophet who is little, except in his own city and in his own house.	And they were offended by him. And Jesus said to them, "There is no prophet who is despised, except in his [own] city and in his [own] house."
58	And he did not many mighty works there because of their unbelief.	And he did not perform there many works of power, because of their unbelief.	And he did not do many miracles there because of their unbelief.

Chapter 14

	KJV	Murdock	Magiera
1	At that time Herod the tetrarch heard of the fame of Jesus,	And at that time Herod the Tetrarch heard the fame of Jesus:	Now in that time, Herod the Tetrarch heard a report about Jesus.
2	And said unto his servants, This is John the Baptist; he is risen from the dead; and therefore mighty works do shew forth themselves in him.	and he said to his servants: This is John the Baptizer: he is risen from the grave: therefore works of power are wrought by him.	And he said to his servants, "This is John the baptizer. He has risen from the dead. Because of this, miracles are done by him."
3	For Herod had laid hold on John, and bound him, and put him in prison for Herodias' sake, his brother Philip's wife.	Now this Herod had seized John, and bound him and cast him into prison; on account of Herodias, the wife of his brother Philip.	For Herod had arrested John and bound him and threw him into prison because of Herodias, the wife of his brother Philip.
4	For John said unto him, It is not lawful for thee to have her.	For John had said to him: It is not lawful for her to be thy wife.	For John was saying to him, "It is unlawful that she be a wife to you."
5	And when he would have put him to death, he feared the multitude, because they counted him as a prophet.	And he had wished to kill him; but he was afraid of the people, seeing that they regarded him as a prophet.	And he was desiring to kill him, but he was afraid of the people, who were regarding him as a prophet.
6	But when Herod's birthday was kept, the daughter of Herodias danced before them, and pleased Herod.	But when Herod's birthday festival occurred, the daughter of Herodias danced before the guests; and she pleased Herod.	Now when the birthday of Herod occurred, the daughter of Herodias danced before the guests and she pleased Herod.

Parallel Translations

MATTHEW *Chapter 14*

	KJV	Murdock	Magiera
7	Whereupon he promised with an oath to give her whatsoever she would ask.	Therefore he swore to her by an oath, that he would give her whatsoever she might ask.	Because of this, with an oath he swore to her that he would give her anything that she asked.
8	And she, being before instructed of her mother, said, Give me here John Baptist's head in a charger.	And she, as she had been instructed by her mother, said: Give me here in a dish the head of John the Baptizer.	And because she was instructed by her mother, she said, "Give me here on a plate the head of John the baptizer."
9	And the king was sorry: nevertheless for the oath's sake, and them which sat with him at meat, he commanded it to be given her.	And it troubled the king: nevertheless, on account of the oath, and the guests, he commanded that it should be given her.	And it saddened the king, but because of the oath and the guests, he commanded that it be given to her.
10	And he sent, and beheaded John in the prison.	And he sent and cut off the head of John in the prison.	And he sent [and] cut off the head of John [in] the prison.
11	And his head was brought in a charger, and given to the damsel: and she brought it to her mother.	And the head was brought in a dish and given to the girl; and she brought it to her mother.	And he brought his head on a plate and it was given to the girl and she brought it to her mother.
12	And his disciples came, and took up the body, and buried it, and went and told Jesus.	And his disciples came and bore away the corpse, and buried [it]; and they went and informed Jesus.	And his disciples came near, took up his corpse, buried [it] and came [and] made [his death] known to Jesus.
13	When Jesus heard of it, he departed thence by ship into a desert place apart: and when the people had heard thereof, they followed him on foot out of the cities.	And Jesus, when he had heard [it], retired alone, in a ship, to a desert place. And when the multitudes heard [of it], they followed him by dry land from the cities.	Now when Jesus heard [this], he went away from there in a ship to a desert place alone. And when the crowds heard [this], they followed him by dry land from the cities.
14	And Jesus went forth, and saw a great multitude, and was moved with compassion toward them, and he healed their sick.	And when Jesus disembarked, he saw great multitudes; and he had compassion on them, and healed their sick.	And Jesus went out [and] saw the large crowds. And he had compassion on them and he healed their diseases.
15	And when it was evening, his disciples came to him, saying, This is a desert place, and the time is now past; send the multitude away, that they may go into the villages, and buy themselves victuals.	And when it was evening, his disciples came to him, and said to him: This is a desert place, and the time is gone; send away the throngs of people, that they may go to the villages, and buy themselves food.	Now when it was evening, his disciples came near to him and said to him, "[This] is a desert place and the time has passed. Dismiss the crowds of people that they may go on to the villages and buy food for themselves."
16	But Jesus said unto them, They need not depart; give ye them to eat.	But he said to them: It is not necessary for them to go; give ye them to eat.	But he said to them, "It is not necessary for them to leave. Give them [food] to eat."
17	And they say unto him, We have here but five loaves, and two fishes.	And they said to him: We have nothing here but five cakes and two fishes.	But they said to him, "We have nothing here, except five [loaves of] bread and two fish."
18	He said, Bring them hither to me.	Jesus said to them: Bring them here to me.	Jesus said to them, "Bring them here to me."

Parallel Translations

MATTHEW *Chapter 14*

	KJV	*Murdock*	*Magiera*
19	And he commanded the multitude to sit down on the grass, and took the five loaves, and the two fishes, and looking up to heaven, he blessed, and brake, and gave the loaves to his disciples, and the disciples to the multitude.	And he commanded the multitudes to recline on the ground: and he took the five cakes and two fishes, and he looked towards heaven, and blessed, and brake, and gave to his disciples; and the disciples placed before the multitudes.	And he commanded the crowds to recline on the ground and he lifted up those five [loaves of] bread and two fish and looked into heaven and blessed and broke [them] and gave [them] to his disciples and the disciples set [the food] before the crowds.
20	And they did all eat, and were filled: and they took up of the fragments that remained twelve baskets full.	And they all ate, and were satisfied: and they took up the broken remains, twelve full baskets.	And all of them ate and were satisfied. And they took up the rest of the fragments, twelve baskets full.
21	And they that had eaten were about five thousand men, beside women and children.	And the men who had eaten were five thousand, besides the women and children.	Now those men who ate were five thousand, besides women and children.
22	And straightway Jesus constrained his disciples to get into a ship, and to go before him unto the other side, while he sent the multitudes away.	And immediately he constrained his disciples to embark in a ship, and to go before him to the other side, while he sent away the multitudes.	And immediately he urged his disciples to board the ship and to go before him to the opposite side, while he dismissed the crowds.
23	And when he had sent the multitudes away, he went up into a mountain apart to pray: and when the evening was come, he was there alone.	And when he had sent the multitudes away, he ascended a mountain alone to pray. And when it was dark, he was there alone.	And when he dismissed the crowds, he went up to a mountain alone to pray. And when it became dark, he was alone there.
24	But the ship was now in the midst of the sea, tossed with waves: for the wind was contrary.	And the ship was distant from land many furlongs: meanwhile it was much tossed by the waves; for the wind was adverse to it.	And the ship was many furlongs away from land, being tossed greatly by the waves, for the wind was against it.
25	And in the fourth watch of the night Jesus went unto them, walking on the sea.	And in the fourth watch of the night, Jesus came up to them, walking upon the waters.	Now in the fourth watch of the night, Jesus came toward them, walking on the water.
26	And when the disciples saw him walking on the sea, they were troubled, saying, It is a spirit; and they cried out for fear.	And his disciples saw him as he walked upon the waters, and they were perturbated: and they said, What we see is a spectre: and they cried out through fear.	And his disciples saw him that he was walking on the water. And they were troubled and were saying, "It is a false vision." And they cried out because of their fear.
27	But straightway Jesus spake unto them, saying, Be of good cheer; it is I; be not afraid.	But Jesus immediately spoke to them, and said: Have courage: it is I; be not afraid.	But Jesus immediately spoke with them and said, "Be encouraged, it is I. Do not be afraid."
28	And Peter answered him and said, Lord, if it be thou, bid me come unto thee on the water.	Cephas replied, and said to him: My Lord, if it be thou, bid me come to thee on the waters.	And Peter answered and said to him, "My Lord, if it is you, command me to come to you on the water."
29	And he said, Come. And when Peter was come down out of the ship, he walked on the water, to go to Jesus.	And Jesus said to him, Come. And Cephas descended from the ship, and walked upon the waters to go to Jesus.	And Jesus said to him, "Come." And Peter got down from the ship and walked on the water to go to Jesus.

MATTHEW Chapter 14

	KJV	Murdock	Magiera
30	But when he saw the wind boisterous, he was afraid; and beginning to sink, he cried, saying, Lord, save me.	But when he saw the wind to be violent, he was afraid, and began to sink. And he raised his voice, and said: My Lord, rescue me.	And when he saw the wind was rough, he feared and began to sink. And he raised his voice and said, "My Lord, save me."
31	And immediately Jesus stretched forth his hand, and caught him, and said unto him, O thou of little faith, wherefore didst thou doubt?	And immediately our Lord reached forth his hand, and caught him, and said to him: O small in faith, why didst thou distrust!	And immediately our Lord reached out his hand and grasped him and said to him, "Little of faith, why did you doubt?"
32	And when they were come into the ship, the wind ceased.	And as they entered the ship, the wind subsided.	And when they boarded the ship, the wind quieted.
33	Then they that were in the ship came and worshipped him, saying, Of a truth thou art the Son of God.	And they that were in the ship, came and worshipped him, and said: Truly thou art the Son of God!	And those who were in the ship came [and] worshipped him and said, "Truly you [are] the Son of God."
34	And when they were gone over, they came into the land of Gennesaret.	And they rowed on, and came to the land of Gennesaret.	And they traveled on and came to the land of Gennesaret.
35	And when the men of that place had knowledge of him, they sent out into all that country round about, and brought unto him all that were diseased;	And the men of that place knew him: and they sent to all the villages around them; and they brought to him all that were very sick;	And the men of that place knew him and they sent [word] to all the villages of the surrounding area. And all those who were very sick came near to him.
36	And besought him that they might only touch the hem of his garment: and as many as touched were made perfectly whole.	and they entreated of him, that they might touch at least the extremity of his garment. And they who touched, were healed.	And they were begging him that they might touch [him], even if only the outer edge of his clothing. And those who touched were healed.

Chapter 15

	KJV	Murdock	Magiera
1	Then came to Jesus scribes and Pharisees, which were of Jerusalem, saying,	Then came to Jesus Pharisees and Scribes that were from Jerusalem, and said:	Then the Pharisees and scribes, who were from Jerusalem, came near to Jesus and said,
2	Why do thy disciples transgress the tradition of the elders? for they wash not their hands when they eat bread.	Why do thy disciples transgress the tradition of the elders, and wash not their hands when they eat bread?	"Why do your disciples cross against the tradition of the elders and do not wash their hands when they eat bread?
3	But he answered and said unto them, Why do ye also transgress the commandment of God by your tradition?	Jesus replied and said to them: Why do ye also transgress the commandment of God, on account of your tradition?	Jesus answered and said to them, "Why do you also cross against the commandment of God because of your tradition?
4	For God commanded, saying, Honour thy father and mother: and, He that curseth father or mother, let him die the death.	For God hath said: Honor thy father, and thy mother; and he that revileth his father or his mother, shall be put to death.	For God said: HONOR YOUR FATHER AND YOUR MOTHER and HE WHO REVILES HIS FATHER AND HIS MOTHER SHOULD INDEED BE PUT TO DEATH.

Parallel Translations

MATTHEW *Chapter 15*

	KJV	Murdock	Magiera
5	But ye say, Whosoever shall say to his father or his mother, It is a gift, by whatsoever thou mightest be profited by me;	But ye say: Whosoever shall say to a father or to a mother, Be that my offering, by which ye get profit from me: then he must not honor his father or his mother.	But you say, 'Anyone who will say to a father or to a mother, [Let] whatever you have gained by me [be] my offering, and [then] he does not [need to] honor his father or his mother.'
6	And honour not his father or his mother, he shall be free. Thus have ye made the commandment of God of none effect by your tradition.	And [thus] ye make void the word of God, for the sake of your tradition.	And you nullify the word of God because of your tradition.
7	Ye hypocrites, well did Esaias prophesy of you, saying,	Ye hypocrites, well did the prophet Isaiah prophesy of you, and say:	Hypocrites! Well did Isaiah prophesy concerning you and say:
8	This people draweth nigh unto me with their mouth, and honoureth me with their lips; but their heart is far from me.	This people honoreth me with the lips, but their heart is far from me.	THIS PEOPLE HONORS ME WITH THEIR LIPS, BUT THEIR HEART IS VERY FAR FROM ME.
9	But in vain they do worship me, teaching for doctrines the commandments of men.	And in vain they pay me homage, while they teach doctrines that are the precepts of men.	AND VAINLY THEY REVERENCE ME, WHILE TEACHING THE DOCTRINES OF THE COMMANDMENTS OF MEN."
10	And he called the multitude, and said unto them, Hear, and understand:	And he called the multitudes, and said to them, Hear and understand.	And he cried out to the crowds and said to them, "Hear and understand.
11	Not that which goeth into the mouth defileth a man; but that which cometh out of the mouth, this defileth a man.	Not that which entereth the mouth, defileth a man; but that which proceedeth from the mouth, that defileth a man.	It is not what enters the mouth [that] corrupts a man, but what comes out of the mouth, that corrupts a man."
12	Then came his disciples, and said unto him, Knowest thou that the Pharisees were offended, after they heard this saying?	Then came his disciples, and said to him: Knowest thou, that the Pharisees were offended when they heard that speech?	Then his disciples came near and said to him, "Do you know that the Pharisees who heard this saying were offended?"
13	But he answered and said, Every plant, which my heavenly Father hath not planted, shall be rooted up.	And he replied, and said to them: Every plant, which my Father who is in heaven hath not planted, shall be eradicated.	Now he answered and said to them, "Every plant that my Father who is in heaven has not planted will be uprooted.
14	Let them alone: they be blind leaders of the blind. And if the blind lead the blind, both shall fall into the ditch.	Let them alone: they are blind leaders of the blind. And if a blind man leadeth one blind, they will both fall into the ditch.	Leave them alone. They are blind leaders of the blind. And if the blind lead the blind, both will fall into a pit."
15	Then answered Peter and said unto him, Declare unto us this parable.	And Simon Cephas answered and said to him: My Lord, explain to us this similitude.	And Simon Peter answered and said to him, "My Lord, explain to us this parable."
16	And Jesus said, Are ye also yet without understanding?	And he said to them: Are ye also, up to this time, without understanding?	And he said to them, "Until now do you also not understand?
17	Do not ye yet understand, that whatsoever entereth in at the mouth goeth into the belly, and is cast out into the draught?	Know ye not, that whatever entereth the mouth, passeth into the belly, and from there is ejected by purgation?	Do you not know that whatever enters the mouth goes to the stomach and from there is cast out [of the body] by a bowel movement?

Parallel Translations

	KJV	*Murdock*	*Magiera*
	MATTHEW *Chapter 15*		
18	But those things which proceed out of the mouth come forth from the heart; and they defile the man.	But that which proceedeth from the mouth, cometh from the heart: and that is what defileth a man.	But what goes out of the mouth goes out of the heart and becomes corrupting to the man.
19	For out of the heart proceed evil thoughts, murders, adulteries, fornications, thefts, false witness, blasphemies:	For, from the heart proceed evil thoughts, adultery, murder, whoredom, theft, false testimony, reviling.	For from the heart go out evil thoughts: adultery, murder, fornication, theft, false witness, [and] blasphemy.
20	These are the things which defile a man: but to eat with unwashen hands defileth not a man.	These are the things that defile a man. But if a man eat while his hands are unwashed, he is not defiled.	These are [the things] that corrupt a man. But if a man eats while his hands are not washed, he is not corrupted."
21	Then Jesus went thence, and departed into the coasts of Tyre and Sidon.	And Jesus departed from there, and went to the confines of Tyre and Sidon.	And Jesus went out from there and came to the border of Tyre and Sidon.
22	And, behold, a woman of Canaan came out of the same coasts, and cried unto him, saying, Have mercy on me, O Lord, thou Son of David; my daughter is grievously vexed with a devil.	And lo, a woman, a Canaanitess from those confines, came forth, calling out and saying: Compassionate me, my Lord, thou son of David: my daughter is grievously distressed by a demon.	And behold, a woman of Canaan from those borders came out crying and saying, "Have compassion on me, my Lord, Son of David. My daughter is seriously oppressed by a demon."
23	But he answered her not a word. And his disciples came and besought him, saying, Send her away; for she crieth after us.	But he answered her not a word. And his disciples came and requested of him, and said: Send her away, for she crieth after us.	But he did not answer her a word. And his disciples came near [and] begged him and said, "Send her away, because she cries after us."
24	But he answered and said, I am not sent but unto the lost sheep of the house of Israel.	But he answered and said to them: I am not sent, except to the sheep that have strayed from the house of Israel.	But he answered and said to them, "I have not been sent, except to the sheep that have strayed from the house of Israel."
25	Then came she and worshipped him, saying, Lord, help me.	And she came, and worshipped him, and said: Help me, my Lord.	And she came [and] worshipped him. And she said, "My Lord, help me."
26	But he answered and said, It is not meet to take the children's bread, and to cast it to dogs.	Jesus said to her: It is not proper, to take the bread of the children and throw it to the dogs.	He said to her, "It is not proper to take the bread of the children and to throw [it] to the dogs."
27	And she said, Truth, Lord: yet the dogs eat of the crumbs which fall from their masters' table.	And she said: Even so, my Lord; yet the dogs eat of the fragments that fall from the tables of their masters, and live.	Now she said, "Yes, my Lord, [but] even the dogs eat from the crumbs that fall from the tables of their lords and live."
28	Then Jesus answered and said unto her, O woman, great is thy faith: be it unto thee even as thou wilt. And her daughter was made whole from that very hour.	Then Jesus said to her: O woman, great is thy faith: be it to thee, as thou desirest. And her daughter was cured from that hour.	Then Jesus said to her, "Oh woman, great is your faith. Let it be to you as you desire." And her daughter was healed at that moment.
29	And Jesus departed from thence, and came nigh unto the sea of Galilee; and went up into a mountain, and sat down there.	And Jesus departed from there, and came to the side of the sea of Galilee: and he ascended a mountain, and sat there.	And Jesus went away from there and came to the shore of the Sea of Galilee. And he climbed a mountain and sat there.

Parallel Translations

	KJV	*Murdock*	*Magiera*
	MATTHEW *Chapter 15*		
30	And great multitudes came unto him, having with them those that were lame, blind, dumb, maimed, and many others, and cast them down at Jesus' feet; and he healed them:	And great multitudes came to him; and with them were the lame, and the blind, and the dumb, and the maimed, and many others: and they laid them at the feet of Jesus, and he healed them.	And large crowds came near to him in which there were the lame and blind and dumb and the maimed and many others. And they laid them at the feet of Jesus and he healed them,
31	Insomuch that the multitude wondered, when they saw the dumb to speak, the maimed to be whole, the lame to walk, and the blind to see: and they glorified the God of Israel.	So that the multitudes were amazed, when they saw the dumb speaking, and the maimed made whole, and the lame walking, and the blind seeing: and they praised the God of Israel.	so that those crowds were amazed who saw the dumb who spoke and the maimed who were made whole and the lame who walked and the blind who saw. And they praised the God of Israel.
32	Then Jesus called his disciples unto him, and said, I have compassion on the multitude, because they continue with me now three days, and have nothing to eat: and I will not send them away fasting, lest they faint in the way.	Then Jesus called his disciples, and said to them: I pity this multitude; for lo, these three days they have continued with me, and they have nothing to eat: and I am unwilling to send them away fasting, lest they faint by the way.	But Jesus called to his disciples and said to them, "I have compassion for this crowd, because, behold, three days they have stayed with me and they do not have anything to eat. And I do not want to send them away fasting, so that they will not lose strength during the journey."
33	And his disciples say unto him, Whence should we have so much bread in the wilderness, as to fill so great a multitude?	His disciples say to him: Whence can we get bread in the wilderness, to satisfy all this multitude?	His disciples were saying to him, "Where is there bread for us in the desert to satisfy this whole crowd?"
34	And Jesus saith unto them, How many loaves have ye? And they said, Seven, and a few little fishes.	Jesus said to them, How many loaves have ye? They said to him, Seven, and a few little fishes.	Jesus said to them, "How many [loaves of] bread do you have?" They said to him, "Seven and a few small fish."
35	And he commanded the multitude to sit down on the ground.	And he commanded the multitudes to recline on the ground.	And he commanded the crowds to recline on the ground.
36	And he took the seven loaves and the fishes, and gave thanks, and brake them, and gave to his disciples, and the disciples to the multitude.	And he took the seven loaves and the fishes, and gave thanks, and brake, and gave to his disciples; and the disciples gave to the multitudes.	And he took those seven [loaves of] bread and the fish and gave thanks and broke [them] into pieces and gave [them] to his disciples and the disciples gave [them] to the crowds.
37	And they did all eat, and were filled: and they took up of the broken meat that was left seven baskets full.	And they all ate, and were satisfied. And they took up the remains of fragments, seven full baskets.	And all of them ate and were satisfied. And they took up the rest of the fragments, seven baskets full.
38	And they that did eat were four thousand men, beside women and children.	And they that had eaten were four thousand men, besides women and children.	Now those who ate were four thousand men, besides women and children.
39	And he sent away the multitude, and took ship, and came into the coasts of Magdala.	And when he had sent away the multitudes, he took ship, and came to the coasts of Magdala.	And when he sent away the crowds, he boarded a ship and came to the border of Magdala.

Parallel Translations

	KJV	*Murdock*	*Magiera*

MATTHEW *Chapter 16*

	KJV	Murdock	Magiera
1	The Pharisees also with the Sadducees came, and tempting desired him that he would shew them a sign from heaven.	And Pharisees and Sadducees came near, tempting him, and asking him to show them a sign from heaven.	And the Pharisees and Sadducees came near, tempting him and asking him to show them a sign from heaven.
2	He answered and said unto them, When it is evening, ye say, It will be fair weather: for the sky is red.	But he answered, and said to them: When it is evening ye say, It will be fair weather; for the heavens are red.	But he answered and said to them, "When it becomes evening, you say, 'It [will be] fair, for the sky is red.'
3	And in the morning, It will be foul weather to day: for the sky is red and lowring. O ye hypocrites, ye can discern the face of the sky; but can ye not discern the signs of the times?	And in the morning ye say, There will be a storm to-day; for the heavens are sadly red. Ye hypocrites, ye are intelligent to discover the aspect of the heavens, but the signs of this time ye have no skill to discern.	And in the morning you say, 'Today it [will be] stormy for the sky is a gloomy red.' Hypocrites! You know [how] to investigate the appearance of the sky, [but] you do not know [how] to discern the signs of this time.
4	A wicked and adulterous generation seeketh after a sign; and there shall no sign be given unto it, but the sign of the prophet Jonas. And he left them, and departed.	A wicked and adulterous generation asketh for a sign; but no sign shall be given it, but the sign of the prophet Jonah. And he left them, and departed.	An evil and adulterous generation seeks for a sign and a sign is not given to it, except the sign of Jonah the prophet." And he left them and went away.
5	And when his disciples were come to the other side, they had forgotten to take bread.	And when his disciples had come to the farther shore, they had forgotten to take bread with them.	And when his disciples came to the other side, they had forgotten to take bread with them.
6	Then Jesus said unto them, Take heed and beware of the leaven of the Pharisees and of the Sadducees.	And he said to them: Take heed, and beware of the leaven of the Pharisees and the Sadducees.	Now he said to them, "Watch. Beware of the leaven of the Pharisees and the Sadducees."
7	And they reasoned among themselves, saying, It is because we have taken no bread.	And they reasoned among themselves, and said, [it was] because they had taken no bread.	And they were reasoning among themselves and said that they had not taken bread.
8	Which when Jesus perceived, he said unto them, O ye of little faith, why reason ye among yourselves, because ye have brought no bread?	But Jesus knew [it] and said to them: O ye small in faith! why reason ye among yourselves because ye have taken no bread?	But Jesus knew and said to them, "What are you thinking to yourselves, little of faith, that [it is because] you did not bring bread?
9	Do ye not yet understand, neither remember the five loaves of the five thousand, and how many baskets ye took up?	Have ye not yet understood? Do ye not remember the five loaves and the five thousand, and the many baskets ye took up?	Do you not yet understand? Do you not remember those five [loaves of] bread for the five thousand and how many baskets you took up?
10	Neither the seven loaves of the four thousand, and how many baskets ye took up?	Nor the seven loaves and the four thousand, and the many baskets ye took up?	Nor those seven [loaves of] bread for the four thousand and how many baskets you took up?

Parallel Translations

	KJV	Murdock	Magiera

MATTHEW *Chapter 16*

	KJV	Murdock	Magiera
11	How is it that ye do not understand that I spake it not to you concerning bread, that ye should beware of the leaven of the Pharisees and of the Sadducees?	How is it that ye do not understand that it was not concerning bread that I spoke to you; but that ye should beware of the leaven of the Pharisees and of the Sadducees?	How do you not understand that it was not about bread [that] I spoke to you, but that you should beware of the leaven of the Pharisees and of the Sadducees?"
12	Then understood they how that he bade them not beware of the leaven of bread, but of the doctrine of the Pharisees and of the Sadducees.	Then understood they, that he did not bid them beware of the leaven of bread, but of the doctrine of the Pharisees and of the Sadducees.	Then they understood that he did not say that they should beware of the leaven of bread, but of the doctrine of the Pharisees and of the Sadducees.
13	When Jesus came into the coasts of Caesarea Philippi, he asked his disciples, saying, Whom do men say that I the Son of man am?	And when Jesus came into the region of Caesarea Philippi, he questioned his disciples, and said: What do men say concerning me, that I the Son of man, am?	And when Jesus came to the region of Caesarea Philippi, he was asking his disciples and said, "What are men saying about me, who is the Son of Man?"
14	And they said, Some say that thou art John the Baptist: some, Elias; and others, Jeremias, or one of the prophets.	And they said: Some say that [thou art] John the Baptizer; but others, Elijah; and others, Jeremiah, or one of the prophets.	And they said, "Some say [that you are] John the baptizer, but others [that you are] Elijah and others Jeremiah or one of the prophets."
15	He saith unto them, But whom say ye that I am?	He said to them: But, who do ye yourselves say that I am?	He said to them, "But who do you say that I am?"
16	And Simon Peter answered and said, Thou art the Christ, the Son of the living God.	Simon Cephas answered and said: Thou art the Messiah, the Son of the living God.	Simon Peter answered and said, "You are the Messiah, the Son of the living God."
17	And Jesus answered and said unto him, Blessed art thou, Simon Barjona: for flesh and blood hath not revealed it unto thee, but my Father which is in heaven.	Jesus answered, and said to him: Blessed art thou, Simon son of Jonas; for flesh and blood have not revealed [it] to thee, but my Father who is in heaven.	Jesus answered and said to him, "You are blessed, Simon, son of Jonah, because flesh and blood did not reveal [this] to you, but my Father who is in heaven.
18	And I say also unto thee, That thou art Peter, and upon this rock I will build my church; and the gates of hell shall not prevail against it.	Also I say to thee, that thou art Cephas: and upon this rock, I will build my church: and the gates of death shall not triumph over it.	Also I say to you, you are a rock and on this rock I will build my church and the gates of Sheol will not subdue it.
19	And I will give unto thee the keys of the kingdom of heaven: and whatsoever thou shalt bind on earth shall be bound in heaven: and whatsoever thou shalt loose on earth shall be loosed in heaven.	To thee will I give the keys of the kingdom of heaven: and whatever thou shalt bind on earth, shall be bound in heaven: and whatever thou shalt unbind on earth, shall be unbound in heaven.	To you I will give the keys of the kingdom of heaven and anything that you bind on earth will be bound in heaven. And that which you loose on earth will be loosed in heaven."
20	Then charged he his disciples that they should tell no man that he was Jesus the Christ.	Then he enjoined on his disciples, that they should tell no man that he was the Messiah.	Then he commanded his disciples that they should not tell anyone that he was the Messiah.

MATTHEW Chapter 16

	KJV	Murdock	Magiera
21	From that time forth began Jesus to shew unto his disciples, how that he must go unto Jerusalem, and suffer many things of the elders and chief priests and scribes, and be killed, and be raised again the third day.	And from that time Jesus began to show to his disciples, that he was to go up to Jerusalem, and to suffer much from the Elders, and from the chief priests and Scribes, and be killed, and on the third day arise.	And from then [on], Jesus began to show his disciples that he would go to Jerusalem and suffer much from the elders and from the chief priests and scribes and [that] he would be killed and on the third day would rise up.
22	Then Peter took him, and began to rebuke him, saying, Be it far from thee, Lord: this shall not be unto thee.	And Cephas took him, and began to rebuke him; and he said: Far be it from thee, my Lord, that this should be to thee.	Yet Peter took him and began to berate him. And he said, "Forbid it to you, my Lord, that this [thing] should happen to you."
23	But he turned, and said unto Peter, Get thee behind me, Satan: thou art an offence unto me: for thou savourest not the things that be of God, but those that be of men.	But he turned, and said to Cephas: Get thee behind me, Satan: Thou art a stumbling block to me; for thou thinkest not the things of God, but the things of men.	But he turned and said to Peter, "Go behind me, Satan! You are a stumbling block to me, because you do not think [the things] of God, but of men."
24	Then said Jesus unto his disciples, If any man will come after me, let him deny himself, and take up his cross, and follow me.	Then said Jesus to his disciples: If any one desireth to come after me, let him deny himself; and let him bear his cross, and come after me.	Then Jesus said to his disciples, "He who wants to follow me should deny himself and take up his cross and follow me.
25	For whosoever will save his life shall lose it: and whosoever will lose his life for my sake shall find it.	For, whoever chooseth to preserve his life, shall lose it; and whoever will lose his life for my sake, shall find it.	For he who wants to save his life will lose it. And he who will lose his life because of me will find it.
26	For what is a man profited, if he shall gain the whole world, and lose his own soul? or what shall a man give in exchange for his soul?	For what will it profit a man, if he shall gain the whole world, and shall lose his soul? Or what will a man give in exchange for his soul?	For what does a man profit if he gains the whole world and loses his life? Or what [thing of] exchange will a man give for his life?
27	For the Son of man shall come in the glory of his Father with his angels; and then he shall reward every man according to his works.	For the Son of man is to come in the glory of his Father, with all his holy angels; and then will he recompense to every man as his deeds are.	For THE SON OF MAN IS ABOUT TO COME IN THE GLORY OF HIS FATHER WITH HIS HOLY ANGELS. And then he will reward each man according to his works.
28	Verily I say unto you, There be some standing here, which shall not taste of death, till they see the Son of man coming in his kingdom.	Verily I say to you: There are some persons standing here, who shall not taste death, till they see the Son of man coming in his kingdom.	Truly I say to you, there are men who are standing here who will not taste death until they will see the Son of Man come in his kingdom."

Chapter 17

	KJV	Murdock	Magiera
1	And after six days Jesus taketh Peter, James, and John his brother, and bringeth them up into an high mountain apart,	And after six days Jesus took Cephas, and James, and John his brother, and conducted them alone to a high mountain.	And after six days, Jesus led Peter and James and John his brother and took them up to a high mountain alone.
2	And was transfigured before them: and his face did shine as the sun, and his raiment was white as the light.	And Jesus was changed before them: and his face shone like the sun; and his vestments became white like the light.	And Jesus was transformed before them and his face was bright like the sun. And his clothes became white like light.
3	And, behold, there appeared unto them Moses and Elias talking with him.	And there appeared to them Moses and Elijah, in conversation with him.	And [there] appeared to them Moses and Elijah speaking with him.

Parallel Translations

	KJV	*Murdock*	*Magiera*

MATTHEW *Chapter 17*

	KJV	Murdock	Magiera
4	Then answered Peter, and said unto Jesus, Lord, it is good for us to be here: if thou wilt, let us make here three tabernacles; one for thee, and one for Moses, and one for Elias.	Then Cephas answered and said to Jesus: My Lord, it is good for us to be here: and, if it please thee, we will make here three booths; one for thee, and one for Moses, and one for Elijah.	And Peter answered and said to Jesus, "My Lord, it is good for us that we were here. And if you want, we will make here three booths, one for you and one for Moses and one for Elijah."
5	While he yet spake, behold, a bright cloud overshadowed them: and behold a voice out of the cloud, which said, This is my beloved Son, in whom I am well pleased; hear ye him.	And while he was yet speaking, lo, a bright cloud overshadowed them: and there was a voice from the cloud which said: This is my beloved Son, in whom I have pleasure; hear ye him.	And while he was speaking, behold, a bright cloud overshadowed them. And a voice came from the cloud that said, "This is my beloved Son in whom I am pleased. Hear him."
6	And when the disciples heard it, they fell on their face, and were sore afraid.	And when the disciples heard [it], they fell on their faces, and were much afraid.	And when the disciples heard [this], they fell on their faces and were very afraid.
7	And Jesus came and touched them, and said, Arise, and be not afraid.	And Jesus came to them and touched them, and said: Arise, and be not afraid.	And Jesus came near to them and touched them and said, "Stand up. Do not be afraid."
8	And when they had lifted up their eyes, they saw no man, save Jesus only.	And they raised their eyes, and they saw no person, except Jesus only.	And they raised their eyes and did not see anyone, except Jesus alone.
9	And as they came down from the mountain, Jesus charged them, saying, Tell the vision to no man, until the Son of man be risen again from the dead.	And as they came down from the mountain, Jesus charged them, and said to them: Speak of this vision before no person, until the Son of man shall have arisen from the dead.	And while they were coming down from the mountain, Jesus commanded them and said to them, "Do not speak [about] this vision in the presence of anyone until the Son of Man rises from the dead."
10	And his disciples asked him, saying, Why then say the scribes that Elias must first come?	And his disciples asked him, and said to him: Why then do the Scribes say, that Elijah must first come?	And his disciples asked him and said to him, "Why then do the scribes say that Elijah ought to come first?"
11	And Jesus answered and said unto them, Elias truly shall first come, and restore all things.	Jesus answered, and said to them: Elijah doth first come, to fulfill every thing.	Jesus answered and said, "Elijah comes first to fulfill everything.
12	But I say unto you, That Elias is come already, and they knew him not, but have done unto him whatsoever they listed. Likewise shall also the Son of man suffer of them.	And I say to you. That, behold, Elijah hath come, and they did not know him; and they have done to him whatever they pleased: and, in like manner, also the Son of man is to suffer from them.	But I say to you, behold, Elijah has come and they did not know him and they did with him whatever they desired. So also the Son of Man is about to suffer from them."
13	Then the disciples understood that he spake unto them of John the Baptist.	Then the disciples understood, that he spake to them of John the Baptizer.	Then the disciples understood that he spoke to them about John the baptizer.
14	And when they were come to the multitude, there came to him a certain man, kneeling down to him, and saying,	And when they came to the multitude, a man approached him, and bowed himself on his knees,	And when they came to the crowd, a man came near to him and bowed down on his knees

Parallel Translations

	KJV	Murdock	Magiera
	MATTHEW *Chapter 17*		
15	Lord, have mercy on my son: for he is lunatick, and sore vexed: for ofttimes he falleth into the fire, and oft into the water.	and said to him: My Lord, compassionate me. I have a son who is a lunatic, and grievously afflicted; for often he falleth into the fire, and often into the water.	and said to him, "My Lord, have compassion on me. My son is one who is insane and he is seriously afflicted, for many times he has fallen into the fire and many times in the water.
16	And I brought him to thy disciples, and they could not cure him.	And I brought him to thy disciples, and they could not heal him.	And I brought him to your disciples and they were not able to heal him."
17	Then Jesus answered and said, O faithless and perverse generation, how long shall I be with you? how long shall I suffer you? bring him hither to me.	Jesus answered and said: O unbelieving and perverse generation! How long shall I be with you? and how long bear with you? Bring him here to me.	Jesus answered and said, "Oh faithless and perverted generation! How long must I be with you and how long must I endure you? Bring him here to me."
18	And Jesus rebuked the devil; and he departed out of him: and the child was cured from that very hour.	And Jesus rebuked the demon, and it departed from him: and from that hour the child was healed.	And Jesus rebuked it and the demon went out of him and the child was healed at that moment.
19	Then came the disciples to Jesus apart, and said, Why could not we cast him out?	Then came the disciples to Jesus, apart, and said to him: Why could not we heal him?	Then the disciples came near to Jesus alone and said to him, "Why were we not able to heal him?"
20	And Jesus said unto them, Because of your unbelief: for verily I say unto you, If ye have faith as a grain of mustard seed, ye shall say unto this mountain, Remove hence to yonder place; and it shall remove; and nothing shall be impossible unto you.	Jesus said to them: Because of your unbelief. For verily I say to you, That if there be in you faith like a grain of mustard seed, ye may say to this mountain, Remove hence, and it will remove: and nothing will be too hard for you.	Jesus said to them, "Because of your unbelief. For truly I say to you, if you have faith like a grain of mustard seed, you can say to this mountain, 'Move from here,' and it will move and nothing will overcome you.
21	Howbeit this kind goeth not out but by prayer and fasting.	But this kind goeth not out, except by fasting and prayer.	But this kind does not go out, except by fasting and by prayer."
22	And while they abode in Galilee, Jesus said unto them, The Son of man shall be betrayed into the hands of men:	And while they were resident in Galilee, Jesus said to them: The Son of man is to be betrayed into the hands of men;	Now while they were traveling in Galilee, Jesus said to them, "The Son of Man is about to be betrayed into the hands of men.
23	And they shall kill him, and the third day he shall be raised again. And they were exceeding sorry.	and they will kill him; and the third day he will arise. And it saddened them much.	And they will kill him and on the third day, he will rise up." And [the saying] saddened them very much.
24	And when they were come to Capernaum, they that received tribute money came to Peter, and said, Doth not your master pay tribute?	And when they came to Capernaum, those who receive the two drachmas of capitation money came to Cephas, and said to him: Doth not your rabbi pay his two drachmas?	And when they came to Capernaum, those who were receiving the two drachmas for the poll tax came near to Peter. And they said to him, "Does not your master give his two drachmas?"

Parallel Translations

	KJV	Murdock	Magiera

MATTHEW *Chapter 17*

	KJV	Murdock	Magiera
25	He saith, Yes. And when he was come into the house, Jesus prevented him, saying, What thinkest thou, Simon? of whom do the kings of the earth take custom or tribute? of their own children, or of strangers?	He said to them, Yes. And when Cephas had entered the house, Jesus anticipated him and said to him: How doth it appear to thee, Simon? The kings of the earth, of whom do they receive tribute and capitation money? of their children, or of aliens?	He said to them, "Yes." And when Peter entered the house, Jesus anticipated him and said to him, "What does it appear to you, Simon? The kings of the earth, from whom do they receive tribute and the poll tax, from their children or from strangers?"
26	Peter saith unto him, Of strangers. Jesus saith unto him, Then are the children free.	Simon said to him: Of aliens. Jesus said to him: Then the children are free.	Simon said to him, "From strangers." Jesus said to him, "Then the children are free.
27	Notwithstanding, lest we should offend them, go thou to the sea, and cast an hook, and take up the fish that first cometh up; and when thou hast opened his mouth, thou shalt find a piece of money: that take, and give unto them for me and thee.	But still, lest they be stumbled with us, go thou to the sea and cast in a fish-hook, and the fish that shall first come up, open its mouth, and thou wilt find a stater: that take, and give for me and for thyself.	But so that [this] should not offend them, go to the sea and cast a fishhook. And the first fish that comes up, open its mouth and you will find a stater. Take that and give [it] for me and for you."

Chapter 18

	KJV	Murdock	Magiera
1	At the same time came the disciples unto Jesus, saying, Who is the greatest in the kingdom of heaven?	In that hour the disciples approached Jesus, and said: Who is the greatest in the kingdom of heaven?	At that time, the disciples came near to Jesus and said, "Who is indeed great in the kingdom of heaven?"
2	And Jesus called a little child unto him, and set him in the midst of them,	And Jesus called a child, and placed him in the midst of them,	And Jesus called a child and set him among them
3	And said, Verily I say unto you, Except ye be converted, and become as little children, ye shall not enter into the kingdom of heaven.	and said: Verily I say to you, that unless ye be converted, and become like children, ye will not enter the kingdom of heaven.	and said, "Truly I say to you, if you do not change and become like children, you will not enter into the kingdom of heaven.
4	Whosoever therefore shall humble himself as this little child, the same is greatest in the kingdom of heaven.	He therefore that shall humble himself like this child, he will be great in the kingdom of heaven.	Therefore, he who humbles himself like this child will be great in the kingdom of heaven.
5	And whoso shall receive one such little child in my name receiveth me.	And he that shall receive in my name [one who is] like to this child, he receiveth me.	And he who receives [one] like this child in my name receives me.
6	But whoso shall offend one of these little ones which believe in me, it were better for him that a millstone were hanged about his neck, and that he were drowned in the depth of the sea.	And whosoever shall stumble one of these little ones that believe in me, it were better for him that a millstone were suspended to his neck, and that he were sunk in the depths of the sea.	And anyone who causes one of these little ones who believe in me to stumble, it would be better for him that the millstone of a donkey would be hung on his neck and he be sunk in the depths of the sea.
7	Woe unto the world because of offences! for it must needs be that offences come; but woe to that man by whom the offence cometh!	Woe to the world because of stumbling blocks! For it must be, that stumbling blocks come. But, woe to the person by whose means the stumbling blocks come.	Woe to the world because of offenses! For it is necessary that offenses should come. But woe to the man by whose hand the offenses come!

Parallel Translations

	KJV	Murdock	Magiera
	MATTHEW Chapter 18		
8	Wherefore if thy hand or thy foot offend thee, cut them off, and cast them from thee: it is better for thee to enter into life halt or maimed, rather than having two hands or two feet to be cast into everlasting fire.	If then thy hand or thy foot make thee stumble, cut it off and cast it from thee: for it is good for thee to enter into life lame or mutilated, and not that, with two hands or two feet, thou fall into eternal fire.	Now if your hand or your foot causes you to stumble, cut it off and throw it away from you. It is better for you to enter life while you are lame or while maimed, and not, while you have two hands or two feet, to fall into everlasting fire.
9	And if thine eye offend thee, pluck it out, and cast it from thee: it is better for thee to enter into life with one eye, rather than having two eyes to be cast into hell fire.	And if thine eye make thee stumble, pluck it out and cast it from thee: for it is good for thee to enter into life with one eye, and not that, with two eyes, thou fall into the hell of fire.	And if your eye causes you to stumble, tear it out and throw it away from you. It is better for you that you enter life with one eye and not, while you have two eyes, to fall into the Gehenna of fire.
10	Take heed that ye despise not one of these little ones; for I say unto you, That in heaven their angels do always behold the face of my Father which is in heaven.	See that ye despise not one of these little ones; for I say to you, That their angels in heaven, at all times, are beholding the face of my Father who is in heaven.	See, you should not despise one of these little ones, for I say to you, their angels that are in heaven always see the face of my Father who is in heaven.
11	For the Son of man is come to save that which was lost.	For the Son of man, hath come to give life to that which was lost.	For the Son of Man has come to make alive that which was perishing.
12	How think ye? if a man have an hundred sheep, and one of them be gone astray, doth he not leave the ninety and nine, and goeth into the mountains, and seeketh that which is gone astray?	How doth it appear to you? If a man should have a hundred sheep, and one of them should go astray, will he not leave the ninety and nine in the mountains, and go and seek the one that strayed?	What does it appear to you? If a man had one hundred sheep and one of them strayed, does he not leave the ninety-nine on the mountain and go [and] seek that which has strayed?
13	And if so be that he find it, verily I say unto you, he rejoiceth more of that sheep, than of the ninety and nine which went not astray.	And if he find it, verily I say to you, that he rejoiceth in it, more than in the ninety and nine that did not stray.	And if he finds it, truly I say to you, he rejoices at it more than the ninety-nine that did not stray.
14	Even so it is not the will of your Father which is in heaven, that one of these little ones should perish.	Just so, it is not the pleasure of your Father who is in heaven, that one of these little ones should perish.	Likewise, it is not the will before your Father who is in heaven that one of these little ones should perish.
15	Moreover if thy brother shall trespass against thee, go and tell him his fault between thee and him alone: if he shall hear thee, thou hast gained thy brother.	Moreover, if thy brother commit an offence against thee, go and admonish him between thee and him only. If he hear thee, thou hast gained thy brother.	Now if your brother offends you, go [and] reprove him between you and him alone. If he hears you, you have gained your brother.
16	But if he will not hear thee, then take with thee one or two more, that in the mouth of two or three witnesses every word may be established.	But if he hear thee not, take with thee one or two, that at the mouth of two or three witnesses every word may be established.	And if he does not hear you, take with you one or two [others] that, AT THE MOUTH OF TWO OR THREE WITNESSES EVERY WORD WILL BE ESTABLISHED.
17	And if he shall neglect to hear them, tell it unto the church: but if he neglect to hear the church, let him be unto thee as an heathen man and a publican.	And if he will also not hear them, tell [it] to the church. And if he will also not hear the church, let him be to thee as a publican and a heathen.	Now if he will not hear them also, tell the church. And if he will not hear the church also, he will be to you like a tax collector and like a heathen.

Parallel Translations

	KJV	*Murdock*	*Magiera*

MATTHEW *Chapter 18*

	KJV	Murdock	Magiera
18	Verily I say unto you, Whatsoever ye shall bind on earth shall be bound in heaven: and whatsoever ye shall loose on earth shall be loosed in heaven.	Verily I say to you, That whatever ye shall bind on earth, shall be bound in heaven: and whatever ye shall unbind on earth, shall be unbound in heaven.	And truly I say to you, anything that you bind on earth will be bound in heaven. And that which you loose on earth will be loosed in heaven.
19	Again I say unto you, That if two of you shall agree on earth as touching any thing that they shall ask, it shall be done for them of my Father which is in heaven.	Again I say to you, That if two of you shall agree on earth concerning any thing that they shall ask, it shall be to them from my Father who is in heaven.	Again I say to you, if two of you agree on earth concerning every matter that they will ask, they will have [an answer] from the presence of my Father who is in heaven.
20	For where two or three are gathered together in my name, there am I in the midst of them.	For where two or three [are] assembled in my name, there [am] I in the midst of them.	For where two or three are gathered in my name, there I am among them."
21	Then came Peter to him, and said, Lord, how oft shall my brother sin against me, and I forgive him? till seven times?	Then Cephas approached him, and said to him: My Lord, how many times, if my brother commit offence against me, shall I forgive him? up to seven times?	Then Peter came near to him and said, "My Lord, if my brother offends me, how many times should I forgive him? Up to seven times?"
22	Jesus saith unto him, I say not unto thee, Until seven times: but, Until seventy times seven.	Jesus said to him: I do not say to thee, up to seven times, but up to seventy times seven.	Jesus said to him, "I do not say to you up to seven [times], but up to seventy times, by sevens.
23	Therefore is the kingdom of heaven likened unto a certain king, which would take account of his servants.	Therefore the kingdom of heaven is like to some king, who wished to have a reckoning with his servants.	Because of this, the kingdom of heaven is compared to a certain king, who wanted to take an accounting of his servants.
24	And when he had begun to reckon, one was brought unto him, which owed him ten thousand talents.	And when he began to reckon, they brought to him one debtor of ten thousand talents.	And when he began to take [the accounting], they brought to him one who owed ten thousand talents.
25	But forasmuch as he had not to pay, his lord commanded him to be sold, and his wife, and children, and all that he had, and payment to be made.	And as he had not wherewith to pay, his lord commanded him to be sold, him and his wife and his children, and all that he possessed, and payment to be made.	And when he had no [way] to repay, his lord commanded that he should be sold and his wife and his children and everything that was his and [that] he should repay [the debt].
26	The servant therefore fell down, and worshipped him, saying, Lord, have patience with me, and I will pay thee all.	And that servant fell down and worshipped him, and said: My lord, have patience with me, and I will pay thee the whole.	And the servant fell down [and] worshipped him and said, 'My lord, be patient with me and I will repay everything to you.'
27	Then the lord of that servant was moved with compassion, and loosed him, and forgave him the debt.	And his lord had compassion on that servant, and set him free, and forgave him his debt.	And the lord of that servant had compassion and sent him away and forgave him his debt.
28	But the same servant went out, and found one of his fellowservants, which owed him an hundred pence: and he laid hands on him, and took him by the throat, saying, Pay me that thou owest.	Then that servant went out, and found one of his fellowservants who owed him a hundred denarii. And he laid hold of him and choked him, and said to him: Pay me what thou owest me.	Now that servant went out and found one of his fellow-servants, who owed him one hundred denarii, and he grabbed him and was choking him, and said to him, 'Give me that which you owe me.'

Parallel Translations

	KJV	Murdock	Magiera
	MATTHEW *Chapter 18*		
29	And his fellowservant fell down at his feet, and besought him, saying, Have patience with me, and I will pay thee all.	And that fellow-servant fell at his feet and entreated him, and said: Have patience with me, and I will pay thee the whole.	And that [man], his fellow-servant, fell at his feet, begged him and said to him, 'Be patient with me and I will repay you.'
30	And he would not: but went and cast him into prison, till he should pay the debt.	But he would not, but went and cast him into prison, until he should pay him what he owed him.	And he did not want [to], but went [and] threw him into prison, until he would pay him what he owed him.
31	So when his fellowservants saw what was done, they were very sorry, and came and told unto their lord all that was done.	And when their fellow-servants saw what was done, it grieved them much; and they came and made known to their lord all that had occurred.	Now when their fellow-servants saw what had happened, it saddened them very much. And they came [and] made known to their lord all that happened.
32	Then his lord, after that he had called him, said unto him, O thou wicked servant, I forgave thee all that debt, because thou desiredst me:	Then his lord called him, and said to him: Thou vile servant! Lo, I forgave thee that whole debt, because thou entreatedst of me:	Then his lord called him and said to that evil servant, "I forgave you all of the debt because you begged me.
33	Shouldest not thou also have had compassion on thy fellowservant, even as I had pity on thee?	oughtest not thou also to have compassion on thy fellow-servant, as I had compassion on thee?	Was it not proper for you also to have mercy toward your fellow-servant, as I had mercy on you?"
34	And his lord was wroth, and delivered him to the tormentors, till he should pay all that was due unto him.	And his lord was angry, and delivered him over to the torturers, until he should pay all he owed him.	And his lord was angry and delivered him to the torturers, until he would repay everything that he owed him.
35	So likewise shall my heavenly Father do also unto you, if ye from your hearts forgive not every one his brother their trespasses.	So will my Father who is in heaven do to you, unless ye from your heart forgive each his brother his offence.	Likewise my Father who is in heaven will do to you, unless you each forgive his brother his offense from your heart."
	Chapter 19		
1	And it came to pass, that when Jesus had finished these sayings, he departed from Galilee, and came into the coasts of Judaea beyond Jordan;	And when Jesus had ended these discourses, he removed from Galilee, and came to the confines of Judaea on the other side of Jordan.	And it happened that when Jesus finished these words, he started from Galilee and came to the border of Judea on the other side of Jordan.
2	And great multitudes followed him; and he healed them there.	And great multitudes followed after him, and he healed them there.	And large crowds followed him and he healed them there.
3	The Pharisees also came unto him, tempting him, and saying unto him, Is it lawful for a man to put away his wife for every cause?	And Pharisees came to him, and tempted him and said: Is it lawful for a man to divorce his wife for every cause?	And the Pharisees came near to him and were tempting him and saying, "Is it lawful for a man to put away his wife on any occasion?"
4	And he answered and said unto them, Have ye not read, that he which made them at the beginning made them male and female,	And he answered and said to them: Have ye not read, that he who made [them] at the beginning, made them a male and a female?	Now he answered and said to them, "Have you not read that he who made [them] from the beginning made them male and female?"

MATTHEW *Chapter 19*

	KJV	*Murdock*	*Magiera*
5	And said, For this cause shall a man leave father and mother, and shall cleave to his wife: and they twain shall be one flesh?	And he said: For this reason, a man shall leave his father and his mother, and adhere to his wife; and they two shall be one flesh.	And he said, "Because of this, A MAN SHOULD LEAVE HIS FATHER AND HIS MOTHER AND SHOULD CLEAVE TO HIS WIFE AND THE TWO OF THEM WILL BECOME ONE FLESH.
6	Wherefore they are no more twain, but one flesh. What therefore God hath joined together, let not man put asunder.	Wherefore they were not two, but one flesh. What therefore God hath united, let not man sunder.	Therefore, they will not be two, but rather, one flesh. Therefore, that which God has united, man should not separate."
7	They say unto him, Why did Moses then command to give a writing of divorcement, and to put her away?	They say to him: Why then did Moses command to give a bill of divorce, and to put her away?	They said to him, "Why then did Moses command to give a writing of divorce and to dismiss her?"
8	He saith unto them, Moses because of the hardness of your hearts suffered you to put away your wives: but from the beginning it was not so.	He said to them: Moses, on account of the hardness of your heart, permitted you to divorce your wives: but from the beginning it was not so.	He said to them, "Moses, because of the hardness of your heart, allowed you to dismiss your wives. But previously it was not so.
9	And I say unto you, Whosoever shall put away his wife, except it be for fornication, and shall marry another, committeth adultery: and whoso marrieth her which is put away doth commit adultery.	And I say to you, That whoever leaveth his wife not being an adulteress, and taketh another, committeth adultery. And whoever taketh her that is divorced, committeth adultery.	But I say to you, he who forsakes his wife, except [for] adultery, and takes another, commits adultery. And he who takes a forsaken woman commits adultery."
10	His disciples say unto him, If the case of the man be so with his wife, it is not good to marry.	His disciples say to him: If such is the case between man and wife, it is not expedient to take a wife.	His disciples said to him, "If such is the case between husband and wife, it is not advantageous to take a wife."
11	But he said unto them, All men cannot receive this saying, save they to whom it is given.	But he said to them: Not every one is capable of that thing, but he only to whom it is given.	But he said to them, "Not every man is fit for this arrangement, except he to whom it is given.
12	For there are some eunuchs, which were so born from their mother's womb: and there are some eunuchs, which were made eunuchs of men: and there be eunuchs, which have made themselves eunuchs for the kingdom of heaven's sake. He that is able to receive it, let him receive it.	For there are some eunuchs, born so from their mother's womb; and there are some eunuchs, who were made eunuchs by men; and there are some eunuchs who have made themselves eunuchs for the sake of the kingdom of heaven. He that can be contented let him be contented.	For there are believers who were born so from the womb of their mother and there are believers who became believers by men and there are believers who made themselves believers for the sake of the kingdom of heaven. He who is able to understand should understand."
13	Then were there brought unto him little children, that he should put his hands on them, and pray: and the disciples rebuked them.	Then they brought children to him, that he might lay his hand upon them and pray. And his disciples rebuked them.	Then children came near to him that he would lay his hand on them and pray. And his disciples berated them.
14	But Jesus said, Suffer little children, and forbid them not, to come unto me: for of such is the kingdom of heaven.	But Jesus said to them: Allow children to come to me, and forbid them not; for of those that are like them is the kingdom of heaven.	But Jesus said to them, "Allow the children [to] come to me and do not hinder them. For of those who are like these is the kingdom of heaven."
15	And he laid his hands on them, and departed thence.	And he laid his hand upon them, and departed from there.	And he laid his hand on them and went away from there.

Parallel Translations

	KJV	*Murdock*	*Magiera*
	MATTHEW *Chapter 19*		
16	And, behold, one came and said unto him, Good Master, what good thing shall I do, that I may have eternal life?	And one came, drew near, and said to him: Good Teacher, what good thing must I do, that eternal life may be mine?	And a certain [man] came [and] approached and said to him, "Good teacher, what good [thing] should I do that I might have eternal life?"
17	And he said unto him, Why callest thou me good? there is none good but one, that is, God: but if thou wilt enter into life, keep the commandments.	And he said to him: Why callest thou me good? There is none good, except one, [namely,] God. But if thou wouldst enter into life, keep the commandments.	Now he said to him, "Why do you call me good? There is no good [one], except one, God. Now if you want to enter life, keep the commandments."
18	He saith unto him, Which? Jesus said, Thou shalt do no murder, Thou shalt not commit adultery, Thou shalt not steal, Thou shalt not bear false witness,	He said to him, Which? And Jesus said to him: Thou shalt not kill; and thou shalt not commit adultery; and thou shalt not steal; and thou shalt not bear false testimony;	He said to him, "Which [ones]?" And Jesus said to him, "DO NOT KILL and DO NOT COMMIT ADULTERY and DO NOT STEAL and DO NOT GIVE FALSE TESTIMONY.
19	Honour thy father and thy mother: and, Thou shalt love thy neighbour as thyself.	and honor thy father and thy mother; and thou shalt love thy neighbor as thyself.	And HONOR YOUR FATHER AND YOUR MOTHER and LOVE YOUR NEIGHBOR AS YOURSELF."
20	The young man saith unto him, All these things have I kept from my youth up: what lack I yet?	The young man saith to him: All these have I kept from my childhood. What do I lack?	That young man said to him, "All these [things] I have kept from my youth. What do I lack?'
21	Jesus said unto him, If thou wilt be perfect, go and sell that thou hast, and give to the poor, and thou shalt have treasure in heaven: and come and follow me.	Jesus saith to him: If thou desirest to be perfect, go, sell thy property, and give to the poor; and there shall be for thee a treasure in heaven; and come thou after me.	Jesus said to him, "If you want to be mature, go, sell your possessions and give [them] to the poor and you will have treasure in heaven and follow me."
22	But when the young man heard that saying, he went away sorrowful: for he had great possessions.	And the young man heard that speech, and he went away in sadness; for he had much property.	And that young man heard this word and went away, feeling sorry for himself, for he had many possessions.
23	Then said Jesus unto his disciples, Verily I say unto you, That a rich man shall hardly enter into the kingdom of heaven.	And Jesus said to his disciples: Verily I say to you, it is difficult for a rich man to enter into the kingdom of heaven.	Now Jesus said to his disciples, "Truly I say to you, it is difficult for a rich man to enter into the kingdom of heaven.
24	And again I say unto you, It is easier for a camel to go through the eye of a needle, than for a rich man to enter into the kingdom of God.	And again, I say to you: It is easier for a camel to enter the aperture of a needle, than for a rich man to enter the kingdom of God	And again I say to you, it is easier for a camel to enter into the eye of a needle than [for] a rich man to enter into the kingdom of God."
25	When his disciples heard it, they were exceedingly amazed, saying, Who then can be saved?	And when the disciples heard [it], they wondered greatly, and said: Who then can attain to life!	And when the disciples heard [him], they were very amazed and said, "Who is indeed able to [gain] life?"
26	But Jesus beheld them, and said unto them, With men this is impossible; but with God all things are possible.	Jesus looked on them, and said to them: With men this is not practicable, but with God every thing is practicable.	Jesus looked at them and said to them, "With men, this is not possible, but with God everything is possible."

Parallel Translations

	KJV	Murdock	Magiera

MATTHEW Chapter 19

	KJV	Murdock	Magiera
27	Then answered Peter and said unto him, Behold, we have forsaken all, and followed thee; what shall we have therefore?	Then answered Cephas, and said to him: Lo, we have forsaken every thing, and come after thee: What therefore shall we receive?	Then answered Peter and said to him, "Behold, we have left everything and have followed you. What indeed will we have?"
28	And Jesus said unto them, Verily I say unto you, That ye which have followed me, in the regeneration when the Son of man shall sit in the throne of his glory, ye also shall sit upon twelve thrones, judging the twelve tribes of Israel.	Jesus said to them: Verily I say to you, that, as for you who have followed me, when the Son of man shall sit on the throne of his glory in the new world, ye also shall sit on twelve seats, and shall judge the twelve tribes of Israel.	Jesus said to them, "Truly I say you, you who have followed me, when the Son of Man sits on the throne of his glory in the new age, you will also sit on twelve seats of state. And you will judge the twelve tribes of Israel.
29	And every one that hath forsaken houses, or brethren, or sisters, or father, or mother, or wife, or children, or lands, for my name's sake, shall receive an hundredfold, and shall inherit everlasting life.	And every man that relinquisheth houses, or brothers or sisters, or father or mother, or wife or children, or lands, for my name's sake, shall receive an hundredfold, and shall inherit eternal life.	And everyone who has left houses or brothers or sisters or father or mother or wife or children or fields on account of my name will receive one hundred[fold] and will inherit eternal life.
30	But many that are first shall be last; and the last shall be first.	But there are many first who shall be last, and last [who shall be] first.	But many [are] first, who will be last, and [many are] last, [who will be] first.

Chapter 20

	KJV	Murdock	Magiera
1	For the kingdom of heaven is like unto a man that is an householder, which went out early in the morning to hire labourers into his vineyard.	For the kingdom of heaven is like a man, the lord of a house, who went out, at dawn of day, to hire laborers for his vineyard.	For the kingdom of heaven is compared to a man, the lord of a house, who went out in the morning to hire laborers for his vineyard.
2	And when he had agreed with the labourers for a penny a day, he sent them into his vineyard.	And he contracted with the labors for a denarius a day: and sent them into his vineyard.	And he made an agreement with the laborers for a denarius per day. And he sent them to his vineyard.
3	And he went out about the third hour, and saw others standing idle in the marketplace,	And he went out at the third hour, and saw others standing idle in the market-place:	And he went out in the third hour and saw others who were standing in the marketplace and were idle.
4	And said unto them; Go ye also into the vineyard, and whatsoever is right I will give you. And they went their way.	and he said to them, Go ye also into my vineyard, and what is right I will give you;	And he said to them, 'Go also to the vineyard and I will give to you whatever is right.'
5	Again he went out about the sixth and ninth hour, and did likewise.	and they went. And again he went out at the sixth and ninth hours, and did the same.	And they went away. And again he came out in the sixth and in the ninth hour and did the same.
6	And about the eleventh hour he went out, and found others standing idle, and saith unto them, Why stand ye here all the day idle?	And about the eleventh hour, he went out and found others who were standing and idle; and he said to them: Why stand ye all the day, and are idle?	And toward the eleventh hour, he went out and found others who were standing and were idle. And he said to them, 'Why are you standing all day and are idle?'
7	They say unto him, Because no man hath hired us. He saith unto them, Go ye also into the vineyard; and whatsoever is right, that shall ye receive.	They say to him, Because no one hath hired us. He saith to them: Go ye also into the vineyard; and what is right ye shall receive.	They said to him, 'No man has hired us.' He said to them, 'Go also to the vineyard and you will receive whatever is right.'

MATTHEW *Chapter 20*

	KJV	Murdock	Magiera
8	So when even was come, the lord of the vineyard saith unto his steward, Call the labourers, and give them their hire, beginning from the last unto the first.	And when it was evening, the lord of the vineyard said to his steward: Call the laborers, and give them their wages; and commence with the last, and proceed to the first.	Now when it was evening, the lord of the vineyard said to his steward, 'Call the laborers and give them their wage and begin from the last and [proceed] up to the first.'
9	And when they came that were hired about the eleventh hour, they received every man a penny.	And those of the eleventh hour came, and received each a denarius.	And those of the eleventh hour came [and] each received a denarius.
10	But when the first came, they supposed that they should have received more; and they likewise received every man a penny.	And when the first came, they supposed they should receive more; but they also received each a denarius.	And when the first came, they thought that they would receive more. And they each received a denarius also.
11	And when they had received it, they murmured against the goodman of the house,	And when they received [it], they murmured against the lord of the house,	And when they received [it], they murmured against the lord of the house.
12	Saying, These last have wrought but one hour, and thou hast made them equal unto us, which have borne the burden and heat of the day.	and said: These last have labored but one hour, and thou hast made them equal with us who have borne the burden of the day and the heat of it.	And they said, 'These last [ones] worked one hour and you made them equal with us who bore the burden of the day and its heat.'
13	But he answered one of them, and said, Friend, I do thee no wrong: didst not thou agree with me for a penny?	But he answered, and said to one of them: My friend, I do thee no injustice: was it not for a denarius that thou didst contract with me?	Now he answered and said to one of them, 'My friend, I did not wrong you. Did you not agree with me for a denarius?
14	Take that thine is, and go thy way: I will give unto this last, even as unto thee.	Take what belongeth to thee, and go: for I am disposed to give to this last, as to thee.	Take your own and go. But I desire to give to this last [one] as to you.
15	Is it not lawful for me to do what I will with mine own? Is thine eye evil, because I am good?	Is it not lawful for me, to do what I please with what belongeth to me; or is thy eye evil, because I am good?	Or is it not lawful for me to do with my own what I want? Or is your eye evil because I am good?
16	So the last shall be first, and the first last: for many be called, but few chosen.	Thus the last shall be first, and the first last: for the called are many, but the chosen are few.	So the last will be first and the first last. For many are called and few chosen."
17	And Jesus going up to Jerusalem took the twelve disciples apart in the way, and said unto them,	And Jesus was about to go up to Jerusalem: and he took his twelve disciples aside, on the way, and said to them:	And Jesus was about to go up to Jerusalem. And he took [aside] his twelve disciples privately on the journey and said to them,
18	Behold, we go up to Jerusalem; and the Son of man shall be betrayed unto the chief priests and unto the scribes, and they shall condemn him to death,	Behold we are going to Jerusalem; and the Son of man will be delivered up to the chief priests and to the Scribes, and they will condemn him to death.	"Behold, we are going up to Jerusalem and the Son of Man will be delivered to the chief priests and to the scribes and they will condemn him to death.
19	And shall deliver him to the Gentiles to mock, and to scourge, and to crucify him: and the third day he shall rise again.	And they will deliver him over to the Gentiles: and they will mock him, and will scourge him, and will crucify him; and the third day, he will arise.	And they will deliver him to the Gentiles and they will mock him and they will beat him and they will crucify him and on the third day, he will rise up."
20	Then came to him the mother of Zebedee's children with her sons, worshipping him, and desiring a certain thing of him.	Then came, to him the mother of Zebedee's children, she and her sons; and she worshipped him, and asked something from him.	Then the mother of the sons of Zebedee came to him, she and her sons. And she worshipped him and was asking him something.

	KJV	Murdock	Magiera
	MATTHEW *Chapter 20*		
21	And he said unto her, What wilt thou? She saith unto him, Grant that these my two sons may sit, the one on thy right hand, and the other on the left, in thy kingdom.	And he said to her, What desirest thou? She said to him: Say, that these my two sons shall sit, the one on thy right hand and the other on thy left, in thy kingdom.	Now he said to her, "What do you want?" She said to him, "Say that these, my two sons, will sit one on your right and one on your left in your kingdom."
22	But Jesus answered and said, Ye know not what ye ask. Are ye able to drink of the cup that I shall drink of, and to be baptized with the baptism that I am baptized with? They say unto him, We are able.	Jesus answered and said: Ye know not what ye ask for. Can ye drink of the cup, of which I am to drink? or be baptized with the baptism, that I am baptized with? They say to him: We can.	Jesus answered and said, "You do not know what you ask. Are you able to drink the cup that I am about to drink or to be baptized [with] the baptism [with] which I [will be] baptized?" They said to him, "We are able."
23	And he saith unto them, Ye shall drink indeed of my cup, and be baptized with the baptism that I am baptized with: but to sit on my right hand, and on my left, is not mine to give, but it shall be given to them for whom it is prepared of my Father.	He saith to them: Ye will [indeed] drink of my cup, and will be baptized with the baptism that I am baptized with: but that ye should sit on my right hand and on my left, is not mine to give, except to those for whom it is prepared by my Father.	He said to them, "You will drink my cup and be baptized [with] the baptism [with] which I [will be] baptized. But that you should sit at my right and at my left is not mine to give, except to those [for] whom it is prepared by my Father."
24	And when the ten heard it, they were moved with indignation against the two brethren.	And when the ten heard [it], they were angry against the two brothers.	And when the ten heard [of this], they were angry at those two brothers.
25	But Jesus called them unto him, and said, Ye know that the princes of the Gentiles exercise dominion over them, and they that are great exercise authority upon them.	And Jesus called them, and said to them: Ye know that the princes of the nations are their lords, and their great men exercise authority over them.	And Jesus called them and said to them, "You know that the rulers of the Gentiles are their lords and their nobles are in authority over them.
26	But it shall not be so among you: but whosoever will be great among you, let him be your minister;	Not so shall it be among you. But whoever among you desireth to be great, let him be to you, a ministerer:	It should not be so among you. But rather, whoever among you wants to be great should be a minister to you.
27	And whosoever will be chief among you, let him be your servant:	and whoever among you desireth to be first, let him be your servant:	And whoever among you wants to be first should be a servant to you,
28	Even as the Son of man came not to be ministered unto, but to minister, and to give his life a ransom for many.	even as the Son of man came, not to be served, but to serve; and to give his life a ransom for many.	even as the Son of Man did not come to be served, but to serve and to give himself [as] a payment on behalf of many."
29	And as they departed from Jericho, a great multitude followed him.	And as Jesus passed out of Jericho, a great multitude followed him.	And when Jesus went out of Jericho, a large crowd was following him.
30	And, behold, two blind men sitting by the way side, when they heard that Jesus passed by, cried out, saying, Have mercy on us, O Lord, thou Son of David.	And lo, two blind men were sitting by the way side. And when they heard that Jesus was passing, they called out, and said: Have compassion on us, my Lord, thou son of David!	And behold, two blind men were sitting on the side of the road. And when they heard that Jesus passed by, they gave a cry and said, "Have compassion on us, my Lord, Son of David."

	KJV	Murdock	Magiera
	MATTHEW *Chapter 20*		
31	And the multitude rebuked them, because they should hold their peace: but they cried the more, saying, Have mercy on us, O Lord, thou Son of David.	And the multitudes rebuked them, that they might be silent. But they raised their voice the more, and said: Our Lord, have compassion on us, thou son of David.	But the crowds were admonishing them to be quiet. And they raised their voice more and said, "Our Lord, have compassion on us, Son of David."
32	And Jesus stood still, and called them, and said, What will ye that I shall do unto you?	And Jesus stopped, and called them, and said: What wish ye, that I should do for you?	And Jesus stopped and called them and said, "What do you want me to do for you?"
33	They say unto him, Lord, that our eyes may be opened.	They said to him: Our Lord, that our eyes may be opened.	They said to him, "Our Lord, that our eyes be opened."
34	So Jesus had compassion on them, and touched their eyes: and immediately their eyes received sight, and they followed him.	And he had compassion on them, and touched their eyes: and immediately their eyes were opened, and they followed him.	And Jesus had compassion on them and touched their eyes and immediately their eyes were opened and they followed him.
	Chapter 21		
1	And when they drew nigh unto Jerusalem, and were come to Bethphage, unto the mount of Olives, then sent Jesus two disciples,	And as he approached Jerusalem, and came to Bethphage, by the side of the mount of Olives, Jesus sent two of his disciples;	And when he came near to Jerusalem and came to Bethphage by the side of the Mount of Olives, Jesus sent two of his disciples
2	Saying unto them, Go into the village over against you, and straightway ye shall find an ass tied, and a colt with her: loose them, and bring them unto me.	and said to them: Go into this village which is over against you, and directly ye will find an ass tied, and a colt with her. Untie and bring [them] to me.	and said to them, "Go to this village that is opposite you and immediately you will find a donkey that is tied and a colt with her. Loose [them and] bring [them] to me.
3	And if any man say ought unto you, ye shall say, The Lord hath need of them; and straightway he will send them.	And if any man say ought to you, tell him, That they are needed by our Lord: and at once he will send them hither.	And if anyone says anything to you, say to him that they are needed for our Lord. And immediately he will send them here."
4	All this was done, that it might be fulfilled which was spoken by the prophet, saying,	Now this whole occurrence was, that so might be fulfilled that which was spoken by the prophet, saying:	Now this which happened [was] so that what was spoken by way of the prophet would be fulfilled, who said:
5	Tell ye the daughter of Sion, Behold, thy King cometh unto thee, meek, and sitting upon an ass, and a colt the foal of an ass.	Tell ye the daughter of Sion, Behold, thy king cometh to thee, meek, and riding on an ass, and on a colt the foal of an ass.	SAY TO THE DAUGHTER OF ZION, BEHOLD, YOUR KING COMES TO YOU MEEK AND MOUNTED ON A DONKEY AND ON A COLT, THE FOAL OF A DONKEY.
6	And the disciples went, and did as Jesus commanded them,	And the disciples went, and did as Jesus commanded them.	And the disciples went and did as Jesus had commanded them.
7	And brought the ass, and the colt, and put on them their clothes, and they set him thereon.	And they brought the ass and the colt. And they placed their garments on the colt, and set Jesus upon it.	And they brought the donkey and the colt and placed their garments on the colt and Jesus mounted it.

Parallel Translations

MATTHEW *Chapter 21*

	KJV	*Murdock*	*Magiera*
8	And a very great multitude spread their garments in the way; others cut down branches from the trees, and strawed them in the way.	And a very great throng strewed their clothes in the path; and others cut branches from the trees, and cast them in the path.	And a large number of crowds were spreading out their clothes in the road. And others were cutting branches from the trees and throwing [them] on the road.
9	And the multitudes that went before, and that followed, cried, saying, Hosanna to the Son of David: Blessed is he that cometh in the name of the Lord; Hosanna in the highest.	And the multitudes that went before him, and that followed after him, shouted and said: Hosanna to the son of David: Blessed is he that cometh in the name of the Lord: Hosanna in the highest.	And the crowds, who were going before him and were following him, were crying out and saying: HOSANNA TO THE SON OF DAVID. BLESSED IS HE WHO COMES IN THE NAME OF THE LORD. HOSANNA IN THE HIGHEST!
10	And when he was come into Jerusalem, all the city was moved, saying, Who is this?	And as he entered Jerusalem, the whole city was in commotion; and they said, Who is this?	And when he entered Jerusalem, the entire city was in turmoil. And they were saying, "Who is this [man]?"
11	And the multitude said, This is Jesus the prophet of Nazareth of Galilee.	And the multitudes said, This is Jesus the prophet, who is from Nazareth of Galilee.	And the crowds were saying, "This is Jesus, the prophet, who is from Nazareth of Galilee."
12	And Jesus went into the temple of God, and cast out all them that sold and bought in the temple, and overthrew the tables of the moneychangers, and the seats of them that sold doves,	And Jesus entered into the temple of God, and expelled all them that bought and sold in the temple, and overset the counters of the money-brokers, and the seats of them that sold doves.	And Jesus entered the temple of God and threw out all who were buying and selling in the temple. And he overturned the tables of the moneychangers and the chairs of those who were selling doves.
13	And said unto them, It is written, My house shall be called the house of prayer; but ye have made it a den of thieves.	And he said to them: It is written, my house shall be called the house of prayer; but ye have made it a den of robbers.	And he said to them, "It is written: MY HOUSE WILL BE CALLED A HOUSE OF PRAYER. But you have made it a den of thieves."
14	And the blind and the lame came to him in the temple; and he healed them.	And there came to him in the temple the blind and the lame; and he healed them.	And the blind and lame came near to him in the temple and he healed them.
15	And when the chief priests and scribes saw the wonderful things that he did, and the children crying in the temple, and saying, Hosanna to the Son of David; they were sore displeased,	And when the chief priests and Pharisees saw the wonderful things which he performed, and the children shouting in the temple and saying, Hosanna to the son of David, their indignation was excited.	Now when the chief priests and the Pharisees saw the wonders that he did and the children who were crying out in the temple and saying, "Hosanna to the Son of David," they were displeased.
16	And said unto him, Hearest thou what these say? And Jesus saith unto them, Yea; have ye never read, Out of the mouth of babes and sucklings thou hast perfected praise?	And they said to him: Hearest thou what these are saying? Jesus said to them: Yes. Have ye never read, Out of the mouth of children and infants thou hast acquired praise?	And they said to him, "Do you hear what these are saying?" Jesus said to them, "Yes. Have you never read: FROM THE MOUTH OF CHILDREN AND INFANTS YOU HAVE FASHIONED PRAISE?"
17	And he left them, and went out of the city into Bethany; and he lodged there.	And he left them, and retired out of the city to Bethany, and lodged there.	And he left them and went away outside of the city to Bethany and lodged there.

Parallel Translations

MATTHEW Chapter 21

	KJV	Murdock	Magiera
18	Now in the morning as he returned into the city, he hungered.	And in the morning, when he returned to the city, he was hungry.	Now in the morning when he returned to the city, he was hungry.
19	And when he saw a fig tree in the way, he came to it, and found nothing thereon, but leaves only, and said unto it, Let no fruit grow on thee henceforward for ever. And presently the fig tree withered away.	And he saw a fig-tree by the way, and came to it and found nothing on it, except leaves only. And he said to it: There shall no more be fruit on thee for ever. And immediately the fig-tree withered.	And he saw a certain fig tree by the road and came to it. And he did not find anything on it, except leaves only. And he said to it, "There will not be fruit on you again forever." And immediately that fig tree dried up.
20	And when the disciples saw it, they marvelled, saying, How soon is the fig tree withered away!	And the disciples saw [it], and admired, and said: How suddenly hath the fig-tree withered!	And the disciples saw and marveled and said, "How quickly the fig tree dried up!"
21	Jesus answered and said unto them, Verily I say unto you, If ye have faith, and doubt not, ye shall not only do this which is done to the fig tree, but also if ye shall say unto this mountain, Be thou removed, and be thou cast into the sea; it shall be done.	Jesus replied and said to them: Verily I say to you, That if there be faith in you, and ye shall not doubt, ye may not only do this thing of the fig-tree, but also if ye shall say to this mountain, be thou lifted up, and fall into the sea, it will be so.	Jesus answered and said to them, "Truly I say to you, if you have faith and do not doubt, not only will you do this [miracle] of the fig, but even if you say to this mountain, 'Be removed and fall into the sea,' it will happen.
22	And all things, whatsoever ye shall ask in prayer, believing, ye shall receive.	And whatsoever ye shall ask in prayer, and shall believe, ye shall receive.	And everything that you ask for in prayer and believe, you will receive."
23	And when he was come into the temple, the chief priests and the elders of the people came unto him as he was teaching, and said, By what authority doest thou these things? and who gave thee this authority?	And when Jesus came to the temple, the chief priests and the Elders of the people came to him as he was teaching, and said to him: By what authority doest thou these things? And who gave thee this authority?	And when Jesus came to the temple, the chief priests and the elders of the people came near to him while he was teaching and said to him, "By what authority do you do these [things]? And who gave you this authority?"
24	And Jesus answered and said unto them, I also will ask you one thing, which if ye tell me, I in like wise will tell you by what authority I do these things.	Jesus replied and said to them: I also will ask you one question, and if ye will tell me, I also will tell you by what authority I do these things.	Jesus answered and said to them, "I will ask you also a certain question and if you answer me, I will also tell you by what authority I do these [things].
25	The baptism of John, whence was it? from heaven, or of men? And they reasoned with themselves, saying, If we shall say, From heaven; he will say unto us, Why did ye not then believe him?	The baptism of John, from whence was it? From heaven, or from men? And they reasoned among themselves, and said: If we should say, From heaven; he will say to us, Why did ye not believe in him?	The baptism of John, from where is it? Is it from heaven or from men?" Now they were reasoning among themselves and said, "If we say from heaven, he will say to us, 'Why did you not believe him?'
26	But if we shall say, Of men; we fear the people; for all hold John as a prophet.	And if we should say, From men; we are afraid of the multitude, for they all hold John as a prophet.	And [if] we say from men, we are afraid of the crowd, for all of them regarded John as a prophet."
27	And they answered Jesus, and said, We cannot tell. And he said unto them, Neither tell I you by what authority I do these things.	And they answered, and said to him: We do not know. Jesus said to them: Neither do I tell you by what authority I do these things.	They answered and said to him, "We do not know." Jesus said to them, "Neither will I tell you by what authority I do these [things].

Parallel Translations

	KJV	Murdock	Magiera
	MATTHEW *Chapter 21*		
28	But what think ye? A certain man had two sons; and he came to the first, and said, Son, go work to day in my vineyard.	But how appeareth it to you? A certain man had two sons; and he came to the first and said to him, My son, go, labor to-day in the vineyard.	But what does it seem to you? A certain man had two sons. And he came near to the first and said to him, 'My son, go today [and] work in the vineyard.'
29	He answered and said, I will not: but afterward he repented, and went.	And he answered and said, I am not willing. But afterwards he repented and went.	Now he answered and said, 'I do not want to.' But later, he regretted [it] and went.
30	And he came to the second, and said likewise. And he answered and said, I go, sir: and went not.	And he came to the other, and said the same to him. And he answered and said: I [go], my lord, but did not go.	And he came near to the other and said to him the same. Now he answered and said, 'I am [going], my lord,' and did not go.
31	Whether of them twain did the will of his father? They say unto him, The first. Jesus saith unto them, Verily I say unto you, That the publicans and the harlots go into the kingdom of God before you.	Which of these two performed the pleasure of his father? They say to him, The first. Jesus said to them: Verily I say to you That publicans and harlots go before you into the kingdom of God.	Which of these two did the will of his father?" They said to him, "That first [son]." Jesus said to them, "Truly I say to you, tax collectors and harlots will precede you in the kingdom of God.
32	For John came unto you in the way of righteousness, and ye believed him not: but the publicans and the harlots believed him: and ye, when ye had seen it, repented not afterward, that ye might believe him.	For John came to you in the way of righteousness, and ye believed him not; but the publicans and harlots believed him: and ye, after ye had seen [it], did not even then repent and believe in him.	For John came to you in the way of uprightness and you did not believe him. But the tax collectors and harlots believed him. But not even when you saw [him], did you finally repent that you might believe in him.
33	Hear another parable: There was a certain householder, which planted a vineyard, and hedged it round about, and digged a winepress in it, and built a tower, and let it out to husbandmen, and went into a far country:	Hear ye another similitude. A certain man, the lord of a house, planted a vineyard, and inclosed it with a hedge, and digged in it a wine-press, and built a tower in it, and leased it to cultivators, and removed to a distance.	Hear another parable. A certain man was a lord of a house. And he planted a vineyard. And he set a fence around it and dug a winepress in it. And he built a tower in it and handed it over to laborers and went on a journey.
34	And when the time of the fruit drew near, he sent his servants to the husbandmen, that they might receive the fruits of it.	And when the time for the fruits arrived, he sent his servants to the cultivators that they might remit to him of the fruits of the vineyard.	Now when the time of harvest arrived, he sent his servants to the laborers that they might send [some] of the fruit of his vineyard to him.
35	And the husbandmen took his servants, and beat one, and killed another, and stoned another.	And the cultivators laid hold of his servants, and beat one, and stoned another and one they slew.	Yet the laborers grabbed his servants and some they beat and some they stoned and some they killed.
36	Again, he sent other servants more than the first: and they did unto them likewise.	And again he sent other servants, more numerous than the first; and they did the like to them.	And again he sent other servants, more than the first, and they did the same to them.
37	But last of all he sent unto them his son, saying, They will reverence my son.	And at last he sent to them his son: for he said, Perhaps they will respect my son.	And lastly, he sent them his son, saying, 'Perhaps they will respect my son.'

MATTHEW *Chapter 21*

	KJV	Murdock	Magiera
38	But when the husbandmen saw the son, they said among themselves, This is the heir; come, let us kill him, and let us seize on his inheritance.	But the cultivators, when they saw the son, said among themselves: This is the heir: Come; let us kill him, and retain his inheritance.	But the laborers, when they saw the son, said among themselves, 'This is the heir. Come, let us kill him and obtain his inheritance.'
39	And they caught him, and cast him out of the vineyard, and slew him.	And they laid hold of him, thrust him out of the vineyard, and slew him.	And they grabbed [him and] took him outside of the vineyard and killed him.
40	When the lord therefore of the vineyard cometh, what will he do unto those husbandmen?	When the lord of the vineyard, therefore, shall come; what will he do to those cultivators?	When, therefore, the lord of the vineyard comes, what should he do to those laborers?"
41	They say unto him, He will miserably destroy those wicked men, and will let out his vineyard unto other husbandmen, which shall render him the fruits in their seasons.	They say to him: He will utterly destroy them; and will lease the vineyard to other cultivators, who will render him the fruits in their seasons.	They said to him, "He will utterly destroy them and he will hand over the vineyard to other laborers, those who will give him the fruit in its season."
42	Jesus saith unto them, Did ye never read in the scriptures, The stone which the builders rejected, the same is become the head of the corner: this is the Lord's doing, and it is marvellous in our eyes?	Jesus said to them: Have ye never read in the scripture, The stone which the builders rejected, hath become the head of the corner: this is from the Lord; and it is marvellous in our eyes?	Jesus said to them, "Have you never read in the scripture of THE STONE THAT THE BUILDERS REJECTED? IT HAS BECOME THE HEAD OF THE CORNER. THIS [STONE] CAME FROM THE PRESENCE OF THE LORD AND IT IS A WONDER IN OUR EYES.
43	Therefore say I unto you, The kingdom of God shall be taken from you, and given to a nation bringing forth the fruits thereof.	Therefore I say to you, That the kingdom of God shall be taken from you, and shall be given to a people that will yield fruits.	Because of this, I say to you, the kingdom of God will be taken away from you and be given to a people who bear fruit.
44	And whosoever shall fall on this stone shall be broken: but on whomsoever it shall fall, it will grind him to powder.	And whoever shall fall upon this stone, will be fractured; but on whomsoever it shall fall, it will crush him to atoms?	And whoever falls on this stone will be bruised, and whomever it falls on, it will blow him away [as chaff]."
45	And when the chief priests and Pharisees had heard his parables, they perceived that he spake of them.	And when the chief priests and Pharisees had heard his similitudes, they understood that he spoke in reference to them.	And when the chief priests and Pharisees heard his parables, they knew that he spoke against them.
46	But when they sought to lay hands on him, they feared the multitude, because they took him for a prophet.	And they sought to apprehend him, but were afraid of the multitude, because they accounted him as a prophet.	And they sought to arrest him, yet they were afraid of the crowd, because they regarded him as a prophet.

Chapter 22

	KJV	Murdock	Magiera
1	And Jesus answered and spake unto them again by parables, and said,	And Jesus answered again by similitudes, and said:	And Jesus answered again in parables and said,
2	The kingdom of heaven is like unto a certain king, which made a marriage for his son,	The kingdom of heaven is like to a royal person, who made a feast for his son.	"The kingdom of heaven is compared to a certain king who prepared a wedding feast for his son.

Parallel Translations

MATTHEW *Chapter 22*

	KJV	*Murdock*	*Magiera*
3	And sent forth his servants to call them that were bidden to the wedding: and they would not come.	And he sent his servants to call those that had been invited, to the feast: and they would not come.	And he sent his servants to call the invited [ones] to the wedding feast and they did not want to come.
4	Again, he sent forth other servants, saying, Tell them which are bidden, Behold, I have prepared my dinner: my oxen and my fatlings are killed, and all things are ready: come unto the marriage.	And again he sent other servants, and said: Tell those invited, Behold, my entertainment is prepared, my oxen and my fatlings are slain, and every thing is prepared; come ye to the feast.	Again he sent other servants and told [them] to say to the invited [ones], 'Behold, my feast is prepared and my oxen and my fat [ones] are killed and everything is ready. Come to the wedding feast.'
5	But they made light of it, and went their ways, one to his farm, another to his merchandise:	But they showed contempt, and went away, one to his farm, and another to his merchandise;	But they scorned [the servants] and went away, one to his field and another to his business.
6	And the remnant took his servants, and entreated them spitefully, and slew them.	and the rest seized his servants, and abused them, and slew them.	Now the rest grabbed his servants and disgraced and killed [them].
7	But when the king heard thereof, he was wroth: and he sent forth his armies, and destroyed those murderers, and burned up their city.	And when the king heard [of it], he was angry; and he sent his military forces, and destroyed those murderers, and burned their city.	Now when the king heard [this], he was angry and sent his armies [and] destroyed those murderers and burned their city.
8	Then saith he to his servants, The wedding is ready, but they which were bidden were not worthy.	Then said he to his servants, The feast is prepared, but they who were invited were unworthy.	Then he said to his servants, 'The wedding feast is prepared and those who were invited were not worthy.
9	Go ye therefore into the highways, and as many as ye shall find, bid to the marriage.	Go ye therefore to the terminations of the streets; and as many as ye find, bid to the feast.	Go, therefore, to the limits of the roads and call whomever you find to the wedding feast.'
10	So those servants went out into the highways, and gathered together all as many as they found, both bad and good: and the wedding was furnished with guests.	And those servants went out into the streets, and collected all they found, both bad and good; and the place of feasting was filled with guests.	And those servants went out to the roads and gathered all whom they found, bad and good, and the banquet house was filled with guests.
11	And when the king came in to see the guests, he saw there a man which had not on a wedding garment:	And the king went in to see the guests: and he saw there a man who was not clad in the festal garments.	And the king entered to see the guests. And he saw there a man who was not wearing wedding clothes.
12	And he saith unto him, Friend, how camest thou in hither not having a wedding garment? And he was speechless.	And he said to him: My friend, how camest thou here without the festal robes? But he was silent.	And he said to him, 'My friend, how did you enter this place, having no wedding garments?' And he was speechless.
13	Then said the king to the servants, Bind him hand and foot, and take him away, and cast him into outer darkness; there shall be weeping and gnashing of teeth.	Then said the king to the servitors: Bind his hands and his feet, and cast him into the outer darkness: there will be weeping and gnashing of teeth.	Then said the king to the servers, 'Bind his hands and his feet and throw him into the outer darkness. Crying and gnashing of teeth will be there.
14	For many are called, but few are chosen.	For the called are many, and the chosen are few.	For many are called, yet few chosen."
15	Then went the Pharisees, and took counsel how they might entangle him in his talk.	Then went the Pharisees and took counsel, how they might ensnare him in discourse.	Then the Pharisees went away [and] took counsel how they might trap him with a question.

Parallel Translations

	KJV	*Murdock*	*Magiera*
	MATTHEW *Chapter 22*		
16	And they sent out unto him their disciples with the Herodians, saying, Master, we know that thou art true, and teachest the way of God in truth, neither carest thou for any man: for thou regardest not the person of men.	And they sent to him their disciples, with domestics of Herod, and said to him: Teacher, we know that thou art veracious, and teachest the way of God with truth, regardless of man, for thou hast no respect of persons.	And they sent him their disciples with the Herodians and said to him, "Teacher, we know that you are true and you teach the way of God with truthfulness and you are not moved by anyone, for you are not a respecter of persons.
17	Tell us therefore, What thinkest thou? Is it lawful to give tribute unto Caesar, or not?	Tell us, therefore, how doth it appear to thee: is it lawful to pay capitation money to Caesar, or not?	Tell us, therefore, how does it seem to you? Is it lawful to give the poll tax to Caesar or not?"
18	But Jesus perceived their wickedness, and said, Why tempt ye me, ye hypocrites?	But Jesus knew their wickedness, and said: Why tempt ye me, ye hypocrites?	Now Jesus knew their evil [counsel] and said, "Why do you tempt me? Hypocrites!
19	Shew me the tribute money. And they brought unto him a penny.	Show me a denarius of the capitation money. And they brought to him a denarius.	Show me the denarius of the poll tax." And they brought to him a denarius.
20	And he saith unto them, Whose is this image and superscription?	And Jesus said to them: Whose is this image and inscription?	And Jesus said to them, "Whose is this image and inscription?"
21	They say unto him, Caesar's. Then saith he unto them, Render therefore unto Caesar the things which are Caesar's; and unto God the things that are God's.	They say, Caesar's. He saith to them: Give then Caesar's things to Caesar, and God's things to God.	They said, "Caesar's." He said to them, "Give, therefore, Caesar's to Caesar and God's to God."
22	When they had heard these words, they marvelled, and left him, and went their way.	And when they heard [it] they were surprised: and they left him, and went away.	And when they heard [this], they were amazed and they left him and went away.
23	The same day came to him the Sadducees, which say that there is no resurrection, and asked him,	The same day came Sadducees, and said to him: There is no life of the dead. And they questioned him,	On the same day, the Sadducees came near and said to him, "There is no resurrection of the dead." And they asked him
24	Saying, Master, Moses said, If a man die, having no children, his brother shall marry his wife, and raise up seed unto his brother.	and said to him: Teacher; Moses commanded us, that if a man should die childless, his brother must take his wife and raise up seed to his brother.	and said to him, "Teacher, Moses said to us, IF A MAN DIES WHILE HE HAS NO SONS, HIS BROTHER SHOULD TAKE HIS WIFE AND RAISE UP SEED FOR HIS BROTHER.
25	Now there were with us seven brethren: and the first, when he had married a wife, deceased, and, having no issue, left his wife unto his brother:	Now there were with us seven brothers. The first took a wife, and deceased; and, as he had no children, he left his wife to his brother.	Now there were seven brothers with us. The first took a wife and died and since he had no sons, he left his wife to his brother.
26	Likewise the second also, and the third, unto the seventh.	In like manner also the second, and the third, and up to the whole seven.	Likewise also, the second and also the third, even up to the seventh.
27	And last of all the woman died also.	And after them all, the woman also herself died.	Now finally, all of them died [and] the woman also.
28	Therefore in the resurrection whose wife shall she be of the seven? for they all had her.	In the resurrection, therefore, to which of those seven will she be the wife? For they all had taken her?	In the resurrection, therefore, to which of those seven [brothers] will she be a wife? For all of them married her."

Parallel Translations

	KJV	Murdock	Magiera

MATTHEW *Chapter 22*

	KJV	Murdock	Magiera
29	Jesus answered and said unto them, Ye do err, not knowing the scriptures, nor the power of God.	Jesus answered, and said to them: Ye do err, from not knowing the scriptures, nor the power of God.	Jesus answered and said to them, "You err, because you do not know the scriptures nor the power of God.
30	For in the resurrection they neither marry, nor are given in marriage, but are as the angels of God in heaven.	For in the resurrection of the dead, they do not take wives, nor are wives given to husbands; but they are as the angels of God in heaven.	For in the resurrection of the dead, [men] do not marry women, nor are women [given] to husbands, but they are as the angels of God in heaven.
31	But as touching the resurrection of the dead, have ye not read that which was spoken unto you by God, saying,	But as to the resurrection of the dead,: have ye not read what was spoken to you by God, who said:	Now concerning the resurrection of the dead, have you not read that which was spoken to you by God, who said:
32	I am the God of Abraham, and the God of Isaac, and the God of Jacob? God is not the God of the dead, but of the living.	I am the God of Abraham, the God of Isaac, the God of Jacob? Now he is not the God of the dead, but of the living.	I AM THE GOD OF ABRAHAM, THE GOD OF ISAAC, [AND] THE GOD OF JACOB? And he is not the God of the dead, but of the living."
33	And when the multitude heard this, they were astonished at his doctrine.	And when the multitude heard [it] they were astonished at his doctrine.	And when the crowds heard [this], they were amazed by his teaching.
34	But when the Pharisees had heard that he had put the Sadducees to silence, they were gathered together.	And when the Pharisees heard that he had put the Sadducees to silence, they assembled together;	Now when the Pharisees heard that he had silenced the Sadducees, they assembled together.
35	Then one of them, which was a lawyer, asked him a question, tempting him, and saying,	and one of them, who was expert in the law, to tempt him, inquired:	And one of them who knew the law asked, tempting him,
36	Master, which is the great commandment in the law?	Teacher, which is the great command in the law?	"Teacher, what commandment is great in the law?"
37	Jesus said unto him, Thou shalt love the Lord thy God with all thy heart, and with all thy soul, and with all thy mind.	Jesus said to him: Thou shalt love the Lord thy God, with all thy heart, and with all thy soul, and with all thy might, and with all thy mind.	And Jesus said to him, "YOU SHOULD LOVE THE LORD YOUR GOD WITH ALL YOUR HEART AND WITH ALL YOUR SOUL AND WITH ALL YOUR STRENGTH AND WITH ALL YOUR MIND.
38	This is the first and great commandment.	This is the great and first command.	This is the great and first commandment.
39	And the second is like unto it, Thou shalt love thy neighbour as thyself.	And the second, which is like it, is, Thou shalt love thy neighbor as thyself.	And the second is like it: YOU SHOULD LOVE YOUR NEIGHBOR AS YOURSELF.
40	On these two commandments hang all the law and the prophets.	On these two commands hang the law and the prophets.	On these two commandments suspend the law and the prophets."
41	While the Pharisees were gathered together, Jesus asked them,	And while the Pharisees were assembled, Jesus questioned them,	Now while the Pharisees were assembled, Jesus asked them
42	Saying, What think ye of Christ? whose son is he? They say unto him, The Son of David.	and said: What say ye respecting, the Messiah? Whose son is he? They say to him; The son of David.	and said, "What do you say about the Messiah? Whose son is he?" They said to him, "The Son of David."

Parallel Translations

MATTHEW *Chapter 22*

	KJV	*Murdock*	*Magiera*
43	He saith unto them, How then doth David in spirit call him Lord, saying,	He saith to them: How then doth David, by the Spirit, call him Lord? for he said:	He said to them, "Yet how does David spiritually call him LORD? For he said:
44	The LORD said unto my Lord, Sit thou on my right hand, till I make thine enemies thy footstool?	The Lord said to my Lord, Seat thyself at my right hand, until I place thy enemies under thy feet.	THE LORD SAID TO MY LORD, SIT AT MY RIGHT UNTIL I PLACE YOUR ENEMIES UNDER YOUR FEET.
45	If David then call him Lord, how is he his son?	If David then call him Lord, how is he his son?	Therefore, if David called him 'LORD,' how is he his son?"
46	And no man was able to answer him a word, neither durst any man from that day forth ask him any more questions.	And no one was able to give him an answer? And from that day, no one dared to question him.	And no man was able to give him an answer. And no man dared to question him again from that day [on].

Chapter 23

	KJV	*Murdock*	*Magiera*
1	Then spake Jesus to the multitude, and to his disciples,	Then Jesus conversed with the multitude and with his disciples,	Then Jesus talked with the crowds and with his disciples.
2	Saying, The scribes and the Pharisees sit in Moses' seat:	and said to them: The Scribes and Pharisees sit in the seat of Moses.	And he said to them, "The scribes and the Pharisees sit on the seat of Moses.
3	All therefore whatsoever they bid you observe, that observe and do; but do not ye after their works: for they say, and do not.	Whatever therefore they tell you to observe, that observe and do. But according to their deeds, practise ye not: for they say, and do not.	Everything, therefore, that they say that you should keep, keep and do. But you should not do according to their deeds. For they speak and do not act.
4	For they bind heavy burdens and grievous to be borne, and lay them on men's shoulders; but they themselves will not move them with one of their fingers.	They tie up heavy burdens, and lay [them] on men's shoulders; but will not themselves touch them with their finger.	And they bind heavy burdens and place [them] on the shoulders of men, but do not want to touch them with their finger[s].
5	But all their works they do for to be seen of men: they make broad their phylacteries, and enlarge the borders of their garments,	And all their works they do, to be seen of men: for they make their phylacteries broad, and extend the fringes of their garments.	And they do all of their deeds to be seen by men. For they broaden their phylacteries and lengthen the fringes of their mantles.
6	And love the uppermost rooms at feasts, and the chief seats in the synagogues,	And they love the highest couches at suppers and the highest seats in the synagogues,	And they love the chief places at festivals and the chief seats in the synagogues
7	And greetings in the markets, and to be called of men, Rabbi, Rabbi.	and the greeting in the market places, and to be addressed by men with Rabbi.	and a greeting in the marketplaces and that they are called Rabbi by men.
8	But be not ye called Rabbi: for one is your Master, even Christ; and all ye are brethren.	But be not ye called Rabbi; for one is your Rabbi, and ye are all brethren.	But you should not be called Rabbi. For one is your Rabbi and all of you are brothers.
9	And call no man your father upon the earth: for one is your Father, which is in heaven.	And ye shall not call yourselves Father on earth; for one is your Father, who is in heaven.	And do not call yourselves father on earth. For one is your Father, who is in heaven.
10	Neither be ye called masters: for one is your Master, even Christ.	And be ye not called guides; for one is your Guide, the Messiah.	And you should not be called leaders, because one is your leader, the Messiah.
11	But he that is greatest among you shall be your servant.	And the great one among you will be your servitor.	But he who is great among you should be a minister to you.

Parallel Translations

	KJV	Murdock	Magiera
	MATTHEW *Chapter 23*		
12	And whosoever shall exalt himself shall be abased; and he that shall humble himself shall be exalted.	For whoever shall] exalt himself, will be abased: and whoever shall abase himself, will be exalted.	For he who elevates himself will be humbled and he who humbles himself will be elevated.
13	But woe unto you, scribes and Pharisees, hypocrites! for ye shut up the kingdom of heaven against men: for ye neither go in yourselves, neither suffer ye them that are entering to go in.	Woe to you, Scribes and Pharisees, hypocrites: for ye devour the houses of widows, under the disguise of protracting your prayers. Therefore ye shall receive greater condemnation.	Woe to you, scribes and Pharisees! Hypocrites! Because you consume the houses of widows with the occasion that you would lengthen your prayers. Because of this, you will receive greater judgment.
14	Woe unto you, scribes and Pharisees, hypocrites! for ye devour widows' houses, and for a pretence make long prayer: therefore ye shall receive the greater damnation.	Woe to you. Scribes and Pharisees, hypocrites: for ye hold the kingdom of heaven closed before men; for ye enter not yourselves, and those that would enter ye suffer not to enter.	Woe to you, scribes and Pharisees! Hypocrites! Because you have held the kingdom of heaven closed before men. For you are not entering and those who would enter, you do not allow to enter.
15	Woe unto you, scribes and Pharisees, hypocrites! for ye compass sea and land to make one proselyte, and when he is made, ye make him twofold more the child of hell than yourselves.	Woe to you, Scribes and Pharisees, hypocrites: for ye traverse sea and land to make one proselyte; and when he is gained, ye make him a child of hell twofold more than yourselves.	Woe to you, scribes and Pharisees! Hypocrites! Because you travel over sea and land to make one convert. And when he has become [a convert], you make him the son of Gehenna more than you.
16	Woe unto you, ye blind guides, which say, Whosoever shall swear by the temple, it is nothing; but whosoever shall swear by the gold of the temple, he is a debtor!	Woe to you, ye blind guides: for ye say, Whoever shall swear by the temple, it is nothing; but whoever shall swear by the gold that is in the temple, he is holden.	Woe to you, blind guides! Because you say that whoever swears by the temple, it is nothing. But he who swears by the gold that is in the temple is guilty.
17	Ye fools and blind: for whether is greater, the gold, or the temple that sanctifieth the gold?	Ye fools, and blind: for which is greater, the gold, or the temple that sanctifieth the gold?	[You are] fools and blind! For what is greater, the gold or the temple? Which sanctifies, the gold?
18	And, Whosoever shall swear by the altar, it is nothing; but whosoever sweareth by the gift that is upon it, he is guilty.	And, whoever shall swear by the altar, it is nothing: but whoever shall swear by the oblation upon it, he is holden.	And [you say], whoever swears by the altar, it is nothing. But he who swears by the offering that is on it is guilty.
19	Ye fools and blind: for whether is greater, the gift, or the altar that sanctifieth the gift?	Ye fools, and blind: for which is greater, the oblation, or the altar that sanctifieth the oblation?	[You are] fools and blind! What is greater, the offering or the altar that is sanctified by the offering?
20	Whoso therefore shall swear by the altar, sweareth by it, and by all things thereon.	He therefore who sweareth by the altar, sweareth by it, and by all that is upon it.	Therefore, he who swears by the altar swears by it and by everything that is on it.
21	And whoso shall swear by the temple, sweareth by it, and by him that dwelleth therein.	And he who sweareth by the temple, sweareth by it, and by him that dwelleth in it.	And he who swears by the temple swears by it and by him who dwells in it.
22	And he that shall swear by heaven, sweareth by the throne of God, and by him that sitteth thereon.	And he who sweareth by heaven, sweareth by throne of God, and by him that sitteth on it.	And he who swears by heaven swears by the throne of God and by him who sits on it.

Parallel Translations

	KJV	*Murdock*	*Magiera*
	MATTHEW *Chapter 23*		
23	Woe unto you, scribes and Pharisees, hypocrites! for ye pay tithe of mint and anise and cummin, and have omitted the weightier matters of the law, judgment, mercy, and faith: these ought ye to have done, and not to leave the other undone.	Woe to you, Scribes and Pharisees, hypocrites: for ye tithe mint, and anise, and cummin, and omit the graver [matters] of the law, judgment, and mercy, and fidelity: these ought ye to do, and those not to omit.	Woe to you, scribes and Pharisees! Hypocrites! Because you tithe the mint and dill and cummin and you overlook the more important [things] of the law, judgment and mercy and faith. Now these were necessary for you to have done and you should not have overlooked those.
24	Ye blind guides, which strain at a gnat, and swallow a camel.	Ye blind guides, who strain out gnats, and swallow down camels.	[You are] blind guides, who strain gnats and swallow camels!
25	Woe unto you, scribes and Pharisees, hypocrites! for ye make clean the outside of the cup and of the platter, but within they are full of extortion and excess.	Woe to you, Scribes and Pharisees, hypocrites: for ye cleanse the outside of the cup and the dish, while within they are full of rapine and wickedness.	Woe to you, scribes and Pharisees! Hypocrites! For you cleanse the outside of the cup and of the dish, but inside are full of violence and wickedness.
26	Thou blind Pharisee, cleanse first that which is within the cup and platter, that the outside of them may be clean also.	Ye blind Pharisees, cleanse first the inside of the cup and dish, that their outside may be clean also.	Blind Pharisees! Cleanse first the inside of the cup and of the dish, so that their outside may also be clean.
27	Woe unto you, scribes and Pharisees, hypocrites! for ye are like unto whited sepulchres, which indeed appear beautiful outward, but are within full of dead men's bones, and of all uncleanness.	Woe to you, Scribes and Pharisees, hypocrites: for ye are like whited sepulchres, which appear comely without, but are within full of bones of the dead and all impurity.	Woe to you, scribes and Pharisees! Hypocrites! Because you are like white graves that on the outside appear beautiful, but on the inside are full of the bones of the dead and all corruption.
28	Even so ye also outwardly appear righteous unto men, but within ye are full of hypocrisy and iniquity.	So ye also, outwardly, appear to men as righteous; but within, ye are full of iniquity and hypocrisy.	So also, on the outside you appear to men as just and on the inside you are full of wickedness and hypocrisy.
29	Woe unto you, scribes and Pharisees, hypocrites! because ye build the tombs of the prophets, and garnish the sepulchres of the righteous,	Woe to you, Scribes and Pharisees, hypocrites: for ye build the tombs of the prophets and ye adorn the sepulchres of the righteous;	Woe to you, scribes and Pharisees! Hypocrites! Because you maintain the graves of the prophets and you adorn the tombs of the just [ones]
30	And say, If we had been in the days of our fathers, we would not have been partakers with them in the blood of the prophets.	and ye say: If we had been in the days of our fathers, we would not have been participators with them in the blood of the prophets.	and you say, 'If we had been in the days of our fathers, we would not have been participants with them in the blood of the prophets.'
31	Wherefore ye be witnesses unto yourselves, that ye are the children of them which killed the prophets.	Wherefore ye are witnesses, against yourselves, that ye are the children of them that killed the prophets.	Thereby you witness against yourselves that you are the sons of those who killed the prophets.
32	Fill ye up then the measure of your fathers.	And as for you, fill ye up the measure of your fathers.	And you also fill up the measure of your fathers.
33	Ye serpents, ye generation of vipers, how can ye escape the damnation of hell?	Ye serpents, ye race of vipers: how can ye escape the condemnation of hell?	[You] snakes! Offspring of vipers! How will you flee from the judgment of Gehenna?

MATTHEW *Chapter 23*

	KJV	Murdock	Magiera
34	Wherefore, behold, I send unto you prophets, and wise men, and scribes: and some of them ye shall kill and crucify; and some of them shall ye scourge in your synagogues, and persecute them from city to city:	Wherefore, behold, I send unto you prophets, and wise men, and scribes; some of whom ye will kill and crucify, and some of them ye will scourge in your synagogues, and will persecute them from city to city:	Because of this, behold, I send to you prophets and wise men and scribes. Some of them you will kill and you will crucify and some of them you will beat in your synagogues and you will pursue them from city to city,
35	That upon you may come all the righteous blood shed upon the earth, from the blood of righteous Abel unto the blood of Zacharias son of Barachias, whom ye slew between the temple and the altar.	so that on you may come all the blood of the righteous, which hath been shed on the earth, from the blood of righteous Abel unto the blood of Zachariah, son of Barachiah, whom ye slew between the temple and the altar.	so that all the blood of the just [ones] that has been shed on the earth will come on you, from the blood of Abel the just up to the blood of Zechariah, the son of Barachiah, whom you killed between the temple [and] the altar.
36	Verily I say unto you, All these things shall come upon this generation.	Verily I say to you, that all these things will come upon this generation.	Truly I say to you, all these [things] will come on this generation.
37	O Jerusalem, Jerusalem, thou that killest the prophets, and stonest them which are sent unto thee, how often would I have gathered thy children together, even as a hen gathereth her chickens under her wings, and ye would not!	O Jerusalem, Jerusalem, who killest the prophets, and stonest them that are sent to thee: how often would I have gathered thy children, as a hen gathereth her young under her wings, and ye would not.	Jerusalem, Jerusalem, you have killed the prophets and you have stoned those who were sent to her. How many times have I wanted to gather your sons like a hen gathers her chicks under her wings and you did not want [to be gathered]?
38	Behold, your house is left unto you desolate.	Behold, your house is left to you desolate!	Behold, your house is left to you desolate.
39	For I say unto you, Ye shall not see me henceforth, till ye shall say, Blessed is he that cometh in the name of the Lord.	For I say to you, That ye shall not see me henceforth, until ye shall say: Blessed is he that cometh in the name of the Lord.	For I say to you, you will not see me from now until you say, BLESSED IS HE WHO COMES IN THE NAME OF THE LORD."

Chapter 24

	KJV	Murdock	Magiera
1	And Jesus went out, and departed from the temple: and his disciples came to him for to shew him the buildings of the temple.	And Jesus passed out of the temple to go away: and his disciples came to him, showing him the structure of the temple.	And Jesus came out of the temple to go away. And his disciples came near [and] were showing him the construction of the temple.
2	And Jesus said unto them, See ye not all these things? verily I say unto you, There shall not be left here one stone upon another, that shall not be thrown down.	And he said to them: See ye not all these? Verily I say to you, There will not be left here a stone upon a stone, that is not demolished.	And he said to them, "Behold, do you not see all these [things]? Truly I say to you, [one] stone here will not be left on [another] stone that will not be demolished."
3	And as he sat upon the mount of Olives, the disciples came unto him privately, saying, Tell us, when shall these things be? and what shall be the sign of thy coming, and of the end of the world?	And as Jesus sat on the mount of Olives, his disciples came, and said between themselves and him: Tell us when these things are to be; and what will be the sign of thy coming, and of the consummation of the world.	And when Jesus sat on the Mount of Olives, his disciples came near and said among themselves and to him, "Tell us when these [things] will be and what is the sign of your coming and of the end of the age."

Parallel Translations

	KJV	Murdock	Magiera
	MATTHEW *Chapter 24*		
4	And Jesus answered and said unto them, Take heed that no man deceive you.	Jesus answered and said to them: Take heed, that no one deceive you.	Jesus answered and said to them, "Beware, [so that] no one will deceive you.
5	For many shall come in my name, saying, I am Christ; and shall deceive many.	For many will come in my name, and will say, I am the Messiah: and they will deceive many.	For many will come in my name and they will say, 'I am the Messiah.' And they will deceive many.
6	And ye shall hear of wars and rumours of wars: see that ye be not troubled: for all these things must come to pass, but the end is not yet.	And ye are to hear of conflicts, and the rumor of battles. See that ye be not disquieted: for all these things must come; but the consummation is not yet.	Now you are about to hear of battles and a report of wars. See [that] you are not disturbed. For it is necessary that all these [things] occur, but the end [is] not yet.
7	For nation shall rise against nation, and kingdom against kingdom: and there shall be famines, and pestilences, and earthquakes, in divers places.	For nation will rise against nation, and kingdom against kingdom; and there will be famines, and pestilences, and earthquakes in divers places.	For people will rise against people and kingdom against kingdom and famines and pestilence and earthquakes will occur in various places.
8	All these are the beginning of sorrows.	But all these are only the commencement of sorrows.	But all these [things] are [only] the beginning of sorrows.
9	Then shall they deliver you up to be afflicted, and shall kill you: and ye shall be hated of all nations for my name's sake.	And they will deliver you up to tribulation, and will kill you: and ye will be hated by all nations, on account of my name.	Then they will deliver you to trials and they will kill you and you will be hated by all nations because of my name.
10	And then shall many be offended, and shall betray one another, and shall hate one another.	Then many will be stumbled: and they will hate one another, and will betray one another.	Then many will be caused to stumble and will hate one another and will betray one another.
11	And many false prophets shall rise, and shall deceive many.	And many false prophets will rise up; and they will deceive many.	And many false prophets will rise up and deceive many.
12	And because iniquity shall abound, the love of many shall wax cold.	And on account of the abounding of iniquity, the love of many will decline.	And because of the abundance of wickedness, the love of many will grow cold.
13	But he that shall endure unto the end, the same shall be saved.	But he that shall persevere to the end, will have life.	But he who endures until the last will have life.
14	And this gospel of the kingdom shall be preached in all the world for a witness unto all nations; and then shall the end come.	And this announcement of the kingdom shall be published in all the world, for a testimony to all nations: and then will come the consummation.	And this gospel of the kingdom will be preached in the entire world for a testimony to all of the nations and then the end will come.
15	When ye therefore shall see the abomination of desolation, spoken of by Daniel the prophet, stand in the holy place, (whoso readeth, let him understand:)	And when ye see the abominable sign of desolation, which was spoken of by Daniel the prophet, standing in the holy place; then let the reader consider;	Now when you see the abominable sign of desecration that was spoken of by Daniel the prophet that will stand in the holy place (he who reads should understand),
16	Then let them which be in Judaea flee into the mountains:	and then let them who are in Judaea, flee to the mountain:	then those who are in Judah should flee to the mountain.
17	Let him which is on the housetop not come down to take any thing out of his house:	and let him who is on the roof, not come down to take what is in his house:	And he who is on the roof should not come down to take that which is in his house.
18	Neither let him which is in the field return back to take his clothes.	and let him who is in the field, not return back to take his clothing.	And he who is in the field should not turn back behind himself to take his clothing.

Parallel Translations

	KJV	*Murdock*	*Magiera*
	MATTHEW *Chapter 24*		
19	And woe unto them that are with child, and to them that give suck in those days!	But woe to those with child, and to them that are nursing, in those days.	But woe to the pregnant women and those who are nursing in those days!
20	But pray ye that your flight be not in the winter, neither on the sabbath day:	And pray ye, that your flight be not in winter, or on the sabbath.	Now pray, so that your flight will not be in the winter, nor on the Sabbath.
21	For then shall be great tribulation, such as was not since the beginning of the world to this time, no, nor ever shall be.	For there will then be great distress, such as hath not been from the commencement of the world, until now, and will not be.	For then a great ordeal will occur, such as has not been from the beginning of the world until now, nor will be.
22	And except those days should be shortened, there should no flesh be saved: but for the elect's sake those days shall be shortened.	And unless those days should be cut short, no flesh would remain alive. But, for the elect's sake, those days will be cut short.	And if those days were not cut short, no flesh would live. But because of the chosen [ones], those days will be cut short.
23	Then if any man shall say unto you, Lo, here is Christ, or there; believe it not.	Then, if any one shall say to you, Lo, the Messiah is here, or is there; give no credence.	Then if anyone should say to you, 'Here is the Messiah or [over] here,' do not believe [him].
24	For there shall arise false Christs, and false prophets, and shall shew great signs and wonders; insomuch that, if it were possible, they shall deceive the very elect.	For there will arise false Messiahs, and mendacious prophets; who will exhibit great signs, so as to deceive, if possible, even the elect.	For false messiahs and lying prophets will rise up and they will produce signs [and] wonders in order to deceive even the chosen [ones], if possible.
25	Behold, I have told you before.	Behold, I have told you beforehand.	Behold, I have told you beforehand.
26	Wherefore if they shall say unto you, Behold, he is in the desert; go not forth: behold, he is in the secret chambers; believe it not.	If therefore they say to you, Behold, he is in the desert; go not out: or, Behold, he is in a secret chamber; give no credence.	Therefore, if they say to you, 'Behold, he is in the wilderness,' do not go out, or 'Behold, he is in an inner chamber,' do not believe [them].
27	For as the lightning cometh out of the east, and shineth even unto the west; so shall also the coming of the Son of man be.	As the lightning cometh out of the east, and shineth unto the west, so will be the coming of the Son of man.	For as the lightning comes out of the east and is visible into the west, so the arrival of the Son of Man will be.
28	For wheresoever the carcase is, there will the eagles be gathered together.	And wherever the carcass may be, there will the eagles be congregated.	Wherever the carcass will be, there the eagles will be gathered.
29	Immediately after the tribulation of those days shall the sun be darkened, and the moon shall not give her light, and the stars shall fall from heaven, and the powers of the heavens shall be shaken:	And immediately after the distress of those days, the sun will be darkened, and the moon will not show her light, and the stars will fall from heaven, and the powers of heaven will be agitated.	And immediately after the ordeal of those days, THE SUN WILL GROW DARK AND THE MOON WILL NOT SHINE ITS LIGHT AND STARS WILL FALL FROM HEAVEN AND THE POWERS OF HEAVEN WILL BE SHAKEN.
30	And then shall appear the sign of the Son of man in heaven: and then shall all the tribes of the earth mourn, and they shall see the Son of man coming in the clouds of heaven with power and great glory.	And then will be seen the signal of the Son of man in heaven: and then will all the tribes of the earth mourn, when they see the Son of man coming on the clouds of heaven, with power and great glory.	And then the standard of the Son of Man will be seen in heaven. And then all the tribes of the earth will mourn and they will see THE SON OF MAN WHO COMES ON THE CLOUDS OF HEAVEN WITH POWER AND GREAT GLORY.

Parallel Translations

	KJV	Murdock	Magiera
	MATTHEW Chapter 24		
31	And he shall send his angels with a great sound of a trumpet, and they shall gather together his elect from the four winds, from one end of heaven to the other.	And he will send his angels with a great trumpet and they will collect together his elect from the four winds, from one extremity of heaven to the other.	And he will send his angels with a great trumpet and they will gather his chosen [ones] from the four winds, from one end of heaven to the other.
32	Now learn a parable of the fig tree; When his branch is yet tender, and putteth forth leaves, ye know that summer is nigh:	And learn ye an illustration from the fig-tree. As soon as its branches become tender and its leaves shoot forth, ye know that summer is coming on.	Now learn an illustration from the fig tree. Immediately when its branches are tender and its leaves bud, you know that summer has arrived.
33	So likewise ye, when ye shall see all these things, know that it is near, even at the doors.	So also ye, when ye perceive all these things, know ye, that he is nigh, [even] at the door.	So also you, when you have seen these [things], will all know that I have arrived at the door.
34	Verily I say unto you, This generation shall not pass, till all these things be fulfilled.	Verily I say to you, That this generation shall not pass away, till all these things shall be.	Truly I say to you, this generation will not pass until all these [things] occur.
35	Heaven and earth shall pass away, but my words shall not pass away.	Heaven and earth will pass away; but my words shall not pass away.	Heaven and earth will pass away, yet my words will not pass away.
36	But of that day and hour knoweth no man, no, not the angels of heaven, but my Father only.	But of that day and of that hour, knoweth no man, nor even the angels of heaven, but the Father only.	But about that day and about that hour, no man knows, not even the angels of heaven, but the Father only.
37	But as the days of Noe were, so shall also the coming of the Son of man be.	And as the days of Noah, so will the coming of the Son of man be.	And as the days of Noah, so will be the arrival of the Son of Man.
38	For as in the days that were before the flood they were eating and drinking, marrying and giving in marriage, until the day that Noe entered into the ark,	For as, before the flood, they were eating and drinking, taking wives and giving to husbands, up to the day that Noah entered the ark,	For as they were before the flood, eating and drinking and marrying women and giving [women in marriage] to men, up to the day [in] which Noah entered the ark,
39	And knew not until the flood came, and took them all away; so shall also the coming of the Son of man be.	and knew not, until the flood came and took them all away; so will the coming of the Son of man be.	and they did not know until the flood came and took all of them, so will be the arrival of the Son of Man.
40	Then shall two be in the field; the one shall be taken, and the other left.	Then will two [men] be in the field; the one will be taken, and the other left.	Then two [men] will be in the field. One will be taken and one will be left.
41	Two women shall be grinding at the mill; the one shall be taken, and the other left.	Two [women] will be grinding at the mill; the one taken, and the other left.	And two [women] will be grinding at the mill. One will be taken and one will be left.
42	Watch therefore: for ye know not what hour your Lord doth come.	Watch, therefore, since ye know not at what hour your Lord cometh.	Therefore, watch, because you do not know in what hour your Lord will come.
43	But know this, that if the goodman of the house had known in what watch the thief would come, he would have watched, and would not have suffered his house to be broken up.	But know this, that if the lord of the house had known in what watch the thief would come, he would have been awake, and would not have suffered his house to be broken into.	But know this, if the master of the house had known in what watch the thief would come, he would have watched and would not have allowed his house to be broken into.

Parallel Translations

	KJV	Murdock	Magiera
MATTHEW	*Chapter 24*		
44	Therefore be ye also ready: for in such an hour as ye think not the Son of man cometh.	Therefore, be ye also ready; for at an hour ye do not expect, the Son of man will come.	Because of this, you should be prepared also, because in an hour that you do not expect, the Son of Man will come.
45	Who then is a faithful and wise servant, whom his lord hath made ruler over his household, to give them meat in due season?	Who then, is that faithful and wise servant, whom his lord hath placed over his domestics, to give them their food in its time?	Who truly is the faithful and wise servant whom his lord has set over his household, to give them food in its time?
46	Blessed is that servant, whom his lord when he cometh shall find so doing.	Happy is that servant, whom, when his lord shall come, he will find so doing.	Blessed [is] that servant who, [when] his lord comes, finds him doing so.
47	Verily I say unto you, That he shall make him ruler over all his goods.	Verily I say to you, He will place him over all that he hath.	Truly I say to you, he will set him over all that he has.
48	But and if that evil servant shall say in his heart, My lord delayeth his coming;	But if that servant, being wicked, shall say in his heart, My lord delayeth his coming;	But if a servant, [being] evil in his heart, says, 'My lord is delaying to come,'
49	And shall begin to smite his fellowservants, and to eat and drink with the drunken;	and shall begin to beat his fellow-servants, and shall be eating and drinking with drunkards;	and begins to beat his fellow-servants and is eating and drinking with drunkards,
50	The lord of that servant shall come in a day when he looketh not for him, and in an hour that he is not aware of,	the lord of that servant will come in a day he will not expect, and in an hour he knoweth not,	the lord of that servant will come in a day that he does not expect and in an hour that he does not know.
51	And shall cut him asunder, and appoint him his portion with the hypocrites: there shall be weeping and gnashing of teeth.	and will cut him asunder, and will assign him his portion with the hypocrites; there will be weeping and gnashing of teeth.	And he will cut him in pieces and assign [him] his portion with the hypocrites. Crying and gnashing of teeth will be there.
Chapter 25			
1	Then shall the kingdom of heaven be likened unto ten virgins, which took their lamps, and went forth to meet the bridegroom.	Then may the kingdom of heaven be shadowed forth by ten virgins, who took their lamps and went out to meet the bridegroom and bride.	Then the kingdom of heaven will be compared to ten virgins, those who took their lamps and went out for the arrival of the bridegroom and bride.
2	And five of them were wise, and five were foolish.	And five of them were wise, and five were foolish.	Now five of them were wise and five were foolish.
3	They that were foolish took their lamps, and took no oil with them:	And the foolish took their lamps, but took no oil with them.	And those foolish [virgins] took their lamps, but did not take oil with them.
4	But the wise took oil in their vessels with their lamps.	But the wise took oil in vessels, with their lamps.	But those wise [virgins] took oil in vessels with their lamps.
5	While the bridegroom tarried, they all slumbered and slept.	And while the bridegroom delayed, they all became sleepy and fell asleep.	Now when the bridegroom was delayed, all of them tired and went to sleep.
6	And at midnight there was a cry made, Behold, the bridegroom cometh; go ye out to meet him.	And at midnight there was an outcry: Behold, the bridegroom cometh; go ye out to meet him.	And at midnight there was a shout, 'Behold, the bridegroom comes. Go out to meet him.'
7	Then all those virgins arose, and trimmed their lamps.	Then all those virgins arose, and trimmed their lamps.	Then all those virgins got up and put their lamps in good order.

Parallel Translations

	KJV	*Murdock*	*Magiera*
	MATTHEW *Chapter 25*		
8	And the foolish said unto the wise, Give us of your oil; for our lamps are gone out.	And the foolish said to the wise; Give us of your oil; for, behold, our lamps have gone out.	And those foolish [virgins] said to the wise, 'Give us [some] of your oil, because, behold, our lamps have gone out.'
9	But the wise answered, saying, Not so; lest there be not enough for us and you: but go ye rather to them that sell, and buy for yourselves.	The wise answered and said: [We must refuse,] lest there should not be enough for us and for you: but go ye to them that sell, and buy for yourselves.	These wise [virgins] answered and said, 'Will there be enough for us and for you? But rather go to those who sell and buy [some] for yourselves.'
10	And while they went to buy, the bridegroom came; and they that were ready went in with him to the marriage: and the door was shut.	And while they went to buy, the bridegroom came; and they that were ready, went with him into the house of the nuptials, and the door was shut.	And while they went to buy, the bridegroom came. And those who were prepared entered with him into the banquet hall and the door was shut.
11	Afterward came also the other virgins, saying, Lord, Lord, open to us.	And at length came also the other virgins, and said: Our lord, our lord, open to us.	Now later, those other virgins also came and said, 'Our Lord, our Lord, open [the door] for us.'
12	But he answered and said, Verily I say unto you, I know you not.	But he answered, and said to them: Verily I say to you, I know you not.	But he answered and said to them, 'Truly I say to you, I do not know you.'
13	Watch therefore, for ye know neither the day nor the hour wherein the Son of man cometh.	Watch, therefore, seeing ye know not the day nor the hour.	Therefore, watch, for you do not know that day or hour.
14	For the kingdom of heaven is as a man travelling into a far country, who called his own servants, and delivered unto them his goods.	For, as a man that took a journey, called his servants and delivered to them his property;	For [the kingdom of heaven is] as a man who went on a journey. He called his servants and delivered his possessions to them.
15	And unto one he gave five talents, to another two, and to another one; to every man according to his several ability; and straightway took his journey.	to one he gave five talents; to another, two; and to another, one: to each, according to his ability: and he immediately departed.	There was one to whom he gave five talents and another two and another one, each according to his ability. And immediately he went on a journey.
16	Then he that had received the five talents went and traded with the same, and made them other five talents.	Then he that received five talents, went and traded with them, and gained five more.	Now he who received five talents went, engaged in business with them, and gained five others.
17	And likewise he that had received two, he also gained other two.	And likewise: the one of two [talents], by trading gained two more.	And in the same manner also, he who [received] two engaged in business [and gained] two others.
18	But he that had received one went and digged in the earth, and hid his lord's money.	But he that received one, went and digged in the earth, and hid his lord's money.	But he who received one [talent] went [and] dug in the ground and hid the money of his lord.
19	After a long time the lord of those servants cometh, and reckoneth with them.	And after a long time, the lord of those servants came, and received account from them.	Now after a long time the lord of those servants came and received an accounting from them.

MATTHEW *Chapter 25*

	KJV	*Murdock*	*Magiera*
20	And so he that had received five talents came and brought other five talents, saying, Lord, thou deliveredst unto me five talents: behold, I have gained beside them five talents more.	And he who had received the five talents, came and brought five others; and said, My lord, thou gavest me five talents; behold, I have gained by trading five more to them.	And he who received five talents came near and brought five others and said, 'My lord, you gave me five talents. Behold, I have engaged in business [and gained] five others with them.'
21	His lord said unto him, Well done, thou good and faithful servant: thou hast been faithful over a few things, I will make thee ruler over many things: enter thou into the joy of thy lord.	His lord said to him: Well done! good and faithful servant: thou hast been faithful with a little; I will set thee over much: enter thou into the joy of thy lord.	His lord said to him, 'Well done, good and faithful servant. You have been faithful over little. I will place you over much. Enter into the joy of your lord.'
22	He also that had received two talents came and said, Lord, thou deliveredst unto me two talents: behold, I have gained two other talents beside them.	And he of the two talents came, and said: My lord, thou gavest me two talents; behold, I have by trading gained two more to them.	And he who [received] two talents came near and said, 'My lord, you gave me two talents. Behold, I have engaged in business [and gained] two others with them.'
23	His lord said unto him, Well done, good and faithful servant; thou hast been faithful over a few things, I will make thee ruler over many things: enter thou into the joy of thy lord.	His lord said to him: Well done! Good and faithful servant: thou hast been faithful with a little; I will set thee over much: enter thou into the joy of thy lord.	His lord said to him, 'Well done, good and faithful servant. You have been faithful over little. I will place you over much. Enter into the joy of your lord.'
24	Then he which had received the one talent came and said, Lord, I knew thee that thou art an hard man, reaping where thou hast not sown, and gathering where thou hast not strawed:	And he also that received the one talent, came and said: My lord, I knew thee, that thou art a hard man, reaping where thou hast not sowed, and gathering where thou hast not scattered;	Now he who received one talent also came near and said, 'My lord, I know that you are a hard man and [that] you reap where you have not sown and [that] you gather from where you have not scattered.
25	And I was afraid, and went and hid thy talent in the earth: lo, there thou hast that is thine.	and I was afraid, and I went and hid thy talent in the earth. Behold, thou hast what is thine.	And I was afraid and went [and] hid your talent in the ground. Behold, you have [what is] yours.'
26	His lord answered and said unto him, Thou wicked and slothful servant, thou knewest that I reap where I sowed not, and gather where I have not strawed:	His lord answered, and said to him: Wicked and slothful servant! Thou knewest me, that I reap where I have not sowed, and gather where I have not scattered!	His lord answered and said to him, 'Wicked and lazy servant, you know that I reap where I have not sown and gather from where I have not scattered.
27	Thou oughtest therefore to have put my money to the exchangers, and then at my coming I should have received mine own with usury.	Thou oughtest to have cast my money into the exchange; and I might have come and demanded my property with its interest.	It would have been right for you to have put my money on the exchange table and I would have come and demanded my own with its interest.
28	Take therefore the talent from him, and give it unto him which hath ten talents.	Take therefore the talent from him, and give it to him that hath ten talents.	Take from him, therefore, the talent and give it to him who has ten talents.
29	For unto every one that hath shall be given, and he shall have abundance: but from him that hath not shall be taken away even that which he hath.	For, to him that hath, shall be given, and he shall have more; but from him that hath not, even what he hath shall be taken away.	For to him who has it will be given and it will be added to him. But he who does not have, even that which he has will be taken from him.

Parallel Translations

MATTHEW *Chapter 25*

	KJV	*Murdock*	*Magiera*
30	And cast ye the unprofitable servant into outer darkness: there shall be weeping and gnashing of teeth.	And cast ye the unprofitable servant into the outer darkness: there will be weeping and gnashing of teeth.	And throw the useless servant into outer darkness. Crying and gnashing of teeth will be there.'
31	When the Son of man shall come in his glory, and all the holy angels with him, then shall he sit upon the throne of his glory:	And when the Son of man shall come in his glory, and all his holy angels with him, then will he sit upon the throne of his glory.	And when the Son of Man comes in his glory and all of his holy angels with him, then he will sit on the throne of his glory.
32	And before him shall be gathered all nations: and he shall separate them one from another, as a shepherd divideth his sheep from the goats:	And before him will be gathered all nations; and he will separate them one from another, as a shepherd severeth the sheep from the goats.	And all the nations will be gathered before him. And he will separate them one from another as a shepherd who separates the sheep from the goats.
33	And he shall set the sheep on his right hand, but the goats on the left.	And he will place the sheep on his right hand, and the goats on his left.	And he will set the sheep on his right and the goats on his left.
34	Then shall the King say unto them on his right hand, Come, ye blessed of my Father, inherit the kingdom prepared for you from the foundation of the world:	Then will the king say to those on his right hand: Come, ye blessed of my Father; inherit the kingdom that was prepared for you from the foundation of the world.	Then the king will say to those who are on his right, 'Come, blessed of my Father, inherit the kingdom that has been prepared for you from the foundations of the world.'
35	For I was an hungred, and ye gave me meat: I was thirsty, and ye gave me drink: I was a stranger, and ye took me in:	For I was hungry, and ye gave me food; I was thirsty, and ye gave me drink; I was a stranger, and ye took me home;	For I was hungry and you gave me to eat. And I was thirsty and you gave me to drink. I was a stranger and you took me in.
36	Naked, and ye clothed me: I was sick, and ye visited me: I was in prison, and ye came unto me.	I was naked, and ye clothed me; I was sick, and ye visited me; I was in prison, and ye came to me.	I was naked and you covered me. I was sick and you visited me. And I was in prison and you came to me.
37	Then shall the righteous answer him, saying, Lord, when saw we thee an hungred, and fed thee? or thirsty, and gave thee drink?	Then will the righteous say to him: Our Lord, when saw we thee hungry, and fed thee? or thirsty, and gave thee drink?	Then those just [ones] will say to him, 'Our Lord, when did we see that you were hungry and feed you, or that you were thirsty and give you drink?
38	When saw we thee a stranger, and took thee in? or naked, and clothed thee?	And when saw we thee a stranger, and took thee home? or naked, and clothed thee?	And when did we see that you were a stranger and take you in or that you were naked and cover you?
39	Or when saw we thee sick, or in prison, and came unto thee?	And when saw we thee sick, or in prison, and came to thee?	And when did we see you sick or in prison and come to you?'
40	And the King shall answer and say unto them, Verily I say unto you, Inasmuch as ye have done it unto one of the least of these my brethren, ye have done it unto me.	And the king will answer, and say to them: Verily I say to you, That inasmuch as ye did so to one of these my little brothers, ye did so to me.	And the king will answer and say to them, 'Truly I say to you, whatever you did for one of these, my little brothers, you did for me.'
41	Then shall he say also unto them on the left hand, Depart from me, ye cursed, into everlasting fire, prepared for the devil and his angels:	Then will he say also to them on his left hand: Go from me, ye accursed, into everlasting fire, which was prepared for the Calumniator and his angels,	Then he will say also to those who are on his left, 'Go away from me, cursed [ones], to the eternal fire that is prepared for the Accuser and his angels.

Parallel Translations

	KJV	Murdock	Magiera
	MATTHEW Chapter 25		
42	For I was an hungred, and ye gave me no meat: I was thirsty, and ye gave me no drink:	For I was hungry, and ye gave me no food; and I was thirsty, and ye gave me no drink;	For I was hungry and you did not give me to eat and I was thirsty and you did not give me drink.
43	I was a stranger, and ye took me not in: naked, and ye clothed me not: sick, and in prison, and ye visited me not.	and I was a stranger, and ye took me not home; and I was naked, and ye clothed me not; and I was sick and in prison, and ye did not visit me.	And I was a stranger and you did not take me in and I was naked and you did not cover me. And I was sick and I was in prison and you did not visit me.'
44	Then shall they also answer him, saying, Lord, when saw we thee an hungred, or athirst, or a stranger, or naked, or sick, or in prison, and did not minister unto thee?	Then will they also answer and say: Our Lord, when saw we thee hungry, or thirsty, or a stranger, or naked, or sick, or in prison, and did not minister to thee?	Then they will also answer and say, 'Our Lord, when did we see you hungry or thirsty or a stranger or naked or sick or in prison and not minister to you?'
45	Then shall he answer them, saying, Verily I say unto you, Inasmuch as ye did it not to one of the least of these, ye did it not to me.	Then will he answer, and say to them: Verily I say to you, That in as much as ye did not so to one of these little ones, ye did not so to me.	Then he will answer and say to them, 'Truly I say to you, whatever you did not do for one of these little ones, you did also not do for me.'
46	And these shall go away into everlasting punishment: but the righteous into life eternal.	And these will go into everlasting torment, and the righteous into everlasting life.	And these will go to eternal torment and the just [ones] to eternal life."
	Chapter 26		
1	And it came to pass, when Jesus had finished all these sayings, he said unto his disciples,	And it came to pass, when Jesus had concluded all these discourses, that he said to his disciples:	And it happened that when Jesus completed all of these sayings, he said to his disciples,
2	Ye know that after two days is the feast of the passover, and the Son of man is betrayed to be crucified.	Ye know that after two days is the Passover; and the Son of man is betrayed to be crucified.	"You know that after two days will be the Passover and the Son of Man will be betrayed to be crucified.
3	Then assembled together the chief priests, and the scribes, and the elders of the people, unto the palace of the high priest, who was called Caiaphas,	Then assembled the chief priests and the Scribes and the Elders of the people, at the hall of the high priest, who was called Caiaphas.	Then the chief priests and scribes and elders of the people were gathered at the court of the high priest, who was called Caiaphas.
4	And consulted that they might take Jesus by subtilty, and kill him.	And they held a counsel against Jesus, that they might take him by guile, and kill him.	And they held counsel against Jesus that they might arrest him by deceit and kill him.
5	But they said, Not on the feast day, lest there be an uproar among the people.	But they said: Not on the festival, lest there be a commotion among the people.	And they were saying, "Not during the festival, lest a riot should occur among the people."
6	Now when Jesus was in Bethany, in the house of Simon the leper,	And when Jesus was at Bethany, in the house of Simon the leper,	And while Jesus was in Bethany in the house of Simon the leper,
7	There came unto him a woman having an alabaster box of very precious ointment, and poured it on his head, as he sat at meat.	there came to him a woman having a vase of aromatic ointment very precious, and she poured it on the head of Jesus as he was reclining.	a woman approached him who had with her an alabaster vase of oil that was very costly perfume. And she poured it on the head of Jesus while he was lying down [to eat].

Parallel Translations

MATTHEW *Chapter 26*

	KJV	*Murdock*	*Magiera*
8	But when his disciples saw it, they had indignation, saying, To what purpose is this waste?	And when his disciples saw [it] they were displeased, and said: Why is this waste?	And his disciples saw [it] and it displeased them. And they said, "Why [was there] this waste?
9	For this ointment might have been sold for much, and given to the poor.	For this [ointment] might have been sold for much, and have been given to the poor.	For this [oil] could have been sold for much and [the money] given to the poor."
10	When Jesus understood it, he said unto them, Why trouble ye the woman? for she hath wrought a good work upon me.	But Jesus knew [their dissatisfaction], and said to them: Why trouble ye the woman? She hath performed a good deed towards me.	But Jesus knew [this] and said to them, "Why are you troubling the woman? She has done a good deed for me.
11	For ye have the poor always with you; but me ye have not always.	For the poor ye have at all times with you; but I am not with you always	For you will always have the poor with you, but you will not always have me.
12	For in that she hath poured this ointment on my body, she did it for my burial.	And this her act, pouring the ointment on my body, she hath done as it were for my burial.	Now this [act], that she poured this oil on my body, she did as though for my burial.
13	Verily I say unto you, Wheresoever this gospel shall be preached in the whole world, there shall also this, that this woman hath done, be told for a memorial of her.	Verily I say to you, That wherever this my gospel shall be proclaimed, in all the world, this thing that she hath done shall be told for a memorial of her.	And truly I say to you, wherever this my gospel is preached in all the world, what she has done will be spoken also for her remembrance."
14	Then one of the twelve, called Judas Iscariot, went unto the chief priests,	Then one of the twelve, named Judas Iscariot, went to the chief priests,	Then one of the twelve, who was called Judas Iscariot, went to the chief priests.
15	And said unto them, What will ye give me, and I will deliver him unto you? And they covenanted with him for thirty pieces of silver.	and said to them: What will ye give me, if I will deliver him to you? And they promised him thirty pieces of silver.	And he said to them, "What do you want to give me? And I will deliver him to you." Now they promised him thirty [pieces] of silver.
16	And from that time he sought opportunity to betray him.	And from that time he sought opportunity to betray him.	And from that time on, he was seeking an occasion to betray him.
17	Now the first day of the feast of unleavened bread the disciples came to Jesus, saying unto him, Where wilt thou that we prepare for thee to eat the passover?	And on the first day of unleavened bread, the disciples came to Jesus, and said to him: Where wilt thou that we prepare for thee to eat the passover?	Now on the first day of the Feast of Unleavened Bread, the disciples came near to Jesus and said to him, "Where do you want us to prepare for you to eat the Passover?"
18	And he said, Go into the city to such a man, and say unto him, The Master saith, My time is at hand; I will keep the passover at thy house with my disciples.	And he said to them: Go ye into the city, to such a man, and say to him: Our Rabbi saith, My time approaches: with thee will I keep the passover with my disciples	And he said to them, "Go to the city to a certain [one] and say to him, 'Our Master says, my time comes.' With you I will serve the Passover with my disciples."
19	And the disciples did as Jesus had appointed them; and they made ready the passover.	And his disciples did as Jesus directed them, and made ready the passover.	And his disciples did as Jesus had commanded them and they prepared the Passover.
20	Now when the even was come, he sat down with the twelve.	And when it was evening, he reclined with his twelve disciples.	And when it was evening, he was lying down [to eat] with his twelve disciples.
21	And as they did eat, he said, Verily I say unto you, that one of you shall betray me.	And as they were eating, he said: Verily I say to you, That one of you will betray me.	And while they were eating, he said, "Truly I say to you, one of you will betray me."

Parallel Translations

MATTHEW *Chapter 26*

	KJV	Murdock	Magiera
22	And they were exceeding sorrowful, and began every one of them to say unto him, Lord, is it I?	And it troubled them much. And they began each one of them to say to him; My Lord is it I?	And it made them very sad. And each one of them began to say to him, "Is it I, my Lord?"
23	And he answered and said, He that dippeth his hand with me in the dish, the same shall betray me.	And he answered and said: One that dippeth his hand with me in the dish, he will betray me.	But he answered and said, "He who dips his hand with me in the dish, he will betray me.
24	The Son of man goeth as it is written of him: but woe unto that man by whom the Son of man is betrayed! it had been good for that man if he had not been born.	And the Son of man goeth, as it is written of him: but woe to that man, by whom the Son of man is betrayed. It would have been better for that man, if he had not been born.	And the Son of Man will go as it is written about him. But woe to the man by whose hand the Son of Man is betrayed! It would be better for that man if he had not been born."
25	Then Judas, which betrayed him, answered and said, Master, is it I? He said unto him, Thou hast said.	Judas the betrayer answered and said: Rabbi, is it I? Jesus said to him: Thou hast said.	Judas, the betrayer, answered and said, "Is it I, my Master?" Jesus said to him, "You have said [it]."
26	And as they were eating, Jesus took bread, and blessed it, and brake it, and gave it to the disciples, and said, Take, eat; this is my body.	And as they were eating, Jesus took bread, and blessed, and brake; and gave to his disciples, and said: Take, eat; this is my body.	And while they were eating, Jesus took up bread and blessed [it] and broke [it] and gave to his disciples and said, "Take, eat, this is my body."
27	And he took the cup, and gave thanks, and gave it to them, saying, Drink ye all of it;	And he took the cup, and offered thanks and gave [it] to them, saying: Take, drink of this all of you.	And he took up a cup and gave thanks and gave [it] to them. And he said, "Take, drink from it, all of you.
28	For this is my blood of the new testament, which is shed for many for the remission of sins.	This is my blood of the new testament, which, in behalf of many, is shed for the remission of sins.	This is my blood of the new covenant that is poured out for many for the forgiveness of sins.
29	But I say unto you, I will not drink henceforth of this fruit of the vine, until that day when I drink it new with you in my Father's kingdom.	But I say to you, that I will henceforth not drink of this product of the vine, until the day in which I shall drink it with you new in the kingdom of God.	And I say to you, I will not drink from now [on] from this fruit of the vine until the day in which I drink it with you anew in the kingdom of my Father."
30	And when they had sung an hymn, they went out into the mount of Olives.	And they sang praises, and went forth to the mount of Olives.	And they offered praise and went out to the Mount of Olives.
31	Then saith Jesus unto them, All ye shall be offended because of me this night: for it is written, I will smite the shepherd, and the sheep of the flock shall be scattered abroad.	Then said Jesus to them: Ye will all be offended in me this night; for it is written, I will smite the shepherd, and the sheep of his flock will be dispersed.	Then Jesus said to them, "All of you will be offended by me in this night, for it is written: I WILL STRIKE THE SHEPHERD AND THE SHEEP OF HIS FLOCK WILL BE SCATTERED.
32	But after I am risen again, I will go before you into Galilee.	But after I am arisen, I will go before you into Galilee.	But after I have risen, I [will go] before you into Galilee."
33	Peter answered and said unto him, Though all men shall be offended because of thee, yet will I never be offended.	Cephas replied, and said to him: Though all men should be offended in thee, I will never be offended in thee.	Peter answered and said to him, "Even if everyone be offended by you, I will never be offended by you."
34	Jesus said unto him, Verily I say unto thee, That this night, before the cock crow, thou shalt deny me thrice.	Jesus said to him: Verily I say to thee, That this night, before the cock crow, thou wilt thrice deny me.	Jesus said to him, "Truly I say to you, in this night before the rooster crows three times, you will deny me."

Parallel Translations

MATTHEW *Chapter 26*

	KJV	*Murdock*	*Magiera*
35	Peter said unto him, Though I should die with thee, yet will I not deny thee. Likewise also said all the disciples.	Cephas said to him: If I were to die with thee, I would not deny thee: and so also said all the disciples.	Peter said to him, "If it be [necessary] for me to die with you, I would not deny you." And so also said all the disciples.
36	Then cometh Jesus with them unto a place called Gethsemane, and saith unto the disciples, Sit ye here, while I go and pray yonder.	Then came Jesus with them to a place called Gethsemane: and he said to his disciples, Sit ye here, while I go and pray.	Then Jesus came with them to a place that was called Gethsemane. And he said to his disciples, "Sit here while I go [and] pray."
37	And he took with him Peter and the two sons of Zebedee, and began to be sorrowful and very heavy.	And he took Cephas and the two sons of Zebedee, and began to be dejected and sorrowful.	And he took Peter and the two sons of Zebedee. And he began to be sad and wearied.
38	Then saith he unto them, My soul is exceeding sorrowful, even unto death: tarry ye here, and watch with me.	And he said to them: There is anguish in my soul, even unto death. Wait for me here; and watch with me.	And he said to them, "There is sadness to my soul unto death. Remain with me here and watch with me."
39	And he went a little further, and fell on his face, and prayed, saying, O my Father, if it be possible, let this cup pass from me: nevertheless not as I will, but as thou wilt.	And retiring a little, he fell on his face, and prayed, and said: My Father, if it can be so, let this cup pass from me. Yet not as I choose, but as thou.	And he went on a little and fell down on his face and was praying and said, "My Father, if it is possible, let this cup pass by me. Nevertheless not as I want, but as you [want]."
40	And he cometh unto the disciples, and findeth them asleep, and saith unto Peter, What, could ye not watch with me one hour?	And he came to his disciples, and found them asleep: and he said to Cephas: So! could ye not watch with me one hour?	And he came to his disciples and found them asleep. And he said to Peter, "What, were you not able to watch with me one hour?
41	Watch and pray, that ye enter not into temptation: the spirit indeed is willing, but the flesh is weak.	Wake ye, and pray, lest ye fall into temptation. The mind is prepared, but the body is infirm.	Watch and pray, so that you will not enter into temptation. The spirit is ready, but the body is weak."
42	He went away again the second time, and prayed, saying, O my Father, if this cup may not pass away from me, except I drink it, thy will be done.	Again he went away the second time, and prayed, and said: My Father, if it cannot be that this cup pass, except I drink it, thy will be done.	Again he went a second time [and] prayed. And he said, "My Father, if it is not possible for this cup to pass over, except I drink it, your desire will be [done]."
43	And he came and found them asleep again: for their eyes were heavy.	And he came again and found them sleeping, for their eyes were heavy.	And he came again [and] found them asleep, for their eyes were heavy.
44	And he left them, and went away again, and prayed the third time, saying the same words.	And he left them, and went again and prayed the third time, and used the same language.	And he left them and went again [and] prayed a third time and he said the same thing.
45	Then cometh he to his disciples, and saith unto them, Sleep on now, and take your rest: behold, the hour is at hand, and the Son of man is betrayed into the hands of sinners.	Then he came to his disciples, and said to them: Sleep on now, and take rest. Behold, the hour is come: and the Son of man is betrayed into the hands of sinners.	Then he came to his disciples and said to them, "Sleep now and be rested. Behold, the hour has arrived and the Son of Man will be delivered into the hands of sinners.
46	Rise, let us be going: behold, he is at hand that doth betray me.	Arise, let us go. Behold, he that betrayeth me hath come.	Rise up, we will go. Behold, he who has betrayed me has arrived."

MATTHEW *Chapter 26*

	KJV	Murdock	Magiera
47	And while he yet spake, lo, Judas, one of the twelve, came, and with him a great multitude with swords and staves, from the chief priests and elders of the people.	And while he was yet speaking, lo, Judas the betrayer, one of the twelve, arrived; and a great multitude with him, with swords and clubs, from the presence of the chief priests and elders of the people.	And while he was speaking, behold, Judas the betrayer, one of the twelve, came and with him [was] a large crowd with swords and staffs, from before the chief priests and elders of the people.
48	Now he that betrayed him gave them a sign, saying, Whomsoever I shall kiss, that same is he: hold him fast.	And Judas the betrayer had given them a sign, saying: He it is, whom I shall kiss: him seize ye.	And Judas the betrayer had given them a sign and said, "It is he whom I kiss. Arrest him."
49	And forthwith he came to Jesus, and said, Hail, master; and kissed him.	And forthwith he approached Jesus, and said: Hail, Rabbi; and kissed him.	And immediately he came near to Jesus and said, "Peace, my Master." And he kissed him.
50	And Jesus said unto him, Friend, wherefore art thou come? Then came they, and laid hands on Jesus, and took him.	And Jesus said to him: My friend, is it for this thou hast come? Then they came up, and laid their hands on Jesus, and took him.	And Jesus said to him, "Did you come for this [purpose], my friend?" Then they came near and placed their hands on Jesus and arrested him.
51	And, behold, one of them which were with Jesus stretched out his hand, and drew his sword, and struck a servant of the high priest's, and smote off his ear.	And lo, one of them with Jesus stretched out his hand, and drew a sword, and smote a servant of the high priest, and cut off his ear.	And behold, one of those who [were] with Jesus stretched out his hand and drew a sword and struck a servant of the high priest and cut off his ear.
52	Then said Jesus unto him, Put up again thy sword into his place: for all they that take the sword shall perish with the sword.	Then Jesus said to him: Return the sword to its place; for all they that take swords, shall die by swords.	Then Jesus said to him, "Return the sword to its place, for all those who take up swords by swords will die.
53	Thinkest thou that I cannot now pray to my Father, and he shall presently give me more than twelve legions of angels?	Supposest thou that I cannot ask of my Father, and he now assign me more than twelve legions of angels?	Or do you think that I am not able to ask of my Father and would he [not] assign to me now more than twelve legions of angels?
54	But how then shall the scriptures be fulfilled, that thus it must be?	But how then would the scriptures be fulfilled, that thus it must be?	How then would the scriptures be fulfilled that so it must be?"
55	In that same hour said Jesus to the multitudes, Are ye come out as against a thief with swords and staves for to take me? I sat daily with you teaching in the temple, and ye laid no hold on me.	At that time Jesus said to the multitude: Have ye come out, as against a cut-throat, with swords and clubs, to take me? I daily sat with you, and taught in the temple, and ye did not apprehend me.	At that moment Jesus said to the crowds, "Have you come out as against a robber with swords and with staffs to arrest me? I was sitting and teaching every day with you in the temple and you did not arrest me.
56	But all this was done, that the scriptures of the prophets might be fulfilled. Then all the disciples forsook him, and fled.	And this occurred, that the writings of the prophets might be fulfilled. Then the disciples all forsook him and fled.	Now this has occurred so that the writings of the prophets would be fulfilled." Then all the disciples deserted him and fled.
57	And they that had laid hold on Jesus led him away to Caiaphas the high priest, where the scribes and the elders were assembled.	And they who apprehended Jesus carried him to Caiaphas the high priest, where the Scribes and Elders were assembled.	And those who arrested Jesus led him to Caiaphas, the high priest, where the scribes and elders were gathering.

Parallel Translations

	KJV	*Murdock*	*Magiera*

MATTHEW *Chapter 26*

	KJV	Murdock	Magiera
58	But Peter followed him afar off unto the high priest's palace, and went in, and sat with the servants, to see the end.	And Simon Cephas followed after him at a distance, unto the high priest's hall, and entered, and sat with the servants within, that he might see the issue.	And Simon Peter was following him from a distance up to the courtyard of the high priest. And he entered [and] sat inside with the guards that he might see the end.
59	Now the chief priests, and elders, and all the council, sought false witness against Jesus, to put him to death;	And the chief priests and the Elders and the whole assembly sought for witnesses against Jesus, that they might put him to death;	Now the chief priests and elders and all the assembly were seeking witnesses against Jesus so that they might kill him
60	But found none: yea, though many false witnesses came, yet found they none. At the last came two false witnesses,	and found them not. And many false witnesses came; and at last, two came forward,	and they did not find [them] and many false witnesses came. But finally, two came near
61	And said, This fellow said, I am able to destroy the temple of God, and to build it in three days.	and said: This man said, I can destroy the temple of God, and in three days rebuild it.	and said, "This [man] said, 'I am able to destroy the temple of God and to rebuild it in three days.'"
62	And the high priest arose, and said unto him, Answerest thou nothing? what is it which these witness against thee?	And the high priest rose up and said to him: Respondest thou nothing? What do these testify against thee?	And the high priest stood up and said to him, "Do you not answer anything [to this] matter? Why do these [men] witness against you?"
63	But Jesus held his peace. And the high priest answered and said unto him, I adjure thee by the living God, that thou tell us whether thou be the Christ, the Son of God.	And Jesus was silent. And the high priest answered, and said to him: I adjure thee by the living God, that thou tell us whether thou art the Messiah, the Son of God.	But Jesus was silent. And the high priest answered and said to him, "I command you by the living God that you tell us if you are the Messiah, the Son of God."
64	Jesus saith unto him, Thou hast said: nevertheless I say unto you, Hereafter shall ye see the Son of man sitting on the right hand of power, and coming in the clouds of heaven.	Jesus saith to him: Thou hast said. And I say to you, That hereafter ye will see the Son of man sitting on the right hand of power, and coming on the clouds of heaven.	Jesus said to him, "You have said. But I say to you, from now on you will see THE SON OF MAN SITTING AT THE RIGHT HAND OF POWER AND COMING ON THE CLOUDS OF HEAVEN."
65	Then the high priest rent his clothes, saying, He hath spoken blasphemy; what further need have we of witnesses? behold, now ye have heard his blasphemy.	Then the high priest rent his clothes, and said: Behold, he hath blasphemed! Why therefore should we seek for witnesses? Behold, ye have now heard his blasphemy.	Then the high priest tore his clothes and said, "Behold, he has blasphemed. Why, therefore, do we need witnesses? Behold, now you have heard his blasphemy.
66	What think ye? They answered and said, He is guilty of death.	What is your pleasure? They answered and said: He is liable to death.	What do you want [to do]?" They answered and were saying, "He is deserving of death."
67	Then did they spit in his face, and buffeted him; and others smote him with the palms of their hands,	Then they spit in his face, and buffeted him, and others smote him,	Then they spit in his face and they were striking him. And others were beating him.
68	Saying, Prophesy unto us, thou Christ, Who is he that smote thee?	and said to him: Prophesy to us, thou Messiah, who is it smote thee?	And they said, "Prophesy to us, Messiah. Who is the one who beat you?"

MATTHEW *Chapter 26*

	KJV	Murdock	Magiera
69	Now Peter sat without in the palace: and a damsel came unto him, saying, Thou also wast with Jesus of Galilee.	And Cephas was sitting without in the hall, and a certain maid approached him, and said to him: Thou also wast with Jesus the Nazarean.	Now Peter was sitting outside in the courtyard and a certain maid came near to him. And she said to him, "You also were with Jesus the Nazarene."
70	But he denied before them all, saying, I know not what thou sayest.	But he denied [it] before them all, and said: I know not what thou sayest.	But he denied [it] before all of them and said, "I do not know what you are saying."
71	And when he was gone out into the porch, another maid saw him, and said unto them that were there, This fellow was also with Jesus of Nazareth.	And as he went out into the porch, another maid saw him, and said to them: This man was also there with Jesus the Nazarean.	And when he went out to the porch, another [maid] saw him and said to them, "This [man] also was there with Jesus the Nazarene."
72	And again he denied with an oath, I do not know the man.	And again he denied, with oaths: I know not that man.	And again he denied [it] with oaths, "I do not know the man."
73	And after a while came unto him they that stood by, and said to Peter, Surely thou also art one of them; for thy speech bewrayeth thee.	And a little after, those standing [there] came up and said to Cephas: Certainly, thou too art one of them; and thy speech maketh thee manifest.	And after a little while, those who were standing by came near and said to Peter, "Surely also you are one of them, for your speech also makes you known."
74	Then began he to curse and to swear, saying, I know not the man. And immediately the cock crew.	Then he began to imprecate and to swear, I know not that man. And in that hour the cock crew.	Then he began to curse and to say, "I do not know the man." And immediately the rooster crowed.
75	And Peter remembered the word of Jesus, which said unto him, Before the cock crow, thou shalt deny me thrice. And he went out, and wept bitterly.	And Cephas remembered the declaration of Jesus, who said to him: Before the cock croweth, thou wilt three times deny me. And he went out, and wept bitterly.	And Peter remembered the word of Jesus who said to him, "Before the rooster crows three times, you will deny me." And he went outside [and] cried bitterly.

Chapter 27

	KJV	Murdock	Magiera
1	When the morning was come, all the chief priests and elders of the people took counsel against Jesus to put him to death:	And when it was morning, the chief priests and the elders of the people held a council against Jesus, how they might put him to death.	Now when it was morning, all the chief priests and elders of the people took counsel against Jesus so that they might put him to death.
2	And when they had bound him, they led him away, and delivered him to Pontius Pilate the governor.	And they bound him, and carried him and delivered him up to Pilate, the president.	And they bound him and took him and delivered him to Pilate the governor.
3	Then Judas, which had betrayed him, when he saw that he was condemned, repented himself, and brought again the thirty pieces of silver to the chief priests and elders,	Then Judas the betrayer, when he saw that Jesus was condemned, repented. And he went and returned the thirty pieces of silver to the chief priests and elders;	Then Judas, the betrayer, when he saw that Jesus was condemned, repented and went [and] returned those thirty [pieces] of silver to the chief priests and to the elders.
4	Saying, I have sinned in that I have betrayed the innocent blood. And they said, What is that to us? see thou to that.	and said: I have sinned, by betraying innocent blood. And they said: What is that to us? See to it thyself.	And he said, "I have sinned, because I have betrayed innocent blood." But they said to him, "What [is it] to us? You know [what to do about it]."

Parallel Translations

	KJV	*Murdock*	*Magiera*
	MATTHEW *Chapter 27*		
5	And he cast down the pieces of silver in the temple, and departed, and went and hanged himself.	And he cast down the silver in the temple, and retiring, went and strangled himself	And he threw down the silver in the temple and left and went [and] strangled himself.
6	And the chief priests took the silver pieces, and said, It is not lawful for to put them into the treasury, because it is the price of blood.	And the chief priests took up the silver, and said: It is not lawful to put it into the treasury, because it is the price of blood.	Now the chief priests picked up the silver and said, "It is not lawful to put [this] in the treasury, because it is the price of blood."
7	And they took counsel, and bought with them the potter's field, to bury strangers in.	And they took counsel, and bought with it the potter's field, for a place to bury strangers.	And they took counsel and bought with it the field of the potter as a cemetery for strangers.
8	Wherefore that field was called, The field of blood, unto this day.	Wherefore that field is called the field of blood, unto this day.	Because of this, that field is called "The Field of Blood" until today.
9	Then was fulfilled that which was spoken by Jeremy the prophet, saying, And they took the thirty pieces of silver, the price of him that was valued, whom they of the children of Israel did value;	Then was fulfilled that which was spoken by the prophet, saying: I took the thirty [shekels] of silver, the price of the precious one, which they of the children of Israel had stipulated;	Then it was fulfilled what was spoken by way of the prophet, who said: I TOOK THE THIRTY [PIECES] OF SILVER, THE PRICE OF THE PRECIOUS [ONE] WHICH [THOSE] FROM THE SONS OF ISRAEL AGREED ON,
10	And gave them for the potter's field, as the Lord appointed me.	and I gave them for the potter's field, as the Lord directed me.	AND I GAVE THEM FOR THE FIELD OF THE POTTER AS THE LORD COMMANDED ME.
11	And Jesus stood before the governor: and the governor asked him, saying, Art thou the King of the Jews? And Jesus said unto him, Thou sayest.	And Jesus stood before the president. And the resident asked him, and said to him: Art thou the king of the Jews? And Jesus said to him: Thou hast said.	Now Jesus stood before the governor. And the governor asked him and said to him, "Are you the king of the Judeans?" Jesus said to him, "You have said."
12	And when he was accused of the chief priests and elders, he answered nothing.	And when the chief priests and elders accused him, he made no reply.	And while the chief priests and elders were accusing him, he did not give any answer.
13	Then said Pilate unto him, Hearest thou not how many things they witness against thee?	Then Pilate said to him: Hearest thou not how much they testify against thee?	Then Pilate said to him, "Do you not hear how much they testify against you?"
14	And he answered him to never a word; insomuch that the governor marvelled greatly.	But he gave him no answer, not even one word: and therefore Pilate wondered greatly.	And he did not give him an answer, not even with one word. And he greatly marveled at this.
15	Now at that feast the governor was wont to release unto the people a prisoner, whom they would.	And at each festival, the president was accustomed to release to the people one prisoner, such as they preferred.	Now at every feast, the governor was accustomed to free one prisoner to the people, whomever they were desiring.
16	And they had then a notable prisoner, called Barabbas.	And they had then in bonds a noted prisoner, called Bar Abas.	And they had imprisoned a well-known prisoner who was called Barabbas.
17	Therefore when they were gathered together, Pilate said unto them, Whom will ye that I release unto you? Barabbas, or Jesus which is called Christ?	And when they were assembled, Pilate said to them: Whom will ye, that I release to you, Bar Abas, or Jesus who is called Messiah?	And when they were gathered, Pilate said to them, "Whom do you want me to free to you, Barabbas or Jesus, who is called the Messiah?"

Parallel Translations

	KJV	Murdock	Magiera

MATTHEW *Chapter 27*

	KJV	Murdock	Magiera
18	For he knew that for envy they had delivered him.	For Pilate knew that it was from enmity they had delivered him up.	For Pilate was realizing that they had delivered him up because of envy.
19	When he was set down on the judgment seat, his wife sent unto him, saying, Have thou nothing to do with that just man: for I have suffered many things this day in a dream because of him.	And as the president was sitting on his tribunal, his wife sent to him, and said: Have thou nothing to do with that just man; for I have suffered much this day in a dream because of him.	Now while the governor sat on his judgment seat, his wife sent to him and said to him, "Have nothing to do with that just [man], for I have suffered much today in my dream because of him."
20	But the chief priests and elders persuaded the multitude that they should ask Barabbas, and destroy Jesus.	But the chief priests and the elders persuaded the multitude that they should demand Bar Abas, and destroy Jesus.	But the chief priests and elders persuaded the crowds to ask for Barabbas and to destroy Jesus.
21	The governor answered and said unto them, Whether of the twain will ye that I release unto you? They said, Barabbas.	And the president answered, and said to them: Which of the two, will ye, that I release to you? And they said: Bar Abas.	And the governor answered and said to them, "Whom do you want me to free to you from the two?" And they said, "Barabbas."
22	Pilate saith unto them, What shall I do then with Jesus which is called Christ? They all say unto him, Let him be crucified.	Pilate said to them: And what shall I do to Jesus who is called Messiah? They all replied: Let him be crucified.	Pilate said to them, "And what should I do to Jesus, who is called the Messiah?" All of them said to him, "He should be crucified!"
23	And the governor said, Why, what evil hath he done? But they cried out the more, saying, Let him be crucified.	The president said to them: But what hath he done, that is evil? And they cried out the more, and said: Let him be crucified.	The governor said to them, "For what has he done that is evil?" But they cried out all the more and said, "He should be crucified!"
24	When Pilate saw that he could prevail nothing, but that rather a tumult was made, he took water, and washed his hands before the multitude, saying, I am innocent of the blood of this just person: see ye to it.	And Pilate, when he saw that it availed nothing, but rather that tumult was produced, took water, and washed his hands before the eyes of the multitude, and said: I am pure from the blood of this just man: see ye to it.	Now Pilate, when he saw that nothing helped, but [that] the clamor was increased, he took water [and] washed his hands before the crowd and said, "I am absolved of the blood of this just [man]. You should do [what you will]."
25	Then answered all the people, and said, His blood be on us, and on our children.	And all the people answered, and said His blood be on us, and on our children!	And all the people answered and said, "His blood [be] on us and on our children."
26	Then released he Barabbas unto them: and when he had scourged Jesus, he delivered him to be crucified.	Then released he to them Bar Abas; and scourged Jesus with whips and delivered him to be crucified.	Then he released Barabbas to them and scourged Jesus with whips and delivered him up to be crucified.
27	Then the soldiers of the governor took Jesus into the common hall, and gathered unto him the whole band of soldiers.	Then the soldiers of the president took Jesus into the Praetorium, and assembled the whole regiment against him.	Then the soldiers of the governor took Jesus to the Praetorium and assembled all the company of soldiers against him.
28	And they stripped him, and put on him a scarlet robe.	And they stripped him, and put on him a scarlet military cloak.	And they stripped him and clothed him with a robe of purple.

Parallel Translations

	KJV	*Murdock*	*Magiera*
	MATTHEW *Chapter 27*		
29	And when they had platted a crown of thorns, they put it upon his head, and a reed in his right hand: and they bowed the knee before him, and mocked him, saying, Hail, King of the Jews!	And they wove a crown of thorns, and set it on his head, and [put] a reed in his hand, and they bowed their knees before him, and mocked him, and said: Hail, thou king of the Jews.	And they wove a crown of thorns and placed [it] on his head and a reed in his right hand and they bowed down on their knees before him and were mocking him and said, "Hail, king of the Judeans."
30	And they spit upon him, and took the reed, and smote him on the head.	And they spit in his face, and took the reed, and smote him on his head.	And they spit in his face and they took the reed and were striking him on his head.
31	And after that they had mocked him, they took the robe off from him, and put his own raiment on him, and led him away to crucify him.	And when they had mocked him, they divested him of the cloak, and clothed him in his own garments, and led him out to be crucified.	And after they had mocked him, they stripped him of the robe and dressed him in his clothes and led him away to be crucified.
32	And as they came out, they found a man of Cyrene, Simon by name: him they compelled to bear his cross.	And as they went out, they found a man of Cyrene whose name was Simon; him they compelled to bear his cross.	And while they were going out, they found a man, a Cyrenian, whose name [was] Simon. They compelled this [man] to carry his cross.
33	And when they were come unto a place called Golgotha, that is to say, a place of a skull,	And they came to a place which is called Golgotha, which is interpreted a skull.	And they came to the place that is called Golgotha, which is interpreted, "The Skull."
34	They gave him vinegar to drink mingled with gall: and when he had tasted thereof, he would not drink.	And they gave him to drink vinegar mixed with gall. And he tasted [it], and would not drink.	And they gave him vinegar that was mixed with gall to drink. And he tasted [it], yet did not want to drink [it].
35	And they crucified him, and parted his garments, casting lots: that it might be fulfilled which was spoken by the prophet, They parted my garments among them, and upon my vesture did they cast lots.	And when they had crucified him, they distributed his garments by lot.	And when they crucified him, they divided his clothes by lot.
36	And sitting down they watched him there;	And they sat down, and watched him there	And they were sitting and watching him there.
37	And set up over his head his accusation written, THIS IS JESUS THE KING OF THE JEWS.	And they placed over his head the cause of his death, in the writing: THIS IS JESUS, THE KING OF THE JEWS.	And they placed over his head the cause of his death in an inscription, "This is Jesus, king of the Judeans."
38	Then were there two thieves crucified with him, one on the right hand, and another on the left.	And there were crucified with him two robbers, the one on his right hand, and the other on his left.	And two thieves were crucified with him, one on his right and one on his left.
39	And they that passed by reviled him, wagging their heads,	And they that passed by reviled him, and shook their heads	And those who were passing by were insulting him and were shaking their heads.
40	And saying, Thou that destroyest the temple, and buildest it in three days, save thyself. If thou be the Son of God, come down from the cross.	and said: Destroyer of the temple, and builder of it in three days, deliver thyself, if thou art the Son of God, and come down from the cross.	And they said, "[You who would] tear down the temple and rebuild it in three days, save yourself if you [are] the Son of God and come down from the cross."

Parallel Translations

MATTHEW *Chapter 27*

	KJV	*Murdock*	*Magiera*
41	Likewise also the chief priests mocking him, with the scribes and elders, said,	So also the chief priests mocked, with the Scribes and Elders and Pharisees,	Likewise, also, the chief priests were mocking [him] with the scribes and elders and Pharisees.
42	He saved others; himself he cannot save. If he be the King of Israel, let him now come down from the cross, and we will believe him.	and said: He gave life to others, his own life he cannot preserve. If he is the king of Israel, let him now descend from the cross, and we will believe in him.	And they said, "He saved others, [but] is not able to save himself. If he is the king of Israel, let him come down now from the cross and we will believe in him.
43	He trusted in God; let him deliver him now, if he will have him: for he said, I am the Son of God.	He trusted in God; let him rescue him now, if he hath pleasure in him: for he said, I am the Son of God.	He put his trust in God. Let him save him now if he is pleased with him, for he said, 'I am the Son of God.'"
44	The thieves also, which were crucified with him, cast the same in his teeth.	In like manner the marauders also, that were crucified with him, reproached him.	Likewise, also, those robbers who were crucified with him were insulting him.
45	Now from the sixth hour there was darkness over all the land unto the ninth hour.	And from the sixth hour there was darkness over all the land, until the ninth hour.	Now from the sixth hour there was darkness over all the land until the ninth hour.
46	And about the ninth hour Jesus cried with a loud voice, saying, Eli, Eli, lama sabachthani? that is to say, My God, my God, why hast thou forsaken me?	And about the ninth hour, Jesus cried with a loud voice and said: O God, O God; why hast thou forsaken me?	And about the ninth hour, Jesus cried with a loud voice and said, "God, God, why have you left me?"
47	Some of them that stood there, when they heard that, said, This man calleth for Elias.	And some of them that stood there, when they heard [it], said: He calleth for Elijah.	And some of those who were standing there, when they heard, were saying, "This [man] calls to Elijah."
48	And straightway one of them ran, and took a spunge, and filled it with vinegar, and put it on a reed, and gave him to drink.	And immediately one of them ran, and took a sponge, and filled it with vinegar, and put it on a reed, and gave him to drink.	And immediately one of them ran and took a sponge and filled it with vinegar and placed it on a reed and offered [a drink] to him.
49	The rest said, Let be, let us see whether Elias will come to save him.	But the rest said: Desist; we will see if Elijah will come to rescue him.	But the rest were saying, "Leave [him]. We will see if Elijah comes to rescue him."
50	Jesus, when he had cried again with a loud voice, yielded up the ghost.	Then Jesus cried again with a loud voice, and yielded up his spirit.	Now Jesus again cried out with a loud voice and gave up his spirit.
51	And, behold, the veil of the temple was rent in twain from the top to the bottom; and the earth did quake, and the rocks rent;	And instantly, the curtain of the door of the temple was torn asunder, from the top to the bottom; and the earth shook; and the rocks rived;	And immediately the curtains of the temple were torn in two from the top to the bottom and the earth was shaken and the rocks were split.
52	And the graves were opened; and many bodies of the saints which slept arose,	and graves were opened; and many bodies of saints who slept, arose,	And the tombs were opened and many bodies of the holy [ones] who were asleep rose up
53	And came out of the graves after his resurrection, and went into the holy city, and appeared unto many.	and came forth; and, after his resurrection, entered into the holy city, and appeared to many.	and went out. And after his resurrection they entered the holy city and were seen by many.

Parallel Translations

	KJV	*Murdock*	*Magiera*
	MATTHEW *Chapter 27*		
54	Now when the centurion, and they that were with him, watching Jesus, saw the earthquake, and those things that were done, they feared greatly, saying, Truly this was the Son of God.	And the centurion, and they that were with him guarding Jesus, when they saw the earthquake and the things that occurred, feared greatly, and said: Verily, this was the Son of God.	And the centurion and those who were watching Jesus with him, when they saw the earthquake and those [things] that had occurred, they were very afraid and said, "Truly this was the Son of God."
55	And many women were there beholding afar off, which followed Jesus from Galilee, ministering unto him:	And many women were there, looking on from a distance; the same who had followed Jesus from Galilee, and had ministered to him.	Now there were also there many women who were watching from a distance, those who had followed Jesus from Galilee and had ministered to him.
56	Among which was Mary Magdalene, and Mary the mother of James and Joses, and the mother of Zebedee's children.	One of them was Mary of Magdala, also Mary the mother of James and Joses, and the mother of Zebedee's children.	One of them [was] Mary Magdalene, and Mary, the mother of James and John, and the mother of the sons of Zebedee.
57	When the even was come, there came a rich man of Arimathaea, named Joseph, who also himself was Jesus' disciple:	And when it was evening, there came a rich man of Ramath, whose name was a Joseph, who was also a disciple of Jesus.	Now when it was evening, a rich man from Ramath came, whose name [was] Joseph, who also was taught by Jesus.
58	He went to Pilate, and begged the body of Jesus. Then Pilate commanded the body to be delivered.	This man went to Pilate, and begged the body of Jesus. And Pilate directed the body to be given him.	This [man] came near to Pilate and asked for the body of Jesus. And Pilate commanded that the body be given to him.
59	And when Joseph had taken the body, he wrapped it in a clean linen cloth,	And Joseph took the body, and wrapped it in a winding-sheet of clean linen;	And Joseph took the body and wrapped it in a cloth of clean linen.
60	And laid it in his own new tomb, which he had hewn out in the rock: and he rolled a great stone to the door of the sepulchre, and departed.	and laid it in his new sepulchre, that was excavated in a rock. And he rolled a great stone against the door of the sepulchre, and departed:	And he placed it in his new tomb that was hewn in rock. And they rolled a large stone [and] placed [it] over the opening of the tomb and they went away.
61	And there was Mary Magdalene, and the other Mary, sitting over against the sepulchre.	And there were present Mary of Magdala, and the other Mary, who sat over against the grave.	Now Mary Magdalene was there and the other Mary, who were sitting opposite the grave.
62	Now the next day, that followed the day of the preparation, the chief priests and Pharisees came together unto Pilate,	And on the day that was next after the preparation, the chief priests and Pharisees assembled before Pilate,	And on the next day that was after the preparation, the chief priests and the Pharisees were gathered with Pilate
63	Saying, Sir, we remember that that deceiver said, while he was yet alive, After three days I will rise again.	and said to him: Our Lord, we remember that this deceiver said, while he was alive, After three days, I shall arise	and said to him, "Our lord, we are reminded that that deceiver was saying while he was alive, 'After three days, I will rise up.'
64	Command therefore that the sepulchre be made sure until the third day, lest his disciples come by night, and steal him away, and say unto the people, He is risen from the dead: so the last error shall be worse than the first.	Command, therefore to guard the sepulchre; until the third day; lest his disciples come and steal him away by night, and say to the people that he hath risen from the dead; and the last delusion be worse than the first.	Command therefore to guard the grave until the third day, so that his disciples will not come [and] steal him in the night and say to the people that he has risen from the dead and the last deception should become more evil than the first."

	KJV	Murdock	Magiera

MATTHEW *Chapter 27*

	KJV	Murdock	Magiera
65	Pilate said unto them, Ye have a watch: go your way, make it as sure as ye can.	Pilate said to them: Ye have soldiers: go and guard it, as ye know how.	Pilate said to them, "You have soldiers. Go, watch as you know [how]."
66	So they went, and made the sepulchre sure, sealing the stone, and setting a watch.	And they went and set a guard to the sepulchre, and sealed the stone.	And they went [and] set a watch on the tomb and sealed that stone, with the soldiers.

Chapter 28

	KJV	Murdock	Magiera
1	In the end of the sabbath, as it began to dawn toward the first day of the week, came Mary Magdalene and the other Mary to see the sepulchre.	And in the close of the sabbath, as the first [day] of the week began to dawn, came Mary of Magdala and the other Mary, to view the sepulchre.	Now in the evening of the Sabbath, as it was twilight [on] the first of the week, Mary Magdalene and the other Mary came to see the grave.
2	And, behold, there was a great earthquake: for the angel of the Lord descended from heaven, and came and rolled back the stone from the door, and sat upon it.	And lo, there was a great earthquake: for an angel of the Lord descended from heaven, and came and rolled away the stone from the door, and sat upon it.	And behold, a great earthquake occurred, for an angel of the LORD came down from heaven and came near [and] rolled the stone from the opening and he was sitting on it.
3	His countenance was like lightning, and his raiment white as snow:	And his aspect was like the lightning; and his raiment white like snow:	And his appearance was like lightning and his clothes were white like snow.
4	And for fear of him the keepers did shake, and became as dead men.	and from fear of him the keepers were astounded, and became as dead men.	And those who were watching, trembled with fear of him and became like dead [men].
5	And the angel answered and said unto the women, Fear not ye: for I know that ye seek Jesus, which was crucified.	And the angel answered, and said to the women: Be not ye afraid, for I know that ye seek Jesus who was crucified.	Now the angel answered and said to the women, "Do not fear, for I know that you seek Jesus who was crucified.
6	He is not here: for he is risen, as he said. Come, see the place where the Lord lay.	He is not here; for he is risen, as he predicted. Come ye, see the place where our Lord was laid.	He is not here, for he has risen, as he said. Come, see the place in which our Lord was laid.
7	And go quickly, and tell his disciples that he is risen from the dead; and, behold, he goeth before you into Galilee; there shall ye see him: lo, I have told you.	And [then] go quickly, tell his disciples, that he is risen from the dead; and lo, he precedeth you to Galilee; there will ye see him. Behold, I have told you.	And go quickly [and] tell his disciples that he has risen from the dead, and behold, [he goes] before you to Galilee. There you will see him. Behold, I have told you."
8	And they departed quickly from the sepulchre with fear and great joy; and did run to bring his disciples word.	And they went quickly from the sepulchre, with fear and great joy, and ran to tell his disciples.	And they went away quickly from the grave with fear and with great joy and ran to tell his disciples.
9	And as they went to tell his disciples, behold, Jesus met them, saying, All hail. And they came and held him by the feet, and worshipped him.	And lo, Jesus met them, and said to them: Hail, ye. And they came and clasped his feet, and worshipped him.	And behold, Jesus met up with them and said to them, "Peace to you." And they came near [and] clasped his feet and worshipped him.
10	Then said Jesus unto them, Be not afraid: go tell my brethren that they go into Galilee, and there shall they see me.	Then Jesus said to them: Be not afraid; but go, tell my brethren, that they go into Galilee, and there they will see me.	Then Jesus said to them, "Do not fear! But go [and] tell my brothers that they should go to Galilee and there they will see me."

	KJV	Murdock	Magiera
	MATTHEW	*Chapter 28*	
11	Now when they were going, behold, some of the watch came into the city, and shewed unto the chief priests all the things that were done.	And while they were going, some of the guards came into the city, and told the chief priests all that had occurred.	Now when they had gone, some of those soldiers came to the city and told the chief priests everything that had occurred.
12	And when they were assembled with the elders, and had taken counsel, they gave large money unto the soldiers,	And they assembled with the Elders, and held a council; and they gave no little money to the guards,	And they were gathered with the elders and took counsel and gave no little money to the soldiers
13	Saying, Say ye, His disciples came by night, and stole him away while we slept.	and said to them: Say ye, that his disciples came and stole him away by night, while we were asleep.	and said to them, "Say that his disciples came [and] stole him in the night while we were asleep.
14	And if this come to the governor's ears, we will persuade him, and secure you.	And if this should be reported before the President, we will pacify him, and cause you not to be troubled.	And if this is heard before the governor, we will persuade him and we will not make trouble for you."
15	So they took the money, and did as they were taught: and this saying is commonly reported among the Jews until this day.	And they, having received the money, did as they were instructed. And this story is current among the Jews to this day.	Now they, when they had received the money, did as they had instructed them. And this report has gone out among the Judeans up to today.
16	Then the eleven disciples went away into Galilee, into a mountain where Jesus had appointed them.	And the eleven disciples went into Galilee, to the mountain which Jesus had appointed for them.	Now the eleven disciples went to Galilee to the mountain where Jesus had arranged [for] them to meet.
17	And when they saw him, they worshipped him: but some doubted.	And when they beheld him, they worshipped him: but some doubted.	And when they saw him, they worshipped him. But some of them were doubting.
18	And Jesus came and spake unto them, saying, All power is given unto me in heaven and in earth.	And Jesus came near, and discoursed with them, and said to them: All authority is given to me, in heaven and on earth. And as my Father sent me, so also I send you.	And Jesus came near [and] spoke with them and said to them, "All authority is given to me in heaven and on earth. And as my Father sent me, I send you.
19	Go ye therefore, and teach all nations, baptizing them in the name of the Father, and of the Son, and of the Holy Ghost:	Go ye, therefore, and instruct all nations; and baptize them in the name of the Father, and of the Son, and of the Holy Spirit.	Go, therefore, disciple all nations and baptize them in the name [of] the Father and the Son and the Holy Spirit.
20	Teaching them to observe all things whatsoever I have commanded you: and, lo, I am with you alway, even unto the end of the world. Amen.	And teach them to observe all that I have commanded you. And, behold, I am with you always, unto the consummation of the worlds Amen.	And teach them to keep all that I commanded you. And behold, I am with you all the days until the end of the world." Amen.

Parallel Translations

MARK *Chapter 1*

	KJV	*Murdock*	*Magiera*
1	The beginning of the gospel of Jesus Christ, the Son of God;	The beginning of the gospel of Jesus the Messiah, the Son of God.	The beginning of the gospel of Jesus Christ, the Son of God.
2	As it is written in the prophets, Behold, I send my messenger before thy face, which shall prepare thy way before thee.	As it is written in Isaiah the prophet: Behold, I send my messenger before thy face, who shall prepare thy way.	As it is written in Isaiah the prophet: BEHOLD I WILL SEND MY MESSENGER BEFORE YOUR FACE THAT HE MIGHT PREPARE YOUR WAY.
3	The voice of one crying in the wilderness, Prepare ye the way of the Lord, make his paths straight.	The voice of one crying in the wilderness: Prepare ye the way of the Lord; make smooth his paths.	A VOICE THAT CRIES IN THE WILDERNESS: PREPARE THE WAY OF THE LORD AND MAKE STRAIGHT HIS PATHS.
4	John did baptize in the wilderness, and preach the baptism of repentance for the remission of sins.	John baptized in the wilderness, and proclaimed the baptism of repentance for the remission of sins.	John was in the wilderness, baptizing and preaching the baptism of repentance for the forgiveness of sins.
5	And there went out unto him all the land of Judaea, and they of Jerusalem, and were all baptized of him in the river of Jordan, confessing their sins.	And there went out to him all the region of Judaea, and all the people of Jerusalem; and he baptized them in the river Jordan, while they confessed their sins.	And the whole region of Judah went out to him and all the sons of Jerusalem, and he was baptizing them in the Jordan [river] as they confessed their sins.
6	And John was clothed with camel's hair, and with a girdle of a skin about his loins; and he did eat locusts and wild honey;	And this John was clad in raiment of camels' hair; and was girded with a cincture of skin about his loins; and his food was locusts and wild honey.	Now John was clothed with clothing of the hair of camels and was bound with a leather girdle around his loins and his food was locusts and wild honey.
7	And preached, saying, There cometh one mightier than I after me, the latchet of whose shoes I am not worthy to stoop down and unloose.	And he proclaimed, and said: Behold, after me cometh one more powerful than I, of whom I am not worthy to stoop and untie the fastenings of his shoes.	And he was preaching and said, "Behold, one comes after me who is more powerful than I, the straps of whose sandals I am not worthy to stoop [and] loosen.
8	I indeed have baptized you with water: but he shall baptize you with the Holy Ghost.	I have baptized you with water; but he will baptize you with the Holy Spirit.	I have baptized you with water, but he will baptize you with the Holy Spirit."
9	And it came to pass in those days, that Jesus came from Nazareth of Galilee, and was baptized of John in Jordan.	And it occurred, in those days, that Jesus came from Nazareth in Galilee, and was baptized in Jordan by John.	And it was in those days [that] Jesus came from Nazareth of Galilee and was baptized in the Jordan [river] by John.
10	And straightway coming up out of the water, he saw the heavens opened, and the Spirit like a dove descending upon him:	And immediately on his coming from the water, he saw the heavens cleft, and the Spirit descending like a dove upon him.	And immediately when he came up from the water, he saw the heavens split and the Spirit, as a dove, came down on him.
11	And there came a voice from heaven, saying, Thou art my beloved Son, in whom I am well pleased.	And there was a voice from the heavens: Thou art my beloved Son, in whom I delight.	And there was a voice from the heavens: "You are my beloved Son. I am pleased with you."
12	And immediately the Spirit driveth him into the wilderness.	And directly the Spirit carried him into the wilderness:	And immediately the Spirit led him out into the wilderness.

Parallel Translations

	KJV	Murdock	Magiera

MARK *Chapter 1*

Verse	KJV	Murdock	Magiera
13	And he was there in the wilderness forty days, tempted of Satan; and was with the wild beasts; and the angels ministered unto him.	and he was there in the wilderness forty days, being tempted by Satan. And he was with the wild beasts; and angels ministered to him.	And he was there in the wilderness [for] forty days, being tempted by Satan. And he was with the wild beasts and angels were ministering to him.
14	Now after that John was put in prison, Jesus came into Galilee, preaching the gospel of the kingdom of God,	After John was delivered up, Jesus came into Galilee, and proclaimed the tidings, of the kingdom of God,	Now after John was delivered up, Jesus came to Galilee and was preaching the gospel of the kingdom of God.
15	And saying, The time is fulfilled, and the kingdom of God is at hand: repent ye, and believe the gospel.	and said: The time is completed, and the kingdom of God is near. Repent ye, and believe the tidings.	And he said, "The time is complete and the kingdom of God has arrived. Repent and believe in the gospel."
16	Now as he walked by the sea of Galilee, he saw Simon and Andrew his brother casting a net into the sea: for they were fishers.	And as he walked near the sea of Galilee, he saw Simon and Andrew his brother casting a net into the sea, for they were fishermen.	And while walking round about the Sea of Galilee, he saw Simon and Andrew, his brother, who were casting nets into the sea, for they were fishermen.
17	And Jesus said unto them, Come ye after me, and I will make you to become fishers of men.	And Jesus said to them: Come after me, and I will make you fishers of men.	And Jesus said to them, "Follow me and I will make you fishermen of men."
18	And straightway they forsook their nets, and followed him.	And immediately they left their nets, and went after him.	And immediately they left their nets and followed him.
19	And when he had gone a little further thence, he saw James the son of Zebedee, and John his brother, who also were in the ship mending their nets.	And as he passed on a little, he saw James the son of Zebedee, and John his brother, who also were in a ship, and mending their nets.	And as he passed on a little further, he saw James, the son of Zebedee, and John, his brother, and they also [were] in a boat mending their nets.
20	And straightway he called them: and they left their father Zebedee in the ship with the hired servants, and went after him.	And he called them: and immediately they left Zebedee their father in the ship, with the hired servants, and went after him.	And he called them and immediately they left Zebedee, their father, in the boat with the hired servants and followed him.
21	And they went into Capernaum; and straightway on the sabbath day he entered into the synagogue, and taught.	And when they entered Capernaum, he immediately taught on the sabbath in their synagogues.	And when they entered Capernaum, immediately he was teaching on the Sabbaths in their synagogues.
22	And they were astonished at his doctrine: for he taught them as one that had authority, and not as the scribes.	And they were astonished at his doctrine; for he taught them, as having authority, and not as their Scribes.	And they were amazed at his teaching, for he was teaching them as an authority and not as their scribes.
23	And there was in their synagogue a man with an unclean spirit; and he cried out,	And in their synagogue was a man, in whom was an unclean spirit; and he cried out,	And in their synagogue there was a man in whom was an unclean spirit. And he called out
24	Saying, Let us alone; what have we to do with thee, thou Jesus of Nazareth? art thou come to destroy us? I know thee who thou art, the Holy One of God.	and said: What have we to do with thee? Jesus thou Nazarean. Hast thou come to destroy us? I know thee, who thou art, the Holy One of God.	and said, "What have we to do with you, Jesus, the Nazarene? Have you come to destroy us? I know who you [are]. You are the Holy [one] of God."
25	And Jesus rebuked him, saying, Hold thy peace, and come out of him.	And Jesus rebuked him, and said: Shut thy mouth, and come out of him.	And Jesus rebuked him and said, "Close your mouth and come out of him."

MARK Chapter 1

	KJV	Murdock	Magiera
26	And when the unclean spirit had torn him, and cried with a loud voice, he came out of him.	And the unclean spirit threw him down, and cried with a loud voice, and came out of him.	And the unclean spirit threw him down and cried out with a loud voice and went out of him.
27	And they were all amazed, insomuch that they questioned among themselves, saying, What thing is this? what new doctrine is this? for with authority commandeth he even the unclean spirits, and they do obey him.	And they were all amazed, and inquired one of another, and said: What is this? What new doctrine is this? For with authority he commandeth the unclean spirits, and they obey him.	And all of them were amazed and were asking each other and saying, "What is this? And what is this new teaching? For with authority he commands even the unclean spirits and they obey him."
28	And immediately his fame spread abroad throughout all the region round about Galilee.	And immediately his fame spread into all the land of Galilee.	And immediately his fame went out into all the land of Galilee.
29	And forthwith, when they were come out of the synagogue, they entered into the house of Simon and Andrew, with James and John.	And he retired from the synagogue, and entered into the house of Simon and Andrew, with James and John.	And they went away from the synagogue and came to the house of Simon and of Andrew, with James and John.
30	But Simon's wife's mother lay sick of a fever, and anon they tell him of her.	And Simon's mother-in-law was lying sick with a fever: and they told him about her.	And the mother-in-law of Simon was sick with a fever and they told him about her.
31	And he came and took her by the hand, and lifted her up; and immediately the fever left her, and she ministered unto them.	And he came, and took her hand, and raised her up; and immediately the fever left her, and she ministered to them.	And he came near [and] took her by her hand and raised her up. And immediately her fever left her and she was ministering to them.
32	And at even, when the sun did set, they brought unto him all that were diseased, and them that were possessed with devils.	And in the evening at the setting of the sun, they brought to him all them that were diseased, and demoniacs.	Now in the evening at the setting of the sun, they brought to him all those who were very ill and possessed.
33	And all the city was gathered together at the door.	And all the city was collected at the door.	And the entire city was gathered at the door.
34	And he healed many that were sick of divers diseases, and cast out many devils; and suffered not the devils to speak, because they knew him.	And he healed many who labored under divers diseases, and cast out many demons; and he suffered not the demons to speak, because they knew him.	And he healed many that were very ill with diverse sicknesses and he cast out many devils. And he did not allow the devils to speak, because they knew him.
35	And in the morning, rising up a great while before day, he went out, and departed into a solitary place, and there prayed.	And in the morning, he rose much before others, and retired to a solitary place, and there prayed.	And in the morning he got up very early and went to a desert place and was praying there.
36	And Simon and they that were with him followed after him.	And Simon and his associates sought for him.	And Simon and those with him were searching for him.
37	And when they had found him, they said unto him, All men seek for thee.	And when they found him, they said to him: Every body is seeking for thee.	And when they found him, they said to him, "Everyone is searching for you."
38	And he said unto them, Let us go into the next towns, that I may preach there also: for therefore came I forth.	And he said to them: Go into the adjacent villages and towns; for there also I will preach, because therefore have I come.	He said to them, "Walk into the villages and into the cities that are nearby, for I will also preach there, for I have come to [do] this."
39	And he preached in their synagogues throughout all Galilee, and cast out devils.	And he preached in all their synagogues, in all Galilee, and cast out demons.	And he was preaching in all their synagogues in all of Galilee and cast out demons.

Parallel Translations

MARK Chapter 1

	KJV	Murdock	Magiera
40	And there came a leper to him, beseeching him, and kneeling down to him, and saying unto him, If thou wilt, thou canst make me clean.	And a leper came to him, and fell at his feet, and entreated him, and said to him: If thou wilt, thou canst make me clean.	And a leper came to him and fell at his feet and was begging him and said to him, "If you want to, you can cleanse me."
41	And Jesus, moved with compassion, put forth his hand, and touched him, and saith unto him, I will; be thou clean.	And Jesus had compassion on him, and stretched out his hand, and touched him, and said: I will; be thou clean.	And Jesus had compassion on him and stretched out his hand, touched him and said, "I want to. Be cleansed."
42	And as soon as he had spoken, immediately the leprosy departed from him, and he was cleansed.	And in that hour, his leprosy departed from him, and he became clean.	And immediately his leprosy went away from him and he was cleansed.
43	And he straitly charged him, and forthwith sent him away;	And he charged him, and sent him away,	And he charged him and sent him out
44	And saith unto him, See thou say nothing to any man: but go thy way, shew thyself to the priest, and offer for thy cleansing those things which Moses commanded, for a testimony unto them.	and he said to him: See that thou tell no person; but go, show thyself to the priests, and offer an oblation on account of thy purification, as Moses commanded, for a testimony to them.	and said to him, "See [that] you do not speak to anyone, but go, show yourself to the priests and offer an offering for your purification, as Moses commanded for their testimony."
45	But he went out, and began to publish it much, and to blaze abroad the matter, insomuch that Jesus could no more openly enter into the city, but was without in desert places: and they came to him from every quarter.	And he, as he went out, began to proclaim [it] much, and to divulge the matter; so that Jesus could not openly go into the city, but was without, in desert places; and they came to him from every quarter.	But when he went away, he began much preaching and made known the event, so that Jesus was not able to openly enter the city, but was outside in a deserted place. And they were coming to him from every place.

Chapter 2

	KJV	Murdock	Magiera
1	And again he entered into Capernaum after some days; and it was noised that he was in the house.	And Jesus again entered into Capernaum, after some days. And when they heard that he was in the house,	And Jesus again entered into Capernaum after [some] days. And when they heard that he was in the house,
2	And straightway many were gathered together, insomuch that there was no room to receive them, no, not so much as about the door: and he preached the word unto them.	many were assembled, so that [the house] could not contain them, not even before the door. And he held discourse with them.	many gathered, so that [the house] was not able to contain them, not even in front of the door. And he was speaking the word with them.
3	And they come unto him, bringing one sick of the palsy, which was borne of four.	And they came to him and brought to him a paralytic, borne between four persons.	And they came to him and brought him a paralytic, bearing him between four [men].
4	And when they could not come nigh unto him for the press, they uncovered the roof where he was: and when they had broken it up, they let down the bed wherein the sick of the palsy lay.	And as they could not come near him on account of the crowd, they ascended to the roof, and removed the covering of the place where Jesus was, and let down the bed on which the paralytic lay.	And because they were not able to draw near to him because of the crowd, they climbed up to the roof and lifted the covering of the place where Jesus was and they lowered the bed on which the paralytic was laid.
5	When Jesus saw their faith, he said unto the sick of the palsy, Son, thy sins be forgiven thee.	And when Jesus saw their faith, he said to the paralytic: My son, thy sins are forgiven thee.	And when Jesus saw their faith, he said to that paralytic, "My son, your sins are forgiven you."

Parallel Translations

MARK *Chapter 2*

	KJV	Murdock	Magiera
6	But there were certain of the scribes sitting there, and reasoning in their hearts,	And there were some Scribes and Pharisees there, who sat and reasoned in their hearts:	Now there were there some scribes and Pharisees, who were sitting and reasoning in their heart[s],
7	Why doth this man thus speak blasphemies? who can forgive sins but God only?	Who is this speaking, blasphemy? Who can forgive sins, except God only?	"Why does this [man] speak blasphemy? Who is able to forgive sins, except one, God?"
8	And immediately when Jesus perceived in his spirit that they so reasoned within themselves, he said unto them, Why reason ye these things in your hearts?	And Jesus knew, in his spirit, that they thus reasoned in themselves; and he said to them: Why reason ye thus in your heart?	But Jesus knew in his spirit that they were reasoning these [things] in themselves and he said to them, "Why do you reason these [things] in your heart[s]?
9	Whether is it easier to say to the sick of the palsy, Thy sins be forgiven thee; or to say, Arise, and take up thy bed, and walk?	Which is the easier, to say to a paralytic, Thy sins are forgiven thee? or to say, Arise, take up thy bed, and walk?	Which is easier to say to the paralytic, 'Your sins are forgiven you' or to say, 'Rise, take up your bed and walk?'
10	But that ye may know that the Son of man hath power on earth to forgive sins, (he saith to the sick of the palsy,)	But that ye may know that the Son of man hath power on earth to forgive sins, he said to the paralytic,	But that you might know that it is lawful [for] the Son of Man to forgive sins on earth," he said to the paralytic,
11	I say unto thee, Arise, and take up thy bed, and go thy way into thine house.	I say to thee, Arise, take thy bed, and go to thy house.	"I say to you, Rise, take up your bed, and go to your house."
12	And immediately he arose, took up the bed, and went forth before them all; insomuch that they were all amazed, and glorified God, saying, We never saw it on this fashion.	And he arose in that hour, took up his bed, and departed in presence of them all: so that they were all amazed, and praised God, saying: We never saw the like.	And he got up immediately and took his bed and went away in the sight of all, so that all of them were amazed and praised God, saying that they had never seen such.
13	And he went forth again by the sea side; and all the multitude resorted unto him, and he taught them.	And he went again to the sea; and all the multitude came to him, and he taught them.	And he went again to the sea and all the crowds were coming to him and he was teaching them.
14	And as he passed by, he saw Levi the son of Alphaeus sitting at the receipt of custom, and said unto him, Follow me. And he arose and followed him.	And as he passed along he saw Levi the son of Alpheus sitting among the publicans. And he said to him: Come after me. And he arose and went after him.	And while passing by, he saw Levi the son of Alphaeus, who was sitting at the customs-house and he said to him, "Follow me." And he got up [and] followed him.
15	And it came to pass, that, as Jesus sat at meat in his house, many publicans and sinners sat also together with Jesus and his disciples: for there were many, and they followed him.	And it was so, that as he reclined in his [Levi's] house, many publicans and sinners reclined with Jesus and with his disciples: for they were many, and they followed him.	And it happened that when he was seated [to eat] in his house, many tax collectors and sinners were seated [to eat] with Jesus and with his disciples, for there were many and they followed him.
16	And when the scribes and Pharisees saw him eat with publicans and sinners, they said unto his disciples, How is it that he eateth and drinketh with publicans and sinners?	And when the Scribes and Pharisees saw that he ate with publicans and with sinners, they said to his disciples: Why doth he eat and drink with publicans and sinners?	And the scribes and the Pharisees, when they saw that he was eating with the tax collectors and with sinners, said to his disciples, "Why does he eat and drink with tax collectors and sinners?"

Parallel Translations

MARK *Chapter 2*

	KJV	*Murdock*	*Magiera*
17	When Jesus heard it, he saith unto them, They that are whole have no need of the physician, but they that are sick: I came not to call the righteous, but sinners to repentance.	When Jesus heard [it], he said to them: The healthy need not a physician, but those laboring under disease: I came, not to call the righteous, but sinners.	But when Jesus heard [this] he said to them, "The whole do not have need for a physician, but those who are very ill. I have not come to call the just, but rather the sinners."
18	And the disciples of John and of the Pharisees used to fast: and they come and say unto him, Why do the disciples of John and of the Pharisees fast, but thy disciples fast not?	And the disciples of John and of the Pharisees were fasters; and they came and said to him: Why are the disciples of John and of the Pharisees fasters, and thy disciples fast not?	Now the disciples of John and the Pharisees were fasting and came and said to him, "Why do the disciples of John and of the Pharisees fast and your disciples do not fast?"
19	And Jesus said unto them, Can the children of the bridechamber fast, while the bridegroom is with them? as long as they have the bridegroom with them, they cannot fast.	Jesus said to them: Can the guests of the nuptial chamber fast so long as the bridegroom is with them? No.	Jesus said to them, "Are the guests of the wedding feast able to fast as long as the bridegroom is with them? No!
20	But the days will come, when the bridegroom shall be taken away from them, and then shall they fast in those days.	But the days will come, when the bridegroom will be taken from them, and then they will fast, in that day.	But the days will come when the bridegroom will be taken away from them. Then they will fast in that day.
21	No man also seweth a piece of new cloth on an old garment: else the new piece that filled it up taketh away from the old, and the rent is made worse.	No one taketh a patch of new cloth and seweth it upon an old garment, lest the supplemental new should take from the old, and the rent become the greater.	No man lays a new patch and sews [it] on an old garment, lest the new addition takes away from the old and the tear becomes worse.
22	And no man putteth new wine into old bottles: else the new wine doth burst the bottles, and the wine is spilled, and the bottles will be marred: but new wine must be put into new bottles.	And no one putteth new wine into old sacks, lest the wine burst the sacks, and the sacks be spoiled, and the wine spilled; but they put new wine into new sacks.	And no man puts new wine into old wineskins, lest the wine burst the wineskins and the wineskins are ruined and the wine is poured out. But they put new wine into new wineskins."
23	And it came to pass, that he went through the corn fields on the sabbath day; and his disciples began, as they went, to pluck the ears of corn.	And it was so, that as Jesus on a sabbath walked in the tillage grounds, his disciples walked and plucked the ears.	And it happened that when Jesus went [through] the sown fields on the Sabbath, his disciples were walking and picking the heads of grain.
24	And the Pharisees said unto him, Behold, why do they on the sabbath day that which is not lawful?	And the Pharisees said to him: See, how on the sabbath, they do that which is not lawful?	And the Pharisees said to him, "See, why are they doing something that is not lawful [to do] on the Sabbath?"
25	And he said unto them, Have ye never read what David did, when he had need, and was an hungred, he, and they that were with him?	Jesus said to them: Have ye never read what David did, when he had need and was hungry, he and his attendants?	Jesus said to them, "Have you never read what David did when he had need and was hungry, [both] he and those with him,
26	How he went into the house of God in the days of Abiathar the high priest, and did eat the shewbread, which is not lawful to eat but for the priests, and gave also to them which were with him?	How he entered the house of God, when Abiathar was high priest, and ate the bread of the Lord's table, which it was not lawful for any but priests to eat, and gave [it] also to those with him?	how he entered the house of God, while Abiathar [was] high priest, and ate the bread of the table of the LORD, which was not lawful to eat except for the priests, and gave also to those who were with him?"

Parallel Translations

	KJV	*Murdock*	*Magiera*

MARK *Chapter 2*

	KJV	Murdock	Magiera
27	And he said unto them, The sabbath was made for man, and not man for the sabbath:	And he said to them: The sabbath was made on man's account, and not man for the sake of the sabbath.	And he said to them, "The Sabbath was made for man and man was not [made] for the Sabbath.
28	Therefore the Son of man is Lord also of the sabbath.	Therefore also the Son of man is lord of the sabbath.	So also, the Son of Man is the Lord of the Sabbath."

Chapter 3

	KJV	Murdock	Magiera
1	And he entered again into the synagogue; and there was a man there which had a withered hand.	And again Jesus entered into a synagogue. And there was a man there, whose hand was withered.	And again Jesus entered into the synagogue, and there was there a certain man whose hand was withered.
2	And they watched him, whether he would heal him on the sabbath day; that they might accuse him.	And they watched him, that if he should heal on the sabbath, they might accuse him.	And they were watching him, so that if he healed him on the Sabbath, they might accuse him.
3	And he saith unto the man which had the withered hand, Stand forth.	And he said to the man of the withered hand: Stand up in the midst.	And he said to that man whose hand was withered, "Stand up in the middle."
4	And he saith unto them, Is it lawful to do good on the sabbath days, or to do evil? to save life, or to kill? But they held their peace.	And he said also to them: Is it lawful to do good on the sabbath, or to do evil? to give life to a person, or to destroy? But they were silent	And he also said to them, "Is it lawful on the Sabbath to do that which is good or that which is evil? To save life or to destroy [it]?" But they were silent.
5	And when he had looked round about on them with anger, being grieved for the hardness of their hearts, he saith unto the man, Stretch forth thine hand. And he stretched it out: and his hand was restored whole as the other.	And he looked on them with indignation, being grieved with the hardness of their heart. And he said to the man: Stretch forth thy hand. And he stretched forth, and his hand was restored.	And he looked on them with anger, being saddened by the hardness of their heart[s]. And he said to that man, "Stretch out your hand." And he stretched [it] out and his hand was restored.
6	And the Pharisees went forth, and straightway took counsel with the Herodians against him, how they might destroy him.	And the Pharisees went out, that very hour, with the domestics of Herod, and held a consultation against him, how they might destroy him.	And the Pharisees went out immediately with the Herodians and took counsel against him, how they might destroy him.
7	But Jesus withdrew himself with his disciples to the sea: and a great multitude from Galilee followed him, and from Judaea,	And Jesus retired with his disciples to the sea. And many people joined him from Galilee, and from Judaea,	And Jesus went with his disciples to the sea and many people were joining with him from Galilee and from Judah
8	And from Jerusalem, and from Idumaea, and from beyond Jordan; and they about Tyre and Sidon, a great multitude, when they had heard what great things he did, came unto him.	and from Jerusalem, and from Idumaea, and from beyond Jordan, and from Tyre, and from Sidon: great multitudes,--- when they heard all that he did, came to him.	and from Jerusalem and from Idumaea and from beyond Jordan and from Tyre and from Sidon. Many crowds who had heard all that he had done came to him.
9	And he spake to his disciples, that a small ship should wait on him because of the multitude, lest they should throng him.	And he told his disciples to bring him a ship, on account of the multitude, lest they should crowd upon him	And he told his disciples to bring him a boat because of the crowds, so that they would not press on him.
10	For he had healed many; insomuch that they pressed upon him for to touch him, as many as had plagues.	For he had healed many, so that they rushed upon him, in order to touch him.	For he had healed so many up until then that they were falling on him in order to touch him.

Parallel Translations

MARK *Chapter 3*

	KJV	*Murdock*	*Magiera*
11	And unclean spirits, when they saw him, fell down before him, and cried, saying, Thou art the Son of God.	And they who were afflicted with unclean spirits, when they saw him, fell down and cried out, and said: Thou art the Son of God.	And those who had torments of unclean spirits, when they saw him, were falling down and crying out and saying, "You are the Son of God."
12	And he straitly charged them that they should not make him known.	And he charged them much, not to make him known.	And he severely rebuked them that they should not reveal him.
13	And he goeth up into a mountain, and calleth unto him whom he would: and they came unto him.	And he ascended a mountain, and called whom he pleased; and they came to him.	And he climbed up a mountain and called those whom he wanted and they came to him.
14	And he ordained twelve, that they should be with him, and that he might send them forth to preach,	And he chose twelve to be with him, whom he would send out to preach,	And he chose twelve to be with him and to send them to preach
15	And to have power to heal sicknesses, and to cast out devils:	and who would have power to heal the sick, and to cast out demons.	and to be authorities to heal the sick and to cast out devils.
16	And Simon he surnamed Peter;	And to Simon he gave the name of Cephas.	And he named Simon the name Peter,
17	And James the son of Zebedee, and John the brother of James; and he surnamed them Boanerges, which is, The sons of thunder:	And to James the son of Zebedee and to John the brother of James, he gave the name of Boanerges, that is, Sons of thunder.	and to James the son of Zebedee and to John the brother of James, he gave them the name Boanerges, which is, sons of thunder.
18	And Andrew, and Philip, and Bartholomew, and Matthew, and Thomas, and James the son of Alphaeus, and Thaddaeus, and Simon the Canaanite,	And [he chose also] Andrew, and Philip, and Bartholomew, and Matthew, and Thomas, and James the son of Alpheus, and Thaddeus, and Simon the Canaanite,	And [he chose] Andrew and Philip and Bartholomew and Matthew and Thomas and James, the son of Alphaeus, and Thaddeus and Simon the Canaanite,
19	And Judas Iscariot, which also betrayed him: and they went into an house.	And Judas Iscariot, who betrayed him. And they came to the house:	and Judas Iscariot, who betrayed him. And they came to a house
20	And the multitude cometh together again, so that they could not so much as eat bread.	and the multitude assembled again, so that they could not eat bread.	and the crowds gathered again, so that they were not able to eat bread.
21	And when his friends heard of it, they went out to lay hold on him: for they said, He is beside himself.	And his kinsmen heard, and went out to take him; for they said: He is out of his reason.	And his relatives heard and went out to seize him, for they were saying that he had gone out of his mind.
22	And the scribes which came down from Jerusalem said, He hath Beelzebub, and by the prince of the devils casteth he out devils.	And those Scribes that had come down from Jerusalem, said: Beelzebub is in him; and by the prince of demons he expelleth demons.	And those scribes who had come down from Jerusalem were saying, "Beelzebub is in him, and he casts out devils by the chief of the devils."
23	And he called them unto him, and said unto them in parables, How can Satan cast out Satan?	And Jesus called them, and said to them, by similitudes: How can Satan cast out Satan?	And Jesus called them and in parables said to them, "How is Satan able to cast out Satan?
24	And if a kingdom be divided against itself, that kingdom cannot stand.	For if a kingdom be divided against itself, that kingdom cannot stand.	For if a kingdom will be divided against itself, that kingdom is not able to stand.
25	And if a house be divided against itself, that house cannot stand.	And if a house be divided against itself, that house cannot stand.	And if a house will be divided against itself, that house is not able to stand.

Parallel Translations

MARK *Chapter 3*

	KJV	*Murdock*	*Magiera*
26	And if Satan rise up against himself, and be divided, he cannot stand, but hath an end.	And if Satan rise up against himself and be divided, he cannot stand, but is at an end.	And if Satan stands against himself and is divided, he is not able to stand, but is [at] his end.
27	No man can enter into a strong man's house, and spoil his goods, except he will first bind the strong man; and then he will spoil his house.	No one can enter the house of a strong man, and plunder his goods, unless he first bind the strong man; and then he may rob his house.	No man is able to enter the house of a strong man and to grab his possessions, except he first binds the strong man and then robs his house.
28	Verily I say unto you, All sins shall be forgiven unto the sons of men, and blasphemies wherewith soever they shall blaspheme:	Verily I say to you: All sins, and the blasphemies that men may utter, may be forgiven them:	Truly I say to you, all the sins and blasphemies that men will blaspheme will be forgiven them,
29	But he that shall blaspheme against the Holy Ghost hath never forgiveness, but is in danger of eternal damnation:	but whoever shall blaspheme against the Holy Spirit, to him for ever there is no forgiveness; but he is obnoxious to eternal judgment.	but he who blasphemes against the Holy Spirit has no forgiveness forever, but is guilty before the judgment that is eternal."
30	Because they said, He hath an unclean spirit.	Because they had said: An unclean spirit is in him.	[This was] because they were saying, "He has an unclean spirit."
31	There came then his brethren and his mother, and, standing without, sent unto him, calling him.	And his mother and his brothers came, and, standing without, sent to call him to them.	And his mother and his brothers came, standing outside, and they sent [someone] to call him to them.
32	And the multitude sat about him, and they said unto him, Behold, thy mother and thy brethren without seek for thee.	And the multitude were sitting around him, and they said to him: Lo, thy mother and thy brothers, without, call for thee.	Now the crowd was sitting around him and they said to him, "Behold, your mother and your brothers [are] outside seeking you."
33	And he answered them, saying, Who is my mother, or my brethren?	He replied, and said to them: Who is my mother? and who are my brothers?	And he answered and said to them, "Who is my mother? And who are my brothers?"
34	And he looked round about on them which sat about him, and said, Behold my mother and my brethren!	And he looked upon those who sat by him, and said: Behold my mother! and, behold my brothers!	And he looked at those who sat with him and said, "Behold, my mother, and behold, my brothers.
35	For whosoever shall do the will of God, the same is my brother, and my sister, and mother.	For whoever shall do the pleasure of God, he is my brother, and my sister, and my mother.	For he who does the will of God is my brother and my sister and my mother."

Chapter 4

	KJV	*Murdock*	*Magiera*
1	And he began again to teach by the sea side: and there was gathered unto him a great multitude, so that he entered into a ship, and sat in the sea; and the whole multitude was by the sea on the land.	And again he began to teach by the side of the sea. And great multitudes were assembled about him; so that he embarked and sat in a ship on the sea, and all the multitude stood on the land by the side of the sea.	And again he began to teach by the shore of the sea. And large crowds were gathered around him so that he boarded [and] sat in a boat on the sea. And the entire crowd was standing on the land by the shore of the sea.
2	And he taught them many things by parables, and said unto them in his doctrine,	And he taught them much by similitudes. And in his teaching, he said:	And he was teaching them in many parables and said in his teaching,
3	Hearken; Behold, there went out a sower to sow:	Hear ye: Behold a sower went forth to sow.	"Listen. Behold, a sower went out to sow

Parallel Translations

	KJV	*Murdock*	*Magiera*
	MARK	*Chapter 4*	
4	And it came to pass, as he sowed, some fell by the way side, and the fowls of the air came and devoured it up.	And as he sowed, some [seed] fell on the side of the path; and a bird came, and devoured it.	and while he sowed, one [seed] fell by the side of the road and a bird came and ate it.
5	And some fell on stony ground, where it had not much earth; and immediately it sprang up, because it had no depth of earth:	And other [seed] fell on a rock, so that it had not much earth; and it soon shot up, because it had no depth of earth.	And another [seed] fell on rock where there was not much earth, and immediately it sprouted because there was no depth of earth.
6	But when the sun was up, it was scorched; and because it had no root, it withered away.	But when the sun was up, it wilted; and because it had no root, it dried up.	But when the sun came up, [the plant] withered and because it had no root, it dried up.
7	And some fell among thorns, and the thorns grew up, and choked it, and it yielded no fruit.	And other [seed] fell among thorns. And the thorns grew up, and choked it, and it yielded no fruits.	And another [seed] fell among the thorns. And the thorns grew up and choked it and it did not bear fruit.
8	And other fell on good ground, and did yield fruit that sprang up and increased; and brought forth, some thirty, and some sixty, and some an hundred.	And other [seed] fell on good ground, and came up, and grew, and yielded fruits; some thirty, some sixty, and some a hundred.	But another [seed] fell on good earth and grew up and matured and bore fruit, some thirty and some sixty and some one hundred[fold]."
9	And he said unto them, He that hath ears to hear, let him hear.	And he said: Whoever hath ears to hear, let him hear.	And he said, "He who has ears to hear should hear."
10	And when he was alone, they that were about him with the twelve asked of him the parable.	And when they were by themselves, those with him, together with the twelve, asked him [concerning] this similitude.	Now when they were alone, those who were with him with his twelve asked him about that parable.
11	And he said unto them, Unto you it is given to know the mystery of the kingdom of God: but unto them that are without, all these things are done in parables:	And Jesus said to them: To you it is given to know the mystery of the kingdom of God; but to them without, all is in similitudes:	And Jesus said to them, "To you is given to know the mystery of the kingdom of God. But to [those] outside, everything is in parables,
12	That seeing they may see, and not perceive; and hearing they may hear, and not understand; lest at any time they should be converted, and their sins should be forgiven them.	that when they see, they may see and not see, and when they hear, they may hear and not understand; lest they should be converted, and their sins be forgiven them.	so that WHEN THEY SEE, THEY WILL SEE YET NOT SEE, AND WHEN THEY HEAR, THEY WILL HEAR YET NOT UNDERSTAND, LEST THEY SHOULD RETURN AND THEIR SINS WOULD BE FORGIVEN THEM."
13	And he said unto them, Know ye not this parable? and how then will ye know all parables?	And he said to them: Do ye not understand this similitude? And how will ye understand all similitudes?	And he said to them, "Do you not understand this parable? Then how will you understand all parables?
14	The sower soweth the word.	The sower that sowed, sowed the word.	The sower, who sowed, sowed the word.
15	And these are they by the way side, where the word is sown; but when they have heard, Satan cometh immediately, and taketh away the word that was sown in their hearts.	And those by the side of the path, are they in whom the word is sown; and as soon as they have heard [it], Satan cometh, and taketh away the word that was sown in their hearts.	And those [seed] that [were] by the side of the road are those in whom the word is sown. And when they have heard, immediately Satan comes and takes away the word that was sown in their heart[s].

MARK *Chapter 4*

	KJV	*Murdock*	*Magiera*
16	And these are they likewise which are sown on stony ground; who, when they have heard the word, immediately receive it with gladness;	And those sown on the rock, are they who, when they hear the word, immediately with joy receive it.	And those that were sown on rock are those that when they have heard the word, immediately receive it with joy.
17	And have no root in themselves, and so endure but for a time: afterward, when affliction or persecution ariseth for the word's sake, immediately they are offended.	And they have no root in them, but are temporary; and when there is affliction or persecution on account of the word, they are quickly stumbled.	And they have no root in themselves, but they are temporary. And when trouble or persecution happens on account of the word, they are quickly offended.
18	And these are they which are sown among thorns; such as hear the word,	And those sown among thorns, are they that hear the word,	And those that were sown among thorns are those who have heard the word
19	And the cares of this world, and the deceitfulness of riches, and the lusts of other things entering in, choke the word, and it becometh unfruitful.	and the cares of this world, and the deceitfulness of riches, and the residue of other lusts enter in and choke the word, and it is without fruits.	and the care of this world and the deceit of riches and the rest of the other lusts enter [and] choke the word, and they are without fruit.
20	And these are they which are sown on good ground; such as hear the word, and receive it, and bring forth fruit, some thirtyfold, some sixty, and some an hundred.	And those sown on good ground are they that hear the word, and receive it, and bear fruits, by thirties, and by sixties, and by hundreds.	And those that were sown on good ground are those who have heard the word and receive [it] and bear fruit thirty and sixty and one hundred[fold]."
21	And he said unto them, Is a candle brought to be put under a bushel, or under a bed? and not to be set on a candlestick?	And he said to them: Is a lamp brought to be placed under a bushel, or under a bed? Is it not to be placed on a light-stand?	And he said to them, "Is there any profit for a lamp to be placed under a basket or under a couch? Should it not be placed on a lamp stand?
22	For there is nothing hid, which shall not be manifested; neither was any thing kept secret, but that it should come abroad.	For there is nothing hid, which will not be exposed; and nothing concealed, which will not be made manifest.	For there is not anything that is hidden that will not be revealed or [anything] occurring in secret and is not revealed.
23	If any man have ears to hear, let him hear.	If any one have ears to hear, let him hear.	If a man has ears to hear, he should hear."
24	And he said unto them, Take heed what ye hear: with what measure ye mete, it shall be measured to you: and unto you that hear shall more be given.	And he said to them: Take heed what ye hear: with what measure ye measure, it shall be measured to you: and there shall more be given to you who hear.	And he said to them, "Notice what you hear. With that measure that you measure, it will be measured to you, and it is accumulated to you who hear.
25	For he that hath, to him shall be given: and he that hath not, from him shall be taken even that which he hath.	For to him that hath, will more be given; and from him that hath not, even what he hath, will be taken from him.	For he who has, it will be given to him. And he who has not, even that which he has will be taken from him."
26	And he said, So is the kingdom of God, as if a man should cast seed into the ground;	And he said: So is the kingdom of God, as if a man should cast seed into the ground,	And he was saying, "Such is the kingdom of God as a man who throws seed on the ground.
27	And should sleep, and rise night and day, and the seed should spring and grow up, he knoweth not how.	and should sleep and rise, by night and by day, and the seed should grow and shoot up, he knoweth not how.	And he will sleep and rise in the night and in the day, and the seed will grow and be tall, as he does not know [how],

	KJV	Murdock	Magiera
	MARK	*Chapter 4*	
28	For the earth bringeth forth fruit of herself; first the blade, then the ear, after that the full corn in the ear.	For the earth bringeth forth the fruit; first the plant, and subsequently the ear, and at last the complete wheat in the ear.	for the ground brings forth the fruit. And first comes the plant, and after it the ear, and finally the full grain in the ear.
29	But when the fruit is brought forth, immediately he putteth in the sickle, because the harvest is come.	And when the fruit is ripe, immediately cometh the sickle, because the harvest hath arrived.	And when the fruit is ripe, immediately the sickle comes, because the harvest has arrived."
30	And he said, Whereunto shall we liken the kingdom of God? or with what comparison shall we compare it?	And he said: To what shall we liken the kingdom of God? and with what similitude shall we compare it?	And he said, "What is the kingdom of God like and with what parable can we compare it?
31	It is like a grain of mustard seed, which, when it is sown in the earth, is less than all the seeds that be in the earth:	It is like a grain of mustard seed which, when it is sown in the earth, is the least of all seeds sown on the earth;	It is as a grain of mustard, which, when it is planted in the ground, is the least of all the small seeds that are on the earth.
32	But when it is sown, it groweth up, and becometh greater than all herbs, and shooteth out great branches; so that the fowls of the air may lodge under the shadow of it.	and when it is sown it springeth up, and becometh greater than all herbs, and produceth great branches, so that birds can lodge under its shadow.	And when it is planted, it grows up and becomes greater than all the herbs and produces great branches, so that a bird is able to nest in its shade."
33	And with many such parables spake he the word unto them, as they were able to hear it.	And by many such similitudes,---similitudes such as they could hear,---Jesus discoursed with the people.	With parables such as these, Jesus was speaking with them, parables such as they were able to hear.
34	But without a parable spake he not unto them: and when they were alone, he expounded all things to his disciples.	And without similitudes he did not converse with them: but to his disciples, between himself and them, he explained every thing.	And without parables, he was not speaking with them. But he was explaining everything to his disciples privately.
35	And the same day, when the even was come, he saith unto them, Let us pass over unto the other side.	And he said to them, the same day at evening: Let us pass over to the other side.	And he said to them on the same day at evening, "Let us cross over to the other shore."
36	And when they had sent away the multitude, they took him even as he was in the ship. And there were also with him other little ships.	And they sent away the multitudes: and they conducted him in the ship as he was. And there were also with him other little ships.	And they left the crowds and conducted him away in a boat, and there were other boats with them.
37	And there arose a great storm of wind, and the waves beat into the ship, so that it was now full.	And there was a great tempest and wind: and the waves beat upon the ship, and it was near being filled.	And there was a great storm and wind, and waves were falling into the boat, and [the boat] was about to be filled.
38	And he was in the hinder part of the ship, asleep on a pillow: and they awake him, and say unto him, Master, carest thou not that we perish?	And Jesus was asleep on a pillow in the hinder part of the ship. And they came and awoke him, and said to him: Our Rabbi, carest thou not, that we perish?	And Jesus was asleep on a cushion in the stern of the boat, and they came [and] woke him and said to him, "Our Master, do you not care that we are being destroyed?"

Parallel Translations

MARK *Chapter 4*

	KJV	*Murdock*	*Magiera*
39	And he arose, and rebuked the wind, and said unto the sea, Peace, be still. And the wind ceased, and there was a great calm.	And he arose, and rebuked the wind, and said to the sea: Cease; be still. And the wind ceased, and there was a great calm.	And he rose up and rebuked the wind and said to the sea, "Cease; be restrained." And the wind ceased and a great calm occurred.
40	And he said unto them, Why are ye so fearful? how is it that ye have no faith?	And he said to them: Why were ye so fearful? and why have ye not faith?	And he said to them, "Why are you fearful in this manner? And why do you not have faith?"
41	And they feared exceedingly, and said one to another, What manner of man is this, that even the wind and the sea obey him?	And they feared with great fear: and they said, one to another: Who is this, that even the winds and the sea obey him!	And they feared a great fear and were saying one to another, "Who indeed is this [man] that the winds and sea obey him?"

Chapter 5

	KJV	*Murdock*	*Magiera*
1	And they came over unto the other side of the sea, into the country of the Gadarenes.	And he came to the other side of the sea, to the country of the Gadarenes.	And he came to the opposite side of the sea to the region of the Gadarenes.
2	And when he was come out of the ship, immediately there met him out of the tombs a man with an unclean spirit,	And as he went out of the ship, there met him from the place of sepulchres a man in whom was an unclean spirit.	And when he disembarked from the boat, he met a man from the tombs who had an unclean spirit.
3	Who had his dwelling among the tombs; and no man could bind him, no, not with chains:	And he dwelt in the place of sepulchres; and no one could confine him with chains:	And he was living in the tombs and no man was able to bind him with chains,
4	Because that he had been often bound with fetters and chains, and the chains had been plucked asunder by him, and the fetters broken in pieces: neither could any man tame him.	because, as often as he had been confined with fetters and chains, he had broken the chains and burst the fetters: and no one could subdue him.	because whenever he was bound with shackles and with chains, he would break the chains and would cut the shackles. And no man was able to subdue him.
5	And always, night and day, he was in the mountains, and in the tombs, crying, and cutting himself with stones.	And continually, by night and by day, he was in the place of sepulchres, and cried and wounded himself with stones.	And always in the night and in the day, he was in the tombs and in the mountains and he was crying and cutting himself with stones.
6	But when he saw Jesus afar off, he ran and worshipped him,	And when he saw Jesus at a distance, he ran and worshipped him;	And when he saw Jesus from a distance, he ran [and] worshipped him.
7	And cried with a loud voice, and said, What have I to do with thee, Jesus, thou Son of the most high God? I adjure thee by God, that thou torment me not.	and cried with a loud voice, and said: What have I to do with thee, Jesus, thou Son of the High God? I adjure thee by God, that thou torment me not.	And he cried with a loud voice and said, "What have I to do with you, Jesus, Son of the Most High God? I urge you by God that you do not torment me."
8	For he said unto him, Come out of the man, thou unclean spirit.	For he had said to him: Come out of the man, thou unclean spirit.	For he was saying to him, "Come out from the man, unclean spirit."
9	And he asked him, What is thy name? And he answered, saying, My name is Legion: for we are many.	And he demanded of him: What is thy name? And he replied to him: Our name is Legion; for we are many.	And he asked him, "What is your name?" He said to him, "Our name [is] Legion, because we are many."
10	And he besought him much that he would not send them away out of the country.	And he besought him much, that he would not send him out of the country.	And he was begging him very much not to send him out of the country.

Parallel Translations

	KJV	Murdock	Magiera
MARK	*Chapter 5*		
11	Now there was there nigh unto the mountains a great herd of swine feeding.	And there was there by the mountain, a great herd of swine grazing.	Now there was there near the mountain a large herd of pigs that were feeding.
12	And all the devils besought him, saying, Send us into the swine, that we may enter into them.	And the demons besought him, and said: Send us upon those swine, that we may enter them.	And those demons were begging him and saying, "Send us against those pigs that we may attack them."
13	And forthwith Jesus gave them leave. And the unclean spirits went out, and entered into the swine: and the herd ran violently down a steep place into the sea, (they were about two thousand;) and were choked in the sea.	And he permitted them. And those unclean spirits went out, and entered the swine: and the herd, of about two thousand, ran to a precipice, and fell into the sea, and were strangled in the waters.	And he allowed them. And those unclean spirits went away and attacked the pigs, and that herd ran to a steep place and fell into the sea and about two thousand [pigs] were drowned in the water.
14	And they that fed the swine fled, and told it in the city, and in the country. And they went out to see what it was that was done.	And they who tended them, fled and told [it] in the city and in the villages: and they came out to see what had occurred.	And those who were tending them fled and reported [it] in the city and also in the villages. And they came out to see what had happened.
15	And they come to Jesus, and see him that was possessed with the devil, and had the legion, sitting, and clothed, and in his right mind: and they were afraid.	And: they came to Jesus, and saw him in whom the demons had been,---him in whom had been the legion,--- clothed, and sober, and sitting; and they were afraid.	And they came to Jesus and saw him, the one possessed of demons, in whom Legion had been, dressed and sober and sitting. And they were afraid.
16	And they that saw it told them how it befell to him that was possessed with the devil, and also concerning the swine.	And those who had seen [it] told them how it occurred to him who had the demons, and also concerning the swine.	And those who had seen related to them how it happened to the one possessed of demons and also about those pigs.
17	And they began to pray him to depart out of their coasts.	And they began to request him, that he would go from their border.	And they began begging him to leave their border.
18	And when he was come into the ship, he that had been possessed with the devil prayed him that he might be with him.	And as he ascended the ship, the late demoniac requested that he might continue with him.	And when he boarded a boat, he who had been possessed of demons was begging him that he might be with him,
19	Howbeit Jesus suffered him not, but saith unto him, Go home to thy friends, and tell them how great things the Lord hath done for thee, and hath had compassion on thee.	And he suffered him not, but said to him: Go home to thy people, and tell them what the Lord hath done for thee, and hath compassionated thee.	yet he did not allow him. On the contrary, he said to him, "Go to your house to your people and tell them what the LORD did for you and how he had compassion on you."
20	And he departed, and began to publish in Decapolis how great things Jesus had done for him: and all men did marvel.	And he went, and began to publish in Decapolis, what Jesus had done for him. And they were all amazed.	And he went and began preaching in the Decapolis what Jesus had done for him, and all of them were amazed.
21	And when Jesus was passed over again by ship unto the other side, much people gathered unto him: and he was nigh unto the sea.	And when Jesus had passed by ship to the other side, great multitudes again assembled about him as he was on the shore of the sea.	And when Jesus had crossed over by boat to that other side, large crowds again were gathered around him while he was by the shore of the sea.

Parallel Translations

	KJV	Murdock	Magiera
	MARK Chapter 5		
22	And, behold, there cometh one of the rulers of the synagogue, Jairus by name; and when he saw him, he fell at his feet,	And one of the rulers of the synagogue, whose name was Jairus, came, and, on seeing him, fell at his feet,	And a certain [man] whose name [was] Jairus came from the rulers of the synagogue. And when he saw him, he fell down at his feet.
23	And besought him greatly, saying, My little daughter lieth at the point of death: I pray thee, come and lay thy hands on her, that she may be healed; and she shall live.	and besought him much, and said to him: My daughter is very sick; but come and lay thy hand on her, and she will be cured, and will live.	And he was begging him very much and said to him, "My daughter is very sick. Come [and] place your hand on her and she will be made whole and live."
24	And Jesus went with him; and much people followed him, and thronged him.	And Jesus went with him; and a great company attended him, and pressed upon him.	And Jesus went away with him and a large crowd followed him and they were pressing on him.
25	And a certain woman, which had an issue of blood twelve years,	And a woman who had had a defluxion of blood twelve years,	And a certain woman, who had a flow of blood [for] twelve years,
26	And had suffered many things of many physicians, and had spent all that she had, and was nothing bettered, but rather grew worse,	and who had suffered much from many physicians, and had expended all she possessed, and was not profited, but was even the more afflicted;	who had suffered much from many doctors and had spent everything that she had and was not some helped, but was afflicted even more,
27	When she had heard of Jesus, came in the press behind, and touched his garment.	when she heard of Jesus, came behind him in the press of the crowd, and touched his garment	when she heard about Jesus, came through the press of the crowd [and] from behind him touched his clothing,
28	For she said, If I may touch but his clothes, I shall be whole.	For she said: If I but touch his garment, I shall live.	for she was saying, "If only I can touch his clothing, I will live."
29	And straightway the fountain of her blood was dried up; and she felt in her body that she was healed of that plague.	And immediately the fountain of her blood dried up; and she felt in her body that she was healed of her plague.	And immediately the flow of her blood dried up and she felt in her body that she had been healed of her sickness.
30	And Jesus, immediately knowing in himself that virtue had gone out of him, turned him about in the press, and said, Who touched my clothes?	And Jesus at once knew in himself, that virtue had issued from him: and he turned to the throng, and said: Who touched my clothes?	Now Jesus immediately knew within himself that power had gone out of him. And he turned to the crowd and said, "Who touched my garments?"
31	And his disciples said unto him, Thou seest the multitude thronging thee, and sayest thou, Who touched me?	And his disciples said to him: Thou seest the throngs that press upon thee; and sayest thou, Who touched me?	And his disciples said to him, "Do you see the crowds that are pressing you, and you say, who touched me?"
32	And he looked round about to see her that had done this thing.	And he looked around, to see who had done this.	And he was looking to see who had done this.
33	But the woman fearing and trembling, knowing what was done in her, came and fell down before him, and told him all the truth.	And the woman, fearing and trembling, for she knew what had taken place in her, came and fell down before him, and told him all the truth.	And that woman, being afraid and trembling, because she knew what had happened to her, came [and] fell down before him and told him all the truth.
34	And he said unto her, Daughter, thy faith hath made thee whole; go in peace, and be whole of thy plague.	And he said to her: My daughter, thy faith hath made thee live: go in peace; and be thou healed of thy plague.	And he said to her, "My daughter, your faith has given you life. Go in peace and be healed from your sickness."

MARK Chapter 5

	KJV	Murdock	Magiera
35	While he yet spake, there came from the ruler of the synagogue's house certain which said, Thy daughter is dead: why troublest thou the Master any further?	And while he was speaking, some domestics of the ruler of the synagogue came, and said: Thy daughter is dead: why therefore troublest thou the teacher?	And while he was speaking they came from the house of the ruler of the synagogue and were saying, "Your daughter is dead. Why therefore are you troubling the teacher?"
36	As soon as Jesus heard the word that was spoken, he saith unto the ruler of the synagogue, Be not afraid, only believe.	But Jesus heard the word they spoke, and said to the ruler of the synagogue: Fear not; only believe.	But Jesus heard the word that they said and said to the ruler of the synagogue, "Do not fear; only believe."
37	And he suffered no man to follow him, save Peter, and James, and John the brother of James.	And he suffered no one to go with him, except Simon Cephas, and James, and John the brother of James.	And he did not allow anyone to go with him, except Simon Peter and James and John, the brother of James.
38	And he cometh to the house of the ruler of the synagogue, and seeth the tumult, and them that wept and wailed greatly.	And they came to the house of the ruler of the synagogue; and he saw, that they were in a tumult, and weeping, and howling.	And they came to the house of that ruler of the synagogue and saw that they were troubled and weeping and wailing.
39	And when he was come in, he saith unto them, Why make ye this ado, and weep? the damsel is not dead, but sleepeth.	And he entered in and said to them: Why are ye in a tumult, and weep? The maid is not dead, but is asleep.	And he entered and said to them, "Why are you troubled and weeping? The girl is not dead, but she is asleep,"
40	And they laughed him to scorn. But when he had put them all out, he taketh the father and the mother of the damsel, and them that were with him, and entereth in where the damsel was lying.	And they laughed at him. But Jesus put them all out. And he took the maids father, and her mother, and those that accompanied him, and entered into where the maid lay.	and they were laughing at him. But he sent all of them out and he took the father of the girl and her mother and those who were with him and entered where the girl was laid.
41	And he took the damsel by the hand, and said unto her, Talitha cumi; which is, being interpreted, Damsel, I say unto thee, arise.	And he took the maid's hand, and said to her: Maiden, arise.	And he took the hand of the girl and said to her, "[Young] girl, rise."
42	And straightway the damsel arose, and walked; for she was of the age of twelve years. And they were astonished with a great astonishment.	And immediately the maid arose, and walked; for she was twelve years old. And they were astonished with a great astonishment.	And immediately the girl rose up and walked, for she was twelve years old. And they were amazed [with] great amazement.
43	And he charged them straitly that no man should know it; and commanded that something should be given her to eat.	And he enjoined it upon them much, that no one should know of it. And he directed, that they should give her to eat.	And he commanded them very much that no one should make this known. And he said that they should give her [something] to eat.

Chapter 6

	KJV	Murdock	Magiera
1	And he went out from thence, and came into his own country; and his disciples follow him.	And Jesus departed from there and came to his own city, and his disciples attended him.	And he went away from there and came to his city and his disciples were following him.

Parallel Translations

	KJV	Murdock	Magiera
	MARK Chapter 6		
2	And when the sabbath day was come, he began to teach in the synagogue: and many hearing him were astonished, saying, From whence hath this man these things? and what wisdom is this which is given unto him, that even such mighty works are wrought by his hands?	And when the sabbath came, he began to teach in the synagogue. And many who heard [him] were astonished, and said: Whence hath he obtained these things? And, what wisdom is this, which is given to him! and that such mighty works are done by his hands!	And when it was the Sabbath, he began to teach in the synagogue. And many who heard were amazed and were saying, "Where [did] this man [learn] these [things]? And what is [this] wisdom that was given to him, that miracles such as these might be done by his hand?
3	Is not this the carpenter, the son of Mary, the brother of James, and Joses, and of Juda, and Simon? and are not his sisters here with us? And they were offended at him.	Is not this the carpenter, the son of Mary, and the brother of James and of Joses and of Judas and of Simon? And are not his sisters here with us? And they were stumbled in him.	Is this not the carpenter, the son of Mary and the brother of James and of Joses and of Judas and of Simon? And behold, are not his sisters here with us?" And they were offended at him.
4	But Jesus said unto them, A prophet is not without honour, but in his own country, and among his own kin, and in his own house.	And Jesus said to them: There is no prophet who is little, except in his own city, and among his kindred, and at home.	And Jesus said to them, "There is no prophet who is dishonored, except in his own city and among his own relatives and in his own house."
5	And he could there do no mighty work, save that he laid his hands upon a few sick folk, and healed them.	And he could not there do even one mighty work, except that he laid his hand on a few sick, and healed them.	And he was not able to do even one miracle there, except that he laid his hand on a few sick and healed [them].
6	And he marvelled because of their unbelief. And he went round about the villages, teaching.	And he wondered at the defect of their faith. And he travelled about the villages and taught.	And he was amazed by the lack of their faith. And he was traveling in the villages while teaching.
7	And he called unto him the twelve, and began to send them forth by two and two; and gave them power over unclean spirits;	And he called his twelve, and began to send them forth, two and two; and he gave them authority over unclean spirits, to cast them out.	And he called his twelve and began to send them in pairs. And he gave them authority over unclean spirits, to cast [them] out.
8	And commanded them that they should take nothing for their journey, save a staff only; no scrip, no bread, no money in their purse:	And he commanded them to take nothing for the journey, except a staff only; neither a wallet, nor bread, nor brass in their purses;	And he commanded them that they should not carry anything for the journey, except only a staff, no bag and no bread and no brass in their purses,
9	But be shod with sandals; and not put on two coats.	but to be shod with sandals, and not put on two coats.	but [that] they should wear sandals and not wear two coats.
10	And he said unto them, In what place soever ye enter into an house, there abide till ye depart from that place.	And he said to them: Into whatever house ye enter, there abide till ye leave the place.	And he said to them, "Into that house, which you enter, there be until you leave there.
11	And whosoever shall not receive you, nor hear you, when ye depart thence, shake off the dust under your feet for a testimony against them. Verily I say unto you, It shall be more tolerable for Sodom and Gomorrha in the day of judgment, than for that city.	And whoever will not receive you, nor hear you, when ye go out from that place shake off the dust that is under your feet, for a testimony to them. Verily I say to you, There will be comfort for Sodom and Gomorrah in the day of judgment rather than for that city.	And whoever does not receive you and does not hear you when you leave from there, shake off the dust that is under the sole of your feet for their witness. And truly I say to you, it will be [more] pleasant for Sodom and for Gomorrah in the day of judgment than for that city.

Parallel Translations

MARK *Chapter 6*

	KJV	*Murdock*	*Magiera*
12	And they went out, and preached that men should repent.	And they went out and proclaimed, that [men] should repent.	And they went out and preached that [men] should repent.
13	And they cast out many devils, and anointed with oil many that were sick, and healed them.	And they cast out many demons, and many of the sick they anointed with oil, and healed them.	And many demons were cast out. And they were anointing with oil many sick [people] and were healing [them].
14	And king Herod heard of him; (for his name was spread abroad:) and he said, That John the Baptist was risen from the dead, and therefore mighty works do shew forth themselves in him.	And Herod the king heard of Jesus,---for his name had become known to him,---and he said: John the Baptizer hath risen from the dead: and therefore it is, mighty deeds are done by him.	And Herod, the king, heard about Jesus, for his name was made known to him. And he was saying [that] John the baptizer had risen from the dead, [and] because of this, miracles are done by him.
15	Others said, That it is Elias. And others said, That it is a prophet, or as one of the prophets.	Others said: He is Elijah: and others: He is a prophet, like one of the prophets.	Others were saying that he was Elijah, and others that he was a prophet like one of the prophets.
16	But when Herod heard thereof, he said, It is John, whom I beheaded: he is risen from the dead.	But when Herod heard [of him], he said: He is that John whose head I struck off: he is risen from the dead.	Now when Herod heard [this] he said, "[It is] John, the one whose head I cut off. He has risen from the dead."
17	For Herod himself had sent forth and laid hold upon John, and bound him in prison for Herodias' sake, his brother Philip's wife: for he had married her.	For Herod had sent and seized John and bound him in prison, on account of Herodias, his brother Philips wife, whom he had taken.	For Herod had sent [and] arrested John and bound him [in] prison because of Herodias, the wife of Philip, his brother, whom he had taken.
18	For John had said unto Herod, It is not lawful for thee to have thy brother's wife.	For John had said to Herod: It is not lawful for thee to take thy brother's wife.	For John had told Herod, "It is unlawful for you to take the wife of your brother."
19	Therefore Herodias had a quarrel against him, and would have killed him; but she could not:	And Herodias herself was an enemy to him, and wished to kill him, but was not able.	Now Herodias was threatened by him and she wanted to kill him and was not able,
20	For Herod feared John, knowing that he was a just man and an holy, and observed him; and when he heard him, he did many things, and heard him gladly.	For Herod was afraid of John, because he knew him to be a just and holy man: and he observed him, and gave ear to him in many things and did [the things], and he heard him with satisfaction.	for Herod was afraid of John, because he knew that he was a just and holy man. And he observed him, and [in] many [things] heard him and did [these things], and gladly heard him.
21	And when a convenient day was come, that Herod on his birthday made a supper to his lords, high captains, and chief estates of Galilee;	And there was a noted day, when Herod made a supper, in the house of his nativity, for his nobles and the chiliarchs and the chiefs of Galilee.	And there was a notable day when Herod made a banquet on his birthday for his nobles and chiliarchs and rulers of Galilee.
22	And when the daughter of the said Herodias came in, and danced, and pleased Herod and them that sat with him, the king said unto the damsel, Ask of me whatsoever thou wilt, and I will give it thee.	And the daughter of Herodias came in, and danced; and she pleased Herod and those reclining with him. And the king said to the maid: Ask of me what thou pleasest, and I will give it thee.	And the daughter of Herodias entered [and] danced and pleased Herod and those who were sitting to eat with him. And the king said to the girl, "Ask me anything that you want and I will give [it] to you."
23	And he sware unto her, Whatsoever thou shalt ask of me, I will give it thee, unto the half of my kingdom.	And he swore to her: Whatever thou shalt ask, I will give thee, even to the half of my kingdom.	And he swore to her, "Whatever you ask, I will give to you, up to half of my kingdom."

Parallel Translations

	KJV	*Murdock*	*Magiera*
	MARK	*Chapter 6*	
24	And she went forth, and said unto her mother, What shall I ask? And she said, The head of John the Baptist.	And she went out, and said to her mother: What shall I ask of him? She said to her: The head of John the Baptizer.	And she went away and said to her mother, "What should I ask of him?" She said to her, "The head of John the baptizer."
25	And she came in straightway with haste unto the king, and asked, saying, I will that thou give me by and by in a charger the head of John the Baptist.	And she soon entered with eagerness to the king, and said: I desire that thou, this hour, give me in a dish the head of John the Baptizer.	And immediately she entered with care to the king and said to him, "I desire right now that you would give me on a platter the head of John the baptizer."
26	And the king was exceeding sorry; yet for his oath's sake, and for their sakes which sat with him, he would not reject her.	And it pained the king greatly; yet, on account of the oath, and on account of the guests, he would not deny her:	And it made the king very sad, but because of the oaths and because of the guests, he did not want to deny her.
27	And immediately the king sent an executioner, and commanded his head to be brought: and he went and beheaded him in the prison,	and the king sent immediately an executioner, and commanded [him] to bring the head of John. And he went, and struck off the head of John in the prison;	But immediately the king sent the executioner and commanded that he should bring the head of John. And he went [and] cut off the head of John [in] prison.
28	And brought his head in a charger, and gave it to the damsel: and the damsel gave it to her mother.	and brought it on a dish, and gave it to the maid; and the maid gave it to her mother.	And he brought [it] on a platter and gave [it] to the girl, and the girl gave [it] to her mother.
29	And when his disciples heard of it, they came and took up his corpse, and laid it in a tomb.	And his disciples heard [of it]; and they came and took up the corpse, and laid it in a sepulchre.	And his disciples heard and came [and] took his body and placed [it] in a grave.
30	And the apostles gathered themselves together unto Jesus, and told him all things, both what they had done, and what they had taught.	And the legates assembled before Jesus, and told him all they had done, and all they had taught.	And the apostles were gathered around Jesus and told him everything they had done and everything they had learned.
31	And he said unto them, Come ye yourselves apart into a desert place, and rest a while: for there were many coming and going, and they had no leisure so much as to eat.	And he said to them: Come, let us go into a desert by ourselves, and rest a little. For there were many going and coming, and they had not opportunity even to eat bread.	And he said to them, "Come, let us go into the desert by ourselves and rest a little," for there were many who were going and coming and they had no opportunity even to eat.
32	And they departed into a desert place by ship privately.	And they went by ship to a desert place by themselves.	And they went away to a deserted place in a boat by themselves.
33	And the people saw them departing, and many knew him, and ran afoot thither out of all cities, and outwent them, and came together unto him.	But many saw them, as they departed, and knew them; and from all the cities, they ran thither by land before him.	And many saw them as they were going away and recognized them. And they ran by land before him, from all the cities, to the place.
34	And Jesus, when he came out, saw much people, and was moved with compassion toward them, because they were as sheep not having a shepherd: and he began to teach them many things.	And Jesus disembarked and saw great multitudes: and he compassionated them, because they were like sheep having no shepherd. And he began to teach them many things.	And Jesus disembarked [and] saw the large crowds and had compassion on them because they were like sheep that did not have a shepherd. And he began to teach them many [things].

Parallel Translations

	KJV	Murdock	Magiera
MARK	*Chapter 6*		
35	And when the day was now far spent, his disciples came unto him, and said, This is a desert place, and now the time is far passed:	And when the time was advanced, his disciples came to him, and said to him: This is a desert place, and the time is advanced.	And when the time grew late, his disciples came to him and said to him, "This is a barren place and the time is late.
36	Send them away, that they may go into the country round about, and into the villages, and buy themselves bread: for they have nothing to eat.	Dismiss them, that they may go into the fields around us and into the villages, and may buy themselves bread; for they have nothing to eat.	Dismiss them to go to the surrounding fields and villages and let them buy bread for themselves, for they do not have anything to eat."
37	He answered and said unto them, Give ye them to eat. And they say unto him, Shall we go and buy two hundred pennyworth of bread, and give them to eat?	And he said to them: Give ye them to eat. They say to him: Shall we go and buy bread of the value of two hundred denarii, and give them to eat?	But he said to them, "Give them to eat." They said to him, "Should we go [and] buy bread [worth] two hundred denarii and give them to eat?"
38	He saith unto them, How many loaves have ye? go and see. And when they knew, they say, Five, and two fishes.	And he said to them: Go, see how many loaves ye have here. And when they had seen, they say to him: Five loaves and two fishes.	And he said to them, "Go [and] see how much bread you have here." And when they saw, they said to him, "Five [loaves of] bread and two fish."
39	And he commanded them to make all sit down by companies upon the green grass.	And he bid them make the people recline on the grass by companies.	And he commanded them to seat everyone by groups on the grass.
40	And they sat down in ranks, by hundreds, and by fifties.	And they reclined, by companies of a hundred, and of fifty.	And they sat [to eat] by groups of hundreds and fifties.
41	And when he had taken the five loaves and the two fishes, he looked up to heaven, and blessed, and brake the loaves, and gave them to his disciples to set before them; and the two fishes divided he among them all.	And he took the five loaves and the two fishes, and looked towards heaven, and blessed and brake the bread, and gave to his disciples to set before them: and they divided [also] the two fishes among them all.	And he took those five [loaves of] bread and two fish, and looked into heaven and blessed and broke the bread, and gave [it] to his disciples to place before them. And they distributed those two fish to all.
42	And they did all eat, and were filled.	And they all ate, and were satisfied.	And all ate and were full.
43	And they took up twelve baskets full of the fragments, and of the fishes.	And they took up twelve baskets full of the fragments and of the fishes.	And they took up the fragments [of bread] and of fish, twelve baskets full.
44	And they that did eat of the loaves were about five thousand men.	And they who had eaten bread were five thousand men.	And those who ate bread were five thousand men.
45	And straightway he constrained his disciples to get into the ship, and to go to the other side before unto Bethsaida, while he sent away the people.	And he immediately constrained his disciples to take ship, and go before him to the other side, to Bethsaida, while he dismissed the multitudes.	And immediately he pressed his disciples to board a boat and to precede him to the opposite shore to Bethsaida while he dismissed the crowds.
46	And when he had sent them away, he departed into a mountain to pray.	And when he had dismissed them, he went to a mountain to pray.	And when he had dismissed them, he went to a mountain to pray.
47	And when even was come, the ship was in the midst of the sea, and he alone on the land.	And when evening came, the ship was in the middle of the sea, and he alone on the land.	And when evening came, the boat was in the middle of the sea and he [was] alone on the land.

Parallel Translations

	KJV	*Murdock*	*Magiera*
	MARK *Chapter 6*		
48	And he saw them toiling in rowing; for the wind was contrary unto them: and about the fourth watch of the night he cometh unto them, walking upon the sea, and would have passed by them.	And he saw them straining themselves in rowing; for the wind was against them. And in the fourth watch of the night, Jesus came to them walking on the waters; and he was disposed to pass by them.	And he saw them straining while rowing, for the wind was against them. And in the fourth watch of the night, Jesus came to them, walking on the water. And he wanted to pass by them.
49	But when they saw him walking upon the sea, they supposed it had been a spirit, and cried out:	And they saw him walking on the waters, and they supposed that the appearance was a spectre: and they cried out.	But they saw him walking on the water, and they thought to themselves that it was a false vision, and they cried out,
50	For they all saw him, and were troubled. And immediately he talked with them, and saith unto them, Be of good cheer: it is I; be not afraid.	For they all saw him, and were afraid. And immediately he spoke with them, and said to them: Take courage; it is I; fear not.	for all of them saw him and were afraid. And immediately he spoke with them and said to them, "Take courage, it is I. Do not be afraid."
51	And he went up unto them into the ship; and the wind ceased: and they were sore amazed in themselves beyond measure, and wondered.	And he entered into the ship to them; and the wind ceased. And they were greatly amazed, and astonished among themselves.	And he climbed into the boat with them and the wind ceased. And they were greatly amazed and astonished among themselves,
52	For they considered not the miracle of the loaves: for their heart was hardened.	For they did not learn by the bread; because their heart was stupid.	for they had not gained insight from that bread, because their heart was hardened.
53	And when they had passed over, they came into the land of Gennesaret, and drew to the shore.	And when they had passed to the other shore, they came to the land of Gennesaret.	And when they had crossed to the other side, they came to the land of Gennesaret.
54	And when they were come out of the ship, straightway they knew him,	And when they went out of the ship, immediately the men of the place knew him.	And after they had disembarked from the boat, immediately the people of the place recognized him.
55	And ran through that whole region round about, and began to carry about in beds those that were sick, where they heard he was.	And they ran through all that region, and began to bring forth them that were sick, bearing them on beds to where they heard he was.	And they ran into that entire region and began to bring those who were very ill, carrying them on pallets to where they heard that he was.
56	And whithersoever he entered, into villages, or cities, or country, they laid the sick in the streets, and besought him that they might touch if it were but the border of his garment: and as many as touched him were made whole.	And wherever he entered into villages or cities, the sick were laid in he streets: and they besought him, that they might touch but the extremity of his raiment. And all they that touched him, were healed.	And wherever he entered into the villages and cities, the sick were placed in the streets. And they were begging him that they might touch even the border of his clothes. And all those who touched him were healed.
	Chapter 7		
1	Then came together unto him the Pharisees, and certain of the scribes, which came from Jerusalem.	And there gathered about him Pharisees and Scribes, who had come from Jerusalem.	And the Pharisees and scribes gathered around him who came from Jerusalem.
2	And when they saw some of his disciples eat bread with defiled, that is to say, with unwashen, hands, they found fault.	And they saw some of his disciples eating bread, with their hands unwashed; and they censured it.	And they saw some of his disciples who were eating bread while their hands were not washed, and they complained.

Parallel Translations

MARK *Chapter 7*

	KJV	*Murdock*	*Magiera*
3	For the Pharisees, and all the Jews, except they wash their hands oft, eat not, holding the tradition of the elders.	For all the Jews and the Pharisees, unless they carefully wash their hands do not eat; because they hold fast the tradition of the Elders.	For all the Judeans and the Pharisees do not eat unless they wash their hands carefully, because they hold to the tradition of the elders.
4	And when they come from the market, except they wash, they eat not. And many other things there be, which they have received to hold, as the washing of cups, and pots, brasen vessels, and of tables.	And [coming] from the market-place, except they baptize, they do not eat. And there are many other things which they have received to observe, [such as] the baptisms of cups, and of pots, and of brazen vessels, and of couches.	And they do not eat [things] from the marketplace unless they are washed. And there are many other [traditions] that they have received to observe, washings of cups and of pots and of brass vessels and of beds.
5	Then the Pharisees and scribes asked him, Why walk not thy disciples according to the tradition of the elders, but eat bread with unwashen hands?	And the Scribes and Pharisees asked him: Why walk not thy disciples according to the tradition of the Elders, but eat bread with their hands unwashed?	And the scribes and the Pharisees asked him, "Why do your disciples not walk according to the tradition of the elders, but they eat bread while their hands are not washed?"
6	He answered and said unto them, Well hath Esaias prophesied of you hypocrites, as it is written, This people honoureth me with their lips, but their heart is far from me.	And he said to them: Well did Isaiah the prophet prophecy concerning you, ye hypocrites; as it is written: This people honoreth me with its lips, but their heart is very far from me.	And he said to them, "Well did Isaiah the prophet prophesy concerning you. Hypocrites! As it is written: THIS PEOPLE HONORS ME WITH ITS LIPS BUT THEIR HEART IS VERY FAR FROM ME.
7	Howbeit in vain do they worship me, teaching for doctrines the commandments of men.	And in vain do they give me reverence, while teaching as doctrines the precepts of men.	AND WITHOUT RESULTS THEY REVERENCE ME WHILE TEACHING THE TEACHINGS OF THE COMMANDMENTS OF MEN.
8	For laying aside the commandment of God, ye hold the tradition of men, as the washing of pots and cups: and many other such like things ye do.	For ye have forsaken the commandment of God, and hold fast the tradition of men, the baptisms of cups, and of pots, and many things like these.	For you have left the commandment of God and you have held to the tradition of men, washings of cups and of pots and many [things] that resemble these."
9	And he said unto them, Full well ye reject the commandment of God, that ye may keep your own tradition.	He said [also] to them: Full well do ye spurn the precept of God, that ye may establish your tradition!	He said to them, "Well did you reject the commandment of God that you might establish your tradition.
10	For Moses said, Honour thy father and thy mother; and, Whoso curseth father or mother, let him die the death:	For Moses said: Honor thy father and thy mother; and whoever shall revile his father or his mother, shall surely die.	For Moses said: HONOR YOUR FATHER AND YOUR MOTHER. And HE WHO REVILES FATHER AND MOTHER SHOULD INDEED DIE.
11	But ye say, If a man shall say to his father or mother, It is Corban, that is to say, a gift, by whatsoever thou mightest be profited by me; he shall be free.	But ye say: If a man say to his father or to his mother, Be it my oblation, whatever thou mayest gain from me:	But you say [that] if a man should say to his father or to his mother, 'My offering [is] what you have gained from me,'
12	And ye suffer him no more to do ought for his father or his mother;	then ye suffer him not to do any thing for his father or his mother.	then you allow him not to do anything for his father or his mother.

MARK *Chapter 7*

	KJV	Murdock	Magiera
13	Making the word of God of none effect through your tradition, which ye have delivered: and many such like things do ye.	And ye reject the word of God, on account of the tradition which ye hand down. And many things like these, ye do.	And you despise the word of God because of the tradition that you have handed down and you do many [things] that resemble these.
14	And when he had called all the people unto him, he said unto them, Hearken unto me every one of you, and understand:	And Jesus called all the multitude, and said to them: Hear, all ye; and understand.	And Jesus called to the entire crowd and said to them, "Hear me, all of you, and understand.
15	There is nothing from without a man, that entering into him can defile him: but the things which come out of him, those are they that defile the man.	There is nothing without a man which, by entering him, can pollute him. But that which cometh out of him, that it is that polluteth a man.	There is nothing that is outside of a man that enters him that is able [to] defile him. But what goes out from him, that defiles a man.
16	If any man have ears to hear, let him hear.	Whoever hath ears to hear, let him hear.	He who has ears to hear should hear."
17	And when he was entered into the house from the people, his disciples asked him concerning the parable.	And when Jesus had entered the house, apart from the multitude, his disciples asked him about this similitude.	And when Jesus entered the house [away] from the crowd, his disciples asked him about that saying.
18	And he saith unto them, Are ye so without understanding also? Do ye not perceive, that whatsoever thing from without entereth into the man, it cannot defile him;	And he said to them: Are ye likewise so undiscerning? Do ye not know, that whatever from without entereth into a man, cannot defile him?	He said to them, "Are you likewise also slow to understand? Do you not know that everything that enters a man from the outside cannot defile him,
19	Because it entereth not into his heart, but into the belly, and goeth out into the draught, purging all meats?	For it doth not enter into his heart, but into his belly, and is thrown into the digestive process, which carries off all that is eaten.	because it does not enter his heart but into his stomach and is cast off by excretion, which purifies all the food?
20	And he said, That which cometh out of the man, that defileth the man.	But that which proceedeth from a man, that defileth a man.	But anything that goes out from a man, that defiles the man.
21	For from within, out of the heart of men, proceed evil thoughts, adulteries, fornications, murders,	For from within, from the heart of men, proceed evil thoughts, adultery, whoredom,	For from within, from the heart of men, evil thoughts proceed: adultery, fornication, theft, murder,
22	Thefts, covetousness, wickedness, deceit, lasciviousness, an evil eye, blasphemy, pride, foolishness:	theft, murder, avarice, malice, deceit, lasciviousness, an evil eye, reviling, haughtiness, folly.	injustice, wickedness, deceit, filthiness, an evil eye, blasphemy, boastfulness, foolishness.
23	All these evil things come from within, and defile the man.	All these evil things come from within, and defile a man.	All these evils proceed from within and defile a man."
24	And from thence he arose, and went into the borders of Tyre and Sidon, and entered into an house, and would have no man know it: but he could not be hid.	Thence Jesus arose, and went to the border of Tyre and Sidon. And he entered a house, and wished no man to know him; but he could not be concealed.	From there Jesus rose up and came to the border of Tyre and Sidon. And he entered a certain house. And he did not want anyone to know about him, yet he was not able to conceal [himself],
25	For a certain woman, whose young daughter had an unclean spirit, heard of him, and came and fell at his feet:	For immediately a woman, whose daughter had an unclean spirit, heard of him; and she came, and fell before his feet,	for immediately a certain woman, whose daughter had an unclean spirit, heard about him and came [and] fell down before his feet.

MARK *Chapter 7*

Verse	KJV	Murdock	Magiera
26	The woman was a Greek, a Syrophenician by nation; and she besought him that he would cast forth the devil out of her daughter.	the woman was a Gentile from Phenicia of Syria, and besought him, that he would expel the demon from her daughter.	Now the woman was a foreigner from Phoenicia of Syria, and she was begging him to cast out the demon from her daughter.
27	But Jesus said unto her, Let the children first be filled: for it is not meet to take the children's bread, and to cast it unto the dogs.	Jesus said to her: Permit the children first to be satisfied; for it is not becoming, to take the children's bread and cast it to dogs.	And Jesus said to her, "Allow first the children to be satisfied, for it is not proper to take the bread of the children and to throw [it] to the dogs."
28	And she answered and said unto him, Yes, Lord: yet the dogs under the table eat of the children's crumbs.	And she replied, and said to him: Yes, my Lord: and yet the dogs under the table eat the children's crumbs.	And she answered and said to him, "Yes, my Lord. Yet even the dogs eat the crumbs of the children from under the tables."
29	And he said unto her, For this saying go thy way; the devil is gone out of thy daughter.	Jesus said to her: Go thou; because of this speech, the demon hath departed from thy daughter.	Jesus said to her, "Go! Because of this saying, the demon has gone out from your daughter."
30	And when she was come to her house, she found the devil gone out, and her daughter laid upon the bed.	And she went to her house, and found her daughter lying on a bed, and the demon gone from her.	And she went to her house and found her daughter lying on a pallet and her demon had left her.
31	And again, departing from the coasts of Tyre and Sidon, he came unto the sea of Galilee, through the midst of the coasts of Decapolis.	Again Jesus departed from the border of Tyre and Sidon, and came to the sea of Galilee, to the border of Decapolis.	Again Jesus went out from the border of Tyre and Sidon and came to the Sea of Galilee, on the border of the Decapolis.
32	And they bring unto him one that was deaf, and had an impediment in his speech; and they beseech him to put his hand upon him.	And they brought to him a deaf and stammering man, and besought him to lay his hand on him.	And they brought him a certain deaf man, a stammerer, and were asking him to place a hand on him.
33	And he took him aside from the multitude, and put his fingers into his ears, and he spit, and touched his tongue;	And he led him aside from the multitude, and put his fingers into his ears, and spit, and touched his tongue,	And he led him away from the crowd privately and placed his fingers in his ears and he spit and touched his tongue.
34	And looking up to heaven, he sighed, and saith unto him, Ephphatha, that is, Be opened.	and looked towards heaven, and sighed, and said to him: Be opened.	And he looked into heaven and sighed and said to him, "Be opened."
35	And straightway his ears were opened, and the string of his tongue was loosed, and he spake plain.	And immediately his ears were opened, and the bond of his tongue was loosed, and he spake plainly.	And immediately his ears were opened and the restriction of his tongue was loosed and he spoke plainly.
36	And he charged them that they should tell no man: but the more he charged them, so much the more a great deal they published it;	And he charged them to tell no man of it: and the more he charged them, the more they proclaimed it.	And he admonished them not to tell anyone. And the more that he was admonishing them, the more they were proclaiming.
37	And were beyond measure astonished, saying, He hath done all things well: he maketh both the deaf to hear, and the dumb to speak.	And they admired exceedingly, and said: He doeth every thing excellently: he maketh the deaf to hear, and the speechless to talk.	And they were exceedingly amazed and were saying, "He does everything well. He makes the deaf to hear, and those not speaking to speak."

Parallel Translations

MARK *Chapter 8*

	KJV	*Murdock*	*Magiera*
1	In those days the multitude being very great, and having nothing to eat, Jesus called his disciples unto him, and saith unto them,	And in those days, when the multitude was great, and had nothing to eat, he called his disciples, and said to them:	Now in those days when there was a large crowd and there was nothing to eat, he called his disciples and said to them,
2	I have compassion on the multitude, because they have now been with me three days, and have nothing to eat:	I compassionate this multitude; for, lo, three days have they continued with me, and they have nothing to eat.	"I have compassion on this crowd because, behold, they have remained with me three days and they do not have anything to eat.
3	And if I send them away fasting to their own houses, they will faint by the way: for divers of them came from far.	And if I send them to their homes fasting, they will faint by the way: for some of them have come from a great distance.	And if I dismiss them to their homes while they are fasting, they will faint along the road, for some of them have come from far away."
4	And his disciples answered him, From whence can a man satisfy these men with bread here in the wilderness?	His disciples say to him: Whence can one, here in the desert, satisfy all these with bread?	His disciples said to him, "[From] where can a man find here in the wilderness bread to satisfy all these [people]?"
5	And he asked them, How many loaves have ye? And they said, Seven.	And he asked them: How many loaves have ye? They say to him, Seven.	And he asked them, "How many [loaves of] bread do you have?" They told him, "Seven."
6	And he commanded the people to sit down on the ground: and he took the seven loaves, and gave thanks, and brake, and gave to his disciples to set before them; and they did set them before the people.	And he directed the multitudes to recline on the ground: and he took the seven loaves, and blessed, and brake, and grave to his disciples to set forth; and they set before the multitudes.	And he commanded the crowds to recline on the ground, and he took those seven [loaves of] bread and blessed and broke [them] and gave [them] to his disciples to set out, and they set [the food] before the crowds.
7	And they had a few small fishes: and he blessed, and commanded to set them also before them.	And there were a few fishes; and them he also blessed, and ordered them set forth.	And there were a few fish and he also blessed them, and said to set them out.
8	So they did eat, and were filled: and they took up of the broken meat that was left seven baskets.	And they ate, and were satisfied: and they took up seven baskets of the remaining fragments.	And they ate and were satisfied. And they took up the remains of the fragments, seven baskets.
9	And they that had eaten were about four thousand: and he sent them away.	And the men who had eaten, were about four thousand: and he sent them away.	And the men who ate were about four thousand.
10	And straightway he entered into a ship with his disciples, and came into the parts of Dalmanutha.	And immediately he entered a ship, with his disciples, and came to the place Dalmanutha.	And he dismissed them, and immediately boarded a boat with his disciples, and came to the region of Dalmanutha.
11	And the Pharisees came forth, and began to question with him, seeking of him a sign from heaven, tempting him.	And the Pharisees came out, and began to dispute with him; and, to tempt him, they demanded of him a sign from heaven.	And the Pharisees came out and began to dispute with him. And they were asking him [for] a sign from heaven, tempting him.
12	And he sighed deeply in his spirit, and saith, Why doth this generation seek after a sign? verily I say unto you, There shall no sign be given unto this generation.	And he sighed with his breath, and said: Why doth this generation seek after a sign? Verily I say to you, No sign will be given to this generation.	And he sighed in his spirit and said, "Why does this generation seek a sign? Truly I say to you, a sign will not be given to this generation."

Parallel Translations

	KJV	*Murdock*	*Magiera*

MARK *Chapter 8*

	KJV	Murdock	Magiera
13	And he left them, and entering into the ship again departed to the other side.	And he left them, and embarked in the ship; and they passed to the other shore.	And he left them and boarded a boat and they went to the other side.
14	Now the disciples had forgotten to take bread, neither had they in the ship with them more than one loaf.	And they had forgotten to take bread with them, and had but a single cake in the ship with them.	And they forgot to take bread. And except [for] one loaf, there was nothing with them in the boat.
15	And he charged them, saying, Take heed, beware of the leaven of the Pharisees, and of the leaven of Herod.	And he charged them, and said to them: Take heed, and beware of the leaven of the Pharisees, and of the leaven of Herod.	And he commanded them and said to them, "Watch out! Beware of the leaven of the Pharisees and of the leaven of Herod."
16	And they reasoned among themselves, saying, It is because we have no bread.	And they reasoned one with another, and said: It is, because we have no bread.	And they were reasoning with each other and saying, "[It is] because we have no bread."
17	And when Jesus knew it, he saith unto them, Why reason ye, because ye have no bread? perceive ye not yet, neither understand? have ye your heart yet hardened?	And Jesus knew [it], and said to them: Why reason ye, because ye have no bread? Do ye still not know, nor understand? How long will your heart be hard?	But Jesus knew [this] and said to them, "Why are you thinking [it is] because you have no bread? Do you still not know and do you not understand? How long will you have a hard heart?
18	Having eyes, see ye not? and having ears, hear ye not? and do ye not remember?	and ye have eyes, but see not? and have ears, but hear not, nor reflect?	And you have eyes and you do not see, and you have ears and you do not hear, and you do not remember.
19	When I brake the five loaves among five thousand, how many baskets full of fragments took ye up? They say unto him, Twelve.	When I broke the five loaves to five thousand, how many baskets full of the fragments took ye up? They say to him: Twelve.	When I broke those five [loaves of] bread for the five thousand, how many baskets full of fragments did you take up?" They told him, "Twelve."
20	And when the seven among four thousand, how many baskets full of fragments took ye up? And they said, Seven.	He saith to them. And when the seven to four thousand, how many baskets full of the fragments took ye up? They say: Seven.	He said to them, "And when seven [loaves] to the four thousand, how many baskets full of fragments did you take up?" They said, "Seven."
21	And he said unto them, How is it that ye do not understand?	He saith to them: Why is it that, to this time, ye do not consider?	He said to them, "Why is it [that] still you do not understand?"
22	And he cometh to Bethsaida; and they bring a blind man unto him, and besought him to touch him.	And he came to Bethsaida: and they brought to him a blind man, and besought him to touch him.	And he came to Bethsaida. And they brought him a blind man and were begging him to touch him.
23	And he took the blind man by the hand, and led him out of the town; and when he had spit on his eyes, and put his hands upon him, he asked him if he saw ought.	And he took the blind man by the hand, and led him out of the village, and spit on his eyes, and laid on his hand: and asked him, what he saw.	And he took the hand of the blind man and led him outside of the village. And he spat on his eyes and laid his hand [on him] and asked him what he saw.
24	And he looked up, and said, I see men as trees, walking.	And he gazed, and said: I see men like trees which walk.	And he looked and said, "I see men as trees that are walking."
25	After that he put his hands again upon his eyes, and made him look up: and he was restored, and saw every man clearly.	Again he laid his hand on his eyes, and he was recovered, and saw every thing plainly.	Again he laid his hand on his eyes and he was restored and was seeing everything clearly.

Parallel Translations

MARK *Chapter 8*

	KJV	*Murdock*	*Magiera*
26	And he sent him away to his house, saying, Neither go into the town, nor tell it to any in the town.	And he sent him to his house, and said to him: Neither enter into the village, nor tell any person in the village.	And he sent him to his house and said, "Neither enter the village nor tell anyone in the village."
27	And Jesus went out, and his disciples, into the towns of Caesarea Philippi: and by the way he asked his disciples, saying unto them, Whom do men say that I am?	And Jesus and his disciples went to the villages of Caesarea Philippi. And he asked his disciples by the way, and said to them: Who, do men say of me, that I am?	And Jesus and his disciples went out to the villages of Caesarea Philippi. And he was asking his disciples along the way and said to them, "What do men say about me, who I am?"
28	And they answered, John the Baptist: but some say, Elias; and others, One of the prophets.	And they said to him: That [thou art] John the Baptizer; and others: That [thou art] Elijah; and others: That [thou art] one of the prophets.	And they said, "John the baptizer, and others Elijah, and others, one of the prophets.
29	And he saith unto them, But whom say ye that I am? And Peter answereth and saith unto him, Thou art the Christ.	Jesus said to them: And who, do ye yourselves say of me, that I am? Simon replied, and said to him: Thou art the Messiah, the Son of the living God.	Jesus said to them, "But what do you say about me, who I am?" Simon answered and said to him, "You are the Messiah, the Son of the living God."
30	And he charged them that they should tell no man of him.	And he charged them, that they should say [this] of him to no person.	And he charged them not to tell anyone about him.
31	And he began to teach them, that the Son of man must suffer many things, and be rejected of the elders, and of the chief priests, and scribes, and be killed, and after three days rise again.	And he began to teach them, that the Son of man was about to suffer much, and be rejected by the Elders and by the chief priests and by the Scribes, and be killed, and rise on the third day.	And he began to teach them that the Son of Man would suffer much, and be rejected by the elders and by the chief priests and by the scribes, and be killed and after three days, rise up.
32	And he spake that saying openly. And Peter took him, and began to rebuke him.	And he spoke out the thing distinctly. And Cephas took him, and began to rebuke him.	And he was speaking publicly [about this] matter. And Peter took him and began to rebuke him.
33	But when he had turned about and looked on his disciples, he rebuked Peter, saying, Get thee behind me, Satan: for thou savourest not the things that be of God, but the things that be of men.	But he turned, and looked upon his disciples, and rebuked Simon, and said: Get thee behind me, Satan: for thou dost not consider what is of God, but what is of men.	But he turned and looked at his disciples and rebuked Simon and said, "Go behind me, Satan, because you do not think about [the things] of God, but [the things] of men!"
34	And when he had called the people unto him with his disciples also, he said unto them, Whosoever will come after me, let him deny himself, and take up his cross, and follow me.	And Jesus called the multitude, together with his disciples, and said to them: Whoever will come after me, let him deny himself, and take up his cross, and come after me.	And Jesus called the crowds with his disciples and said to them, "He who wants to follow me should deny himself and take up his cross and follow me.
35	For whosoever will save his life shall lose it; but whosoever shall lose his life for my sake and the gospel's, the same shall save it.	For, whoever will preserve his life, shall lose it; and whoever will lose his life on my account, and on account of my tidings, shall preserve it.	For everyone who wants to save his soul will lose it. And anyone who will lose his soul because of me and because of my gospel will save it.
36	For what shall it profit a man, if he shall gain the whole world, and lose his own soul?	For, what will a man be profited, if he gain the whole world, and lose his life?	For what is a man profited if he should gain the entire world and should lose his soul?

	KJV	*Murdock*	*Magiera*
	MARK *Chapter 8*		
37	Or what shall a man give in exchange for his soul?	Or what will a man give in exchange for his life?	Or what will a man give in exchange of his soul?
38	Whosoever therefore shall be ashamed of me and of my words in this adulterous and sinful generation; of him also shall the Son of man be ashamed, when he cometh in the glory of his Father with the holy angels.	For, whoever shall be ashamed of me, and of my words, in this sinful and adulterous generation, of him also will the Son of man be ashamed, when he cometh in the glory of his Father, with his holy angels.	For anyone who is ashamed of me and my words in this sinful and adulterous generation, the Son of Man will also be ashamed of him when he comes in the glory of his Father with his holy angels."
	Chapter 9		
1	And he said unto them, Verily I say unto you, That there be some of them that stand here, which shall not taste of death, till they have seen the kingdom of God come with power.	And he said to them: Verily I say to you, There are some standing here, who will not taste of death, until they shall see the kingdom of God to be coming with power.	And he was saying to them, "Truly I say to you, there are some that are standing here who will not taste death until they see the kingdom of God that has come in power."
2	And after six days Jesus taketh with him Peter, and James, and John, and leadeth them up into an high mountain apart by themselves: and he was transfigured before them.	And after six days, Jesus took Cephas and James and John, and led them to a high mountain, apart; and was transformed before them.	And after six days, Jesus led Peter and James and John and took them up into a high mountain privately and he was changed before their eyes.
3	And his raiment became shining, exceeding white as snow; so as no fuller on earth can white them.	And his raiment shone and was very white, like snow, so as men on earth can never whiten.	And his clothing was bright and became very white like snow, such that men are not able to make white on earth.
4	And there appeared unto them Elias with Moses: and they were talking with Jesus.	And there appeared to them Moses and Elijah, in conversation with Jesus.	And Elijah and Moses were seen by them, speaking with Jesus.
5	And Peter answered and said to Jesus, Master, it is good for us to be here: and let us make three tabernacles; one for thee, and one for Moses, and one for Elias.	And Cephas said to him: Rabbi, it is delightful for us to be here. And let us make three booths; one for thee, and one for Moses, and one for Elijah.	And Peter said to him, "My Master, it is good for us to be here. And let us make three booths, one for you and one for Moses and one for Elijah."
6	For he wist not what to say; for they were sore afraid.	But he did not know what he said, for they were in trepidation.	And he did not know what he was saying, for they were in fear.
7	And there was a cloud that overshadowed them: and a voice came out of the cloud, saying, This is my beloved Son: hear him.	And there was a cloud, and it overshadowed them. And a voice issued from the cloud, which said: This is my beloved Son. Hear ye him.	And a cloud came and overshadowed them, and a voice [came] from the cloud that said, "This is my beloved Son; hear him."
8	And suddenly, when they had looked round about, they saw no man any more, save Jesus only with themselves.	And suddenly, when the disciples looked up, they saw no one with them, except Jesus only.	And suddenly, when the disciples looked up, they did not see anyone except Jesus only with them.
9	And as they came down from the mountain, he charged them that they should tell no man what things they had seen, till the Son of man were risen from the dead.	And as they descended the mountain, he commanded them to tell no man what they had seen, till after the Son of man should be risen from the dead.	And while they were descending from the mountain, he was commanding them that they should not tell anyone what they saw until after the Son of Man had risen from the dead.

Parallel Translations

	KJV	*Murdock*	*Magiera*
	MARK	*Chapter 9*	
10	And they kept that saying with themselves, questioning one with another what the rising from the dead should mean.	And they kept that saying in their mind; and inquired, What doth this saying mean: "When he shall be risen from the dead!"	And they kept the saying to themselves and were inquiring, "What is this saying, 'When he is raised from the dead?'"
11	And they asked him, saying, Why say the scribes that Elias must first come?	And they asked him, and said: Why then do the Scribes say, that Elijah must first come?	And they were asking him and saying, "Why then do the scribes say that Elijah must come first?"
12	And he answered and told them, Elias verily cometh first, and restoreth all things; and how it is written of the Son of man, that he must suffer many things, and be set at nought.	He said to them: Elijah [truly] first cometh, to prepare all things: and, as it is written of the Son of man, he will suffer much, and be rejected.	He said to them, "Elijah will come first in order to prepare everything and as it is written about the Son of Man: HE WILL SUFFER MUCH AND BE REJECTED.
13	But I say unto you, That Elias is indeed come, and they have done unto him whatsoever they listed, as it is written of him.	But I say to you: That Elijah hath come; and they have done to him all that they desired, as it was written of him.	But I say to you, indeed Elijah has come and they did with him whatever they desired, as it was written about him."
14	And when he came to his disciples, he saw a great multitude about them, and the scribes questioning with them.	And when he came to his disciples, he saw a great multitude with them, and the Scribes disputing with them.	And when he came to the disciples, he saw a large crowd with them and the scribes disputing with them.
15	And straightway all the people, when they beheld him, were greatly amazed, and running to him saluted him.	And immediately the multitude saw him, and were surprised: and they ran and saluted him.	And immediately all the crowds saw him and were amazed, and they ran [and] greeted him.
16	And he asked the scribes, What question ye with them?	And he asked the Scribes: What were ye disputing with them?	And he asked the scribes, "What are you disputing with them?"
17	And one of the multitude answered and said, Master, I have brought unto thee my son, which hath a dumb spirit;	And one of the multitude replied, and said: Teacher, I have brought to thee my son, who hath a spirit that will not speak.	And one of the crowd answered and said, "Teacher, I brought my son to you, because he has a spirit that does not speak.
18	And wheresoever he taketh him, he teareth him: and he foameth, and gnasheth with his teeth, and pineth away: and I spake to thy disciples that they should cast him out; and they could not.	And wherever he seizeth him, he shaketh and teareth him: and he gnasheth his teeth, and pineth away. And I spoke to thy disciples, to cast him out; and they could not.	And sometimes it grabs him, it knocks him down and he foams and gnashes his teeth and he languishes. And I asked your disciples to cast it out, and they were not able."
19	He answereth him, and saith, O faithless generation, how long shall I be with you? how long shall I suffer you? bring him unto me.	Jesus answered, and said to them: O incredulous generation! How long shall I be with you? how long bear with you? Bring him to me.	Jesus answered and said to him, "Oh faithless generation! How long must I be with you and how long must I endure you? Bring him to me."
20	And they brought him unto him: and when he saw him, straightway the spirit tare him; and he fell on the ground, and wallowed foaming.	And they brought him to him. And when the spirit saw him, immediately he shook him; and he fell upon the ground, and wallowed and foamed.	And they brought him to him. And when the spirit saw him, immediately it knocked him down and he fell on the ground and was violently shaken, and he foamed.
21	And he asked his father, How long is it ago since this came unto him? And he said, Of a child.	And Jesus asked his father, how long a time he had been thus. He said to him: Lo, from his childhood.	And Jesus asked his father, "How long [has it been] since [he was] this way?" He said to him, "Since his youth.

Parallel Translations

	KJV	Murdock	Magiera
	MARK Chapter 9		
22	And ofttimes it hath cast him into the fire, and into the waters, to destroy him: but if thou canst do any thing, have compassion on us, and help us.	And many times it hath thrown him into the fire, and into the water, to destroy him. But, if thou canst do any thing, aid me and have compassion on me.	And many times it has thrown him into the fire and into the water to destroy him, but whatever you are able [to do], help me and have compassion on us."
23	Jesus said unto him, If thou canst believe, all things are possible to him that believeth.	Jesus said to him: If thou canst believe; every thing can be, to him that believeth.	Jesus said to him, "If you are able to believe, everything will be possible to him who believes."
24	And straightway the father of the child cried out, and said with tears, Lord, I believe; help thou mine unbelief.	And immediately the father of the child cried out, while he wept and said: I believe; aid thou the defect of my faith.	And immediately the father of the boy cried out, mourning, and said, "I believe, my Lord! Help the lack of my faith."
25	When Jesus saw that the people came running together, he rebuked the foul spirit, saying unto him, Thou dumb and deaf spirit, I charge thee, come out of him, and enter no more into him.	And when Jesus saw that the people were, running and collecting around him, he rebuked the unclean spirit, and said to him: Thou deaf and unspeaking spirit, I command thee, come out of him; and no more enter him.	And when Jesus saw that the people ran and gathered about him, he rebuked that unclean spirit and said to it, "Dumb spirit that does not speak, I command you, come out of him and do not enter him again."
26	And the spirit cried, and rent him sore, and came out of him: and he was as one dead; insomuch that many said, He is dead.	And the demon cried out greatly, and bruised him, and came out. And he was as a dead person; so that many would say, he is dead.	And that demon cried out and he bruised him much and came out. And he was like a dead man, so that many said, "He is dead."
27	But Jesus took him by the hand, and lifted him up; and he arose.	And Jesus took him by the hand, and raised him up.	But Jesus took him by his hand and raised him up.
28	And when he was come into the house, his disciples asked him privately, Why could not we cast him out?	And when Jesus entered the house, his disciples asked him privately: Why could not we cast him out?	Now when Jesus entered the house, his disciples asked him privately, "Why were we not able to cast it out?"
29	And he said unto them, This kind can come forth by nothing, but by prayer and fasting.	He saith to them: This kind can come out, by nothing but fasting and prayer.	He said to them, "This kind cannot be cast out by anything except by fasting and by prayer."
30	And they departed thence, and passed through Galilee; and he would not that any man should know it.	And when he departed from there, they passed through Galilee: and he desired that no one might know him.	And when he went away from there, they were passing through Galilee. And he did not want anyone to know about him,
31	For he taught his disciples, and said unto them, The Son of man is delivered into the hands of men, and they shall kill him; and after that he is killed, he shall rise the third day.	For he taught his disciples, and said to them: The Son of man is delivered into the hands of men, and they will kill him; and when he is killed, on the third day, he will rise.	For he was teaching his disciples and said to them, "The Son of Man will be delivered into the hands of man, and they will kill him, and after he has been killed, on the third day he will rise up."
32	But they understood not that saying, and were afraid to ask him.	But they did not understand that speech; and they were afraid to ask him.	And they did not understand the meaning, yet were afraid to ask him.

	KJV	Murdock	Magiera
	MARK	*Chapter 9*	
33	And he came to Capernaum: and being in the house he asked them, What was it that ye disputed among yourselves by the way?	And they came to Capernaum. And when they entered the house, he asked them: What disputed ye among yourselves by the way?	And they came to Capernaum and when they had entered the house, he asked them, "What were you discussing among yourselves on the way?"
34	But they held their peace: for by the way they had disputed among themselves, who should be the greatest.	And they were silent; for by the way they had contended with one another, which should be the great among them.	But they were silent, for they were arguing on the way with each other, who was the greater among them.
35	And he sat down, and called the twelve, and saith unto them, If any man desire to be first, the same shall be last of all, and servant of all.	And Jesus sat down, and called the twelve, and said to them: Whoever would be first, let him be last of all, and servitor to all.	And Jesus sat down and called the twelve and said to them, "He who wants to be first should be the last of all men and a servant of all men."
36	And he took a child, and set him in the midst of them: and when he had taken him in his arms, he said unto them,	And he took a child, and set him in the midst, and took him in his arms and said to them:	And he took a certain child and set him in the middle [of them] and took him into his arms and said to them,
37	Whosoever shall receive one of such children in my name, receiveth me: and whosoever shall receive me, receiveth not me, but him that sent me.	Whoever receiveth one in my name, like this child, he receiveth me; and he that receiveth me, receiveth not me [only], but him that sent me.	Whoever receives like this child in my name receives me. And he who receives me does not receive me, but him who sent me.
38	And John answered him, saying, Master, we saw one casting out devils in thy name, and he followeth not us: and we forbad him, because he followeth not us.	John said to him: Rabbi, we saw one casting out demons in thy name, and we forbad him, because he adhereth not to us.	John said to him, "My Master, we saw a man who was casting out demons in your name and we stopped him, because he did not follow us."
39	But Jesus said, Forbid him not: for there is no man which shall do a miracle in my name, that can lightly speak evil of me.	Jesus said to them: Forbid him not; for there is no one who doeth mighty works in my name, that can readily speak evil of me.	Jesus said to them, "Do not stop him, for there is no one who does miracles in my name and is readily able [to] speak wickedly about me.
40	For he that is not against us is on our part.	Whoever therefore is not against you, is for you.	Therefore, he who is not against you is for you.
41	For whosoever shall give you a cup of water to drink in my name, because ye belong to Christ, verily I say unto you, he shall not lose his reward.	For whoever shall give you to drink a cup of water only, on the ground that ye are Messiah's [followers], verily I say to you, he will not lose his reward.	But anyone who gives you only a cup of water to drink because you are in the name of the Messiah, truly I say to you, 'he will not lose his reward.'
42	And whosoever shall offend one of these little ones that believe in me, it is better for him that a millstone were hanged about his neck, and he were cast into the sea.	And whoever shall cause one of these little ones that believe in me to stumble, it were better for him, if a millstone were put to his neck, and he cast into the sea.	And whoever causes one of these little ones who believe in me to stumble, it would be better for him if the millstone of a donkey were placed on his neck and he were thrown into the sea.
43	And if thy hand offend thee, cut it off: it is better for thee to enter into life maimed, than having two hands to go into hell, into the fire that never shall be quenched:	And if thy hand make thee offend, cut it off: it is better for thee to enter into life maimed, than, having two hands, to go into hell;	Now if your hand offends you, cut it off. It is better for you to enter life maimed, than although you have two hands, to go to Gehenna,
44	Where their worm dieth not, and the fire is not quenched.	where their worm dieth not, and their fire is not extinguished.	where their worm does not die and their fire does not go out.

	KJV	Murdock	Magiera
MARK	*Chapter 9*		
45	And if thy foot offend thee, cut it off: it is better for thee to enter halt into life, than having two feet to be cast into hell, into the fire that never shall be quenched:	And if thy foot make thee offend, cut it off: it is better for thee to enter into life lamed, than, having two feet, to fall into hell;	And if your foot offends you, cut if off. It is better for you to enter life lame, than although you have two feet, to fall in Gehenna,
46	Where their worm dieth not, and the fire is not quenched.	where their worm dieth not, and their fire is not extinguished.	where their worm does not die and their fire does not go out.
47	And if thine eye offend thee, pluck it out: it is better for thee to enter into the kingdom of God with one eye, than having two eyes to be cast into hell fire:	And if thy eye make thee offend, pluck it out: it is better for thee to enter with one eye into the kingdom of God, than, having two eyes, to fall into the hell of fire;	And if your eye offends you, pick it out. It is better for you to enter into the kingdom of God with one of your eye[s], than although you have two eyes, to fall in the Gehenna of fire,
48	Where their worm dieth not, and the fire is not quenched.	where their worm dieth not, and their fire is not extinguished.	where their worm does not die and their fire does not go out.
49	For every one shall be salted with fire, and every sacrifice shall be salted with salt.	For every thing will be salted with fire; and every sacrifice will be salted with salt.	For everything will be salted with fire and every sacrifice will be salted with salt.
50	Salt is good: but if the salt have lost his saltness, wherewith will ye season it? Have salt in yourselves, and have peace one with another.	Salt is a good thing: but if the salt become insipid, with what will it be salted? Let there be salt in you: and be ye in peace, one with another.	Salt is good, but if the salt should lose its flavor, with what will it be salted? Let salt be in you and be in harmony with each other."
Chapter 10			
1	And he arose from thence, and cometh into the coasts of Judaea by the farther side of Jordan: and the people resort unto him again; and, as he was wont, he taught them again.	And he arose from there, and came to the border of Judaea, on the other side the Jordan. And great multitudes came to him there; and again he instructed them, as he was accustomed.	And he rose up from there and came to the border of Judea to the crossing of the Jordan and large crowds went there with him. And he was teaching them again, as he was accustomed.
2	And the Pharisees came to him, and asked him, Is it lawful for a man to put away his wife? tempting him.	And the Pharisees came to him, and, tempting him, inquired if it were lawful for a man to divorce his wife.	And the Pharisees approached, tempting him, and were asking if it was lawful for a man to divorce his wife.
3	And he answered and said unto them, What did Moses command you?	He said to them: What did Moses command you?	He said to them, "What did Moses command you?"
4	And they said, Moses suffered to write a bill of divorcement, and to put her away.	They said: Moses permitted us to write a bill of divorce, and send [her] away.	And they said, "Moses allowed us to write a decree of divorce and to send [her] away."
5	And Jesus answered and said unto them, For the hardness of your heart he wrote you this precept.	Jesus answered and said to them: On account of the hardness of your heart, Moses wrote you this precept.	Jesus answered and said to them, "In contrast to the hardness of your heart, he wrote this commandment for you,
6	But from the beginning of the creation God made them male and female.	But, from the beginning, God made them a male and a female.	but from the beginning GOD MADE THEM MALE AND FEMALE.
7	For this cause shall a man leave his father and mother, and cleave to his wife;	Therefore shall a man leave his father and his mother, and adhere to his wife:	Because of this, A MAN WILL LEAVE HIS FATHER AND HIS MOTHER AND JOIN TO HIS WIFE

Parallel Translations

MARK *Chapter 10*

	KJV	*Murdock*	*Magiera*
8	And they twain shall be one flesh: so then they are no more twain, but one flesh.	and they two shall be one flesh. Wherefore they are not two, but one flesh.	AND THE TWO OF THEM WILL BECOME ONE FLESH. So then, they are not two, but one flesh.
9	What therefore God hath joined together, let not man put asunder.	What therefore God hath conjoined, let not man separate.	Therefore, that which God has joined together, man should not separate."
10	And in the house his disciples asked him again of the same matter.	And in the house, the disciples asked him again of this matter.	And his disciples asked him again in the house about this [matter].
11	And he saith unto them, Whosoever shall put away his wife, and marry another, committeth adultery against her.	And he said to them: Whoever shall divorce his wife, and take another, committeth adultery.	And he said to them, "Whoever dismisses his wife and takes another commits adultery.
12	And if a woman shall put away her husband, and be married to another, she committeth adultery.	And if a woman shall leave her husband, and marry another, she committeth adultery.	And if a woman should dismiss her husband and be [a wife] to another, she commits adultery."
13	And they brought young children to him, that he should touch them: and his disciples rebuked those that brought them.	And they brought little children to him, that he might touch them. But his disciples rebuked those who brought them.	And children were approaching him so that he would touch them, but his disciples were rebuking those who were bringing them.
14	But when Jesus saw it, he was much displeased, and said unto them, Suffer the little children to come unto me, and forbid them not: for of such is the kingdom of God.	And when Jesus saw it, he was displeased; and he said to them, Suffer little children to come to me, and forbid them not; for of those like them is the kingdom of God.	And Jesus saw [it] and was offended and said to them, "Allow the children [to] come to me and do not hinder them, for because of those who are as these are, the kingdom of God exists.
15	Verily I say unto you, Whosoever shall not receive the kingdom of God as a little child, he shall not enter therein.	Verily I say to you, That whoever doth not receive the kingdom of God, like a little child, shall not enter it.	Truly I say to you, anyone who does not receive the kingdom of God like a child will not enter it."
16	And he took them up in his arms, put his hands upon them, and blessed them.	And he took them in his arms, and laid his hand on them and blessed them.	And he took them into his arms and placed his hand on them and blessed them.
17	And when he was gone forth into the way, there came one running, and kneeled to him, and asked him, Good Master, what shall I do that I may inherit eternal life?	And as he walked in the way, one ran and fell upon his knees, and asked him, and said: Good Teacher, what must I do, to inherit eternal life?	And while he was traveling on the road, a certain [man] ran [and] fell on his knees and asked him and said, "Good teacher, what should I do to gain eternal life?"
18	And Jesus said unto him, Why callest thou me good? there is none good but one, that is, God.	Jesus saith to him: Why callest thou me good? There is none good, but one, God.	Jesus said to him, "Why do you call me good? There is no [one] good, except one, God.
19	Thou knowest the commandments, Do not commit adultery, Do not kill, Do not steal, Do not bear false witness, Defraud not, Honour thy father and mother.	Thou knowest the commandments; thou shalt not commit adultery, thou shalt not steal, thou shalt not kill, thou shalt not give false testimony, thou shalt not defraud; honor thy father and thy mother.	You know the commandments: DO NOT COMMIT ADULTERY, DO NOT STEAL, DO NOT KILL AND DO NOT BEAR FALSE WITNESS, DO NOT DEFRAUD, HONOR YOUR FATHER AND YOUR MOTHER."

Parallel Translations

MARK *Chapter 10*

	KJV	Murdock	Magiera
20	And he answered and said unto him, Master, all these have I observed from my youth.	And he answered, and said to him: Teacher, all these have I kept from my childhood.	And he answered and said to him, "Teacher, I have kept all of these [things] from my youth."
21	Then Jesus beholding him loved him, and said unto him, One thing thou lackest: go thy way, sell whatsoever thou hast, and give to the poor, and thou shalt have treasure in heaven: and come, take up the cross, and follow me.	And Jesus looked on him, and loved him, and said to him: One thing thou lackest. Go, sell all that thou possessest, and give to the poor, and there will be a treasure for thee in heaven; and take thy cross, and come after me.	And Jesus looked at him and loved him and said to him, "You lack one [thing]. Go [and] sell everything that you have and give to the poor and you will have treasure in heaven and take up a cross and follow me."
22	And he was sad at that saying, and went away grieved: for he had great possessions.	And he was made sad by that speech, and went away sorrowing: for he possessed great riches.	And he was sad at this saying and went away, being grieved, for he had many possessions.
23	And Jesus looked round about, and saith unto his disciples, How hardly shall they that have riches enter into the kingdom of God!	And Jesus looked upon his disciples, and said to them: How hard for those who possess wealth, to enter into the kingdom of God!	And Jesus looked at his disciples and said to them, "How difficult [it is] for those who have possessions to enter the kingdom of God."
24	And the disciples were astonished at his words. But Jesus answereth again, and saith unto them, Children, how hard is it for them that trust in riches to enter into the kingdom of God!	And the disciples wondered at the remark. And Jesus, replied again, and said to them: My children, how hard it is, for those who trust in riches, to enter into the kingdom of God.	And the disciples were wondering at his words, and Jesus answered again and said to them, "My sons, how difficult [it is] for those who trust in their possessions to enter the kingdom of God.
25	It is easier for a camel to go through the eye of a needle, than for a rich man to enter into the kingdom of God.	It is easier for a camel to enter the eye of a needle, than for a rich man to enter the kingdom of God.	It is easier for a camel to enter through the eye of the needle than [for] a rich man to enter the kingdom of God."
26	And they were astonished out of measure, saying among themselves, Who then can be saved?	And they wondered the more, and said among themselves: Who can obtain life!	And they were all the more wondering and saying among themselves, "Who is able to [gain] life?"
27	And Jesus looking upon them saith, With men it is impossible, but not with God: for with God all things are possible.	And Jesus looked on them again, and said to them: With men, this is not possible, but with God [it is]; for with God all things are possible.	And Jesus looked at them and said to them, "With men this is not possible, but with God [it is]. For everything is possible with God."
28	Then Peter began to say unto him, Lo, we have left all, and have followed thee.	And Cephas began to say: Lo, we have left every thing, and have cleaved to thee.	And Peter began to say, "Behold, we have left everything and followed you."
29	And Jesus answered and said, Verily I say unto you, There is no man that hath left house, or brethren, or sisters, or father, or mother, or wife, or children, or lands, for my sake, and the gospel's,	Jesus answered and said: Verily I say to you, There is no man that leaveth houses, or brothers or sisters, or father or mother, or wife or children, for my sake, and for the sake of my tidings,	Jesus answered and said, "Truly I say to you, there is no man who has left houses or brothers or sisters or father or mother or wife or children or fields because of me and because of my gospel,

MARK *Chapter 10*

	KJV	*Murdock*	*Magiera*
30	But he shall receive an hundredfold now in this time, houses, and brethren, and sisters, and mothers, and children, and lands, with persecutions; and in the world to come eternal life.	who will not receive a hundredfold, here in the present time,---houses, and brothers and sisters, and mothers and children, and lands, with persecution; and in the world to come eternal life.	and will not receive a hundredth part now in this time, houses and brothers and sisters and mothers and children and fields with persecution. Yet in the age to come, [he will receive] eternal life.
31	But many that are first shall be last; and the last first.	But many are first, who will be last; and last, [who will be] first.	And [there will be] many first who will be last, and last, first."
32	And they were in the way going up to Jerusalem; and Jesus went before them: and they were amazed; and as they followed, they were afraid. And he took again the twelve, and began to tell them what things should happen unto him,	And as they were in the way, going up to Jerusalem, Jesus went before them: and they were amazed, and walked after him with trembling. And he took his twelve, and began to tell them what was to befall him.	And while they were climbing up on the road to Jerusalem, Jesus was before them. And they were amazed and were following him, although they were afraid. And he took his twelve and began to tell them what would happen to him.
33	Saying, Behold, we go up to Jerusalem; and the Son of man shall be delivered unto the chief priests, and unto the scribes; and they shall condemn him to death, and shall deliver him to the Gentiles:	Behold, we are going to Jerusalem; and the Son of man will be delivered up to the chief priests and the Scribes; and they will condemn him to die, and will deliver him over to the Gentiles.	"Behold, we will go up to Jerusalem, and the Son of Man will be delivered to the chief priests and to the scribes, and they will condemn him to death and deliver him to the Gentiles.
34	And they shall mock him, and shall scourge him, and shall spit upon him, and shall kill him: and the third day he shall rise again.	And they will mock him, and will scourge him, and will spit in his face, and will kill him; and on the third day he will arise.	And they will mock him and beat him and spit in his face and kill him and on the third day, he will rise up."
35	And James and John, the sons of Zebedee, come unto him, saying, Master, we would that thou shouldest do for us whatsoever we shall desire.	And James and John, the sons of Zebedee, came to him, and said to him: Teacher, we desire that thou wouldst do for us all that we ask.	And James and John, the sons of Zebedee, approached him and said to him, "Teacher, we want you to do for us all that we ask."
36	And he said unto them, What would ye that I should do for you?	He saith to them: What would ye, that I should do for you?	He said to them, "What do you want me to do for you?"
37	They said unto him, Grant unto us that we may sit, one on thy right hand, and the other on thy left hand, in thy glory.	They say to him: Grant to us, that one may sit on thy right hand, and the other on thy left, in thy glory.	They said to him, "Grant us that one sit on your right and one on your left in your glory."
38	But Jesus said unto them, Ye know not what ye ask: can ye drink of the cup that I drink of? and be baptized with the baptism that I am baptized with?	But he said to them: Ye know not what ye ask. Are ye able to drink the cup, of which I drink? and to be baptized with the baptism, that I am baptized with?	But he said to them, "You do not know what you ask. Are you able to drink the cup that I drink and to be baptized with the baptism [with] which I am baptized?"
39	And they said unto him, We can. And Jesus said unto them, Ye shall indeed drink of the cup that I drink of; and with the baptism that I am baptized withal shall ye be baptized:	They say to him: We are able. Jesus saith to them: The cup that I drink, ye will drink, and the baptism that I am baptized with, ye will be baptized with:	They said to him, "We are able." Jesus said to them, "The cup that I drink, you will drink, and the baptism [with] which I am baptized, you will be baptized,
40	But to sit on my right hand and on my left hand is not mine to give; but it shall be given to them for whom it is prepared.	But that ye should sit on my right hand and on my left, is not mine to give, except to those for whom it is prepared.	but that you may sit at my right and at my left is not mine to give, except to those for whom it is prepared."

Parallel Translations

	KJV	Murdock	Magiera
	MARK *Chapter 10*		
41	And when the ten heard it, they began to be much displeased with James and John.	And when the ten heard [it], they began to murmur against James and John.	And when the ten heard [it], they began murmuring against James and John.
42	But Jesus called them to him, and saith unto them, Ye know that they which are accounted to rule over the Gentiles exercise lordship over them; and their great ones exercise authority upon them.	And Jesus called them, and said to them: Ye know, that they who are accounted chiefs of the nations, are their lords; and their great men have authority over them.	And Jesus called them and said to them, "You know that those who are counted as chiefs of the nations are their lords and their great men are in authority over them.
43	But so shall it not be among you: but whosoever will be great among you, shall be your minister:	But it shall not be so among you: but he that would be great among you, must be a servitor to you.	But it should not be so among you, but rather he who wants to be great among you should be a minister to you.
44	And whosoever of you will be the chiefest, shall be servant of all.	And he of you that would be first, must be servant to every one.	And whoever of you wants to be first should be a servant of everyone.
45	For even the Son of man came not to be ministered unto, but to minister, and to give his life a ransom for many.	And also the Son of man came, not to be served, but to serve; and to give his life a ransom for many.	For even the Son of Man did not come to be served, but rather to serve and to give himself [as] a ransom for many."
46	And they came to Jericho: and as he went out of Jericho with his disciples and a great number of people, blind Bartimaeus, the son of Timaeus, sat by the highway side begging.	And they came to Jericho. And as Jesus went out of Jericho, he and his disciples and a great multitude; Timeus, the son of Timeus, a blind man, was sitting by the side of the way, and begging.	And they came to Jericho. And when Jesus went out from Jericho and his disciples and a large crowd, Timaeus, the son of Timaeus, a blind man, was sitting by the side of the road and begging.
47	And when he heard that it was Jesus of Nazareth, he began to cry out, and say, Jesus, thou Son of David, have mercy on me.	And he heard that it was Jesus the Nazarean; and he began to cry out, and to say: Thou Son of David, have mercy on me.	And he heard that it was Jesus the Nazarene and he began to cry out and to say, "Son of David, have compassion on me."
48	And many charged him that he should hold his peace: but he cried the more a great deal, Thou Son of David, have mercy on me.	And many rebuked him, that he might be silent. But he cried out the more, and said: Thou Son of David, have mercy on me.	Many were reproving him to be silent, but he was crying out all the more and said, "Son of David, have compassion on me."
49	And Jesus stood still, and commanded him to be called. And they call the blind man, saying unto him, Be of good comfort, rise; he calleth thee.	And Jesus stood, and directed him to be called. And they called the blind man, and said to him: Take courage: arise, he calleth thee.	And Jesus stopped and commanded that they call him. And they called the blind man and said to him, "Take courage [and] rise up. He calls you."
50	And he, casting away his garment, rose, and came to Jesus.	And the blind man cast off his garment and arose, and went to Jesus.	And the blind man threw off his garment and rose up [and] came to Jesus.
51	And Jesus answered and said unto him, What wilt thou that I should do unto thee? The blind man said unto him, Lord, that I might receive my sight.	Jesus said to him: What wilt thou, that I do for thee? And the blind man said to him: Rabbi, that I may have sight.	Jesus said to him, "What do you want me to do for you?" And the blind man said to him, "My Master, that I may see."

Parallel Translations

	KJV	*Murdock*	*Magiera*
	MARK	*Chapter 10*	
52	And Jesus said unto him, Go thy way; thy faith hath made thee whole. And immediately he received his sight, and followed Jesus in the way.	And Jesus said to him: Go; thy faith hath procured thee life. And immediately his sight was restored; and he followed after him.	And Jesus said to him, "See! Your faith has made you whole." And immediately he received sight and went on [his] way.
	Chapter 11		
1	And when they came nigh to Jerusalem, unto Bethphage and Bethany, at the mount of Olives, he sendeth forth two of his disciples,	And as they approached Jerusalem, near by Bethphage and Bethany, at the mount of Olives, he sent two of his disciples,	And when he came near to Jerusalem by the side of Bethphage and Bethany toward the Mount of Olives, he sent two of his disciples
2	And saith unto them, Go your way into the village over against you: and as soon as ye be entered into it, ye shall find a colt tied, whereon never man sat; loose him, and bring him.	and said to them: Go ye to the village that is over against us, and as soon as ye enter it, ye will find a colt tied, on which no person hath ridden: loose [him], and bring him hither.	and said to them, "Go to that village opposite us. And immediately when you enter it, you will find a colt that is tied that no man has ridden. Untie [it] [and] bring it.
3	And if any man say unto you, Why do ye this? say ye that the Lord hath need of him; and straightway he will send him hither.	And, if any one say to you, Why do ye this? Say ye to him: Because our Lord hath need of him. And immediately he will send him hither.	And if anyone should say to you, 'Why are you doing this?' say to him, 'It is necessary for our Lord,' and immediately he will send it here."
4	And they went their way, and found the colt tied by the door without in a place where two ways met; and they loose him.	And they went, and they found the colt tied, by the door, without in the street. And as they were loosing [him],	And they went [and] found a colt that was tied at the door outside on the street. And while they were untying it,
5	And certain of them that stood there said unto them, What do ye, loosing the colt?	some of those standing there, said to them: What do ye, untying the colt?	some of those who were standing [there] said to them, "What are you doing untying the colt?"
6	And they said unto them even as Jesus had commanded: and they let them go.	And they said to them, as Jesus had commanded them; and they permitted them.	And they said to them as Jesus had commanded and they allowed them.
7	And they brought the colt to Jesus, and cast their garments on him; and he sat upon him.	And they brought the colt to Jesus, and cast their garments upon him, and set Jesus upon him.	And they brought the colt to Jesus and placed their garments on it and Jesus rode on it.
8	And many spread their garments in the way: and others cut down branches off the trees, and strawed them in the way.	And many spread their garments in the way; and others cut branches from the trees, and strewed them in the way.	And many were spreading their garments on the road and others were cutting branches from trees and spreading [them] on the road.
9	And they that went before, and they that followed, cried, saying, Hosanna; Blessed is he that cometh in the name of the Lord:	And those preceding him, and those following him shouted and said: Hosanna: Blessed is he that cometh in the name of the Lord.	And those who were before him and those who were behind him were crying out and saying: "HOSANNA! BLESSED IS HE WHO COMES IN THE NAME OF THE LORD.
10	Blessed be the kingdom of our father David, that cometh in the name of the Lord: Hosanna in the highest.	And blessed is the advancing kingdom of our father David. Hosanna in the highest [heavens].	And BLESSED IS THE KINGDOM OF OUR FATHER DAVID THAT IS COMING! HOSANNA ON HIGH!

Parallel Translations

MARK *Chapter 11*

	KJV	*Murdock*	*Magiera*
11	And Jesus entered into Jerusalem, and into the temple: and when he had looked round about upon all things, and now the eventide was come, he went out unto Bethany with the twelve.	And Jesus entered Jerusalem and the temple, and surveyed every thing. And when evening arrived, he went out to Bethany with the twelve.	And Jesus entered Jerusalem [and] the temple and saw everything. And when evening time came, he went out to Bethany with the twelve.
12	And on the morrow, when they were come from Bethany, he was hungry:	And the following day, as he left Bethany, he was hungry:	And on the next day, when he went out from Bethany, he was hungry.
13	And seeing a fig tree afar off having leaves, he came, if haply he might find any thing thereon: and when he came to it, he found nothing but leaves; for the time of figs was not yet.	and he saw a fig-tree at a distance, on which were leaves, and he came to it, if he could find somewhat on it. And when he had come, he found on it only leaves; for the time of figs had not arrived.	And he saw a certain fig tree from a distance that had leaves on it. And he came to it [to see] if he could find anything on it. And when he arrived, he did not find [anything] on it except leaves, for the time of figs had not [yet] come.
14	And Jesus answered and said unto it, No man eat fruit of thee hereafter for ever. And his disciples heard it.	And he said to it: Henceforth and for ever, let no man eat fruit from thee: and the disciples heard it. And they came to Jerusalem.	And he said to it, "Now and forever man will not eat fruit from you." And his disciples heard [it]. And they came to Jerusalem.
15	And they come to Jerusalem: and Jesus went into the temple, and began to cast out them that sold and bought in the temple, and overthrew the tables of the moneychangers, and the seats of them that sold doves;	And Jesus entered the temple of God: and he began to cast out those who bought and sold in the temple; and he overturned the counters of the money-brokers, and the seats of them that sold doves.	And Jesus entered the temple of God and began to drive out those who were buying and selling in the temple. And he turned over the tables of the moneychangers and the seats of those who were selling doves.
16	And would not suffer that any man should carry any vessel through the temple.	And he suffered no one to carry goods through the temple.	And he did not allow anyone to carry goods inside the temple.
17	And he taught, saying unto them, Is it not written, My house shall be called of all nations the house of prayer? but ye have made it a den of thieves.	And he taught them, and said: Is it not written, My house shall be called the house of prayer for all nations? But ye have made it a den of robbers.	And he was teaching and said to them, "Is it not written: MY HOUSE WILL BE CALLED A HOUSE OF PRAYER FOR ALL NATIONS? But you have made it a den of robbers."
18	And the scribes and chief priests heard it, and sought how they might destroy him: for they feared him, because all the people was astonished at his doctrine.	And the chief priests and the Scribes heard [him], and they sought how they might destroy him; for they were afraid of him, because all the people admired his doctrine.	And the chief priests and scribes heard [it] and were seeking how they might destroy him, for they were afraid of him because all the people were astonished at his teaching.
19	And when even was come, he went out of the city.	And when it was evening, they went out from the city.	And when it was evening, they went out of the city.
20	And in the morning, as they passed by, they saw the fig tree dried up from the roots.	And in the morning, as they passed by, they saw the fig-tree dried up, as it were, from its root.	And in the morning while they were passing by, they saw that fig tree dried up from its root.
21	And Peter calling to remembrance saith unto him, Master, behold, the fig tree which thou cursedst is withered away.	And Simon remembered, and said to him: Rabbi; behold, the fig-tree which thou cursedst, is dried up.	And Simon remembered and said to him, "My Master, behold, that fig tree that you cursed has dried up."

	KJV	Murdock	Magiera

MARK *Chapter 11*

	KJV	Murdock	Magiera
22	And Jesus answering saith unto them, Have faith in God.	And Jesus replied, and said to them: Have faith in God.	And Jesus answered and said to them, "You should have faith of God.
23	For verily I say unto you, That whosoever shall say unto this mountain, Be thou removed, and be thou cast into the sea; and shall not doubt in his heart, but shall believe that those things which he saith shall come to pass; he shall have whatsoever he saith.	Verily I say to you, That whoever shall say to this mountain, Be thou removed, and fall into the sea; and shall not doubt in his heart, but shall believe that what he said will occur, to him will be the thing he spoke.	For truly I say to you, whoever says to this mountain, 'Be lifted up and fall into the sea,' and is not divided in his heart, but believes that what he said will happen, he will have what he said.
24	Therefore I say unto you, What things soever ye desire, when ye pray, believe that ye receive them, and ye shall have them.	Therefore I say to you, That whatsoever ye shall pray and ask for, believe that it will be, and it will be to you.	Because of this, I say to you, everything that you pray and you ask [for], believe that you will receive [it], and you will have [it].
25	And when ye stand praying, forgive, if ye have ought against any: that your Father also which is in heaven may forgive you your trespasses.	And when ye stand up to pray, forgive what ye have against any one; that your Father who is in heaven may also forgive your offences.	And when you stand to pray, forgive anything that you have against anyone, so that your Father, who is in heaven, will also forgive you your transgressions.
26	But if ye do not forgive, neither will your Father which is in heaven forgive your trespasses.	For if ye forgive not, your Father also who is in heaven will not forgive you your offences.	And if you do not forgive, neither will your Father who is in heaven forgive you your transgressions."
27	And they come again to Jerusalem: and as he was walking in the temple, there come to him the chief priests, and the scribes, and the elders,	And they came again to Jerusalem. And as he was walking in the temple, the chief priests and Scribes and Elders came to him,	And they came again to Jerusalem. And while he was walking in the temple, the chief priests and scribes and elders came to him.
28	And say unto him, By what authority doest thou these things? and who gave thee this authority to do these things?	and said to him: By what authority doest thou these things? And who gave thee the authority to do these things?	And they said to him, "With what authority do you do these [things]? And who gave you this authority to do these [things]?"
29	And Jesus answered and said unto them, I will also ask of you one question, and answer me, and I will tell you by what authority I do these things.	And Jesus said to them: I also will ask you one thing, that ye may tell me, and I will tell you by what authority I do these things.	And Jesus said to them, "I will ask you also a certain question that you might answer me. And I will tell you with what authority I do these [things].
30	The baptism of John, was it from heaven, or of men? answer me.	The baptism of John, whence was it? from heaven, or from men? Tell me.	The baptism of John, from where was it, from heaven or from men? Tell me."
31	And they reasoned with themselves, saying, If we shall say, From heaven; he will say, Why then did ye not believe him?	And they reasoned with themselves, and said: If we should say to him, From heaven; he will say to us, Why then did ye not believe him?	And they reasoned among themselves and said, "If we say to him that [it was] from heaven, he will say to us, 'Then why did you not believe him?'
32	But if we shall say, Of men; they feared the people: for all men counted John, that he was a prophet indeed.	But if we should say, From men; there is fear from the people; for they have all held John to be truly a prophet.	And [if] we say from men, there is the fear of the people, for all of them were regarding John to be truly a prophet."

MARK — Chapter 11

	KJV	Murdock	Magiera
33	And they answered and said unto Jesus, We cannot tell. And Jesus answering saith unto them, Neither do I tell you by what authority I do these things.	And they answered, and said to Jesus: We do not know. He said to them: Neither do I tell you by what authority I do these things.	And they answered and said to Jesus, "We do not know." He said to them, "Neither will I tell you by what authority I do these [things]."

Chapter 12

	KJV	Murdock	Magiera
1	And he began to speak unto them by parables. A certain man planted a vineyard, and set an hedge about it, and digged a place for the winefat, and built a tower, and let it out to husbandmen, and went into a far country.	And he began to discourse with them in similitudes. A certain man planted a vineyard, and inclosed it with a hedge, and dug in it a wine vat, and built a tower in it, and put it into the hands of husbandmen, and removed to a distance.	And he began to speak with them in parables. "A certain man planted a vineyard and surrounded it [with] a hedge, and dug a wine press in it, and built a tower in it, and handed it over to workers and went on a journey.
2	And at the season he sent to the husbandmen a servant, that he might receive from the husbandmen of the fruit of the vineyard.	And at the proper time, he sent his servant to the husbandmen, to receive of the fruits of the vineyard.	And in time he sent his servant to the workers to receive from the fruit of the vineyard.
3	And they caught him, and beat him, and sent him away empty.	And they beat him, and sent him away empty.	But they beat him and sent him away empty.
4	And again he sent unto them another servant; and at him they cast stones, and wounded him in the head, and sent him away shamefully handled.	And again he sent to them another servant; and him also they stoned, and wounded, and sent him away under indignities.	And he sent again to them another servant and they also stoned and wounded that one and they sent him away in shame.
5	And again he sent another; and him they killed, and many others; beating some, and killing some.	And again he sent another; and him they killed. And he sent many other servants, some of whom they beat, and some they killed.	And he sent again another also, whom they killed. And he sent many other servants and they beat some and killed some.
6	Having yet therefore one son, his wellbeloved, he sent him also last unto them, saying, They will reverence my son.	At last, having an only and dear son, he sent him to them; for he said, Perhaps they will respect my son.	And [at] the end, he had one beloved son and he sent him to them finally, for he said, 'Perhaps they will respect my son.'
7	But those husbandmen said among themselves, This is the heir; come, let us kill him, and the inheritance shall be ours.	But those husbandmen said among themselves: This is the heir; come, let us kill him, and the inheritance will be ours.	But those workers said among themselves, 'This is the heir. Come, let us kill him and the inheritance will be ours.'
8	And they took him, and killed him, and cast him out of the vineyard.	And they took him, and slew [him], and cast [him] out of the vineyard.	And they took [and] killed him and they drove him outside of the vineyard.
9	What shall therefore the lord of the vineyard do? he will come and destroy the husbandmen, and will give the vineyard unto others.	What therefore will the lord of the vineyard do? He will come and destroy those husbandmen, and transfer the vineyard to others.	What then will the lord of the vineyard do? He will come to destroy those workers and give the vineyard to others.
10	And have ye not read this scripture; The stone which the builders rejected is become the head of the corner:	And have ye not read this scripture, The stone which the builders rejected, hath become the head of the corner:	And have you not even read this scripture: THE STONE THAT THE BUILDERS REJECTED HAS BECOME THE HEAD OF THE CORNER?

Parallel Translations

MARK *Chapter 12*

	KJV	*Murdock*	*Magiera*
11	This was the Lord's doing, and it is marvellous in our eyes?	From the Lord, was this; and it is wonderful in our eyes?	THIS CAME FROM THE PRESENCE OF THE LORD AND IT IS A WONDER IN OUR EYES."
12	And they sought to lay hold on him, but feared the people: for they knew that he had spoken the parable against them: and they left him, and went their way.	And they sought to apprehend him, but were afraid of the people; for they knew that he spoke this similitude against them. And they left him, and went away.	And they sought to arrest him, yet they were afraid of the people, for they knew that he spoke this parable about them, and they left him and went away.
13	And they send unto him certain of the Pharisees and of the Herodians, to catch him in his words.	And they sent to him some of the Scribes and of the household of Herod, to ensnare him in discourse.	And they sent him some of the scribes and [some] of the Herodians to ensnare him in speech.
14	And when they were come, they say unto him, Master, we know that thou art true, and carest for no man: for thou regardest not the person of men, but teachest the way of God in truth: Is it lawful to give tribute to Caesar, or not?	And these came, and asked him: Teacher; we know that thou art veracious, and hast no fear of man; for thou regardest not the face of men, but teachest the way of God in truth. Is it lawful to give capitation money to Caesar; or not? Shall we give, or not give?	And they came and asked him, "Teacher, we know that you are true and [that] you are not moved by anyone, for you do not look on the faces of men, but in truth you teach the way of God. Is it lawful to give the poll tax to Caesar or not? Should we give or should we not give [it]?
15	Shall we give, or shall we not give? But he, knowing their hypocrisy, said unto them, Why tempt ye me? bring me a penny, that I may see it.	And he knew their wile, and said to them: Why tempt ye me? Bring me a denarius, that I may see it.	But he knew their trickery and said to them, "Why do you tempt me? Bring me a denarius to see."
16	And they brought it. And he saith unto them, Whose is this image and superscription? And they said unto him, Caesar's.	And they brought [one] to him. And he said to them: Whose is this image and inscription? They said to him: Caesar's.	And they brought [one] to him. He said to them, "Whose image and inscription is this?" And they said, "Caesar's."
17	And Jesus answering said unto them, Render to Caesar the things that are Caesar's, and to God the things that are God's. And they marvelled at him.	Jesus said to them: What is Caesar's, give to Caesar; and what is God's, [give] to God. And they wondered at him.	Jesus said to them, "That which is of Caesar give to Caesar and that which is of God to God." And they were marveling at him.
18	Then come unto him the Sadducees, which say there is no resurrection; and they asked him, saying,	Then came to him Sadducees, who say that there is no resurrection; and they asked him, and said:	And the Sadducees came to him, those who say that there is no resurrection, and were asking him and saying,
19	Master, Moses wrote unto us, If a man's brother die, and leave his wife behind him, and leave no children, that his brother should take his wife, and raise up seed unto his brother.	Teacher: Moses wrote to us, that if a man's brother die, and leave a widow, but leave no children, his brother shall take his widow, and raise up seed to his brother.	"Teacher, Moses wrote to us: IF THE BROTHER OF A MAN DIES AND LEAVES A WIFE AND DOES NOT LEAVE SONS, HIS BROTHER SHOULD TAKE HIS WIFE AND RAISE UP SEED FOR HIS BROTHER.
20	Now there were seven brethren: and the first took a wife, and dying left no seed.	There were seven brothers: and the first took a wife, and died, and left no seed.	There were seven brothers. The first took a wife and died and did not leave [any] seed.
21	And the second took her, and died, neither left he any seed: and the third likewise.	And the second took her, and died, and he also left no seed: and the third in like manner.	And the second took her and died, although also he did not leave [any] seed, and the third likewise.

Parallel Translations

	KJV	Murdock	Magiera
	MARK	*Chapter 12*	
22	And the seven had her, and left no seed: last of all the woman died also.	And the seven took her, and left no seed. Last of all, the woman also died.	And the seven of them took her and did not leave [any] seed. Last of all of them, the wife also died.
23	In the resurrection therefore, when they shall rise, whose wife shall she be of them? for the seven had her to wife.	In the resurrection, therefore, of which of them will she be the wife? For all the seven took her.	Therefore, in the resurrection, whose wife will she be? For the seven of them took her."
24	And Jesus answering said unto them, Do ye not therefore err, because ye know not the scriptures, neither the power of God?	Jesus said to them: Is it not on this account that ye err, because ye understand not the scriptures, nor the power of God?	Jesus said to them, "Is it not because of this you err? For you do not know the scriptures nor the power of God.
25	For when they shall rise from the dead, they neither marry, nor are given in marriage; but are as the angels which are in heaven.	For when they rise from the dead, they do not take wives, nor are wives given to husbands; but they are as the angels that are in heaven.	For when they rise up from the dead, they do not marry women nor are women with men, but rather they are as the angels that are in heaven.
26	And as touching the dead, that they rise: have ye not read in the book of Moses, how in the bush God spake unto him, saying, I am the God of Abraham, and the God of Isaac, and the God of Jacob?	But concerning the dead, that they rise, have ye not read in a book of Moses, how God said to him from the bush: I am the God of Abraham, and the God of Isaac, and the God of Jacob?	Now about the dead who will rise up, have you not read in the book of Moses how God spoke to him from the bush: I AM THE GOD OF ABRAHAM AND THE GOD OF ISAAC AND THE GOD OF JACOB?
27	He is not the God of the dead, but the God of the living: ye therefore do greatly err.	He is not the God of the dead, but of the living. Ye, therefore, do err greatly.	And he is not the God of the dead, but of the living. Therefore you err greatly."
28	And one of the scribes came, and having heard them reasoning together, and perceiving that he had answered them well, asked him, Which is the first commandment of all?	And one of the Scribes came, and heard them as they discussed, and he saw that he gave them an excellent answer; and he asked him, Which is the first of all the commandments?	And one of the scribes approached and heard them disputing and saw that he answered the matter well for them. And he asked, "What is the most important commandment?"
29	And Jesus answered him, The first of all the commandments is, Hear, O Israel; The Lord our God is one Lord:	Jesus said to him: The first of all the commandments [is]: Hear, O Israel; the Lord our God is one Lord:	Jesus said to him, "The most important of all the commandments [is]: HEAR, ISRAEL, THE LORD OUR GOD IS ONE LORD
30	And thou shalt love the Lord thy God with all thy heart, and with all thy soul, and with all thy mind, and with all thy strength: this is the first commandment.	and thou shalt love the Lord thy God, with all thy heart, and with all thy soul, and with all thy mind, and with all thy might. This is the first commandment.	and YOU SHOULD LOVE THE LORD YOUR GOD WITH ALL YOUR HEART AND WITH ALL YOUR SOUL AND WITH ALL YOUR MIND AND WITH ALL YOUR MIGHT. This is the most important commandment.
31	And the second is like, namely this, Thou shalt love thy neighbour as thyself. There is none other commandment greater than these.	And the second, which is like it, [is]: Thou shalt love thy neighbor, as thyself. There is no other commandment greater than these.	And the second that is like it [is]: YOU SHOULD LOVE YOUR NEIGHBOR AS YOURSELF. There is no other commandment that is greater than these."

	KJV	*Murdock*	*Magiera*
	MARK	*Chapter 12*	
32	And the scribe said unto him, Well, Master, thou hast said the truth: for there is one God; and there is none other but he:	The Scribe said to him: Excellently! Rabbi; thou hast spoken the truth; for he is one [God], and there is no other beside him.	The scribe said to him, "Well [said], my Master. You have spoken in truth, because he is one and there are no others outside of him.
33	And to love him with all the heart, and with all the understanding, and with all the soul, and with all the strength, and to love his neighbour as himself, is more than all whole burnt offerings and sacrifices.	And for a man to love him, with all the heart, and with all the mind, and with all the soul, and with all the might; and to love his neighbor, as himself; is better than all holocausts and sacrifices.	And that a man should love him with all the heart and with all the mind and with all the soul and with all might, and that he should love his neighbor as himself, greater is [this] than all the burnt offerings and sacrifices."
34	And when Jesus saw that he answered discreetly, he said unto him, Thou art not far from the kingdom of God. And no man after that durst ask him any question.	And Jesus perceived that he replied wisely; and he answered, and said to him: Thou art not far from the kingdom of God.---And no one dared again to question him.	And Jesus saw that he responded to the matter wisely. He answered and said to him, "You are not far from the kingdom of God." And no man dared to question him again.
35	And Jesus answered and said, while he taught in the temple, How say the scribes that Christ is the Son of David?	And as Jesus was teaching in the temple, he answered and said: How can the Scribes say, that Messiah is the son of David?	And Jesus answered and said while [he was] teaching in the temple, "In what way do the scribes say that the Messiah is the Son of David?
36	For David himself said by the Holy Ghost, The LORD said to my Lord, Sit thou on my right hand, till I make thine enemies thy footstool.	For David himself saith, by the Holy Spirit: The Lord said to my Lord; Seat thyself on my right hand, until I place thy enemies as a footstool beneath thy feet.	For David spoke by the Holy Spirit: THE LORD SAID TO MY LORD, SIT ON MY RIGHT [HAND] UNTIL I PLACE YOUR ENEMIES [AS] A FOOTSTOOL UNDER YOUR FEET.
37	David therefore himself calleth him Lord; and whence is he then his son? And the common people heard him gladly.	David therefore calleth him "My Lord;" and how is he his son? And all the multitude heard him with pleasure.	Since David called him, 'My Lord,' then how is he his Son?" And the whole crowd was hearing him gladly.
38	And he said unto them in his doctrine, Beware of the scribes, which love to go in long clothing, and love salutations in the marketplaces,	And he said to them in his teaching: Beware of the Scribes, who choose to walk in long robes, and love the salutation in the streets,	And in his teaching he was saying to them, "Beware of the scribes who want to walk in robes and love a greeting in the streets
39	And the chief seats in the synagogues, and the uppermost rooms at feasts:	and the chief seats in the synagogues, and the chief couches at feasts.	and the chief seats in the synagogues and the chief places at banquets,
40	Which devour widows' houses, and for a pretence make long prayers: these shall receive greater damnation.	They devour the houses of widows, under pretence that they prolong their prayers. These shall receive a greater condemnation.	those who devour the house of widows with the pretext that they lengthen their prayers. Those will receive the greater judgment."
41	And Jesus sat over against the treasury, and beheld how the people cast money into the treasury: and many that were rich cast in much.	And as Jesus sat over against the treasury-room, he saw how the multitude cast money into the treasury. And many rich ones cast in much.	And when Jesus sat near the treasury, he considered how the crowds were putting money into the treasury. And many rich men were putting in much.
42	And there came a certain poor widow, and she threw in two mites, which make a farthing.	And a poor widow came, and cast in two mites, which are a brass farthing.	And a certain poor widow came [and] put in two lepta that are very small coins.

	KJV	*Murdock*	*Magiera*
	MARK *Chapter 12*		
43	And he called unto him his disciples, and saith unto them, Verily I say unto you, That this poor widow hath cast more in, than all they which have cast into the treasury:	And Jesus called his disciples, and said to them: Verily I say to you, That this poor widow hath cast into the treasury more than all they that cast in.	And Jesus called his disciples and said to them, "Truly I say to you, this poor widow has put in more than everyone who put in the treasury.
44	For all they did cast in of their abundance; but she of her want did cast in all that she had, even all her living.	For they all cast in of that which abounded to them, but she, of her poverty, hath cast in all that she possessed, the whole of her property.	For all of them put in from what abounded to them, but this one, from her need, put in everything that she had, her entire wealth."
	Chapter 13		
1	And as he went out of the temple, one of his disciples saith unto him, Master, see what manner of stones and what buildings are here!	And as Jesus retired from the temple, one of his disciples said to him: Teacher; behold; see these stones, and these structures!	And when Jesus went out from the temple, one of his disciples said to him, "Teacher, behold, look at those stones and those buildings."
2	And Jesus answering said unto him, Seest thou these great buildings? there shall not be left one stone upon another, that shall not be thrown down.	And Jesus said to him: Admirest thou these great structures? There will not be left here one stone upon another, not demolished.	But Jesus said to him, "Do you see these great buildings? One stone on another will not be left here that will not be torn down."
3	And as he sat upon the mount of Olives over against the temple, Peter and James and John and Andrew asked him privately,	And as Jesus was sitting on the mount of Olives, over against the temple, Cephas and James and John and Andrew asked him, privately:	And while Jesus sat on the Mount of Olives opposite the temple, Peter and James and John and Andrew asked him privately,
4	Tell us, when shall these things be? and what shall be the sign when all these things shall be fulfilled?	Tell us, when will these things be? and what [will be] the sign that these things approach their consummation?	Tell us when these [things] will be. And what [is] the sign when all these [things] are close to being fulfilled?
5	And Jesus answering them began to say, Take heed lest any man deceive you:	And Jesus began to say to them Beware, that no one mislead you:	And Jesus began to say to them, "Beware, so that no one will deceive you.
6	For many shall come in my name, saying, I am Christ; and shall deceive many.	for many will come in my name, and will say: I am he. And they will mislead many.	For many will come in my name and say, 'I am [he],' and will deceive many.
7	And when ye shall hear of wars and rumours of wars, be ye not troubled: for such things must needs be; but the end shall not be yet.	But when ye shall hear of battles, and the rumor of battles, be not afraid; for this must be; but the end is not yet.	But when you hear of wars and a rumor of battles, do not be afraid, for it is about to occur, but the end [is] not yet.
8	For nation shall rise against nation, and kingdom against kingdom: and there shall be earthquakes in divers places, and there shall be famines and troubles: these are the beginnings of sorrows.	For nation will rise against nation, and kingdom against kingdom, and there will be earthquakes in several places, and there will be famines and insurrections. These are the beginning of sorrows.	For people will rise up against people and kingdom against kingdom. And there will be earthquakes in various places and there will be famines and riots. These [things] are the beginning of sorrows.
9	But take heed to yourselves: for they shall deliver you up to councils; and in the synagogues ye shall be beaten: and ye shall be brought before rulers and kings for my sake, for a testimony against them.	And take heed to yourselves; for they will deliver you up to the tribunals; and ye will be beaten in the synagogues, and ye will stand before kings and governors, on my account, for a testimony to them.	But watch out for yourselves, for they will deliver you to the judges, and in the synagogues you will be beaten, and you will stand before kings and governors because of me, as a testimony to them.

Parallel Translations

	KJV	*Murdock*	*Magiera*

MARK *Chapter 13*

	KJV	Murdock	Magiera
10	And the gospel must first be published among all nations.	And my tidings must first be proclaimed among all the nations.	But first my gospel will be preached among all the nations.
11	But when they shall lead you, and deliver you up, take no thought beforehand what ye shall speak, neither do ye premeditate: but whatsoever shall be given you in that hour, that speak ye: for it is not ye that speak, but the Holy Ghost.	And when they shall lead you to deliver you up, be not solicitous beforehand what ye shall say, neither premeditate; but, that which shall be given you in that hour, speak ye; for it is not ye that speak, but the Holy Spirit.	And when they bring you to deliver you up, do not be anxious beforehand about what you will say or think, but what is given to you at that moment, that speak. For you are not speaking, but the Holy Spirit.
12	Now the brother shall betray the brother to death, and the father the son; and children shall rise up against their parents, and shall cause them to be put to death.	And brother will deliver up his brother to death, and the father his son; and children will rise up against their parents, and will kill them.	And brother will deliver his brother to death and a father his son and children will rise up against their parents and will put them to death.
13	And ye shall be hated of all men for my name's sake: but he that shall endure unto the end, the same shall be saved.	And ye will be hated of every man, on account of my name. But whoever shall persevere to the end, shall live.	And you will be hated by all men because of my name. But he who endures until the end will live.
14	But when ye shall see the abomination of desolation, spoken of by Daniel the prophet, standing where it ought not, (let him that readeth understand,) then let them that be in Judaea flee to the mountains:	And when ye see the profane sign of desolation, which was mentioned by Daniel the prophet, standing where it ought not;---(let him that readeth, understand;) then let those that are in Judaea, flee to the mountain:	And when you see the abominable sign of desecration that was spoken of by Daniel the prophet that will stand where it should not be (he who reads should understand) then those who are in Judah should flee to the mountain.
15	And let him that is on the housetop not go down into the house, neither enter therein, to take any thing out of his house:	and let him that is on the roof, not come down and enter [it], to take any thing from his house:	And he who is on the roof should not come down nor enter to take anything from his house.
16	And let him that is in the field not turn back again for to take up his garment.	and let him that is in the field, not return back to take his clothing.	And he who is in the field should not turn back to pick up his clothing.
17	But woe to them that are with child, and to them that give suck in those days!	But, woe to those with child, and to those who nurse children, in those days!	And woe to pregnant women and to those who are nursing in those days!
18	And pray ye that your flight be not in the winter.	And pray ye, that your flight be not in winter.	Now pray, so that your flight will not be in winter.
19	For in those days shall be affliction, such as was not from the beginning of the creation which God created unto this time, neither shall be.	For in those days will be affliction, such as hath not been from the beginning of the creation that God made until now, and shall not be.	For an ordeal will come in those days such as has not occurred from the beginning of the creation that God created until now, nor will be [again].
20	And except that the Lord had shortened those days, no flesh should be saved: but for the elect's sake, whom he hath chosen, he hath shortened the days.	And, unless God should shorten those days, no flesh would live. But, on account of the elect whom he hath chosen, he hath shortened those days.	And if the LORD had not shortened those days, no flesh would live. But because of the chosen [ones] that he chose, he shortened those days.
21	And then if any man shall say to you, Lo, here is Christ; or, lo, he is there; believe him not:	Then, if any one shall say to you: Lo, here is Messiah, or lo, there; give not credence.	Then, if anyone says to you, 'Behold, here is the Messiah and behold, [over] here,' do not believe [him].

Parallel Translations

	KJV	*Murdock*	*Magiera*
	MARK	*Chapter 13*	
22	For false Christs and false prophets shall rise, and shall shew signs and wonders, to seduce, if it were possible, even the elect.	For false Messiahs will arise, and lying prophets; and they will give signs and wonders; and will deceive, if possible, even the elect.	For false messiahs and lying prophets will rise up and they will produce signs and wonders and will deceive even the chosen [ones], if possible.
23	But take ye heed: behold, I have foretold you all things.	But take ye heed. Lo, I have told you the whole beforehand.	But watch out! Behold, I have told you everything beforehand.
24	But in those days, after that tribulation, the sun shall be darkened, and the moon shall not give her light,	And in those days, after that affliction, the sun will be darkened; and the moon will not give her light;	And in those days after that ordeal, THE SUN WILL DARKEN AND THE MOON WILL NOT GIVE ITS LIGHT.
25	And the stars of heaven shall fall, and the powers that are in heaven shall be shaken.	and the stars will fall from heaven; and the powers of heaven will be shaken.	AND THE STARS WILL FALL FROM HEAVEN AND THE POWERS OF HEAVEN WILL BE SHAKEN.
26	And then shall they see the Son of man coming in the clouds with great power and glory.	And then will they see the Son of man coming in the clouds, with great power and glory.	And then they will see THE SON OF MAN COMING IN THE CLOUDS WITH GREAT POWER AND WITH GLORY.
27	And then shall he send his angels, and shall gather together his elect from the four winds, from the uttermost part of the earth to the uttermost part of heaven.	And then will he send forth his angels, and will assemble his elect from the four winds, from the extremity of earth to the extremity of heaven.	Then he will send his angels and gather his chosen [ones] from the four winds, from one end of the earth to the end of heaven.
28	Now learn a parable of the fig tree; When her branch is yet tender, and putteth forth leaves, ye know that summer is near:	And, from the fig-tree learn ye a simile. When its twigs are tender, and its leaves bud forth, ye know that summer approacheth.	Now learn an illustration from the fig tree that when its branches are tender and its leaves bud, you know that summer has arrived.
29	So ye in like manner, when ye shall see these things come to pass, know that it is nigh, even at the doors.	So also, when ye shall see these occurrences, know ye, that it is near, at the door.	So also, when you have seen these [things] that are going to be, know that it is near, at the door.
30	Verily I say unto you, that this generation shall not pass, till all these things be done.	Verily I say to you, That this generation shall not pass away, until all these things occur.	Truly I say to you, this generation will not pass away until all these [things] occur.
31	Heaven and earth shall pass away: but my words shall not pass away.	Heaven and earth will pass away, but my words will not pass away.	Heaven and earth will pass away, yet my words will not pass away.
32	But of that day and that hour knoweth no man, no, not the angels which are in heaven, neither the Son, but the Father.	But of that day and that hour, knoweth no man; nor the angels of heaven; neither the Son, but the Father.	But about that day and about that hour, no man knows, not even the angels of heaven, nor the Son, but only the Father.
33	Take ye heed, watch and pray: for ye know not when the time is.	Take heed, watch, and pray; for ye know not when the time is.	Watch, be alert and pray, for you do not know when the time is.
34	For the Son of man is as a man taking a far journey, who left his house, and gave authority to his servants, and to every man his work, and commanded the porter to watch.	For it is as a man, who took a journey, and left his home; and he gave authority to his servants, and to each his service; and he commanded the porter to be watchful.	For [it is] like a man who went on a journey and left his house and gave authority to his servants and to each man his work and commanded the porter to be alert.

MARK *Chapter 13*

	KJV	Murdock	Magiera
35	Watch ye therefore: for ye know not when the master of the house cometh, at even, or at midnight, or at the cockcrowing, or in the morning:	Watch ye, therefore; for ye know not when the lord of the house cometh; at evening, or at midnight, or at the cock-crowing, or in the morning:	Be alert, therefore, because you do not know when the lord of the house will come, in the evening or in the middle of the night or at the rooster crow or in the morning,
36	Lest coming suddenly he find you sleeping.	lest he come suddenly, and find you sleeping.	lest he comes suddenly and finds you sleeping.
37	And what I say unto you I say unto all, Watch.	And what I say to you, I say to you all: Be ye watchful.	Now what I say to you, I say to all of you, 'Be alert.'"

Chapter 14

	KJV	Murdock	Magiera
1	After two days was the feast of the passover, and of unleavened bread: and the chief priests and the scribes sought how they might take him by craft, and put him to death.	And after two days, was the passover of unleavened cakes. And the chief priests and the Scribes sought how they might take him by stratagem, and kill him.	Now after two days was the Passover of the unleavened bread, and the chief priests and scribes were seeking how they might arrest [him] with trickery and kill him.
2	But they said, Not on the feast day, lest there be an uproar of the people.	But they said: Not on the festival, lest there be commotion among the people.	And they were saying, "Not during the feast, so that a riot will not occur among the people."
3	And being in Bethany in the house of Simon the leper, as he sat at meat, there came a woman having an alabaster box of ointment of spikenard very precious; and she brake the box, and poured it on his head.	And when he was at Bethany in the house of Simon the leper, as he reclined, a woman came having an alabaster box of precious ointment of spikenard, of great price; and she opened and poured upon the head of Jesus.	And while he was in Bethany in the house of Simon the leper while reclining, a woman came who had near her an alabaster box of perfume of spikenard, the best, very costly, and she opened it and poured it on the head of Jesus.
4	And there were some that had indignation within themselves, and said, Why was this waste of the ointment made?	And there were certain of the disciples, who were dissatisfied among themselves, and said: Why was this waste of the ointment?	And there were some of the disciples who were offended among themselves and said, "Why was [there] the waste of this perfume?
5	For it might have been sold for more than three hundred pence, and have been given to the poor. And they murmured against her.	For it might have been sold for more than three hundred denarii, and been given to the poor. And they were indignant at her.	For it was possible to be sold [for] more than three hundred denarii and be given to the poor." And they were angry with him.
6	And Jesus said, Let her alone; why trouble ye her? she hath wrought a good work on me.	But Jesus said: Let her alone; why trouble ye her? She hath done an excellent act towards me.	But Jesus said, "Leave her alone. Why are you troubling her? She has done a proper act for me.
7	For ye have the poor with you always, and whensoever ye will ye may do them good: but me ye have not always.	For the poor ye have always with you; and when ye please, ye can do them kind offices: but I am not always with you.	For you always have the poor with you, and whenever you want, you are able to do for them what is proper, but I am not always with you.
8	She hath done what she could: she is come aforehand to anoint my body to the burying.	What was in her power, she hath done; and by anticipation, hath perfumed my body, as if for burial.	She did this of what she had and she has perfumed my body as for burial beforehand.

	KJV	Murdock	Magiera
	MARK *Chapter 14*		
9	Verily I say unto you, Wheresoever this gospel shall be preached throughout the whole world, this also that she hath done shall be spoken of for a memorial of her.	Verily I say to you, That wherever this my gospel shall be proclaimed, in all the world, this also which she hath done shall be told in memory of her.	And truly I say to you, wherever this, my gospel, is preached in all the world, also the thing that she has done will be spoken for her remembrance."
10	And Judas Iscariot, one of the twelve, went unto the chief priests, to betray him unto them.	And Judas Iscariot, one of the twelve, went to the chief priests, in order to betray Jesus to them.	And Judas Iscariot, one of the twelve, went to the chief priests to betray Jesus to them.
11	And when they heard it, they were glad, and promised to give him money. And he sought how he might conveniently betray him.	And when they heard [him], they rejoiced; and they promised to give him money. And he sought for opportunity to betray him.	And they, when they heard [him], rejoiced and promised to give him money. And he was seeking for himself an opportunity to betray him.
12	And the first day of unleavened bread, when they killed the passover, his disciples said unto him, Where wilt thou that we go and prepare that thou mayest eat the passover?	And on the first day of unleavened cakes, on which the Jews slay the passover, his disciples said to him: Where wilt thou that we go, and prepare for thee to eat the passover?	And on the first day of unleavened bread on which the Judeans slay the Passover, his disciples were saying to him, "Where do you want us to go to prepare for you to eat the Passover?"
13	And he sendeth forth two of his disciples, and saith unto them, Go ye into the city, and there shall meet you a man bearing a pitcher of water: follow him.	And he sent two of his disciples, and said to them: Go ye to the city, and behold, there will meet you a man bearing a pitcher of water. Go ye after him,	And he sent two of his disciples and said to them, "Go to the city and behold, a man who is carrying a vessel of water will meet you. Follow him.
14	And wheresoever he shall go in, say ye to the goodman of the house, The Master saith, Where is the guestchamber, where I shall eat the passover with my disciples?	and where he entereth in, say ye to the lord of the house: Our Rabbi saith, Where is the place of refreshment, in which I may eat the passover with my disciples?	And wherever he enters, say to the lord of the house, 'Our Master said, Where is the guest house where I may eat the Passover with my disciples?'
15	And he will shew you a large upper room furnished and prepared: there make ready for us.	And lo, he will show you a large upper room, furnished and prepared: there make ready for us.	And behold, he will show you a large upper room that is furnished and prepared. There make ready for us."
16	And his disciples went forth, and came into the city, and found as he had said unto them: and they made ready the passover.	And his disciples went, and entered the city, and found as he had told them: and they made ready the passover.	And his disciples went out and came to the city and found as he had said to them and they prepared the Passover.
17	And in the evening he cometh with the twelve.	And when it was evening, he came with his twelve.	And when evening came, he came with his twelve.
18	And as they sat and did eat, Jesus said, Verily I say unto you, One of you which eateth with me shall betray me.	And as they reclined and ate, Jesus said: Verily I say to you, That one of you that eateth with me, will betray me.	And while they were reclining and eating, Jesus said, "Truly I say to you, one of you who eats with me will betray me."
19	And they began to be sorrowful, and to say unto him one by one, Is it I? and another said, Is it I?	And they began to be distressed. And they said to him, one by one, Is it I?	And they began to be grieved and were saying to him, one by one, "Is it I?"
20	And he answered and said unto them, It is one of the twelve, that dippeth with me in the dish.	And he said to them: It is one of the twelve that dippeth with me in the dish.	And he said to them, "[It is] one of the twelve who dips with me in the dish.

	KJV	Murdock	Magiera
MARK	*Chapter 14*		
21	The Son of man indeed goeth, as it is written of him: but woe to that man by whom the Son of man is betrayed! good were it for that man if he had never been born.	And the Son of man goeth, as it is written of him: but woe to that man, by whom the Son of man is betrayed. Better would it have been for that man, if he had not been born.	And the Son of Man will die as it is written about him. But woe to that man by whose hand the Son of Man is delivered up! It would be better for that man if he had not been born."
22	And as they did eat, Jesus took bread, and blessed, and brake it, and gave to them, and said, Take, eat: this is my body.	And as they were eating, Jesus took bread, and blessed, and brake, and gave to them, and said to them: Take; this is my body.	And while they were eating, Jesus took bread and blessed [it] and broke [it] and gave [it] to them. And he said to them, "Take, this is my body."
23	And he took the cup, and when he had given thanks, he gave it to them: and they all drank of it.	And he took the cup, and gave thanks, and blessed, and gave to them. And they all drank of it.	And he took a cup and gave thanks and blessed [it] and gave [it] to them, and they all drank from it.
24	And he said unto them, This is my blood of the new testament, which is shed for many.	And he said to them: This is my blood of the new testament, which is shed in behalf of many.	And he said to them, "This is my blood of the new covenant that is shed on behalf of many.
25	Verily I say unto you, I will drink no more of the fruit of the vine, until that day that I drink it new in the kingdom of God.	Verily I say to you, That I will not drink again of the product of the vine, until the day in which I shall drink it anew in the kingdom of God.	Truly I say to you, I will not drink again from the fruit of the vine until that day in which I will drink it anew in the kingdom of God."
26	And when they had sung an hymn, they went out into the mount of Olives.	And they sang praise, and went out to the mount of Olives.	And they offered praise and went out to the Mount of Olives.
27	And Jesus saith unto them, All ye shall be offended because of me this night: for it is written, I will smite the shepherd, and the sheep shall be scattered.	And Jesus said to them: All of you will this night be stumbled in me: for it is written, "I will smite the shepherd, and his sheep will be scattered."	And Jesus said to them, "All of you will be offended at me in this night, for it is written: I WILL STRIKE THE SHEPHERD AND HIS LAMBS WILL BE SCATTERED.
28	But after that I am risen, I will go before you into Galilee.	And when I am risen, I will precede you into Galilee.	But when I have risen, I will go before you into Galilee."
29	But Peter said unto him, Although all shall be offended, yet will not I.	And Cephas said to him: Though they all should be stumbled, yet I will not be.	Peter said to him, "Though all of them be offended, I [will] not [be]."
30	And Jesus saith unto him, Verily I say unto thee, That this day, even in this night, before the cock crow twice, thou shalt deny me thrice.	Jesus said to him: Verily I say to thee, That this day, on this night, before the cock shall crow twice, thou wilt thrice deny me.	Jesus said to him, "Truly I say to you, today in this night, before the rooster will crow two times, you will deny me three [times]."
31	But he spake the more vehemently, If I should die with thee, I will not deny thee in any wise. Likewise also said they all.	And he said, in addition: If I were to die with thee, I will not deny thee, my Lord. And like him, spake all the disciples.	And all the more he was saying, "If I must die with you, I will not deny you, my Lord." And all of them also spoke likewise.
32	And they came to a place which was named Gethsemane: and he saith to his disciples, Sit ye here, while I shall pray.	And they came to the place called Gethsemane; and he said to his disciples, Sit ye here, while I pray.	And they came to a place that was called Gethsemane, and he said to his disciples, "Sit here while I pray."
33	And he taketh with him Peter and James and John, and began to be sore amazed, and to be very heavy;	And he took with him Cephas and James and John, and began to be gloomy and distressed.	And he took with him Peter and James and John and began to be sad and to grieve.

Parallel Translations

MARK *Chapter 14*

	KJV	*Murdock*	*Magiera*
34	And saith unto them, My soul is exceeding sorrowful unto death: tarry ye here, and watch.	And he said to them: My soul hath anguish, even to death. Wait for me here, and be watchful.	And he said to them, "It is grievous to my soul unto death. Remain here and be watchful."
35	And he went forward a little, and fell on the ground, and prayed that, if it were possible, the hour might pass from him.	And he advanced a little, and fell upon the ground, and prayed that, if it were possible, the hour might pass from him.	And he went on a little and fell on the ground and was praying that if it was possible, [this] hour might pass from him.
36	And he said, Abba, Father, all things are possible unto thee; take away this cup from me: nevertheless not what I will, but what thou wilt.	And he said: Father, my Father, thou canst do all things. Let this cup pass from me. Yet not my pleasure, but thine.	And he said, "Father, my Father, you can [do] everything. Make this cup pass from me. Yet not my own will, but yours."
37	And he cometh, and findeth them sleeping, and saith unto Peter, Simon, sleepest thou? couldest not thou watch one hour?	And he came and found them sleeping. And he said to Cephas: Sleepest thou, Simon? Couldst thou not watch with me one hour?	And he came [and] found them sleeping. And he said to Peter, "Simon, are you sleeping? Are you not able to be watchful for one hour?
38	Watch ye and pray, lest ye enter into temptation. The spirit truly is ready, but the flesh is weak.	Watch and pray, lest ye enter into temptation. The spirit is willing and ready, but the body is weak.	Be watchful and pray, so that you might not enter into temptation. The spirit is willing and ready, but the body is weak."
39	And again he went away, and prayed, and spake the same words.	And he went again and prayed, speaking the same language.	And he went again [and] prayed and he said the same thing.
40	And when he returned, he found them asleep again, (for their eyes were heavy,) neither wist they what to answer him.	And returning he came again and found them sleeping, for their eyes were heavy. And they knew not what to say to him.	And he returned [and] came [and] again found them sleeping, because their eyes were heavy, and they did not know what to say to him.
41	And he cometh the third time, and saith unto them, Sleep on now, and take your rest: it is enough, the hour is come; behold, the Son of man is betrayed into the hands of sinners.	And he came the third time, and said to them: Sleep on now, and take rest. The end is near; the hour is come; and lo, the Son of man is betrayed into the hands of sinners.	And he came a third time and said to them, "Sleep now, and rest. The end has arrived and the hour has come and behold, the Son of Man is delivered into the hands of sinners.
42	Rise up, let us go; lo, he that betrayeth me is at hand.	Arise ye; let us go. Lo, he that betrayeth me is at hand.	Rise up, let us go. Behold, he who has delivered me draws near."
43	And immediately, while he yet spake, cometh Judas, one of the twelve, and with him a great multitude with swords and staves, from the chief priests and the scribes and the elders.	And while he was yet speaking, Judas Iscariot, one of the twelve, arrived, and much people, with swords and clubs, from before the chief priests and Scribes and Elders.	And while he was speaking, Judas Iscariot, one of the twelve, and many people with swords and rods, came from being with the chief priests and scribes and elders.
44	And he that betrayed him had given them a token, saying, Whomsoever I shall kiss, that same is he; take him, and lead him away safely.	And the traitor who betrayed [him], had given them a sign, and said: He whom I shall kiss is the man. Seize promptly, and lead him away.	And the traitor who betrayed [him] had given them a sign and had said, "Whomever I kiss is he. Arrest him securely and take him away."
45	And as soon as he was come, he goeth straightway to him, and saith, Master, master; and kissed him.	And immediately he came up, and said to him: Rabbi, Rabbi; and kissed him.	And immediately he drew near and said to him, "My Master, my Master," and he kissed him.

	KJV	*Murdock*	*Magiera*
	MARK	*Chapter 14*	
46	And they laid their hands on him, and took him.	And they laid hands on him and took him.	And they placed [their] hands on him and arrested him.
47	And one of them that stood by drew a sword, and smote a servant of the high priest, and cut off his ear.	And one of them that stood by, drew a sword, and smote a servant of the high priest, and cut off his ear.	And one of those who were standing [there] drew a sword and struck the servant of the high priest and took off his ear.
48	And Jesus answered and said unto them, Are ye come out, as against a thief, with swords and with staves to take me?	And Jesus answered and said to them: Have ye come out against me, as against a robber; with swords and clubs, to apprehend me?	And Jesus answered and said to them, "Do you come out as against a robber with swords and rods to arrest me?
49	I was daily with you in the temple teaching, and ye took me not: but the scriptures must be fulfilled.	I was daily with you, while I taught in the temple, and ye seized me not. But this occurs, that the scriptures may be fulfilled.	Every day I was with you while I was teaching in the temple and you did not arrest me. But this has occurred that the scriptures would be fulfilled."
50	And they all forsook him, and fled.	Then his disciples left him and fled.	Then his disciples left him and fled.
51	And there followed him a certain young man, having a linen cloth cast about his naked body; and the young men laid hold on him:	And a young man followed after him, who was clad with a linen cloth on [his] naked [body]: and they laid hold of him.	And a certain young man followed him, and a linen cloth was wrapped around [his] naked [body], and they grabbed him.
52	And he left the linen cloth, and fled from them naked.	And he left the linen cloth, and fled naked.	And he left the linen cloth and fled naked.
53	And they led Jesus away to the high priest: and with him were assembled all the chief priests and the elders and the scribes.	And they led away Jesus to Caiaphas the high priest. And with him were assembled all the chief priests and the Scribes and the Elders.	And they took Jesus to Caiaphas, the high priest, and all the chief priests and scribes and elders were gathered with him.
54	And Peter followed him afar off, even into the palace of the high priest: and he sat with the servants, and warmed himself at the fire.	And Simon followed after him, at a distance; into the hall of the high priest; and he sat with the servants, and warmed himself by the fire.	And Simon was following him from a distance as far as the inside of the courtyard of the high priest. And he was sitting with the servants and was warming [himself] near the fire.
55	And the chief priests and all the council sought for witness against Jesus to put him to death; and found none.	And the chief priests and all the assembly sought for testimony against Jesus, to put him to death: but they found it not.	And the chief priests and all their assembly were seeking testimony against Jesus, so that they might kill him, but they did not find [any].
56	For many bare false witness against him, but their witness agreed not together.	For while many testified against him, their testimonies were inadequate.	For although many were testifying against him, their testimony was not agreeing.
57	And there arose certain, and bare false witness against him, saying,	And some false witnesses stood up against him, and said:	And some false witnesses stood up against him and said,
58	We heard him say, I will destroy this temple that is made with hands, and within three days I will build another made without hands.	We have heard him say: I will destroy this temple, which is made with hands; and in three days I will build another not made with hands.	"We heard him when he said, 'I will destroy this temple that was made with hands, and after three days I will build another that is not made with hands.'"
59	But neither so did their witness agree together.	Nor even thus were their testimonies adequate.	But even so, their testimony was not agreeing.

Parallel Translations

	KJV	Murdock	Magiera
	MARK	*Chapter 14*	
60	And the high priest stood up in the midst, and asked Jesus, saying, Answerest thou nothing? what is it which these witness against thee?	And the high priest arose in the midst, and interrogated Jesus and said: Returnest thou no answer? What do these testify against thee?	And the high priest stood up in the middle [of them] and questioned Jesus and said, "Do you not answer the accusation? Why are they testifying these [things] against you?"
61	But he held his peace, and answered nothing. Again the high priest asked him, and said unto him, Art thou the Christ, the Son of the Blessed?	And Jesus was silent, and made no reply. And again the chief priest interrogated him, and said: Art thou the Messiah, the Son of the Blessed?	But he was silent and did not answer him anything. And again the high priest questioned him and said, "Are you the Messiah, the Son of the Blessed One?"
62	And Jesus said, I am: and ye shall see the Son of man sitting on the right hand of power, and coming in the clouds of heaven.	And Jesus said to him: I am. And ye will see the Son of man sitting on the right hand of power, and he will come on the clouds of heaven.	And Jesus said to him, "I am. And you will see THE SON OF MAN WHEN HE SITS ON THE RIGHT [HAND] OF POWER and COMES ON THE CLOUDS OF HEAVEN."
63	Then the high priest rent his clothes, and saith, What need we any further witnesses?	And the high priest rent his tunic, and said: What need of witnesses have we, any more?	And the high priest tore his robe and said, "Why now are we seeking witnesses?
64	Ye have heard the blasphemy: what think ye? And they all condemned him to be guilty of death.	Behold, from his own mouth ye have heard blasphemy. How doth it appear to you? And they all decided, that he deserved to die.	Behold, from his mouth you have heard blasphemy. What do you think?" And all of them judged that he was deserving of death.
65	And some began to spit on him, and to cover his face, and to buffet him, and to say unto him, Prophesy: and the servants did strike him with the palms of their hands.	And some began to spit in his face, and to buffet him, saying: Prophesy thou. And the servants smote him on the cheeks.	And some began spitting in his face. And they covered his face and were striking him and saying, "Prophesy!" And the guards were striking him on his cheeks.
66	And as Peter was beneath in the palace, there cometh one of the maids of the high priest:	And as Simon was below in the court, a maid of the high priest came,	And while Simon was below in the courtyard, a certain maiden of the high priest came.
67	And when she saw Peter warming himself, she looked upon him, and said, And thou also wast with Jesus of Nazareth.	and saw him warming himself; and she looked upon him, and said to him: And thou too wast with Jesus the Nazarean.	She saw him while he was warming [himself] and she looked at him and said to him, "And you also were with Jesus the Nazarene."
68	But he denied, saying, I know not, neither understand I what thou sayest. And he went out into the porch; and the cock crew.	But he denied, and said: I know not what thou sayest. And he went out into the porch; and the cock crew.	But he denied [it] and said, "I do not know what you are saying." And he went outside to the porch and the rooster crowed.
69	And a maid saw him again, and began to say to them that stood by, This is one of them.	And the maid saw him again, and she began to say to those standing by, This man also is one of them.	And again the maiden saw him and she began to tell those who were standing [there], "This one also is one of them."
70	And he denied it again. And a little after, they that stood by said again to Peter, Surely thou art one of them: for thou art a Galilaean, and thy speech agreeth thereto.	And he again denied [it]. And a little after, those standing there said again to Cephas: Surely, thou art one of them; for thou art likewise a Galilean, and thy speech answers to it.	But again he denied [it]. And after a little [time] again those who were standing [there] said to Peter, "Truly you are one of them, for you are also a Galilean and your speech is like [theirs]."

Parallel Translations

	KJV	Murdock	Magiera
	MARK *Chapter 14*		
71	But he began to curse and to swear, saying, I know not this man of whom ye speak.	And he began to imprecate, and swore: I know not that man, of whom ye speak.	And he began to curse and swore, "I do not know this man of whom you speak!"
72	And the second time the cock crew. And Peter called to mind the word that Jesus said unto him, Before the cock crow twice, thou shalt deny me thrice. And when he thought thereon, he wept.	And immediately the cock crew the second time. And Simon remembered the declaration of Jesus, who said to him: Before the cock shall crow twice, thou wilt thrice deny me. And he began to weep.	And immediately, the rooster crowed the second time, and Simon remembered the saying of Jesus, who had said to him, "Before the rooster crows two times, you will deny me three [times]," and he began to cry.
	Chapter 15		
1	And straightway in the morning the chief priests held a consultation with the elders and scribes and the whole council, and bound Jesus, and carried him away, and delivered him to Pilate.	And forthwith, in the morning, the chief priests with the Elders and the Scribes, and the whole Sanhedrim, held a consultation. And they bound Jesus, and led him away, and delivered him over to Pilate the president.	And immediately in the morning the chief priests took counsel with the elders and with the scribes and with the entire assembly. And they bound Jesus and led him away. And they delivered him to Pilate.
2	And Pilate asked him, Art thou the King of the Jews? And he answering said unto him, Thou sayest it.	And Pilate asked him: Art thou the king of the Jews? He replied and said to him: Thou hast said.	And Pilate asked him, "Are you the king of the Judeans?" And he answered and said to him, "You have said [it]."
3	And the chief priests accused him of many things: but he answered nothing.	And the chief priests accused him of many things.	And the chief priests were accusing him of many [things].
4	And Pilate asked him again, saying, Answerest thou nothing? behold how many things they witness against thee.	And Pilate again questioned him, and said to him: Makest thou no reply? See how much they testify against thee!	And Pilate again asked him and said to him, "Will you not answer the accusation? See how many are testifying against you!"
5	But Jesus yet answered nothing; so that Pilate marvelled.	But Jesus gave no answer; so that Pilate wondered.	But Jesus did not give any answer, so that Pilate was amazed.
6	Now at that feast he released unto them one prisoner, whomsoever they desired.	And it was his custom, at each festival, to release to them one prisoner, whom they might desire.	Now he was accustomed during every feast to release one prisoner to them, whomever they requested.
7	And there was one named Barabbas, which lay bound with them that had made insurrection with him, who had committed murder in the insurrection.	And there was one named Bar Abas, who was confined with the movers of sedition, who had committed murder in the insurrection.	And there was one who was called Barabbas who was a prisoner with the ones who had caused an insurrection, those who had committed murder in the insurrection.
8	And the multitude crying aloud began to desire him to do as he had ever done unto them.	And the people clamored, and began to demand, that he should do to them as he was accustomed.	And the people cried out and began to request he do [this] for them as he was accustomed.
9	But Pilate answered them, saying, Will ye that I release unto you the King of the Jews?	And Pilate answered, and said: Will ye, that I release to you the king of the Jews?	But Pilate answered and said, "Do you want me to release to you the king of the Judeans?"
10	For he knew that the chief priests had delivered him for envy.	For Pilate knew that the chief priests, from envy, had delivered him up.	(For Pilate knew that the chief priests had delivered him up out of envy.)

Parallel Translations

MARK *Chapter 15*

	KJV	*Murdock*	*Magiera*
11	But the chief priests moved the people, that he should rather release Barabbas unto them.	But the chief priests further persuaded the multitudes, that Bar Abas should be released to them.	And the chief priests all the more exhorted the crowds [to ask] that he should release Barabbas to them.
12	And Pilate answered and said again unto them, What will ye then that I shall do unto him whom ye call the King of the Jews?	And Pilate said to them: What will ye, therefore, that I do to him whom ye call king of the Jews?	And Pilate said to them, "What then do you want me to do to this one whom you call king of the Judeans?"
13	And they cried out again, Crucify him.	And they again cried out: Crucify him.	And again they cried out, "Crucify him!"
14	Then Pilate said unto them, Why, what evil hath he done? And they cried out the more exceedingly, Crucify him.	And Pilate said to them: But what evil hath he done? And they cried out the more: Crucify him.	And Pilate said to them, "What evil has he done?" And they were crying out all the more, "Crucify him!"
15	And so Pilate, willing to content the people, released Barabbas unto them, and delivered Jesus, when he had scourged him, to be crucified.	And Pilate was willing to gratify the wishes of the multitudes; and he released to them Bar Abas; and, having scourged Jesus, he delivered him to them to be crucified.	And Pilate wanted to do the will of the crowds and he released Barabbas to them and he delivered Jesus to them, after he had scourged [him], to be crucified.
16	And the soldiers led him away into the hall, called Praetorium; and they call together the whole band.	And the soldiers led him into the hall which was the Praetorium; and they called together the whole regiment;	And the soldiers led him away inside the hall that was the Praetorium and they called the whole company of soldiers.
17	And they clothed him with purple, and platted a crown of thorns, and put it about his head,	and they clothed him in purple, and braided a crown of thorns and put upon him;	And they put purple clothes on him and wove [and] placed on him a crown of thorns.
18	And began to salute him, Hail, King of the Jews!	and began to salute him with, "Hail, king of the Jews!"	And they began to salute him [with], "Hail, king of the Judeans."
19	And they smote him on the head with a reed, and did spit upon him, and bowing their knees worshipped him.	And they smote him on the head with a reed and spit in his face, and bowed upon their knees and worshipped him.	And they were striking him on his head with a reed and were spitting in his face and were kneeling on their knees and bowing to him.
20	And when they had mocked him, they took off the purple from him, and put his own clothes on him, and led him out to crucify him.	And having mocked him, they divested him of the purple, and clothed him in his own garments, and led him forth to crucify him.	And after they had mocked him, they stripped off the purple clothes and put on his own garments and took him out to crucify him.
21	And they compel one Simon a Cyrenian, who passed by, coming out of the country, the father of Alexander and Rufus, to bear his cross.	And they compelled a passer-by, Simon the Cyrenian, the father of Alexander and Rufus, who was coming from the fields, to bear his cross.	And they compelled one who was passing by, Simon, a Cyrenian, who had come from the country, the father of Alexander and of Rufus, to carry his cross.
22	And they bring him unto the place Golgotha, which is, being interpreted, The place of a skull.	And they brought him to Golgotha, the place which is interpreted a Skull.	And they brought him to Golgotha, the place that is interpreted, The Skull.
23	And they gave him to drink wine mingled with myrrh: but he received it not.	And they gave him to drink wine in which myrrh was mixed; and he would not receive it.	And they gave him wine in which was mixed myrrh to drink, but he did not take [it].

Parallel Translations

	KJV	Murdock	Magiera
	MARK	*Chapter 15*	
24	And when they had crucified him, they parted his garments, casting lots upon them, what every man should take.	And when they had crucified him, they divided his garments; and cast the lot upon them, what each should take.	And after they had crucified him, they divided his garments and cast lots for them, what each should take.
25	And it was the third hour, and they crucified him.	And it was the third hour when they crucified him.	And it was the third hour when they crucified him.
26	And the superscription of his accusation was written over, THE KING OF THE JEWS.	And the cause of his death was written in the inscription: THIS IS THE KING OF THE JEWS.	And the cause of his death was written in the inscription, "This is the king of the Judeans."
27	And with him they crucify two thieves; the one on his right hand, and the other on his left.	And they crucified with him two robbers, the one on his right hand, and the other on his left.	And they crucified with him two robbers, one on his right and one on his left.
28	And the scripture was fulfilled, which saith, And he was numbered with the transgressors.	And the scripture was fulfilled which saith: He was accounted among the wicked.	And the scripture was fulfilled that said: HE WAS COUNTED WITH THE WICKED.
29	And they that passed by railed on him, wagging their heads, and saying, Ah, thou that destroyest the temple, and buildest it in three days,	And they also that passed by, reviled him; and, nodding their heads, they said: Aha, thou that destroyest the temple and buildest it in three days,	And also those who were passing by were reviling him and shaking their heads and saying, "Oh indeed! [He said] he will destroy the temple and build it after three days.
30	Save thyself, and come down from the cross.	rescue thyself, and come down from the cross.	Save yourself and come down from the cross."
31	Likewise also the chief priests mocking said among themselves with the scribes, He saved others; himself he cannot save.	And so also the chief priests, jeering one with another, and the Scribes, said: He gave life to others, his own life he cannot save.	And likewise also the chief priests and the scribes were laughing with each other and saying, "Others he saved. Himself he is not able to save.
32	Let Christ the King of Israel descend now from the cross, that we may see and believe. And they that were crucified with him reviled him.	Let Messiah, the king of the Jews, now descend from the cross, that we may see [it] and believe in him. And those also who were crucified with him, derided him.	Let the Messiah, the King of Israel, come down now from the cross that we might see and believe in him." And those also who were crucified with him were reviling him.
33	And when the sixth hour was come, there was darkness over the whole land until the ninth hour.	And when the sixth hour was come, there was darkness over all the land until the ninth hour.	And when the sixth hour came, there was darkness over all the land until the ninth hour.
34	And at the ninth hour Jesus cried with a loud voice, saying, Eloi, Eloi, lama sabachthani? which is, being interpreted, My God, my God, why hast thou forsaken me?	And at the ninth hour, Jesus cried with a loud voice, and said: Il, Il, lemono shebakthone; that is: My God, my God; why hast thou forsaken me?	And in the ninth hour Jesus cried out with a loud voice and said, "Eil, Eil, lmana shavaqtani," which is [interpreted], "MY GOD, MY GOD, WHY HAVE YOU LEFT ME?"
35	And some of them that stood by, when they heard it, said, Behold, he calleth Elias.	And some of them that stood by, when they heard it, said: He calleth for Elijah.	And some of those who were standing [there] who heard were saying, "He calls to Elijah."
36	And one ran and filled a spunge full of vinegar, and put it on a reed, and gave him to drink, saying, Let alone; let us see whether Elias will come to take him down.	And one ran and filled a sponge with vinegar, and tied it on a reed, to offer him drink. And they said: Desist; let us see if Elijah will come to take him down.	And one ran and filled a sponge [with] vinegar and fastened [it] on a reed to give him to drink. And they said, "Leave [him]! Let us see if Elijah will come to take him down."

Parallel Translations

MARK *Chapter 15*

	KJV	*Murdock*	*Magiera*
37	And Jesus cried with a loud voice, and gave up the ghost.	And Jesus cried with a loud voice, and expired.	And Jesus cried out with a loud voice and died.
38	And the veil of the temple was rent in twain from the top to the bottom.	And the curtain of the door of the temple was rent, from the top to the bottom.	And the veil of the temple was torn into two [pieces], from the top to the bottom.
39	And when the centurion, which stood over against him, saw that he so cried out, and gave up the ghost, he said, Truly this man was the Son of God.	And when the centurion, who was standing near him, saw that he so cried and expired, he said: Verily, this was the Son of God.	Now when the centurion who was standing near him saw that he cried out so and died, he said, "Truly this man was the Son of God."
40	There were also women looking on afar off: among whom was Mary Magdalene, and Mary the mother of James the less and of Joses, and Salome;	And there were women looking on, from a distance, Mary Magdalena, and Mary the mother of James the less and of Joses, and Salome;	And there were also women who were watching from afar, Mary Magdalene and Mary the mother of James the less and of Joses and Salome,
41	(Who also, when he was in Galilee, followed him, and ministered unto him;) and many other women which came up with him unto Jerusalem.	who, when he was in Galilee adhered to him, and ministered to him; and many other women, who had come up with him to Jerusalem.	those who, when he was in Galilee, were following him and ministering to him, and many others who had gone up with him to Jerusalem.
42	And now when the even was come, because it was the preparation, that is, the day before the sabbath,	And, as it was the eve of preparation, which precedeth the sabbath,	And when the evening of the preparation had come, that was before the Sabbath,
43	Joseph of Arimathaea, an honourable counsellor, which also waited for the kingdom of God, came, and went in boldly unto Pilate, and craved the body of Jesus.	Joseph of Ramath, an honorable counsellor, who also himself waited for the kingdom of God, came, and assuming courage, went to Pilate, and begged the body of Jesus.	Joseph who was from Arimathaea, an honorable counselor who also was waiting for the kingdom of God, came and was bold and approached Pilate and requested the body of Jesus.
44	And Pilate marvelled if he were already dead: and calling unto him the centurion, he asked him whether he had been any while dead.	And Pilate wondered that he should be already dead. And he called the centurion, and inquired if he had been any time dead.	And Pilate marveled that he had already died. And he called the centurion and asked him if he had already died.
45	And when he knew it of the centurion, he gave the body to Joseph.	And when he learned it, he gave his body to Joseph.	And when he learned [it], he gave his body to Joseph.
46	And he bought fine linen, and took him down, and wrapped him in the linen, and laid him in a sepulchre which was hewn out of a rock, and rolled a stone unto the door of the sepulchre.	And Joseph bought fine linen, and took it down, and wrapped it in the linen, and deposited it in a sepulchre that was hewed in a rock, and rolled a stone against the door of the sepulchre.	And Joseph bought linen cloth and took him down and wrapped him in it and placed him in a grave that was hewn out in the rock and he rolled a stone on the door of the grave.
47	And Mary Magdalene and Mary the mother of Joses beheld where he was laid.	And Mary Magdalena and Mary [the mother] of Joses saw where he was laid.	And Mary Magdalene and Mary the [mother] of Joses saw where he was laid.

Parallel Translations

	KJV	*Murdock*	*Magiera*
MARK	*Chapter 16*		
1	And when the sabbath was past, Mary Magdalene, and Mary the mother of James, and Salome, had bought sweet spices, that they might come and anoint him.	And when the sabbath had passed, Mary Magdalena, and Mary [the mother] of James, and Salome, bought aromatics, that they might come and anoint him.	And when the Sabbath had passed, Mary Magdalene and Mary [the mother] of James and Salome bought spices that they might come to anoint him.
2	And very early in the morning the first day of the week, they came unto the sepulchre at the rising of the sun.	And in the morning of the first day of the week, they came to the sepulchre as the sun arose.	And early on the first [day] of the week, they came to the tomb while the sun was rising.
3	And they said among themselves, Who shall roll us away the stone from the door of the sepulchre?	And they said among themselves: Who will roll back for us the stone from the door of the sepulchre?	And they were saying among themselves, "Who [will] roll the stone from the door of the tomb for us?"
4	And when they looked, they saw that the stone was rolled away: for it was very great.	And they looked, and saw that the stone was rolled away; for it was very great.	And they looked [and] saw that the stone was rolled away, for it was very great.
5	And entering into the sepulchre, they saw a young man sitting on the right side, clothed in a long white garment; and they were affrighted.	And entering the sepulchre, they saw a youth sitting on the right hand, and clothed in a white robe: and they were in perturbation.	And they entered the tomb and saw a young man who was sitting on the right [side] and wrapped around [him] was a white robe, and they were amazed.
6	And he saith unto them, Be not affrighted: Ye seek Jesus of Nazareth, which was crucified: he is risen; he is not here: behold the place where they laid him.	But he said to them: Be not affrighted. Ye are seeking Jesus the Nazarean, who was crucified. He is risen; he is not here. Behold the place where he was laid.	And he said to them, "Do not be afraid. You seek Jesus the Nazarene who was crucified. He has risen. He is not here. Behold the place where he was laid.
7	But go your way, tell his disciples and Peter that he goeth before you into Galilee: there shall ye see him, as he said unto you.	But go, tell his disciples and Cephas: Lo, he precedeth you into Galilee; there will ye see him, as he said to you.	But go [and] tell his disciples and Peter that behold, [he goes] before you to Galilee. There you will see him as he said to you."
8	And they went out quickly, and fled from the sepulchre; for they trembled and were amazed: neither said they any thing to any man; for they were afraid.	And when they heard, they fled and left the sepulchre; for astonishment and trembling had seized them; and they said nothing to any one, for they were in fear.	And when they had heard, they fled and went out of the grave, for amazement and trembling had taken hold on them and they did not speak anything to anyone, for they were afraid.
9	Now when Jesus was risen early the first day of the week, he appeared first to Mary Magdalene, out of whom he had cast seven devils.	And in the morning of the first day of the week, he arose; and he appeared first to Mary Magdalena, from whom he had cast out seven demons.	And early on the first of the week he had risen and appeared first to Mary Magdalene from whom he had cast out seven demons.
10	And she went and told them that had been with him, as they mourned and wept.	And she went and told them that had been with him, while they were mourning and weeping.	And she went [and] brought hope to those who had been with him who were mourning and weeping.
11	And they, when they had heard that he was alive, and had been seen of her, believed not.	And they, when they heard [the women] say that he was alive, and that he had appeared to them, did not believe them.	And when they heard what they were saying, that he was alive and had appeared to them, they did not believe them.

Parallel Translations

MARK *Chapter 16*

	KJV	*Murdock*	*Magiera*
12	After that he appeared in another form unto two of them, as they walked, and went into the country.	After this he appeared, under another aspect, to two of them as they walked and went into the country.	After these [things] he appeared to two of them in another form while they were walking and traveling to a village.
13	And they went and told it unto the residue: neither believed they them.	And these went and told the rest; but they would not believe them	And those went [and] told the rest. They did not even believe them.
14	Afterward he appeared unto the eleven as they sat at meat, and upbraided them with their unbelief and hardness of heart, because they believed not them which had seen him after he was risen.	And at last, he appeared to the eleven: as they reclined at table; and he reproved the slenderness of their faith, and the hardness of their heart; because they believed not those who had seen him actually risen.	And finally he appeared to the eleven while they were eating. And he reproved the lack of their faith and the hardness of their heart, since they had not believed those who had seen that he had risen.
15	And he said unto them, Go ye into all the world, and preach the gospel to every creature.	And he said to them: Go ye into all the world, and proclaim my tidings in the whole creation.	And he said to them, "Go to all the world and preach my gospel in all of creation.
16	He that believeth and is baptized shall be saved; but he that believeth not shall be damned.	He that believeth, and is baptized, liveth; but he that believeth not, is condemned.	Whoever believes and is baptized will live, and whoever does not believe is condemned.
17	And these signs shall follow them that believe; In my name shall they cast out devils; they shall speak with new tongues;	And these signs shall attend them that believe: In my name, they will cast out demons; and in new tongues will they speak.	And these signs will follow those who believe. In my name they will cast out demons and they will speak with new tongues.
18	They shall take up serpents; and if they drink any deadly thing, it shall not hurt them; they shall lay hands on the sick, and they shall recover.	And they will take up serpents; and if they should drink a deadly poison, it will not harm them; and they will lay their hands on the sick, and they will be healed.	And they will capture snakes, and if they should drink a deadly poison, it will harm not them and they will place their hands on the sick and they will be made whole."
19	So then after the Lord had spoken unto them, he was received up into heaven, and sat on the right hand of God.	And Jesus, our Lord, after he had conversed with them, ascended to heaven, and sat on the right hand of God.	And Jesus, our Lord, after speaking with them, went up to heaven and sat on the right hand of God.
20	And they went forth, and preached every where, the Lord working with them, and confirming the word with signs following. Amen.	And they went forth, and preached everywhere: and our Lord aided them, and confirmed their discourses by the signs which they wrought.	And they went out and preached in every place and our Lord was helping them and establishing their words by the signs that they were doing.

Parallel Translations

	KJV	Murdock	Magiera
	LUKE	*Chapter 1*	
1	Forasmuch as many have taken in hand to set forth in order a declaration of those things which are most surely believed among us,	Since many have been disposed to write narratives of those events, of which we have full assurance,	Because many have wanted to write the accounts of the works of which we are persuaded,
2	Even as they delivered them unto us, which from the beginning were eyewitnesses, and ministers of the word;	as they delivered them to us, who from the first were eye-witnesses and ministers of the word;	according to what they delivered to us, those who were eye-witnesses and ministers of the word at the first,
3	It seemed good to me also, having had perfect understanding of all things from the very first, to write unto thee in order, most excellent Theophilus,	it seemed proper for me also, as I had examined them all accurately, to write out the whole, methodically, for thee, excellent Theophilus:	it seemed [good] to me also, because I had carefully attended to all of them that I should write down everything in order for you, noble Theophilus,
4	That thou mightest know the certainty of those things, wherein thou hast been instructed.	that thou mayest know the truth of the statements, which thou hast been taught.	that you would know the truth of the words by which you were taught.
5	There was in the days of Herod, the king of Judaea, a certain priest named Zacharias, of the course of Abia: and his wife was of the daughters of Aaron, and her name was Elisabeth.	In the days of Herod the king of Judaea, there was a certain priest, whose name was Zachariah, of the ministration of the house of Abijah; and his wife was of the daughters of Aaron, and her name was Elisabeth.	In the days of Herod, the king of Judea, there was a certain priest, whose name was Zachariah, from the course of the house of Abia, and his wife, from the daughters of Aaron, whose name was Elizabeth.
6	And they were both righteous before God, walking in all the commandments and ordinances of the Lord blameless.	And they were both upright before God, and walked in all his commandments, and in the righteousness of the Lord, without reproach.	Now both of them were just before God and were walking in all his commandments and in the uprightness of the LORD without blame.
7	And they had no child, because that Elisabeth was barren, and they both were now well stricken in years.	But they had no child, because Elisabeth was barren: and they were both advanced in life.	But they had no son because Elizabeth was barren and both of them were advanced in their days.
8	And it came to pass, that while he executed the priest's office before God in the order of his course,	And it occurred, that as he performed the priestly functions in the order of his ministration before the Lord,	And it happened, while he was serving as priest in the order of his ministering before God,
9	According to the custom of the priest's office, his lot was to burn incense when he went into the temple of the Lord.	according to the usage of the priesthood, it fell to him to offer the incense. And he went into the temple of the Lord,	in the custom of the priesthood, it arrived that he was to place the incense. And he entered the temple of the LORD
10	And the whole multitude of the people were praying without at the time of incense.	and the whole multitude of the people were praying without, at the time of incense.	and the whole assembly of people was praying outside at the time of the incense.
11	And there appeared unto him an angel of the Lord standing on the right side of the altar of incense.	And the angel of the Lord appeared to Zachariah, standing on the right side of the altar of incense.	And an angel of the LORD appeared to Zachariah, who stood on the right [side] of the altar of incense,

Parallel Translations

LUKE *Chapter 1*

	KJV	*Murdock*	*Magiera*
12	And when Zacharias saw him, he was troubled, and fear fell upon him.	And when Zachariah saw him, he was agitated, and fear fell upon him.	and Zachariah was agitated when he saw him, and fear fell on him.
13	But the angel said unto him, Fear not, Zacharias: for thy prayer is heard; and thy wife Elisabeth shall bear thee a son, and thou shalt call his name John.	And the angel said to him: Fear not, Zachariah; for thy prayer is heard, and thy wife Elisabeth will bear thee a son, and thou shalt call his name John.	And the angel said to him, "Do not fear, Zachariah, because your prayer has been heard, and your wife, Elizabeth, will bear you a son, and you will call his name John,
14	And thou shalt have joy and gladness; and many shall rejoice at his birth.	And thou wilt have joy and gladness: and many will rejoice at his birth.	and you will have joy and gladness, and many will rejoice at his birth.
15	For he shall be great in the sight of the Lord, and shall drink neither wine nor strong drink; and he shall be filled with the Holy Ghost, even from his mother's womb.	For he will be great before the Lord; and he will not drink wine nor strong drink, and will be filled with the Holy Spirit even from his mother's womb.	For he will be great before the LORD, and he will not drink wine or strong drink, and he will be filled with the Holy Spirit while he is in the womb of his mother,
16	And many of the children of Israel shall he turn to the Lord their God.	And many of the children of Israel will he convert to the Lord their God.	and he will turn many of the sons of Israel to the LORD their God,
17	And he shall go before him in the spirit and power of Elias, to turn the hearts of the fathers to the children, and the disobedient to the wisdom of the just; to make ready a people prepared for the Lord.	And he will go before him, in the spirit and power of Elijah the prophet, and will turn the heart of the fathers unto the children, and them that are disobedient to the knowledge of the righteous, and will prepare a perfect people for the Lord.	and he will go before him in the spirit and in the power of Elijah the prophet, that he might turn the heart of the parents to the children and those who are disobedient to the knowledge of the upright, and he will prepare a mature people for the LORD."
18	And Zacharias said unto the angel, Whereby shall I know this? for I am an old man, and my wife well stricken in years.	And Zachariah said to the angel: How shall I know this? For I am old, and my wife is advanced in life.	And Zachariah said to the angel, "How will I know this? For I am old and my wife is advanced in her days."
19	And the angel answering said unto him, I am Gabriel, that stand in the presence of God; and am sent to speak unto thee, and to shew thee these glad tidings.	The angel answered, and said to him: I am Gabriel, who stand before God; and I am sent to converse with thee, and to tell thee these things.	And the angel answered and said to him, "I am Gabriel, for I stand before God. And I have been sent to speak with you and to declare to you these [things].
20	And, behold, thou shalt be dumb, and not able to speak, until the day that these things shall be performed, because thou believest not my words, which shall be fulfilled in their season.	Henceforth thou wilt be dumb, and unable to speak, until the day when these things take place: because thou believedst not my words, which will be fulfilled in their time.	From now on, you will be silent and not able to speak until the day that these [things] occur, because you did not believe my words that will be fulfilled in their season."
21	And the people waited for Zacharias, and marvelled that he tarried so long in the temple.	And the people were standing and waiting for Zachariah; and they wondered at his tarrying so long in the temple.	Now the people were standing and waiting for Zachariah and they were wondering about his delay in the temple.
22	And when he came out, he could not speak unto them: and they perceived that he had seen a vision in the temple: for he beckoned unto them, and remained speechless.	And when Zachariah came forth, he could not speak with them: and they understood that he had seen a vision in the temple: and he made many signs to them, and remained speechless.	And when Zachariah came out, he was not able to speak with them and they perceived that he had seen a vision in the temple. And he continually made signs to them, yet remained mute.

Parallel Translations

	KJV	Murdock	Magiera
	LUKE *Chapter 1*		
23	And it came to pass, that, as soon as the days of his ministration were accomplished, he departed to his own house.	And when the days of his ministration were accomplished, he came to his house.	And when the days of his service were completed, he went to his house.
24	And after those days his wife Elisabeth conceived, and hid herself five months, saying,	And it was after those days, that Elisabeth his wife conceived. And she secluded herself five months; and she said:	And it happened after those days [that] Elizabeth, his wife, conceived. And she hid herself [for] five months, and she said,
25	Thus hath the Lord dealt with me in the days wherein he looked on me, to take away my reproach among men.	These things hath the Lord done for me, in the days when he looked upon me to take away my reproach among men.	"These [things] the LORD has done for me in the days that he looked on me to remove my reproach that was among men."
26	And in the sixth month the angel Gabriel was sent from God unto a city of Galilee, named Nazareth,	And in the sixth month, the angel Gabriel was sent by God into Galilee, to a city named Nazareth,	Now in the sixth month, the angel Gabriel was sent from before God to Galilee, to a city by the name of Nazareth,
27	To a virgin espoused to a man whose name was Joseph, of the house of David; and the virgin's name was Mary.	to a virgin espoused to a man whose name was Joseph, of the house of David; and the virgin's name was Mary.	to a virgin who was engaged to a man whose name [was] Joseph from the house of David. And the name of the virgin [was] Mary.
28	And the angel came in unto her, and said, Hail, thou that art highly favoured, the Lord is with thee: blessed art thou among women.	And the angel entered the house, and said to her: Peace to thee, thou full of grace! The Lord is with thee: and blessed art thou among women.	And the angel approached her and said to her, "Peace to you, [one] full of grace! Our Lord [is] with you, blessed [one] of women."
29	And when she saw him, she was troubled at his saying, and cast in her mind what manner of salutation this should be.	And when she saw [him], she was agitated by his speech; and she pondered, what this salutation could mean.	Now when she saw [him], she was shocked at his saying and wondered, "What is this greeting?"
30	And the angel said unto her, Fear not, Mary: for thou hast found favour with God.	And the angel said to her: Fear not, Mary; for thou hast found favor with God.	And the angel said to her, "Do not be afraid, Mary, for you have found grace with God.
31	And, behold, thou shalt conceive in thy womb, and bring forth a son, and shalt call his name JESUS.	For lo, thou wilt conceive in thy womb, and wilt bear a son, and wilt call his name Jesus.	For behold, you will conceive and give birth to a son and you will call his name Jesus.
32	He shall be great, and shall be called the Son of the Highest: and the Lord God shall give unto him the throne of his father David:	He will be great, and will be called the Son of the Most High, and the Lord God will give him the throne of his father David.	He will be great, and he will be called the Son of the Most High, and the LORD God will give to him the throne of David, his father,
33	And he shall reign over the house of Jacob for ever; and of his kingdom there shall be no end.	And he will reign over the house of Jacob for ever; and of his reign there will be no end.	and he will reign over the house of Jacob forever, and there will not be a boundary to his kingdom."
34	Then said Mary unto the angel, How shall this be, seeing I know not a man?	And Mary said to the angel: How can this be, as I have not known a man?	Mary said to the angel, "How can this be? Because no man has known me."

LUKE *Chapter 1*

	KJV	*Murdock*	*Magiera*
35	And the angel answered and said unto her, The Holy Ghost shall come upon thee, and the power of the Highest shall overshadow thee: therefore also that holy thing which shall be born of thee shall be called the Son of God.	The angel replied, and said to her: The Holy Spirit will come, and the power of the Most High will overshadow thee; therefore he that is born of thee is holy, and will be called the Son of God.	The angel answered and said to her, "The Holy Spirit will come and the power of the Most High will overshadow you. Because of this, the one who is begotten in you will be holy and will be called the Son of God.
36	And, behold, thy cousin Elisabeth, she hath also conceived a son in her old age: and this is the sixth month with her, who was called barren.	And lo, Elisabeth thy kinswoman, even she too hath conceived a son in her old age; and this is the sixth month with her who is called barren.	And behold, Elizabeth, your kinswoman, is also pregnant with a son in her old age and this [is] the sixth month for her who was called barren,
37	For with God nothing shall be impossible.	Because nothing is difficult for God.	because nothing [is] difficult for God."
38	And Mary said, Behold the handmaid of the Lord; be it unto me according to thy word. And the angel departed from her.	Mary said: Behold, I am the handmaid of the Lord; be it to me, according to thy word. And the angel departed from her.	Mary said, "Behold, I am the handmaid of the LORD. It will happen to me according to your word." And the angel left her.
39	And Mary arose in those days, and went into the hill country with haste, into a city of Juda;	And Mary arose in those days, and went hastily to the mountain [district], to a city of Judaea;	And Mary rose up in those days and went quickly to a mountain, to a city of Judea.
40	And entered into the house of Zacharias, and saluted Elisabeth.	and entered the house of Zachariah, and saluted Elisabeth.	And she entered the house of Zachariah and greeted Elizabeth.
41	And it came to pass, that, when Elisabeth heard the salutation of Mary, the babe leaped in her womb; and Elisabeth was filled with the Holy Ghost:	And it was so, that when Elisabeth heard the salutation of Mary, the child leaped in her womb, and she was filled with the Holy Spirit.	And it happened that when Elizabeth heard the greeting of Mary, the baby leaped in her womb, and Elizabeth was filled with the Holy Spirit
42	And she spake out with a loud voice, and said, Blessed art thou among women, and blessed is the fruit of thy womb.	And she cried out with a loud voice, and said to Mary: Blessed art thou among women; and blessed is the fruit of thy womb.	and she cried out in a loud voice and said to Mary, "You are blessed among women, and blessed is the fruit that is in your womb.
43	And whence is this to me, that the mother of my Lord should come to me?	And whence is this to me, that the mother of my Lord should come to me?	How did this [happen] to me that the mother of my Lord would come to me?
44	For, lo, as soon as the voice of thy salutation sounded in mine ears, the babe leaped in my womb for joy.	For lo, as the voice of thy salutation fell upon my ears, with great joy the child leaped in my womb.	For behold, when the sound of your greeting fell on my ears, the baby in my womb leaped with great joy.
45	And blessed is she that believed: for there shall be a performance of those things which were told her from the Lord.	And happy is she that believed; for there will be a fulfillment of those things that were told her by the Lord.	And blessed [is] she who believed, because there will be a completion of those [things] that were spoken with her in the presence of the LORD."
46	And Mary said, My soul doth magnify the Lord,	And Mary said: My soul doth magnify the Lord:	And Mary said, "My soul magnifies the LORD
47	And my spirit hath rejoiced in God my Saviour.	and my spirit rejoiceth in God the author of my life.	and my spirit has rejoiced in God, my Life-giver,

	KJV	*Murdock*	*Magiera*
	LUKE	*Chapter 1*	
48	For he hath regarded the low estate of his handmaiden: for, behold, from henceforth all generations shall call me blessed.	For he hath looked upon the humble condition of his hand maid; and lo, henceforth all generations will ascribe blessedness to me.	because he has looked at the humiliation of his handmaid. For behold, from now on, all generations will give me a blessing,
49	For he that is mighty hath done to me great things; and holy is his name.	And He that is mighty hath done for me great things; and holy is his name.	because he who is mighty has done great [things] with me and his name [is] holy
50	And his mercy is on them that fear him from generation to generation.	And his mercy is on them that fear him, for generations and posterities.	and his mercy [is] on those who fear him for ages and generations.
51	He hath shewed strength with his arm; he hath scattered the proud in the imagination of their hearts.	He hath wrought victory with his arm; and hath scattered the proud in the imagination of their heart.	He has accomplished victory with his arm and has scattered the proud in the thought of their heart[s].
52	He hath put down the mighty from their seats, and exalted them of low degree.	He hath cast down the mighty from their thrones, and hath exalted the lowly.	He has thrown down the mighty from the seats and elevated the humble.
53	He hath filled the hungry with good things; and the rich he hath sent empty away.	The hungry hath he satisfied with good things, and the rich hath he sent away empty.	The hungry he has satisfied with good [things] and the rich he has sent away empty-handed.
54	He hath holpen his servant Israel, in remembrance of his mercy;	He hath aided Israel his servant, and remembered his mercy,	He has aided Israel his servant and remembered his mercy,
55	As he spake to our fathers, to Abraham, and to his seed for ever.	(as he spoke with the fathers,) with Abraham and his seed, for ever.	as he spoke with our fathers, with Abraham and with his seed forever."
56	And Mary abode with her about three months, and returned to her own house.	And Mary remained with Elisabeth about three months, and returned to her home.	And Mary stayed with Elizabeth for three months and she returned to her house.
57	Now Elisabeth's full time came that she should be delivered; and she brought forth a son.	And Elisabeth's time of bringing forth arrived; and she bore a son.	Now [concerning] Elizabeth, the time came that she should give birth and she bore a son.
58	And her neighbours and her cousins heard how the Lord had shewed great mercy upon her; and they rejoiced with her.	And her neighbors and relatives heard that the Lord had magnified his mercy to her, and they rejoiced with her.	And her neighbors and her relatives heard that God had increased his mercy toward her and they rejoiced with her.
59	And it came to pass, that on the eighth day they came to circumcise the child; and they called him Zacharias, after the name of his father.	And it occurred, that on the eighth day they came to circumcise the child. And they called him by the name of his father, Zachariah.	And it happened on the eighth day and they came to circumcise the young boy and they were going to call him by the name of his father, Zachariah.
60	And his mother answered and said, Not so; but he shall be called John.	And his mother answered and said: Not so; but John, shall he be called.	But his mother answered and said to them, "Not so, but he will be called John."
61	And they said unto her, There is none of thy kindred that is called by this name.	And they said to her: There is no one among thy kindred called by that name.	And they said to her, "There is no man in your tribe who is called by this name."
62	And they made signs to his father, how he would have him called.	And they made signs to his father, how he would have him named.	And they made signs to his father as to what he wanted to name him.

Parallel Translations

	KJV	Murdock	Magiera

LUKE Chapter 1

	KJV	Murdock	Magiera
63	And he asked for a writing table, and wrote, saying, His name is John. And they marvelled all.	And he asked for a tablet, and wrote, and said: John is his name. And every one was surprised.	And he asked for a writing tablet and wrote and said, "His name is John." And everyone marveled.
64	And his mouth was opened immediately, and his tongue loosed, and he spake, and praised God.	And immediately his mouth was opened, and his tongue; and he spoke, and praised God.	And immediately his mouth was opened and his tongue [was loosed] and he spoke and blessed God.
65	And fear came on all that dwelt round about them: and all these sayings were noised abroad throughout all the hill country of Judaea.	And fear came upon all their neighbors; and these things were talked of in all the mountain [district] of Judaea.	And fear came over all their neighbors, and in all the mountain of Judea these [things] were spoken.
66	And all they that heard them laid them up in their hearts, saying, What manner of child shall this be! And the hand of the Lord was with him.	And all who heard, pondered them in their heart, and said: What will this child be? And the hand of the Lord was with him.	And all that heard were pondering in their heart[s] and saying, "What indeed will this child be?" And the hand of the LORD was with him.
67	And his father Zacharias was filled with the Holy Ghost, and prophesied, saying,	And Zachariah his father was filled with the Holy Spirit, and prophesied, and said:	And Zachariah, his father, was filled with the Holy Spirit and prophesied and said,
68	Blessed be the Lord God of Israel; for he hath visited and redeemed his people,	Blessed be the Lord God of Israel, who hath visited his people, and wrought redemption for them:	"The LORD is blessed, the God of Israel, who has visited his nation and brought redemption for it.
69	And hath raised up an horn of salvation for us in the house of his servant David;	And hath raised up a horn of redemption for us, in the house of David his servant:	And he has raised up for us a horn of redemption in the house of David his servant,
70	As he spake by the mouth of his holy prophets, which have been since the world began:	as he spake by the mouth of his holy prophets, who were of old,	as he spoke by the mouth of his holy prophets who were from old,
71	That we should be saved from our enemies, and from the hand of all that hate us;	that he would redeem us from our enemies, and from the hand of all that hate us.	that he would redeem us from our enemies and from the hand of all our adversaries.
72	To perform the mercy promised to our fathers, and to remember his holy covenant;	And he hath exercised his mercy to our fathers, and hath remembered his holy covenants,	And he has performed his mercy with our fathers and has remembered his holy covenants
73	The oath which he sware to our father Abraham,	and the oath that he sware to Abraham our father, that he would grant to us,	and the oaths that he swore to Abraham, our father, that he would give to us,
74	That he would grant unto us, that we being delivered out of the hand of our enemies might serve him without fear,	to be redeemed from the hand of our enemies; and that we should worship before him, without fear,	so that we would be redeemed from the hand of our enemies and [that] without fear we might serve before him
75	In holiness and righteousness before him, all the days of our life.	all our days, in rectitude and uprightness.	all our days in uprightness and justification.
76	And thou, child, shalt be called the prophet of the Highest: for thou shalt go before the face of the Lord to prepare his ways;	And thou, child, wilt be called a prophet of the Most High; for thou wilt go before the face of the Lord, to prepare his way,	And you, [oh] child, will be called the prophet of the Most High, for you will go before the face of the LORD to prepare his way,
77	To give knowledge of salvation unto his people by the remission of their sins,	that he may give the knowledge of life to his people, and forgiveness of their sins,	so that he may give the knowledge of life to his people in the forgiveness of their sins,

Parallel Translations

	KJV	Murdock	Magiera
	LUKE *Chapter 1*		
78	Through the tender mercy of our God; whereby the dayspring from on high hath visited us,	through the compassion of the mercy of our God; whereby the day-spring from on high will visit us,	by the bowels of mercy of our God, by which the dawn from on high will visit us,
79	To give light to them that sit in darkness and in the shadow of death, to guide our feet into the way of peace.	to give light to them that sit in darkness, and in the shadow of death; and to guide our feet into the way of peace.	to enlighten those who sit in darkness and in the shadows of death, that he may direct our feet in the way of peace."
80	And the child grew, and waxed strong in spirit, and was in the deserts till the day of his shewing unto Israel.	And the child grew, and was strengthened in spirit. And he was in the wilderness, until the day of his manifestation to Israel.	And the child grew and was strengthened by the Spirit and he was in the wilderness until the day of his appearance to Israel.
	Chapter 2		
1	And it came to pass in those days, that there went out a decree from Caesar Augustus, that all the world should be taxed.	And in those days it occurred, that a decree went forth from Augustus Caesar, that all the people of his dominion should be enrolled.	And it happened [that] in those days a decree went out from Caesar Augustus that every nation of his jurisdiction should be enrolled.
2	(And this taxing was first made when Cyrenius was governor of Syria.)	And this enrollment was first made under the presidency of Quirinus in Syria.	This was the first enrollment during the governorship of Quirinius in Syria.
3	And all went to be taxed, every one into his own city.	And everyone went to his own city to be enrolled.	And everyone went to his city to be enrolled.
4	And Joseph also went up from Galilee, out of the city of Nazareth, into Judaea, unto the city of David, which is called Bethlehem; (because he was of the house and lineage of David:)	And Joseph also went up from Nazareth of Galilee to Judaea, to the city of David which is called Bethlehem, because he was of the house and lineage of David,	And Joseph also went up from Nazareth, a city of Galilee, into Judea to the city of David that is called Bethlehem, because he was from the house and from the tribe of David,
5	To be taxed with Mary his espoused wife, being great with child.	with Mary his espoused, then pregnant, to be enrolled.	with Mary, his pregnant wife, to be enrolled there.
6	And so it was, that, while they were there, the days were accomplished that she should be delivered.	And it was while they were there, that the days for her to bring forth were completed.	And it happened that while they were there, her days were fulfilled that she should give birth,
7	And she brought forth her firstborn son, and wrapped him in swaddling clothes, and laid him in a manger; because there was no room for them in the inn.	And she brought forth her firstborn son, and wrapped him in bandages, and laid him in the stall; for they had no place where they could lodge.	and she bore her firstborn son and wrapped him in swaddling clothes and laid him in a manger, because they had no place where they were staying.
8	And there were in the same country shepherds abiding in the field, keeping watch over their flock by night.	And there were shepherds in that region, who abode there and kept watch of their flocks by night.	And there were shepherds in that region who were abiding there and keeping watch over their flocks at night.
9	And, lo, the angel of the Lord came upon them, and the glory of the Lord shone round about them: and they were sore afraid.	And lo, the angel of God came to them, and the glory of the Lord shone upon them: and they feared with great fear.	And behold, an angel of God came to them and the glory of the LORD shone on them and they were very afraid.
10	And the angel said unto them, Fear not: for, behold, I bring you good tidings of great joy, which shall be to all people.	And the angel said to them: Fear not; for, behold I announce to you great joy, which will be to all the world.	And the angel said to them, "Do not be afraid, for behold, I announce to you great joy that will be to all the world.

Parallel Translations

	KJV	*Murdock*	*Magiera*

LUKE *Chapter 2*

	KJV	Murdock	Magiera
11	For unto you is born this day in the city of David a Saviour, which is Christ the Lord.	For there is born to you this day a deliverer, who is the Lord Messiah, in the city of David	For today the deliverer, who is the LORD the Messiah, is born to you in the city of David.
12	And this shall be a sign unto you; Ye shall find the babe wrapped in swaddling clothes, lying in a manger.	And this is the sign for you: Ye will find the babe wrapped in bandages, and placed in a stall.	And this [is] a sign to you, you will find a baby who is wrapped in swaddling clothes and laid in a manger."
13	And suddenly there was with the angel a multitude of the heavenly host praising God, and saying,	And instantly there were seen with the angel, the many hosts of heaven, praising God, and saying:	And suddenly the great hosts of heaven appeared with the angel, praising God and saying,
14	Glory to God in the highest, and on earth peace, good will toward men.	Glory to God in the highest [heavens], and on earth peace and good hope for men.	"Glory to God in the highest and on earth, peace and a good hope to men."
15	And it came to pass, as the angels were gone away from them into heaven, the shepherds said one to another, Let us now go even unto Bethlehem, and see this thing which is come to pass, which the Lord hath made known unto us.	And it was so, that when the angels had gone from them into heaven, the shepherds conferred with one another, and said: Let us go down to Bethlehem, and see this thing which hath occurred, as the Lord hath made known to us.	And it happened that after the angels had gone away from them to heaven, the shepherds spoke with each other and said, "Let us journey to Bethlehem and see this matter that has happened as the LORD has made known to us."
16	And they came with haste, and found Mary, and Joseph, and the babe lying in a manger.	And they came hastily, and found Mary and Joseph, and the babe laid in the stall.	And they came quickly and found Mary and Joseph and the baby, who was laid in the manger.
17	And when they had seen it, they made known abroad the saying which was told them concerning this child.	And when they saw, they made known the information which was given to them concerning the child.	And after they had seen [him], they made known the message that had been told to them about the child.
18	And all they that heard it wondered at those things which were told them by the shepherds.	And all that heard, wondered at the things that were told them by the shepherds.	And all who heard [it] marveled at those [things] that were spoken to them by the shepherds.
19	But Mary kept all these things, and pondered them in her heart.	And Mary laid up all these things, and pondered them in her heart.	But Mary kept all those words and was pondering [them] in her heart.
20	And the shepherds returned, glorifying and praising God for all the things that they had heard and seen, as it was told unto them.	And the shepherds returned glorifying and praising God for all that they had seen and heard, as it was told them.	And those shepherds returned, glorifying and praising God for all that they had seen and heard as it was told to them.
21	And when eight days were accomplished for the circumcising of the child, his name was called JESUS, which was so named of the angel before he was conceived in the womb.	And when the eight days for the circumcision of the child were completed, his name was called JESUS; as he was named by the angel, before he was conceived in the womb.	And when eight days were completed so that the boy could be circumcised, his name was called Jesus as he had been named by the angel before he was conceived in the womb.
22	And when the days of her purification according to the law of Moses were accomplished, they brought him to Jerusalem, to present him to the Lord;	And when the days of their purification were completed, according to the law of Moses, they carried him to Jerusalem, to present him before the Lord:	And when the days of their purification were fulfilled according to the law of Moses, they took him up to Jerusalem to present him to the LORD,

LUKE *Chapter 2*

	KJV	*Murdock*	*Magiera*
23	(As it is written in the law of the Lord, Every male that openeth the womb shall be called holy to the Lord;)	(as it is written in the law of the Lord, that every male opening the womb shall be called holy to the Lord:)	according to what was written in the law of the LORD: EVERY MALE [WHO] OPENS THE WOMB WILL BE CALLED A HOLY ONE OF THE LORD,
24	And to offer a sacrifice according to that which is said in the law of the Lord, A pair of turtledoves, or two young pigeons.	and to offer a sacrifice, according as it is written in the law of the Lord, A pair of turtle-doves, or two young pigeons.	and to give a sacrifice, as is said in the law of the LORD, A PAIR OF TURTLEDOVES OR TWO CHICKS OF A DOVE.
25	And, behold, there was a man in Jerusalem, whose name was Simeon; and the same man was just and devout, waiting for the consolation of Israel: and the Holy Ghost was upon him.	And there was a certain man in Jerusalem, whose name was Simeon. This man was upright and just, and was waiting for the consolation of Israel, and the Holy Spirit was upon him.	Now there was a certain man in Jerusalem whose name was Simeon. And this man was upright and just and was waiting for the comfort of Israel and the Holy Spirit was on him.
26	And it was revealed unto him by the Holy Ghost, that he should not see death, before he had seen the Lord's Christ.	And it had been told him by the Holy Spirit, that he would not see death, until he should see the Messiah of the Lord.	And it had been spoken to him by the Holy Spirit that he would not see death until he would see the Messiah of the LORD.
27	And he came by the Spirit into the temple: and when the parents brought in the child Jesus, to do for him after the custom of the law,	This man came, by the Spirit, into the temple; and when his parents brought in the child Jesus, to do for him as is commanded in the law,	This [man] came by the Spirit to the temple and when his parents brought the child Jesus to do for him as was commanded in the law,
28	Then took he him up in his arms, and blessed God, and said,	he took him in his arms, and blessed God, and said:	he took him up in his arms and blessed God and said,
29	Lord, now lettest thou thy servant depart in peace, according to thy word:	My Lord, now release thou thy servant in peace, as thou hast said:	"Now, my Lord, dismiss your servant in peace according to your word.
30	For mine eyes have seen thy salvation,	for lo, my eyes have seen thy mercy,	For behold, my eyes have seen your mercy
31	Which thou hast prepared before the face of all people;	which thou hast prepared in the presence of all nations,	that you have prepared in the presence of all nations,
32	A light to lighten the Gentiles, and the glory of thy people Israel.	a light for a revelation to the Gentiles, and a glory for thy people Israel.	a light for a revelation to the Gentiles and a glory to your people, Israel."
33	And Joseph and his mother marvelled at those things which were spoken of him.	And Joseph and his mother were astonished at those things which were spoken concerning him.	And Joseph and his mother marveled at these [things] that were spoken about him.
34	And Simeon blessed them, and said unto Mary his mother, Behold, this child is set for the fall and rising again of many in Israel; and for a sign which shall be spoken against;	And Simeon blessed them, and said to Mary his mother: Behold, this [child] is set forth for the fall and for the rising of many in Israel, and for a standard of contention;	And Simeon blessed them and said to Mary his mother, "Behold, this [man] is set for the fall and the rising of many in Israel and for a sign of contention,
35	(Yea, a sword shall pierce through thy own soul also,) that the thoughts of many hearts may be revealed.	(and also a dart will pierce thy own soul); that the thoughts of the hearts of many may be disclosed.	(and a spear will pass through your soul) so that the thoughts of many hearts may be revealed."

LUKE *Chapter 2*

	KJV	Murdock	Magiera
36	And there was one Anna, a prophetess, the daughter of Phanuel, of the tribe of Aser: she was of a great age, and had lived with an husband seven years from her virginity;	And Hanna, a prophetess, the daughter of Phanuel, of the tribe of Asher,---she also was aged in days, and, from her maidenhood, had lived seven years with her husband,	And Anna, a prophetess, the daughter of Phanuel, from the tribe of Asher, was also advanced in her years. And she had lived [for] seven years with her husband from her maidenhood.
37	And she was a widow of about fourscore and four years, which departed not from the temple, but served God with fastings and prayers night and day.	and was a widow of about eighty and four years, and departed not from the temple, but worshipped by day and by night with fasting and prayer;	And she was a widow for about eighty-four years and she did not go out of the temple and she served in fasting and in prayer both day and night.
38	And she coming in that instant gave thanks likewise unto the Lord, and spake of him to all them that looked for redemption in Jerusalem.	and she too stood up, in that hour, and gave thanks to the Lord, and spoke of him to every one that waited for the redemption of Jerusalem.	And she also stood up immediately and gave thanks to the LORD and spoke about him to everyone who waited for the redemption of Jerusalem.
39	And when they had performed all things according to the law of the Lord, they returned into Galilee, to their own city Nazareth.	And when they had accomplished all things, according to the law of the Lord, they returned to Galilee, to their city Nazareth.	And when they had completed everything according to in the law of the LORD, they returned to Galilee, to their city Nazareth.
40	And the child grew, and waxed strong in spirit, filled with wisdom: and the grace of God was upon him.	And the child grew, and was strengthened in spirit, and was filled with wisdom; and the grace of God was upon him.	And the child grew and was strengthened by the Spirit and was filled with wisdom and the grace of God was on him.
41	Now his parents went to Jerusalem every year at the feast of the passover.	And his people went up to Jerusalem every year, at the feast of the passover.	And his relatives, during every year, went to Jerusalem for the celebration of the feast of Passover.
42	And when he was twelve years old, they went up to Jerusalem after the custom of the feast.	And when he was twelve years old, they went up to the feast, as they were accustomed.	And when he was twelve years old, they went up, as they were accustomed, for the celebration.
43	And when they had fulfilled the days, as they returned, the child Jesus tarried behind in Jerusalem; and Joseph and his mother knew not of it.	And when the days were completed, they returned: but the child Jesus remained at Jerusalem, and Joseph and his mother knew not [of it];	And after the [feast] days were completed, they returned. But the child Jesus remained in Jerusalem and Joseph and his mother did not know [it],
44	But they, supposing him to have been in the company, went a day's journey; and they sought him among their kinsfolk and acquaintance.	for they supposed he was with his companions. And when they had travelled a day's journey, they sought him among their people, and [inquired] of every one that knew them.	for they thought that he was with their companions. And after they had journeyed one day, they searched for him among their relatives and among anyone who knew them
45	And when they found him not, they turned back again to Jerusalem, seeking him.	And they did not find him. And they returned again to Jerusalem, searching for him.	and they did not find him. So they returned again to Jerusalem and searched for him.
46	And it came to pass, that after three days they found him in the temple, sitting in the midst of the doctors, both hearing them, and asking them questions.	And after three days, they found him in the temple, sitting in the midst of the teachers, and listening to them, and asking them questions.	And after three days, they found him in the temple, sitting in the middle of the teachers. And he was listening to them and questioning them.

Parallel Translations

LUKE Chapter 2

	KJV	Murdock	Magiera
47	And all that heard him were astonished at his understanding and answers.	And all they that heard him, were astonished at his wisdom and his answers.	And all those who heard him were amazed by his wisdom and his answers.
48	And when they saw him, they were amazed: and his mother said unto him, Son, why hast thou thus dealt with us? behold, thy father and I have sought thee sorrowing.	And when they saw him they were amazed. And his mother said to him: My son, why hast thou done so to us? For lo, I and thy father have been seeking for thee with great anxiety.	And when they saw him, they were amazed and his mother said to him, "My son, why have you acted toward us in this manner? For behold, your father and I have been searching for you with much anxiety."
49	And he said unto them, How is it that ye sought me? wist ye not that I must be about my Father's business?	He said to them: Why did ye seek me? Do ye not know, that it behooveth me to be in my Father's house?	He said to them, "Why were you searching for me? Do you not know that it is necessary for me to be in the house of my Father?"
50	And they understood not the saying which he spake unto them.	But they did not comprehend the word that he spoke to them.	But they did not understand the saying that he had told them.
51	And he went down with them, and came to Nazareth, and was subject unto them: but his mother kept all these sayings in her heart.	And he went down with them, and came to Nazareth, and was obedient to them. And his mother laid up all these things in her heart.	And he went down with them and came to Nazareth and was subject to them. And his mother kept all the words in her heart.
52	And Jesus increased in wisdom and stature, and in favour with God and man.	And Jesus increased in stature, and in wisdom, and in grace, before God and men.	And Jesus grew in his stature and in his wisdom and in favor with God and men.

Chapter 3

	KJV	Murdock	Magiera
1	Now in the fifteenth year of the reign of Tiberius Caesar, Pontius Pilate being governor of Judaea, and Herod being tetrarch of Galilee, and his brother Philip tetrarch of Ituraea and of the region of Trachonitis, and Lysanias the tetrarch of Abilene,	And in the fifteenth year of the reign of Tiberius Caesar, in the presidency of Pontius Pilate in Judaea, while Herod was Tetrarch in Galilee, and Philip his brother Tetrarch in Ituraea and in the region of Trachonitis, and Lysanias Tetrarch of Abilene,	Now in the fifteenth year of the reign of Tiberius Caesar, in the governorship of Pontius Pilate in Judea, while Herod [was] tetrarch in Galilee and Philip, his brother, [was] tetrarch in Ituraea and in the region of Trachonitis, and Lysanias [was] tetrarch of Abilene,
2	Annas and Caiaphas being the high priests, the word of God came unto John the son of Zacharias in the wilderness.	in the high priesthood of Annas and of Caiaphas; the word of God was upon John the son of Zachariah, in the wilderness.	during the high priesthood of Annas and Caiaphas, the word of God came to John, the son of Zachariah, in the wilderness.
3	And he came into all the country about Jordan, preaching the baptism of repentance for the remission of sins;	And he came into all the region about the Jordan, proclaiming the baptism of repentance for the forgiveness of sins.	And he came into all the region that was around the Jordan, proclaiming the baptism of repentance for the forgiveness of sins,
4	As it is written in the book of the words of Esaias the prophet, saying, The voice of one crying in the wilderness, Prepare ye the way of the Lord, make his paths straight.	As it is written in the book of the discourses of Isaiah the prophet, who said: The voice of one crying in the wilderness, Prepare ye the way of the Lord; and make straight paths in the plain for our God.	as it is written in the book of the words of Isaiah the prophet who said: THE VOICE THAT CALLS IN THE WILDERNESS: PREPARE THE WAY OF THE LORD AND MAKE STRAIGHT PATHS IN THE PLAIN FOR OUR GOD.

Parallel Translations

LUKE *Chapter 3*

	KJV	*Murdock*	*Magiera*
5	Every valley shall be filled, and every mountain and hill shall be brought low; and the crooked shall be made straight, and the rough ways shall be made smooth;	All valleys shall be filled up, and all mountains and hills be lowered; and the hillock shall be levelled down, and the rough place become smooth.	ALL THE VALLEYS WILL BE FILLED AND ALL THE MOUNTAINS AND HILLS WILL BE LEVELED AND THE RUGGED [PLACE] WILL BE CLEARED AND THE ROUGH LAND, A PLAIN.
6	And all flesh shall see the salvation of God.	And all flesh shall see the life which is of God.	AND ALL FLESH WILL SEE THE LIFE OF GOD.
7	Then said he to the multitude that came forth to be baptized of him, O generation of vipers, who hath warned you to flee from the wrath to come?	And he said to the multitudes, who came to him to be baptized: Ye progeny of vipers, who hath instructed you to flee from the future wrath?	And he said to those crowds that had come to him to be baptized, "Generation of vipers, who has shown you to flee from the wrath that is to come?
8	Bring forth therefore fruits worthy of repentance, and begin not to say within yourselves, We have Abraham to our father: for I say unto you, That God is able of these stones to raise up children unto Abraham.	Bring forth, therefore, fruits comporting with repentance. And begin not to say in yourselves: We have Abraham for our father; for I say to you, that God can, from these stones, raise up sons to Abraham.	Produce therefore fruit that is worthy for repentance and do not begin to say within yourselves, 'We have Abraham [for] a father.' For I say to you, 'From these stones, God is able to raise up sons to Abraham.'
9	And now also the axe is laid unto the root of the trees: every tree therefore which bringeth not forth good fruit is hewn down, and cast into the fire.	And lo, the ax is put to the root of trees. Every tree therefore that beareth not good fruits, is hewed down, and falleth into the fire.	And behold, the ax is laid on the root of the trees. Therefore, every tree that does not produce good fruit will be cut off and will fall into the fire."
10	And the people asked him, saying, What shall we do then?	And the multitudes asked him, and said: What, then, shall we do?	And the crowds were asking him and saying, "What then should we do?"
11	He answereth and saith unto them, He that hath two coats, let him impart to him that hath none; and he that hath meat, let him do likewise.	He answered and said to them: Whoever hath two tunics, let him give [one] to him that hath none; and whoever hath food, let him do the same.	He answered and said to them, "He who has two coats should give to him who does not have [any] and he who has food should do likewise."
12	Then came also publicans to be baptized, and said unto him, Master, what shall we do?	And publicans also came to be baptized. And they said to him: Teacher, what shall we do?	And the tax collectors also came to be baptized and were saying to him, "Teacher, what should we do?"
13	And he said unto them, Exact no more than that which is appointed you.	And he said to them: Exact no more than ye are required to exact.	And he said to them, "Do not require anything more than what is commanded to you to require."
14	And the soldiers likewise demanded of him, saying, And what shall we do? And he said unto them, Do violence to no man, neither accuse any falsely; and be content with your wages.	And those serving in war inquired of him, and said: And what shall we do? He said to them: Be insolent to no one, and oppress no one, and let your pay satisfy you.	And the soldiers were asking him and said, "What should we also do?" He said to them, "Do not deal harshly with anyone and do not accuse anyone and let your rations be sufficient for you."
15	And as the people were in expectation, and all men mused in their hearts of John, whether he were the Christ, or not;	And while the people were thinking of John, and all pondered in their heart, whether he were the Messiah;	And as the nation was thinking about John and all were considering in their heart that perhaps he was the Messiah,

Parallel Translations

LUKE *Chapter 3*

	KJV	*Murdock*	*Magiera*
16	John answered, saying unto them all, I indeed baptize you with water; but one mightier than I cometh, the latchet of whose shoes I am not worthy to unloose: he shall baptize you with the Holy Ghost and with fire:	John answered and said to them: Behold, I baptize you with water; but after me cometh one mightier than I, the strings of whose shoes I am not worthy to untie; he will baptize you with the Holy Spirit and with fire.	John answered and said to them, "Behold, I baptize you with water, but one who is greater than I will come, the straps of whose sandals I am not worthy to loosen. He will baptize you with the Holy Spirit and with fire,
17	Whose fan is in his hand, and he will throughly purge his floor, and will gather the wheat into his garner; but the chaff he will burn with fire unquenchable.	He holdeth his winnowing shovel in his hand, and he will make clean his threshing floor; and the wheat he gathereth into his garners, and the chaff he will burn with fire not extinguished.	he who holds a winnowing fan in his hand and has cleaned his threshing floors. And he will gather the wheat into his granaries and he will burn the chaff with a fire that will not go out."
18	And many other things in his exhortation preached he unto the people.	And many other things also, he taught and proclaimed to the people.	Now also many other [things] he was teaching and declaring to the people.
19	But Herod the tetrarch, being reproved by him for Herodias his brother Philip's wife, and for all the evils which Herod had done,	But Herod the Tetrarch, because he was reproved by John, on account of Herodias the wife of his brother Philip, and on account of all the evil things he had done,	But Herod, the tetrarch, because he had been reproved by John on account of Herodias, the wife of Philip, his brother, and on account of all the evil [things] that he had done,
20	Added yet this above all, that he shut up John in prison.	added this also to them all, that he shut up John in prison.	added this also above all of them, that he shut up John [in] prison.
21	Now when all the people were baptized, it came to pass, that Jesus also being baptized, and praying, the heaven was opened,	And it occurred, when all the people were baptized, that Jesus also was baptized. And as he prayed, the heavens were opened;	Now it happened while he baptized all the people, he also baptized Jesus. And while he prayed, the sky opened,
22	And the Holy Ghost descended in a bodily shape like a dove upon him, and a voice came from heaven, which said, Thou art my beloved Son; in thee I am well pleased.	and the Holy Spirit descended upon him, in the bodily likeness of a dove: and there was a voice from heaven, which said: Thou art my beloved Son, in whom I have delight.	and the Holy Spirit came down on him in the likeness of the form of a dove. And a voice came from heaven that said, "You are my beloved Son in whom I am pleased."
23	And Jesus himself began to be about thirty years of age, being (as was supposed) the son of Joseph, which was the son of Heli,	And Jesus was about thirty years old. And he was accounted the son of Joseph, the son of Heli,	And Jesus was about thirty years old and was thought [to be] the son of Joseph, the son of Heli,
24	Which was the son of Matthat, which was the son of Levi, which was the son of Melchi, which was the son of Janna, which was the son of Joseph,	the son of Matthat, the son of Levi, the son of Melchi, the son of Janna, the son of Joseph,	the son of Matthat, the son of Levi, the son of Melki, the son of Janni, the son of Joseph,
25	Which was the son of Mattathias, which was the son of Amos, which was the son of Naum, which was the son of Esli, which was the son of Nagge,	the son of Mattathias, the son of Amos, the son of Nahum, the son of Esli, the son of Naggai,	the son of Mattathias, the son of Amos, the son of Nahum, the son of Esli, the son of Naggai,

	KJV	Murdock	Magiera

LUKE *Chapter 3*

	KJV	Murdock	Magiera
26	Which was the son of Maath, which was the son of Mattathias, which was the son of Semei, which was the son of Joseph, which was the son of Juda,	the son of Maath, the son of Mattathias, the son of Shimei, the son of Joseph, the son of Judah,	the son of Maath, the son of Mattathias, the son of Semein, the son of Joseph, the son of Judah,
27	Which was the son of Joanna, which was the son of Rhesa, which was the son of Zorobabel, which was the son of Salathiel, which was the son of Neri,	the son of Joanna, the son of Rhesa, the son of Zorubbabel, the son of Salathiel, the son of Neri,	the son of Joanan, the son of Rhesa, the son of Zerabbabel, the son of Shealtiel, the son of Neri,
28	Which was the son of Melchi, which was the son of Addi, which was the son of Cosam, which was the son of Elmodam, which was the son of Er,	the son of Melchi, the son of Addi, the son of Cosam, the son of Elmodam, the son of Er,	the son of Melki, the son of Addi, the son of Cosam, the son of Elmodam, the son of Er,
29	Which was the son of Jose, which was the son of Eliezer, which was the son of Jorim, which was the son of Matthat, which was the son of Levi,	the son of Joses, the son of Eliezer, the son of Joram, the son of Matthat, the son of Levi,	the son of Jose, the son of Eliezer, the son of Jorim, the son of Matthat, the son of Levi,
30	Which was the son of Simeon, which was the son of Juda, which was the son of Joseph, which was the son of Jonan, which was the son of Eliakim,	the son of Simeon, the son of Judah, the son of Joseph, the son of Jonam, the son of Eliakim,	the son of Simeon, the son of Juda, the son of Joseph, the son of Jonam, the son of Eliakim,
31	Which was the son of Melea, which was the son of Menan, which was the son of Mattatha, which was the son of Nathan, which was the son of David,	the son of Melcah, the son of Mainan, the son of Mattatha, the son of Nathan, the son of David,	the son of Melea, the son of Menna, the son of Mattatha, the son of Nathan, the son of David,
32	Which was the son of Jesse, which was the son of Obed, which was the son of Booz, which was the son of Salmon, which was the son of Naasson,	the son of Jesse, the son of Obed, the son of Boaz, the son of Salmon, the son of Nahshon	the son of Jesse, the son of Obed, the son of Boaz, the son of Salmon, the son of Nahshon,
33	Which was the son of Aminadab, which was the son of Aram, which was the son of Esrom, which was the son of Phares, which was the son of Juda,	the son of Amminadab, the son of Ram, the son of Hezron, the son of Pharez, the son of Judah	the son of Aminadab, the son of Aram, the son of Hezron, the son of Perez, the son of Judah,
34	Which was the son of Jacob, which was the son of Isaac, which was the son of Abraham, which was the son of Thara, which was the son of Nachor,	the son of Jacob, the son of Isaac, the son of Abraham, the son of Terah, the son of Nahor,	the son of Jacob, the son of Isaac, the son of Abraham, the son of Terah, the son of Nahor,
35	Which was the son of Saruch, which was the son of Ragau, which was the son of Phalec, which was the son of Heber, which was the son of Sala,	the son of Serug, the son of Reu, the son of Peleg, the son of Eber, the son of Salah,	the son of Serug, the son of Reu, the son of Peleg, the son of Eber, the son of Shelah,
36	Which was the son of Cainan, which was the son of Arphaxad, which was the son of Sem, which was the son of Noe, which was the son of Lamech,	the son of Cainan, the son of Arphaxad, the son of Shem, the son of Noah, the son of Lamech,	the son of Cainan, the son of Arphaxad, the son of Shem, the son of Noah, the son of Lamech,

Parallel Translations

	KJV	*Murdock*	*Magiera*
LUKE *Chapter 3*			
37	Which was the son of Mathusala, which was the son of Enoch, which was the son of Jared, which was the son of Maleleel, which was the son of Cainan,	the son of Methuselah, the son of Enoch, the son of Jared, the son of Mehalaleel, the son of Cainan,	the son of Methuselah, the son of Enoch, the son of Jared, the son of Mahalalel, the son of Kenan,
38	Which was the son of Enos, which was the son of Seth, which was the son of Adam, which was the son of God.	the son of Enos, the son of Seth, the son of Adam, the son of God.	the son of Enosh, the son of Seth, the son of Adam, who [was] from God.
Chapter 4			
1	And Jesus being full of the Holy Ghost returned from Jordan, and was led by the Spirit into the wilderness,	And Jesus, being full of the Holy Spirit, returned from the Jordan. And the Spirit led him into the wilderness,	And Jesus, being full of the Holy Spirit, returned from the Jordan. And the Spirit led him to the wilderness
2	Being forty days tempted of the devil. And in those days he did eat nothing: and when they were ended, he afterward hungered.	forty days, to be tempted by the Calumniator. And during those days, he ate nothing; and when he had completed them, he was at last hungry.	[for] forty days to be tempted by the Accuser. And he did not eat anything in those days, and when he had completed them, at the end he was hungry.
3	And the devil said unto him, If thou be the Son of God, command this stone that it be made bread.	And the Calumniator said to him: If thou art the Son of God, command this stone to become bread.	And the Accuser said to him, "If you are the Son of God, tell this stone to become bread."
4	And Jesus answered him, saying, It is written, That man shall not live by bread alone, but by every word of God.	Jesus replied, and said to him: It is written, Not by bread only, doth man live; but by every thing of God.	Jesus answered and said to him, "It is written: MAN SHOULD NOT LIVE BY BREAD ALONE, BUT BY EVERY ANSWER OF GOD."
5	And the devil, taking him up into an high mountain, shewed unto him all the kingdoms of the world in a moment of time.	And Satan conducted him to a high mountain and showed him all the kingdoms of the land, in a little time.	And Satan took him up to a high mountain and showed him all the kingdoms of the earth in a short period of time.
6	And the devil said unto him, All this power will I give thee, and the glory of them: for that is delivered unto me; and to whomsoever I will I give it.	And the Calumniator said to him: To thee will I give all this dominion, and the glory of it, which is committed to me, and to whom I please, I give it:	And the Accuser said to him, "I will give you all this authority and its glory that is delivered to me and to whom I want, I give it.
7	If thou therefore wilt worship me, all shall be thine.	if therefore thou wilt worship before me, the whole shall be thine.	Therefore, if you worship before me, all of it will be yours."
8	And Jesus answered and said unto him, Get thee behind me, Satan: for it is written, Thou shalt worship the Lord thy God, and him only shalt thou serve.	But Jesus replied, and said to him: It is written Thou shalt worship the Lord thy God, and him only shalt thou serve.	Jesus answered and said to him, "It is written: YOU SHOULD WORSHIP THE LORD YOUR GOD AND YOU SHOULD SERVE HIM ALONE."
9	And he brought him to Jerusalem, and set him on a pinnacle of the temple, and said unto him, If thou be the Son of God, cast thyself down from hence:	And he brought him to Jerusalem, and set him on a pinnacle of the temple, and said to him: If thou art the Son of God, cast thyself down hence:	And he brought him to Jerusalem and placed him on the edge of the temple and said to him, "If you are the Son of God, throw yourself down from here to the bottom.

Parallel Translations

	KJV	*Murdock*	*Magiera*
	LUKE *Chapter 4*		
10	For it is written, He shall give his angels charge over thee, to keep thee:	for it is written, He will give his angels charge over thee, to keep thee:	For it is written: HE WILL COMMAND HIS ANGELS CONCERNING YOU TO KEEP YOU
11	And in their hands they shall bear thee up, lest at any time thou dash thy foot against a stone.	and in their arms will they sustain thee, lest thou strike thy foot against a stone.	AND BEAR YOU IN THEIR ARMS, SO THAT YOUR FOOT WILL NOT STUMBLE ON A STONE."
12	And Jesus answering said unto him, It is said, Thou shalt not tempt the Lord thy God.	And Jesus replied and said to him: It is said, Thou shalt not tempt the Lord thy God.	And Jesus answered and said to him, "It is said: YOU SHOULD NOT TEMPT THE LORD YOUR GOD."
13	And when the devil had ended all the temptation, he departed from him for a season.	And when the Calumniator had finished all his temptations, he departed from him for a time.	And after the Accuser had finished all his temptations, he left his presence for a while.
14	And Jesus returned in the power of the Spirit into Galilee: and there went out a fame of him through all the region round about.	And Jesus returned, in the power of the Spirit, to Galilee; and fame concerning him spread in all the region around them.	And Jesus returned in the power of the Spirit to Galilee and a report about him went out into every region around them.
15	And he taught in their synagogues, being glorified of all.	And he taught in their synagogues, and was lauded by every one.	And he was teaching in their synagogues and was being praised by everyone.
16	And he came to Nazareth, where he had been brought up: and, as his custom was, he went into the synagogue on the sabbath day, and stood up for to read.	And he came to Nazareth, where he had been brought up: and he went, as he was accustomed, into the synagogue on the sabbath day, and rose up to read.	And he came to Nazareth where he had been raised. And he entered into the synagogue as he was accustomed on the day of the Sabbath and stood up to read.
17	And there was delivered unto him the book of the prophet Esaias. And when he had opened the book, he found the place where it was written,	And there was delivered to him the book of Isaiah the prophet. And Jesus opened the book, and found the place where it is written:	And the scroll of Isaiah the prophet was given to him and Jesus opened the scroll and found the place where it was written:
18	The Spirit of the Lord is upon me, because he hath anointed me to preach the gospel to the poor; he hath sent me to heal the brokenhearted, to preach deliverance to the captives, and recovering of sight to the blind, to set at liberty them that are bruised,	The Spirit of the Lord is upon me; and therefore he hath anointed me to proclaim tidings to the poor; and hath sent me to heal the contrite in heart, and to proclaim release to the captives, and sight to the blind; and to send away the contrite with forgiveness [of their sins];	THE SPIRIT OF THE LORD [IS] ON ME AND BECAUSE OF THIS, HE HAS ANOINTED ME TO PREACH TO THE POOR AND HAS SENT ME TO HEAL THE BROKEN-HEARTED AND TO PREACH FORGIVENESS TO THE CAPTIVES AND SIGHT TO THE BLIND AND TO STRENGTHEN THE BROKEN WITH FORGIVENESS
19	To preach the acceptable year of the Lord.	and to proclaim the acceptable year of the Lord.	AND TO PREACH THE ACCEPTABLE YEAR OF THE LORD."
20	And he closed the book, and he gave it again to the minister, and sat down. And the eyes of all them that were in the synagogue were fastened on him.	And he rolled up the book, and gave it to the servitor, and went and sat down. And the eyes of all in the synagogue were gazing upon him.	And he rolled up the scroll and gave it to the minister and went [and] sat down. And the eyes of all of them in the synagogue were fixed on him.

	KJV	*Murdock*	*Magiera*
	LUKE	*Chapter 4*	
21	And he began to say unto them, This day is this scripture fulfilled in your ears.	And he began to say to them: This day, is this scripture which ye have heard, fulfilled.	And he began to speak to them, "Today this scripture is fulfilled in your ears."
22	And all bare him witness, and wondered at the gracious words which proceeded out of his mouth. And they said, Is not this Joseph's son?	And all bare him witness, and admired the gracious words which proceeded from his mouth; and they said: Is not this the son of Joseph?	And all were witnessing to him and were amazed at the words of blessing that were coming out of his mouth. And they were saying, "Is not this [man] the son of Joseph?"
23	And he said unto them, Ye will surely say unto me this proverb, Physician, heal thyself: whatsoever we have heard done in Capernaum, do also here in thy country.	Jesus said to them: Perhaps, ye will speak to me this proverb, Physician, heal thyself: and whatever we have heard of thy doing in Capernaum, do thou here also in thy city.	Jesus said to them, "Perhaps you will tell me this proverb: 'Physician, heal yourself,' and all that we have heard that you did in Capernaum, do also here in your city."
24	And he said, Verily I say unto you, No prophet is accepted in his own country.	And he said to them: Verily I say to you, There is no prophet who is acceptable in his own city.	But he said, "Truly, I say to you, there is no prophet that is received in his city.
25	But I tell you of a truth, many widows were in Israel in the days of Elias, when the heaven was shut up three years and six months, when great famine was throughout all the land;	And I tell you the truth, that there were many widows in the house of Israel, in the days of Elijah the prophet, when the heavens were closed up three years and six months, and there was a great famine in all the land:	For I tell you the truth, that there were many widows in Israel in the days of Elijah the prophet, while the heavens were closed [for] three years and six months and a great famine was in all the land.
26	But unto none of them was Elias sent, save unto Sarepta, a city of Sidon, unto a woman that was a widow.	but to no one of them was Elijah sent, except to Sarepta of Sidon, unto a widow woman.	And Elijah was not sent to one of them, except to Zarephath of Sidon, to a widow woman.
27	And many lepers were in Israel in the time of Eliseus the prophet; and none of them was cleansed, saving Naaman the Syrian.	And there were many leprous in the house of Israel, in the days of Elisha the prophet; but none of them was cleansed, except Naaman the Syrian.	And there were many lepers [in] Israel in the days of Elisha the prophet, yet not one of them was cleansed, except Naaman the Syrian."
28	And all they in the synagogue, when they heard these things, were filled with wrath,	And when they heard these things, those in the synagogue were all filled with wrath.	And when they heard these [things], all that were in the synagogue were filled with anger.
29	And rose up, and thrust him out of the city, and led him unto the brow of the hill whereon their city was built, that they might cast him down headlong.	And they rose up, and thrust him out of the city, and brought him to the top of the hill on which the city was built, that they might cast him down from the rock.	And they rose up [and] threw him outside of the city. And they brought him up to the top of the mountain on which their city was built to throw him down from the steep place.
30	But he passing through the midst of them went his way,	But he passed through the midst of them, and went away.	But he passed through them and went away.
31	And came down to Capernaum, a city of Galilee, and taught them on the sabbath days.	And he went down to Capernaum, a city of Galilee; and taught them on sabbath days.	And he went down to Capernaum, a city of Galilee, and taught them on the Sabbaths.
32	And they were astonished at his doctrine: for his word was with power.	And they were astonished at his teaching, for his word was authoritative.	And they were astonished at his teaching, because his message had power.

LUKE *Chapter 4*

	KJV	*Murdock*	*Magiera*
33	And in the synagogue there was a man, which had a spirit of an unclean devil, and cried out with a loud voice,	And there was in the synagogue a man, in whom was an unclean demon: and he cried out, with a loud voice,	And there was in the synagogue a man who had the spirit of an unclean demon and he cried out with a loud voice
34	Saying, Let us alone; what have we to do with thee, thou Jesus of Nazareth? art thou come to destroy us? I know thee who thou art; the Holy One of God.	and said: Let me alone: What have I to do with thee, Jesus, thou Nazarean? Hast thou come to destroy us? I know thee, who thou art, the Holy One of God.	and said, "Leave me. What do we have in common, Jesus the Nazarene? Have you come to destroy us? I know you, who you are, the Holy [one] of God."
35	And Jesus rebuked him, saying, Hold thy peace, and come out of him. And when the devil had thrown him in the midst, he came out of him, and hurt him not.	And Jesus rebuked him, and said: Shut thy mouth; and come out of him. And the demon threw him down in the midst, and came out of him, having not harmed him at all.	And Jesus rebuked him and said, "Shut your mouth and go out of him." And the demon threw him down in the middle and went out of him, not harming him at all.
36	And they were all amazed, and spake among themselves, saying, What a word is this! for with authority and power he commandeth the unclean spirits, and they come out.	And wonder seized every one, and they talked together, and said: What a word is this! For, with authority and efficiency, he commandeth the unclean spirits, and they come out	And great amazement took hold of everyone and they were speaking with each other and saying, "What indeed is this message, because with authority and power he commands the unclean spirits and they go out?"
37	And the fame of him went out into every place of the country round about.	And his fame went out into all the surrounding region.	And a report went out about him into the entire region surrounding them.
38	And he arose out of the synagogue, and entered into Simon's house. And Simon's wife's mother was taken with a great fever; and they besought him for her.	And when Jesus went out of the synagogue, he entered the house of Simon. And the mother-in-law of Simon was afflicted with a severe fever: and they besought him in her behalf .	And after Jesus went out of the synagogue, he entered the house of Simon, and the mother-in-law of Simon was tormented with a great fever, and they begged him on account of her.
39	And he stood over her, and rebuked the fever; and it left her: and immediately she arose and ministered unto them.	And he stood over her, and rebuked the fever; and it left her. And immediately she arose and ministered to them.	And he stood over her and rebuked her fever and it left her. And immediately she rose up and served them.
40	Now when the sun was setting, all they that had any sick with divers diseases brought them unto him; and he laid his hands on every one of them, and healed them.	And when the sun was set, all those that had sick persons, afflicted with divers diseases, brought them to him; and he laid his hand on every one of them, and healed them.	And [at] the setting of the sun all those who had sick who were sick with various sicknesses brought them to him. And he placed his hand on each of them and healed them.
41	And devils also came out of many, crying out, and saying, Thou art Christ the Son of God. And he rebuking them suffered them not to speak: for they knew that he was Christ.	And demons went out of many, crying out and saying: Thou art the Messiah, the Son of God. And he rebuked them, and suffered them not to say, that they knew him to be Messiah.	And also demons were going out of many, crying out and saying, "You are the Messiah, the Son of God." And he rebuked them and did not allow them to say that they knew he was the Messiah.

Parallel Translations

LUKE *Chapter 4*

	KJV	*Murdock*	*Magiera*
42	And when it was day, he departed and went into a desert place: and the people sought him, and came unto him, and stayed him, that he should not depart from them.	And at the dawn of day, he went out and retired to a desert place. And the multitudes sought him, and went out to him, and held him fast, that he might not retire from them.	And on the morning of the day he went out [and] journeyed to a deserted place. And the crowds were seeking him and came up to him and were holding him captive so that he would not go away from them.
43	And he said unto them, I must preach the kingdom of God to other cities also: for therefore am I sent.	And Jesus said to them: It behooveth me to announce the kingdom of God to other cities also; for therefore was I sent.	But Jesus said to them, "It is necessary for me also to preach to other cities the kingdom of God, because for this I was sent."
44	And he preached in the synagogues of Galilee.	And he preached in the synagogues of Galilee.	And he was preaching in the synagogues of Galilee.

Chapter 5

	KJV	*Murdock*	*Magiera*
1	And it came to pass, that, as the people pressed upon him to hear the word of God, he stood by the lake of Gennesaret,	And it occurred, that a multitude gathered about him, to hear the word of God. And he was standing by the side of the sea of Gennesaret,	And it happened [that] as the crowd gathered around him to hear the word of God and he was standing on the shore of the lake of Gennesaret,
2	And saw two ships standing by the lake: but the fishermen were gone out of them, and were washing their nets.	and he saw two ships standing near the sea, and the fishermen were gone out of them, and were washing their nets.	he saw two ships that were standing at the edge of the lake and the fishermen that had come down from them and they were washing their nets.
3	And he entered into one of the ships, which was Simon's, and prayed him that he would thrust out a little from the land. And he sat down, and taught the people out of the ship.	And one of them belonged to Simon Cephas: and Jesus entered and sat in it. And he told them to draw off a little from the shore, into the sea: and he seated himself, and taught the multitude from the ship.	And one of them belonged to Simon Peter. And Jesus boarded [and] sat in it and told [them] to take him a little way from dry land on the water. And he sat and taught the crowd from the ship.
4	Now when he had left speaking, he said unto Simon, Launch out into the deep, and let down your nets for a draught.	And when he ceased from speaking, he said to Simon: Launch out into the deep, and cast your net for a draught.	And after he stopped speaking, he said to Simon, "Row to deep [water] and cast your net for a catch."
5	And Simon answering said unto him, Master, we have toiled all the night, and have taken nothing: nevertheless at thy word I will let down the net.	Simon answered, and said to him: Rabbi, all the night we have toiled, and have caught nothing: but, at thy bidding, I will cast the net.	Simon answered and said to him, "My Master, we have labored all night and have not caught anything. But at your word I will cast the net."
6	And when they had this done, they inclosed a great multitude of fishes: and their net brake.	And when they had done so, they inclosed very many fishes, so that the net was rent.	And after they did this, they caught a great many fish and their net was tearing.
7	And they beckoned unto their partners, which were in the other ship, that they should come and help them. And they came, and filled both the ships, so that they began to sink.	And they made signs to their associates, in the other ship, to come and help them. And when they came, they filled both the ships, so that they were near to sinking.	And they made signs to their friends who were in the other ship to come to help them. And after they had come, they filled both ships, so that they were close to sinking.
8	When Simon Peter saw it, he fell down at Jesus' knees, saying, Depart from me; for I am a sinful man, O Lord.	And when Simon Cephas saw [it], he fell before the feet of Jesus, and said to him: I beseech thee, my Lord, that thou leave me, for I am a sinful man.	And when Simon Peter saw [this], he fell down before the feet of Jesus and said to him, "I beg you, my Lord, go away from me, for I am a sinful man."

Parallel Translations

	KJV	Murdock	Magiera
	LUKE	*Chapter 5*	
9	For he was astonished, and all that were with him, at the draught of the fishes which they had taken:	For astonishment had seized him, and all that were with him, at the draught of fishes which they had caught:	For amazement had taken hold of him and all who were with him, because of that catch of fish that they had caught,
10	And so was also James, and John, the sons of Zebedee, which were partners with Simon. And Jesus said unto Simon, Fear not; from henceforth thou shalt catch men.	and in like manner also James and John, the sons of Zebedee, who were partners of Simon. But Jesus said: Fear thou not; henceforth thou shalt catch men unto life.	and so also James and John, the sons of Zebedee, who were partners of Simon. And Jesus said to Simon, "Do not be afraid. From now on, you will catch men to life."
11	And when they had brought their ships to land, they forsook all, and followed him.	And they brought the vessels to the land: and they left all and followed him.	And they brought those ships to land and left everything and followed him.
12	And it came to pass, when he was in a certain city, behold a man full of leprosy: who seeing Jesus fell on his face, and besought him, saying, Lord, if thou wilt, thou canst make me clean.	And when Jesus was in one of the cities, a man came all full of leprosy and seeing Jesus, he fell upon his face, and besought him, and said to him: My Lord, if thou wilt, thou canst cleanse me.	And when Jesus was in one of the cities, a man who was completely covered with leprosy came. He saw Jesus and fell on his face and begged him and said to him, "My Lord, if you want to, you are able to cleanse me."
13	And he put forth his hand, and touched him, saying, I will: be thou clean. And immediately the leprosy departed from him.	And Jesus put forth his hand, and touched him, and said to him: I will [it]; be thou clean. And immediately his leprosy went from him.	And Jesus stretched out his hand [and] touched him and said to him, "I want to. Be cleansed." And immediately his leprosy went away from him and he was cleansed.
14	And he charged him to tell no man: but go, and shew thyself to the priest, and offer for thy cleansing, according as Moses commanded, for a testimony unto them.	And he charged him: Speak to no one; but go and show thyself to the priests, and offer the oblation for thy purification, as Moses hath commanded, for a testimony to them.	And he commanded him, "Do not tell anyone, but go [and] show yourself to the priests and offer for your purification, as Moses commanded for their witness."
15	But so much the more went there a fame abroad of him: and great multitudes came together to hear, and to be healed by him of their infirmities.	And his fame spread abroad still more: and much people assembled to hear him, and to be cured of their diseases.	And a report about him went out all the more and a large crowd was gathered to hear from him and to be healed from their sicknesses.
16	And he withdrew himself into the wilderness, and prayed.	And he retired into a desert, and prayed.	And he went away to the desert land and was praying.
17	And it came to pass on a certain day, as he was teaching, that there were Pharisees and doctors of the law sitting by, which were come out of every town of Galilee, and Judaea, and Jerusalem: and the power of the Lord was present to heal them.	And it occurred, on one of the days when Jesus was teaching, that Pharisees and Doctors of the law were sitting by, who had come from all the villages of Galilee and of Judaea, and Jerusalem: and the power of the Lord was present to heal them.	And it happened [that] on a certain day while Jesus was teaching, Pharisees and teachers of the law were sitting [there] who had come from all the villages of Galilee and of Judea and of Jerusalem, and there was the power of the LORD to heal them.
18	And, behold, men brought in a bed a man which was taken with a palsy: and they sought means to bring him in, and to lay him before him.	And some persons brought a paralytic man, on a couch, and sought to bring him in, and to place him before him.	And men brought on a pallet a certain paralyzed man and were seeking to bring [him] in to lay him before him.

Parallel Translations

	KJV	*Murdock*	*Magiera*
	LUKE	*Chapter 5*	
19	And when they could not find by what way they might bring him in because of the multitude, they went upon the housetop, and let him down through the tiling with his couch into the midst before Jesus.	And when they could not thus introduce him, because of the multitude of the people, they ascended to the roof, and let him down with the couch, from the covering, into the midst, before Jesus.	And when they could not find how to bring him in because of the multitude of people, they went up to the roof and let him down on his pallet from the roof floor into the middle before Jesus.
20	And when he saw their faith, he said unto him, Man, thy sins are forgiven thee.	And when Jesus saw their faith, he said to the paralytic: Man, thy sins are forgiven thee.	And when Jesus saw their faith, he said to that paralyzed man, "Your sins are forgiven."
21	And the scribes and the Pharisees began to reason, saying, Who is this which speaketh blasphemies? Who can forgive sins, but God alone?	And the Scribes and Pharisees began to reason, and to say: Who is this that speaketh blasphemy? Who can forgive sins, but God only?	And the scribes and Pharisees began reasoning and saying, "Who is this [man] who speaks blasphemy? Who is able to forgive sins, except God alone?"
22	But when Jesus perceived their thoughts, he answering said unto them, What reason ye in your hearts?	And Jesus knew their thoughts, and said to them: What think ye in your heart?	But Jesus knew their reasonings and answered and said to them, "Why are you reasoning in your heart?
23	Whether is easier, to say, Thy sins be forgiven thee; or to say, Rise up and walk?	Which is the easier, to say, Thy sins are forgiven thee, or to say, Arise and walk?	Which [thing] is easier to say, 'Your sins are forgiven' or to say, 'Rise up, walk?'
24	But that ye may know that the Son of man hath power upon earth to forgive sins, (he said unto the sick of the palsy,) I say unto thee, Arise, and take up thy couch, and go into thine house.	But that ye may know, that the Son of man is competent to forgive sins on the earth,---he said to the paralytic: I say to thee, Arise, take up thy couch, and go to thy home.	But that you will know that it is lawful for the Son of Man to forgive sins on earth," he said to the paralytic, "I say to you, rise up, take up your pallet and go to your house."
25	And immediately he rose up before them, and took up that whereon he lay, and departed to his own house, glorifying God.	And instantly, he rose up before their eyes, and took up his couch, and went home, glorifying God.	And immediately he rose up before their eyes and took up his pallet and went to his house, praising God.
26	And they were all amazed, and they glorified God, and were filled with fear, saying, We have seen strange things to day.	And astonishment seized every one; and they Praised God; and they were filled with awe, and said: We have seen wonders today.	And amazement took hold of everyone and they were praising God and were filled with fear and were saying, "We have seen wonders today."
27	And after these things he went forth, and saw a publican, named Levi, sitting at the receipt of custom: and he said unto him, Follow me.	And after these things, Jesus went out and saw a publican, named Levi, sitting among the publicans; and he said to him: Come after me.	After these [things], Jesus went out and saw a tax collector, whose name was Levi, who was sitting at the customs-house, and he said to him, "Follow me."
28	And he left all, rose up, and followed him.	And he left every thing, and arose, and went after him.	And he left everything and stood up [and] followed him.
29	And Levi made him a great feast in his own house: and there was a great company of publicans and of others that sat down with them.	And Levi made a great entertainment for him at his house; and there was a numerous company of publicans and others who reclined with them.	And Levi made for him a great feast in his house, and there was a large crowd of tax collectors and of others who were eating with them.

LUKE *Chapter 5*

	KJV	*Murdock*	*Magiera*
30	But their scribes and Pharisees murmured against his disciples, saying, Why do ye eat and drink with publicans and sinners?	And the Scribes and Pharisees murmured, and said to his disciples: Why do ye eat and drink with publicans and sinners?	And the scribes and Pharisees were murmuring and saying to his disciples, "Why are you eating and drinking with tax collectors and sinners?"
31	And Jesus answering said unto them, They that are whole need not a physician; but they that are sick.	And Jesus answered and said to them: A physician is not sought after for the well, but for those very sick.	And Jesus answered and said to them, "The physician is not needed by the healthy, but by those who are very sick.
32	I came not to call the righteous, but sinners to repentance.	I came not to call the righteous, but sinners, to repentance.	I did not come to call the just, but sinners to repentance."
33	And they said unto him, Why do the disciples of John fast often, and make prayers, and likewise the disciples of the Pharisees; but thine eat and drink?	And they said to him: Why do the disciples of John fast often, and pray, and also [those] of the Pharisees; but thine eat and drink?	And those were saying to him, "Why are the disciples of John, also of the Pharisees, fasting and praying continually, but yours are eating and drinking?"
34	And he said unto them, Can ye make the children of the bridechamber fast, while the bridegroom is with them?	And he said to them: Ye cannot make the guests of the nuptial chamber fast, while the bridegroom is with them.	And he said to them, "You cannot make the wedding guests fast as long as the bridegroom [is] with them.
35	But the days will come, when the bridegroom shall be taken away from them, and then shall they fast in those days.	But the days will come, when the bridegroom will be taken up from them, and then will they fast, in those days.	But the days will come when the bridegroom will be taken up from them. Then, in those days, they will fast."
36	And he spake also a parable unto them; No man putteth a piece of a new garment upon an old; if otherwise, then both the new maketh a rent, and the piece that was taken out of the new agreeth not with the old.	And he spoke a similitude to them: No one teareth a patch from a new garment, and putteth it to an old garment; lest he tear the new, and the patch from the new cease to make the old [garment] whole.	And he told them a parable: "No one cuts off a piece of cloth from a new garment and lays [it] on an old garment, lest he cuts off the new and the patch that is from the new does not repair the old.
37	And no man putteth new wine into old bottles; else the new wine will burst the bottles, and be spilled, and the bottles shall perish.	And no one putteth new wine into old sacks; otherwise, the new wine will burst the sacks, and the wine will run out, and the sacks be ruined.	And no one puts new wine into old wineskins, lest the new wine will burst the wineskins and the wine should be poured out and the wineskins ruined.
38	But new wine must be put into new bottles; and both are preserved.	But they put new wine into new sacks, and both are preserved.	On the contrary, they put new wine into new wineskins and both of them are preserved.
39	No man also having drunk old wine straightway desireth new: for he saith, The old is better.	And no one drinketh old wine, and immediately calleth for new; for he saith, The old is the delicious.	And no one drinks old wine and immediately desires new, for he says, 'The old is delicious.'"

Chapter 6

	KJV	*Murdock*	*Magiera*
1	And it came to pass on the second sabbath after the first, that he went through the corn fields; and his disciples plucked the ears of corn, and did eat, rubbing them in their hands.	And on a sabbath it occurred, as Jesus walked among the tilled grounds, that his disciples plucked ears, and rubbed them in their hands and ate.	And it happened [that] on the Sabbath, while Jesus was walking [in] the sown fields, his disciples were picking the heads of grain and rubbing [them] in their hands and eating [them].
2	And certain of the Pharisees said unto them, Why do ye that which is not lawful to do on the sabbath days?	And some of the Pharisees said to them: Why do ye that, which it is not lawful to do on the sabbath?	And some of the Pharisees were saying to them, "Why are you doing that which is not lawful to do on the Sabbath?"

Parallel Translations

LUKE *Chapter 6*

	KJV	*Murdock*	*Magiera*
3	And Jesus answering them said, Have ye not read so much as this, what David did, when himself was an hungred, and they which were with him;	Jesus replied, and said to them: Have ye not read what David did, when he was hungry, he and those with him?	Jesus answered and said to them, "And have you not read what David did when he was hungry, and those who were with him,
4	How he went into the house of God, and did take and eat the shewbread, and gave also to them that were with him; which it is not lawful to eat but for the priests alone?	How he entered into the house of God, and took and ate the bread of the Lord's table, and gave [it] to those that were with him; which it was not lawful, except for the priests only, to eat?	how he entered the house of God and took the bread of the table of the LORD [and] ate and gave to those who were with him, that which was not lawful for [anyone] to eat, but only the priests alone?"
5	And he said unto them, That the Son of man is Lord also of the sabbath.	And he said to them: The Son of man is lord of the sabbath.	And he said to them, "The Lord of the Sabbath is the Son of Man."
6	And it came to pass also on another sabbath, that he entered into the synagogue and taught: and there was a man whose right hand was withered.	And on another sabbath, he entered a synagogue and taught. And a man was there, whose right hand was withered.	And it happened [that] on another Sabbath he entered the synagogue and was teaching. And there was there a man whose right hand was withered.
7	And the scribes and Pharisees watched him, whether he would heal on the sabbath day; that they might find an accusation against him.	And the Scribes and Pharisees watched him, whether he would heal on the sabbath; that they might be able to accuse him.	And the scribes and Pharisees were watching him, if he would heal on the Sabbath, so that they would be able to accuse him.
8	But he knew their thoughts, and said to the man which had the withered hand, Rise up, and stand forth in the midst. And he arose and stood forth.	And as he knew their thoughts, he said to the man with a withered hand: Rise and come into the midst of the congregation. And when he came and stood [there],	And he knew their thoughts and said to that man whose hand was withered, "Stand up. Come to the middle of the synagogue." And when he came and stood,
9	Then said Jesus unto them, I will ask you one thing; Is it lawful on the sabbath days to do good, or to do evil? to save life, or to destroy it?	Jesus said to them: I ask you, What is it lawful to do on the sabbath? that which is good? or that which is evil? to save life or to destroy [it]?	Jesus said to them, "I will ask you, is it lawful on the Sabbath to do good or evil, to cause a soul to live or to destroy [it]?"
10	And looking round about upon them all, he said unto the man, Stretch forth thy hand. And he did so: and his hand was restored whole as the other.	And he looked upon them all; and [then] said to him, Stretch forth thy hand. And he stretched out his hand, and it was restored like the other.	And he gazed at all of them and said to him, "Stretch out your hand." And he stretched [it] out and his hand was restored like the other.
11	And they were filled with madness; and communed one with another what they might do to Jesus.	And they were filled with envy; and they conferred one with another, what they should do to Jesus.	And they were filled with envy and were speaking with each other about what they should do to Jesus.
12	And it came to pass in those days, that he went out into a mountain to pray, and continued all night in prayer to God.	And in those days, Jesus retired to a mountain to pray; and he passed the night there, in prayer to God.	And it happened [that] in those days Jesus went out to a mountain to pray. And there he spent the night in prayer to God.
13	And when it was day, he called unto him his disciples: and of them he chose twelve, whom also he named apostles;	And when the day dawned, he called his disciples, and selected from them twelve, whom he named Legates :	And when [day] dawned, he called his disciples and chose twelve of them, those whom he named apostles:

Parallel Translations

	KJV	Murdock	Magiera
	LUKE	*Chapter 6*	
14	Simon, (whom he also named Peter,) and Andrew his brother, James and John, Philip and Bartholomew,	Simon whom he named Cephas, and Andrew his brother, and James, and John, and Philip, and Bartholomew,	Simon, whom he called Peter, and Andrew, his brother, and James and John and Philip and Bartholomew
15	Matthew and Thomas, James the son of Alphaeus, and Simon called Zelotes,	and Matthew, and Thomas, and James the son of Alpheus, and Simon who was called Zelotes,	and Matthew and Thomas and James, the son of Alphaeus, and Simon, who was called the zealot,
16	And Judas the brother of James, and Judas Iscariot, which also was the traitor.	and Judas the son of James, and Judas Iscariot, who became a traitor.	and Judas, the son of James, and Judas Iscariot, who was the betrayer.
17	And he came down with them, and stood in the plain, and the company of his disciples, and a great multitude of people out of all Judaea and Jerusalem, and from the sea coast of Tyre and Sidon, which came to hear him, and to be healed of their diseases;	And Jesus descended with them, and stood in the plain; and a great company of his disciples, and a multitude of assembled people, from all Judaea, and from Jerusalem and from the seashore of Tyre and Sidon; who came to hear his discourse, and to be healed of their diseases;	And Jesus came down with them and stood in the plain with a large crowd of his disciples and a multitude of a crowd of people from all Judea and from Jerusalem and from the sea coast of Tyre and of Sidon,
18	And they that were vexed with unclean spirits: and they were healed.	and they who were afflicted by unclean spirits: and they were healed.	who had come to hear his message and to be healed of their sicknesses, and those who were tormented by unclean spirits, and they were healed.
19	And the whole multitude sought to touch him: for there went virtue out of him, and healed them all.	And the whole multitude sought to touch him; for there went a virtue out of him and healed them all.	And the whole crowd was seeking to touch him, for power was going out of him, and he was healing all of them.
20	And he lifted up his eyes on his disciples, and said, Blessed be ye poor: for yours is the kingdom of God.	And he lifted his eyes upon his disciples, and said: Blessed are ye poor; for the kingdom of God is yours.	And he lifted up his eyes to his disciples and said, "Blessed are you poor, because yours is the kingdom of God.
21	Blessed are ye that hunger now: for ye shall be filled. Blessed are ye that weep now: for ye shall laugh.	Blessed are ye that hunger now; for ye will be satisfied. Blessed are ye that weep now; for ye will laugh.	Blessed are you who are hungry now, because you will be satisfied. Blessed are you who are weeping now, because you will laugh.
22	Blessed are ye, when men shall hate you, and when they shall separate you from their company, and shall reproach you, and cast out your name as evil, for the Son of man's sake.	Blessed are ye, when men shall hate you, and repel you, and revile you, and cast out your names as base, for the Son of man's sake.	Blessed are you when men hate you and discriminate against you and reproach you and cast out your name as evil for the sake of the Son of Man.
23	Rejoice ye in that day, and leap for joy: for, behold, your reward is great in heaven: for in the like manner did their fathers unto the prophets.	Rejoice in that day and exult, for your reward is great in heaven; for so did their fathers to the prophets.	Rejoice in that day and leap for joy, because your reward is great in heaven, for their fathers did the same to the prophets.
24	But woe unto you that are rich! for ye have received your consolation.	But, woe to you that are rich; for ye have received your consolation.	But woe to you, rich [ones], because you have received your comfort!

	KJV	Murdock	Magiera
	LUKE	*Chapter 6*	
25	Woe unto you that are full! for ye shall hunger. Woe unto you that laugh now! for ye shall mourn and weep.	Woe to you that are full; for ye will hunger. Woe to you that laugh now, for ye will weep and mourn.	Woe to you, satisfied [ones], because you will hunger! Woe to you who are laughing now, because you will cry and you will mourn!
26	Woe unto you, when all men shall speak well of you! for so did their fathers to the false prophets.	Woe to you, when men shall speak your praise; for so did their fathers to the false prophets.	Woe to you, when men will speak what is good about you, for their fathers did so to the false prophets!
27	But I say unto you which hear, Love your enemies, do good to them which hate you,	And to you who hear, I say: Love your enemies; and do favors to them that hate you;	But to you who hear, I say, 'Love your enemies and do that which is good to those who hate you.
28	Bless them that curse you, and pray for them which despitefully use you.	and bless them that curse you; and pray for them that drag you with violence.	And bless those who curse you and pray for those who take you by force.
29	And unto him that smiteth thee on the one cheek offer also the other; and him that taketh away thy cloke forbid not to take thy coat also.	To him that smiteth thee on thy cheek, offer the other: and from him that taketh away thy cloak, keep not back thy tunic.	And to him, who strikes you on your cheek, offer to him the other, and from him who takes away your outer cloak, do not hold back your tunic also.
30	Give to every man that asketh of thee; and of him that taketh away thy goods ask them not again.	To every one that asketh of thee, give thou: and from him that taketh thy property, demand it not.	To everyone who asks you, give to him, and from him, who takes away your [things], do not demand [them] back.
31	And as ye would that men should do to you, do ye also to them likewise.	And as ye would that men should do to you, so do ye also to them.	And whatever you desire men to do to you, do the same to them also.
32	For if ye love them which love you, what thank have ye? for sinners also love those that love them.	For, if ye love them that love you, what goodness is it in you? For even sinners love those that love them.	For if you love those who love you, what is your goodness? For even sinners love those who love them.
33	And if ye do good to them which do good to you, what thank have ye? for sinners also do even the same.	And if ye do good to them that do good to you, what goodness is it in you? For even sinners do the same.	And if you do that which is good to those who do good to you, what is your goodness? For even sinners do the same.
34	And if ye lend to them of whom ye hope to receive, what thank have ye? for sinners also lend to sinners, to receive as much again.	And if ye lend to one from whom ye expect recompense, what goodness is it in you? For sinners also lend to sinners, to receive adequate recompense.	And if you lend to [those] from whom you expect to be repaid, what is your goodness? For even sinners lend to sinners, that in the same way they might be repaid.
35	But love ye your enemies, and do good, and lend, hoping for nothing again; and your reward shall be great, and ye shall be the children of the Highest: for he is kind unto the unthankful and to the evil.	But love ye your enemies, and do them good; and lend ye, and disappoint the hopes of no one: and great will be your reward, and ye will be children of the Highest; for he is kind to the evil, and to the unthankful.	But love your enemies and do good to them and lend and do not cut off the hope of anyone, and your reward will be increased and you will be the sons of the Most High, because he is kind to the evil and to the unthankful.
36	Be ye therefore merciful, as your Father also is merciful.	Be ye therefore merciful, as also your Father is merciful.	Therefore be merciful, as your Father also is merciful.

Parallel Translations

	KJV	Murdock	Magiera
	LUKE Chapter 6		
37	Judge not, and ye shall not be judged: condemn not, and ye shall not be condemned: forgive, and ye shall be forgiven:	Judge not, and ye will not be judged: condemn not, and ye will not be condemned: release, and ye will be released.	Do not judge and you will not be judged. Do not condemn and you will not be condemned. Forgive and you will be forgiven.
38	Give, and it shall be given unto you; good measure, pressed down, and shaken together, and running over, shall men give into your bosom. For with the same measure that ye mete withal it shall be measured to you again.	Give ye, and it will be given to you; in good measure, pressed down, and running over, will they cast into your lap. For, with what measure ye measure, it will be measured to you.	Give and it will be given to you. With good and pressed down and abundant measure they will throw into your laps. For with the same measure that you measure, it will be measured to you."
39	And he spake a parable unto them, Can the blind lead the blind? shall they not both fall into the ditch?	And he spake a similitude to them: Can a blind man lead a blind? Will not both fall into the ditch?	And he told them a parable, "Are the blind able to lead the blind? Would not they both fall in a ditch?
40	The disciple is not above his master: but every one that is perfect shall be as his master.	No disciple is better than his teacher; for whoever is perfect, will be like his teacher.	There is no disciple who is greater than his master, for everyone who is mature should be as his master [is].
41	And why beholdest thou the mote that is in thy brother's eye, but perceivest not the beam that is in thine own eye?	And why observest thou the straw that is in thy brother's eye, but regardest not the beam that is in thy own eye?	And why do you see the straw that is in the eye of your brother, but the plank that is in your [own] eye is not seen by you?
42	Either how canst thou say to thy brother, Brother, let me pull out the mote that is in thine eye, when thou thyself beholdest not the beam that is in thine own eye? Thou hypocrite, cast out first the beam out of thine own eye, and then shalt thou see clearly to pull out the mote that is in thy brother's eye.	Or how canst thou say to thy brothers, My brother, allow me to pluck the straw from thy eye; when, lo, the beam that is in thy own eye, thou regardest not. Hypocrite! first cast the beam out thy eye, and then thy vision will be clear to pluck the straw from thy brother's eye.	Or how are you able to say to your brother, 'My brother, allow me to take out the straw from your eye,' when behold, the plank that is in your own eye is not seen by you? Hypocrite! First take out the plank from your [own] eye and then it will be clear for you to take out the straw from the eye of your brother.
43	For a good tree bringeth not forth corrupt fruit; neither doth a corrupt tree bring forth good fruit.	There is no good tree, that beareth bad fruits; nor a bad tree, that beareth good fruits.	There is not a good tree that produces bad fruit or a bad tree that produces good fruit.
44	For every tree is known by his own fruit. For of thorns men do not gather figs, nor of a bramble bush gather they grapes.	For every tree is known by its fruits. Do men gather figs from thorn-bushes? So, neither do they pluck grapes from brambles.	For every tree is known by its fruit. For they do not gather figs from thorn-bushes, nor do they gather grapes from a bramble-bush.
45	A good man out of the good treasure of his heart bringeth forth that which is good; and an evil man out of the evil treasure of his heart bringeth forth that which is evil: for of the abundance of the heart his mouth speaketh.	A good man, from the good treasure that is in his heart, bringeth out good things: and a bad man, from the bad treasure that is in his heart, bringeth out bad things. For, from the abundance of the heart, the lips speak.	A good man, from the good treasures that are in his heart, produces good things, and an evil man, from the evil treasures that are in his heart, produces evil things. For from the abundant [things] of the heart the lips speak.
46	And why call ye me, Lord, Lord, and do not the things which I say?	And why call ye me, My Lord, my Lord; while ye do not that which I command you?	Why do you call me, 'My Lord, my Lord,' and you do not do what I say?

	KJV	*Murdock*	*Magiera*

LUKE *Chapter 6*

	KJV	Murdock	Magiera
47	Whosoever cometh to me, and heareth my sayings, and doeth them, I will shew you to whom he is like:	Every one that cometh to me, and heareth my words, and doeth them, I will show to whom he is like:	I will show you what each one who comes to me and hears my words and does them is like.
48	He is like a man which built an house, and digged deep, and laid the foundation on a rock: and when the flood arose, the stream beat vehemently upon that house, and could not shake it: for it was founded upon a rock.	He is like a man that built a house; and he dug and went deep, and laid the foundations on a rock: and when a flood occurred, the flood rushed upon that house, and could not move it, for its foundation rested on a rock.	He is like the man who built a house and dug and went deep and laid the foundations on rock. And when there was a flood, the flood beat on that house and it was not able to shake it, for its foundation was placed on rock.
49	But he that heareth, and doeth not, is like a man that without a foundation built an house upon the earth; against which the stream did beat vehemently, and immediately it fell; and the ruin of that house was great.	But he that heareth and doeth not, is like a man that built his house upon the earth, without a foundation; and when the torrent rushed upon it, it fell immediately, and the ruin of that house was great.	And whoever hears [my words] and does not do [them] is like the man who built his house on ground without a foundation. And when the river beat on it, immediately it fell, and the fall of that house was great."

Chapter 7

	KJV	Murdock	Magiera
1	Now when he had ended all his sayings in the audience of the people, he entered into Capernaum.	And when he had finished all these discourses in the audience of the people, Jesus entered into Capernaum.	And when he completed all the sayings for the hearing of the people, Jesus entered Capernaum.
2	And a certain centurion's servant, who was dear unto him, was sick, and ready to die.	And the servant of a centurion, who was dear to him, was very sick, and near to death.	And the servant of a certain centurion, who was dear to him, was very sick and was about to die.
3	And when he heard of Jesus, he sent unto him the elders of the Jews, beseeching him that he would come and heal his servant.	And he heard of Jesus, and sent the Elders of the Jews to him, and requested of him that he would come and save the life of his servant.	And he heard about Jesus and sent to him elders of the Judeans and was begging him to come [and] give life to his servant.
4	And when they came to Jesus, they besought him instantly, saying, That he was worthy for whom he should do this:	And when they came to Jesus, they entreated him earnestly, and said: He is worthy that thou shouldst do this for him;	And when they came to Jesus, they were begging him earnestly and saying, "He is worthy that you do this for him,
5	For he loveth our nation, and he hath built us a synagogue.	for he loveth our nation, and hath also built us a house of assembly.	for he loves our people and has even built a synagogue for us."
6	Then Jesus went with them. And when he was now not far from the house, the centurion sent friends to him, saying unto him, Lord, trouble not thyself: for I am not worthy that thou shouldest enter under my roof:	And Jesus went with them. And when he was not far from the house, the centurion sent his friends to him, and said to him: My Lord, trouble not thyself, for I am not worthy that thou shouldst come under my roof:	And Jesus went with them. And when he was not very far from the house, the centurion sent his friends to him and said to him, "My Lord, do not trouble [yourself], for I am not worthy that you should come under my roof,
7	Wherefore neither thought I myself worthy to come unto thee: but say in a word, and my servant shall be healed.	therefore I deemed myself not worthy to approach thee myself; but speak the word only, and my young man will be healed.	[and] on account of that, I am not worthy to come to you. But speak with a word and my young man will be healed,

Parallel Translations

	KJV	*Murdock*	*Magiera*
	LUKE	*Chapter 7*	
8	For I also am a man set under authority, having under me soldiers, and I say unto one, Go, and he goeth; and to another, Come, and he cometh; and to my servant, Do this, and he doeth it.	For I also am a man subjected to authority; and I have soldiers under my command; and I say to this one, Go; and he goeth: and to another, Come; and he cometh: and to my servant, Do this; and he doeth [it.]	for I also am a man who is subject to authority and there are soldiers under my hand. And I say to this one, 'Go,' and he goes, and to another, 'Come,' and he comes, and to my servant, 'Do this,' and he does [it]."
9	When Jesus heard these things, he marvelled at him, and turned him about, and said unto the people that followed him, I say unto you, I have not found so great faith, no, not in Israel.	And when Jesus heard these things, he admired him; and he turned, and said to the throng that followed him: I say to you, I have not found faith like this even in Israel.	And when Jesus heard these [things], he marveled at him. And he turned and said to the crowd that was following him, "I say to you, not even [in] Israel have I found faith like this."
10	And they that were sent, returning to the house, found the servant whole that had been sick.	And they that were sent, returned to the house; and they found the servant that had been sick, now well.	And those who were sent returned to the house and found that servant who was sick made whole.
11	And it came to pass the day after, that he went into a city called Nain; and many of his disciples went with him, and much people.	And the following day, he went to a city called Nain; and his disciples [were] with him, and a great multitude.	And it happened on the day that followed, [that] he went to a city by the name of Nain and his disciples and a large crowd [were] with him.
12	Now when he came nigh to the gate of the city, behold, there was a dead man carried out, the only son of his mother, and she was a widow: and much people of the city was with her.	And as he approached the gate of the city, he saw a procession bearing a dead man, the only son of his mother, and she a widow; and a great company of the people of the city were with her.	And when he approached the gate of the city, he saw a dead man being brought who was the only [son] of his mother, and his mother was a widow, and a large crowd of citizens [was] with her.
13	And when the Lord saw her, he had compassion on her, and said unto her, Weep not.	And Jesus looked upon her, and had compassion on her; and he said to her, Weep not.	And Jesus saw her and had compassion on her and said to her, "Do not cry."
14	And he came and touched the bier: and they that bare him stood still. And he said, Young man, I say unto thee, Arise.	And he went, and touched the bier; and they that bore him stood still. And he said: Young man, I say to thee, Arise.	And he went [and] touched the pallet. And those who were carrying it stood, and he said, "Young man, I say to you, rise up."
15	And he that was dead sat up, and began to speak. And he delivered him to his mother.	And the dead man sat up, and began to speak: and he delivered him to his mother.	And that dead man sat up and began to speak and he gave him to his mother.
16	And there came a fear on all: and they glorified God, saying, That a great prophet is risen up among us; and, That God hath visited his people.	And awe seized all the people; and they glorified God, and said: A great prophet hath arisen among us, and God hath visited his people.	And fear took hold of all men and they were praising God and saying, "A great prophet has risen up among us and God has visited his people."
17	And this rumour of him went forth throughout all Judaea, and throughout all the region round about.	And that saying respecting him went out through all Judaea and all the surrounding region.	And this saying went out about him into all Judea and into all the region around them,
18	And the disciples of John shewed him of all these things.	And the disciples of John told him all these things.	and his disciples reported all these [things] to John.

Parallel Translations

	KJV	*Murdock*	*Magiera*
LUKE	*Chapter 7*		
19	And John calling unto him two of his disciples sent them to Jesus, saying, Art thou he that should come? or look we for another?	And John called two of his disciples, and sent them to Jesus, and said: Art thou he that cometh, or shall we look for another?	And John called two of his disciples and sent them to Jesus and said, "Are you that one who is to come or should we wait for another?"
20	When the men were come unto him, they said, John Baptist hath sent us unto thee, saying, Art thou he that should come? or look we for another?	And they came to Jesus, and said to him: John the Baptizer hath sent us to thee, and saith: Art thou he that cometh, or shall we look for another?	And they came to Jesus and said to him, John the baptizer sent us to you and said, "Are you that one who is to come or should we wait for another?"
21	And in that same hour he cured many of their infirmities and plagues, and of evil spirits; and unto many that were blind he gave sight.	And in that hour he healed many persons of their diseases, and of plagues, and of unclean spirits, and gave sight to many blind persons.	And in that same hour he healed many of sicknesses and of plagues and of evil spirits and he gave sight to many blind.
22	Then Jesus answering said unto them, Go your way, and tell John what things ye have seen and heard; how that the blind see, the lame walk, the lepers are cleansed, the deaf hear, the dead are raised, to the poor the gospel is preached.	And Jesus replied, and said to them: Go ye, and tell John all that ye have seen and heard; that the blind see, and the lame walk, and the leprous are cleansed, and the deaf hear, and the dead arise, and to the poor good news is proclaimed:	And Jesus answered and said to them, "Go [and] tell John everything that you have seen and heard, that the blind see and the lame walk and the lepers are cleansed and the deaf hear and the dead rise up and the poor receive good news.
23	And blessed is he, whosoever shall not be offended in me.	and blessed is he that is not stumbled in me.	And blessed is he who is not offended at me."
24	And when the messengers of John were departed, he began to speak unto the people concerning John, What went ye out into the wilderness for to see? A reed shaken with the wind?	And when John's disciples were gone, Jesus began to say to the multitude, concerning John: What went ye into the wilderness to see?---a reed agitated by the wind?	And when the disciples of John went away, he began to speak to the crowds about John: "What did you go out to the desert to see, a reed that was shaken by the wind?
25	But what went ye out for to see? A man clothed in soft raiment? Behold, they which are gorgeously apparelled, and live delicately, are in kings' courts.	Or if not; what went ye out to see?---a man clad in soft raiment? Lo, they that use splendid garments and luxuries, are in kings' palaces.	And if not, what did you go out to see, a man clothed with soft garments? Behold, those who are with fancy clothes and luxuries are [in] the house of kings.
26	But what went ye out for to see? A prophet? Yea, I say unto you, and much more than a prophet.	Or if not; what went ye out to see?---a prophet? Yea, say I to you; and more than a prophet.	And if not, what did you go out to see, a prophet? Yes, I say to you, even greater than the prophets.
27	This is he, of whom it is written, Behold, I send my messenger before thy face, which shall prepare thy way before thee.	[For] this is he, of whom it is written: Behold I send my messenger before thy face, to prepare thy way before thee.	This is he about whom it is written: BEHOLD, I WILL SEND MY MESSENGER BEFORE YOUR FACE TO PREPARE THE WAY BEFORE YOU.
28	For I say unto you, Among those that are born of women there is not a greater prophet than John the Baptist: but he that is least in the kingdom of God is greater than he.	I say to you, that no prophet, among those born of women, was greater than John the Baptizer: and yet the little one in the kingdom of God, is greater than he.	I say to you, there is no prophet among those born of women who is greater than John the baptizer, but the least in the kingdom of God is greater than he."

Parallel Translations

	KJV	*Murdock*	*Magiera*
LUKE	*Chapter 7*		
29	And all the people that heard him, and the publicans, justified God, being baptized with the baptism of John.	And all the people that heard him, justified God, as they had been baptized with John's baptism.	And all the people who heard, even the tax collectors, declared God [to be] just, because they had been baptized [with] the baptism of John.
30	But the Pharisees and lawyers rejected the counsel of God against themselves, being not baptized of him.	But the Pharisees and Scribes rejected the good pleasure of God, against themselves; as they were not baptized by him.	And the Pharisees and the scribes rejected in themselves the will of God, because they were not baptized by him.
31	And the Lord said, Whereunto then shall I liken the men of this generation? and to what are they like?	To what, therefore, shall I compare this generation? and to what are they like?	"To what therefore can I liken the men of this generation and to what are they like?
32	They are like unto children sitting in the marketplace, and calling one to another, and saying, We have piped unto you, and ye have not danced; we have mourned to you, and ye have not wept.	They are like children, that sit in the market-place, and call to their fellows and say: We have piped to you, and ye did not dance; we have howled to you, and ye did not weep.	They are like young boys who sit in the marketplace and call out to their friends and say, 'We have played music for you and you did not dance and we mourned for you and you did not weep.'
33	For John the Baptist came neither eating bread nor drinking wine; and ye say, He hath a devil.	For John the Baptizer came, not eating bread, and not drinking wine; and ye say: He hath a demon.	For John the baptizer came neither eating bread nor drinking wine and you said, 'There is a demon in him.'
34	The Son of man is come eating and drinking; and ye say, Behold a gluttonous man, and a winebibber, a friend of publicans and sinners!	The Son of man came, eating and drinking; and ye say: Behold, a gluttonous man, and a wine drinker, and one fond of publicans and sinners.	The Son of Man came eating and drinking and you say, 'Behold, a gluttonous man and [one] drinking wine and a friend of tax collectors and sinners.'
35	But wisdom is justified of all her children.	But wisdom is justified by all her children.	Yet wisdom is declared just by all its children."
36	And one of the Pharisees desired him that he would eat with him. And he went into the Pharisee's house, and sat down to meat.	And one of the Pharisees came, and asked him to eat with him. And he entered the house of the Pharisee, and reclined.	Now one of the Pharisees came [and] begged him to eat with him. And he entered the house of that Pharisee and sat to eat.
37	And, behold, a woman in the city, which was a sinner, when she knew that Jesus sat at meat in the Pharisee's house, brought an alabaster box of ointment,	And there was a woman in the city, who was a sinner; and when she learned that he reclined in the Pharisee's house, she took an alabaster box of perfume,	And there was a woman [who was] a sinner in that city. And when she learned that he was reclining in the house of that Pharisee, she took an alabaster box of ointment
38	And stood at his feet behind him weeping, and began to wash his feet with tears, and did wipe them with the hairs of her head, and kissed his feet, and anointed them with the ointment.	and stood behind him, at his feet, and wept; and she began to bathe his feet with her tears, and to wipe them with the hair of her head; and she kissed his feet, and anointed [them] with the perfume.	and stood behind him at his feet and she was crying. And she began washing his feet with her tears and wiping them with the hair of her head. And she was kissing his feet and anointed [them] with ointment.

Parallel Translations

LUKE *Chapter 7*

	KJV	Murdock	Magiera
39	Now when the Pharisee which had bidden him saw it, he spake within himself, saying, This man, if he were a prophet, would have known who and what manner of woman this is that toucheth him: for she is a sinner.	And when the Pharisee that invited him, saw it, he thought within himself, and said: If this man were a prophet, he would know who she is, and what is her reputation; for the woman that toucheth him, is a sinner.	Now when that Pharisee who had invited him saw [this], he reasoned within himself and said, "This man, if he were a prophet, would have known who she is and what her reputation [is], because the woman who touched him is a sinner."
40	And Jesus answering said unto him, Simon, I have somewhat to say unto thee. And he saith, Master, say on.	And Jesus answered, and said to him: Simon, I have something to say to thee. He said to him: Say it, Rabbi. Jesus said to him:	But Jesus answered and said to him, "Simon, I have something to say to you." And he said to him, "Speak, my Master." Jesus said to him,
41	There was a certain creditor which had two debtors: the one owed five hundred pence, and the other fifty.	There were two debtors to a certain creditor; the one owed him five hundred denarii, and the other fifty denarii.	"There were two debtors to a certain lender. One owed five hundred denarii and the other fifty denarii.
42	And when they had nothing to pay, he frankly forgave them both. Tell me therefore, which of them will love him most?	And as they had not the means of pay, he released them both. Which of them, therefore will love him most?	And because they had no way to repay, he forgave both of them. Now then, which of them will love him more?"
43	Simon answered and said, I suppose that he, to whom he forgave most. And he said unto him, Thou hast rightly judged.	Simon replied, and said: I suppose he to whom most was released. Jesus said to him: Thou hast judged correctly.	Simon answered and said, "I suppose that the one who was forgiven the most." Jesus said to him, "You have judged correctly."
44	And he turned to the woman, and said unto Simon, Seest thou this woman? I entered into thine house, thou gavest me no water for my feet: but she hath washed my feet with tears, and wiped them with the hairs of her head.	And he turned to the woman, and said to Simon: Seest thou this woman? I entered thy house, and thou gavest [me] no water for my feet; but she hath bathed my feet with her tears, and wiped them with her hair.	Then he turned to that woman and said to Simon, "Do you see this woman? I entered your house [and] you did not give [me] water for my feet, but this [woman] has washed my feet with her tears and she has dried them with her hair.
45	Thou gavest me no kiss: but this woman since the time I came in hath not ceased to kiss my feet.	Thou gavest me no kiss; but this woman, since she came in, hath not ceased to kiss my feet.	You did not kiss me, but behold, this [woman], since I entered, has not ceased to kiss my feet.
46	My head with oil thou didst not anoint: but this woman hath anointed my feet with ointment.	Thou didst not anoint my head with perfume; but she hath anointed my feet with perfumed ointment.	You did not anoint my head [with] oil, but this [woman] has anointed my feet with perfumed ointment.
47	Wherefore I say unto thee, Her sins, which are many, are forgiven; for she loved much: but to whom little is forgiven, the same loveth little.	I therefore say to thee: Her many sins are forgiven her, for she loveth much. But he, to whom little is forgiven, loveth little.	Because of this I say to you, her many sins are forgiven, because she has loved much. But he to whom little is forgiven loves little."
48	And he said unto her, Thy sins are forgiven.	And he said to the woman: Thy sins are forgiven thee.	And he said to that woman, "Your sins are forgiven."
49	And they that sat at meat with him began to say within themselves, Who is this that forgiveth sins also?	And they that were reclining, began to say in themselves: Who is this, that even forgiveth sins?	And those who were sitting to eat began saying among themselves, "Who is this who even forgives sins?"

	KJV	Murdock	Magiera
LUKE *Chapter 7*			
50	And he said to the woman, Thy faith hath saved thee; go in peace.	And Jesus said to the woman: Thy faith hath given thee life. Go, in peace.	But Jesus said to that woman, "Your faith has given you life. Go in peace."
Chapter 8			
1	And it came to pass afterward, that he went throughout every city and village, preaching and shewing the glad tidings of the kingdom of God: and the twelve were with him,	And after these things Jesus travelled about the cities and the villages, and proclaimed and announced the kingdom of God. And with him were his twelve [disciples],	And it happened [that] after these [things] Jesus was going around in the cities and in the villages and he was preaching and declaring the kingdom of God. And his twelve [were] with him
2	And certain women, which had been healed of evil spirits and infirmities, Mary called Magdalene, out of whom went seven devils,	and those women who were healed of infirmities and of unclean spirits, Mary called Magdalena, out of whom went seven demons,	and those women who had been healed of sicknesses and of evil spirits: Mary who was called Magdalene, from whom seven demons had gone out,
3	And Joanna the wife of Chuza Herod's steward, and Susanna, and many others, which ministered unto him of their substance.	and Joanna the wife of Chusa, Herod's steward, and Susanna, and many others, who ministered to them of their property.	and Joanna the wife of Chuza, the steward of Herod, and Susanna, and many others who were ministering to them from their properties.
4	And when much people were gathered together, and were come to him out of every city, he spake by a parable:	And when a great multitude was assembled, and people came to him from all the cities, he said, in similitudes:	And when a large crowd had gathered and they were coming to him from all the cities, he spoke in parables:
5	A sower went out to sow his seed: and as he sowed, some fell by the way side; and it was trodden down, and the fowls of the air devoured it.	A sower went out to sow his seed: and as he sowed, some fell by the side of the path, and was trodden upon, and a bird devoured it.	"A sower went to sow his seed, and as he sowed, some fell by the side of the road and was trampled and a bird ate it.
6	And some fell upon a rock; and as soon as it was sprung up, it withered away, because it lacked moisture.	And other fell upon a rock, and sprung up forthwith; but, as it lacked moisture, it dried up.	And other [seed] fell on rock. And immediately it sprang up, but because it did not have moisture, it withered.
7	And some fell among thorns; and the thorns sprang up with it, and choked it.	And other fell among thorns, and the thorns sprung up with it, and choked it.	And other [seed] fell among thorns and the thorns sprang up with it and choked it.
8	And other fell on good ground, and sprang up, and bare fruit an hundredfold. And when he had said these things, he cried, He that hath ears to hear, let him hear.	And other fell on good and fair ground, and sprung up, and bore fruits, a hundred for one. Having said these things, he cried: He that hath ears to hear, let him hear.	And other [seed] fell on good and fertile earth and sprang up and produced fruit one hundred[fold]. When he had said these [things], he cried out, "He who has ears to hear should hear."
9	And his disciples asked him, saying, What might this parable be?	And his disciples asked him: what meaneth this similitude?	And his disciples asked him, "What is [the meaning of] this parable?"

Parallel Translations

	KJV	Murdock	Magiera
	LUKE *Chapter 8*		
10	And he said, Unto you it is given to know the mysteries of the kingdom of God: but to others in parables; that seeing they might not see, and hearing they might not understand.	And he said to them: To you it is given, to know the mysteries of the kingdom of God; but to others, it is spoken in allegories; that, while seeing, they may not see, and while hearing, may not understand.	And he said to them, "To you it is given to know the secret of the kingdom of God. But to the rest, it is spoken in comparisons: BECAUSE ALTHOUGH THEY SEE, THEY WILL NOT SEE AND ALTHOUGH THEY HEAR, THEY WILL NOT UNDERSTAND.
11	Now the parable is this: The seed is the word of God.	But this is the similitude: The seed is the word of God.	Now, this is [the meaning of] the parable. The seed is the word of God.
12	Those by the way side are they that hear; then cometh the devil, and taketh away the word out of their hearts, lest they should believe and be saved.	And those by the side of the path, are they that hear the word, and the enemy cometh and taketh the word out of their heart, that they may not believe and live.	And those [seeds] that [fell] by the side of the road are those who hear the word, yet the enemy comes [and] takes the word from their heart[s],so that they will not believe and live.
13	They on the rock are they, which, when they hear, receive the word with joy; and these have no root, which for a while believe, and in time of temptation fall away.	And those upon the rock, are they who, when they hear, receive the word with joy: but they have no root in them, and their faith is temporary, and in time of temptation they are stumbled.	And those [seeds] that [fell] on rock are those that when they hear, receive the word with joy. But they have no root. On the contrary, their faith is for a while, yet in the time of temptation, they are offended.
14	And that which fell among thorns are they, which, when they have heard, go forth, and are choked with cares and riches and pleasures of this life, and bring no fruit to perfection.	And that which fell among thorns, are those who hear the word, but are choked by cares, and by riches, and by worldly desires, and bear no fruits.	And that [seed] which fell among thorns are those who hear the word and are choked with the care and wealth and lusts of the world and they do not bear fruit.
15	But that on the good ground are they, which in an honest and good heart, having heard the word, keep it, and bring forth fruit with patience.	And that on good ground, are those who, with a humble and good heart, hear the word, and retain it, and with patience bring forth fruits.	And that [seed] which [fell] on good ground are those who with an honest and good heart hear the word and adhere [to it] and bear fruit with patience.
16	No man, when he hath lighted a candle, covereth it with a vessel, or putteth it under a bed; but setteth it on a candlestick, that they which enter in may see the light.	No one lighteth a lamp, and covereth it with a vessel, or placeth it under a bed, but setteth it upon a light-stand, that all who come in, may see the light of it.	No one lights a lamp and hides it in a vessel or places it under a bed. On the contrary, he places it on a lamp stand, so that all who enter will see its light.
17	For nothing is secret, that shall not be made manifest; neither any thing hid, that shall not be known and come abroad.	For there is nothing covered, that shall not be uncovered; nor concealed, that shall not be known and become manifest.	For there is not anything that is covered that will not be revealed or that is hidden that will not be known and come [out] openly.
18	Take heed therefore how ye hear: for whosoever hath, to him shall be given; and whosoever hath not, from him shall be taken even that which he seemeth to have.	Take heed how ye hear: for to him that hath, shall be given; and from him that hath not, shall be taken even what he thinketh he hath.	Take heed how you hear, for whoever has, it will be given to him, and whoever does not have, even that which he thinks he has, will be taken from him."

LUKE *Chapter 8*

	KJV	*Murdock*	*Magiera*
19	Then came to him his mother and his brethren, and could not come at him for the press.	And his mother and his brothers came to him, and they could not speak with him, because of the multitude.	Now his mother and his brothers came to him and were not able to speak with him because of the crowd.
20	And it was told him by certain which said, Thy mother and thy brethren stand without, desiring to see thee.	And they say to him: Thy mother and thy brothers stand without, and wish to see thee.	And they said to him, "Your mother and your brothers are standing outside and want to see you."
21	And he answered and said unto them, My mother and my brethren are these which hear the word of God, and do it.	And he answered and said: My mother and my brothers, are they who hear the word of God, and do it.	But he answered and said to them, "My mother and my brothers are those who hear the word of God and do it."
22	Now it came to pass on a certain day, that he went into a ship with his disciples: and he said unto them, Let us go over unto the other side of the lake. And they launched forth.	And on a certain day Jesus embarked and sat in a ship, he and his disciples. And he said to them; Let us pass over to the other side of the sea.	And it happened [that] on a certain day Jesus boarded [and] sat in a boat, he and his disciples, and he said to them, "Let us cross over to the other side of the lake."
23	But as they sailed he fell asleep: and there came down a storm of wind on the lake; and they were filled with water, and were in jeopardy.	And while they were rowing, Jesus fell asleep. And there was a tempest of wind on the sea; and the ship was near to sinking.	And while they were journeying, Jesus was asleep. And there was a sudden wind storm on the lake and the boat was about to sink.
24	And they came to him, and awoke him, saying, Master, master, we perish. Then he arose, and rebuked the wind and the raging of the water: and they ceased, and there was a calm.	And they came and awaked him, and said to him: Our Rabbi, our Rabbi, we are perishing! And he arose, and rebuked the winds and the agitations of the water; and they ceased, and there was a calm.	And they came near [and] woke him and said to him, "Our Master, our Master, we are being destroyed." And he stood up and rebuked the winds and the waves of the sea and they ceased and there was calm.
25	And he said unto them, Where is your faith? And they being afraid wondered, saying one to another, What manner of man is this! for he commandeth even the winds and water, and they obey him.	And he said to them: Where is your faith? And they being in awe, wondered, and said one to another: Who is this, that commandeth even the winds, and the waves, and the sea; and they obey him?	And he said to them, "Where is your faith?" And, being afraid, they were amazed and said one to another, "Who indeed is this [man] who commands even the winds and the waves and the sea and they obey him?"
26	And they arrived at the country of the Gadarenes, which is over against Galilee.	And they rowed on, and came to the country of the Gadarenes, which lieth over against Galilee.	And they journeyed and came to the region of the Gadarenes that is on the shore opposite Galilee.
27	And when he went forth to land, there met him out of the city a certain man, which had devils long time, and ware no clothes, neither abode in any house, but in the tombs.	And when he went out upon the land, there, met him a man of the city, in whom had been a demon for a long time; and he wore no clothing, and did not reside in a house, but among the tombs.	And when he had come onto the land, he met a certain man from the city who had had a devil for a long time. And he did not wear clothes and did not live in a house, but in the tombs.
28	When he saw Jesus, he cried out, and fell down before him, and with a loud voice said, What have I to do with thee, Jesus, thou Son of God most high? I beseech thee, torment me not.	And when he saw Jesus, he cried out, and fell down before him, and said, with a loud voice: What have we to do with thee? Jesus, thou Son of the exalted God. I entreat of thee, torment me not.	And when he saw Jesus, he cried out and fell down before him and spoke with a loud voice, "What do we have in common, Jesus, Son of the Most High God? I beg you, do not torment me."

Parallel Translations

LUKE Chapter 8

	KJV	Murdock	Magiera
29	(For he had commanded the unclean spirit to come out of the man. For oftentimes it had caught him: and he was kept bound with chains and in fetters; and he brake the bands, and was driven of the devil into the wilderness.)	For Jesus had commanded the unclean spirit, to come out of the man: for, of a long time he had been held captive by him; and he had been bound with chains, and held in fetters; but he had burst the bonds, and had been driven by the demon into the desert.	For Jesus was commanding the unclean spirit to go out of the man, for a long time had passed since he was [first] held captive by him. And he had been bound with chains and restrained with fetters, but he broke his bonds and was driven by the demon into the wilderness.
30	And Jesus asked him, saying, What is thy name? And he said, Legion: because many devils were entered into him.	And Jesus demanded of him: What is thy name? And he said to him: Legion: because many demons had entered into him.	And Jesus asked him, "What is your name?" He said to him, "Legion," because many devils had entered into him.
31	And they besought him that he would not command them to go out into the deep.	And they besought him, not to command them to depart into the abyss.	And they were begging him that he would not command them to go to the abyss.
32	And there was there an herd of many swine feeding on the mountain: and they besought him that he would suffer them to enter into them. And he suffered them.	And there was a herd of many swine grazing on the mountain. And they besought him, that he would permit them to enter the swine. And he permitted them.	And there was there a herd of many pigs that was feeding on the mountain. And they were begging him to permit them to attack the pigs and he permitted them.
33	Then went the devils out of the man, and entered into the swine: and the herd ran violently down a steep place into the lake, and were choked.	And the demons went out of the man, and entered the swine; and the whole herd ran to a precipice, and plunged into the sea, and were strangled.	And the demons went out from the man and attacked the pigs and that whole herd rushed to a steep place and fell into the lake and was drowned.
34	When they that fed them saw what was done, they fled, and went and told it in the city and in the country.	And when the herdmen saw what had occurred, they fled, and told [it] in the cities and the villages.	And when the herdsmen saw what had happened, they fled and reported [it] in the cities and villages.
35	Then they went out to see what was done; and came to Jesus, and found the man, out of whom the devils were departed, sitting at the feet of Jesus, clothed, and in his right mind: and they were afraid.	And the men went out to see what was done. And they came to Jesus, and found the man, out of whom the demons had gone, now clothed, and modest, and sitting at the feet of Jesus; and they were awed.	And the men came out to see what had happened. And they came to Jesus and found the man, whose demons had gone out, clothed and sober and sitting at the feet of Jesus, and they were afraid.
36	They also which saw it told them by what means he that was possessed of the devils was healed.	And they that saw [it], related to them in what manner the demoniac was cured.	And those who had seen [it] reported to them how he healed the man possessed with a devil.
37	Then the whole multitude of the country of the Gadarenes round about besought him to depart from them; for they were taken with great fear: and he went up into the ship, and returned back again.	And the whole throng of the Gadarenes requested him, that he would depart from them: for great fear had seized them. And Jesus embarked in a ship, and retired from among them.	And all the assembly of the Gadarenes begged him to go away from them, because great fear had taken hold of them. And Jesus boarded a ship and turned away from them.
38	Now the man out of whom the devils were departed besought him that he might be with him: but Jesus sent him away, saying,	And the man, from whom the demons had gone out, requested that he might remain with him. But Jesus dismissed him, and said to him:	And that man from whom the demons went out begged him that he might remain with him. But Jesus sent him away and said to him,

Parallel Translations

	KJV	Murdock	Magiera
	LUKE	*Chapter 8*	
39	Return to thine own house, and shew how great things God hath done unto thee. And he went his way, and published throughout the whole city how great things Jesus had done unto him.	Return to thy home, and relate what God hath done for thee. And he went away, and proclaimed through all the city what Jesus had done for him.	"Return to your house and report what God has done for you." And he went and was preaching in the whole city what Jesus had done for him.
40	And it came to pass, that, when Jesus was returned, the people gladly received him: for they were all waiting for him.	And when Jesus returned, a great multitude received him; for all were looking for him.	And when Jesus returned, a large crowd received him, for all were looking for him.
41	And, behold, there came a man named Jairus, and he was a ruler of the synagogue: and he fell down at Jesus' feet, and besought him that he would come into his house:	And a man, whose name was Jairus, a chief of the synagogue, fell down at the feet of Jesus, and besought him to enter his house;	And a certain man whose name [was] Jairus, a chief of the synagogue, fell before the feet of Jesus and begged him to enter his house,
42	For he had one only daughter, about twelve years of age, and she lay a dying. But as he went the people thronged him.	for he had an only daughter, about twelve years old, and she was near dying. And as Jesus went with him, a great multitude pressed upon him.	for he had an only daughter about twelve years old and she was about to die. And while Jesus went with him, a large crowd thronged him.
43	And a woman having an issue of blood twelve years, which had spent all her living upon physicians, neither could be healed of any,	And a certain woman, whose blood had flowed twelve years, and who had expended all her property among physicians, and could not be cured by any one,	And a certain woman, whose blood had been flowing [for] twelve years, who had spent all her wealth among the doctors, but was not able to be healed by man,
44	Came behind him, and touched the border of his garment: and immediately her issue of blood stanched.	came up behind him, and touched the border of his garment; and immediately the flow of her blood stopped.	approached from behind him and touched the outer edge of his garment. And immediately the flow of her blood stopped.
45	And Jesus said, Who touched me? When all denied, Peter and they that were with him said, Master, the multitude throng thee and press thee, and sayest thou, Who touched me?	And Jesus said: Who touched me? And when all denied, Simon Cephas and those with him said to him: Our Rabbi, crowds press upon thee and sayest thou, Who touched me?	And Jesus said, "Who touched me?" And while all were denying [it], Simon Peter and those with him said to him, "Our Master, the crowds are pressing and thronging you, yet you say, 'Who touched me?'"
46	And Jesus said, Somebody hath touched me: for I perceive that virtue is gone out of me.	And he said: Some one touched me; for I perceive, that energy hath gone out from me.	And he said, "Someone touched me, for I know that power went out of me."
47	And when the woman saw that she was not hid, she came trembling, and falling down before him, she declared unto him before all the people for what cause she had touched him, and how she was healed immediately.	And the woman, when she saw that she had not escaped his notice, came trembling, and fell down and worshipped him. And in the presence of all the people, she declared for what cause she had touched him, and that she was instantly healed.	Now when that woman saw that she had not escaped his notice, she came trembling and fell down [and] worshipped him. And she declared before all the people for what reason she had touched [him] and how she was immediately healed.
48	And he said unto her, Daughter, be of good comfort: thy faith hath made thee whole; go in peace.	And Jesus said to her: Take courage, my daughter: Thy faith hath given thee life: Go in peace.	And Jesus said to her, "Be encouraged, my daughter. Your faith has given you life. Go in peace."

	KJV	Murdock	Magiera
	LUKE *Chapter 8*		
49	While he yet spake, there cometh one from the ruler of the synagogue's house, saying to him, Thy daughter is dead; trouble not the Master.	And while he was speaking, one came from the house of the chief of the synagogue, and said to him: Thy daughter is dead; trouble not the teacher.	And while he was speaking, a man from the house of the chief of the synagogue came and said to him, "Your daughter has died. Do not trouble the teacher."
50	But when Jesus heard it, he answered him, saying, Fear not: believe only, and she shall be made whole.	And Jesus heard [it], and said to the father of the maid: Fear not; believe only, and she will live.	But Jesus heard [it] and said to the father of the girl, "Do not fear, believe only and she will live."
51	And when he came into the house, he suffered no man to go in, save Peter, and James, and John, and the father and the mother of the maiden.	And Jesus came to the house; and he suffered none to go in with him, except Simon, and James, and John, and the father and mother of the maid.	And Jesus came to the house and did not allow anyone to enter with him, except Simon and James and John and the father of the girl and her mother.
52	And all wept, and bewailed her: but he said, Weep not; she is not dead, but sleepeth.	And all were weeping and wailing over her. And Jesus said: Weep not; for she is not dead, but sleepeth	And all were weeping and mourning over her. But Jesus said, "Do not weep, for she has not died, but sleeps."
53	And they laughed him to scorn, knowing that she was dead.	And they derided him, knowing that she was dead.	And they were laughing at him, because they knew that she had died.
54	And he put them all out, and took her by the hand, and called, saying, Maid, arise.	And he put every one out, and took her by the hand, and called, and said: Maid, arise.	And he put everyone outside and took her by her hand and called her and said, "Young girl, rise up."
55	And her spirit came again, and she arose straightway: and he commanded to give her meat.	And her spirit returned, and she instantly arose. And he directed them to give her food.	And her spirit returned and immediately she rose up. And he commanded them to give her [something] to eat.
56	And her parents were astonished: but he charged them that they should tell no man what was done.	And her parents were astonished: and he charged them to tell no one what had occurred.	And her parents were astonished. And he warned them not to tell anyone what had happened.
	Chapter 9		
1	Then he called his twelve disciples together, and gave them power and authority over all devils, and to cure diseases.	And Jesus called his twelve, and gave them power and authority over all demons and diseases, to heal [them].	And Jesus called his twelve and gave them power and authority over all demons and to heal sicknesses.
2	And he sent them to preach the kingdom of God, and to heal the sick.	And he sent them forth, to proclaim the kingdom of God, and to heal the sick.	And he sent them to preach the kingdom of God and to heal the sick.
3	And he said unto them, Take nothing for your journey, neither staves, nor scrip, neither bread, neither money; neither have two coats apiece.	And he said to them: Take nothing for the journey, neither a staff, nor a wallet, nor bread, nor money; neither have two tunics.	And he said to them, "Do not take anything on the journey, neither staff nor bag nor bread nor money nor should you have two coats.
4	And whatsoever house ye enter into, there abide, and thence depart.	And into whatever house ye enter, there stay, and thence depart.	And in whatever house you enter, remain there and leave from there.

	KJV	*Murdock*	*Magiera*
	LUKE	*Chapter 9*	
5	And whosoever will not receive you, when ye go out of that city, shake off the very dust from your feet for a testimony against them.	And against them that receive you not, when ye go out of that city, shake off even the dust of your feet against them, for a testimony.	And whoever does not receive you, when you leave that city, shake off even the dust from your feet for a witness against them."
6	And they departed, and went through the towns, preaching the gospel, and healing every where.	And the Legates went forth, and travelled about the villages and cities, and preached and healed everywhere.	And the apostles left and were going around in the villages and cities and were preaching and healing in every place.
7	Now Herod the tetrarch heard of all that was done by him: and he was perplexed, because that it was said of some, that John was risen from the dead;	And Herod the Tetrarch heard of all the things done by him, and he was disturbed; because some said, that John had arisen from the dead.	Now Herod the tetrarch heard of all [the things] that were done by his hand and he was wondering, because some were saying that John had risen from the dead.
8	And of some, that Elias had appeared; and of others, that one of the old prophets was risen again.	But others said, that Elijah hath appeared; and others, that a prophet from among the ancient prophets hath arisen.	And others were saying that Elijah had appeared and others that a prophet from the first prophets had risen.
9	And Herod said, John have I beheaded: but who is this, of whom I hear such things? And he desired to see him.	And Herod said: The head of John, I have cut off; but who is this, of whom I hear these things? And he was desirous to see him.	And Herod said, "I cut off the head of John, but who is this [man] about whom I hear these [things]?" And he wanted to see him.
10	And the apostles, when they were returned, told him all that they had done. And he took them, and went aside privately into a desert place belonging to the city called Bethsaida.	And when the Legates returned, they narrated, to Jesus all they had done. And he took them aside, to the desert part of Bethsaida.	And when the apostles returned, they reported to Jesus everything that they had done. And he took them privately to a desert place of Bethsaida.
11	And the people, when they knew it, followed him: and he received them, and spake unto them of the kingdom of God, and healed them that had need of healing.	And when the multitude knew [it], they followed him: and he received them, and conversed with them respecting the kingdom of God: and such as had need of healing, he healed.	And when the crowds knew [it], they followed him. And he received them and spoke with them about the kingdom of God. And those who had a need for healing, he healed.
12	And when the day began to wear away, then came the twelve, and said unto him, Send the multitude away, that they may go into the towns and country round about, and lodge, and get victuals: for we are here in a desert place.	And when the day began to decline, his disciples came near, and said to him: Send away the multitude, that they may go to the villages around us and to the towns, to lodge in them, and to procure themselves food, for we are in a desert place.	And when the day began to fade, his disciples came near and were saying to him, "Send away the crowds that they may go to the villages and to the towns around us to stay in them and to find food for themselves, because we are in a desert place.
13	But he said unto them, Give ye them to eat. And they said, We have no more but five loaves and two fishes; except we should go and buy meat for all this people.	Jesus said to then: Give ye them to eat. And they say: We have no more than five loaves and two fishes; unless we go and buy food for all this people:	Jesus said to them, "You give them [something] to eat." But they were saying, "We do not have more than five [loaves of] bread and two fish, unless we go and buy food for all this people,"
14	For they were about five thousand men. And he said to his disciples, Make them sit down by fifties in a company.	for they were about five thousand men. Jesus said to them: Make them recline by companies, fifty persons in a company.	for there were about five thousand men. Jesus said to them, "Cause them to sit to eat [in] groups, fifty men in a group."

	KJV	Murdock	Magiera

LUKE *Chapter 9*

	KJV	Murdock	Magiera
15	And they did so, and made them all sit down.	And the disciples did so, and made them all recline.	And the disciples did so and caused them all to sit to eat.
16	Then he took the five loaves and the two fishes, and looking up to heaven, he blessed them, and brake, and gave to the disciples to set before the multitude.	And Jesus took the five loaves and two fishes, and looked towards heaven, and blessed, and brake, and gave to his disciples to set before the multitudes.	And Jesus took those five [loaves of] bread and two fish and gazed into heaven and blessed and broke [them] and gave [them] to his disciples to set before the crowds.
17	And they did eat, and were all filled: and there was taken up of fragments that remained to them twelve baskets.	And they all ate, and were satisfied: and they took up the fragments of remains, twelve baskets.	And all ate and were satisfied and they took up the fragments that were left over, twelve baskets.
18	And it came to pass, as he was alone praying, his disciples were with him: and he asked them, saying, Whom say the people that I am?	And as he was praying in private with his disciples, he asked them, and said: Who, do the multitudes say of me, that I am?	And while he was praying alone and his disciples with him, he asked them and said, "What do the crowds say about me, who I am?"
19	They answering said, John the Baptist; but some say, Elias; and others say, that one of the old prophets is risen again.	They answer and say to him: John the Baptizer; others, Elijah and others, a prophet, one of the ancient prophets arisen.	They answered and were saying to him, "John the baptizer, and others, Elijah, and others, that a certain prophet from the first prophets has risen."
20	He said unto them, But whom say ye that I am? Peter answering said, The Christ of God.	He said to them: But who, do ye say, that I am? Simon answered, and said: The Messiah of God.	He said to them, "But who do you say that I am?" Simon answered and said, "The Messiah of God."
21	And he straitly charged them, and commanded them to tell no man that thing;	And he chided them, and charged them, that they should say this to no one.	And he reproved them and warned them not to say this to anyone.
22	Saying, The Son of man must suffer many things, and be rejected of the elders and chief priests and scribes, and be slain, and be raised the third day.	And he said to them: The Son of man is to suffer many things, and to be rejected by the Elders and the chief priests and Scribes; and they will kill him; and on the third day, he will arise.	And he said to them that the Son of Man would suffer many things and he would be rejected by the elders and the chief priests and scribes and they would kill him and on the third day he would rise up.
23	And he said to them all, If any man will come after me, let him deny himself, and take up his cross daily, and follow me.	And he said before all the people: He that would follow me, must deny himself, and take up his cross daily, and [so] come after me.	And he said before everyone, "He who wants to follow me should deny himself and take up his cross every day and follow me.
24	For whosoever will save his life shall lose it: but whosoever will lose his life for my sake, the same shall save it.	For he that will preserve his life, shall lose it; but he that shall lose his life, for my sake, will preserve it.	For he who wants to save his soul will lose it, but he who will lose his soul because of me, this one will save it.
25	For what is a man advantaged, if he gain the whole world, and lose himself, or be cast away?	For, what will a man be profited, if he gain the whole world, and lose his life or be deprived [of it]?	For what is a man helped who gains the whole world, but will lose or is deprived of his soul?
26	For whosoever shall be ashamed of me and of my words, of him shall the Son of man be ashamed, when he shall come in his own glory, and in his Father's, and of the holy angels.	And whoever shall be ashamed of me and of my words, of him will the Son of man be ashamed, when he cometh in the glory of his Father, with his holy angels.	And whoever will be ashamed of me and of my words, the Son of Man will be ashamed of him when he comes in the glory of his Father with his holy angels.

Parallel Translations

LUKE *Chapter 9*

	KJV	*Murdock*	*Magiera*
27	But I tell you of a truth, there be some standing here, which shall not taste of death, till they see the kingdom of God.	I tell you the truth, that there are some standing here, who will not taste death, until they shall see the kingdom of God.	I say the truth to you, there are men who stand here who will not taste death until they see the kingdom of God."
28	And it came to pass about an eight days after these sayings, he took Peter and John and James, and went up into a mountain to pray.	And it was about eight days after these discourses, that Jesus took Simon and James and John, and went up a mountain to pray.	And it happened [that] about eight days after these words, Jesus took Simon and James and John and climbed a mountain to pray.
29	And as he prayed, the fashion of his countenance was altered, and his raiment was white and glistering.	And while he prayed, the aspect of his countenance was changed, and his garments became white and brilliant.	And while he was praying, the appearance of his face was changed and his clothes were whitened and made to shine.
30	And, behold, there talked with him two men, which were Moses and Elias:	And lo, two men were talking with him: and they were Moses and Elijah,	And behold, two men were talking with him, who were Moses and Elijah,
31	Who appeared in glory, and spake of his decease which he should accomplish at Jerusalem.	who appeared in glory. And they were conversing on his departure, which was to be consummated at Jerusalem.	who appeared in glory. And they were talking about his departure that was about to be accomplished in Jerusalem.
32	But Peter and they that were with him were heavy with sleep: and when they were awake, they saw his glory, and the two men that stood with him.	And Simon and those with him were oppressed with drowsiness; and being scarcely awake, they saw his glory, and those two men who stood near him.	And Simon and those who were with him were heavy with sleep and scarcely awake and they saw his glory and those two men who were standing with him.
33	And it came to pass, as they departed from him, Peter said unto Jesus, Master, it is good for us to be here: and let us make three tabernacles; one for thee, and one for Moses, and one for Elias: not knowing what he said.	And when they began to retire from him, Simon said to Jesus: Rabbi, it is delightful for us to be here. And let us make here three booths, one for thee, and one for Moses, and one for Elijah. But he knew not what he said.	And when they began to go away from him, Simon said to Jesus, "My Master, it is good for us that we were here. Yet let us make three booths, one for you and one for Moses and one for Elijah," and he did not know what he said.
34	While he thus spake, there came a cloud, and overshadowed them: and they feared as they entered into the cloud.	And as he thus spoke, there was a cloud; and it overshadowed them; and they were afraid, when they saw Moses and Elijah go up into the cloud.	And when he said these [things], a cloud came and overshadowed them. And they were afraid when they saw that Moses and Elijah entered into the cloud.
35	And there came a voice out of the cloud, saying, This is my beloved Son: hear him.	And there was a voice from the cloud, which said: This is my beloved Son; hear ye him.	And a voice came from the cloud that said, "This is my beloved Son. Hear him."
36	And when the voice was past, Jesus was found alone. And they kept it close, and told no man in those days any of those things which they had seen.	And when the voice had passed, Jesus was found to be alone.---And they kept silence, and told no one in those days what they had seen.	And after the voice came, Jesus was found alone and they kept silent and did not tell anyone in those days anything that they had seen.
37	And it came to pass, that on the next day, when they were come down from the hill, much people met him.	And the next day, as they came down from the mountain, a great multitude met them.	And it happened [that] on the next day when they came down from the mountain, a large crowd met them.

LUKE *Chapter 9*

	KJV	*Murdock*	*Magiera*
38	And, behold, a man of the company cried out, saying, Master, I beseech thee, look upon my son: for he is mine only child.	And a man from the throng cried out, and said: Teacher, I beseech thee, turn thyself to me. Here is my only son:	And a certain man from that crowd cried out and said, "Teacher, I beg you, take notice of me. He is my only son
39	And, lo, a spirit taketh him, and he suddenly crieth out; and it teareth him that he foameth again, and bruising him hardly departeth from him.	and a spirit cometh upon him, and he suddenly crieth out, and gnasheth his teeth, and foameth; and he hardly leaveth him, when he hath crushed him.	and a spirit quickly comes over him and suddenly he cries out and gnashes his teeth and foams and with difficulty does it go out of him when it has harassed him.
40	And I besought thy disciples to cast him out; and they could not.	And I requested thy disciples to expel him; and they could not.	And I begged your disciples to cast it out and they were not able."
41	And Jesus answering said, O faithless and perverse generation, how long shall I be with you, and suffer you? Bring thy son hither.	And Jesus answered, and said: O the unbelieving and perverse generation! How long shall I be with you, and bear with you? Bring hither thy son.	And Jesus answered and said, "Oh faithless and perverted generation! How long should I be with you and endure you? Bring your son here."
42	And as he was yet a coming, the devil threw him down, and tare him. And Jesus rebuked the unclean spirit, and healed the child, and delivered him again to his father.	And while he was bringing him, the demon threw him down, and convulsed him. And Jesus rebuked the unclean spirit, and healed the lad, and delivered him to his father.	And while he was bringing him, that devil cast him down and convulsed him. And Jesus rebuked that unclean spirit and he healed the young boy and gave him to his father.
43	And they were all amazed at the mighty power of God. But while they wondered every one at all things which Jesus did, he said unto his disciples,	And they were all amazed at the majesty of God.---And while every one admired at all that Jesus did, he said to his disciples:	And they were all amazed at the greatness of God. And while everyone was wondering about all that Jesus had done, he said to his disciples,
44	Let these sayings sink down into your ears: for the Son of man shall be delivered into the hands of men.	Lay up these words in your minds: for the Son of man is to be delivered into the hands of men.	Set these words in your ears, for the Son of Man is about to be delivered into the hands of men.
45	But they understood not this saying, and it was hid from them, that they perceived it not: and they feared to ask him of that saying.	But they understood not that speech; because it was hidden from them, that they should not know it: and they feared to ask him concerning that speech.	But they did not understand this saying, because it was hidden from them so that they did not know it, and they were afraid to ask him about this saying.
46	Then there arose a reasoning among them, which of them should be greatest.	And the thought arose among them, which of them [was to be] the greatest.	And the thought entered into them [as to] who was indeed great among them.
47	And Jesus, perceiving the thought of their heart, took a child, and set him by him,	And Jesus knew the thought of their heart: and he took a child, and placed him near to him;	And Jesus knew the thought of their heart[s] and he took a young child and set him by him.
48	And said unto them, Whosoever shall receive this child in my name receiveth me: and whosoever shall receive me receiveth him that sent me: for he that is least among you all, the same shall be great.	and said to them: Whoever receiveth a child like this, in my name, receiveth me; and he that receiveth me, receiveth him that sent me. For he that shall be least among you all, he will be the great one.	And he said to them, "He who receives a child like this in my name, receives me. And he who receives me, receives him who sent me. For whoever is least among all of you, this one will be great."

Parallel Translations

	KJV	*Murdock*	*Magiera*
	LUKE	*Chapter 9*	
49	And John answered and said, Master, we saw one casting out devils in thy name; and we forbad him, because he followeth not with us.	And John answered, and said: Our Rabbi, we saw a man casting out demons in thy name; and we forbad him, because he doth not, with us, follow thee.	And John answered and said, "Our Master, we saw a man who was casting out devils in your name and we prohibited him, because he did not follow you with us."
50	And Jesus said unto him, Forbid him not: for he that is not against us is for us.	Jesus said to them: Forbid not: for, whoever is not against you, is for you.	Jesus said to them, "Do not prohibit [him], for he who is not against you is for you."
51	And it came to pass, when the time was come that he should be received up, he stedfastly set his face to go to Jerusalem,	And when the days for his ascension were completed, so it was, that he set his face to go up to Jerusalem.	And it happened that when the days of his offering up were fulfilled, he directed his face to go to Jerusalem.
52	And sent messengers before his face: and they went, and entered into a village of the Samaritans, to make ready for him.	And he sent messengers before his face; and they went, and entered a village of the Samaritans, to prepare [lodgings] for him.	And he sent messengers before his face and they went [and] entered a village of the Samaritans in order to prepare for him.
53	And they did not receive him, because his face was as though he would go to Jerusalem.	And they received him not, because he had set his face to go up to Jerusalem.	And they did not receive him because his face was set to go to Jerusalem.
54	And when his disciples James and John saw this, they said, Lord, wilt thou that we command fire to come down from heaven, and consume them, even as Elias did?	And when his disciples James and John saw [it], they said to him: Our Lord, wilt thou that we speak, and fire come down from heaven, and consume them, as also did Elijah?	And when James and John, his disciples, saw [it], they said to him, "Our Lord, do you want us to speak and have fire come down from heaven and consume them as also Elijah did?"
55	But he turned, and rebuked them, and said, Ye know not what manner of spirit ye are of.	And he turned and rebuked them, and said: Ye know not of what spirit ye are.	And he turned and rebuked them and said, "You do not know of what spirit you are.
56	For the Son of man is not come to destroy men's lives, but to save them. And they went to another village.	For the Son of man hath not come to destroy souls; but to quicken [them]. And they went to another village.	For the Son of Man did not come to destroy souls, but to make [them] to live." And they went to another village.
57	And it came to pass, that, as they went in the way, a certain man said unto him, Lord, I will follow thee whithersoever thou goest.	And as they went by the way, one said to him: I will follow thee to whatever place thou goest, my Lord.	And while they were traveling on the road, a man said to him, "I will follow you wherever you go, my Lord."
58	And Jesus said unto him, Foxes have holes, and birds of the air have nests; but the Son of man hath not where to lay his head.	Jesus said to him: The foxes have holes, and the birds of heaven have coverts; but the Son of man hath not where he may lay his head.	Jesus said to him, "Foxes have holes and a bird of heaven a shelter, but the Son of Man has no where to lay his head."
59	And he said unto another, Follow me. But he said, Lord, suffer me first to go and bury my father.	And he said to another: Come thou after me. And he said to him: My Lord, permit me first to go and bury my father.	And he said to another, "Follow me." And he said to him, "My Lord, allow me first to go [and] bury my father."
60	Jesus said unto him, Let the dead bury their dead: but go thou and preach the kingdom of God.	And Jesus said to him: Allow the dead to bury their dead; and go thou and proclaim the kingdom of God.	Jesus said to him, "Leave the dead burying their dead and go [and] preach the kingdom of God."

Parallel Translations

	KJV	Murdock	Magiera

LUKE *Chapter 9*

	KJV	Murdock	Magiera
61	And another also said, Lord, I will follow thee; but let me first go bid them farewell, which are at home at my house.	Another said to him: I will follow thee, my Lord; but allow me first to bid adieu to my household, and I will come.	Another said to him, "I will follow you, my Lord, but first allow me to go [and] say goodbye to my household and [then] I will come."
62	And Jesus said unto him, No man, having put his hand to the plough, and looking back, is fit for the kingdom of God.	Jesus said to him: No man putting his hand to the ox-plough, and looking backward, is fit for the kingdom of God.	Jesus said to him, "No one places his hand on the handle of a plow and looks back and is useful for the kingdom of God."

Chapter 10

	KJV	Murdock	Magiera
1	After these things the Lord appointed other seventy also, and sent them two and two before his face into every city and place, whither he himself would come.	And after these things, Jesus separated from among his disciples seventy other persons, and sent them, two and two, before his face, to every place and city whither he was to go.	After these [things], Jesus appointed from his disciples seventy others and sent them two by two before his face to every region and city that he was about to go.
2	Therefore said he unto them, The harvest truly is great, but the labourers are few: pray ye therefore the Lord of the harvest, that he would send forth labourers into his harvest.	And he said to them: The harvest is great, and the laborers few: pray ye, therefore, the lord of the harvest that he would send laborers into his harvest.	And he said to them, "The harvest is great and the workers are few. Therefore, pray the Lord [of] the harvest to send out workers for his harvest.
3	Go your ways: behold, I send you forth as lambs among wolves.	Go ye: lo, I send you forth, as sheep among wolves.	Go! Behold, I send you as lambs among wolves.
4	Carry neither purse, nor scrip, nor shoes: and salute no man by the way.	Take to you no purses, nor wallets, nor shoes; and salute no man by the way.	Do not carry bags or sacks or shoes and do not greet anyone on the way.
5	And into whatsoever house ye enter, first say, Peace be to this house.	And into whatever house ye enter, first say: Peace be to this house.	And in whatever house you enter, first say, 'Peace to this house.'
6	And if the son of peace be there, your peace shall rest upon it: if not, it shall turn to you again.	And if the son of peace is there, your salutation will rest upon it; but if not, your salutation will return to you.	And if there is there a man of peace, your peace will rest on him, but if not, it will return on you.
7	And in the same house remain, eating and drinking such things as they give: for the labourer is worthy of his hire. Go not from house to house.	And remain in that house, eating and drinking of what it affords; for the laborer is worthy of his hire. And pass not from house to house.	And remain in the same house, eating and drinking from their [food], for the worker is worthy of his wage and do not move from house to house.
8	And into whatsoever city ye enter, and they receive you, eat such things as are set before you:	And into whatever city ye enter, and they receive you; eat that which set before you.	And in whatever city you enter and they receive you, eat what is placed before you.
9	And heal the sick that are therein, and say unto them, The kingdom of God is come nigh unto you.	And heal them that are sick in it; and say to them: The kingdom of God hath come near you.	And heal those who are sick in it and say to them, 'The kingdom of God has come near to you.'
10	But into whatsoever city ye enter, and they receive you not, go your ways out into the streets of the same, and say,	And into whatever city ye enter, and they receive you not; go out into the street, and say:	But in whatever city you enter and they do not receive you, go out in the marketplace and say,

Parallel Translations

	KJV	*Murdock*	*Magiera*
	LUKE	*Chapter 10*	
11	Even the very dust of your city, which cleaveth on us, we do wipe off against you: notwithstanding be ye sure of this, that the kingdom of God is come nigh unto you.	Even the dust of your city which adhereth to our feet, we shake off against you: but this know ye, that the kingdom of God hath come near to you.	'Even the dust that sticks to us on our feet from your city, we shake off against you, but know this, that the kingdom of God has come near to you.'
12	But I say unto you, that it shall be more tolerable in that day for Sodom, than for that city.	I say to you, that for Sodom there will be comfort in that day, rather than for that city.	I say to you, it will be [more] pleasant for Sodom in that day than for that city.
13	Woe unto thee, Chorazin! woe unto thee, Bethsaida! for if the mighty works had been done in Tyre and Sidon, which have been done in you, they had a great while ago repented, sitting in sackcloth and ashes.	Woe to thee, Chorazin; woe to thee, Bethsaida; for if in Tyre and Sidon there had been the mighty deeds, that were in you, they would long ago have repented in sackcloth and ashes.	Woe to you, Chorazin! Woe to you, Bethsaida! Because if the miracles that happened in you had happened in Tyre and Sidon, they would have long ago repented in sackclothes and in ash.
14	But it shall be more tolerable for Tyre and Sidon at the judgment, than for you.	But for Tyre and Sidon there will be comfort in the day of judgment, rather than for you.	But for Tyre and Sidon it will be [more] pleasant in the judgment than for you.
15	And thou, Capernaum, which art exalted to heaven, shalt be thrust down to hell.	And thou Capernaum, that art lifted up to heaven, shalt be brought down to hell.	And you, Capernaum, who are lifted up to heaven will be brought down low to Sheol.
16	He that heareth you heareth me; and he that despiseth you despiseth me; and he that despiseth me despiseth him that sent me.	He that heareth you, heareth me; and he that despiseth you, despiseth me; and he that despiseth me, despiseth him that sent me.	He who hears you hears me. And he who rejects you rejects me and he who rejects me rejects him who sent me."
17	And the seventy returned again with joy, saying, Lord, even the devils are subject unto us through thy name.	And the seventy whom he sent forth, returned with great joy, and say to him: Our Lord, even the demons were subject to us, in thy name.	And those seventy whom he had sent returned with great joy and said to him, "Our Lord, even the demons were subject to us in your name."
18	And he said unto them, I beheld Satan as lightning fall from heaven.	And he said to them: I saw Satan fall, like the lightning from heaven.	And he said to them, "I was seeing Satan fall like lightning from heaven.
19	Behold, I give unto you power to tread on serpents and scorpions, and over all the power of the enemy: and nothing shall by any means hurt you.	Behold, I give you authority to tread on serpents, and scorpions, and on all the power of the adversary: and nothing shall harm you.	Behold, I give to you authority to trample on serpents and scorpions and all the power of the enemy and nothing will hurt you.
20	Notwithstanding in this rejoice not, that the spirits are subject unto you; but rather rejoice, because your names are written in heaven.	Yet rejoice not in this, that the demons are subject to you; but rejoice, that your names are written in heaven.	But do not rejoice in this, that demons are subject to you, but rather rejoice that your names are written in heaven."
21	In that hour Jesus rejoiced in spirit, and said, I thank thee, O Father, Lord of heaven and earth, that thou hast hid these things from the wise and prudent, and hast revealed them unto babes: even so, Father; for so it seemed good in thy sight.	In that hour Jesus exulted in the Holy Spirit, and said: I thank thee, my Father, thou Lord of heaven and earth, that thou hast hid these things from the wise and intelligent, and hast revealed them to babes: yes, my Father, for such was thy good pleasure.	Immediately, Jesus was joyful in the Holy Spirit and said, "I thank you, my Father, Lord of heaven and earth, that you have hidden these [things] from wise and intelligent [ones] and have revealed them to infants, yes, my Father, because so was the will before you."

	KJV	*Murdock*	*Magiera*
	LUKE	*Chapter 10*	
22	All things are delivered to me of my Father: and no man knoweth who the Son is, but the Father; and who the Father is, but the Son, and he to whom the Son will reveal him.	And he turned himself to his disciples, and said to them: Every thing is committed to me by my Father: and no one knoweth who the Son is, but the Father; or who the Father is, but the Son, and he to whom the Son is pleased to reveal [him].	And he turned toward his disciples and said to them, "Everything is delivered to me from my Father and no man knows who is the Son, except the Father and who is the Father, except the Son and to whom the Son wants to reveal [him]?"
23	And he turned him unto his disciples, and said privately, Blessed are the eyes which see the things that ye see:	And he turned to his disciples, privately, and said: Blessed are the eyes that see, what ye see.	And he turned toward his disciples privately and said, "Blessed are the eyes that see what you see.
24	For I tell you, that many prophets and kings have desired to see those things which ye see, and have not seen them; and to hear those things which ye hear, and have not heard them.	For I say to you, that many prophets and kings desired to see what ye see, and did not see [it]; and to hear what ye hear, and did not hear [it].	For I say to you, many prophets and kings have wanted to see what you see and have not seen, and to hear what you hear and have not heard."
25	And, behold, a certain lawyer stood up, and tempted him, saying, Master, what shall I do to inherit eternal life?	And behold, a Scribe stood up to try him, and said: Teacher, what must I do, to inherit eternal life?	And behold, a certain scribe stood up to tempt him and said, "Teacher, what must I do to inherit eternal life?"
26	He said unto him, What is written in the law? how readest thou?	And Jesus said to him: How is it written in the law? How readest thou?	And Jesus said to him, "How is it written in the law? How do you read?"
27	And he answering said, Thou shalt love the Lord thy God with all thy heart, and with all thy soul, and with all thy strength, and with all thy mind; and thy neighbour as thyself.	He answered and said to him: Thou shalt love the Lord thy God, with all thy heart, and with all thy soul, and with all thy might, and with all thy mind; and thy neighbor, as thyself.	He answered and said to him: YOU SHOULD LOVE THE LORD YOUR GOD WITH ALL YOUR HEART AND WITH ALL YOUR SOUL AND WITH ALL YOUR STRENGTH AND WITH ALL YOUR MIND, and YOUR NEIGHBOR AS YOURSELF.
28	And he said unto him, Thou hast answered right: this do, and thou shalt live.	Jesus said to him: Thou hast said correctly; do thus, and thou wilt live.	Jesus said to him, "You have spoken correctly; do this and you will live."
29	But he, willing to justify himself, said unto Jesus, And who is my neighbour?	And he, being disposed to justify himself, said: And who is my neighbor?	But wanting to justify himself, he said to him, "And who is my neighbor?"
30	And Jesus answering said, A certain man went down from Jerusalem to Jericho, and fell among thieves, which stripped him of his raiment, and wounded him, and departed, leaving him half dead.	Jesus said to him: A certain man was going down from Jerusalem to Jericho, and robbers fell upon him, and plundered him, and smote him, and left him with little life in him, and went their way.	Jesus said to him, "A certain man went down from Jerusalem to Jericho, and robbers fell on him and they stripped him and beat him and left him when little life remained in him and they went away.
31	And by chance there came down a certain priest that way: and when he saw him, he passed by on the other side.	And a certain priest went down by that way; and he saw him, and passed on.	And a certain priest happened to be going down on that road and he saw him and passed by.
32	And likewise a Levite, when he was at the place, came and looked on him, and passed by on the other side.	So also a Levite came, approached the spot, and saw him, and passed on.	And so also a Levite came [and] arrived at that place and saw him and passed by.

Parallel Translations

LUKE Chapter 10

	KJV	Murdock	Magiera
33	But a certain Samaritan, as he journeyed, came where he was: and when he saw him, he had compassion on him,	But a Samaritan, as he travelled, came where he was, and saw him, and took pity on him,	Now a Samaritan man, while he was journeying, came where he was, and he saw him and had compassion on him.
34	And went to him, and bound up his wounds, pouring in oil and wine, and set him on his own beast, and brought him to an inn, and took care of him.	and went to him, and bound up his wounds, and poured wine and oil on them, and placed him upon his ass, and brought him to the inn, and took care of him.	And he came near and bandaged his wounds and poured wine and oil on them and placed him on his donkey and brought him to an inn and took care of him.
35	And on the morrow when he departed, he took out two pence, and gave them to the host, and said unto him, Take care of him; and whatsoever thou spendest more, when I come again, I will repay thee.	And on the morning of the [next] day, he took out two denarii and gave to the host, and said: Take good care of him; and if thou expendest any more, when I return, I will repay thee.	And at the break of the day he went away, he gave two denarii to the innkeeper and said to him 'Care for him. And if you spend anything more, when I return I will give [it] to you.'
36	Which now of these three, thinkest thou, was neighbour unto him that fell among the thieves?	Which therefore of these three, appears to thee, to have been neighbor to him that fell into the hands of marauders?	Therefore, which of these three seems to you to have been a neighbor to him who fell into the hands of robbers?"
37	And he said, He that shewed mercy on him. Then said Jesus unto him, Go, and do thou likewise.	And he said: He that had pity on him. Jesus said to him: Go, and do thou also the like.	And he said, "The one who had compassion on him." Jesus said to him, "Go, you should also do the same."
38	Now it came to pass, as they went, that he entered into a certain village: and a certain woman named Martha received him into her house.	And it occurred, as they travelled by the way, that he entered a certain village, and a woman whose name was Martha, received him at her house.	And it happened that while they were journeying on the road, he entered a certain village and a woman whose name [was] Martha received him into her house.
39	And she had a sister called Mary, which also sat at Jesus' feet, and heard his word.	And she had a sister whose name, was Mary: and she came and seated herself at the feet of our Lord, and listened to his discourses.	And she had a sister whose name [was] Mary. And she came [and] seated herself at the feet of our Lord and was listening to his words.
40	But Martha was cumbered about much serving, and came to him, and said, Lord, dost thou not care that my sister hath left me to serve alone? bid her therefore that she help me.	But Martha was occupied with much service; and she came, and said to him: My Lord, hast thou no concern, that my sister hath left me to serve alone? Bid her assist me.	But Martha was occupied with much service and came [and] said to him, "My Lord, do you not care that my sister has left me alone to serve? Tell her to help me."
41	And Jesus answered and said unto her, Martha, Martha, thou art careful and troubled about many things:	Jesus answered, and said to her: Martha, Martha, thou art anxious and troubled about many things:	But Jesus answered and said to her, "Martha, Martha, you are anxious and troubled about many [things].
42	But one thing is needful: and Mary hath chosen that good part, which shall not be taken away from her.	yet but one thing is necessary; and Mary hath chosen for herself the good part, which shall not be taken from her.	But there is one [thing] that is necessary and Mary has chosen that good part for herself that will not be taken from her."

Parallel Translations

LUKE *Chapter 11*

	KJV	*Murdock*	*Magiera*
1	And it came to pass, that, as he was praying in a certain place, when he ceased, one of his disciples said unto him, Lord, teach us to pray, as John also taught his disciples.	And as he was praying in a certain place, it occurred, that when he ceased, one of his disciples said to him: Our Lord, teach us to pray, as John also taught his disciples.	And it happened that while he was praying in a certain place, when he had finished, one of his disciples said to him, "Our Lord, teach us to pray, as John also taught his disciples."
2	And he said unto them, When ye pray, say, Our Father which art in heaven, Hallowed be thy name. Thy kingdom come. Thy will be done, as in heaven, so in earth.	Jesus said to them: When ye pray, thus speak ye: Our Father who art in heaven, hallow be thy name; thy kingdom come; thy pleasure be done, as in heaven, so on earth;	Jesus said to them, "When you pray, you should speak so: Our Father who is in heaven, your name will be made holy, your kingdom will come, your desire will occur, as in heaven, even also on earth.
3	Give us day by day our daily bread.	give us daily the bread we need;	Give us the bread of our necessity every day,
4	And forgive us our sins; for we also forgive every one that is indebted to us. And lead us not into temptation; but deliver us from evil.	and remit to us our sins, for we also remit to all that are indebted to us; and bring us not into trials, but deliver us from evil.	and forgive us [of] our sins, for we also forgive all who have wronged us. And do not let us enter into temptation, but deliver us from the Evil [one]."
5	And he said unto them, Which of you shall have a friend, and shall go unto him at midnight, and say unto him, Friend, lend me three loaves;	And he said to them: Which of you shall have a friend, that shall come to him at midnight and say to him, My friend, lend me three cakes;	And he said to them, "Who is among you who has a friend and would go to him at midnight and say to him, 'My friend, lend me three loaves,
6	For a friend of mine in his journey is come to me, and I have nothing to set before him?	for a friend hath come to me from a journey, and I have nothing to set before him?	because a friend has come to me from a journey and I have nothing to place before him;'
7	And he from within shall answer and say, Trouble me not: the door is now shut, and my children are with me in bed; I cannot rise and give thee.	And his friend within shall answer, and say to him: Do not disturb me, for lo, the door is closed, and my children with me in bed; I cannot rise and give thee.	and his friend would answer from within and say to him, 'Do not trouble me, for behold, the door is shut and my children are with me in bed. I am not able to rise and give to you.'
8	I say unto you, Though he will not rise and give him, because he is his friend, yet because of his importunity he will rise and give him as many as he needeth.	I say to you: If he give him not, on account of friendship, yet on account of [his] importunity, he will arise and give [him] as much as he asketh.	I say to you, if on account of friendship he will not give to him, because of his persistence, he will rise up and give to him as much as is needed by him.
9	And I say unto you, Ask, and it shall be given you; seek, and ye shall find; knock, and it shall be opened unto you.	I say also to you: Ask, and it will be given you; seek, and ye will find; knock, and it will be opened to you.	I say to you also, 'Ask and it will be given to you, seek and you will find, knock and it will be opened to you,'
10	For every one that asketh receiveth; and he that seeketh findeth; and to him that knocketh it shall be opened.	For every one that asketh, receiveth; and he that seeketh, findeth; and to him that knocketh, it is opened.	for everyone who asks will receive and whoever seeks will find and who knocks, it will be opened to him.
11	If a son shall ask bread of any of you that is a father, will he give him a stone? or if he ask a fish, will he for a fish give him a serpent?	For which of you being a father, if his son shall ask him for bread, will he reach to him a stone? Or, if he ask of him a fish, will he, instead of a fish, reach to him a serpent?	For what father among you whose son asks him for bread will offer him a stone? And if he asks him for a fish, instead of a fish will he offer him a serpent?

Parallel Translations

	KJV	Murdock	Magiera
	LUKE *Chapter 11*		
12	Or if he shall ask an egg, will he offer him a scorpion?	Or, if he ask of him an egg, will he reach to him a scorpion?	And if he asks him for an egg, will he offer him a scorpion?
13	If ye then, being evil, know how to give good gifts unto your children: how much more shall your heavenly Father give the Holy Spirit to them that ask him?	And if ye, who are evil, know how to give good gifts to your children, how much more will your Father from heaven give the Holy Spirit to them that ask him?	And if you who are evil know to give good gifts to your children, how much more will your Father from heaven give the Holy Spirit to those who ask him?"
14	And he was casting out a devil, and it was dumb. And it came to pass, when the devil was gone out, the dumb spake; and the people wondered.	And as he was casting out a demon that was dumb, it occurred, that when the demon had gone out, the dumb [man] conversed: and the multitudes admired.	And as he was casting out a demon because he was dumb, it occurred that after that demon went out that dumb [man] spoke and the crowds were amazed.
15	But some of them said, He casteth out devils through Beelzebub the chief of the devils.	But some of them said: It is by Beelzebub, the prince of demons, that he casteth out demons.	And some of them said, "This [man] casts out devils by Beelzebub, the prince of devils."
16	And others, tempting him, sought of him a sign from heaven.	And others, to tempt him, asked of him a sign from heaven.	And others, tempting him, were asking him for a sign from heaven.
17	But he, knowing their thoughts, said unto them, Every kingdom divided against itself is brought to desolation; and a house divided against a house falleth.	But Jesus, as he knew their thoughts, said to them: Every kingdom that is divided against itself, will become a desolation: and a house that is divided against itself, will fall.	But Jesus, who knew their thoughts, said to them, "Every kingdom that is divided against itself will be ruined and a house that is separated from its essential [foundation] will fall.
18	If Satan also be divided against himself, how shall his kingdom stand? because ye say that I cast out devils through Beelzebub.	And if Satan be divided against himself, how will his kingdom stand? since ye say, that I by Beelzebub cast out demons.	And if Satan is divided against himself, how will his kingdom stand? For you say that I cast out devils by Beelzebub.
19	And if I by Beelzebub cast out devils, by whom do your sons cast them out? therefore shall they be your judges.	And if I, by Beelzebub, cast out demons, by whom do your sons cast [them] out? Therefore will they be to you judges.	And if I cast out devils by Beelzebub, by whom do your sons cast [them] out? Because of this, they will be judges to you.
20	But if I with the finger of God cast out devils, no doubt the kingdom of God is come upon you.	But if I, by the finger of God, cast out demons, the kingdom of God hath come near to you.	But if I cast out devils by the finger of God, the kingdom of God has come near to you.
21	When a strong man armed keepeth his palace, his goods are in peace:	When a strong man armed keepeth his doorway, his property rests securely.	When a strong man, being armed, guards his courtyard, his property is in quietness.
22	But when a stronger than he shall come upon him, and overcome him, he taketh from him all his armour wherein he trusted, and divideth his spoils.	But if a stronger than he come and overpower him, he taketh away all his arms on which he relied, and divideth the spoil of him.	But if one who is stronger than him should come, he will conquer him [and] he will capture all of his armor on which he had relied and he will distribute his spoil.
23	He that is not with me is against me: and he that gathereth not with me scattereth.	He that is not for me, is against me; and he that gathereth not with me, actually scattereth.	He who is not with me is against me and he who does not gather with me actually scatters.

	KJV	Murdock	Magiera
24	When the unclean spirit is gone out of a man, he walketh through dry places, seeking rest; and finding none, he saith, I will return unto my house whence I came out.	An unclean spirit, when he goeth out of a man, goeth wandering in places where no water is, in order to find rest; and, as he cannot find [it] he saith: I will return to my habitation, from which I came.	When an unclean spirit leaves a man, it goes [and] wanders around in places in which there is no water to seek rest for itself. And when it does not find [rest], it says, "I will return to my house from where I left."
25	And when he cometh, he findeth it swept and garnished.	And when he cometh, he findeth it swept clean and set in order.	And if it comes [and] finds that it is swept and furnished,
26	Then goeth he, and taketh to him seven other spirits more wicked than himself; and they enter in, and dwell there: and the last state of that man is worse than the first.	Then he goeth and taketh seven other spirits, worse than himself, and they enter in and dwell there; and the last state of that man is worse than the first.	then it goes [and] leads seven other spirits more evil that it and they enter and live there and the end [state] of that man becomes worse than his first [state]."
27	And it came to pass, as he spake these things, a certain woman of the company lifted up her voice, and said unto him, Blessed is the womb that bare thee, and the paps which thou hast sucked.	And while he was saying these things, a certain woman from the crowd, lifted up her voice, and said to him: Blessed is the womb that carried thee, and the breasts that nursed thee.	And while he was speaking these [things], a certain woman raised up her voice from the crowd and said to him, "Blessed is the womb that bore you and the breasts that nursed you."
28	But he said, Yea rather, blessed are they that hear the word of God, and keep it.	He said to her: Blessed are they who hear the word of God, and keep it.	He said to her, "Blessed are those who have heard the word of God and keep it."
29	And when the people were gathered thick together, he began to say, This is an evil generation: they seek a sign; and there shall no sign be given it, but the sign of Jonas the prophet.	And when multitudes were assembled, he began to say: This evil generation seeketh a sign; and no sign will be given it, but the sign of Jonah the prophet.	And when the crowds were gathered, he began to say, "This evil generation seeks a sign and a sign will not be given to it, except the sign of Jonah the prophet.
30	For as Jonas was a sign unto the Ninevites, so shall also the Son of man be to this generation.	For as Jonah was a sign to the Ninevites, so also will the Son of man be a sign to this generation.	For as Jonah was a sign to the Ninevites, so also the Son of Man will be [a sign] to this generation.
31	The queen of the south shall rise up in the judgment with the men of this generation, and condemn them: for she came from the utmost parts of the earth to hear the wisdom of Solomon; and, behold, a greater than Solomon is here.	The queen of the south will stand up in the judgment with the men of this generation, and will condemn them; for she came from the other side of the earth, to hear the wisdom of Solomon, and lo, one superior to Solomon is here.	The queen of the south will stand in the judgment concerning the men of this generation and will condemn them, because she came from the far sides of the earth to hear the wisdom of Solomon, and behold, one who is greater than Solomon [is] here.
32	The men of Nineve shall rise up in the judgment with this generation, and shall condemn it: for they repented at the preaching of Jonas; and, behold, a greater than Jonas is here.	The men of Nineveh will stand up in the judgment with this generation, and will condemn it; for they repented at the preaching of Jonah, and lo, one superior to Jonah is here.	The Ninevite men will stand in the judgment concerning this generation and will condemn it, because they repented at the preaching of Jonah, and behold, one who is greater than Jonah [is] here.

Parallel Translations

LUKE *Chapter 11*

	KJV	*Murdock*	*Magiera*
33	No man, when he hath lighted a candle, putteth it in a secret place, neither under a bushel, but on a candlestick, that they which come in may see the light.	No one lighteth a lamp, and putteth it in a secret place, or under a bushel, but upon a light-stand; that they who come in, may see its light.	No one lights a lamp and places it in a hidden place or under a basket, but rather [he places it] on a lamp stand, so that those who enter will see its light.
34	The light of the body is the eye: therefore when thine eye is single, thy whole body also is full of light; but when thine eye is evil, thy body also is full of darkness.	The lamp of thy body is thy eye. Therefore, when thy eye is sound, thy whole body will be enlightened; but if it be bad, thy body also will be dark.	The lamp of your body is the eye. So when your eye is simple, your whole body will also be lightened. But if it is evil, your [whole] body will also be darkened.
35	Take heed therefore that the light which is in thee be not darkness.	See to it, therefore, lest the light that is in thee, be darkness.	Therefore, beware that the light that is in you is not darkness.
36	If thy whole body therefore be full of light, having no part dark, the whole shall be full of light, as when the bright shining of a candle doth give thee light.	For if thy whole body be enlightened, and no part in it be dark, the whole will be luminous, as if a lamp enlightened thee by its radiance.	Now if your whole body is lightened and does not have any dark portion, all of it will be giving light, as a lamp by its flame gives you light."
37	And as he spake, a certain Pharisee besought him to dine with him: and he went in, and sat down to meat.	And while he was speaking, a certain Pharisee requested him to dine with him: and he went in, and reclined.	And while he was speaking, a certain Pharisee asked him to eat with him and he entered [and] sat to eat.
38	And when the Pharisee saw it, he marvelled that he had not first washed before dinner.	And the Pharisee noticing him, wondered that he did not previously baptize before dinner.	And that Pharisee, when he saw him, was amazed that he had not washed first before his meal.
39	And the Lord said unto him, Now do ye Pharisees make clean the outside of the cup and the platter; but your inward part is full of ravening and wickedness.	And Jesus said to him: Now ye Pharisees make clean the exterior of the cup and the dish; but your interior is full of extortion and wickedness.	And Jesus said to him, "Now you Pharisees cleanse the outside of the cup and of the dish, but your inside is full of rape and evil.
40	Ye fools, did not he that made that which is without make that which is within also?	Ye deficient in understanding! did not he who made the exterior, make also the interior?	Fools! Did not he who made the outside also make the inside?
41	But rather give alms of such things as ye have; and, behold, all things are clean unto you.	But, give ye alms from what ye possess; and lo, every thing will be clean to you.	But what you have, give in alms, and behold, everything will be clean to you.
42	But woe unto you, Pharisees! for ye tithe mint and rue and all manner of herbs, and pass over judgment and the love of God: these ought ye to have done, and not to leave the other undone.	But woe to you, Pharisees! for ye tithe mint and rue, and every pot-herb; but pass over justice and the love of God. Now ye ought to do these things, and not to omit those.	But woe to you, Pharisees, because you tithe of mint and rue and every herb, yet you pass over justice and the love of God. Now these [things] you ought to do and these [things] you should not leave out.
43	Woe unto you, Pharisees! for ye love the uppermost seats in the synagogues, and greetings in the markets.	Woe to you, Pharisees! who love the chief seats in the synagogues, and a salutation in the streets.	Woe to you, Pharisees, because you love the chief seats in the synagogues and a greeting in the streets.
44	Woe unto you, scribes and Pharisees, hypocrites! for ye are as graves which appear not, and the men that walk over them are not aware of them.	Woe to you, Scribes and Pharisees, hypocrites! for ye are like graves that are unknown, and men walk over them and do not know [it].	Woe to you, scribes and Pharisees, hypocrites, because you are like graves that are unknown and men walk over them and do not know [it]."

Parallel Translations

	KJV	*Murdock*	*Magiera*
LUKE	*Chapter 11*		
45	Then answered one of the lawyers, and said unto him, Master, thus saying thou reproachest us also.	And one of the Scribes replied, and said to him: Teacher, while saying these things, thou reproachest us also.	And one of the scribes answered and said to him, "Teacher, when you say these [things], you reproach us also."
46	And he said, Woe unto you also, ye lawyers! for ye lade men with burdens grievous to be borne, and ye yourselves touch not the burdens with one of your fingers.	And he said: Woe to you also! ye Scribes, who lade men with heavy burdens; yet ye yourselves will not touch those burdens with one of your fingers.	And he said, "Woe also to you, scribes, because you make men carry heavy burdens, yet you do not touch the burdens with one of your fingers.
47	Woe unto you! for ye build the sepulchres of the prophets, and your fathers killed them.	Woe to you! who build the sepulchres of the prophets, whom your fathers slew.	Woe to you, because you build tombs for the prophets whom your fathers killed.
48	Truly ye bear witness that ye allow the deeds of your fathers: for they indeed killed them, and ye build their sepulchres.	Thus ye testify, that ye acquiesce in the deeds of your fathers; for they slew them, and ye build their sepulchres.	Therefore, you bear witness to and approve of the works of your fathers, because they killed them and you build their graves.
49	Therefore also said the wisdom of God, I will send them prophets and apostles, and some of them they shall slay and persecute:	Therefore hath wisdom said: Lo, I will send to them prophets and legates; and some of them they will persecute and slay;	Because of this, the wisdom of God also said, 'Behold, I will send them prophets and apostles, some of whom they will persecute and kill,'
50	That the blood of all the prophets, which was shed from the foundation of the world, may be required of this generation;	that from this generation may be required, the blood of all the prophets, which hath been shed since the world was created;	so that the blood of all the prophets that was shed from when the world was established will be required from this generation,
51	From the blood of Abel unto the blood of Zacharias, which perished between the altar and the temple: verily I say unto you, It shall be required of this generation.	from the blood of Abel, to the blood of Zachariah who was slain between the temple and the altar. Yea, say I to you: It will be required of this generation.	from the blood of Abel up to the blood of Zacharias, who was killed between the temple [and] the altar, yes, I say to you, it will be required from this generation.
52	Woe unto you, lawyers! for ye have taken away the key of knowledge: ye entered not in yourselves, and them that were entering in ye hindered.	Woe to you, Scribes; for ye have taken away the keys of knowledge: ye yourselves enter not, and them that are entering ye hinder.	Woe to you, scribes, because you have taken away the keys of knowledge. You have not entered and you have hindered those who were entering."
53	And as he said these things unto them, the scribes and the Pharisees began to urge him vehemently, and to provoke him to speak of many things:	And when he had said these things to them, the Scribes and Pharisees began to be offended, and became angry, and carped at his discourses,	And while he was speaking these [things] to them, the scribes and Pharisees began to be offended and they grew angry and were criticizing his words.
54	Laying wait for him, and seeking to catch something out of his mouth, that they might accuse him.	and practised many wiles upon him, seeking to catch some thing from his lips, that they might accuse him.	And they were plotting against him in many [ways], seeking to catch something from his mouth in order to be able to accuse him.

LUKE *Chapter 12*

	KJV	*Murdock*	*Magiera*
1	In the mean time, when there were gathered together an innumerable multitude of people, insomuch that they trode one upon another, he began to say unto his disciples first of all, Beware ye of the leaven of the Pharisees, which is hypocrisy.	And when great multitudes were assembled by myriads, so that they trod one upon another, Jesus began to say to his disciples: First of all, beware for yourselves of that leaven of the Pharisees, which is hypocrisy.	And when very large crowds were gathered, so that they were trampling one another, Jesus began to say to his disciples, "First, beware among yourselves of the leaven of the Pharisees, which is hypocrisy.
2	For there is nothing covered, that shall not be revealed; neither hid, that shall not be known.	For there is nothing hidden, which will not be revealed; nor concealed, that will not be known.	And there is not anything that is covered that will not be revealed or that is hidden that will not be known.
3	Therefore whatsoever ye have spoken in darkness shall be heard in the light; and that which ye have spoken in the ear in closets shall be proclaimed upon the housetops.	For whatever ye speak in the dark, will be heard in the light; and what in secret chambers, ye whisper in the ear, will be proclaimed on the house-tops.	For everything that you speak in darkness will be heard in the light, and what you murmur in closets into ears will be proclaimed on the roofs.
4	And I say unto you my friends, Be not afraid of them that kill the body, and after that have no more that they can do.	And to you, my friends, I say: Be not afraid of them that kill the body, and afterwards have nothing more they can do.	And I say to you, my friends, 'Do not fear those who kill the body and afterwards have nothing more to do.'
5	But I will forewarn you whom ye shall fear: Fear him, which after he hath killed hath power to cast into hell; yea, I say unto you, Fear him.	But I will show you, of whom to be afraid: of him who, after he hath killed, hath authority to cast into hell. Yea, say I to you: be afraid of him.	But I will show you whom you should fear, him who after he has killed, has authority to send into Gehenna, yes, I say to you, 'Fear this [one].'
6	Are not five sparrows sold for two farthings, and not one of them is forgotten before God?	Are not five sparrows sold for two assarii? and not one of them is forgotten before God.	Are not five birds sold for two coins? And one of them is not forgotten before God.
7	But even the very hairs of your head are all numbered. Fear not therefore: ye are of more value than many sparrows.	And as for you, the very hairs of your head are all numbered. Fear not, therefore; for ye are superior to many sparrows.	But even the separate hairs of your head are all numbered. Do not fear, therefore, because you are more valuable than a multitude of birds.
8	Also I say unto you, Whosoever shall confess me before men, him shall the Son of man also confess before the angels of God:	And I say to you, that every one that shall confess me before men, the Son of man will also confess him before the angels of God.	And I say to you, whoever will confess me before men, the Son of Man also will confess him before the angels of God.
9	But he that denieth me before men shall be denied before the angels of God.	But he that shall deny me before men, shall himself be denied before the angels of God.	But he who denies me before men will be denied himself before the angels of God.
10	And whosoever shall speak a word against the Son of man, it shall be forgiven him: but unto him that blasphemeth against the Holy Ghost it shall not be forgiven.	And every one that shall speak a word against the Son of man, it shall be forgiven him: but he that shall reproach the Holy Spirit, it will not be forgiven him.	And whoever speaks a word against the Son of Man will be forgiven, but he who blasphemes against the Holy Spirit will not be forgiven.
11	And when they bring you unto the synagogues, and unto magistrates, and powers, take ye no thought how or what thing ye shall answer, or what ye shall say:	And when they shall bring you into the synagogues, before chiefs and men in authority, be not anxious how ye shall make defence, or what ye shall say;	And when they bring you to the synagogues before chiefs and rulers, do not be anxious how you should answer or what you should say,

Parallel Translations

	KJV	Murdock	Magiera
	LUKE *Chapter 12*		
12	For the Holy Ghost shall teach you in the same hour what ye ought to say.	for the Holy Spirit will, in that hour, instruct you what to say.	for the Holy Spirit will teach you at that moment what you ought to say."
13	And one of the company said unto him, Master, speak to my brother, that he divide the inheritance with me.	And one of the assembly said to him: Teacher, tell my brother, to divide the inheritance with me.	And one of that crowd said to him, "Teacher, tell my brother to divide the inheritance with me."
14	And he said unto him, Man, who made me a judge or a divider over you?	But Jesus said to him: Man, who established me a judge and distributor over you?	And Jesus said to him, "Man, who set me [as] a judge and distributor over you?"
15	And he said unto them, Take heed, and beware of covetousness: for a man's life consisteth not in the abundance of the things which he possesseth.	And he said to his disciples: Beware of all avarice, for life consisteth not in abundance of riches.	And he said to his disciples, "Beware of all greediness, because life is not in the abundance of possessions."
16	And he spake a parable unto them, saying, The ground of a certain rich man brought forth plentifully:	And he spoke to them a similitude: The land of a certain rich man brought forth produce in abundance.	And he spoke a parable to them, "A certain rich man's land brought to him many crops.
17	And he thought within himself, saying, What shall I do, because I have no room where to bestow my fruits?	And he considered with himself, and said: What shall I do; for I have not where I can store up my produce?	And he thought within himself and said, 'What shall I do, because I do not have anywhere I can gather in my crops?'
18	And he said, This will I do: I will pull down my barns, and build greater; and there will I bestow all my fruits and my goods.	And he said : This will I do; I will pull down my storehouses, and build them larger; and there will I store up all my corn and my good things:	And he said, 'I will do this. I will pull down my storehouses and I will build and enlarge them and I will gather in there all my harvest and my goods.'
19	And I will say to my soul, Soul, thou hast much goods laid up for many years; take thine ease, eat, drink, and be merry.	and I will say to my soul: My soul, thou hast good things in abundance, which are stored up for many years; take thy ease; eat, drink, and live in pleasure.	And I will say to my soul, 'My soul, you have many goods that are laid up for many years. Take rest, eat, drink [and] be merry.'
20	But God said unto him, Thou fool, this night thy soul shall be required of thee: then whose shall those things be, which thou hast provided?	But God said to him: Thou void of reason! This night, thy soul will be required of thee; and to whom will belong these things provided by thee?	But God said to him, 'Fool! In this night they will require your soul from you, and those [things] that you have prepared, for whom will they be?'
21	So is he that layeth up treasure for himself, and is not rich toward God.	Such is he that layeth up treasures for himself, and is not rich in God.	So is he who lays up for himself treasures and does not abound in God."
22	And he said unto his disciples, Therefore I say unto you, Take no thought for your life, what ye shall eat; neither for the body, what ye shall put on.	And he said to his disciples: Therefore I tell you, Be not anxious for your life, what ye shall eat; nor for your body, what ye shall put on.	And he said to his disciples, "Because of this, I say to you, do not be anxious for yourselves, what you will eat or for your body, what you will wear,
23	The life is more than meat, and the body is more than raiment.	For the life is more important than food, and the body than raiment.	for the soul is more than food, and the body than clothes.

Parallel Translations

LUKE *Chapter 12*

	KJV	Murdock	Magiera
24	Consider the ravens: for they neither sow nor reap; which neither have storehouse nor barn; and God feedeth them: how much more are ye better than the fowls?	Consider the ravens, which sow not, nor reap, nor have cellars and storehouses; yet God provideth them food. How much more important now are ye, than the birds!	Consider the ravens, for they neither sow nor reap and they do not have rooms and storehouses, yet God provides for them. Therefore, how much more important are you than birds?
25	And which of you with taking thought can add to his stature one cubit?	And which of you, by taking pains, can add one cubit to his stature?	And which of you, being anxious, is able to add one cubit to his stature?
26	If ye then be not able to do that thing which is least, why take ye thought for the rest?	And if ye are impotent for that which is least, why are ye anxious about the rest?	And if you are not even capable of a small [thing], why are you anxious about the rest?
27	Consider the lilies how they grow: they toil not, they spin not; and yet I say unto you, that Solomon in all his glory was not arrayed like one of these.	Consider the lilies, how they grow: they toil not, nor do they spin. Yet I say to you, that not even Solomon in all his glory, was clothed like one of these.	Consider how the lilies grow, for they neither labor nor spin, but I say to you, not even Solomon in all his glory was covered as one of these.
28	If then God so clothe the grass, which is to day in the field, and to morrow is cast into the oven; how much more will he clothe you, O ye of little faith?	And if God so clothe the herb, which to-day exists in the field, and to-morrow falls into the oven, how much more you, ye little in faith?	And if God so clothes the grass that today is in the field and tomorrow falls into the oven, how much more you, [oh] little of faith?
29	And seek not ye what ye shall eat, or what ye shall drink, neither be ye of doubtful mind.	And inquire not, what ye shall eat, or what ye shall drink; nor let your mind wander upon these things.	And you should not seek what you will eat and what you will drink and your mind should not wander in these [things].
30	For all these things do the nations of the world seek after: and your Father knoweth that ye have need of these things.	For all these things the people of the world seek after; and your father knoweth that, for you also, these things are needful.	For all these [things] the Gentiles of the world seek. Now your Father also knows that these [things] are necessary for you.
31	But rather seek ye the kingdom of God; and all these things shall be added unto you.	But seek ye the kingdom of God, and all these things will be added to you.	But seek the kingdom of God and all these [things] will be added to you.
32	Fear not, little flock; for it is your Father's good pleasure to give you the kingdom.	Fear not, little flock; for your Father is disposed to give you the kingdom.	Do not fear, little flock, because your Father wants to give you the kingdom.
33	Sell that ye have, and give alms; provide yourselves bags which wax not old, a treasure in the heavens that faileth not, where no thief approacheth, neither moth corrupteth.	Sell your property, and give alms: make for yourselves bags that do not become old, and a treasure that is not transient, in the heavens; where no thief approacheth, and no moth eateth.	Sell your possessions and give alms. Make for yourselves bags that do not grow old and a treasure that does not fail in heaven, where a thief does not approach and moth does not corrupt.
34	For where your treasure is, there will your heart be also.	For where your treasure is, there also will your heart be.	For wherever your treasure is, there will your heart be also.
35	Let your loins be girded about, and your lights burning;	Let your loins be girded, and your lamps burning.	Your loins should be girded and your lamps lit.
36	And ye yourselves like unto men that wait for their lord, when he will return from the wedding; that when he cometh and knocketh, they may open unto him immediately.	And be ye like persons who are waiting for their lord, when he shall return from the house of feasting, that, when he shall come and knock, they may open to him immediately.	And you should be like men who wait for their lord at that time when he returns from the wedding feast, so that when he comes and knocks, they may immediately open [the door] for him.

	KJV	Murdock	Magiera
	LUKE	*Chapter 12*	
37	Blessed are those servants, whom the lord when he cometh shall find watching: verily I say unto you, that he shall gird himself, and make them to sit down to meat, and will come forth and serve them.	Happy are those servants, whom their lord, when he cometh, shall find so doing. Verily I say to you: He will gird his loins, and make them recline, and will pass around and serve them.	Blessed are those servants whose lord comes and finds them awake. Truly I say to you, he will gird up his loins and cause them to sit to eat and will cross over [and] serve them.
38	And if he shall come in the second watch, or come in the third watch, and find them so, blessed are those servants.	And if in the second watch, or in the third, he shall come and so find [them], happy are those servants.	And if he comes in the second or third watch and finds [them] so, blessed are those servants.
39	And this know, that if the goodman of the house had known what hour the thief would come, he would have watched, and not have suffered his house to be broken through.	And this know ye, that if the lord of the house had known at what watch the thief would come, he would have been awake and would not have suffered his house to be broken into.	Now know this, that if the lord of the house had known in what watch the thief would come, he would have watched and would not have allowed his house to be broken into.
40	Be ye therefore ready also: for the Son of man cometh at an hour when ye think not.	Therefore be ye also ready; for at an hour that ye think not, the Son of man cometh.	Therefore, you should also be prepared, because the Son of Man will come at that moment that you do not expect."
41	Then Peter said unto him, Lord, speakest thou this parable unto us, or even to all?	Simon Cephas saith to him: Our Lord, speakest thou this similitude to us, or also to all men?	Simon Peter said to him, "Our Lord, do you speak this parable to us or also to everyone?"
42	And the Lord said, Who then is that faithful and wise steward, whom his lord shall make ruler over his household, to give them their portion of meat in due season?	Jesus said to him: Who then is that faithful and wise steward, whom his lord will place over all his domestics, to give them their portion in due time?	Jesus said to him, "Who indeed is the faithful and wise steward, whose lord will place him over his service that he should give [him] a measured portion in its time?
43	Blessed is that servant, whom his lord when he cometh shall find so doing.	Happy is that servant whom his lord, when he cometh, shall find so doing.	Blessed is that servant whose lord comes [and] finds that he does so.
44	Of a truth I say unto you, that he will make him ruler over all that he hath.	Verily I say to you: He will place him over all his possessions.	Truly I say to you, he will place him over all his possessions.
45	But and if that servant say in his heart, My lord delayeth his coming; and shall begin to beat the menservants and maidens, and to eat and drink, and to be drunken;	But if that servant shall say in his heart, My lord delayeth his coming; and shall begin to smite the servants and the maidens of his lord; and shall begin to eat and to drink and be drunk;	But if that servant says in his heart, 'My lord delays to come,' and begins to beat the servants and the handmaids of his lord and begins to eat and to drink and to be drunk,
46	The lord of that servant will come in a day when he looketh not for him, and at an hour when he is not aware, and will cut him in sunder, and will appoint him his portion with the unbelievers.	the lord of that servant will come in a day he thinketh not, and in an hour he knoweth not, and will cut him in two; and will assign him his portion with them that are unfaithful.	the lord of that servant will come in a day that he does not expect and in an hour that he does not know and will separate him and place his lot with those who are not faithful.
47	And that servant, which knew his lord's will, and prepared not himself, neither did according to his will, shall be beaten with many stripes.	And the servant that knew his lord's pleasure, and did not prepare for him according to his pleasure, shall be beaten with many [stripes].	And the servant, who knows the will of his lord and does not prepare for him according to his will, will be beaten with many [stripes].

Parallel Translations

	KJV	Murdock	Magiera
	LUKE	*Chapter 12*	
48	But he that knew not, and did commit things worthy of stripes, shall be beaten with few stripes. For unto whomsoever much is given, of him shall be much required: and to whom men have committed much, of him they will ask the more.	But he that knew not, yet did that which deserved stripes, shall be beaten with few stripes. For to whomsoever much is given, from him will much be required; and to whom much is committed, the more will be required at his hand.	But he who did not know, yet did something that was worthy of stripes, will be beaten with a few stripes, for anyone who is given much, much is required, and to whom they have committed much, they will require more by his hand.
49	I am come to send fire on the earth; and what will I, if it be already kindled?	I have come to cast fire on the earth; and I would, that it already burned.	I have come to send fire on the earth and I want to. Oh that it was already kindled!
50	But I have a baptism to be baptized with; and how am I straitened till it be accomplished!	And I have a baptism to be baptized with; and I am much pressed until it be accomplished.	And I have a baptism that I am baptized [with] and I am greatly pressured, until it is fulfilled.
51	Suppose ye that I am come to give peace on earth? I tell you, Nay; but rather division:	Suppose ye, that I have come to produce tranquillity on the earth? I tell you, No: but division.	Do you think that I have come to bring harmony on earth? I say to you, 'No, but rather division.'
52	For from henceforth there shall be five in one house divided, three against two, and two against three.	For from this time, there will be five [persons] in one house, who will be divided, three against two, and two against three.	For from now on, there will be five in one house who are divided, three against two and two against three.
53	The father shall be divided against the son, and the son against the father; the mother against the daughter, and the daughter against the mother; the mother in law against her daughter in law, and the daughter in law against her mother in law.	For a father will be divided against his son, and a son against his father; a mother against her daughter, and a daughter against her mother; a mother-in-law against her daughter-in-law, and a daughter-in-law against her mother-in-law.	For father will be divided against his son and son against his father, mother against her daughter, and daughter against her mother, mother-in-law against her daughter-in-law, and daughter-in-law against her mother-in-law."
54	And he said also to the people, When ye see a cloud rise out of the west, straightway ye say, There cometh a shower; and so it is.	And he said to the multitudes: When you see a cloud rising out of the west, ye at once say: Rain is coming; and it is so.	And he said to the crowds, "When you see a cloud that rises from the west immediately you say, 'Rain will come,' and it happens so.
55	And when ye see the south wind blow, ye say, There will be heat; and it cometh to pass.	And when a south wind bloweth, ye say: It will be hot: and it is so.	And when the south [wind] blows, you say, 'There will be heat,' and it happens.
56	Ye hypocrites, ye can discern the face of the sky and of the earth; but how is it that ye do not discern this time?	Ye hypocrites, ye know how to distinguish the aspect of the heavens and the earth; and why can ye not distinguish the present time?	Hypocrites! You know [how] to distinguish the appearance of the earth and of heaven. So how do you not distinguish this time?
57	Yea, and why even of yourselves judge ye not what is right?	And why do ye not, of yourselves, judge correctly?	And why of yourselves do you not judge [with] truthfulness?
58	When thou goest with thine adversary to the magistrate, as thou art in the way, give diligence that thou mayest be delivered from him; lest he hale thee to the judge, and the judge deliver thee to the officer, and the officer cast thee into prison.	And when thou goest with thy adversary to the ruler, while on the way, make effort to be released by him; lest he bring thee to the judge and the judge deliver thee to the exactor, and the exactor cast thee into prison.	For when you go with your adversary to the ruler, while you are on the road, make terms [with him] and be quit of him, so that he will not conduct you to the judge and the judge deliver you to the official and the official cast you in prison.

	KJV	Murdock	Magiera
	LUKE *Chapter 12*		
59	I tell thee, thou shalt not depart thence, till thou hast paid the very last mite.	For verily I say to thee: Thou wilt not come out thence, until thou pay the last mite.	And I say to you, you will not leave there until you give back the last coin."
	Chapter 13		
1	There were present at that season some that told him of the Galilaeans, whose blood Pilate had mingled with their sacrifices.	And at that time, some came and told him of those Galileans, whose blood Pilate had mingled with their sacrifices.	Now at that time, men came [and] told him about those Galileans, whose blood Pilate had mingled with their sacrifices.
2	And Jesus answering said unto them, Suppose ye that these Galilaeans were sinners above all the Galilaeans, because they suffered such things?	And Jesus replied, and said to them: Suppose ye, that these Galileans were sinners beyond all the Galileans, because this occurred to them?	And Jesus answered and said to them, "Do you think that these Galileans were sinners more than all the Galileans because it happened to them so?
3	I tell you, Nay: but, except ye repent, ye shall all likewise perish.	No. And I say to you, That all of you also, unless ye repent, will likewise perish.	No! And I say to you, but all of you will also be destroyed likewise, [if] you do [not] repent.
4	Or those eighteen, upon whom the tower in Siloam fell, and slew them, think ye that they were sinners above all men that dwelt in Jerusalem?	Or those eighteen, on whom the tower in Siloam fell, and slew them, suppose ye, that they were sinners beyond all the men inhabiting Jerusalem?	Or those eighteen, on whom the tower fell in Siloam and killed them, do you think that they were sinners more than all the men who lived in Jerusalem?
5	I tell you, Nay: but, except ye repent, ye shall all likewise perish.	No. And I say to you, That except ye repent, ye like them will all of you perish.	No! And I say to you, except all of you repent like them, you will be destroyed."
6	He spake also this parable; A certain man had a fig tree planted in his vineyard; and he came and sought fruit thereon, and found none.	And he spoke this similitude: A man had a fig-tree that was planted in his vineyard: and he came, seeking fruits upon it, and found none.	And he spoke this parable, "A man had a fig tree that was planted in his vineyard, and he came [and] looked on it for fruit and did not find [any].
7	Then said he unto the dresser of his vineyard, Behold, these three years I come seeking fruit on this fig tree, and find none: cut it down; why cumbereth it the ground?	And he said to the cultivator: Lo, these three years, I have come seeking fruits on this fig-tree, and I find none. Cut it down: why should it cumber the ground?	And he said to the laborer, 'Behold, [for] three years I have come [and] I looked for fruit on this fig tree and I have not found [any]. Cut it down. Why should the ground be wasted?'
8	And he answering said unto him, Lord, let it alone this year also, till I shall dig about it, and dung it:	The cultivator said to him: My Lord, spare it this year also, until I shall work about it, and manure it.	The laborer said to him, 'My lord, leave it even this year, until I work with it and manure it
9	And if it bear fruit, well: and if not, then after that thou shalt cut it down.	And if it bear fruits, [well;] and if not, thou wilt cut it down: why should it live?	and perhaps it will produce fruit. Yet if not, next year you may cut it down.'"
10	And he was teaching in one of the synagogues on the sabbath.	And when Jesus was teaching in one of the synagogues, on the sabbath,	And while Jesus was teaching on the Sabbath in one of the synagogues,
11	And, behold, there was a woman which had a spirit of infirmity eighteen years, and was bowed together, and could in no wise lift up herself.	a woman was there who had had a spirit of infirmity eighteen years; and she was bent over, and could not straighten herself at all.	there was a woman there who had had a spirit of infirmity [for] eighteen years and she was bent over and was not able to straighten at all.

LUKE *Chapter 13*

	KJV	Murdock	Magiera
12	And when Jesus saw her, he called her to him, and said unto her, Woman, thou art loosed from thine infirmity.	And Jesus saw her, and called her, and said to her: Woman, thou art released from thy infirmity.	And Jesus saw her and called her and said to her, "Woman, you are free from your infirmity."
13	And he laid his hands on her: and immediately she was made straight, and glorified God.	And he put his hand upon her; and immediately she straightened her self up, and glorified God.	And he placed his hand on her and immediately she straightened and praised God.
14	And the ruler of the synagogue answered with indignation, because that Jesus had healed on the sabbath day, and said unto the people, There are six days in which men ought to work: in them therefore come and be healed, and not on the sabbath day.	And the chief of the synagogue, being angry that Jesus had healed on the sabbath, answered, and said to the multitude: There are six days, on which it is lawful to work; on them come ye, and be healed, and not on the sabbath day.	And the ruler of the synagogue, being angered because Jesus had healed on the Sabbath, answered and said to the crowds, "There are six days in which you ought to work. You should come [and] be healed in them and not on the day of the Sabbath."
15	The Lord then answered him, and said, Thou hypocrite, doth not each one of you on the sabbath loose his ox or his ass from the stall, and lead him away to watering?	But Jesus replied, and said to him: Thou hypocrite! Doth not every one of you, on the sabbath, loose his ox or his ass from the stall, and lead him to water?	And Jesus answered and said to him, "Hypocrite! What one of you on the Sabbath does not untie his ox or his donkey from the stall and go [and] water [it]?
16	And ought not this woman, being a daughter of Abraham, whom Satan hath bound, lo, these eighteen years, be loosed from this bond on the sabbath day?	And this woman, a daughter of Abraham, whom the Calumniator hath bound, lo, these eighteen years, ought she not to be loosed from this bond on the sabbath day?	And this [woman], because she is a daughter of Abraham, and the Accuser has bound her, behold, eighteen years, is it not right that she should be freed from this bondage on the day of the Sabbath?"
17	And when he had said these things, all his adversaries were ashamed: and all the people rejoiced for all the glorious things that were done by him.	And when he had said these things, all those that stood up against him were ashamed: and all the people rejoiced in all the miracles that were wrought by his hand.	And when he said these [things], all those who were opposing were ashamed and all the people were rejoicing at all the wonders that occurred by his hand.
18	Then said he, Unto what is the kingdom of God like? and whereunto shall I resemble it?	And Jesus said: To what is the kingdom of God like? and with what shall I compare it?	And Jesus said, "What is the kingdom of God like and to what can I compare it?
19	It is like a grain of mustard seed, which a man took, and cast into his garden; and it grew, and waxed a great tree; and the fowls of the air lodged in the branches of it.	It is like a grain of mustard, which a man took and cast into his garden; and it grew, and became a large tree; and a bird of heaven made her nest in its branches.	It is like a grain of mustard seed, which a man took [and] threw into his garden. And it grew and became a large tree and a bird of heaven built a nest in its branches."
20	And again he said, Whereunto shall I liken the kingdom of God?	Jesus said again: With what shall I compare the kingdom of God?	Jesus again said, "To what can I compare the kingdom of God?
21	It is like leaven, which a woman took and hid in three measures of meal, till the whole was leavened.	It is like leaven, which a woman took and hid in three seahs of meal, until the whole was fermented.	It is like leaven that a woman took and hid in three measures [of] flour until all was leavened."
22	And he went through the cities and villages, teaching, and journeying toward Jerusalem.	And he travelled through the villages and cities, teaching and going towards Jerusalem.	And he traveled into the villages and cities while teaching and going to Jerusalem.

Parallel Translations

	KJV	Murdock	Magiera
LUKE	*Chapter 13*		
23	Then said one unto him, Lord, are there few that be saved? And he said unto them,	And a person asked him, whether they were few who would have life?	And a man asked him whether those who will live are few.
24	Strive to enter in at the strait gate: for many, I say unto you, will seek to enter in, and shall not be able.	And Jesus said to them: Strive to enter the narrow gate: for I say to you, many will seek to enter, and will not be able.	And Jesus said to them, "Strive to enter through the narrow door, for I say to you, many will seek to enter and not be able.
25	When once the master of the house is risen up, and hath shut to the door, and ye begin to stand without, and to knock at the door, saying, Lord, Lord, open unto us; and he shall answer and say unto you, I know you not whence ye are:	From the time that the lord of the house shall rise and close the door, then ye will stand without, and knock at the door; and ye will begin to say: Our Lord, our Lord, open to us and he will answer, and say: I tell you, I know you not, whence ye are.	From the time that the lord [of] the house will rise and shut the door, then you will stand outside and knock on the door and begin to say, 'Our lord, our lord, open to us,' and he will answer and say, 'I say to you, I do not know you. From where are you?'
26	Then shall ye begin to say, We have eaten and drunk in thy presence, and thou hast taught in our streets.	And ye will begin to say: We have eaten and drunken before thee; and thou hast taught in our streets.	And you will begin to say, 'We have eaten and we drank before you and you have taught in our streets.'
27	But he shall say, I tell you, I know you not whence ye are; depart from me, all ye workers of iniquity.	And he will say to you: I know you not, whence ye are: depart from me, ye doers of falsehood.	And he will say to you, 'I do not know you. From where are you? DEPART FROM ME, WORKERS OF FALSEHOOD.'
28	There shall be weeping and gnashing of teeth, when ye shall see Abraham, and Isaac, and Jacob, and all the prophets, in the kingdom of God, and you yourselves thrust out.	There will be weeping and gnashing of teeth, when ye will see Abraham, and Isaac, and Jacob, and all the prophets, in the kingdom of God; and yourselves will be thrust out.	There will be there weeping and gnashing of teeth when you see Abraham and Isaac and Jacob and all the prophets in the kingdom of God, but you will be thrown outside.
29	And they shall come from the east, and from the west, and from the north, and from the south, and shall sit down in the kingdom of God.	And they will come from the east and from the west, and from the south and from the north, and will recline in the kingdom of God.	And they will come from the east and from the west and from the south and from the north and will sit to eat in the kingdom of God.
30	And, behold, there are last which shall be first, and there are first which shall be last.	And lo, there are last that will be first, and there are first that will be last.	And behold, there are last who will be first and there are first who will be last."
31	The same day there came certain of the Pharisees, saying unto him, Get thee out, and depart hence: for Herod will kill thee.	On the same day came some of the Pharisees, and said to him: Go, depart hence; for Herod purposeth to kill thee.	On the same day, some of the Pharisees approached and were saying to him, "Go away, leave here, because Herod wants to kill you."
32	And he said unto them, Go ye, and tell that fox, Behold, I cast out devils, and I do cures to day and to morrow, and the third day I shall be perfected.	Jesus said to them: Go ye and tell that fox, Behold, I cast out demons and perform cures, to-day and to-morrow, and on the third day I shall be consummated.	Jesus said to them, "Go, tell this fox, 'Behold, I will cast out demons and do healings today and tomorrow and on the third day I will be finished.'
33	Nevertheless I must walk to day, and to morrow, and the day following: for it cannot be that a prophet perish out of Jerusalem.	But I must labor to-day and to-morrow, and on the following day I will go; because it cannot be, that a prophet should perish away from Jerusalem.	Nevertheless, it is right for me to heal today and tomorrow and I will go on another day, because it is not possible that the prophet should be hurt outside of Jerusalem.

LUKE *Chapter 13*

	KJV	*Murdock*	*Magiera*
34	O Jerusalem, Jerusalem, which killest the prophets, and stonest them that are sent unto thee; how often would I have gathered thy children together, as a hen doth gather her brood under her wings, and ye would not!	O Jerusalem, Jerusalem, that killest the prophets, and stonest them that are sent to thee; how many times would I have gathered thy children, as a hen that gathereth her young under her wings, and ye would not?	Jerusalem, Jerusalem, she has killed the prophets and stoned those who were sent to her. How many times did I want to gather your children as a hen who gathers her chicks under her wings and you did not want [it]?
35	Behold, your house is left unto you desolate: and verily I say unto you, Ye shall not see me, until the time come when ye shall say, Blessed is he that cometh in the name of the Lord.	Behold, your house is left to you desolate. For I say to you: Ye will not see me, until ye will say, Blessed is he that cometh in the name of the Lord.	Behold, your house is left desolate, for I say to you, you will not see me until you say, 'Blessed is he who comes in the name of the LORD.'"

Chapter 14

	KJV	*Murdock*	*Magiera*
1	And it came to pass, as he went into the house of one of the chief Pharisees to eat bread on the sabbath day, that they watched him.	And it occurred, that, as he entered the house of one of the chief Pharisees to eat bread, on the sabbath day, they watched him.	And it happened that when he entered the house of one of the rulers of the Pharisees to eat bread on the day of the Sabbath, they were watching him.
2	And, behold, there was a certain man before him which had the dropsy.	And lo, a dropsical man was before him.	And behold, there was a certain man before him who was swollen with water.
3	And Jesus answering spake unto the lawyers and Pharisees, saying, Is it lawful to heal on the sabbath day?	And Jesus answered, and said to the Scribes and Pharisees: Is it lawful to heal on the sabbath?	And Jesus spoke out and said to the scribes and Pharisees, "Is it lawful to heal on the Sabbath?"
4	And they held their peace. And he took him, and healed him, and let him go;	And they were silent. And he took him, and healed him, and dismissed him.	And they were quiet and he took him and healed him and let him go.
5	And answered them, saying, Which of you shall have an ass or an ox fallen into a pit, and will not straightway pull him out on the sabbath day?	And he said to them: Which of you, if his son or his ox fall into a pit on the sabbath day, doth not immediately lift and draw him out?	And he said to them, "Which of you whose son or ox falls into a well on the day of the Sabbath does not immediately draw up [and] lift him out?"
6	And they could not answer him again to these things.	And they could give him no answer to that.	And they did not find an answer to give to him about this.
7	And he put forth a parable to those which were bidden, when he marked how they chose out the chief rooms; saying unto them,	And he spoke a similitude to the guests that were present, as he noticed how they chose places on the highest couches.	And he spoke a parable to those who were invited there because he saw those who were choosing the places that were the best seats.
8	When thou art bidden of any man to a wedding, sit not down in the highest room; lest a more honourable man than thou be bidden of him;	When thou art invited by any one to a house of feasting, go not and recline on the highest couch; lest there should be invited there, one more honorable than thou;	When you are invited by someone to a banquet, do not go [and] seat yourself in the best seat, lest someone who is more honorable than you should be invited there,
9	And he that bade thee and him come and say to thee, Give this man place; and thou begin with shame to take the lowest room.	and he that invited both him and thee come and say to thee, Give place to this man; and thou be ashamed, when thou risest, and takest a lower couch.	And he who called you and him will come and say to you, 'Give place to this [man].' And you will be ashamed as you stand and take the last place.

	KJV	Murdock	Magiera
	LUKE	*Chapter 14*	
10	But when thou art bidden, go and sit down in the lowest room; that when he that bade thee cometh, he may say unto thee, Friend, go up higher: then shalt thou have worship in the presence of them that sit at meat with thee.	But when thou art invited, go and recline on the lowest [couch]; that when he who invited thee come, he may say to thee: My friend, come up higher and recline. And thou wilt have honor, before all that recline with thee.	On the contrary, when you are invited, go [and] seat yourself at the end, so that when he who called you comes, he will say to you, 'My friend, move yourself up higher and be seated,' and you will have praise before all who sit to eat with you,
11	For whosoever exalteth himself shall be abased; and he that humbleth himself shall be exalted.	For, every one that exalteth himself, will be humbled: and every one that humbleth himself, will be exalted.	because everyone who elevates himself will be humbled, and everyone who humbles himself will be raised up."
12	Then said he also to him that bade him, When thou makest a dinner or a supper, call not thy friends, nor thy brethren, neither thy kinsmen, nor thy rich neighbours; lest they also bid thee again, and a recompence be made thee.	And he said to him that invited him: When thou makest a dinner or a supper, invite not thy friends, nor thy brothers, nor thy relatives, nor thy rich neighbors; lest they also invite thee, and thou have this recompense.	And he spoke also to him who invited him, "When you make a meal or a dinner, do not call your friends, not even your brothers or your kinsmen, and not your rich neighbors, lest they also invite you and you have this payment.
13	But when thou makest a feast, call the poor, the maimed, the lame, the blind:	But when thou makest a feast, invite the poor, the maimed, the lame, the blind.	On the contrary, when you make a feast, call the poor, the hurt, the lame, [and] the blind.
14	And thou shalt be blessed; for they cannot recompense thee: for thou shalt be recompensed at the resurrection of the just.	And thou wilt be blessed. For they cannot recompense thee; but thy recompense will be at the resurrection of the just.	And you [will have] blessing, because they have nothing to repay you, for your payment will be in the resurrection of the just."
15	And when one of them that sat at meat with him heard these things, he said unto him, Blessed is he that shall eat bread in the kingdom of God.	And when one of those reclining heard these things, he said to him: Blessed is he that shall eat bread in the kingdom of God.	And when one of those who were seated to eat heard these [things], he said to him, "Blessed is he who will eat bread in the kingdom of God."
16	Then said he unto him, A certain man made a great supper, and bade many:	Jesus said to him: A certain man made a great supper, and invited many.	Jesus said to him, "A certain man made a great supper and called many.
17	And sent his servant at supper time to say to them that were bidden, Come; for all things are now ready.	And at the time for supper, he sent his servant to say to those invited: Lo, every thing is ready for you; come.	And he sent his servant at the time of the supper to tell those who were called, 'Behold, everything is prepared for you. Come.'
18	And they all with one consent began to make excuse. The first said unto him, I have bought a piece of ground, and I must needs go and see it: I pray thee have me excused.	And they all to a man, began to excuse themselves. The first said to him: I have bought a field, and am constrained to go out and see it. I pray thee, allow me to be excused.	And all began as one to excuse themselves. The first said to him, 'I have bought a field and I need to go out [and] see it. I beg you, allow me to be excused.'
19	And another said, I have bought five yoke of oxen, and I go to prove them: I pray thee have me excused.	Another said: I have bought five yoke of oxen, and I go to inspect them. I pray thee, allow me to be excused.	Another said, 'I have bought five yoke [of] oxen and I am going to prove them. I beg you, allow me to be excused.'
20	And another said, I have married a wife, and therefore I cannot come.	Another said: I have married a wife, and on this account I cannot come.	And another said, 'I have taken a wife and because of this, I am not able to come.'

Parallel Translations

	KJV	Murdock	Magiera
	LUKE *Chapter 14*		
21	So that servant came, and shewed his lord these things. Then the master of the house being angry said to his servant, Go out quickly into the streets and lanes of the city, and bring in hither the poor, and the maimed, and the halt, and the blind.	And the servant came, and told his lord these things. Then the lord of the house was angry: and he said to his servant, Go out quickly into the market-places and streets of the city, and bring in hither the poor, and the diseased, and the lame, and the blind.	And that servant came and told his lord these [things]. Then the lord of the house was angry and said to his servant, 'Go out quickly into the marketplaces and streets of the city and bring here the poor and the afflicted and the lame and the blind.'
22	And the servant said, Lord, it is done as thou hast commanded, and yet there is room.	And the servant said: My lord, it is done as thou commandedst; and still there is room.	And the servant said, 'My lord, it is as you commanded and yet there is room.'
23	And the lord said unto the servant, Go out into the highways and hedges, and compel them to come in, that my house may be filled.	And the lord said to his servant: Go out to the by-paths, and among the hedges, and constrain them to come in; that my house may be filled.	And the lord said to his servant, 'Go out into the roads and among the hedges and urge them to enter, so that my house may be full,
24	For I say unto you, That none of those men which were bidden shall taste of my supper.	For I declare to you, that not one of those men that were invited, shall taste of my supper.	for I say to you, not one of those men who were called will taste of my supper.'"
25	And there went great multitudes with him: and he turned, and said unto them,	And when great multitudes were travelling with him, he turned himself, and said to them:	And while large crowds were going with him, he turned and said to them,
26	If any man come to me, and hate not his father, and mother, and wife, and children, and brethren, and sisters, yea, and his own life also, he cannot be my disciple.	He that cometh to me, and hateth not his father and his mother, and his brothers and his sisters, and his wife and his children, and his own life also, cannot become a disciple to me.	"He who comes to me and does not hate his father and his mother and his brothers and his sisters and his wife and his children and also himself is not able to be a disciple of me.
27	And whosoever doth not bear his cross, and come after me, cannot be my disciple.	And he that doth not take up his cross and come after me, cannot become a disciple to me.	And he who does not bear his cross and follow me is not able to be a disciple of me.
28	For which of you, intending to build a tower, sitteth not down first, and counteth the cost, whether he have sufficient to finish it?	For, which of you, wishing to build a tower, doth not first sit down and compute the expense, whether he have the means to complete it?	For which of you who wants to build a tower does not first sit down [and] think about his expenses, whether he has [enough] to complete it,
29	Lest haply, after he hath laid the foundation, and is not able to finish it, all that behold it begin to mock him,	lest, when he hath laid the foundation, and is unable to finish, all that see it begin to deride him;	so that when he has not laid the foundation and is not able to finish [it], all who see will mock him
30	Saying, This man began to build, and was not able to finish.	and say: This man began to build, and was unable to finish.	and say, 'This man began to build and was not able to finish [it]'?
31	Or what king, going to make war against another king, sitteth not down first, and consulteth whether he be able with ten thousand to meet him that cometh against him with twenty thousand?	Or what king, that is going to contend in battle with his neighbor king, doth not first consider, whether he is able, with ten thousand, to meet him that is coming against him with twenty thousand?	Or what king who goes to war to fight with his neighboring king does not first think whether he is able to meet with ten thousand, him who comes against him with twenty thousand?

Parallel Translations

	KJV	*Murdock*	*Magiera*

LUKE *Chapter 14*

	KJV	Murdock	Magiera
32	Or else, while the other is yet a great way off, he sendeth an ambassage, and desireth conditions of peace.	and if not; while he is yet far from him, he sendeth envoys, and sueth for peace.	And if not, while he is far away from him, he will send an ambassador and ask for peace.
33	So likewise, whosoever he be of you that forsaketh not all that he hath, he cannot be my disciple.	So every one of you who doth not give up all his possessions, cannot be my disciple.	So, every one of you who does not forsake all his wealth is not able to be a disciple of me.
34	Salt is good: but if the salt have lost his savour, wherewith shall it be seasoned?	Salt is a good thing: but if the salt itself hath become insipid, wherewith shall it be salted?	Salt is good, but if even the salt should lose its flavor, with what will it be salted?
35	It is neither fit for the land, nor yet for the dunghill; but men cast it out. He that hath ears to hear, let him hear.	It is fit for neither the earth, nor the dunghill. They cast it away.---He that hath ears to hear, let him hear.	It is fit neither for the land nor for the dung-heap. They put it outside. He who has ears to hear should hear."

Chapter 15

	KJV	Murdock	Magiera
1	Then drew near unto him all the publicans and sinners for to hear him.	And publicans and sinners came to him, to hear him.	Now the tax collectors and sinners came near to him in order to hear him.
2	And the Pharisees and scribes murmured, saying, This man receiveth sinners, and eateth with them.	And the Scribes and Pharisees murmured, and said: This man receiveth sinners, and eateth with them.	And the scribes and Pharisees were murmuring and saying, "This [man] receives sinners and eats with them."
3	And he spake this parable unto them, saying,	And Jesus spoke to them this similitude:	And Jesus told them this parable.
4	What man of you, having an hundred sheep, if he lose one of them, doth not leave the ninety and nine in the wilderness, and go after that which is lost, until he find it?	What man among you, that hath a hundred sheep, if he lose one of them, doth not leave the ninety and nine in the desert, and go and seek for that which is lost, until he find it?	"What man among you who has one hundred sheep and if one of them should be lost, does not leave the ninety-nine in the open country and go [and] seek that one which is lost until he finds it?
5	And when he hath found it, he layeth it on his shoulders, rejoicing.	And when he findeth it, he rejoiceth, and taketh it upon his shoulders;	And when he has found it, he will rejoice and take it on his shoulders
6	And when he cometh home, he calleth together his friends and neighbours, saying unto them, Rejoice with me; for I have found my sheep which was lost.	and he cometh home, and he calleth together his friends and neighbors, and saith to them: Rejoice with me; for I have found my sheep that was lost.	and come to his house and call to his friends and his neighbors and say to them, 'Rejoice with me, because I have found my sheep that was lost.'
7	I say unto you, that likewise joy shall be in heaven over one sinner that repenteth, more than over ninety and nine just persons, which need no repentance.	I say to you, that there will thus be joy in heaven, over one sinner that repenteth, more than over ninety and nine just ones, to whom repentance was not necessary.	I say to you, so there will be [more] joy in heaven for one sinner who repents than for ninety-nine just [ones] who do not need repentance.
8	Either what woman having ten pieces of silver, if she lose one piece, doth not light a candle, and sweep the house, and seek diligently till she find it?	Or what woman is there, who, if she have ten drachmas, and lose one of them, doth not light a lamp, and sweep the house, and search for it carefully, until she find it?	Or what woman, who has ten coins and loses one of them, does not light a lamp and sweep the house and search for it carefully until she finds it?

Parallel Translations

	KJV	*Murdock*	*Magiera*
	LUKE	*Chapter 15*	
9	And when she hath found it, she calleth her friends and her neighbours together, saying, Rejoice with me; for I have found the piece which I had lost.	And when she hath found it, she calleth together her friends and neighbors, and saith to them: Rejoice with me, for I have found my drachma that was lost.	And when she has found it, she will call her friends and her neighbors and say to them, 'Rejoice with me, because I have found my coin that was lost.'
10	Likewise, I say unto you, there is joy in the presence of the angels of God over one sinner that repenteth.	I say to you, That there will thus be joy, before the angels of God, over one sinner that repenteth.	I say to you, so there will be joy before the angels of God over one sinner that repents."
11	And he said, A certain man had two sons:	And Jesus said to them again: A certain man had two sons.	And Jesus spoke again to them,, "A certain man had two sons.
12	And the younger of them said to his father, Father, give me the portion of goods that falleth to me. And he divided unto them his living.	And his younger son said to him: My father, give me the portion that falleth to me from thy house. And he divided to them his property.	And his younger son said to him, 'My father, give me the portion that is coming to me from your house, and he divided to them his wealth.'
13	And not many days after the younger son gathered all together, and took his journey into a far country, and there wasted his substance with riotous living.	And after a few days, the younger son collected together all that fell to him, and went to a distant place and there squandered his property, by living in dissipation.	And after a few days, his younger son gathered up everything that came to him and went to a region far away and there spent his wealth living wastefully.
14	And when he had spent all, there arose a mighty famine in that land; and he began to be in want.	And when he had consumed all that he had, there occurred a great famine in that place; and he began to be in want.	And when he had used up everything that he had, a great famine occurred in that region and he began to have need.
15	And he went and joined himself to a citizen of that country; and he sent him into his fields to feed swine.	And he went and connected himself with one of the citizens of that place: and he sent him into the field to tend swine.	And he went [and] joined himself to one of the citizens of that land and he sent him into the field to tend the pigs.
16	And he would fain have filled his belly with the husks that the swine did eat: and no man gave unto him.	And he longed to fill his belly with those pods which the swine ate: and no one gave to him.	And he desired to fill his stomach from the carob husks that the pigs were eating, and no one gave to him.
17	And when he came to himself, he said, How many hired servants of my father's have bread enough and to spare, and I perish with hunger!	And when he came to himself, he said: How many hired servants are now at my father's house, who have bread enough, and I am here perishing with hunger.	And when he came to himself, he said, 'How many hired servants are now [at] my father's house who have an abundance of bread and I am perishing here with my hunger?'
18	I will arise and go to my father, and will say unto him, Father, I have sinned against heaven, and before thee,	I will arise and go to my father, and say to him: My father, I have sinned against heaven, and before thee;	I will rise up [and] go to my father and say to him, 'My father, I have sinned against heaven and before you,
19	And am no more worthy to be called thy son: make me as one of thy hired servants.	and am no longer worthy to be called thy son. Make me like one of thy hired servants.	and therefore I am not worthy to be called your son. Make me like one of your hired servants.'

Parallel Translations

	KJV	*Murdock*	*Magiera*

LUKE *Chapter 15*

	KJV	Murdock	Magiera
20	And he arose, and came to his father. But when he was yet a great way off, his father saw him, and had compassion, and ran, and fell on his neck, and kissed him.	And he arose and went towards his father. And he was yet at a distance, when his father saw him; and he pitied him, and ran, and fell upon his neck and kissed him.	And he rose up [and] came to his father. And while he was far away, his father saw him and had compassion on him and ran [and] fell on his neck and kissed him.
21	And the son said unto him, Father, I have sinned against heaven, and in thy sight, and am no more worthy to be called thy son.	And his son said to him: My father, I have sinned against heaven, and before thee, and am not worthy to be called thy son.	And his son said to him, 'My father, I have sinned against heaven and before you and I am not worthy to be called your son.'
22	But the father said to his servants, Bring forth the best robe, and put it on him; and put a ring on his hand, and shoes on his feet:	But his father said to his servants: Bring forth the best robe, and clothe him, and put a ring on his hand, and supply him with shoes.	And his father said to his servants, 'Bring out the best robe, clothe him, and place a ring on his hand and put shoes on him
23	And bring hither the fatted calf, and kill it; and let us eat, and be merry:	And bring forth and slay the fatted bullock; and let us eat, and be merry.	and bring [and] kill the ox that is fattened and let us eat and be merry,
24	For this my son was dead, and is alive again; he was lost, and is found. And they began to be merry.	For, this my son was dead, and is alive; he was lost and is found. And they began to be merry.	because this, my son, was dead and [now] is alive, and he was lost and [now] is found,' and they began to be merry.
25	Now his elder son was in the field: and as he came and drew nigh to the house, he heard musick and dancing.	But his elder son was in the field; and as he came and drew near to the house, he heard the sound of the singing of many.	Now his oldest son was in the field and when he arrived and came near to the house, he heard the sound of the singing of many.
26	And he called one of the servants, and asked what these things meant.	And he called to one of the boys, and asked him what it meant.	And he called to one of the boys and asked him, 'What is this?'
27	And he said unto him, Thy brother is come; and thy father hath killed the fatted calf, because he hath received him safe and sound.	And he said to him: Thy brother hath come; and thy father hath killed the fatted bullock, because he hath received him in health.	He said to him, 'Your brother has come and your father has killed the ox that is fattened, because he has received him [back] healthy.'
28	And he was angry, and would not go in: therefore came his father out, and intreated him.	And he was angry, and would not go in: and his father went out and entreated him.	And he was angry and did not want to enter. So his father came out [and] begged him.
29	And he answering said to his father, Lo, these many years do I serve thee, neither transgressed I at any time thy commandment: and yet thou never gavest me a kid, that I might make merry with my friends:	And he said to his father: Lo, these many years have I labored in thy service, and never transgressed thy command; and thou never gavest me a kid, that I might make merry with my friends.	And he said to his father, 'Behold, how many years have I worked for you [in] service and never transgressed your commandment, yet during all this time you did not give me a goat to make merry with my friends.
30	But as soon as this thy son was come, which hath devoured thy living with harlots, thou hast killed for him the fatted calf.	But for this thy son, when he had dissipated thy property with harlots, and came [home], thou hast slain the fatted bullock for him.	But for this your son, after he has squandered your wealth with harlots and has come [home], you kill for him the ox that is fattened.'
31	And he said unto him, Son, thou art ever with me, and all that I have is thine.	His father said to him: My son, thou hast been ever with me, and all that I have, is thine.	His father said to him, 'My son, you always are with me and everything of mine is yours,

Parallel Translations

	KJV	*Murdock*	*Magiera*
LUKE	*Chapter 15*		
32	It was meet that we should make merry, and be glad: for this thy brother was dead, and is alive again; and was lost, and is found.	But it was proper for us to be merry, and to rejoice; because this thy brother was dead, and is alive; he was lost, and is found.	but it is right for us to make merry and to rejoice, because your brother was dead, yet [now] is alive and was lost, yet [now] is found."
Chapter 16			
1	And he said also unto his disciples, There was a certain rich man, which had a steward; and the same was accused unto him that he had wasted his goods.	And he spoke a parable to his disciples. There was a certain rich man, who had a steward; and accusations were brought to him of him, that he squandered his property.	And he spoke a parable to his disciples, "There was a certain rich man, and he had a steward, and they had accused him of squandering his wealth.
2	And he called him, and said unto him, How is it that I hear this of thee? give an account of thy stewardship; for thou mayest be no longer steward.	And his lord called him, and said to him: What is this that I hear of thee? Render to me an account of thy stewardship; for thou canst no longer be my steward.	And his lord called him and said to him, 'What is this that I hear about you? Give me an accounting of your stewardship, for you can no longer be a steward for me.'
3	Then the steward said within himself, What shall I do? for my lord taketh away from me the stewardship: I cannot dig; to beg I am ashamed.	And the steward said with himself: What shall I do, since my lord is about to take from me the stewardship? To dig, I am unable; and to become a beggar, I am ashamed.	That steward said to himself, 'What should I do, for my lord has taken from me the stewardship? I am not able to dig, and I am ashamed to beg.
4	I am resolved what to do, that, when I am put out of the stewardship, they may receive me into their houses.	I know what to do, that, when I am put out of the stewardship, they may receive me to their houses.	I know what I will do so that when I am dismissed from the stewardship, they will receive me into their houses.'
5	So he called every one of his lord's debtors unto him, and said unto the first, How much owest thou unto my lord?	And he called each one of his lord's debtors; and he said to the first, How much owest thou to my lord?	And he called each one of his lord's debtors and said to the first, 'How much do you owe my lord?'
6	And he said, An hundred measures of oil. And he said unto him, Take thy bill, and sit down quickly, and write fifty.	And he said to him, One hundred measures of oil. And he said to him: Take thy bill, and sit down quickly, and write Fifty measures.	He said to him, 'One hundred measures [of] oil.' He said to him, 'Take your book and sit down quickly; write fifty measures.'
7	Then said he to another, And how much owest thou? And he said, An hundred measures of wheat. And he said unto him, Take thy bill, and write fourscore.	And he said to another: And how much owest thou to my lord? And he said to him, One hundred cors of wheat. And he said to him: Take thy bill, and sit down, and write Eighty cors.	And he said to another, 'And what do you owe my lord?' He said to him, 'One hundred cors [of] wheat.' He said to him, 'Take your book and sit down; write eighty cors.'
8	And the lord commended the unjust steward, because he had done wisely: for the children of this world are in their generation wiser than the children of light.	And our Lord praised the unrighteous steward, for having acted sagaciously: for the children of this world are more sagacious than the children of light, in this their generation.	And our Lord praised the unjust steward because he had acted wisely, for the sons of this world are wiser than the sons of light, in this, their generation.
9	And I say unto you, Make to yourselves friends of the mammon of unrighteousness; that, when ye fail, they may receive you into everlasting habitations.	And I also say to you: Make to yourselves friends, with this unrighteous mammon; so that when it is finished, they may receive you to their everlasting tabernacles.	And also I say to you, 'Make friends for yourself from this wealth of evil that when it is fully spent, they may welcome you into their everlasting shelters.'

LUKE *Chapter 16*

	KJV	*Murdock*	*Magiera*
10	He that is faithful in that which is least is faithful also in much: and he that is unjust in the least is unjust also in much.	He that is faithful in the little, is also faithful in the much; and he that is unjust in the little, is also unjust in the much.	He who is trustworthy in little also is trustworthy in much, and he who is unjust in little also is unjust in much.
11	If therefore ye have not been faithful in the unrighteous mammon, who will commit to your trust the true riches?	If therefore ye have not been faithful in the unrighteous mammon, who will intrust to you the reality?	If therefore you are not trustworthy [ones] with the wealth of evil, who will entrust the truth to you?
12	And if ye have not been faithful in that which is another man's, who shall give you that which is your own?	And if ye have not been found faithful in that which is not yours, who will give to you that which is yours?	And if you have not been found trustworthy [ones] in that which is not yours, who will give to you your own?"
13	No servant can serve two masters: for either he will hate the one, and love the other; or else he will hold to the one, and despise the other. Ye cannot serve God and mammon.	There is no servant, who can serve two lords. For, either he will hate the one and love the other, or he will honor the one and despise the other. Ye cannot serve God and mammon.	There is no servant that is able to serve two masters, for either he will hate the one and love the other or honor the one and despise the other. You are not able to serve God and wealth.
14	And the Pharisees also, who were covetous, heard all these things: and they derided him.	And the Pharisees, when they heard all these things, because they loved money, derided him.	Now the Pharisees, when they heard all these [things], because they loved money, were mocking him.
15	And he said unto them, Ye are they which justify yourselves before men; but God knoweth your hearts: for that which is highly esteemed among men is abomination in the sight of God.	And Jesus said to them: Ye are such as justify yourselves before men; but God knoweth your heart: for that which is exalted among men, is abominable before God.	And Jesus said to them, "You are those who justify themselves before men. But God knows your hearts, because what is esteemed among men is abominable before God.
16	The law and the prophets were until John: since that time the kingdom of God is preached, and every man presseth into it.	The law and the prophets were until John: since then, the kingdom of God is proclaimed, and every one presseth it to enter in.	The law and the prophets [were] until John. Since then, the kingdom of God is preached and all crowd to enter it.
17	And it is easier for heaven and earth to pass, than one tittle of the law to fail.	And it is easier for heaven and earth to pass away, than for one letter to pass from the law.	And it is easier for heaven and earth to pass away than [for] one letter of the law to pass away.
18	Whosoever putteth away his wife, and marrieth another, committeth adultery: and whosoever marrieth her that is put away from her husband committeth adultery.	Whoever putteth away his wife, and taketh another, committeth adultery; and whoever taketh her that is put away, committeth adultery.	Everyone who dismisses his wife and marries another commits adultery, and everyone who marries a forsaken woman commits adultery.
19	There was a certain rich man, which was clothed in purple and fine linen, and fared sumptuously every day:	And there was a certain rich man, who was clothed in fine linen and scarlet, and passed every day in splendid luxury.	Now there was a certain rich man and he wore linen and purple. And every day he lived in pleasure splendidly.
20	And there was a certain beggar named Lazarus, which was laid at his gate, full of sores,	And there was a certain poor man, whose name was Lazarus; and he was laid at the gate of the rich man, smitten with ulcers.	And there was a certain poor man whose name was Lazarus. And he lay at the gate of that rich man, stricken with boils.

Parallel Translations

	KJV	*Murdock*	*Magiera*
	LUKE	*Chapter 16*	
21	And desiring to be fed with the crumbs which fell from the rich man's table: moreover the dogs came and licked his sores.	And he desired to fill his belly with the fragments that fell from the rich man's table: and the dogs also came and licked his ulcers.	And he longed to fill his stomach from the crumbs that fell from the table of that rich man. But even the dogs came [and] licked his boils.
22	And it came to pass, that the beggar died, and was carried by the angels into Abraham's bosom: the rich man also died, and was buried;	And so it was, that the poor man died; and angels transported him to Abraham's bosom. The rich man also died, and was buried.	Now it happened and that poor [man] died and the angels carried him to the bosom of Abraham. And also that rich man died and was buried.
23	And in hell he lift up his eyes, being in torments, and seeth Abraham afar off, and Lazarus in his bosom.	And being tormented in hell, he raised his eyes from afar off, and saw Abraham, and Lazarus in his bosom.	And while he was tormented in Sheol, he lifted up his eyes from far away and saw Abraham and Lazarus in his bosom.
24	And he cried and said, Father Abraham, have mercy on me, and send Lazarus, that he may dip the tip of his finger in water, and cool my tongue; for I am tormented in this flame.	And he called with a loud voice, and said: Abraham, my father, have pity on me; and send Lazarus, that he may dip the tip of his finger in water, and moisten my tongue; for, lo, I am tormented in this flame.	And he cried with a loud voice and said, 'My father Abraham, have compassion on me and send Lazarus to dip the tip of his finger in water and to moisten my tongue for me, for, behold, I am tormented in this flame.'
25	But Abraham said, Son, remember that thou in thy lifetime receivedst thy good things, and likewise Lazarus evil things: but now he is comforted, and thou art tormented.	And Abraham said to him: My son, remember, that thou receivedst thy good things in thy lifetime, and Lazarus his evil things: and now, behold he is here at rest, and thou art tormented.	Abraham said to him, 'My son, remember that you received your good [things] during your life and Lazarus his bad [things] and now, behold, he is refreshed here and you are tormented.
26	And beside all this, between us and you there is a great gulf fixed: so that they which would pass from hence to you cannot; neither can they pass to us, that would come from thence.	And with all these, there is a great barrier between us and you; so that they who would pass from here to you, cannot; neither [can they] pass from there to us	And with all these [things] a great chasm is placed between us and you, so that those who want to pass over from here to you are not able, nor from there to pass over to us.'
27	Then he said, I pray thee therefore, father, that thou wouldest send him to my father's house:	He said to him: I pray thee, therefore, my father, that thou wouldst send him to my father's house;	Then he said to him, 'I beg of you, my father, to send him to the house of my father,
28	For I have five brethren; that he may testify unto them, lest they also come into this place of torment.	for I have five brothers; that he may go and protest to them; lest they also come to this place of torment.	for I have five brothers. Let him go [and] witness to them so that they will not also come to this place of torment.'
29	Abraham saith unto him, They have Moses and the prophets; let them hear them.	Abraham said to him: They have Moses and the prophets, let them hear them.	Abraham said to him, 'They have Moses and the prophets. They should hear them.'
30	And he said, Nay, father Abraham: but if one went unto them from the dead, they will repent.	But he said to him: No, my father Abraham: but if one shall go to them from the dead, they will repent.	And he said to him, 'No, my father Abraham, but if someone from the dead would go to them, they would repent.'
31	And he said unto him, If they hear not Moses and the prophets, neither will they be persuaded, though one rose from the dead.	Abraham said to him: If they hear not Moses and the prophets, they will not believe, though one should rise from the dead.	Abraham said to him, 'If they will not hear Moses and the prophets, even if someone would rise from the dead, they will not believe him.'"

Chapter 17

	KJV	Murdock	Magiera
1	Then said he unto the disciples, It is impossible but that offences will come: but woe unto him, through whom they come!	And Jesus said to his disciples: It cannot be, but that offences will come: but woe to him, by whom they come.	And Jesus said to his disciples, "It is not possible that offenses not come, but woe to him by whose hand they come!
2	It were better for him that a millstone were hanged about his neck, and he cast into the sea, than that he should offend one of these little ones.	Better for him were it, if a millstone were suspended to his neck, and he cast into the sea, than that he should cause one of these little ones to stumble.	It would be better for him if a millstone of a donkey were hung on his neck and he were thrown into the sea, than to cause one of these little ones to stumble.
3	Take heed to yourselves: If thy brother trespass against thee, rebuke him; and if he repent, forgive him.	Take heed to yourselves.---If thy brother transgress, rebuke him; and if he repent, forgive him.	Take heed to yourselves. If your brother sins, reprove him. And if he repents, forgive him.
4	And if he trespass against thee seven times in a day, and seven times in a day turn again to thee, saying, I repent; thou shalt forgive him.	And if he shall offend against thee seven times in a day, and, seven times in a day, shall turn himself to thee, and say, I repent; forgive him.	And if he offends you seven times in a day and in a day seven times he turns to you and says, 'I repent,' forgive him."
5	And the apostles said unto the Lord, Increase our faith.	And the Legates said to our Lord: Increase our faith.	And the apostles said to our Lord, "Increase faith to us."
6	And the Lord said, If ye had faith as a grain of mustard seed, ye might say unto this sycamine tree, Be thou plucked up by the root, and be thou planted in the sea; and it should obey you.	He said to them: If ye had faith like a grain of mustard seed, ye might say to this mulberry-tree, Be thou torn up by the roots, and be thou planted in the sea; and it would obey you.	He said to them, "If you have faith like a grain of mustard seed, you could say to this tree, 'Be uprooted and be planted in the sea,' and it will obey you.
7	But which of you, having a servant plowing or feeding cattle, will say unto him by and by, when he is come from the field, Go and sit down to meat?	Which of you, having a servant driving a yoke of oxen, or tending sheep, will say to him when he cometh from the field, Pass on at once, and recline for supper?	And which of you who has a servant who plows or tends a flock, and when he comes from the field says immediately to him, 'Pass through, sit down to eat?'
8	And will not rather say unto him, Make ready wherewith I may sup, and gird thyself, and serve me, till I have eaten and drunken; and afterward thou shalt eat and drink?	But he will say to him: Prepare for me what I may sup upon, and gird thy loins and serve me, until I have eaten and drunken; and afterwards thou shalt eat and drink.	On the contrary, he says to him, 'Prepare something to eat for me and gird up your loins [and] serve me until I have eaten and drunk, and afterwards you also may eat and drink.'
9	Doth he thank that servant because he did the things that were commanded him? I trow not.	Hath he thanks for him, because the servant did what was commanded him? I think not.	Does that servant receive his thanks because he did what was commanded him? I think not.
10	So likewise ye, when ye shall have done all those things which are commanded you, say, We are unprofitable servants: we have done that which was our duty to do.	So also ye, when ye have done all the things commanded you, say: We are unprofitable servants, for we have done only what we were obligated to do.	So also, when you do all these [things] that are commanded to you, say, 'We are unprofitable servant[s],' because what we ought to do we have done."
11	And it came to pass, as he went to Jerusalem, that he passed through the midst of Samaria and Galilee.	And it occurred as Jesus advanced towards Jerusalem, that he passed among the Samaritans into Galilee.	And it happened that when Jesus went to Jerusalem he passed through the Samaritans to Galilee.

Parallel Translations

	KJV	Murdock	Magiera
LUKE	*Chapter 17*		
12	And as he entered into a certain village, there met him ten men that were lepers, which stood afar off:	And when he drew near to enter a certain village, there met him ten leprous men; and they stood at a distance,	And when he was about to enter a certain village, ten men, lepers, met him and stood at a distance.
13	And they lifted up their voices, and said, Jesus, Master, have mercy on us.	and raised their voice, and said: Our Rabbi, Jesus, have compassion upon us.	And they lifted their voice[s] and said, "Our Master, Jesus, have compassion on us."
14	And when he saw them, he said unto them, Go shew yourselves unto the priests. And it came to pass, that, as they went, they were cleansed.	And when he had looked upon them, he said to them: Go, show yourselves to the priests. And as they were going, they were cleansed.	And when he saw them, he said to them, "Go [and] show yourselves to the priests." And as they went, they were cleansed.
15	And one of them, when he saw that he was healed, turned back, and with a loud voice glorified God,	And one of them, when he saw that he was cleansed, returned, and with a loud voice, glorified God.	And one of them, when he saw that he was cleansed, returned and with a loud voice was praising God.
16	And fell down on his face at his feet, giving him thanks: and he was a Samaritan.	And he fell on his face, at the feet of Jesus, and thanked him. And he was a Samaritan.	And he fell on his face before the feet of Jesus, giving him thanks, and this [man] was a Samaritan.
17	And Jesus answering said, Were there not ten cleansed? but where are the nine?	And Jesus answered, and said: Were they not ten who were cleansed? Where are the nine?	And Jesus answered and said, "Were there not ten who were cleansed? Where are the nine?
18	There are not found that returned to give glory to God, save this stranger.	Have they so gone as not to come and give glory to God; except this one, who is of another nation?	Did [no one else] determine to come [and] give praise to God, except this [one] who is from a foreign nation?"
19	And he said unto him, Arise, go thy way: thy faith hath made thee whole.	And he said to him; Arise, and go: thy faith hath given thee life.	And he said to him, "Stand up [and] go! Your faith has given you life."
20	And when he was demanded of the Pharisees, when the kingdom of God should come, he answered them and said, The kingdom of God cometh not with observation:	And as [some] of the Pharisees asked him, When the kingdom of God would come; he answered, and said to them: The kingdom of God will not come with observables.	And when some of the Pharisees asked Jesus when the kingdom of God would come, he answered and said to them, "The kingdom of God does not come with watching,"
21	Neither shall they say, Lo here! or, lo there! for, behold, the kingdom of God is within you.	And they will not say: Behold, here it is! or, Behold, it is there! For lo, the kingdom of God is within you	nor should they say, 'Behold, here it is,' and 'Behold, there it is,' for behold, the kingdom of God is in the middle of you."
22	And he said unto the disciples, The days will come, when ye shall desire to see one of the days of the Son of man, and ye shall not see it.	And he said to his disciples: The days will come, when ye will long to see one of the days of the Son of man, and ye will not see [them].	And he said to his disciples, "The days will come when you will desire to see one of the days of the Son of Man and you will not see.
23	And they shall say to you, See here; or, see there: go not after them, nor follow them.	And if they shall say to you: Lo, here he is! or, Lo, there he is! go not forth.	And if they say to you, 'Behold, here he is,' and 'Behold, there he is,' you should not go.
24	For as the lightning, that lighteneth out of the one part under heaven, shineth unto the other part under heaven; so shall also the Son of man be in his day.	For, as the lightning darteth from the heavens, and illuminateth all beneath the heavens; so will the Son of man be, in his day.	For as lightning shines from heaven and all under heaven is lightened, so the Son of Man will be in his day,
25	But first must he suffer many things, and be rejected of this generation.	But, previously, he is to suffer many things, and to be rejected by this generation.	but first he is going to suffer many [things] and be rejected by this generation.

Parallel Translations

	KJV	Murdock	Magiera

LUKE Chapter 17

	KJV	Murdock	Magiera
26	And as it was in the days of Noe, so shall it be also in the days of the Son of man.	And as it was in the days of Noah, so will it be in the days of the Son of man.	And as it was in the days of Noah, so will it be in the days of the Son of Man,
27	They did eat, they drank, they married wives, they were given in marriage, until the day that Noe entered into the ark, and the flood came, and destroyed them all.	They ate and drank, they took wives and were given to husbands, until the day that Noah entered the ark; and the flood came, and destroyed every one.	for they were eating and drinking and taking wives and being given to husbands, until the day that Noah entered the ark and the flood came and destroyed everyone.
28	Likewise also as it was in the days of Lot; they did eat, they drank, they bought, they sold, they planted, they builded;	And again, as it was in the days of Lot; they ate and drank, bought and sold, planted and built.	And [it will be] again as it was in the days of Lot, when they were eating and drinking and buying and selling and planting and building.
29	But the same day that Lot went out of Sodom it rained fire and brimstone from heaven, and destroyed them all.	But in the day that Lot went out of Sodom, the Lord rained fire and sulphur from heaven, and destroyed them all.	And on the day that Lot went out from Sodom, the LORD rained fire and sulphur from heaven and destroyed all of them.
30	Even thus shall it be in the day when the Son of man is revealed.	Thus will it be, in the day when the Son of man shall be revealed.	So it will be in the day that the Son of Man is revealed.
31	In that day, he which shall be upon the housetop, and his stuff in the house, let him not come down to take it away: and he that is in the field, let him likewise not return back.	In that day, let him that is on the house-top, and his goods in the house, not come down to take them: and let him that is in the field, not return [after what is] behind him.	In that day, he who is on the roof and his goods are in the house should not come down to take them, and he who is in the field should not turn back.
32	Remember Lot's wife.	Remember Lot's wife.	Remember the wife of Lot.
33	Whosoever shall seek to save his life shall lose it; and whosoever shall lose his life shall preserve it.	He that desireth to preserve his life, will lose it; and he that will lose his life, shall preserve it.	He who wants to save his soul will lose it, and he who loses his soul will save it.
34	I tell you, in that night there shall be two men in one bed; the one shall be taken, and the other shall be left.	I tell you, that, in that night, two will be in one bed; one will be taken, and the other left.	I say to you, in that night, two will be in one bed. One will be taken and the other will be left.
35	Two women shall be grinding together; the one shall be taken, and the other left.	And two females will be grinding together; one will be taken, and the other left.	Two [women] will be grinding together. One will be taken and the other will be left.
36	Two men shall be in the field; the one shall be taken, and the other left.	Two men will be in the field; one will be taken, and the other left.	Two [men] will be in the field. One will be taken and the other will be left."
37	And they answered and said unto him, Where, Lord? And he said unto them, Wheresoever the body is, thither will the eagles be gathered together.	They answered, and said to him: Whither, our Lord? He said to them: Where the body is, there will the eagles assemble themselves.	They answered and said to him, "To where, our Lord?" He said to them, "Where the body [is], there the eagles will be gathered."

Chapter 18

	KJV	Murdock	Magiera
1	And he spake a parable unto them to this end, that men ought always to pray, and not to faint;	And he spoke to them a similitude also, that men should pray at all times, and not become weary.	And he also spoke to them a parable that at all times they should pray and not be weary.

LUKE *Chapter 18*

	KJV	*Murdock*	*Magiera*
2	Saying, There was in a city a judge, which feared not God, neither regarded man:	There was a judge in a certain city, who feared not God, and regarded not men.	"There was a certain judge in a certain city who did not fear God and did not reverence men.
3	And there was a widow in that city; and she came unto him, saying, Avenge me of mine adversary.	And there was a certain widow in that city; and she came to him, and said: Vindicate me against my adversary.	And there was a certain widow in that city and she came to him and said, 'Avenge me of my adversary.'
4	And he would not for a while: but afterward he said within himself, Though I fear not God, nor regard man;	And he would not, for a long time: but afterwards, he said to himself: Though I fear not God, and regard not men,	And he did not want to [for] a long time, but afterwards he said to himself, 'Although I do not fear God and I do not reverence men,
5	Yet because this widow troubleth me, I will avenge her, lest by her continual coming she weary me.	yet, because this widow troubleth me, I will vindicate her; that she may not be always coming and troubling me.	yet, because this widow troubles me, I will avenge her, so that she is not coming continually [and] annoying me.'"
6	And the Lord said, Hear what the unjust judge saith.	And our Lord said: Hear what the unjust judge saith.	And our Lord said, "Hear what the unjust judge said.
7	And shall not God avenge his own elect, which cry day and night unto him, though he bear long with them?	And will not God, much more, vindicate his chosen, who call upon him by day and by night; and have patience with them?	And will not God perform vengeance even more for his chosen [ones], who call on him by day and by night, and be long-suffering with them?
8	I tell you that he will avenge them speedily. Nevertheless when the Son of man cometh, shall he find faith on the earth?	I tell you, He will vindicate them speedily. Yet the Son of man will come; and will he find faith on the earth?	I say to you, he will perform their vengeance quickly. Nevertheless, will the Son of Man come and will he indeed find faith on the earth?"
9	And he spake this parable unto certain which trusted in themselves that they were righteous, and despised others:	And he spake this similitude, against certain persons, who had confidence in themselves that they were righteous, and despised every one.	And he spoke this parable against those men who were confident in themselves that they were just and were despising everyone.
10	Two men went up into the temple to pray; the one a Pharisee, and the other a publican.	Two men went up to the temple to pray; the one a Pharisee, and the other a publican.	"Two men went up to the temple to pray. One [was] a Pharisee and the other a tax collector.
11	The Pharisee stood and prayed thus with himself, God, I thank thee, that I am not as other men are, extortioners, unjust, adulterers, or even as this publican.	And the Pharisee stood by himself, and prayed thus: God, I thank thee that I have not been like the rest of men, rapacious, oppressive, and adulterous; nor like this publican.	And that Pharisee was standing by himself and so was praying, 'God, I thank you that I am not like the rest of men, extortioners and greedy [ones] and adulterers, nor like this tax collector.
12	I fast twice in the week, I give tithes of all that I possess.	But I fast twice in a week, and tithe all I possess.	On the contrary, I fast twice in a week and I tithe everything that I gain.'
13	And the publican, standing afar off, would not lift up so much as his eyes unto heaven, but smote upon his breast, saying, God be merciful to me a sinner.	And the publican stood afar off, and would not even lift his eyes to heaven, but smote upon his breast, and said: God, be merciful to me, a sinner.	But that tax collector was standing far away and did not even want to raise his eyes to heaven, but was beating on his breast and saying, 'God, have mercy on me, a sinner.'

LUKE *Chapter 18*

	KJV	Murdock	Magiera
14	I tell you, this man went down to his house justified rather than the other: for every one that exalteth himself shall be abased; and he that humbleth himself shall be exalted.	I say to you, that this [man] went down to his house justified, rather than the Pharisee. For every one that exalteth himself, will be humbled; and every one that humbleth himself, will be exalted.	I say to you, this [man] went down to his house more justified than that Pharisee, for everyone who raises himself up will be humbled, and everyone who humbles himself will be raised up."
15	And they brought unto him also infants, that he would touch them: but when his disciples saw it, they rebuked them.	And they brought to him infants, that he might touch them: and his disciples saw them, and rebuked them.	And they also brought him infants that he would touch them, and his disciples saw them and rebuked them.
16	But Jesus called them unto him, and said, Suffer little children to come unto me, and forbid them not: for of such is the kingdom of God.	But Jesus called them, and said to them: Suffer little children to come to me, and forbid them not; for of those that are like them, of such is the kingdom of heaven.	And Jesus called them and said to them, "Let the children come to me, and do not hinder them, for the kingdom of heaven belongs to those who are like these.
17	Verily I say unto you, Whosoever shall not receive the kingdom of God as a little child shall in no wise enter therein.	Verily I say to you, That he who shall not receive the kingdom of God, as a little child, will not enter it.	Truly I say to you, whoever does not receive the kingdom of God as a child will not enter it."
18	And a certain ruler asked him, saying, Good Master, what shall I do to inherit eternal life?	And one of the chiefs asked him, and said to him: Good Teacher, what shall I do, that I may inherit eternal life?	And one of the rulers asked him and said to him, "Good teacher, what must I do to inherit eternal life?"
19	And Jesus said unto him, Why callest thou me good? none is good, save one, that is, God.	Jesus said to him: Why callest thou me, good? For, there is none good, except one; God.	Jesus said to him, "Why do you call me good? There is none good, except one, God.
20	Thou knowest the commandments, Do not commit adultery, Do not kill, Do not steal, Do not bear false witness, Honour thy father and thy mother.	Thou knowest the commandments: Thou shalt not kill; and thou shalt not commit adultery; and thou shalt not steal; and thou shalt not testify a false testimony; honor thy father and thy mother.	You know the commandments: DO NOT KILL, and DO NOT COMMIT ADULTERY, and DO NOT STEAL, and DO NOT BEAR WITNESS THAT IS FALSE. HONOR YOUR FATHER AND YOUR MOTHER."
21	And he said, All these have I kept from my youth up.	He said to him: All these have I kept, from my childhood.	He said to him, "All these [things] I have kept from my youth."
22	Now when Jesus heard these things, he said unto him, Yet lackest thou one thing: sell all that thou hast, and distribute unto the poor, and thou shalt have treasure in heaven: and come, follow me.	And when Jesus heard these [words], he said to him: One thing is lacking to thee: go, sell all that thou hast, and give to the poor; and thou wilt have a treasure in heaven; and come after me.	And when Jesus heard these [things] he said to him, "You lack one [thing]. Go [and] sell everything that you have and give to the poor and you will have a treasure in heaven and follow me."
23	And when he heard this, he was very sorrowful: for he was very rich.	And he, when he heard these [words], was dejected; for he was very rich.	But when he heard these [things], he was sad, for he was very rich.
24	And when Jesus saw that he was very sorrowful, he said, How hardly shall they that have riches enter into the kingdom of God!	And when Jesus saw that he was dejected, he said: How difficult [it is], for those that have wealth to enter into the kingdom of God!	And when Jesus saw that he was sad, he said, "How difficult [it is] for those who have possessions to enter the kingdom of God,

	KJV	Murdock	Magiera
	LUKE	*Chapter 18*	
25	For it is easier for a camel to go through a needle's eye, than for a rich man to enter into the kingdom of God.	It is easier for a camel to enter the eye of a needle, than a rich man the kingdom of God.	because it is easier for a camel to enter through the eye of a needle, than [for] a rich man [to enter] the kingdom of God."
26	And they that heard it said, Who then can be saved?	They who heard [it], said to him: Who then can have life?	Those who heard were saying to him, "Then who is able to have life?"
27	And he said, The things which are impossible with men are possible with God.	And Jesus said: Those things which, with men, cannot be, with God, can be.	And Jesus said, "Those [things] that with men are not possible, with God are possible."
28	Then Peter said, Lo, we have left all, and followed thee.	Simon Cephas said to him: Lo, we have left every thing, and come after thee.	Simon Peter said to him, "Behold, we have left everything and have followed you."
29	And he said unto them, Verily I say unto you, There is no man that hath left house, or parents, or brethren, or wife, or children, for the kingdom of God's sake,	Jesus said to him: Verily I say to you: There is no man, who hath left houses, or parents, or brothers, or wife, or children, for the sake of the kingdom of God,	Jesus said to him, "Truly I say to you, there is no man who has left houses or parents or brothers or wife or children because of the kingdom of God
30	Who shall not receive manifold more in this present time, and in the world to come life everlasting.	that shall not receive manifold in the present time, and, in the coming world, eternal life.	and will not receive doubly many [things] in this time, and in the age to come, eternal life."
31	Then he took unto him the twelve, and said unto them, Behold, we go up to Jerusalem, and all things that are written by the prophets concerning the Son of man shall be accomplished.	And Jesus took his twelve, and said to them: Behold, we are going up to Jerusalem; and all the things written in the prophets, concerning the Son of man, will be fulfilled.	And Jesus took his twelve and said to them, "Behold, we go up to Jerusalem and all the things that are written in the prophets about the Son of Man will be fulfilled,
32	For he shall be delivered unto the Gentiles, and shall be mocked, and spitefully entreated, and spitted on:	For he will be delivered over to the Gentiles; and they will mock him, and spit in his face;	for he will be delivered to the Gentiles and they will mock him and they will spit in his face.
33	And they shall scourge him, and put him to death: and the third day he shall rise again.	and will scourge him, and will treat him with ignominy, and will kill him; and, the third day, he will arise.	And they will beat him and they will despise him and they will kill him, and on the third day he will rise up."
34	And they understood none of these things: and this saying was hid from them, neither knew they the things which were spoken.	But not one of these things, did they understand; but this subject was hidden from them, and they knew not the things told to them.	And they did not understand any of these [things], but this saying was hidden from them and they did not know these [things] that were spoken to them.
35	And it came to pass, that as he was come nigh unto Jericho, a certain blind man sat by the way side begging:	And as they came near to Jericho, a blind man was sitting by the side of the way, begging.	And when he was near to Jericho, a certain blind man was sitting by the side of the road, begging.
36	And hearing the multitude pass by, he asked what it meant.	And he heard the noise of the multitude that passed, and inquired what it was.	And he heard the sound of the crowd that was passing by and he asked, "Who is this [man]?"
37	And they told him, that Jesus of Nazareth passeth by.	They say to him: Jesus the Nazarean is passing by.	They said to him, "Jesus the Nazarene is passing by."
38	And he cried, saying, Jesus, thou Son of David, have mercy on me.	And he called out, and said: Jesus, Son of David, have mercy on me.	And he cried out and said, "Jesus, Son of David, have compassion on me."

Parallel Translations

	KJV	*Murdock*	*Magiera*

LUKE *Chapter 18*

	KJV	Murdock	Magiera
39	And they which went before rebuked him, that he should hold his peace: but he cried so much the more, Thou Son of David, have mercy on me.	And they that went before Jesus rebuked him, that he might be silent. But he cried out the more, Son of David, have mercy on me.	And those who were preceding Jesus rebuked him that he should be silent, but he cried out all the more, "Son of David, have compassion on me."
40	And Jesus stood, and commanded him to be brought unto him: and when he was come near, he asked him,	And Jesus stood, and commanded him to be called to him. And when he came to him, he asked him,	And Jesus stopped and commanded that they bring him to him. And when he was near to him, he asked him
41	Saying, What wilt thou that I shall do unto thee? And he said, Lord, that I may receive my sight.	and said to him: What wilt thou, that I do for thee? And he said: My Lord, that I may see.	and said to him, "What do you want me to do for you?" And he said, "My Lord, that I may see."
42	And Jesus said unto him, Receive thy sight: thy faith hath saved thee.	And Jesus said to him: See thou; thy faith hath vivified thee.	And Jesus said to him, "See! Your faith has given you life."
43	And immediately he received his sight, and followed him, glorifying God: and all the people, when they saw it, gave praise unto God.	And immediately he saw. And he followed after him, and glorified God. And all the people who beheld, gave glory to God.	And immediately, he saw and followed him and praised God. And all the people who saw [it] were giving glory to God.

Chapter 19

	KJV	Murdock	Magiera
1	And Jesus entered and passed through Jericho.	And as Jesus entered and passed through Jericho,	And when Jesus entered and passed through into Jericho,
2	And, behold, there was a man named Zacchaeus, which was the chief among the publicans, and he was rich.	[there was] a certain man, whose name was Zaccheus, who was rich, and chief of the publicans;	there was a certain man whose name was Zacchaeus, a rich man and the chief of the tax collectors.
3	And he sought to see Jesus who he was; and could not for the press, because he was little of stature.	and he wished to see Jesus, who he was; and could not, on account of the crowd; because Zaccheus was small in stature.	And he wanted to see who Jesus was, and was not able to from the crowd, because Zacchaeus was small in his stature.
4	And he ran before, and climbed up into a sycomore tree to see him: for he was to pass that way.	And he ran forward of Jesus, and climbed a wild fig-tree, in order to see him; for he was to pass that way.	And he ran before Jesus and climbed up a barren fig tree to see him, because he was going to pass by that way.
5	And when Jesus came to the place, he looked up, and saw him, and said unto him, Zacchaeus, make haste, and come down; for to day I must abide at thy house.	And when Jesus came to the place, he saw him, and said to him: Make haste and come down, Zaccheus; for I must be at thy house to-day.	And when Jesus came to that place, he saw him and said to him, "Hurry, come down, Zacchaeus, for today I must be in your house."
6	And he made haste, and came down, and received him joyfully.	And he hastened, and came down, and received him with gladness.	And he hurried [and] came down and received him, rejoicing.
7	And when they saw it, they all murmured, saying, That he was gone to be guest with a man that is a sinner.	And when they all saw [it], they murmured, and said: He hath gone in to be guest with a man that is a sinner.	And when all of them saw, they were murmuring and saying that he had entered [and] lodged with a sinful man.

Parallel Translations

LUKE *Chapter 19*

	KJV	Murdock	Magiera
8	And Zacchaeus stood, and said unto the Lord; Behold, Lord, the half of my goods I give to the poor; and if I have taken any thing from any man by false accusation, I restore him fourfold.	And Zaccheus stood up, and said to Jesus: Behold, my Lord, the half of my riches I give to the poor; and to every man, whom I have wronged in any thing, I restore fourfold.	And Zacchaeus stood up and said to Jesus, "Behold, my Lord, half of my possessions I give to the poor and to everyone I have defrauded anything I repay fourfold."
9	And Jesus said unto him, This day is salvation come to this house, forsomuch as he also is a son of Abraham.	Jesus said to him: This day, life is to this house; for he also is a son of Abraham.	Jesus said to him, "Today life has come to this house, because this [man] also is a son of Abraham,
10	For the Son of man is come to seek and to save that which was lost.	For the Son of man came, to seek and to vivify that which was lost.	for the Son of Man is come to seek and to give life to him who was perishing."
11	And as they heard these things, he added and spake a parable, because he was nigh to Jerusalem, and because they thought that the kingdom of God should immediately appear.	And when they heard these things, he proceeded to utter a similitude; because he was near to Jerusalem, and they supposed that the kingdom of God was to be soon developed.	And when they heard these [things], he went on to speak a parable because he was near to Jerusalem and they thought that the kingdom of God was going to be revealed at that time.
12	He said therefore, A certain nobleman went into a far country to receive for himself a kingdom, and to return.	And he said: A certain man of high birth was going to a distant place, to obtain royalty, and return again.	And he said, "A certain man, a great nobleman, went to a far country to receive a kingdom for himself and [then] to return.
13	And he called his ten servants, and delivered them ten pounds, and said unto them, Occupy till I come.	And he called his ten servants, and gave them ten pounds: and he said to them, Traffic until I come.	And he called his ten servants and gave them ten coins, and said to them, 'Do business until I come.'
14	But his citizens hated him, and sent a message after him, saying, We will not have this man to reign over us.	But the inhabitants of his city hated him; and they sent envoys after him, saying: We wish this man not to reign over us.	But his citizens hated him, and sent ambassadors after him and were saying, 'We do not want this [man] to rule over us.'
15	And it came to pass, that when he was returned, having received the kingdom, then he commanded these servants to be called unto him, to whom he had given the money, that he might know how much every man had gained by trading.	And when he had obtained the royalty, and had returned, he commanded those servants to be called, to whom he had committed his money; that he might know what each of them had gained by trading.	And when he received the kingdom and was returning, he said that they should call to him those [of] his servants to whom he had given money, to know what each and every one of them had gained.
16	Then came the first, saying, Lord, thy pound hath gained ten pounds.	And the first came, and said: My Lord, thy pound hath gained ten pounds.	And the first came said, 'My lord, your coin has gained ten coins.'
17	And he said unto him, Well, thou good servant: because thou hast been faithful in a very little, have thou authority over ten cities.	He said to him: Well done, good servant! As thou hast been faithful over a little, thou shalt have authority over ten towns.	He said to him, 'Well done, good servant. Because you have been found faithful with little, you will be a ruler over ten walled cities.'
18	And the second came, saying, Lord, thy pound hath gained five pounds.	And the second came, and said: My lord, thy pound hath produced five pounds.	And the second came and said, 'My lord, your coin has made five coins.'
19	And he said likewise to him, Be thou also over five cities.	He said likewise to him: Thou also shalt have authority over five towns.	He also said to this [man], 'You also will be a ruler over five walled cities.'

Parallel Translations

	KJV	*Murdock*	*Magiera*

LUKE *Chapter 19*

	KJV	Murdock	Magiera
20	And another came, saying, Lord, behold, here is thy pound, which I have kept laid up in a napkin:	And another came, and said: My lord, lo, this is thy pound, which hath been with me, laid up in fine linen.	And another came and said, 'My lord, behold, your coin has been with me since it was placed in a linen cloth,
21	For I feared thee, because thou art an austere man: thou takest up that thou layedst not down, and reapest that thou didst not sow.	For I was afraid of thee, because thou art a hard man, and takest up that which thou layedst not down, and reapest that which thou sowedst not.	for I feared you because you are a harsh man and you take up what you have not laid down and you reap what you have not sown.'
22	And he saith unto him, Out of thine own mouth will I judge thee, thou wicked servant. Thou knewest that I was an austere man, taking up that I laid not down, and reaping that I did not sow:	He said to him: Out of thy own mouth will I judge thee, thou evil servant. Thou knewest me, that I am a hard man, and that I take up what I laid not down, and reap what I sowed not!	He said to him, 'From your mouth I will judge you, evil servant. You knew me, that I am a harsh man and [that] I take up what I have not laid down and [that] I reap what I have not sown.
23	Wherefore then gavest not thou my money into the bank, that at my coming I might have required mine own with usury?	Why didst thou not put my money into the broker's hands, that when I came, I might have demanded it with interest?	Why did you not give my money to the exchange and I could come [and] demand it with its interest?'
24	And he said unto them that stood by, Take from him the pound, and give it to him that hath ten pounds.	And he said to them that stood before him: Take from him the pound, and give it to him with whom are the ten pounds.	And to those who were standing before him, he said, 'Take from him the coin and give [it] to the one who has ten coins.'
25	(And they said unto him, Lord, he hath ten pounds.)	They say to him: Our lord, there are with him ten pounds.	They were saying to him, 'Our lord, he has ten coins.'
26	For I say unto you, That unto every one which hath shall be given; and from him that hath not, even that he hath shall be taken away from him.	He said to them: I tell you, that to every one that hath, will be given; and from him that hath not, even what he hath will be taken away.	He said to them, 'I say to you, to whomever has, it will be given, and whoever does not have, even that which he has will be taken from him.
27	But those mine enemies, which would not that I should reign over them, bring hither, and slay them before me.	But as for those my enemies, who would not have me to reign over them, bring them and slay them before me.	But my enemies, those who did not want me to rule over them, bring them and kill them before me.'"
28	And when he had thus spoken, he went before, ascending up to Jerusalem.	And when Jesus had spoken these things, he went forward, to go to Jerusalem.	And when he had said these [things], Jesus left to travel on to Jerusalem.
29	And it came to pass, when he was come nigh to Bethphage and Bethany, at the mount called the mount of Olives, he sent two of his disciples,	And when he arrived at Bethphage and Bethany, near to the mount called the place of Olives, he sent two of his disciples,	And when he arrived at Bethphage and Bethany on the side of the mountain that is called the Mount of Olives, he sent two of his disciples.
30	Saying, Go ye into the village over against you; in the which at your entering ye shall find a colt tied, whereon yet never man sat: loose him, and bring him hither.	and said to them: Go ye to the village that is over against us, and as ye enter [it], ye will find a colt tied, on which no man ever rode; loose [him] and bring [him].	And he said to them, "Go to the village that is opposite us, and when you enter it, behold, you will find a colt that is tied, on which a man has never ridden. Untie [and] bring it.
31	And if any man ask you, Why do ye loose him? thus shall ye say unto him, Because the Lord hath need of him.	And if any man ask you, Why do ye loose him? say to him: Our Lord needeth him.	And if anyone asks you, 'Why are you untying it,' say thus to him, 'Our Lord needs [it].'"

Parallel Translations

LUKE *Chapter 19*

	KJV	*Murdock*	*Magiera*
32	And they that were sent went their way, and found even as he had said unto them.	And they went who were sent, and they found, as he said to them.	And those, who were sent, went and found [it] as he had told them.
33	And as they were loosing the colt, the owners thereof said unto them, Why loose ye the colt?	And as they loosed the colt, the owner of him said to them: Why do ye loose that colt?	And while they were untying the colt, its owners said to them, "Why are you untying that colt?"
34	And they said, The Lord hath need of him.	And they said: Because our Lord needeth him.	And they said to them, "Our Lord needs [it]."
35	And they brought him to Jesus: and they cast their garments upon the colt, and they set Jesus thereon.	And they brought him to Jesus. And they cast their garments upon the colt, and set Jesus upon him.	And they brought it to Jesus and they threw their garments on the colt and mounted Jesus on it.
36	And as he went, they spread their clothes in the way.	And as he went, they spread their garments in the way.	And as he went along, they were spreading their garments on the road.
37	And when he was come nigh, even now at the descent of the mount of Olives, the whole multitude of the disciples began to rejoice and praise God with a loud voice for all the mighty works that they had seen;	And when he came near to the descent of the place of Olives, the whole multitude of the disciples began to rejoice, and to praise God, with a loud voice, for all the mighty deeds which they had seen.	And when he came near to the descent of the Mount of Olives, the whole crowd of disciples began rejoicing and praising God with a loud voice for all the miracles that they had seen.
38	Saying, Blessed be the King that cometh in the name of the Lord: peace in heaven, and glory in the highest.	And they said: Blessed be the king, that cometh in the name of the Lord: peace in heaven, and glory on high.	And they were saying: BLESSED IS THE KING WHO HAS COME IN THE NAME OF THE LORD. PEACE IN HEAVEN AND GLORY IN THE HIGHEST.
39	And some of the Pharisees from among the multitude said unto him, Master, rebuke thy disciples.	And some of the Pharisees from among the crowd, said to him: Rabbi, rebuke thy disciples.	And some of the Pharisees from among the crowds were saying to him, "My Master, rebuke your disciples."
40	And he answered and said unto them, I tell you that, if these should hold their peace, the stones would immediately cry out.	He said to them: I tell you, that, if these should be silent, the stones would cry out.	He said to them, "I say to you, if these would be quiet, the stones would cry out."
41	And when he was come near, he beheld the city, and wept over it,	And as he drew near, and beheld the city, he wept over it:	And when he came near and saw the city, he wept over it.
42	Saying, If thou hadst known, even thou, at least in this thy day, the things which belong unto thy peace! but now they are hid from thine eyes.	and said: O, hadst thou known the things that are of thy peace, at least in this thy day: but now they are hidden from thy eyes.	And he said, "Would that you had known those [things] that were for your peace, even in this your day, but now they are hidden from your eyes.
43	For the days shall come upon thee, that thine enemies shall cast a trench about thee, and compass thee round, and keep thee in on every side,	For the days will come upon thee, when thy enemies will encompass thee, and besiege thee on every side.	But the days will come to you when your enemies will surround you and will pressure you on every side.
44	And shall lay thee even with the ground, and thy children within thee; and they shall not leave in thee one stone upon another; because thou knewest not the time of thy visitation.	And they will destroy thee, and thy children within thee; and will not leave in thee one stone upon another; because thou knewest not the time of thy visitation.	And they will overthrow you and your children within you and they will not leave a stone on a stone in you, for you did not know the time of your visitation."

Parallel Translations

	KJV	Murdock	Magiera
	LUKE Chapter 19		
45	And he went into the temple, and began to cast out them that sold therein, and them that bought;	And when he entered the temple, he began to expel those who bought and sold in it.	And when he entered the temple, he began to throw out those who were selling and buying in it.
46	Saying unto them, It is written, My house is the house of prayer: but ye have made it a den of thieves.	And he said to them: It is written, My house is a house of prayer; but ye have made it a den of robbers.	And he said to them, "It is written: MY HOUSE IS A HOUSE OF PRAYER, but you have made it a den of robbers."
47	And he taught daily in the temple. But the chief priests and the scribes and the chief of the people sought to destroy him,	And he taught daily in the temple: and the chief priests and Scribes and Elders of the people, sought to destroy him.	And he taught everyday in the temple and the chief priests and scribes and elders of the people were seeking to destroy him.
48	And could not find what they might do: for all the people were very attentive to hear him.	But they found not, what they could do to him; for all the people hung upon him to hear him.	And they were not able to find to do to him, for all the people were intent to hear him.
	Chapter 20		
1	And it came to pass, that on one of those days, as he taught the people in the temple, and preached the gospel, the chief priests and the scribes came upon him with the elders,	And on one of those days, as he was teaching the people in the temple, and preaching, the chief priests and Scribes, with the Elders, came upon him,	And it happened [that] on one of the days when he was teaching to the people in the temple and preaching, the chief priests and scribes with the elders rose up against him.
2	And spake unto him, saying, Tell us, by what authority doest thou these things? or who is he that gave thee this authority?	and said to him: Tell us, by what authority thou doest these things? And who is it, that gave thee this authority?	And they were saying to him, "Tell us with what authority you do these [things] and who is it who gave you this authority?"
3	And he answered and said unto them, I will also ask you one thing; and answer me:	Jesus answered, and said to them: I also will ask you a word, and tell ye me.	Jesus answered and said to them, "I will also ask you a question and [you] tell me,
4	The baptism of John, was it from heaven, or of men?	The baptism of John, was it from heaven, or from men?	the baptism of John, was it from heaven or from men?"
5	And they reasoned with themselves, saying, If we shall say, From heaven; he will say, Why then believed ye him not?	And they reasoned with themselves, and said: If we say, From heaven; he will say to us, And why did ye not believe him?	And they were reasoning among themselves and were saying, "If we say from heaven, he will say to us, 'Then why do you not believe him?'
6	But and if we say, Of men; all the people will stone us: for they be persuaded that John was a prophet.	But if we say, From men; all the people will stone us; for they are persuaded that John was a prophet.	And if we say from men, the people will stone us, for they all are convinced that John was a prophet."
7	And they answered, that they could not tell whence it was.	And they said to him: We do not know, whence it was.	And they said to him, "We do not know from where it is."
8	And Jesus said unto them, Neither tell I you by what authority I do these things.	Jesus said to them: Neither do I tell you, by what authority I do these things.	Jesus said to them, "Neither will I tell you with what authority I do these [things]."
9	Then began he to speak to the people this parable; A certain man planted a vineyard, and let it forth to husbandmen, and went into a far country for a long time.	And he began to utter this similitude to the people: A certain man planted a vineyard, and leased it to cultivators, and went abroad for a long time.	And he began to speak this parable to the people. "A certain man planted a vineyard and handed it over to workers and stayed away [for] a long time.

Parallel Translations

LUKE *Chapter 20*

	KJV	*Murdock*	*Magiera*
10	And at the season he sent a servant to the husbandmen, that they should give him of the fruit of the vineyard: but the husbandmen beat him, and sent him away empty.	And in time, he sent his servant to the cultivators, that they might give him of the fruits of the vineyard. But the cultivators beat him, and sent him away empty.	And in time, he sent his servant to the workers that they should give him of the fruit of the vineyard. But the workers beat him and sent him away empty-handed.
11	And again he sent another servant: and they beat him also, and entreated him shamefully, and sent him away empty.	And again he sent another servant; and him also they beat, and treated with rudeness, and sent empty away.	And in addition he sent another servant. And they also beat that one and shamefully treated him and sent him away empty-handed.
12	And again he sent a third: and they wounded him also, and cast him out.	And again he sent the third. And they wounded him, and cast him out.	And in addition he sent a third. And also they wounded that one and threw him out.
13	Then said the lord of the vineyard, What shall I do? I will send my beloved son: it may be they will reverence him when they see him.	The lord of the vineyard said: What shall I do? I will send my dear son. Perhaps they will look upon him, and be ashamed.	The lord of the vineyard said, 'What should I do? I will send my beloved son. Perhaps they will see him and respect [him].'
14	But when the husbandmen saw him, they reasoned among themselves, saying, This is the heir: come, let us kill him, that the inheritance may be ours.	But when the cultivators saw him, they reasoned with themselves, and said: This is the heir; come, let us kill him, and the inheritance will be ours.	But when the workers saw him they were reasoning among themselves and were saying, 'This is the heir. Come, let us kill him and the inheritance will be ours.'
15	So they cast him out of the vineyard, and killed him. What therefore shall the lord of the vineyard do unto them?	And they cast him out of the vineyard, and slew him. What therefore will the lord of the vineyard do to them?	And they threw him outside of the vineyard and killed him. Therefore what should the lord of the vineyard do to them?
16	He shall come and destroy these husbandmen, and shall give the vineyard to others. And when they heard it, they said, God forbid.	He will come, and destroy those cultivators, and will lease the vineyard to others. And when they heard [it], they said: This shall not be.	He will come and destroy those workers and will give the vineyard to others." And when they heard [it] they said, "This should not be."
17	And he beheld them, and said, What is this then that is written, The stone which the builders rejected, the same is become the head of the corner?	And he looked upon them, and said: What is that which is written, The stone, which the builders rejected, is become the chief corner stone?	And he gazed at them and said, "And what is that which is written: THE STONE THAT THE BUILDERS REJECTED HAS BECOME THE HEAD OF THE CORNER OF THE CORNERSTONE?
18	Whosoever shall fall upon that stone shall be broken; but on whomsoever it shall fall, it will grind him to powder.	And whoever shall fall upon this stone, will be broken; and on whomsoever it shall fall, it will crush him in pieces.	And whoever will fall on that stone will be bruised, and whomever it falls on, it will blow him away [as chaff]."
19	And the chief priests and the scribes the same hour sought to lay hands on him; and they feared the people: for they perceived that he had spoken this parable against them.	And the chief priests and Scribes sought to lay hands on him, at that time; but they were afraid of the people; for they knew, that he spoke this similitude against them.	And the chief priests and scribes were wanting to lay hands on him at that time, yet they were afraid of the people, for they knew that he had spoken this parable against them.

Parallel Translations

	KJV	Murdock	Magiera
LUKE	*Chapter 20*		
20	And they watched him, and sent forth spies, which should feign themselves just men, that they might take hold of his words, that so they might deliver him unto the power and authority of the governor.	And they sent to him spies, who feigned themselves righteous men, that they might insnare him in discourse, and deliver him up to a court, and to the authority of the president.	And they sent to him spies who were acting like just [men] to catch him in speech and to deliver him to the judge and to the authority of the governor.
21	And they asked him, saying, Master, we know that thou sayest and teachest rightly, neither acceptest thou the person of any, but teachest the way of God truly:	And they questioned him, and said to him: Teacher, we know that thou speakest and teachest correctly, and hast no respect of persons, but teachest the way of God in truth.	And they asked him and said to him, "Teacher, we know that you speak and teach rightly and do not respect persons, but rather you teach the way of God with truthfulness.
22	Is it lawful for us to give tribute unto Caesar, or no?	Is it lawful for us to pay head-money to Caesar, or not?	Is it lawful for us to give the poll tax to Caesar or not?"
23	But he perceived their craftiness, and said unto them, Why tempt ye me?	But he perceived their craftiness, and said: Why tempt ye me?	But he perceived their craftiness and said, "Why do you tempt me?
24	Shew me a penny. Whose image and superscription hath it? They answered and said, Caesar's.	Show me a denarius. Whose is this image and superscription upon it? They said to him, Caesar's.	Show me a denarius. Whose image and inscriptions are on it?" And they said, "That of Caesar."
25	And he said unto them, Render therefore unto Caesar the things which be Caesar's, and unto God the things which be God's.	Jesus said to them: Then, give to Caesar what is Caesar's, and to God what is God's.	Jesus said to them, "Give therefore that which is of Caesar to Caesar and that which is of God to God."
26	And they could not take hold of his words before the people: and they marvelled at his answer, and held their peace.	And they could not catch from him a word [of accusation] before the people: and they were surprised at his answers, and were silent.	And they were not able to capture a word from him before the people, and they marveled at his answer and were silent.
27	Then came to him certain of the Sadducees, which deny that there is any resurrection; and they asked him,	And some of the Sadducees, who say there is no resurrection, came and questioned him,	And some of the Sadducees came near, those who were saying that there is no resurrection, and they asked him
28	Saying, Master, Moses wrote unto us, If any man's brother die, having a wife, and he die without children, that his brother should take his wife, and raise up seed unto his brother.	and said to him: Teacher, Moses wrote to us, that if a man's brother die, who had a wife without children, his [surviving] brother shall take his wife, and raise up seed to his [deceased] brother.	and said to him, "Teacher, Moses wrote to us, 'If a brother of a man, who has a wife, should die without children, he should take the wife of his brother and raise up seed for his brother.'
29	There were therefore seven brethren: and the first took a wife, and died without children.	Now, there were seven brothers; and the first took a wife, and died without children.	Now there were seven brothers. The first took a wife and died without children.
30	And the second took her to wife, and he died childless.	And the second took her to wife; and he died without children.	And the second took her for his wife, and this [one] died without children.
31	And the third took her; and in like manner the seven also: and they left no children, and died.	And again, the third took her, and in like manner also all the seven; and they died, and left no children.	And the third took her again, and so also the seven of them. And they died and did not leave children.
32	Last of all the woman died also.	At last, the woman likewise died.	And finally the woman also died.

Parallel Translations

	KJV	Murdock	Magiera
	LUKE	*Chapter 20*	
33	Therefore in the resurrection whose wife of them is she? for seven had her to wife.	In the resurrection, therefore, of which of them will she be the wife, for the seven took her?	Therefore, in the resurrection, whose wife will she be, for seven of them married her?"
34	And Jesus answering said unto them, The children of this world marry, and are given in marriage:	Jesus said to them: The children of this world take wives, and wives are given to husbands.	Jesus said to them, "The children of this world take women and women are [given] to men,
35	But they which shall be accounted worthy to obtain that world, and the resurrection from the dead, neither marry, nor are given in marriage:	But they who are worthy of that world, and of the resurrection from the dead, do not take wives, nor are wives given to husbands.	but those who are worthy of that world and of the resurrection that is from the dead neither take women nor are women [given] to men.
36	Neither can they die any more: for they are equal unto the angels; and are the children of God, being the children of the resurrection.	Neither can they die any more; for they are as the angels, and are the children of God, because they are children of the resurrection.	For neither are they able to die again, for they are like the angels and are sons of God, because they are sons of the resurrection.
37	Now that the dead are raised, even Moses shewed at the bush, when he calleth the Lord the God of Abraham, and the God of Isaac, and the God of Jacob.	But that the dead will arise, even Moses showed; for, at the bush, he maketh mention, while he saith: The Lord, the God of Abraham, the God of Isaac, and the God of Jacob.	Now that the dead will rise even Moses showed, for he mentioned [it] at the bush when he said: THE LORD, THE GOD OF ABRAHAM AND THE GOD OF ISAAC AND THE GOD OF JACOB.
38	For he is not a God of the dead, but of the living: for all live unto him.	Now God is not [the God] of the dead, but of the living; for they all live to him.	And he is not the God of the dead, but of the living, for all are alive to him."
39	Then certain of the scribes answering said, Master, thou hast well said.	And some of the Scribes answered, and said to him: Teacher, thou hast spoken well.	And some of the scribes answered and said to him, "Teacher, you have spoken well."
40	And after that they durst not ask him any question at all.	And they did not again venture to question him, on any matter.	And they did not dare to ask him about anything again.
41	And he said unto them, How say they that Christ is David's son?	And he said also to them: How do the Scribes say of Messiah, that he is the son of David?	And he said to them, "In what way do the scribes say concerning the Messiah that he is the Son of David?
42	And David himself saith in the book of Psalms, The LORD said unto my Lord, Sit thou on my right hand,	And David himself said, in the book of Psalms: The Lord said to my Lord, seat thyself at my right hand,	Even David said in the book of Psalms: THE LORD SAID TO MY LORD, SIT AT MY RIGHT [HAND]
43	Till I make thine enemies thy footstool.	until I shall place thy foes under thy feet.	UNTIL I PLACE YOUR ENEMIES UNDER YOUR FEET.
44	David therefore calleth him Lord, how is he then his son?	If David, therefore, called him, My Lord; how is he his son?	If therefore David called him, 'My Lord,' how is he his son?"
45	Then in the audience of all the people he said unto his disciples,	And while all the people heard, he said to his disciples:	And while all the people were listening, he said to his disciples,
46	Beware of the scribes, which desire to walk in long robes, and love greetings in the markets, and the highest seats in the synagogues, and the chief rooms at feasts;	Beware of the Scribes, who choose to walk in long robes, and love a salutation in the streets, and the chief seats in the synagogues, and the chief couches at suppers:	"Beware of the scribes who want to walk in robes and love a greeting in the streets and the chief places in the synagogues and the best seats at meals.

	KJV	Murdock	Magiera
	LUKE Chapter 20		
47	Which devour widows' houses, and for a shew make long prayers: the same shall receive greater damnation.	who eat up the houses of widows, under pretence that they prolong their prayers. They will receive a greater condemnation.	Those who devour the houses of widows with the pretext of lengthening their prayers, the same will receive a greater judgment."
	Chapter 21		
1	And he looked up, and saw the rich men casting their gifts into the treasury.	And Jesus looked upon the rich, who cast their oblations into the treasury.	And Jesus looked at the rich [men] who were putting their gifts in the treasury.
2	And he saw also a certain poor widow casting in thither two mites.	And he saw also a certain poor widow, who cast in two mites.	And he also saw a certain poor widow who put in two small coins.
3	And he said, Of a truth I say unto you, that this poor widow hath cast in more than they all:	And he said: Truly I say to you, that this poor widow hath cast in more than any one.	And he said, "I speak the truth to you that this poor widow has put in more than everyone.
4	For all these have of their abundance cast in unto the offerings of God: but she of her penury hath cast in all the living that she had.	For all they, from what was superfluous to them, have cast into the receptacle of oblations to God; but she, from her penury, hath cast in all that she possessed.	For all of these have put into the place of the offerings of God from what was left over to them, but this [widow] from her need has put in all that she owned."
5	And as some spake of the temple, how it was adorned with goodly stones and gifts, he said,	And when some spoke of the temple, as adorned with goodly stones and oblations, Jesus said to them:	And while some were speaking about the temple, how it was adorned with beautiful stones and with gifts, Jesus said to them,
6	As for these things which ye behold, the days will come, in the which there shall not be left one stone upon another, that shall not be thrown down.	[As for] these things, on which ye gaze, the days will come, in which there will not be left a stone upon a stone, that is not cast down.	These [things] that you see, the days will come in which [one] stone will not be left on [another] stone that is not pulled down.
7	And they asked him, saying, Master, but when shall these things be? and what sign will there be when these things shall come to pass?	And they questioned him, and said: Teacher, when will these things be? And what is the sign that they are near to take place?	And they asked him and said, "Teacher, when will these [things] be and what is the sign when these [things] are about to happen?"
8	And he said, Take heed that ye be not deceived: for many shall come in my name, saying, I am Christ; and the time draweth near: go ye not therefore after them.	And he said to them: See, that ye be not deceived; for many will come in my name, and will say: I am Messiah and the time is near. But go ye not after them.	And he said to them, "See [that] you are not deceived, for many will come in my name and will say, 'I am the Messiah, and the time draws near,' but you should not follow them.
9	But when ye shall hear of wars and commotions, be not terrified: for these things must first come to pass; but the end is not by and by.	And when ye shall hear of wars and commotions, be not afraid; for these things are previously to take place, but the end is not yet come.	And when you hear of wars and riots, do not fear, for these [things] are going to happen first, but the end will not yet have arrived,
10	Then said he unto them, Nation shall rise against nation, and kingdom against kingdom:	For nation will rise against nation, and kingdom against kingdom;	for nation will rise against nation and kingdom against kingdom

Parallel Translations

LUKE *Chapter 21*

	KJV	Murdock	Magiera
11	And great earthquakes shall be in divers places, and famines, and pestilences; and fearful sights and great signs shall there be from heaven.	and great earthquakes will occur in several places, and famines, and pestilences; and there will be terrors, and trepidations, and great signs from heaven will be seen, and there will be great tempests.	and great earthquakes will occur in various places, and famines and plagues, and there will be fears and panic, and great signs from heaven will be seen and there will be much foul weather.
12	But before all these, they shall lay their hands on you, and persecute you, delivering you up to the synagogues, and into prisons, being brought before kings and rulers for my name's sake.	But before all these things, they will lay hands upon you, and will persecute you, and will deliver you up to councils and to prison, and will arraign you before kings and governors, on account of my name.	But before all these [things], they will lay hands on you and persecute you and deliver you to the synagogues and to prison, and they will bring you before kings and governors on account of my name.
13	And it shall turn to you for a testimony.	But it will be to you for a testimony.	But it will happen to you for a testimony.
14	Settle it therefore in your hearts, not to meditate before what ye shall answer:	And settle it in your hearts, that ye will not previously seek instruction for making a defence.	And put [it] in your heart[s] that you should not be learning to make a defense,
15	For I will give you a mouth and wisdom, which all your adversaries shall not be able to gainsay nor resist.	For I will give you a mouth and wisdom, which all your enemies will be unable to withstand.	for I will give to you a mouth and wisdom, so that all your enemies will not be able to stand against it.
16	And ye shall be betrayed both by parents, and brethren, and kinsfolks, and friends; and some of you shall they cause to be put to death.	And your parents, and your brothers, and your relatives, and your friends, will deliver you up, and cause some of you to die.	And your fathers and your brothers and your kinsmen and your friends will betray you and they will kill some of you.
17	And ye shall be hated of all men for my name's sake.	And ye will be hated by every one, on account of my name.	And you will be hated by everyone on account of my name,
18	But there shall not an hair of your head perish.	But a hair of your head shall not perish.	yet not a hair from your head will be hurt.
19	In your patience possess ye your souls.	And by your patience, will ye preserve your souls.	And by your patience you will gain your life.
20	And when ye shall see Jerusalem compassed with armies, then know that the desolation thereof is nigh.	And when ye shall see Jerusalem with an army encompassing it, then know ye, that its destruction draweth nigh.	And when you see Jerusalem [with] an army surrounding it, then know that its destruction draws near.
21	Then let them which are in Judaea flee to the mountains; and let them which are in the midst of it depart out; and let not them that are in the countries enter thereinto.	Then let them who shall be in Judaea, flee to the mountain [district]; and let them, who are in the midst of it, flee away; and those in the fields, not enter it.	Then those who are in Judea should flee to the mountain and those who are within it should flee and [those] in the villages should not enter it,
22	For these be the days of vengeance, that all things which are written may be fulfilled.	For these are days of vengeance, to fulfill all that is written.	because these are the days of vengeance that everything that is written will be fulfilled.
23	But woe unto them that are with child, and to them that give suck, in those days! for there shall be great distress in the land, and wrath upon this people.	But woe to them that are with child, and to them that nurse children, in those days; for then will be great distress in the land, and wrath upon this people.	And woe to those who are pregnant and to those who are nursing in those days, for there will be a great torment in the land and wrath on this people.

	KJV	Murdock	Magiera
	LUKE	*Chapter 21*	
24	And they shall fall by the edge of the sword, and shall be led away captive into all nations: and Jerusalem shall be trodden down of the Gentiles, until the times of the Gentiles be fulfilled.	And they will fall by the edge of the sword, and be carried captive to every place. And Jerusalem will be trodden down by the Gentiles, until the times of the Gentiles shall be completed.	And they will fall by the edge of the sword and be led away captive to every land. And Jerusalem will be trampled by the Gentiles until the times of the Gentiles will be fulfilled.
25	And there shall be signs in the sun, and in the moon, and in the stars; and upon the earth distress of nations, with perplexity; the sea and the waves roaring;	And there will be signs in the sun, and in the moon, and in the stars; and distress of nations on the earth; and clasping of hands, from astonishment at the noise of the sea;	And there will be signs in the sun and in the moon and in the stars, and on the earth the torment of the nations and anxiety from the roaring of the sea,
26	Men's hearts failing them for fear, and for looking after those things which are coming on the earth: for the powers of heaven shall be shaken.	and dismay that driveth out the souls of men, from fear of that which is to come on the earth; and the powers of heaven will be moved.	and a shaking that draws out the lives of men from the fear of what is about to come on the earth, and the powers of heaven will be shaken.
27	And then shall they see the Son of man coming in a cloud with power and great glory.	And then will they see the Son of man coming in the clouds, with much power, and with great glory.	And then they will see THE SON OF MAN WHO WILL COME IN THE CLOUDS with much power and great glory.
28	And when these things begin to come to pass, then look up, and lift up your heads; for your redemption draweth nigh.	And when these things shall begin to be, take courage, and lift up your heads, for your deliverance draweth nigh.	And when these [things] begin to happen, take heart and lift up your heads, because your deliverance is near."
29	And he spake to them a parable; Behold the fig tree, and all the trees;	And he uttered a similitude to them. Look at the fig-tree, and all the trees.	And he told them a parable: "Look at the fig tree and all the trees,
30	When they now shoot forth, ye see and know of your own selves that summer is now nigh at hand.	When they bud forth, ye at once understand from them that summer approacheth.	because when they bud, you understand immediately from them that summer is near.
31	So likewise ye, when ye see these things come to pass, know ye that the kingdom of God is nigh at hand.	So also, when ye shall see all these things take place, know ye that the kingdom of God is near.	Likewise also, when you see these [things] that are happening, know that the kingdom of God is near.
32	Verily I say unto you, This generation shall not pass away, till all be fulfilled.	Verily I say to you, That this generation will not pass away, until all these things occur.	Truly I say to you, this generation will not pass away until all these [things] happen.
33	Heaven and earth shall pass away: but my words shall not pass away.	Heaven and earth will pass away; but my word will not pass away.	Heaven and earth will pass away, yet my words will not pass away.
34	And take heed to yourselves, lest at any time your hearts be overcharged with surfeiting, and drunkenness, and cares of this life, and so that day come upon you unawares.	Take heed to yourselves, that your hearts be, at no time, stupefied by gluttony and ebriety and worldly care; and so that day come upon you unawares.	And take heed to yourselves that your hearts should never become heavy in excess and in drunkenness and in the anxiety of the world, and that day should come suddenly on you.
35	For as a snare shall it come on all them that dwell on the face of the whole earth.	For, like a hunter's snare, it will spring upon all them that dwell upon the face of the whole land.	For as a snare it will ensnare all those who live on the face of all the earth.

LUKE Chapter 21

	KJV	Murdock	Magiera
36	Watch ye therefore, and pray always, that ye may be accounted worthy to escape all these things that shall come to pass, and to stand before the Son of man.	Be ye therefore vigilant, at all times, and prayerful; that ye may be worthy to escape the things that are to take place, and may stand before the Son of man .	Therefore, watch always and pray that you will be worthy to escape these [things] that are going to happen and [that] you will stand before the Son of Man."
37	And in the day time he was teaching in the temple; and at night he went out, and abode in the mount that is called the mount of Olives.	And, in the daytime he taught in the temple, and at night he went out and lodged in the mount, called the Place of Olives.	And in the daytime, he was teaching in the temple and at night he went out [and] was staying in the mountain that was called the Mount of Olives.
38	And all the people came early in the morning to him in the temple, for to hear him.	And all the people came early to him in the temple, to hear his discourse.	And all the people were preceding him to the temple to hear his word.

Chapter 22

	KJV	Murdock	Magiera
1	Now the feast of unleavened bread drew nigh, which is called the Passover.	And the feast of unleavened cakes, which is called the passover, drew near.	Now the Feast of Unleavened Bread, that is called the Passover, was near
2	And the chief priests and scribes sought how they might kill him; for they feared the people.	And the chief priests and Scribes sought how they might kill him, for they were afraid of the people.	and the chief priests and scribes were seeking how to kill him, for they were afraid of the people.
3	Then entered Satan into Judas surnamed Iscariot, being of the number of the twelve.	And Satan entered into Judas called Iscariot, who was of the number of the twelve.	And Satan entered into Judas, who was called Iscariot, who was from the number of the twelve.
4	And he went his way, and communed with the chief priests and captains, how he might betray him unto them.	And he went and conferred with the chief priests and Scribes, and the military commanders of the temple, how he might betray him to them.	And he went [and] talked with the chief priests and scribes and captains of the temple about how he might deliver him to them.
5	And they were glad, and covenanted to give him money.	And they were glad, and covenanted to give him money.	And they rejoiced and pledged to give him money.
6	And he promised, and sought opportunity to betray him unto them in the absence of the multitude.	And he promised them, and sought opportunity to betray him to them, in the absence of the multitude.	And he promised them and sought an opportunity to deliver him to them apart from the crowd.
7	Then came the day of unleavened bread, when the passover must be killed.	And the day of unleavened cakes arrived, on which it was customary for the passover to be slain.	And the day of the Feast of Unleavened Bread arrived, during which was the custom that the Passover be killed.
8	And he sent Peter and John, saying, Go and prepare us the passover, that we may eat.	And Jesus sent Cephas and John, and said to them; Go, prepare for us the passover, that we may eat it.	And Jesus sent Peter and John and said to them, "Go [and] prepare for us the Passover that we may eat."
9	And they said unto him, Where wilt thou that we prepare?	And they said to him: Where wilt thou, that we prepare?	And they said to him, "Where do you want us to prepare [it]?"
10	And he said unto them, Behold, when ye are entered into the city, there shall a man meet you, bearing a pitcher of water; follow him into the house where he entereth in.	He said to them: Lo, when ye enter the city, there will a man meet you, bearing a vessel of water. Go after him;	He said to them, "Behold, when you enter the city, a man will meet you who is bearing a jar of water. Follow him.

Parallel Translations

LUKE *Chapter 22*

	KJV	*Murdock*	*Magiera*
11	And ye shall say unto the goodman of the house, The Master saith unto thee, Where is the guestchamber, where I shall eat the passover with my disciples?	and where he entereth, say ye to the lord of the house: Our Rabbi saith, Is there a place of refreshment, in which I may eat the Passover, with my disciples?	And where he enters, say to the lord of the house, 'Our Master says, Where is a place of lodging where I may eat the Passover with my disciples?'
12	And he shall shew you a large upper room furnished: there make ready.	And lo, he will show you a large upper room that is furnished; there prepare ye.	And behold, he will show you a certain large upper room that is furnished. There make ready."
13	And they went, and found as he had said unto them: and they made ready the passover.	And they went, and found as he had said to them: and they made ready the passover.	And they went [and] found [the man] as he had told them and they prepared the Passover.
14	And when the hour was come, he sat down, and the twelve apostles with him.	And when the time arrived, Jesus came and reclined; and the twelve Legates with him.	And when the time was come, Jesus and the twelve apostles with him came [and] sat to eat.
15	And he said unto them, With desire I have desired to eat this passover with you before I suffer:	And he said to them: I have greatly desired to eat this passover with you, before I suffer.	And he said to them, "I have greatly desired to eat this Passover with you before I suffer.
16	For I say unto you, I will not any more eat thereof, until it be fulfilled in the kingdom of God.	For I say to you, That henceforth I shall not eat it, until it be fulfilled in the kingdom of God.	For I say to you, from now on I will not eat until it is fulfilled in the kingdom of God."
17	And he took the cup, and gave thanks, and said, Take this, and divide it among yourselves:	[And he took the cup, and gave thanks, and said: Take this, and divide it among you.	OMITTED IN PESHITTA TEXT
18	For I say unto you, I will not drink of the fruit of the vine, until the kingdom of God shall come.	For I say to you, That I shall not drink of the product of the vine, until the kingdom of God shall come.]	OMITTED IN PESHITTA TEXT
19	And he took bread, and gave thanks, and brake it, and gave unto them, saying, This is my body which is given for you: this do in remembrance of me.	And he took bread, and gave thanks, and brake, and gave to them, and said: This is my body, which is given for your sakes. This do ye, in remembrance of me.	And he took bread and gave thanks and broke [it] and gave [it] to them and said, "This is my body that is given for your sakes. This do for my remembrance."
20	Likewise also the cup after supper, saying, This cup is the new testament in my blood, which is shed for you.	And in like manner also concerning the cup, after they had supped, he said: This cup is the new testament in my blood, which, for your sakes, is poured out!	And likewise also, concerning the cup, after they had eaten supper he said, "This cup [is] the new covenant in my blood that is shed on behalf of you.
21	But, behold, the hand of him that betrayeth me is with me on the table.	But, behold, the hand of him that betrayeth me is on the table.	But, behold, the hand of my betrayer [is] on the table
22	And truly the Son of man goeth, as it was determined: but woe unto that man by whom he is betrayed!	And the Son of man goeth, as it was determined; but woe to that man, by whom he is betrayed.	and the Son of Man dies as it was determined. But woe to that man by whose hand he is betrayed!"
23	And they began to enquire among themselves, which of them it was that should do this thing.	And they began to inquire among themselves, which of them it was, that would do this.	And they began to examine among themselves which one of them indeed it was who was going to do this.

Parallel Translations

	KJV	*Murdock*	*Magiera*
	LUKE *Chapter 22*		
24	And there was also a strife among them, which of them should be accounted the greatest.	And there was contention also among them, who among them would be greatest.	And there was also a conflict among them about which of them was the greatest.
25	And he said unto them, The kings of the Gentiles exercise lordship over them; and they that exercise authority upon them are called benefactors.	And Jesus said to them: The kings of the nations, are their lords; and those exercising authority over them, are called benefactors.	And Jesus said to them, "The kings of the Gentiles are their lords and those who are authorities over them are called workers of good.
26	But ye shall not be so: but he that is greatest among you, let him be as the younger; and he that is chief, as he that doth serve.	But ye, not so: but he that is great among you, must be as the least; and he that is chief, as the servitor.	But you are not so, but he who is the greatest among you must be as the least and he who is chief as a servant.
27	For whether is greater, he that sitteth at meat, or he that serveth? is not he that sitteth at meat? but I am among you as he that serveth.	For, which is the greater, he that reclineth, or he that serveth? Is not he that reclineth? But I am among you, as he that serveth.	For who is greater, he who sits to eat or he who serves? Is it not he who sits to eat? But I am among you as one who serves.
28	Ye are they which have continued with me in my temptations.	Ye are they who have continued with me in my trials:	But you are those who have continued with me in my trials.
29	And I appoint unto you a kingdom, as my Father hath appointed unto me;	and I promise to you, as my Father hath promised to me, a kingdom:	And I promise to you, as my Father has promised a kingdom to me,
30	That ye may eat and drink at my table in my kingdom, and sit on thrones judging the twelve tribes of Israel.	that ye may eat and drink at the table of my kingdom, and may sit on thrones, and judge the twelve tribes of Israel.	that you will eat and drink at the table of my kingdom and you will sit on thrones and you will judge the twelve tribes of Israel."
31	And the Lord said, Simon, Simon, behold, Satan hath desired to have you, that he may sift you as wheat:	And Jesus said to Simon: Simon, lo, Satan hath desired to sift thee, as wheat:	And Jesus said to Simon, "Simon, behold, Satan is resigned to sift you like wheat.
32	But I have prayed for thee, that thy faith fail not: and when thou art converted, strengthen thy brethren.	but I have prayed for thee, that thy faith may not fail. And thou also, in time, turn; and confirm thy brethren.	And I have prayed for you that your faith would not be lacking. You also in time will turn and strengthen your brothers."
33	And he said unto him, Lord, I am ready to go with thee, both into prison, and to death.	And Simon said to him: My Lord, with thee I am ready, both for prison and for death.	And Simon said to him, "My Lord, I am ready [to go] with you even to prison and to death."
34	And he said, I tell thee, Peter, the cock shall not crow this day, before that thou shalt thrice deny that thou knowest me.	Jesus said to him: I tell thee, Simon, the cock will not crow this day, until thou hast three times denied that thou knowest me.	Jesus said to him, "I say to you, Simon, that the rooster will not crow today before you insist three times that you do not know me."
35	And he said unto them, When I sent you without purse, and scrip, and shoes, lacked ye any thing? And they said, Nothing.	And he said to them: When I sent you without purses, without wallets and shoes, lacked ye any thing? They say to him: Nothing.	And he said to them, "When I sent you out without purses and without bags and shoes, what did you lack?" They said to him, "Nothing."

	KJV	Murdock	Magiera
	LUKE	*Chapter 22*	
36	Then said he unto them, But now, he that hath a purse, let him take it, and likewise his scrip: and he that hath no sword, let him sell his garment, and buy one.	He said to them: Henceforth, let him that hath a purse, take it; and so likewise a wallet. And let him that hath no sword, sell his garment, and buy himself a sword.	He said to them, "From now on, he who has a purse should take [it] and likewise also a bag. And he who does not have a sword should sell his garment and buy a sword for himself.
37	For I say unto you, that this that is written must yet be accomplished in me, And he was reckoned among the transgressors: for the things concerning me have an end.	For I say to you, That this also, which was written, must be fulfilled in me: I shall be numbered with transgressors. For, all that relates to me, will be fulfilled.	For I say to you, this also that was written must be fulfilled in me: I WILL BE NUMBERED WITH THE UNJUST, for all [things] that concern me will be fulfilled."
38	And they said, Lord, behold, here are two swords. And he said unto them, It is enough.	And they said to him: Our Lord, lo, here are two swords. He said to them: They are sufficient.	And they said to him, "Our Lord, behold, here are two swords." He said to them, "They are sufficient."
39	And he came out, and went, as he was wont, to the mount of Olives; and his disciples also followed him.	And he went out, and proceeded, as was his custom, to the mount of the place of Olives; and his disciples followed him.	And he left and traveled (as he was accustomed) to the Mount of Olives and his disciples also followed him.
40	And when he was at the place, he said unto them, Pray that ye enter not into temptation.	And when he arrived at the place, he said to them: Pray ye, that ye enter not into temptation.	And when he arrived at the place, he said to them, "Pray, so that you should not enter into temptation."
41	And he was withdrawn from them about a stone's cast, and kneeled down, and prayed,	And he retired from them, about a stone's throw; and kneeled down, and prayed,	And he went away from them about [the distance] one throws a stone and he knelt and was praying.
42	Saying, Father, if thou be willing, remove this cup from me: nevertheless not my will, but thine, be done.	and said: Father, if it please thee, let this cup pass from me. Yet not my pleasure, but thine, be done.	And he said, "Father, if you want, let this cup pass by me. Nevertheless, not my will, but yours be done."
43	And there appeared an angel unto him from heaven, strengthening him.	And there appeared to him an angel from heaven, who strengthened him.	And an angel from heaven appeared to him to strengthen him.
44	And being in an agony he prayed more earnestly: and his sweat was as it were great drops of blood falling down to the ground.	And as he was in fear, he prayed earnestly; and his sweat was like drops of blood; and it fell on the ground.	And being in fear, he prayed earnestly and his sweat was as drops of blood and he fell down on the ground.
45	And when he rose up from prayer, and was come to his disciples, he found them sleeping for sorrow,	And he arose from his prayer, and came to his disciples: and he found them sleeping, from sorrow.	And he rose up from his prayer and came to his disciples and found them asleep from sorrow.
46	And said unto them, Why sleep ye? rise and pray, lest ye enter into temptation.	And he said to them: Why sleep ye? Arise, and pray, lest ye enter into temptation.	And he said to them, "Why are you sleeping? Rise up [and] pray, so that you should not enter into temptation."

Parallel Translations

	KJV	Murdock	Magiera
LUKE	*Chapter 22*		
47	And while he yet spake, behold a multitude, and he that was called Judas, one of the twelve, went before them, and drew near unto Jesus to kiss him.	And while he was speaking, lo, a multitude, and he that was called Judas, one of the twelve, came at their head. And he came up to Jesus, and kissed him. For he had given them this sign: Whom I shall kiss, he it is.	And while he was speaking, behold, a crowd with him who was called Judas, one of the twelve, came before them. And he came near to Jesus and kissed him, for he had given this sign to them, "Whomever I kiss is him."
48	But Jesus said unto him, Judas, betrayest thou the Son of man with a kiss?	Jesus said to him: Judas, is it with a kiss thou betrayest the Son of man?	Jesus said to him, "Judas, do you betray the Son of Man with a kiss?"
49	When they which were about him saw what would follow, they said unto him, Lord, shall we smite with the sword?	And when they that were with him, saw what occurred, they said to him: Our Lord, shall we smite them with the sword?	And when those who were with him saw what happened, they said to him, "Our Lord, should we strike them with swords?"
50	And one of them smote the servant of the high priest, and cut off his right ear.	And one of them smote a servant of the high priest, and took off his right ear.	And one of them struck the servant of the chief priests and took off his right ear.
51	And Jesus answered and said, Suffer ye thus far. And he touched his ear, and healed him.	And Jesus answered and said: Sufficient, thus far. And he touched the ear of him that was smitten, and healed him.	And Jesus answered and said, "This is enough." And he touched the ear of the one who was wounded and healed him.
52	Then Jesus said unto the chief priests, and captains of the temple, and the elders, which were come to him, Be ye come out, as against a thief, with swords and staves?	And Jesus said to those who had come upon him, the chief priests and Elders and military captains of the temple: Have ye come out against me, as against a robber, with swords, and with clubs, to take me?	And Jesus said to those who had come against him, the chief priests and the elders and the captains of the temple, "Do you come out against me as against a robber with swords and with clubs to arrest me?
53	When I was daily with you in the temple, ye stretched forth no hands against me: but this is your hour, and the power of darkness.	I was with you daily in the temple, and ye laid not hands upon me. But this is your hour, and the reign of darkness.	Every day I was with you in the temple and you did not lay hands on me. But this is your hour and the power of darkness."
54	Then took they him, and led him, and brought him into the high priest's house. And Peter followed afar off.	And they took him, and conducted him to the house of the high priest. And Simon followed after him, at a distance.	And they arrested [him and] brought him to the house of the high priest and Simon followed him from a distance.
55	And when they had kindled a fire in the midst of the hall, and were set down together, Peter sat down among them.	And they kindled a fire in the middle of the court, and sat around it; and Simon also sat among them.	And they kindled a fire in the middle of the enclosure and they were sitting around it and Simon also was sitting among them.
56	But a certain maid beheld him as he sat by the fire, and earnestly looked upon him, and said, This man was also with him.	And a certain maid saw him sitting at the fire, and she looked upon him, and said: This man also was with him.	And a certain young woman saw him while he was sitting by the fire and she looked at him and said, "This [man] was also with him."
57	And he denied him, saying, Woman, I know him not.	But he denied, and said: Woman, I have not known him.	And he denied [it] and said, "Woman, I do not know him."
58	And after a little while another saw him, and said, Thou art also of them. And Peter said, Man, I am not.	And a little after, another [person] saw him, and said to him: Thou too art one of them. And Cephas said: I am not.	And after a little while another saw him and said to him, "You also are of them," but Peter said, "I am not."

	KJV	Murdock	Magiera

LUKE *Chapter 22*

	KJV	Murdock	Magiera
59	And about the space of one hour after another confidently affirmed, saying, Of a truth this fellow also was with him: for he is a Galilaean.	And an hour after, another contended and said: Certainly, this man also was with him, for he likewise is a Galilean.	And after one hour another argued and said, "Truly this [man] also was with him, for he is also a Galilean."
60	And Peter said, Man, I know not what thou sayest. And immediately, while he yet spake, the cock crew.	Cephas said: Man, I know not what thou sayest. And immediately, while he was speaking, the cock crew.	Peter said, "Man, I do not know what you are talking about." And immediately while he was speaking the rooster crowed.
61	And the Lord turned, and looked upon Peter. And Peter remembered the word of the Lord, how he had said unto him, Before the cock crow, thou shalt deny me thrice.	And Jesus turned, and looked upon Cephas. And Simon remembered the word of our Lord, which he spoke to him: Before the cock shall crow, thou wilt deny me three times.	And Jesus turned and looked at Peter, and Simon remembered the word of our Lord that he had spoken to him, "Before the rooster will crow, you will deny me three times."
62	And Peter went out, and wept bitterly.	And Simon went out, and wept bitterly.	And Simon went outside [and] cried bitterly.
63	And the men that held Jesus mocked him, and smote him.	And the men who had taken Jesus, insulted him, and blinded him,	And the men who held Jesus captive were mocking him and were covering him
64	And when they had blindfolded him, they struck him on the face, and asked him, saying, Prophesy, who is it that smote thee?	and smote him on his face, and said: Prophesy thou, who smote thee?	and were striking him on his face and saying, "Prophesy who struck you."
65	And many other things blasphemously spake they against him.	And many other things they revilingly uttered, and spoke against him.	And many other [things] they were reviling and saying against him.
66	And as soon as it was day, the elders of the people and the chief priests and the scribes came together, and led him into their council, saying,	And when the day dawned, the Elders and chief priests and Scribes assembled together; and they led him to the place of their meeting,	And when [day] dawned, the elders and chief priests and scribes were gathered together and they took him to their council.
67	Art thou the Christ? tell us. And he said unto them, If I tell you, ye will not believe:	and said to him: If thou art the Messiah, tell us. He said to them: If I tell you, ye will not believe in me.	And they said to him, "If you are the Messiah, tell us." He said to them, "If I tell you, you will not believe me.
68	And if I also ask you, ye will not answer me, nor let me go.	And if I should ask you, ye will not return me an answer; nor will ye release me.	And if I ask you, you will not restore or will you release me.
69	Hereafter shall the Son of man sit on the right hand of the power of God.	From this time, the Son of man will sit on the right hand of the majesty of God.	From now on, the Son of Man will be seated at the right [hand] of the power of God."
70	Then said they all, Art thou then the Son of God? And he said unto them, Ye say that I am.	And they all said: Thou art then, the Son of God? Jesus said to them: Ye say that I am.	And all of them were saying, "Are you therefore the Son of God?" Jesus said to them, "You say that I am."
71	And they said, What need we any further witness? for we ourselves have heard of his own mouth.	They say: What further need have we of witnesses? For we have heard from his own mouth.	They said, "Why do we need more witnesses? For we have heard [it] from his mouth."

Chapter 23

	KJV	Murdock	Magiera
1	And the whole multitude of them arose, and led him unto Pilate.	And the whole company of them arose, and carried him before Pilate.	And the whole company of them rose up and brought him to Pilate.
2	And they began to accuse him, saying, We found this fellow perverting the nation, and forbidding to give tribute to Caesar, saying that he himself is Christ a King.	And they began to accuse him, and said: We have found this man seducing our people, and forbidding to pay the capitation money to Caesar, and declaring himself to be king Messiah.	And they began to accuse him and say, "We have found that this [man] is deceiving our nation and he denies that the poll tax should be given to Caesar. And he says about himself that he is a king, the Messiah."
3	And Pilate asked him, saying, Art thou the King of the Jews? And he answered him and said, Thou sayest it.	And Pilate interrogated him, and said to him: Art thou king of the Jews? He said to him: Thou hast said.	And Pilate asked him and said to him, "Are you the king of the Judeans?" He said to him, "You have said [it]."
4	Then said Pilate to the chief priests and to the people, I find no fault in this man.	And Pilate said to the chief priests and the company: I find no crime upon this man.	And Pilate said to the chief priests and to the crowd, "I do not find any cause against this man."
5	And they were the more fierce, saying, He stirreth up the people, teaching throughout all Jewry, beginning from Galilee to this place.	And they vociferated, and said: He raiseth disturbance among our people, by teaching in all Judaea, commencing from Galilee, and quite to this place.	And they were shouting and saying, "He incites our nation, teaching in all of Judea. And he began from Galilee up to here."
6	When Pilate heard of Galilee, he asked whether the man were a Galilaean.	And Pilate, when he heard the name Galilee, inquired if the man were a Galilean.	And Pilate, when he heard the name of Galilee, asked if the man was a Galilean.
7	And as soon as he knew that he belonged unto Herod's jurisdiction, he sent him to Herod, who himself also was at Jerusalem at that time.	And having learned that he was from under Herod's jurisdiction, he sent him to Herod; for he was at Jerusalem on those days.	And when he knew that he was under the authority of Herod, he sent him to Herod, because he was in Jerusalem in those days.
8	And when Herod saw Jesus, he was exceeding glad: for he was desirous to see him of a long season, because he had heard many things of him; and he hoped to have seen some miracle done by him.	And Herod rejoiced greatly when he saw Jesus, for he had been desirous to see him for a long time, because he had heard many things of him, and he hoped to see some sign from him.	And Herod, when he saw Jesus, was very glad, for he had wanted to see him for a long time because he had heard many [things] about him, and he thought that he might see some sign from him.
9	Then he questioned with him in many words; but he answered him nothing.	And he asked him many questions; but Jesus gave him no reply.	And he asked him many questions, but Jesus did not give him any answer.
10	And the chief priests and scribes stood and vehemently accused him.	And the chief priests and Scribes stood up, and accused him vehemently.	And the chief priests and scribes rose up and were vehemently accusing him.
11	And Herod with his men of war set him at nought, and mocked him, and arrayed him in a gorgeous robe, and sent him again to Pilate.	And Herod and his warriors contemned him. And when he had mocked him, he clothed him in a purple robe, and sent him to Pilate.	And Herod and his soldiers treated him with contempt and when he had mocked [him], he clothed him with garments of purple and sent him to Pilate.

Parallel Translations

	KJV	*Murdock*	*Magiera*
	LUKE *Chapter 23*		
12	And the same day Pilate and Herod were made friends together: for before they were at enmity between themselves.	And on that day, Pilate and Herod became friends to each other; for there had previously been enmity between them.	And in that day Pilate and Herod became friends with one another, for there had been a conflict between them from the start.
13	And Pilate, when he had called together the chief priests and the rulers and the people,	And Pilate called the chief priests and the rulers of the people,	And Pilate called the chief priests and the rulers and the people
14	Said unto them, Ye have brought this man unto me, as one that perverteth the people: and, behold, I, having examined him before you, have found no fault in this man touching those things whereof ye accuse him:	and said to them: Ye have brought this man before me, as a disturber of your people; and lo, I have examined him before you, and I find in the man no crime, among all that ye charge upon him.	and he said to them, "You have brought me this man as a rebel against of your nation and behold, I have examined him before your eyes and I have not found any fault in this man of all you have accused him.
15	No, nor yet Herod: for I sent you to him; and, lo, nothing worthy of death is done unto him.	Neither yet Herod: for I sent him to him, and lo, nothing deserving death hath been done by him.	Not even Herod [found anything], for I sent him to him and behold, nothing that is worthy of death has been done by him.
16	I will therefore chastise him, and release him.	I will therefore chastise him, and release him.	I will therefore punish him and let him go."
17	(For of necessity he must release one unto them at the feast.)	For it was a custom, that he should release one at the festival.	For it was a custom that he would release one [prisoner] to them at the feast.
18	And they cried out all at once, saying, Away with this man, and release unto us Barabbas:	And all the company vociferated, and said: Away with this man; and release to us Barabbas.	And the whole crowd cried out and said, "Take this [man] away and release Barabbas to us,"
19	(Who for a certain sedition made in the city, and for murder, was cast into prison.)	He was one who had been thrown into prison, on account of a sedition and murder which had occurred in the city.	him who was thrown into prison because of insurrection and murder that had happened in the city.
20	Pilate therefore, willing to release Jesus, spake again to them.	And Pilate, being disposed to release Jesus, conversed with them again.	And again Pilate spoke to them, wanting to release Jesus.
21	But they cried, saying, Crucify him, crucify him.	But they cried out, and said: Crucify him; crucify him.	But they cried out and said, "Crucify him, crucify him."
22	And he said unto them the third time, Why, what evil hath he done? I have found no cause of death in him: I will therefore chastise him, and let him go.	And he said to them the third time: But, what evil hath he done? I find no crime in him deserving of death. I will scourge him, therefore, and release him.	And the third time he said to them, "For what evil has this [man] done? I have not found any cause that is worthy of death in him. Therefore, I will punish him and let him go."
23	And they were instant with loud voices, requiring that he might be crucified. And the voices of them and of the chief priests prevailed.	But they were urgent, with a loud voice; and demanded of him, that they might crucify him.	But they were insisting with a loud voice and asking him to crucify him. And their voice and [that] of the chief priests prevailed.
24	And Pilate gave sentence that it should be as they required.	And Pilate decreed, that their request be granted.	And Pilate commanded that their request be done.

LUKE *Chapter 23*

	KJV	*Murdock*	*Magiera*
25	And he released unto them him that for sedition and murder was cast into prison, whom they had desired; but he delivered Jesus to their will.	And he released to them him, who for sedition and murder had been cast into prison, for whom they petitioned; and he delivered up Jesus to their pleasure.	And he released to them him who because of insurrection and murder was thrown into prison, whom they had requested, but he delivered Jesus to their will.
26	And as they led him away, they laid hold upon one Simon, a Cyrenian, coming out of the country, and on him they laid the cross, that he might bear it after Jesus.	And as they led him away, they seized Simon the Cyrenian, coming from the fields. and laid upon him the cross, to bear [it] after Jesus.	And as they were leading him, they took hold of Simon, a Cyrenian, who was coming from the country, and set the cross on him to carry [it] after Jesus.
27	And there followed him a great company of people, and of women, which also bewailed and lamented him.	And there followed after him a great multitude of people; and those women [also] who wailed and lamented over him.	And a large group of people were following him and women who were lamenting and mourning for him.
28	But Jesus turning unto them said, Daughters of Jerusalem, weep not for me, but weep for yourselves, and for your children.	And Jesus turned to them, and said to them: Daughters of Jerusalem, weep not for me; but weep rather for yourselves, and for your children.	And Jesus turned to them and said, "Daughters of Jerusalem, do not weep for me, but weep for yourselves and for your sons.
29	For, behold, the days are coming, in the which they shall say, Blessed are the barren, and the wombs that never bare, and the paps which never gave suck.	For lo, the days are coming, in which they will say: Happy the barren, and the wombs that never bore, and the breasts that never nursed.	For behold, the days are coming in which they will say, 'Blessed are the barren and the wombs that have not given birth and the breasts that have not nursed.'
30	Then shall they begin to say to the mountains, Fall on us; and to the hills, Cover us.	Then will they begin to say to the mountains, Fall upon us! and to the hills, Cover us!	THEN YOU WILL BEGIN TO SAY TO THE MOUNTAINS, 'FALL ON US,' AND TO THE HILLS, 'COVER US.'
31	For if they do these things in a green tree, what shall be done in the dry?	For if they do these things in a green tree, what will be in the dry?	For if they do these [things] in a green tree, what will happen in the dry?"
32	And there were also two other, malefactors, led with him to be put to death.	And there went along with him two others, malefactors, to be crucified.	And two others, evildoers were coming with him to be killed.
33	And when they were come to the place, which is called Calvary, there they crucified him, and the malefactors, one on the right hand, and the other on the left.	And when they came to a certain place which is called a Skull, they crucified him there; and the two malefactors, the one on his right hand, and the other on his left.	And when they had come to a certain place that was called 'The Skull,' they crucified him there, and those evildoers, one on his right and one on his left.
34	Then said Jesus, Father, forgive them; for they know not what they do. And they parted his raiment, and cast lots.	And Jesus said: Father, forgive them; for they know not what they do. And they divided his garments, casting a lot upon them.	And Jesus said, "Father, forgive them, for they do not know what they are doing." And they divided his garments and cast a lot for them.
35	And the people stood beholding. And the rulers also with them derided him, saying, He saved others; let him save himself, if he be Christ, the chosen of God.	And the people stood and looked on; and the rulers also derided him, and said: He quickened others; let him quicken himself, if he is the Messiah, the chosen of God.	And the people were standing and observing and the rulers also were mocking him and saying, "He saved others. Let him save himself if he is the Messiah, the chosen of God."

Parallel Translations

	KJV	*Murdock*	*Magiera*

LUKE *Chapter 23*

	KJV	Murdock	Magiera
36	And the soldiers also mocked him, coming to him, and offering him vinegar,	And the soldiers like wise mocked him, coming to him and offering him vinegar,	And the soldiers were also mocking him, while drawing near to him and offering him vinegar.
37	And saying, If thou be the king of the Jews, save thyself.	and saying to him: If thou art the king of the Jews, quicken thyself.	And they were saying to him, "If you are the king of the Judeans, save yourself."
38	And a superscription also was written over him in letters of Greek, and Latin, and Hebrew, THIS IS THE KING OF THE JEWS.	And there was likewise a superscription over him, written in Greek, and Latin, and Hebrew: THIS IS THE KING OF THE JEWS.	And there was also an inscription that was written over him in Greek and Latin and Hebrew: "This is the king of the Judeans."
39	And one of the malefactors which were hanged railed on him, saying, If thou be Christ, save thyself and us.	And one of the malefactors who were crucified with him, reproached him, and said: If thou art the Messiah, rescue thyself, and rescue us.	And one of those evildoers who was crucified with him was blaspheming against him and said, "If you are the Messiah, rescue yourself and rescue us also."
40	But the other answering rebuked him, saying, Dost not thou fear God, seeing thou art in the same condemnation?	But his fellow [Malefactor] rebuked him, said to him: Art thou not afraid even of God, seeing thou art under the same sentence?	And his companion rebuked him and said to him, "Are you not afraid even of God, because indeed you are in the same judgment?
41	And we indeed justly; for we receive the due reward of our deeds: but this man hath done nothing amiss.	And we justly; for we have a retribution according to our deserts, and according to our deeds; but nothing hateful hath been done by him.	And we justly, for as we deserve and as we have done we have been repaid, but nothing that is hateful has been done by this [man]."
42	And he said unto Jesus, Lord, remember me when thou comest into thy kingdom.	And he said to Jesus: My Lord, remember me, when thou comest into thy kingdom.	And he said to Jesus, "Remember me, my Lord, when you come in your kingdom."
43	And Jesus said unto him, Verily I say unto thee, To day shalt thou be with me in paradise.	Jesus said to him: Verily I say to you, That this day thou shalt be with me in paradise.	Jesus said to him, "Truly I say to you, today you will be with me in paradise."
44	And it was about the sixth hour, and there was a darkness over all the earth until the ninth hour.	And it was about the sixth hour; and darkness was over all the land, until the ninth hour.	Now it was about the sixth hour and darkness was on all the land until the ninth hour.
45	And the sun was darkened, and the veil of the temple was rent in the midst.	And the sun was darkened, and the curtain of the door of the temple was rent through its middle.	And the sun was dark and the veil of the temple was torn from the middle of it.
46	And when Jesus had cried with a loud voice, he said, Father, into thy hands I commend my spirit: and having said thus, he gave up the ghost.	And Jesus cried with a loud voice, and said: My Father, into thy hand I commit my spirit. Thus he spake, and expired.	And Jesus cried out with a loud voice and said, "MY FATHER, INTO YOUR HANDS I PLACE MY SPIRIT." He said this and died.
47	Now when the centurion saw what was done, he glorified God, saying, Certainly this was a righteous man.	And when the centurion saw what occurred, he glorified God and said: Certainly, this was a righteous man.	And when the centurion saw what had happened, he praised God and said, "Truly this man was just."
48	And all the people that came together to that sight, beholding the things which were done, smote their breasts, and returned.	And all the multitudes who had assembled at this spectacle, on seeing what occurred, returned, smiting upon their breasts.	And all the crowds, who were gathered for this sight, when they saw what had happened, returned, beating their breast[s].

LUKE *Chapter 23*

	KJV	*Murdock*	*Magiera*
49	And all his acquaintance, and the women that followed him from Galilee, stood afar off, beholding these things.	And there were standing at a distance, all they that knew Jesus, and those women who came with him from Galilee; and they beheld these things.	And all the acquaintances of Jesus were standing at a distance, and the women, who had come with him from Galilee, and they saw these [things].
50	And, behold, there was a man named Joseph, a counsellor; and he was a good man, and a just:	And there was a certain man, whose name was Joseph, a counsellor, from Ramath a city of Judaea, who was a good man and righteous;	And a certain man, whose name [was] Joseph, a counselor from Arimathaea, a city of Judea, was a good and just man.
51	(The same had not consented to the counsel and deed of them;) he was of Arimathaea, a city of the Jews: who also himself waited for the kingdom of God.	and he had not consented to their decision and deed; and he was waiting for the kingdom of God.	This [man] did not agree with their will and with their deed and was waiting for the kingdom of God.
52	This man went unto Pilate, and begged the body of Jesus.	This man went to Pilate, and begged the body of Jesus.	This [man] came near to Pilate and asked for the body of Jesus.
53	And he took it down, and wrapped it in linen, and laid it in a sepulchre that was hewn in stone, wherein never man before was laid.	And he took it down, and wrapped it in a winding-sheet of linen; and laid it in an excavated sepulchre, in which no one had hitherto been laid.	And he took it down and wrapped it in a sheet of linen and placed it in a hewn tomb in which no man yet had been placed.
54	And that day was the preparation, and the sabbath drew on.	And it was the day of preparation, and the sabbath began to dawn.	And it was the preparation day and the Sabbath was dawning.
55	And the women also, which came with him from Galilee, followed after, and beheld the sepulchre, and how his body was laid.	And those women who came with him from Galilee, approached, and viewed the sepulchre, and the manner in which the body was deposited.	And the women who had come with him from Galilee were near and they saw the grave and how his body had been placed.
56	And they returned, and prepared spices and ointments; and rested the sabbath day according to the commandment.	And they returned, and prepared perfumes and aromatics; and they rested on the sabbath, as it is commanded.	And they returned [and] prepared spices and ointments and rested on the Sabbath as was commanded.

Chapter 24

	KJV	*Murdock*	*Magiera*
1	Now upon the first day of the week, very early in the morning, they came unto the sepulchre, bringing the spices which they had prepared, and certain others with them.	And on the first day of the week, in the morning, while it was yet dark, they came to the sepulchre, and brought the aromatics they had prepared. And there were other women with them.	Now on the first [day] of the week, at dawn while [it was] dark, they came to the tomb and brought the spices they had prepared, and there were with them other women.
2	And they found the stone rolled away from the sepulchre.	And they found the stone rolled from the sepulchre.	And they found the stone that was rolled from the tomb.
3	And they entered in, and found not the body of the Lord Jesus.	And they entered, and found not the body of Jesus.	And they entered, yet did not find the body of Jesus.
4	And it came to pass, as they were much perplexed thereabout, behold, two men stood by them in shining garments:	And as they wondered at this, behold, two men stood opposite them; and their raiment was effulgent.	And it happened that while they were astonished about this, behold, two men stood above them and their clothing was shining.

KJV | *Murdock* | *Magiera*

LUKE *Chapter 24*

	KJV	Murdock	Magiera
5	And as they were afraid, and bowed down their faces to the earth, they said unto them, Why seek ye the living among the dead?	And they were in fear, and bowed their faces to the ground. And the men said to them: Why seek ye the living among the dead?	And they were in fear and bowed their faces to the ground. And they said to them, "Why do you seek the living with the dead?
6	He is not here, but is risen: remember how he spake unto you when he was yet in Galilee,	He is not here; he is risen. Remember how he conversed with you, when he was in Galilee,	He is not here. He has risen! Remember what he spoke to you while he was in Galilee
7	Saying, The Son of man must be delivered into the hands of sinful men, and be crucified, and the third day rise again.	and said, That the Son of man was to be delivered into the hands of sinful men, and to be crucified, and to rise on the third day.	and he said that the Son of Man will be delivered into the hands of men [who are] sinners and would be crucified, and after three days would rise?"
8	And they remembered his words,	And they remembered his words.	And they remembered his words.
9	And returned from the sepulchre, and told all these things unto the eleven, and to all the rest.	And they returned from the sepulchre, and related all these things to the eleven, and to the rest.	And they returned from the grave and told all these [things] to the eleven and to the rest.
10	It was Mary Magdalene, and Joanna, and Mary the mother of James, and other women that were with them, which told these things unto the apostles.	Now they were Mary Magdalena, and Joanna, and Mary the mother of James, and the others with them, who related these things to the Legates.	Now there was Mary Magdalene and Joanna and Mary the mother of James and the rest who were with them, who had told the apostles.
11	And their words seemed to them as idle tales, and they believed them not.	And these words appeared in their eyes as dreams: and they believed them not.	And these words seemed crazy in their eyes and they did not believe them.
12	Then arose Peter, and ran unto the sepulchre; and stooping down, he beheld the linen clothes laid by themselves, and departed, wondering in himself at that which was come to pass.	But Simon arose, and ran to the sepulchre, and looked in, and saw the linen lying by itself: and he went away wondering in himself at what had occurred.	And Simon stood up and ran to the grave and looked in [and] saw the linen clothes placed alone, and went away wondering in himself about what had happened.
13	And, behold, two of them went that same day to a village called Emmaus, which was from Jerusalem about threescore furlongs.	And lo, two of them, on the same day, were going to a village named Emmaus, distant sixty furlongs from Jerusalem.	And behold, two of them on the same day went to a village by the name of Emmaus, and it was sixty furlongs distant from Jerusalem.
14	And they talked together of all these things which had happened.	And they talked together of all that had occurred.	And they were speaking with each other about all those [things] that had happened.
15	And it came to pass, that, while they communed together and reasoned, Jesus himself drew near, and went with them.	And as they conversed, and questioned each other, Jesus came, and drew near, and walked with them.	And while they were speaking and questioning one another, Jesus came and approached them and was walking with them.
16	But their eyes were holden that they should not know him.	And their eyes were held, that they did not recognize him.	And their eyes were closed so that they did not recognize him.
17	And he said unto them, What manner of communications are these that ye have one to another, as ye walk, and are sad?	And he said to them: What are these discourses, which ye hold with each other, as ye walk and are sad?	And he said to them, "What are these words that you are speaking with each other while you walk and are sad?"

Parallel Translations

LUKE Chapter 24

	KJV	Murdock	Magiera
18	And the one of them, whose name was Cleopas, answering said unto him, Art thou only a stranger in Jerusalem, and hast not known the things which are come to pass there in these days?	And one of them, whose name was Cleopas, answered and said to him: Art thou only a stranger in Jerusalem, that thou knowest not the things that have occurred there in these days?	One of them whose name was Cleopas answered and said to him, "Are you indeed only a stranger from Jerusalem that you do not know what has happened in it in these days?"
19	And he said unto them, What things? And they said unto him, Concerning Jesus of Nazareth, which was a prophet mighty in deed and word before God and all the people:	He said to them: What things? They say to him: In regard to Jesus of Nazareth, a man who was a prophet, and mighty in discourse and in action, before God, and before all the people.	He said to them, "What [things]?" They said to him, "About Jesus who was from Nazareth, a man who was a prophet and was mighty in word and in deeds before God and before all the people.
20	And how the chief priests and our rulers delivered him to be condemned to death, and have crucified him.	And the chief priests and Elders delivered him up to a sentence of death, and crucified him.	And the chief priests and elders delivered him to the judgment of death and they crucified him.
21	But we trusted that it had been he which should have redeemed Israel: and beside all this, to day is the third day since these things were done.	But we expected that he was to deliver Israel. And lo, three days [have passed], since all these things occurred.	But we had hoped that he was going to deliver Israel and behold, three days [have passed] since all these [things] happened.
22	Yea, and certain women also of our company made us astonished, which were early at the sepulchre;	And moreover, certain women of ours astonished us; for they went early to the sepulchre;	But also [some of] our women astonished us, for they went early to the tomb
23	And when they found not his body, they came, saying, that they had also seen a vision of angels, which said that he was alive.	and as they did not find the body, they came and said to us: We saw angels there, and they said that he is alive.	and when they did not find his body, they came [and] told us, 'We saw angels there and they said about him that he is alive.'
24	And certain of them which were with us went to the sepulchre, and found it even so as the women had said: but him they saw not.	And also some of us went to the sepulchre; and they found, as the women reported; but him they saw not.	And also, [some of] our men went to the tomb and found the same as what the women had said, but they did not see him."
25	Then he said unto them, O fools, and slow of heart to believe all that the prophets have spoken:	Then Jesus said to them: O deficient in understanding, and slow of heart to believe all the things that the prophets uttered.	Then Jesus said to them, "Oh fools and dull of heart to believe in all those [things] that the prophets spoke!
26	Ought not Christ to have suffered these things, and to enter into his glory?	Were not these things to be; that the Messiah should suffer and that he should enter into his glory?	Were not for these [things] Messiah intended to endure and to enter into his glory?"
27	And beginning at Moses and all the prophets, he expounded unto them in all the scriptures the things concerning himself.	Then he began from Moses, and from all the prophets, and expounded to them concerning himself from all the scriptures.	And he began from Moses and from all the prophets and expounded to them about himself from all the scriptures.
28	And they drew nigh unto the village, whither they went: and he made as though he would have gone further.	And they drew near to the village to which they were going; and he made them feel, as if he would go to a more distant place.	And they came near the village to which they were going and he caused them to think that he was going to a more distant place.

LUKE *Chapter 24*

	KJV	Murdock	Magiera
29	But they constrained him, saying, Abide with us: for it is toward evening, and the day is far spent. And he went in to tarry with them.	And they urged him, and said to him: Tarry with us, for the day inclineth towards dark. And he went in to remain with them.	And they constrained him and said to him, "Remain with us because the day now is at an end [and it is starting] to become dark." And he entered to continue with them.
30	And it came to pass, as he sat at meat with them, he took bread, and blessed it, and brake, and gave to them.	And it occurred, while he reclined with them, that he took bread, and blessed, and brake, and gave to them.	And it happened that while he sat to eat with them, he took bread and blessed [it] and broke [it] and gave [it] to them.
31	And their eyes were opened, and they knew him; and he vanished out of their sight.	And instantly, their eyes were opened, and, they knew him. And he took himself from them.	And immediately their eyes were opened and they knew him. And he was taken from them.
32	And they said one to another, Did not our heart burn within us, while he talked with us by the way, and while he opened to us the scriptures?	And they said one to another: Did not our heart burn within us, while he talked with us by the way, and explained to us the scriptures?	And they said one to another, "Were not our heart[s] heavy within us while he talked with us along the road and expounded to us the scriptures?"
33	And they rose up the same hour, and returned to Jerusalem, and found the eleven gathered together, and them that were with them,	And they arose, the same hour, and returned: to Jerusalem. And they found the eleven assembled, and those with them,	And they rose up immediately and returned to Jerusalem. And they found the eleven, who were gathered together and those who were with them,
34	Saying, The Lord is risen indeed, and hath appeared to Simon.	who were saying: Certainly, our Lord hath risen; and he hath appeared to Simon.	saying, "Truly our Lord has risen and appeared to Simon."
35	And they told what things were done in the way, and how he was known of them in breaking of bread.	And they also related what occurred by the way, and how he became known to them, when he broke bread.	And those also related these [things] that had happened on the road and how he was made known to them while breaking bread.
36	And as they thus spake, Jesus himself stood in the midst of them, and saith unto them, Peace be unto you.	And while they were talking of these things, Jesus stood in the midst of them, and said to them: Peace be with you! It is I; be not afraid.	And while they were saying these [things], Jesus stood among them and said to them, "Peace [be] with you. It is I. Do not be afraid."
37	But they were terrified and affrighted, and supposed that they had seen a spirit.	And they were in trepidation and fear, for they supposed they saw a spirit.	And they were astonished and were in fear, for they supposed that they had seen a spirit.
38	And he said unto them, Why are ye troubled? and why do thoughts arise in your hearts?	Jesus said to them: Why are ye agitated? And why do imaginations arise in your hearts?	And Jesus said to them, "Why are you troubled and why do thoughts well up in your hearts?
39	Behold my hands and my feet, that it is I myself: handle me, and see; for a spirit hath not flesh and bones, as ye see me have.	Look at my hands and my feet, that it is myself. Handle me, and know; for a spirit hath not flesh and bones, as ye see me have.	Look at my hands and my feet, for it is I. Touch me and know that a spirit has no flesh and bones as you see that I have."
40	And when he had thus spoken, he shewed them his hands and his feet.	And as he said thus, he showed them his hands and his feet.	And while he said these [things], he showed them his hands and his feet.

Parallel Translations

	KJV	*Murdock*	*Magiera*
	LUKE	*Chapter 24*	
41	And while they yet believed not for joy, and wondered, he said unto them, Have ye here any meat?	And while they still believed not, for their joy, and were astonished; he said to them: Have ye here any thing to eat?	And while they did still not believe from their joy and were astonished, he said to them, "Do you have anything here to eat?"
42	And they gave him a piece of a broiled fish, and of an honeycomb.	And they gave him a piece of broiled fish, and of honeycomb.	And they gave him a portion of fish that was broiled and of a comb of honey.
43	And he took it, and did eat before them.	And he took, [and] ate before them.	And he took [and] ate [it] before them.
44	And he said unto them, These are the words which I spake unto you, while I was yet with you, that all things must be fulfilled, which were written in the law of Moses, and in the prophets, and in the psalms, concerning me.	And he said to them: These are the things which I said to you while I was with you, That all things written of me, in the law of Moses and in the prophets and in the psalms, must be fulfilled.	And he said to them, "These are the words that I spoke to you while I was with you, that it was necessary that everything be fulfilled that was written in the law of Moses and in the prophets and in the Psalms about me."
45	Then opened he their understanding, that they might understand the scriptures,	Then he opened their mind to understand the scriptures.	Then he opened their minds to understand the scriptures.
46	And said unto them, Thus it is written, and thus it behoved Christ to suffer, and to rise from the dead the third day:	And he said to them: Thus it is written, and thus it was right for Messiah to suffer, and rise from the dead on the third day;	And he said to them, "So it is written and so it was right that the Messiah should suffer and rise from the dead after three days
47	And that repentance and remission of sins should be preached in his name among all nations, beginning at Jerusalem.	and that, in his name, repentance for the remission of sins should be preached among all nations, and that the commencement be at Jerusalem.	and that repentance will be preached through his name for the forgiveness of sins in all the nations and [that] the beginning will be from Jerusalem.
48	And ye are witnesses of these things.	And ye are the witnesses of these things.	And you are a witness of these [things]
49	And, behold, I send the promise of my Father upon you: but tarry ye in the city of Jerusalem, until ye be endued with power from on high.	And I will send upon you the promise of my Father. But remain ye at Jerusalem until ye shall be clothed with energy from on high.	and I will send to you the promise of my Father. But remain in the city, Jerusalem, until you be clothed with power from on high."
50	And he led them out as far as to Bethany, and he lifted up his hands, and blessed them.	And he led them out as far as Bethany, and lifted his hands, and blessed them.	And he took them out up to Bethany and raised his hands and blessed them.
51	And it came to pass, while he blessed them, he was parted from them, and carried up into heaven.	And it occurred, while he blessed them, that he was separated from them, and ascended to heaven.	And it happened that while he blessed them, he was separated from them and taken up to heaven.
52	And they worshipped him, and returned to Jerusalem with great joy:	And they worshipped him, and returned to Jerusalem with great joy.	And they worshipped him and returned to Jerusalem with great joy.
53	And were continually in the temple, praising and blessing God. Amen.	And they were continually in the temple, praising and blessing God. Amen.	And they were always in the temple praising and blessing God. Amen.

Parallel Translations

JOHN *Chapter 1*

	KJV	*Murdock*	*Magiera*
1	In the beginning was the Word, and the Word was with God, and the Word was God.	In the beginning, was the Word; and the Word was with God; and the Word was God.	In the beginning was the word and that word was with God and God was that word.
2	The same was in the beginning with God.	He was in the beginning with God.	This [word] was in the beginning with God.
3	All things were made by him; and without him was not any thing made that was made.	Every thing was by his hand; and without him, was not any thing whatever that existed.	Everything existed by his hand and without him not even one [thing] existed [of] that which existed.
4	In him was life; and the life was the light of men.	In him was life; and the life was the light of man.	In him was life and the life was the light of men.
5	And the light shineth in darkness; and the darkness comprehended it not.	And this light shineth in the darkness; and the darkness apprehended it not.	And that light brought light in the darkness and the darkness did not overtake it.
6	There was a man sent from God, whose name was John.	There was a man sent from God, whose name was John.	There was a man who was sent from God whose name [was] John.
7	The same came for a witness, to bear witness of the Light, that all men through him might believe.	He came for testimony, to bear witness concerning the light.	This [man] came for a witness to bear witness concerning the light that everyone would believe by his hand.
8	He was not that Light, but was sent to bear witness of that Light.	He was not himself the light, but [came] to bear witness concerning the light.	He was not the light, but rather [he came] to bear witness concerning the light.
9	That was the true Light, which lighteth every man that cometh into the world.	The true light was that, which enlighteneth every man who cometh into the world.	For the light of truth was that which brings light to everyone who comes into the world.
10	He was in the world, and the world was made by him, and the world knew him not.	He was in the world; and the world was by his hand; and the world did not know him.	He was in the world and the world was by his hand and the world did not know him.
11	He came unto his own, and his own received him not.	He came to his own [people]; and his own [people] received him not.	He came to his own and his own did not receive him.
12	But as many as received him, to them gave he power to become the sons of God, even to them that believe on his name:	But such as received him, to them gave he the prerogative to be children of God; [even] to them that believe on his name;	But those who did receive him, to those who believed in his name, he gave authority to be sons of God,
13	Which were born, not of blood, nor of the will of the flesh, nor of the will of man, but of God.	who are born, not of blood, nor of the pleasure of the flesh, nor of the pleasure of man, but of God.	those who were birthed, not by blood, nor by the will of flesh, nor by the will of man, but rather by God.
14	And the Word was made flesh, and dwelt among us, (and we beheld his glory, the glory as of the only begotten of the Father,) full of grace and truth.	And the: Word became flesh, and tabernacled with us: and we saw his glory, a glory as of the only begotten from the Father, that he was full of grace and truth.	And the word became flesh and lived among us and we saw his glory, the glory as of the unique one who was from the Father, who is full of grace and truthfulness.
15	John bare witness of him, and cried, saying, This was he of whom I spake, He that cometh after me is preferred before me: for he was before me.	John testified of him, and cried, and said: This is he, of whom I said, That he cometh after me, and is before me; for he was prior to me.	John witnessed about him and cried out and said, "This is he, who I said would follow me, yet be before me, because he was earlier than me.

Parallel Translations

JOHN Chapter 1

	KJV	Murdock	Magiera
16	And of his fulness have all we received, and grace for grace.	And of his plenitude have we all received, and grace for grace.	And from his fullness we all have received and grace on account of grace,
17	For the law was given by Moses, but grace and truth came by Jesus Christ.	For the law was given by the hand of Moses; but the reality and grace was by the hand of Jesus Messiah.	because the law was given by way of Moses, but truth and grace was by way of Jesus Christ.
18	No man hath seen God at any time; the only begotten Son, which is in the bosom of the Father, he hath declared him.	No man hath ever seen God; the only begotten God, he who is in the bosom of his Father, he hath declared [him].	No man has ever seen God. The unique one [of] God, who was in the bosom of his Father, has declared [him].
19	And this is the record of John, when the Jews sent priests and Levites from Jerusalem to ask him, Who art thou?	And this is the testimony of John, when the Jews of Jerusalem sent to him priests and Levites, to ask him, Who art thou?	And this is the witness of John, when the Judeans from Jerusalem sent to him priests and Levites to ask him, "Who are you?"
20	And he confessed, and denied not; but confessed, I am not the Christ.	And he confessed, and denied not, but confessed I am not the Messiah.	And he confessed and did not deny, but confessed, "I am not the Messiah."
21	And they asked him, What then? Art thou Elias? And he saith, I am not. Art thou that prophet? And he answered, No.	And they asked him again: Who then? Art thou Elijah? And he said: I am not. Art thou a prophet? And he said, No.	And they asked him again, "Who then? Are you Elijah?" And he said, "I am not." "Are you a prophet?" And he said, "No."
22	Then said they unto him, Who art thou? that we may give an answer to them that sent us. What sayest thou of thyself?	And they said to him: Who art thou? that we may give answer to them that sent us. What sayest thou of thyself?	And they said to him, "Then who are you that we may give an answer to those who sent us? What do you say about yourself?"
23	He said, I am the voice of one crying in the wilderness, Make straight the way of the Lord, as said the prophet Esaias.	He said: I am the voice of one crying in the wilderness, Make smooth the way of the Lord; as said the prophet Isaiah.	He said, "I AM THE VOICE THAT CRIES IN THE WILDERNESS, MAKE SMOOTH THE WAY OF THE LORD, as Isaiah the prophet said."
24	And they which were sent were of the Pharisees.	And they who were sent, were of the Pharisees.	And they who were sent were from the Pharisees.
25	And they asked him, and said unto him, Why baptizest thou then, if thou be not that Christ, nor Elias, neither that prophet?	And they asked him, and said to him: Why then baptizest thou, if thou art not the Messiah, nor Elijah, nor a prophet?	And they asked him and said to him, "Why then do you baptize, if you are neither the Messiah nor Elijah nor a prophet?"
26	John answered them, saying, I baptize with water: but there standeth one among you, whom ye know not;	John answered, and said to them; I baptize with water; but among you standeth one, whom ye do not know.	John answered and said to them, "I baptize with water, but among you stands him whom you do not know.
27	He it is, who coming after me is preferred before me, whose shoe's latchet I am not worthy to unloose.	He it is that cometh after me, and was before me, whose shoe-strings I am not worthy to untie.	This is he who will follow me, yet was before me, the straps of whose sandals I am not worthy to loosen."
28	These things were done in Bethabara beyond Jordan, where John was baptizing.	These things occurred in Bethany, where John was baptizing.	These [things] happened in Bethany at the crossing of the Jordan where John was baptizing.

JOHN *Chapter 1*

	KJV	*Murdock*	*Magiera*
29	The next day John seeth Jesus coming unto him, and saith, Behold the Lamb of God, which taketh away the sin of the world.	The day after, John saw Jesus coming towards him, and said: Behold, the Lamb of God, that beareth the sin of the world.	And on the next day, John saw Jesus, who was coming towards him and said, "Behold, the Lamb of God who takes away the sin of the world.
30	This is he of whom I said, After me cometh a man which is preferred before me: for he was before me.	This is he of whom I said, After me cometh a man, who is before me, for he was prior to me.	This is he about whom I said, 'A man will follow me, yet he was before me, because he was earlier than me.'
31	And I knew him not: but that he should be made manifest to Israel, therefore am I come baptizing with water.	And I knew him not; but that he might be known to Israel, therefore am I come baptizing with water.	And I did not know him, except that he would be made known to Israel. Because of this, I have come to baptize with water."
32	And John bare record, saying, I saw the Spirit descending from heaven like a dove, and it abode upon him.	And John testified, and said: I saw the Spirit descend from heaven, as a dove, and rest upon him.	And John testified and said, "I saw the Spirit coming down from heaven as a dove and it remained on him.
33	And I knew him not: but he that sent me to baptize with water, the same said unto me, Upon whom thou shalt see the Spirit descending, and remaining on him, the same is he which baptizeth with the Holy Ghost.	And I did not know him; but he who sent me to baptize with water, he said to me, On whom thou seest the Spirit descend, and rest upon him, he baptizeth with the Holy Spirit.	And I did not know him, but he who sent me to baptize with water said to me, 'Him on whom you see the Spirit come down and remain, this [one] will baptize with the Holy Spirit.'
34	And I saw, and bare record that this is the Son of God.	And I saw; and I testify, that this is the Son of God.	And I have seen and testify that this is the Son of God."
35	Again the next day after John stood, and two of his disciples;	And the next day, John was standing, and two of his disciples.	And on another day John was standing, and two of his disciples,
36	And looking upon Jesus as he walked, he saith, Behold the Lamb of God!	And he looked upon Jesus as he walked, and said: Behold, the Lamb of God!	and he looked at Jesus as he was walking and said, "Behold, the Lamb of God."
37	And the two disciples heard him speak, and they followed Jesus.	And his two disciples heard him when he said [it], and they went after Jesus.	And two of his disciples heard [him] when he spoke and they followed Jesus.
38	Then Jesus turned, and saw them following, and saith unto them, What seek ye? They said unto him, Rabbi, (which is to say, being interpreted, Master,) where dwellest thou?	And Jesus turned, and saw them coming after him, and he said to them: What seek ye? They said to him: Our Rabbi, where stayest thou?	And Jesus turned and saw them who were following and said to them, "What do you want?" They said to him, "Our Master, where do you live?"
39	He saith unto them, Come and see. They came and saw where he dwelt, and abode with him that day: for it was about the tenth hour.	He said to them: Come, and see. And they came and saw where he lodged; and they were with him that day, for it was about the tenth hour.	He said to them, "Come and you will see." And they came and saw where he was and they were with him that day and it was about the tenth hour.
40	One of the two which heard John speak, and followed him, was Andrew, Simon Peter's brother.	And one of those who heard John and went after Jesus was Andrew, the brother of Simon.	And one of those who had heard from John and followed Jesus was Andrew, the brother of Simon.
41	He first findeth his own brother Simon, and saith unto him, We have found the Messias, which is, being interpreted, the Christ.	He first saw Simon his brother, and said to him: We have found the Messiah.	This [one] first saw Simon his brother and said to him, "I have found the Messiah."

Parallel Translations

	KJV	*Murdock*	*Magiera*
	JOHN *Chapter 1*		
42	And he brought him to Jesus. And when Jesus beheld him, he said, Thou art Simon the son of Jona: thou shalt be called Cephas, which is by interpretation, A stone.	And he brought him to Jesus. And Jesus looked upon him, and said Thou art Simon the son of Jona; thou shalt be called Cephas.	And he brought him to Jesus. And Jesus looked at him and said, "You are Simon, the son of Jonas. You will be called Peter."
43	The day following Jesus would go forth into Galilee, and findeth Philip, and saith unto him, Follow me.	The next day, Jesus was disposed to depart for Galilee: and he found Philip and said to him, Come after me.	And on another day, Jesus wanted to go to Galilee. And he found Philip and said to him, "Follow me."
44	Now Philip was of Bethsaida, the city of Andrew and Peter.	And Philip was of Bethsaida, the city of Andrew and Simon.	Now Philip was from Bethsaida, from the city of Andrew and of Simon.
45	Philip findeth Nathanael, and saith unto him, We have found him, of whom Moses in the law, and the prophets, did write, Jesus of Nazareth, the son of Joseph.	And Philip found Nathaniel, and said to him: We have found him, of whom Moses wrote in the law, and the prophets, Jesus the son of Joseph, who is of Nazareth.	And Philip found Nathaniel and said to him, "We have found him about whom Moses wrote in the law and the prophets, that he is Jesus the son of Joseph from Nazareth."
46	And Nathanael said unto him, Can there any good thing come out of Nazareth? Philip saith unto him, Come and see.	Nathaniel said to him: Can there be any good thing from Nazareth? Philip said to him: Come, and see.	Nathaniel said to him, "Is it possible for anything good to be from Nazareth?" Philip said to him, "Come and you will see."
47	Jesus saw Nathanael coming to him, and saith of him, Behold an Israelite indeed, in whom is no guile!	And Jesus saw Nathaniel coming towards him, and said of him: Behold a real Israelite, in whom is no deceit.	And Jesus saw Nathaniel coming towards him and said about him, "Behold, truly a son of Israel in whom there is no deceit."
48	Nathanael saith unto him, Whence knowest thou me? Jesus answered and said unto him, Before that Philip called thee, when thou wast under the fig tree, I saw thee.	Nathaniel said to him: Whence knowest thou me? Jesus said to him: Before Philip called thee when thou wast under the fig-tree, I saw thee.	Nathaniel said to him, "From where do you know me?" Jesus said to him, "Before Philip called you, while you were under the fig tree, I saw you."
49	Nathanael answered and saith unto him, Rabbi, thou art the Son of God; thou art the King of Israel.	Nathaniel answered, and said to him: Rabbi; thou art the Son of God; thou art the King of Israel.	Nathaniel answered and said to him, "My Master, you are the Son of God. You are the King of Israel."
50	Jesus answered and said unto him, Because I said unto thee, I saw thee under the fig tree, believest thou? thou shalt see greater things than these.	Jesus said to him: Because I said to thee, that I saw thee under the fig-tree, believest thou? Thou wilt see greater things than these.	Jesus said to him, "Because I told you that I saw you under the fig tree, do you believe? For you will see greater [things] than these."
51	And he saith unto him, Verily, verily, I say unto you, Hereafter ye shall see heaven open, and the angels of God ascending and descending upon the Son of man.	He said to him: Verily, verily, I say to you, That hereafter ye will see heaven opened, and the angels of God ascending and descending unto the Son of man.	He said to him, "Truly, truly I say to you, from now on you will see heaven opening and the angels of God ascending and descending to the Son of Man."
	Chapter 2		
1	And the third day there was a marriage in Cana of Galilee; and the mother of Jesus was there:	And on the third day there was a feast in Cana, a city of Galilee: and the mother of Jesus was there.	And on the third day there was a wedding feast in Cana, a city of Galilee, and the mother of Jesus was there.

Parallel Translations

	KJV	Murdock	Magiera

JOHN Chapter 2

	KJV	Murdock	Magiera
2	And both Jesus was called, and his disciples, to the marriage.	And also Jesus and his disciples were invited to the feast.	And Jesus and his disciples were also invited to the wedding feast.
3	And when they wanted wine, the mother of Jesus saith unto him, They have no wine.	And the wine fell short: and his mother said to Jesus: They have no wine.	And the wine was running out and his mother said to Jesus, "They have no wine."
4	Jesus saith unto her, Woman, what have I to do with thee? mine hour is not yet come.	Jesus said to her: What is [in common] to me and thee? Not yet hath my hour come.	Jesus said to her, "What do you want from me, woman? My hour has not yet come."
5	His mother saith unto the servants, Whatsoever he saith unto you, do it.	His mother said to the waiters: Whatever he saith to you, do [it].	His mother said to the servants, "Whatever he tells you, do."
6	And there were set there six waterpots of stone, after the manner of the purifying of the Jews, containing two or three firkins apiece.	And there were there six waterpots of stone, set for the purification of Jews, containing each two or three quadrantalia.	And there were there six water pots of stone, which were placed for the purification of the Judeans that each held two or three liquid measures.
7	Jesus saith unto them, Fill the waterpots with water. And they filled them up to the brim.	Jesus said to them: Fill those water-pots with water. And they filled them to the top.	Jesus said to them, "Fill the water pots [with] water." And they filled them up to the top.
8	And he saith unto them, Draw out now, and bear unto the governor of the feast. And they bare it.	He said to them: Draw now, and carry to the master of the feast. And they carried.	He said to them, "Draw [the wine] now and take [it] to the chief of the feast." And they took [it].
9	When the ruler of the feast had tasted the water that was made wine, and knew not whence it was: (but the servants which drew the water knew;) the governor of the feast called the bridegroom,	And when the master of the feast tasted the water that had become wine, and did not know whence it came, although the waiters knew, as they had filled the pots with water, the master of the feast called the bridegroom,	And when the chief of the feast had tasted that water that had become wine and did not know from where it came (but the servants knew, because they had filled the water) the chief of the feast called the bridegroom
10	And saith unto him, Every man at the beginning doth set forth good wine; and when men have well drunk, then that which is worse: but thou hast kept the good wine until now.	and said to him: Every man first bringeth forward the good wine, and when they are satiated, then that which is inferior; but thou hast kept the good wine till now.	and said to him, "Everyone first brings good wine and when they are drunk, then that which is inferior. But you have kept the good wine until now."
11	This beginning of miracles did Jesus in Cana of Galilee, and manifested forth his glory; and his disciples believed on him.	This is the first sign, which Jesus wrought at Cana in Galilee, and manifested his glory: and his disciples believed on him.	This was the first sign that Jesus did in Cana of Galilee. And he made known his glory and his disciples believed in him.
12	After this he went down to Capernaum, he, and his mother, and his brethren, and his disciples: and they continued there not many days.	Afterwards he went down to Capernaum, he and his mother and his brothers and his disciples; and they were there a few days.	After this, he went down to Capernaum, he and his mother and his brothers and his disciples and they stayed there a few days.
13	And the Jews' passover was at hand, and Jesus went up to Jerusalem,	And the pass over of the Jews drew near; and Jesus went up to Jerusalem.	And the feast of the Passover of the Judeans was near and Jesus went up to Jerusalem.
14	And found in the temple those that sold oxen and sheep and doves, and the changers of money sitting:	And he found in the temple those who sold beeves and sheep and doves, and the money-changers sitting [there].	And he found in the temple those who were selling oxen and sheep and doves and moneychangers who were sitting.

JOHN Chapter 2

	KJV	Murdock	Magiera
15	And when he had made a scourge of small cords, he drove them all out of the temple, and the sheep, and the oxen; and poured out the changers' money, and overthrew the tables;	And he made himself a whip from a cord, and turned them all out of the temple, and the sheep and the beeves and the money-changers; and he poured out their money, and overset their tables:	And he made himself a whip from a rope and drove out all of them from the temple, even the sheep and oxen and the moneychangers. And he poured out their money and turned over their tables.
16	And said unto them that sold doves, Take these things hence; make not my Father's house an house of merchandise.	and he said to them that sold doves, Take away these things; and make not my Father's house a house of traffic.	And to those who were selling doves, he said, "Take these away [from] here and do not make the house of my Father a house of merchandise."
17	And his disciples remembered that it was written, The zeal of thine house hath eaten me up.	And his disciples remembered, that it is written: The zeal of thy house hath devoured me.	And his disciples remembered that it was written: THE ZEAL OF YOUR HOUSE HAS CONSUMED ME.
18	Then answered the Jews and said unto him, What sign shewest thou unto us, seeing that thou doest these things?	But the Jews replied, and said to him: What sign showest thou to us, since thou doest these things?	Now the Judeans answered and said to him, "What sign do you show us, because you do these [things]?"
19	Jesus answered and said unto them, Destroy this temple, and in three days I will raise it up.	Jesus answered, and said to them: Demolish this temple, and in three days I will again erect it.	Jesus answered and said to them, "Tear down this temple and after three days, I will raise it."
20	Then said the Jews, Forty and six years was this temple in building, and wilt thou rear it up in three days?	The Jews said to him: Forty and six years, this temple was building; and wilt thou build it again in three days?	The Judeans said to him, "This temple was being built for forty-six years and after three days you will raise it?"
21	But he spake of the temple of his body.	But he spake of the temple of his body.	But he was speaking about the temple of his body.
22	When therefore he was risen from the dead, his disciples remembered that he had said this unto them; and they believed the scripture, and the word which Jesus had said.	And when he was arisen from the dead, his disciples remembered, that he spoke this: and they believed the scriptures, and the word that Jesus spake.	And when he rose from the dead, his disciples remembered that he had said this and they believed the scriptures and the word that Jesus had said.
23	Now when he was in Jerusalem at the passover, in the feast day, many believed in his name, when they saw the miracles which he did.	And while Jesus was in Jerusalem, at the feast of the passover, many believed on him, because they saw the signs he wrought.	Now while Jesus was in Jerusalem at the feast of the Passover, during the feast many believed in him when they saw the signs that he did.
24	But Jesus did not commit himself unto them, because he knew all men,	But Jesus did not confide himself to them; because he knew all men:	But Jesus did not entrust himself to them, because he knew all men
25	And needed not that any should testify of man: for he knew what was in man.	And he needed not that any one should testify to him respecting any man; for he himself knew what is in man.	and he did not need a man to testify to him about anyone, for he knew what was in man.

Chapter 3

	KJV	Murdock	Magiera
1	There was a man of the Pharisees, named Nicodemus, a ruler of the Jews:	And there was a man of the Pharisees there, whose name was Nicodemus, a ruler of the Jews.	Now there was a certain man there from the Pharisees. His name was Nicodemus, a ruler of the Judeans.

Parallel Translations

	KJV	Murdock	Magiera
	JOHN	*Chapter 3*	
2	The same came to Jesus by night, and said unto him, Rabbi, we know that thou art a teacher come from God: for no man can do these miracles that thou doest, except God be with him.	And he came to Jesus by night, and said to him: Rabbi, we know that thou art a teacher sent from God; for no one can work those signs which thou workest, unless God be with him.	This [man] came to Jesus at night and said to him, "My Master, we know that you were sent from God [as] a teacher, for no man is able to do these signs that you do, but he with whom God [is]."
3	Jesus answered and said unto him, Verily, verily, I say unto thee, Except a man be born again, he cannot see the kingdom of God.	Jesus replied, and said to him: Verily, verily, I say to thee, That, unless a man be born anew, he cannot behold the kingdom of God.	Jesus answered and said to him, "Truly, truly I say to you, if a man is not born again, he is not able to see the kingdom of God."
4	Nicodemus saith unto him, How can a man be born when he is old? can he enter the second time into his mother's womb, and be born?	Nicodemus said to him: How can an old man be born? Can he enter a second time into his mother's womb and be born?	Nicodemus said to him, "How is it possible for an old man to be born? Is it possible to enter the womb of his mother again a second time and to be born?"
5	Jesus answered, Verily, verily, I say unto thee, Except a man be born of water and of the Spirit, he cannot enter into the kingdom of God.	Jesus replied, and said to him Verily, verily, I say to thee, That, unless a man be born of water and the Spirit, he cannot enter the kingdom of God.	Jesus answered and said to him, "Truly, truly I say to you, if a man is not born from water and Spirit, he is not able to enter into the kingdom of God.
6	That which is born of the flesh is flesh; and that which is born of the Spirit is spirit.	That which is born of the flesh, is flesh; and that which is born of the Spirit, is spirit.	What is born from the flesh is flesh and what is born from the Spirit is Spirit.
7	Marvel not that I said unto thee, Ye must be born again.	Be not surprised that I said to thee, Ye must be born anew.	Do not marvel that I say to you that it is necessary for you to be born again.
8	The wind bloweth where it listeth, and thou hearest the sound thereof, but canst not tell whence it cometh, and whither it goeth: so is every one that is born of the Spirit.	The wind bloweth where it chooseth; and thou hearest its sound, but knowest not whence it cometh, and whither it goeth: so is every one, that is born of the Spirit.	The wind will blow where it wants and you hear its sound, but you do not know [from] where it comes and to where it goes. So is everyone who is born from the Spirit."
9	Nicodemus answered and said unto him, How can these things be?	Nicodemus answered, and said to him: How can these things be?	Nicodemus answered and said to him, "How can these [things] be?"
10	Jesus answered and said unto him, Art thou a master of Israel, and knowest not these things?	Jesus answered, and said to him: Art thou a teacher of Israel, and knowest not these things?	Jesus answered and said to him, "You are a teacher of Israel and you do not know these [things]?
11	Verily, verily, I say unto thee, We speak that we do know, and testify that we have seen; and ye receive not our witness.	Verily, verily, I say to thee: We speak, what we know; and we testify to what we have seen; but ye receive not our testimony.	Truly, truly I say to you, what we know, we speak, and what we see, we witness [to], and you do not receive our witness.
12	If I have told you earthly things, and ye believe not, how shall ye believe, if I tell you of heavenly things?	If I have spoken to you of things on earth, and ye believe not; how will ye believe, if I speak of things in heaven?	If I have spoken to you about [things] on the earth and you do not believe, how will you believe me if I speak to you about [things] in heaven?
13	And no man hath ascended up to heaven, but he that came down from heaven, even the Son of man which is in heaven.	And no one hath ascended to heaven, but he that descended from heaven, the Son of man who is in heaven.	And no man has ascended into heaven, but he who descended from heaven, the Son of Man who is in heaven.

Parallel Translations

JOHN *Chapter 3*

	KJV	*Murdock*	*Magiera*
14	And as Moses lifted up the serpent in the wilderness, even so must the Son of man be lifted up:	And as Moses elevated the serpent in the wilderness, so must the Son of man be lifted up:	And as Moses raised up the serpent in the wilderness, so the Son of Man is going to be raised up,
15	That whosoever believeth in him should not perish, but have eternal life.	that every one who believeth in him, may not perish, but may have life eternal.	so that everyone who believes in him will not be destroyed, but will have eternal life.
16	For God so loved the world, that he gave his only begotten Son, that whosoever believeth in him should not perish, but have everlasting life.	For God so loved the world, that he gave his only begotten Son, that whosoever believeth on him, should not perish, but should have life eternal.	For God so loved the world, even that he would give his unique Son, that whoever will believe in him will not be destroyed, but will have eternal life,
17	For God sent not his Son into the world to condemn the world; but that the world through him might be saved.	For God sent not his Son into the world, to condemn the world; but that the world might live by means of him.	for God did not send his Son into the world to condemn the world, but to give life to the world by his hand.
18	He that believeth on him is not condemned: but he that believeth not is condemned already, because he hath not believed in the name of the only begotten Son of God.	He that believeth on him is not condemned; but he that believeth not, is already condemned; because he hath not believed on the name of the only begotten Son of God.	He who believes in him is not judged and he who does not believe is judged already, because he does not believe in the name of the unique Son of God.
19	And this is the condemnation, that light is come into the world, and men loved darkness rather than light, because their deeds were evil.	And this is the [ground of] condemnation, that light hath come into the world, and men have loved darkness rather than light, for their deeds have been evil.	Now this is the judgment, because the light has come to the world and men loved darkness more than the light, for their works are evil.
20	For every one that doeth evil hateth the light, neither cometh to the light, lest his deeds should be reproved.	For every one that doeth abominable things, hateth the light, and cometh not to the light, lest his deeds should be reproved.	For everyone who does hateful [things] hates the light and does not come to the light, so that his works will not be reproved.
21	But he that doeth truth cometh to the light, that his deeds may be made manifest, that they are wrought in God.	But he that doeth right, cometh to the light, that his works may be known to be done in God.	But he who does truth[ful things] comes to the light, so that his works may be known that they are done in God."
22	After these things came Jesus and his disciples into the land of Judaea; and there he tarried with them, and baptized.	After these things, came Jesus and his disciples into the land of Judaea; and there he abode with them, and baptized.	After these [things] Jesus and his disciples went to the land of Judea and he was living with them there and baptizing.
23	And John also was baptizing in Aenon near to Salim, because there was much water there: and they came, and were baptized.	And John also was baptizing in Ænon, which is near to Salim, because there were many waters there: and the people came, and were baptized.	Now John was also baptizing at Aenon, which was beside Salim, because there was plenty of water there and they were coming and being baptized,
24	For John was not yet cast into prison.	For John had not yet fallen into prison.	for John had not yet been cast into prison.
25	Then there arose a question between some of John's disciples and the Jews about purifying.	And one of John's disciples and a certain Jew had disputed respecting purification.	Now there was a question with a certain Judean to one of the disciples of John about purification.

JOHN Chapter 3

	KJV	Murdock	Magiera
26	And they came unto John, and said unto him, Rabbi, he that was with thee beyond Jordan, to whom thou barest witness, behold, the same baptizeth, and all men come to him.	And they came to John, and said to him: Our Rabbi, he who was with thee beyond Jordan, and of whom thou gavest testimony, lo, he also baptizeth; and many go after him.	And they came to John and said to him, "Our Master, he who was with you at the crossing of the Jordan about whom you witnessed, behold, he is also baptizing and many are coming to him."
27	John answered and said, A man can receive nothing, except it be given him from heaven.	John answered, and said to them: A man cannot take any thing by his own choice, unless it be given him from heaven.	John answered and said to them, "No man is able to receive anything of his own desire, except it be given to him from heaven.
28	Ye yourselves bear me witness, that I said, I am not the Christ, but that I am sent before him.	Ye are witnesses for me, that I said: I am not the Messiah, but am sent to go before him.	You are my witnesses that I said that I am not the Messiah, but I am a messenger who is before him.
29	He that hath the bride is the bridegroom: but the friend of the bridegroom, which standeth and heareth him, rejoiceth greatly because of the bridegroom's voice: this my joy therefore is fulfilled.	He that hath the bride, is the bridegroom: and the friend of the bridegroom, who standeth and listeneth to him, rejoiceth with great joy on account of the bridegroom's voice: this my joy, therefore, lo, it is full.	He who has the bride is the bridegroom, but the friend of the bridegroom who stands and listens for him rejoices [with] a great joy, because of the voice of the bridegroom. Therefore, this my joy, behold, is full.
30	He must increase, but I must decrease.	To him must be increase, and to me decrease.	It is necessary for him to increase and for me to decrease.
31	He that cometh from above is above all: he that is of the earth is earthly, and speaketh of the earth: he that cometh from heaven is above all.	For he that cometh from above, is above all; and he that is from the earth, is of the earth, and talketh of the earth. He that cometh from heaven, is above all;	For he who has come from above is above all and he who is from the earth is from the earth and speaks from the earth. He who has come from heaven is above all.
32	And what he hath seen and heard, that he testifieth; and no man receiveth his testimony.	and what he hath seen and heard, he testifieth; and his testimony, no one receiveth.	And what he has seen and heard he witnesses, yet no man receives his witness.
33	He that hath received his testimony hath set to his seal that God is true.	But he that receiveth his testimony, hath set his seal, that God is true.	But he who receives his witness confirms that God is true.
34	For he whom God hath sent speaketh the words of God: for God giveth not the Spirit by measure unto him.	For he whom God hath sent, speaketh the words of God; for God hath not given the Spirit by measure [to him].	For he whom God sent speaks the words of God, for God did not give the Spirit with measure.
35	The Father loveth the Son, and hath given all things into his hand.	The Father loveth the Son, and hath given every thing into his hands.	The Father loves the Son and has given everything into his hands.
36	He that believeth on the Son hath everlasting life: and he that believeth not the Son shall not see life; but the wrath of God abideth on him.	He that believeth on the Son, hath life eternal; but he who obeyeth not the Son, shall not see life. but the wrath of God will abide upon him.	He who believes in the Son has eternal life and he who does not obey the Son will not see life. On the contrary, the wrath of God will continue against him."

Parallel Translations

JOHN Chapter 4

	KJV	*Murdock*	*Magiera*
1	When therefore the Lord knew how the Pharisees had heard that Jesus made and baptized more disciples than John,	And Jesus knew, that the Pharisees had heard; that he made many disciples, and baptized more than John.	Now Jesus knew that the Pharisees had heard that he made many disciples and was baptizing more than John,
2	(Though Jesus himself baptized not, but his disciples,)	Yet Jesus himself did not baptize but his disciples.	although Jesus was not baptizing, but rather his disciples [were].
3	He left Judaea, and departed again into Galilee.	And he left Judaea, and went again into Galilee.	And he left Judea and went again to Galilee
4	And he must needs go through Samaria.	And in going, he had occasion to pass through the midst of the Samaritans.	and he was planning to pass through Samaria.
5	Then cometh he to a city of Samaria, which is called Sychar, near to the parcel of ground that Jacob gave to his son Joseph.	And he came to a city of the Samaritans called Sychar, near the field which Jacob gave to his son Joseph.	And he came to a city of the Samaritans that was called Sychar, by the edge of the field that Jacob had given to Joseph, his son.
6	Now Jacob's well was there. Jesus therefore, being wearied with his journey, sat thus on the well: and it was about the sixth hour.	And Jacob's well of water was there. And Jesus was weary with the toil of travelling, and seated himself by the well: and it was at the sixth hour.	And there was there a well of water that [had belonged to] Jacob. And Jesus was tired from the toil of the journey and was sitting by the well and it was the sixth hour.
7	There cometh a woman of Samaria to draw water: Jesus saith unto her, Give me to drink.	And a woman from Samaria came to draw water. And Jesus said to her: Give me water to drink.	And a woman from Samaria came to draw water. And Jesus said to her, "Give me water to drink,"
8	(For his disciples were gone away unto the city to buy meat.)	And his disciples had gone to the city, to buy themselves food.	for his disciples had entered the city to buy food for them.
9	Then saith the woman of Samaria unto him, How is it that thou, being a Jew, askest drink of me, which am a woman of Samaria? for the Jews have no dealings with the Samaritans.	The Samaritan woman said to him: How dost thou, a Jew, ask drink of me, who am a Samaritan woman? For the Jews have no familiarity with Samaritans.	That Samaritan woman said to him, "How is it [since] you are a Judean, yet you ask to drink of me, who am a Samaritan woman? For the Judeans do not deal with the Samaritans."
10	Jesus answered and said unto her, If thou knewest the gift of God, and who it is that saith to thee, Give me to drink; thou wouldest have asked of him, and he would have given thee living water.	Jesus replied and said to her: If thou hadst known the gift of God, and who it is that saith to thee, Give me to drink, thou wouldest have asked of him, and he would have given thee living waters.	Jesus answered and said to her, "If you were aware of the gift of God and who this is who said to you, 'Give me to drink,' you would ask him and he would give you living water."
11	The woman saith unto him, Sir, thou hast nothing to draw with, and the well is deep: from whence then hast thou that living water?	The woman said to him: My lord, thou hast no bucket, and the well is deep.; how hast thou living waters?	That woman said to him, "My Lord, you have no water pot and the well is deep. Where [is] your living water?
12	Art thou greater than our father Jacob, which gave us the well, and drank thereof himself, and his children, and his cattle?	Art thou greater than our father Jacob, who gave us this well, and drank from it himself, and his children, and his flocks?	Are you greater than our father Jacob, who gave us this well and from which he and his sons and his flocks drank?"
13	Jesus answered and said unto her, Whosoever drinketh of this water shall thirst again:	Jesus replied and said to her: Whoever shall drink of these waters, will thirst again;	Jesus answered and said to her, "Everyone who drinks from this water will thirst again,

Parallel Translations

	KJV	Murdock	Magiera
	JOHN *Chapter 4*		
14	But whosoever drinketh of the water that I shall give him shall never thirst; but the water that I shall give him shall be in him a well of water springing up into everlasting life.	but whoever shall drink of the waters which I shall give him, will not thirst for ever; but the waters, which I shall give him, will be in him a fountain of waters, springing up unto life eternal.	but everyone who drinks from the water that I give him will not thirst forever. But that water that I give him will be in him a spring of water that will bubble up to eternal life."
15	The woman saith unto him, Sir, give me this water, that I thirst not, neither come hither to draw.	The woman said to him: My lord, give me of these waters, that I may not thirst again, and may not come to draw from here.	That woman said to him, "My Lord, give to me from this water, so that I will not thirst again nor have to come [and] draw [water] from here."
16	Jesus saith unto her, Go, call thy husband, and come hither.	Jesus said to her: Go, call thy husband, and come hither.	Jesus said to her, "Go, call your husband and come here."
17	The woman answered and said, I have no husband. Jesus said unto her, Thou hast well said, I have no husband:	She said to him: I have no husband. Jesus said to her: Thou hast well said, I have no husband;	She said to him, "I have no husband." Jesus said to her, "You have spoken well, 'I have no husband,'
18	For thou hast had five husbands; and he whom thou now hast is not thy husband: in that saidst thou truly.	for thou hast had five husbands, and he whom thou now hast, is not thy husband. In this thou didst speak truly.	for you have had five husbands and this [one] that you have now is not your husband. This you have said [is] true."
19	The woman saith unto him, Sir, I perceive that thou art a prophet.	The woman said to him: My lord, I perceive thou art a prophet.	That woman said to him, "My Lord, I perceive that you are a prophet.
20	Our fathers worshipped in this mountain; and ye say, that in Jerusalem is the place where men ought to worship.	Our fathers worshipped in this mountain; but ye say, that in Jerusalem is the place where it is proper to worship.	Our fathers worshipped on this mountain, yet you say that in Jerusalem is the place that it is proper to worship."
21	Jesus saith unto her, Woman, believe me, the hour cometh, when ye shall neither in this mountain, nor yet at Jerusalem, worship the Father.	Jesus said to her: Woman, believe me, the hour cometh, when neither in this mountain, nor in Jerusalem, ye will worship the Father.	Jesus said to her, "Woman, believe me that the hour comes, when not on this mountain, nor even in Jerusalem will they worship the Father.
22	Ye worship ye know not what: we know what we worship: for salvation is of the Jews.	Ye worship, ye know not what; but we worship what we know; for life is from the Jews.	You worship that which you do not know, but we worship what we know, because life is from the Judeans.
23	But the hour cometh, and now is, when the true worshippers shall worship the Father in spirit and in truth: for the Father seeketh such to worship him.	But the hour cometh, and now is, when the true worshippers will worship the Father in spirit and in truth; for the Father requireth that worshippers be such.	But the hour comes and now is, when the true worshipper will worship the Father by the Spirit and with the truth, for the Father also seeks worshippers who are like these.
24	God is a Spirit: and they that worship him must worship him in spirit and in truth.	For God is a Spirit; and they that worship him, should worship in spirit and in truth.	For God is a Spirit and those who worship him must worship by the Spirit and with truth."
25	The woman saith unto him, I know that Messias cometh, which is called Christ: when he is come, he will tell us all things.	The woman said to him: I know that Messiah will come; and when he cometh, he will teach us every thing.	That woman said to him, "I know that the Messiah will come and when he comes, he will teach us everything."
26	Jesus saith unto her, I that speak unto thee am he.	Jesus said to her: I, who talk with thee, am he.	Jesus said to her, "I who speak with you am [he]."

Parallel Translations

JOHN *Chapter 4*

	KJV	*Murdock*	*Magiera*
27	And upon this came his disciples, and marvelled that he talked with the woman: yet no man said, What seekest thou? or, Why talkest thou with her?	And while he was speaking, his disciples came. And they wondered that he would converse with the woman; yet no one said, What seekest thou? or, Why talkest thou with her?	And while he spoke, his disciples came and were amazed that he spoke with a woman, but no one said, "What do you ask?" or, "Why do you speak with her?"
28	The woman then left her waterpot, and went her way into the city, and saith to the men,	And the woman left her water-pot, and went to the city, and said [to the people]:	And the woman left her water pitcher and went to the city and told the men,
29	Come, see a man, which told me all things that ever I did: is not this the Christ?	Come, see a man that told me every thing I ever did: is not this the Messiah?	"Come, see the man who told me everything that I have done. Is he the Messiah?"
30	Then they went out of the city, and came unto him.	And the people went out of the city, and came to him.	And the men went out of the city and they were coming to him.
31	In the mean while his disciples prayed him, saying, Master, eat.	In the mean time, his disciples entreated him, and said to him: Our Rabbi, eat.	And in the middle of these [things] his disciples were begging him and saying to him, "Our Master, eat."
32	But he said unto them, I have meat to eat that ye know not of.	But he said to them: I have food to eat, of which ye are ignorant.	But he said to them, "I have food to eat that you do not know."
33	Therefore said the disciples one to another, Hath any man brought him ought to eat?	The disciples said among themselves: Hath any one brought him something to eat?	The disciples spoke among themselves, "Has someone brought him something to eat?"
34	Jesus saith unto them, My meat is to do the will of him that sent me, and to finish his work.	Jesus said to them: My food is to do the pleasure of him that sent me, and to accomplish his work.	Jesus said to them, "My food is to do the will of him who sent me and [that] I complete his work.
35	Say not ye, There are yet four months, and then cometh harvest? behold, I say unto you, Lift up your eyes, and look on the fields; for they are white already to harvest.	Do ye not say, that after four months cometh the harvest? Behold, I say to you, and lift up your eyes, and look upon the grounds, that they are white, and have already come to the harvest.	Do you not say that after four months comes the harvest? Behold, I say to you, 'Lift up your eyes and see the fields that are white and have arrived at the harvest already.'
36	And he that reapeth receiveth wages, and gathereth fruit unto life eternal: that both he that soweth and he that reapeth may rejoice together.	And he that reapeth, receiveth wages, and gathereth fruits unto life eternal; and the sower and the reaper equally rejoice.	And he who reaps receives a wage and gathers fruit for eternal life and the sower and the reaper will rejoice together.
37	And herein is that saying true, One soweth, and another reapeth.	For in this, is the proverb true, that one is the sower, and another the reaper.	For in this is a word of truth: SOMEONE SOWS AND ANOTHER REAPS.
38	I sent you to reap that whereon ye bestowed no labour: other men laboured, and ye are entered into their labours.	I sent you to reap that, on which ye labored not: for others toiled, and ye entered into their labor.	I have sent you to reap in what you did not labor, for others labored and you have entered into their toil."
39	And many of the Samaritans of that city believed on him for the saying of the woman, which testified, He told me all that ever I did.	And many Samaritans of that city believed on him, because of the discourse of the woman, who testified, He told me all that I ever did.	And many Samaritans from that city believed in him, because of the word of that woman who had testified, "He told me everything that I have done."

JOHN *Chapter 4*

	KJV	Murdock	Magiera
40	So when the Samaritans were come unto him, they besought him that he would tarry with them: and he abode there two days.	And when these Samaritans came to him, they requested him to tarry with them; and he remained with them two days.	And when those Samaritans came to him, they begged him to stay with them and he stayed with them [for] two days.
41	And many more believed because of his own word;	And many believed on him, because of his discourse.	And many believed in him, because of his word.
42	And said unto the woman, Now we believe, not because of thy saying: for we have heard him ourselves, and know that this is indeed the Christ, the Saviour of the world.	And they said to the woman: Henceforth we believe in him, not on account of thy word; for we have heard him ourselves, and we know that he truly is the Messiah, the Life-Giver of the world.	And they were saying to that woman, "From now on, we do not believe in him [only] because of your word, for we have heard and know that this is truly the Messiah, the Savior of the world."
43	Now after two days he departed thence, and went into Galilee.	And after two days Jesus departed from there and went into Galilee.	And after two days, Jesus went away from there and traveled to Galilee,
44	For Jesus himself testified, that a prophet hath no honour in his own country.	For Jesus himself testified, that a prophet is not honored in his own city.	for Jesus had testified that a prophet is not honored in his [own] city.
45	Then when he was come into Galilee, the Galilaeans received him, having seen all the things that he did at Jerusalem at the feast: for they also went unto the feast.	And when he came to Galilee, the Galileans received him, having seen all the signs which he wrought in Jerusalem at the feast, for they too had gone to the feast.	And when he came to Galilee, the Galileans received him who had seen all the signs that he had done in Jerusalem during the feast, for they also had gone to the feast.
46	So Jesus came again into Cana of Galilee, where he made the water wine. And there was a certain nobleman, whose son was sick at Capernaum.	And Jesus came again to Cana of Galilee, where he made the water wine. And there was at Capernaum a king's servant, whose son was sick.	And Jesus came again to Cana of Galilee, where he had made the water wine. And in Capernaum there was a servant of a certain king whose son was sick.
47	When he heard that Jesus was come out of Judaea into Galilee, he went unto him, and besought him that he would come down, and heal his son: for he was at the point of death.	He heard that Jesus had come from Judaea to Galilee; and he went to him, and besought him that he would come down and heal his son; for he was near dying.	This [man] heard that Jesus had come from Judea to Galilee, and he went to him and was begging him to come down and to heal his son, for he was close to dying.
48	Then said Jesus unto him, Except ye see signs and wonders, ye will not believe.	Jesus said to him: Unless ye see signs and wonders, ye will not believe.	Jesus said to him, "If you do not see signs and wonders, you do not believe."
49	The nobleman saith unto him, Sir, come down ere my child die.	The king's servant said to him: My lord, come down, before the child dieth.	That servant of the king said to him, "My Lord, come down before the boy dies."
50	Jesus saith unto him, Go thy way; thy son liveth. And the man believed the word that Jesus had spoken unto him, and he went his way.	Jesus said to him: Go, thy son liveth. And the man believed the word which Jesus spake to him, and went away.	Jesus said to him, "Go! Your son is alive." And that man believed in the word that Jesus spoke to him and he went away.
51	And as he was now going down, his servants met him, and told him, saying, Thy son liveth.	And as he was going down, his servants met him, and informed him and said to him: Thy son liveth.	And while he was going down, his servants met him and brought him good news and said to him, "Your son lives."

JOHN Chapter 4

	KJV	Murdock	Magiera
52	Then enquired he of them the hour when he began to amend. And they said unto him, Yesterday at the seventh hour the fever left him.	And he asked them, at what time he recovered. And they said to him: Yesterday, at the seventh hour the fever left him.	And he asked them at what time he was healed. They said to him, "Yesterday, in the seventh hour the fever left him."
53	So the father knew that it was at the same hour, in the which Jesus said unto him, Thy son liveth: and himself believed, and his whole house.	And his father knew, that it was at the hour in which Jesus said to him, Thy son liveth. And he believed, and all his house.	And his father knew that [it was] at that moment in which Jesus had said to him, "Your son lives." And he and his whole house believed.
54	This is again the second miracle that Jesus did, when he was come out of Judaea into Galilee.	This again was the second sign that Jesus wrought, when he came from Judaea to Galilee.	Furthermore, this [was] the second sign Jesus did after he came from Judea to Galilee.

Chapter 5

	KJV	Murdock	Magiera
1	After this there was a feast of the Jews; and Jesus went up to Jerusalem.	After these things there was a feast of the Jews, and Jesus went up to Jerusalem.	After these [things] was the feast of the Judeans and Jesus went up to Jerusalem.
2	Now there is at Jerusalem by the sheep market a pool, which is called in the Hebrew tongue Bethesda, having five porches.	And there was there in Jerusalem a certain place of baptizing, which was called in Hebrew Bethesda; and there were in it five porches.	Now there was in Jerusalem there a certain pool of baptizing, which is called in Hebrew, Bethesda, and it had five porches in it.
3	In these lay a great multitude of impotent folk, of blind, halt, withered, waiting for the moving of the water.	And in them were laid a great multitude of the sick, and the blind, and the lame, and the withered, waiting for the moving of the waters.	And many people were lying in these [porches] who were sick and blind and lame and crippled and they were waiting for the movement of the water,
4	For an angel went down at a certain season into the pool, and troubled the water: whosoever then first after the troubling of the water stepped in was made whole of whatsoever disease he had.	For an angel, from time to time, descended into the baptistery, and moved the waters; and he who first went in, after the moving of the waters, was cured of whatever disease he had.	for an angel came down at various times to the pool and moved the water. And whoever would go down first after the movement of the water was healed [of] every pain that he had.
5	And a certain man was there, which had an infirmity thirty and eight years.	And a certain man was there, who had been diseased thirty and eight years.	Now there was there a certain man who had had an infirmity [for] thirty-eight years.
6	When Jesus saw him lie, and knew that he had been now a long time in that case, he saith unto him, Wilt thou be made whole?	Jesus saw him lying, and knew that [his disease] had been a long time upon him, and said to him: Desirest thou to be healed?	Jesus saw this [man] who was lying [there] and knew that he had been [infirm] a long time. And he said to him, 'Do you want to be healed?"
7	The impotent man answered him, Sir, I have no man, when the water is troubled, to put me into the pool: but while I am coming, another steppeth down before me.	And the sick man answered and said: Yes, my lord; but I have no one who, when the water is moved, will put me into the baptistery; but while I am coming, another descendeth before me.	That sick man answered and said, "Yes, my Lord, but I have no one to place me in the pool when the water is moved. But before I go [down], another comes down before me."
8	Jesus saith unto him, Rise, take up thy bed, and walk.	Jesus said to him: Arise, take up thy bed, and walk.	Jesus said to him, "Rise, pick up your bed and walk."

Parallel Translations

	KJV	Murdock	Magiera
	JOHN *Chapter 5*		
9	And immediately the man was made whole, and took up his bed, and walked: and on the same day was the sabbath.	And immediately the man was healed; and he arose, took up his bed, and walked; and it was the sabbath day.	And immediately that man was healed and he rose up, picked up his bed and walked. And that same day was the Sabbath.
10	The Jews therefore said unto him that was cured, It is the sabbath day: it is not lawful for thee to carry thy bed.	And the Jews said to him that was healed: It is the sabbath; it is not lawful for thee to bear thy bed.	And the Judeans said to him who was healed, "It is the Sabbath. It is not lawful for you to carry your bed."
11	He answered them, He that made me whole, the same said unto me, Take up thy bed, and walk.	But he answered, and said to them: He that made me whole, he said to me, Take up thy bed and walk.	But he answered and said to them, "He who made me whole said to me, 'Pick up your bed and walk.'"
12	Then asked they him, What man is that which said unto thee, Take up thy bed, and walk?	And they asked him: Who is the man that said to thee, Take up thy bed and walk?	And they asked him, "Who is this man who told you to pick up your bed and walk?"
13	And he that was healed wist not who it was: for Jesus had conveyed himself away, a multitude being in that place.	But the man that was healed, knew not who it was; for Jesus had slid away, in the great multitude that was in the place.	And he who was healed did not know who he was, for Jesus had withdrawn from the large crowd that was in that place.
14	Afterward Jesus findeth him in the temple, and said unto him, Behold, thou art made whole: sin no more, lest a worse thing come unto thee.	After a time, Jesus found him in the temple, and said to him: Lo, thou art healed; sin not again, lest something worse come upon thee than before.	After a time, Jesus found him in the temple and said to him, "Behold, you are whole. Do not sin again, lest something that is worse than before should happen to you."
15	The man departed, and told the Jews that it was Jesus, which had made him whole.	And the man went and told the Jews, that it was Jesus who had cured him.	And that man went and told the Judeans that it was Jesus who had healed him.
16	And therefore did the Jews persecute Jesus, and sought to slay him, because he had done these things on the sabbath day.	And for this cause the Jews persecuted Jesus, and sought to kill him; because he had done these things on the sabbath.	And because of this, the Judeans were persecuting Jesus and seeking to kill him, because he had done these [things] on the Sabbath.
17	But Jesus answered them, My Father worketh hitherto, and I work.	But Jesus said to them: My Father worketh until now, and I work.	But Jesus said to them, "My Father works until now. I also work."
18	Therefore the Jews sought the more to kill him, because he not only had broken the sabbath, but said also that God was his Father, making himself equal with God.	And for this, the Jews sought the more to kill him, not only because he had broken the sabbath, but because he had said of God, that he was his Father, and had equalled himself with God.	And because of this, the Judeans were seeking to kill him even more, not only because he had broken the Sabbath, but also because he was saying about God that he was his Father and was equating himself with God.
19	Then answered Jesus and said unto them, Verily, verily, I say unto you, The Son can do nothing of himself, but what he seeth the Father do: for what things soever he doeth, these also doeth the Son likewise.	And Jesus answered, and said to them: Verily, verily, I say to you: The Son can do nothing, of his own pleasure, but what he seeth the Father do: for what things the Father doeth, these in like manner doeth the Son.	Now Jesus answered and said to them, "Truly, truly I say to you, the Son is not able to do anything by his own will, but what he sees the Father [do], that he does. For those [things] that the Father does, these also the Son does likewise.

Parallel Translations

	KJV	*Murdock*	*Magiera*
	JOHN *Chapter 5*		
20	For the Father loveth the Son, and sheweth him all things that himself doeth: and he will shew him greater works than these, that ye may marvel.	For the Father loveth his Son, and showeth him every thing he doeth: and greater works than these, will he show him, that ye may wonder.	For the Father loves his Son and everything that he does, he shows him and he will show him greater than these works, so that you will marvel.
21	For as the Father raiseth up the dead, and quickeneth them; even so the Son quickeneth whom he will.	For as the Father raiseth the dead, and vivifieth them; so also the Son vivifieth whom he pleaseth.	For as the Father raises the dead and makes them alive, so also the Son will make alive those whom he wants.
22	For the Father judgeth no man, but hath committed all judgment unto the Son:	For neither doth the Father judge any one, but hath given all judgment to the Son:	For the Father does not judge anyone, but has given all judgment to the Son,
23	That all men should honour the Son, even as they honour the Father. He that honoureth not the Son honoureth not the Father which hath sent him.	that every man may honor the Son, as he honoreth the Father. He that honoreth not the Son, honoreth not the Father that sent him.	so that everyone should honor the Son as he honors the Father. He who does not honor the Son does not honor the Father who sent him.
24	Verily, verily, I say unto you, He that heareth my word, and believeth on him that sent me, hath everlasting life, and shall not come into condemnation; but is passed from death unto life.	Verily, verily, I say to you, That he who heareth my word, and believeth on him that sent me, hath life eternal, and will not come into condemnation, but hath passed from death to life.	Truly, truly I say to you, whoever hears my word and believes on him who sent me has eternal life and does not come to judgment, but has removed himself from death to life.
25	Verily, verily, I say unto you, The hour is coming, and now is, when the dead shall hear the voice of the Son of God: and they that hear shall live.	Verily, verily, I say to you, That the hour cometh, and even now come, when the dead will hear the voice of the Son of God; and they that hear, will live.	Truly, truly I say to you, the hour comes, even now is, when the dead will hear the voice of the Son of God and those who hear [it] will live.
26	For as the Father hath life in himself; so hath he given to the Son to have life in himself;	For, as the Father hath life in himself, so hath he given to the Son also, to have life in himself:	For as the Father has life in himself, so he also gave to the Son to have life in himself
27	And hath given him authority to execute judgment also, because he is the Son of man.	and hath moreover given him authority to execute judgment. But that he is the Son of man,	and he gave him authority to also execute judgment.
28	Marvel not at this: for the hour is coming, in the which all that are in the graves shall hear his voice,	wonder not at this; for the hour cometh when all that are in their graves will hear his voice;	Now because he is the Son of Man, do not marvel at this, because the hour will come when all those who are in the graves will hear his voice.
29	And shall come forth; they that have done good, unto the resurrection of life; and they that have done evil, unto the resurrection of damnation.	and will come forth; they that have done good, to the resurrection of life, and they that have done evil, to the resurrection of condemnation.	And those who have done good [things] will go out to the resurrection of life and those who have done evil [things] to the resurrection of judgment.
30	I can of mine own self do nothing: as I hear, I judge: and my judgment is just; because I seek not mine own will, but the will of the Father which hath sent me.	I can do nothing of my own pleasure; but as I hear, so I judge. And my judgment is just; for I seek not my own pleasure, but the pleasure of him that sent me.	I cannot do anything of my own will, but as I hear, I judge, and my judgment is upright, for I do not seek my will, but the will of him who sent me.
31	If I bear witness of myself, my witness is not true.	If I should bear testimony respecting myself, my testimony would not be valid.	If I testify about myself, my testimony is not true.

Parallel Translations

JOHN *Chapter 5*

	KJV	*Murdock*	*Magiera*
32	There is another that beareth witness of me; and I know that the witness which he witnesseth of me is true.	There is another that beareth testimony concerning me; and I know that the testimony which he beareth concerning me is true.	There is another who bears testimony about me and I know that his testimony that he testifies about me is true.
33	Ye sent unto John, and he bare witness unto the truth.	Ye sent unto John; and he bore testimony to the truth.	You sent to John and he testified concerning the truth.
34	But I receive not testimony from man: but these things I say, that ye might be saved.	And I have not received testimony from men: but these things I say, that ye may live.	And I did not receive the testimony from man, but I say these [things] that you may live.
35	He was a burning and a shining light: and ye were willing for a season to rejoice in his light.	He was a burning and shining lamp; and ye were willing for a time, to glory in his light.	That [man] was a lamp that shone and brought light and you were willing to boast for a time in his light.
36	But I have greater witness than that of John: for the works which the Father hath given me to finish, the same works that I do, bear witness of me, that the Father hath sent me.	But I have a testimony, which is greater than that of John; for the works which my Father hath given me to accomplish, these works which I do, testify of me that the Father hath sent me.	But I have a testimony that is greater than [that] of John, for the works that my Father gave to me to finish, those works that I do, testify concerning me that the Father sent me.
37	And the Father himself, which hath sent me, hath borne witness of me. Ye have neither heard his voice at any time, nor seen his shape.	And the Father who sent me, he testifieth of me. Ye have not at any time heard his voice, nor have ye seen his visage.	And the Father who sent me testifies about me. You have not ever heard his voice, nor have you seen his appearance.
38	And ye have not his word abiding in you: for whom he hath sent, him ye believe not.	And his word abideth not in you, because ye believe not in him whom he hath sent.	And his word does not remain in you, because you do not believe in him whom he sent.
39	Search the scriptures; for in them ye think ye have eternal life: and they are they which testify of me.	Search the scriptures; for in them, ye think, there is life eternal for you; and they testify of me.	Search the scriptures, because in them you think that you have eternal life and they testify about me.
40	And ye will not come to me, that ye might have life.	And ye are unwilling to come to me, that life eternal may be yours.	And you are not desiring to come to me that you might have eternal life.
41	I receive not honour from men.	I do not receive glory from men.	I do not receive praise from men,
42	But I know you, that ye have not the love of God in you.	But I know you, that the love of God is not in you.	but I know you, that the love of God is not in you.
43	I am come in my Father's name, and ye receive me not: if another shall come in his own name, him ye will receive.	I came in the name of my Father, and ye receive me not: if another shall come in his own name, him ye will receive.	I have come in the name of my Father and you have not received me. Yet if another would come in his own name, you would receive him.
44	How can ye believe, which receive honour one of another, and seek not the honour that cometh from God only?	How can ye believe, who receive glory from one another, and seek not the glory which cometh from God only?	How are you able to believe, who receive praise from one another, yet you do not seek the praise that is from God alone?
45	Do not think that I will accuse you to the Father: there is one that accuseth you, even Moses, in whom ye trust.	Do ye suppose, that I shall accuse you before the Father? There is one that will accuse you, that Moses, on whom ye rely.	Do you think that I will accuse you before the Father? There is one who accuses you, Moses, in whom you trust,

JOHN *Chapter 5*

	KJV	Murdock	Magiera
46	For had ye believed Moses, ye would have believed me: for he wrote of me.	For, if ye believed Moses, ye would also believe me; for Moses wrote concerning me.	for if you believe in Moses, you would also believe in me, for Moses wrote about me.
47	But if ye believe not his writings, how shall ye believe my words?	But if ye believe not his writings, how will ye believe my words?	And if you do not believe his writings, how will you believe my words?"

Chapter 6

	KJV	Murdock	Magiera
1	After these things Jesus went over the sea of Galilee, which is the sea of Tiberias.	After these things, Jesus went to the other side of the sea of Galilee [or] of Tiberias.	After these [things], Jesus went to the other shore of the Sea of Galilee, which is Tiberias.
2	And a great multitude followed him, because they saw his miracles which he did on them that were diseased.	And great multitudes went after him; because they had seen the signs which he wrought upon the sick.	And large crowds followed him, because they had seen the signs that he did with the sick.
3	And Jesus went up into a mountain, and there he sat with his disciples.	And Jesus ascended a mountain, and there he seated himself with his disciples.	And Jesus went up to a mountain and was sitting there with his disciples.
4	And the passover, a feast of the Jews, was nigh.	And the feast of the Jewish passover was near.	And the feast of the Passover of the Judeans was near.
5	When Jesus then lifted up his eyes, and saw a great company come unto him, he saith unto Philip, Whence shall we buy bread, that these may eat?	And Jesus raised his eyes, and saw a great multitude coming towards him; and he said to Philip: Whence shall we buy bread, that these may eat?	And Jesus raised his eyes and saw a large crowd that came towards him. And he said to Philip, "Where will we buy bread that these may eat?"
6	And this he said to prove him: for he himself knew what he would do.	And this he said, to try him; for he knew what he was about to do.	And he said this, testing him, for he knew what he was going to do.
7	Philip answered him, Two hundred pennyworth of bread is not sufficient for them, that every one of them may take a little.	Philip said to him: Two hundred denarii in bread would not suffice them, that each might take but a little.	Philip said to him, "Two hundred denarii [of] bread is not sufficient for them, [even] when each of them would [only] take a little."
8	One of his disciples, Andrew, Simon Peter's brother, saith unto him,	One of his disciples, Andrew, the brother of Simon Cephas, said to him:	Andrew, the brother of Simon Peter, one of his disciples, said to him,
9	There is a lad here, which hath five barley loaves, and two small fishes: but what are they among so many?	There is a lad here, who hath with him five cakes of barley, and two fishes; but what are these for all those [people]?	"There is a certain boy here who has five loaves of barley and two fish with him, but what are these for all those [people]?"
10	And Jesus said, Make the men sit down. Now there was much grass in the place. So the men sat down, in number about five thousand.	Jesus said to them: Make all the people recline. Now there was much grass in that place: and the people reclined, in number five thousand.	Jesus said to them, "Make all the men to sit to eat." Now there was much grass in that place and the men sat to eat, five thousand in number.
11	And Jesus took the loaves; and when he had given thanks, he distributed to the disciples, and the disciples to them that were set down; and likewise of the fishes as much as they would.	And Jesus took the bread, and blessed, and distributed to them that reclined. And so also, with the fish; as much as they desired.	And Jesus took the bread and blessed [it] and distributed [it] to those who sat to eat, and so also from the fish, as much as they wanted.

Parallel Translations

	KJV	Murdock	Magiera

JOHN *Chapter 6*

	KJV	Murdock	Magiera
12	When they were filled, he said unto his disciples, Gather up the fragments that remain, that nothing be lost.	And when they were satisfied, he said to his disciples: Gather up the fragments which remain, that nothing be lost.	And when they were satisfied, he said to his disciples, "Gather the fragments that remain, so that nothing will be lost."
13	Therefore they gathered them together, and filled twelve baskets with the fragments of the five barley loaves, which remained over and above unto them that had eaten.	And they collected and filled twelve baskets, with fragments of what remained to them that had eaten of the five barley cakes.	And they gathered [them] and filled twelve baskets [with] those fragments that remained to them who had eaten from the five loaves of barley.
14	Then those men, when they had seen the miracle that Jesus did, said, This is of a truth that prophet that should come into the world.	And those people, when they saw the sign which Jesus had wrought, said: Certainly, this is that prophet who was to come into the world.	Now those men who had seen the sign that Jesus had done were saying, "Truly this is the prophet who has come into the world."
15	When Jesus therefore perceived that they would come and take him by force, to make him a king, he departed again into a mountain himself alone.	And Jesus knew, that they were about to come and take him by force, and make him king: and he retired into a mountain alone.	But Jesus knew that they were going to come [and] grab him and to make him a king and he went out to a mountain alone.
16	And when even was now come, his disciples went down unto the sea,	And when it was evening, his disciples went down to the sea,	And when evening came, his disciples went down to the sea.
17	And entered into a ship, and went over the sea toward Capernaum. And it was now dark, and Jesus was not come to them.	and sat in a ship, and were going over to Capernaum. And darkness came on, and Jesus had not come to them.	And they took a ship and were going to the other shore, to Capernaum. And it was dark and Jesus had not come to them.
18	And the sea arose by reason of a great wind that blew.	And the sea was boisterous against them, for a violent wind was blowing.	And the sea was lifted up against them, because a fierce wind was blowing.
19	So when they had rowed about five and twenty or thirty furlongs, they see Jesus walking on the sea, and drawing nigh unto the ship: and they were afraid.	And they had gone about five and twenty or thirty furlongs, when they saw Jesus walking upon the sea: and as he drew near to the ship, they were afraid.	And they went onward about twenty-five or thirty furlongs and they saw Jesus walking on the lake. And as he came near to their ship, they were afraid.
20	But he saith unto them, It is I; be not afraid.	But Jesus said to them: It is I; be not afraid.	And Jesus said to them, "It is I. Do not be afraid."
21	Then they willingly received him into the ship: and immediately the ship was at the land whither they went.	And they were glad to receive him into the ship. And, directly, the ship was at the land to which they were going.	And they wanted to receive him into the ship and immediately, that ship was at the land [to] which they were going.
22	The day following, when the people which stood on the other side of the sea saw that there was none other boat there, save that one whereinto his disciples were entered, and that Jesus went not with his disciples into the boat, but that his disciples were gone away alone;	And the next day, the multitude, who had remained on the other side of the sea, saw that there was no other ship there, except that in which the disciples embarked, and that Jesus did not embark in that ship with his disciples;	And on the next day that crowd that remained on the other side of the sea saw that there was no other ship there, except that one which the disciples had boarded and that Jesus had not entered the ship with his disciples.

JOHN *Chapter 6*

	KJV	*Murdock*	*Magiera*
23	(Howbeit there came other boats from Tiberias nigh unto the place where they did eat bread, after that the Lord had given thanks:)	yet that other ships had come from Tiberias, near to the place where they ate the bread when Jesus blessed [it].	But other boats had come from Tiberias to the shore of the place in which they ate bread after Jesus had blessed [it],
24	When the people therefore saw that Jesus was not there, neither his disciples, they also took shipping, and came to Capernaum, seeking for Jesus.	And when the multitude saw, that Jesus was not there, nor his disciples; they embarked in ships, and came to Capernaum, and sought for Jesus.	and when that crowd saw that neither Jesus was there nor his disciples, they boarded these boats and came to Capernaum and were seeking Jesus.
25	And when they had found him on the other side of the sea, they said unto him, Rabbi, when camest thou hither?	And when they found him on the other side of the sea, they said to him: Our Rabbi, when camest thou hither?	And when they found him on the other shore of the sea, they said to him, "Our Master, when did you come here?"
26	Jesus answered them and said, Verily, verily, I say unto you, Ye seek me, not because ye saw the miracles, but because ye did eat of the loaves, and were filled.	Jesus replied and said to them: Verily, verily, I say to you, Ye seek me, not because ye saw the signs, but because ye ate the bread and were satisfied.	Jesus answered and said to them, "Truly, truly I say to you, you are seeking me, not because you saw the miracles, but because you ate bread and were satisfied.
27	Labour not for the meat which perisheth, but for that meat which endureth unto everlasting life, which the Son of man shall give unto you: for him hath God the Father sealed.	Labor not for the food that perisheth, but for the food that abideth unto life eternal, which the Son of man will give to you; for him hath God the Father sealed.	Do not labor for food that is destroyed, but [for] food that lasts for life forever, that which the Son of Man will give to you, for this the Father, God, has confirmed."
28	Then said they unto him, What shall we do, that we might work the works of God?	They said to him: What shall we do, in order to work the works of God?	They said to him, "What should we do to labor for the works of God?"
29	Jesus answered and said unto them, This is the work of God, that ye believe on him whom he hath sent.	Jesus replied and said to them: This is the work of God, that ye believe on him whom he hath sent.	Jesus answered and said to them, "This is the work of God, that you should believe in him whom he sent."
30	They said therefore unto him, What sign shewest thou then, that we may see, and believe thee? what dost thou work?	They say to him: What sign doest thou, that we may see and believe in thee? What workest thou?	They said to him, "What sign have you done that we may see and believe in you? What have you performed?
31	Our fathers did eat manna in the desert; as it is written, He gave them bread from heaven to eat.	Our fathers ate the manna, in the wilderness; as it is written, He gave them bread from heaven to eat.	Our fathers ate manna in the wilderness, as it is written: HE GAVE THEM BREAD FROM HEAVEN TO EAT."
32	Then Jesus said unto them, Verily, verily, I say unto you, Moses gave you not that bread from heaven; but my Father giveth you the true bread from heaven.	Jesus said to them: Verily, verily, I say to you, Moses gave you not the bread from heaven; but my Father giveth you the real bread from heaven.	Jesus said to them, "Truly, truly I say to you, Moses did not give you bread from heaven, but my Father gave you the truthful bread from heaven.
33	For the bread of God is he which cometh down from heaven, and giveth life unto the world.	For the bread of God is, he that came down from heaven, and giveth life to the world.	For the bread of God is he who has come down from heaven and gives life to the world."
34	Then said they unto him, Lord, evermore give us this bread.	They say to him: Our Lord, give us at all times this bread.	They said to him, "Our Lord, give us this bread always."

Parallel Translations

	KJV	Murdock	Magiera
	JOHN Chapter 6		
35	And Jesus said unto them, I am the bread of life: he that cometh to me shall never hunger; and he that believeth on me shall never thirst.	Jesus said to them: I am the bread of life: he that cometh to me, shall not hunger; and he that believeth on me, shall not thirst, for ever.	Jesus said to them, "I am the bread of life. He who comes to me will not hunger and he who believes in me will not thirst forever.
36	But I said unto you, That ye also have seen me, and believe not.	But I said to you, That ye have seen me, and do not believe.	But I said to you, 'You have seen me, yet you do not believe.'
37	All that the Father giveth me shall come to me; and him that cometh to me I will in no wise cast out.	All that my Father gave me, will come to me: and him, that cometh to me, I will not cast out.	All whom my Father has given to me will come to me and whoever will come to me I will not throw out,
38	For I came down from heaven, not to do mine own will, but the will of him that sent me.	For I came down from heaven, not to do my own pleasure, but the pleasure of him that sent me.	because I came down from heaven, not to do my will, but to do the will of him who sent me.
39	And this is the Father's will which hath sent me, that of all which he hath given me I should lose nothing, but should raise it up again at the last day.	And this is the pleasure of him that sent me, that whatever he hath given me, I should lose nothing of it, but should raise it up at the last day.	And this is the will of him who sent me, that I do not lose anyone [of] all whom he has given me, but I will raise him up in the last day.
40	And this is the will of him that sent me, that every one which seeth the Son, and believeth on him, may have everlasting life: and I will raise him up at the last day.	For this is the pleasure of my Father, that every one who seeth the Son, and believeth on him, should have life eternal; and I will raise him up at the last day.	For this is the will of my Father, that all who see the Son and believe in him will have eternal life and I will raise him up in the last day."
41	The Jews then murmured at him, because he said, I am the bread which came down from heaven.	Then the Jews murmured at him, because he said: I am the bread, who have descended from heaven.	And the Judeans were murmuring against him, because he said, "I am the bread that came down from heaven."
42	And they said, Is not this Jesus, the son of Joseph, whose father and mother we know? how is it then that he saith, I came down from heaven?	And they said: Is not this Jesus the son of Joseph, whose father and mother we know? And how doth he say: I came down from heaven?	And they were saying, "Is not this Jesus the son of Joseph, him whose father and mother we know? Yet how does this [man] say, 'I came down from heaven?'"
43	Jesus therefore answered and said unto them, Murmur not among yourselves.	Jesus replied and said to them: Murmur not, one with another.	Jesus answered and said to them, "Do not murmur to each other.
44	No man can come to me, except the Father which hath sent me draw him: and I will raise him up at the last day.	No man can come to me, unless the Father who sent me, shall draw him; and I will raise him up at the last day.	No one is able to come to me, unless the Father who sent me draws him and I will raise him up in the last day,
45	It is written in the prophets, And they shall be all taught of God. Every man therefore that hath heard, and hath learned of the Father, cometh unto me.	For it is written, in the prophet: And they shall all be taught of God. Whoever, therefore, heareth from the Father, and learneth from him, cometh to me.	for it is written in the prophet: ALL OF THEM WILL BE TAUGHT OF GOD. Everyone who hears, therefore, from the Father and learns from him will come to me.
46	Not that any man hath seen the Father, save he which is of God, he hath seen the Father.	Not that any one hath seen the Father, except him who hath come from God; he it is, hath seen the Father.	There is no one who will see the Father, but rather he who is from God is that one [who] sees the Father.

Parallel Translations

JOHN *Chapter 6*

	KJV	*Murdock*	*Magiera*
47	Verily, verily, I say unto you, He that believeth on me hath everlasting life.	Verily, verily, I say to you: That, to him who believeth in me, there is life eternal.	Truly, truly I say to you, he who believes in me has eternal life.
48	I am that bread of life.	I am the bread of life.	I am the bread of life.
49	Your fathers did eat manna in the wilderness, and are dead.	Your fathers ate the manna, in the wilderness, and they died.	Your fathers ate manna in the wilderness and they died.
50	This is the bread which cometh down from heaven, that a man may eat thereof, and not die.	But this is the bread which cometh from heaven, that a man may eat of it, and not die.	Now this is the bread that came down from heaven, that a man may eat of it and not die.
51	I am the living bread which came down from heaven: if any man eat of this bread, he shall live for ever: and the bread that I will give is my flesh, which I will give for the life of the world.	I am the bread of life, who have come down from heaven: and if a man shall eat of this bread, he will live for ever. And the bread which I shall give, is my body, which I give for the life of the world.	I am the living bread, who came down from heaven and if a man should eat of this bread, he will live forever. And the bread that I give is my body, which I give for the life of the world."
52	The Jews therefore strove among themselves, saying, How can this man give us his flesh to eat?	Then the Jews contended one with another, and said: How can he give us his body to eat?	And the Judeans were arguing with each other and saying, "How can this [man] give us his body to eat?"
53	Then Jesus said unto them, Verily, verily, I say unto you, Except ye eat the flesh of the Son of man, and drink his blood, ye have no life in you.	And Jesus said to them: Verily, verily, I say to you, That, unless ye eat the body of the Son of man, and drink his blood, ye have no life within you.	And Jesus said to them, "Truly, truly I say to you, unless you eat the body of the Son of Man and drink his blood, you do not have life in yourselves.
54	Whoso eateth my flesh, and drinketh my blood, hath eternal life; and I will raise him up at the last day.	But he that eateth of my body, and drinketh of my blood, to him is life eternal; and I will raise him up at the last day	And he who eats of my body and drinks of my blood has eternal life and I will raise him up in the last day.
55	For my flesh is meat indeed, and my blood is drink indeed.	For my body truly is food, and my blood truly is drink.	For my body truly is food and my blood truly is drink.
56	He that eateth my flesh, and drinketh my blood, dwelleth in me, and I in him.	He that eateth my body, and drinketh my blood, abideth in me, and I in him	He who eats my body and drinks my blood remains in me and I in him.
57	As the living Father hath sent me, and I live by the Father: so he that eateth me, even he shall live by me.	As the living Father hath sent me, and I live because of the Father; so he that shall eat me, he also will live because of me.	As the living Father has sent me and I live because of the Father, [so] he who eats me will also live because of me.
58	This is that bread which came down from heaven: not as your fathers did eat manna, and are dead: he that eateth of this bread shall live for ever.	This is the bread that came down from heaven: not as your fathers ate the manna, and died; whoever shall eat of this bead, will live for ever.	This is the bread that came down from heaven, not as your fathers ate manna and died. He who eats this bread will live forever."
59	These things said he in the synagogue, as he taught in Capernaum.	These things he uttered in the synagogue, while teaching at Capernaum.	These [things] he said in the synagogue while teaching in Capernaum.
60	Many therefore of his disciples, when they had heard this, said, This is an hard saying; who can hear it?	And many of his disciples who heard [him], said: This is a hard speech, who can hear it.	And many of his disciples who heard [him] said, "This saying is hard. Who is able to hear it?"
61	When Jesus knew in himself that his disciples murmured at it, he said unto them, Doth this offend you?	And Jesus knew in himself, that his disciples murmured at this; and he said to them, Doth this stumble you?	Now Jesus knew in himself that his disciples were murmuring about this [saying] and he said to them, "[Does] this offend you?

Parallel Translations

JOHN *Chapter 6*

	KJV	Murdock	Magiera
62	What and if ye shall see the Son of man ascend up where he was before?	If then, ye were to see the Son of man ascend, to where he was from the beginning!	[What] if then you see the Son of Man ascending to the place where he was before?
63	It is the spirit that quickeneth; the flesh profiteth nothing: the words that I speak unto you, they are spirit, and they are life.	It is the Spirit that vivifieth; the body profiteth nothing. The words which I have used with you, they are spirit, and they are life.	It is the Spirit that makes alive. The body does not profit anything. The words that I speak with you are spirit and they are life.
64	But there are some of you that believe not. For Jesus knew from the beginning who they were that believed not, and who should betray him.	But there are some of you, that believe not. For Jesus knew, from the beginning, who they were that believed not, and who it was that would betray him.	But there are some of you who do not believe." (For Jesus knew previously who those were who did not believe and who it was who would betray him.)
65	And he said, Therefore said I unto you, that no man can come unto me, except it were given unto him of my Father.	And he said to them: For this reason, I said to you, That no one can come to me, unless it be given to him by my Father.	And he was saying to them, "Because of this, I told you that no one is able to come to me, unless it is given to him by my Father."
66	From that time many of his disciples went back, and walked no more with him.	On account of this speech, many of his disciples turned back, and walked not with him.	Because of this saying, many of his disciples turned their back[s] and did not walk with him.
67	Then said Jesus unto the twelve, Will ye also go away?	And Jesus said to the twelve: Are ye also disposed to go away?	And Jesus said to his twelve, "Do you also want to go?"
68	Then Simon Peter answered him, Lord, to whom shall we go? thou hast the words of eternal life.	Simon Cephas replied, and said: My Lord, to whom shall we go? The words of life eternal are with thee.	Simon Peter answered and said, "My Lord, to whom would we go? You have the words of eternal life.
69	And we believe and are sure that thou art that Christ, the Son of the living God.	And we believe, and know, that thou art the Messiah, the Son of the living God.	And we believe and know that you are the Messiah, the Son of the living God."
70	Jesus answered them, Have not I chosen you twelve, and one of you is a devil?	Jesus said to them: Have not I chosen you twelve? Yet one of you is a devil.	Jesus said to them, "Did not I choose you twelve? Yet one of you is an opponent."
71	He spake of Judas Iscariot the son of Simon: for he it was that should betray him, being one of the twelve.	This he spoke of Judas Iscariot, the son of Simon; for he was afterwards to betray him, being one of the twelve.	Now he was speaking about Judas, the son of Simon Iscariot, for he was going to betray him, one of the twelve.

Chapter 7

	KJV	Murdock	Magiera
1	After these things Jesus walked in Galilee: for he would not walk in Jewry, because the Jews sought to kill him.	After these things Jesus walked in Galilee, for he would not walk in Judaea, because the Jews sought to slay him.	After these [things], Jesus was walking in Galilee, for he did not want to walk in Judea, because the Judeans were seeking to kill him.
2	Now the Jews' feast of tabernacles was at hand.	And the Jewish feast of tabernacles drew near.	And the Feast of Tabernacles of the Judeans was near.
3	His brethren therefore said unto him, Depart hence, and go into Judaea, that thy disciples also may see the works that thou doest.	And the brothers of Jesus said to him: Leave here, and go into Judaea; that thy disciples may see the works thou doest.	And his brothers said to Jesus, "Leave here and go to Judea, so that your disciples may see the works that you are doing,

Parallel Translations

	KJV	Murdock	Magiera
	JOHN	*Chapter 7*	
4	For there is no man that doeth any thing in secret, and he himself seeketh to be known openly. If thou do these things, shew thyself to the world.	For there is no one who doeth any thing in secret, while he wisheth to become public. If thou doest these things, show thyself to the world.	for there is no one who does anything secretly, yet desires that it be [known] openly. If you do these [things], show yourself to the world."
5	For neither did his brethren believe in him.	For even his brothers did not believe in Jesus.	For not even his brothers believed in Jesus.
6	Then Jesus said unto them, My time is not yet come: but your time is alway ready.	Jesus said to them: My time hath not yet come: but your time is always ready.	Jesus said to them, "My time has not yet arrived, but your time has always been ready.
7	The world cannot hate you; but me it hateth, because I testify of it, that the works thereof are evil.	The world cannot hate you, but me it hateth; because I testify of it, that its deeds are evil.	The world is not able to hate you, but it hates me, because I testify against it that its works are evil.
8	Go ye up unto this feast: I go not up yet unto this feast; for my time is not yet full come.	Go ye up to the feast; I do not go up to this feast now, because my time is not yet completed.	Go up to this feast. I will not go up to this feast now, because my time is still not finished."
9	When he had said these words unto them, he abode still in Galilee.	These things he said, and remained still in Galilee.	He said these [things] and he stayed in Galilee.
10	But when his brethren were gone up, then went he also up unto the feast, not openly, but as it were in secret.	But when his brothers had gone up to the feast, then he also went up, not openly, but as it were secretly.	Now after his brothers had gone up to the feast, then he also went up, not openly, but secretly.
11	Then the Jews sought him at the feast, and said, Where is he?	And the Jews sought for him at the feast; and they said, Where is he?	And the Judeans were seeking him at the feast and were saying, "Where is he?"
12	And there was much murmuring among the people concerning him: for some said, He is a good man: others said, Nay; but he deceiveth the people.	And there was much altercation among the people respecting him; for some said, He is a good man; while others said, No, but he deceiveth the people.	And there was much murmuring in the crowd because of him, for there were [those] who said, "He is good," and others were saying, "Not so, but rather he deceives the people."
13	Howbeit no man spake openly of him for fear of the Jews.	Yet no one spoke openly of him, from fear of the Jews.	But no one was speaking openly about him, because of fear of the Judeans.
14	Now about the midst of the feast Jesus went up into the temple, and taught.	And in the midst of the days of the feast, Jesus went into the temple, and taught.	Now when the days of the feast were half gone, Jesus went up to the temple and was teaching.
15	And the Jews marvelled, saying, How knoweth this man letters, having never learned?	And the Jews wondered, and said: How knoweth this man literature, having not been educated?	And the Judeans were amazed and said, "How does this [man] know the writings, when he has not learned [them]?"
16	Jesus answered them, and said, My doctrine is not mine, but his that sent me.	Jesus answered and said: My doctrine is not from me, but from him that sent me.	Jesus answered and said, "My teaching is not mine, but his who sent me.
17	If any man will do his will, he shall know of the doctrine, whether it be of God, or whether I speak of myself.	He that wisheth to do his pleasure, will understand my doctrine, whether it is from God, or whether I speak from my own pleasure.	He who wants to do his will, will understand my teaching, if it is from God or [if] I speak from my own will.

	KJV	*Murdock*	*Magiera*
	JOHN	*Chapter 7*	
18	He that speaketh of himself seeketh his own glory: but he that seeketh his glory that sent him, the same is true, and no unrighteousness is in him.	He that speaketh according to the pleasure of his own mind, seeketh glory for himself: but he who seeketh the glory of him that sent him, is veracious, and evil is not in his heart.	He who speaks from the will of his [own] mind seeks glory for himself. Now he who seeks the glory of him who sent him is true and has no wickedness in his heart.
19	Did not Moses give you the law, and yet none of you keepeth the law? Why go ye about to kill me?	Did not Moses give you the law? Yet no one of you observeth the law.	Did not Moses give you the law? Yet not one of you keeps the law.
20	The people answered and said, Thou hast a devil: who goeth about to kill thee?	Why do ye seek to kill me? The multitude answered and said: Thou hast a demon: who seeketh to kill thee?	Why do you seek to kill me?" The crowd answered and said, "You have a devil. Who wants to kill you?"
21	Jesus answered and said unto them, I have done one work, and ye all marvel.	Jesus replied, and said to them: I have wrought one work, and ye all wonder.	Jesus answered and said to them, "I have done one work and all of you are amazed.
22	Moses therefore gave unto you circumcision; (not because it is of Moses, but of the fathers;) and ye on the sabbath day circumcise a man.	Because Moses gave you circumcision, not that it was from Moses, but it was from the fathers, ye circumcise a child on the sabbath.	On account of this, Moses gave you circumcision, not because it was from Moses, but because it was from the forefathers, and on the Sabbath you circumcise a man.
23	If a man on the sabbath day receive circumcision, that the law of Moses should not be broken; are ye angry at me, because I have made a man every whit whole on the sabbath day?	And if a child is circumcised on the sabbath day, that the law of Moses may not be violated, do ye murmur at me, because I have made a man entirely sound on the sabbath day?	If a man is circumcised on the day of the Sabbath [and] because of [this] the law of Moses is not broken, [why] are you murmuring against me, because I have healed the man on the day of the Sabbath?
24	Judge not according to the appearance, but judge righteous judgment.	Judge not, with a respect for persons; but judge ye a righteous judgment.	Do not judge with respect of persons, but rather judge [with an] upright judgment."
25	Then said some of them of Jerusalem, Is not this he, whom they seek to kill?	And some from Jerusalem said: Is not this he, whom they seek to kill?	And some from Jerusalem were saying, "Is this not him whom they seek to kill?
26	But, lo, he speaketh boldly, and they say nothing unto him. Do the rulers know indeed that this is the very Christ?	And lo, he discourseth publicly, and they say nothing to him. Do our Elders know, that he really is the Messiah?	And behold, he speaks openly and they do not say anything to him. Do our elders know that this is truly the Messiah?
27	Howbeit we know this man whence he is: but when Christ cometh, no man knoweth whence he is.	Yet we know this man, whence he is; the Messiah, when he shall come, no one knoweth whence he is.	But we know from where he is. And the Messiah, when he comes, no man will know from where he is."
28	Then cried Jesus in the temple as he taught, saying, Ye both know me, and ye know whence I am: and I am not come of myself, but he that sent me is true, whom ye know not.	And Jesus, while teaching in the temple, raised his voice and said: Ye both know me, and ye know from whence I am. And I did not come of my own accord; but he that sent me is true. Him ye know not;	And Jesus lifted up his voice as he taught in the temple and said, "You both know me and you know from where I [am]. And I did not come by my own will, but he is true who sent me, whom you do not know.
29	But I know him: for I am from him, and he hath sent me.	but I know him; because I am from him, and he sent me.	But I know him, because I [am] from his presence and he has sent me."

Parallel Translations

	KJV	*Murdock*	*Magiera*
	JOHN	*Chapter 7*	
30	Then they sought to take him: but no man laid hands on him, because his hour was not yet come.	And they sought to apprehend him; but no one laid hands on him, because his hour was not yet come.	And they wanted to arrest him, yet no one laid hands on him, because his hour had not yet come.
31	And many of the people believed on him, and said, When Christ cometh, will he do more miracles than these which this man hath done?	And many of the multitude believed on him, and said: When the Messiah cometh, will he work greater signs than these which this man doeth?	Now many from the crowd believed in him and said, "When the Messiah comes, will he do more than these miracles this [man] has done?"
32	The Pharisees heard that the people murmured such things concerning him; and the Pharisees and the chief priests sent officers to take him.	And the Pharisees heard the multitude say these things of him: and they and the chief priests sent constables to take him.	And the Pharisees heard the crowds who were saying these [things] about him and they and the chief priests sent guards to arrest him.
33	Then said Jesus unto them, Yet a little while am I with you, and then I go unto him that sent me.	And Jesus said: A little while longer I am with you, and then I go to him that sent me.	And Jesus said, "Yet a little time I [am] with you, and I will go to him who sent me.
34	Ye shall seek me, and shall not find me: and where I am, thither ye cannot come.	And ye will seek me, and will not find me; and where I am, ye cannot come.	And you will seek me and you will not find me and where I am [going], you are not able to come."
35	Then said the Jews among themselves, Whither will he go, that we shall not find him? will he go unto the dispersed among the Gentiles, and teach the Gentiles?	The Jews said among themselves: Whither is he about to go, that we cannot find him? Will he go to some region of the Gentiles, and teach the profane?	The Judeans said among themselves, "Where is this [man] about to go that we cannot find him? Is he about to go, perhaps, to the regions of the Gentiles and to teach the heathens?
36	What manner of saying is this that he said, Ye shall seek me, and shall not find me: and where I am, thither ye cannot come?	What means this speech he uttered: Ye will seek me, and will not find me; and where I am, ye cannot come?	What is this saying that he said, 'You will seek me and you will not find me and where I am [going], you are not able to come?'"
37	In the last day, that great day of the feast, Jesus stood and cried, saying, If any man thirst, let him come unto me, and drink.	And on the great day, which was the last of the feast, Jesus stood and cried, and said: If any man thirst, let him come to me and drink.	And on the high day, which is the last [day] of the feast, Jesus was standing and he cried out and said, "If anyone is thirsty, he should come to me and drink.
38	He that believeth on me, as the scripture hath said, out of his belly shall flow rivers of living water.	Whoever believeth in me, as the scriptures have said, Out of his belly shall flow rivers of living waters.	Whoever believes in me, as the scriptures have said, rivers of living water will flow from his inner part."
39	(But this spake he of the Spirit, which they that believe on him should receive: for the Holy Ghost was not yet given; because that Jesus was not yet glorified.)	This he said of the Spirit, which they who believe in him were to receive: for the Spirit had not yet been given, because Jesus was not yet glorified.	Now he said this about the Spirit that those who believed in him were about to receive, for the Spirit was not yet given, because Jesus was not yet glorified.
40	Many of the people therefore, when they heard this saying, said, Of a truth this is the Prophet.	And many of the multitude who heard his discourses, said: Certainly, he is a prophet.	And many from the crowds who heard his words were saying, "This is truly a prophet."
41	Others said, This is the Christ. But some said, Shall Christ come out of Galilee?	Others said: He is the Messiah. Others said: Doth Messiah come from Galilee?	Others were saying, "This is the Messiah." Others were saying, "Does the Messiah come from Galilee?

	KJV	Murdock	Magiera
	JOHN *Chapter 7*		
42	Hath not the scripture said, That Christ cometh of the seed of David, and out of the town of Bethlehem, where David was?	Doth not the scriptures say, That Messiah cometh of the seed of David, and from Bethlehem the town of David?	Does not the scripture say that the Messiah will come from the seed of David and from Bethlehem, the village of David?"
43	So there was a division among the people because of him.	And there was a division among the multitude respecting him.	And there was division in the crowds because of him.
44	And some of them would have taken him; but no man laid hands on him.	And there were some of them who wished to apprehend him. But no one laid hands on him.	And there were some of them who wanted to arrest him, but no one laid hands on him.
45	Then came the officers to the chief priests and Pharisees; and they said unto them, Why have ye not brought him?	And the constables came to the chief priests and Pharisees; and the priests said to them: Why have ye not brought him?	And those guards came to the chief priests and the Pharisees and the priests said to them, "Why have you not brought him?"
46	The officers answered, Never man spake like this man.	The constables say to them: Never did a man speak, as this man speaketh.	The guards said to them, "Never has a man spoken so, as this man speaks."
47	Then answered them the Pharisees, Are ye also deceived?	The Pharisees said to them: Are ye also deceived?	The Pharisees said to them, "Are you also deceived?
48	Have any of the rulers or of the Pharisees believed on him?	Have any of the chiefs, or of the Pharisees, believed in him?	Have any of the leaders or of the Pharisees believed in him,
49	But this people who knoweth not the law are cursed.	But this people, who know not the law, are accursed.	except only this cursed people, who do not know the law?"
50	Nicodemus saith unto them, (he that came to Jesus by night, being one of them,)	One of them: Nicodemus, he who came to Jesus by night, said to them:	Nicodemus, one of them, who had come to Jesus in the night, said to them,
51	Doth our law judge any man, before it hear him, and know what he doeth?	Doth our law condemn a man, unless it first hear him, and know what he hath done?	"Does our law condemn a man, unless it hears from him first and knows what he has done?"
52	They answered and said unto him, Art thou also of Galilee? Search, and look: for out of Galilee ariseth no prophet.	They answered, and said to him: Art thou also from Galilee? Search, and see, that no prophet ariseth from Galilee.	They answered and said to him, "Are you also from Galilee? Search and see that the prophet will not rise up from Galilee."
53	And every man went unto his own house.	So they went every one to his own house.*	Then each one went to his house.
	Chapter 8		
1	Jesus went unto the mount of Olives.	And Jesus went to the mount of Olives.	And Jesus went to the Mount of Olives.
2	And early in the morning he came again into the temple, and all the people came unto him; and he sat down, and taught them.	And in the morning he came again to the temple; and all the people came to him, and he sat down and taught them.	And in the morning he came again to the temple and all the people came to him. And while he was sitting, he was teaching them.
3	And the scribes and Pharisees brought unto him a woman taken in adultery; and when they had set her in the midst,	And the Scribes and Pharisees brought forward a woman that was caught in adultery. And when they had placed her in the midst,	And the scribes and Pharisees brought a woman who was caught in adultery. And placing her in the middle,
4	They say unto him, Master, this woman was taken in adultery, in the very act.	they say to him: Teacher, this woman was caught openly in the act of adultery.	they said to him, "Teacher, this woman was caught openly in the act of adultery.

Parallel Translations

	KJV	*Murdock*	*Magiera*
JOHN	*Chapter 8*		
5	Now Moses in the law commanded us, that such should be stoned: but what sayest thou?	And in the law of Moses, [God] hath commanded us to stone such persons. What therefore dost thou say?	And in the law of Moses, he commanded that we stone those who are like these. Therefore, what do you say?"
6	This they said, tempting him, that they might have to accuse him. But Jesus stooped down, and with his finger wrote on the ground, as though he heard them not.	And this they said, tempting him, so that they might have [ground] to accuse him. But Jesus having stooped down, was writing on the ground.	They said this tempting him, so that they would have [cause] to accuse him. But Jesus, after he had stooped down, wrote on the ground.
7	So when they continued asking him, he lifted up himself, and said unto them, He that is without sin among you, let him first cast a stone at her.	And as they continued asking him, he straightened himself up, and said to them: Whoever among you is without sin, let him first cast a stone at her.	And when they continued asking him, he straightened himself and said to them, "Whoever is without sin may throw a stone at her first."
8	And again he stooped down, and wrote on the ground.	And, having again stooped down, he wrote on the ground.	And again after he had stooped down, he wrote on the ground.
9	And they which heard it, being convicted by their own conscience, went out one by one, beginning at the eldest, even unto the last: and Jesus was left alone, and the woman standing in the midst.	And they, when they heard [it], went out one by one, beginning with the older; and the woman was left, alone where she had stood in the midst.	And when they heard [it], they went out one by one beginning with the elders. And the woman was left by herself, being in the middle.
10	When Jesus had lifted up himself, and saw none but the woman, he said unto her, Woman, where are those thine accusers? hath no man condemned thee?	And when Jesus had straightened himself up, he said to the woman: Where are they? Doth no one condemn thee?	And after Jesus straightened himself, he said to the woman, "Where are they? Does no man condemn you?"
11	She said, No man, Lord. And Jesus said unto her, Neither do I condemn thee: go, and sin no more.	And she said: No man, Lord. And Jesus said: Neither do I condemn thee. Go thou, and henceforth sin no more.	And that [one] said, "No man, LORD." And Jesus said, "Neither do I condemn you. Go and from now on, do not sin again."
12	Then spake Jesus again unto them, saying, I am the light of the world: he that followeth me shall not walk in darkness, but shall have the light of life.	And Jesus again conversed with them, and said: I am the light of the world: he that cometh to me, will not walk in darkness; but will find for himself the light of life.	Now again Jesus spoke to them and said, "I am the light of the world. He who follows me will not walk in darkness, but he will find for himself the light of life."
13	The Pharisees therefore said unto him, Thou bearest record of thyself; thy record is not true.	The Pharisees said to him: Thou bearest witness of thyself, thy testimony is not certain.	The Pharisees said to him, "You testify concerning yourself. Your testimony is not true."
14	Jesus answered and said unto them, Though I bear record of myself, yet my record is true: for I know whence I came, and whither I go; but ye cannot tell whence I come, and whither I go.	Jesus answered and said to them: Although I bear witness of myself, my testimony is certain, because I know whence I came, and whither I go. But ye do not know, whence I came, and whither I go.	Jesus answered and said to them, "Even if I testify concerning myself, my testimony is true, because I know from where I came and to where I am going. But you do not know from where I came or to where I am going.
15	Ye judge after the flesh; I judge no man.	Ye judge according to the flesh: I judge no one.	You judge according to the flesh. I do not judge anyone.

Parallel Translations

	KJV	Murdock	Magiera
	JOHN Chapter 8		
16	And yet if I judge, my judgment is true: for I am not alone, but I and the Father that sent me.	Yet if I judge, my judgment is certain, because I am not alone, but I and my Father who sent me.	Yet now if I do judge, my judgment is true, because I am not alone. But rather, I and my Father who sent me [judge].
17	It is also written in your law, that the testimony of two men is true.	And in your law it is written, that the testimony of two persons is certain.	And now in your law it is written that the testimony of two men is true.
18	I am one that bear witness of myself, and the Father that sent me beareth witness of me.	I am one: who bear witness of myself, and my Father who sent me, beareth witness of me.	I am [one] who testifies concerning myself and my Father who sent me testifies concerning me."
19	Then said they unto him, Where is thy Father? Jesus answered, Ye neither know me, nor my Father: if ye had known me, ye should have known my Father also.	They say to him: Where is thy Father? Jesus replied, and said to them: Ye neither know me nor my Father. If ye had known me, ye would also have known my Father.	They said to him, "Where is your father?" Jesus answered and said to them, "You know neither me nor my Father. If you would know me, you would also know my Father."
20	These words spake Jesus in the treasury, as he taught in the temple: and no man laid hands on him; for his hour was not yet come.	These words spake Jesus in the treasury, as he taught in the temple: and no one laid hands on him, because his hour was not yet come.	He spoke these words [in] the treasury while he taught in the temple. And no one arrested him, for his hour had not yet come.
21	Then said Jesus again unto them, I go my way, and ye shall seek me, and shall die in your sins: whither I go, ye cannot come.	Again Jesus said to them: I go away, and ye will seek me, and will die in your sins. And whither I go, ye cannot come.	Again Jesus said to them, "I will go and you will seek me and you will die in your sins. And where I am going, you are not able to come."
22	Then said the Jews, Will he kill himself? because he saith, Whither I go, ye cannot come.	The Jews said: Is he about to kill himself, that he should say, Whither I go ye cannot come?	The Judeans said, "Will he perhaps kill himself?" because he said, "Where I am going, you are not able to come."
23	And he said unto them, Ye are from beneath; I am from above: ye are of this world; I am not of this world.	And he said to them: Ye are from below, I am from above; ye are of this world, I am not of this world	And he said to them, "You are from below and I am from above. You are from this world. I am not from this world.
24	I said therefore unto you, that ye shall die in your sins: for if ye believe not that I am he, ye shall die in your sins.	I said to you, That ye will die in your sins; for if ye believe not that I am he, ye will die in your sins.	I told you that you will die in your sins, for unless you believe that I am [he], you will die in your sins."
25	Then said they unto him, Who art thou? And Jesus saith unto them, Even the same that I said unto you from the beginning.	The Jews said to him: Who art thou? Jesus said to them: Although I have begun to converse with you,	The Judeans said, "Who are you?" Jesus said to them, "Although I have [just] begun to speak to you,
26	I have many things to say and to judge of you: but he that sent me is true; and I speak to the world those things which I have heard of him.	I have yet many things to say and to Judge concerning you. But he that sent me is true: and the things which I have heard from him, them I speak in the world.	I have much to say and to judge against you, but he who sent me is true and those [things] that I have heard from him, I speak in the world."
27	They understood not that he spake to them of the Father.	And they did not know, that he spake to them of the Father.	And they did not know that he spoke to them about the Father.

Parallel Translations

JOHN Chapter 8

	KJV	Murdock	Magiera
28	Then said Jesus unto them, When ye have lifted up the Son of man, then shall ye know that I am he, and that I do nothing of myself; but as my Father hath taught me, I speak these things.	Jesus said to them again: When ye shall have lifted up the Son of man, then will ye know that I am he, and that I do nothing from my own pleasure, but as my Father taught me, so I speak.	Jesus said to them again, "When you have lifted up the Son of Man, then you will know that I am [he] and [that] I did not do anything of my own will, but as my Father has taught me, so I speak.
29	And he that sent me is with me: the Father hath not left me alone; for I do always those things that please him.	And he that sent me, is with me; and my Father hath not left me alone, because I do, at all times, that which pleaseth him.	And he who sent me is with me and my Father does not leave me alone, because I always do that which pleases him."
30	As he spake these words, many believed on him.	And when he had spoken these things, many believed on him.	While he was speaking these [things], many believed in him.
31	Then said Jesus to those Jews which believed on him, If ye continue in my word, then are ye my disciples indeed;	And Jesus said to those Jews who believed on him: If ye continue in my word, ye will be truly my disciples.	And Jesus said to those Judeans who believed in him, "If you will remain in my word, you [are] truly my disciples.
32	And ye shall know the truth, and the truth shall make you free.	And ye will know the truth; and the truth will make you free.	And you will know the truth and that truth will set you free."
33	They answered him, We be Abraham's seed, and were never in bondage to any man: how sayest thou, Ye shall be made free?	They say to him: We are the seed of Abraham, and never were in servitude to any man; and how sayest thou, Ye will be freemen?	They said to him, "We [are] the seed of Abraham and bondage has not ever been served by us to anyone. How can you say, 'You will be free men?'"
34	Jesus answered them, Verily, verily, I say unto you, Whosoever committeth sin is the servant of sin.	Jesus said to them: Verily, verily, I say to you, That whoever committeth sin, is the servant of sin.	Jesus said to them, "Truly, truly I say to you, everyone who commits sin is the servant of sin.
35	And the servant abideth not in the house for ever: but the Son abideth ever.	And a servant abideth not for ever in the house; but the Son abideth for ever.	And a servant does not remain in the house forever, but the Son remains forever.
36	If the Son therefore shall make you free, ye shall be free indeed.	If therefore the Son shall make you free, ye will really be free men.	Therefore, if the Son should free you, you will truly be free men.
37	I know that ye are Abraham's seed; but ye seek to kill me, because my word hath no place in you.	I know that ye are the children of Abraham; but ye seek to kill me, because ye do not acquiesce in my word.	I know that you [are] the seed of Abraham, but you are seeking to kill me, because you do not empty yourselves [to make room] for my word.
38	I speak that which I have seen with my Father: and ye do that which ye have seen with your father.	I speak that which I have seen with my Father, and ye do that which ye have seen with your father.	What I have seen with my Father, I speak, and what you have seen with your father, you do."
39	They answered and said unto him, Abraham is our father. Jesus saith unto them, If ye were Abraham's children, ye would do the works of Abraham.	They answered, and said to him: Our father is Abraham. Jesus said to them: If ye were children of Abraham, ye would do the works of Abraham.	They answered and said to him, "Our father is Abraham." Jesus said to them, "If you were the children of Abraham, you would do the works of Abraham.
40	But now ye seek to kill me, a man that hath told you the truth, which I have heard of God: this did not Abraham.	But now ye seek to kill me, a man who hath told you the truth, which I have heard from God: this did not Abraham.	But now, behold, you are seeking to kill me, a man who has spoken the truth with you, that which I have heard from God. Abraham did not do this,

Parallel Translations

JOHN Chapter 8

	KJV	Murdock	Magiera
41	Ye do the deeds of your father. Then said they to him, We be not born of fornication; we have one Father, even God.	But ye do the works of your father. They say to him: We are not [the offspring] of whoredom; we have one Father, God.	but you are doing the works of your father." They said to him, "We were not [born] of fornication. We have one Father, God."
42	Jesus said unto them, If God were your Father, ye would love me: for I proceeded forth and came from God; neither came I of myself, but he sent me.	Jesus said to them: If God were your Father, ye would love me; for I proceeded and came from God: I did not come of my own accord, but he sent me.	Jesus said to them, "If God was your Father, you would love me, for I have gone out and I have come from God and it was not of my own will, but rather he sent me.
43	Why do ye not understand my speech? even because ye cannot hear my word.	Why do ye not understand my speech? It is because ye cannot hear my speech.	Why do you not understand my word concerning [this]? Because you are not able to hear my word.
44	Ye are of your father the devil, and the lusts of your father ye will do. He was a murderer from the beginning, and abode not in the truth, because there is no truth in him. When he speaketh a lie, he speaketh of his own: for he is a liar, and the father of it.	Ye are of your father, the calumniator; and the lust of your father ye are disposed to do. He was from the beginning a manslayer, and abode not in the truth; for the truth is not in him, and when he speaketh a lie he speaketh from himself, for he is a liar, and the father of it.	You are from [your] father, the Accuser. And you desire to do the lust of your father, he who from the beginning killed men and he [who] does not stand in the truth, because he has no truth. When he speaks a lie, he speaks from himself, because he [is] a liar, even its originator.
45	And because I tell you the truth, ye believe me not.	But me, because I speak the truth, ye believe me not.	Now because I speak the truth, you do not believe me.
46	Which of you convinceth me of sin? And if I say the truth, why do ye not believe me?	Which of you convicteth me of sin? And if I speak the truth, why do ye not believe me?	Which of you rebukes me concerning sin? And if I speak the truth, why do you not believe me?
47	He that is of God heareth God's words: ye therefore hear them not, because ye are not of God.	He that is of God, heareth the words of God. Therefore ye do not hear, because ye are not of God.	He who is of God hears the words of God. Because of this, you do not hear, because you are not of God."
48	Then answered the Jews, and said unto him, Say we not well that thou art a Samaritan, and hast a devil?	The Jews answered, and said to him: Did we not well say, that thou art a Samaritan, and hast a demon?	The Judeans answered and said to him, "Did we not well say that you are a Samaritan and you have a devil?"
49	Jesus answered, I have not a devil; but I honour my Father, and ye do dishonour me.	Jesus said to them: I have no demon: but I honor God; and ye contemn me.	Jesus said to them, "I do not have a devil. But rather, I honor my Father and you curse me.
50	And I seek not mine own glory: there is one that seeketh and judgeth.	But I seek not my own glory: there is one that seeketh [it], and judgeth.	And I do not seek my [own] glory. There is one who seeks [it] and judges.
51	Verily, verily, I say unto you, If a man keep my saying, he shall never see death.	Verily, verily, I say to you: He that keepeth my word, will never see death.	Truly, truly I say to you, he who keeps my word will not see death forever."
52	Then said the Jews unto him, Now we know that thou hast a devil. Abraham is dead, and the prophets; and thou sayest, If a man keep my saying, he shall never taste of death.	The Jews say to him: Now we know, that thou hast a demon. Abraham is dead, and the prophets; yet thou sayest: He that keepeth my word, will never taste death.	The Judeans said to him, "Now we know that you have a devil. Abraham and the prophets died and you say, 'Whoever keeps my word will not taste death forever.'

	KJV	*Murdock*	*Magiera*
	JOHN *Chapter 8*		
53	Art thou greater than our father Abraham, which is dead? and the prophets are dead: whom makest thou thyself?	Art thou greater than our father Abraham who is dead, or than the prophets who died? What dost thou make thyself?	Are you greater than our father Abraham who died and the prophets who died? Whom do you make yourself?"
54	Jesus answered, If I honour myself, my honour is nothing: it is my Father that honoureth me; of whom ye say, that he is your God:	Jesus said to them: If I glorify myself, my glory is nothing. It is my Father that glorifieth me, of whom ye say, He is our God.	Jesus said to them "If I praise myself, my praise is nothing. My Father is the one who praises me, [of] whom you say, 'He is our God.'
55	Yet ye have not known him; but I know him: and if I should say, I know him not, I shall be a liar like unto you: but I know him, and keep his saying.	And ye know him not. But I know him; and if I should say, I know him not, I should be a liar, like you: but I do know him, and I observe his word.	And you do not know him, but I know him. And if I say that I do not know him, I would be a liar like you. But I know him and I keep his word.
56	Your father Abraham rejoiced to see my day: and he saw it, and was glad.	Abraham your father desired to see my day: and he saw it, and rejoiced.	Abraham, your father, was longing to see my day and he saw [it] and rejoiced."
57	Then said the Jews unto him, Thou art not yet fifty years old, and hast thou seen Abraham?	The Jews say to him: Thou art not yet fifty years old, and hast thou seen Abraham?	The Judeans said to him, "You are not yet fifty years old and you have seen Abraham?"
58	Jesus said unto them, Verily, verily, I say unto you, Before Abraham was, I am.	Jesus said to them: Verily, verily I say to you, That before Abraham existed, I was.	Jesus said to them, "Truly, truly I say to you, before Abraham was, I was."
59	Then took they up stones to cast at him: but Jesus hid himself, and went out of the temple, going through the midst of them, and so passed by.	And they took up stones to stone him. But Jesus concealed himself, and went out of the temple, and passed along among them, and went away.	And they took up rocks to stone him, yet Jesus hid himself and went away from the temple and passed among them and left.
	Chapter 9		
1	And as Jesus passed by, he saw a man which was blind from his birth.	And while passing, he saw a man blind from his mother's womb.	And as he passed by, he saw a man who was blind from the womb of his mother.
2	And his disciples asked him, saying, Master, who did sin, this man, or his parents, that he was born blind?	And his disciples asked him, and said: Our Rabbi, who sinned, this man or his parents, that he was born blind?	And his disciples asked him and said, "Our Master, who sinned, this [man] or his parents, that he was born being blind?"
3	Jesus answered, Neither hath this man sinned, nor his parents: but that the works of God should be made manifest in him.	Jesus said to them: Neither did he sin, nor his parents; but that the works of God might be seen in him.	Jesus said to them, "He did not sin, nor his parents, but that the works of God may be seen in him.
4	I must work the works of him that sent me, while it is day: the night cometh, when no man can work.	I must work the works of him that sent me, while it is day; the night cometh, in which no one can work.	It is necessary for me to work the works of him who sent me while it is day. The night will come when no one will be able to serve.
5	As long as I am in the world, I am the light of the world.	So long as I am in the world, I am the light of the world.	As long as I am in the world, I am the light of the world."
6	When he had thus spoken, he spat on the ground, and made clay of the spittle, and he anointed the eyes of the blind man with the clay,	And having spoken thus, he spit on the ground, and made mud with the spittle, and spread it on the eyes of the blind man;	And while he said these [things], he spat on the ground and formed clay from his saliva and he rubbed [it] on the eyes of that blind man.

JOHN *Chapter 9*

	KJV	Murdock	Magiera
7	And said unto him, Go, wash in the pool of Siloam, (which is by interpretation, Sent.) He went his way therefore, and washed, and came seeing.	and said to him: Go, wash in the baptistery of Siloam. And he went, and washed, and came away seeing.	And he said to him, "Go [and] wash in the pool of Siloam." And he went [and] washed and he came seeing.
8	The neighbours therefore, and they which before had seen him that he was blind, said, Is not this he that sat and begged?	And his neighbors, and they by whom he had before been seen begging, said: Is not this he, who sat and begged?	Now his neighbors and those who previously had seen him begging were saying, "Is this [man] not he who was sitting and begging?"
9	Some said, This is he: others said, He is like him: but he said, I am he.	Some said, It is he: and others said, No; but he is very like him. But he said: I am he.	[There were] some who were saying, "This was he," yet [others] who were saying, "No, but he really resembles him." Now he said, "I am [he]."
10	Therefore said they unto him, How were thine eyes opened?	And they said to him: How were thy eyes opened?	They said to him, "How were your eyes opened?"
11	He answered and said, A man that is called Jesus made clay, and anointed mine eyes, and said unto me, Go to the pool of Siloam, and wash: and I went and washed, and I received sight.	He answered, and said to them: A man whose name is Jesus, made mud and spread it on my eyes, and said to me, Go, wash in the waters of Siloam. And I went, and washed, and my sight was restored.	He answered and said to them, "A man whose name is Jesus made clay and rubbed [it] on me, on my eyes, and said to me, "Go [and] wash in the water of Siloam." And I went, I washed and I began to see.
12	Then said they unto him, Where is he? He said, I know not.	They said to him: Where is he? He said to them: I know not.	They said to him, "Where is he?" He said to them, "I do not know."
13	They brought to the Pharisees him that aforetime was blind.	And they brought him that had been blind, before the Pharisees.	And they brought him who previously was blind to the Pharisees.
14	And it was the sabbath day when Jesus made the clay, and opened his eyes.	Now it was on the sabbath that Jesus made the mud, and opened his eyes.	Now it was the Sabbath when Jesus made the clay and opened his eyes for him.
15	Then again the Pharisees also asked him how he had received his sight. He said unto them, He put clay upon mine eyes, and I washed, and do see.	And again the Pharisees asked him: How was thy sight restored? And he said to them: He put mud upon my eyes, and I washed, and my sight was restored.	And again the Pharisees asked him, "How did you begin to see?" And he said to them, "He placed clay on my eyes and I washed and I began to see."
16	Therefore said some of the Pharisees, This man is not of God, because he keepeth not the sabbath day. Others said, How can a man that is a sinner do such miracles? And there was a division among them.	And some of the Pharisees said: This man is not of God, for he doth not observe the sabbath. But others said: How can a man that is a sinner, work these signs? And there was a division among them.	And some of the Pharisees were saying, "This man is not from God, who does not keep the Sabbath." But others were saying, "How is a man [who is] a sinner able to do these miracles?" And there was division among them.
17	They say unto the blind man again, What sayest thou of him, that he hath opened thine eyes? He said, He is a prophet.	They say again to the blind man: What sayest thou of him, seeing he hath opened thy eyes? He said to them: I say, that he is a prophet.	Again they said to that blind man, "What do you say about him who opened your eyes for you?" He said to them, "I say that he is a prophet."

Parallel Translations

JOHN *Chapter 9*

	KJV	Murdock	Magiera
18	But the Jews did not believe concerning him, that he had been blind, and received his sight, until they called the parents of him that had received his sight.	And the Jews would not believe concerning him, that he had been blind, and recovered sight, until they called the parents of him who recovered sight.	But the Judeans did not believe that he was blind and [then] saw, until they called the parents of him who saw.
19	And they asked them, saying, Is this your son, who ye say was born blind? how then doth he now see?	And they asked them: Is this your son, of whom ye say that he was born blind? And how doth he now see?	And they asked them, "Is this your son whom you say was born being blind? How does he now see?"
20	His parents answered them and said, We know that this is our son, and that he was born blind:	And his parents answered and said: We know that this is our son, and that he was born blind;	Now his parents answered and said, "We know that this is our son and that he was born being blind,
21	But by what means he now seeth, we know not; or who hath opened his eyes, we know not: he is of age; ask him: he shall speak for himself.	but how he now seeth, or who opened his eyes, we know not. He hath come to his years, ask him; he will speak for himself.	but how he now sees or who opened his eyes for him, we do not know. Indeed, he is of age. Ask him. He will speak for himself."
22	These words spake his parents, because they feared the Jews: for the Jews had agreed already, that if any man did confess that he was Christ, he should be put out of the synagogue.	These things said his parents, because they feared the Jews: for the Jews had decided, that if any one should confess him to be Messiah, they would expel him from the synagogue.	His parents said these [things], because they were afraid of the Judeans, for the Judeans had decided that if anyone would confess him, that he was the Messiah, they would put him out of the synagogue.
23	Therefore said his parents, He is of age; ask him.	For this reason his parents said, He hath come to his years, ask him.	Because of this, his parents said, "He is of age. Ask him."
24	Then again called they the man that was blind, and said unto him, Give God the praise: we know that this man is a sinner.	And they called a second time the man who had been blind, and said to him: Give glory to God; for we know that this man is a sinner.	And they called the man who was blind a second time and said to him, "Give glory to God, for we know that this man is a sinner."
25	He answered and said, Whether he be a sinner or no, I know not: one thing I know, that, whereas I was blind, now I see.	He replied, and said to them: Whether he is a sinner, I know not; but, one thing I know, that I was blind, and lo, now I see.	He answered and said to them, "If he is a sinner, I do not know, but one [thing] I do know, I was blind and now, behold, I see."
26	Then said they to him again, What did he to thee? how opened he thine eyes?	They said to him again: What did he to thee? How did he open thy eyes?	Again they said to him, "What did he do to you? How did he open your eyes for you?"
27	He answered them, I have told you already, and ye did not hear: wherefore would ye hear it again? will ye also be his disciples?	He said to them: I have told you, and ye did not hear. Why would ye hear again? Do ye also wish to become his disciples?	He said to them, "I told you and you did not hear. What do you want to hear again? Do you also want to become his disciples?"
28	Then they reviled him, and said, Thou art his disciple; but we are Moses' disciples.	But they reproached him, and said to him: Thou art his disciple, but we are the disciples of Moses.	And they reviled him and said to him, "You are his disciple, but we are disciples of Moses.
29	We know that God spake unto Moses: as for this fellow, we know not from whence he is.	And we know that God conversed with Moses; but as for this man, we know not whence he is.	And we know that God spoke with Moses, but this [man], we do not know from where he is."

Parallel Translations

	KJV	*Murdock*	*Magiera*

JOHN *Chapter 9*

	KJV	Murdock	Magiera
30	The man answered and said unto them, Why herein is a marvellous thing, that ye know not from whence he is, and yet he hath opened mine eyes.	The man replied and said to them: In this therefore is [something] to be admired, that ye know not whence he is, and yet he hath opened my eyes.	That man answered and said to them, "In this there is therefore [something] to be amazed at, because you do not know from where he is, yet he opened my eyes.
31	Now we know that God heareth not sinners: but if any man be a worshipper of God, and doeth his will, him he heareth.	Now we know, that God heareth not the voice of sinners; but him that feareth him, and doeth his pleasure, him he heareth.	Now we know that God does not hear the voice of sinners, but whoever fears him and does his will, he hears.
32	Since the world began was it not heard that any man opened the eyes of one that was born blind.	Never hath it been heard, that any one opened the eyes of one born blind.	Never before has it been heard that anyone has opened the eyes of one who was born blind.
33	If this man were not of God, he could do nothing.	If this man were not of God, he could not do this thing.	If this [man] was not from God, he would not be able to do this."
34	They answered and said unto him, Thou wast altogether born in sins, and dost thou teach us? And they cast him out.	They replied, and said to him: Thou wast wholly born in sins; and dost thou teach us? And they expelled him.	They answered and said to him, "You were born entirely in sins, yet you teach us?" And they put him out.
35	Jesus heard that they had cast him out; and when he had found him, he said unto him, Dost thou believe on the Son of God?	And Jesus heard that they had expelled him; and he found him, and said to him: Believest thou on the Son of God?	And Jesus heard that they had put him out and he found him and said to him, "Do you believe in the Son of God?"
36	He answered and said, Who is he, Lord, that I might believe on him?	And he that was healed, answered and said: My Lord, who is he, that I may believe on him?	That one who was healed answered and said, "Who is he, my Lord, that I may believe in him?"
37	And Jesus said unto him, Thou hast both seen him, and it is he that talketh with thee.	Jesus said to him: Thou hast seen him, and it is he that talketh with thee.	Jesus said to him, "You have seen him and he who speaks with you is him."
38	And he said, Lord, I believe. And he worshipped him.	And he said: My Lord, I believe: and he fell down, and worshipped him.	And he said, "I believe, my Lord." And he fell down [and] worshipped him.
39	And Jesus said, For judgment I am come into this world, that they which see not might see; and that they which see might be made blind.	And Jesus said: For the judgment of this world, have I come; that they who see not, might see; and that they who see, might become blind.	And Jesus said, "I have come for the judgment of this world, so that those who do not see may see and those who see may become blind."
40	And some of the Pharisees which were with him heard these words, and said unto him, Are we blind also?	And [some] of those Pharisees who were with him, heard these things; and they said to him: How? Are we also blind?	And those of the Pharisees who were with him heard these [things] and said to him, "Are we also blind?"
41	Jesus said unto them, If ye were blind, ye should have no sin: but now ye say, We see; therefore your sin remaineth.	Jesus said to them: If ye were blind, ye would be without sin; but now ye say, We see; therefore your sin is established.	Jesus said to them, "If you were [only] blind, you would have no sin." But now you say, "We see. Because of this, your sin is established."

Parallel Translations

JOHN Chapter 10

	KJV	Murdock	Magiera
1	Verily, verily, I say unto you, He that entereth not by the door into the sheepfold, but climbeth up some other way, the same is a thief and a robber.	Verily, verily, I say to you, That he who doth not enter by the door into the fold of the flock, but climbeth up in some other place, he is a thief and a robber.	Truly, truly, I say to you, whoever does not enter the sheepfold of the flock by the gate, but climbs up by another place, that [man] is a thief and a robber.
2	But he that entereth in by the door is the shepherd of the sheep.	But he that entereth by the door, is the shepherd of the flock.	But he who enters by the gate is the shepherd of the flock,
3	To him the porter openeth; and the sheep hear his voice: and he calleth his own sheep by name, and leadeth them out.	And to him the door-keeper openeth the door; and the sheep hear his voice. And he calleth the sheep by their names, and leadeth them out.	and for this [man], the keeper of the gate opens the gate. And the flock hears his voice and he calls his sheep by their names and leads them out.
4	And when he putteth forth his own sheep, he goeth before them, and the sheep follow him: for they know his voice.	And when he hath led out his flock, he goeth before it; and his sheep follow him, because they know his voice.	And when he leads out his flock, he goes before it and his sheep follow him, because they know his voice.
5	And a stranger will they not follow, but will flee from him: for they know not the voice of strangers.	But after a stranger the flock will not follow, but it fleeth from him; because it knoweth not the voice of a stranger.	Now the flock will not follow a stranger, but rather it flees from him, because it does not know the voice of a stranger."
6	This parable spake Jesus unto them: but they understood not what things they were which he spake unto them.	This allegory spake Jesus to them; but they knew not what he said to them.	Jesus told them this parable, but they did not understand what he said to them.
7	Then said Jesus unto them again, Verily, verily, I say unto you, I am the door of the sheep.	And Jesus said to them again: Verily, verily, I say to you, That I am the door of the flock.	Now again Jesus said to them, "Truly, truly I say to you, I am the gate of the flock.
8	All that ever came before me are thieves and robbers: but the sheep did not hear them.	All those who have come, were thieves and robbers: but the flock did not hear them.	And all those who come are thieves and robbers, unless the flock hears them.
9	I am the door: by me if any man enter in, he shall be saved, and shall go in and out, and find pasture.	I am the door: and if any enter by me, he will live, and will come in and go out, and will find pasture.	I am the gate and if anyone should enter by me, he will live. And he will enter and he will go out and find pasture.
10	The thief cometh not, but for to steal, and to kill, and to destroy: I am come that they might have life, and that they might have it more abundantly.	The thief cometh not, but that he may steal, and kill, and destroy. I have come, that they may have life, and may have that which is excellent.	A thief does not come, except to steal and to kill and to destroy. I have come that they may have life and [that] they may have that which is abundant.
11	I am the good shepherd: the good shepherd giveth his life for the sheep.	I am a good shepherd. A good shepherd exposeth his life for the sheep.	I am the good shepherd. A good shepherd lays down his life on behalf of his flock.
12	But he that is an hireling, and not the shepherd, whose own the sheep are not, seeth the wolf coming, and leaveth the sheep, and fleeth: and the wolf catcheth them, and scattereth the sheep.	But a hireling, who is not the shepherd, and to whom the sheep do not belong, when he seeth the wolf coming, leaveth the flock, and fleeth; and the wolf cometh, and teareth, and disperseth the flock.	But a hired servant, who is not the shepherd nor are the sheep his, when he sees a wolf coming, leaves the flock and flees. And the wolf comes [and] plunders and scatters the flock.

Parallel Translations

	KJV	*Murdock*	*Magiera*
	JOHN	*Chapter 10*	
13	The hireling fleeth, because he is an hireling, and careth not for the sheep.	And a hireling fleeth, because he is a hireling, and hath no concern for the flock.	Now a hired servant flees, because he is a hired servant and he does not care about the flock.
14	I am the good shepherd, and know my sheep, and am known of mine.	I am a good shepherd; and I know my own [sheep], and am known by my own.	I am the good shepherd and I know my own and I am known by my own,
15	As the Father knoweth me, even so know I the Father: and I lay down my life for the sheep.	As my Father knoweth me, so know I my Father; and I expose my life for the flock.	as my Father knows me and I know my Father and I lay down my life on behalf of the flock.
16	And other sheep I have, which are not of this fold: them also I must bring, and they shall hear my voice; and there shall be one fold, and one shepherd.	And I have other sheep, which are not of this fold: and them also I must bring; and they will hear my voice; and the whole will be one flock, and one shepherd.	Now I also have other sheep, those that are not from this sheepfold, and it is also necessary for me to bring them. And they will hear my voice and all the flock will become one and [have] one shepherd.
17	Therefore doth my Father love me, because I lay down my life, that I might take it again.	For this cause my Father loveth me, that I lay down my life, to resume it again.	Because of this, my Father loves me, because I lay down my life that I may take it up again.
18	No man taketh it from me, but I lay it down of myself. I have power to lay it down, and I have power to take it again. This commandment have I received of my Father.	There is no one that taketh it from me; but I lay it down of my own pleasure: for I have authority to lay it down, and authority to resume it again; because I have received this command from my Father.	No one takes it away from me, but rather I lay it down by my [own] will, for I have authority to lay it down and I have authority to take it up again, for I have received this command from my Father."
19	There was a division therefore again among the Jews for these sayings.	And again there was a division among the Jews, on account of these sayings.	And again there was division among the Judeans, because of these words.
20	And many of them said, He hath a devil, and is mad; why hear ye him?	And many of them said: He hath a demon, and is wholly beside himself; why hear ye him?	And many of them were saying, "He has a devil and is quite insane. Why do you listen to him?"
21	Others said, These are not the words of him that hath a devil. Can a devil open the eyes of the blind?	But others said: These are not the discourses of a demoniac: can a demon open the eyes of one blind?	But others were saying, "These are not the words of a possessed [man]. Is a devil able to open the eyes of a blind man?"
22	And it was at Jerusalem the feast of the dedication, and it was winter.	And the feast of the dedication was [held] at Jerusalem, and it was winter.	Now the feast of dedication was in Jerusalem and it was winter.
23	And Jesus walked in the temple in Solomon's porch.	And Jesus walked in the temple, in the porch of Solomon.	And Jesus was walking in the temple, in the porch of Solomon.
24	Then came the Jews round about him, and said unto him, How long dost thou make us to doubt? If thou be the Christ, tell us plainly.	And the Jews gathered around him; and said to him: how long holdest thou our mind in suspense? If thou art the Messiah, tell us plainly.	And the Judeans gathered around him and said to him, "How long will you keep us [waiting]? If you are the Messiah, tell us openly."

Parallel Translations

JOHN *Chapter 10*

	KJV	Murdock	Magiera
25	Jesus answered them, I told you, and ye believed not: the works that I do in my Father's name, they bear witness of me.	Jesus answered, and said to them: I have told you, and ye did not believe. The works which I do in the name of my Father, they testify of me	Jesus answered and said to them, "I told you and you do not believe and the works that I do in the name of my Father testify about me.
26	But ye believe not, because ye are not of my sheep, as I said unto you.	But ye do not believe, because ye are not of my sheep, as I have said to you.	But you do not believe, because you are not of my sheep, as I said to you.
27	My sheep hear my voice, and I know them, and they follow me:	My sheep hear my voice: and I know them: and they go after me.	My sheep hear my voice and I know them and they follow me.
28	And I give unto them eternal life; and they shall never perish, neither shall any man pluck them out of my hand.	And I give to them life eternal: and they will never be lost: nor will any one pluck them from my hand.	And I give them eternal life and they will not be destroyed forever and no one will seize them out of my hands.
29	My Father, which gave them me, is greater than all; and no man is able to pluck them out of my Father's hand.	For my Father, who gave [them] to me, is greater than all; nor can any pluck from my Father's hand.	For my Father who gave [them] to me is greater than all and no one is able to seize [them] out of the hand of my Father.
30	I and my Father are one.	I and my Father are one.	I and my Father are one."
31	Then the Jews took up stones again to stone him.	And again the Jews took up stones, to stone him.	And again the Judeans took up rocks to stone him.
32	Jesus answered them, Many good works have I shewed you from my Father; for which of those works do ye stone me?	Jesus said to them: Many good works have I showed you from my Father; for which of those works do ye stone me?	Jesus said to them, "I have shown you many good works from my Father. Because of which work of them do you stone me?"
33	The Jews answered him, saying, For a good work we stone thee not; but for blasphemy; and because that thou, being a man, makest thyself God.	The Jews said to him: It is not on account of good works, that we stone thee: but because thou blasphemest; and, whilst thou art a man, thou makest thyself God.	The Judeans said to him, "We do not stone you because of the good works, but rather because you have blasphemed, and being a man, you make yourself God."
34	Jesus answered them, Is it not written in your law, I said, Ye are gods?	Jesus said to them: Is it not written in your law, I have said, Ye are gods?	Jesus said to them, "Is it not so written in your law: I HAVE SAID, YOU ARE GODS?
35	If he called them gods, unto whom the word of God came, and the scripture cannot be broken;	If he called them gods, because the word of God was with them, and the scripture cannot be nullified;	If he called those [people] gods, because the word of God was with them and the scripture is not able to be broken,
36	Say ye of him, whom the Father hath sanctified, and sent into the world, Thou blasphemest; because I said, I am the Son of God?	do ye say to him, whom the Father, hath sanctified and sent into the world, Thou blasphemest; because I said to you, I am the Son of God?	to him whom the Father made holy and sent to the world do you say, 'You blaspheme,' because I told you that I [am] the Son of God?
37	If I do not the works of my Father, believe me not.	And if I do not the works of my Father, believe me not.	Unless I do the works of my Father, do not believe me.
38	But if I do, though ye believe not me, believe the works: that ye may know, and believe, that the Father is in me, and I in him.	But if I do [them], although ye believe not me, yet believe the works; that ye may know and believe, that my Father is in me, and I in my Father.	But if I do, even if you do not believe me, believe the works, that you may know and believe that my Father [is] in me and I [am] in my Father."

JOHN Chapter 10

	KJV	Murdock	Magiera
39	Therefore they sought again to take him: but he escaped out of their hand,	And again they sought to lay hold of him; but he escaped out of their hands;	And they were seeking to arrest him again, yet he escaped from their hands.
40	And went away again beyond Jordan into the place where John at first baptized; and there he abode.	and retired to the other side of the Jordan, to the place where John at first baptized, and tarried there.	And he went to the crossing of the Jordan, to the place where John had been previously when he was baptizing and he stayed there.
41	And many resorted unto him, and said, John did no miracle: but all things that John spake of this man were true.	And many persons came to him: and they said, John indeed wrought not even one sign; but every thing that John said of his man, was true.	And many men came to him and were saying, "John did not even do one sign, but everything that John said about this man is true."
42	And many believed on him there.	And many believed on him.	And many believed in him.

Chapter 11

	KJV	Murdock	Magiera
1	Now a certain man was sick, named Lazarus, of Bethany, the town of Mary and her sister Martha.	And a certain man was sick, Lazarus of the town of Bethany, the brother of Mary and Martha.	Now there was a certain [man] who was sick, Lazarus from the town [of] Bethany, the brother of Mary and Martha.
2	(It was that Mary which anointed the Lord with ointment, and wiped his feet with her hair, whose brother Lazarus was sick.)	It was that Mary who anointed the feet of Jesus with perfume, and wiped [them] with her hair, whose brother Lazarus was sick.	And it was this Mary who anointed the feet of Jesus with perfume and wiped [them] with her hair. Lazarus who was sick was the brother of this [one].
3	Therefore his sisters sent unto him, saying, Lord, behold, he whom thou lovest is sick.	And his two sisters sent to Jesus, and said: Our Lord, he whom thou lovest is sick.	And his two sisters sent to Jesus and said, "Our Lord, behold, he whom you love is sick."
4	When Jesus heard that, he said, This sickness is not unto death, but for the glory of God, that the Son of God might be glorified thereby.	And Jesus said: This sickness is not that of death, but for the glory of God, that the Son of God may be glorified by means of it.	Now Jesus said, "This sickness is not to death, but rather for the glory of God, so that the Son of God may be glorified because of him."
5	Now Jesus loved Martha, and her sister, and Lazarus.	Now Jesus loved Martha and Mary, and Lazarus.	Now Jesus loved Martha and Mary and Lazarus.
6	When he had heard therefore that he was sick, he abode two days still in the same place where he was.	And when he heard that he was sick, he remained in the place where he was two days.	And when he heard that he was sick, he remained in the place that he was [for] two days.
7	Then after that saith he to his disciples, Let us go into Judaea again.	And afterwards he said to his disciples: Come, let us go again into Judaea.	And afterwards he said to his disciples, "Come, let us go again to Judea."
8	His disciples say unto him, Master, the Jews of late sought to stone thee; and goest thou thither again?	His disciples say to him: Our Rabbi, the Jews have just sought to stone thee; and goest thou again thither.	His disciples said to him, "Our Master, the Judeans now are seeking to stone you and you are going there again?"
9	Jesus answered, Are there not twelve hours in the day? If any man walk in the day, he stumbleth not, because he seeth the light of this world.	Jesus said to them: Are there not twelve hours in the day? And if a man walk in the daytime, he stumbleth not; because he seeth the light of the world.	Jesus said to them, "Are [there] not twelve hours in a day? And if a man walks in the day he will not stumble, because he sees the light of this world.

Parallel Translations

	KJV	*Murdock*	*Magiera*
	JOHN	*Chapter 11*	
10	But if a man walk in the night, he stumbleth, because there is no light in him.	But if one walk in the night, he stumbleth; because there is no light in him.	But if a man should walk in the night, he will stumble, because he has no illumination."
11	These things said he: and after that he saith unto them, Our friend Lazarus sleepeth; but I go, that I may awake him out of sleep.	These things said Jesus, and afterwards he said to them: Lazarus our friend reposeth. But I go to awake him.	These [things] Jesus said and afterward he said to them, "Lazarus, our friend, sleeps, but I am going to wake him."
12	Then said his disciples, Lord, if he sleep, he shall do well.	His disciples say to him: Our Lord, if he sleepeth, he is recovering.	His disciples said to him, "Our Lord, if he sleeps, he will be healed."
13	Howbeit Jesus spake of his death: but they thought that he had spoken of taking of rest in sleep.	But Jesus spoke of his death; and they thought, he spoke of the sleep of repose.	But Jesus spoke about his death, yet they thought that he spoke about sleeping on a bed.
14	Then said Jesus unto them plainly, Lazarus is dead.	Then Jesus said to them explicitly; Lazarus is dead.	Then Jesus said to them plainly, "Lazarus has died.
15	And I am glad for your sakes that I was not there, to the intent ye may believe; nevertheless let us go unto him.	And I rejoice, for your sakes, that I was not there; that ye may believe. But let us go there.	And I rejoice that I was not there for your sakes, so that you may believe. But let us walk there."
16	Then said Thomas, which is called Didymus, unto his fellowdisciples, Let us also go, that we may die with him.	Thomas, who is called the Twin, said to his fellow-disciples: Let us also go [and] die with him.	[Then] Thomas, who was called the Twin, said to his fellow disciples, "Let us also go [and] die with him."
17	Then when Jesus came, he found that he had lain in the grave four days already.	And Jesus came to Bethany, and found that he had been in the grave four days.	And Jesus came to Bethany and found him to have been in the tomb for four days.
18	Now Bethany was nigh unto Jerusalem, about fifteen furlongs off:	Now Bethany was near to Jerusalem, distant from it about fifteen furlongs.	Now Bethany was near to Jerusalem, being about fifteen furlongs away from it.
19	And many of the Jews came to Martha and Mary, to comfort them concerning their brother.	And many of the Jews had come to Martha and Mary, to comfort them concerning their brother.	And many of the Judeans were coming to Martha and Mary to comfort their heart[s] because of their brother.
20	Then Martha, as soon as she heard that Jesus was coming, went and met him: but Mary sat still in the house.	And Martha, when she heard that Jesus was coming, went out to meet him; but Mary was sitting in the house.	And Martha, when she had heard that Jesus had come, went out to meet him, but Mary was sitting in the house.
21	Then said Martha unto Jesus, Lord, if thou hadst been here, my brother had not died.	And Martha said to Jesus: My Lord, if thou hadst been here, my brother had not died.	And Martha said to Jesus, "My Lord, if only you would have been here, my brother would not have died.
22	But I know, that even now, whatsoever thou wilt ask of God, God will give it thee.	But even now, I know, that whatever thou wilt ask of God, he will give it thee.	But even now, I know that whatever you ask God he will give to you."
23	Jesus saith unto her, Thy brother shall rise again.	Jesus said to her: Thy brother will rise.	Jesus said to her, "Your brother will rise up."
24	Martha saith unto him, I know that he shall rise again in the resurrection at the last day.	Martha said to him: I know, that he will rise in the consolation, at the last day.	Martha said to him, "I know that he will rise up in the resurrection in the last day."
25	Jesus said unto her, I am the resurrection, and the life: he that believeth in me, though he were dead, yet shall he live:	Jesus said to her: I am the consolation, and life. And he that believeth in me, though he should die, will live.	Jesus said to her, "I am the resurrection and the life. He who believes in me, even if he should die, will live.

JOHN Chapter 11

	KJV	Murdock	Magiera
26	And whosoever liveth and believeth in me shall never die. Believest thou this?	And every one that liveth, and believeth in me, will not die for ever. Believest thou this?	And everyone who is alive and believes in me will not ever die. Do you believe this?"
27	She saith unto him, Yea, Lord: I believe that thou art the Christ, the Son of God, which should come into the world.	She said to him: Yes, my Lord; I believe, that thou art the Messiah, the Son of God, that cometh into the world.	She said to him, "Yes, my Lord. I am a believer that you are the Messiah, the Son of God, who has come into the world."
28	And when she had so said, she went her way, and called Mary her sister secretly, saying, The Master is come, and calleth for thee.	And when she had thus said, she went and called her sister Mary, secretly, and said to her: Our Rabbi hath come, and calleth for thee.	And when she had said these [things], she went [and] called Mary her sister secretly and said to her, "Our Master has come and calls for you."
29	As soon as she heard that, she arose quickly, and came unto him.	And Mary, when she heard [it], rose up quickly, and went to meet him.	And Mary, when she heard [it], rose up quickly and came to him.
30	Now Jesus was not yet come into the town, but was in that place where Martha met him.	And Jesus had not yet entered the village, but was in the place where Martha met him.	Now Jesus had not yet come into the village, but was in that place that he met Martha.
31	The Jews then which were with her in the house, and comforted her, when they saw Mary, that she rose up hastily and went out, followed her, saying, She goeth unto the grave to weep there.	Those Jews also, who were with her in the house and consoled her, when they saw that Mary rose up quickly and went out, followed after her; for they supposed, she was going to the grave to weep.	And those Judeans also who were with her in the house, who were comforting her, when they saw Mary, that she quickly rose [and] went out, followed her. For they thought that she was going to the grave to weep.
32	Then when Mary was come where Jesus was, and saw him, she fell down at his feet, saying unto him, Lord, if thou hadst been here, my brother had not died.	And Mary, when she came where Jesus was and saw him, fell at his feet, and said to him: If thou hadst been here, my Lord, my brother had not died.	But Mary, when she came [to] where Jesus was and saw him, fell down at his feet and said to him, "If only you had been here, my Lord, my brother would not have died."
33	When Jesus therefore saw her weeping, and the Jews also weeping which came with her, he groaned in the spirit, and was troubled,	And when Jesus saw her weeping, and the Jews weeping who came with her, he was moved in spirit, and was agitated.	And when Jesus saw her weeping and those Judeans who had come with her who were weeping, he groaned in his spirit and was moved [in] his soul.
34	And said, Where have ye laid him? They said unto him, Lord, come and see.	And he said: Where have ye laid him? They say to him: Our Lord, come, and see.	And he said, "Where have you laid him?" And they said to him, "Our Lord, come [and] see."
35	Jesus wept.	And the tears of Jesus came.	And the tears of Jesus came.
36	Then said the Jews, Behold how he loved him!	And the Jews said: See, how much he loved him.	And the Judeans were saying, "See how much he loved him."
37	And some of them said, Could not this man, which opened the eyes of the blind, have caused that even this man should not have died?	And some of them said: Could not he who opened the eyes of the blind man, have caused that this also should not have died?	Now some of them said, "Was not this [one] able, who opened the eyes of that blind man, to do [something], so that this [man] would not have died also?"

Parallel Translations

	KJV	Murdock	Magiera
	JOHN Chapter 11		
38	Jesus therefore again groaning in himself cometh to the grave. It was a cave, and a stone lay upon it.	And Jesus, still agitated within, came to the grave. Now the grave was a cave, and a stone was laid upon its entrance.	And Jesus, groaning in himself, came to the tomb. And that tomb was a cave and a stone was placed on its entrance.
39	Jesus said, Take ye away the stone. Martha, the sister of him that was dead, saith unto him, Lord, by this time he stinketh: for he hath been dead four days.	And Jesus said: Take away this stone. Martha, the sister of the deceased, said to him: My Lord, by this time he is putrid; for four days have elapsed.	And Jesus said, "Take away this stone." Martha, the sister of that dead man, said to him, "My Lord, he already stinks, for it is the fourth day."
40	Jesus saith unto her, Said I not unto thee, that, if thou wouldest believe, thou shouldest see the glory of God?	Jesus said to her: Did I not tell thee, that if thou wouldst believe, thou shouldst see the glory of God?	Jesus said to her, "Did I not tell you that if you would believe, you would see the glory of God?"
41	Then they took away the stone from the place where the dead was laid. And Jesus lifted up his eyes, and said, Father, I thank thee that thou hast heard me.	And they took away the stone. And Jesus raised his eyes on high, and said: Father, I thank thee that thou hast heard me.	And they took away that stone and Jesus raised up his eyes and said, "Father, I thank you that you have heard me.
42	And I knew that thou hearest me always: but because of the people which stand by I said it, that they may believe that thou hast sent me.	And I know that thou hearest me always; but on account of this multitude that standeth here, I say these things; that they may believe, that thou hast sent me.	And I know that you always hear me, but because of this crowd that stands [here] I have said these [things], so that they will believe that you have sent me."
43	And when he thus had spoken, he cried with a loud voice, Lazarus, come forth.	And when he had thus spoken, he called with a loud voice: Lazarus, come forth!	And when he had said these [things], he cried out with a loud voice, "Lazarus, come outside."
44	And he that was dead came forth, bound hand and foot with graveclothes: and his face was bound about with a napkin. Jesus saith unto them, Loose him, and let him go.	And the dead man came forth, with his hands and his feet swathed with bandages, and his face with a napkin. Jesus said to them: Loose him, and let him go.	And that dead man came out, his hands and feet being bound in swathing and his face bound in burial cloth. Jesus said to them, "Untie him and allow [him] to go."
45	Then many of the Jews which came to Mary, and had seen the things which Jesus did, believed on him.	And many of the Jews who had come to Mary, when they saw what Jesus did, believed on him.	And many of the Judeans who had come with Mary, when they saw what Jesus had done, believed in him.
46	But some of them went their ways to the Pharisees, and told them what things Jesus had done.	But some of them went to the Pharisees, and told them all that Jesus had done.	And some of them went to the Pharisees and told them what Jesus had done.
47	Then gathered the chief priests and the Pharisees a council, and said, What do we? for this man doeth many miracles.	And the chief priests and Pharisees assembled together, and said: What shall we do? For this man worketh many signs.	And the chief priests and the Pharisees were gathered together and were saying, "What will we do? For this man does many signs,
48	If we let him thus alone, all men will believe on him: and the Romans shall come and take away both our place and nation.	And if we thus let him alone, all the people will believe in him; and the Romans will come, and will take away our place and our nation.	and if we allow him [to continue] like this, all men will believe in him and the Romans will come [and] take away our land and our nation."

Parallel Translations

	KJV	*Murdock*	*Magiera*
	JOHN *Chapter 11*		
49	And one of them, named Caiaphas, being the high priest that same year, said unto them, Ye know nothing at all,	But, one of them, named Caiaphas, was the high priest of that year; and he said to them: Ye know not any thing.	But one of them, whose name [was] Caiaphas, was the high priest for that year and he said to them, "You do not know anything.
50	Nor consider that it is expedient for us, that one man should die for the people, and that the whole nation perish not.	Neither do ye consider, that it is expedient for us, that one man die for the people, and not that this whole people perish.	And do you not realize that it is better for us that one man should die for the nation, than [that] the whole nation should be destroyed?"
51	And this spake he not of himself: but being high priest that year, he prophesied that Jesus should die for that nation;	This he said, however, not from the promptings of his own mind; but being the high priest of that year, he prophesied, that Jesus was about to die for the people:	Now he did not say this from his own will. But because he was the high priest for that year, he prophesied that Jesus was going to die for the nation,
52	And not for that nation only, but that also he should gather together in one the children of God that were scattered abroad.	and not only for the people, but also that he might collect together the sons of God that were dispersed.	and not only for the nation, but that he should also gather together into one the sons of God who are scattered.
53	Then from that day forth they took counsel together for to put him to death.	And from that day, they plotted to kill him.	And from that day, they decided to kill him.
54	Jesus therefore walked no more openly among the Jews; but went thence unto a country near to the wilderness, into a city called Ephraim, and there continued with his disciples.	And Jesus did not walk openly among the Jews; but retired from them to a place near the wilderness, to a town called Ephraim; and there he abode with his disciples.	Now Jesus did not walk openly among the Judeans, but he went from there to a place that was near the wilderness, to a walled city that was called Ephraim. And there he was staying with his disciples.
55	And the Jews' passover was nigh at hand: and many went out of the country up to Jerusalem before the passover, to purify themselves.	And the passover of the Jews drew near: and many went up from the villages to Jerusalem, before the feast, that they might purify themselves.	Now the Passover of the Judeans was near. And many from the villages went up to Jerusalem before the feast to purify themselves.
56	Then sought they for Jesus, and spake among themselves, as they stood in the temple, What think ye, that he will not come to the feast?	And they sought for Jesus; and they said one to another, in the temple: What think ye? that he will not come to the feast?	And they were seeking Jesus and were saying one to another in the temple, "What do you think? Will he not come to the feast?"
57	Now both the chief priests and the Pharisees had given a commandment, that, if any man knew where he were, he should shew it, that they might take him.	And the chief priests and the Pharisees had commanded that if any one knew where he was, he should make it known to them, that they might take him.	Now the chief priests and the Pharisees had commanded that if anyone knew where he was, he should show [it] to them, so that they could arrest him.
	Chapter 12		
1	Then Jesus six days before the passover came to Bethany, where Lazarus was which had been dead, whom he raised from the dead.	And six days before the passover, Jesus came to Bethany, where was that Lazarus whom Jesus raised from the dead.	Now six days before the Passover, Jesus came to Bethany where Lazarus was, whom Jesus had raised from the dead.
2	There they made him a supper; and Martha served: but Lazarus was one of them that sat at the table with him.	And they made a supper for him there: and Martha served, and Lazarus was one of the guests with him.	And they made a dinner for him there and Martha was serving and Lazarus was one of the guests who [were] with him.

Parallel Translations

JOHN *Chapter 12*

	KJV	*Murdock*	*Magiera*
3	Then took Mary a pound of ointment of spikenard, very costly, and anointed the feet of Jesus, and wiped his feet with her hair: and the house was filled with the odour of the ointment.	And Mary took an alabaster box of perfume of choice spikenard, of great price; and anointed the feet of Jesus; and she wiped his feet with her hair. And the house was filled with the odor of the perfume.	And Mary took an alabaster vase of perfume of the best spikenard, very expensive, and anointed the feet of Jesus and wiped his feet with her hair and the house was filled with the smell of the perfume.
4	Then saith one of his disciples, Judas Iscariot, Simon's son, which should betray him,	Then said Judas Iscariot, one of the disciples, he that was about to betray him:	And Judas Iscariot, one of his disciples, he who was about to betray him, said,
5	Why was not this ointment sold for three hundred pence, and given to the poor?	Why was not this ointment sold for three hundred denarii, and given to the poor?	"Why was this oil not sold for three hundred denarii and given to the poor?"
6	This he said, not that he cared for the poor; but because he was a thief, and had the bag, and bare what was put therein.	And this he said, not be cause he cared for the poor, but because he was thief, and held the purse, and carried what was put in it.	Now he said this, not because he cared for the poor, but because he was a thief and the bag was with him and he was carrying whatever fell into it.
7	Then said Jesus, Let her alone: against the day of my burying hath she kept this.	But Jesus said: Let her alone; she hath kept it for the day of my burial.	But Jesus said, "Leave her. She has kept it for the day of my burial,
8	For the poor always ye have with you; but me ye have not always.	For the poor are always with you, but I am not with you always.	for you always have the poor with you, but you do not always have me."
9	Much people of the Jews therefore knew that he was there: and they came not for Jesus' sake only, but that they might see Lazarus also, whom he had raised from the dead.	And great multitudes of the Jews heard that he was there: and they came, not only on account of Jesus, but also that they might see Lazarus, whom he raised from the dead.	And large crowds of the Judeans heard that Jesus was there and came, not because of Jesus alone, but also to see Lazarus who was raised from the dead.
10	But the chief priests consulted that they might put Lazarus also to death;	And the chief priests deliberated about killing even Lazarus:	And the chief priests were thinking that they should also kill Lazarus,
11	Because that by reason of him many of the Jews went away, and believed on Jesus.	because many of the Jews, on his account, went and believed in Jesus.	because many of the Judeans, on account of him, went away and were believing in Jesus.
12	On the next day much people that were come to the feast, when they heard that Jesus was coming to Jerusalem,	And the next day, a great multitude who had come to the feast, when they heard that Jesus was coming to Jerusalem,	And on the next day a large crowd that had come to the feast, when they heard that Jesus was coming to Jerusalem,
13	Took branches of palm trees, and went forth to meet him, and cried, Hosanna: Blessed is the King of Israel that cometh in the name of the Lord.	took boughs of palm-trees, and went out to meet him. And they cried, and said: Hosanna, Blessed is he that cometh in the name of the Lord, the king of Israel!	took branches of palm trees and went out to meet him. And they were crying out and saying: HOSANNA, BLESSED IS HE WHO COMES IN THE NAME OF THE LORD, THE KING OF ISRAEL.
14	And Jesus, when he had found a young ass, sat thereon; as it is written,	And Jesus found an ass, and sat upon it; as it is written	And Jesus found a donkey and sat on it, as it was written:

Parallel Translations

	KJV	*Murdock*	*Magiera*
	JOHN	*Chapter 12*	
15	Fear not, daughter of Sion: behold, thy King cometh, sitting on an ass's colt.	Fear not, daughter of Sion. Behold, thy king cometh to thee; and he rideth upon a colt, the foal of an ass.	DO NOT FEAR, DAUGHTER OF ZION. BEHOLD, YOUR KING COMES TO YOU AND IS MOUNTED ON A COLT, THE FOAL OF A DONKEY.
16	These things understood not his disciples at the first: but when Jesus was glorified, then remembered they that these things were written of him, and that they had done these things unto him.	These things understood not his disciples, at that time; but when Jesus was glorified, then his disciples remembered that these things were written of him, and that they did them to him.	Now these [things] his disciples did not understand at that time, but when Jesus was glorified, his disciples remembered that these [things] were written about him and [that] they had done these [things] to him.
17	The people therefore that was with him when he called Lazarus out of his grave, and raised him from the dead, bare record.	And the multitude that had been with him, testified that he had called Lazarus from the grave, and raised him from the dead.	And the crowd that was with him was bearing testimony that he had called Lazarus from the grave and raised him from the dead.
18	For this cause the people also met him, for that they heard that he had done this miracle.	And for this reason, great multitudes went out to meet him, as they had heard that he wrought this sign.	And because of this, large crowds went out to meet him, because they heard that he had done this sign.
19	The Pharisees therefore said among themselves, Perceive ye how ye prevail nothing? behold, the world is gone after him.	But the Pharisees said, one to another: Do ye see, that ye are gaining nothing? For, lo, the whole world is going after him.	Now the Pharisees were saying to each other, "Do you see that you do not gain anything? For behold, the whole world goes after him.
20	And there were certain Greeks among them that came up to worship at the feast:	And there were also among the people, some who had come up to worship at the feast.	And there were also some of the Gentiles, men among them who had gone up to worship at the feast.
21	The same came therefore to Philip, which was of Bethsaida of Galilee, and desired him, saying, Sir, we would see Jesus.	These came, and approached Philip, who was of Bethsaida in Galilee, and said to him: My lord, we are desirous to see Jesus.	These [men] came [and] drew near to Philip who [was] from Bethsaida of Galilee and asked him and said to him, "My lord, we want to see Jesus."
22	Philip cometh and telleth Andrew: and again Andrew and Philip tell Jesus.	Philip came and told Andrew; and Andrew and Philip told Jesus.	And Philip came and told Andrew and Andrew and Philip told Jesus.
23	And Jesus answered them, saying, The hour is come, that the Son of man should be glorified.	And Jesus answered, and said to them: The hour is come that the Son of man should be glorified.	And Jesus answered and said to them, "The hour has come for the Son of Man to be glorified.
24	Verily, verily, I say unto you, Except a corn of wheat fall into the ground and die, it abideth alone: but if it die, it bringeth forth much fruit.	Verily, verily, I say to you, That a kernel of wheat, unless it fall and die in the ground, remaineth alone; but if it die, it produceth numerous fruits.	Truly, truly I say to you, a grain of wheat, except it fall and die in the ground, remains alone. But if it dies, it will produce much fruit.
25	He that loveth his life shall lose it; and he that hateth his life in this world shall keep it unto life eternal.	He that loveth his life, will lose it; and he that hateth his life, in this world, will preserve it unto life everlasting.	He who loves his life will lose it, and he who hates his life in this world will keep it to eternal life.

Parallel Translations

JOHN *Chapter 12*

	KJV	*Murdock*	*Magiera*
26	If any man serve me, let him follow me; and where I am, there shall also my servant be: if any man serve me, him will my Father honour.	If any one is servant to me, he will come after me; and where I am, there also will my servant be. Him that serveth me, will the Father honor.	If anyone serves me, he should follow me. And wherever I am, there will my servant be also. He who serves me, the Father will honor him.
27	Now is my soul troubled; and what shall I say? Father, save me from this hour: but for this cause came I unto this hour.	Behold, now is my soul troubled; and what shall I say? My Father, deliver me from this hour? But for this very cause, came I to this hour.	Now behold, my soul is troubled. And what do I say, 'My Father, deliver me from this hour?' On the contrary, because of this, I have come to this hour.
28	Father, glorify thy name. Then came there a voice from heaven, saying, I have both glorified it, and will glorify it again.	Father, glorify thy name! And a voice was heard from heaven: I have glorified [it]; and I will glorify [it] again.	[I will say] 'Father, glorify your name.'" And a voice was heard from heaven, "I have glorified [it] and again I will glorify [it]."
29	The people therefore, that stood by, and heard it, said that it thundered: others said, An angel spake to him.	And the multitude standing by, heard [it]; and they said: There was thunder. But others said: An angel spoke with him.	And the crowd that was standing by heard [it] and said, "It was thunder." But others said, "An angel spoke with him."
30	Jesus answered and said, This voice came not because of me, but for your sakes.	Jesus answered, and said to them: This voice was not for my sake, but for yours.	Jesus answered and said to them, "This voice was not for me, but it was for you.
31	Now is the judgment of this world: now shall the prince of this world be cast out.	Now is the judgment of this world: now the ruler of this world is cast out.	Now is the judgment of this world. Now the ruler of this world is cast outside.
32	And I, if I be lifted up from the earth, will draw all men unto me.	And I, when I am lifted up from the earth, will draw all men to me.	And when I am lifted up from the earth, I will draw all men to me."
33	This he said, signifying what death he should die.	And this he said, to show by what manner of death, he was to die.	And this he said to show by what death he would die.
34	The people answered him, We have heard out of the law that Christ abideth for ever: and how sayest thou, The Son of man must be lifted up? who is this Son of man?	The multitude said to him: We have heard from the law, that the Messiah abideth for ever: [and] how sayest thou, that the Son of man is to be lifted up? Who is this Son of man?	The crowds said to him, "We have heard from the law that the Messiah remains forever. How do you say that the Son of Man is going to be lifted up? Who is this Son of Man?"
35	Then Jesus said unto them, Yet a little while is the light with you. Walk while ye have the light, lest darkness come upon you: for he that walketh in darkness knoweth not whither he goeth.	Jesus said to them: A short time longer, the light is with you. Walk, while ye have the light, lest the darkness overtake you. He that walketh in the dark, knoweth not whither he goeth.	Jesus said to them, "The light is with you a little while longer. Walk while you have light, so that the darkness will not overtake you. And he who walks in darkness does not know to where he goes.
36	While ye have light, believe in the light, that ye may be the children of light. These things spake Jesus, and departed, and did hide himself from them.	While the light is with you, confide in the light; that ye may be children of the light. These things said Jesus, and departed, and concealed himself from them.	While you have the light, believe in the light that you may become sons of light." Jesus spoke these [things] and went [and] hid from them.
37	But though he had done so many miracles before them, yet they believed not on him:	And although he wrought all these signs before them, they believed him not;	And although he did all these miracles before them, they did not believe in him,

Parallel Translations

	KJV	Murdock	Magiera

JOHN Chapter 12

	KJV	Murdock	Magiera
38	That the saying of Esaias the prophet might be fulfilled, which he spake, Lord, who hath believed our report? and to whom hath the arm of the Lord been revealed?	that the word of Isaiah the prophet might be fulfilled, who said: My Lord; who hath believed our report? And to whom is the arm of the Lord revealed?	that the word of Isaiah the prophet would be fulfilled, who said: MY LORD, WHO HAS BELIEVED OUR REPORT AND TO WHOM HAS THE ARM OF THE LORD BEEN REVEALED?
39	Therefore they could not believe, because that Esaias said again,	For this reason they could not believe, because Isaiah said again:	Because of this, they were not able to believe, because again Isaiah said:
40	He hath blinded their eyes, and hardened their heart; that they should not see with their eyes, nor understand with their heart, and be converted, and I should heal them.	They have blinded their eyes, and darkened their hearts; that they might not see with their eyes, and understand with their heart, and be converted; and I should heal them.	THEY HAVE BLINDED THEIR EYES AND HAVE DARKENED THEIR HEART[S], SO THAT THEY WOULD NOT SEE WITH THEIR EYES AND WOULD UNDERSTAND WITH THEIR HEART[S] AND WOULD REPENT AND I WOULD HEAL THEM.
41	These things said Esaias, when he saw his glory, and spake of him.	These things spake Isaiah, when he saw his glory, and spoke of him.	These [things] Isaiah said, when he saw his glory and spoke about him.
42	Nevertheless among the chief rulers also many believed on him; but because of the Pharisees they did not confess him, lest they should be put out of the synagogue:	And of the chiefs also, many believed on him; but on account of the Pharisees, they did not confess [him], lest they should be put out of the synagogue;	Now many of the rulers also believed in him, but because of the Pharisees, they did not confess [him], lest they should be [put] out of the synagogue,
43	For they loved the praise of men more than the praise of God.	for they loved the praise of men, more than the praise of God.	for they loved the praise of men more than the praise of God.
44	Jesus cried and said, He that believeth on me, believeth not on me, but on him that sent me.	And Jesus cried, and said: He that believeth in me, believeth not in me, but in him that sent me.	Now Jesus cried out and said, "He who believes in me does not believe in me, but in him who sent me.
45	And he that seeth me seeth him that sent me.	And he that seeth me, seeth him that sent me.	And he who sees me, sees him who sent me.
46	I am come a light into the world, that whosoever believeth on me should not abide in darkness.	I have come into the world, a light, that whoever believeth in me, might not abide in darkness.	I have come [as] a light to the world that all who believe in me would not remain in darkness.
47	And if any man hear my words, and believe not, I judge him not: for I came not to judge the world, but to save the world.	And whoever shall hear my words, and not observe them, I judge him not; for I did not come to judge the world, but to vivify the world.	And he who hears my words, yet does not keep them, I do not judge, for I did not come to judge the world, but to give life to the world.
48	He that rejecteth me, and receiveth not my words, hath one that judgeth him: the word that I have spoken, the same shall judge him in the last day.	Whoever rejecteth me, and receiveth not my words, there is one to judge him; the word which I speak, will judge him, at the last day.	He who rejects me and does not receive my words, there is something that judges him. The word that I speak will judge him in the last day,

Parallel Translations

	KJV	*Murdock*	*Magiera*
	JOHN	*Chapter 12*	
49	For I have not spoken of myself; but the Father which sent me, he gave me a commandment, what I should say, and what I should speak.	For I have not spoken from myself; but the Father who sent me, he gave me commandment, what I should speak, and what I should say.	because I do not speak from myself, but rather the Father who sent me gave me a command, what I [should] say and what I [should] speak.
50	And I know that his commandment is life everlasting: whatsoever I speak therefore, even as the Father said unto me, so I speak.	And I know that his commandment is life eternal. Therefore, these things which I speak, as my Father hath said to me, so I speak.	And I know that his command is eternal life. Therefore, these [things] that I speak, as my Father told me, so I speak."
	Chapter 13		
1	Now before the feast of the passover, when Jesus knew that his hour was come that he should depart out of this world unto the Father, having loved his own which were in the world, he loved them unto the end.	And before the feast of the passover, Jesus knew that the hour had come when he should depart from this world unto the Father. And he loved his own [people], who were in the world; and he loved them unto the end.	Now before the Feast of the Passover, Jesus knew that the hour had arrived that he would go out of this world to his Father. And he loved his own who were in this world and he loved them until the end.
2	And supper being ended, the devil having now put into the heart of Judas Iscariot, Simon's son, to betray him;	And when the supper was passed, it had been injected by Satan into the heart of Judas Iscariot, the son of Simon, to betray him.	And when it was supper, it was placed by Satan in the heart of Judas, the son of Simon Iscariot, that he should betray him.
3	Jesus knowing that the Father had given all things into his hands, and that he was come from God, and went to God;	And Jesus, because he knew that the Father had given all things into his hands; and that he came out from the Father, and was going to God;	And Jesus, because he knew that the Father had given everything into his hands and that he had proceeded from God and was going to God,
4	He riseth from supper, and laid aside his garments; and took a towel, and girded himself.	arose from the supper, and laid aside his long garments, and took a linen cloth, and wrapped it about his loins;	rose up from the supper and lay aside his garments and took a cloth [and] girded his loins.
5	After that he poureth water into a bason, and began to wash the disciples' feet, and to wipe them with the towel wherewith he was girded.	and poured water into a wash-basin, and began to wash the feet of his disciples: and he wiped them with the linen cloth with which he had girded his loins.	And he poured water into a bowl and began to wash the feet of his disciples and he was wiping [them] with the cloth that girded his loins.
6	Then cometh he to Simon Peter: and Peter saith unto him, Lord, dost thou wash my feet?	And when he came to Simon Cephas, Simon said to him: Dost thou, my Lord, wash my feet for me?	Now when he came to Simon Peter, Simon said to him, "My Lord, do you wash my feet for me?"
7	Jesus answered and said unto him, What I do thou knowest not now; but thou shalt know hereafter.	Jesus answered, and said to him: What I do, thou understandest not now: but hereafter thou wilt understand.	Jesus answered and said to him, "What I am doing you do not understand now, but afterwards you will understand."
8	Peter saith unto him, Thou shalt never wash my feet. Jesus answered him, If I wash thee not, thou hast no part with me.	Simon Cephas said to him: Never shalt thou wash my feet. Jesus said to him: Unless I wash thee, thou hast no part with me.	Simon Peter said to him, "You will not ever wash my feet for me." Jesus said to him, "Unless I wash you, you have no portion with me."
9	Simon Peter saith unto him, Lord, not my feet only, but also my hands and my head.	Simon Cephas said to him: Then, my Lord, not my feet only shalt thou wash, but also my hands and my head.	Simon Peter said to him, "Then, my Lord, wash not only my feet for me, but also my hands, even my head."

	KJV	Murdock	Magiera
10	Jesus saith to him, He that is washed needeth not save to wash his feet, but is clean every whit: and ye are clean, but not all.	Jesus said to him: He that hath bathed, needeth not but to wash his feet; for he is all clean. And ye also are clean; but not all of you.	Jesus said to him, "He who has bathed does not need [to wash his whole body], but to only wash his feet, for all of him is clean. Also, all of you are clean, but not all of you."
11	For he knew who should betray him; therefore said he, Ye are not all clean.	For Jesus knew, who would betray him: therefore he said, Ye are not all clean.	For Jesus knew him who would betray him. Because of this, he said, "Not all of you are clean."
12	So after he had washed their feet, and had taken his garments, and was set down again, he said unto them, Know ye what I have done to you?	And when he had washed their feet, he resumed his long garments, and reclined. And he said to them: Understand ye what I have done to you?	And after he had washed their feet, he took up his garments and sat and said to them, "Do you know what I have done to you?
13	Ye call me Master and Lord: and ye say well; for so I am.	Ye call me, Our Rabbi, and Our Lord; and ye speak well; for I am so.	You call me 'our Master and our Lord' and you speak well, for I am.
14	If I then, your Lord and Master, have washed your feet; ye also ought to wash one another's feet.	If then I, your Lord and your Rabbi, have washed your feet, how much more ought ye to wash the feet of one another?	If therefore I, your Lord and your Master, have washed your feet for you, how much more ought you to wash the feet of one another?
15	For I have given you an example, that ye should do as I have done to you.	For I have given you this example, that ye might do, as I have done to you.	For I have given you this example, that you should also do as I have done for you.
16	Verily, verily, I say unto you, The servant is not greater than his lord; neither he that is sent greater than he that sent him.	Verily, verily, I say to you, That no servant is greater than his lord; and no legate is greater than he who sent him.	Truly, truly I say to you, there is no servant who is greater than his lord and there is no apostle who is greater than him who sent him.
17	If ye know these things, happy are ye if ye do them.	If ye know these things, happy will ye be if ye do them.	If you understand these [things], you are blessed if you will do them.
18	I speak not of you all: I know whom I have chosen: but that the scripture may be fulfilled, He that eateth bread with me hath lifted up his heel against me.	Not of you all, do I speak: I know whom I have chosen. But that the scripture may be fulfilled, He that eateth bread with me, hath lifted his heel against me.	I do not speak concerning all of you, for I know those whom I have chosen, but rather [I speak] because the scripture will be fulfilled: HE WHO EATS BREAD WITH ME HAS LIFTED HIS HEEL AGAINST ME.
19	Now I tell you before it come, that, when it is come to pass, ye may believe that I am he.	From this time, I tell you, before it occurs, that when it shall occur, ye may know that I am he.	I tell you from now on before it happens, so that when it happens, you will believe that I am [he].
20	Verily, verily, I say unto you, He that receiveth whomsoever I send receiveth me; and he that receiveth me receiveth him that sent me.	Verily, verily, I say to you: He that receiveth him whom I send, receiveth me; and he that receiveth me, receiveth him that sent me.	Truly, truly I say to you, he who receives him whom I send receives me, and he who receives me receives him who sent me.
21	When Jesus had thus said, he was troubled in spirit, and testified, and said, Verily, verily, I say unto you, that one of you shall betray me.	These things said Jesus, and he was agitated in his spirit; and he testified, and said: Verily, verily, I say to you, That one of you will betray me.	Jesus said these [things] and he groaned in his spirit and testified and said, "Truly, truly I say to you, one of you will betray me."

Parallel Translations

	KJV	*Murdock*	*Magiera*

JOHN *Chapter 13*

	KJV	Murdock	Magiera
22	Then the disciples looked one on another, doubting of whom he spake.	And the disciples stared at one another; because they knew not, of whom he spake.	And the disciples looked at each other, because they did not know about whom he spoke.
23	Now there was leaning on Jesus' bosom one of his disciples, whom Jesus loved.	And there was one of his disciples, who was reclining on his bosom, he whom Jesus loved;	Now there was one of his disciples who was reclining on his bosom, he whom Jesus loved.
24	Simon Peter therefore beckoned to him, that he should ask who it should be of whom he spake.	to him Simon Cephas beckoned, that he should ask him, who it was of whom he spoke.	Simon Peter waved to this [one] that he should ask him who it was about whom he spoke.
25	He then lying on Jesus' breast saith unto him, Lord, who is it?	And that disciple fell upon the breast of Jesus, and said to him: My Lord, which is he?	And that disciple fell on the breast of Jesus and said to him, "My Lord, who is this [man]?"
26	Jesus answered, He it is, to whom I shall give a sop, when I have dipped it. And when he had dipped the sop, he gave it to Judas Iscariot, the son of Simon.	Jesus answered and said: He it is, to whom I give the bread when I have dipped it. And Jesus dipped the bread, and gave it to Judas Iscariot, the son of Simon.	Jesus answered and said, "He [is] the one to whom I give the bread that I dip." And Jesus dipped the bread and gave [it] to Judas, son of Simon Iscariot.
27	And after the sop Satan entered into him. Then said Jesus unto him, That thou doest, do quickly.	And after the bread, then Satan entered into him. And Jesus said to him: What thou doest, do quickly.	And after the bread, then Satan entered him and Jesus said to him, "What you do, do quickly."
28	Now no man at the table knew for what intent he spake this unto him.	And no one of those reclining, knew, wherefore he said this to him.	Now not one of those guests understood what he said to him.
29	For some of them thought, because Judas had the bag, that Jesus had said unto him, Buy those things that we have need of against the feast; or, that he should give something to the poor.	For some of them supposed, because the purse was in the hands of Judas, that Jesus expressly charged him to buy something needful for the feast, or that he should give something to the poor.	For some thought because Judas had the bag with him that he had expressly commanded him to buy something that was needed for the feast or to give something to the poor.
30	He then having received the sop went immediately out: and it was night.	And Judas took the bread at once, and went out of the house. And it was night when he went out.	Now Judas took the bread immediately and went outside. And it was night when he went out.
31	Therefore, when he was gone out, Jesus said, Now is the Son of man glorified, and God is glorified in him.	And Jesus said: Now is the Son of man glorified; and God is glorified in him.	And Jesus said, "Now the Son of Man is glorified and God is glorified in him.
32	If God be glorified in him, God shall also glorify him in himself, and shall straightway glorify him.	And if God is glorified in him, God will glorify him in himself; and will glorify him speedily.	And if God is glorified in him, God also will glorify him in himself and will glorify him at once.
33	Little children, yet a little while I am with you. Ye shall seek me: and as I said unto the Jews, Whither I go, ye cannot come; so now I say to you.	My children, a little longer I am with you; and ye will seek for me; and, as I said to the Jews, Whither I go ye cannot come, so I now say to you.	My sons, a little while longer I am with you and you will seek me and as I said to the Judeans, 'Where I go, you are not able to come,' yet even now I say to you.

	KJV	*Murdock*	*Magiera*
	JOHN	*Chapter 13*	
34	A new commandment I give unto you, That ye love one another; as I have loved you, that ye also love one another.	A new commandment I give to you, that ye be affectionate to each other. As I have loved you, do ye also love one another.	A new commandment I give to you, be loving one to another. As I loved you, you should also love one another.
35	By this shall all men know that ye are my disciples, if ye have love one to another.	By this will every one know that ye are my disciples, if ye have love for each other.	By this everyone will know that you [are] my disciples, if love be among you one toward another."
36	Simon Peter said unto him, Lord, whither goest thou? Jesus answered him, Whither I go, thou canst not follow me now; but thou shalt follow me afterwards.	Simon Cephas said to him: Our Lord, whither goest thou? Jesus answered, and said to him: Whither I go, thou canst not now come after me; but thou wilt at last come.	Simon Peter said to him, "Our Lord, where are you going?" Jesus answered and said to him, "Where I go you are not now able to follow me, but you will come [after me] at the end."
37	Peter said unto him, Lord, why cannot I follow thee now? I will lay down my life for thy sake.	Simon Cephas said to him: My Lord, why can I not come after thee? I would lay down my life for thee.	Simon Peter said to him, "My Lord, why am I not able to follow you now? I will lay down my life for you."
38	Jesus answered him, Wilt thou lay down thy life for my sake? Verily, verily, I say unto thee, The cock shall not crow, till thou hast denied me thrice.	Jesus said to him: Wouldst thou lay down thy life for me? Verily, verily, I say to thee, The cock will not crow, until thou hast three times denied me.	Jesus said to him, "Will you lay down your life for me? Truly, truly I say to you, the rooster will not crow until you deny me three times."
	Chapter 14		
1	Let not your heart be troubled: ye believe in God, believe also in me.	Let not your heart be troubled: believe in God, and, believe in me.	"Let your heart not be troubled. Believe in God and believe in me.
2	In my Father's house are many mansions: if it were not so, I would have told you. I go to prepare a place for you.	There are many mansions in the house of my Father: and if not, I would have told you; for I go to prepare a place for you.	There are many rooms [in] the house of my Father. And [if] not, I would have told you, for I go to prepare a place for you.
3	And if I go and prepare a place for you, I will come again, and receive you unto myself; that where I am, there ye may be also.	And if I go to prepare for you a place, I will come again and take you to myself; that where I am, there ye may be also.	And if I go [and] prepare a place for you, I will come again and I will take you with me, so that where I am you may be also.
4	And whither I go ye know, and the way ye know.	And whither I go, ye know; and the way ye know.	And to where I go, you know and the way you know."
5	Thomas saith unto him, Lord, we know not whither thou goest; and how can we know the way?	Thomas said to him: Our Lord, we know not whither thou goest; and how can we know the way?	Thomas said to him, "Our Lord, we do not know where you are going and how are we able to know the way?"
6	Jesus saith unto him, I am the way, the truth, and the life: no man cometh unto the Father, but by me.	Jesus said to him: I am the way, and truth, and life: no one cometh unto my Father, but by me.	Jesus said to him, "I am the way and truth and life. No one comes to my Father except by me.
7	If ye had known me, ye should have known my Father also: and from henceforth ye know him, and have seen him.	If ye had known me, ye would also have known my Father: and henceforth, ye know him, and have seen him.	If you knew me, you would also know my Father. And from now on, you will know him and you have seen him."
8	Philip saith unto him, Lord, shew us the Father, and it sufficeth us.	Philip said to him: Our Lord, show us the Father, and it will suffice for us.	Philip said to him, "Our Lord, show us the Father and it will satisfy us."

Parallel Translations

	KJV	*Murdock*	*Magiera*
JOHN	*Chapter 14*		
9	Jesus saith unto him, Have I been so long time with you, and yet hast thou not known me, Philip? he that hath seen me hath seen the Father; and how sayest thou then, Shew us the Father?	Jesus said to him: Have I been all this time with you, and hast thou not known me, Philip? He that seeth me, seeth the Father: and how sayest thou, Show us the Father?	Jesus said to him, "[Have] I [been] with you all this time and you do not know me, Philip? He who sees me sees the Father. And how do you say, 'Show us the Father?'
10	Believest thou not that I am in the Father, and the Father in me? the words that I speak unto you I speak not of myself: but the Father that dwelleth in me, he doeth the works.	Believest thou not, that I am in my Father, and my Father in me? And the words which I speak, I speak not from myself: but my Father, who dwelleth in me, he doeth these works.	Do you not believe that I [am] in my Father and my Father [is] in me? These words that I speak, I do not speak of myself, but my Father who lives in me works these works.
11	Believe me that I am in the Father, and the Father in me: or else believe me for the very works' sake.	Believe, that I am in my Father, and my Father in me. And if not, believe, at least, on account of the works.	Believe that I [am] in my Father and my Father [is] in me. Otherwise, believe also because of the works.
12	Verily, verily, I say unto you, He that believeth on me, the works that I do shall he do also; and greater works than these shall he do; because I go unto my Father.	Verily, verily, I say to you: He that believeth in me, the works which I do, will he also do. And greater than these will he do, because I go unto my Father.	Truly, truly I say to you, whoever believes in me, these works that I do, he also will do and more than these will he do, because I go to the Father.
13	And whatsoever ye shall ask in my name, that will I do, that the Father may be glorified in the Son.	And what ye shall ask in my name, I will do for you; that the Father may be glorified in his Son.	And whatever you ask in my name, I will do for you, so that the Father will be glorified by his Son.
14	If ye shall ask any thing in my name, I will do it.	And if ye shall ask of me, in my name, I will do [it].	And if you ask of me in my name, I will do [it].
15	If ye love me, keep my commandments.	If ye love me, keep my commands.	If you love me, keep my commandments.
16	And I will pray the Father, and he shall give you another Comforter, that he may abide with you for ever;	And I will ask of my Father, and he will give you another Comforter, that he may be with you for ever,	And I will ask of my Father and he will give you another Deliverer, who will be with you forever,
17	Even the Spirit of truth; whom the world cannot receive, because it seeth him not, neither knoweth him: but ye know him; for he dwelleth with you, and shall be in you.	the Spirit of truth; whom the world cannot receive, because it seeth him not, and knoweth him not: but ye know him, because he abideth with you, and is in you.	the Spirit of truth that the world is not able to receive, because it has not seen him and does not know him. But you know him, because he lives with you and he [is] in you.
18	I will not leave you comfortless: I will come to you.	I shall not leave you orphans: for I shall come to you in a little while.	I will not leave you [as] orphans, for I will come to you in a little while.
19	Yet a little while, and the world seeth me no more; but ye see me: because I live, ye shall live also.	And the world will not see me; but ye will see me. Because I live, ye will live also.	And the world will not see me, but you will see me. Because I live, you also will live.
20	At that day ye shall know that I am in my Father, and ye in me, and I in you.	In that day ye will know, that I am in my Father; and that ye are in me, and I in you.	In that day you will know that I [am] in my Father and you [are] in me and I [am] in you.
21	He that hath my commandments, and keepeth them, he it is that loveth me: and he that loveth me shall be loved of my Father, and I will love him, and will manifest myself to him.	He, with whom are my commands, and who keepeth them, he it is that loveth me. And he that loveth me, will be loved by my Father: and I will love him, and will manifest myself to him.	He who has my commandments with him and keeps them, that [one] loves me. And he who loves me will be loved by my Father and I will love him and I will show myself to him."

	KJV	Murdock	Magiera

JOHN Chapter 14

	KJV	Murdock	Magiera
22	Judas saith unto him, not Iscariot, Lord, how is it that thou wilt manifest thyself unto us, and not unto the world?	Judas, not Iscariot, said to him: My Lord, how is it that thou art to manifest thyself to us, and not to the world?	Judas, not Iscariot, said to him, "My Lord, why is it you are going to show yourself to us and not to the world?"
23	Jesus answered and said unto him, If a man love me, he will keep my words: and my Father will love him, and we will come unto him, and make our abode with him.	Jesus answered, and said to him: He that loveth me, observeth my instruction; and my Father will love him, and we will come to him, and make our abode with him.	Jesus answered and said to him, "He who loves me will keep my word and my Father will love him and we will come to him and we will make a dwelling with him.
24	He that loveth me not keepeth not my sayings: and the word which ye hear is not mine, but the Father's which sent me.	But he that loveth me not, observeth not my instruction. And the instruction which ye hear, is not mine, but the Father's who sent me.	But he who does not love me will not keep my word. And this word that you have heard is not mine, but rather of the Father who sent me.
25	These things have I spoken unto you, being yet present with you.	These things have I said to you, while I was with you.	I have spoken these [things] with you while I am with you.
26	But the Comforter, which is the Holy Ghost, whom the Father will send in my name, he shall teach you all things, and bring all things to your remembrance, whatsoever I have said unto you.	But the Comforter, the Holy Spirit, whom the Father will send in my name, he will teach you every thing, and will remind you of all that I say to you.	But that Deliverer, the Holy Spirit, whom my Father will send in my name, will teach you everything and will remind you of all that I said to you.
27	Peace I leave with you, my peace I give unto you: not as the world giveth, give I unto you. Let not your heart be troubled, neither let it be afraid.	Peace I leave with you; my peace I give to you. It is not as the world giveth, that I give to you. Let not your heart be troubled, nor be afraid.	I leave you peace, my own peace I give to you. Not as the world gives, do I give to you. Let not your heart[s] be troubled and do not fear.
28	Ye have heard how I said unto you, I go away, and come again unto you. If ye loved me, ye would rejoice, because I said, I go unto the Father: for my Father is greater than I.	Ye have heard what I said to you that I go away, and come [again] to you. If ye had loved me, ye would have rejoiced, that I go to my Father; for my Father is greater than I.	You have heard that I have said to you that I will go [away] and I will come to you. If you love me, you would have rejoiced that I go to my Father, because my Father is greater than I [am].
29	And now I have told you before it come to pass, that, when it is come to pass, ye might believe.	And now, lo, I have told you, before it occurreth; so that when it shall have occurred, ye may believe.	And now, behold, I have told you before it happens, so that when it happens you will believe.
30	Hereafter I will not talk much with you: for the prince of this world cometh, and hath nothing in me.	Hereafter I shall not converse much with you; for the ruler of this world cometh, and hath nothing in me.	After this, I will not speak many [things] with you, for the ruler of the world comes and he does not have anything in me.
31	But that the world may know that I love the Father; and as the Father gave me commandment, even so I do. Arise, let us go hence.	But that the world may know, that I love my Father, and as my Father commanded me, so I do. Arise; let us go hence.	But that the world may know that I love my Father and as my Father has commanded me, so I do. Rise up, let us go from here.

Chapter 15

	KJV	Murdock	Magiera
1	I am the true vine, and my Father is the husbandman.	I am the true vine; and my Father is the cultivator.	I am the vine of truth and my Father is the vine-dresser.

Parallel Translations

JOHN *Chapter 15*

	KJV	Murdock	Magiera
2	Every branch in me that beareth not fruit he taketh away: and every branch that beareth fruit, he purgeth it, that it may bring forth more fruit.	Every branch in me, which yieldeth not fruits, he taketh it away: and that which yieldeth fruits, he cleanseth it, that it may yield more fruits.	Every branch that is on me [that] does not bear fruit he takes away. And that which bears fruit, he prunes, so that it may produce much fruit.
3	Now ye are clean through the word which I have spoken unto you.	Ye henceforth are clean, on account of the discourse I have held with you .	You are pruned already, because of the word that I have spoken with you.
4	Abide in me, and I in you. As the branch cannot bear fruit of itself, except it abide in the vine; no more can ye, except ye abide in me.	Abide in me, and I in you. As the branch cannot yield fruits of itself, unless it abide in the vine; so also, neither can ye, unless ye abide in me.	Remain in me and I [will remain] in you. As the branch is not able to produce fruit of itself, unless it will remain in the vine, so neither [will] you, unless you remain in me.
5	I am the vine, ye are the branches: He that abideth in me, and I in him, the same bringeth forth much fruit: for without me ye can do nothing.	I am the vine, and ye are the branches. He that abideth in me, and I in him, he yieldeth much fruit; for without me, ye can do nothing.	I am the vine and you [are] the branches. He who remains in me and I in him, this [one] will bring much fruit, because without me you are not able to do anything.
6	If a man abide not in me, he is cast forth as a branch, and is withered; and men gather them, and cast them into the fire, and they are burned.	And if a man abide not in me, he is cast forth as a withered branch; and they gather it up, and cast it into the fire to be burned.	Now except a man remains in me, he is thrown outside like a branch that has withered and they gather and place it in the fire that it may burn.
7	If ye abide in me, and my words abide in you, ye shall ask what ye will, and it shall be done unto you.	But if ye shall abide in me, and my instructions shall abide in you, whatever ye shall be pleased to ask, it will be given to you.	But if you remain in me and my words remain in you, whatever you want to ask, you will have.
8	Herein is my Father glorified, that ye bear much fruit; so shall ye be my disciples.	In this is the Father glorified, that ye bear much fruit; and ye will be my disciples.	In this the Father is glorified, that you bear much fruit and be my disciples.
9	As the Father hath loved me, so have I loved you: continue ye in my love.	As my Father hath loved me, I also have loved you: abide ye in the love of me.	As my Father has loved me, so also I have loved you. Remain in my compassion.
10	If ye keep my commandments, ye shall abide in my love; even as I have kept my Father's commandments, and abide in his love.	If ye shall keep my commands, ye will abide in the love of me, as I have kept the commands of my Father, and abide in his love.	If you keep my commandments, you will remain in my love, as I have kept the commandments of my Father and remain in his love.
11	These things have I spoken unto you, that my joy might remain in you, and that your joy might be full.	These things have I spoken to you, that my joy may be in you, and that your joy may be complete.	These [things] I have spoken with you, so that my joy would be in you and [that] your joy would be made full.
12	This is my commandment, That ye love one another, as I have loved you.	This is my command, that ye love one another, as I have loved you.	This is my commandment, that you love one another as I have loved you.
13	Greater love hath no man than this, that a man lay down his life for his friends.	There is no greater love than this, that a man lay down his life for his friends.	There is no love that is greater than this, that a man would lay down his life for his friends.
14	Ye are my friends, if ye do whatsoever I command you.	Ye are my friends, if ye do all that I command you.	You are my friends, if you do all that I command you.

Parallel Translations

	KJV	Murdock	Magiera
	JOHN	*Chapter 15*	
15	Henceforth I call you not servants; for the servant knoweth not what his lord doeth: but I have called you friends; for all things that I have heard of my Father I have made known unto you.	I no longer call you servants; because a servant knoweth not what his lord doeth; but I have called you my friends; because, whatever I have heard from my Father, I have made known to you.	No longer do I call you servants, because a servant does not know what his lord does, but I have called you my friends, because everything that I have heard from my Father I have made known to you.
16	Ye have not chosen me, but I have chosen you, and ordained you, that ye should go and bring forth fruit, and that your fruit should remain: that whatsoever ye shall ask of the Father in my name, he may give it you.	It is not ye that chose me, but I that have chosen you; and I have appointed you, that ye also should go and yield fruits, and that your fruits should continue; so that whatever ye may ask of my Father in my name, he may give it you.	You did not choose me, but I have chosen you and I have appointed you that you also should go [and] bear fruit and [that] your fruit should remain, so that whatever you ask of my Father in my name, he will give to you.
17	These things I command you, that ye love one another.	These things I command you, that ye should love one another.	These [things] I command you, that you should love one another.
18	If the world hate you, ye know that it hated me before it hated you.	And if the world hate you, know ye, that it hated me before you.	And if the world hates you, know that it hated me before you.
19	If ye were of the world, the world would love his own: but because ye are not of the world, but I have chosen you out of the world, therefore the world hateth you.	And if ye were of the world, the world would love what is of it. But ye are not of the world, for I have chosen you out of the world; for this cause, the world hateth you.	Now if you are of the world, the world would love its own. But you are not of the world, for I have chosen you out of the world. Because of this, the world hates you.
20	Remember the word that I said unto you, The servant is not greater than his lord. If they have persecuted me, they will also persecute you; if they have kept my saying, they will keep yours also.	Remember the word that I spoke to you, That there is no servant, who is greater than his lord. If they have persecuted me, they will also persecute you; and if they have observed my teaching, they will also observe yours.	Remember the saying that I told you, 'There is no servant who is greater than his lord.' If they persecute me, they will also persecute you. And if they keep my word, they will also keep yours.
21	But all these things will they do unto you for my name's sake, because they know not him that sent me.	But all these things will they do to you, on account of my name, because they know not him that sent me.	But all these [things] they will do to you because of my name, because they do not know him who sent me.
22	If I had not come and spoken unto them, they had not had sin: but now they have no cloke for their sin.	If I had not come and discoursed with them, sin would not have been to them; but now there is no excuse for their sins.	If I had not come [and] spoken with them, they would have no sin. But now they have no excuse for their sin.
23	He that hateth me hateth my Father also.	He that hateth me, hateth my Father also.	He who hates me also hates my Father.
24	If I had not done among them the works which none other man did, they had not had sin: but now have they both seen and hated both me and my Father.	If I had not wrought before them works which no other person ever did, sin would not have been to them: but now they have seen, and have hated, both me and my Father;	And if I had not done deeds before their eyes that another man did not do, they would have no sin. But now they have seen and have hated both me and also my Father,
25	But this cometh to pass, that the word might be fulfilled that is written in their law, They hated me without a cause.	so that in them will be fulfilled the word which is written in their law: They hated me, without a cause.	that the word that is written in their law would be fulfilled: THEY HATED ME WITHOUT A CAUSE.

Parallel Translations

	KJV	Murdock	Magiera
	JOHN	*Chapter 15*	
26	But when the Comforter is come, whom I will send unto you from the Father, even the Spirit of truth, which proceedeth from the Father, he shall testify of me:	But when the Comforter shall come, whom I will send to you from my Father, that Spirit of truth who proceedeth from the Father, He will testify of me.	Now when the Deliverer comes, whom I will send to you from my Father, the Spirit of truth who has proceeded from my Father, he will testify about me.
27	And ye also shall bear witness, because ye have been with me from the beginning.	And do ye also testify; for ye have been with me from the beginning.	You also will testify, because you [were] with me from the beginning.
	Chapter 16		
1	These things have I spoken unto you, that ye should not be offended.	. These things have I said to you, that ye may not be stumbled.	These [things] I have spoken with you, so that you will not be offended.
2	They shall put you out of the synagogues: yea, the time cometh, that whosoever killeth you will think that he doeth God service.	For they will eject you from their synagogues; and the hour will come, that whoever shall kill you, will suppose that he presenteth an offering to God.	For they will put you out of their synagogues and the hour will come when all who kill you will think that he offers an offering to God.
3	And these things will they do unto you, because they have not known the Father, nor me.	And these things will they do, because they have not known either my Father, or me.	And they will do these [things], because they do not know either my Father or me.
4	But these things have I told you, that when the time shall come, ye may remember that I told you of them. And these things I said not unto you at the beginning, because I was with you.	These things have I spoken to you, that when the time of them cometh, ye may recollect, that I told you of them. And I did not tell you these things from the beginning, because I was with you.	These [things] I have spoken with you, so that when their time has come, you will remember that I told you. Now I did not tell you these [things] previously, because I was with you.
5	But now I go my way to him that sent me; and none of you asketh me, Whither goest thou?	But now, I am going to Him that sent me; and none of you asketh me, Whither goest thou?	But now I go to him who sent me, yet not one of you asks me, 'Where are you going?'
6	But because I have said these things unto you, sorrow hath filled your heart.	And because I have told you these things, sorrow hath come and hath filled your hearts.	For I have told you these [things] and sorrow has come and filled your hearts.
7	Nevertheless I tell you the truth; It is expedient for you that I go away: for if I go not away, the Comforter will not come unto you; but if I depart, I will send him unto you.	But I tell you the truth, that it is profitable for you that I go away; for, if I go not away, the Comforter will not come to you; but if I go, I will send him to you.	But I tell you the truth, it is profitable for you that I go, for if I do not go, the Deliverer will not come to you. But if [I] go, I will send him to you.
8	And when he is come, he will reprove the world of sin, and of righteousness, and of judgment:	And when he is come, he will convict the world of sin, and of righteousness, and of judgment.	And when he has come, he will reprove the world concerning sin and concerning justification and concerning judgment--
9	Of sin, because they believe not on me;	Of sin because they believe not in me:	concerning sin, because they do not believe in me,
10	Of righteousness, because I go to my Father, and ye see me no more;	and of righteousness, because I go to my Father, and ye see me no more:	and concerning justification, because I go to my Father and you will not see me again,
11	Of judgment, because the prince of this world is judged.	and of Judgment, because the ruler of this world is judged.	and concerning judgment, because the ruler of this world is judged.
12	I have yet many things to say unto you, but ye cannot bear them now.	Moreover, I have much to say to you: but ye cannot comprehend [it] now.	Again, I have much to say to you, but you are not able to accept [it] now.

	KJV	Murdock	Magiera
	JOHN Chapter 16		
13	Howbeit when he, the Spirit of truth, is come, he will guide you into all truth: for he shall not speak of himself; but whatsoever he shall hear, that shall he speak: and he will shew you things to come.	But when the Spirit of truth shall come, he will lead you into all the truth. For he will not speak from his own mind; but whatever he heareth, that will he speak: and he will make known to you things to come.	But when the Spirit of truth comes, he will lead you into all truth, for he will not speak of his own mind. But everything that he hears, he will speak and he will make known to you future [things].
14	He shall glorify me: for he shall receive of mine, and shall shew it unto you.	He will glorify me; because he will receive of what is mine, and will show [it] to you.	And he will glorify me, because he will receive from me and will show [it[to you.
15	All things that the Father hath are mine: therefore said I, that he shall take of mine, and shall shew it unto you.	Whatever the Father hath, is mine: therefore said I to you that he will receive of what is mine, and will show [it] to you.	Everything that belongs to my Father is mine. Because of this, I have told you that he will receive from me and will show [it] to you.
16	A little while, and ye shall not see me: and again, a little while, and ye shall see me, because I go to the Father.	A little while, and ye will not see me; and again a little while, and ye will see me; because I go to the Father.	A little while and you will not see me and again a little while and you will see me, because I go to the Father."
17	Then said some of his disciples among themselves, What is this that he saith unto us, A little while, and ye shall not see me: and again, a little while, and ye shall see me: and, Because I go to the Father?	And his disciples said one to another: What is this that he saith to us, A little while, and ye will not see me and again a little while, and ye will see me, because I go to my Father?	And his disciples said to one another, "What is this that he tells us, 'A little while and you will not see me and again a little while and you will see me,' and, 'I go to my Father?'"
18	They said therefore, What is this that he saith, A little while? we cannot tell what he saith.	And they said: What is this little while, of which he speaketh? We know not what he saith.	And they were saying, "What is this little while that he spoke of? We do not understand what he says."
19	Now Jesus knew that they were desirous to ask him, and said unto them, Do ye enquire among yourselves of that I said, A little while, and ye shall not see me: and again, a little while, and ye shall see me?	And Jesus knew, that they desired to ask him; and he said to them: Are ye debating with each other, of what I said to you, A little while, and ye will not see me, and again a little while, and ye will see me?	Now Jesus knew that they wanted to ask him and he said to them, "Are you questioning each other about this, because I said to you, 'A little while and you will not see me and again a little while and you will see me'?
20	Verily, verily, I say unto you, That ye shall weep and lament, but the world shall rejoice: and ye shall be sorrowful, but your sorrow shall be turned into joy.	Verily, verily, I say to you, That ye will weep and lament: And the world will rejoice, while to you will be sorrow. But your sorrow will be turned to joy.	Truly, truly I say to you, you will weep and you will mourn, yet the world will rejoice. And you will have sadness, but your sorrow will become joy.
21	A woman when she is in travail hath sorrow, because her hour is come: but as soon as she is delivered of the child, she remembereth no more the anguish, for joy that a man is born into the world.	A woman, in bringing forth, hath sorrow, for the day of her travail hath come: but when she hath brought forth a son, she remembereth not her anguish, because of the joy that a human being is born into the world.	A woman, when she gives birth, has sadness, because the day of her birthing has come. But when she has given birth to a son, she does not remember her ordeal, because of the joy that a man has been born into the world.
22	And ye now therefore have sorrow: but I will see you again, and your heart shall rejoice, and your joy no man taketh from you.	Ye also now have sorrow; but I will see you again, and your heart will rejoice, and no one will deprive you of your joy.	You also now have sadness, but I will see you again and your heart[s] will rejoice and no one will take your joy from you.

Parallel Translations

JOHN — Chapter 16

	KJV	Murdock	Magiera
23	And in that day ye shall ask me nothing. Verily, verily, I say unto you, Whatsoever ye shall ask the Father in my name, he will give it you.	And in that day ye will ask me nothing. Verily, verily, I say to you, That whatsoever ye shall ask of my Father in my name, he will give to you.	And in that day you will not ask me anything. Truly, truly I say to you, everything that you ask of my Father in my name, he will give to you.
24	Hitherto have ye asked nothing in my name: ask, and ye shall receive, that your joy may be full.	Hitherto ye have asked nothing in my name. Ask, and ye will receive; that your joy may be complete.	Until now you have not asked for anything in my name. Ask and you will receive, so that your joy may be full.
25	These things have I spoken unto you in proverbs: but the time cometh, when I shall no more speak unto you in proverbs, but I shall shew you plainly of the Father.	These things have I spoken to you in allegories: but the hour will come, when I shall not speak to you in allegories, but I will speak to you plainly of the Father.	These [things] I have spoken with you with comparisons. But the hour comes when I will not speak to you with comparisons, but I will openly make known to you about the Father.
26	At that day ye shall ask in my name: and I say not unto you, that I will pray the Father for you:	In that day ye will ask in my name; and I do not say to you, that I will pray to the Father for you;	In that day, you will ask in my name and I will not say to you that I will ask the Father for you.
27	For the Father himself loveth you, because ye have loved me, and have believed that I came out from God.	for the Father himself loveth you, because ye have loved me, and have believed that I proceeded from the presence of the Father.	For the Father loves you, because you have loved me and you have believed that I proceeded from before God.
28	I came forth from the Father, and am come into the world: again, I leave the world, and go to the Father.	I proceeded forth from before the Father, and came into the world; and again I leave the world, and go to the Father.	I proceeded from before the Father and came to the world and again I will leave the world and I will go to the Father."
29	His disciples said unto him, Lo, now speakest thou plainly, and speakest no proverb.	His disciples say to him: Lo, now thou speakest plainly, and thou utterest no allegory.	His disciples were saying to him, "Behold, now you speak clearly and you do not speak one comparison.
30	Now are we sure that thou knowest all things, and needest not that any man should ask thee: by this we believe that thou camest forth from God.	Now know we, that thou knowest every thing; and thou hast no need, that any one should ask thee: by this we believe, that thou didst proceed from God.	Now we know that you know everything and have no need of a man to ask you. In this we believe that you proceeded from God."
31	Jesus answered them, Do ye now believe?	Jesus said to them: Do ye believe?	Jesus said to them, "Believe,
32	Behold, the hour cometh, yea, is now come, that ye shall be scattered, every man to his own, and shall leave me alone: and yet I am not alone, because the Father is with me.	Behold, the hour cometh, and hath now come, when ye will be dispersed, each to his place; and ye will leave me alone. But I am not alone, for the Father is with me.	for behold, the hour comes and now has come, when you will be scattered, [each] man to his place and you will leave me alone. Yet I will not be alone, because the Father is with me.
33	These things I have spoken unto you, that in me ye might have peace. In the world ye shall have tribulation: but be of good cheer; I have overcome the world.	These things have I said to you, that in me ye might have peace. In the world ye will have trouble: but, take courage, I have vanquished the world.	These [things] I have told you, so that you may have peace about me. In the world you will have affliction, but take courage, I have conquered the world."

Parallel Translations

	KJV	*Murdock*	*Magiera*
	JOHN	***Chapter 17***	
1	These words spake Jesus, and lifted up his eyes to heaven, and said, Father, the hour is come; glorify thy Son, that thy Son also may glorify thee:	These things spake Jesus, and lifted up his eyes to heaven, and said: My Father, the hour is come: glorify thy Son, that thy Son may glorify thee.	These [things] Jesus spoke and he raised his eyes to heaven and said, "My Father, the hour has come. Glorify your Son, so that your Son may glorify you.
2	As thou hast given him power over all flesh, that he should give eternal life to as many as thou hast given him.	As thou hast given him authority over all flesh, that he might give life eternal to as many as thou hast given him.	According as you have given him authority over all flesh, to whomever you have given him, he will give eternal life.
3	And this is life eternal, that they might know thee the only true God, and Jesus Christ, whom thou hast sent.	And this is life eternal, that they may know thee, that thou art the only true God, and whom thou hast sent, Jesus Messiah.	Now this is eternal life, that they will know you, that you alone are the God of truth and he whom you have sent [is] Jesus the Messiah.
4	I have glorified thee on the earth: I have finished the work which thou gavest me to do.	I have glorified thee on the earth; the work which thou gavest me to do, I have finished.	I have glorified you on the earth. The work that you gave me to do I have completed.
5	And now, O Father, glorify thou me with thine own self with the glory which I had with thee before the world was.	And now, my Father, glorify thou me, with that glory which I had with thee before the world was.	And now, my Father, glorify me with you with that glory that I had with you before the world was.
6	I have manifested thy name unto the men which thou gavest me out of the world: thine they were, and thou gavest them me; and they have kept thy word.	I have made known thy name to the men, whom thou gavest me from the world: thine they were, and thou gavest them to me; and they have kept thy word.	I have made known your name to the men whom you gave to me from the world. They were yours and you gave them to me and they have kept your word.
7	Now they have known that all things whatsoever thou hast given me are of thee.	Now I have known, that whatever thou hast given me, was from thee.	Now I know that whatever you gave me was from before you,
8	For I have given unto them the words which thou gavest me; and they have received them, and have known surely that I came out from thee, and they have believed that thou didst send me.	For, the words thou gavest to me, I have given to them; and they have received them, and have known certainly, that I came from thy presence; and they have believed that thou didst send me.	for the words that you gave me, I gave to them and they received [them] and they know truly that I have proceeded from before you and they believe that you sent me.
9	I pray for them: I pray not for the world, but for them which thou hast given me; for they are thine.	And I pray for them; it is not for the world that I pray, but for them whom thou hast given me, for they are thine.	And I pray for them. I do not pray for the world, but for those whom you gave me, because they are yours.
10	And all mine are thine, and thine are mine; and I am glorified in them.	And all that is mine is thine, and what is thine is mine; and I am glorified in them.	And everything that is mine is yours and yours is mine and I am glorified by them.
11	And now I am no more in the world, but these are in the world, and I come to thee. Holy Father, keep through thine own name those whom thou hast given me, that they may be one, as we are.	Henceforth I am not in the world; but these are in the world, and I go to thee. Holy Father, keep them in that thy name, which thou hast given to me; that they may be one, as we are.	From now on, I will not be in the world, yet these are in the world and I am coming to you, holy Father. Keep them in your name, [those] whom you gave me, so that they be one as we [are].

Parallel Translations

JOHN Chapter 17

	KJV	Murdock	Magiera
12	While I was with them in the world, I kept them in thy name: those that thou gavest me I have kept, and none of them is lost, but the son of perdition; that the scripture might be fulfilled.	While I have been with them in the world, I have kept them in thy name. Those thou gavest me, have I kept; and none of them is lost, but the son of perdition, that the scripture might be fulfilled.	While I was with them in the world, I have kept them in your name. Those whom you gave me, I have kept and not one of them is lost, except for the son of destruction, that the scripture would be fulfilled.
13	And now come I to thee; and these things I speak in the world, that they might have my joy fulfilled in themselves.	But now I come to thee; and these things I speak in the world, that my joy may be complete in them.	But now I come to you. And these [things] I speak in the world, so that my joy will be full in them.
14	I have given them thy word; and the world hath hated them, because they are not of the world, even as I am not of the world.	I have given them thy word: and the world hath hated them, because they are not of the world, even as I am not of the world.	I have given them your word and the world hates them, because they are not of the world, as I am not of the world.
15	I pray not that thou shouldest take them out of the world, but that thou shouldest keep them from the evil.	I pray not, that thou wouldst take them out of the world, but that thou wouldst keep them from evil:	I do not pray that you should take them from the world, but that you would keep them from the Evil [one],
16	They are not of the world, even as I am not of the world.	for they are not of the world, even as I am not of the world.	for they are not of the world, as I am not of the world.
17	Sanctify them through thy truth: thy word is truth.	Father, sanctify them by thy truth, thy word is the truth.	Father, set them apart by your truth, for your word is truth.
18	As thou hast sent me into the world, even so have I also sent them into the world.	As thou didst send me into the world, so have I also sent them into the world.	As you sent me into the world, so also I send them into the world.
19	And for their sakes I sanctify myself, that they also might be sanctified through the truth.	And for their sakes I sanctify myself, that they also may be sanctified by the truth.	And for their sakes I set myself apart, so that they also may be set apart in truth.
20	Neither pray I for these alone, but for them also which shall believe on me through their word;	And it is not for them only that I pray, but also for those who shall believe in me through their discourse;	And I do not pray for the sake of these only, but also for the sake of those who will believe in me through their word,
21	That they all may be one; as thou, Father, art in me, and I in thee, that they also may be one in us: that the world may believe that thou hast sent me.	that they all may be one; as thou, my Father, [art] in me, and I in thee; that they also may be one in us; so that the world may believe, that thou didst send me.	so that all of them may be one as you [are], my Father in me and I in you, so that they also may be one in us, so that the world may believe that you have sent me.
22	And the glory which thou gavest me I have given them; that they may be one, even as we are one:	And the glory which thou gavest me, I have given them; that they may be one, as we are one.	And the glory that you gave me, I gave to them, so that they may be one as we are one,
23	I in them, and thou in me, that they may be made perfect in one; and that the world may know that thou hast sent me, and hast loved them, as thou hast loved me.	I in them, and thou in me; that they may be perfected into one; and that the world may know that thou didst send me, and that thou hast loved them as also thou hast loved me.	I in them and you in me, that they be perfected into one, and that the world may know that you have sent me and that you have loved them, as also you have loved me.

Parallel Translations

	KJV	Murdock	Magiera
	JOHN	*Chapter 17*	
24	Father, I will that they also, whom thou hast given me, be with me where I am; that they may behold my glory, which thou hast given me: for thou lovedst me before the foundation of the world.	Father, I desire that those whom thou hast given me, may also be with me where I am; that they may see that glory of mine which thou hast given me, as thou lovedst me before the foundation of the world.	Father, I desire that those whom you gave me may also be with me where I am, so that they may see my glory that you gave me, because you loved me from before the foundations of the world.
25	O righteous Father, the world hath not known thee: but I have known thee, and these have known that thou hast sent me.	My righteous Father, the world hath not known thee; but I have known thee, and these have known, that thou didst send me.	My upright Father, the world has not known you, but I know you and they know that you sent me.
26	And I have declared unto them thy name, and will declare it: that the love wherewith thou hast loved me may be in them, and I in them.	And I have made known to them thy name; and I will make it known; so that the love, with which thou lovedst me, may be in them, and I in them.	And I have made known your name to them and I will make [it] known, so that the love [with] which you loved me will be in them and I will be in them."
	Chapter 18		
1	When Jesus had spoken these words, he went forth with his disciples over the brook Cedron, where was a garden, into the which he entered, and his disciples.	These things spake Jesus, and went forth with his disciples over the brook Cedron, where there was a garden, into which he and his disciples entered.	These [things] Jesus spoke and he went out with his disciples to the other side of the brook of Kidron, a place that had a garden, where he entered, he and his disciples.
2	And Judas also, which betrayed him, knew the place: for Jesus ofttimes resorted thither with his disciples.	And Judas also, the betrayer, knew the place; because Jesus often there met with his disciples.	Now Judas, the betrayer, also knew that location, because Jesus had gathered there many times with his disciples.
3	Judas then, having received a band of men and officers from the chief priests and Pharisees, cometh thither with lanterns and torches and weapons.	Then Judas received a regiment, and from the presence of the chief priests and Pharisees he had officials; and he came to the place with lanterns and lamps and weapons.	Therefore, Judas took a company of soldiers and he took guards from the chief priests and the Pharisees and came there with torches and lamps and weapons.
4	Jesus therefore, knowing all things that should come upon him, went forth, and said unto them, Whom seek ye?	And Jesus, as he knew every thing that was to befall him, went forth and said to them: Whom seek ye?	Now Jesus, because he knew everything that was coming concerning him, went out and said to them, "Whom do you seek?"
5	They answered him, Jesus of Nazareth. Jesus saith unto them, I am he. And Judas also, which betrayed him, stood with them.	They say to him: Jesus the Nazarean. Jesus said to them: I am he. And Judas the betrayer was also standing with them.	They said to him, "Jesus, the Nazarene." Jesus said to them, "I am [he]." Now Judas, the betrayer, was also standing with them.
6	As soon then as he had said unto them, I am he, they went backward, and fell to the ground.	And when Jesus said to them, I am he, they drew back and fell upon the ground.	And when Jesus said to them, "I am [he]," they went backwards and fell on the ground.
7	Then asked he them again, Whom seek ye? And they said, Jesus of Nazareth.	And again Jesus asked them: Whom seek ye? And they said: Jesus the Nazarean.	Jesus again asked them, "Whom do you seek?" And they said, "Jesus, the Nazarene."
8	Jesus answered, I have told you that I am he: if therefore ye seek me, let these go their way:	Jesus said to them: I have told you that I am he; and if ye seek me, let these go away:	Jesus said to them, "I told you that I am [he] and if you seek me, allow these to go,"

	KJV	Murdock	Magiera
	JOHN	*Chapter 18*	
9	That the saying might be fulfilled, which he spake, Of them which thou gavest me have I lost none.	that the speech might be fulfilled, which he uttered: Of them, whom thou hast given me, I have lost not even one.	that the word that he had said would be fulfilled, "I have not lost any of those whom you gave me, not even one."
10	Then Simon Peter having a sword drew it, and smote the high priest's servant, and cut off his right ear. The servant's name was Malchus.	And Simon Cephas had upon him a sword; and he drew it, and smote a servant of the high priest, and cut off his right ear. And the servant's name was Malchus.	But Simon Peter had a sword on him and he drew it and struck the servant of the high priest and took off his right ear. Now the name of the servant [was] Malchus.
11	Then said Jesus unto Peter, Put up thy sword into the sheath: the cup which my Father hath given me, shall I not drink it?	And Jesus said to Cephas: Put the sword into its sheath. The cup which my Father hath given me, shall I not drink it?	And Jesus said to Peter, "Place the sword into its sheath. Should I not drink the cup that my Father has given to me?"
12	Then the band and the captain and officers of the Jews took Jesus, and bound him,	Then the regiment and the chiliarchs and the officials of the Jews laid hold of Jesus, and bound him;	Then the company of soldiers and the captains and the guards of the Judeans arrested Jesus and bound him.
13	And led him away to Annas first; for he was father in law to Caiaphas, which was the high priest that same year.	and they led him first to the presence of Annas; for he was father-in-law to Caiaphas, who was the high priest of that year.	And they brought him to Annas first, because he was the father-in-law of Caiaphas, who was the high priest of that year.
14	Now Caiaphas was he, which gave counsel to the Jews, that it was expedient that one man should die for the people.	And it was Caiaphas who counselled the Jews, that it was expedient, one man should die for the people.	(Now Caiaphas was he who had counseled the Judeans that it was expedient that one man should die on behalf of the people.)
15	And Simon Peter followed Jesus, and so did another disciple: that disciple was known unto the high priest, and went in with Jesus into the palace of the high priest.	And Simon Cephas and one other of the disciples went after Jesus. And that other disciple knew the high priest; and he entered with Jesus into the hall.	Now Simon Peter and one of the other disciples were following Jesus. And that disciple knew the high priest and he entered the hall with Jesus.
16	But Peter stood at the door without. Then went out that other disciple, which was known unto the high priest, and spake unto her that kept the door, and brought in Peter.	But Simon stood without at the door; and that other disciple, who knew the high priest, went out and spoke to the doorkeeper and brought in Simon.	But Simon was standing outside by the gate. And that other disciple, who knew the high priest, went out and spoke to the keeper of the gate and brought in Simon.
17	Then saith the damsel that kept the door unto Peter, Art not thou also one of this man's disciples? He saith, I am not.	And the maid who kept the door, said to Simon: Art not thou also one of this man's disciples? And he said: I am not.	And the young woman, the keeper of the gate, said to Simon, "Are you also [one] of the disciples of this man?" He said to her, "No."
18	And the servants and officers stood there, who had made a fire of coals; for it was cold: and they warmed themselves: and Peter stood with them, and warmed himself.	And the servants and officials were standing, and had placed a fire to warm themselves	And the servants and guards were standing and had made a fire to warm themselves because it was cold. Now Simon was also standing with them and warming himself.
19	The high priest then asked Jesus of his disciples, and of his doctrine.	And the high priest interrogated Jesus respecting his disciples, and respecting his doctrine.	And the high priest asked Jesus about his disciples and about his teaching.

Parallel Translations

JOHN — *Chapter 18*

	KJV	*Murdock*	*Magiera*
20	Jesus answered him, I spake openly to the world; I ever taught in the synagogue, and in the temple, whither the Jews always resort; and in secret have I said nothing.	And Jesus said to him: I have discoursed openly with the people, and have at all times taught in the synagogue and in the temple, where all the Jews assemble; and I have uttered nothing in private.	And Jesus said to him, "I spoke openly with the people and I always taught in the synagogue and in the temple, where all the Judeans are gathered and I did not say anything in secret.
21	Why askest thou me? ask them which heard me, what I have said unto them: behold, they know what I said.	Why dost thou interrogate me? Ask them who have heard, what I said to them: lo, they know what I have said.	Why do you ask me? Ask those who heard what I spoke with them. Behold, they know everything that I have said."
22	And when he had thus spoken, one of the officers which stood by struck Jesus with the palm of his hand, saying, Answerest thou the high priest so?	And as he said these things, one of the officials standing by, smote the cheek of Jesus, and said to him: Givest thou such an answer to the high priest?	And when he had said these [things], one of the guards who was standing [there] struck Jesus on his cheek and said to him, "Do you give such an answer to the high priest?"
23	Jesus answered him, If I have spoken evil, bear witness of the evil: but if well, why smitest thou me?	Jesus replied, and said to him: If I have spoken evil bear witness of that evil; but if well, why smitest thou me?	Jesus answered and said to him, "If I have spoken wickedly, bear witness against the wickedness, yet if [I have spoken] well, why do you strike me?"
24	Now Annas had sent him bound unto Caiaphas the high priest.	Now Annas had sent Jesus bound to Caiaphas the high priest.	Now Annas sent Jesus bound to Caiaphas, the high priest.
25	And Simon Peter stood and warmed himself. They said therefore unto him, Art not thou also one of his disciples? He denied it, and said, I am not.	And Simon Cephas was standing and warming himself; and they said to him: Art not thou also one of his disciples? And he denied, and said: I am not.	And Simon Peter was standing and warming himself and they said to him, "Are you not also one of his disciples?" And he denied [it] and said, "I am not."
26	One of the servants of the high priest, being his kinsman whose ear Peter cut off, saith, Did not I see thee in the garden with him?	And one of the servants of the high priest, a kinsman of him whose ear Simon cut off, said to him: Did I not see thee with him in the garden?	One of the servants of the high priest, a kinsman of him whose ear Simon had cut off, said to him, "Did I not see you with him in the garden?"
27	Peter then denied again: and immediately the cock crew.	And again Simon denied: and at that moment the cock crew.	And again Simon denied [it] and immediately the rooster crowed.
28	Then led they Jesus from Caiaphas unto the hall of judgment: and it was early; and they themselves went not into the judgment hall, lest they should be defiled; but that they might eat the passover.	And they led Jesus from the presence of Caiaphas unto the Praetorium; and it was morning. But they did not enter the Praetorium, lest they should defile themselves before they had eaten the passover.	Now they brought Jesus from Caiaphas into the judgment hall and it was daybreak. And they did not enter into the judgment hall, so that they would not be defiled before they had eaten the Passover.
29	Pilate then went out unto them, and said, What accusation bring ye against this man?	And Pilate went forth to them without, and said to them: What accusation have ye against this man?	And Pilate went outside to them and said to them, "What accusation do you have against this man?"
30	They answered and said unto him, If he were not a malefactor, we would not have delivered him up unto thee.	They replied, and said to him: If he were not a malefactor, we should not have delivered him up to thee.	They answered and said to him, "If he was not a doer of evil, we would not even have delivered him to you."

Parallel Translations

	KJV	*Murdock*	*Magiera*
	JOHN	*Chapter 18*	
31	Then said Pilate unto them, Take ye him, and judge him according to your law. The Jews therefore said unto him, It is not lawful for us to put any man to death:	Pilate said to them: Take ye him, and judge him according to your law. The Jews said to him: It is not lawful for us to put a man to death:	Pilate said to them, "Take him and judge him according to your law. The Judeans said to him, "It is not lawful for us to kill a man,"
32	That the saying of Jesus might be fulfilled, which he spake, signifying what death he should die.	that the speech of Jesus might be fulfilled, when he made known by what death he was to die.	that the word would be fulfilled that Jesus said when he made known with what death he was going to die.
33	Then Pilate entered into the judgment hall again, and called Jesus, and said unto him, Art thou the King of the Jews?	And Pilate went into the Praetorium, and called Jesus, and said to him: Art thou the king of the Jews?	Now Pilate entered the judgment hall and called Jesus and said to him, "Are you the king of the Judeans?"
34	Jesus answered him, Sayest thou this thing of thyself, or did others tell it thee of me?	Jesus said to him: Sayest thou this of thyself, or have others said [it] to thee of me?	Jesus said to him, "Do you say this of yourself or have others told you about me?"
35	Pilate answered, Am I a Jew? Thine own nation and the chief priests have delivered thee unto me: what hast thou done?	Pilate said to him: Am I a Jew? Thy countrymen and the chief priests have delivered thee to me. What hast thou done?	Pilate said to him, "Am I a Judean? Your countrymen and the chief priests have delivered you to me. What have you done?"
36	Jesus answered, My kingdom is not of this world: if my kingdom were of this world, then would my servants fight, that I should not be delivered to the Jews: but now is my kingdom not from hence.	Jesus said to him: My kingdom is not of this world. If my kingdom were of this world, my servants would have fought, that I might not be delivered up to the Jews: but now, my kingdom is not from hence.	Jesus said to him, "My kingdom is not of this world. If my kingdom were of this world, my servants would have fought, so that I would not be delivered to the Judeans. But now my kingdom is not from here."
37	Pilate therefore said unto him, Art thou a king then? Jesus answered, Thou sayest that I am a king. To this end was I born, and for this cause came I into the world, that I should bear witness unto the truth. Every one that is of the truth heareth my voice.	Pilate said to him . Then thou art a king? Jesus said to him: Thou hast said, that I am a king. For this was I born; and for this came I into the world, that I might bear testimony to the truth. Every one that is of the truth, heareth my voice.	Pilate said to him, "Then [are] you a king?" Jesus said to him, "You have said that I am a king. I was born for this and for this I came into the world that I would testify concerning the truth. Everyone who is of the truth hears my voice."
38	Pilate saith unto him, What is truth? And when he had said this, he went out again unto the Jews, and saith unto them, I find in him no fault at all.	Pilate said to him: What is the truth? And as he said this, he went out again to the Jews, and said to them: I find not any crime in him.	Pilate said to him, "What is truth?" And after he had said this, he went out again to the Judeans and said to them, "I do not find even one fault in him.
39	But ye have a custom, that I should release unto you one at the passover: will ye therefore that I release unto you the King of the Jews?	And ye have a custom that I should release one to you at the passover; will ye, therefore, that I release to you this king of the Jews?	But you have a custom that I should release someone to you during the Passover. Therefore, do you want me to release to you this king of the Judeans?"
40	Then cried they all again, saying, Not this man, but Barabbas. Now Barabbas was a robber.	And they all cried out, and said: Not this man, but Barabbas. Now this Barabbas was a robber.	And all of them cried out and said, "Not this [man], but Barabbas." Now this Barabbas was a thief.
	Chapter 19		
1	Then Pilate therefore took Jesus, and scourged him.	Then Pilate scourged Jesus.	Then Pilate scourged Jesus.

Parallel Translations

	KJV	*Murdock*	*Magiera*
	JOHN	*Chapter 19*	
2	And the soldiers platted a crown of thorns, and put it on his head, and they put on him a purple robe,	And the soldiers braided a crown of thorns, and put it on his head; and they clothed him in purple garments:	And the soldiers wove a crown of thorns and they placed it on his head and covered him with robes of purple.
3	And said, Hail, King of the Jews! and they smote him with their hands.	and they said: Hail, king of the Jews! and smote him on his cheeks.	And they were saying, "Peace [be] to you, king of the Judeans, and they were striking him on his cheeks."
4	Pilate therefore went forth again, and saith unto them, Behold, I bring him forth to you, that ye may know that I find no fault in him.	And Pilate went out again, and said to them: Lo, I bring him out to you, that ye may know that I find against him no offence whatever.	And Pilate went outside again and said to them, "Behold, I will bring him outside to you, so that you may know that I can find not even one fault against him."
5	Then came Jesus forth, wearing the crown of thorns, and the purple robe. And Pilate saith unto them, Behold the man!	And Jesus went forth, having on him the crown of thorns, and the purple garments. And Pilate said to them: Behold, the man!	And Jesus went outside while the crown of thorns and robes of purple were on him and Pilate said to them, "Behold, the man."
6	When the chief priests therefore and officers saw him, they cried out, saying, Crucify him, crucify him. Pilate saith unto them, Take ye him, and crucify him: for I find no fault in him.	And when the chief priests and officials saw him, they cried out, and said: Hang him; hang him. Pilate said to them: Take ye him, and crucify him; for I find no offence in him.	Now when the chief priests and guards saw him, they cried out and said, "Crucify him, crucify him." Pilate said to them, "You take and crucify him, for I am not able to find a fault in him."
7	The Jews answered him, We have a law, and by our law he ought to die, because he made himself the Son of God.	The Jews say to him: We have a law, and, according to our law, he deserveth death, because he made himself the Son of God.	The Judeans said to him, "We have a law and according to that which is in our law, he is deserving of death, because he made himself the Son of God."
8	When Pilate therefore heard that saying, he was the more afraid;	And when Pilate heard that declaration, he feared the more.	And when Pilate heard this saying, he was more afraid.
9	And went again into the judgment hall, and saith unto Jesus, Whence art thou? But Jesus gave him no answer.	And he went again into the Praetorium; and he said to Jesus: Whence art thou? And Jesus gave him no answer.	And he entered again into the judgment hall and said to Jesus, "Where [are] you from?" But Jesus did not give him an answer.
10	Then saith Pilate unto him, Speakest thou not unto me? knowest thou not that I have power to crucify thee, and have power to release thee?	Pilate said to him: Wilt thou not speak to me? Knowest thou not, that I have authority to release thee, and have authority to crucify thee?	Pilate said to him, "Are you not speaking to me? Do you not know that I have the authority to release you and I have the authority to crucify you?"
11	Jesus answered, Thou couldest have no power at all against me, except it were given thee from above: therefore he that delivered me unto thee hath the greater sin.	Jesus said to him: Thou wouldst have no authority at all over me, if it were not given to thee from on high: therefore his sin who delivered me up to thee, is greater than thine.	Jesus said to him, "You would have no authority over me at all if it had not been given to you from above. Because of this, his sin who delivered me to you is greater than yours."
12	And from thenceforth Pilate sought to release him: but the Jews cried out, saying, If thou let this man go, thou art not Caesar's friend: whosoever maketh himself a king speaketh against Caesar.	And for this reason, Pilate was disposed to release him. But the Jews cried out: If thou release this man, thou art not Caesar's friend: for whoever maketh himself a king, is the adversary of Caesar.	And because of this, Pilate wanted to release him, but the Judeans were crying out, "If you release this [man], you are not the friend of Caesar, for everyone who makes himself a king is an opponent of Caesar."

Parallel Translations

JOHN *Chapter 19*

	KJV	*Murdock*	*Magiera*
13	When Pilate therefore heard that saying, he brought Jesus forth, and sat down in the judgment seat in a place that is called the Pavement, but in the Hebrew, Gabbatha.	And when Pilate heard this declaration, he brought Jesus forth, and sat upon the tribunal, in a place called the pavement of stones; but in Hebrew it is called Gabbatha.	Now when Pilate heard this saying, he brought Jesus outside and sat on the judgment seat in a place that is called "The Pavement of Stones," but in Hebrew is called Gabbatha.
14	And it was the preparation of the passover, and about the sixth hour: and he saith unto the Jews, Behold your King!	And it was the preparation for the passover; and it was about the sixth hour. And he said to the Jews: Behold, your king.	And it was the day of preparation of the Passover and it was about the sixth hour. And he said to the Judeans, "Behold, your king."
15	But they cried out, Away with him, away with him, crucify him. Pilate saith unto them, Shall I crucify your King? The chief priests answered, We have no king but Caesar.	But they cried out: Away with him, away with him; hang him, hang him. Pilate said to them: Shall I crucify your king? The chief priests said to him: We have no king, but Caesar.	And they were crying out, "Take him away, take him away. Crucify him, crucify him." Pilate said to them, "Should I crucify your king?" The chief priests were saying, "We have no king, except Caesar."
16	Then delivered he him therefore unto them to be crucified. And they took Jesus, and led him away.	Then he delivered him to them, that they might crucify him. And they took Jesus, and led him away,	Then he delivered him to them that they might crucify him. And they led Jesus out and took him,
17	And he bearing his cross went forth into a place called the place of a skull, which is called in the Hebrew Golgotha:	bearing his cross, to a place called a Skull, and in Hebrew called Golgotha;	bearing his cross, to a place that was called 'The Skull,' but in Hebrew is called Golgotha,
18	Where they crucified him, and two other with him, on either side one, and Jesus in the midst.	where they crucified him; and two others with him, the one on this side, and the other on that, and Jesus in the middle.	where they crucified him and with him two others, one on one side and one on the other and Jesus in the center.
19	And Pilate wrote a title, and put it on the cross. And the writing was, JESUS OF NAZARETH THE KING OF THE JEWS.	And Pilate also wrote a tablet, and affixed it to his cross. And thus it was written: THIS IS JESUS THE NAZAREAN, KING OF THE JEWS.	And Pilate also wrote a tablet and placed [it] on his cross. Now it was written like this, "Jesus, the Nazarene, the king of the Judeans."
20	This title then read many of the Jews: for the place where Jesus was crucified was nigh to the city: and it was written in Hebrew, and Greek, and Latin.	And many of the Jews read this label; because the place where Jesus was crucified, was near to Jerusalem; and it was written in Hebrew and Greek and Latin.	And many of the Judeans read this board, because the place at which Jesus was crucified was near to the city and it was written in Hebrew and in Greek and in Latin.
21	Then said the chief priests of the Jews to Pilate, Write not, The King of the Jews; but that he said, I am King of the Jews.	And the chief priests said to Pilate: Write not that he is king of the Jews, but that he said I am king of the Jews.	And the chief priests said to Pilate, "Do not write that he is king of the Judeans, but rather, 'He said I [am] the king of the Judeans.'"
22	Pilate answered, What I have written I have written.	Pilate said: What I have written, I have written.	Pilate said, "What I have written, I have written."
23	Then the soldiers, when they had crucified Jesus, took his garments, and made four parts, to every soldier a part; and also his coat: now the coat was without seam, woven from the top throughout.	And the soldiers, when they had crucified Jesus, took his garments and made four parcels of them, a parcel for each of the soldiers. And his tunic was without seam from the top, woven throughout.	Now the soldiers, after they had crucified Jesus, took his garments and made four pieces, a piece for each of the soldiers. But his robe was without seam from the top, completely woven.

JOHN *Chapter 19*

	KJV	*Murdock*	*Magiera*
24	They said therefore among themselves, Let us not rend it, but cast lots for it, whose it shall be: that the scripture might be fulfilled, which saith, They parted my raiment among them, and for my vesture they did cast lots. These things therefore the soldiers did.	And they said one to another: We will not rend it, but will cast the lot upon it, whose it shall he. And the scripture was fulfilled, which said: They divided my garments among them; and upon my vesture they cast the lot. These things did the soldiers.	And they said to one another, "Let us not tear it, but let us cast lots for it, whose it will be." And the scripture was fulfilled that said: THEY DIVIDED MY GARMENTS AMONG THEMSELVES AND FOR MY CLOTHES THEY CAST A LOT. These [things] the soldiers did.
25	Now there stood by the cross of Jesus his mother, and his mother's sister, Mary the wife of Cleophas, and Mary Magdalene.	And there were standing near the cross of Jesus, his mother, and his mother's sister, and Mary [the wife] of Cleophas, and Mary Magdalena.	Now standing at the cross of Jesus were his mother and the sister of his mother and Mary, who [was the wife] of Cleophas, and Mary Magdalene.
26	When Jesus therefore saw his mother, and the disciple standing by, whom he loved, he saith unto his mother, Woman, behold thy son!	And Jesus saw his mother, and that disciple whom he loved, standing by, and he said to his mother: Woman, behold, thy son.	And Jesus saw his mother and the disciple whom he loved who was standing [there] and he said to his mother, "Woman, behold your son."
27	Then saith he to the disciple, Behold thy mother! And from that hour that disciple took her unto his own home.	And he said to that disciple: Behold, thy mother. And from that hour, the disciple took her near himself.	And he said to that disciple, "Behold, your mother." And from that time, that disciple took her with him.
28	After this, Jesus knowing that all things were now accomplished, that the scripture might be fulfilled, saith, I thirst.	After these things, Jesus knew that every thing was finished; and, that the scripture might be fulfilled, he said: I thirst.	After these [things], Jesus knew that everything was fulfilled. And so that the scripture would be fulfilled, he said, "I am thirsty."
29	Now there was set a vessel full of vinegar: and they filled a spunge with vinegar, and put it upon hyssop, and put it to his mouth.	And a vessel was standing there, full of vinegar. And they filled a sponge with the vinegar, and put it on a hyssop [stalk], and bore it to his mouth.	And a vessel was placed [there] that was full of vinegar. And they filled a sponge with the vinegar and placed [it] on hyssop and brought [it] to his mouth.
30	When Jesus therefore had received the vinegar, he said, It is finished: and he bowed his head, and gave up the ghost.	And when Jesus had received the vinegar, he said: Lo; Done. And he bowed his head, and yielded up his spirit.	And after he had taken that vinegar, Jesus said, "Behold, it is finished." And he bowed his head and gave up his spirit.
31	The Jews therefore, because it was the preparation, that the bodies should not remain upon the cross on the sabbath day, (for that sabbath day was an high day,) besought Pilate that their legs might be broken, and that they might be taken away.	And because it was the preparation, the Jews said: These bodies must not remain all night upon the cross: because the sabbath was dawning; and the day of that sabbath was a great day. And they requested of Pilate, that they should break the legs of those crucified, and take them down.	Now the Judeans, because it was the day of preparation, said, "These bodies should not remain on their crosses, because the Sabbath is dawning, for the day of that Sabbath was a high day. And they begged Pilate that they might break the legs of those [who were] crucified and take them down.
32	Then came the soldiers, and brake the legs of the first, and of the other which was crucified with him.	And the soldiers came, and broke the legs of the first, and of the other that was crucified with him.	And the soldiers came and broke the legs of the first and of that other [one] who was crucified with him.

Parallel Translations

JOHN Chapter 19

	KJV	Murdock	Magiera
33	But when they came to Jesus, and saw that he was dead already, they brake not his legs:	But when they came to Jesus, they saw that he was already dead; and they broke not his legs.	And when they came to Jesus, they saw that he was dead already and did not break his legs.
34	But one of the soldiers with a spear pierced his side, and forthwith came there out blood and water.	But one of the soldiers thrust a spear into his side; and immediately there issued out blood and water.	But one of the soldiers struck him in his side with a spear and immediately blood and water came out
35	And he that saw it bare record, and his record is true: and he knoweth that he saith true, that ye might believe.	And he who saw [it], hath testified: and his testimony is true: and he knoweth, that he speaketh the truth, that ye also may believe.	and the one who saw [it] testified and his testimony is true. And he knows that he spoke the truth that you also may believe.
36	For these things were done, that the scripture should be fulfilled, A bone of him shall not be broken.	For these things occurred, that the scripture might be fulfilled, which said: A bone of him shall not be broken.	For these [things] happened that the scripture would be fulfilled that said: A BONE OF HIM WILL NOT BE BROKEN.
37	And again another scripture saith, They shall look on him whom they pierced.	And again another scripture, which saith: They will look on him, whom they pierced.	And again another scripture that said: THEY WILL GAZE AT HIM WHOM THEY PIERCED.
38	And after this Joseph of Arimathaea, being a disciple of Jesus, but secretly for fear of the Jews, besought Pilate that he might take away the body of Jesus: and Pilate gave him leave. He came therefore, and took the body of Jesus.	After these things, Joseph of Ramath, for he was a disciple of Jesus, and kept concealed through fear of the Jews, requested of Pilate, that he might take away the body of Jesus. And Pilate permitted. And he came, and bore away the body of Jesus.	After these [things], Joseph, who was from Arimathaea, requested from Pilate, because he was a disciple of Jesus and was hiding for fear of the Judeans, that he might take away the body of Jesus. And Pilate gave permission and he came and took the body of Jesus.
39	And there came also Nicodemus, which at the first came to Jesus by night, and brought a mixture of myrrh and aloes, about an hundred pound weight.	And there came also Nicodemus, he who previously came to Jesus by night, and he brought with him a compound of myrrh and aloes, about a hundred pounds.	And Nicodemus also came, who previously had come to Jesus during the night, and he brought with him a mixture of spices of myrrh and of aloe, about one hundred Roman libras.
40	Then took they the body of Jesus, and wound it in linen clothes with the spices, as the manner of the Jews is to bury.	and they bore away the body of Jesus, and wound it in linens and aromatics, as it is the custom of the Jews to bury.	And they took the body of Jesus and wrapped it in linen and with spices, as is the custom for the Judeans when they bury.
41	Now in the place where he was crucified there was a garden; and in the garden a new sepulchre, wherein was never man yet laid.	And there was a garden in the place where Jesus was crucified, and in the garden a new sepulchre in which no person had ever been laid.	Now there was a garden in that location in which Jesus was crucified and in that garden, a new tomb in which no one had yet been placed.
42	There laid they Jesus therefore because of the Jews' preparation day; for the sepulchre was nigh at hand.	And there they laid Jesus, because the sabbath had commenced, and because the sepulchre was near.	And they placed Jesus there, because the Sabbath was beginning and because the grave was nearby.

Parallel Translations

	KJV	*Murdock*	*Magiera*

JOHN *Chapter 20*

Verse	KJV	Murdock	Magiera
1	The first day of the week cometh Mary Magdalene early, when it was yet dark, unto the sepulchre, and seeth the stone taken away from the sepulchre.	And the first day of the week, in the morning, while it was yet dark, Mary Magdalena came to the sepulchre: and she saw that the stone was removed from the grave.	Now on the first of the week, Mary Magdalene came in the early morning while it was dark to the tomb. And she saw the stone that it was taken away from the grave.
2	Then she runneth, and cometh to Simon Peter, and to the other disciple, whom Jesus loved, and saith unto them, They have taken away the Lord out of the sepulchre, and we know not where they have laid him.	And she ran, and came to Simon Cephas, and to that other disciple whom Jesus loved, and said to them: They have taken away our Lord from the sepulchre, and I know not where they have laid him.	And she ran [and] came to Simon Peter and to that other disciple whom Jesus loved and she said to them, "They have taken our Lord from the tomb and I do not know where they have put him."
3	Peter therefore went forth, and that other disciple, and came to the sepulchre.	And Simon set out, and the other disciple, and they were going to the sepulchre.	And Simon went and that other disciple and they came to the tomb.
4	So they ran both together: and the other disciple did outrun Peter, and came first to the sepulchre.	And they both ran together; but that disciple outran Simon, and came first to the sepulchre.	And both of them were running together, but that disciple ran before Simon and came to the tomb first.
5	And he stooping down, and looking in, saw the linen clothes lying; yet went he not in.	And he looked in, and saw the linen cloths lying: but he did not go in.	And he looked in [and] saw the linen clothes laid [there], but he did not indeed enter.
6	Then cometh Simon Peter following him, and went into the sepulchre, and seeth the linen clothes lie,	And after him came Simon; and he entered the sepulchre, and saw the linen cloths lying;	Now Simon came after him and entered the tomb and saw the linen clothes laid [there]
7	And the napkin, that was about his head, not lying with the linen clothes, but wrapped together in a place by itself.	and the napkin, that had been wrapped about his head, was not with the linen cloths, but was folded up, and laid in a place by itself.	and the cloth that had been bound around his head, not with the linen clothes, but folded and placed aside in a certain place.
8	Then went in also that other disciple, which came first to the sepulchre, and he saw, and believed.	Then entered also the disciple who came first to the sepulchre; and he saw, and believed.	Then that disciple who had come to the tomb first entered also and he saw and believed,
9	For as yet they knew not the scripture, that he must rise again from the dead.	For they had not yet learned from the scriptures, that he was to arise from the dead.	for they did not yet know from the scriptures that he was going to rise from the dead.
10	Then the disciples went away again unto their own home.	And those disciples went away again to their place.	And those disciples went away again to their place.
11	But Mary stood without at the sepulchre weeping: and as she wept, she stooped down, and looked into the sepulchre,	But Mary remained standing at the sepulchre, and weeping; and as she wept, she looked into the sepulchre	Now Mary was standing by the grave and was crying. And as she cried, she looked into the grave.
12	And seeth two angels in white sitting, the one at the head, and the other at the feet, where the body of Jesus had lain.	and saw two angels in white, who were sitting, one at the pillows and one at the feet, where the body of Jesus was laid.	And she saw two angels in white who were sitting, one by his pillows and one at his feet, where the body of Jesus had been laid.

JOHN *Chapter 20*

	KJV	*Murdock*	*Magiera*
13	And they say unto her, Woman, why weepest thou? She saith unto them, Because they have taken away my Lord, and I know not where they have laid him.	And they said to her: Woman, why weepest thou? She said to them: Because they have taken away my Lord, and I know not where they have laid him	And they said to her, "Woman, why are you crying?" She said to them, "Because they have taken away my Lord and I do not know where they have put him."
14	And when she had thus said, she turned herself back, and saw Jesus standing, and knew not that it was Jesus.	Having said this, she turned round, and saw Jesus standing, but did not know that it was Jesus.	She said this and she turned back and saw Jesus standing [there]. And she did not know that it was Jesus.
15	Jesus saith unto her, Woman, why weepest thou? whom seekest thou? She, supposing him to be the gardener, saith unto him, Sir, if thou have borne him hence, tell me where thou hast laid him, and I will take him away.	Jesus said to her: Woman, why weepest thou? and, whom dost thou seek? And she supposed that he was the gardener: and she said to him: My lord, if thou hast borne him away, tell me where thou hast laid him, [and] I will go and take him away.	Jesus said to her, "Woman, why are you crying and whom do you seek?" Now she thought that he was the gardener and said to him, "My lord, if you have taken him, tell me where you have put him. I will go [and] take him away."
16	Jesus saith unto her, Mary. She turned herself, and saith unto him, Rabboni; which is to say, Master.	Jesus said to her: Mary! And she turned, and said to him in Hebrew: Rabbuni; which is interpreted Teacher.	Jesus said to her, "Mary." And she turned around and said to him in Hebrew, "Rabbuli," which means Teacher.
17	Jesus saith unto her, Touch me not; for I am not yet ascended to my Father: but go to my brethren, and say unto them, I ascend unto my Father, and your Father; and to my God, and your God.	Jesus said to her: Touch me not; for not yet have I ascended to my Father. But go to my brethren, and say to them: I ascend to my Father and your Father, and to my God and your God.	Jesus said to her, "Do not touch me, for I have not yet ascended to my Father. But go to my brothers and tell them [that] I ascend to my Father and your Father, and [to] my God and your God."
18	Mary Magdalene came and told the disciples that she had seen the Lord, and that he had spoken these things unto her.	Then came Mary Magdalena, and told the disciples that she had seen our Lord; and that he had said these things to her.	Then Mary Magdalene came and declared to the disciples that she had seen our Lord and that he had told her these [things].
19	Then the same day at evening, being the first day of the week, when the doors were shut where the disciples were assembled for fear of the Jews, came Jesus and stood in the midst, and saith unto them, Peace be unto you.	And on the evening of that first day of the week, the doors being shut where the disciples were, for fear of the Jews, Jesus came, and stood in the midst of them, and said to them: Peace be with you.	Now when it was the evening of that first day in the week and the doors were shut where the disciples were because of fear of the Judeans, Jesus came [and] stood among them and said to them, "Peace [be] with you."
20	And when he had so said, he shewed unto them his hands and his side. Then were the disciples glad, when they saw the Lord.	Having said this, he showed them his hands and his side. And the disciples rejoiced, when they saw our Lord.	He said this and showed them his hands and his side and the disciples rejoiced that they had seen our Lord.
21	Then said Jesus to them again, Peace be unto you: as my Father hath sent me, even so send I you.	And Jesus said to them; Peace be with you. As my Father hath sent me, I also send you.	And Jesus said to them again, "Peace [be] with you. As my Father has sent me, I also send you."
22	And when he had said this, he breathed on them, and saith unto them, Receive ye the Holy Ghost:	And as he said these things, he breathed on them, and said to them: Receive ye the Holy Spirit.	And when he had said these [things], he breathed on them and said to them, "Receive the Holy Spirit.

JOHN Chapter 20

	KJV	Murdock	Magiera
23	Whose soever sins ye remit, they are remitted unto them; and whose soever sins ye retain, they are retained.	If ye shall remit sins to any one, they will be remitted to him; and if ye shall retain [those] of any one, they will be retained.	If you forgive sins of anyone, they will be forgiven him, and if you retain [the sins] of anyone, they will be retained."
24	But Thomas, one of the twelve, called Didymus, was not with them when Jesus came.	But Thomas, who was called the Twin, one of the twelve, was not there with them, when Jesus came.	Now Thomas, one of the twelve who was called the Twin, was not there with them when Jesus came.
25	The other disciples therefore said unto him, We have seen the Lord. But he said unto them, Except I shall see in his hands the print of the nails, and put my finger into the print of the nails, and thrust my hand into his side, I will not believe.	And the disciples said to him: We have seen our Lord. But he said to them: Unless I see in his hands the places of the nails, and put my fingers into them, and extend my hand to his side, I will not believe.	And the disciples told him, "We have seen our Lord." But he said to them, "Unless I see in his hands the locations of the nails and place my fingers in them and stretch out my hand on his side, I will not believe."
26	And after eight days again his disciples were within, and Thomas with them: then came Jesus, the doors being shut, and stood in the midst, and said, Peace be unto you.	And after eight days, the disciples were again within, and Thomas with them: and Jesus came, while the doors were closed, stood in the midst, and said to them: Peace be with you.	And after eight days the disciples again were inside and Thomas [was] with them. And while the doors were closed, Jesus came [and] stood in the middle and said to them, "Peace [be] with you."
27	Then saith he to Thomas, Reach hither thy finger, and behold my hands; and reach hither thy hand, and thrust it into my side: and be not faithless, but believing.	And he said to Thomas: Reach hither thy finger, and look at my hands; and reach out thy hand and extend it to my side: and be not incredulous, but believing.	And he said to Thomas, "Reach your finger here and see my hands. And reach your hand and stretch [it] out on my side and do not be an unbeliever, but a believer."
28	And Thomas answered and said unto him, My Lord and my God.	And Thomas answered, and said to him: My Lord, and my God!	And Thomas answered and said to him, "My Lord and my God."
29	Jesus saith unto him, Thomas, because thou hast seen me, thou hast believed: blessed are they that have not seen, and yet have believed.	Jesus said to him: Now, when thou hast seen me, thou believest: blessed are they, who have not seen me, yet believe.	Jesus said to him, "Now that you have seen me, you have believed. Blessed [are] those who have not seen me and believe."
30	And many other signs truly did Jesus in the presence of his disciples, which are not written in this book:	And many other signs did Jesus before his disciples, which are not written in this book.	Now Jesus did many other signs before his disciples that are not written in this book.
31	But these are written, that ye might believe that Jesus is the Christ, the Son of God; and that believing ye might have life through his name.	But these are written, that ye may believe that Jesus is the Messiah, the Son of God; and that when ye believe, ye may have life eternal by his name.	But even these [things] were written that you would believe that Jesus is the Messiah, the Son of God, and [that] when you believe, you would have eternal life through his name.

Chapter 21

	KJV	Murdock	Magiera
1	After these things Jesus shewed himself again to the disciples at the sea of Tiberias; and on this wise shewed he himself.	After these things, Jesus showed himself again to his disciples, at the sea of Tiberias: and he showed himself thus:	After these [things], Jesus showed himself again to his disciples by the sea of Tiberias. And he appeared like this.

Parallel Translations

JOHN Chapter 21

	KJV	Murdock	Magiera
2	There were together Simon Peter, and Thomas called Didymus, and Nathanael of Cana in Galilee, and the sons of Zebedee, and two other of his disciples.	There were together, Simon Cephas, and Thomas called the Twin, and Nathaniel who was of Cana in Galilee, and the sons of Zebedee, and two other of the disciples.	There were together, Simon Peter and Thomas who was called the Twin, and Nathaniel, who was from Cana of Galilee, and the sons of Zebedee and two of the other disciples.
3	Simon Peter saith unto them, I go a fishing. They say unto him, We also go with thee. They went forth, and entered into a ship immediately; and that night they caught nothing.	Simon Cephas said to them: I will go [and] catch fishes. They said to him: We will go with thee. And they went, and embarked in a ship: and that night, they caught nothing.	Simon Peter said to them, "I am going to catch fish." They said to him, "We will also come with you." And they went out and boarded a ship. And during that night they did not catch anything.
4	But when the morning was now come, Jesus stood on the shore: but the disciples knew not that it was Jesus.	And when it was morning, Jesus stood on the shore of the sea: and the disciples did not know that it was Jesus.	Now when it was morning, Jesus stood on the shore of the sea. And the disciples did not know that it was Jesus.
5	Then Jesus saith unto them, Children, have ye any meat? They answered him, No.	And Jesus said to them: Lads, have ye any thing to eat? They say to him: No.	And Jesus said to them, "Children, do you have anything to eat?" They said to him, "No."
6	And he said unto them, Cast the net on the right side of the ship, and ye shall find. They cast therefore, and now they were not able to draw it for the multitude of fishes.	He said to them: Cast your net on the right side of the ship, and ye will find them. And they cast; and they could not draw up the net, because of the multitude of fishes it contained.	He said to them, "Cast your net from the right side of the boat and you will find." And they cast [it] and they were not able to drag in the net from the great number of fish that it had caught.
7	Therefore that disciple whom Jesus loved saith unto Peter, It is the Lord. Now when Simon Peter heard that it was the Lord, he girt his fisher's coat unto him, (for he was naked,) and did cast himself into the sea.	And that disciple whom Jesus loved, said to Cephas: That is our Lord. And Simon, when he heard that it was our Lord, took his tunic, and girded his loins, for he had been naked, and threw himself into the sea, to go to Jesus.	And that disciple whom Jesus loved said to Peter, "This [man] is our Lord." Now Simon, when he heard that it was our Lord, took his garment [and] girded his loins, because he was naked, and threw himself in the sea to come to Jesus.
8	And the other disciples came in a little ship; (for they were not far from land, but as it were two hundred cubits,) dragging the net with fishes.	But the other disciples came in the ship, for they were not very far from the land, only about two hundred cubits, and they dragged the net with the fishes.	But the other disciples came in the boat, for they were not very far from the land, but [only] about two hundred cubits and they were dragging in that net of fish.
9	As soon then as they were come to land, they saw a fire of coals there, and fish laid thereon, and bread.	And when they came upon the land, they saw coals placed, and fish laid on them, and bread.	And when they had climbed up to the land, they saw burning coals placed [there] and fish placed on them and bread.
10	Jesus saith unto them, Bring of the fish which ye have now caught.	And Jesus said to them: Bring [some] of the fishes, which ye have just caught.	And Jesus said to them, "Bring some of those fish that you have just now caught."
11	Simon Peter went up, and drew the net to land full of great fishes, an hundred and fifty and three: and for all there were so many, yet was not the net broken.	And Simon Cephas embarked, and drew the net to land, full of huge fishes, one hundred and fifty and three. And with all this weight, the net was not rent.	And Simon Peter boarded [the boat] and dragged the net to land, full of large fish, one hundred fifty-three. And with this entire load, that net was not torn.

	KJV	*Murdock*	*Magiera*
	JOHN	*Chapter 21*	
12	Jesus saith unto them, Come and dine. And none of the disciples durst ask him, Who art thou? knowing that it was the Lord.	And Jesus said to them: Come and dine. And no one of the disciples presumed to ask him, who he was; for they knew that it was our Lord.	And Jesus said to them, "Come [and] eat." And not one of the disciples dared to ask him who he was, because they knew that he was our Lord.
13	Jesus then cometh, and taketh bread, and giveth them, and fish likewise.	And Jesus came, and took bread and fishes, and gave to his disciples.	Now Jesus came near and took the bread and fish and gave to them.
14	This is now the third time that Jesus shewed himself to his disciples, after that he was risen from the dead.	This is the third time that Jesus appeared to his disciples when he had arisen from the dead.	This [was] the third time Jesus had appeared to his disciples after he had risen from the dead.
15	So when they had dined, Jesus saith to Simon Peter, Simon, son of Jonas, lovest thou me more than these? He saith unto him, Yea, Lord; thou knowest that I love thee. He saith unto him, Feed my lambs.	And when they had dined, Jesus said to Simon Cephas: Simon, son of Jonas, lovest thou me, more than these do? He said to him: Yes, my Lord: thou knowest that I love thee. Jesus said to him: Feed my lambs for me.	Now after they had eaten, Jesus said to Simon Peter, "Simon, son of Jonas, do you love me more than these?" He said to him, "Yes, my Lord, you know that I love you." He said to him, "Feed my lambs for me."
16	He saith to him again the second time, Simon, son of Jonas, lovest thou me? He saith unto him, Yea, Lord; thou knowest that I love thee. He saith unto him, Feed my sheep.	Again, he said to him the second time: Simon, son of Jonas, lovest thou me? He said to him: Yes, my Lord; thou knowest that I love thee. Jesus said to him: Feed my sheep for me.	He said to him again a second time, "Simon, son of Jonas, do you love me?" He said to him, "Yes, my Lord, you know that I love you." Jesus said to him, "Feed my sheep for me."
17	He saith unto him the third time, Simon, son of Jonas, lovest thou me? Peter was grieved because he said unto him the third time, Lovest thou me? And he said unto him, Lord, thou knowest all things; thou knowest that I love thee. Jesus saith unto him, Feed my sheep.	Again, Jesus said to him the third time: Simon, son of Jonas, lovest thou me? And it grieved Cephas, that he said to him the third time, Lovest thou me; and he said to him: My Lord, thou understandest all things, thou knowest that I love thee. Jesus said to him: Feed my sheep for me.	He said to him a third time, "Simon, son of Jonas, do you love me?" And Peter was sad, because he had said to him a third time, "Do you love me?" And he said to him, "My Lord, you know everything. You know that I love you." Jesus said to him, "Feed my ewes for me.
18	Verily, verily, I say unto thee, When thou wast young, thou girdedst thyself, and walkedst whither thou wouldest: but when thou shalt be old, thou shalt stretch forth thy hands, and another shall gird thee, and carry thee whither thou wouldest not.	Verily, verily, I say to thee: When thou wast young, thou girdedst thy own loins, and walkedst whither it pleased thee: but when thou shalt be old, thou wilt extend thy hands, and another will gird thy loins for thee, and will conduct thee whither thou wouldst not.	Truly, truly I say to you, when you were a boy, you girded your loins by yourself and you walked to where you wanted, but when you grow old, you will stretch out your hands and another will gird your loins for you and conduct you to where you do not want [to go]."
19	This spake he, signifying by what death he should glorify God. And when he had spoken this, he saith unto him, Follow me.	And this he said, to show by what death he was to glorify God. And having said these things, he said to him: Follow me.	Now he said this to show by what death he would glorify God. And after he had said these [things], he said to him, "Follow me."
20	Then Peter, turning about, seeth the disciple whom Jesus loved following; which also leaned on his breast at supper, and said, Lord, which is he that betrayeth thee?	And Simon turned himself, and saw coming after him, that disciple whom Jesus loved, who fell on the breast of Jesus at the supper, and said, My Lord, who is it will betray thee?	And Simon Peter turned and saw the disciple whom Jesus loved who followed him, who fell on the breast of Jesus during the supper and said, 'My Lord, who will betray you?"

Parallel Translations

JOHN *Chapter 21*

	KJV	Murdock	Magiera
21	Peter seeing him saith to Jesus, Lord, and what shall this man do?	Him Cephas saw, and said to Jesus: My Lord, as for this man, what?	When Peter saw this [man], he said to Jesus, "My Lord, and what [of] this [man]?"
22	Jesus saith unto him, If I will that he tarry till I come, what is that to thee? follow thou me.	Jesus said to him: If I will, that he abide here until I come, what [is that] to thee? Follow thou me.	Jesus said to him, "If I desire that this [man] should remain until I come, what is it to you? Follow me."
23	Then went this saying abroad among the brethren, that that disciple should not die: yet Jesus said not unto him, He shall not die; but, If I will that he tarry till I come, what is that to thee?	And this saying went forth among the brethren, that this disciple would not die. Yet Jesus did not say, that he would not die; but, If I will that he abide here until I come, what [is that] to thee.	And this saying went out among the brothers that that disciple would not die. But Jesus did not say that he would not die, but rather, "If I desire that this [man] should remain until I come, what is it to you?"
24	This is the disciple which testifieth of these things, and wrote these things: and we know that his testimony is true.	This is the disciple who hath testified of all these things, and hath written them: and we know, that his testimony is true.	This is the disciple who testified about all these [things] and also wrote them and we know that his testimony is true.
25	And there are also many other things which Jesus did, the which, if they should be written every one, I suppose that even the world itself could not contain the books that should be written. Amen.	And there are also many other things, which Jesus did; which, if written out with particularity, the world itself, as I suppose, would not suffice for the books that would be written.	Now there are also many other [things] that Jesus did, which if they were written one by one, not even the world (as I suppose) would be sufficient for the books that would be written.

Parallel Translations

	KJV	*Murdock*	*Magiera*
ACTS	*Chapter 1*		
1	The former treatise have I made, O Theophilus, of all that Jesus began both to do and teach,	The former book have I written, O Theophilus concerning all the things which our Lord Jesus Messiah began to do and teach,	I wrote the former book, oh Theophilus, concerning all those [things] that our Lord Jesus Christ began to do and to teach,
2	Until the day in which he was taken up, after that he through the Holy Ghost had given commandments unto the apostles whom he had chosen:	until the day when he was taken up, after he had instructed those legates whom he had chosen by the Holy Spirit.	until that day in which he was taken up, after he had commanded the apostles, those whom he had chosen by the Holy Spirit,
3	To whom also he shewed himself alive after his passion by many infallible proofs, being seen of them forty days, and speaking of the things pertaining to the kingdom of God:	To whom also he showed himself alive after he had suffered, by numerous signs, during forty days, while he was seen by them, and spoke of the kingdom of God.	those to whom he also showed himself alive after he had suffered with many signs for forty days, while he was seen by them and spoke about the kingdom of God.
4	And, being assembled together with them, commanded them that they should not depart from Jerusalem, but wait for the promise of the Father, which, saith he, ye have heard of me.	And when he had eaten bread with them, he instructed them not to depart from Jerusalem, but to wait for the promise of the Father, which (said he) ye have heard from me.	And as he ate bread with them, he commanded them that they should not leave Jerusalem, but that they should wait for the promise of the Father [about] which [he said], "You have heard from me.
5	For John truly baptized with water; but ye shall be baptized with the Holy Ghost not many days hence.	For John baptized with water; but ye will be baptized with the Holy Spirit after not many days.	For John baptized with water, yet you will be baptized with the Holy Spirit after not many days."
6	When they therefore were come together, they asked of him, saying, Lord, wilt thou at this time restore again the kingdom to Israel?	And they, when assembled, asked him and said to him: Our Lord, wilt thou at this time restore the kingdom to Israel?	Now while they were assembled, they asked him and said to him, "Our Lord, at this time will you restore the kingdom to Israel?"
7	And he said unto them, It is not for you to know the times or the seasons, which the Father hath put in his own power.	He said to them: It is not yours, to know the time or times which God hath placed in his own power.	He said to them, "This is not yours to know the time or these times that the Father has placed in his own authority.
8	But ye shall receive power, after that the Holy Ghost is come upon you: and ye shall be witnesses unto me both in Jerusalem, and in all Judaea, and in Samaria, and unto the uttermost part of the earth.	But when the Holy Spirit shall come upon you, ye will receive energy, and will be witnesses for me in Jerusalem, and in all Judaea, and also among the Samaritans, and unto the ends of the earth.	But when the Holy Spirit comes on you, you will receive power and you will be witnesses for me in Jerusalem and in all Judea and also among the Samaritans, even to the ends of the earth."
9	And when he had spoken these things, while they beheld, he was taken up; and a cloud received him out of their sight.	And when he had said these things, while they beheld him, he was taken up, and a cloud received him, and he was hidden from their eyes.	And after he said these [things], while they watched him, he was taken up and a cloud received him and he was hidden from their eyes.
10	And while they looked stedfastly toward heaven as he went up, behold, two men stood by them in white apparel;	And while they were looking toward heaven, as he departed, two men were found standing near them, in white garments,	And while they were staring into heaven as he was going away, two men were found standing near them in white clothing.

Parallel Translations

	KJV	Murdock	Magiera
	ACTS Chapter 1		
11	Which also said, Ye men of Galilee, why stand ye gazing up into heaven? this same Jesus, which is taken up from you into heaven, shall so come in like manner as ye have seen him go into heaven.	and saying to them: Ye Galilean men, why stand ye and look toward heaven? This Jesus, who is taken up from you to heaven, will so come, as ye have seen him ascend to heaven.	And they said to them, "Galilean men, why are you standing and staring into heaven? This Jesus, who was taken up from you into heaven, will come in the same manner as you have seen him who went up to heaven."
12	Then returned they unto Jerusalem from the mount called Olivet, which is from Jerusalem a sabbath day's journey.	And afterwards they returned to Jerusalem from the mount called the place of Olives, which was near to Jerusalem, and distant from it about seven furlongs.	And afterwards, they returned to Jerusalem from the mountain that is called the Mount of Olives, which was near Jerusalem and distant from it about seven furlongs.
13	And when they were come in, they went up into an upper room, where abode both Peter, and James, and John, and Andrew, Philip, and Thomas, Bartholomew, and Matthew, James the son of Alphaeus, and Simon Zelotes, and Judas the brother of James.	And when they had entered, they went to an upper chamber; where were Peter, and John, and James, and Andrew, and Philip, and Thomas, and Matthew, and Bartholomew, and James the son of Alpheus, and Simon Zelotes, and Judas the son of James.	And after they entered, they went up to an upper room, in which Peter and John and James and Andrew and Philip and Thomas and Matthew and Bartholomew and James, the son of Alphaeus, and Simon, the zealot, and Judas, the son of James were staying.
14	These all continued with one accord in prayer and supplication, with the women, and Mary the mother of Jesus, and with his brethren.	All these unitedly persevered in prayer, with one soul, together with the women, and with Mary the mother of Jesus, and with his brothers.	All of these as one were steadfast in prayer with one soul with the women and with Mary, the mother of Jesus, and with his brothers.
15	And in those days Peter stood up in the midst of the disciples, and said, (the number of names together were about an hundred and twenty,)	And in those days stood up Simon Cephas in the midst of the disciples, (the persons there assembled being about one hundred and twenty,) and said:	And among them in those days, Simon Peter stood up in the middle of the disciples (now there was a gathering there of about one hundred and twenty men) and he said,
16	Men and brethren, this scripture must needs have been fulfilled, which the Holy Ghost by the mouth of David spake before concerning Judas, which was guide to them that took Jesus.	Men, brethren, it was right that the scripture should be fulfilled, which the Holy Spirit spake, by the mouth of David, concerning Judas who was guide to them that apprehended Jesus.	"Men, our brothers, it was right that the scripture should be fulfilled, which the Holy Spirit foretold by the mouth of David, about Judas who was a guide to those who arrested Jesus,
17	For he was numbered with us, and had obtained part of this ministry.	For he was numbered with us, and had a part in this ministry.	because he was numbered with us and he had a portion in this ministry.
18	Now this man purchased a field with the reward of iniquity; and falling headlong, he burst asunder in the midst, and all his bowels gushed out.	He purchased a field with the wages of sin; and he fell upon his face on the ground, and burst in the middle, and all his entrails were poured out.	This is he who acquired a field for himself from the wage of sin and fell on his face on the ground and burst from his middle and all his insides poured out.
19	And it was known unto all the dwellers at Jerusalem; insomuch as that field is called in their proper tongue, Aceldama, that is to say, The field of blood.	And this was known to all that dwelt at Jerusalem; so that the field was called, in the language of the country, Aceldama, which is interpreted Field of Blood.	And this was known to all who lived in Jerusalem and so that field was called in the language of the country, "Akeldama," which [by] interpretation is, "Field of Blood."

	KJV	Murdock	Magiera
	ACTS Chapter 1		
20	For it is written in the book of Psalms, Let his habitation be desolate, and let no man dwell therein: and his bishoprick let another take.	For it is written, in the book of Psalms: Let his habitation be desolate, and let no resident be in it; and let another take his service.	For it is written in the book of Psalms: LET HIS HABITATION BE DESOLATE and LET NO ONE BE A DWELLER IN IT AND LET ANOTHER TAKE HIS MINISTRY.
21	Wherefore of these men which have companied with us all the time that the Lord Jesus went in and out among us,	It should therefore be, that one of these persons, who have been with us all the time that our Lord Jesus went in and out with us,	It is right, therefore, for one of these men who were with us during this whole time in which our Lord Jesus entered and went out among us,
22	Beginning from the baptism of John, unto that same day that he was taken up from us, must one be ordained to be a witness with us of his resurrection.	commencing from the baptism of John, unto the day he was taken up from us,---should be, with us, a witness of his resurrection.	who began from the baptism of John until the day that he was taken up from [being] with us, to be a witness of his resurrection with us."
23	And they appointed two, Joseph called Barsabas, who was surnamed Justus, and Matthias.	And they proposed two, Joseph called Barsabas, whose surname was Justus, and Matthias.	And they caused two to stand, Joseph, who was called Barsabas, who was named Justus, and Matthias.
24	And they prayed, and said, Thou, Lord, which knowest the hearts of all men, shew whether of these two thou hast chosen,	And when they had prayed, they said: Thou, Lord, knowest what is in the hearts of all, manifest which thou hast chosen of these two,	And when they prayed, they said, "LORD, you know what is in the hearts of all. Reveal the one that you have chosen of these two,
25	That he may take part of this ministry and apostleship, from which Judas by transgression fell, that he might go to his own place.	that he should take part in this ministry and legateship, from which Judas broke away, that he might go to his own place.	that he should receive a portion of the ministry and apostleship from which Judas left to go to his place.
26	And they gave forth their lots; and the lot fell upon Matthias; and he was numbered with the eleven apostles.	And they cast lots, and it came upon Matthias; and he was numbered with the eleven legates.	And they cast lots and it fell on Matthias and he was numbered with the eleven apostles.
	Chapter 2		
1	And when the day of Pentecost was fully come, they were all with one accord in one place.	And when the days of pentecost were fully come, while they were all assembled together,	And when the days of Pentecost were fulfilled as all were assembled together,
2	And suddenly there came a sound from heaven as of a rushing mighty wind, and it filled all the house where they were sitting.	suddenly there was a sound from heaven, as of a violent wind; and the whole house where they were sitting was filled with it.	suddenly there was a sound from heaven as a powerful wind and the whole house in which they were sitting was filled with it.
3	And there appeared unto them cloven tongues like as of fire, and it sat upon each of them.	And there appeared to them tongues, which were divided like flame; and they rested upon each of them.	And tongues that were divided appeared to them as fire and sat on each one of them.
4	And they were all filled with the Holy Ghost, and began to speak with other tongues, as the Spirit gave them utterance.	And they were all filled with the Holy Spirit, and began to speak in diverse languages, as the Spirit gave them to speak.	And all of them were filled with the Holy Spirit and they began to speak in different languages, as the Spirit gave them to speak.

Parallel Translations

	KJV	*Murdock*	*Magiera*

ACTS *Chapter 2*

	KJV	Murdock	Magiera
5	And there were dwelling at Jerusalem Jews, devout men, out of every nation under heaven.	Now there were resident at Jerusalem persons who feared God, Jews from all the nations under heaven.	And there were men who were living in Jerusalem who feared God, Judeans from all the nations that are under heaven.
6	Now when this was noised abroad, the multitude came together, and were confounded, because that every man heard them speak in his own language.	And when that sound occurred, all the people collected together; and they were agitated, because they every one heard them speaking in their own languages.	And when that sound occurred, all the people gathered and were troubled, because each one of them heard that they were speaking in their [own] languages.
7	And they were all amazed and marvelled, saying one to another, Behold, are not all these which speak Galilaeans?	And they were all astonished, and wondered, saying one to another: All these who speak behold, are they not Galileans?	And all of them were amazed and wondered, saying to each other, "All these who are speaking, behold, are they not Galileans?
8	And how hear we every man in our own tongue, wherein we were born?	And how do we hear, each his own language, in which we were born?	How do we each hear the language into which we were born?
9	Parthians, and Medes, and Elamites, and the dwellers in Mesopotamia, and in Judaea, and Cappadocia, in Pontus, and Asia,	Parthians, and Medes, and Elamites, and those dwelling between the rivers, Jews and Cappadocians, and those from the region of Pontus and of Asia,	Parthians and Medes and Elamites, and those who dwell in Mesopotamia, Judeans and Cappadocians and those from the region of Pontus and of Asia,
10	Phrygia, and Pamphylia, in Egypt, and in the parts of Libya about Cyrene, and strangers of Rome, Jews and proselytes,	and those from the region of Phrygia, and of Pamphylia, and of Egypt, and of the parts of Lybia near Cyrene, and those who have come from Rome, Jews and proselytes;	and those from the region of Phrygia and of Pamphylia and of Egypt and of the regions of Libya that are near to Cyrene, and those who have come from Rome, Judeans and proselytes,
11	Cretes and Arabians, we do hear them speak in our tongues the wonderful works of God.	and those from Crete, and Arabians.---Lo, we hear them speak in our own languages the wonders of God.	and those from Crete, and Arabians, behold, we hear them, that they are speaking in our languages the wonders of God."
12	And they were all amazed, and were in doubt, saying one to another, What meaneth this?	And they all wondered and were astonished, saying one to another: From whom is this thing?	And all of them were amazed and wondered, saying to one another, "What is this event?"
13	Others mocking said, These men are full of new wine.	Others however ridiculed them, saying: They have drunken new wine, and are intoxicated.	And others were mocking them, saying, "These [men] have drunk new wine and are intoxicated."
14	But Peter, standing up with the eleven, lifted up his voice, and said unto them, Ye men of Judaea, and all ye that dwell at Jerusalem, be this known unto you, and hearken to my words:	And afterwards Simon Cephas rose up, with the eleven legates, and elevated his voice, and said to them: Men, Jews, and all ye that reside at Jerusalem; be this known to you, and hearken ye to my words.	Afterward, Simon Peter stood up with the eleven apostles and raised his voice and said to them, "Men, Judeans, and all who live in Jerusalem, let this be known to you and listen to my words.
15	For these are not drunken, as ye suppose, seeing it is but the third hour of the day.	For these are not intoxicated, as ye suppose: for lo, it is yet but the third hour.	For these [men] are not intoxicated, as you suppose, for behold, it is still only the third hour.

	KJV	*Murdock*	*Magiera*

ACTS *Chapter 2*

Verse	KJV	Murdock	Magiera
16	But this is that which was spoken by the prophet Joel;	But this is what was spoken by Joel the prophet:	But this is that which was spoken by Joel the prophet:
17	And it shall come to pass in the last days, saith God, I will pour out of my Spirit upon all flesh: and your sons and your daughters shall prophesy, and your young men shall see visions, and your old men shall dream dreams:	It shall be in the last days, saith God, that I will pour my Spirit upon all flesh: and your sons shall prophesy, and your daughters and your young men shall see visions, and your old men shall dream dreams.	IT WILL BE IN THE LAST DAYS, said God, [THAT] I WILL POUR OUT MY SPIRIT ON ALL FLESH. YOUR SONS WILL PROPHESY AND YOUR DAUGHTERS AND YOUR YOUNG MEN WILL SEE VISIONS, AND YOUR OLD MEN WILL DREAM DREAMS.
18	And on my servants and on my handmaidens I will pour out in those days of my Spirit; and they shall prophesy:	And upon my servants and my handmaids will I pour my Spirit, in those days, and they shall prophesy.	AND ON MY SERVANTS AND ON MY HANDMAIDENS I WILL POUR OUT MY SPIRIT IN THOSE DAYS AND THEY WILL PROPHESY.
19	And I will shew wonders in heaven above, and signs in the earth beneath; blood, and fire, and vapour of smoke:	And I will give signs in heaven, and prodigies on earth, blood, and fire, and vapor of smoke.	AND I WILL GIVE SIGNS IN HEAVEN AND MIGHTY WORKS ON THE EARTH, BLOOD AND FIRE AND VAPOR OF SMOKE.
20	The sun shall be turned into darkness, and the moon into blood, before that great and notable day of the Lord come:	And the sun shall be turned into darkness, and the moon into blood, before that great and fearful day of the Lord come.	THE SUN WILL BE TURNED TO DARKNESS AND THE MOON INTO BLOOD BEFORE THE GREAT AND TERRIBLE DAY OF THE LORD WILL COME.
21	And it shall come to pass, that whosoever shall call on the name of the Lord shall be saved.	And it shall be, that whoever will call on the name of the Lord, shall live.	AND IT WILL BE [THAT] EVERYONE WHO CALLS ON THE NAME OF THE LORD WILL LIVE.
22	Ye men of Israel, hear these words; Jesus of Nazareth, a man approved of God among you by miracles and wonders and signs, which God did by him in the midst of you, as ye yourselves also know:	Men, sons of Israel, hear ye these words: Jesus the Nazarean, a man made manifest among you by God, by those deeds of power and prodigies which God wrought among you by his hand, as ye yourselves know;	Men, sons of Israel, hear these words! Jesus the Nazarene, a man who was shown to you by God with miracles and with signs and with mighty works that God did among you by his hand, as you know,
23	Him, being delivered by the determinate counsel and foreknowledge of God, ye have taken, and by wicked hands have crucified and slain:	him, being hereto appointed by the prescience and the good pleasure of God,---ye have delivered into the hands of the wicked; and have crucified and slain.	this [man], who was set apart for this by the foreknowledge and will of God, you delivered into the hands of ungodly [men] and you crucified and you killed.
24	Whom God hath raised up, having loosed the pains of death: because it was not possible that he should be holden of it.	But God hath resuscitated him, and hath loosed the cords of the grave; because it could not be, that he should be held in the grave.	But God raised him and released the cords of Sheol, because it was not possible that he should be held captive in Sheol.
25	For David speaketh concerning him, I foresaw the Lord always before my face, for he is on my right hand, that I should not be moved:	For David said of him: I foresaw my Lord at all times; for he is on my right hand, so that I shall not be moved.	For David spoke about him, I FORESAW MY LORD AT ALL TIMES, FOR HE IS AT MY RIGHT HAND, SO THAT I WILL NOT BE MOVED.

Parallel Translations

	KJV	*Murdock*	*Magiera*
ACTS	*Chapter 2*		
26	Therefore did my heart rejoice, and my tongue was glad; moreover also my flesh shall rest in hope:	Therefore my heart doth rejoice, and my glory exult, and also my body shall abide in hope.	BECAUSE OF THIS, MY HEART REJOICES AND MY PRAISE FLOURISHES AND ALSO MY BODY WILL LIE DOWN IN HOPE,
27	Because thou wilt not leave my soul in hell, neither wilt thou suffer thine Holy One to see corruption.	For thou wilt not leave my soul in the grave, nor wilt thou give thy pious one to see corruption.	BECAUSE YOU WILL NOT LEAVE MY SOUL IN SHEOL, NEITHER WILL YOU ALLOW YOUR INNOCENT [ONE] TO SEE CORRUPTION.
28	Thou hast made known to me the ways of life; thou shalt make me full of joy with thy countenance.	Thou hast revealed to me the path of life; thou wilt fill me with joy with thy presence.	YOU HAVE REVEALED TO ME THE WAY OF LIFE. YOU WILL FILL ME WITH GLADNESS WITH YOUR PRESENCE.
29	Men and brethren, let me freely speak unto you of the patriarch David, that he is both dead and buried, and his sepulchre is with us unto this day.	Men, brethren, I may speak to you explicitly of the patriarch David, that he died, and also was buried; and his sepulchre is with us to this day.	Men, our brothers, allow [me] to speak boldly with you about the patriarch David, who is dead and also buried and whose tomb is with us until today.
30	Therefore being a prophet, and knowing that God had sworn with an oath to him, that of the fruit of his loins, according to the flesh, he would raise up Christ to sit on his throne;	For he was a prophet, and he knew, that God had sworn to him by an oath: Of the fruit of thy bowels, I will seat [one] on thy throne.	For he was a prophet and knew that God had sworn oaths to him: OF THE FRUIT OF YOUR LOINS I WILL ESTABLISH [ONE] ON YOUR THRONE.
31	He seeing this before spake of the resurrection of Christ, that his soul was not left in hell, neither his flesh did see corruption.	And he foresaw, and spoke of the resurrection of Messiah, that he was not left in the grave, neither did his body see corruption.	And he foresaw and spoke about the resurrection of Christ: HE WAS NOT LEFT IN SHEOL, NEITHER DID HIS BODY SEE CORRUPTION.
32	This Jesus hath God raised up, whereof we all are witnesses.	This Jesus hath God resuscitated; and we all are his witnesses.	This Jesus has God raised and all of us are his witnesses.
33	Therefore being by the right hand of God exalted, and having received of the Father the promise of the Holy Ghost, he hath shed forth this, which ye now see and hear.	And he it is, who is exalted by the right hand of God, and hath received from the Father a promise respecting the Holy Spirit, and hath sent this gift which, lo, ye see and hear.	And this is he who is elevated at the right hand of God and received from the Father the promise concerning the Holy Spirit. And he has poured out this gift that behold, you see and you hear.
34	For David is not ascended into the heavens: but he saith himself, The LORD said unto my Lord, Sit thou on my right hand,	For David hath not ascended into heaven; because he himself said: The Lord said to my Lord, seat thyself at my right hand,	For David did not ascend into heaven, because he said, THE LORD SAID TO MY LORD, SIT AT MY RIGHT HAND
35	Until I make thy foes thy footstool.	until I shall place thy enemies a footstool to thy feet.	UNTIL I PLACE YOUR ENEMIES [AS] A FOOTSTOOL FOR YOUR FEET.
36	Therefore let all the house of Israel know assuredly, that God hath made that same Jesus, whom ye have crucified, both Lord and Christ.	Therefore, let all the house of Israel know, assuredly, that God hath made that Jesus whom ye crucified, to be Lord and Messiah.	Therefore, all the house of Israel should truly know that God has made this Jesus, whom you crucified, LORD and Christ."

Parallel Translations

	KJV	*Murdock*	*Magiera*
ACTS	*Chapter 2*		
37	Now when they heard this, they were pricked in their heart, and said unto Peter and to the rest of the apostles, Men and brethren, what shall we do?	And when they heard these things, they were agitated in their heart; and they said to Simon and to the rest of the legates: Brethren, what shall we do?	And when they heard these [things], they were moved in their heart[s] and said to Simon and to the rest of the apostles, "What should we do, our brothers?"
38	Then Peter said unto them, Repent, and be baptized every one of you in the name of Jesus Christ for the remission of sins, and ye shall receive the gift of the Holy Ghost.	Simon said to them: Repent, and be baptized every one of you, in the name of the Lord Jesus, for the remission of sins; so that ye may receive the gift of the Holy Spirit.	Simon said to them, "Repent and be baptized, each one of you, in the name of the LORD Jesus for the forgiveness of sins, so that you will receive the gift of the Holy Spirit.
39	For the promise is unto you, and to your children, and to all that are afar off, even as many as the Lord our God shall call.	For the promise is to you, and to your children, and to all those afar off whom God will call.	For the promise is to you and to your children and to all those who are far away, those whom God will call."
40	And with many other words did he testify and exhort, saying, Save yourselves from this untoward generation.	And in many other words he testified to them, and entreated of them, saying: Live ye from this perverse generation.	And with many other words he testified to them and begged them, saying, "Live apart from this perverse generation."
41	Then they that gladly received his word were baptized: and the same day there were added unto them about three thousand souls.	And some of them readily received his discourse, and believed, and were baptized. And there were added, on that day, about three thousand souls.	And some of them willingly received his word and believed and were baptized. And there were added in that day about three thousand people.
42	And they continued stedfastly in the apostles' doctrine and fellowship, and in breaking of bread, and in prayers.	And they persevered in the doctrine of the legates; and were associated together in prayer, and in breaking the eucharist.	And they were steadfast in the teaching of the apostles and were fellowshipping in prayer and in the breaking [of the bread] of communion.
43	And fear came upon every soul: and many wonders and signs were done by the apostles.	And fear was on every mind: and many signs and prodigies were [wrought] by the hand of the legates in Jerusalem.	And fear was to every person and many signs and mighty works occurred by way of the apostles in Jerusalem.
44	And all that believed were together, and had all things common;	And all they who believed, were together; and whatever belonged to them, was of the community.	And all those who had believed were as one and everything that they had was held in common.
45	And sold their possessions and goods, and parted them to all men, as every man had need.	And they who had a possession, sold it, and divided to each one as he had need.	And those who had wealth sold it and distributed to each one according to whatever was needed.
46	And they, continuing daily with one accord in the temple, and breaking bread from house to house, did eat their meat with gladness and singleness of heart,	And they continued daily in the temple, with one soul: and at home, they broke bread and took food rejoicing, and in the simplicity of their heart.	And every day they were steadfast in the temple with one soul and at home they were breaking bread and were receiving food, rejoicing. And in the simplicity of their heart[s]
47	Praising God, and having favour with all the people. And the Lord added to the church daily such as should be saved.	And they praised God, and had favor with all the people. And our Lord added daily to the assembly those who became alive.	they were praising God, while giving mercies before all the people. And our Lord added every day those who were being given life in the church.

Parallel Translations

ACTS *Chapter 3*

	KJV	*Murdock*	*Magiera*
1	Now Peter and John went up together into the temple at the hour of prayer, being the ninth hour.	And it occurred, as Simon Cephas and John went together up to the temple, at the time of prayer, being the ninth hour,	And it happened that while Simon Peter and John were going up together to the temple at the time of prayer at the ninth hour,
2	And a certain man lame from his mother's womb was carried, whom they laid daily at the gate of the temple which is called Beautiful, to ask alms of them that entered into the temple;	that, lo, those accustomed to bring a man lame from his mother's womb, brought him and laid him at the gate of the temple called Beautiful; that he might ask alms of those going into the temple.	and behold, men were carrying a certain man who was lame from the womb of his mother. These [were men] who were accustomed to bringing and laying him at the gate of the temple, which was called Beautiful, so that he could ask alms from those who were entering the temple.
3	Who seeing Peter and John about to go into the temple asked an alms.	This man, when he saw Simon and John going into the temple, asked them to give him alms.	This [man], when he saw Simon and John entering the temple, begged them to give him alms.
4	And Peter, fastening his eyes upon him with John, said, Look on us.	And Simon and John looked on him, and said to him: Look on us.	And Simon and John looked at him and said to him, "Look at us."
5	And he gave heed unto them, expecting to receive something of them.	And he looked on them, expecting to receive something from them.	And he looked at them, expecting to receive something from them.
6	Then Peter said, Silver and gold have I none; but such as I have give I thee: In the name of Jesus Christ of Nazareth rise up and walk.	Simon said to him: Gold and silver, I have not; but what I have, I give to thee; in the name of our Lord Jesus Messiah, the Nazarean, rise up and walk.	Simon said to him, "I have no gold and silver, but what I have I will give to you. In the name of Jesus Christ the Nazarene, rise up [and] walk."
7	And he took him by the right hand, and lifted him up: and immediately his feet and ankle bones received strength.	And he took him by the right hand, and raised him up: and forthwith, his feet and his heels recovered strength.	And he took him by his right hand and raised him up. And immediately his feet and his ankles were strengthened.
8	And he leaping up stood, and walked, and entered with them into the temple, walking, and leaping, and praising God.	And he sprang, stood up, and walked: and he entered with them into the temple, walking, and leaping, and praising God.	And he leaped up [and] stood and walked and entered with them into the temple, walking and leaping and praising God.
9	And all the people saw him walking and praising God:	And all the people saw him, as he walked and praised God.	And all the people saw him walking and praising God.
10	And they knew that it was he which sat for alms at the Beautiful gate of the temple: and they were filled with wonder and amazement at that which had happened unto him.	And they knew that he was the beggar, who sat daily and asked alms, at the gate called Beautiful: and they were filled with wonder and admiration at what had occurred.	And they recognized that he was that beggar who sat every day and asked alms at the gate that was called Beautiful. And they were filled with amazement and wonder at what had happened.
11	And as the lame man which was healed held Peter and John, all the people ran together unto them in the porch that is called Solomon's, greatly wondering.	And as he held fast to Simon and John, all the people admiring ran to them at the portico called Solomon's.	And while he held Simon and John, all the people, being amazed, ran to them, to the porch that was called Solomon's [Porch].

Parallel Translations

	KJV	Murdock	Magiera

ACTS *Chapter 3*

Verse	KJV	Murdock	Magiera
12	And when Peter saw it, he answered unto the people, Ye men of Israel, why marvel ye at this? or why look ye so earnestly on us, as though by our own power or holiness we had made this man to walk?	And when Simon saw [it], he answered and said to them: Men, sons of Israel, why do ye wonder at this? or why do ye gaze on us, as if by our own power or authority we had made this man to walk?	And when Simon saw [it], he answered and said to them, "Men, sons of Israel, why do you wonder at this [man]? Or why do you look at us as if by our own power or by our authority we did this, so that this [man] would walk?
13	The God of Abraham, and of Isaac, and of Jacob, the God of our fathers, hath glorified his Son Jesus; whom ye delivered up, and denied him in the presence of Pilate, when he was determined to let him go.	The God of Abraham and of Isaac and of Jacob, the God of our fathers, hath glorified his Son Jesus; whom ye delivered up, and denied in the presence of Pilate, when he would have justified him and set him free.	The God of Abraham and of Isaac and of Jacob, the God of our fathers, has glorified his Son Jesus, whom you delivered up and denied in the presence of Pilate, after he had thought it right to let him go.
14	But ye denied the Holy One and the Just, and desired a murderer to be granted unto you;	But ye denied the holy and just One, and demanded that a murderer should be released to you.	But you denied the Holy and Just [one] and requested that a murderer should be given to you.
15	And killed the Prince of life, whom God hath raised from the dead; whereof we are witnesses.	And that Prince of life ye slew; and him, hath God raised from the dead, and all of us are witnesses of it.	And you killed that Prince of Life, whom God raised from the dead. And we all are his witnesses.
16	And his name through faith in his name hath made this man strong, whom ye see and know: yea, the faith which is by him hath given him this perfect soundness in the presence of you all.	And, by the faith in his name, he hath strengthened and cured this man, whom ye see and know; and faith in him hath given the man this soundness before you all.	And by the faith of his name he has strengthened and healed this [man], whom you see and know, and faith that is in him has given him this wholeness before all of you.
17	And now, brethren, I wot that through ignorance ye did it, as did also your rulers.	And now, my brethren, I know that through misapprehensions ye did this, as did also your chiefs:	But now, our brothers, I know that through ignorance you did this, as did your leaders.
18	But those things, which God before had shewed by the mouth of all his prophets, that Christ should suffer, he hath so fulfilled.	and God, according as he had previously announced by the mouth of all the prophets that the Messiah would suffer, hath in this manner fulfilled [it].	And God, according to what he preached beforehand by the mouth of all the prophets, that his Messiah would suffer, has fulfilled [it] in this manner.
19	Repent ye therefore, and be converted, that your sins may be blotted out, when the times of refreshing shall come from the presence of the Lord;	Repent, therefore, and be converted; that so your sins may be blotted out, and times of rest may come to you from before the face of the Lord;	Repent, therefore, and be converted, so that your sins will be blotted out and times of rest will come to you from the presence of the LORD.
20	And he shall send Jesus Christ, which before was preached unto you:	and he may send to you him, who was made ready for you, Jesus the Messiah:	And he will send to you him who was prepared for you, Jesus Christ,
21	Whom the heaven must receive until the times of restitution of all things, which God hath spoken by the mouth of all his holy prophets since the world began.	whom the heavens must retain, until the completion of the times of those things, which God hath spoken by the mouth of his holy prophets of old.	whom it is required for heaven to retain, until the fullness of the times of all those [things] that God spoke by the mouth of his holy prophets of old.

Parallel Translations

ACTS Chapter 3

	KJV	Murdock	Magiera
22	For Moses truly said unto the fathers, A prophet shall the Lord your God raise up unto you of your brethren, like unto me; him shall ye hear in all things whatsoever he shall say unto you.	For Moses said: A prophet, like me, will the Lord raise up to you, from among your brethren; to him hearken ye, in all that he shall say to you.	For Moses said: THE LORD WILL RAISE UP A PROPHET FOR YOU FROM YOUR BROTHERS LIKE ME. HEAR HIM IN WHATEVER HE SPEAKS TO YOU.
23	And it shall come to pass, that every soul, which will not hear that prophet, shall be destroyed from among the people.	And it will be, that every soul who will not hearken to that prophet, that soul shall perish from his people.	AND IT WILL BE [THAT] EVERY PERSON THAT DOES NOT HEAR THAT PROPHET, THAT PERSON WILL PERISH FROM HIS PEOPLE.
24	Yea, and all the prophets from Samuel and those that follow after, as many as have spoken, have likewise foretold of these days.	And all the prophets that have been, from Samuel and those after him, have spoken and proclaimed of these days.	And all the prophets from Samuel and those who were after him spoke and preached about those days.
25	Ye are the children of the prophets, and of the covenant which God made with our fathers, saying unto Abraham, And in thy seed shall all the kindreds of the earth be blessed.	Ye are the children of the prophets: and that covenant which God made with our fathers,---when he said to Abraham, that in thy seed shall all the families of the earth be blessed,	You are the sons of the prophets and of the covenant that God established with our fathers, when he said to Abraham: IN YOUR SEED ALL THE FAMILIES OF THE EARTH WILL BE BLESSED.
26	Unto you first God, having raised up his Son Jesus, sent him to bless you, in turning away every one of you from his iniquities.	he hath first established to you: and God hath sent his Son to bless you, if ye will be converted, and repent of your wickedness.	He has first appointed to you and God has sent his Son to bless you, if you will be converted and repent from your evil [ways].

Chapter 4

	KJV	Murdock	Magiera
1	And as they spake unto the people, the priests, and the captain of the temple, and the Sadducees, came upon them,	And while they were speaking these words to the people, the priests and the Sadducees and the rulers of the temple rose up against them;	And while they were speaking these words to the people, the priests and the Sadducees and the rulers of the temple stood up against them,
2	Being grieved that they taught the people, and preached through Jesus the resurrection from the dead.	being angry with them, that they taught the people, and preached a resurrection from the dead by the Messiah.	being furious at them that they taught the people and preached about Christ concerning the resurrection from the dead.
3	And they laid hands on them, and put them in hold unto the next day: for it was now eventide.	And they laid hands on them, and kept them until the next day; because evening was drawing near.	And they seized them and kept them for the next day, because evening was drawing near.
4	Howbeit many of them which heard the word believed; and the number of the men was about five thousand.	And many who had heard the word, believed; and they were, in number, about five thousand men.	And many who heard the word believed. And there were about five thousand men in number.
5	And it came to pass on the morrow, that their rulers, and elders, and scribes,	And the next day, the rulers and the Elders and the Scribes assembled;	And on the next day, the rulers and elders and scribes were gathered together,

	KJV	*Murdock*	*Magiera*
6	And Annas the high priest, and Caiaphas, and John, and Alexander, and as many as were of the kindred of the high priest, were gathered together at Jerusalem.	and also Annas the high priest, and Caiaphas, and John, and Alexander, and they who were of the kindred of the high priests.	and also Annas, the high priest, and Caiaphas and John and Alexander and those who were of the family of the chief priests.
7	And when they had set them in the midst, they asked, By what power, or by what name, have ye done this?	And when they had set them in the midst, they interrogated them: By what power or what name, have ye done this?	And after they had placed them in the middle, they asked them, "By what power or in what name have you done this?"
8	Then Peter, filled with the Holy Ghost, said unto them, Ye rulers of the people, and elders of Israel,	Then Simon Cephas was filled with the Holy Spirit, and said to them: Ye rulers of the people, and Elders of the house of Israel, hear ye.	Then Simon Peter was filled with the Holy Spirit and said to them, "Rulers of the people and elders of the house of Israel, hear [me].
9	If we this day be examined of the good deed done to the impotent man, by what means he is made whole;	If we are judged by you this day, respecting the good deed done to the infirm man, by what means he was healed;	If today we are judged by you concerning the good [thing] that happened to the sick man, by what [means] this [man] was healed,
10	Be it known unto you all, and to all the people of Israel, that by the name of Jesus Christ of Nazareth, whom ye crucified, whom God raised from the dead, even by him doth this man stand here before you whole.	be it known to you, and to all the people of Israel, that by the name of Jesus Messiah the Nazarean, whom ye crucified, and whom God hath raised from the dead, lo, by him, doth this [man] stand here before you recovered.	let this be known to you and to all the people of Israel, that in the name of Jesus Christ the Nazarene, whom you crucified, whom God raised from the dead, by that same [one], behold, this [man] stands before you whole.
11	This is the stone which was set at nought of you builders, which is become the head of the corner.	This is the stone, which ye builders rejected; and it hath become the head of the corner.	This is THE STONE THAT YOU BUILDERS REJECTED AND HE HAS BECOME THE HEAD OF THE CORNER.
12	Neither is there salvation in any other: for there is none other name under heaven given among men, whereby we must be saved.	Neither is there deliverance in any other; for there is not another name under heaven, which is given to men, whereby to live.	And there is no deliverance by another man, for there is no other name under heaven that is given to men by which it is possible to have life."
13	Now when they saw the boldness of Peter and John, and perceived that they were unlearned and ignorant men, they marvelled; and they took knowledge of them, that they had been with Jesus.	And when they heard the speech of Simon and John, which they pronounced confidently, they reflected that these were unlearned and plebeian men, and they were surprised at them, and recognized them as having been conversant with Jesus.	And when they heard the word of Simon and of John that they spoke boldly, they perceived that they were unlearned and ignorant. And they marveled at them and recognized that they had associated with Jesus.
14	And beholding the man which was healed standing with them, they could say nothing against it.	And they saw that the lame man, who had been healed, stood near them; and they could say nothing to confront them.	And they saw the lame [man], who had been healed, standing with them and they were not able to say anything against them.
15	But when they had commanded them to go aside out of the council, they conferred among themselves,	Then they commanded to remove them from the presence of the council; and said one to another:	Then they commanded that they should remove them from their assembly. And they were saying to each other,

Parallel Translations

ACTS Chapter 4

	KJV	Murdock	Magiera
16	Saying, What shall we do to these men? for that indeed a notable miracle hath been done by them is manifest to all them that dwell in Jerusalem; and we cannot deny it.	What shall we do to these men? For lo, that a manifest sign hath been wrought by them, is known to all that reside at Jerusalem, and we cannot deny it.	"What should we do to these men? For behold, a visible sign that has happened by their hands is known to all the inhabitants of Jerusalem and we are not able to deny [it].
17	But that it spread no further among the people, let us straitly threaten them, that they speak henceforth to no man in this name.	But that the fame of it spread no further, let us interdict their speaking any more to any man in this name.	But so that this rumor does not spread any more among the people, we should threaten them that they should not speak again to anyone among men in this name."
18	And they called them, and commanded them not to speak at all nor teach in the name of Jesus.	And they called them, and commanded them not to speak nor to teach at all in the name of Jesus.	And they called them and commanded them that they should absolutely not speak or teach in the name of Jesus.
19	But Peter and John answered and said unto them, Whether it be right in the sight of God to hearken unto you more than unto God, judge ye.	Simon Cephas and John answered, and said to them: Whether it be right before God, that we hearken to you more than to God, judge ye.	Simon Peter and John answered and said to them, "You judge if it is right before God that we should obey you more than God.
20	For we cannot but speak the things which we have seen and heard.	For we cannot but speak that which we have seen and heard.	For we are not able not to speak what we have seen and heard."
21	So when they had further threatened them, they let them go, finding nothing how they might punish them, because of the people: for all men glorified God for that which was done.	And they threatened them, and dismissed them. For they found no ground for punishing them, because of the people: for every one praised God for what had been done;	And they threatened them and released them, for they did not find a cause for which to punish them because of the people, for everyone was glorifying God for what had happened.
22	For the man was above forty years old, on whom this miracle of healing was shewed.	for the man, on whom this sign of healing had been wrought, was more than forty years old.	For that man, on whom this sign of healing happened, was more than forty years old.
23	And being let go, they went to their own company, and reported all that the chief priests and elders had said unto them.	And when they were dismissed, they went to their brethren, and told them all that the priests and Elders had said.	And when they were released, they went to their brothers and told them all that the priests and elders had said.
24	And when they heard that, they lifted up their voice to God with one accord, and said, Lord, thou art God, which hast made heaven, and earth, and the sea, and all that in them is:	And they, when they heard [it], unitedly lifted up their voice to God and said: Lord, thou art God, who hast made heaven, and earth, and seas, and every thing in them.	And when they heard [it], they raised their voice as one to God and said, "LORD, you are God, who made the heaven and earth and seas and everything that is in them.
25	Who by the mouth of thy servant David hast said, Why did the heathen rage, and the people imagine vain things?	And it is thou who hast said, by the Holy Spirit in the mouth of David thy servant: Why do the nations rage, and the people imagine a vain thing?	And it is you who spoke by way of the Holy Spirit by the mouth of David your servant: WHY DO THE NATIONS RAGE AND THE PEOPLE CONSIDER VANITY?
26	The kings of the earth stood up, and the rulers were gathered together against the Lord, and against his Christ.	The kings of the earth and the potentates stood up, and they consulted together, against the Lord, and against his anointed.	THE KINGS OF THE EARTH AND THE RULERS HAVE RISEN UP AND HAVE DELIBERATED AS ONE AGAINST THE LORD AND AGAINST HIS MESSIAH.

Parallel Translations

	KJV	*Murdock*	*Magiera*
ACTS	*Chapter 4*		
27	For of a truth against thy holy child Jesus, whom thou hast anointed, both Herod, and Pontius Pilate, with the Gentiles, and the people of Israel, were gathered together,	For, in reality, against thy holy Son Jesus whom thou hast anointed, Herod and Pilate, with the Gentiles and the congregation of Israel, have been combined together in this city,	For truly Herod and Pilate with the Gentiles and the congregation of Israel were gathered together in this city against the Holy [one], your Son, Jesus, whom you anointed,
28	For to do whatsoever thy hand and thy counsel determined before to be done.	to do whatever thy hand and thy pleasure previously marked out to be done.	to do everything that your hand and your will foreordained to be [done].
29	And now, Lord, behold their threatenings: and grant unto thy servants, that with all boldness they may speak thy word,	And also now, Lord, behold and see their menaces: and grant to thy servants, that they may proclaim thy word boldly,	And also now, LORD, look and see their threats and allow your servants to boldly preach your word,
30	By stretching forth thine hand to heal; and that signs and wonders may be done by the name of thy holy child Jesus.	while thou extendest thy hand for cures and prodigies, to be done in the name of thy holy Son Jesus.	while you extend your hand for healings and mighty works and signs to be [done] in the name of your holy Son, Jesus."
31	And when they had prayed, the place was shaken where they were assembled together; and they were all filled with the Holy Ghost, and they spake the word of God with boldness.	And when they had prayed and made supplications, the place in which they were assembled was shaken; and they were all filled with the Holy Spirit, and spoke the word of God boldly.	And after they had prayed and made [this] request, the place in which they were gathered was shaken and all of them were filled with the Holy Spirit and were boldly speaking the word of God.
32	And the multitude of them that believed were of one heart and of one soul: neither said any of them that ought of the things which he possessed was his own; but they had all things common.	And in the assembly of the persons that believed, there was one soul, and one mind: and no one of them said, of the property he possessed, that it was his own; but whatever was theirs, it was the community's.	And the assembly of men who believed had one soul and one mind and not one of them said concerning the possessions that he owned that they were his, but everything that they had was held in common.
33	And with great power gave the apostles witness of the resurrection of the Lord Jesus: and great grace was upon them all.	And with great power, the legates testified to the resurrection of Jesus Messiah: and great grace was with them all.	And with great power the apostles witnessed about the resurrection of Jesus Christ and great grace was with all of them.
34	Neither was there any among them that lacked: for as many as were possessors of lands or houses sold them, and brought the prices of the things that were sold,	And no one among them was destitute; for those who possessed lands or houses, sold, and brought the price of what was sold,	And there was no one among them who was lacking, for those who owned fields and houses sold [them] and brought the price of what was sold
35	And laid them down at the apostles' feet: and distribution was made unto every man according as he had need.	and placed [it] at the feet of the legates; and distribution was made to every one, as he had need.	and placed [it] at the feet of the apostles and it was given to each one according to what he needed.
36	And Joses, who by the apostles was surnamed Barnabas, (which is, being interpreted, The son of consolation,) a Levite, and of the country of Cyprus,	And Joseph, who by the legates was surnamed Barnabas, (which is interpreted Son of Consolation,) a Levite of the country of Cyprus,	And Joseph, who was called Barnabas by the apostles, which is interpreted, "son of comfort," a Levite from the region of Cyprus,
37	Having land, sold it, and brought the money, and laid it at the apostles' feet.	had a field: and he sold it, and brought the price of it, and laid [it] before the feet of the legates.	had a field. And he sold it and brought its price and placed [it] before the feet of the apostles.

Parallel Translations

ACTS *Chapter 5*

	KJV	*Murdock*	*Magiera*
1	But a certain man named Ananias, with Sapphira his wife, sold a possession,	And a certain man whose name was Ananias, with his wife whose name was Sapphira, sold his field,	And a certain man whose name was Ananias, with his wife, whose name was Sapphira, sold his field
2	And kept back part of the price, his wife also being privy to it, and brought a certain part, and laid it at the apostles' feet.	and carried away [part] of the price and concealed it, his wife consenting; and he brought [a part] of the money, and laid [it] before the feet of the legates.	and took [some] of its price and hid [it], his wife being aware of it. And he brought a part of the money and placed [it] before the feet of the apostles.
3	But Peter said, Ananias, why hath Satan filled thine heart to lie to the Holy Ghost, and to keep back part of the price of the land?	And Simon said to him: Ananias, why hath Satan so filled thy heart, that thou shouldst lie against the Holy Spirit, and conceal of the money of the price of the field?	And Simon said to him, Ananias, why is it that Satan has so filled your heart that you should lie to the Holy Spirit and hide some of the money of the sale of the field?
4	Whiles it remained, was it not thine own? and after it was sold, was it not in thine own power? why hast thou conceived this thing in thine heart? thou hast not lied unto men, but unto God.	Was it not thine own before it was sold? And when sold, again thou hadst authority over the price of it. Why hast thou set thy heart to do this purpose? Thou hast not lied against men, but against God.	Was it not yours before it was sold? And after it was sold, again you were in control of its sale. Why have you decided in your heart to do this thing? You have not lied to men, but to God.
5	And Ananias hearing these words fell down, and gave up the ghost: and great fear came on all them that heard these things.	And when Ananias heard these words, he fell down, and died. And great fear was upon all them that heard [of it].	And when Ananias heard these words, he fell down and died. And there was great fear among all those who heard.
6	And the young men arose, wound him up, and carried him out, and buried him.	And the young men among them arose, and gathered him up, and carried [him] out, and buried him.	And those who were young among them rose up and gathered him up and took [and] buried him.
7	And it was about the space of three hours after, when his wife, not knowing what was done, came in.	And when three hours had passed, his wife also came in, without knowing what had occurred.	And after three hours had passed, his wife also entered, not knowing what had happened.
8	And Peter answered unto her, Tell me whether ye sold the land for so much? And she said, Yea, for so much.	Simon said to her: Tell me, if ye sold the field for this price? And she said: Yes, for this price.	Simon said to her, "Tell me if you sold the field for this sale price?" And she said, "Yes, for this sale price."
9	Then Peter said unto her, How is it that ye have agreed together to tempt the Spirit of the Lord? behold, the feet of them which have buried thy husband are at the door, and shall carry thee out.	Simon said to her: Since ye have been equals in tempting the Spirit of the Lord, lo, the feet of the buriers of thy husband are at the door, and they will carry thee out.	Simon said to her, "Because you have agreed to tempt the Spirit of the LORD, behold, the feet of the grave diggers of your husband [are] at the door and they will take you out."
10	Then fell she down straightway at his feet, and yielded up the ghost: and the young men came in, and found her dead, and, carrying her forth, buried her by her husband.	And immediately she fell before their feet, and died. And those young men came in, and found her dead; and they took up, carried forth, and buried her by the side of her husband.	And immediately, she fell before their feet and died. And those young men entered and found her dead. And they gathered [her] up, took [and] buried her by the side of her husband.
11	And great fear came upon all the church, and upon as many as heard these things.	And great fear was on all the assembly, and on all them that heard [it].	And there was great fear in all the church and among all those who heard.

Parallel Translations

	KJV	*Murdock*	*Magiera*
	ACTS	*Chapter 5*	
12	And by the hands of the apostles were many signs and wonders wrought among the people; (and they were all with one accord in Solomon's porch.	And there were many signs and prodigies wrought by the legates among the people. And they were all assembled together in the porch of Solomon.	And by way of the apostles many signs and mighty works occurred among the people. And they were all assembled together in Solomon's Porch.
13	And of the rest durst no man join himself to them: but the people magnified them.	And of the others, no one ventured to come near them; but the people magnified them.	And of other men, no one dared to come near to them, but the people magnified them.
14	And believers were the more added to the Lord, multitudes both of men and women.)	And the more were those added who feared the Lord, a multitude both of men and of women.	And more were added who believed in the LORD, a crowd of men and of women,
15	Insomuch that they brought forth the sick into the streets, and laid them on beds and couches, that at the least the shadow of Peter passing by might overshadow some of them.	So that they brought out into the streets the sick, laid on beds, that when Simon should pass, at least his shadow might cover them.	so that they brought out the sick into the streets, lying on pallets, that when Simon should come by, at least his shadow would cover them.
16	There came also a multitude out of the cities round about unto Jerusalem, bringing sick folks, and them which were vexed with unclean spirits: and they were healed every one.	And many came to them from other cities around Jerusalem, bringing the sick and those who had unclean spirits; and they were all cured.	And many came to them from other cities that were around Jerusalem, bringing the sick and those who had unclean spirits and all of them were healed.
17	Then the high priest rose up, and all they that were with him, (which is the sect of the Sadducees,) and were filled with indignation,	And the high priest was filled with indignation, and all those with him who were of the doctrine of the Sadducees.	And the high priest and all who were with him who were of the teaching of the Sadducees were filled with envy.
18	And laid their hands on the apostles, and put them in the common prison.	And they laid hands on the legates, and took and bound them in prison.	And they seized the apostles and arrested [and] bound them [in] prison.
19	But the angel of the Lord by night opened the prison doors, and brought them forth, and said,	Then the angel of the Lord, by night, opened the door of the prison, and let them out; and said to them:	Then, during the night, an angel of the LORD opened the door of the prison and took them out and said to them,
20	Go, stand and speak in the temple to the people all the words of this life.	Go, stand in the temple, and speak to the people all these words of life.	"Go! Stand in the temple and speak to the people all these words of life."
21	And when they heard that, they entered into the temple early in the morning, and taught. But the high priest came, and they that were with him, and called the council together, and all the senate of the children of Israel, and sent to the prison to have them brought.	And in the morning, they went and entered into the temple, and taught. And the high priest and those with him, convoked their associates and the Elders of Israel, and sent to the prison to bring forth the legates.	And they went out at daybreak and entered the temple and were teaching. And the high priest and those who were with him called for their companions and the elders of Israel and sent to the prison to bring out the apostles.
22	But when the officers came, and found them not in the prison, they returned, and told,	And when those sent by them went, they found them not in the prison; and they returned and came back,	And when those who had been sent by them went, they could not find them [in] prison, and they turned [and] came [back],

Parallel Translations

	KJV	*Murdock*	*Magiera*

ACTS *Chapter 5*

	KJV	Murdock	Magiera
23	Saying, The prison truly found we shut with all safety, and the keepers standing without before the doors: but when we had opened, we found no man within.	and said: We found the prison carefully closed, and also the keepers standing before the doors; and we opened, but found no one there.	saying, "We found the prison that was securely closed, and also the guards who were standing at the doors. And we opened [them], yet we did not find anyone there."
24	Now when the high priest and the captain of the temple and the chief priests heard these things, they doubted of them whereunto this would grow.	And when the chief priests and rulers of the temple heard these words, they were astonished at them; and they studied what this could mean.	And when the chief priests and rulers of the temple heard these words, they were amazed at them and were reasoning, "What is this?"
25	Then came one and told them, saying, Behold, the men whom ye put in prison are standing in the temple, and teaching the people.	And one came and informed them: Those men, whom ye shut up in the prison, lo, they are standing in the temple, and teaching the people.	Then a man came [and] told them, "Those men that you confined [in] prison, behold, they are standing in the temple and teaching the people."
26	Then went the captain with the officers, and brought them without violence: for they feared the people, lest they should have been stoned.	Then went the rulers with attendants, to bring them without violence; for they feared, lest the people should stone them.	Then the rulers with the guards went to have them brought, [but] not with violence, for they feared lest the people would stone them.
27	And when they had brought them, they set them before the council: and the high priest asked them,	And when they had brought them, they placed them before the whole council; and the high priest began to say to them:	And when they had brought them, they caused them to stand them before all the assembly and the high priest began to speak to them.
28	Saying, Did not we straitly command you that ye should not teach in this name? and, behold, ye have filled Jerusalem with your doctrine, and intend to bring this man's blood upon us.	Did we not strictly charge you, to teach no person in this name? And behold, ye have filled Jerusalem with your doctrine; and ye would bring the blood of this man upon us.	"Did we not particularly command you that you should not teach anyone in this name? Now behold, you have filled Jerusalem with your teaching. And you want to bring the blood of this man on us."
29	Then Peter and the other apostles answered and said, We ought to obey God rather than men.	And Simon, with the legates, answered and said to them: God is to be obeyed, rather than men.	Simon answered with the apostles and said to them, "It is right to be persuaded by God, more than by men.
30	The God of our fathers raised up Jesus, whom ye slew and hanged on a tree.	The God of our fathers hath raised up that Jesus, whom ye slew when ye hanged him on a tree.	The God of our fathers raised Jesus, whom you killed when you hung him on the tree.
31	Him hath God exalted with his right hand to be a Prince and a Saviour, for to give repentance to Israel, and forgiveness of sins.	Him hath God established as a head and vivifier; and hath exalted him to his own right hand, so that he might give repentance and remission of sins to Israel.	God has established this [man as] a leader and savior and has elevated him by his right hand to give repentance and forgiveness of sins to Israel.
32	And we are his witnesses of these things; and so is also the Holy Ghost, whom God hath given to them that obey him.	And we are the witnesses of these things; and also the Holy Spirit, whom God giveth to them that believe in him.	And we are witnesses of these words and [so] is the Holy Spirit that God gives to those who believe in him."
33	When they heard that, they were cut to the heart, and took counsel to slay them.	And when they heard these things, they burned with indignation, and thought of putting them to death.	And when they heard these words, they were inflamed with anger and planned to kill them.

	KJV	Murdock	Magiera
	ACTS Chapter 5		
34	Then stood there up one in the council, a Pharisee, named Gamaliel, a doctor of the law, had in reputation among all the people, and commanded to put the apostles forth a little space;	Then rose up one of the Pharisees whose name was Gamaliel, a teacher of the law, and honored by all the people; and he directed them to put the legates aside for a short time.	And one of the Pharisees stood up, whose name was Gamaliel, a teacher of the law and honored by all the people. And he commanded that they should take the apostles outside [for] a short time.
35	And said unto them, Ye men of Israel, take heed to yourselves what ye intend to do as touching these men.	And he said, to them: Men, sons of Israel, take heed to yourselves, and consider what ye ought to do in regard to these men.	And he said to them, "Men, sons of Israel, take precaution among yourselves and look at what you ought to do about these men.
36	For before these days rose up Theudas, boasting himself to be somebody; to whom a number of men, about four hundred, joined themselves: who was slain; and all, as many as obeyed him, were scattered, and brought to nought.	For before this time, rose up Theudas, and said of himself, that he was some great one; and there went after him about four hundred men. And he was slain; and they who went after him, were dispersed and became as nothing.	For before this time, Theudas rose up and said about himself that he was someone great. And about four hundred men followed him. And he was killed and those who followed him were scattered and became as nothing.
37	After this man rose up Judas of Galilee in the days of the taxing, and drew away much people after him: he also perished; and all, even as many as obeyed him, were dispersed.	And after him, rose up Judas a Galilean, in the days when the people were enrolled for the capitation tax; and he seduced much people after him. And he died, and all they that went after him were dispersed.	And Judas the Galilean rose up after him in the days that men were registered for the poll tax and caused many people to turn after him. And he died and all those who followed him were scattered.
38	And now I say unto you, Refrain from these men, and let them alone: for if this counsel or this work be of men, it will come to nought:	And now, I say to you: Desist from these men, and let them alone. For if this device and this work originate from men, they will dissolve and come to nothing.	And now I say to you, 'Separate yourselves from these men and leave them alone,' for if this thought and this work is of men they will be dismissed and pass away.
39	But if it be of God, ye cannot overthrow it; lest haply ye be found even to fight against God.	But if it be from God, it is not in your power to frustrate it: that ye may not be found placing yourselves in opposition to God.---And they assented to him.	But if it is from God, you are not able to stop it with your hands, lest you should be found standing against God.'"
40	And to him they agreed: and when they had called the apostles, and beaten them, they commanded that they should not speak in the name of Jesus, and let them go.	And they called the legates, and scourged them, and commanded them not to teach in the name of Jesus, and dismissed them.	And they were persuaded by him. And they called the apostles and beat them and commanded them that they should not speak in the name of Jesus and released them.
41	And they departed from the presence of the council, rejoicing that they were counted worthy to suffer shame for his name.	And they went from before them, rejoicing that they were worthy to suffer abuse on account of that name.	And they left their presence, rejoicing that they were worthy to be despised because of the name.
42	And daily in the temple, and in every house, they ceased not to teach and preach Jesus Christ.	And they ceased not to teach daily, in the temple and at home, and to preach concerning our Lord Jesus Messiah.	And they did not cease to teach every day in the temple and at home and to preach about our Lord Jesus Christ.

ACTS *Chapter 6*

	KJV	*Murdock*	*Magiera*
1	And in those days, when the number of the disciples was multiplied, there arose a murmuring of the Grecians against the Hebrews, because their widows were neglected in the daily ministration.	And in those days, when the disciples had become numerous, the Grecian disciples murmured against the Hebrew, because their widows were neglected in the daily ministration [to the needy].	And in those days as the disciples multiplied, the Greek disciples were murmuring against the Hebrews that their widows were neglected in the daily service.
2	Then the twelve called the multitude of the disciples unto them, and said, It is not reason that we should leave the word of God, and serve tables.	And the twelve legates convoked the whole company of the disciples, and said to them: It is not proper, that we should neglect the word of God, and serve tables.	And the twelve apostles called the whole assembly of disciples and said to them, "It is not good that we should leave the word of God and serve tables.
3	Wherefore, brethren, look ye out among you seven men of honest report, full of the Holy Ghost and wisdom, whom we may appoint over this business.	Therefore brethren, search out, and elect from among you, seven men of whom there is good testimony, men full of the Spirit of the Lord, and of wisdom; that we may place them over this business:	Therefore, my brothers, search out and choose seven men from among you about whom there is a [good] testimony and [who] are full of the Spirit of the LORD and wisdom, and we will set them over this matter.
4	But we will give ourselves continually to prayer, and to the ministry of the word.	and we will continue in prayer, and in the ministration of the word.	And we will be steadfast in prayer and in the ministering of the word."
5	And the saying pleased the whole multitude: and they chose Stephen, a man full of faith and of the Holy Ghost, and Philip, and Prochorus, and Nicanor, and Timon, and Parmenas, and Nicolas a proselyte of Antioch:	And this proposal was acceptable before all the people. And they elected Stephen, a man who was full of faith and of the Holy Spirit; and Philip, and Prochorus, and Nicanor, and Timon, and Parmenas, and Nicolas an Antiochian proselyte.	And this saying was good before all the people, and they chose Stephen, a man who was full of faith and the Holy Spirit, and Philip and Prochorus and Nicanor and Timon and Parmenes and Nicolas, an Antiochene proselyte.
6	Whom they set before the apostles: and when they had prayed, they laid their hands on them.	These stood before the legates; and when they had prayed, they laid the hand on them.	These stood before the apostles and after they had prayed, they laid a hand on them.
7	And the word of God increased; and the number of the disciples multiplied in Jerusalem greatly; and a great company of the priests were obedient to the faith.	And the word of God increased, and the number of disciples was enlarged at Jerusalem greatly; and many people from among the Jews, were obedient to the faith.	And the word of God grew and the number of disciples in Jerusalem multiplied greatly and many people of the Judeans were obedient to the faith.
8	And Stephen, full of faith and power, did great wonders and miracles among the people.	And Stephen was full of grace and energy; and he wrought signs and prodigies among the people.	Now Stephen was full of grace and power and did signs and wonders among the people.
9	Then there arose certain of the synagogue, which is called the synagogue of the Libertines, and Cyrenians, and Alexandrians, and of them of Cilicia and of Asia, disputing with Stephen.	And there rose up some of the synagogue which is called that of the freed men, Cyrenians, and Alexandrians, and persons from Cilicia and from Asia; and they disputed with Stephen.	And men from the synagogue, which was called that of the Libertine, rose up, along with the Cyrenians and Alexandrians and those from Cilicia and from Asia, and they were disputing with Stephen.

	KJV	Murdock	Magiera
ACTS	Chapter 6		
10	And they were not able to resist the wisdom and the spirit by which he spake.	And they could not withstand the wisdom and the Spirit that spoke by him.	And they were not able to stand against the wisdom and the Spirit by which he spoke.
11	Then they suborned men, which said, We have heard him speak blasphemous words against Moses, and against God.	Then they sent men, and instructed them to say: We have heard him speak words of blasphemy, against Moses and against God.	Then they sent men and instructed them to say, "We have heard him speak words of blasphemy against Moses and against God."
12	And they stirred up the people, and the elders, and the scribes, and came upon him, and caught him, and brought him to the council,	And they excited the people, and the Elders, and the Scribes; and they came, and rose upon him, and seized him, and carried him into the midst of the council.	And they stirred up the people and the elders and the scribes and came and stood against him and seized [and] brought him into the middle of the council.
13	And set up false witnesses, which said, This man ceaseth not to speak blasphemous words against this holy place, and the law:	And they set up false witnesses, who said: This man ceaseth not to utter words contrary to the law, and against this holy place.	And they set up false witnesses who said, "This man does not cease to speak words against the law and against this holy place.
14	For we have heard him say, that this Jesus of Nazareth shall destroy this place, and shall change the customs which Moses delivered us.	For we have heard him say, that this Jesus the Nazarean will destroy this place, and will change the rites which Moses delivered to you.	For we have heard him say that this Jesus, the Nazarene, will destroy this place and will change the customs that Moses delivered to you."
15	And all that sat in the council, looking stedfastly on him, saw his face as it had been the face of an angel.	And all they who were sitting in the council looked upon him, and they beheld his face, as the face of an angel.	And all those who were sitting in the synagogue looked at him and saw his face as the face of an angel.
Chapter 7			
1	Then said the high priest, Are these things so?	And the high priest asked him: Are these things so?	And the high priest asked him if these [things] were so.
2	And he said, Men, brethren, and fathers, hearken; The God of glory appeared unto our father Abraham, when he was in Mesopotamia, before he dwelt in Charran,	And he said: Men, brethren, and our fathers, hear ye. The God of glory appeared to our father Abraham, when he was between the rivers, before he came to reside in Charran;	And he said, "Men, our brothers and our fathers, listen. The God of glory appeared to our father Abraham when he was in Mesopotamia before he came to live in Haran.
3	And said unto him, Get thee out of thy country, and from thy kindred, and come into the land which I shall shew thee.	and he said to him: Depart from thy country, and from thy kindred, and go to a land which I will show to thee.	And he said to him: DEPART FROM YOUR COUNTRY AND FROM AMONG YOUR KINSMEN, AND GO TO THE COUNTRY THAT I WILL SHOW YOU.
4	Then came he out of the land of the Chaldaeans, and dwelt in Charran: and from thence, when his father was dead, he removed him into this land, wherein ye now dwell.	And then Abraham departed from the land of the Chaldeans, and came and dwelt in Charran. And from there, after his father had died, God removed him to this land, in which ye this day dwell.	And then Abraham left the land of the Chaldeans and came [and] lived in Haran. And from there, after his father had died, God moved him to this land in which you live today.

ACTS *Chapter 7*

	KJV	*Murdock*	*Magiera*
5	And he gave him none inheritance in it, no, not so much as to set his foot on: yet he promised that he would give it to him for a possession, and to his seed after him, when as yet he had no child.	And he did not give him an inheritance in it, not even a foot-track: but he promised that he would give it him, as an inheritance to him and to his seed, when as yet he had no son.	And he did not give him an inheritance in it, not even a place to stand for [his] feet. And he promised that he would give it to him to inherit it, to him and to his seed, when he had no son.
6	And God spake on this wise, That his seed should sojourn in a strange land; and that they should bring them into bondage, and entreat them evil four hundred years.	And God conversed with him, and said to him: Thy seed will be a sojourner in a foreign land; and they will reduce it to servitude, and will treat it ill, during four hundred years.	And God spoke with him, saying to him: YOUR SEED WILL BE A SETTLER IN A STRANGE LAND, AND THEY WILL SUBJECT HIM AND TREAT HIM WICKEDLY [FOR] FOUR HUNDRED YEARS.
7	And the nation to whom they shall be in bondage will I judge, said God: and after that shall they come forth, and serve me in this place.	And the nation, to whom they perform bondservice, I will judge saith God. And afterwards, they will go out, and will worship me in this land.	AND I WILL JUDGE THE PEOPLE WHOM THEY WILL SERVE [IN] BONDAGE, said God. AND AFTER THESE [THINGS] THEY WILL GO OUT AND SERVE ME IN THIS LAND.
8	And he gave him the covenant of circumcision: and so Abraham begat Isaac, and circumcised him the eighth day; and Isaac begat Jacob; and Jacob begat the twelve patriarchs.	And he gave them the covenant of circumcision. And then he begat Isaac, and circumcised him the eighth day. And Isaac begat Jacob: and Jacob begat our twelve fathers.	And he gave him the covenant of circumcision. And then he fathered Isaac and circumcised him on the eighth day. And Isaac fathered Jacob and Jacob fathered our twelve fathers.
9	And the patriarchs, moved with envy, sold Joseph into Egypt: but God was with him,	And those our fathers envied Joseph, and sold him into Egypt: but God was with him,	And our fathers were jealous of Joseph and sold him into Egypt, yet God was with him.
10	And delivered him out of all his afflictions, and gave him favour and wisdom in the sight of Pharaoh king of Egypt; and he made him governor over Egypt and all his house.	and delivered him from all his afflictions; and gave him favor and wisdom before Pharaoh, king of Egypt, and he made him chief over Egypt, and over all his house.	And he delivered him from all of his adversities and gave him grace and wisdom before Pharoah, the king of Egypt, and he made him ruler over Egypt and over all his house.
11	Now there came a dearth over all the land of Egypt and Chanaan, and great affliction: and our fathers found no sustenance.	And there was a famine and great distress in all Egypt, and in the land of Canaan, and our fathers lacked food.	And there was a famine and great calamity in all of Egypt and in the land of Canaan and there was nothing to sustain our fathers.
12	But when Jacob heard that there was corn in Egypt, he sent out our fathers first.	And when Jacob heard that there was bread-stuff in Egypt, he sent our fathers a first time.	And when Jacob heard that there was food in Egypt, he sent our fathers the first [time].
13	And at the second time Joseph was made known to his brethren; and Joseph's kindred was made known unto Pharaoh.	And when they went the second time, Joseph made himself known to his brethren; and the kindred of Joseph was known to Pharaoh.	And as they were going away the second time, Joseph made himself known to his brothers and the family of Joseph was made known to Pharoah.
14	Then sent Joseph, and called his father Jacob to him, and all his kindred, threescore and fifteen souls.	And Joseph sent and brought is father Jacob, and all his family; and they were in number seventy and five souls.	And Joseph sent and brought his father, Jacob, and all his family. And they were seventy-five people in number.
15	So Jacob went down into Egypt, and died, he, and our fathers,	And Jacob went down into Egypt; and he died there, he and our fathers.	And Jacob went down to Egypt and died there, he and our fathers.

Parallel Translations

	KJV	Murdock	Magiera
	ACTS *Chapter 7*		
16	And were carried over into Sychem, and laid in the sepulchre that Abraham bought for a sum of money of the sons of Emmor the father of Sychem.	And he was transported to Sychem, and was deposited in the sepulchre which Abraham bought with money of the sons of Emmor.	And he was moved to Shechem and placed in the grave that Abraham had bought with money from the sons of Hamor.
17	But when the time of the promise drew nigh, which God had sworn to Abraham, the people grew and multiplied in Egypt,	And when the time arrived for that which God had promised to Abraham with an oath, the people had multiplied and become strong, in Egypt:	And when the time arrived for what God had promised to Abraham with oaths, the people had multiplied and grown strong in Egypt,
18	Till another king arose, which knew not Joseph.	until there arose another king over Egypt, who knew not Joseph.	until another king rose up over Egypt, who did not know Joseph.
19	The same dealt subtilly with our kindred, and evil entreated our fathers, so that they cast out their young children, to the end they might not live.	And he dealt craftily with our kindred, and ill-treated our fathers, and gave orders that their infants should be cast away, and should not live.	And he plotted against our family and dealt wickedly with our fathers and commanded that their infant boys should be cast away so that they would not live.
20	In which time Moses was born, and was exceeding fair, and nourished up in his father's house three months:	At that time was Moses born; and he was lovely to God: and he was nursed three months in his father's house.	At that time Moses was born and he was loved by God. And he was nurtured three months [in] the house of his father.
21	And when he was cast out, Pharaoh's daughter took him up, and nourished him for her own son.	And when he was cast out, by his people, the daughter of Pharaoh found him, and brought him up for her own son.	And when he was cast away by his mother, the daughter of Pharoah found him and raised him for herself as a son.
22	And Moses was learned in all the wisdom of the Egyptians, and was mighty in words and in deeds.	And Moses was instructed in all the wisdom of the Egyptians; and he was eminent in his words, and also in his deeds.	And Moses was instructed in all the wisdom of the Egyptians and he was prepared in his words and also in his actions.
23	And when he was full forty years old, it came into his heart to visit his brethren the children of Israel.	And when he was forty years old, it came into his heart to visit his brethren, the children of Israel.	And when he was forty years old, it came into his heart to visit his brothers, the sons of Israel.
24	And seeing one of them suffer wrong, he defended him, and avenged him that was oppressed, and smote the Egyptian:	And he saw one of the race of his kindred treated with violence; and he avenged him, and did him justice, and killed the Egyptian who had abused him.	And he saw one of the sons of his tribe who was treated with violence and he avenged him and executed judgment on him and killed the Egyptian who had wronged him.
25	For he supposed his brethren would have understood how that God by his hand would deliver them: but they understood not.	And he supposed that his brethren the sons of Israel would have understood, that by his hand God would give them deliverance; but they understood not.	And he supposed that his brothers, the sons of Israel, would understand that God by his hand would give them deliverance, yet they did not understand.
26	And the next day he shewed himself unto them as they strove, and would have set them at one again, saying, Sirs, ye are brethren; why do ye wrong one to another?	And on another day, he appeared to them, as they were quarrelling one with another. And he exhorted them to become reconciled, saying: Men, ye are brethren; why do ye seek to harm each other?	And on another day, he was seen by them while they were quarreling with one another and he was persuading them to be reconciled, saying, 'Men, you are brothers. Why do you wrong one another?'

Parallel Translations

ACTS *Chapter 7*

	KJV	*Murdock*	*Magiera*
27	But he that did his neighbour wrong thrust him away, saying, Who made thee a ruler and a judge over us?	But he who did the wrong to his fellow, repulsed him from him, and said to him: Who constituted thee a ruler and a judge over us?	But he who was wronging his neighbor, pushed him away from him and said to him: WHO HAS SET YOU OVER US [AS] A RULER AND JUDGE?
28	Wilt thou kill me, as thou diddest the Egyptian yesterday?	Dost thou seek to kill me, as thou killedst the Egyptian yesterday?	WILL YOU SEEK TO KILL ME AS YOU KILLED THE EGYPTIAN YESTERDAY?
29	Then fled Moses at this saying, and was a stranger in the land of Midian, where he begat two sons.	And Moses fled at that speech, and became a sojourner in the land of Midian. And he had two sons.	And Moses fled at this saying and was a settler in the land of Midian and he had two sons.
30	And when forty years were expired, there appeared to him in the wilderness of mount Sina an angel of the Lord in a flame of fire in a bush.	And when forty years had been passed by him there, the angel of the Lord appeared to him in the wilderness of mount Sinai, in a fire that burned in a bush.	And after forty years were completed there, an angel of the LORD appeared to him in the wilderness of Mount Sinai in a fire that burned in a bush.
31	When Moses saw it, he wondered at the sight: and as he drew near to behold it, the voice of the Lord came unto him,	And when Moses saw [it], he admired the sight: and as he drew near to behold [it], the Lord said to him, audibly:	And when Moses saw [it] he was amazed at the vision and as he came near to see [it], the LORD said to him in a voice:
32	Saying, I am the God of thy fathers, the God of Abraham, and the God of Isaac, and the God of Jacob. Then Moses trembled, and durst not behold.	I am the God of thy fathers, the God of Abraham, and of Isaac, and of Jacob. And Moses trembled, and dared not to gaze at the sight.	I AM THE GOD OF YOUR FATHERS, THE GOD OF ABRAHAM AND OF ISAAC AND OF JACOB. And as he was trembling, Moses did not dare to look at the vision.
33	Then said the Lord to him, Put off thy shoes from thy feet: for the place where thou standest is holy ground.	And the Lord said to him: Loose thy shoes from thy feet; for the ground on which thou standest is holy.	And the LORD said to him: LOOSEN YOUR SANDALS FROM YOUR FEET, FOR THE GROUND ON WHICH YOU STAND IS HOLY.
34	I have seen, I have seen the affliction of my people which is in Egypt, and I have heard their groaning, and am come down to deliver them. And now come, I will send thee into Egypt.	I have attentively seen the affliction of my people, who are in Egypt; and I have heard their groans, and have come down to deliver them. And now, come, I will send thee to Egypt.	I HAVE INDEED SEEN THE TORMENT OF MY PEOPLE WHO ARE IN EGYPT AND I HAVE HEARD THEIR GROANS AND I HAVE COME DOWN TO DELIVER THEM. AND NOW COME, I WILL SEND YOU TO EGYPT.
35	This Moses whom they refused, saying, Who made thee a ruler and a judge? the same did God send to be a ruler and a deliverer by the hand of the angel which appeared to him in the bush.	This Moses, whom they rejected, saying, Who constituted thee a ruler and judge over us? this same did God, by the hand of the angel that appeared to him in the bush, send to them to be their captain and deliverer.	This [is] Moses, whom they denied, saying, 'Who set you over us [as] a ruler and judge? This [man] God sent to them [as] a ruler and deliverer by the hands of an angel who appeared to him in a bush.
36	He brought them out, after that he had shewed wonders and signs in the land of Egypt, and in the Red sea, and in the wilderness forty years.	He it was that brought them out, working signs and wonders and prodigies in the land of Egypt, and at the sea of rushes, and in the desert, forty years.	This is he who brought them out after he had done signs and wonders and mighty works in the land of Egypt and in the sea of reeds and in the wilderness [for] forty years.

ACTS *Chapter 7*

	KJV	*Murdock*	*Magiera*
37	This is that Moses, which said unto the children of Israel, A prophet shall the Lord your God raise up unto you of your brethren, like unto me; him shall ye hear.	This Moses is the man who said to the children of Israel: A prophet, like me, will the Lord God raise up to you from among your brethren; to him give ear.	This is Moses, who said to the sons of Israel, 'The LORD God will raise up a prophet for you from your brothers like me. Hear him.'
38	This is he, that was in the church in the wilderness with the angel which spake to him in the mount Sina, and with our fathers: who received the lively oracles to give unto us:	He it was, who was in the congregation in the wilderness, with the angel that conversed with him and with our fathers at mount Sinai; and he it was, received the living words to give [them] to us.	This is he who was in the assembly in the wilderness with the angel who spoke with him and with our fathers in the mountain of Sinai. And he is the one who received the living words to give to us.
39	To whom our fathers would not obey, but thrust him from them, and in their hearts turned back again into Egypt,	And our fathers would not hearken to him, but forsook him, and in their hearts returned again to Egypt;	And our fathers did not want to follow to him, but left him and in their hearts returned to Egypt,
40	Saying unto Aaron, Make us gods to go before us: for as for this Moses, which brought us out of the land of Egypt, we wot not what is become of him.	when they said to Aaron: Make us gods who may go before us; because, as for this Moses who brought us from the land of Egypt, we know not what hath become of him.	saying to Aaron: MAKE US GODS TO PRECEDE US, BECAUSE THIS MOSES, WHO BROUGHT US OUT OF THE LAND OF EGYPT, WE DO NOT KNOW WHAT HAS HAPPENED TO HIM.
41	And they made a calf in those days, and offered sacrifice unto the idol, and rejoiced in the works of their own hands.	And he made them a calf in those days; and they offered sacrifices to idols, and were voluptuous with the work of their hands.	And they made for themselves a calf in those days and they sacrificed sacrifices to the idols and they were rejoicing in the work of their hands.
42	Then God turned, and gave them up to worship the host of heaven; as it is written in the book of the prophets, O ye house of Israel, have ye offered to me slain beasts and sacrifices by the space of forty years in the wilderness?	And God turned away, and gave them up to worship the hosts of heaven: as it is written in the book of the prophets: Did ye, for forty years, in the wilderness, present to me a slain animal or a sacrifice, ye sons of Israel?	And God turned away and delivered them to serve the powers of heaven, as it is written in the book of the prophets: [FOR] FORTY YEARS IN THE WILDERNESS DID YOU OFFER ME A SLAIN ANIMAL OR A SACRIFICE, SONS OF ISRAEL?
43	Yea, ye took up the tabernacle of Moloch, and the star of your god Remphan, figures which ye made to worship them: and I will carry you away beyond Babylon.	But ye bore the tabernacle of Malchum, and the star of the god Rephon, images which ye had made, that ye might bow down to them. I will transport you beyond Babylon.	BUT YOU CARRIED THE TABERNACLE OF MOLOCH AND THE STAR OF THE GOD OF REPHAN, IMAGES THAT YOU MADE TO WORSHIP. I WILL REMOVE YOU BEYOND BABYLON.
44	Our fathers had the tabernacle of witness in the wilderness, as he had appointed, speaking unto Moses, that he should make it according to the fashion that he had seen.	Lo, the tabernacle of the testimony of our fathers, was in the wilderness; as he who talked with Moses, commanded to make it after the form which he showed him.	Behold, the tabernacle of the testimony of our fathers was in the wilderness, as he who spoke with Moses commanded to make it in the likeness that he showed him.

ACTS *Chapter 7*

	KJV	*Murdock*	*Magiera*
45	Which also our fathers that came after brought in with Jesus into the possession of the Gentiles, whom God drave out before the face of our fathers, unto the days of David;	And this same tabernacle, our fathers, with Joshua, actually brought into the land which God gave to them for an inheritance from those nations which he drove out before them; and it was borne about, until the days of David.	And our fathers, with Joshua, indeed brought this tabernacle also into the land that God gave them [as] an inheritance from those nations that he threw out from before them. And it was carried about until the days of David,
46	Who found favour before God, and desired to find a tabernacle for the God of Jacob.	He found favor before God; and he requested, that he might find a residence for the God of Jacob.	who found mercy before God and requested that he find a tabernacle for the God of Jacob.
47	But Solomon built him an house.	But Solomon built the house.	But Solomon built the house.
48	Howbeit the most High dwelleth not in temples made with hands; as saith the prophet,	Yet the most High lodgeth not in a work of [human] hands; as saith the prophet:	And the Most High does not dwell in a work of hands, as the prophet said:
49	Heaven is my throne, and earth is my footstool: what house will ye build me? saith the Lord: or what is the place of my rest?	Heaven is my throne, and earth the footstool under my feet. What is the house, ye will build for me? saith the Lord: or, what is the place of my repose?	HEAVEN [IS] MY THRONE AND EARTH A FOOTSTOOL THAT IS UNDER MY FEET. WHAT IS THE HOUSE THAT YOU WILL BUILD FOR ME? says the LORD. OR WHAT IS THE PLACE OF MY REST?
50	Hath not my hand made all these things?	Lo, hath not my hand made all these things?	BEHOLD, DID NOT MY HAND MAKE ALL THESE [THINGS]?
51	Ye stiffnecked and uncircumcised in heart and ears, ye do always resist the Holy Ghost: as your fathers did, so do ye.	O ye stiff of neck, and uncircumcised in their heart, and in their hearing; ye do always set yourselves against the Holy Spirit; as your fathers, so also ye.	Oh stiff of neck and without circumcision in their heart[s] and in their hearing! You always stand against the Holy Spirit. As your fathers [were], you [are] also.
52	Which of the prophets have not your fathers persecuted? and they have slain them which shewed before of the coming of the Just One; of whom ye have been now the betrayers and murderers:	For, which of the prophets did not your fathers persecute and kill, [even] them, who foretold the coming of the Just One, whom ye delivered up and slew?	For which of the prophets have your fathers not persecuted and killed, those who foretold about the coming of the Just [one], whom you delivered up and killed?
53	Who have received the law by the disposition of angels, and have not kept it.	And ye have received the law by the ordination of angels, and have not kept it.	And you have received the law by way of the command of angels and have not kept it."
54	When they heard these things, they were cut to the heart, and they gnashed on him with their teeth.	And when they heard these things, they were filled with rage in their souls; and they gnashed their teeth against him.	And when they heard these [things], they were filled with anger in themselves, and they gnashed their teeth against him.
55	But he, being full of the Holy Ghost, looked up stedfastly into heaven, and saw the glory of God, and Jesus standing on the right hand of God,	And he, as he was full of faith and of the Holy Spirit, looked towards heaven, and saw the glory of God, and Jesus standing at the right hand of God.	And being full of faith and the Holy Spirit, he looked into heaven and saw the glory of God and Jesus standing at the right hand of God.
56	And said, Behold, I see the heavens opened, and the Son of man standing on the right hand of God.	And he said: Lo, I see heaven open, and the Son of man standing on the right hand of God.	And he said, "Behold, I see heaven opened and the Son of Man standing at the right hand of God."

Parallel Translations

	KJV	Murdock	Magiera
	ACTS	*Chapter 7*	
57	Then they cried out with a loud voice, and stopped their ears, and ran upon him with one accord,	And they cried out with a loud voice, and stopped their ears, and all rushed upon him.	And they cried out with a loud voice and closed their ears and all of them rushed on him.
58	And cast him out of the city, and stoned him: and the witnesses laid down their clothes at a young man's feet, whose name was Saul.	And they seized him, and hurried him out of the city, and stoned him. And they who testified against him, laid their clothes at the feet of a certain young man who was called Saul.	And they arrested [and] took him outside of the city and stoned him. And those who witnessed against him laid their garments at the feet of a certain young man who was called Saul.
59	And they stoned Stephen, calling upon God, and saying, Lord Jesus, receive my spirit.	And they stoned Stephen, while he prayed and said: Our Lord Jesus, receive my spirit.	And they stoned Stephen while he prayed and he said, "Our Lord Jesus, receive my spirit."
60	And he kneeled down, and cried with a loud voice, Lord, lay not this sin to their charge. And when he had said this, he fell asleep.	And when he had kneeled down, he cried with a loud voice, and said: Our Lord, establish not this sin against them. And when he had said this, he fell asleep.	And while he was kneeling down, he cried out with a loud voice and said, "Our Lord, do not cause this sin to stand against them." And after he said this, he fell asleep.
	Chapter 8		
1	And Saul was consenting unto his death. And at that time there was a great persecution against the church which was at Jerusalem; and they were all scattered abroad throughout the regions of Judaea and Samaria, except the apostles.	And Saul was consenting and participating in his death.---And there was, in that day, a great persecution against the church that was at Jerusalem; and they were all dispersed, except the legates, among the villages of Judaea and likewise among the Samaritans.	And Saul was consenting and participating in his murder. And there was in that day a great persecution of the church that was in Jerusalem. And all were scattered into the villages of Judea and also among the Samaritans, except for the apostles only.
2	And devout men carried Stephen to his burial, and made great lamentation over him.	And believing men gathered up and buried Stephen. And they lamented over him greatly.	And faithful men gathered up [and] buried Stephen and they mourned over him greatly.
3	As for Saul, he made havock of the church, entering into every house, and haling men and women committed them to prison.	And Saul persecuted the church of God, entering houses, and dragging forth men and women and committing them to prison.	And Saul was persecuting the church of God, entering into houses and dragging away men and women and delivering [them] to prison.
4	Therefore they that were scattered abroad went every where preaching the word.	And they who were dispersed, travelled about, and preached the word of God.	And those who were scattered, traveled around and preached the word of God.
5	Then Philip went down to the city of Samaria, and preached Christ unto them.	And Philip went down to a city of the Samaritans, and preached concerning the Messiah.	Now Philip went down to a city of the Samaritans and was preaching to them about Christ.
6	And the people with one accord gave heed unto those things which Philip spake, hearing and seeing the miracles which he did.	And when the people who were there heard his discourse, they gave ear to him, and acquiesced in all that he said; because they saw the signs which he wrought.	And when they heard his word, the men who were there listened to him and were persuaded by all that he said, because they saw the signs that he did.

Parallel Translations

	KJV	*Murdock*	*Magiera*
	ACTS	*Chapter 8*	
7	For unclean spirits, crying with loud voice, came out of many that were possessed with them: and many taken with palsies, and that were lame, were healed.	For many who were possessed by unclean spirits, cried with a loud voice, and came out of them: and others, who were paralytic and lame, were healed.	For many, who were possessed with unclean spirits, cried out with a loud voice, and they came out of them. And others, paralytics and lame, were healed.
8	And there was great joy in that city.	And there was great joy in that city.	And there was great joy in that city.
9	But there was a certain man, called Simon, which beforetime in the same city used sorcery, and bewitched the people of Samaria, giving out that himself was some great one:	And there was a certain man there, whose name was Simon, who had resided in that city a long time, and who seduced the people of the Samaritans by his sorceries, magnifying himself, and saying, I am a great personage.	And there was there a certain man whose name was Simon. And he had lived in that city a long time. And he was seducing the nation of the Samaritans with his sorceries, magnifying himself and saying, "I am a great [man]."
10	To whom they all gave heed, from the least to the greatest, saying, This man is the great power of God.	And they all inclined towards him, great and small; and they said, This is the mighty power of God.	And all of them were praying to him, great and small, and were saying, "This is the mighty power of God."
11	And to him they had regard, because that of long time he had bewitched them with sorceries.	And they acquiesced in him, because for a long time he had astonished them by his sorceries.	And all of them were persuaded by him, because he had astonished them a long time with his sorceries.
12	But when they believed Philip preaching the things concerning the kingdom of God, and the name of Jesus Christ, they were baptized, both men and women.	But when they gave credence to Philip, as he preached the kingdom of God, in the name of our Lord Jesus Messiah; they were baptized, both men and women.	But when they believed Philip, who was preaching the kingdom of God in the name of our Lord Jesus Christ, they were baptized, men and women.
13	Then Simon himself believed also: and when he was baptized, he continued with Philip, and wondered, beholding the miracles and signs which were done.	And Simon himself also believed, and was baptized, and adhered to Philip. And when he saw the signs and mighty deeds which were wrought by his hand, he was surprised and astonished.	And even Simon believed and was baptized and was following Philip. And when he had seen the signs and the great miracles that happened by his hand, he was amazed and marveled.
14	Now when the apostles which were at Jerusalem heard that Samaria had received the word of God, they sent unto them Peter and John:	And when the legates at Jerusalem, heard that the people of the Samaritans had received the word of God, they sent out to them Simon Cephas and John.	And when the apostles who were in Jerusalem heard that the nation of the Samaritans had received the word of God, they sent Simon Peter and John to them.
15	Who, when they were come down, prayed for them, that they might receive the Holy Ghost:	And they went down, and prayed over them, that they might receive the Holy Spirit.	And they went down and prayed for them, so that they would receive the Holy Spirit.
16	(For as yet he was fallen upon none of them: only they were baptized in the name of the Lord Jesus.)	For he was not yet on any one of them; and they had only been baptized in the name of our Lord Jesus.	For it was not yet on any of them, but they were only baptized in the name of our Lord Jesus.
17	Then laid they their hands on them, and they received the Holy Ghost.	Then they laid the hand on them; and they received the Holy Spirit.	Then they placed a hand on them and they received the Holy Spirit.

ACTS *Chapter 8*

	KJV	Murdock	Magiera
18	And when Simon saw that through laying on of the apostles' hands the Holy Ghost was given, he offered them money,	And when Simon saw that, by the imposition of a hand of the legates, the Holy Spirit was given, he offered them money,	And when Simon saw that by the placing of a hand of the apostles the Holy Spirit was given, he offered them money,
19	Saying, Give me also this power, that on whomsoever I lay hands, he may receive the Holy Ghost.	saying: Give me also this prerogative, that he on whom I impose a hand, may receive the Holy Spirit.	saying, "Give me also this authority that on whom I place a hand, he will receive the Holy Spirit."
20	But Peter said unto him, Thy money perish with thee, because thou hast thought that the gift of God may be purchased with money.	Simon Cephas said to him: Thy money go with thee to perdition! because thou hast supposed, that the gift of God may be purchased by a worldly substance.	Simon Peter said to him, "Your money will go with you to destruction, because you thought that the gift of God could be obtained with the wealth of the world.
21	Thou hast neither part nor lot in this matter: for thy heart is not right in the sight of God.	Thou hast no part nor lot in this faith; because thy heart is not right before God.	You have no part or portion in this faith, because your heart is not straight before God.
22	Repent therefore of this thy wickedness, and pray God, if perhaps the thought of thine heart may be forgiven thee.	Nevertheless, repent of this thy wickedness, and entreat of God, if perhaps the guile of thy heart may be forgiven thee.	But repent from this, your evil, and implore God that somehow the treachery of your heart will be forgiven you.
23	For I perceive that thou art in the gall of bitterness, and in the bond of iniquity.	For I perceive that thou art in the bitter gall and in the bonds of iniquity.	For I see that you are in bitter anger and in the bonds of wickedness."
24	Then answered Simon, and said, Pray ye to the Lord for me, that none of these things which ye have spoken come upon me.	Simon answered and said: Intercede ye with God for me, that nothing of which ye have mentioned may come upon me.	Simon answered and said, "Implore God on my behalf that none of these [things] you have said will come on me."
25	And they, when they had testified and preached the word of the Lord, returned to Jerusalem, and preached the gospel in many villages of the Samaritans.	And Simon and John, when they had testified, and had taught them the word of God, returned to Jerusalem. And they had preached in many villages of the Samaritans.	And Simon and John, when they had witnessed and taught the word of God, returned to Jerusalem and preached in many villages of the Samaritans.
26	And the angel of the Lord spake unto Philip, saying, Arise, and go toward the south unto the way that goeth down from Jerusalem unto Gaza, which is desert.	And the angel of the Lord spake with Philip, and said to him: Arise, go to the south, along the desert way that leadeth down from Jerusalem to Gaza.	And an angel of the LORD spoke with Philip and said to him, "Rise up [and] go to the south on the desert road that goes down from Jerusalem to Gaza."
27	And he arose and went: and, behold, a man of Ethiopia, an eunuch of great authority under Candace queen of the Ethiopians, who had the charge of all her treasure, and had come to Jerusalem for to worship,	And he arose and went. And there met him a eunuch, who had come from Cush, an officer of Candace, queen of the Cushites, who had charge of all her treasure; and he had come to worship at Jerusalem.	And he rose up [and] went. And he met a certain eunuch, who had come from Ethiopia, an official of Candace, queen of the Ethiopians. And he was responsible for all of her treasure and had come to worship in Jerusalem.
28	Was returning, and sitting in his chariot read Esaias the prophet.	And as he turned to go, he was sitting in his chariot, and was reading in Isaiah the prophet.	And as he turned to go, he was sitting in a chariot and was reading in Isaiah the prophet.
29	Then the Spirit said unto Philip, Go near, and join thyself to this chariot.	And the Holy Spirit said to Philip: Go near, and join thyself to the chariot.	And the Spirit said to Philip, "Go near and follow the chariot."

ACTS *Chapter 8*

	KJV	Murdock	Magiera
30	And Philip ran thither to him, and heard him read the prophet Esaias, and said, Understandest thou what thou readest?	And when he came near, he heard him reading in Isaiah the prophet; and he said to him: Understandest thou what thou readest?	And when he had gone near, he heard that he was reading in Isaiah the prophet and said to him, "Do you understand what you are reading?"
31	And he said, How can I, except some man should guide me? And he desired Philip that he would come up and sit with him.	And he said: How can I understand, unless some one instruct me? And he requested of Philip, that he would come up and sit with him.	And he said, "How am I able to understand, unless someone instructs me?" And he begged Philip to come up and sit with him.
32	The place of the scripture which he read was this, He was led as a sheep to the slaughter; and like a lamb dumb before his shearer, so opened he not his mouth:	And the section of scripture in which he was reading, was this: As a lamb to the slaughter he was led away, and as a sheep before the shearer is silent, so also he in his humility opened not his mouth.	And the section of the scripture which he was reading was this, AS A LAMB HE WAS LED TO THE SLAUGHTER AND AS A SHEEP BEFORE THE SHEARER IS SILENT, EVEN SO HE DID NOT OPEN HIS MOUTH.
33	In his humiliation his judgment was taken away: and who shall declare his generation? for his life is taken from the earth.	From prison and from judgment he was carried: and his generation, who will declare? for his life is taken away from the earth.	IN HIS HUMILITY HE WAS LED FROM PRISON AND FROM JUDGMENT AND HIS GENERATION, WHO WILL DECLARE [IT]? FOR HIS LIFE HAS BEEN TAKEN FROM THE EARTH.
34	And the eunuch answered Philip, and said, I pray thee, of whom speaketh the prophet this? of himself, or of some other man?	And the eunuch said to Philip: I pray thee, of whom speaketh the prophet this? of himself, or of some other person?	And that eunuch said to Philip, "I ask of you, concerning whom did the prophet speak this, of himself or of another man?"
35	Then Philip opened his mouth, and began at the same scripture, and preached unto him Jesus.	Then Philip opened his mouth and, from that scripture, began to preach to him concerning our Lord Jesus.	Then Philip opened his mouth and from this same scripture began to preach to him about our Lord Jesus.
36	And as they went on their way, they came unto a certain water: and the eunuch said, See, here is water; what doth hinder me to be baptized?	And as they proceeded on the way, they came to a certain place in which there was water. And the eunuch said: Lo, [here is] water; what doth forbid, that I should be baptized?	And as they traveled on the road, they arrived at a certain place where there was water. And that eunuch said, "Behold, [here is] water. What is the hindrance that I may be baptized?"
37	And Philip said, If thou believest with all thine heart, thou mayest. And he answered and said, I believe that Jesus Christ is the Son of God.	[And Philip said: If thou believest with all thy heart, it is allowable. And he answered, and said: I believe that Jesus Messiah is the Son of God.]	OMITTED IN THE WESTERN PESHITTA TEXT
38	And he commanded the chariot to stand still: and they went down both into the water, both Philip and the eunuch; and he baptized him.	And he commanded the chariot to stop; and they both went down to the water, and Philip baptized the eunuch.	And he commanded the chariot to stop and the two of them went down into the water and Philip baptized that eunuch.
39	And when they were come up out of the water, the Spirit of the Lord caught away Philip, that the eunuch saw him no more: and he went on his way rejoicing.	And when they came up from the water, the Spirit of the Lord caught away Philip; and the eunuch saw him no more; but he went on his way rejoicing.	And when they came up from the water, the Spirit of the LORD caught up Philip and that eunuch did not see him again, but went on his way, rejoicing.

Parallel Translations

	KJV	*Murdock*	*Magiera*
ACTS *Chapter 8*			
40	But Philip was found at Azotus: and passing through he preached in all the cities, till he came to Caesarea.	And Philip was found at Azotus; and from there he travelled about, and preached in all the cities, until he came to Caesarea.	And Philip was found at Azotus and from there was traveling around and preaching in all the cities, until he came to Caesarea.
Chapter 9			
1	And Saul, yet breathing out threatenings and slaughter against the disciples of the Lord, went unto the high priest,	And Saul was still full of threats and deadly hatred against the disciples of our Lord.	And Saul was still full of threatening and the anger of murder against the disciples of our Lord.
2	And desired of him letters to Damascus to the synagogues, that if he found any of this way, whether they were men or women, he might bring them bound unto Jerusalem.	And he requested that a letter from the high priest might be given him unto Damascus to the synagogues; that if he should find persons pursuing this course, men or women, he might bind and bring them to Jerusalem.	And he asked for letters from the high priest to give to Damascus to the synagogues, that if he should find any who were following in this way, men or women, he could bind [and] bring them to Jerusalem.
3	And as he journeyed, he came near Damascus: and suddenly there shined round about him a light from heaven:	And as he was going, and began to approach Damascus, suddenly there was poured upon him a light from heaven.	And as he went and approached Damascus, suddenly a light from heaven shone on him.
4	And he fell to the earth, and heard a voice saying unto him, Saul, Saul, why persecutest thou me?	And he fell to the ground; and he heard a voice which said to him: Saul! Saul! why persecutest thou me? It will be hard for thee to kick against the goads.	And he fell on the ground and heard a voice that said to him, "Saul, Saul, why are you persecuting me? It is hard for you to kick at the goads."
5	And he said, Who art thou, Lord? And the Lord said, I am Jesus whom thou persecutest: it is hard for thee to kick against the pricks.	He replied, and said: Who art thou, my Lord? And our Lord said: I am Jesus the Nazarean, whom thou persecutest.	He answered and said, "Who are you, my Lord?" And our Lord said, "I am Jesus, the Nazarene, whom you are persecuting.
6	And he trembling and astonished said, Lord, what wilt thou have me to do? And the Lord said unto him, Arise, and go into the city, and it shall be told thee what thou must do.	But arise and go into the city, and there it will be told thee what thou oughtest to do.	But rise up, enter the city, and there you will be told about what you ought to do."
7	And the men which journeyed with him stood speechless, hearing a voice, but seeing no man.	And the men who travelled with him in the way, stood amazed; for they heard merely the voice, and no one was visible to them.	And the men who were traveling with him on the journey were standing amazed, because they were hearing a voice only, but no one was visible to them.
8	And Saul arose from the earth; and when his eyes were opened, he saw no man: but they led him by the hand, and brought him into Damascus.	And Saul arose from the ground; and nothing was visible to him, with his eyes opened. And they took him by the hand, and led him into Damascus.	And Saul got up from the ground and he was not seeing anything, although his eyes were open. And holding [him] by his hands, they brought him to Damascus.
9	And he was three days without sight, and neither did eat nor drink.	And he had no sight for three days; and he neither ate nor drank.	And he was not seeing [for] three days and he did not eat or drink.

Parallel Translations

	KJV	*Murdock*	*Magiera*
	ACTS	*Chapter 9*	
10	And there was a certain disciple at Damascus, named Ananias; and to him said the Lord in a vision, Ananias. And he said, Behold, I am here, Lord.	And there was in Damascus a certain disciple, whose name was Ananias. And the Lord said to him, in a vision: Ananias! And he said: Lo, I [am here], my Lord.	And there was a certain disciple in Damascus, whose name was Ananias. And the LORD said to him in a vision, "Ananias." And he said, "Behold, I [am here], my Lord."
11	And the Lord said unto him, Arise, and go into the street which is called Straight, and enquire in the house of Judas for one called Saul, of Tarsus: for, behold, he prayeth,	And our Lord said to him: Arise, go to the street which is called Straight; and inquire in the house of Judas, for Saul who is from the city of Tarsus: for, lo, while he prayed,	And our Lord said to him, "Rise up! Go to the street that is called Straight and ask at the house of Judas for Saul, who is from the city [of] Tarsus, for behold, while he was praying,
12	And hath seen in a vision a man named Ananias coming in, and putting his hand on him, that he might receive his sight.	he saw in vision a man named Ananias, who came and laid his hand upon him, that his eyes might be opened.	he saw in a vision that a man whose name [was] Ananias entered and placed a hand on him, so that his eyes would be opened."
13	Then Ananias answered, Lord, I have heard by many of this man, how much evil he hath done to thy saints at Jerusalem:	And Ananias said: My Lord, I have heard of this man, from many, how much evil he hath perpetrated towards thy saints at Jerusalem.	And Ananias said, "My Lord, I have heard from many about this man, how many evil [things] he has inflicted on your holy [ones] in Jerusalem.
14	And here he hath authority from the chief priests to bind all that call on thy name.	And, lo, here also, he hath authority from the chief priests, to bind all them that call on thy name.	And behold, also here, he has authority from the chief priests to bind all those who call on your name."
15	But the Lord said unto him, Go thy way: for he is a chosen vessel unto me, to bear my name before the Gentiles, and kings, and the children of Israel:	The Lord said to him: Arise and go; for he is to me a chosen vessel, to carry my name to the Gentiles, and to kings, and among the sons of Israel.	And the LORD said to him, "Rise up [and] go, because he is a chosen vessel for me to carry my name to the Gentiles and to kings and among the sons of Israel,
16	For I will shew him how great things he must suffer for my name's sake.	For I will show him, how much he is to suffer on account of my name.	for I will show him how much he will suffer on account of my name."
17	And Ananias went his way, and entered into the house; and putting his hands on him said, Brother Saul, the Lord, even Jesus, that appeared unto thee in the way as thou camest, hath sent me, that thou mightest receive thy sight, and be filled with the Holy Ghost.	Then Ananias went to the house to him; and he laid his hand upon him, and said to him: Saul, my brother, our Lord Jesus, he who appeared to thee by the way as thou camest, hath sent me, that thy eyes might be opened, and thou be filled with the Holy Spirit.	Then Ananias went to him to the house and placed a hand on him and said to him, "Saul, my brother, our Lord Jesus, who appeared to you while you were coming on the road, has sent me, so that your eyes would be opened and you would be filled with the Holy Spirit."
18	And immediately there fell from his eyes as it had been scales: and he received sight forthwith, and arose, and was baptized.	And immediately there fell from his eyes something like a scab; and his eyes were opened. And he arose and was baptized.	And immediately, something like scales fell from his eyes and his eyes were opened. And he rose up [and] was baptized
19	And when he had received meat, he was strengthened. Then was Saul certain days with the disciples which were at Damascus.	And he took food, and was invigorated.---And he was [some] days with the disciples of Damascus.	and he received food and was strengthened. And he was [some] days with the disciples who were in Damascus.

Parallel Translations

	KJV	Murdock	Magiera
ACTS	*Chapter 9*		
20	And straightway he preached Christ in the synagogues, that he is the Son of God.	And forthwith he announced Jesus, in the synagogues of the Jews, that he is the Son of God.	And immediately, he was preaching in the synagogues of the Judeans about Jesus, that he was the Son of God.
21	But all that heard him were amazed, and said; Is not this he that destroyed them which called on this name in Jerusalem, and came hither for that intent, that he might bring them bound unto the chief priests?	And all they that heard him were amazed; and they said: Is not this he, who persecuted all them that call on this name in Jerusalem? And lo, for this very thing also, was he sent hither, that he might bind and carry them to the chief priests.	And all those who heard him were amazed and were saying, "Is this not he who persecuted all those who called on this name in Jerusalem? Also, he was sent here for this same [thing], to bind and bring them to the chief priests."
22	But Saul increased the more in strength, and confounded the Jews which dwelt at Damascus, proving that this is very Christ.	But Saul was the more strengthened; and he confounded those Jews who dwelt at Damascus, while he demonstrated that this is the Messiah.	But Saul was strengthened even more and confounded the Judeans, those who lived in Damascus, showing that this is the Christ.
23	And after that many days were fulfilled, the Jews took counsel to kill him:	And when he had been there many days, the Jews formed a conspiracy against him, to kill him.	And after he had been there many days, the Judeans planned treachery against him to kill him.
24	But their laying await was known of Saul. And they watched the gates day and night to kill him.	And the plot which they sought to execute upon him, was made known to Saul: and they watched the gates of the city by day and by night, in order to kill him.	But the plot that they were seeking to do to him was made known to Saul. And they watched the gates of the city, day and night, to kill him.
25	Then the disciples took him by night, and let him down by the wall in a basket.	Then the disciples placed him in a basket, and let him down from the wall by night.	Then the disciples placed him in a basket and let him down from the wall during the night.
26	And when Saul was come to Jerusalem, he assayed to join himself to the disciples: but they were all afraid of him, and believed not that he was a disciple.	And he went to Jerusalem; and he wished to join himself with the disciples, but they were all afraid of him, and did not believe that he was a disciple.	And he went to Jerusalem and wanted to join himself to the disciples, yet all were afraid of him and did not believe that he was a disciple.
27	But Barnabas took him, and brought him to the apostles, and declared unto them how he had seen the Lord in the way, and that he had spoken to him, and how he had preached boldly at Damascus in the name of Jesus.	But Barnabas took him, and brought him to the legates, and related to them how the Lord appeared to him in the way, and how he conversed with him; and how, in Damascus, he had discoursed openly in the name of Jesus.	But Barnabas took him and brought him to the apostles and related to them, how on the road he had seen the LORD and how he spoke with him and how in Damascus he had spoken boldly in the name of Jesus.
28	And he was with them coming in and going out at Jerusalem.	And he went in and out with them, at Jerusalem.	And he entered in and went out with them in Jerusalem.
29	And he spake boldly in the name of the Lord Jesus, and disputed against the Grecians: but they went about to slay him.	And he spoke openly in the name of Jesus and disputed with those Jews who understood Greek. But they wished to kill him:	And he was speaking in the name of Jesus boldly and disputing with the Judeans who understood in Greek. But they wanted to kill him
30	Which when the brethren knew, they brought him down to Caesarea, and sent him forth to Tarsus.	and when the brethren knew [it], they conducted him by night to Caesarea, and from there they sent him to Tarsus.	and when the brothers knew [this], they brought him to Caesarea by night and from there they sent him to Tarsus.

Parallel Translations

ACTS Chapter 9

	KJV	Murdock	Magiera
31	Then had the churches rest throughout all Judaea and Galilee and Samaria, and were edified; and walking in the fear of the Lord, and in the comfort of the Holy Ghost, were multiplied.	Moreover the church, in all Judaea, and in Galilee, and in Samaria, had peace and was edified; and it walked in the fear of God, and abounded in the consolation of the Holy Spirit.	Nevertheless the church that was in all Judea and in Galilee and in Samaria had peace, being edified, and were proceeding in the fear of God and were abounding in the comfort of the Holy Spirit.
32	And it came to pass, as Peter passed throughout all quarters, he came down also to the saints which dwelt at Lydda.	And it occurred, that, as Simon travelled about the cities, he came down to the saints also who dwelt in the city of Lydda.	And it happened that as Simon was traveling around in the cities, he came down also to the holy [ones] who lived in the city [of] Lydda.
33	And there he found a certain man named Aeneas, which had kept his bed eight years, and was sick of the palsy.	And he found a certain man whose name was Æneas, who had lain on a bed and been paralytic eight years.	And he found a certain man whose name [was] Aeneas who was lying on a pallet and was paralyzed [for] eight years.
34	And Peter said unto him, Aeneas, Jesus Christ maketh thee whole: arise, and make thy bed. And he arose immediately.	And Simon said to him: Æneas, Jesus the Messiah doth heal thee; arise, and spread thy bed. And he rose up immediately.	And Simon said to him, "Aeneas, Jesus Christ heals you. Rise up and smooth out your pallet." And immediately he rose up.
35	And all that dwelt at Lydda and Saron saw him, and turned to the Lord.	And all they that dwelt at Lydda and Saron, saw him; and they turned to God.	And all who lived in Lydda and in Saron saw him and turned to God.
36	Now there was at Joppa a certain disciple named Tabitha, which by interpretation is called Dorcas: this woman was full of good works and almsdeeds which she did.	And there was in the city of Joppa, a certain female disciple named Tabitha; [and] she was rich in good works, and in the alms which she did.	And there was a certain disciple in the city [of] Joppa, whose name was Tabitha. This [one] was rich in good deeds and in the charitable works that she did.
37	And it came to pass in those days, that she was sick, and died: whom when they had washed, they laid her in an upper chamber.	And she fell sick in those days, and died; and they washed her, and laid her in an upper room.	And she became sick in those days and died. And they washed her and laid her in an upper room.
38	And forasmuch as Lydda was nigh to Joppa, and the disciples had heard that Peter was there, they sent unto him two men, desiring him that he would not delay to come to them.	And the disciples heard that Simon was in the city of Lydda, which is near to Joppa; and they sent two men to him, to request of him that he would not delay to come to them.	And the disciples heard that Simon was in the city [of] Lydda, which was near Joppa. And they sent two men to him to ask him to come with them, [if] it was not tedious for him.
39	Then Peter arose and went with them. When he was come, they brought him into the upper chamber: and all the widows stood by him weeping, and shewing the coats and garments which Dorcas made, while she was with them.	And Simon arose and went with them. And when he arrived, they conducted him to the chamber; and there were assembled around her all the widows, weeping, and showing him the tunics and the cloaks which Tabitha had given them when alive.	And Simon rose up [and] went with them. And when he had come, they took him up to the upper room and all the widows gathered [and] stood around him, weeping and showing him the tunics and coats that Tabitha had given to them while she was alive.
40	But Peter put them all forth, and kneeled down, and prayed; and turning him to the body said, Tabitha, arise. And she opened her eyes: and when she saw Peter, she sat up.	And Simon put all the people out, and fell on his knees and prayed; and he turned to the corpse and said: Tabitha, arise. And she opened her eyes; and when she saw Simon, she sat up.	Now Simon put all the people outside and he kneeled down and prayed. And he turned to the dead body and said, "Tabitha, rise up." And she opened her eyes and when she saw Simon, she sat up.

Parallel Translations

	KJV	*Murdock*	*Magiera*
	ACTS	*Chapter 9*	
41	And he gave her his hand, and lifted her up, and when he had called the saints and widows, presented her alive.	And he reached to her his hand, and raised her up: and he called the saints and the widows, and presented her to them alive.	And he stretched out his hand to her and raised her up. And called for the holy [ones] and widows and presented her to them alive.
42	And it was known throughout all Joppa; and many believed in the Lord.	And this became known throughout the city; and many believed on our Lord.	And this was known in all the city and many believed in our Lord.
43	And it came to pass, that he tarried many days in Joppa with one Simon a tanner.	And he tarried in Joppa not a few days: and he lodged in the house of Simon a tanner.	And he was in Joppa not a few days, lodging in the house of Simon, a tanner.
	Chapter 10		
1	There was a certain man in Caesarea called Cornelius, a centurion of the band called the Italian band,	And there was a certain man in Caesarea, whose name was Cornelius, a centurion of the regiment called the Italian.	And there was a certain man in Caesarea, a centurion, whose name was Cornelius from the band of soldiers that was called the Italian.
2	A devout man, and one that feared God with all his house, which gave much alms to the people, and prayed to God alway.	And he was righteous, and feared God, he and all his house; [and] he did much alms among the people, and prayed to God at all times.	And he was just and feared God, he and all his house. And he did many charitable works among the people and was always seeking God.
3	He saw in a vision evidently about the ninth hour of the day an angel of God coming in to him, and saying unto him, Cornelius.	This man distinctly saw, in a vision, about the ninth hour of the day, an angel of God, who came in to him and said to him: Cornelius!	This [man] clearly saw an angel of God in a vision [about] the ninth hour of the day, who came toward him and said to him, "Cornelius."
4	And when he looked on him, he was afraid, and said, What is it, Lord? And he said unto him, Thy prayers and thine alms are come up for a memorial before God.	And he looked upon him, and was afraid; and he said: What, my Lord? And the angel said to him: Thy prayers and thy alms have come up in remembrance before God.	And he looked at him and was afraid and said, "What, my Lord?" And the angel said to him, "Your prayers and your charity have come up for a remembrance before God.
5	And now send men to Joppa, and call for one Simon, whose surname is Peter:	And now, send men to the city of Joppa, and bring Simon who is called Cephas.	And now send men to the city [of] Joppa and bring Simon, who is called Peter.
6	He lodgeth with one Simon a tanner, whose house is by the sea side: he shall tell thee what thou oughtest to do.	Lo, he lodgeth in the house of Simon the tanner, which is by the side of the sea.	Behold, he is living in the house of Simon, the tanner, which is on the shore of the sea."
7	And when the angel which spake unto Cornelius was departed, he called two of his household servants, and a devout soldier of them that waited on him continually;	And when the angel that talked with him was gone, he called two of his household, and a soldier who feared God and was obedient to him.	And as the angel who had talked with him was going away, he called two of his household and a certain servant, who feared God, one who obeyed him,
8	And when he had declared all these things unto them, he sent them to Joppa.	And he related to them all that he had seen, and sent them to Joppa.	and told them everything that he had seen and sent them to Joppa.
9	On the morrow, as they went on their journey, and drew nigh unto the city, Peter went up upon the housetop to pray about the sixth hour:	And the next day, as they travelled the road and approached the city, Simon ascended the roof to pray, at the sixth hour.	And on the next day, while they were traveling on the journey and approaching the city, Simon went up to the roof to pray at the sixth hour.

Parallel Translations

	KJV	*Murdock*	*Magiera*
	ACTS	*Chapter 10*	
10	And he became very hungry, and would have eaten: but while they made ready, he fell into a trance,	And he became hungry, and desired to eat. And while they were providing for him, he fell into a trance.	And he was hungry and wanted to eat. And while they were preparing for him, astonishment came on him
11	And saw heaven opened, and a certain vessel descending unto him, as it had been a great sheet knit at the four corners, and let down to the earth:	And he saw the heavens opened, and a certain vessel fastened at the four corners, and it was like a great sheet; and it descended from heaven to the earth.	and he saw heaven opened and a certain garment being held by four corners. And it was like a large linen cloth and it was coming down from heaven to the earth.
12	Wherein were all manner of fourfooted beasts of the earth, and wild beasts, and creeping things, and fowls of the air.	And there were in it all fourfooted animals, and creeping things of the earth, and fowls of heaven.	And in it there were many four-footed animals and creeping things of the earth and birds of heaven.
13	And there came a voice to him, Rise, Peter; kill, and eat.	And a voice came to him, which said: Simon, arise, slay and eat.	And a voice came to him that said, "Simon, rise up, kill and eat."
14	But Peter said, Not so, Lord; for I have never eaten any thing that is common or unclean.	And Simon said: Far be it, my Lord: for never have I eaten any thing unclean and polluted.	And Simon said, "Let it not be so, my Lord, because I have never eaten anything that is corrupt and unclean."
15	And the voice spake unto him again the second time, What God hath cleansed, that call not thou common.	And again the second time, there was a voice to him: What God hath cleansed, make thou not unclean.	And again a second time, a voice came to him, "That which God has cleansed, do not regard as corrupt."
16	This was done thrice: and the vessel was received up again into heaven.	And this was done three times; and the vessel was taken up to heaven.	And this happened three times and the garment was lifted up to heaven.
17	Now while Peter doubted in himself what this vision which he had seen should mean, behold, the men which were sent from Cornelius had made enquiry for Simon's house, and stood before the gate,	And while Simon was wondering with himself, what the vision he had seen could denote, the men who were sent by Cornelius arrived; and they inquired for the house in which Simon lodged, and came and stood at the gate of the court.	And while Simon wondered in himself what was the vision that he had seen, those men who had been sent by Cornelius arrived. And they asked for the house in which Simon lodged and they came and stood at the gate of the courtyard.
18	And called, and asked whether Simon, which was surnamed Peter, were lodged there.	And there they called out, and asked if Simon who is called Cephas lodged there?	And they called there and asked, "Is Simon, who is called Peter, lodged here?"
19	While Peter thought on the vision, the Spirit said unto him, Behold, three men seek thee.	And while Simon was reflecting on the vision, the Spirit said to him: Lo, three men are inquiring for thee.	And while Simon thought on the vision, the Spirit said to him, "Behold, three men seek you.
20	Arise therefore, and get thee down, and go with them, doubting nothing: for I have sent them.	Arise, go down, and accompany them; and let not thy mind hesitate, for I have sent them.	Rise up, get down, and go with them, not letting your mind doubt, because I have sent them."
21	Then Peter went down to the men which were sent unto him from Cornelius; and said, Behold, I am he whom ye seek: what is the cause wherefore ye are come?	Then Simon went down to the men, and said to them: I am he for whom ye inquire: what is the cause for which ye have come?	Then Simon went down to those men and said to them, "I am he whom you seek. What is the reason for which you have come?"

Parallel Translations

	KJV	*Murdock*	*Magiera*

ACTS *Chapter 10*

	KJV	Murdock	Magiera
22	And they said, Cornelius the centurion, a just man, and one that feareth God, and of good report among all the nation of the Jews, was warned from God by an holy angel to send for thee into his house, and to hear words of thee.	They say to him: A certain man whose name is Cornelius, a centurion fearing God, and of whom all the people of the Jews bear good report, was told in vision, by a holy angel, to send and bring thee to his house, that he might hear discourse from thee.	They said to him, "A certain man whose name [is] Cornelius, a centurion, an upright [man] who fears God and about whom all the people of the Judeans give testimony, was told in a vision from a holy angel to send [and] bring you to his house and to hear a word from you.
23	Then called he them in, and lodged them. And on the morrow Peter went away with them, and certain brethren from Joppa accompanied him.	And Simon led them in, and entertained them where he lodged. And the following day, he arose, departed, and went with them: and some of the brethren of Joppa also went with them.	And Simon brought them in and received them where he lodged. And he rose up on the following day and left [and] went with them. And some of the brothers of Joppa went with him.
24	And the morrow after they entered into Caesarea. And Cornelius waited for them, and had called together his kinsmen and near friends.	And the next day, they entered Caesarea. And Cornelius was expecting them: and all the kindred of his family, and also such intimate friends as he had, were assembled with him.	And on the next day, he entered Caesarea and Cornelius was waiting for them, all his kinsmen and also beloved friends that he had being assembled with him.
25	And as Peter was coming in, Cornelius met him, and fell down at his feet, and worshipped him.	And as Simon came up, Cornelius met him, and fell down worshipping at his feet.	And as Simon was entering, Cornelius met him and fell down [and] worshipped at his feet.
26	But Peter took him up, saying, Stand up; I myself also am a man.	And Simon raised him up, and said to him: Arise; I also am a man.	And Simon raised him up and said to him, "Stand up. I am a man also."
27	And as he talked with him, he went in, and found many that were come together.	And as he talked with him, he went in, and found that many had come there.	And while he was talking with him, he entered and found many who had come there.
28	And he said unto them, Ye know how that it is an unlawful thing for a man that is a Jew to keep company, or come unto one of another nation; but God hath shewed me that I should not call any man common or unclean.	And he said to them: Ye know, that it is not lawful for a Jewish man, to associate with an alien who is not of his race: but God hath showed me, that I should not say of any one, that he is defiled or unclean.	And he said to them, "You know that it is not lawful for a Judean man to associate with an alien man who is not [of] his race, yet God showed me that I should not say about anyone that he is unclean or corrupt.
29	Therefore came I unto you without gainsaying, as soon as I was sent for: I ask therefore for what intent ye have sent for me?	Therefore I came readily, when ye sent for me. But, I ask you, for what cause did ye send for me?	Because of this, I came promptly when you sent for me. But I ask you, 'Why did you send for me?'"
30	And Cornelius said, Four days ago I was fasting until this hour; and at the ninth hour I prayed in my house, and, behold, a man stood before me in bright clothing,	And Cornelius said to him: It is four days ago, that, lo, I was fasting; and at the ninth hour, while I was praying in my house, a certain man stood before me, clothed in white,	Cornelius said to him, "Four days have passed, since behold, I was fasting, and in the ninth hour while I was praying in my house, a certain man stood before me, wearing white [clothes]."
31	And said, Cornelius, thy prayer is heard, and thine alms are had in remembrance in the sight of God.	and said to me: Cornelius, thy prayer is heard, and there is remembrance of thy alms before God.	And he said to me, "Cornelius, your prayer has been heard and there is a remembrance of your charity before God.

ACTS Chapter 10

	KJV	Murdock	Magiera
32	Send therefore to Joppa, and call hither Simon, whose surname is Peter; he is lodged in the house of one Simon a tanner by the sea side: who, when he cometh, shall speak unto thee.	But send to the city of Joppa, and bring Simon who is called Cephas: lo, he lodgeth in the house of Simon the tanner, which is by the side of the sea. And he will come and converse with thee.	But send to the city [of] Joppa and bring Simon, who is called Peter. Behold, he is living in the house of Simon, the tanner, which is on the shore of the sea. And he will come to speak to you.
33	Immediately therefore I sent to thee; and thou hast well done that thou art come. Now therefore are we all here present before God, to hear all things that are commanded thee of God.	And immediately I sent to thee; and thou hast done well to come: and lo, we are all of us before thee, and desirous to hear whatever is commanded thee from God.	And immediately I sent to you and you have done well that you came. Now behold, all of us [are] before you and we want to hear all that has been commanded to you from God."
34	Then Peter opened his mouth, and said, Of a truth I perceive that God is no respecter of persons:	And Simon opened his mouth, and said: Truly I discover that God is no respecter of persons.	And Simon opened his mouth and said, "In truth, I perceive that God is not a respecter of persons,
35	But in every nation he that feareth him, and worketh righteousness, is accepted with him.	but, among all the nations, he who feareth him, and worketh righteousness, is acceptable with him.	but among all the nations, he who fears him and works uprightness is acceptable to him.
36	The word which God sent unto the children of Israel, preaching peace by Jesus Christ: (he is Lord of all:)	For [this is] the word, which he sent to the sons of Israel, announcing to them peace and rest by Jesus Messiah,---He is Lord of all;	For [this is] the word that he sent to the sons of Israel and declared to them: Peace and harmony by way of Jesus Christ, who is the LORD of all.
37	That word, I say, ye know, which was published throughout all Judaea, and began from Galilee, after the baptism which John preached;	and ye also know the word, which was in all Judaea, which commenced from Galilee, after the baptism that John preached,	And you also know about the word that was in all Judea that went out from Galilee after the baptism that John preached
38	How God anointed Jesus of Nazareth with the Holy Ghost and with power: who went about doing good, and healing all that were oppressed of the devil; for God was with him.	concerning Jesus, who was of Nazareth, whom God anointed with the Holy Spirit and with power. And he it was, who went about and healed those that were suffering from evil, because God was with him.	concerning Jesus, who was from Nazareth, whom God anointed with the Holy Spirit and with power. And this is he who traveled around and healed those who were oppressed by the Evil [one], because God was with him.
39	And we are witnesses of all things which he did both in the land of the Jews, and in Jerusalem; whom they slew and hanged on a tree:	And we [are] his witnesses, as to whatever he did in all the region of Judaea and in Jerusalem. This same person the Jews hanged on a tree, and slew him.	And we are his witnesses concerning all that he did in all the region of Judea and of Jerusalem. This same [one] the Judeans hung on a tree and killed.
40	Him God raised up the third day, and shewed him openly;	And him did God raise up, on the third day; and caused him to be seen with naked eyes;	And God raised him after three days and allowed him to be seen openly.
41	Not to all the people, but unto witnesses chosen before of God, even to us, who did eat and drink with him after he rose from the dead.	not indeed by all the people, but by us, who were chosen of God to be his witnesses, [and] who ate and drank with him after his resurrection from the dead.	Now [he was] not [seen] by all the people, but by us, those who were chosen by God to be witnesses for him, for we ate and drank with him after his resurrection that was from the dead.

	KJV	Murdock	Magiera
	ACTS *Chapter 10*		
42	And he commanded us to preach unto the people, and to testify that it is he which was ordained of God to be the Judge of quick and dead.	And he commanded us to proclaim and testify to the people, that he is appointed of God to be judge of the living and of the dead.	And he commanded us to preach and to witness to the people that he was the one who was appointed by God [as] the judge of the living and of the dead.
43	To him give all the prophets witness, that through his name whosoever believeth in him shall receive remission of sins.	And of him all the prophets testify, that whoever believeth in his name, will receive remission of sins.	And concerning him all the prophets witness, so that whoever believes on his name will receive forgiveness of sins."
44	While Peter yet spake these words, the Holy Ghost fell on all them which heard the word.	And while Simon was uttering these things, the Holy Spirit overshadowed all them that were hearing the word.	And while Simon was speaking these words, the Holy Spirit overshadowed all who were hearing the word.
45	And they of the circumcision which believed were astonished, as many as came with Peter, because that on the Gentiles also was poured out the gift of the Holy Ghost.	And the circumcised brethren who came with him, were amazed and astonished, that the gift of the Holy Spirit was poured out upon the Gentiles also.	And the circumcised brothers who had come with him were amazed and astonished that the gift of the Holy Spirit was poured out on the Gentiles also,
46	For they heard them speak with tongues, and magnify God. Then answered Peter,	For they heard them speak with diverse tongues, and magnify God.	for they heard them speaking in various languages and magnifying God. And Simon said,
47	Can any man forbid water, that these should not be baptized, which have received the Holy Ghost as well as we?	And Simon said: Can any one forbid water, that those should not be baptized, they who have received, lo, the Holy Spirit, as well as we?	"Can anyone forbid water, so that those who, behold, have received the Holy Spirit as we, should not be baptized?"
48	And he commanded them to be baptized in the name of the Lord. Then prayed they him to tarry certain days.	Then he commanded them to be baptized in the name of our Lord Jesus Messiah. And they requested him to remain with them [some] days.	Then he commanded them to be baptized in the name of our Lord Jesus Christ. And they begged him to stay with them [some] days.
	Chapter 11		
1	And the apostles and brethren that were in Judaea heard that the Gentiles had also received the word of God.	And it was reported to the legates and the brethren in Judaea, that the Gentiles also had received the word of God.	And it was heard by the apostles and the brothers who were in Judea that the Gentiles had also received the word of God.
2	And when Peter was come up to Jerusalem, they that were of the circumcision contended with him,	And when Simon went up to Jerusalem, they who were of the circumcision contended with him,	And when Simon went up to Jerusalem, those who were from the circumcision were arguing with him,
3	Saying, Thou wentest in to men uncircumcised, and didst eat with them.	saying; that he had gone in to be with uncircumcised persons, and had eaten with them.	saying that he had gone in with uncircumcised men and eaten with them.
4	But Peter rehearsed the matter from the beginning, and expounded it by order unto them, saying,	And Simon began to address them methodically:	And Simon began in order to say to them,

	KJV	*Murdock*	*Magiera*
	ACTS	*Chapter 11*	
5	I was in the city of Joppa praying: and in a trance I saw a vision, A certain vessel descend, as it had been a great sheet, let down from heaven by four corners; and it came even to me:	As I was in Joppa, praying, I saw in vision, that a certain vessel descended, which was like a sheet, and it was tied at its four corners; and it descended from heaven and came to me.	"While I was praying in Joppa, I saw in a vision a certain garment, which resembled a linen cloth, that came down. And it was held by its four corners and it was lowered down from heaven and came all the way to me.
6	Upon the which when I had fastened mine eyes, I considered, and saw fourfooted beasts of the earth, and wild beasts, and creeping things, and fowls of the air.	And I looked upon it, and I saw that in it were fourfooted animals, and reptiles of the earth, and fowls of heaven.	And I looked at it and saw that in it there were four-footed animals and creeping things of the earth and also birds of heaven.
7	And I heard a voice saying unto me, Arise, Peter; slay and eat.	And I heard a voice, which said to me: Simon, arise, slay and eat.	And I heard a voice that said to me, 'Simon, rise up, kill and eat.'
8	But I said, Not so, Lord: for nothing common or unclean hath at any time entered into my mouth.	And I said: Far be it, my Lord. For never hath any thing polluted or unclean entered my mouth.	And I said, 'Let it not be so, my Lord, because that which is unclean and corrupt has never entered my mouth.'
9	But the voice answered me again from heaven, What God hath cleansed, that call not thou common.	And again, a voice from heaven said to me: What God hath cleansed, make thou not unclean.	And again a voice said to me from heaven, 'That which God has cleansed, do not regard as corrupt.'
10	And this was done three times: and all were drawn up again into heaven.	And this was done three times: and the whole was taken up to heaven.	This happened three times and everything was taken up to heaven.
11	And, behold, immediately there were three men already come unto the house where I was, sent from Caesarea unto me.	And at the same instant, three men, who were sent to me by Cornelius from Caesarea, came and stood at the gate of the court where I lodged.	And immediately, three men, who were sent to me by Cornelius of Caesarea, came and stood at the gate of the courtyard in which I lodged.
12	And the Spirit bade me go with them, nothing doubting. Moreover these six brethren accompanied me, and we entered into the man's house:	And the Spirit said to me: Go with them, without hesitation. And these six brethren went also with me, and we entered the man's house.	And the Spirit said to me, 'Go with them without doubt.' And these six brothers also came with me and we entered the house of the man.
13	And he shewed us how he had seen an angel in his house, which stood and said unto him, Send men to Joppa, and call for Simon, whose surname is Peter;	And he related to us, how he had seen an angel in his house, who stood and said to him: Send to the city of Joppa, and bring Simon who is called Cephas;	And he related to us how he saw an angel in his house, who stood and said to him, 'Send to the city [of] Joppa and bring Simon, who is called Peter.
14	Who shall tell thee words, whereby thou and all thy house shall be saved.	and he will utter to thee discourses, by which thou wilt live, thou and all thy house.	And he will speak to you words by which you will have life, you and all your house.'
15	And as I began to speak, the Holy Ghost fell on them, as on us at the beginning.	And when I there commenced speaking, the Holy Spirit overshadowed them, as it did us from the beginning.	And as I began to speak there, the Holy Spirit overshadowed them, as [it had] previously on us.
16	Then remembered I the word of the Lord, how that he said, John indeed baptized with water; but ye shall be baptized with the Holy Ghost.	And I remembered the word of our Lord, when he said: John baptized with water, but ye shall be baptized with the Holy Spirit.	And I remembered the word of our Lord, who said, 'John baptized with water, but you will be baptized with the Holy Spirit.'

Parallel Translations

ACTS Chapter 11

	KJV	Murdock	Magiera
17	Forasmuch then as God gave them the like gift as he did unto us, who believed on the Lord Jesus Christ; what was I, that I could withstand God?	If then God equally gave the gift to the Gentiles that believed in our Lord Jesus Messiah, as he did to us: who was I, that I could forbid God?	Therefore, if God equally gave the gift to the Gentiles that believed in our Lord Jesus Christ, as also to us, who was I that I should be able to hinder God?"
18	When they heard these things, they held their peace, and glorified God, saying, Then hath God also to the Gentiles granted repentance unto life.	And when they heard these words, they desisted; and they glorified God and said: Now to the Gentiles also doth God give repentance unto life.	And after they had heard these words, they were quiet and praised God and were saying, "Doubtless, God has also given repentance to life to the Gentiles."
19	Now they which were scattered abroad upon the persecution that arose about Stephen travelled as far as Phenice, and Cyprus, and Antioch, preaching the word to none but unto the Jews only.	And they who were dispersed, by the oppression which occurred on account of Stephen, travelled as far as Phenicia, and even to the country of Cyprus, and to Antioch, speaking the word to none except to Jews only.	Now those who were scattered by the persecution that happened on account of Stephen, approached as far as Phoenicia and also to the region of Cyprus and to Antioch, speaking the word to no one, but to the Judeans only.
20	And some of them were men of Cyprus and Cyrene, which, when they were come to Antioch, spake unto the Grecians, preaching the Lord Jesus.	And there were some of them from Cyprus and from Cyrene, who went up to Antioch, and spoke to the Greeks, and preached concerning our Lord Jesus.	And there were men of them from Cyprus and from Cyrene. These entered Antioch and were speaking to the Greeks and preaching about our Lord Jesus.
21	And the hand of the Lord was with them: and a great number believed, and turned unto the Lord.	And the hand of the Lord was with them; and many believed, and turned to the Lord.	And the hand of the LORD was with them and many believed and turned to the LORD.
22	Then tidings of these things came unto the ears of the church which was in Jerusalem: and they sent forth Barnabas, that he should go as far as Antioch.	And this came to the ears of the sons of the church at Jerusalem: and they sent Barnabas to Antioch.	And this was heard by the ears of the clergy that were in Jerusalem. And they sent Barnabas to Antioch.
23	Who, when he came, and had seen the grace of God, was glad, and exhorted them all, that with purpose of heart they would cleave unto the Lord.	And when he came there, and saw the grace of God, he rejoiced: and he entreated them, that with all their heart, they would adhere to our Lord.	And when he came there and saw the grace of God, he rejoiced and begged them that with all their heart[s], they should follow our Lord,
24	For he was a good man, and full of the Holy Ghost and of faith: and much people was added unto the Lord.	For he was a good man, and was full of the Holy Spirit, and of faith. And many people were added to our Lord.	because he was a good man and filled with the Holy Spirit and with faith. And many people were added to our Lord.
25	Then departed Barnabas to Tarsus, for to seek Saul:	And he went away to Tarsus, to seek for Saul.	And he went away to Tarsus to seek Saul.
26	And when he had found him, he brought him unto Antioch. And it came to pass, that a whole year they assembled themselves with the church, and taught much people. And the disciples were called Christians first in Antioch.	And when he had found him, he brought him with him to Antioch. And a whole year they met together in the church, and instructed many people.---From that time forth, the disciples were first called CHRISTIANS, at Antioch.	And when he had found him, he brought him with him to Antioch. And they were gathered together with the church a whole year and they taught many people. From that time, the disciples were first called Christians in Antioch.
27	And in these days came prophets from Jerusalem unto Antioch.	In those days came prophets thither from Jerusalem.	And in those days, prophets came there from Jerusalem.

	KJV	Murdock	Magiera
	ACTS	*Chapter 11*	
28	And there stood up one of them named Agabus, and signified by the Spirit that there should be great dearth throughout all the world: which came to pass in the days of Claudius Caesar.	And one of them whose name was Agabus, stood up and informed them, by the Spirit, that there would be a great famine in all the country. And that famine occurred in the days of Claudius Caesar.	And one of them, whose name was Agabus, stood up and informed them spiritually that a great famine would occur in all the land. And this famine happened in the days of Claudius Caesar.
29	Then the disciples, every man according to his ability, determined to send relief unto the brethren which dwelt in Judaea:	And moreover the disciples, each of them according to his several ability, determined to send to the relief of the brethren who dwelt in Judaea.	But nevertheless, the disciples, each one of them according to what he had, determined to send to the assistance of the brothers who were living in Judea.
30	Which also they did, and sent it to the elders by the hands of Barnabas and Saul.	And they sent, by the hand of Barnabas and Saul, unto the Elders there.	And they sent, by way of Barnabas and Saul, to the elders who were there.
	Chapter 12		
1	Now about that time Herod the king stretched forth his hands to vex certain of the church.	And at that time Herod the king, who was surnamed Agrippa, laid hands on some of the church, to maltreat them.	Now at that time, Herod the king, who was named Agrippa, laid hands on some who were in the church to wrongfully treat them.
2	And he killed James the brother of John with the sword.	And he killed James the brother of John with the sword.	And he killed James, the brother of John, with a sword.
3	And because he saw it pleased the Jews, he proceeded further to take Peter also. (Then were the days of unleavened bread.)	And when he saw that this pleased the Jews, he proceeded also to arrest Simon Cephas. And the days of unleavened bread were then passing.	And when he saw that this pleased the Judeans, he proceeded to arrest Simon Peter also. And [these] were the days of the Feast of Unleavened Bread.
4	And when he had apprehended him, he put him in prison, and delivered him to four quaternions of soldiers to keep him; intending after Easter to bring him forth to the people.	He seized him and cast him into prison, and delivered him to sixteen soldiers, who were to guard him; that he might, after the passover, deliver him up to the people of the Jews.	And he arrested him and threw him in prison and delivered him [to] sixteen soldiers to keep him, so that after the feast of the Passover, he could deliver him to the people of the Judeans.
5	Peter therefore was kept in prison: but prayer was made without ceasing of the church unto God for him.	And while Simon was in custody in the prison, continual prayer to God in his behalf, was offered to God by the church.	And while Simon was kept in prison, steadfast prayer was offered to God by the church on his behalf.
6	And when Herod would have brought him forth, the same night Peter was sleeping between two soldiers, bound with two chains: and the keepers before the door kept the prison.	And on the night before the morning in which he was to be delivered up, while Simon was sleeping between two soldiers, and was bound with two chains, and others were guarding the doors of the prison;	And in that night toward daybreak [when] he was going to deliver him up, while Simon was asleep between two soldiers and was bound by two chains and others were keeping the doors of the prison,
7	And, behold, the angel of the Lord came upon him, and a light shined in the prison: and he smote Peter on the side, and raised him up, saying, Arise up quickly. And his chains fell off from his hands.	an angel of the Lord stood over him, and a light shone in all the building; and he pricked his side, and awaked him, and said to him: Arise, instantly. And the chains fell from his hands.	an angel of the LORD stood above him and a light shown in all the building. And he hit him on his side and woke him and said to him, "Rise up quickly." And the chains fell from his hands.

Parallel Translations

	KJV	*Murdock*	*Magiera*

ACTS *Chapter 12*

	KJV	Murdock	Magiera
8	And the angel said unto him, Gird thyself, and bind on thy sandals. And so he did. And he saith unto him, Cast thy garment about thee, and follow me.	And the angel said to him: Gird thy loins, and put on thy sandals. And he did so. And again he said to him: Wrap thyself in thy cloak, and come after me.	And the angel said to him, "Gird up your loins and put on your sandals." And he did so. And again he said to him, "Wrap yourself in your outer garment and follow me."
9	And he went out, and followed him; and wist not that it was true which was done by the angel; but thought he saw a vision.	And he went out and followed him, not knowing that what had been done by the angel was a reality; for he supposed, that he saw a vision.	And he went out and followed him, not knowing that what was occurring by way of the angel was true, for he supposed that he was seeing a vision.
10	When they were past the first and the second ward, they came unto the iron gate that leadeth unto the city; which opened to them of his own accord: and they went out, and passed on through one street; and forthwith the angel departed from him.	And when the first ward was passed and the second, they came to the iron gate, and it opened to them of its own accord. And when they had gone out, and had passed one street, the angel departed from him.	And after they had passed the first watch and the second, they came up to the gate of iron and it was opened to them of its own accord. And after they had gone out and passed one street, the angel left him.
11	And when Peter was come to himself, he said, Now I know of a surety, that the Lord hath sent his angel, and hath delivered me out of the hand of Herod, and from all the expectation of the people of the Jews.	Then Simon recognized [where he was]; and he said: Now I know, in reality, that God hath sent his angel, and delivered me from the hand of Herod the king, and from what the Jews were devising against me.	Then Simon realized [what happened] and said, "Now I know with truthfulness that the LORD sent his angel and delivered me from the hand of Herod the king and from what the Judeans had planned against me."
12	And when he had considered the thing, he came to the house of Mary the mother of John, whose surname was Mark; where many were gathered together praying.	And when he had considered, he went to the house of Mary, the mother of John surnamed Mark; because many brethren were assembled there and praying.	And when he understood, he came to the house of Mary, the mother of John who was called Mark, because many brothers were gathered and praying there.
13	And as Peter knocked at the door of the gate, a damsel came to hearken, named Rhoda.	And he knocked at the gate of the court; and a maid named Rhoda came to reply to him.	And he knocked at the gate of the courtyard and a young girl, whose name [was] Rhoda, went out to answer him.
14	And when she knew Peter's voice, she opened not the gate for gladness, but ran in, and told how Peter stood before the gate.	And she recognized the voice of Simon: and, In her joy, she did not open to him the gate, but ran back, and told them: Lo, Simon is standing at the gate of the court.	And she recognized the voice of Simon and in her joy, she did not open the gate for him, but turned back quickly and said to them, "Behold, Simon is standing at the gate of the courtyard."
15	And they said unto her, Thou art mad. But she constantly affirmed that it was even so. Then said they, It is his angel.	They said to her: Thou art delirious. But she maintained that it was a fact. They said to her: Perhaps it is his ghost.	They said to her, "You are indeed confused." Yet she was affirming that this was so. They said to her, "Perhaps it is his angel."
16	But Peter continued knocking: and when they had opened the door, and saw him, they were astonished.	And Simon was knocking at the gate; and they went out, saw him, and were astonished.	And Simon was knocking at the gate and they went out, saw him, and were amazed.

Parallel Translations

	KJV	*Murdock*	*Magiera*
	ACTS	*Chapter 12*	
17	But he, beckoning unto them with the hand to hold their peace, declared unto them how the Lord had brought him out of the prison. And he said, Go shew these things unto James, and to the brethren. And he departed, and went into another place.	And he beckoned to them with the hand to be still; and he went in, and related to them how the Lord had released him from the prison. And he said to them: Tell these things to James and to the brethren. And he went out, and departed to another place.	And he motioned with his hand to them to be quiet. And he entered and told them how the LORD had brought him out of the prison. And he said to them, "Tell these [things] to James and the brothers." And he left [and] went to another place.
18	Now as soon as it was day, there was no small stir among the soldiers, what was become of Peter.	And when it was morning, there was a great dispute among the soldiers concerning Simon, what had become of him.	And when it was morning, there was a great uproar among the soldiers about Simon about what had happened to him.
19	And when Herod had sought for him, and found him not, he examined the keepers, and commanded that they should be put to death. And he went down from Judaea to Caesarea, and there abode.	And Herod, when he sought him, and could not find him, arraigned the keepers, and sentenced them to die. And he went from Judaea, and resided at Caesarea.	And Herod, when he searched for him and could not find him, judged the keepers and commanded that they should die. And he went away from Judea and was in Caesarea.
20	And Herod was highly displeased with them of Tyre and Sidon: but they came with one accord to him, and, having made Blastus the king's chamberlain their friend, desired peace; because their country was nourished by the king's country.	And because he was angry against the Tyrians and Sidonians, they assembled and came to him in a body; and having persuaded Blastus, the king's chamberlain, they begged of him that they might have peace; because the supplies of their country were derived from the kingdom of Herod.	And because he was angry at the Tyrians and at the Sidonians, they gathered together and came to him. And they persuaded Blastus, the chamberlain of the king and they asked him for a peace treaty, because the supply of their country was from the kingdom of Herod.
21	And upon a set day Herod, arrayed in royal apparel, sat upon his throne, and made an oration unto them.	And on a day appointed, Herod was arrayed in royal apparel, and sat on a tribunal, and made a speech to the assembly.	And on a particular day, Herod was clothed in the clothing of the kingdom and sat on the judgment seat and was speaking to the crowd.
22	And the people gave a shout, saying, It is the voice of a god, and not of a man.	And all the people shouted, and said: These are the utterances of a God, and not of a mortal.	And all the people cried out and said, "These are the voices of a god and are not of men!"
23	And immediately the angel of the Lord smote him, because he gave not God the glory: and he was eaten of worms, and gave up the ghost.	And, because he gave not the glory to God, immediately the angel of God smote him; and he was eaten of worms, and died.	And because he did not give glory to God, immediately the angel of the LORD struck him and he rotted with worms and died.
24	But the word of God grew and multiplied.	And the gospel of God was proclaimed, and made progress.	And the gospel of God was preached and it increased.
25	And Barnabas and Saul returned from Jerusalem, when they had fulfilled their ministry, and took with them John, whose surname was Mark.	And Barnabas and Saul, after they had completed their ministration, returned from Jerusalem to Antioch. And they took with them John, who was surnamed Mark.	And Barnabas and Saul returned from Jerusalem to Antioch, after they had completed their service. And they took with them John who was called Mark.

Parallel Translations

ACTS *Chapter 13*

	KJV	Murdock	Magiera
1	Now there were in the church that was at Antioch certain prophets and teachers; as Barnabas, and Simeon that was called Niger, and Lucius of Cyrene, and Manaen, which had been brought up with Herod the tetrarch, and Saul.	Now there were in the church at Antioch, [several] prophets and teachers; Barnabas, and Simon called Niger, and Lucius who was from the city Cyrene, and Menaen, a son of the guardians of Herod the Tetrarch, and Saul.	And there were in the church of Antioch, prophets and teachers, Barnabas, and Simon, who was called Niger, and Lucius who was from the city [of] Cyrene, and Manaen, a foster-brother of Herod the tetrarch, and Saul.
2	As they ministered to the Lord, and fasted, the Holy Ghost said, Separate me Barnabas and Saul for the work whereunto I have called them.	And while they were fasting and making supplication to God, the Holy Spirit said to them: Separate to me Saul and Barnabas, for the work to which I have called them.	And while they were fasting and making intercession to God, the Holy Spirit said to them, "Appoint to me Saul and Barnabas for the work [to] which I have called them."
3	And when they had fasted and prayed, and laid their hands on them, they sent them away.	And after they had fasted and prayed, they laid the hand on them, and sent them away.	And after they had fasted and prayed, they laid a hand on them and sent them.
4	So they, being sent forth by the Holy Ghost, departed unto Seleucia; and from thence they sailed to Cyprus.	And they, being sent forth by the Holy Spirit, went down to Seleucia, and from there they went by sea as far as Cyprus.	And being sent by the Holy Spirit, they went down to Seleucia and from there journeyed by sea up to Cyprus.
5	And when they were at Salamis, they preached the word of God in the synagogues of the Jews: and they had also John to their minister.	And when they entered the city of Salamis, they announced the word of our Lord in the synagogues of the Jews. And John ministered to them.	And after they entered the city [of] Salamis, they were preaching the word of our Lord in the synagogues of the Judeans. And John was ministering to them.
6	And when they had gone through the isle unto Paphos, they found a certain sorcerer, a false prophet, a Jew, whose name was Barjesus:	And when they had travelled over the whole island as far as the city Paphos, they found a certain man, a sorcerer, a Jew, who was a false prophet, and whose name was Bar-Suma.	And when they had traveled around all the island as far as the city [of] Paphos, they found a certain man, a Judean sorcerer, who was a false prophet, whose name was Barshuma.
7	Which was with the deputy of the country, Sergius Paulus, a prudent man; who called for Barnabas and Saul, and desired to hear the word of God.	He adhered to a wise man, who was the proconsul, and was called Sergius Paulus. And the proconsul sent for Saul and Barnabas, and requested to hear from them the word of God.	This [man] attended a wise man, who was the proconsul and was called Sergius Paulus. And the proconsul called for Saul and Barnabas and asked to hear the word of God from them.
8	But Elymas the sorcerer (for so is his name by interpretation) withstood them, seeking to turn away the deputy from the faith.	And this sorcerer, Bar-Suma, (whose name is interpreted, Elymas,) withstood them; because he wished to divert the proconsul from the faith.	And this sorcerer, Barshuma, whose name is interpreted Elymas, was standing against them, because he wanted to turn the proconsul away from the faith.
9	Then Saul, (who also is called Paul,) filled with the Holy Ghost, set his eyes on him,	And Saul who is called Paul, was filled with the Holy Spirit; and he looked upon him,	But Saul, who was called Paul, was filled with the Holy Spirit and looked at him

	KJV	Murdock	Magiera
	ACTS	*Chapter 13*	
10	And said, O full of all subtilty and all mischief, thou child of the devil, thou enemy of all righteousness, wilt thou not cease to pervert the right ways of the Lord?	and said: O thou full of all subtilties, and all mischiefs, thou child of the calumniator, and enemy of all righteousness; wilt thou not cease to pervert the right ways of the Lord?	and said, "Oh full of all treacheries and all evil [things], son of the Accuser and enemy of all uprightness, will you not cease to pervert the straight ways of the LORD?
11	And now, behold, the hand of the Lord is upon thee, and thou shalt be blind, not seeing the sun for a season. And immediately there fell on him a mist and a darkness; and he went about seeking some to lead him by the hand.	And now, the hand of the Lord is upon thee, and thou shalt be blind, and shalt not see the sun for a time. And immediately there fell upon him a mist and darkness; and he went about, inquiring who would take him by the hand.	And now the hand of the LORD [is] on you and you will be blind and you will not see the sun for a time." And immediately a thick darkness and blindness fell on him and he wandered around and looked for one who would take [him] by his hand.
12	Then the deputy, when he saw what was done, believed, being astonished at the doctrine of the Lord.	And when the proconsul saw what occurred, he was astonished; and he believed the doctrine of the Lord.	And when the proconsul saw what had happened, he was amazed and believed in the teaching of the LORD.
13	Now when Paul and his company loosed from Paphos, they came to Perga in Pamphylia: and John departing from them returned to Jerusalem.	And Paul and Barnabas went by sea, from the city of Paphos, and came to Perga, a city of Pamphylia. And John separated from them, and went away to Jerusalem.	And Paul and Barnabas traveled by sea from the city [of] Paphos and came to Perga, a city of Pamphylia. And John separated from them and went to Jerusalem.
14	But when they departed from Perga, they came to Antioch in Pisidia, and went into the synagogue on the sabbath day, and sat down.	And they departed from Perga, and came to Antioch, a city of Pisidia: and they entered the synagogue, on the sabbath day, and sat down.	And they went away from Perga and came to Antioch, a city of Pisidia. And they entered the synagogue on a Sabbath day and sat down.
15	And after the reading of the law and the prophets the rulers of the synagogue sent unto them, saying, Ye men and brethren, if ye have any word of exhortation for the people, say on.	And after the law had been read, and the prophets, the Elders of the synagogue sent to them, and said: Men, brethren, if ye have a word of exhortation, address the people.	And after the law and the prophets were read, the elders of the synagogue sent for them and said, "Men, our brothers, if you have a word of comfort, speak with the people."
16	Then Paul stood up, and beckoning with his hand said, Men of Israel, and ye that fear God, give audience.	And Paul arose, and waved his hand, and said: Men, sons of Israel, and ye that fear God, hear ye.	And Paul stood up and waved his hand and said, "Men, sons of Israel and those who fear God, listen.
17	The God of this people of Israel chose our fathers, and exalted the people when they dwelt as strangers in the land of Egypt, and with an high arm brought he them out of it.	The God of this people chose our fathers, and raised them up, and multiplied them, when they resided in the land of Egypt; and, with a high arm, he brought them out of it.	The God of this people chose our fathers and lifted up and multiplied them while they were settlers in the land of Egypt and with a strong arm he brought them out of it.
18	And about the time of forty years suffered he their manners in the wilderness.	And he fed them in the wilderness forty years.	And he fed them in the wilderness [for] forty years.
19	And when he had destroyed seven nations in the land of Chanaan, he divided their land to them by lot.	And he extirpated seven nations in the land of Canaan, and gave them their land for an inheritance.	And he destroyed seven nations in the land of Canaan and gave them their land for an inheritance.
20	And after that he gave unto them judges about the space of four hundred and fifty years, until Samuel the prophet.	And for four hundred and fifty years he gave them judges, until Samuel the prophet.	And [for] four hundred and fifty years, he gave them judges until Samuel the prophet.

Parallel Translations

ACTS *Chapter 13*

	KJV	*Murdock*	*Magiera*
21	And afterward they desired a king: and God gave unto them Saul the son of Cis, a man of the tribe of Benjamin, by the space of forty years.	And then they asked for themselves a king: and God gave them Saul the son of Kish, a man of the tribe of Benjamin, during forty years.	And then they asked for a king. And God gave them Saul, the son of Kish, a man from the tribe of Benjamin, [for] forty years.
22	And when he had removed him, he raised up unto them David to be their king; to whom also he gave testimony, and said, I have found David the son of Jesse, a man after mine own heart, which shall fulfil all my will.	And he removed him, and raised up to them David as king: and he testified of him, and said: I have found David the son of Jesse, a man after my heart: he will do all my pleasure.	And he removed him and raised up for them David the king. And he testified about him and said: I HAVE FOUND DAVID, THE SON OF JESSE, [TO BE] A MAN ACCORDING TO MY HEART. HE WILL DO ALL OF MY DESIRES.
23	Of this man's seed hath God according to his promise raised unto Israel a Saviour, Jesus:	From the seed of this man, hath God raised up to Israel, as he promised, Jesus a deliverer.	From the seed of this [man], God raised up for Israel as was promised, Jesus the redeemer.
24	When John had first preached before his coming the baptism of repentance to all the people of Israel.	And, before his advent, he sent John to proclaim the baptism of repentance to all the people of Israel.	And he sent John before his coming to preach the baptism of repentance to all the people of Israel.
25	And as John fulfilled his course, he said, Whom think ye that I am? I am not he. But, behold, there cometh one after me, whose shoes of his feet I am not worthy to loose.	And while John was fulfilling his ministry, he said: Who, suppose ye, that I am? I am not he. But lo, he cometh after me; of whom I am not worthy to untie his shoe-strings.	And while John was completing his ministry, he said, 'Whom do you think that I am? I am not [he]. But behold, he follows me, the straps of whose sandals I am not worthy to loosen.'
26	Men and brethren, children of the stock of Abraham, and whosoever among you feareth God, to you is the word of this salvation sent.	Men, brethren, children of the stock of Abraham, and all who, with you, fear God, to you is this word of life sent.	Men, our brothers, sons of the family of Abraham and those with you who fear God, to you is the word of life sent.
27	For they that dwell at Jerusalem, and their rulers, because they knew him not, nor yet the voices of the prophets which are read every sabbath day, they have fulfilled them in condemning him.	For, those inhabitants of Jerusalem and their chiefs, did not apprehend it; neither [did they apprehend] also the writings of the prophets, which are read every sabbath; but they condemned him, and fulfilled all the things written.	For those inhabitants of Jerusalem and their rulers did not acknowledge him or even the writings of the prophets that are read on every Sabbath. But they condemned him and fulfilled those [things] that were written.
28	And though they found no cause of death in him, yet desired they Pilate that he should be slain.	And while they found no ground for [his] death, they desired of Pilate that they might kill him.	And although they could not find any cause for death, they asked [permission] of Pilate to kill him.
29	And when they had fulfilled all that was written of him, they took him down from the tree, and laid him in a sepulchre.	And when they had fulfilled all that was written concerning him, they took him down from the cross, and laid him in a sepulchre.	And after they had completed everything that was written about him, they took him down from the cross and laid him in a tomb.
30	But God raised him from the dead:	But God raised him from the dead.	But God raised him from the dead.
31	And he was seen many days of them which came up with him from Galilee to Jerusalem, who are his witnesses unto the people.	And he was seen many days, by them who came up with him from Galilee to Jerusalem; and they are now his witnesses to the people.	And he appeared many days to those who had gone up with him from Galilee to Jerusalem. And they are now his witnesses to the people.

Parallel Translations

	KJV	*Murdock*	*Magiera*
ACTS *Chapter 13*			
32	And we declare unto you glad tidings, how that the promise which was made unto the fathers,	And lo, we also announce to you, that the promise, which was made to our fathers,	And also, behold, we declare to you that the promise that was to our fathers,
33	God hath fulfilled the same unto us their children, in that he hath raised up Jesus again; as it is also written in the second psalm, Thou art my Son, this day have I begotten thee.	lo, God hath fulfilled it to us their children, in that he raised up Jesus; as it is written in the second psalm: Thou art my Son; this day have I begotten thee.	behold, God has fulfilled it to us, their sons, that he raised up Jesus, as it was written in the second Psalm: YOU ARE MY SON, THIS DAY I HAVE FATHERED YOU.
34	And as concerning that he raised him up from the dead, now no more to return to corruption, he said on this wise, I will give you the sure mercies of David.	And God hath so raised him from the dead, that he will not return again and see corruption; as he said: I will give to you the sure grace of David.	And so God raised him from the dead, so that he will not return again [and] see corruption as he said: I WILL GIVE YOU THE FAITHFUL GRACE OF DAVID.
35	Wherefore he saith also in another psalm, Thou shalt not suffer thine Holy One to see corruption.	And again he said, in another place: Thou hast not given thy devout one to see corruption.	And again he said in another place: YOU WILL NOT ALLOW YOUR INNOCENT [ONE] TO SEE CORRUPTION.
36	For David, after he had served his own generation by the will of God, fell on sleep, and was laid unto his fathers, and saw corruption:	For David, in his generation, served the pleasure of God, and went to rest, and was added to his fathers, and saw corruption.	For David in his generation ministered the will of God and slept and was added to his forefathers and saw corruption.
37	But he, whom God raised again, saw no corruption.	But this person, whom God raised up, did not see corruption.	But this [man], whom God raised, did not see corruption.
38	Be it known unto you therefore, men and brethren, that through this man is preached unto you the forgiveness of sins:	Know therefore, brethren, that through this man remission of sins is proclaimed to you.	Therefore know, my brothers, that by this [man] forgiveness of sins is preached to you.
39	And by him all that believe are justified from all things, from which ye could not be justified by the law of Moses.	And every one that believeth in this man, is made just from all things, from which ye could not be made just by the law of Moses.	And by this [man], everyone who believes is justified from all that which you could not be justified by the law of Moses.
40	Beware therefore, lest that come upon you, which is spoken of in the prophets;	Beware, therefore, lest that come upon you, which is written in the prophets:	Beware, therefore, so that what is written in the prophets should not come on you:
41	Behold, ye despisers, and wonder, and perish: for I work a work in your days, a work which ye shall in no wise believe, though a man declare it unto you.	Behold, ye despisers, and wonder, and perish; for I work a work in your days, which ye will not believe, though a man relate it to you.	SEE [YOU] DESPISERS AND BE ASTONISHED AND BE DESTROYED, FOR I WILL WORK A WORK IN YOUR DAYS WHICH YOU WILL NOT BELIEVE, ALTHOUGH SOMEONE TELLS YOU."
42	And when the Jews were gone out of the synagogue, the Gentiles besought that these words might be preached to them the next sabbath.	And when they had gone from them, they besought them to speak the same things to them the next sabbath day.	And while they were leaving their presence, they begged them that on the next Sabbath they would speak to them these words.

Parallel Translations

	KJV	*Murdock*	*Magiera*
	ACTS	*Chapter 13*	
43	Now when the congregation was broken up, many of the Jews and religious proselytes followed Paul and Barnabas: who, speaking to them, persuaded them to continue in the grace of God.	And when the synagogue was dismissed, many Jews went after them, and likewise proselytes who feared God. And they conversed with them, and persuaded them to adhere to the grace of God.	And after the synagogue was dismissed, many Judeans followed them and also proselytes who feared God. And they were speaking and persuading them to be follower[s] of the grace of God.
44	And the next sabbath day came almost the whole city together to hear the word of God.	And the next sabbath, the whole city assembled to hear the word of God.	And on the next Sabbath [day], the whole city was gathered to hear the word of God.
45	But when the Jews saw the multitudes, they were filled with envy, and spake against those things which were spoken by Paul, contradicting and blaspheming.	And when the Jews saw the great assembly, they were filled with envy, and set themselves against the words which Paul spoke, and blasphemed.	And when the Judeans saw the large crowd, they were filled with envy and stood against the words that Paul spoke and they were blaspheming.
46	Then Paul and Barnabas waxed bold, and said, It was necessary that the word of God should first have been spoken to you: but seeing ye put it from you, and judge yourselves unworthy of everlasting life, lo, we turn to the Gentiles.	And Paul and Barnabas said openly: To you first, ought the word of God to be spoken; but because ye repel it from you, and decide, against yourselves, that ye are not worthy of life eternal, lo, we turn ourselves to the Gentiles.	And Paul and Barnabas spoke boldly, "It was necessary that the word of God be spoken to you first, but because you have pushed it away from you and have decided about yourselves that you are not worthy of eternal life, behold, we turn to the Gentiles.
47	For so hath the Lord commanded us, saying, I have set thee to be a light of the Gentiles, that thou shouldest be for salvation unto the ends of the earth.	For so hath our Lord commanded us; as it is written: I have set thee a light to the Gentiles; that thou shouldst be for life unto the ends of the earth.	For so our Lord commanded us, as it is written: I HAVE SET YOU [AS] A LIGHT TO THE GENTILES THAT YOU WOULD BE FOR LIFE TO THE ENDS OF THE EARTH."
48	And when the Gentiles heard this, they were glad, and glorified the word of the Lord: and as many as were ordained to eternal life believed.	And when the Gentiles heard [this], they rejoiced and glorified God. And those believed, who were appointed to life eternal.	And when the Gentiles heard, they rejoiced and praised God and those who were ordained to eternal life believed.
49	And the word of the Lord was published throughout all the region.	And the word of the Lord was talked of in all that region.	And the word of the LORD was spoken in that whole place.
50	But the Jews stirred up the devout and honourable women, and the chief men of the city, and raised persecution against Paul and Barnabas, and expelled them out of their coasts.	But the Jews stirred up the chiefs of the city, and the opulent women who with them feared God, and set up a persecution against Paul and against Barnabas, and expelled them from their borders.	But the Judeans stirred up the rulers of the city and the rich women, those who feared God with them and they instigated a persecution against Paul and against Barnabas. And they expelled them from their borders.
51	But they shook off the dust of their feet against them, and came unto Iconium.	And when they went out, they shook off the dust of their feet against them, and went to the city of Iconium.	And after they had gone out, they shook off the dust of their feet against them and came to the city [of] Iconium.
52	And the disciples were filled with joy, and with the Holy Ghost.	And the disciples were filled with joy, and with the Holy Spirit.	And the disciples were filled with joy and the Holy Spirit.

Parallel Translations

	KJV	*Murdock*	*Magiera*
	ACTS	*Chapter 14*	
1	And it came to pass in Iconium, that they went both together into the synagogue of the Jews, and so spake, that a great multitude both of the Jews and also of the Greeks believed.	And they came and entered into the synagogue of the Jews, and so spoke with them, that many of the Jews and of the Greeks believed.	And they came and entered the synagogue of the Judeans. And they spoke with them such that many of the Judeans and of the Greeks believed.
2	But the unbelieving Jews stirred up the Gentiles, and made their minds evil affected against the brethren.	But Jews of the class of unbelievers, excited the Gentiles, to maltreat the brethren.	But the Judeans who were not persuaded stirred up the Gentiles to mistreat the brothers.
3	Long time therefore abode they speaking boldly in the Lord, which gave testimony unto the word of his grace, and granted signs and wonders to be done by their hands.	And they continued there a long time, and spoke openly concerning the Lord; and he gave testimony to the word of his grace, by the signs and prodigies which he wrought by their hands.	And they were there a long time and were boldly speaking about the LORD. And he gave witness concerning the word of his grace by the signs and by the wonders that he was doing by their hands.
4	But the multitude of the city was divided: and part held with the Jews, and part with the apostles.	And the whole multitude of the city was divided; and a part were with the Jews, and a part adhered to the legates.	And all the multitude of the city was divided. Some of them were with the Judeans and some of them were following the apostles.
5	And when there was an assault made both of the Gentiles, and also of the Jews with their rulers, to use them despitefully, and to stone them,	And an assault was made on them, by the Gentiles, and by the Jews and their chiefs, to insult them, and to stone them with stones.	And there was an assault against them by the Gentiles and by the Judeans and their rulers to disgrace them and to stone them with rocks.
6	They were ware of it, and fled unto Lystra and Derbe, cities of Lycaonia, and unto the region that lieth round about:	And when they knew [it], they departed and fled to the cities of Lycaonia and Lystra and Derbe, and to the villages around them;	And after they knew [it], they went away and took refuge in the cities of Lycaonia, Lystra, and Derbe and the villages that surrounded them.
7	And there they preached the gospel.	and there they preached.	And they were preaching there.
8	And there sat a certain man at Lystra, impotent in his feet, being a cripple from his mother's womb, who never had walked:	And a certain man dwelt in the city Lystra, who was afflicted in his feet, a cripple from his mother's womb, who had never walked.	And a certain man was sitting in the city [of] Lystra, who was hurt in his feet, lame from the womb of his mother, who had never walked.
9	The same heard Paul speak: who stedfastly beholding him, and perceiving that he had faith to be healed,	He heard Paul speak: and when Paul saw him, and knew that he had faith to live;	This [man] heard Paul speak. And when Paul saw him and knew that he had faith to have life,
10	Said with a loud voice, Stand upright on thy feet. And he leaped and walked.	he said to him, with a loud voice: In the name of our Lord Jesus Messiah, I say to thee, Rise upon thy feet. And he sprang up, stood, and walked.	he said to him in a loud voice, "To you, I say in the name of our Lord Jesus Christ, stand up on your feet." And he leaped up, stood, and walked.
11	And when the people saw what Paul had done, they lifted up their voices, saying in the speech of Lycaonia, The gods are come down to us in the likeness of men.	And the assembly of people, when they saw what Paul had done, raised their voice, and said, in the language of the country: The gods have assumed the likeness of men, and have come down to us.	And the crowd of people, when they saw what Paul had done, raised up their voice[s] in the language of the country and were saying, "The gods have put on the likeness of men and come down to us."

Parallel Translations

	KJV	Murdock	Magiera
ACTS	*Chapter 14*		
12	And they called Barnabas, Jupiter; and Paul, Mercurius, because he was the chief speaker.	And they named Barnabas the Lord of the Gods; and Paul Hermes, because he commenced the speaking.	And they called Barnabas, Jupiter, and Paul, Hermes, because he began the speaking.
13	Then the priest of Jupiter, which was before their city, brought oxen and garlands unto the gates, and would have done sacrifice with the people.	And the priest of the Lord of the Gods, who was without the city, brought oxen and garlands to the gate of the court where they lodged, and was disposed to offer sacrifices to them.	And the priest of Jupiter, who was outside of the city, brought oxen and crowns to the gate of the courtyard where they lodged and wanted to sacrifice to them.
14	Which when the apostles, Barnabas and Paul, heard of, they rent their clothes, and ran in among the people, crying out,	But Barnabas and Paul, when they heard [it], rent their garments, and sprang and went among the throng,	But Barnabas and Paul, when they heard, tore their garments and leaped up and went out to the crowd and cried out
15	And saying, Sirs, why do ye these things? We also are men of like passions with you, and preach unto you that ye should turn from these vanities unto the living God, which made heaven, and earth, and the sea, and all things that are therein:	and called out, and said: Men, what do ye? We also are frail mortals like yourselves, who preach to you, that ye should turn from these useless things, unto the living God, who made heaven and earth and seas, and whatever is in them.	and were saying, "Men, what are you doing? We also are men [having] feelings like you, who preach to you that you should turn from these idle [things] to the living God, who made heaven and earth and the seas and all that is in them,
16	Who in times past suffered all nations to walk in their own ways.	He, in former ages, left all the nations to go in their own ways:	[This is] who in former generations allowed all the nations to go in their own ways,
17	Nevertheless he left not himself without witness, in that he did good, and gave us rain from heaven, and fruitful seasons, filling our hearts with food and gladness.	although he did not leave himself without testimony, while he did them good from heaven, and sent down the rain, and made the fruits to grow in their seasons, and filled their hearts with food and pleasure.	although he did not leave himself without a testimony, in that he did for them good [things] from heaven and caused rain to fall on them and caused the fruit to mature in their seasons and filled their hearts with food and gladness."
18	And with these sayings scarce restrained they the people, that they had not done sacrifice unto them.	And, by saying these things, they with difficulty prevented the people from offering sacrifice to them.	And while they were saying these [things], with difficulty did they restrain the people, so that no one sacrificed to them.
19	And there came thither certain Jews from Antioch and Iconium, who persuaded the people, and, having stoned Paul, drew him out of the city, supposing he had been dead.	But Jews came hither from Iconium and Antioch, and excited the people against them. And they stoned Paul, and dragged him out of the city, supposing that he was dead.	But the Judeans from Iconium and from Antioch came there and stirred up the people against them and they stoned Paul and dragged him outside of the city, because they supposed that he was dead.
20	Howbeit, as the disciples stood round about him, he rose up, and came into the city: and the next day he departed with Barnabas to Derbe.	And the disciples assembled around him; and he arose, and went into the city.---And the next day, he departed from there, with Barnabas; and they came to the city of Derbe.	And the disciples gathered about him and he rose up [and] entered the city. And on the next day, he went away from there with Barnabas and they went to the city [of] Derbe.
21	And when they had preached the gospel to that city, and had taught many, they returned again to Lystra, and to Iconium, and Antioch,	And while they were preaching to the inhabitants of that city, they made many disciples. And turning back, they came to the city Lystra, and to Iconium, and to Antioch,	And while they were preaching to the citizens, they made many disciples. And they returned [and] came to the city [of] Lystra and to Iconium and to Antioch,

Parallel Translations

	KJV	*Murdock*	*Magiera*
ACTS	*Chapter 14*		
22	Confirming the souls of the disciples, and exhorting them to continue in the faith, and that we must through much tribulation enter into the kingdom of God.	confirming the souls of the disciples, and entreating them to persevere in the faith; and they told them, that it was necessary, through much affliction, to enter into the kingdom of God.	establishing the lives of the disciples and begging them to remain in the faith and telling them that it is necessary to enter the kingdom of God with much trial.
23	And when they had ordained them elders in every church, and had prayed with fasting, they commended them to the Lord, on whom they believed.	And they established for them Elders in each church, while they fasted with them, and prayed, and commended them to our Lord in whom they believed.	And they ordained elders for them in every church, while they fasted with them and prayed and commended them to our Lord in whom they believed.
24	And after they had passed throughout Pisidia, they came to Pamphylia.	And when they had travelled over the region of Pisidia they came to Pamphylia.	And after they had traveled around in the region of Pisidia, they came to Pamphylia.
25	And when they had preached the word in Perga, they went down into Attalia:	And when they had spoken the word of the Lord in the city of Perga, they went down to Attalia.	And after they had spoken the word of the LORD in the city [of] Perga, they went down to Attalia.
26	And thence sailed to Antioch, from whence they had been recommended to the grace of God for the work which they fulfilled.	And thence they proceeded by sea, and came to Antioch; because from there they had been commended to the grace of the Lord, for that work which they had accomplished.	And from there they journeyed by sea and came to Antioch, because from there they had been commended to the grace of the LORD for the work that they had accomplished.
27	And when they were come, and had gathered the church together, they rehearsed all that God had done with them, and how he had opened the door of faith unto the Gentiles.	And when they had collected together the whole church, they narrated all that God had wrought with them, and that he had opened a door of faith to the Gentiles.	And after they had gathered the whole church, they were narrating everything that God had done with them and that he had opened a door of faith to the Gentiles.
28	And there they abode long time with the disciples.	And they remained there a long time with the disciples.	And they were there a long time with the disciples.
Chapter 15			
1	And certain men which came down from Judaea taught the brethren, and said, Except ye be circumcised after the manner of Moses, ye cannot be saved.	And certain men came down from Judaea, and taught the brethren, that unless ye be circumcised, in accordance with the rite of the law, ye cannot have life.	And men came down from Judea and were teaching the brothers [saying], "Unless you are circumcised according to the custom of the law, you are not able to have life."
2	When therefore Paul and Barnabas had no small dissension and disputation with them, they determined that Paul and Barnabas, and certain other of them, should go up to Jerusalem unto the apostles and elders about this question.	And Paul and Barnabas had much trouble and disputation with them. And it resulted, that Paul and Barnabas, and others with them, went up to the legates and Elders at Jerusalem, because of this matter.	And Paul and Barnabas had much strife and dispute with them. And it happened that they sent up Paul and Barnabas and others with them to the apostles and elders who were in Jerusalem, because of this dispute.

Parallel Translations

	KJV	Murdock	Magiera
	ACTS	*Chapter 15*	
3	And being brought on their way by the church, they passed through Phenice and Samaria, declaring the conversion of the Gentiles: and they caused great joy unto all the brethren.	And the church waited on them, and sent them away; and they travelled through all Phenicia and the territory of the Samaritans, narrating the conversion of the Gentiles, and causing great joy to all the brethren.	And the church escorted [and] sent them. And they were traveling in all of Phoenicia and also among the Samaritans, narrating about the conversion of the Gentiles and causing great joy to all the brothers.
4	And when they were come to Jerusalem, they were received of the church, and of the apostles and elders, and they declared all things that God had done with them.	And when they came to Jerusalem, they were received by the church, and by the Elders, and by the legates; and they recounted all that God had wrought by them.	And when they came to Jerusalem, they were received by the church and by the apostles and by the elders and they narrated to them all that God had done with them.
5	But there rose up certain of the sect of the Pharisees which believed, saying, That it was needful to circumcise them, and to command them to keep the law of Moses.	And some who from the sect of the Pharisees had believed, rose up and said: It is necessary for you to circumcise them, and to command them to observe the law of Moses.	And some stood up, those from the doctrine of the Pharisees who had believed, and they were saying, "It is necessary for you to circumcise them and you should command them to keep the law of Moses."
6	And the apostles and elders came together for to consider of this matter.	And the legates and Elders assembled, to look into this matter.	And the apostles and elders were gathered to look into this matter.
7	And when there had been much disputing, Peter rose up, and said unto them, Men and brethren, ye know how that a good while ago God made choice among us, that the Gentiles by my mouth should hear the word of the gospel, and believe.	And when there had been much discussion, Simon arose and said to them: Men, brethren, ye know that, from the earlier days, God chose that from my mouth the Gentiles should hear the word of the gospel, and should believe.	And after there had been much debate, Simon stood up and said to them, "Men, our brothers, you know that from the first days, by my mouth, God chose that the Gentiles should hear the word of the gospel and believe.
8	And God, which knoweth the hearts, bare them witness, giving them the Holy Ghost, even as he did unto us;	And God, who knoweth what is in hearts, bore testimony concerning them, and gave the Holy Spirit to them, even as to us.	And God, who knows what is in hearts, gave testimony concerning them and gave them the Holy Spirit as [he did] to us.
9	And put no difference between us and them, purifying their hearts by faith.	And he made no distinction between them and us; because he purified their hearts by faith.	And he made no distinction between us and them, because he cleansed their hearts by faith.
10	Now therefore why tempt ye God, to put a yoke upon the neck of the disciples, which neither our fathers nor we were able to bear?	And now, why tempt ye God, by putting a yoke on the necks of the disciples, which neither our fathers nor we could bear?	And now, why do you tempt God as you place a yoke on the necks of these disciples, which neither our fathers nor we were able to bear?
11	But we believe that through the grace of the Lord Jesus Christ we shall be saved, even as they.	But we believe, that we as well as they, are to have life by the grace of our Lord Jesus Messiah.	But by the grace of our Lord Jesus Christ, we believe to have life, as they [do]."
12	Then all the multitude kept silence, and gave audience to Barnabas and Paul, declaring what miracles and wonders God had wrought among the Gentiles by them.	And the whole assembly were silent, and listened to Paul and Barnabas, who related how God by their hands had wrought signs and prodigies among the Gentiles.	And the whole assembly was silent and listened to Paul and Barnabas who were narrating everything God had done by their hands, signs and mighty works among the Gentiles.

Parallel Translations

	KJV	*Murdock*	*Magiera*
	ACTS	*Chapter 15*	
13	And after they had held their peace, James answered, saying, Men and brethren, hearken unto me:	And after they ceased, James arose and said: Men, brethren, hearken to me.	And after they were silent, James stood up and said, "Men, our brothers, hear me.
14	Simeon hath declared how God at the first did visit the Gentiles, to take out of them a people for his name.	Simon hath related to you, how God hath begun to elect a people for his name from among the Gentiles.	Simon narrated to you how God began to choose from the Gentiles a people for his name.
15	And to this agree the words of the prophets; as it is written,	And with this the words of the prophets accord, as it is written:	And to this the words of the prophets agree, as it is written:
16	After this I will return, and will build again the tabernacle of David, which is fallen down; and I will build again the ruins thereof, and I will set it up:	After these things I will return, and will set up the tabernacle of David that had fallen; and will build that which was in ruins in it, and will raise it up:	AFTER THESE [THINGS] I WILL RETURN AND SET UP THE TABERNACLE OF DAVID WHICH HAS FALLEN AND I WILL REBUILD WHAT HAS FALLEN OF IT AND I WILL RAISE IT UP,
17	That the residue of men might seek after the Lord, and all the Gentiles, upon whom my name is called, saith the Lord, who doeth all these things.	so that the residue of men may seek the Lord, and all the nations on whom my name is called; saith the Lord, who doth all these things.	SO THAT THE REMNANT OF MEN WILL SEEK THE LORD, AND ALL THE GENTILES, ON WHOM MY NAME IS CALLED, SAYS THE LORD WHO DID ALL THESE [THINGS].
18	Known unto God are all his works from the beginning of the world.	Known, from of old, are the works of God.	THE WORKS OF GOD ARE KNOWN FROM OLD.
19	Wherefore my sentence is, that we trouble not them, which from among the Gentiles are turned to God:	Therefore I say to you, let them not crush those who from among the Gentiles have turned unto God.	Because of this, I say, 'They should not harass those have turned to God from the Gentiles.'
20	But that we write unto them, that they abstain from pollutions of idols, and from fornication, and from things strangled, and from blood.	But let word be sent to them, that they keep aloof from the defilement of a sacrifice [to idols], and from whoredom, and from what is strangled, and from blood.	But let it be sent to them that they should stay away from the uncleanness of that which is sacrificed and from fornication and from that which is strangled and from blood.
21	For Moses of old time hath in every city them that preach him, being read in the synagogues every sabbath day.	For in every city, from former ages, Moses hath heralds in the synagogues, who read him every sabbath.	For Moses, from the first generations, had preachers in the synagogues, in every city, who read him on every Sabbath."
22	Then pleased it the apostles and elders, with the whole church, to send chosen men of their own company to Antioch with Paul and Barnabas; namely, Judas surnamed Barsabas, and Silas, chief men among the brethren:	Then the legates and Elders, with all the church, chose men from among themselves, and sent them to Antioch, with Paul and Barnabas; [namely], Jude, who was called Barsabas, and Silas, men who were chiefs among the brethren.	Then the apostles and elders, with all the church, chose men from them and sent [them] to Antioch, with Paul and Barnabas, Judas who was called Barsabas, and Silas, men who were chiefs among the brothers.
23	And they wrote letters by them after this manner; The apostles and elders and brethren send greeting unto the brethren which are of the Gentiles in Antioch and Syria and Cilicia:	And they wrote a letter by them, thus: The legates and Elders and brethren, to them that are in Antioch, and in Syria, and in Cilicia, brethren who are from the Gentiles, greeting:	And they wrote a letter by their hands, [saying] thus, "The apostles and elders and brothers, to those who are in Antioch and in Syria and in Cilicia, brothers who are from the Gentiles, peace.

ACTS *Chapter 15*

	KJV	*Murdock*	*Magiera*
24	Forasmuch as we have heard, that certain which went out from us have troubled you with words, subverting your souls, saying, Ye must be circumcised, and keep the law: to whom we gave no such commandment:	We have heard, that some have gone from us and disquieted you, by discourses, and have subverted your minds, by saying, That ye must be circumcised and keep the law; things which we have not commanded them.	It has been heard by us that men from us have gone out and disturbed you with words and have upset your souls, saying that you should be circumcised and keep the law, those [things] that we did not command them.
25	It seemed good unto us, being assembled with one accord, to send chosen men unto you with our beloved Barnabas and Paul,	Therefore we all have thought fit, when assembled, to choose and send men to you, with our beloved Paul and Barnabas,	Because of this, all of us, being gathered together, purposed and chose men and sent [them] to you, with our beloved Paul and Barnabas
26	Men that have hazarded their lives for the name of our Lord Jesus Christ.	men who have given up their lives for the name of our Lord Jesus Messiah.	(men who have committed themselves on behalf of the name of our Lord Jesus Christ).
27	We have sent therefore Judas and Silas, who shall also tell you the same things by mouth.	And we have sent with them Jude and Silas, that they may tell you the same things orally.	And we have sent with them Judas and Silas, who will tell you these same [things] by word:
28	For it seemed good to the Holy Ghost, and to us, to lay upon you no greater burden than these necessary things;	For it was pleasing to the Holy Spirit, and to us, that there should not be laid upon you any additional burden, besides these necessary things:	For it was the will of the Holy Spirit and also of us that a greater burden should not be placed on you, outside of those [things] that are necessary,
29	That ye abstain from meats offered to idols, and from blood, and from things strangled, and from fornication: from which if ye keep yourselves, ye shall do well. Fare ye well.	that ye keep aloof from a sacrifice [to idols], and from blood, and from what is strangled, and from whoredom. And if ye keep yourselves from these, ye will do well. Be ye steadfast in the Lord.	that you should stay away from that which is sacrificed and from blood and from [that which] is strangled and from fornication, that as you keep yourselves from these [things], you will [do] well. Be steadfast in our Lord."
30	So when they were dismissed, they came to Antioch: and when they had gathered the multitude together, they delivered the epistle:	And they who were sent, came to Antioch, and assembled all the people, and delivered the letter.	And those who were sent came to Antioch and gathered all the people and delivered the letter.
31	Which when they had read, they rejoiced for the consolation.	And when they had read [it], they rejoiced and were comforted.	And after they had read [it], they rejoiced and were comforted.
32	And Judas and Silas, being prophets also themselves, exhorted the brethren with many words, and confirmed them.	And with abundant discourse they strengthened the brethren; and the associates of Jude and Silas established them, because they also were prophets.	And with an abundance of the word Judas and Silas strengthened the brothers and established those of the household, because they also were prophets.
33	And after they had tarried there a space, they were let go in peace from the brethren unto the apostles.	And when, they had been there some time, the brethren dismissed them in peace to the legates.	And after they were there a while, the brothers dismissed them in peace to the apostles.
34	Notwithstanding it pleased Silas to abide there still.	[But it was the pleasure of Silas to remain there.]	OMITTED IN THE WESTERN PESHITTA TEXT

Parallel Translations

ACTS Chapter 15

	KJV	Murdock	Magiera
35	Paul also and Barnabas continued in Antioch, teaching and preaching the word of the Lord, with many others also.	Paul also and Barnabas remained at Antioch; and they taught and proclaimed, with many others, the word of God.	Now Paul and Barnabas remained in Antioch and were teaching and preaching the word of God with many others.
36	And some days after Paul said unto Barnabas, Let us go again and visit our brethren in every city where we have preached the word of the Lord, and see how they do.	And after [some] days, Paul said to Barnabas: Let us return, and visit the brethren in every city, in which we have preached the word of God; and let us see what they are doing.	And after [some] days, Paul said to Barnabas, "Let us return and visit the brothers who are in every city in which we have preached the word of God and let us see what they are doing."
37	And Barnabas determined to take with them John, whose surname was Mark.	And Barnabas was disposed to take John, who was surnamed Mark.	And Barnabas wanted to take John, who was called Mark.
38	But Paul thought not good to take him with them, who departed from them from Pamphylia, and went not with them to the work.	But Paul was not willing to take him with them; because he left them when they were in Pamphylia, and went not with them.	But Paul did not want to take him with them, because he had left them while they were in Pamphylia and had not gone with them.
39	And the contention was so sharp between them, that they departed asunder one from the other: and so Barnabas took Mark, and sailed unto Cyprus;	In, consequence of this strife, they separated from each other: and Barnabas took Mark, and they travelled by sea and went to Cyprus.	Because of this contention, they separated from each other and Barnabas took Mark and journeyed by sea and traveled to Cyprus.
40	And Paul chose Silas, and departed, being recommended by the brethren unto the grace of God.	But Paul chose Silas for his companion, and departed, being commended by the brethren to the grace of God.	Now Paul chose Silas and went away, being commended by the brothers to the grace of God.
41	And he went through Syria and Cilicia, confirming the churches.	And he travelled through Syria, and through Cilicia, and strengthened the churches.	And he traveled in Syria and in Cilicia and established the churches.

Chapter 16

	KJV	Murdock	Magiera
1	Then came he to Derbe and Lystra: and, behold, a certain disciple was there, named Timotheus, the son of a certain woman, which was a Jewess, and believed; but his father was a Greek:	And he came to the city Derbe, and to Lystra. And there was a certain disciple there, whose name was Timothy, the son of a believing Jewess, but his father was a Gentile.	And he arrived at the city [of] Derbe and of Lystra. And there was a certain disciple there, whose name [was] Timothy, the son of a certain faithful Judean woman and his father was an Aramean.
2	Which was well reported of by the brethren that were at Lystra and Iconium.	And all the disciples of Lystra and Iconium gave good testimony of him.	And all the disciples who were from Lystra and from Iconium gave testimony concerning him.
3	Him would Paul have to go forth with him; and took and circumcised him because of the Jews which were in those quarters: for they knew all that his father was a Greek.	Him Paul was disposed to take with him: and he took him, and circumcised him, because of the Jews that were in that region; for they all knew that his father was a Gentile.	Paul wanted to take this [man] with him, so he took [and] circumcised him because of the Judeans that were in the place, for all of them knew his father was an Aramean.
4	And as they went through the cities, they delivered them the decrees for to keep, that were ordained of the apostles and elders which were at Jerusalem.	And as they went among the cities, they preached and taught them, that they should observe those injunctions which the legates and Elders at Jerusalem had written.	And while they went among the cities, they were preaching and teaching them to be keeping the commandments which the apostles and elders who were in Jerusalem had written.

ACTS *Chapter 16*

	KJV	Murdock	Magiera
5	And so were the churches established in the faith, and increased in number daily.	And so were the churches established in the faith, and were increased in number daily.	Yet the churches were established in faith and increased in number every day.
6	Now when they had gone throughout Phrygia and the region of Galatia, and were forbidden of the Holy Ghost to preach the word in Asia,	And they travelled through the regions of Phrygia and Galatia; and the Holy Spirit forbid them to speak the word of God in Asia.	And they walked in the regions of Phrygia and of Galatia and the Holy Spirit hindered them from speaking the word of God in Asia.
7	After they were come to Mysia, they assayed to go into Bithynia: but the Spirit suffered them not.	And when they came into the region of Mysia, they were disposed to go from there into Bithynia, but the Spirit of Jesus permitted them not.	And after they had come to the region [of] Mysia, they wanted to go from there to Bithynia, yet the Spirit of Jesus did not permit them.
8	And they passing by Mysia came down to Troas.	And when they departed from Mysia, they came down to the region of Troas.	And after they had gone out from Mysia, they went down to the region [of] Troas.
9	And a vision appeared to Paul in the night; There stood a man of Macedonia, and prayed him, saying, Come over into Macedonia, and help us.	And in a vision of the night, there appeared unto Paul, a man of Macedonia, who stood and besought him, saying: Come to Macedonia and help us.	And in a vision during the night, there appeared to Paul (as [it were]) a certain Macedonian man who was standing and begging him, saying, "Come to Macedonia and help us."
10	And after he had seen the vision, immediately we endeavoured to go into Macedonia, assuredly gathering that the Lord had called us for to preach the gospel unto them.	And when Paul had seen this vision, immediately we were desirous to depart for Macedonia; because we inferred, that our Lord called us to preach to them.	And after Paul had seen this vision, immediately we wanted to leave for Macedonia, because we understood that our Lord had called us to preach to them.
11	Therefore loosing from Troas, we came with a straight course to Samothracia, and the next day to Neapolis;	And we sailed from Troas, and came direct to Samothrace; and from there, on the following day, we came to the city Neapolis.	And we traveled from Troas and headed straight for Samothracia and from there on the next day, we came to the city [of] Neapolis,
12	And from thence to Philippi, which is the chief city of that part of Macedonia, and a colony: and we were in that city abiding certain days.	And from there to Philippi, which is the chief [city] of Macedonia, and is a colony. And we remained in that city certain days.	and from there to Philippi, which is the chief [city] of Macedonia and is a colony. And we were in that city certain days.
13	And on the sabbath we went out of the city by a river side, where prayer was wont to be made; and we sat down, and spake unto the women which resorted thither.	And on the sabbath day, we went without the gate of the city to the side of a river, because a house of prayer was seen there. And when we were seated, we conversed with the women who there assembled.	And we went out on the day of the Sabbath outside of the gate of the city by the edge of a river, because a house of prayer was seen there. And after we were seated, we were speaking with the women who were gathered there.
14	And a certain woman named Lydia, a seller of purple, of the city of Thyatira, which worshipped God, heard us: whose heart the Lord opened, that she attended unto the things which were spoken of Paul.	And a certain woman who feared God, a seller of purple, whose name was Lydia, from the city of Thyatira, [was there]. Her heart our Lord opened, and she hearkened to what Paul spake.	And a certain woman, a seller of purple cloth, who feared God [was there]. Her name was Lydia, from the city [of] Thyatira. Our Lord opened the heart of this [woman] and she heard what Paul said.

Parallel Translations

ACTS *Chapter 16*

	KJV	Murdock	Magiera
15	And when she was baptized, and her household, she besought us, saying, If ye have judged me to be faithful to the Lord, come into my house, and abide there. And she constrained us.	And she was baptized, and her household. And she entreated us, saying: If ye are really persuaded that I have believed in our Lord, come and take lodging in my house. And she urged us much.	And she was baptized, she and her household. And she begged us and was saying, "If you are truly confident that I believe in our Lord, come, lodge in my house." And she constrained us much.
16	And it came to pass, as we went to prayer, a certain damsel possessed with a spirit of divination met us, which brought her masters much gain by soothsaying:	And it occurred that, as we were going to the house of prayer, a certain maid met us, who had a spirit of divination, and who procured for her lords great gain by the divination which she performed.	And it happened that while we were going to the house of prayer, a certain young woman met us who had a spirit of divinations. And she earned a large profit for her masters by the divination that she was divining.
17	The same followed Paul and us, and cried, saying, These men are the servants of the most high God, which shew unto us the way of salvation.	And she followed after Paul and us, and cried, saying: These men are the servants of the Most High God, and they announce to you the way of life.	And she was following Paul and us and was crying out and saying, "These men are the servants of the Most High God and are declaring to you the way of life."
18	And this did she many days. But Paul, being grieved, turned and said to the spirit, I command thee in the name of Jesus Christ to come out of her. And he came out the same hour.	And this she did many days. And Paul was indignant; and he said to that spirit, I command thee, in the name of Jesus Messiah, that thou come out of her. And it came out the same hour.	And so she did many days. And Paul was provoked and said to that spirit, "I command you in the name of Jesus Christ to come out of her. And immediately it went away.
19	And when her masters saw that the hope of their gains was gone, they caught Paul and Silas, and drew them into the marketplace unto the rulers,	And when her lords saw that the prospect of their gain from her was gone, they seized Paul and Silas, and dragging them along brought them to the market-place,	And when her masters saw that the hope of their profit had gone out of her, they arrested Paul and Silas and dragged [and] brought them to the marketplace.
20	And brought them to the magistrates, saying, These men, being Jews, do exceedingly trouble our city,	and set them before the prefects and chiefs of the city, and said: These men disturb our city; for they are Jews,	And they brought them to the magistrates and to the rulers of the city and were saying, "These men are troubling our city, because they are Judeans
21	And teach customs, which are not lawful for us to receive, neither to observe, being Romans.	and they preach to us customs, which it is not lawful for us to receive and to practise, because we are Romans.	and are preaching to us customs that are not permitted for us to receive and to do because we are Romans."
22	And the multitude rose up together against them: and the magistrates rent off their clothes, and commanded to beat them.	And a great company was collected against them. Then the prefects rent their garments, and commanded to scourge them.	And a large crowd gathered against them. Then the magistrates tore their garments and commanded to beat them.
23	And when they had laid many stripes upon them, they cast them into prison, charging the jailor to keep them safely:	And when they had scourged them much, they cast them into the prison, and commanded the keeper of the prison to keep them with care.	And after they had beaten them much, they threw them into prison and commanded the keeper of the prison to keep them carefully.

	KJV	Murdock	Magiera
	ACTS	*Chapter 16*	
24	Who, having received such a charge, thrust them into the inner prison, and made their feet fast in the stocks.	And he, having received this command, carried and immured them in the inner part of the prison, and confined their feet in the stocks.	Now when he received this command, he brought [them] in [and] confined them in the inner room of the prison and fastened their feet in stocks.
25	And at midnight Paul and Silas prayed, and sang praises unto God: and the prisoners heard them.	And at midnight Paul and Silas were praying and glorifying God: and the prisoners heard them.	And in the middle of the night, Paul and Silas were praying and praising God and the prisoners were listening to them.
26	And suddenly there was a great earthquake, so that the foundations of the prison were shaken: and immediately all the doors were opened, and every one's bands were loosed.	And suddenly there was a great shaking, and the foundations of the prison were moved; and at once all the doors opened, and the bands of all were loosed.	And suddenly, there was a great earthquake and the foundations of the prison were shaken and immediately, all the doors were opened and the fastenings of all were released.
27	And the keeper of the prison awaking out of his sleep, and seeing the prison doors open, he drew out his sword, and would have killed himself, supposing that the prisoners had been fled.	And when the keeper of the prison awoke, and saw that the doors of the prison were open, he took a sword and sought to kill himself; because he supposed the prisoners had escaped.	And when the keeper of the prison was awakened and saw that the doors of the prison were opened, he took a sword and wanted to kill himself, because he thought that the prisoners had fled.
28	But Paul cried with a loud voice, saying, Do thyself no harm: for we are all here.	But Paul called to him, in a loud voice, and said: Do thyself no harm, for we are all here.	And Paul called to him with a loud voice and said to him, "Do not do to yourself anything evil, because all of us are here."
29	Then he called for a light, and sprang in, and came trembling, and fell down before Paul and Silas,	And he lighted for himself a lamp, and sprang and came in, trembling, and fell at the feet of Paul and Silas.	And he lit a lamp for himself and sprang up and entered, trembling, and fell at the feet of Paul and of Silas.
30	And brought them out, and said, Sirs, what must I do to be saved?	And he brought them out, and said to them: My lords, what must I do, that I may have life?	And he brought them outside and said to them, "My lords, what is necessary for me to do, so that I may have life?"
31	And they said, Believe on the Lord Jesus Christ, and thou shalt be saved, and thy house.	And they said to him: Believe on the name of our Lord Jesus Messiah, and thou wilt have life, thou and thy house.	And they said to him, "Believe in our Lord Jesus Christ and you will have life, you and your house."
32	And they spake unto him the word of the Lord, and to all that were in his house.	And they spoke the word of the Lord to him, and to all the members of his house.	And they spoke to him the word of the LORD and to all his household.
33	And he took them the same hour of the night, and washed their stripes; and was baptized, he and all his, straightway.	And the same hour of the night, he took and washed them from their stripes; and he was baptized immediately, he and all the members of his house.	And immediately in the night, he took [and] washed them of their wounds and immediately he was baptized, he and all his household.
34	And when he had brought them into his house, he set meat before them, and rejoiced, believing in God with all his house.	And he took them and brought them into his house, and set a table for them; and he rejoiced in the faith of God, he and all the members of his house.	And he took [and] brought them up to his house and set a table for them and was rejoicing, he and his household, in the faith of God.

Parallel Translations

ACTS Chapter 16

	KJV	Murdock	Magiera
35	And when it was day, the magistrates sent the serjeants, saying, Let those men go.	And when it was morning, the prefects sent rod-bearers to say to the superior of the prison: Let those men loose.	And when it was morning, the magistrates sent sergeants to say to the ruler of the prisoners, "Release those men."
36	And the keeper of the prison told this saying to Paul, The magistrates have sent to let you go: now therefore depart, and go in peace.	And when the superior of the prison heard [it], he went in, and said the same thing to Paul; [namely], that the prefects have sent [word] that ye be set free. And now, [said he,] Go ye out, and depart in peace.	And when the ruler of the prison heard about [it], he told Paul this message, "The magistrates have sent [a message] that you should be released, and now leave, go in peace."
37	But Paul said unto them, They have beaten us openly uncondemned, being Romans, and have cast us into prison; and now do they thrust us out privily? nay verily; but let them come themselves and fetch us out.	But Paul said to him: They have scourged us, unoffending men, and Romans, before all the world, and have cast us into prison; and now, do they secretly let us out? No, surely: but let them come themselves and bring us out.	Paul said to him, "They have beaten Roman men without fault before the eye of the whole world and have put [them] into prison and now secretly do they send us away? Indeed not! Rather, they should come [and] send us away."
38	And the serjeants told these words unto the magistrates: and they feared, when they heard that they were Romans.	And the rod-bearers went and told to the prefects the words which were told to them: and when they heard that they were Romans, they were afraid,	And the sergeants went and told the magistrates these words that were said to them. And when they heard that they were Romans, they were afraid.
39	And they came and besought them, and brought them out, and desired them to depart out of the city.	and came to them, and entreated of them that they would come out, and that they would leave the city.	And they came to them and begged them to go out and to leave the city.
40	And they went out of the prison, and entered into the house of Lydia: and when they had seen the brethren, they comforted them, and departed.	And when they came out from the prison, they entered the house of Lydia; and there they saw the brethren, and comforted them, and departed.	And after they had gone out of the prison, they entered [the house of] Lydia and saw the brothers there and comforted them and left.

Chapter 17

	KJV	Murdock	Magiera
1	Now when they had passed through Amphipolis and Apollonia, they came to Thessalonica, where was a synagogue of the Jews:	And they passed through the cities of Amphipolis and Apollonia, and came to Thessalonica, where was a synagogue of the Jews.	And they passed by the cities [of] Amphipolis and Apollonia and came to Thessalonica, where there was a synagogue of the Judeans.
2	And Paul, as his manner was, went in unto them, and three sabbath days reasoned with them out of the scriptures,	And Paul, as was his custom, went in to them; and during three sabbaths he discoursed with them from the scriptures;	And Paul, as he was accustomed, went in to them and [for] three Sabbaths, spoke with them from the scriptures,
3	Opening and alleging, that Christ must needs have suffered, and risen again from the dead; and that this Jesus, whom I preach unto you, is Christ.	expounding and showing, that the Messiah was to suffer, and to arise from the dead, and that this Jesus whom I announce to you is the Messiah.	explaining and demonstrating that Christ had to suffer and to rise from the dead and [saying], "This Jesus is the Messiah whom I declare to you."

Parallel Translations

	KJV	*Murdock*	*Magiera*
	ACTS	*Chapter 17*	
4	And some of them believed, and consorted with Paul and Silas; and of the devout Greeks a great multitude, and of the chief women not a few.	And some of them believed, and adhered to Paul and Silas; and of those Greeks who feared God, a great many; and also of noted women, not a few.	And some of them believed and followed Paul and Silas and many of the Greeks who feared God and also notable women, not a few, [followed Paul].
5	But the Jews which believed not, moved with envy, took unto them certain lewd fellows of the baser sort, and gathered a company, and set all the city on an uproar, and assaulted the house of Jason, and sought to bring them out to the people.	But the Jews were indignant, and gathered to themselves evil men from the market-place of the city, and formed a great mob; and they alarmed the city, and came and assaulted the house of Jason, and sought to draw them from it, and to deliver them up to the mob.	And the Judeans were jealous and gathered to themselves evil men from the streets of the city and formed a large mob and disturbed the city and came and assaulted the house of Jason and wanted to take them from there and deliver them to the mob.
6	And when they found them not, they drew Jason and certain brethren unto the rulers of the city, crying, These that have turned the world upside down are come hither also;	And when they found them not there, they drew Jason and the brethren who were there, and brought them before the chiefs of the city, crying out: These are they who have terrified all the country; and lo, they have come hither also:	And when they did not find them there, they dragged away Jason and the brothers who were there and brought them to the rulers of the city, crying, "These are they who have disturbed the whole region and behold, they have come here also.
7	Whom Jason hath received: and these all do contrary to the decrees of Caesar, saying that there is another king, one Jesus.	and this Jason is their entertainer: and they all resist the commands of Caesar, saying that there is another king, one Jesus.	And this is Jason, their host, and all of these stand against the commandments of Caesar, saying, 'There is another king, Jesus.'"
8	And they troubled the people and the rulers of the city, when they heard these things.	And the chiefs of the city and all the people, were alarmed when they heard these things.	And the rulers of the city and all of the people were troubled after they had heard these [things].
9	And when they had taken security of Jason, and of the other, they let them go.	And they took sureties from Jason, and also from the brethren, and then released them.	And they took bail from Jason and also from the brothers and then released them.
10	And the brethren immediately sent away Paul and Silas by night unto Berea: who coming thither went into the synagogue of the Jews.	And the brethren immediately, on the same night, sent away Paul and Silas to the city of Berea. And when they came there, they entered into the synagogue of the Jews.	Now the brothers immediately in the night sent Paul and Silas to the city [of] Berea. And when they had come there, they entered the synagogue of the Judeans.
11	These were more noble than those in Thessalonica, in that they received the word with all readiness of mind, and searched the scriptures daily, whether those things were so.	For the Jews there were more liberal than the Jews of Thessalonica; and they gladly heard the word from them daily, and searched from the scriptures whether these things were so.	For those Judeans who were there were nobler than those Judeans in Thessalonica. And they gladly heard the word from them every day, discerning from the scriptures whether these [things] were so.
12	Therefore many of them believed; also of honourable women which were Greeks, and of men, not a few.	And many of them believed; and so likewise of the Greeks, many men, and women of note.	And many of them believed and likewise also from the Greeks, many men and notable women [believed].

Parallel Translations

	KJV	*Murdock*	*Magiera*
	ACTS	*Chapter 17*	
13	But when the Jews of Thessalonica had knowledge that the word of God was preached of Paul at Berea, they came thither also, and stirred up the people.	And when the Jews of Thessalonica had knowledge that the word of God was preached by Paul in the city of Berea, they came thither also, and they ceased not to excite and alarm the people.	And when those Judeans who were from Thessalonica knew that the word of God was preached by Paul in the city [of] Berea, they came there also and did not cease to stir up and to trouble the people.
14	And then immediately the brethren sent away Paul to go as it were to the sea: but Silas and Timotheus abode there still.	And the brethren sent away Paul, that he might go down to the sea. But Silas and Timothy abode in that city.	And the brothers sent Paul away to go down to the sea and Silas and Timothy remained in that city.
15	And they that conducted Paul brought him unto Athens: and receiving a commandment unto Silas and Timotheus for to come to him with all speed, they departed.	And they who conducted Paul, went with him to the city of Athens. And when they departed from him, they received an epistle from him to Silas and Timothy, that they should come to him speedily.	And those who escorted Paul went with him as far as the city [of] Athens. And when they went away from his presence, they took a letter from him to Silas and Timothy that they should travel to him quickly.
16	Now while Paul waited for them at Athens, his spirit was stirred in him, when he saw the city wholly given to idolatry.	And while Paul was waiting [for them] at Athens, he was pained in his spirit; because he saw that the whole city was full of idols.	Now Paul, while waiting in Athens, was grieved in his spirit, when he saw that the whole city was full of idols.
17	Therefore disputed he in the synagogue with the Jews, and with the devout persons, and in the market daily with them that met with him.	And in the synagogue he spoke with the Jews, and with those that feared God, and in the market-place with them who daily assembled there.	And he spoke in the synagogue with the Judeans and with those who feared God and in the marketplace with those who were present every day.
18	Then certain philosophers of the Epicureans, and of the Stoicks, encountered him. And some said, What will this babbler say? other some, He seemeth to be a setter forth of strange gods: because he preached unto them Jesus, and the resurrection.	And also philosophers of the sect of Epicureans, and others who were called Stoics, disputed with him. And one and another of them said: What doth this word-monger mean? Others said: He announceth foreign deities; because he preached to them Jesus and his resurrection.	And also philosophers, who were from the teaching of Epicurus and others who were called Stoics, were debating with him. And every one of them were saying, "What does this babbler want?" And others were saying, "He preaches strange gods," because he was preaching Jesus and his resurrection to them.
19	And they took him, and brought him unto Areopagus, saying, May we know what this new doctrine, whereof thou speakest, is?	And they took him and brought him to the place of judgments called Areopagus, and said to him: May we know what this new doctrine which thou preachest is?	And they arrested him and brought him to the judgment hall that was called Areopagus, saying to him, "Can we know what this new teaching is that you preach?
20	For thou bringest certain strange things to our ears: we would know therefore what these things mean.	For thou scatterest in our ears strange words; and we wish to know what they are.	For you are sowing strange words in our hearing and we want to know what these [things] are."
21	(For all the Athenians and strangers which were there spent their time in nothing else, but either to tell, or to hear some new thing.)	For all the Athenians and the foreigners residing there, cared for nothing else but to tell or to hear something new.	Now all the Athenians and those strangers who came there did not care for anything else, except to say and to hear something new.

Parallel Translations

	KJV	*Murdock*	*Magiera*
	ACTS	*Chapter 17*	
22	Then Paul stood in the midst of Mars' hill, and said, Ye men of Athens, I perceive that in all things ye are too superstitious.	And as Paul stood in the Areopagus, he said: Men, Athenians, I perceive that in all things ye are excessive in the worship of demons.	And as Paul stood in the Areopagus, he said, "Men, Athenians, I see that in all [things] you are abundant in the worship of demons.
23	For as I passed by, and beheld your devotions, I found an altar with this inscription, TO THE UNKNOWN GOD. Whom therefore ye ignorantly worship, him declare I unto you.	For, as I was rambling about, and viewing the temples of your worship, I met with an altar, on which was inscribed, TO THE HIDDEN GOD. Him, therefore, whom ye worship while ye know him not, the very same I announce to you.	For while I was traveling around and seeing the place of your worship, I found a certain altar on which was inscribed, 'The unknown god.' Therefore, although you do not know whom you worship, I will preach about this one to you.
24	God that made the world and all things therein, seeing that he is Lord of heaven and earth, dwelleth not in temples made with hands;	For the God who made the world and all that is in it, and who is Lord of heaven and of earth, dwelleth not in temples made with hands.	For the God, who made the world and all that is in it and is the Lord of heaven and of earth, does not live in temples that hands have made.
25	Neither is worshipped with men's hands, as though he needed any thing, seeing he giveth to all life, and breath, and all things;	Nor is he ministered to by human hands, neither hath he any wants; for he it is giveth life and breath to every man.	And he is not served by the hands of men and he does not lack in anything, because he has given life and soul to every man.
26	And hath made of one blood all nations of men for to dwell on all the face of the earth, and hath determined the times before appointed, and the bounds of their habitation;	And of one blood hath he made the whole world of men, that they might dwell on the face of all the earth: and he hath separated the seasons by his ordinance; and hath set bounds to the residence of men:	And from one blood he made the whole world of men to be living on the face of all the earth. And he appointed the seasons by his commandment and set boundaries for the habitation of men,
27	That they should seek the Lord, if haply they might feel after him, and find him, though he be not far from every one of us:	that they might inquire and search after God, and, by means of his creations, might find him; because he is not afar off from each one of us:	that they would seek and inquire after God and by his creations find him, because he is also not far from all of us.
28	For in him we live, and move, and have our being; as certain also of your own poets have said, For we are also his offspring.	for in him it is we live, and move, and exist: as one of your own wise men hath said: From him is our descent.	For it is in him we live and move and are, as also one of the wise [men] who is with you said, 'From him is our origin.'
29	Forasmuch then as we are the offspring of God, we ought not to think that the Godhead is like unto gold, or silver, or stone, graven by art and man's device.	Therefore we, whose descent is from God, ought not to suppose that the Deity hath the likeness of gold, or silver, or stone, sculptured by the art and skill of men.	Therefore, men, because our origin is from God, we ought not to think that the divine is likened to gold or to silver or to stone that is engraved by the workmanship and by the knowledge of man.
30	And the times of this ignorance God winked at; but now commandeth all men every where to repent:	And the times of this error God hath made to pass away; and at the present time, he commandeth all men, that each individual, in every place, should repent.	For God has caused the times of ignorance to pass. And in this time he has commanded all men that every man in every place should repent,

Parallel Translations

ACTS Chapter 17

	KJV	Murdock	Magiera
31	Because he hath appointed a day, in the which he will judge the world in righteousness by that man whom he hath ordained; whereof he hath given assurance unto all men, in that he hath raised him from the dead.	Because he hath appointed a day, in which he will judge all the earth, with righteousness, by the man whom he hath designated: and he turneth every man to faith in him, in that he raised him from the dead.	because he has established a day in which he is going to judge the whole earth with justice by way of the man whom he appointed. And he has caused everyone to turn to his faith, in that he raised him from the dead."
32	And when they heard of the resurrection of the dead, some mocked: and others said, We will hear thee again of this matter.	And when they heard of the resurrection from the dead, some of them ridiculed, and others of them said: At another time, we will hear thee on this matter.	And when they heard of the resurrection that is from the dead, some of them mocked, and some of them said, "At another time we will hear you about this."
33	So Paul departed from among them.	And so Paul departed from among them.	And so Paul went away from among them.
34	Howbeit certain men clave unto him, and believed: among the which was Dionysius the Areopagite, and a woman named Damaris, and others with them.	And some of them adhered to him, and believed; one of these was Dionysius from among the judges of Areopagus, and a woman named Damaris, and others with them.	And some of them followed after him and believed. And one of them was Dionysius of the judges of Areopagus, and a certain woman whose name was Damaris, and others with them.

Chapter 18

	KJV	Murdock	Magiera
1	After these things Paul departed from Athens, and came to Corinth;	And when Paul departed from Athens, he went to Corinth.	And after Paul went away from Athens, he came to Corinth.
2	And found a certain Jew named Aquila, born in Pontus, lately come from Italy, with his wife Priscilla; (because that Claudius had commanded all Jews to depart from Rome:) and came unto them.	And he found there a man, a Jew, whose name was Aquila, who was from the region of Pontus, and had just then arrived from the country of Italy, he and Priscilla his wife, because Claudius Caesar had commanded that all Jews should depart from Rome. And he went to them;	And he found there a certain Judean man whose name was Aquila, who was from the region [of] Pontus, who in that time had come from the region of Italy, he and Priscilla his wife, because Claudius Caesar had commanded all the Judeans to leave Rome. And he approached them
3	And because he was of the same craft, he abode with them, and wrought: for by their occupation they were tentmakers.	and, because he was of a their trade, he took lodgings with them, and worked with them; for by their trade they were tent-makers.	and because he was their fellow craftsman, he lodged with them and was working with them. And by their craft, they were makers of tent cloth.
4	And he reasoned in the synagogue every sabbath, and persuaded the Jews and the Greeks.	And he spoke in the synagogue every sabbath, and persuaded the Jews and Gentiles.	And he spoke in the synagogue on every Sabbath and persuaded the Judeans and heathens.
5	And when Silas and Timotheus were come from Macedonia, Paul was pressed in the spirit, and testified to the Jews that Jesus was Christ.	And when Silas and Timothy had come from Macedonia, Paul was impeded in discourse, because the Jews stood up against him, and reviled, as he testified to them that Jesus is the Messiah.	And after Silas and Timothy had come from Macedonia, Paul was pressured in the word because the Judeans were opposing him and blaspheming while he was witnessing to them that Jesus was the Messiah.

Parallel Translations

	KJV	Murdock	Magiera

ACTS Chapter 18

	KJV	Murdock	Magiera
6	And when they opposed themselves, and blasphemed, he shook his raiment, and said unto them, Your blood be upon your own heads; I am clean: from henceforth I will go unto the Gentiles.	And he shook his garments, and said to them: Henceforth I am clean; I betake myself to the Gentiles.	And he shook his garments and said to them, "From now on, I am clean. I am going to the Gentiles."
7	And he departed thence, and entered into a certain man's house, named Justus, one that worshipped God, whose house joined hard to the synagogue.	And he went away, and entered into the house of a certain man named Titus, one who feared God, and whose house adjoined the synagogue.	And he went away from there and entered the house of a man whose name [was] Titus, who feared God. And his house was attached to the synagogue.
8	And Crispus, the chief ruler of the synagogue, believed on the Lord with all his house; and many of the Corinthians hearing believed, and were baptized.	And Crispus, the president of the synagogue, believed on our Lord, he and all the members of his house. And many Corinthians gave ear, and believed in God and were baptized.	And Crispus, the ruler of the synagogue, believed in our Lord, he and all his household. And many Corinthians heard and believed in God and were baptized.
9	Then spake the Lord to Paul in the night by a vision, Be not afraid, but speak, and hold not thy peace:	And the Lord said to Paul in a vision: Fear not, but speak and be not silent:	And the LORD said to Paul in a vision, "Do not fear, but speak and do not keep silent,
10	For I am with thee, and no man shall set on thee to hurt thee: for I have much people in this city.	for I am with thee, and no one is able to harm thee; and I have much people in this city.	because I am with you, and no man is able to harm you, and I have many people in this city."
11	And he continued there a year and six months, teaching the word of God among them.	And he resided in Corinth a year and six months, and taught them the word of God.	And he stayed in Corinth [for] one year and six months and taught them the word of God.
12	And when Gallio was the deputy of Achaia, the Jews made insurrection with one accord against Paul, and brought him to the judgment seat,	And when Gallio was proconsul of Achaia, the Jews assembled together against Paul; and they brought him before the judgment-seat,	And when Gallio was proconsul of Achaia, the Judeans were gathered together against Paul. And they brought him before the judgment seat,
13	Saying, This fellow persuadeth men to worship God contrary to the law.	saying: This man persuadeth the people to worship God contrary to the law.	saying, "This [man] persuades men to be fearing God, beyond the law."
14	And when Paul was now about to open his mouth, Gallio said unto the Jews, If it were a matter of wrong or wicked lewdness, O ye Jews, reason would that I should bear with you:	And when Paul requested that he might open his mouth and speak, Gallio said to the Jews: If your accusation, O Jews, related to any wrong done, or any fraud, or base act, I would listen to you suitably.	And while Paul was requesting to open his mouth and to speak, Gallio said to the Judeans, "If you were accusing about a matter of evil or of deceit or of hatred, oh Judeans, of necessity I would receive you.
15	But if it be a question of words and names, and of your law, look ye to it; for I will be no judge of such matters.	But if the contests are about words, and about names, and concerning your law, ye must see to it among yourselves, for I am not disposed to be a judge of such matters.	But if the questions are about word[s] and about names and about your law, you should understand [them] among yourselves, for I do not want to be a judge of these issues."
16	And he drave them from the judgment seat.	And he repelled them from his judgment-seat.	And he expelled them from his judgment seat.

Parallel Translations

	KJV	*Murdock*	*Magiera*
	ACTS	*Chapter 18*	
17	Then all the Greeks took Sosthenes, the chief ruler of the synagogue, and beat him before the judgment seat. And Gallio cared for none of those things.	And all the Gentiles laid hold of Sosthenes an Elder of the synagogue, and smote him before the judgment-seat. And Gallio disregarded these things.	And all the heathens arrested Sosthenes, an elder of the synagogue, and beat him before the judgment seat. And Gallio overlooked these [things].
18	And Paul after this tarried there yet a good while, and then took his leave of the brethren, and sailed thence into Syria, and with him Priscilla and Aquila; having shorn his head in Cenchrea: for he had a vow.	And when Paul had been there many days, he bid adieu to the brethren, and departed by sea to go to Syria. And with him went Priscilla and Aquila, when he had shaved his head at Cenchrea, because he had vowed a vow.	And after Paul was there many days, he gave a farewell to the brothers and journeyed by sea to go to Syria. And Priscilla and Aquila went with him, after he had shaved his head in Cenchrea, because a vow was vowed by him.
19	And he came to Ephesus, and left them there: but he himself entered into the synagogue, and reasoned with the Jews.	And they came to Ephesus; and Paul entered the synagogue, and discoursed with the Jews.	And they arrived at Ephesus. And Paul entered the synagogue and was speaking with the Judeans.
20	When they desired him to tarry longer time with them, he consented not;	And they requested him to tarry with them: but he could not be persuaded.	And they begged him to extend the time with them, yet he was not persuaded,
21	But bade them farewell, saying, I must by all means keep this feast that cometh in Jerusalem: but I will return again unto you, if God will. And he sailed from Ephesus.	For he said: I must certainly keep the approaching feast at Jerusalem. But, if it please God, I will come again to you.	saying, "It is right for me certainly, that I should keep the feast that is coming in Jerusalem. But if God wills, I will return again to you." And he left Aquila and Priscilla in Ephesus.
22	And when he had landed at Caesarea, and gone up, and saluted the church, he went down to Antioch.	And Aquila and Priscilla he left at Ephesus, and he himself proceeded by sea and came to Caesarea. And he went up and saluted the members of the church, and went on to Antioch.	And he journeyed by sea and came to Caesarea. And he went up and greeted the clergy and went to Antioch.
23	And after he had spent some time there, he departed, and went over all the country of Galatia and Phrygia in order, strengthening all the disciples.	And when he had been there some days, he departed, and travelled from place to place in the regions of Phrygia and Galatia, establishing all the disciples.	And after he was there some days, he went away and traveled around in order in the region of Galatia and of Phrygia, establishing all the disciples.
24	And a certain Jew named Apollos, born at Alexandria, an eloquent man, and mighty in the scriptures, came to Ephesus.	And a certain man named Apollos, a Jew, a native of Alexandria, who was trained to eloquence, and well taught in the scriptures, came to Ephesus.	And a certain man whose name was Apollos, a Judean who was a native of Alexandria and was trained in speech and observant in the scriptures, came to Ephesus.
25	This man was instructed in the way of the Lord; and being fervent in the spirit, he spake and taught diligently the things of the Lord, knowing only the baptism of John.	He had been instructed in the ways of the Lord, and was fervent in spirit; and he discoursed and taught fully respecting Jesus, while yet he knew nothing except the baptism of John.	This [man] was instructed in the way of the LORD and was spiritually fervent and was speaking and teaching fully about Jesus, while not knowing anything except the baptism of John.

ACTS Chapter 18

	KJV	Murdock	Magiera
26	And he began to speak boldly in the synagogue: whom when Aquila and Priscilla had heard, they took him unto them, and expounded unto him the way of God more perfectly.	And he began to speak boldly in the synagogue. And when Aquila and Priscilla heard him, they took him to their house, and fully showed him the way of the Lord.	And he began to speak boldly in the synagogue. And when Aquila and Priscilla heard him, they brought him to their house and fully showed him the way of the LORD.
27	And when he was disposed to pass into Achaia, the brethren wrote, exhorting the disciples to receive him: who, when he was come, helped them much which had believed through grace:	And when he was disposed to go to Achaia, the brethren anticipated him, and wrote to the disciples to receive him. And, by going, through grace, he greatly assisted all them that believed.	And when he wanted to go to Achaia, the brothers encouraged him and wrote to the disciples to receive him. And after he had gone, through grace, he greatly aided all the believers,
28	For he mightily convinced the Jews, and that publickly, shewing by the scriptures that Jesus was Christ.	For he reasoned powerfully against the Jews, before the congregation; and showed from the scriptures, respecting Jesus, that he is the Messiah.	for he debated mightily against the Judeans before the crowds, showing from the scriptures concerning Jesus, that he is the Messiah.

Chapter 19

	KJV	Murdock	Magiera
1	And it came to pass, that, while Apollos was at Corinth, Paul having passed through the upper coasts came to Ephesus: and finding certain disciples,	And while Apollos was at Corinth, Paul travelled over the upper countries to Ephesus. And he inquired of the disciples whom he found there,	And while Apollos was in Corinth, Paul traveled around in the upper regions and came to Ephesus. And he asked the disciples whom he found there,
2	He said unto them, Have ye received the Holy Ghost since ye believed? And they said unto him, We have not so much as heard whether there be any Holy Ghost.	Have ye received the Holy Spirit, since ye believed? They answered and said to him: If there be a Holy Spirit, it hath not come to our hearing.	"Did you receive the Holy Spirit when you believed?" They answered and said to him, "We have not even heard if there is a Holy Spirit."
3	And he said unto them, Unto what then were ye baptized? And they said, Unto John's baptism.	He said to them: Into what then were ye baptized? They say: Into the baptism of John.	He said to them, "Then into what were you baptized?" They said, "Into the baptism of John."
4	Then said Paul, John verily baptized with the baptism of repentance, saying unto the people, that they should believe on him which should come after him, that is, on Christ Jesus.	Paul said to them: John baptized the people with the baptism of repentance, while he told them to believe in him who was to come after him, that is, in Jesus the Messiah.	Paul said to them, "John baptized the people with the baptism of repentance, telling [them] to believe in him who would follow him, who is Jesus Christ."
5	When they heard this, they were baptized in the name of the Lord Jesus.	And when they heard these things, they were baptized in the name of our Lord Jesus Messiah.	And after they heard these [things], they were baptized in the name of our Lord Jesus Christ.
6	And when Paul had laid his hands upon them, the Holy Ghost came on them; and they spake with tongues, and prophesied.	And Paul laid [his] hand on them; and the Holy Spirit came upon them, and they spoke in various tongues, and prophesied.	And Paul laid a hand on them and the Holy Spirit came on them and they spoke in different languages and prophesied.
7	And all the men were about twelve.	And all the persons were twelve.	And all the men were twelve.
8	And he went into the synagogue, and spake boldly for the space of three months, disputing and persuading the things concerning the kingdom of God.	And Paul entered into the synagogue, and spoke boldly three months, persuading in regard to the kingdom of God.	And Paul entered the synagogue and spoke boldly [for] three months and was persuading [them] about the kingdom of God.

Parallel Translations

	KJV	Murdock	Magiera
	ACTS	*Chapter 19*	
9	But when divers were hardened, and believed not, but spake evil of that way before the multitude, he departed from them, and separated the disciples, disputing daily in the school of one Tyrannus.	And some of them were hardened, and disputatious, and reviled the way of God before the assembly of the people. Then Paul withdrew himself, and separated the disciples from them. And he discoursed with them daily in the school of a man named Tyrannus.	And some of them were hardened and were striving against and reviling the way of God before the assembly of the Gentiles. Then Paul distanced [himself] and separated the disciples from them. And every day he was speaking to them in the school of a man whose name [was] Tyrannus.
10	And this continued by the space of two years; so that all they which dwelt in Asia heard the word of the Lord Jesus, both Jews and Greeks.	And this continued for two years, until all who resided in [Proconsular] Asia, both Jews and Gentiles, heard the word of the Lord.	And this continued [for] two years, until all who lived in Asia, Judeans and Arameans, heard the word of the LORD.
11	And God wrought special miracles by the hands of Paul:	And God wrought very great miracles by the hand of Paul:	And God was doing great miracles by the hand of Paul,
12	So that from his body were brought unto the sick handkerchiefs or aprons, and the diseases departed from them, and the evil spirits went out of them.	so that, from the clothes on his body, napkins and rags were carried and laid upon the sick, and the diseases left them, and demons also went out.	so that even from the coats that were on his body, handkerchiefs or pieces of cloth were brought and placed on the sick and the sicknesses went away from them and demons also went out.
13	Then certain of the vagabond Jews, exorcists, took upon them to call over them which had evil spirits the name of the Lord Jesus, saying, We adjure you by Jesus whom Paul preacheth.	And moreover certain Jews, who went about exorcising demons, were disposed to exorcise in the name of our Lord Jesus over those who had unclean spirits, by saying: We adjure you, in the name of that Jesus whom Paul announceth.	And some Judeans, who traveled about and exorcised demons, were also wanting to exorcise in the name of our Lord Jesus those who had unclean spirits, saying, "We exorcise you in the name of the Jesus whom Paul preaches."
14	And there were seven sons of one Sceva, a Jew, and chief of the priests, which did so.	And there were seven sons of one Sceva, a Jew, and chief of the priests, who did this.	And there were seven sons of a certain Judean man, a chief priest whose name was Sceva, who were doing this.
15	And the evil spirit answered and said, Jesus I know, and Paul I know; but who are ye?	And the evil demon answered and said to them: Jesus I well know, and Paul I know, but as for you, who are ye?	And that wicked demon answered and said to them, "Jesus I know and Paul I know, but who are you?"
16	And the man in whom the evil spirit was leaped on them, and overcame them, and prevailed against them, so that they fled out of that house naked and wounded.	And the man in whom was the evil demon leaped upon them, and overpowered them, and threw them down: and they fled out of the house denuded and bruised.	And that man who had the evil spirit leaped on them and overcame them and cast them down. And being naked and wounded, they fled from that house.
17	And this was known to all the Jews and Greeks also dwelling at Ephesus; and fear fell on them all, and the name of the Lord Jesus was magnified.	And this became known to all the Jews and Gentiles, who resided at Ephesus. And fear fell on them all, and the name of our Lord Jesus Messiah was exalted.	And this was known by all the Judeans and Arameans who lived in Ephesus. And fear fell on all of them and the name of our Lord Jesus Christ was lifted up.

	KJV	*Murdock*	*Magiera*

ACTS *Chapter 19*

	KJV	Murdock	Magiera
18	And many that believed came, and confessed, and shewed their deeds.	And many of them that believed, came and narrated their faults, and confessed what they had done.	And many of those who believed came and declared their faults and confessed what they had done.
19	Many of them also which used curious arts brought their books together, and burned them before all men: and they counted the price of them, and found it fifty thousand pieces of silver.	And also many magicians collected their books, and brought and burned them before every body: and they computed the cost of them, and it amounted to fifty thousand [pieces] of silver.	And many sorcerers also gathered their books and brought [and] burned them before everyone. And they counted their price and the silver amounted to five thousand [pieces].
20	So mightily grew the word of God and prevailed.	And thus with great power was the faith of God strengthened and increased.	And so with great power the faith of God grew strong and increased.
21	After these things were ended, Paul purposed in the spirit, when he had passed through Macedonia and Achaia, to go to Jerusalem, saying, After I have been there, I must also see Rome.	And when these things had been accomplished, Paul purposed in his mind, to make the circuit of all Macedonia and Achaia, and [then] go to Jerusalem. And he said: After I have gone thither, I must also see Rome.	And after these [things] had been accomplished, Paul set in his mind to travel around in all of Macedonia and in Achaia and [then] to go to Jerusalem. And he said, "When I have gone there, it is right for me to also see Rome."
22	So he sent into Macedonia two of them that ministered unto him, Timotheus and Erastus; but he himself stayed in Asia for a season.	And he sent two persons, of those that ministered to him, Timothy and Erastus, into Macedonia; but he himself remained for a time in Asia.	And he sent two men from those who ministered to him to Macedonia, Timothy and Erastus. But he remained a time in Asia.
23	And the same time there arose no small stir about that way.	And at that time there was great commotion respecting the way of God.	And during that time a great uproar occurred about the way of God.
24	For a certain man named Demetrius, a silversmith, which made silver shrines for Diana, brought no small gain unto the craftsmen;	For a certain silversmith was there, named Demetrius, who made silver shrines for Diana, and afforded great profits to the artisans of his trade.	And there was there a certain worker of silver, whose name was Demetrius who was making shrines of silver for Artemis and he brought great profit to his fellow craftsmen.
25	Whom he called together with the workmen of like occupation, and said, Sirs, ye know that by this craft we have our wealth.	He assembled all the artisans of his trade, and those who labored with them, and said to them: Gentlemen, ye know that our gains are all from this manufacture.	This [man] gathered all his fellow craftsmen and those who worked with them and said to them, "Men, you know that all our trade is from this occupation.
26	Moreover ye see and hear, that not alone at Ephesus, but almost throughout all Asia, this Paul hath persuaded and turned away much people, saying that they be no gods, which are made with hands:	And ye also know and see, that not only the citizens of Ephesus, but also the mass of all Asia, this Paul hath persuaded and enticed away, by saying, that those are not gods, which are made by the hands of men.	And you have also heard and you have seen that this Paul has persuaded and turned away, not only the citizens of Ephesus, but also a multitude of all of Asia, saying that those are not gods that are made by the hands of men.

ACTS *Chapter 19*

	KJV	Murdock	Magiera
27	So that not only this our craft is in danger to be set at nought; but also that the temple of the great goddess Diana should be despised, and her magnificence should be destroyed, whom all Asia and the world worshippeth.	And not only is this occupation slandered and impeded, but also the temple of the great goddess Diana is accounted as nothing; and likewise the goddess herself of all Asia, and whom all nations worship, is contemned.	And not only this business is being shamed and brought to nothing, but also the temple of the great goddess Artemis is counted as nothing, and also the goddess, whom all Asia and all the Gentiles worship, is despised."
28	And when they heard these sayings, they were full of wrath, and cried out, saying, Great is Diana of the Ephesians.	And when they heard these things they were filled with wrath; and they cried out, and said: Great is Diana of the Ephesians.	And when they heard these [things], they were filled with fury and cried out and said, "Great is Artemis of the Ephesians."
29	And the whole city was filled with confusion: and having caught Gaius and Aristarchus, men of Macedonia, Paul's companions in travel, they rushed with one accord into the theatre.	And the whole city was in commotion; and they ran together, and entered the theatre. And they caught, and bore along with them, Gaius and Aristarchus, men of Macedonia, and associates of Paul.	And the whole city was stirred up. And they ran together and went to the theater. And they seized [and] took along with them, Gaius and Aristarchus, Macedonian men, the companions of Paul.
30	And when Paul would have entered in unto the people, the disciples suffered him not.	And Paul was disposed to go into the theatre: but the disciples restrained him.	And Paul wanted to enter the theater, yet the disciples prevented him.
31	And certain of the chief of Asia, which were his friends, sent unto him, desiring him that he would not adventure himself into the theatre.	And likewise the chiefs of Asia, because they were his friends, sent and requested of him, that he would not expose himself by going into the theatre.	And also the chiefs of Asia, because they were his friends, sent [and] begged him not to give up his life to enter the theater.
32	Some therefore cried one thing, and some another: for the assembly was confused; and the more part knew not wherefore they were come together.	And the multitudes that were in the theatre were in great confusion, and cried, some one thing, and some another: and many of them knew not for what cause they had come together.	And the crowds that were in the theater were very confused and were crying one thing and [then] another, for many of them did not know why they had been gathered.
33	And they drew Alexander out of the multitude, the Jews putting him forward. And Alexander beckoned with the hand, and would have made his defence unto the people.	And the Jewish people who were there, brought forward one of their men, a Jew, named Alexander. And he, rising up, waved his hand, and wished to make a defence before the people.	And the people of the Judeans who were there put forward a Judean man of them whose name was Alexander. And when he stood up, he waved his hand and wanted to make a defense to the people.
34	But when they knew that he was a Jew, all with one voice about the space of two hours cried out, Great is Diana of the Ephesians.	But they knowing him to be a Jew, all cried out with one voice, about two hours: Great is Diana of the Ephesians.	And knowing that he was a Judean, all of them cried out with one voice [for] about two hours, "Great is Artemis of the Ephesians."
35	And when the townclerk had appeased the people, he said, Ye men of Ephesus, what man is there that knoweth not how that the city of the Ephesians is a worshipper of the great goddess Diana, and of the image which fell down from Jupiter?	But the chief of the city tranquillized them, by saying: Men of Ephesus, What person is there, among men, who doth not know the city of the Ephesians to be devoted to the worship of the great Diana, and of her image that descended from heaven?	And the ruler of the city quieted them, saying, "Men, Ephesians, for who are the men who do not know that the city of the Ephesians is the priestess of the great Artemis and her image that came down from heaven?

Parallel Translations

	KJV	Murdock	Magiera

ACTS Chapter 19

	KJV	Murdock	Magiera
36	Seeing then that these things cannot be spoken against, ye ought to be quiet, and to do nothing rashly.	Since therefore no one can gainsay this, ye ought to be tranquil, and to do nothing with precipitancy.	Therefore, because no one can speak against this, you ought to be quiet and not do anything in haste,
37	For ye have brought hither these men, which are neither robbers of churches, nor yet blasphemers of your goddess.	For ye have brought forward these men, when they have robbed no temples, and have not reviled our goddess.	for you have brought these men [here], although they have not stolen from the temples, nor reviled our goddess.
38	Wherefore if Demetrius, and the craftsmen which are with him, have a matter against any man, the law is open, and there are deputies: let them implead one another.	But if Demetrius and the men of his trade have a controversy with any one, lo, there is a proconsul in the city, they are men of dexterity, let them approach and litigate with one another.	Now if this Demetrius and his fellow craftsmen have a controversy with someone, behold, the proconsul [is] in the city. They are craftsmen, [so] they should go near and judge one with the other.
39	But if ye enquire any thing concerning other matters, it shall be determined in a lawful assembly.	Or if you desire any other thing, it may be determined in the place assigned by law for an assembly.	And if you are seeking something else, let it be settled in a place that is given by the law for an assembly,
40	For we are in danger to be called in question for this day's uproar, there being no cause whereby we may give an account of this concourse.	Because too we are now in danger of being accused as seditious, since we cannot give a reason for the meeting of this day, because we have assembled needlessly, and been tumultuous without a cause.	because now we also stand in danger of being accused as troublemakers, because we are not able to give a reason for the crowd of this day, because we have been assembled needlessly and made an uproar without a cause."
41	And when he had thus spoken, he dismissed the assembly.	And having said these things, he dismissed the assembly.	And after he had said these [things], he dismissed the crowd.

Chapter 20

	KJV	Murdock	Magiera
1	And after the uproar was ceased, Paul called unto him the disciples, and embraced them, and departed for to go into Macedonia.	And after the tumult had subsided, Paul called the disciples to him, and comforted them, and kissed them, and departed, and went into Macedonia.	And after the uproar had subsided, Paul called for the disciples and comforted them and kissed them and left [and] went to Macedonia.
2	And when he had gone over those parts, and had given them much exhortation, he came into Greece,	And when he had travelled over those regions, and had comforted them with many discourses, he proceeded to the country of Greece.	And when he had gone about those regions and had comforted them with many words, he came to the country [of] Greece.
3	And there abode three months. And when the Jews laid wait for him, as he was about to sail into Syria, he purposed to return through Macedonia.	And he was there three months. And the Jews formed a plot against him, when he was about to go to Syria: and he contemplated returning to Macedonia.	And he was there [for] three months. But the Judeans planned treachery against him when he was about to go to Syria and he thought that he should return to Macedonia.

Parallel Translations

	KJV	Murdock	Magiera
	ACTS	*Chapter 20*	
4	And there accompanied him into Asia Sopater of Berea; and of the Thessalonians, Aristarchus and Secundus; and Gaius of Derbe, and Timotheus; and of Asia, Tychicus and Trophimus.	And there departed with him, as far as Asia, Sopater of the city Berea, and Aristarchus and Secundus who were of Thessalonica, and Gaius who was of the city of Derbe, and Timothy of Lystra, and of Asia Tychicus and Trophimus.	And Sopater, who was from the city [of] Berea, and Aristarchus and Secundus, who were of the Thessalonians, and Trophimus and Gaius, who were from the city [of] Derbe, and Timothy, who was from Lystra, and Tychicus and Trophimus from Asia went away with him as far as Asia.
5	These going before tarried for us at Troas.	These proceeded on before us, and waited for us at Troas.	These went on before us and waited for us at Troas.
6	And we sailed away from Philippi after the days of unleavened bread, and came unto them to Troas in five days; where we abode seven days.	And we departed from Philippi, a city of the Macedonians, after the days of unleavened bread; and proceeded by water and arrived at Troas in five days, and remained there seven days.	But we left Philippi, a city of the Macedonians, after the days of the Feast of Unleavened Bread, and traveled by sea and arrived at Troas in five days. And we were there [for] seven days.
7	And upon the first day of the week, when the disciples came together to break bread, Paul preached unto them, ready to depart on the morrow; and continued his speech until midnight.	And on the first day of the week, when we assembled to break the eucharist, Paul discoursed with them, because he was to depart the next day; and he continued his discourse till midnight.	And on the first day of the week when we were assembled to break [the bread of] communion, Paul spoke with them, because the next day he was going to leave and he continued to speak until the middle of the night.
8	And there were many lights in the upper chamber, where they were gathered together.	And there were many lamps burning in the chamber where we were assembled.	And there were many lamps burning there in that upper room where we were gathered.
9	And there sat in a window a certain young man named Eutychus, being fallen into a deep sleep: and as Paul was long preaching, he sunk down with sleep, and fell down from the third loft, and was taken up dead.	And a young man named Eutychus was sitting in a window and listening. And while Paul prolonged his discourse, he sunk into a deep sleep; and, in his sleep, he fell from the third loft, and was taken up as dead.	And a certain young man, whose name was Eutychus, was sitting in a window and listening. And he sunk into a deep sleep while Paul was continuing the speech, and in his sleep he fell from the third loft and was taken up as dead.
10	And Paul went down, and fell on him, and embracing him said, Trouble not yourselves; for his life is in him.	And Paul went down, and bent over him and embraced him, and said: Be not agitated, for his soul is in him.	And Paul went down [and] fell on him and embraced him. And he said, "Do not be troubled, because his life is in him."
11	When he therefore was come up again, and had broken bread, and eaten, and talked a long while, even till break of day, so he departed.	And when he had gone up, he broke the bread and tasted [it], and discoursed until the morning dawned. And then he departed to go by land.	Now when he had gone [back] up, he broke bread and ate and continued speaking until the morning dawned. And then he left to go on by land.
12	And they brought the young man alive, and were not a little comforted.	And they brought the young man alive, and rejoiced over him greatly.	And they led out the young man alive and rejoiced in him greatly.

Parallel Translations

	KJV	*Murdock*	*Magiera*
	ACTS	*Chapter 20*	
13	And we went before to ship, and sailed unto Assos, there intending to take in Paul: for so had he appointed, minding himself to go afoot.	And we went on board the ship, and sailed to the port of Thesos; because, there we were to take in Paul: for so had he bidden us, when he proceeded on by land.	And we went down to the ship and sailed to the port of Assos, because there we had arranged to meet Paul. For so he had commanded us, when he had gone on by land.
14	And when he met with us at Assos, we took him in, and came to Mitylene.	And when we had received him at Thesos, we took him on board ship and proceeded to Mitylene.	Now when we met him at Assos, we boarded the ship and came to Mitylene.
15	And we sailed thence, and came the next day over against Chios; and the next day we arrived at Samos, and tarried at Trogyllium; and the next day we came to Miletus.	And from there, the next day, we sailed over against the island Chios; and again, the next day we arrived at Samos, and stopped at Trogyllium; and on the following day we arrived at Miletus.	And from there, the next day we sailed toward the island [of] Chios. And again, the next day we came to Samos and remained at Trogyllium. And the next day we came to Miletus,
16	For Paul had determined to sail by Ephesus, because he would not spend the time in Asia: for he hasted, if it were possible for him, to be at Jerusalem the day of Pentecost.	For Paul had determined with himself to pass by Ephesus, lest he should be delayed there; because he hasted on, if possible, to keep the day of pentecost in Jerusalem.	for Paul was determined to pass by Ephesus, lest he should be delayed there, because he was hurrying, so that if possible, he would celebrate the day of Pentecost in Jerusalem.
17	And from Miletus he sent to Ephesus, and called the elders of the church.	And from Miletus, he sent and called the Elders of the church at Ephesus.	And from Miletus, he sent to bring the elders of the church at Ephesus.
18	And when they were come to him, he said unto them, Ye know, from the first day that I came into Asia, after what manner I have been with you at all seasons,	And when they had come to him, he said to them: Ye yourselves know, how, at all times, since the first day that I entered Asia, I have been with you;	And when they came to him, he said to them, "You know, since the first day that I entered Asia, how I was with you all the time,
19	Serving the Lord with all humility of mind, and with many tears, and temptations, which befell me by the lying in wait of the Jews:	laboring for God, in great humility, and with tears, amid the trials which beset me from the plottings of Jews:	as I was serving God with great meekness and with tears and in the trials that came on me by the treacheries of the Judeans.
20	And how I kept back nothing that was profitable unto you, but have shewed you, and have taught you publickly, and from house to house,	and I shunned not that which was advantageous to your souls, that I might preach to you, and teach in the streets and in houses,	And I did not avoid what was profitable for your lives to preach to you and teach in the streets and in houses,
21	Testifying both to the Jews, and also to the Greeks, repentance toward God, and faith toward our Lord Jesus Christ.	while I testified to Jews and to Gentiles, as to repentance towards God and faith in our Lord Jesus Messiah.	witnessing to the Judeans and to the Arameans concerning repentance towards God and the faith that is in our Lord Jesus Christ.
22	And now, behold, I go bound in the spirit unto Jerusalem, not knowing the things that shall befall me there:	And now I am bound in spirit, and I go to Jerusalem; and I know not what will befall me there;	And now I am bound by the Spirit and I am traveling to Jerusalem and I do not know what will happen to me in it.
23	Save that the Holy Ghost witnesseth in every city, saying that bonds and afflictions abide me.	except that the Holy Spirit in every city, testifieth to me and saith: Bonds and afflictions await thee.	Nevertheless, the Holy Spirit witnesses in every city to me and has said, 'Bonds and trials are prepared for you.'

Parallel Translations

ACTS *Chapter 20*

	KJV	*Murdock*	*Magiera*
24	But none of these things move me, neither count I my life dear unto myself, so that I might finish my course with joy, and the ministry, which I have received of the Lord Jesus, to testify the gospel of the grace of God.	But my life is accounted by me as nothing, so that I may but finish my course, and the ministration which I have received from our Lord Jesus, to bear testimony to the gospel of the grace of God.	But I have not counted my life [as] anything, so that I may complete my course and the ministry that I have received from our Lord Jesus, that I may witness concerning the gospel of the grace of God.
25	And now, behold, I know that ye all, among whom I have gone preaching the kingdom of God, shall see my face no more.	And now, I know that ye will see my face no more, all of you among whom I have travelled and preached the kingdom of God.	And now I know that you will not see my face again, all of you for whom I have traveled [and] preached the kingdom.
26	Wherefore I take you to record this day, that I am pure from the blood of all men.	I therefore protest to you, this day, that I am pure from the blood of you all.	And because of this, I witness to you this very day that I am pure from the blood of all of you.
27	For I have not shunned to declare unto you all the counsel of God.	For I have not shunned to acquaint you with all the will of God.	For I have not refused to make known to you all the will of God.
28	Take heed therefore unto yourselves, and to all the flock, over the which the Holy Ghost hath made you overseers, to feed the church of God, which he hath purchased with his own blood.	Take heed therefore to yourselves, and to all the flock over which the Holy Spirit hath established you bishops; that ye feed the church of God, which he hath acquired by his blood.	Watch, therefore, over yourselves and over all the flock over which the Holy Spirit has appointed you overseers, to feed the church of God that he purchased with his blood.
29	For I know this, that after my departing shall grievous wolves enter in among you, not sparing the flock.	For I know, that after I am gone, fierce wolves will come in among you, and will have no mercy on the flock.	I know that after I am gone fierce wolves will enter among you without mercy on the flock.
30	Also of your own selves shall men arise, speaking perverse things, to draw away disciples after them.	And also, from among yourselves, there will rise up men speaking perverse things, that they may turn away the disciples to go after them.	And also, from yourselves [there] will rise up men speaking perverse [things] to turn away the disciples to follow them.
31	Therefore watch, and remember, that by the space of three years I ceased not to warn every one night and day with tears.	Therefore be ye vigilant; and remember, that for three years I ceased not to admonish each one of you, by day and by night, with tears.	Because of this, you should be vigilant and remember that [for] three years I did not stop, by night and by day, admonishing each one of you with tears.
32	And now, brethren, I commend you to God, and to the word of his grace, which is able to build you up, and to give you an inheritance among all them which are sanctified.	And now I commend you to God, and to the word of his grace, which is able to build you up, and to give you an inheritance among all the saints.	And now I commend you to God and to the word of his grace that is able to build you up and to give you an inheritance with all the holy [ones].
33	I have coveted no man's silver, or gold, or apparel.	Silver, or gold, or garments, I have not coveted.	Silver or gold or garments I have not desired.
34	Yea, ye yourselves know, that these hands have ministered unto my necessities, and to them that were with me.	And ye yourselves, know, that these hands ministered to my wants, and to them that were with me.	And you know that these hands ministered to my necessity and to those who were with me.

Parallel Translations

ACTS *Chapter 20*

	KJV	Murdock	Magiera
35	I have shewed you all things, how that so labouring ye ought to support the weak, and to remember the words of the Lord Jesus, how he said, It is more blessed to give than to receive.	And I have showed you all things; that thus it is a duty to labor, and to care for the infirm, and to remember the words of our Lord Jesus; for he hath said, That he is more blessed who giveth, than he who receiveth.	And I demonstrated everything to you, that so it is right to labor and to care for those who are weak and to remember the words of our Lord Jesus, because he said, 'He who gives is more blessed than he who receives.'"
36	And when he had thus spoken, he kneeled down, and prayed with them all.	And when he had said these things, he fell on his knees and prayed, and all the people with him.	And when he said these [things], he kneeled down and prayed and everyone with him.
37	And they all wept sore, and fell on Paul's neck, and kissed him,	And there was great weeping among them all. And they embraced him, and kissed him.	And there was great weeping among all of them and they embraced him and kissed him.
38	Sorrowing most of all for the words which he spake, that they should see his face no more. And they accompanied him unto the ship.	And they had the most anguish, because of the word he uttered, that they would see his face no more. And they accompanied him to the ship.	But they were most anguished about that word that he said, that they were not going to see his face again. And they accompanied him as far as the ship.

Chapter 21

	KJV	Murdock	Magiera
1	And it came to pass, that after we were gotten from them, and had launched, we came with a straight course unto Coos, and the day following unto Rhodes, and from thence unto Patara:	And we separated from them, and proceeded in a straight course to the island of Coos: and the next day, we reached Rhodes, and from there Patara.	And we separated from them and journeyed directly to the island [of] Coos. And the next day we came to Rhodes and from there to Patara.
2	And finding a ship sailing over unto Phenicia, we went aboard, and set forth.	And we found there a ship going to Phenicia; and we entered it, and proceeded on.	And we found a ship there that was going to Phoenicia and we boarded it and proceeded.
3	Now when we had discovered Cyprus, we left it on the left hand, and sailed into Syria, and landed at Tyre: for there the ship was to unlade her burden.	And we came up with the island of Cyprus, and leaving it on the left we came to Syria; and from there we went to Tyre, for there the ship was to discharge her cargo.	And we came as far as the island [of] Cyprus and passed it by on the left hand and came to Syria. And from there we arrived at Tyre, for there the ship was to unload her cargo.
4	And finding disciples, we tarried there seven days: who said to Paul through the Spirit, that he should not go up to Jerusalem.	And, as we found disciples there, we tarried with them seven days: and they, by the Spirit, told Paul not to go to Jerusalem.	And finding disciples there, we remained with them seven days and they were saying every day to Paul spiritually that he should not go to Jerusalem.
5	And when we had accomplished those days, we departed and went our way; and they all brought us on our way, with wives and children, till we were out of the city: and we kneeled down on the shore, and prayed.	And after those days, we departed and went on [our] way; and they all clung to us, they and their wives and their children, until [we were] without the city; and they fell on their knees by the seaside, and prayed.	And after those days, we left to go on the journey and they all accompanied us, with their wives and their children, until [we were] outside of the city. Then they kneeled down by the shore of the sea and prayed.
6	And when we had taken our leave one of another, we took ship; and they returned home again.	And we kissed one another: and we embarked in the ship, and they returned to their homes.	And we kissed each other and we boarded the ship and they returned to their houses.

Parallel Translations

ACTS Chapter 21

	KJV	Murdock	Magiera
7	And when we had finished our course from Tyre, we came to Ptolemais, and saluted the brethren, and abode with them one day.	And we sailed from Tyre, and arrived at the city Acco; and we saluted the brethren there, and stopped with them one day.	Now we sailed from Tyre and came to the city [of] Accho. And we greeted the brothers there and lodged with them one day.
8	And the next day we that were of Paul's company departed, and came unto Caesarea: and we entered into the house of Philip the evangelist, which was one of the seven; and abode with him.	And the next day, we departed and came to Cesarea; and we went in and put up in the house of Philip the Evangelist, who was one of the seven.	And on the next day we left and came to Caesarea. And we entered [and] lodged in the house of Philip the evangelist, who was [one] of the seven.
9	And the same man had four daughters, virgins, which did prophesy.	He had four virgin daughters, who were prophetesses.	And he had four unmarried daughters who prophesied.
10	And as we tarried there many days, there came down from Judaea a certain prophet, named Agabus.	And as we were there many days, a certain prophet came down from Judaea, whose name was Agabus.	And while we were there many days, a certain prophet came down from Judea, whose name was Agabus.
11	And when he was come unto us, he took Paul's girdle, and bound his own hands and feet, and said, Thus saith the Holy Ghost, So shall the Jews at Jerusalem bind the man that owneth this girdle, and shall deliver him into the hands of the Gentiles.	And he came in to us, and took the girdle of Paul's loins, and bound his own feet and hands, and said: Thus saith the Holy Spirit, So will the Jews in Jerusalem bind the man, who owns this girdle; and they will deliver him into the hands of the Gentiles.	And he came in to us and took the girdle of the loins of Paul and bound his own feet and his hands and said, "Thus says the Holy Spirit, so the Judeans in Jerusalem will bind the man [who is] the owner of this girdle and will deliver him into the hands of the Gentiles."
12	And when we heard these things, both we, and they of that place, besought him not to go up to Jerusalem.	And when we heard these words, we and the residents of the place begged of him, that he would not go to Jerusalem.	And when we heard these words, we and the residents begged him that he would not go to Jerusalem.
13	Then Paul answered, What mean ye to weep and to break mine heart? for I am ready not to be bound only, but also to die at Jerusalem for the name of the Lord Jesus.	Then Paul answered and said: What do ye, weeping and crushing my heart? For I am prepared, not only to be bound, but also to die at Jerusalem, for the name of our Lord Jesus Messiah.	Then Paul answered and said, "What are you doing, that you are weeping and breaking my heart? For I am ready not to be bound only, but also to die in Jerusalem for the name of our Lord Jesus."
14	And when he would not be persuaded, we ceased, saying, The will of the Lord be done.	And as he was not to be persuaded by us, we desisted; and we said: Let the pleasure of our Lord take place.	And when he was not persuaded by us, we ceased and we said that the will of our Lord will happen.
15	And after those days we took up our carriages, and went up to Jerusalem.	And after those days, we prepared ourselves and went up to Jerusalem.	And after those days, we prepared ourselves and went up to Jerusalem.
16	There went with us also certain of the disciples of Caesarea, and brought with them one Mnason of Cyprus, an old disciple, with whom we should lodge.	And some disciples of Caesarea went along with us, taking with them a brother from among the earlier disciples, whose name was Mnason, and who was from Cyprus; that he might entertain us at his house.	And some of the disciples from Caesarea came with us, bringing with them a brother, one of the first disciples whose name was Mnason and was from Cyprus, so that he might receive us in his house.
17	And when we were come to Jerusalem, the brethren received us gladly.	And when we arrived at Jerusalem, the brethren received us joyfully.	And when we arrived at Jerusalem, the brothers received us gladly.

Parallel Translations

	KJV	Murdock	Magiera
	ACTS	*Chapter 21*	
18	And the day following Paul went in with us unto James; and all the elders were present.	And the next day, with Paul, we went unto James, when all the Elders were with him.	And the next day we went in with Paul to James, as all of the elders were with him.
19	And when he had saluted them, he declared particularly what things God had wrought among the Gentiles by his ministry.	And we gave them salutation: and Paul narrated to them, with particularity what God had wrought among the Gentiles by his ministry.	And we greeted them and Paul was narrating to them in order all that God had done among the Gentiles by his ministry.
20	And when they heard it, they glorified the Lord, and said unto him, Thou seest, brother, how many thousands of Jews there are which believe; and they are all zealous of the law:	And when they heard [it] they glorified God. And they said to him: Our brother, Thou seest how many myriads there are in Judaea who have believed: and these are all zealous for the law.	And after they heard, they praised God and said to him, "Our brother, you see how many thousands there are in Judea who have believed and all of these are zealots of the law.
21	And they are informed of thee, that thou teachest all the Jews which are among the Gentiles to forsake Moses, saying that they ought not to circumcise their children, neither to walk after the customs.	And it hath been told them, of thee, that thou teachest all the Jews that are among the Gentiles to depart from Moses, by telling them not to circumcise their children, and not to observe the rites of the law.	Now it was said to them about you, that you are teaching that all of the Judeans who are with the Gentiles should break away from Moses, saying that they should not circumcise their children and they should not walk in the customs of the law.
22	What is it therefore? the multitude must needs come together: for they will hear that thou art come.	Now, because they have heard that thou hast arrived here,	Therefore, because they have heard that you have come here,
23	Do therefore this that we say to thee: We have four men which have a vow on them;	do thou what we tell thee. We have four men, who have vowed to purify themselves.	do what we tell you. We have four men who have made a vow to be purified.
24	Them take, and purify thyself with them, and be at charges with them, that they may shave their heads: and all may know that those things, whereof they were informed concerning thee, are nothing; but that thou thyself also walkest orderly, and keepest the law.	Take them, and go and purify thyself with them, and pay the expenses along with them, as they shall shave their heads; that every one may know, that what is said against thee is false, and that thou fulfillest and observest the law.	Lead them and go, be purified with them and pay the expenses with them, as they will shave their heads. And it will be known to everyone that what is said about you is false and [that] you fulfill and keep the law.
25	As touching the Gentiles which believe, we have written and concluded that they observe no such thing, save only that they keep themselves from things offered to idols, and from blood, and from strangled, and from fornication.	As to those of the Gentiles who have believed, we have written, that they should keep themselves from [an idol's] sacrifice, and from whoredom, and from what is strangled, and from blood.	Now about those who believed of the Gentiles, we have written that they should be keeping themselves away from that which is sacrificed and from fornication and from [that which] is strangled and from blood."
26	Then Paul took the men, and the next day purifying himself with them entered into the temple, to signify the accomplishment of the days of purification, until that an offering should be offered for every one of them.	Then Paul took those men, on the following day, and was purified with them; and he entered and went into the temple, manifesting to them the completion of the days of the purification, up to the presentation of the offering by each of them.	Then Paul took these men the next day and was purified with them. And he entered [and] went into the temple, informing them [of] the completion of the days of purification, until the offering of each one of them was offered.

Parallel Translations

ACTS Chapter 21

	KJV	Murdock	Magiera
27	And when the seven days were almost ended, the Jews which were of Asia, when they saw him in the temple, stirred up all the people, and laid hands on him,	And when the seventh day arrived, the Jews from Asia saw him in the temple: and they excited all the people against him, and laid hands on him,	And when the seventh day arrived, the Judeans who were from Asia saw him in the temple and incited all of the people against him and they laid hands on him,
28	Crying out, Men of Israel, help: This is the man, that teacheth all men every where against the people, and the law, and this place: and further brought Greeks also into the temple, and hath polluted this holy place.	crying out and saying: Men, sons of Israel; help. This is the man, who teacheth in every place, against our people, and against the law, and against this place; and he hath also brought Gentiles into the temple, and hath polluted this holy place.	crying out and saying, "Men of Israel, help! This is the man who is against our own people, teaching in every location against the law and against this place. And he has also brought Arameans into the temple and defiled this holy place."
29	(For they had seen before with him in the city Trophimus an Ephesian, whom they supposed that Paul had brought into the temple.)	For they had previously seen with him in the city Trophimus the Ephesian; and they supposed, that he had entered the temple with Paul.	For previously they had seen Trophimus, an Ephesian, with him in the city, and were supposing that he had entered the temple with Paul.
30	And all the city was moved, and the people ran together: and they took Paul, and drew him out of the temple: and forthwith the doors were shut.	And the whole city was in commotion; and all the people assembled together, and laid hold of Paul, and dragged him out of the temple: and instantly the gates were closed.	And the city was stirred up and all of the people were gathered. And they took hold of Paul and dragged him outside of the temple and immediately the gates were shut.
31	And as they went about to kill him, tidings came unto the chief captain of the band, that all Jerusalem was in an uproar.	And while the multitude were seeking to kill him, it was reported to the Chiliarch of the cohort, that the whole city was in uproar.	And as the crowd was seeking to kill him, it was reported to the chiliarch of the military guard that all of the city was stirred up.
32	Who immediately took soldiers and centurions, and ran down unto them: and when they saw the chief captain and the soldiers, they left beating of Paul.	And immediately he took a centurion and many soldiers, and they ran upon them. And when they saw the Chiliarch and the soldiers, they desisted from beating Paul.	And immediately he took a centurion and many soldiers and they ran to them. And when they saw the chiliarch and the soldiers, they stopped beating Paul.
33	Then the chief captain came near, and took him, and commanded him to be bound with two chains; and demanded who he was, and what he had done.	And the Chiliarch came up to him, and seized him, and ordered him to be bound with two chains: and he inquired respecting him, who he was, and what he had done.	And the chiliarch came toward him and held him and commanded that they should bind him with two chains. And he asked about him, who he was and what he had done.
34	And some cried one thing, some another, among the multitude: and when he could not know the certainty for the tumult, he commanded him to be carried into the castle.	And persons from the throng vociferated against him this thing and that. And, because he could not, on account of their clamor, learn what the truth was, he commanded to conduct him to the castle.	And some of the mob cried out various [things] about him, yet because of their noise, he was not able to know what was the truth. And he commanded that they should conduct him to the military camp.
35	And when he came upon the stairs, so it was, that he was borne of the soldiers for the violence of the people.	And when Paul came to the stairs, the soldiers bore him along, because of the violence of the people.	And when Paul reached the stairs, the soldiers carried him because of the violence of the people.

ACTS *Chapter 21*

	KJV	Murdock	Magiera
36	For the multitude of the people followed after, crying, Away with him.	For a great many people followed after him, and cried out, saying: Away with him.	For many people followed him and they cried out and were saying, "Take him away!"
37	And as Paul was to be led into the castle, he said unto the chief captain, May I speak unto thee? Who said, Canst thou speak Greek?	And when he came near to entering the castle, Paul said to the Chiliarch: Wilt thou permit me to speak with thee? And he said to him: Dost thou know Greek?	And when he arrived at the entrance to the military camp, Paul said to the chiliarch, "Will you allow me to speak with you?" And he said to him, "Do you know Greek?
38	Art not thou that Egyptian, which before these days madest an uproar, and leddest out into the wilderness four thousand men that were murderers?	Art not thou that Egyptian who, before these days, madest insurrection, and leadest out into the desert four thousand men, doers of evil?	Are you not that Egyptian, who before these days stirred up and led out to the wilderness four thousand men, doers of evil [things]?"
39	But Paul said, I am a man which am a Jew of Tarsus, a city in Cilicia, a citizen of no mean city: and, I beseech thee, suffer me to speak unto the people.	Paul said to him: I am a Jew, a man of Tarsus, a noted city in Cilicia, in which I was born: I pray thee, suffer me to speak to the people.	Paul said to him, "I am a Judean man from Tarsus, the notable city of Cilicia in which I was born. I beg you [to] allow me to speak to the people."
40	And when he had given him licence, Paul stood on the stairs, and beckoned with the hand unto the people. And when there was made a great silence, he spake unto them in the Hebrew tongue, saying,	And when he permitted him, Paul stood upon the stairs, and waved to them his hand; and when they were quiet, he addressed them in Hebrew, and said to them:	And when he allowed him, Paul stood on the stairs and was motioning to them with his hand. And when they quieted down, he spoke with them in Hebrew and said to them,

Chapter 22

	KJV	Murdock	Magiera
1	Men, brethren, and fathers, hear ye my defence which I make now unto you.	Brethren, and fathers, hearken to my defence before you.	"Brothers and fathers, hear a defense that is to you."
2	(And when they heard that he spake in the Hebrew tongue to them, they kept the more silence: and he saith,)	And when they perceived that he addressed them in Hebrew, they were the more quiet: and he said to them:	And when they heard that he was speaking with them in Hebrew, they quieted down more. And he said to them,
3	I am verily a man which am a Jew, born in Tarsus, a city in Cilicia, yet brought up in this city at the feet of Gamaliel, and taught according to the perfect manner of the law of the fathers, and was zealous toward God, as ye all are this day.	I am a man who am a Jew; and I was born in Tarsus of Cilicia, but was brought up in this city, at the feet of Gamaliel, and instructed perfectly in the law of our fathers; and I was zealous for God, as ye also all are.	"I am a Judean man and I was born in Tarsus of Cilicia, but I was educated in this city beside the feet of Gamaliel and was instructed perfectly in the law of our fathers. And I was zealous of God, even as also all of you are.
4	And I persecuted this way unto the death, binding and delivering into prisons both men and women.	And I persecuted this way, even to death; for I bound, and delivered up to prison, [both] men and women.	And I persecuted this way to the death, binding and delivering men and women to prison.
5	As also the high priest doth bear me witness, and all the estate of the elders: from whom also I received letters unto the brethren, and went to Damascus, to bring them which were there bound unto Jerusalem, for to be punished.	As the high priest is my witness, and likewise all the Elders; from whom I received letters, that I might go to the brethren in Damascus, and bring those who were there prisoners to Jerusalem, to receive capital punishment.	As the chief priests and all of the elders witness about me, from them I received letters to go to the brothers that are in Damascus, that I should also bring those who were there to Jerusalem, being bound and to receive punishment.

Parallel Translations

	KJV	Murdock	Magiera
	ACTS	*Chapter 22*	
6	And it came to pass, that, as I made my journey, and was come nigh unto Damascus about noon, suddenly there shone from heaven a great light round about me.	And as I travelled and began to approach Damascus, at noonday, from amidst tranquillity, a great light from heaven burst upon me.	And as I was traveling and began to approach Damascus in the middle of the day, suddenly a great light from heaven shone on me.
7	And I fell unto the ground, and heard a voice saying unto me, Saul, Saul, why persecutest thou me?	And I fell to the earth: and I heard a voice, which said to me: Saul, Saul! why persecutest thou me?	And I fell on the ground and I heard a voice that said to me, 'Saul, Saul, why are you persecuting me?'
8	And I answered, Who art thou, Lord? And he said unto me, I am Jesus of Nazareth, whom thou persecutest.	And I answered and said: Who art thou, my Lord? And he said to me: I am Jesus the Nazarean, whom thou persecutest.	And I answered and said, 'Who are you, my Lord?' And he said to me, 'I am Jesus, the Nazarene, whom you are persecuting.'
9	And they that were with me saw indeed the light, and were afraid; but they heard not the voice of him that spake to me.	And the men who were with me, saw the light, but heard not the voice that talked with me.	And the men who were with me saw the light, but they did not hear the voice that was speaking with me.
10	And I said, What shall I do, Lord? And the Lord said unto me, Arise, and go into Damascus; and there it shall be told thee of all things which are appointed for thee to do.	And I said: My Lord, what must I do? And our Lord said to me: Arise, go to Damascus; and there will be told thee, all that it is commanded thee to do.	And I said, 'What should I do, my Lord?' And our Lord said to me, 'Stand up [and] go to Damascus and there it will be told you about everything that is commanded you to do.'
11	And when I could not see for the glory of that light, being led by the hand of them that were with me, I came into Damascus.	And as I could see nothing, because of the glory of that light, those with me took me by the hand, and I entered Damascus.	And when I did not see because of the glory of that light, those who were with me took hold of my hands and I entered Damascus.
12	And one Ananias, a devout man according to the law, having a good report of all the Jews which dwelt there,	And a certain man, Ananias, who was upright according to the law, as all the Jews there testified concerning him, came to me.	And a certain man, Ananias, upright in the law, as all of the Judeans there witnessed about him,
13	Came unto me, and stood, and said unto me, Brother Saul, receive thy sight. And the same hour I looked up upon him.	And he said to me: My brother Saul! open thine eyes. And instantly my eyes were opened; and I looked upon him.	came to me and said to me, 'Saul, my brother, open your eyes!' And immediately my eyes were opened and I looked at him.
14	And he said, The God of our fathers hath chosen thee, that thou shouldest know his will, and see that Just One, and shouldest hear the voice of his mouth.	And he said to me: The God of our fathers hath ordained thee to know his will, and to behold the Just One, and to hear the voice of his mouth.	And he said to me, 'The God of our fathers has appointed you to know his will and to see the Just [one] and to hear the voice from his mouth.
15	For thou shalt be his witness unto all men of what thou hast seen and heard.	And thou shalt be a witness for him before all men, concerning all that thou hast seen and heard.	And you will be a witness for him to all men about all that you have seen and heard.
16	And now why tarriest thou? arise, and be baptized, and wash away thy sins, calling on the name of the Lord.	And now, why delayest thou? Arise, be baptized, and be cleansed from thy sins, while thou invokest his name.	And now, why are you wasting time? Rise up [and] be baptized and be cleansed from your sins, as you call on his name.'

Parallel Translations

	KJV	Murdock	Magiera
	ACTS	*Chapter 22*	
17	And it came to pass, that, when I was come again to Jerusalem, even while I prayed in the temple, I was in a trance;	And I returned and came hither to Jerusalem. And I prayed in the temple.	And I returned [and] came here to Jerusalem and I prayed in the temple.
18	And saw him saying unto me, Make haste, and get thee quickly out of Jerusalem: for they will not receive thy testimony concerning me.	And I saw him in a vision, when he said to me: Make haste, and get thee out of Jerusalem; for they will not receive thy testimony concerning me.	And I saw in a vision as he said to me, 'Hurry and go out from Jerusalem, because they will not receive your witness concerning me.'
19	And I said, Lord, they know that I imprisoned and beat in every synagogue them that believed on thee:	And I said: My Lord, they well know that I have delivered up to prison, and have scourged in all synagogues, those who believed in thee.	And I said, 'My Lord, they also know that I delivered to prison and beat those who believed in you in all our synagogues.
20	And when the blood of thy martyr Stephen was shed, I also was standing by, and consenting unto his death, and kept the raiment of them that slew him.	And when the blood of thy martyr Stephen was shed, I also was standing with them, and performed the pleasure of his slayers, and took charge of the garments of those that stoned him.	And when the blood of Stephen your witness was shed, I was also standing with them. And I approved the desire of the murderers and kept the garments of those who were stoning him.'
21	And he said unto me, Depart: for I will send thee far hence unto the Gentiles.	But he said to me: Depart; for I send thee afar, to preach to the Gentiles.	And he said to me, 'Go, for I am sending you to a far place to preach to the Gentiles.'"
22	And they gave him audience unto this word, and then lifted up their voices, and said, Away with such a fellow from the earth: for it is not fit that he should live.	And when they had heard Paul as far as this sentence, they raised their voice, and cried out: Away with such a man from the earth! for he ought not to live!	And after they had listened to Paul up to this word, they raised their voice[s] and cried out, "This [one] should be cut off from the earth, for thus it is not right for him to live!"
23	And as they cried out, and cast off their clothes, and threw dust into the air,	And as they vociferated, and cast off their garments, and threw dust into the air,	And as they were calling out and putting off their garments and throwing dust up into the sky,
24	The chief captain commanded him to be brought into the castle, and bade that he should be examined by scourging; that he might know wherefore they cried so against him.	the Chiliarch gave orders, to carry him into the castle: and he commanded, that he should be examined with stripes; that he might know, for what cause they cried out against him.	the chiliarch commanded that they should carry him to the military camp and commanded that he should be interrogated with stripes, so that he would know for what cause they cried out against him.
25	And as they bound him with thongs, Paul said unto the centurion that stood by, Is it lawful for you to scourge a man that is a Roman, and uncondemned?	And as they were stretching him with ropes, Paul said to the centurion who stood over him: Is it lawful for you to scourge a man, who is a Roman, and not yet found guilty?	And while they stretched him with leather straps, Paul said to the centurion who was standing over him, "Is it permissible for you to beat a Roman man who is not condemned?"
26	When the centurion heard that, he went and told the chief captain, saying, Take heed what thou doest: for this man is a Roman.	And when the centurion heard [it], he went to the Chiliarch, and said to him: What doest thou? For this man is a Roman.	And when the centurion heard [this], he came near to the chiliarch and said to him, "What are you doing? For this man is a Roman."
27	Then the chief captain came, and said unto him, Tell me, art thou a Roman? He said, Yea.	And the Chiliarch came to him, and said to him: Tell me; Art thou a Roman? And he said to him: Yes.	And the chiliarch came near to him and said to him, "Tell me, are you a Roman?" And he said to him, "Yes."

Parallel Translations

ACTS — Chapter 22

	KJV	Murdock	Magiera
28	And the chief captain answered, With a great sum obtained I this freedom. And Paul said, But I was free born.	The Chiliarch replied and said to him: With much money I acquired Roman citizenship. Paul said to him: And I was born in it.	And the chiliarch answered and said, "I obtained Roman citizenship with much money." Paul said to him, "But I was even born in it."
29	Then straightway they departed from him which should have examined him: and the chief captain also was afraid, after he knew that he was a Roman, and because he had bound him.	And immediately they who were intending to scourge him, fled from him: and the Chiliarch was afraid, when he learned that he was a Roman, because he had stretched him [for scourging].	And immediately those who were wanting to beat him went away from him and the chiliarch was afraid after he learned that he was a Roman, because he had bound him.
30	On the morrow, because he would have known the certainty wherefore he was accused of the Jews, he loosed him from his bands, and commanded the chief priests and all their council to appear, and brought Paul down, and set him before them.	And the next day, he wished to know truly what the accusation was, which the Jews brought against him: and he unbound him, and commanded the chief priests, and the whole company of their head-men, to assemble; and he took Paul, and brought him down, and placed him among them.	And the next day, he desired to know truly, what the accusation was that the Judeans were bringing against him. And he released him and commanded that the chief priests and all the assembly of their rulers should come. And he took Paul and brought [him] down [and] put him forward among them.

Chapter 23

	KJV	Murdock	Magiera
1	And Paul, earnestly beholding the council, said, Men and brethren, I have lived in all good conscience before God until this day.	And when Paul had looked on the assembly of them, he said: Men, my brethren; I have lived in all good conscience before God up to this day.	And when Paul looked at their assembly, he said, "Men, my brothers, in all good conscience, I have conducted myself before God up to this day."
2	And the high priest Ananias commanded them that stood by him to smite him on the mouth.	And Ananias, the priest, commanded those who stood by his side, to smite Paul on the mouth.	And Ananias, the priest, commanded those who were standing by his side to strike Paul on his mouth.
3	Then said Paul unto him, God shall smite thee, thou whited wall: for sittest thou to judge me after the law, and commandest me to be smitten contrary to the law?	And Paul said to him: God is hereafter to smite thee, [thou] Whited Wall! For, sittest thou judging me agreeably to law, while thou transgressest the law, and commandest to smite me?	And Paul said to him, "God is going to strike you, whitened wall! And are you sitting [and] judging me according to the law when you are transgressing the law and commanding that they should strike me?"
4	And they that stood by said, Revilest thou God's high priest?	And those standing by, said to him: Dost thou reproach the priest of God!	And those who were standing there said to him, "Are you speaking evil of the priest of God?"
5	Then said Paul, I wist not, brethren, that he was the high priest: for it is written, Thou shalt not speak evil of the ruler of thy people.	Paul said to them: I was not aware, my brethren, that he was the priest: for it is written, Thou shalt not curse the ruler of thy people.	Paul said to them, "I did not know, my brothers, that he was a priest, for it is written: YOU SHOULD NOT CURSE THE LEADER OF YOUR PEOPLE.

Parallel Translations

	KJV	*Murdock*	*Magiera*
ACTS	*Chapter 23*		
6	But when Paul perceived that the one part were Sadducees, and the other Pharisees, he cried out in the council, Men and brethren, I am a Pharisee, the son of a Pharisee: of the hope and resurrection of the dead I am called in question.	And, as Paul knew that a part of the people were of the Sadducees, and a part of the Pharisees, he cried out, in the assembly: Men, my brethren; I am a Pharisee, the son of a Pharisee; and for the hope of the resurrection of the dead, I am judged.	And after Paul knew that some of the people were of the Sadducees and some [were] of the Pharisees, he cried out in the assembly, "Men, my brothers, I am a Pharisee, the son of Pharisees and concerning the hope of the resurrection of the dead, I am being judged."
7	And when he had so said, there arose a dissension between the Pharisees and the Sadducees: and the multitude was divided.	And when he had said this, the Pharisees and Sadducees fell upon one another, and the people were divided.	And when he had said this, the Pharisees and Sadducees fell on one another and the people were divided.
8	For the Sadducees say that there is no resurrection, neither angel, nor spirit: but the Pharisees confess both.	For the Sadducees say that there is no resurrection, nor angels, nor a spirit: but the Pharisees confess all these.	For the Sadducees said that there was no resurrection and no angels and no spirit, but the Pharisees professed all of these.
9	And there arose a great cry: and the scribes that were of the Pharisees' part arose, and strove, saying, We find no evil in this man: but if a spirit or an angel hath spoken to him, let us not fight against God.	And there was great vociferation. And some Scribes of the party of the Pharisees rose up, and contended with them, and said. We have found nothing evil in this man: for if a spirit or an angel hath conversed with him, what is there in that?	And there was a loud cry and some scribes of the side of the Pharisees rose up and were striving with them and said, "We have not found anything that is evil in this man. Now if a spirit or an angel has spoken with him, what is in this?"
10	And when there arose a great dissension, the chief captain, fearing lest Paul should have been pulled in pieces of them, commanded the soldiers to go down, and to take him by force from among them, and to bring him into the castle.	And, as there was great commotion among them, the Chiliarch was afraid lest they should tear Paul in pieces. And he sent Romans, to go and pluck him from their midst, and bring him into the castle.	And as there was a huge uproar among them, the chiliarch was afraid lest they should tear Paul apart. And he sent Romans to go to seize him in the middle of them and bring him to the military camp.
11	And the night following the Lord stood by him, and said, Be of good cheer, Paul: for as thou hast testified of me in Jerusalem, so must thou bear witness also at Rome.	And when night came, our Lord appeared to Paul, and said to him: Be strong; for as thou hast testified of me in Jerusalem, so also art thou to testify at Rome.	And when it was night, our Lord appeared to Paul and said to him, "Be strengthened, because as you have witnessed about me in Jerusalem, so you are also going to witness in Rome."
12	And when it was day, certain of the Jews banded together, and bound themselves under a curse, saying that they would neither eat nor drink till they had killed Paul.	And when it was morning, several of the Jews assembled together, and bound themselves by imprecations that they would neither eat nor drink until they had slain Paul.	And when it was daybreak, men from the Judeans were assembled and they vowed to themselves that they would neither eat nor drink until they had killed Paul.
13	And they were more than forty which had made this conspiracy.	And they who had established this compact by oath, were more than forty persons.	Now there were more than forty men who had confirmed this pact by oaths.

Parallel Translations

ACTS *Chapter 23*

	KJV	*Murdock*	*Magiera*
14	And they came to the chief priests and elders, and said, We have bound ourselves under a great curse, that we will eat nothing until we have slain Paul.	And they went to the priests and Elders, and said: We have bound ourselves by imprecations, that we will taste of nothing, until we shall have slain Paul.	And they approached the priests and the elders and said, "We have vowed a vow to ourselves that we will taste nothing, until we have killed Paul.
15	Now therefore ye with the council signify to the chief captain that he bring him down unto you to morrow, as though ye would enquire something more perfectly concerning him: and we, or ever he come near, are ready to kill him.	And now, do ye and the chiefs of the congregation request of the Chiliarch, that he would bring him unto you, as if ye were desirous to investigate truly his conduct: and we are prepared to slay him, ere he shall come to you.	And now you and the rulers of the synagogue request of the chiliarch, that he should bring him to you as if you were seeking to truly examine his circumstance, and we are prepared to kill him before he would arrive to you."
16	And when Paul's sister's son heard of their lying in wait, he went and entered into the castle, and told Paul.	And the son of Paul's sister, heard of this plot: and he went into the castle, and informed Paul.	And the son of the sister of Paul heard of this plot. And he entered the military camp and informed Paul.
17	Then Paul called one of the centurions unto him, and said, Bring this young man unto the chief captain: for he hath a certain thing to tell him.	And Paul sent and called one of the centurions, and said to him: Conduct this youth to the Chiliarch; for he hath something to tell him.	And Paul sent [and] called for one of the centurions and said to him, "Conduct this young man to the chiliarch, for he has something to say to him."
18	So he took him, and brought him to the chief captain, and said, Paul the prisoner called me unto him, and prayed me to bring this young man unto thee, who hath something to say unto thee.	And the centurion took the young man, and introduced him to the Chiliarch, and said: Paul the prisoner called me, and requested me to bring this youth to thee, for he hath something to tell thee.	And the centurion took the young man and brought him to the chiliarch and he said, "Paul, the prisoner, called me and asked me to bring this young man to you, who has something to say to you."
19	Then the chief captain took him by the hand, and went with him aside privately, and asked him, What is that thou hast to tell me?	And the Chiliarch took the young man by his hand, and led him one side, and asked him: What hast thou to tell me?	And the chiliarch held the young man by the hand and led him to one side and asked him, "What do you have to say to me?"
20	And he said, The Jews have agreed to desire thee that thou wouldest bring down Paul to morrow into the council, as though they would enquire somewhat of him more perfectly.	And the young man said to him: The Jews have projected to ask thee to bring down Paul to-morrow to their assembly, as if wishing to learn something more from him.	And the young man said to him, "The Judeans have purposed to ask you to bring Paul down tomorrow to their synagogue, as though they wish to learn something more from him.
21	But do not thou yield unto them: for there lie in wait for him of them more than forty men, which have bound themselves with an oath, that they will neither eat nor drink till they have killed him: and now are they ready, looking for a promise from thee.	But be not thou persuaded by them: for, lo, more than forty persons of them watch for him in ambush, and have bound themselves by imprecations, that they will neither eat nor drink until they shall have slain him: and lo, they are prepared, and are waiting for thy promise.	However, you should not be persuaded by them, for behold, more than forty men of them are watching for him in ambush and have vowed to themselves that they will neither eat nor drink until they will have killed him. And behold, they are ready and are waiting for your promise."
22	So the chief captain then let the young man depart, and charged him, See thou tell no man that thou hast shewed these things to me.	And the Chiliarch dismissed the young man, after charging him: Let no man know, that thou hast showed me these things.	And the chiliarch dismissed the young man after he had charged him, "Let no man know that you have shown me these [things]."

Parallel Translations

	KJV	*Murdock*	*Magiera*
	ACTS	*Chapter 23*	
23	And he called unto him two centurions, saying, Make ready two hundred soldiers to go to Caesarea, and horsemen threescore and ten, and spearmen two hundred, at the third hour of the night;	And he called two centurions, and said to them: Go and prepare two hundred Romans to go to Caesarea, and seventy horsemen, and shooters with the right hand two hundred; and let them set out at the third hour of the night.	And he called two centurions and said to them, "Go [and] prepare two hundred Romans to go to Caesarea and seventy horsemen and two hundred archers with the right hand to leave at the third hour of the night.
24	And provide them beasts, that they may set Paul on, and bring him safe unto Felix the governor.	And provide also a saddle beast, that they may set Paul on it, and carry him safely to Felix the governor.	And also provide a beast of burden to set Paul on and deliver him to Felix the governor."
25	And he wrote a letter after this manner:	And he wrote a letter and gave them, in which was, thus:	And he wrote a letter [and] gave [it] to them in which was the following:
26	Claudius Lysias unto the most excellent governor Felix sendeth greeting.	Claudius Lysias to the excellent governor Felix; greeting.	Claudius Lysias to Felix, the noble governor: "Greeting.
27	This man was taken of the Jews, and should have been killed of them: then came I with an army, and rescued him, having understood that he was a Roman.	The Jews seized this man, in order to kill him; but I came with Romans, and rescued him, when I learned that he was a Roman.	The Judeans arrested this man so that they could kill him and I aided [him] with Romans and rescued him when I learned that he was a Roman.
28	And when I would have known the cause wherefore they accused him, I brought him forth into their council:	And as I wished to know the offence, for which they criminated him, I brought him to their assembly.	And as I was seeking to know the charge for which they accused him, I brought him to their synagogue.
29	Whom I perceived to be accused of questions of their law, but to have nothing laid to his charge worthy of death or of bonds.	And I found, that it was about questions of their law they accused him, and that an offence worthy of bonds or of death, was not upon him.	And I found out that they accused him about questions of their law and there was not a charge toward him that was worthy of bonds or death.
30	And when it was told me how that the Jews laid wait for the man, I sent straightway to thee, and gave commandment to his accusers also to say before thee what they had against him. Farewell.	And when the wiles of a plot formed by the Jews against him came to my knowledge, I forthwith sent him to thee. And I have directed his accusers, to go and contend with him, before thee. Farewell.	And when I was informed of a plot by an ambush that the Judeans had planned against him, immediately I sent him to you and commanded his accusers to come and speak with him before you. Farewell."
31	Then the soldiers, as it was commanded them, took Paul, and brought him by night to Antipatris.	Then the Romans, as they had been commanded, took Paul by night, and brought him to the city of Antipatris.	Then the Romans, as they were commanded, led Paul by night and brought him to the city [of] Antipatris.
32	On the morrow they left the horsemen to go with him, and returned to the castle:	And the next day, the horsemen dismissed the footmen their associates, that they might return to the castle.	And the next day, the horsemen sent away the foot soldiers, their associates, to return to the military camp.
33	Who, when they came to Caesarea, and delivered the epistle to the governor, presented Paul also before him.	And they brought him to Caesarea: and they delivered the letter to the governor, and set Paul before him.	And they brought him to Caesarea and gave the letter to the governor and they placed Paul before him.
34	And when the governor had read the letter, he asked of what province he was. And when he understood that he was of Cilicia;	And when he had read the letter, he asked him of what province he was? And when he learned that he was of Cilicia,	And when he read the letter, he asked him from what province he was. And when he learned that he was from Cilicia,

Parallel Translations

	KJV	Murdock	Magiera

ACTS Chapter 23

	KJV	Murdock	Magiera
35	I will hear thee, said he, when thine accusers are also come. And he commanded him to be kept in Herod's judgment hall.	he said to him: I will give thee audience, when thy accusers arrive. And he ordered him to be kept in the Praetorium of Herod.	he said to him, "I will hear you, when your accusers are come." And he commanded that they should keep him in the judgment hall of Herod.

Chapter 24

	KJV	Murdock	Magiera
1	And after five days Ananias the high priest descended with the elders, and with a certain orator named Tertullus, who informed the governor against Paul.	And after five days, Ananias the high priest, with the Elders, and with Tertullus the orator, went down, and made a communication to the governor against Paul.	And after five days, Ananias the high priest went down, with the elders and with Tertullus the orator, and they informed the governor concerning Paul.
2	And when he was called forth, Tertullus began to accuse him, saying, Seeing that by thee we enjoy great quietness, and that very worthy deeds are done unto this nation by thy providence,	And when he had been called, Tertullus began to accuse him, and to say: Through thee, we dwell in much tranquillity; and many reforms have come to this nation, under thy administration;	And when he was called, Tertullus began to accuse him and said, "We live in abundance of quietness because of you and many reforms have been [made] for this people in the discharge of your care.
3	We accept it always, and in all places, most noble Felix, with all thankfulness.	and we all, in every place, receive thy grace, excellent Felix.	And all of us in every place receive your favor, noble Felix.
4	Notwithstanding, that I be not further tedious unto thee, I pray thee that thou wouldest hear us of thy clemency a few words.	But, not to weary thee with numerous [particulars], I pray thee to hear our humbleness, in brief.	But lest you should be wearied with many [things], I beg you to hear our humility with few words.
5	For we have found this man a pestilent fellow, and a mover of sedition among all the Jews throughout the world, and a ringleader of the sect of the Nazarenes:	For we have found this man to be an assassin, and a mover of sedition among all Jews in the whole land: for he is a ringleader of the sect of the Nazareans.	For we have found this man to be one who is corrupt and stirs up sedition among all the Judeans in all the land. For he is the leader of the teaching of the Nazarenes
6	Who also hath gone about to profane the temple: whom we took, and would have judged according to our law.	And he was disposed to pollute our temple. And having seized him we wished to judge him according to our law.	and he wanted to defile our temple. After we arrested him, we wanted to judge him according to our law,
7	But the chief captain Lysias came upon us, and with great violence took him away out of our hands,	But Lysias the Chiliarch came, and with great violence took him out of our hands, and sent him to thee.	but Lysias the chiliarch came and with great violence, grabbed him out of our hands and sent him to you.
8	Commanding his accusers to come unto thee: by examining of whom thyself mayest take knowledge of all these things, whereof we accuse him.	And he commanded his accusers to come before thee. And if thou wilt interrogate him, thou canst learn from him respecting all these things of which we accuse him.	And he commanded his accusers to come before you. And you will find when you ask him, that you will learn from him about all these [things] of which we are accusing him."
9	And the Jews also assented, saying that these things were so.	And the Jews also pleaded against him, saying that these things were so.	And the Judeans also cried out against him, saying that these [things] were so.

Parallel Translations

ACTS *Chapter 24*

	KJV	*Murdock*	*Magiera*
10	Then Paul, after that the governor had beckoned unto him to speak, answered, Forasmuch as I know that thou hast been of many years a judge unto this nation, I do the more cheerfully answer for myself:	Then the governor made signs to Paul, that he should speak. And Paul answered and said: I know thee to have been a judge of this nation for many years, and I therefore cheerfully enter upon a defence of myself.	And the governor signaled to Paul to speak. And Paul answered and said, "For many years, I know that you have been a judge of this people and because of this, I make a defense for myself gladly.
11	Because that thou mayest understand, that there are yet but twelve days since I went up to Jerusalem for to worship.	Because thou canst understand, that there have been but twelve days, since I went up to Jerusalem to worship.	As you may know, there has not been more than twelve days since I went up to Jerusalem to worship.
12	And they neither found me in the temple disputing with any man, neither raising up the people, neither in the synagogues, nor in the city:	And they did not find me talking with any person in the temple, nor collecting any company, either in their synagogues, or in the city.	And they did not find me speaking with anyone in the temple, nor gathering a crowd, not in their synagogue or in the city.
13	Neither can they prove the things whereof they now accuse me.	Nor have they the power to prove, before thee, the things of which they now accuse me.	And they will not be able to prove before you what they are now accusing me.
14	But this I confess unto thee, that after the way which they call heresy, so worship I the God of my fathers, believing all things which are written in the law and in the prophets:	But this indeed I acknowledge, that in that same doctrine of which they speak, I do serve the God of my fathers, believing all the things written in the law and in the prophets.	Nevertheless, this I do confess, that in this teaching about which they speak, I serve the God of my fathers, believing all the things that are written in the law and in the prophets.
15	And have hope toward God, which they themselves also allow, that there shall be a resurrection of the dead, both of the just and unjust.	And I have a hope in God, which they also themselves expect,---that there is to be a resurrection of the dead, both of the righteous and the wicked.	And I have hope of God, which they themselves also are hoping, that there is going to be a resurrection from the dead of the upright and of the wicked.
16	And herein do I exercise myself, to have always a conscience void of offence toward God, and toward men.	And for this reason, I also labor to have always a pure conscience before God, and before men.	Because of this also, I am laboring to have a pure conscience before God and before men always.
17	Now after many years I came to bring alms to my nation, and offerings.	And, after many years, I came to the people of my own nation, to impart alms, and to present an offering.	Now after many years, I came to my own people to give charity and to bring an offering.
18	Whereupon certain Jews from Asia found me purified in the temple, neither with multitude, nor with tumult.	And when I had purified myself, these men found me in the temple; not with a throng, nor with a tumult.	And these [men] found me in the temple as I was purifying myself, not with a crowd nor in a riot.
19	Who ought to have been here before thee, and object, if they had ought against me.	But certain Jews, who came from Asia, were tumultuous; who ought, with me, to stand before thee, and make accusation of their own affair.	But if certain Judeans who came from Asia stirred up [the riot], these ought to stand with me before you and accuse [me of] whatever they have [against me].
20	Or else let these same here say, if they have found any evil doing in me, while I stood before the council,	Or let these here present say, whether they found any offence in me, when I stood before their assembly;	Or these should say what offense they found in me, when I stood before their assembly.

Parallel Translations

ACTS Chapter 24

	KJV	Murdock	Magiera
21	Except it be for this one voice, that I cried standing among them, Touching the resurrection of the dead I am called in question by you this day.	except this one thing, that I cried, while standing in the midst of them: Concerning the resurrection of the dead, am I this day on trial before you.	[There was no offense] except this one word that I cried out when I stood among them, 'Concerning the resurrection of the dead I am being judged before you today.'"
22	And when Felix heard these things, having more perfect knowledge of that way, he deferred them, and said, When Lysias the chief captain shall come down, I will know the uttermost of your matter.	And Felix, because he understood that way fully, deferred them, saying: When the Chiliarch shall come, I will give hearing between you.	Now Felix, because he knew of this way fully, put them off, saying, "When the chiliarch comes, I will hear between you."
23	And he commanded a centurion to keep Paul, and to let him have liberty, and that he should forbid none of his acquaintance to minister or come unto him.	And he commanded a centurion to keep Paul, at rest; and that no one of his acquaintances should be forbidden to minister to him.	And he commanded a centurion to keep Paul at ease and that none of his associates would be forbidden to minister to him.
24	And after certain days, when Felix came with his wife Drusilla, which was a Jewess, he sent for Paul, and heard him concerning the faith in Christ.	And after a few days, Felix, and Drusilla his wife who was a Jewess, sent and called for Paul; and they heard him concerning faith in the Messiah.	And after a few days, Felix and Drusilla his wife, who was a Judean, sent and called for Paul and heard from him about the faith of Christ.
25	And as he reasoned of righteousness, temperance, and judgment to come, Felix trembled, and answered, Go thy way for this time; when I have a convenient season, I will call for thee.	And while he was discoursing with them on righteousness, and on holiness, and on the future judgment, Felix was filled with fear; and he said: For the present time, go: and when I have opportunity, I will send for thee.	And while he was speaking with them about justification and about sanctification and about the judgment of the future, Felix was filled with fear. And he said, "Now go, and when I have time, I will send for you."
26	He hoped also that money should have been given him of Paul, that he might loose him: wherefore he sent for him the oftener, and communed with him.	He hoped, moreover, that a present would be given him by Paul; [and] therefore, he often sent for him, and conversed with him.	For he was hoping that a bribe would be given to him by Paul. Because of this, he also continually sent for him to come and speak with him.
27	But after two years Porcius Festus came into Felix' room: and Felix, willing to shew the Jews a pleasure, left Paul bound.	And when two years were fulfilled to him, another governor, whose name was Porcius Festus, came into his place. And Felix, that he might do the Jews a favor, left Paul a prisoner.	And after two years were concluded, another governor came into his position, who was called Porcius Festus. Now Felix, so that he would gain favor with the Judeans, left Paul bound.

Chapter 25

	KJV	Murdock	Magiera
1	Now when Festus was come into the province, after three days he ascended from Caesarea to Jerusalem.	And when Festus arrived at Caesarea, he, after three days, went up to Jerusalem.	And when Festus came to Caesarea, after three days, he went up to Jerusalem.
2	Then the high priest and the chief of the Jews informed him against Paul, and besought him,	And the chief priests and the head men of the Jews made representations to him concerning Paul.	And the chief priests and the rulers of the Judeans informed him about Paul. And they begged him,

ACTS Chapter 25

	KJV	Murdock	Magiera
3	And desired favour against him, that he would send for him to Jerusalem, laying wait in the way to kill him.	And they petitioned him, asking of him the favor, that he would send for him to come to Jerusalem; they placing an ambush to slay him by the way.	asking him this favor, that he would summon him to be brought to Jerusalem, as they were setting ambushes along the road to kill him.
4	But Festus answered, that Paul should be kept at Caesarea, and that he himself would depart shortly thither.	But Festus made answer: Paul is in custody at Caesarea, whither I am in haste to go.	And Festus gave an answer, "Paul will be kept at Caesarea and I will hasten to journey [there].
5	Let them therefore, said he, which among you are able, go down with me, and accuse this man, if there be any wickedness in him.	Therefore, let those among you who are able, go down with us, and make presentment of every offence there is in the man.	Therefore, those who are with you, who are able to come down with us, should accuse [him] concerning every offense that is in the man."
6	And when he had tarried among them more than ten days, he went down unto Caesarea; and the next day sitting on the judgment seat commanded Paul to be brought.	And when he had been there eight or ten days, he came down to Caesarea. And the next day, he sat on the tribunal, and commanded Paul to be brought.	And when he had been there eight or ten days, he went down to Caesarea. And on the next day he sat on the judgment seat and commanded that they should bring Paul.
7	And when he was come, the Jews which came down from Jerusalem stood round about, and laid many and grievous complaints against Paul, which they could not prove.	And when he came, the Jews who had come from Jerusalem surrounded him, and preferred against him many and weighty charges, which they were unable to substantiate.	And after he arrived, the Judeans, who had come down from Jerusalem, surrounded him and the leaders brought many harsh [things] against him, which they were not able to prove,
8	While he answered for himself, Neither against the law of the Jews, neither against the temple, nor yet against Caesar, have I offended any thing at all.	Meanwhile Paul maintained, that he had committed no offence, either against the Jewish law, or against the temple, or against Caesar.	and after Paul made a defense that he had not offended [in] anything, neither in the law of the Judeans, nor in the temple, nor against Caesar.
9	But Festus, willing to do the Jews a pleasure, answered Paul, and said, Wilt thou go up to Jerusalem, and there be judged of these things before me?	But Festus, because he was disposed to conciliate the favor of the Jews, said to Paul: Wilt thou go up to Jerusalem, and there be tried before me for these things?	But Festus, because he was willing to grant a favor to the Judeans, said to Paul, "Are you willing to go up to Jerusalem and there to be judged before me about these [things]?"
10	Then said Paul, I stand at Caesar's judgment seat, where I ought to be judged: to the Jews have I done no wrong, as thou very well knowest.	Paul replied, and said: I stand before Caesar's tribunal: here I ought to be tried. Against the Jews I have committed no offence, as thou also well knowest.	Paul answered and said, "I stand on the judgment seat of Caesar. Here it is right for me to be judged. I have not committed any sin against the Judeans, as you also know.
11	For if I be an offender, or have committed any thing worthy of death, I refuse not to die: but if there be none of these things whereof these accuse me, no man may deliver me unto them. I appeal unto Caesar.	If I had committed any crime, or done any thing worthy of death, I would not refuse to die. But if none of the things of which they accuse me, is upon me, no one may sacrifice me to their pleasure. I announce an appeal to Caesar.	And if I had committed an offense or anything worthy of death, I would not refuse death. But if there is nothing against me of these [things] that they are accusing me, no one should give me to them [as] a gift. I make an appeal to Caesar."

Parallel Translations

	KJV	*Murdock*	*Magiera*
	ACTS	*Chapter 25*	
12	Then Festus, when he had conferred with the council, answered, Hast thou appealed unto Caesar? unto Caesar shalt thou go.	Then Festus conferred with his counsellors, and said: Hast thou declared an appeal to Caesar? Unto Caesar shalt thou go.	Then Festus spoke with his counselors. And he said, "Have you made an appeal [to] Caesar? To Caesar you will go."
13	And after certain days king Agrippa and Bernice came unto Caesarea to salute Festus.	And when [some] days had passed, Agrippa the king, and Bernice, came down to Caesarea to salute Festus.	And after there were [some] days, Agrippa the king and Bernice came down to Caesarea to greet Festus.
14	And when they had been there many days, Festus declared Paul's cause unto the king, saying, There is a certain man left in bonds by Felix:	And when they had been with him: [some] days, Festus related to the king the case of Paul, saying: A certain man was left a prisoner by Felix:	And after they were with him [some] days, Festus narrated the case of Paul to the king, saying, "A certain man was left a prisoner by the hands of Felix.
15	About whom, when I was at Jerusalem, the chief priests and the elders of the Jews informed me, desiring to have judgment against him.	And when I was at Jerusalem, the: chief priests and the Elders of the Jews informed me respecting him, and desired that I would pass judgment upon him in their favor.	And when I was in Jerusalem, the chief priests and elders of the Judeans informed me regarding him and desired that I would give them judgment against him."
16	To whom I answered, It is not the manner of the Romans to deliver any man to die, before that he which is accused have the accusers face to face, and have licence to answer for himself concerning the crime laid against him.	And I told them, It is not the custom of the Romans, to give up a man gratuitously to be slain; until his accuser appeareth and chargeth him to his face, and opportunity is afforded him to make defence respecting what is charged upon him.	And I said to them, "It is not the custom of the Romans to give a man [as] a gift for murder, until his opponent at law should come and charge him to his face and an opportunity is given to him to make a defense regarding that for which he is accused.
17	Therefore, when they were come hither, without any delay on the morrow I sat on the judgment seat, and commanded the man to be brought forth.	And: when I had come hither, without delay, I the next day sat on the tribunal, and commanded the man to be brought before me.	And when I came here, without delay, the next day I sat on the judgment seat and commanded them to bring me the man.
18	Against whom when the accusers stood up, they brought none accusation of such things as I supposed:	And his accusers stood up with him; and they were not able to substantiate any criminal charge against him, as I had expected;	And his accusers stood with him and they were not able to prove any evil accusation against him, even as I had supposed.
19	But had certain questions against him of their own superstition, and of one Jesus, which was dead, whom Paul affirmed to be alive.	but they had certain controversies with him respecting their worship, and respecting one Jesus, who died, but who, as Paul said, was alive.	But they had various questions to him concerning their religion and concerning Jesus, a man who died, whom Paul was saying was alive.
20	And because I doubted of such manner of questions, I asked him whether he would go to Jerusalem, and there be judged of these matters.	And because I was not well established in regard to these questions, I said to Paul: Dost thou ask to go to Jerusalem, and there be judged concerning these matters?	And because I did not establish [anything] about the dispute of these [things], I had said to Paul, 'Do you desire to go to Jerusalem and there to be judged concerning these [things]?'

	KJV	*Murdock*	*Magiera*
ACTS	*Chapter 25*		
21	But when Paul had appealed to be reserved unto the hearing of Augustus, I commanded him to be kept till I might send him to Caesar.	But he requested to be reserved for a trial before Caesar: and I ordered him to be kept, till I could send him to Caesar.	But he requested to be kept for judgment before Caesar and I commanded that he should be kept until I would send him to Caesar."
22	Then Agrippa said unto Festus, I would also hear the man myself. To morrow, said he, thou shalt hear him.	And Agrippa said: I should like to hear that man. And Festus said: To-morrow thou shalt hear him.	And Agrippa said, "I desire to hear this man." And Festus said, "Tomorrow you will hear him."
23	And on the morrow, when Agrippa was come, and Bernice, with great pomp, and was entered into the place of hearing, with the chief captains, and principal men of the city, at Festus' commandment Paul was brought forth.	And the next day, came Agrippa and Bernice, with great pomp, and entered the house of trials, with the Chiliarchs and chiefs of the city: and Festus commanded, and Paul came.	And the next day Agrippa and Bernice came with great ceremony and entered the judgment hall with the chiliarchs and rulers of the city and Festus commanded and Paul came.
24	And Festus said, King Agrippa, and all men which are here present with us, ye see this man, about whom all the multitude of the Jews have dealt with me, both at Jerusalem, and also here, crying that he ought not to live any longer.	And Festus said: King Agrippa, and all persons present with us; concerning this man whom ye see, all the people of the Jews applied to me, at Jerusalem and also here, crying out, that he ought no longer to live.	And Festus said, "Agrippa, the king, and all men who are with us, concerning this man whom you see, all the people of the Judeans have complained to me in Jerusalem and here, crying out that it is no longer right for this [man] to live.
25	But when I found that he had committed nothing worthy of death, and that he himself hath appealed to Augustus, I have determined to send him.	Yet on investigation, I found that he hath done nothing deserving death. But, because he requested to be reserved for the hearing of Caesar, I have ordered him to be sent.	But I have found that he has not done anything that is worthy of death. And because he requested to be kept for judgment before Caesar, I have commanded that he should be sent.
26	Of whom I have no certain thing to write unto my lord. Wherefore I have brought him forth before you, and specially before thee, O king Agrippa, that, after examination had, I might have somewhat to write.	And I know not what I can write to Caesar, in regard to him: and therefore I wished to bring him before you, and especially before thee, king Agrippa; that when his case shall have been heard, I may find what to write.	And I do not know what to write about him to Caesar. Because of this, I desired to bring him before you and especially before you, King Agrippa, that when his case will be examined, I will be able to write what [it is].
27	For it seemeth to me unreasonable to send a prisoner, and not withal to signify the crimes laid against him.	For it is unsuitable, when we send up a prisoner, not to designate his offence.	For it is not proper, when we send a man [as] a prisoner, not to write his offense."
Chapter 26			
1	Then Agrippa said unto Paul, Thou art permitted to speak for thyself. Then Paul stretched forth the hand, and answered for himself:	And Agrippa said to Paul: Thou art permitted to speak in thy own behalf. Then Paul extended his hand, and made defence, saying:	And Agrippa said to Paul, "You are permitted to speak for yourself." Then Paul stretched out his hand and made a defense and said,
2	I think myself happy, king Agrippa, because I shall answer for myself this day before thee touching all the things whereof I am accused of the Jews:	In regard to all the things of which I am accused by the Jews, king Agrippa, I consider myself highly favored, that I may this day make defence before thee:	"Concerning all of which I am accused by the Judeans, King Agrippa, I consider myself blessed that I may make a defense before you today,

Parallel Translations

	KJV	*Murdock*	*Magiera*

ACTS *Chapter 26*

	KJV	Murdock	Magiera
3	Especially because I know thee to be expert in all customs and questions which are among the Jews: wherefore I beseech thee to hear me patiently.	especially, as I know thee to be expert in all the controversies and laws of the Jews. I therefore request thee to hear me with indulgence.	especially because I know that you are acquainted with all the questions and laws of the Judeans. Because of this, I beg you to hear me with long-suffering.
4	My manner of life from my youth, which was at the first among mine own nation at Jerusalem, know all the Jews;	The Jews themselves, if they would testify, know well my course of life from my childhood, which from the beginning was among my nation and in Jerusalem.	For those Judeans also know, if they were willing to testify, [that] my manner of life was from my childhood, from the beginning, among my people and in Jerusalem,
5	Which knew me from the beginning, if they would testify, that after the most straitest sect of our religion I lived a Pharisee.	For they have long been persuaded of me, and have known, that I lived in the princely doctrine of the Pharisees.	because from long ago they were aware of me and know that I lived in the best teaching of the Pharisees.
6	And now I stand and am judged for the hope of the promise made of God unto our fathers:	And now, for the hope of the promise which was made by God to our fathers, I stand and am judged.	And now, concerning the hope of the promise that was [given] to our fathers from God, I stand and am judged.
7	Unto which promise our twelve tribes, instantly serving God day and night, hope to come. For which hope's sake, king Agrippa, I am accused of the Jews.	To this hope, our twelve tribes hope to come, with earnest prayers by day and by night: and for this same hope, king Agrippa, I am accused by the Jews.	For concerning this hope our twelve tribes hope to come, with diligent prayers by day and by night. And concerning this hope, I am accused by the hands of the Judeans, King Agrippa.
8	Why should it be thought a thing incredible with you, that God should raise the dead?	How judge ye? Are we not to believe, that God will raise the dead?	What are you judging? Is it not right that we believe that God raises the dead?
9	I verily thought with myself, that I ought to do many things contrary to the name of Jesus of Nazareth.	For I myself, at first, resolved in my own mind, that I would perpetrate many adverse things against the name of Jesus the Nazarean.	For formerly, I had set in my mind that I would do many adverse [things] against the name of Jesus the Nazarene.
10	Which thing I also did in Jerusalem: and many of the saints did I shut up in prison, having received authority from the chief priests; and when they were put to death, I gave my voice against them.	Which I also did at Jerusalem; and by the authority I received from the chief priests, I cast many of the saints into prison and when they were put to death by them, I took part with those that condemned them.	This I also did in Jerusalem and I threw many holy [ones] in prison by the authority that I received from the chief priests. And when they were killed by them, I shared fully with those who condemned them.
11	And I punished them oft in every synagogue, and compelled them to blaspheme; and being exceedingly mad against them, I persecuted them even unto strange cities.	And in every synagogue I tortured them, while I pressed them to become revilers of the name of Jesus. And in the great wrath, with which I was filled against them, I also went to other cities to persecute them.	And in every synagogue I tortured them, compelling [them] to blaspheme in the name of Jesus. And with the great anger that I was filled with against them, I also went to other cities to persecute them.
12	Whereupon as I went to Damascus with authority and commission from the chief priests,	And, as I was going for this purpose to Damascus, with the authority and license of the chief priests,	And when I was going for this purpose to Damascus with the authority and permission of the chief priests,

	KJV	Murdock	Magiera
	ACTS *Chapter 26*		
13	At midday, O king, I saw in the way a light from heaven, above the brightness of the sun, shining round about me and them which journeyed with me.	at mid-day, on the road, I saw, O king, a light exceeding that of the sun, beaming from heaven upon me, and upon all those with me.	in the middle of the day on the road, I saw from heaven, oh King, a light that was greater than the sun that shone on me and on all who were with me.
14	And when we were all fallen to the earth, I heard a voice speaking unto me, and saying in the Hebrew tongue, Saul, Saul, why persecutest thou me? it is hard for thee to kick against the pricks.	And we all fell to the ground; and I heard a voice, which said to me, in Hebrew: Saul, Saul! why persecutest thou me? It will be a hard thing for thee to kick against the goads.	And we all fell on the ground. And I heard a voice saying to me in Hebrew, 'Saul, Saul, why are you persecuting me? It is hard for you to kick against the goads.'
15	And I said, Who art thou, Lord? And he said, I am Jesus whom thou persecutest.	And I said: My Lord, who art thou? And our Lord said to me: I am Jesus the Nazarean, whom thou persecutest.	And I said, 'Who are you, my Lord?' And our Lord said to me, 'I am Jesus, the Nazarene, whom you are persecuting.'
16	But rise, and stand upon thy feet: for I have appeared unto thee for this purpose, to make thee a minister and a witness both of these things which thou hast seen, and of those things in the which I will appear unto thee;	And he said to me: Stand upon thy feet; for I have appeared to thee, for this purpose, to constitute thee a minister and a witness of this thy seeing me, and of thy seeing me hereafter.	And he said to me, 'Stand on your feet. For I have appeared to you because of this, to ordain you [as] a minister and a witness that you have seen me and that you are going to see me.
17	Delivering thee from the people, and from the Gentiles, unto whom now I send thee,	And I will deliver thee from the people of the Jews, and from other nations; to whom I send thee,	And I will deliver you from the people of the Judeans and from other Gentiles, to whom I send you,
18	To open their eyes, and to turn them from darkness to light, and from the power of Satan unto God, that they may receive forgiveness of sins, and inheritance among them which are sanctified by faith that is in me.	to open their eyes; that they may turn from darkness to the light, and from the dominion of Satan unto God; and may receive remission of sins, and a portion with the saints, by faith in me.	that you should open their eyes, so that they will turn from darkness to the light and from the authority of Satan to God and they will receive forgiveness of sins and a portion with the holy [ones] by faith that [is] in me.'
19	Whereupon, O king Agrippa, I was not disobedient unto the heavenly vision:	Wherefore, king Agrippa, I did not contumaciously withstand the heavenly vision:	Because of this, King Agrippa, I did not oppose the heavenly vision with dispute,
20	But shewed first unto them of Damascus, and at Jerusalem, and throughout all the coasts of Judaea, and then to the Gentiles, that they should repent and turn to God, and do works meet for repentance.	but I preached from the first to them in Damascus, and to them in Jerusalem and in all the villages of Judaea; and I preached also to the Gentiles, that they should repent, and should turn to God, and should do the works suitable to repentance.	but I preached from the first to those of Damascus and to those who were in Jerusalem and in all the villages of Judea and also to the Gentiles. I preached that they should repent and should turn back to God and should perform works that are suitable to repentance.
21	For these causes the Jews caught me in the temple, and went about to kill me.	And on account of these things, the Jews seized me in the temple, and sought to kill me.	And on account of these [things], the Judeans arrested me in the temple and desired to kill me.

Parallel Translations

	KJV	*Murdock*	*Magiera*
	ACTS	*Chapter 26*	
22	Having therefore obtained help of God, I continue unto this day, witnessing both to small and great, saying none other things than those which the prophets and Moses did say should come:	But unto this day God hath helped me; and lo, I stand and bear testimony, to the small and to the great; yet saying nothing aside from Moses and the prophets, but the very things which they declared were to take place:	But God helped me to this day and behold, I stand and testify to the small and to the great, not saying anything outside of Moses and the prophets, but those [things] that they said that were going to happen,
23	That Christ should suffer, and that he should be the first that should rise from the dead, and should shew light unto the people, and to the Gentiles.	[namely,] that Messiah would suffer, and would become the first fruits of the resurrection from the dead; and that he would proclaim light to the people and to the Gentiles.	that the Messiah would suffer and would become the first[fruit] of the resurrection from the dead and that he would preach light to the people and to the Gentiles."
24	And as he thus spake for himself, Festus said with a loud voice, Paul, thou art beside thyself; much learning doth make thee mad.	And when Paul had extended his defence thus far, Festus cried, with a loud voice: Paul, thou art deranged: much study hath deranged thee.	And as Paul was thus making a defense, Festus cried out with a loud voice, "Paul, you are mad! Much learning has caused you to be mad!"
25	But he said, I am not mad, most noble Festus; but speak forth the words of truth and soberness.	Paul replied to him: I am not deranged, excellent Festus; but speak words of truth and rectitude.	Paul said, "I am not mad, noble Festus, but I am speaking words of truth and integrity.
26	For the king knoweth of these things, before whom also I speak freely: for I am persuaded that none of these things are hidden from him; for this thing was not done in a corner.	And king Agrippa is also well acquainted with these things; and I therefore speak confidently before him, because I suppose not one of these things hath escaped his knowledge; for they were not done in secret.	And also, King Agrippa especially knows about these [things], and because of this, I speak boldly before him, because I think that not one of these words has escaped his notice, for it was not performed secretly.
27	King Agrippa, believest thou the prophets? I know that thou believest.	King Agrippa, believest thou the prophets? I know that thou believest.	Do you believe the prophets, King Agrippa? I know that you do believe."
28	Then Agrippa said unto Paul, Almost thou persuadest me to be a Christian.	King Agrippa said to him: Almost, thou persuadest me to become a Christian.	Agrippa said to him, "You are very nearly persuading me to become a Christian."
29	And Paul said, I would to God, that not only thou, but also all that hear me this day, were both almost, and altogether such as I am, except these bonds.	And Paul said: I would to God, that not only thou, but likewise all that hear me this day, were almost, and altogether, as I am, aside from these bonds.	And Paul said, "I have asked God in little and in much, not only for you to be, but also all those who hear me today, that they should be like me, except for these bonds."
30	And when he had thus spoken, the king rose up, and the governor, and Bernice, and they that sat with them:	And the king rose up, and the governor, and Bernice, and those who sat with them.	And the king stood up and the governor and Bernice and those who were sitting with them.
31	And when they were gone aside, they talked between themselves, saying, This man doeth nothing worthy of death or of bonds.	And when they had gone out, they conversed with one another, and said: This man hath done nothing worthy of death or of bonds.	And after they had gone out from there, they spoke with each other and said, "This man has not done anything that is worthy of death or bonds."
32	Then said Agrippa unto Festus, This man might have been set at liberty, if he had not appealed unto Caesar.	And Agrippa said to Festus: The man might be set at liberty, if he had not announced an appeal to Caesar.	And Agrippa said to Festus, "It is possible that this man could have been freed, if he had not appealed to Caesar."

Parallel Translations

	KJV	Murdock	Magiera
	ACTS Chapter 27		
1	And when it was determined that we should sail into Italy, they delivered Paul and certain other prisoners unto one named Julius, a centurion of Augustus' band.	And Festus commanded, respecting him, that he should be sent to Italy, unto Caesar. And he delivered Paul, and other prisoners with him, to a certain man, a centurion of the Augustan cohort, whose name was Julius.	And Festus commanded concerning him that he should be sent to Caesar to Italy. And he delivered Paul and other prisoners with him to a certain man, a centurion from the Augustan cohort, whose name was Julius.
2	And entering into a ship of Adramyttium, we launched, meaning to sail by the coasts of Asia; one Aristarchus, a Macedonian of Thessalonica, being with us.	And when we were to depart, we embarked in a ship which was from the city of Adramyttium, and was going to the country of Asia. And there embarked with us in the ship, Aristarchus, a Macedonian of the city of Thessalonica.	And when it was ready to sail, we went down to a ship that was from the city [of] Adramyttium and was traveling to the region of Asia. And Aristarchus, a Macedonian who was from the city [of] Thessalonica, came on the ship with us.
3	And the next day we touched at Sidon. And Julius courteously entreated Paul, and gave him liberty to go unto his friends to refresh himself.	And the next day, we arrived at Zidon. And the centurion treated Paul with kindness, and permitted him to visit his friends and be refreshed.	And the next day we arrived at Sidon. And the centurion treated Paul with compassion and allowed him to go to his friends and to be refreshed.
4	And when we had launched from thence, we sailed under Cyprus, because the winds were contrary.	And on sailing from there, because the winds were against us, we sailed around to Cyprus.	And we sailed from there and because the winds were contrary to us, we followed a course near Cyprus.
5	And when we had sailed over the sea of Cilicia and Pamphylia, we came to Myra, a city of Lycia.	And we passed over the sea of Cilicia and Pamphylia, and arrived at Myra, a city of Lycia.	And we crossed over the sea of Cilicia and Pamphylia and arrived at the city [of] Myra, of Lycia.
6	And there the centurion found a ship of Alexandria sailing into Italy; and he put us therein.	And there the centurion found a ship of Alexandria, which was going to Italy; and he set us on board of it.	And there the centurion found a ship from Alexandria that was traveling to Italy and they settled us on it.
7	And when we had sailed slowly many days, and scarce were come over against Cnidus, the wind not suffering us, we sailed under Crete, over against Salmone;	And as it was hard navigating, we had scarcely arrived, after many days, over against the isle of Cnidos. And, because the wind would not allow us to pursue a straight course, we sailed around by Crete, [and came] opposite the city of Salmone.	And because we were sailing under heavy [seas], after many days we barely reached the island [of] Cnidus. And because the wind did not allow us to proceed by a straight course, we kept a heading near Crete towards the city [of] Salmone.
8	And, hardly passing it, came unto a place which is called The fair havens; nigh whereunto was the city of Lasea.	And with difficulty, after sailing about it, we arrived at a place called the Fair Havens, near to which was the city called Lassa.	And after we had sailed around it with difficulty, we arrived at a place that was called Fair Havens, [that] was near to a city by the name of Lasea.
9	Now when much time was spent, and when sailing was now dangerous, because the fast was now already past, Paul admonished them,	And we were there a long time, and till after the day of the Jewish fast. And it was hazardous [then] for any one to go by sea; and Paul counselled them,	And we were there a long time until even the day of the fast of the Judeans was past. And it was dangerous for anyone to travel by sea and Paul counseled them

Parallel Translations

	KJV	*Murdock*	*Magiera*
	ACTS	*Chapter 27*	
10	And said unto them, Sirs, I perceive that this voyage will be with hurt and much damage, not only of the lading and ship, but also of our lives.	and said: Men, I perceive that our voyage will be [attended] with peril, and with much loss, not only of the cargo of our ship, but also of our lives.	and said, "Men, I perceive that our voyage will occur with calamity and with much loss, not only of the cargo of our ship, but also of our own lives."
11	Nevertheless the centurion believed the master and the owner of the ship, more than those things which were spoken by Paul.	But the centurion listened to the pilot, and to the owner of the ship, more than to the words of Paul.	But the centurion listened to the shipmaster and the captain of the ship, rather than the words of Paul.
12	And because the haven was not commodious to winter in, the more part advised to depart thence also, if by any means they might attain to Phenice, and there to winter; which is an haven of Crete, and lieth toward the south west and north west.	And, because that harbor was not commodious for wintering in, many of us were desirous to sail from it, and if possible, to reach and to winter in a certain harbor of Crete, which was called Phenice, and which opened towards the south.	And because that port was not suitable to winter in foul weather, many of us wanted to travel from there and if possible, to reach and winter in a certain port that was in Crete and was called Phenice and looked to the south.
13	And when the south wind blew softly, supposing that they had obtained their purpose, loosing thence, they sailed close by Crete.	And when the south wind breezed up, and they hoped to arrive as they desired, we began to sail around Crete.	And after the south wind blew and they thought that we would arrive according to their desire, they followed a course on the side of Crete.
14	But not long after there arose against it a tempestuous wind, called Euroclydon.	And shortly after, a tempest of wind arose upon us, called Typhonic Euroclydon.	And shortly after we left, a sudden blast of wind [came] on us that was called a typhoon Euroclydon.
15	And when the ship was caught, and could not bear up into the wind, we let her drive.	And the ship was whirled about by the wind, and could not keep head to it; and we resigned [the ship] to its power.	And the ship was caught up and was not able to bear up against the wind and we yielded control of it.
16	And running under a certain island which is called Clauda, we had much work to come by the boat:	And when we had passed a certain island, called Cyra, we could hardly retain the boat.	And as we passed by a certain island that was called Cauda, we were hardly able to keep hold of the longboat.
17	Which when they had taken up, they used helps, undergirding the ship; and, fearing lest they should fall into the quicksands, strake sail, and so were driven.	And after hoisting it [on board], we girded the ship around [the waist], and made it strong. And, because we were afraid of falling upon a precipice of the sea, we pulled down the sail; and so we drifted.	And after we had taken it up [on board], we undergirded and prepared the ship. And because we were afraid, lest we should fall in the downward rapids of the sea, we pulled down the sail and so we drifted.
18	And we being exceedingly tossed with a tempest, the next day they lightened the ship;	And as the storm raged violently upon us, we the next day threw goods into the sea.	And as the violent storm raged against us, the next day we threw goods in the sea.
19	And the third day we cast out with our own hands the tackling of the ship.	And on the third day, with our own hands, we threw away the tackling of the ship.	And the third day, we cast overboard the ship's own riggings with our hands.
20	And when neither sun nor stars in many days appeared, and no small tempest lay on us, all hope that we should be saved was then taken away.	And as the storm held on for many days, and as no sun was visible, nor moon, nor stars, all hope of our surviving was wholly cut off.	And as the tempest continued more days and the sun was not visible nor the moon nor stars, all hope of our living was completely cut off.

ACTS *Chapter 27*

	KJV	*Murdock*	*Magiera*
21	But after long abstinence Paul stood forth in the midst of them, and said, Sirs, ye should have hearkened unto me, and not have loosed from Crete, and to have gained this harm and loss.	And as no one had taken a meal of food, Paul now stood up in the midst of them, and said: If ye had given heed to me, O men, we should not have sailed from Crete, and we should have been exempt from this loss and peril.	And as no one had eaten anything, then Paul stood up among them and said, "If you had been persuaded by me, men, we would not have sailed from Crete and we would have been spared from loss and from this calamity.
22	And now I exhort you to be of good cheer: for there shall be no loss of any man's life among you, but of the ship.	And now, I counsel you to be without anxiety; for not a soul of you will be lost, but only the ship.	And now, I counsel that you should be without distress, for not one of you will be destroyed, but only the ship.
23	For there stood by me this night the angel of God, whose I am, and whom I serve,	For there appeared to me this night, the angel of that God whose I am, and whom I serve;	For there appeared to me in this night, an angel of that God whose I am and whom I serve.
24	Saying, Fear not, Paul; thou must be brought before Caesar: and, lo, God hath given thee all them that sail with thee.	and he said to me: Fear not, Paul; for thou art yet to stand before Caesar; and, lo, God hath made a gift to thee of all them that sail with thee.	And he said to me, 'Fear not, Paul, it is prepared for you to stand before Caesar and behold, God has given to you [as a] gift, all who sail with you.'
25	Wherefore, sirs, be of good cheer: for I believe God, that it shall be even as it was told me.	Therefore, men, be ye courageous; for I confide in God, that it will be as was told to me.	Because of this, be encouraged, men, for I believe in God that it will be so even as it was communicated with me.
26	Howbeit we must be cast upon a certain island.	Yet we are to be cast upon a certain island.	Nevertheless, we have to be thrown on a certain island."
27	But when the fourteenth night was come, as we were driven up and down in Adria, about midnight the shipmen deemed that they drew near to some country;	And after the fourteen days of our roaming and tossing on the Adriatic sea, at midnight, the sailors conceived that they approached land.	And after fourteen days that we were wandering and were buffeted in the Adriatic Sea, at midnight, the sailors thought that they were coming near land.
28	And sounded, and found it twenty fathoms: and when they had gone a little further, they sounded again, and found it fifteen fathoms.	And they cast the lead, and found twenty fathoms. And again they advanced a little, and they found fifteen fathoms.	And they put out the anchors and found twenty fathoms, and again they went forward a little, and found fifteen fathoms.
29	Then fearing lest we should have fallen upon rocks, they cast four anchors out of the stern, and wished for the day.	And as we feared lest we should be caught in places where were rocks, they cast four anchors from the stern of the ship, and prayed for the morning.	And being afraid lest we should be found the places where there were rocks, they put out four anchors from the stern of the ship and prayed that it would be day.
30	And as the shipmen were about to flee out of the ship, when they had let down the boat into the sea, under colour as though they would have cast anchors out of the foreship,	And the sailors sought to flee out of the ship. And from it they lowered down the boat into the sea, under pretence that they were going in it to make fast the ship to the land.	Now the sailors tried to flee from the ship and they lowered the longboat to the sea on the pretext that they would go in it to secure the ship on the land.
31	Paul said to the centurion and to the soldiers, Except these abide in the ship, ye cannot be saved.	And when Paul saw [it], he said to the centurion and to the soldiers: Unless these remain in the ship, ye cannot be saved.	And Paul seeing [this], said to the centurion and to the soldiers, "If these do not remain in the ship, you will not be able to be saved."

Parallel Translations

	KJV	Murdock	Magiera
	ACTS	*Chapter 27*	
32	Then the soldiers cut off the ropes of the boat, and let her fall off.	Then the soldiers cut the boat-rope from the ship, and let the boat go adrift.	Then the soldiers cut off the ropes of the longboat from the ship and allowed it to go adrift.
33	And while the day was coming on, Paul besought them all to take meat, saying, This day is the fourteenth day that ye have tarried and continued fasting, having taken nothing.	And while it was not yet morning, Paul advised them all to take food, saying to them: In consequence of the peril, it is now the fourteenth day that ye have tasted nothing.	But Paul, when it was almost daybreak, convinced all of them that to take [some] nourishment, saying to them, "Behold, today [it has been] fourteen days since you have eaten anything on account of the danger.
34	Wherefore I pray you to take some meat: for this is for your health: for there shall not an hair fall from the head of any of you.	Therefore I entreat you, to take food for the sustenance of your life; for not a hair from the head of any of you, will perish.	Because of this, I beg you to take food for the strengthening of your life, for not a hair from the head of any of you will be hurt."
35	And when he had thus spoken, he took bread, and gave thanks to God in presence of them all: and when he had broken it, he began to eat.	And having said these things, he took bread, and gave glory to God before them all; and he broke [it], and began to eat.	And as he said these [things], he took bread and praised God before all of them and he broke [the bread] and began to eat.
36	Then were they all of good cheer, and they also took some meat.	And they were all consoled; and they took nourishment.	And they were all comforted and they received sustenance.
37	And we were in all in the ship two hundred threescore and sixteen souls.	And there were of us in the ship two hundred and seventy-six souls.	Now there were two hundred and seventy-six people in the ship.
38	And when they had eaten enough, they lightened the ship, and cast out the wheat into the sea.	And when they were satisfied with food, they lightened the ship, and took the wheat and cast it into the sea.	And when they were satisfied with the food, they lightened the ship and took the wheat and threw [it] in the sea.
39	And when it was day, they knew not the land: but they discovered a certain creek with a shore, into the which they were minded, if it were possible, to thrust in the ship.	And when it was day, the sailors knew not what land it was: but they saw on the margin of the land an inlet of the sea; whither, if possible they intended to drive the ship.	And when it was day, the sailors did not recognize what land it was, but they saw by the shore of the dry land a certain bay of the sea, where they thought that, if possible, they could thrust the ship.
40	And when they had taken up the anchors, they committed themselves unto the sea, and loosed the rudder bands, and hoised up the mainsail to the wind, and made toward shore.	And they cut away the anchors from the ship, and left them in the sea. And they loosened the bands of the rudder, and hoisted a small sail to the breeze, and made way towards the land.	And they cut off the anchors from the ship and they left them in the sea. And they released the bands of the rudders and hoisted the small sail to the wind that was blowing and they proceeded toward the dry land.
41	And falling into a place where two seas met, they ran the ship aground; and the forepart stuck fast, and remained unmoveable, but the hinder part was broken with the violence of the waves.	And the ship struck upon a shoal between two channels of the sea, and stuck fast upon it. And the forward part rested upon it, and was immovable; but the after part was shattered by the violence of the waves.	And the ship struck on a place that was high between two deep [parts] of the sea and it was stuck on it. And the forward part of it stayed on it and was not to be moved, but the back part of it was broken to pieces by the violence of the waves.

Parallel Translations

	KJV	*Murdock*	*Magiera*
	ACTS *Chapter 27*		
42	And the soldiers' counsel was to kill the prisoners, lest any of them should swim out, and escape.	And the soldiers were disposed to slay the prisoners; lest they should resort to swimming, and escape from them.	And the soldiers wanted to kill the prisoners, so that they would not jump in swimming and would escape from them.
43	But the centurion, willing to save Paul, kept them from their purpose; and commanded that they which could swim should cast themselves first into the sea, and get to land:	But the centurion kept them from it, because he was desirous to preserve Paul. And those who were able to swim, he commanded to swim off first, and pass to the land.	And the centurion prevented them from this, because he wanted to save Paul. And those who were able to jump in swimming, he commanded to swim first and to pass over to the land.
44	And the rest, some on boards, and some on broken pieces of the ship. And so it came to pass, that they escaped all safe to land.	And the rest, he made to transport themselves on planks, and on other timbers of the ship. And so they all escaped safe to land.	And the rest crossed over on boards and on other wood pieces of the ship. And so all of them escaped safely to the land.
	Chapter 28		
1	And when they were escaped, then they knew that the island was called Melita.	And we afterwards learned, that the island was called Melita.	And afterwards, they learned that the island was called Melita.
2	And the barbarous people shewed us no little kindness: for they kindled a fire, and received us every one, because of the present rain, and because of the cold.	And the barbarians who inhabited it, showed us many kindnesses. And they kindled a fire, and called us all to warm ourselves, because of the great rain and cold at that time.	And the barbarians who were living on it showed us many kindnesses and they kindled a fire and called to all of us that we should warm ourselves, because there was a great rain and [it was] cold.
3	And when Paul had gathered a bundle of sticks, and laid them on the fire, there came a viper out of the heat, and fastened on his hand.	And Paul took up a bundle of fagots and laid them on the fire: and a viper, [driven] by the heat, came out of them, and bit his hand.	And Paul picked up a large bundle of sticks and placed [them] on the fire and a viper came out of them because of the heat of the fire and bit his hand.
4	And when the barbarians saw the venomous beast hang on his hand, they said among themselves, No doubt this man is a murderer, whom, though he hath escaped the sea, yet vengeance suffereth not to live.	And when the barbarians saw it hanging on his hand, they said: Doubtless, this man is a murderer; whom, though delivered from the sea, justice will not suffer to live.	And when the barbarians saw that it was hanging on his hand, they said, "Perhaps this man is a murderer, so that even though he was rescued from the sea, justice will not allow him to live."
5	And he shook off the beast into the fire, and felt no harm.	But Paul shook his hand, and threw the viper into the fire: and he received no harm.	But Paul shook his hand and threw the viper in the fire and it did not harm him.
6	Howbeit they looked when he should have swollen, or fallen down dead suddenly: but after they had looked a great while, and saw no harm come to him, they changed their minds, and said that he was a god.	And the barbarians expected, that he would suddenly swell, and fall dead on the ground. And when they had looked a long time, and saw that he received no harm; they changed their language, and said, that he was a god.	Now the barbarians expected that immediately he would swell up and fall dying on the ground. And after they waited a long time and saw that it did not harm him, they changed their words and said, "He is a god."

Parallel Translations

	KJV	*Murdock*	*Magiera*

ACTS *Chapter 28*

	KJV	Murdock	Magiera
7	In the same quarters were possessions of the chief man of the island, whose name was Publius; who received us, and lodged us three days courteously.	And there were lands in that quarter, belonging to a man named Publius, who was the chief man of the island: and he cheerfully received us at his house three days.	Now there were fields in that place [that belonged] to a certain man, whose name was Publius, who was the ruler of the island. And he gladly received us in his house [for] three days.
8	And it came to pass, that the father of Publius lay sick of a fever and of a bloody flux: to whom Paul entered in, and prayed, and laid his hands on him, and healed him.	And the father of Publius was sick with a fever and dysentery. And Paul went in to him, and prayed, and laid his hand on him, and healed him.	Now the father of Publius was sick with fever and with pain in the bowels. And Paul went in to him and prayed and laid his hand on him and healed him.
9	So when this was done, others also, which had diseases in the island, came, and were healed:	And after this event, others also in the island who were sick, came to him and were healed.	And after this happened, the rest of those who were also sick on the island came to him and they were healed.
10	Who also honoured us with many honours; and when we departed, they laded us with such things as were necessary.	And they honored us with great honors: and when we left the place, they supplied us with necessaries.	And they honored us [with] great honors and after we left there, they supplied us with provisions.
11	And after three months we departed in a ship of Alexandria, which had wintered in the isle, whose sign was Castor and Pollux.	And after three months we departed, sailing in a ship of Alexandria, which had wintered in the island, and which bore the signal of the Twins.	Now after three months, we left and sailed in a ship [of] Alexandria that had wintered in the island and the sign of the Twins was on it.
12	And landing at Syracuse, we tarried there three days.	And we came to the city of Syracuse; and remained there three days.	And we came to the city [of] Syracuse and remained there [for] three days.
13	And from thence we fetched a compass, and came to Rhegium: and after one day the south wind blew, and we came the next day to Puteoli:	And from there we made a circuit, and arrived at the city Rhegium. And, after one day, the south wind blew [favorably] for us, and in two days we came to Puteoli, a city of Italy.	And from there we took a course and arrived at the city [of] Rhegium. And after one day, the south wind blew for us and in two days we came to Puteoli, a city of Italy.
14	Where we found brethren, and were desired to tarry with them seven days: and so we went toward Rome.	And there we found brethren; and they invited us, and we remained with them seven days: and then we proceeded towards Rome.	And we found brothers there and they asked us [to stay] and we were with them [for] seven days and then we went on to Rome.
15	And from thence, when the brethren heard of us, they came to meet us as far as Appii forum, and The three taverns: whom when Paul saw, he thanked God, and took courage.	And the brethren there, hearing [of our approach], came out to meet us as far as the village called Appii Forum, and as far as the Three Taverns. And when Paul saw them, he gave thanks to God, and was encouraged.	And when the brothers who were there heard [of our coming], they went out to meet us as far as the square that was called Appii Forum and as far as the Three Taverns. And when Paul saw them, he gave thanks to God and was strengthened.
16	And when we came to Rome, the centurion delivered the prisoners to the captain of the guard: but Paul was suffered to dwell by himself with a soldier that kept him.	And we went on to Rome. And the centurion allowed Paul to reside where he pleased, with a soldier who guarded him.	And we entered Rome and the centurion allowed Paul to lodge where he wanted, with a soldier who guarded him.

	KJV	*Murdock*	*Magiera*

ACTS *Chapter 28*

	KJV	Murdock	Magiera
17	And it came to pass, that after three days Paul called the chief of the Jews together: and when they were come together, he said unto them, Men and brethren, though I have committed nothing against the people, or customs of our fathers, yet was I delivered prisoner from Jerusalem into the hands of the Romans.	And after three days, Paul sent and called for the principal Jews. And when they were assembled, he said to them: Men, my brethren, although I had in nothing risen up against the people or the law of my fathers, I was at Jerusalem delivered over in bonds to the Romans:	And after three days, Paul sent [and] called for the rulers of the Judeans. And when they were gathered, he said to them, "Men, my brothers, although in nothing I stood against the people and the law of my fathers, I was delivered in bonds at Jerusalem into the hand of the Romans."
18	Who, when they had examined me, would have let me go, because there was no cause of death in me.	and they, when they had examined me, were disposed to release me, because they found in me no offence deserving death.	And after they examined me, they wanted to release me, because they did not find any fault against me that was worthy of death.
19	But when the Jews spake against it, I was constrained to appeal unto Caesar; not that I had ought to accuse my nation of.	And, as the Jews withstood me, I was compelled to utter an appeal to Caesar; but not because I had any thing of which to accuse the people of my nation.	"And as the Judeans stood against me, I was compelled to appeal to Caesar, [but] not because I had anything of which I would accuse the sons of my people.
20	For this cause therefore have I called for you, to see you, and to speak with you: because that for the hope of Israel I am bound with this chain.	For this reason I sent for you to come, that I might see you, and might state these things to you: for it is on account of the hope of Israel, that I am bound with this chain.	Because of this, I asked you to come and to see you and to narrate these [things] to you, for because of the hope of Israel, I am bound with this chain."
21	And they said unto him, We neither received letters out of Judaea concerning thee, neither any of the brethren that came shewed or spake any harm of thee.	They said to him: We have received no epistle from Judaea against thee; and none of the brethren who have come from Jerusalem, have told us any evil thing of thee.	They said to him, "We have not received a letter about you from Judea and none of the brothers who have come from Jerusalem have told us anything that is evil about you.
22	But we desire to hear of thee what thou thinkest: for as concerning this sect, we know that every where it is spoken against.	But we are desirous to hear from thee what thou thinkest; for this doctrine, we know, is not received by any one.	Now we want to hear from you what you think, because we know that this teaching is not accepted by men."
23	And when they had appointed him a day, there came many to him into his lodging; to whom he expounded and testified the kingdom of God, persuading them concerning Jesus, both out of the law of Moses, and out of the prophets, from morning till evening.	And they appointed him a day; and many assembled, and came to him at his lodgings. And he explained to them respecting the kingdom of God, testifying and persuading them concerning Jesus, out of the law of Moses, and out of the prophets, from morning till evening.	And they appointed him a day and they gathered together. And many came to him where he was lodging and he made known to them about the kingdom of God, witnessing and persuading them about Jesus, from the law of Moses and from the prophets, from morning until evening.
24	And some believed the things which were spoken, and some believed not.	And some of them assented to his discourses, and others did not assent.	And some of them were convinced of his words and others were not convinced.

Parallel Translations

ACTS Chapter 28

	KJV	Murdock	Magiera
25	And when they agreed not among themselves, they departed, after that Paul had spoken one word, Well spake the Holy Ghost by Esaias the prophet unto our fathers,	And they went out from him, disagreeing among themselves. And Paul addressed to them this speech: Well did the Holy Spirit, by the mouth of Isaiah the prophet, speak concerning your fathers,	And they left him, disagreeing with one another. And Paul said to them this word, "Well did the Holy Spirit speak by the mouth of Isaiah the prophet against your fathers,
26	Saying, Go unto this people, and say, Hearing ye shall hear, and shall not understand; and seeing ye shall see, and not perceive:	saying: Go unto this people, and say to them, Hearing ye will hear, and will not understand; and ye will see, and will not comprehend.	saying: GO TO THIS PEOPLE AND SAY TO THEM, HEARING, YOU WILL HEAR AND YOU WILL NOT UNDERSTAND AND YOU WILL SEE AND YOU WILL NOT COMPREHEND.
27	For the heart of this people is waxed gross, and their ears are dull of hearing, and their eyes have they closed; lest they should see with their eyes, and hear with their ears, and understand with their heart, and should be converted, and I should heal them.	For the heart of this people is stupefied, and their hearing they have made heavy, and their eyes they have closed; lest they should see with their eyes, and hear with their ears, and understand with their hearts, and be converted unto me, and I should forgive them.	FOR THE HEART OF THIS PEOPLE HAS BECOME DENSE AND THEY HAVE MADE HEAVY THEIR HEARING AND THEY HAVE CLOSED THEIR EYES, LEST THEY SHOULD SEE WITH THEIR EYES AND HEAR WITH THEIR EARS AND SHOULD UNDERSTAND IN THEIR HEART[S] AND SHOULD RETURN TO ME AND I SHOULD FORGIVE THEM.
28	Be it known therefore unto you, that the salvation of God is sent unto the Gentiles, and that they will hear it.	Therefore, be this known to you, that to the Gentiles is this redemption of God sent: and, moreover, they will hear it.	Therefore, be this known to you, that to the Gentiles is this redemption of God being sent. For they also are hearing it."
29	And when he had said these words, the Jews departed, and had great reasoning among themselves.	And when he had thus said, the Jews retired; and there were great disputations among them.	OMITTED IN THE WESTERN PESHITTA TEXT
30	And Paul dwelt two whole years in his own hired house, and received all that came in unto him,	And Paul hired a house, at his own cost, and resided in it two years; and there he received all that came to him.	And Paul hired a house for himself at his own [cost] and was in it [for] two years. And there he received all those who came to him.
31	Preaching the kingdom of God, and teaching those things which concern the Lord Jesus Christ, with all confidence, no man forbidding him.	And he preached concerning the kingdom of God, and taught boldly concerning our Lord Jesus Messiah, without hinderance.	And he was preaching about the kingdom of God and teaching boldly about our Lord Jesus Christ without hindrance.

Parallel Translations

ROMANS *Chapter 1*

	KJV	*Murdock*	*Magiera*
1	Paul, a servant of Jesus Christ, called to be an apostle, separated unto the gospel of God,	Paul, a servant of Jesus the Messiah, called and sent; and separated unto the gospel of God,	Paul, a servant of Jesus Christ, a called [one] and an apostle, who was set apart for the gospel of God
2	(Which he had promised afore by his prophets in the holy scriptures,)	(which he had before promised, by his prophets, in the holy scriptures,	that he had promised previously by way of his prophets in the holy scriptures,
3	Concerning his Son Jesus Christ our Lord, which was made of the seed of David according to the flesh;	concerning his Son, (who was born in the flesh, of seed of the house of David,	concerning his Son, who was born in the flesh of the seed of the house of David
4	And declared to be the Son of God with power, according to the spirit of holiness, by the resurrection from the dead:	and was made known as the Son of God, by power, and by the Holy Spirit,) who arose from the dead, Jesus Messiah, our Lord,	and was made known [as] the Son of God by power and by the Holy Spirit, who raised Jesus Christ our Lord from the dead,
5	By whom we have received grace and apostleship, for obedience to the faith among all nations, for his name:	by whom we have received grace, and a mission among all the Gentiles, to the end that they may obey the faith in his name;	by whom we have received grace and apostleship among all the Gentiles, so that they would obey the faith of his name,
6	Among whom are ye also the called of Jesus Christ:	among whom, ye also are called by Jesus Messiah;)	that you also from them are called [ones] in Jesus Christ.
7	To all that be in Rome, beloved of God, called to be saints: Grace to you and peace from God our Father, and the Lord Jesus Christ.	to all those who are at Rome, beloved of God, called and sanctified: Peace and grace be with you, from God our Father, and from our Lord Jesus Messiah.	To all who are in Rome, beloved of God, called and holy [ones]: Peace and grace [be] with you from God our Father and from our Lord Jesus Christ.
8	First, I thank my God through Jesus Christ for you all, that your faith is spoken of throughout the whole world.	In the first place, I give thanks to God by Jesus Messiah, on account of you all; because your faith is heard of in all the world.	First, I thank my God in Jesus Christ for all of you that your faith is heard in all the world.
9	For God is my witness, whom I serve with my spirit in the gospel of his Son, that without ceasing I make mention of you always in my prayers;	And God, whom in spirit I serve in the gospel of his Son, is my witness, that I unceasingly make mention of you, at all times, in my prayers.	For God is a witness to me, whom I am spiritually serving in the gospel of his Son, that without ceasing at all times, I remember you in my prayers.
10	Making request, if by any means now at length I might have a prosperous journey by the will of God to come unto you.	And I likewise supplicate, that hereafter a door may be opened to me, by the good pleasure of God, to come unto you.	And I am imploring that perhaps even now a way would be opened to me by the will of God to come to you,
11	For I long to see you, that I may impart unto you some spiritual gift, to the end ye may be established;	For I long much to see you; and to impart to you the gift of the Spirit, whereby ye may be established;	because I greatly long to see you and to give you a spiritual gift by which you may be strengthened
12	That is, that I may be comforted together with you by the mutual faith both of you and me.	and that we may have comfort together, in the faith of both yourselves and me.	and together we will be comforted by your and my own faith.

	KJV	Murdock	Magiera

ROMANS *Chapter 1*

	KJV	Murdock	Magiera
13	Now I would not have you ignorant, brethren, that oftentimes I purposed to come unto you, (but was let hitherto,) that I might have some fruit among you also, even as among other Gentiles.	And I wish you to know, my brethren, that I have many times desired to come to you, (though prevented hitherto,) that I might have some fruit among you also; even as among other Gentiles,	Now I want you to know, my brothers, that many times I wanted to come to you (yet I was hindered until now) that I would also have fruit among you, as among the rest of the Gentiles,
14	I am debtor both to the Greeks, and to the Barbarians; both to the wise, and to the unwise.	Greeks and barbarians, the wise and the unwise: for to every man am I a debtor, to preach [to him].	Greeks and barbarians, the wise and the foolish, because I am a debtor to preach to every man.
15	So, as much as in me is, I am ready to preach the gospel to you that are at Rome also.	And so I am eager to preach to you also who are at Rome.	And so I am concerned that I should declare [the gospel] to you who are in Rome also.
16	For I am not ashamed of the gospel of Christ: for it is the power of God unto salvation to every one that believeth; to the Jew first, and also to the Greek.	For I am not ashamed of the gospel; for it is the power of God unto life, to all who believe in it; whether first they are of the Jews, or whether they are of the Gentiles.	For I am not ashamed of the gospel, because it is the power of God for the life of all who believe in it, whether [they are] from the Judeans first or from the heathens.
17	For therein is the righteousness of God revealed from faith to faith: as it is written, The just shall live by faith.	For in it is revealed the righteousness of God, from faith to faith; as it is written, The righteous by faith, shall live.	For the uprightness of God is revealed in it from faith to faith, as it is written: THE UPRIGHT [ONE] WILL LIVE BY FAITH.
18	For the wrath of God is revealed from heaven against all ungodliness and unrighteousness of men, who hold the truth in unrighteousness;	For the wrath of God from heaven is revealed against all the iniquity and wickedness of men, who hold the truth in iniquity.	For the wrath of God is revealed from heaven on all the wickedness and the ungodliness of men, those who close off truthfulness with wickedness,
19	Because that which may be known of God is manifest in them; for God hath shewed it unto them.	Because a knowledge of God is manifest in them; for God hath manifested it in them.	because the knowledge of God is revealed among them, for God revealed it among them.
20	For the invisible things of him from the creation of the world are clearly seen, being understood by the things that are made, even his eternal power and Godhead; so that they are without excuse:	For, from the foundations of the world, the occult things of God are seen, by the intellect, in the things he created, even his eternal power and divinity; so that they might be without excuse;	For the hidden [things] of God were made evident from the foundations of the world by his created [things] in [his] wisdom and his power and his Godhead that is eternal, so that they would be without defense,
21	Because that, when they knew God, they glorified him not as God, neither were thankful; but became vain in their imaginations, and their foolish heart was darkened.	because they knew God, and did not glorify him and give thanks to him as God, but became vain in their imaginings, and their unwise heart was darkened.	because they knew God and they did not glorify him as God and give thanks to him, but rather they became fruitless in their reasonings, and their heart without understanding was darkened.
22	Professing themselves to be wise, they became fools,	And, while they thought within themselves that they were wise, they became fools.	And while they were thinking in themselves that they were wise, they were foolish.

	KJV	Murdock	Magiera

ROMANS *Chapter 1*

	KJV	Murdock	Magiera
23	And changed the glory of the uncorruptible God into an image made like to corruptible man, and to birds, and fourfooted beasts, and creeping things.	And they changed the glory of the incorruptible God into a likeness to the image of a corruptible man, and into the likeness of birds and quadrupeds and reptiles on the earth.	And they changed the magnificence of the incorruptible God into the likeness of the image of corruptible man and into the likeness of birds and of four-footed [animals] and of creeping things of the earth.
24	Wherefore God also gave them up to uncleanness through the lusts of their own hearts, to dishonour their own bodies between themselves:	For this cause, God gave them up to the filthy lusts of their heart, to dishonor their bodies with them.	Because of this, God delivered them to the polluted desires of their heart[s] to dishonor their bodies by them.
25	Who changed the truth of God into a lie, and worshipped and served the creature more than the Creator, who is blessed for ever. Amen.	And they changed the truth of God into a lie; and worshipped and served the created things, much more than the Creator of them, to whom belong glory and blessing, for ever and ever: Amen.	And they changed the truth of God into a lie and they reverenced and served the created [things] more than their creator, to whom [be] our praises and our blessings, forever and ever. Amen.
26	For this cause God gave them up unto vile affections: for even their women did change the natural use into that which is against nature:	For this cause, God gave them up to vile passions: for their females changed the use of their natures, and employed that which is unnatural.	Because of this, God delivered them to passions of shame. For their women changed the [natural] use of their sex and used what was not natural.
27	And likewise also the men, leaving the natural use of the woman, burned in their lust one toward another; men with men working that which is unseemly, and receiving in themselves that recompence of their error which was meet.	And so also their males forsook the use of females, which is natural, and burned with lust toward one another; and, male with male, they did what is shameful, and received in themselves the just recompense of their error.	And so also their men left the [natural] use of the sex of women and ran riotously in lust for each other. And male with male, they acted with shame and received in themselves the payment for their error that was just.
28	And even as they did not like to retain God in their knowledge, God gave them over to a reprobate mind, to do those things which are not convenient;	And as they did not determine with themselves to know God, God gave them over to a vain mind; that they might do what they ought not,	And since they had not determined in themselves to know God, God delivered them to a mind of emptiness, that they would do what is not right,
29	Being filled with all unrighteousness, fornication, wickedness, covetousness, maliciousness; full of envy, murder, debate, deceit, malignity; whisperers,	being full of all iniquity, and lewdness, and bitterness, and malice, and covetousness, and envy, and slaughter, and strife, and guile, and evil machinations,	being filled with all wickedness and fornication and bitterness and evil and greed and envy and murder and strife and deceit and evil reasonings
30	Backbiters, haters of God, despiteful, proud, boasters, inventors of evil things, disobedient to parents,	and backbiting, and slander; and being haters of God, scoffers, proud, vain-glorious, devisers of evil things, destitute of reason, disregardful of parents,	and murmuring and slander. And [they are] haters of God, insolent, prideful, boastful, inventors of evil [things], ignorant [ones], who are not obedient to their parents
31	Without understanding, covenantbreakers, without natural affection, implacable, unmerciful:	and to whom a covenant is nothing, neither affection, nor peace, and in whom is no compassion.	and who do not have stability, nor love, nor quietness, nor is there tenderness in them.

Parallel Translations

	KJV	*Murdock*	*Magiera*
	ROMANS	*Chapter 1*	
32	Who knowing the judgment of God, that they which commit such things are worthy of death, not only do the same, but have pleasure in them that do them.	These, while they know the judgment of God, that he condemneth those to death who perpetrate such things, are not only doers of them, but the companions of such as do them.	[They are] those who, although they know the judgment of God that those who act like this he condemns to death, not only are doing these [things], but also fellowship with those who are doing these [things].
	Chapter 2		
1	Therefore thou art inexcusable, O man, whosoever thou art that judgest: for wherein thou judgest another, thou condemnest thyself; for thou that judgest doest the same things.	There is therefore no excuse for thee, O man, that judgest thy neighbor; for by judging thy neighbor, thou condemnest thyself; for thou that judgest, dost practise the same things.	Because of this, you have no defense, oh man [who] judges his neighbor, for by that which you judge your neighbor, you condemn yourself. For you who judge are also occupied in these [things].
2	But we are sure that the judgment of God is according to truth against them which commit such things.	And we know that the judgment of God is in accordance with truth, in regard to those who practise these things.	And we know that the judgment of God is with truthfulness against those who are occupied in these [things].
3	And thinkest thou this, O man, that judgest them which do such things, and doest the same, that thou shalt escape the judgment of God?	And what thinkest thou, O man, that judgest those who practise these things, while practising them thyself, that thou wilt escape the judgment of God?	But what do you think, oh man, you who judge those who are occupied in these [things], while you also are occupied in these [things], that you will escape from the judgment of God?
4	Or despisest thou the riches of his goodness and forbearance and longsuffering; not knowing that the goodness of God leadeth thee to repentance?	Or wilt thou abuse the riches of his benevolence, and his long suffering, and the opportunity which he giveth thee? And dost thou not know, that the benevolence of God should bring thee to repentance?	Or are you presumptuous against the riches of his kindness and against his long-suffering and against the advantage that he gave to you? And do you not know that the kindness of God brings you to repentance?
5	But after thy hardness and impenitent heart treasurest up unto thyself wrath against the day of wrath and revelation of the righteous judgment of God;	But, because of the hardness of thy unrepenting heart, thou art treasuring up a store of wrath against the day of wrath, and against the revelation of the righteous judgment of God:	But because of the hardness of your heart that does not repent, you lay up for yourself a treasure of wrath for the day of wrath and for the revelation of the upright judgment of God,
6	Who will render to every man according to his deeds:	who will recompense to every man, according to his deeds;	who repays everyone according to his works.
7	To them who by patient continuance in well doing seek for glory and honour and immortality, eternal life:	to them who, by perseverance in good works, seek for glory and honor and immortality, to them he will give life eternal;	To those, who in the patience of good works seek glory and honor and incorruptibility, he gives eternal life.
8	But unto them that are contentious, and do not obey the truth, but obey unrighteousness, indignation and wrath,	but to them who are obstinate and obey not the truth, but obey iniquity, to them he will retribute wrath and ire.	But [to] those who are stubborn and do not obey the truth, but obey wickedness, he will repay wrath and fury
9	Tribulation and anguish, upon every soul of man that doeth evil, of the Jew first, and also of the Gentile;	And tribulation and anguish [will be] to every man that doeth evil; to the Jews first, and also to the Gentiles:	and pressure and trouble, to everyone who does evil [things], first to the Judeans and [then] to the heathens.

Parallel Translations

	KJV	Murdock	Magiera
	ROMANS *Chapter 2*		
10	But glory, honour, and peace, to every man that worketh good, to the Jew first, and also to the Gentile:	but glory and honor and peace to every one that doeth good; to the Jews first, and also to the Gentiles.	But glory and honor and peace [will be] to all who do good [things], first to the Judeans and [then] to the heathens.
11	For there is no respect of persons with God.	For there is no respect of persons with God:	For there is no respect of persons with God.
12	For as many as have sinned without law shall also perish without law: and as many as have sinned in the law shall be judged by the law;	for those without law, who sin, will also perish without law; and those under the law, who sin, will be judged by the law,	For those who have sinned without the law will also be destroyed without the law, and those who have sinned in the law will be judged from the law,
13	(For not the hearers of the law are just before God, but the doers of the law shall be justified.	(for not the hearers of the law, are righteous before God; but the doers of the law are justified;	for the hearers of the law are not upright before God, but the doers of the law are justified
14	For when the Gentiles, which have not the law, do by nature the things contained in the law, these, having not the law, are a law unto themselves:	for if Gentiles who have not the law, shall, by their nature, do the things of the law; they, while without the law, become a law to themselves:	(for if the Gentiles, who did not have the law, naturally did [the things] of the law, who although they did not have the law, have a law for themselves
15	Which shew the work of the law written in their hearts, their conscience also bearing witness, and their thoughts the mean while accusing or else excusing one another;)	and they show the work of the law, as it is inscribed on their heart; and their conscience beareth testimony to them, their own reflections rebuking or vindicating one another,)	and they show the work of the law as it is written on their heart[s] and their conscience testifies concerning them, while their reasonings rebuke or defend each other)
16	In the day when God shall judge the secrets of men by Jesus Christ according to my gospel.	in the day in which God will judge the secret [actions] of men, as my gospel [teacheth], by Jesus the Messiah.	in the day when God judges the secret [things] of men according to my gospel by way of Jesus Christ.
17	Behold, thou art called a Jew, and restest in the law, and makest thy boast of God,	But if thou, who art called a Jew, and reposest thyself on the law, and gloriest in God,	Now if you who are called a Judean and you take rest in the law and you boast in God
18	And knowest his will, and approvest the things that are more excellent, being instructed out of the law;	that thou knowest his good pleasure, and discernest obligations, because thou art instructed in the law;	that you know his will and you distinguish the proper [things] that you learned from the law
19	And art confident that thou thyself art a guide of the blind, a light of them which are in darkness,	and hast confidence in thyself, that thou art a guide to the blind, and a light to them who are in darkness,	and are confident about yourself that you are a leader of the blind and a light for those who are in darkness
20	An instructor of the foolish, a teacher of babes, which hast the form of knowledge and of the truth in the law.	and an instructor of those lacking knowledge, and a preceptor to the young; and thou hast the appearance of knowledge and of verity in the law:	and a guide of ignorant [ones] and a teacher of children and you have an example of knowledge and of truth in the law,
21	Thou therefore which teachest another, teachest thou not thyself? thou that preachest a man should not steal, dost thou steal?	Thou therefore, who teachest others, teachest thou not thyself? And thou who teachest that men must not steal, dost thou steal?	then you who teach others, do you not teach yourself? And you who preach that they should not steal, do you steal?
22	Thou that sayest a man should not commit adultery, dost thou commit adultery? thou that abhorrest idols, dost thou commit sacrilege?	And thou who sayest, Men must not commit adultery, dost thou commit adultery? And thou who contemnest idols, dost thou plunder the sanctuary?	And you who say that they should not commit adultery, do you commit adultery? And you who despise idols, do you spoil the sanctuary?

Parallel Translations

	KJV	Murdock	Magiera
	ROMANS *Chapter 2*		
23	Thou that makest thy boast of the law, through breaking the law dishonourest thou God?	And thou who gloriest in the law, dost thou, by acting contrary to the law, insult God himself?	And you who boast in the same law when you transgress the law, do you dishonor God?
24	For the name of God is blasphemed among the Gentiles through you, as it is written.	For, the name of God, as it is written, is reviled among the Gentiles on your account.	FOR BECAUSE OF YOU THE NAME OF GOD IS DEFAMED AMONG THE GENTILES, as it is written.
25	For circumcision verily profiteth, if thou keep the law: but if thou be a breaker of the law, thy circumcision is made uncircumcision.	For circumcision profiteth, indeed, if thou fulfillest the law: but if thou departest from the law, thy circumcision becometh uncircumcision.	For circumcision is beneficial if you thoroughly perform the law, but if you transgress the law, your circumcision becomes uncircumcision.
26	Therefore if the uncircumcision keep the righteousness of the law, shall not his uncircumcision be counted for circumcision?	And if uncircumcision should keep the precepts of the law, would not that uncircumcision be accounted as circumcision?	Now if the uncircumcision keeps the commandment of the law, behold, should not the uncircumcision be counted circumcision?
27	And shall not uncircumcision which is by nature, if it fulfil the law, judge thee, who by the letter and circumcision dost transgress the law?	And the uncircumcision, which from its nature fulfilleth the law, will judge thee; who, with the scripture, and with circumcision, transgressest against the law.	And the uncircumcision, which fulfills the law by its nature, will judge you who with the scripture and with circumcision transgress the law.
28	For he is not a Jew, which is one outwardly; neither is that circumcision, which is outward in the flesh:	For he is not a Jew, who is so in what is external: nor is that circumcision, which is visible in the flesh.	For he is not a Judean who is one in appearance, nor [is] what is made visible in the flesh circumcision.
29	But he is a Jew, which is one inwardly; and circumcision is that of the heart, in the spirit, and not in the letter; whose praise is not of men, but of God.	But he is a Jew, who is so in what is hidden: and circumcision is that of the heart, in the spirit, and not in the letter, whose praise is not from men, but from God.	But that one is a Judean, who is one secretly and circumcision is that of the heart spiritually and not literally, whose praise is not from men, but from God.
	Chapter 3		
1	What advantage then hath the Jew? or what profit is there of circumcision?	What then is the superiority of the Jew? Or what is the advantage of circumcision?	Therefore, what is the advantage of the Judean or what [is] the profit of circumcision?
2	Much every way: chiefly, because that unto them were committed the oracles of God.	Much, every way. And first, because to them were intrusted the oracles of God.	Much in everything. [It is] that they were first entrusted with the words of God.
3	For what if some did not believe? shall their unbelief make the faith of God without effect?	For if some of them have not believed, have they, by their not believing, made the faith of God inefficient?	For if some of them did not believe, did they make void the faith of God in that they did not believe?
4	God forbid: yea, let God be true, but every man a liar; as it is written, That thou mightest be justified in thy sayings, and mightest overcome when thou art judged.	Far be it: for God is veracious, and every man false: as it is written: That thou mightest be upright, in thy declarations; and be found pure, when they judge thee.	Let it not be so! For God is true and every man [is] false, as it is written: YOU SHOULD BE UPRIGHT IN YOUR WORDS AND BE INNOCENT WHEN THEY JUDGE YOU.

Parallel Translations

	KJV	Murdock	Magiera

ROMANS *Chapter 3*

Verse	KJV	Murdock	Magiera
5	But if our unrighteousness commend the righteousness of God, what shall we say? Is God unrighteous who taketh vengeance? (I speak as a man)	But if our iniquity establish the rectitude of God, what shall we say? Is God unrighteous, when he inflicteth wrath? (I speak as a man.)	But if our wickedness establishes the uprightness of God, what should we say? Is God wicked who brings his wrath? (I speak as a man.)
6	God forbid: for then how shall God judge the world?	Far from it. Otherwise how will God judge the world?	Let it not be so! Yet if not, how will God judge the world?
7	For if the truth of God hath more abounded through my lie unto his glory; why yet am I also judged as a sinner?	But if the truth of God hath been furthered by my falsehood, to his glory; why am I then condemned as a sinner?	For if the truth of God was increased by my falsehood for his glory, am I therefore judged as a sinner?
8	And not rather, (as we be slanderously reported, and as some affirm that we say,) Let us do evil, that good may come? whose damnation is just.	Or shall we say as some have slanderously reported us to say: We will do evil things, that good [results] may come? The condemnation of such is reserved for justice.	Or perhaps [we should say], as they blaspheme about us and say that we say, "We will do evil, so that good may come." Their judgment is kept for justice.
9	What then? are we better than they? No, in no wise: for we have before proved both Jews and Gentiles, that they are all under sin;	What then, have WE the superiority, when we have before decided as to both Jews and Gentiles, that all of them are under sin?	What then? Do we have the superiority, although we previously determined about the Judeans and about the heathens that they were all under sin?
10	As it is written, There is none righteous, no, not one:	As it is written: There is none righteous; no, no one:	As it is written: THERE IS NO ONE UPRIGHT, NOT EVEN ONE,
11	There is none that understandeth, there is none that seeketh after God.	and none that understandeth; nor that seeketh after God.	NOR ONE WHO UNDERSTANDS, NOR WHO SEEKS GOD.
12	They are all gone out of the way, they are together become unprofitable; there is none that doeth good, no, not one.	They have all turned aside, together; and become reprobates. There is none that doeth good; no, not one.	ALL OF THEM HAVE TURNED ASIDE TOGETHER AND HAVE REJECTED [GOD] AND THERE IS NO ONE WHO DOES GOOD, NOT EVEN ONE.
13	Their throat is an open sepulchre; with their tongues they have used deceit; the poison of asps is under their lips:	Their throats are open sepulchres, and their tongues treacherous; and the venom of the asp is under their lips.	THEIR THROATS [ARE] OPEN GRAVES AND THEIR TONGUES ARE DECEITFUL AND THE POISON OF THE ASP [IS] UNDER THEIR LIPS.
14	Whose mouth is full of cursing and bitterness:	Their mouth is full of cursing and bitterness;	THEIR MOUTH IS FULL OF CURSING AND BITTERNESS
15	Their feet are swift to shed blood:	and their feet are swift to shed blood.	AND THEIR FEET ARE SWIFT TO SHED BLOOD.
16	Destruction and misery are in their ways:	Destruction and anguish are in their paths:	ADVERSITY AND MISERY [ARE] IN THEIR PATHS
17	And the way of peace have they not known:	and the path of peacefulness they have not known:	AND THEY DO NOT KNOW THE PATH OF PEACE
18	There is no fear of God before their eyes.	and the fear of God is not before their eyes.	AND THERE IS NO FEAR OF GOD BEFORE THEIR EYES.
19	Now we know that what things soever the law saith, it saith to them who are under the law: that every mouth may be stopped, and all the world may become guilty before God.	Now we know, that whatever the law saith, it saith to them who are under the law; that every mouth may be stopped, and all the world be guilty before God.	But we know that what the law said, it said to those who are in the law, so that every mouth may be shut and all the world may be found guilty before God,

Parallel Translations

	KJV	Murdock	Magiera

ROMANS Chapter 3

Verse	KJV	Murdock	Magiera
20	Therefore by the deeds of the law there shall no flesh be justified in his sight: for by the law is the knowledge of sin.	Wherefore, by the deeds of the law, no flesh is justified before him: for, by the law, sin is known.	because by the deeds of the law no flesh is justified before him, for by the law sin is known.
21	But now the righteousness of God without the law is manifested, being witnessed by the law and the prophets;	But now, the righteousness of God without the law, is manifested; and the law and the prophets testify of it:	But now, without the law, the uprightness of God is revealed and the law and the prophets testify about it.
22	Even the righteousness of God which is by faith of Jesus Christ unto all and upon all them that believe: for there is no difference:	even the righteousness of God, which is by faith in Jesus Messiah, for every one, and on every one, that believeth in him: for there is no distinction;	But the uprightness of God is by way of the faith of Jesus Christ to everyone, even on everyone who believes in him, (for there is no distinction,
23	For all have sinned, and come short of the glory of God;	for they have all sinned, and failed of the glory of God.	because all have sinned and are deficient compared to the glory of God)
24	Being justified freely by his grace through the redemption that is in Christ Jesus:	And they are justified gratuitously, by grace, and by the redemption which is in Jesus Messiah;	and they are freely justified by grace and by the redemption that is in Jesus Christ
25	Whom God hath set forth to be a propitiation through faith in his blood, to declare his righteousness for the remission of sins that are past, through the forbearance of God;	whom God hath preconstituted a propitiation, by faith in his blood, because of our sins, which we before committed,	(this [one] whom God determined beforehand [to be] a pardon by the faith of his blood because of our sins that we had previously sinned).
26	To declare, I say, at this time his righteousness: that he might be just, and the justifier of him which believeth in Jesus.	in the space which God in his long suffering gave to us, for the manifestation of his righteousness at the present time; that he might be righteous, and might with righteousness justify him who is in the faith of our Lord Jesus Messiah.	[It is] by the advantage that God in his long-suffering gave to us for the clear showing of his uprightness that is at this time, that he would be upright and would justify with uprightness him who is in the faith of our Lord Jesus Christ.
27	Where is boasting then? It is excluded. By what law? of works? Nay: but by the law of faith.	Where then is glorying? It is annihilated. By what law? by that of works? Nay: but by the law of faith.	Then where is boasting? It has been stopped. By what? The law of works? No, but by the law of faith.
28	Therefore we conclude that a man is justified by faith without the deeds of the law.	We therefore conclude, that it is by faith a man is justified, and not by the works of the law.	Therefore, we conclude that a man is justified by faith and not by the works of the law.
29	Is he the God of the Jews only? is he not also of the Gentiles? Yes, of the Gentiles also:	For, is he the God of the Jews only, and not of the Gentiles? Nay: of the Gentiles also.	For is he the God of the Judeans only and not of the Gentiles? Yes, also of the Gentiles,
30	Seeing it is one God, which shall justify the circumcision by faith, and uncircumcision through faith.	Because there is, one God, who justifieth the circumcision by faith, and the uncircumcision by the same faith.	because there is one God who justifies the circumcision by faith [and] also the uncircumcision by the same faith.
31	Do we then make void the law through faith? God forbid: yea, we establish the law.	Do, we then nullify the law by faith? Far be it. On the contrary, we establish the law.	Therefore, do we make the law of none effect by faith? Let it not be so! Rather, we establish the law.

Parallel Translations

ROMANS *Chapter 4*

	KJV	*Murdock*	*Magiera*
1	What shall we say then that Abraham our father, as pertaining to the flesh, hath found?	What then shall we say concerning Abraham the patriarch, that by the flesh he obtained?	What then? Are we saying about Abraham the patriarch that he obtained [justification] by the flesh?
2	For if Abraham were justified by works, he hath whereof to glory; but not before God.	But if Abraham was justified by works, he had [ground of] glorying; yet not before God.	For if Abraham was justified by works, he had [a reason for] boasting, but not toward God.
3	For what saith the scripture? Abraham believed God, and it was counted unto him for righteousness.	For what saith the scripture? That Abraham believed God, and it was accounted to him for righteousness.	For what does the scripture say? ABRAHAM BELIEVED IN GOD AND IT WAS COUNTED TO HIM FOR JUSTIFICATION.
4	Now to him that worketh is the reward not reckoned of grace, but of debt.	But to him that worketh, the reward is not reckoned as of grace, but as a debt to him.	Now to him who labors, his wage is not counted to him as by grace, but as that which is owed to him.
5	But to him that worketh not, but believeth on him that justifieth the ungodly, his faith is counted for righteousness.	Whereas, to him that worketh not, but only believeth in him that justifieth sinners, his faith is accounted to him for righteousness.	But to him who does not labor, but believes only in him who justifies sinners, his faith is counted to him for uprightness.
6	Even as David also describeth the blessedness of the man, unto whom God imputeth righteousness without works,	As David also speaketh of the blessedness of the man, to whom God reckoneth righteousness without works,	As David also said concerning the blessing of the man to whom God counts justification without works, saying:
7	Saying, Blessed are they whose iniquities are forgiven, and whose sins are covered.	saying: Blessed are they, whose iniquity is forgiven, and whose sins are covered up:	BLESSED ARE THEY WHOSE WICKEDNESS IS FORGIVEN AND WHOSE SINS ARE COVERED
8	Blessed is the man to whom the Lord will not impute sin.	and, Blessed is the man, to whom God will not reckon his sin.	and BLESSED IS THE MAN TO WHOM GOD WILL NOT COUNT HIS SIN.
9	Cometh this blessedness then upon the circumcision only, or upon the uncircumcision also? for we say that faith was reckoned to Abraham for righteousness.	This blessedness, therefore, is it on the circumcision? or on the uncircumcision? For we say, that Abraham's faith was reckoned to him for righteousness.	Therefore, [is] this blessing on the circumcision or on the uncircumcision? For we say that his faith was counted to Abraham for uprightness.
10	How was it then reckoned? when he was in circumcision, or in uncircumcision? Not in circumcision, but in uncircumcision.	How then was it reckoned to him? In circumcision, or in uncircumcision? Not in circumcision, but in uncircumcision.	How then was it counted to him, in circumcision or in uncircumcision? It was not in circumcision, but in uncircumcision.
11	And he received the sign of circumcision, a seal of the righteousness of the faith which he had yet being uncircumcised: that he might be the father of all them that believe, though they be not circumcised; that righteousness might be imputed unto them also:	For he received circumcision, as the sign and the seal of the righteousness of his faith while in uncircumcision: that he might become the father of all them of the uncircumcision who believe; and that it might be reckoned to them also for righteousness:	For he received circumcision [as] a sign and seal of the uprightness of his faith that was in uncircumcision, so that he would become the father to all those who believe from the uncircumcision (that it would be counted to them for uprightness also)

Parallel Translations

ROMANS *Chapter 4*

	KJV	Murdock	Magiera
12	And the father of circumcision to them who are not of the circumcision only, but who also walk in the steps of that faith of our father Abraham, which he had being yet uncircumcised.	and the father of the circumcision; not to them only who are of the circumcision, but to them also who fulfill the steps of the faith of our father Abraham in [his] uncircumcision.	and the father to the circumcision, not to those who are from the circumcision only, but also to those who follow in the footsteps of the faith of the uncircumcision of our father Abraham.
13	For the promise, that he should be the heir of the world, was not to Abraham, or to his seed, through the law, but through the righteousness of faith.	For the promise to Abraham and to his seed, that he should become the heir of the world, was not by the law, but by the righteousness of his faith.	For the promise to Abraham and to his seed that he would be the heir to the world was not by the law, but by the uprightness of his faith.
14	For if they which are of the law be heirs, faith is made void, and the promise made of none effect:	For if they who are of the law were heirs, faith would be made void, and the promise of no force.	For if those who are from the law become heirs, faith becomes void and the promise is being made of no effect.
15	Because the law worketh wrath: for where no law is, there is no transgression.	For the law is a worker of wrath; because where no law is, there is no transgression of law.	For the law is a worker of wrath, for where there is no law, neither [is there] transgression of the law.
16	Therefore it is of faith, that it might be by grace; to the end the promise might be sure to all the seed; not to that only which is of the law, but to that also which is of the faith of Abraham; who is the father of us all,	Wherefore, it is by the faith which is by grace, that we are justified: so that the promise may be sure to all the seed; not to that only which is of the law, but also to that which is of the faith of Abraham, who is the father of us all:	Because of this, [it is] by faith that we will be justified by grace and the promise will be sure to all his seed, not to those who are from the law only, but also to those who are from the faith of Abraham, who is the father of all of us.
17	(As it is written, I have made thee a father of many nations,) before him whom he believed, even God, who quickeneth the dead, and calleth those things which be not as though they were.	as it is written: "I have constituted thee a father to a multitude of nations;" [namely] before God, in whom thou hast believed; who quickeneth the dead, and calleth those things which are not, as if they were.	As it is written: I HAVE PLACED YOU [AS] A FATHER TO A MULTITUDE OF THE GENTILES, BEFORE GOD IN WHOM YOU BELIEVED, WHO MAKES ALIVE THE DEAD AND CALLS THOSE [THINGS] THAT ARE NOT AS THOUGH THEY ARE.
18	Who against hope believed in hope, that he might become the father of many nations, according to that which was spoken, So shall thy seed be.	And without hope, he confided in the hope of becoming the father of a multitude of nations; (as it is written: So will thy seed be.)	And without hope, he believed for the hope that he would be a father to a multitude of the Gentiles, as it is written: SO YOUR SEED WILL BE.
19	And being not weak in faith, he considered not his own body now dead, when he was about an hundred years old, neither yet the deadness of Sara's womb:	And he was not sickly in his faith, while contemplating his inert body, (for he was a hundred years old,) and the inert womb of Sarah.	And he was not weak in his faith, considering his dead body that was one hundred years old and the dead womb of Sarah.
20	He staggered not at the promise of God through unbelief; but was strong in faith, giving glory to God;	And he did not hesitate at the promise of God, as one lacking faith; but he was strong in faith, and gave glory to God;	And he did not doubt the promise of God as [one] lacking faith, but was strong in faith and gave praise to God.
21	And being fully persuaded that, what he had promised, he was able also to perform.	and felt assured, that what God had promised to him, he was able to fulfill.	And he was convinced that God was able to complete what he had promised to him.
22	And therefore it was imputed to him for righteousness.	And therefore it was accounted to him for righteousness.	Because of this, it was counted to him for uprightness.

ROMANS *Chapter 4*

	KJV	Murdock	Magiera
23	Now it was not written for his sake alone, that it was imputed to him;	And not for his sake alone, was it written, that his faith was accounted for righteousness;	And not on his behalf only was this written: HIS FAITH WAS COUNTED FOR UPRIGHTNESS,
24	But for us also, to whom it shall be imputed, if we believe on him that raised up Jesus our Lord from the dead;	but for our sakes also; because it is to be accounted [so] to us, who believe in him that raised our Lord Jesus Messiah from the dead;	but also on our behalf, because he is also prepared to count [uprightness to] those who believe in him who raised our Lord Jesus Christ from the dead,
25	Who was delivered for our offences, and was raised again for our justification.	who was delivered up, on account of our sins; and arose, that he might justify us.	who was delivered up for our sins and rose in order to justify us.

Chapter 5

	KJV	Murdock	Magiera
1	Therefore being justified by faith, we have peace with God through our Lord Jesus Christ:	Therefore, because we are justified by faith, we shall have peace with God, through our Lord Jesus Messiah.	Therefore, because we are justified by faith, we have peace toward God by our Lord Jesus Christ,
2	By whom also we have access by faith into this grace wherein we stand, and rejoice in hope of the glory of God.	By whom we are brought by faith into this grace, in which we stand and rejoice in the hope of the glory of God.	by whom we were brought by faith to this grace in which we stand and boast in the hope of the glory of God.
3	And not only so, but we glory in tribulations also: knowing that tribulation worketh patience;	And not only so, but we also rejoice in afflictions; because we know that affliction perfecteth in us patience;	And not only so, but we also boast in our adversities, because we know that adversity perfects patience in us,
4	And patience, experience; and experience, hope:	and patience, experience; and experience, hope:	and patience, experience, and experience, hope.
5	And hope maketh not ashamed; because the love of God is shed abroad in our hearts by the Holy Ghost which is given unto us.	and hope maketh not ashamed because the love of God is diffused in our hearts, by the Holy Spirit who is given to us.	And hope does not put [us] to shame, because the love of God is poured out in our hearts by the Holy Spirit that was given to us.
6	For when we were yet without strength, in due time Christ died for the ungodly.	And if at this time, on account of our weakness, Messiah died for the ungodly:	Now if Christ at this time, because of our weakness, died for the ungodly,
7	For scarcely for a righteous man will one die: yet peradventure for a good man some would even dare to die.	(for rarely doth one die for the ungodly; though for the good, some one perhaps might venture to die:)	(for seldom does anyone die for the ungodly, although for good [ones] perhaps some would dare to die)
8	But God commendeth his love toward us, in that, while we were yet sinners, Christ died for us.	God hath here manifested his love towards us. Because, if when we were sinners, Messiah died for us;	here God has manifested his love that is toward us, because if when we were sinners, Christ died for us,
9	Much more then, being now justified by his blood, we shall be saved from wrath through him.	how much more, shall we now be justified by his blood and be rescued from wrath by him?	then how much more will we be justified now by his blood and be rescued from wrath by him?
10	For if, when we were enemies, we were reconciled to God by the death of his Son, much more, being reconciled, we shall be saved by his life.	For if when we were enemies, God was reconciled with us by the death of his Son; how much more shall we, in his reconciliation, live by his life?	For if when we were enemies God was reconciled with us by the death of his Son, then how much more will we by his reconciliation live by his life?

Parallel Translations

	KJV	*Murdock*	*Magiera*
	ROMANS *Chapter 5*		
11	And not only so, but we also joy in God through our Lord Jesus Christ, by whom we have now received the atonement.	And not only so, but we also rejoice in God, by means of our Lord Jesus Messiah, through whom we have now received the reconciliation.	And not only so, but also we boast in God by way of our Lord Jesus Christ, in whom we have now received reconciliation.
12	Wherefore, as by one man sin entered into the world, and death by sin; and so death passed upon all men, for that all have sinned:	As by means of one man, sin entered into the world, and, by means of sin, death; and so death passed upon all the sons of men, inasmuch as they all have sinned:	For as by way of one man sin entered the world and by way of sin, death, even so death passed on all men, in that all of them have sinned.
13	(For until the law sin was in the world: but sin is not imputed when there is no law.	For until the law, sin, although it was in the world, was not accounted sin, because there was no law.	For until the law, sin, although it was in the world, was not counted sin, because there was no law.
14	Nevertheless death reigned from Adam to Moses, even over them that had not sinned after the similitude of Adam's transgression, who is the figure of him that was to come.	Yet death reigned from Adam until Moses, even over those who had not sinned after the likeness of the transgression of the command by Adam, who was the type of him that was to come.	But death reigned from Adam until Moses, even over those who had not sinned in the likeness of the transgression of the law of Adam, who was the likeness of him who was to come.
15	But not as the offence, so also is the free gift. For if through the offence of one many be dead, much more the grace of God, and the gift by grace, which is by one man, Jesus Christ, hath abounded unto many.	But not, as the fault, so also the free gift. For if, on account of the fault of one, many died; how much more, will the grace of God and his free gift, on account of one man, Jesus Messiah, abound unto many?	But not as the offense, so also was the gift. For if because of the offense of one, many died, then how much more the grace of God and his gift, because of one man, Jesus Christ, will be made to increase in many?
16	And not as it was by one that sinned, so is the gift: for the judgment was by one to condemnation, but the free gift is of many offences unto justification.	And not, as the offence of one, so also the free gift. For the judgment, which was of one [offence], was unto condemnation; but the free gift was, of many sins, unto righteousness.	And not as the error of one, so also [was] the gift. For the judgment that was from one resulted in condemnation, but the gift resulted in uprightness from many sins.
17	For if by one man's offence death reigned by one; much more they which receive abundance of grace and of the gift of righteousness shall reign in life by one, Jesus Christ.)	For if, on account of the offence of one, death reigned; still more, they who receive the abundance of the grace, and the free gift, and the righteousness, will reign in life, by means of one, Jesus Messiah.	For if because of the error of one, death reigned, much more those who receive the abundance of grace and of the gift and of uprightness will reign in life by way of one, Jesus Christ.
18	Therefore as by the offence of one judgment came upon all men to condemnation; even so by the righteousness of one the free gift came upon all men unto justification of life.	Therefore, as on account of the offence of one, condemnation was to all men; so on account of the righteousness of one, will the victory unto life be to all men.	In like manner, therefore, because of the error of one, condemnation was to all men, so also because of the uprightness of one, the victory for life will be to all men.
19	For as by one man's disobedience many were made sinners, so by the obedience of one shall many be made righteous.	For as, on account of the disobedience of one man, many became sinners; so also, on account of the obedience of one, many become righteous.	For as because of the disobedience of one man, many became sinners, so also because of the obedience of one, many will become upright [ones].

Parallel Translations

	KJV	Murdock	Magiera

ROMANS *Chapter 5*

	KJV	Murdock	Magiera
20	Moreover the law entered, that the offence might abound. But where sin abounded, grace did much more abound:	And the entrance given to the law, was that sin might increase: and where sin increased, there grace abounded.	Now the entrance that the law had [was] that sin should be multiplied. And where sin multiplied, there grace increased,
21	That as sin hath reigned unto death, even so might grace reign through righteousness unto eternal life by Jesus Christ our Lord.	So that, as sin had reigned in death, so grace might reign in righteousness unto life eternal, by means of our Lord Jesus Messiah.	because as sin reigned in death, so also grace will reign in uprightness to eternal life by way of our Lord Jesus Christ.

Chapter 6

	KJV	Murdock	Magiera
1	What shall we say then? Shall we continue in sin, that grace may abound?	What shall we then say? Shall we continue in sin, that grace may abound?	What then should we say? Should we continue in sin that grace would increase?
2	God forbid. How shall we, that are dead to sin, live any longer therein?	Far be it: for if we are persons that have died to sin, how can we again live in it?	Let it not be so! For [we are] those who are dead to sin. How can we live in it again?
3	Know ye not, that so many of us as were baptized into Jesus Christ were baptized into his death?	Or do ye not know, that we who are baptized into Jesus Messiah, are baptized into his death?	Or do you not know that we who are baptized in Jesus Christ are baptized in his death?
4	Therefore we are buried with him by baptism into death: that like as Christ was raised up from the dead by the glory of the Father, even so we also should walk in newness of life.	For we are buried with him in baptism unto death; that as Jesus Messiah arose from the dead into the glory of his Father, so also we, to walk in a new life.	We are buried with him in baptism to death, that as Jesus Christ rose up from the dead in the glory of his Father, so we will also walk in new life.
5	For if we have been planted together in the likeness of his death, we shall be also in the likeness of his resurrection:	For if we have been planted together with him into the likeness of his death, so shall we be also into his resurrection.	For if we were planted together with him in the likeness of his death, so we will also be in [the likeness of] his resurrection.
6	Knowing this, that our old man is crucified with him, that the body of sin might be destroyed, that henceforth we should not serve sin.	For we know, that our old man is crucified with him; that the body of sin might be abolished, and we be no more servants to sin:	For we know that our old man was crucified with him that the body of sin should be annulled, so that we should no longer serve sin.
7	For he that is dead is freed from sin.	for he that is dead [to it], is emancipated from sin.	For he who is dead is set free from sin.
8	Now if we be dead with Christ, we believe that we shall also live with him:	If then we are dead with Messiah, let us believe that we shall live with the same Messiah.	If then we are dead with Christ, we should believe that we will live with Christ.
9	Knowing that Christ being raised from the dead dieth no more; death hath no more dominion over him.	For we know that Messiah rose from the dead, and no more dieth; death hath no dominion over him.	For we know that Christ rose up from the dead and will not die again and death does not have authority over him.
10	For in that he died, he died unto sin once: but in that he liveth, he liveth unto God.	For in dying, he died for sin, once; and in living, he liveth unto God.	For in dying, he died to sin one time, and in living, he lives to God.
11	Likewise reckon ye also yourselves to be dead indeed unto sin, but alive unto God through Jesus Christ our Lord.	So also do ye account yourselves as being dead to sin, and alive to God, through our Lord Jesus Messiah.	So also you should count yourselves that you are dead to sin and alive to God in our Lord Jesus Christ.

Parallel Translations

	KJV	Murdock	Magiera
	ROMANS *Chapter 6*		
12	Let not sin therefore reign in your mortal body, that ye should obey it in the lusts thereof.	Therefore let not sin reign in your dead body, so that ye obey its lusts.	Therefore, let not sin reign in your dead body, so that you would obey its desires.
13	Neither yield ye your members as instruments of unrighteousness unto sin: but yield yourselves unto God, as those that are alive from the dead, and your members as instruments of righteousness unto God.	And also give not up your members as instruments of evil unto sin, but give up yourselves to God, as those who have been resuscitated from the dead; and let your members be instruments for the righteousness of God.	And also do not present your members as an instrument of wickedness for sin, but present yourselves to God as men who have life from the dead and let your members be an instrument for the uprightness of God.
14	For sin shall not have dominion over you: for ye are not under the law, but under grace.	And sin shall not have dominion over you; for ye are not under the law, but under grace.	And sin will not have authority over you, for you are not under the law, but under grace.
15	What then? shall we sin, because we are not under the law, but under grace? God forbid.	What then? Shall we sin, because we are not under the law, but under grace? Far be it.	What then? Should we sin because we are not under the law but under grace? Let it not be so!
16	Know ye not, that to whom ye yield yourselves servants to obey, his servants ye are to whom ye obey; whether of sin unto death, or of obedience unto righteousness?	Know ye not, that to whomsoever ye give up yourselves to serve in bondage, his servants ye are, whom ye serve; whether it be to sin, or whether it be to righteousness, that ye give ear?	Do you not know that you must obey him to whom you present yourself for his service? You are the servants of that one whom you obey, whether to sin or to the obedience of uprightness.
17	But God be thanked, that ye were the servants of sin, but ye have obeyed from the heart that form of doctrine which was delivered you.	But thanks be to God, that ye were [once] the servants of sin but have [now] from the heart obeyed that form of doctrine to which ye are devoted.	But thanks [be] to God, because you were a servant of sin, yet [now] you have obeyed from the heart the likeness of the teaching to which you are committed.
18	Being then made free from sin, ye became the servants of righteousness.	And when ye were emancipated from sin, ye became servants to righteousness.	And when you were freed from sin, you were made subject to uprightness
19	I speak after the manner of men because of the infirmity of your flesh: for as ye have yielded your members servants to uncleanness and to iniquity unto iniquity; even so now yield your members servants to righteousness unto holiness.	—(I speak as among men, because of the infirmity of your flesh.)—As ye [once] gave up your members to the servitude of pollution and iniquity, so also now give ye up your members to the servitude of righteousness and sanctity.	(I speak as among men, because of the weakness of your flesh) that in the same manner that you presented your members for the service of uncleanness and of wickedness, so also now present your members for the service of uprightness and of holiness.
20	For when ye were the servants of sin, ye were free from righteousness.	For when ye were the servants of sin, ye were emancipated from righteousness.	For when you were the servants of sin, you were free from uprightness.
21	What fruit had ye then in those things whereof ye are now ashamed? for the end of those things is death.	And what harvest had ye then, in that of which ye are now ashamed? For the result thereof is death.	And what kind of result did you have at that time of which today you are ashamed? For its end is death.
22	But now being made free from sin, and become servants to God, ye have your fruit unto holiness, and the end everlasting life.	And now, as ye have been emancipated from sin, and have become servants to God, your fruits are holy; and the result thereof is life everlasting.	And now that you have been freed from sin and you are servants to God, you have holy fruit, whose end [is] eternal life.

Parallel Translations

	KJV	Murdock	Magiera

ROMANS Chapter 6

Verse	KJV	Murdock	Magiera
23	For the wages of sin is death; but the gift of God is eternal life through Jesus Christ our Lord.	For the wages of sin is death; but the free gift of God is life eternal, through our Lord Jesus Messiah.	Now the wage of sin is death and the gift of God [is] eternal life in our Lord Jesus Christ.

Chapter 7

Verse	KJV	Murdock	Magiera
1	Know ye not, brethren, (for I speak to them that know the law,) how that the law hath dominion over a man as long as he liveth?	Or do ye not know, my Brethren.—(for I am speaking to them that know the law,)—that the law hath dominion over a man, as long as he is alive?	Or do you not know, my brothers, (for I speak to learned [ones] of the law) that the law has authority over a man as long as he is alive?
2	For the woman which hath an husband is bound by the law to her husband so long as he liveth; but if the husband be dead, she is loosed from the law of her husband.	Just as a woman, by the law, is bound to her husband, as long as he is alive: but if her husband should die, she is freed from the law of her husband.	[It is] as a woman who is bound by the law to her husband as long as he is alive, but if her husband dies, she is freed from the law of her husband.
3	So then if, while her husband liveth, she be married to another man, she shall be called an adulteress: but if her husband be dead, she is free from that law; so that she is no adulteress, though she be married to another man.	And if, while her husband is alive, she should adhere to another man, she would become an adulteress: but if her husband should die, she is freed from the law; and would not be an adulteress though joined to another man.	And if while her husband is alive, she has intercourse with another man, she becomes an adulteress. But if her husband dies, she is freed from the law and she is not an adulteress if she marries another man.
4	Wherefore, my brethren, ye also are become dead to the law by the body of Christ; that ye should be married to another, even to him who is raised from the dead, that we should bring forth fruit unto God.	And now, my brethren, ye also have become dead to the law, by the body of Messiah; that ye might be joined to another, [even] to him who arose from the dead; and might yield fruits unto God.	And now, my brothers, you are also dead to the law in the body of Christ that you would be [married] to another, him who rose up from the dead, so that you would bear fruit to God.
5	For when we were in the flesh, the motions of sins, which were by the law, did work in our members to bring forth fruit unto death.	For while we were in the flesh, the emotions of sin which are by the law, were active in our members, that we should bear fruits unto death.	For while we were in the flesh, the passions of sins that are by the law were working in our members, so that we would bear fruit to death.
6	But now we are delivered from the law, that being dead wherein we were held; that we should serve in newness of spirit, and not in the oldness of the letter.	But now we are absolved from the law, and are dead to that which held us in its grasp: that we might henceforth serve in the newness of the spirit, and not in the oldness of the letter.	But now we are absolved from the law and we are dead to that which was holding us captive, that from now on, we should serve in the newness of the Spirit and not in the oldness of the writing.
7	What shall we say then? Is the law sin? God forbid. Nay, I had not known sin, but by the law: for I had not known lust, except the law had said, Thou shalt not covet.	What shall we say then? Is the law sin?, Far be it. For I had not learned sin, except by means of the law: for I had not known concupiscence, had not the law said, Thou shalt not covet:	What then are we saying? Is the law sin? Let it not be so! But I did not learn sin, except by way of the law. For I had not known lust, except that the law said: DO NOT LUST.
8	But sin, taking occasion by the commandment, wrought in me all manner of concupiscence. For without the law sin was dead.	and by this commandment, sin found occasion, and perfected in me all concupiscence: for without the law, sin was dead.	And by this commandment, sin found opportunity and perfected in me every lust, for without the law sin was dead.

Parallel Translations

ROMANS *Chapter 7*

	KJV	Murdock	Magiera
9	For I was alive without the law once: but when the commandment came, sin revived, and I died.	And I, without the law, was alive formerly; but when the commandment came, sin became alive, and I died;	Now I was alive previously without the law. But when the commandment came, sin lived and I died.
10	And the commandment, which was ordained to life, I found to be unto death.	and the commandment of life was found by me [to be] unto death.	And I found that commandment of life [to be] to death.
11	For sin, taking occasion by the commandment, deceived me, and by it slew me.	For sin, by the occasion which it found by means of the commandment, seduced me; and thereby slew me.	For sin, by the opportunity that it found by way of the commandment, caused me to err and by it killed me.
12	Wherefore the law is holy, and the commandment holy, and just, and good.	Wherefore, the law is holy; and the commandment is holy, and righteous, and good.	Then the law is holy and the commandment is holy and upright and good.
13	Was then that which is good made death unto me? God forbid. But sin, that it might appear sin, working death in me by that which is good; that sin by the commandment might become exceeding sinful.	Did that which is good, therefore, become death to me? Far be it. But sin, that it might be seen to be sin, perfected death in me by means of that good [law]; that sin might the more be condemned, by means of the commandment.	Did a good [thing] therefore become death to me? Let it not be so! But sin, that it would be seen as sin, perfected death in me by a good [thing], so that sin would be more condemned by the commandment.
14	For we know that the law is spiritual: but I am carnal, sold under sin.	For we know, that the law is spiritual; but I am carnal, and sold to sin.	For we know that the law is spiritual, but I am of the flesh and I am sold to sin.
15	For that which I do I allow not: for what I would, that do I not; but what I hate, that do I.	For what I am doing, I know not: and what I would, I do not perform; but what I hate, that I do.	For that which I perform, I know not. And that which I desire, I do not do, but that which I hate, that I do.
16	If then I do that which I would not, I consent unto the law that it is good.	And if I do what I would not, I testify of the law, that it is right.	And if I do that which I do not desire, I am testifying concerning the law that it is good.
17	Now then it is no more I that do it, but sin that dwelleth in me.	And then, it is no more I who do that thing; but sin, which dwelleth in me.	But now, I am not performing this, but sin that lives in me.
18	For I know that in me (that is, in my flesh,) dwelleth no good thing: for to will is present with me; but how to perform that which is good I find not.	For I know, that in me, (that is, in my flesh,) good dwelleth not: because, to approve the good, is easy for me; but to do it, I am unable.	For I know that good does not live in me (but that is in my flesh). For to desire the good is easy for me, but to perform it, I am not able.
19	For the good that I would I do not: but the evil which I would not, that I do.	For I do not perform the good, which I would perform; but the bad, which I would not perform, that I do perform.	For I do not do the good that I desire to do, but the evil that I do not desire to do, I do it.
20	Now if I do that I would not, it is no more I that do it, but sin that dwelleth in me.	And if I do what I would not, it is not I that do it, but sin which dwelleth in me.	And if that which I do not desire, I do, I am not doing [it], but sin that lives in me.
21	I find then a law, that, when I would do good, evil is present with me.	I find therefore a law coinciding with my conscience, which assenteth to my doing good, whereas evil is near to me.	Therefore, I find a law that agrees with my mind that desires to do good, because evil is near to me.
22	For I delight in the law of God after the inward man:	For I rejoice in the law of God, in the interior man.	For I rejoice in the law of God in the inward man.

Parallel Translations

ROMANS *Chapter 7*

	KJV	*Murdock*	*Magiera*
23	But I see another law in my members, warring against the law of my mind, and bringing me into captivity to the law of sin which is in my members.	But I see another law in my members, which warreth against the law of my conscience, and maketh me a captive to the law of sin which existeth in my members	But I see another law in my members that wars against the law of my mind and makes me captive to the law of sin that is in my members.
24	O wretched man that I am! who shall deliver me from the body of this death?	O, a miserable man, am I! Who will rescue me from this body of death?	I am a miserable man! Who will rescue me from this body of death?
25	I thank God through Jesus Christ our Lord. So then with the mind I myself serve the law of God; but with the flesh the law of sin.	I thank God; by means of our Lord Jesus Messiah [I shall be rescued.] Now, therefore, in my conscience, I am a servant of the law of God; but in my flesh, I am a servant of the law of sin.	I thank God by way of our Lord Jesus Christ. Now therefore, in my mind, I am a servant of the law of God, but in my flesh, I am a servant of the law of sin.

Chapter 8

	KJV	*Murdock*	*Magiera*
1	There is therefore now no condemnation to them which are in Christ Jesus, who walk not after the flesh, but after the Spirit.	There is therefore no condemnation, to them who, in Jesus Messiah, walk not after the flesh.	From now on, there is no condemnation to those who in Jesus Christ do not walk in the flesh.
2	For the law of the Spirit of life in Christ Jesus hath made me free from the law of sin and death.	For the law of the spirit of life, which is in Jesus Messiah, hath emancipated thee from the law of sin and death.	For the law of the Spirit of life that is in Jesus Christ has freed you from the law of sin and of death.
3	For what the law could not do, in that it was weak through the flesh, God sending his own Son in the likeness of sinful flesh, and for sin, condemned sin in the flesh:	Inasmuch as the law was impotent, by means of the weakness of the flesh, God sent his Son in the likeness of sinful flesh, on account of sin; that He might, in his flesh, condemn sin;	For because the law was weak by way of the frailty of the flesh, God sent his Son in the likeness of the flesh of sin, because of sin, to condemn sin in the flesh,
4	That the righteousness of the law might be fulfilled in us, who walk not after the flesh, but after the Spirit.	so that the righteousness of the law might be fulfilled in us; since it is not in the flesh that we walk, but in the Spirit.	so that the uprightness of the law would be completed in us, who do not walk carnally but spiritually.
5	For they that are after the flesh do mind the things of the flesh; but they that are after the Spirit the things of the Spirit.	For they who are in the flesh, do mind the things of the flesh: and they who are of the Spirit, do mind the things of the Spirit.	For those who are [walking] carnally are carnally minded and those who are [walking] spiritually are spiritually minded.
6	For to be carnally minded is death; but to be spiritually minded is life and peace.	For minding the things of the flesh, is death; but minding the things of the Spirit, is life and peace.	For the thinking of the flesh is death, yet the thinking of the Spirit [is] life and peace,
7	Because the carnal mind is enmity against God: for it is not subject to the law of God, neither indeed can be.	Because minding the things of the flesh, is enmity towards God: for it doth not subject itself to the law of God, because it is not possible.	because the thinking of the flesh is an enemy to God, for it is not subject to the law of God, because it is impossible.
8	So then they that are in the flesh cannot please God.	And they who are in the flesh cannot please God.	And those who are carnal are not able to please God.

Parallel Translations

	KJV	*Murdock*	*Magiera*
	ROMANS *Chapter 8*		
9	But ye are not in the flesh, but in the Spirit, if so be that the Spirit of God dwell in you. Now if any man have not the Spirit of Christ, he is none of his.	Ye, however, are not in the flesh, but in the Spirit; if the Spirit of God truly dwelleth in you. And if in any one there is not the Spirit of Messiah he is none of his.	Now you are not [walking] carnally, but spiritually, if truly the Spirit of God lives in you. But if anyone does not have the Spirit of Christ, this [one] is not his.
10	And if Christ be in you, the body is dead because of sin; but the Spirit is life because of righteousness.	But if Messiah is in you, the body is dead, in regard to sin; and the Spirit is alive in regard to righteousness.	Now if Christ [is] in you, the body is dead because of sin, but the Spirit is life because of uprightness.
11	But if the Spirit of him that raised up Jesus from the dead dwell in you, he that raised up Christ from the dead shall also quicken your mortal bodies by his Spirit that dwelleth in you.	And if the Spirit of him, who raised our Lord Jesus Messiah from the dead, dwelleth in you; he who raised our Lord Jesus Messiah from the dead, will also vivify your dead bodies, because of his Spirit that dwelleth in you.	And if the Spirit of that one who raised our Lord Jesus Christ from the dead lives in you, that one who raised Jesus Christ from the dead will also make alive your dead bodies because of his Spirit that lives in you.
12	Therefore, brethren, we are debtors, not to the flesh, to live after the flesh.	Now we are debtors, my Brethren, not to the flesh, that we should walk according to the flesh:	Now, my brothers, we are not debtors to the flesh that we should walk in the flesh.
13	For if ye live after the flesh, ye shall die: but if ye through the Spirit do mortify the deeds of the body, ye shall live.	(For if ye live according to the flesh, ye are to die. But if, by the Spirit, ye mortify the practices of the body, ye will live.	For if you live by the flesh, you are going to die. And if spiritually you put to death the habits of the body, you will have life.
14	For as many as are led by the Spirit of God, they are the sons of God.	For they who are led by the Spirit of God, they are the sons of God:)	For those who are led by the Spirit of God are the sons of God.
15	For ye have not received the spirit of bondage again to fear; but ye have received the Spirit of adoption, whereby we cry, Abba, Father.	For ye have not received the spirit of bondage, again to fear; but ye have received the Spirit of adoption, by which we cry, Father, our Father.	For you have not received the spirit of bondage again to fear, but you have received the Spirit of adoption by which we call, "Father, our Father."
16	The Spirit itself beareth witness with our spirit, that we are the children of God:	And this Spirit testifieth to our spirit, that we are the sons of God.	And the Spirit gives testimony to our spirit that we are the sons of God.
17	And if children, then heirs; heirs of God, and joint-heirs with Christ; if so be that we suffer with him, that we may be also glorified together.	And if sons, then heirs; heirs of God, and participators of the inheritance of Jesus Messiah: so that, if we suffer with him, we shall also be glorified with him.	And if [we are] sons, [then] also heirs, heirs of God and fellow-heirs of Jesus Christ, that if we suffer with him, we will also be glorified with him.
18	For I reckon that the sufferings of this present time are not worthy to be compared with the glory which shall be revealed in us.	For I reckon, that the sufferings of the present time, are not comparable with the glory which is to be developed in us.	For I consider that the sufferings of this time are not equal to the glory that will be revealed in us.
19	For the earnest expectation of the creature waiteth for the manifestation of the sons of God.	For the whole creation is hoping and waiting for the development of the sons of God.	For all the creation hopes and waits for the revelation of the sons of God.
20	For the creature was made subject to vanity, not willingly, but by reason of him who hath subjected the same in hope,	For the creation was subjected to vanity, not by its own choice, but because of him who subjected it,	For the creation was made subject to emptiness, not by its will, but because of him who subjected it, to the hope

	KJV	Murdock	Magiera
	ROMANS *Chapter 8*		
21	Because the creature itself also shall be delivered from the bondage of corruption into the glorious liberty of the children of God.	in the hope, that also the creation itself would be emancipated from the bondage of corruption, into the liberty of the glory of the sons of God.	that also the creation will be freed from the bondage of corruption to the freedoms of the glory of the sons of God.
22	For we know that the whole creation groaneth and travaileth in pain together until now.	For we know, that all the creatures are groaning and travailing in pain unto this day.	For we know that all created [things] groan and labor in childbirth until today.
23	And not only they, but ourselves also, which have the firstfruits of the Spirit, even we ourselves groan within ourselves, waiting for the adoption, to wit, the redemption of our body.	And not only they, but we also in whom are the first fruits of the Spirit, we groan within ourselves, and look anxiously for the adoption of sons, the redemption of our bodies.	And they are not alone, but we also who have the first[fruit] of the Spirit groan within ourselves and we wait for the adoption and the redemption of our bodies,
24	For we are saved by hope: but hope that is seen is not hope: for what a man seeth, why doth he yet hope for?	Because we live in hope. But hope that is seen, is not hope: for if we saw it, how should we hope for it?	because we live in hope. But hope that is seen is not hope. For if we see it, why do we wait for it?
25	But if we hope for that we see not, then do we with patience wait for it.	But if we hope for that which is not seen, we are in patient waiting.	But if we hope for something that is not seen, we continue with endurance.
26	Likewise the Spirit also helpeth our infirmities: for we know not what we should pray for as we ought: but the Spirit itself maketh intercession for us with groanings which cannot be uttered.	So also the Spirit aideth our weakness. For we know not what to pray for, in a proper manner; but the Spirit prayeth for us, with groans not expressible:	So also, the Spirit aids our weakness, for we do not know what is right to pray for. But the Spirit prays on our behalf with groans that are not describable.
27	And he that searcheth the hearts knoweth what is the mind of the Spirit, because he maketh intercession for the saints according to the will of God.	and the explorer of hearts, he knoweth what is the mind of the Spirit; because he prayeth for the saints, agreeably to the good pleasure of God.	Now he who searches the hearts knows what is the thinking of the Spirit that prays on behalf of the holy [ones] according to the will of God.
28	And we know that all things work together for good to them that love God, to them who are the called according to his purpose.	And we know that he aideth him in all things, for good, who love God; them whom he predestined to be called.	But we know that those who love God, he aids in everything for good, those whom he determined beforehand to be called [ones].
29	For whom he did foreknow, he also did predestinate to be conformed to the image of his Son, that he might be the firstborn among many brethren.	And he knew them, previously; and he sealed them with the likeness of the image of his Son; that He might be the first-born of many brothers.	And from the first he knew them and marked them out with the likeness of the image of his Son, that he would be the firstborn of many brothers.
30	Moreover whom he did predestinate, them he also called: and whom he called, them he also justified: and whom he justified, them he also glorified.	And those whom he previously sealed, them he called: and those whom he called, them he justified: and those whom he justified, them he glorified.	And those whom he marked out beforehand, he called, and those whom he called, he justified, and those whom he justified, he glorified.
31	What shall we then say to these things? If God be for us, who can be against us?	What then shall we say of these things? If God [is] for us; who [is] against us?	What then should we say about these [things]? If God [is] for us, who is against us?
32	He that spared not his own Son, but delivered him up for us all, how shall he not with him also freely give us all things?	And, if he spared not his Son, but gave him up for us all, how shall he not give us all things, with him?	And if he did not spare his Son, but delivered him up for all of us, how will he not give us everything with him?

ROMANS Chapter 8

	KJV	Murdock	Magiera
33	Who shall lay any thing to the charge of God's elect? It is God that justifieth.	Who will set himself against the chosen of God? It is God who justifieth.	Who can accuse the chosen [ones] of God? God justifies.
34	Who is he that condemneth? It is Christ that died, yea rather, that is risen again, who is even at the right hand of God, who also maketh intercession for us.	Who is it that condemneth? Messiah died, and arose, and is on the right hand of God, and maketh intercession for us.	Who condemns? Christ died and rose and is at the right hand of God and makes petition on our behalf.
35	Who shall separate us from the love of Christ? shall tribulation, or distress, or persecution, or famine, or nakedness, or peril, or sword?	What will sever me from the love of Messiah? Will affliction? or distress? or persecution? or famine? or nakedness? or peril? or the sword?	What will separate me from the love of Christ? [Is it] trial or distress or persecution or famine or nakedness or peril or sword?
36	As it is written, For thy sake we are killed all the day long; we are accounted as sheep for the slaughter.	As it is written: For thy sake, we die daily: and, we are accounted as sheep for the slaughter.	As it is written: BECAUSE OF YOU EVERY DAY WE ARE DYING AND WE ARE COUNTED AS LAMBS TO SLAUGHTER.
37	Nay, in all these things we are more than conquerors through him that loved us.	But in all these things we are victorious, by means of him who loved us.	On the contrary, in all these [things] we are victorious by way of him who loved us.
38	For I am persuaded, that neither death, nor life, nor angels, nor principalities, nor powers, nor things present, nor things to come,	For I am persuaded, that neither death, nor life, nor angels, nor principalities, nor powers, nor things present, nor things to come,	For I am persuaded that neither death nor life nor angels nor authorities nor powers nor those [things] present nor future
39	Nor height, nor depth, nor any other creature, shall be able to separate us from the love of God, which is in Christ Jesus our Lord.	nor height, nor depth, nor any other creature, will be able to sever me from the love of God, which is in our Lord Jesus Messiah.	nor height nor depth, neither any other created [thing] will be able to separate me from the love of God that is in our Lord Jesus Christ.

Chapter 9

	KJV	Murdock	Magiera
1	I say the truth in Christ, I lie not, my conscience also bearing me witness in the Holy Ghost,	I say the truth in Messiah, and do not misrepresent; and my conscience beareth me witness in the Holy Spirit;	I am speaking [with] truthfulness in Christ and I am not lying and my mind bears witness concerning me by the Holy Spirit
2	That I have great heaviness and continual sorrow in my heart.	that I have great sorrow, and the sadness of my heart is unceasing.	that I have great sorrow and the grief that is from my heart does not cease.
3	For I could wish that myself were accursed from Christ for my brethren, my kinsmen according to the flesh:	For I have prayed, that I myself might be accursed from Messiah, for my brethren and my kinsmen in the flesh:	For I have prayed that I myself would be cursed from Christ, instead of my brothers and my kinsmen who are in the flesh,
4	Who are Israelites; to whom pertaineth the adoption, and the glory, and the covenants, and the giving of the law, and the service of God, and the promises;	who are sons of Israel, to whom belonged the adoption of sons, and the glory, and the covenants, and the law, and the ministration, and the promises, and the fathers;	who are the sons of Israel, to whom belong the adoption and the glory and the covenants and the law and the service that is in it and the promises

Parallel Translations

	KJV	*Murdock*	*Magiera*
	ROMANS *Chapter 9*		
5	Whose are the fathers, and of whom as concerning the flesh Christ came, who is over all, God blessed for ever. Amen.	and from among whom, Messiah appeared in the flesh, who is God over all; to whom be praises and benediction, for ever and ever; Amen.	and the fathers and from whom Christ was seen in the flesh. He who is God who is over all, to him [be] our praises and our blessings forever and ever. Amen.
6	Not as though the word of God hath taken none effect. For they are not all Israel, which are of Israel:	Not, however, that the word of God hath actually failed. For all are not Israel, who are of Israel.	Now the word of God has indeed not failed, for not all who are from Israel are Israel.
7	Neither, because they are the seed of Abraham, are they all children: but, In Isaac shall thy seed be called.	Neither are they all sons, because they are of the seed of Abraham: for it was said, In Isaac shall thy seed be called.	Neither are all of them sons because [they are] from the seed of Abraham, because it was said: IN ISAAC THE SEED WILL BE CALLED TO YOU.
8	That is, They which are the children of the flesh, these are not the children of God: but the children of the promise are counted for the seed.	That is, it is not the children of the flesh, who are the children of God; but the children of the promise, are accounted for the seed.	Now this is [the truth]: the sons of the flesh are not the sons of God, but the sons of the promise are counted for the seed.
9	For this is the word of promise, At this time will I come, and Sara shall have a son.	For the word of promise was this: At that time will I come, and Sarah shall have a son.	For the word of promise is this: IN THIS SEASON I WILL COME AND SARAH WILL HAVE A SON.
10	And not only this; but when Rebecca also had conceived by one, even by our father Isaac;	Nor this only; but Rebecca also, when she had cohabited with one [man], our father Isaac,	And not this only, but also when Rebecca had intercourse with one [man], our father Isaac,
11	(For the children being not yet born, neither having done any good or evil, that the purpose of God according to election might stand, not of works, but of him that calleth;)	before her children were born, or: had done good or evil, the choice of God was predeclared; that it might stand, not of works, but of him who called.	before her sons were born and they had not done good or evil, the calling of God was already made known that it should not remain by works, but by way of him who called.
12	It was said unto her, The elder shall serve the younger.	For it was said: The elder shall be servant to the younger.	For it was said: THE ELDER WILL BE A SERVANT TO THE YOUNGER.
13	As it is written, Jacob have I loved, but Esau have I hated.	As it is written: Jacob have I loved, and Esau have I hated.	As it is written: JACOB I HAVE LOVED AND ESAU I HAVE HATED.
14	What shall we say then? Is there unrighteousness with God? God forbid.	What shall we say then? Is there iniquity with God? Far be it.	What then should we say? Is there wickedness with God? Let it not be so!
15	For he saith to Moses, I will have mercy on whom I will have mercy, and I will have compassion on whom I will have compassion.	Behold, to Moses also he said: I will have pity, on whom I will have pity; and I will be merciful, to whom I will be merciful.	Behold, to Moses he also said: I WILL HAVE MERCY ON WHOM I WILL HAVE MERCY AND I WILL PITY WHOM I PITY.
16	So then it is not of him that willeth, nor of him that runneth, but of God that sheweth mercy.	Therefore, it is not of him who is willing, nor of him who runneth, but of the merciful God.	Therefore [it is] not by the hands of him who wills, nor by the hands of him who strives, but by the hands of the merciful God.

Parallel Translations

ROMANS *Chapter 9*

	KJV	Murdock	Magiera
17	For the scripture saith unto Pharaoh, Even for this same purpose have I raised thee up, that I might shew my power in thee, and that my name might be declared throughout all the earth.	For in the scripture, he said to Pharaoh: For this very thing, have I raised thee up; that I might shew my power in thee, and that my name might be proclaimed in all the earth.	For he said in the scripture to Pharaoh: FOR THIS I HAVE APPOINTED YOU, THAT I MAY DEMONSTRATE MY POWER BY YOU AND THAT MY NAME MAY BE PREACHED IN THE WHOLE EARTH.
18	Therefore hath he mercy on whom he will have mercy, and whom he will he hardeneth.	Wherefore, he hath pity upon whom he pleaseth; and whom he pleaseth, he hardeneth.	Then with whom he wills, he has mercy, and with whom he wills, he deals harshly.
19	Thou wilt say then unto me, Why doth he yet find fault? For who hath resisted his will?	But, perhaps thou wilt say: Of what [then] doth he complain? For, who hath resisted his pleasure?	And perhaps you will say, "Why does he complain? For who can stand against his will?"
20	Nay but, O man, who art thou that repliest against God? Shall the thing formed say to him that formed it, Why hast thou made me thus?	Thou, thus! Who art thou? O man; that thou repliest against God! Shall the potter's vessel say to the former of it, Why hast thou formed me so?	Therefore, who are you, oh man, that you are giving an answer to God? Does [the thing] formed say to him who formed it, "Why have you so formed me?"
21	Hath not the potter power over the clay, of the same lump to make one vessel unto honour, and another unto dishonour?	Hath not the potter dominion over his clay out of the same mass to make vessels, one for honor, and another for dishonor?	Or does not the potter have authority over his clay, that from the [same] lump he makes utensils, one to honor and another to dishonor?
22	What if God, willing to shew his wrath, and to make his power known, endured with much longsuffering the vessels of wrath fitted to destruction:	And if God, being disposed to exhibit his wrath and to make known his power, in abundance of long-suffering, brought wrath upon the vessels of wrath which were complete for destruction;	Now if God wanted to display his wrath and to make known his power, he would have brought, in the abundance of his long-suffering, wrath on the utensils of wrath that were made for destruction
23	And that he might make known the riches of his glory on the vessels of mercy, which he had afore prepared unto glory,	and made his mercy flow forth upon the vessels of mercy, which were prepared by God for glory;	and poured out his mercy on the utensils of mercy that were prepared by God for glory,
24	Even us, whom he hath called, not of the Jews only, but also of the Gentiles?	namely, upon us who are called, not of the Jews only, but also of the Gentiles:	which we are, the called [ones], not only from the Judeans, but also from the Gentiles.
25	As he saith also in Osee, I will call them my people, which were not my people; and her beloved, which was not beloved.	As also he said in Hosea: I will call them my people, who were not my people; and will pity, whom I have not pitied:	As also he said in Hosea: I WILL CALL THOSE WHO WERE NOT MY PEOPLE, MY OWN PEOPLE, AND TO WHOM I HAVE NOT SHOWN MERCY, I WILL SHOW MERCY.
26	And it shall come to pass, that in the place where it was said unto them, Ye are not my people; there shall they be called the children of the living God.	For it shall be, that in the place where they were called: Not my people, there shall they be called: The children of the living God.	For it will be [that] in the place where they were called "NOT MY PEOPLE," there they will be called the sons of the living God.

	KJV	Murdock	Magiera
	ROMANS *Chapter 9*		
27	Esaias also crieth concerning Israel, Though the number of the children of Israel be as the sand of the sea, a remnant shall be saved:	And Isaiah proclaimed concerning the children of Israel: Though the number of the children of Israel should be as the sand on the sea, a remnant of them will live.	And Isaiah preached concerning the sons of Israel: EVEN THOUGH THE NUMBER OF THE SONS OF ISRAEL SHOULD BE AS THE SAND THAT IS IN THE SEA, [ONLY] A REMNANT OF THEM WILL BE SAVED.
28	For he will finish the work, and cut it short in righteousness: because a short work will the Lord make upon the earth.	He hath finished and cut short the matter: and the Lord will do it on the earth.	HE HAS DECIDED AND DETERMINED THE MATTER AND THE LORD WILL ACCOMPLISH IT ON THE EARTH.
29	And as Esaias said before, Except the Lord of Sabaoth had left us a seed, we had been as Sodoma, and been made like unto Gomorrha.	And according to what Isaiah had before said: If the Lord of hosts had not favored us with a residue, we had been as Sodom, and had been like Gomorrha.	And [it is] as what Isaiah previously said: IF THE LORD OF HOSTS HAD NOT LEFT US A SURVIVOR, WE WOULD HAVE BEEN AS SODOM AND WOULD HAVE RESEMBLED GOMORRAH.
30	What shall we say then? That the Gentiles, which followed not after righteousness, have attained to righteousness, even the righteousness which is of faith.	What shall we say then? That the Gentiles, who ran not after righteousness, have found righteousness, even the righteousness which is by faith:	What then should we say? The Gentiles who were not following after uprightness have obtained uprightness, even the uprightness that is from faith.
31	But Israel, which followed after the law of righteousness, hath not attained to the law of righteousness.	But Israel, who ran after the law of righteousness, hath not found the law of righteousness.	But Israel, who was following after the law of uprightness, did not obtain the law of uprightness.
32	Wherefore? Because they sought it not by faith, but as it were by the works of the law. For they stumbled at that stumblingstone;	And why? Because [they sought it], not by faith, but by the works of the law. For they stumbled at that stumbling-stone:	Because of what? Because it was not from faith, but from the works of the law, for they stumbled at the stone of stumbling.
33	As it is written, Behold, I lay in Sion a stumblingstone and rock of offence: and whosoever believeth on him shall not be ashamed.	As it is written, Behold, I lay in Zion a stumbling-stone, and a stone of offence: and he who believeth in him, shall not be ashamed.	As it is written: BEHOLD, I HAVE SET IN ZION A STONE OF STUMBLING AND A STONE OF OFFENSE AND HE WHO BELIEVES IN IT WILL NOT BE ASHAMED.
	Chapter 10		
1	Brethren, my heart's desire and prayer to God for Israel is, that they might be saved.	My Brethren, The desire of my heart, and my intercession with God for them, is, that they might have life.	My brothers, the desire of my heart and my request to God for them [is] that they would be saved.
2	For I bear them record that they have a zeal of God, but not according to knowledge.	For I bear them witness, that there is in them a zeal for God; but it is not according to knowledge.	For I testify about them that they have the zeal of God, but not with knowledge.

Parallel Translations

	KJV	*Murdock*	*Magiera*

ROMANS *Chapter 10*

Verse	KJV	Murdock	Magiera
3	For they being ignorant of God's righteousness, and going about to establish their own righteousness, have not submitted themselves unto the righteousness of God.	For they know not the righteousness of God, but seek to establish their own righteousness: and therefore they have not submitted themselves to the righteousness of God.	For they do not know the uprightness of God, but they seek to establish an uprightness of their own, and because of this, they are not subject to the uprightness of God.
4	For Christ is the end of the law for righteousness to every one that believeth.	For Messiah is the aim of the law, for righteousness, unto every one that believeth in him.	For Christ is the consummation of the law for uprightness to all who believe.
5	For Moses describeth the righteousness which is of the law, That the man which doeth those things shall live by them.	For Moses describeth the righteousness, which is by the law, thus: Whoever shall do these things, shall live by them.	For Moses so wrote [about] the uprightness that is by the law: HE WHO DOES THESE [THINGS] WILL LIVE BY THEM.
6	But the righteousness which is of faith speaketh on this wise, Say not in thine heart, Who shall ascend into heaven? (that is, to bring Christ down from above:)	But the righteousness which is by faith, saith thus: Thou shalt not say in thy heart, Who ascendeth to heaven, and bringeth Messiah down?	Now the uprightness that is by faith so says: DO NOT SAY IN YOUR HEART, "WHO HAS ASCENDED TO HEAVEN AND BROUGHT DOWN CHRIST?
7	Or, Who shall descend into the deep? (that is, to bring up Christ again from the dead.)	Or, Who descendeth to the abyss of the grave, and bringeth up Messiah from the place of the dead?	AND WHO HAS GONE DOWN TO THE DEPTH OF SHEOL AND BROUGHT UP CHRIST FROM THE DEAD?"
8	But what saith it? The word is nigh thee, even in thy mouth, and in thy heart: that is, the word of faith, which we preach;	But what saith it? The thing is near to thy mouth, and to thy heart: that is, the word of faith, which we proclaim.	BUT WHAT DOES IT SAY? THE ANSWER IS NEAR TO YOU, TO YOUR MOUTH AND TO YOUR HEART, which is the word of faith that we preach.
9	That if thou shalt confess with thy mouth the Lord Jesus, and shalt believe in thine heart that God hath raised him from the dead, thou shalt be saved.	And if thou shalt confess with thy mouth our Lord Jesus, and shalt believe with thy heart, that God hath raised him from the dead; thou shalt live.	And if you confess with your mouth our Lord Jesus and you believe in your heart that God raised him from the dead, you will have life.
10	For with the heart man believeth unto righteousness; and with the mouth confession is made unto salvation.	For the heart that believeth in him, is justified; and the mouth that confesseth him, is restored to life.	For the heart that believes in him is justified and the mouth that confesses him has life.
11	For the scripture saith, Whosoever believeth on him shall not be ashamed.	For the scripture saith: Every one that believeth in him, shall not be ashamed.	For the scripture said: ALL WHO BELIEVE IN HIM WILL NOT BE ASHAMED.
12	For there is no difference between the Jew and the Greek: for the same Lord over all is rich unto all that call upon him.	And in this, it discriminateth neither Jews nor Gentiles. For there is one Lord over them all, who is rich, towards every one that calleth on him.	And in this it does not discriminate either against Judeans or against the heathens, for the LORD of all of them is one who is abundant with all who call on him.
13	For whosoever shall call upon the name of the Lord shall be saved.	For every one that shall call on the name of the Lord, will have life.	For ALL WHO WILL CALL [ON] THE NAME OF THE LORD WILL HAVE LIFE.

Parallel Translations

	KJV	*Murdock*	*Magiera*
ROMANS *Chapter 10*			
14	How then shall they call on him in whom they have not believed? and how shall they believe in him of whom they have not heard? and how shall they hear without a preacher?	How then shall they call on him, in whom they have not believed? Or, how shall they believe in him, of whom they have not heard? Or, how shall they hear, without a preacher?	How then will they call who have not believed in him? Or how will they believe on him whom they have not heard? Or how will they hear without a preacher?
15	And how shall they preach, except they be sent? as it is written, How beautiful are the feet of them that preach the gospel of peace, and bring glad tidings of good things!	Or, how shall they preach, if they are not sent forth? As it is written: How beautiful are the feet of the heralds of peace, and of the heralds of good things?	Or how will they preach if they are not sent? As it is written: HOW BEAUTIFUL [ARE] THE FEET OF THE MESSENGERS OF PEACE AND OF THE MESSENGERS OF GOOD [THINGS].
16	But they have not all obeyed the gospel. For Esaias saith, Lord, who hath believed our report?	But all of them have not obeyed the proclamation of the gospel. (For, Isaiah said: My Lord, who hath believed our proclamation?)	But not all of them have obeyed the message of the gospel. For Isaiah said: MY LORD, WHO HAS BELIEVED OUR REPORT?
17	So then faith cometh by hearing, and hearing by the word of God.	Therefore, faith is from the hearing of the ear; and the hearing of the ear, is from the word of God.	Then, faith is by obedience and obedience by the word of God.
18	But I say, Have they not heard? Yes verily, their sound went into all the earth, and their words unto the ends of the world.	But I say: Have they not heard? And, lo, their proclamation hath gone out into all the earth; and their words to the ends of the world.	But I say, "Have they not heard?" And behold, THEIR REPORT HAS GONE OUT INTO ALL THE EARTH AND THEIR WORDS INTO THE OUTMOST BORDERS OF THE INHABITED WORLD.
19	But I say, Did not Israel know? First Moses saith, I will provoke you to jealousy by them that are no people, and by a foolish nation I will anger you.	But I say: Did not Israel know? First, Moses said, thus: I will awaken your emulation, by a people which is not a people; and by a disobedient people, I will provoke you.	But I say, "Did not Israel know?" First Moses so said: I WILL MAKE YOU JEALOUS BY A NATION THAT IS NOT A NATION, AND BY A NATION THAT IS DISOBEDIENT, I WILL ANGER YOU.
20	But Esaias is very bold, and saith, I was found of them that sought me not; I was made manifest unto them that asked not after me.	And Isaiah was bold, and said: I was seen by those who sought me not; and I was found by those who inquired not for me.	And Isaiah was bold and said: I WAS SEEN BY THOSE WHO DID NOT SEEK ME AND I WAS FOUND BY THOSE WHO DID NOT ASK FOR ME.
21	But to Israel he saith, All day long I have stretched forth my hands unto a disobedient and gainsaying people.	But to Israel, he said: All the day, have I stretched out my hands to a contentious and disobedient people.	But to Israel he said: I HAVE STRETCHED OUT MY HANDS ALL DAY TOWARD A NATION WHO IS CONTENTIOUS AND DISOBEDIENT.
Chapter 11			
1	I say then, Hath God cast away his people? God forbid. For I also am an Israelite, of the seed of Abraham, of the tribe of Benjamin.	But I say: Hath God cast off his people? Far be it. For I also am of Israel, of the seed of Abraham, of the tribe of Benjamin.	But I say, "Has God rejected his people?" Let it not be so! For I am also from Israel. I am from the seed of Abraham, from the tribe of Benjamin.

	KJV	Murdock	Magiera

ROMANS Chapter 11

Verse	KJV	Murdock	Magiera
2	God hath not cast away his people which he foreknew. Wot ye not what the scripture saith of Elias? how he maketh intercession to God against Israel, saying,	God hath not cast off those his people whom he before knew. Do ye not know, what, in the scripture of God, he said to Elijah? When he had complained to God against Israel, and said:	God has not rejected his people, who previously were known by him. Or do you not know what he said in the scripture about Elijah when he was complaining to God about Israel? And he said:
3	Lord, they have killed thy prophets, and digged down thine altars; and I am left alone, and they seek my life.	My Lord, they have slain thy prophets, and have thrown down thy altars; and I am left alone; and they seek my life.	MY LORD, THEY HAVE KILLED YOUR PROPHETS AND HAVE PULLED DOWN YOUR ALTARS AND I AM LEFT ALONE AND THEY SEEK MY LIFE.
4	But what saith the answer of God unto him? I have reserved to myself seven thousand men, who have not bowed the knee to the image of Baal.	And it was said to him, by revelation: Behold, I have reserved for myself seven thousand men, who have not bowed their knees, and have not worshipped Baal.	And it was said to him by revelation: BEHOLD, I HAVE RESERVED FOR MYSELF SEVEN THOUSAND MEN WHO HAVE NOT KNEELED ON THEIR KNEES AND HAVE NOT WORSHIPPED BAAL.
5	Even so then at this present time also there is a remnant according to the election of grace.	So also at the present time, a remnant is preserved, by the election of grace.	So also in this time, a remnant is left by the calling of grace.
6	And if by grace, then is it no more of works: otherwise grace is no more grace. But if it be of works, then is it no more grace: otherwise work is no more work.	But if by grace, it is not by works: otherwise, grace is not grace. And if by works, it is not by grace: Otherwise, work is not work.	Now if by grace, it is not by works, unless grace is not grace. And if by works, it is not by grace, unless work is not work.
7	What then? Israel hath not obtained that which he seeketh for; but the election hath obtained it, and the rest were blinded	What then? Israel did not obtain that which it sought: but the election obtained it; and the rest of them were blinded in their heart,	What then? Israel did not find what it was seeking, but the called [ones] found [it] and the rest of them were blinded in their heart[s].
8	(According as it is written, God hath given them the spirit of slumber, eyes that they should not see, and ears that they should not hear;) unto this day.	—(as it is written: God gave them a stupid spirit, and eyes to see not, and ears to hear not), unto this very day.	As it is written: GOD GAVE THEM A BLINDING SPIRIT AND EYES THAT THEY WOULD NOT EXAMINE AND EARS THAT THEY WOULD NOT HEAR UNTIL THIS VERY DAY.
9	And David saith, Let their table be made a snare, and a trap, and a stumblingblock, and a recompence unto them:	And again, David said: Let their table become a snare before them; and let their recompense be a stumbling block.	And David again said: THEIR TABLE WILL BE A SNARE BEFORE THEM AND THEIR REWARD [WILL BE] STUMBLING.
10	Let their eyes be darkened, that they may not see, and bow down their back alway.	Let their eyes be darkened, that they see not; and let their back, at all times, be bowed down.	THEIR EYES WILL BE DARKENED, SO THAT THEY WILL NOT SEE AND THEIR BACK WILL ALWAYS BE BOWED.
11	I say then, Have they stumbled that they should fall? God forbid: but rather through their fall salvation is come unto the Gentiles, for to provoke them to jealousy.	But I say: Have they so stumbled as to fall entirely? Far be it. Rather, by their stumbling, life hath come to the Gentiles, for [awakening] their jealousy.	Now I say, "Have they stumbled so as to fall?" Let it not be so! But in their stumbling, life has come to the Gentiles for their jealousy.

	KJV	*Murdock*	*Magiera*

ROMANS *Chapter 11*

	KJV	Murdock	Magiera
12	Now if the fall of them be the riches of the world, and the diminishing of them the riches of the Gentiles; how much more their fulness?	And if their stumbling was riches to the world, and their condemnation riches to the Gentiles; how much more their completeness?	And if their stumbling became riches for the world, and their loss, riches to the Gentiles, how much more then their fullness?
13	For I speak to you Gentiles, inasmuch as I am the apostle of the Gentiles, I magnify mine office:	But [it is] to you Gentiles, I am speaking: as I am a legate to the Gentiles, I honor my ministry;	But I speak to you Gentiles, I who am the apostle of the Gentiles. I am glorifying my ministry,
14	If by any means I may provoke to emulation them which are my flesh, and might save some of them.	if, perhaps, I may provoke emulation in the children of my flesh, and may vivify some of them.	so that perhaps I may provoke my kinsmen to jealousy and may give life to some of them.
15	For if the casting away of them be the reconciling of the world, what shall the receiving of them be, but life from the dead?	For if the rejection of them, was a reconciliation of the world; what will their conversion be, but life from the dead?	For if their rejection was reconciliation to the world, then how much more their return, but life that is from the dead?
16	For if the firstfruit be holy, the lump is also holy: and if the root be holy, so are the branches.	For, if the first-fruits [are] holy, then the mass [is] also: and if the root is holy, then also the branches.	Now if the original part [is] holy, the thing formed [is holy] also. And if the root is holy, the branches [are] also.
17	And if some of the branches be broken off, and thou, being a wild olive tree, wert graffed in among them, and with them partakest of the root and fatness of the olive tree;	And if some of the branches were plucked off; and thou, an olive from the desert, wast in-grafted in their place, and hast become a participator of the root and fatness of the olive-tree;	And if some branches were broken off and you who are a wild olive [tree] were grafted into their places and became a sharer of the root and of the fatness of the olive [tree],
18	Boast not against the branches. But if thou boast, thou bearest not the root, but the root thee.	do not glory over the branches. For if thou gloriest, thou sustainest not the root, but the root sustaineth thee.	do not pride yourself about the branches. Now if you pride yourself, you are not bearing the root, but the root bears you.
19	Thou wilt say then, The branches were broken off, that I might be graffed in.	And shouldst thou say, The branches were plucked off, that I might be grafted into their place.	And it may be [that] you should say of the branches that were broken off, "I will be grafted in their places."
20	Well; because of unbelief they were broken off, and thou standest by faith. Be not highminded, but fear:	Very true. They were plucked off, because they believed not; and thou standest by faith. Be not exalted in thy mind, but fear.	These [things] are good. They were broken off because they did not believe, but you stand by faith. Do not be elevated in your mind, but have reverence,
21	For if God spared not the natural branches, take heed lest he also spare not thee.	For if God spared not the natural branches, perhaps he will not spare you.	for if God did not spare the natural branches, perhaps he will also not spare you.
22	Behold therefore the goodness and severity of God: on them which fell, severity; but toward thee, goodness, if thou continue in his goodness: otherwise thou also shalt be cut off.	Behold now the benignity and the severity of God: on them who fell, severity; but on thee, benignity, if thou continuest in that benignity; and if not, thou also wilt be plucked off.	See then the gentleness and the harshness of God. On those who fell, harshness. But on you, gentleness, if you remain in the gentleness, and if not, you will also be broken off.
23	And they also, if they abide not still in unbelief, shall be graffed in: for God is able to graff them in again.	And they, if they do not continue in their destitution of faith, even they will be grafted in; for God is able to graft them in again.	And those, if they do not remain in their lack of faith, will also be grafted in, for God is able to graft them in again.

	KJV	*Murdock*	*Magiera*

ROMANS *Chapter 11*

	KJV	Murdock	Magiera
24	For if thou wert cut out of the olive tree which is wild by nature, and wert graffed contrary to nature into a good olive tree: how much more shall these, which be the natural branches, be graffed into their own olive tree?	For if thou wast plucked from the wild olive-tree, which was natural to thee, and wast grafted, contrary to thy nature, into a good olive-tree; how much more may they be grafted into their natural olive-tree?	For if you, who are from the olive [tree] that was wild by your nature, were cut off and were grafted contrary to your nature in the good olive [tree], then how much more those, if they be grafted in their natural olive [tree]?
25	For I would not, brethren, that ye should be ignorant of this mystery, lest ye should be wise in your own conceits; that blindness in part is happened to Israel, until the fulness of the Gentiles be come in.	And that ye, my brethren, may not be wise in your own apprehension, I wish you to know this mystery, that blindness of heart hath in some measure befallen Israel, until the fullness of the Gentiles shall come in:	For I want you to know this mystery, my brothers, so that you will not be wise in your own mind, that blindness of the heart in part has happened to Israel until the fullness of the Gentiles should come in.
26	And so all Israel shall be saved: as it is written, There shall come out of Sion the Deliverer, and shall turn away ungodliness from Jacob:	and then, will all Israel live. As it is written: A deliverer will come from Zion, and will turn away iniquity from Jacob.	And then all Israel will have life, as it is written: FROM ZION A DELIVERER WILL COME AND TURN WICKEDNESS FROM JACOB.
27	For this is my covenant unto them, when I shall take away their sins.	And then will they have the covenant that proceedeth from me, when I shall have forgiven their sins.	AND THEN THEY WILL HAVE THE COVENANT THAT IS FROM ME, WHEN I FORGIVE THEM THEIR SINS.
28	As concerning the gospel, they are enemies for your sakes: but as touching the election, they are beloved for the fathers' sakes.	Now, in the gospel, they are enemies for your sake; but in the election, they are beloved for the fathers' sake.	Now in the gospel, they are enemies because of you, and in the calling, they are beloved because of the fathers,
29	For the gifts and calling of God are without repentance.	For God is not changeable in his free gift and in his calling.	for God does not repent in his gift and in his calling.
30	For as ye in times past have not believed God, yet have now obtained mercy through their unbelief:	For as ye too were formerly disobedient to God, and have now obtained mercy, because of their disobedience;	For as you were also disobedient to God previously and now have obtained favor because of their disobedience,
31	Even so have these also now not believed, that through your mercy they also may obtain mercy.	so also are they now disobedient to the mercy, which is upon you, that there may be mercy on them likewise.	so also these are disobedient now to the mercies that are on you, that mercies may also be on them.
32	For God hath concluded them all in unbelief, that he might have mercy upon all.	For God hath shut up all men in disobedience, that upon all men he might have mercy.	For God has confined everyone in disobedience, so that he could have mercy on everyone.
33	O the depth of the riches both of the wisdom and knowledge of God! how unsearchable are his judgments, and his ways past finding out!	O the depth of the riches, and the wisdom, and the knowledge of God! For man hath not searched out his judgments; and his ways are inscrutable.	Oh the depth of the riches and wisdom and knowledge of God,because no one has explored his judgments and his ways are untraceable!
34	For who hath known the mind of the Lord? or who hath been his counsellor?	For who hath known the mind of the Lord? Or who hath been a counsellor to him?	FOR WHO KNOWS THE MIND OF THE LORD? OR WHO IS A COUNSELOR TO HIM?
35	Or who hath first given to him, and it shall be recompensed unto him again?	Or who hath first given to him, and then received from him?	And WHO FIRST GIVES TO HIM AND THEN RECEIVES FROM HIM?

Parallel Translations

	KJV	*Murdock*	*Magiera*
	ROMANS *Chapter 11*		
36	For of him, and through him, and to him, are all things: to whom be glory for ever. Amen.	Because, all is from him, and all by him, and all through him: to whom be praises and benedictions, for ever and ever: Amen.	Because all [is] from him, and all [is] by him, and all [is] by his hand, to whom [be] our praises and our blessings forever and ever. Amen.
	Chapter 12		
1	I beseech you therefore, brethren, by the mercies of God, that ye present your bodies a living sacrifice, holy, acceptable unto God, which is your reasonable service.	I beseech you, therefore, my brethren, by the mercies of God, that ye present your bodies a living sacrifice, holy and acceptable to God, by a rational service [of him].	Therefore, I beg you, my brothers, by the mercies of God, to present your bodies a living and holy and acceptable sacrifice to God in reasonable service.
2	And be not conformed to this world: but be ye transformed by the renewing of your mind, that ye may prove what is that good, and acceptable, and perfect, will of God.	And be not conformed to this world; but be ye transformed, by the renovation of your minds: and discern ye what is the good and acceptable and perfect pleasure of God.	And do not imitate this world, but be turned the other way by the renewal of your minds and distinguish what is the good and acceptable and perfect will of God.
3	For I say, through the grace given unto me, to every man that is among you, not to think of himself more highly than he ought to think; but to think soberly, according as God hath dealt to every man the measure of faith.	And, by the grace given to me, I say to you all: Do not carry thoughts, beyond what ye ought to think; but think with modesty, as God hath distributed to each one his measure of faith.	Now I say by the grace that was given to me for all of you, you should not think outside of what is right to think, but everyone should think soberly, according to faith in the measure God has distributed to him.
4	For as we have many members in one body, and all members have not the same office:	For as we [severally] have many members in one body, and all those members have not the same functions;	For as in one body we have many members and all members do not have one function,
5	So we, being many, are one body in Christ, and every one members one of another.	so also we, who are [collectively] many persons, are one body in Messiah, and are naturally members of each other.	so also we who are many are one body in Christ and each one of us are members of one another.
6	Having then gifts differing according to the grace that is given to us, whether prophecy, let us prophesy according to the proportion of faith;	But we have different gifts, according to the grace given to us. There is that of prophecy, according to the measure of his faith.	But we have various gifts according to the grace that is given to us. There is [giving] of prophecy according to the measure of his faith,
7	Or ministry, let us wait on our ministering: or he that teacheth, on teaching;	And there is that of ministration, possessed by one in his ministry. And there is that of a teacher, in his teaching.	and there is [giving] of ministering one has in his ministering, and there is [giving] of a teacher in his teaching,
8	Or he that exhorteth, on exhortation: he that giveth, let him do it with simplicity; he that ruleth, with diligence; he that sheweth mercy, with cheerfulness.	And there is that of a consoler, in his consoling: And that of a giver, with simplicity: And that of a presider, with dexterity: And of a sympathizer, with cheerfulness.	and there is [giving] of a comforter in his comforting, and of one who gives, with simplicity, and of one who presides, with diligence, and of one who is merciful, with cheerfulness.
9	Let love be without dissimulation. Abhor that which is evil; cleave to that which is good.	Let not your love be guileful: but be haters of evil things, and adherers to good things.	And let not your love be deceitful, but hate evil and adhere to good.

Parallel Translations

ROMANS *Chapter 12*

	KJV	*Murdock*	*Magiera*
10	Be kindly affectioned one to another with brotherly love; in honour preferring one another;	Be affectionate to your brethren: and love one another. Be foremost in honoring one another.	Be compassionate to your brothers and love one another. Prefer one another in honor.
11	Not slothful in business; fervent in spirit; serving the Lord;	Be active; and not slothful. Be fervent in spirit. Be laborers for our Lord.	Be diligent and not lazy. Be fervent in spirit. Labor for your Lord.
12	Rejoicing in hope; patient in tribulation; continuing instant in prayer;	Be joyful in your hope. Be patient under your afflictions. Be persevering in prayer.	Rejoice in your hope. Endure your trials. Be steadfast in prayer.
13	Distributing to the necessity of saints; given to hospitality.	Be communicators to the wants of the saints. Be kind to strangers.	Share toward the need of the holy [ones]. Be compassionate [to] strangers.
14	Bless them which persecute you: bless, and curse not.	Bless your persecutors: bless, and curse not.	Bless your persecutors. Bless and do not curse.
15	Rejoice with them that do rejoice, and weep with them that weep.	Rejoice with them who rejoice: and weep with them who weep.	Rejoice with [those] who are rejoicing and weep with [those] who are weeping.
16	Be of the same mind one toward another. Mind not high things, but condescend to men of low estate. Be not wise in your own conceits.	What estimation ye make of yourselves, [make] also of your brethren. And indulge not high thoughts; but unite yourselves with the lowly minded. And be not wise in your own estimation.	And what you think about yourself, also [think] about your brothers. And do not think [with] a proud mind, but associate with those who are meek. And do not be wise in your own mind.
17	Recompense to no man evil for evil. Provide things honest in the sight of all men.	And repay to no man evil for evil: but let it be your study to do good before all men.	And do not repay anyone evil [things] for evil [things], but be diligent to do good [things] before all men.
18	If it be possible, as much as lieth in you, live peaceably with all men.	And if possible, so far as it dependeth on you, live in peace with every man.	And if it is possible, according to what is in you, be at peace with everyone.
19	Dearly beloved, avenge not yourselves, but rather give place unto wrath: for it is written, Vengeance is mine; I will repay, saith the Lord.	And be ye not avengers of yourselves, my beloved: but give place to wrath. For it is written: If thou dost not execute judgment for thyself, I will execute judgment for thee, saith God.	And do not avenge yourselves, my beloved, but give place to anger, for it is written: IF YOU WILL NOT PERFORM JUDGMENT FOR YOURSELF, I WILL PERFORM YOUR JUDGMENT, says God.
20	Therefore if thine enemy hunger, feed him; if he thirst, give him drink: for in so doing thou shalt heap coals of fire on his head.	And if thy adversary be hungry, feed him: and if he be thirsty, give him drink. For if thou doest these things to him, thou wilt heap coals of fire on his head.	And IF YOUR ENEMY IS HUNGRY, FEED HIM AND IF HE IS THIRSTY, GIVE HIM DRINK AND IF YOU DO THESE [THINGS] TO HIM, YOU WILL HEAP COALS OF FIRE ON HIS HEAD.
21	Be not overcome of evil, but overcome evil with good.	Be ye not overcome by evil; but overcome evil with good.	Do not let evil [things] overcome you, but overcome evil [things] with good [things].

Parallel Translations

ROMANS *Chapter 13*

	KJV	*Murdock*	*Magiera*
1	Let every soul be subject unto the higher powers. For there is no power but of God: the powers that be are ordained of God.	Let every soul be subject to the authorities of magistracy. For there is no authority which is not from God: and the authorities which exist, are established by God.	Every one should be subject to greater authorities, for there is no authority that is not from God and these who are authorities were ordained by God.
2	Whosoever therefore resisteth the power, resisteth the ordinance of God: and they that resist shall receive to themselves damnation.	He therefore who opposeth the authority, opposeth the establishment of God; and they who oppose them, shall receive judgment.	Therefore, he who stands against an authority stands against an ordinance of God and those who stand against them will receive judgment.
3	For rulers are not a terror to good works, but to the evil. Wilt thou then not be afraid of the power? do that which is good, and thou shalt have praise of the same:	For judges are not a terror to good deeds, but to evil deeds. Wouldst thou then not be afraid of the authority? Do good, and thou shalt have praise from it.	For judges are not fearful for good works, but for evil. So do you want to not be afraid of an authority? Do good and you will have praise from him.
4	For he is the minister of God to thee for good. But if thou do that which is evil, be afraid; for he beareth not the sword in vain: for he is the minister of God, a revenger to execute wrath upon him that doeth evil.	For he is the minister of God; but it is to thee for good. But if thou doest evil, be afraid; for he is not girded with the sword in vain; for he is a minister of God, and an avenger of wrath to them that do evil things.	For he is a minister of God, but to you for good. And if you do evil [things], fear, for he is not girded with the sword in vain. For he is a minister of God and an avenger of wrath to those who do evil [things].
5	Wherefore ye must needs be subject, not only for wrath, but also for conscience sake.	And therefore, it is necessary for us to be obedient, not only on account of wrath, but likewise on account of our consciences.	And because of this, it is necessary for us to be subject, not only because of wrath, but also because of our conscience.
6	For this cause pay ye tribute also: for they are God's ministers, attending continually upon this very thing.	For this cause also ye pay tribute money; for they are the ministers of God, established for these same objects.	Because of this, you should also give tribute, for they are the ministers of God, who for these same [things] are established.
7	Render therefore to all their dues: tribute to whom tribute is due; custom to whom custom; fear to whom fear; honour to whom honour.	Render therefore to every one, as is due to him; tribute-money, to whom tribute-money; and excise, to whom excise; and fear, to whom fear; and honor, to whom honor.	Therefore, repay everyone as is owed to him, to whom tribute [is due], tribute, and to whom tax [is due], tax, and to whom reverence [is due], reverence, and to whom honor [is due], honor.
8	Owe no man any thing, but to love one another: for he that loveth another hath fulfilled the law.	And owe nothing to any one; but to love one another. For he that loveth his neighbor, hath fulfilled the law.	And do not owe anyone anything, but to love each other. For he who loves his neighbor has fulfilled the law.
9	For this, Thou shalt not commit adultery, Thou shalt not kill, Thou shalt not steal, Thou shalt not bear false witness, Thou shalt not covet; and if there be any other commandment, it is briefly comprehended in this saying, namely, Thou shalt love thy neighbor as thyself.	For this likewise, which it saith: Thou shalt not kill; nor commit adultery; nor steal; nor covet; and if there is any other commandment, it is completed in this sentence: Thou shalt love thy neighbor as thyself.	For this [is] also what is said: DO NOT COMMIT ADULTERY AND DO NOT KILL AND DO NOT STEAL AND DO NOT LUST, and if there is another commandment, it is fulfilled in this saying: LOVE YOUR NEIGHBOR AS YOURSELF.

ROMANS *Chapter 13*

	KJV	*Murdock*	*Magiera*
10	Love worketh no ill to his neighbour: therefore love is the fulfilling of the law.	Love doeth no evil to one's neighbor; because love is the fulfillment of the law.	Love does not do evil [things] to his neighbor, because love is the fulfillment of the law.
11	And that, knowing the time, that now it is high time to awake out of sleep: for now is our salvation nearer than when we believed.	And this also know ye, that it is the time and the hour, that we should henceforth be awake from our sleep. For now our life hath come nearer to us, than when we believed.	And also know this, that it is the time and the hour that from now on we should be awakened from our sleep. For now our life has come nearer to us than when we believed.
12	The night is far spent, the day is at hand: let us therefore cast off the works of darkness, and let us put on the armour of light.	The night now passeth away, and the day draweth near. Let us therefore cast from us the works of darkness; and let us put on the armor of light.	Then the night is passed and the day is near. So we should lay aside from us the works of darkness and we should put on the armor of light.
13	Let us walk honestly, as in the day; not in rioting and drunkenness, not in chambering and wantonness, not in strife and envying.	And let us walk decorously, as in daylight; not in merriment, nor in drunkenness, nor in impurity of the bed, nor in envy and strife.	And we should walk in [this] manner, as in the day, not in reveling and not in drunkenness and not in a defiled bed and not in envy and in strife.
14	But put ye on the Lord Jesus Christ, and make not provision for the flesh, to fulfil the lusts thereof.	But clothe yourselves with our Lord Jesus Messiah: and be not thoughtful about your flesh, for the indulgence of appetites.	But put on our Lord Jesus Christ and do not have regard for the desires that are in your flesh.

Chapter 14

	KJV	*Murdock*	*Magiera*
1	Him that is weak in the faith receive ye, but not to doubtful disputations.	To him who is feeble in the faith, reach forth the hand. And be not divided in your thoughts.	Now to him who is weak in faith, give a hand, and do not have doubt in your reasonings.
2	For one believeth that he may eat all things: another, who is weak, eateth herbs.	For one man believeth, that he may eat every thing: and he that is feeble, eateth herbs.	For there is one who believes that he may eat everything, yet he who is weak eats herbs.
3	Let not him that eateth despise him that eateth not; and let not him which eateth not judge him that eateth: for God hath received him.	And he that eateth, should not despise him that eateth not; and he that eateth not, should not judge him that eateth, for God hath received him.	Now that one who eats should not treat with contempt him who does not eat, and that one who does not eat should not judge him who eats, for God has received him.
4	Who art thou that judgest another man's servant? to his own master he standeth or falleth. Yea, he shall be holden up: for God is able to make him stand.	Who art thou, that thou judgest a servant not thine; and who, if he standeth, he standeth to his Lord; and if he falleth, he falleth to his Lord? But he will assuredly stand; for his Lord hath power to establish him.	Who are you that you judge a servant who is not your own, who, if he stands, stands before his lord and if he falls, falls before his lord? But he will indeed stand, for it will be by the hands of his lord that he will be established.
5	One man esteemeth one day above another: another esteemeth every day alike. Let every man be fully persuaded in his own mind.	One man discriminateth between days; and another judgeth all days alike. But let every one be sure, in regard to his knowledge.	There is one who judges a day from a day and there is one who judges all days. But everyone should be assured in his own mind.

ROMANS *Chapter 14*

	KJV	Murdock	Magiera
6	He that regardeth the day, regardeth it unto the Lord; and he that regardeth not the day, to the Lord he doth not regard it. He that eateth, eateth to the Lord, for he giveth God thanks; and he that eateth not, to the Lord he eateth not, and giveth God thanks.	He that esteemeth a day, esteemeth [it] for his Lord: and he that esteemeth not a day, for his Lord, he doth not esteem [it.] And he that eateth, eateth to his Lord, and giveth thanks to God: and he that eateth not, to his Lord he eateth not, and giveth thanks to God.	He who is mindful of a day is mindful [of it] before his Lord. And everyone who is not mindful of a day is not mindful [of it] before his Lord. And whoever eats, eats before his Lord and thanks God. And he who does not eat, does not eat before his Lord and thanks God.
7	For none of us liveth to himself, and no man dieth to himself.	For there is not one of us, who liveth for himself: and there is not one, who dieth for himself.	For there is not one of us who lives for himself and there is not one who dies for himself,
8	For whether we live, we live unto the Lord; and whether we die, we die unto the Lord: whether we live therefore, or die, we are the Lord's.	Because, if we live, to our Lord it is we live; or if we die, to our Lord it is we die. Whether we live, therefore, or whether we die, we are our Lord's.	because if we live, we live for our Lord and if we die, we die for our Lord. And therefore, whether we live or whether we die, we belong to our Lord.
9	For to this end Christ both died, and rose, and revived, that he might be Lord both of the dead and living.	Moreover, for this cause Messiah died, and revived, and arose; that he might be Lord of the dead and of the living.	Because of this, Christ also died and is alive and is risen that he would be the LORD for the dead and for the living.
10	But why dost thou judge thy brother? or why dost thou set at nought thy brother? for we shall all stand before the judgment seat of Christ.	But thou, why dost thou judge thy brother? or, why dost thou despise thy brother? For we must all stand before the judgment seat of Messiah,	Now why do you judge your brother? Or why do you also treat your brother with contempt? For all of us are going to stand before the judgment seat of Christ,
11	For it is written, As I live, saith the Lord, every knee shall bow to me, and every tongue shall confess to God.	as it is written: As I live, saith the Lord, to me every knee shall bow; and to me every tongue shall give praise.	as it is written: I LIVE, says the LORD, EVERY KNEE WILL BOW TO ME AND EVERY TONGUE WILL CONFESS ME.
12	So then every one of us shall give account of himself to God.	So then, every one of us must give account of himself to God.	So then, every one of us will give an answer for himself to God.
13	Let us not therefore judge one another any more: but judge this rather, that no man put a stumblingblock or an occasion to fall in his brother's way.	Henceforth, judge ye not one another; but rather, judge ye this, that thou erect not a stumbling-block for thy brother.	So then, we should not judge each other, but rather determine this more, that you will not place a stumbling block before your brother.
14	I know, and am persuaded by the Lord Jesus, that there is nothing unclean of itself: but to him that esteemeth any thing to be unclean, to him it is unclean.	I know indeed, and am persuaded by the Lord Jesus, that there is nothing which is unclean in itself; but to him who thinketh any thing to be unclean, to him only it is defiled.	For I know and am persuaded in the LORD Jesus that there is not anything that is defiled of itself. But to him who thinks that something is unclean, to him alone it is unclean.
15	But if thy brother be grieved with thy meat, now walkest thou not charitably. Destroy not him with thy meat, for whom Christ died.	But if thou grievest thy brother, because of food, thou walkest not in love. On account of food, destroy not him for whom Messiah died.	And if you grieve your brother because of food, you are not walking in love. Do not hurt him by your food for whose sake Christ died.
16	Let not then your good be evil spoken of:	And let not our good thing be matter of reproach.	And let not our good be defamed.

Parallel Translations

	KJV	Murdock	Magiera
	ROMANS	*Chapter 14*	
17	For the kingdom of God is not meat and drink; but righteousness, and peace, and joy in the Holy Ghost.	For the kingdom of God, is not food and drink; but is righteousness, and peace, and joy in the Holy Spirit.	For the kingdom of God is not food and drink, but uprightness and peace and joy by the Holy Spirit.
18	For he that in these things serveth Christ is acceptable to God, and approved of men.	For he who is in these things a servant of Messiah, is pleasing to God, and approved before men.	For he who serves Christ in these [things] pleases God and stands approved [before] men.
19	Let us therefore follow after the things which make for peace, and things wherewith one may edify another.	Now let us strive after peace, and after the edification of one another.	Now we should follow after peace and after edifying each other.
20	For meat destroy not the work of God. All things indeed are pure; but it is evil for that man who eateth with offence.	And let us not, on account of food, destroy the work of God. For every thing is, [indeed,] pure; yet it is evil, to the man who eateth with stumbling.	And we should not depart from the works of God because of food. For everything is pure, but it is wrong for a man who eats with stumbling.
21	It is good neither to eat flesh, nor to drink wine, nor any thing whereby thy brother stumbleth, or is offended, or is made weak.	It is proper, that we neither eat flesh, nor drink wine, nor [do] any thing, whereby our brother is stumbled.	It is good that we should neither eat flesh nor drink wine nor [do] anything by which our brother stumbles.
22	Hast thou faith? have it to thyself before God. Happy is he that condemneth not himself in that thing which he alloweth.	Thou art one in whom there is faith; keep it to thyself, before God. Blessed is he, who doth not condemn himself, in that thing which he alloweth.	You who have faith, keep it in yourself before God. Blessed is he who does not judge himself in what he distinguishes.
23	And he that doubteth is damned if he eat, because he eateth not of faith: for whatsoever is not of faith is sin.	For he who eateth and doubteth, is condemned; because [he eateth] not in faith. For every thing which is not of faith, is sin.	For he who doubts and eats is condemned, because it is not in faith, for everything that is not from faith is sin.
	Chapter 15		
1	We then that are strong ought to bear the infirmities of the weak, and not to please ourselves.	We then who are strong, ought to bear the infirmity of the weak, and not to please ourselves.	Therefore, we, the strong [ones], ought to bear the infirmity of the weak [ones] and not to please ourselves.
2	Let every one of us please his neighbour for his good to edification.	But each of us should please his neighbor, in good things, as conducive to edification.	But, each of us should please his neighbor in good [things] for edification,
3	For even Christ pleased not himself; but, as it is written, The reproaches of them that reproached thee fell on me.	Because Messiah also did not please himself; but, as it is written: The reviling of thy revilers fell upon me.	because Christ also did not please himself. But as it is written: THE REVILING OF YOUR REVILERS HAS FALLEN ON ME.
4	For whatsoever things were written aforetime were written for our learning, that we through patience and comfort of the scriptures might have hope.	For every thing written of old, was written for our instruction; that we, by patience and by the consolation of the scriptures, might possess hope.	For everything that was previously written is for our instruction. It was written so that by the patience and by the comfort of the scriptures we would have hope.
5	Now the God of patience and consolation grant you to be likeminded one toward another according to Christ Jesus:	And may the God of patience and of consolation, grant to you, to think in harmony one with another, in Jesus Messiah;	Now the God of patience and of comfort grant you to think in harmony with each other, in Jesus Christ,

ROMANS *Chapter 15*

	KJV	Murdock	Magiera
6	That ye may with one mind and one mouth glorify God, even the Father of our Lord Jesus Christ.	so that with one mind and one mouth, ye may glorify God, the Father of our Lord Jesus Messiah.	that with one mind and with one mouth you may praise God, the Father of our Lord Jesus Christ.
7	Wherefore receive ye one another, as Christ also received us to the glory of God.	Wherefore, receive ye and bear up one another, as also Messiah received you, to the glory of God.	Because of this, draw near to and bear up each other, as also Christ has drawn near to you for the glory of God.
8	Now I say that Jesus Christ was a minister of the circumcision for the truth of God, to confirm the promises made unto the fathers:	Now I say, that Jesus Messiah ministered to the circumcision, in behalf of the truth of God, in order to confirm the promise [made] to the fathers;	Now I say that Jesus Christ served the circumcision on behalf of the truth of God to confirm the promise of the fathers
9	And that the Gentiles might glorify God for his mercy; as it is written, For this cause I will confess to thee among the Gentiles, and sing unto thy name.	and that the Gentiles might glorify God for his mercies upon them, as it is written: I will confess to thee among the Gentiles, and to thy name will I sing psalms.	and [that] the Gentiles would glorify God for the mercies that came on them. As it is written: I WILL CONFESS YOU AMONG THE GENTILES AND I WILL SING TO YOUR NAME.
10	And again he saith, Rejoice, ye Gentiles, with his people.	And again he said: Rejoice, ye Gentiles, with his people.	And again he said: REJOICE, GENTILES, WITH HIS PEOPLE.
11	And again, Praise the Lord, all ye Gentiles; and laud him, all ye people.	And again he said: Praise the Lord, all ye Gentiles; [and] laud him, all ye nations.	And again he said: PRAISE THE LORD, ALL YOU GENTILES. PRAISE HIM, ALL PEOPLE.
12	And again, Esaias saith, There shall be a root of Jesse, and he that shall rise to reign over the Gentiles; in him shall the Gentiles trust.	And again Isaiah said: There will be a root of Jesse; and he that shall arise, will be a prince for the Gentiles; and in him will the Gentiles hope.	And again Isaiah said: THERE WILL BE A ROOT TO JESSE AND HE WHO WILL RISE UP WILL BE A RULER TO THE GENTILES AND ON HIM THE GENTILES WILL HOPE.
13	Now the God of hope fill you with all joy and peace in believing, that ye may abound in hope, through the power of the Holy Ghost.	Now may the God of hope fill you with all joy and peace, by faith; that ye may abound in his hope, by the power of the Holy Spirit.	Now the God of hope fill you with all joy and peace in faith, so that you may abound in his hope by the power of the Holy Spirit.
14	And I myself also am persuaded of you, my brethren, that ye also are full of goodness, filled with all knowledge, able also to admonish one another.	Now I am persuaded, my Brethren, even I, concerning you; that ye too are full of goodness, and are replenished with all knowledge, and are able also to instruct others.	Now I also am persuaded concerning you, my brothers, that you are also full of goodness and are completed with all knowledge and are also able to admonish others.
15	Nevertheless, brethren, I have written the more boldly unto you in some sort, as putting you in mind, because of the grace that is given to me of God,	Yet I have written rather boldly to you, my Brethren, that I might put you in remembrance; because of the grace which is given to me by God,	Now I have written somewhat boldly to you, my brothers, to remind you of the grace that was given to me from God,
16	That I should be the minister of Jesus Christ to the Gentiles, ministering the gospel of God, that the offering up of the Gentiles might be acceptable, being sanctified by the Holy Ghost.	that I should be a minister of Jesus Messiah among the Gentiles, and should subserve the gospel of God, that the oblation of the Gentiles might be acceptable, and be sanctified by the Holy Spirit.	that I should be a minister to Jesus Christ among the Gentiles and I should labor for the gospel of God, so that the offering of the Gentiles would be acceptable and made holy by the Holy Spirit.

ROMANS Chapter 15

	KJV	Murdock	Magiera
17	I have therefore whereof I may glory through Jesus Christ in those things which pertain to God.	I have therefore a glorying in Jesus Messiah, before God.	Therefore, I have boasting in Jesus Christ to God.
18	For I will not dare to speak of any of those things which Christ hath not wrought by me, to make the Gentiles obedient, by word and deed,	Yet I presume not to speak of any thing [done] for the obedience of the Gentiles, which Messiah hath not wrought by me, in word and in deeds,	For I do not presume to speak of anything that Christ has not accomplished by my hands for the obedience of the Gentiles, in word and in deeds,
19	Through mighty signs and wonders, by the power of the Spirit of God; so that from Jerusalem, and round about unto Illyricum, I have fully preached the gospel of Christ.	by the power of signs and wonders, and by the power of the Holy Spirit; so that from Jerusalem I have made a circuit quite to Illyricum, and have fulfilled the announcement of the Messiah;	by the power of signs and of wonders and by the power of the Spirit of God. From Jerusalem I have traveled all the way to Illyricum and I have fulfilled the gospel of Christ,
20	Yea, so have I strived to preach the gospel, not where Christ was named, lest I should build upon another man's foundation:	while I was careful not to preach where the name of Messiah had been invoked, lest I should build upon another man's foundation;	being careful not to preach where the name of Christ was called, so that I would not build on a strange foundation,
21	But as it is written, To whom he was not spoken of, they shall see: and they that have not heard shall understand.	but, it is written: They, to whom mention of him had not been made, will see him; and they, who had not heard, will be obedient.	but rather, as it is written: THOSE WHO WERE NOT TOLD ABOUT HIM WILL SEE HIM AND THOSE WHO HAVE NOT HEARD WILL BE PERSUADED.
22	For which cause also I have been much hindered from coming to you.	And on this account, I have been many times prevented from coming to you.	Because of this, I have been prevented many times [from] coming to you.
23	But now having no more place in these parts, and having a great desire these many years to come unto you;	But now, since I have no place in these regions, and as I have been desirous for many years past to come to you,	But now, because I have no place in these regions and I have desired for many years to come to you,
24	Whensoever I take my journey into Spain, I will come to you: for I trust to see you in my journey, and to be brought on my way thitherward by you, if first I be somewhat filled with your company.	when I go to Spain, I hope to come and see you; and that ye will accompany me thither, when I shall have been satisfied, in some measure, with visiting you.	when I go to Spain, I hope to come and see you and [that] you will accompany me there when I have been a little refreshed by the sight of you.
25	But now I go unto Jerusalem to minister unto the saints.	But I am now going to Jerusalem, to minister to the saints.	But now, I am going to Jerusalem to minister to the holy [ones],
26	For it hath pleased them of Macedonia and Achaia to make a certain contribution for the poor saints which are at Jerusalem.	For they of Macedonia and Achaia, have been willing to make up a contribution for the needy saints who are at Jerusalem.	for those who are in Macedonia and in Achaia desired to be a partner with the poor holy [ones] who are in Jerusalem.
27	It hath pleased them verily; and their debtors they are. For if the Gentiles have been made partakers of their spiritual things, their duty is also to minister unto them in carnal things.	They were willing, because they were also debtors to them: for if the Gentiles have been participators with them in the Spirit, they are debtors to serve them also in things of the flesh.	They desired [this], because they are also indebted to them. For if the Gentiles have partnered with them in spiritual [things], they are indebted also to serve them in fleshly [things].

Parallel Translations

	KJV	*Murdock*	*Magiera*
ROMANS	*Chapter 15*		
28	When therefore I have performed this, and have sealed to them this fruit, I will come by you into Spain.	When therefore, I shall have accomplished this, and shall have sealed to them this fruit, I will pass by you into Spain.	Therefore, when I have finished this and have impressed on them this fruit, I will cross over to you [on my way] to Spain.
29	And I am sure that, when I come unto you, I shall come in the fulness of the blessing of the gospel of Christ.	And I know that when I come to you, I shall come in the fullness of the blessing of the gospel of Messiah.	And I know that when I come to you, I will come in the fullness of the blessing of the gospel of Christ.
30	Now I beseech you, brethren, for the Lord Jesus Christ's sake, and for the love of the Spirit, that ye strive together with me in your prayers to God for me;	And I beseech you, my Brethren, by our Lord Jesus Messiah, and by the love of the Spirit, that ye labor with me in prayer to God for me;	Now I beg you, my brothers, by our Lord Jesus Christ and by love of the Spirit, to labor with me in prayer to God for me,
31	That I may be delivered from them that do not believe in Judaea; and that my service which I have for Jerusalem may be accepted of the saints;	that I may be delivered from them in Judaea, who believe not and that the ministration, which I carry to the saints in Jerusalem, may be well received;	that I may be delivered from those who are not persuaded who are in Judea, and [that] the service that I carry to the holy [ones] that are in Jerusalem will be received well,
32	That I may come unto you with joy by the will of God, and may with you be refreshed.	and that, by the good pleasure of God, I may come to you with joy, and may take comfort with you.	and [that] I may come to you with joy by the will of God and be refreshed with you.
33	Now the God of peace be with you all. Amen.	And may the God of peace be with you all: Amen.	Now the God of peace be with all of you. Amen.
Chapter 16			
1	I commend unto you Phebe our sister, which is a servant of the church which is at Cenchrea:	And I commend to you Phebe, our sister, who is a servant of the church in Cenchrea:	Now I commend to you Phoebe, our sister, who is a minister of the church of Cenchrea,
2	That ye receive her in the Lord, as becometh saints, and that ye assist her in whatsoever business she hath need of you: for she hath been a succourer of many, and of myself also.	that ye may receive her in our Lord, as is just for saints; and that ye may assist her, in whatever thing she may ask of you: for she also hath been assistant to many, and to me also.	that you should receive her in our Lord as is just for holy [ones] and you should assist her in every matter that she asks of you, because she has been an assistant both to many [and] also to me.
3	Greet Priscilla and Aquila my helpers in Christ Jesus:	Salute ye Priscilla and Aquila, my fellow-laborers in Jesus Messiah;	Greet Priscilla and Aquila, workers with me in Jesus Christ,
4	Who have for my life laid down their own necks: unto whom not only I give thanks, but also all the churches of the Gentiles.	who, for my life, surrendered their own necks; and to whom, not only I am grateful, but also all the churches of the Gentiles.	because these same ones risked their necks for my life. And not only I am thankful for them, but also all the churches of the Gentiles [are thankful].
5	Likewise greet the church that is in their house. Salute my wellbeloved Epaenetus, who is the firstfruits of Achaia unto Christ.	And give a salutation to the church which is in their house. Salute my beloved Epenetus, who was the first-fruits of Achaia in Messiah.	And greet the church that is in their house. Greet my beloved Epaenetus, who was the first[fruit] of Achaia in Christ.
6	Greet Mary, who bestowed much labour on us.	Salute Mary, who hath toiled much with you.	Greet Mary who has toiled much among you.

Parallel Translations

	KJV	*Murdock*	*Magiera*
	ROMANS	***Chapter 16***	
7	Salute Andronicus and Junia, my kinsmen, and my fellowprisoners, who are of note among the apostles, who also were in Christ before me.	Salute Andronicus and Junia, my relatives, who were in captivity with me, and are of note among the legates, and were in Messiah before me.	Greet Andronicus and Junia, my brothers, who were captives with me and are known by the apostles and were in Christ before me.
8	Greet Amplias my beloved in the Lord.	Salute Amplias, my beloved in our Lord.	Greet Amplias, my beloved in our Lord.
9	Salute Urbane, our helper in Christ, and Stachys my beloved.	Salute Urbanus, a laborer with us in Messiah; and my beloved Stachys.	Greet Urbane, a worker who is with us in Christ, and my beloved Stachys.
10	Salute Apelles approved in Christ. Salute them which are of Aristobulus' household.	Salute Apelles, chosen in our Lord. Salute the members of the house of Aristobulus.	Greet Apelles, chosen in our Lord. Greet the household of Aristobulus.
11	Salute Herodion my kinsman. Greet them that be of the household of Narcissus, which are in the Lord.	Salute Herodion, my kinsman. Salute the members of the house of Narcissus, who are in our Lord.	Greet Herodion, my kinsman. Greet the household of Narcissus, who are in our Lord.
12	Salute Tryphena and Tryphosa, who labour in the Lord. Salute the beloved Persis, which laboured much in the Lord.	Salute Tryphena and Tryphosa, who toil in our Lord. Salute my beloved Persis, who toiled much in our Lord.	Greet Tryphena and Tryphosa who labor in our Lord. Greet my beloved Persis, who labored much in our Lord.
13	Salute Rufus chosen in the Lord, and his mother and mine.	Salute Rufus, chosen in our Lord; and his and my mother.	Greet Rufus, chosen in our Lord, and his own mother and mine.
14	Salute Asyncritus, Phlegon, Hermas, Patrobas, Hermes, and the brethren which are with them.	Salute Asyncritus, and Phlegon, and Hermas, and Patrobas, and Hermes, and the brethren who are with them.	Greet Asyncritus and Phlegon and Hermas and Patrobas and Hermes and the brothers who are with them.
15	Salute Philologus, and Julia, Nereus, and his sister, and Olympas, and all the saints which are with them.	Salute Philologus and Julia, Nereus and his sister, and Olympas, and all the saints who are with them.	Greet Philologus and Julia and Nereus and his sister and Olympas and all of the holy [ones] who are with them.
16	Salute one another with an holy kiss. The churches of Christ salute you.	Salute one another, with a holy kiss. All the churches of Messiah salute you.	Greet each other with a holy kiss. All of the churches of Christ greet you.
17	Now I beseech you, brethren, mark them which cause divisions and offences contrary to the doctrine which ye have learned; and avoid them.	And I beseech you, my Brethren, that ye beware of them who cause divisions and stumblings [among you], aside from the doctrine which ye have learned: and that ye stand aloof from them.	Now I beg you, my brothers, to beware of those who cause divisions and scandals outside of the teaching that you have learned, that you keep away from them.
18	For they that are such serve not our Lord Jesus Christ, but their own belly; and by good words and fair speeches deceive the hearts of the simple.	For they who are such, do not serve our Lord Jesus Messiah, but their own belly: and by bland speeches and good wishes, they beguile the hearts of the simple.	For those who are like this do not serve our Lord Jesus Christ, but their belly. And with sweet words and with blessings, they turn away the hearts of the simple.
19	For your obedience is come abroad unto all men. I am glad therefore on your behalf: but yet I would have you wise unto that which is good, and simple concerning evil.	But your obedience is known to every one. I therefore rejoice in you: and I would have you be wise in what is good, and blameless in what is evil.	But your obedience is known to everyone. I rejoice, therefore, in you and want you to be wise to good [things] and innocent to evil [things].

ROMANS *Chapter 16*

	KJV	Murdock	Magiera
20	And the God of peace shall bruise Satan under your feet shortly. The grace of our Lord Jesus Christ be with you. Amen.	And the God of peace will soon crush Satan under your feet. The grace of our Lord Jesus Messiah, be with you.	And the God of peace will soon crush Satan under your feet. The grace of our Lord Jesus Christ be with you.
21	Timotheus my workfellow, and Lucius, and Jason, and Sosipater, my kinsmen, salute you.	Timothy, my fellow-laborer, and Lucius, and Jason, and Sosipater, my kinsmen, salute you.	Timothy, a worker with me, greets you, and Lucius and Jason and Sosipater, my brothers.
22	I Tertius, who wrote this epistle, salute you in the Lord.	I Tertius, who have written this epistle, salute you in the Lord.	I, Tertius, who wrote the letter, greet you in our Lord.
23	Gaius mine host, and of the whole church, saluteth you. Erastus the chamberlain of the city saluteth you, and Quartus a brother.	Gaius, hospitable to me and to all the church, saluteth you. Erastus, the steward of the city, and Quartus a brother, salute you.	Gaius, my host and [a host] of all the church, greets you. Erastus, the steward of the city, and Quartus, a brother, greet you.
24	The grace of our Lord Jesus Christ be with you all. Amen.	Now unto God, who is able to establish you,— (according to my gospel, which is proclaimed concerning Jesus Messiah; and according to the revelation of the mystery, which was hidden from the times that are past,	Now to God, who is able to establish you in my gospel that is proclaimed about Jesus Christ by the revelation of the mystery that was hidden from the times of the ages,
25	Now to him that is of power to stablish you according to my gospel, and the preaching of Jesus Christ, according to the revelation of the mystery, which was kept secret since the world began,	but is at this time revealed, by means of the scriptures of the prophets; and by the command of the eternal God, is made known to all the Gentiles, for the obedience of faith;)	but is revealed in this time by way of the writings of the prophets, and by the commandment of the eternal God is made known to all the Gentiles for the obedience of the faith,
26	But now is made manifest, and by the scriptures of the prophets, according to the commandment of the everlasting God, made known to all nations for the obedience of faith:	[to him] who only is wise, be glory, through Jesus Messiah, for ever and ever: Amen.	who alone is wise, [be] glory by way of Jesus Christ forever and ever. Amen.
27	To God only wise, be glory through Jesus Christ for ever. Amen.	The grace of our Lord Jesus Messiah, be with you all: Amen.	The grace of our Lord Jesus Christ [be] with all of you. Amen.

Parallel Translations

I CORINTHIANS *Chapter 1*

	KJV	*Murdock*	*Magiera*
1	Paul, called to be an apostle of Jesus Christ through the will of God, and Sosthenes our brother,	Paul, called and sent by Jesus Messiah in the good pleasure of God; and Sosthenes, a brother;	Paul, a called [one] and an apostle by Jesus Christ by the will of God, and Sosthenes, a brother,
2	Unto the church of God which is at Corinth, to them that are sanctified in Christ Jesus, called to be saints, with all that in every place call upon the name of Jesus Christ our Lord, both theirs and ours:	to the church of God which is at Corinth, to the [people] called and sanctified, who are sanctified in Jesus Messiah; and to all them, in every place, who invoke the name of our Lord Jesus Messiah, their and our [Lord]:	to the church of God that is in Corinth, called [ones] and holy [ones] who are made holy in Jesus Christ, and to all who call on the name of our Lord Jesus Christ in every place, theirs and ours:
3	Grace be unto you, and peace, from God our Father, and from the Lord Jesus Christ.	Grace [be] with you, and peace; from God our Father, and from our Lord Jesus Messiah.	Grace [be] with you and peace from God our Father and from our Lord Jesus Christ.
4	I thank my God always on your behalf, for the grace of God which is given you by Jesus Christ;	I thank my God at all times on your behalf, for the grace of God which is given to you in Jesus Messiah;	I give thanks to my God at all times on behalf of you for the grace of God that was given to you in Jesus Christ,
5	That in every thing ye are enriched by him, in all utterance, and in all knowledge;	that in every thing ye are enriched by him, in all discourse, and in all knowledge;	that in everything you may grow rich in him in every word and in all knowledge,
6	Even as the testimony of Christ was confirmed in you:	even as the testimony of Messiah was confirmed among you:	as the witness of Christ is established in you,
7	So that ye come behind in no gift; waiting for the coming of our Lord Jesus Christ:	so that ye are not inferior in any one of his gifts; but are waiting for the manifestation of our Lord Jesus Messiah:	so that you do not lack in any one of his gifts, but you are waiting for the appearance of our Lord Jesus Christ,
8	Who shall also confirm you unto the end, that ye may be blameless in the day of our Lord Jesus Christ.	who will confirm you unto the end, so that ye may be blameless in the day of our Lord Jesus Messiah.	who will establish you up to the end, so that you may be without blame in the day of our Lord Jesus Christ.
9	God is faithful, by whom ye were called unto the fellowship of his Son Jesus Christ our Lord.	God is faithful; by whom ye have been called into the fellowship of his Son, Jesus Messiah, our Lord.	God is faithful, by whom you were called to the fellowship of his Son, Jesus Christ, our Lord.
10	Now I beseech you, brethren, by the name of our Lord Jesus Christ, that ye all speak the same thing, and that there be no divisions among you; but that ye be perfectly joined together in the same mind and in the same judgment.	And I beseech you, my Brethren, by the name of our Lord Jesus Messiah, that to you all there may be one language; and that there may be no divisions among you: but that ye may become perfectly of one mind, and of one way of thinking.	Now I beg you, my brothers, in the name of our Lord Jesus Christ, that you have one word to all and [that] there should be no divisions among you, but [that] you may be perfected in one purpose and in one mind.
11	For it hath been declared unto me of you, my brethren, by them which are of the house of Chloe, that there are contentions among you.	For concerning you, my Brethren, it hath been reported to me by the house of Chloe, that there are contentions among you.	For they sent a message to me about you, my brothers, from the house of Chloe, that there are disputes among you.

Parallel Translations

	KJV	*Murdock*	*Magiera*

I CORINTHIANS *Chapter 1*

	KJV	Murdock	Magiera
12	Now this I say, that every one of you saith, I am of Paul; and I of Apollos; and I of Cephas; and I of Christ.	And this I state: That one of you saith, I am of Paul; and another saith, I am of Apollos; and another saith, I am of Cephas; and another saith, I am of Messiah.	Now I say this because there is one of you who says, "I am of Paul," and there is one who says, "I am of Apollos," and there is one who says, "I am of Peter," and there is one who says, "I am of Christ."
13	Is Christ divided? was Paul crucified for you? or were ye baptized in the name of Paul?	Now was Messiah divided? Or was Paul crucified for you? Or were ye baptized in the name of Paul?	Is Christ divided? Or was Paul crucified for your sake? Or were you baptized in the name of Paul?
14	I thank God that I baptized none of you, but Crispus and Gaius;	I thank my God that I baptized none of you, except Crispus and Gaius;	I thank God that I did not baptize any of you, except Crispus and Gaius,
15	Lest any should say that I had baptized in mine own name.	lest any one should say, that I baptized in my own name.	so that no one would say that I baptized in my name.
16	And I baptized also the household of Stephanas: besides, I know not whether I baptized any other.	I moreover baptized the household of Stephanas: but further, I know not that I baptized any other.	Now I also baptized the household of Stephanas. But besides [them], I do not know if I baptized anyone else.
17	For Christ sent me not to baptize, but to preach the gospel: not with wisdom of words, lest the cross of Christ should be made of none effect.	For Messiah did not send me to baptize, but to preach; not with wisdom of words, lest the cross of Messiah should be inefficient.	For Christ did not send me to baptize, but to preach, not with wisdom of words, so that the cross of Christ would not be made void.
18	For the preaching of the cross is to them that perish foolishness; but unto us which are saved it is the power of God.	For a discourse concerning the cross is, to them who perish, foolishness; but to us who live, it is the energy of God.	For the word regarding the cross is foolishness to the perishing [ones], but to us who are living, it is the power of God.
19	For it is written, I will destroy the wisdom of the wise, and will bring to nothing the understanding of the prudent.	For it is written: I will destroy the wisdom of the wise; and I will dissipate the intelligence of the sagacious.	For it is written: I WILL DESTROY THE WISDOM OF THE WISE AND I WILL TAKE AWAY THE UNDERSTANDING OF THE INTELLIGENT.
20	Where is the wise? where is the scribe? where is the disputer of this world? hath not God made foolish the wisdom of this world?	Where is the wise? Or where is the scribe? Or where is the disputant of this world? Lo, hath not God showed, that the wisdom of this world is folly?	Where is the wise? Or where is the scribe? Or where is the analyzer of this world? Behold, has not God made foolish the wisdom of this world?
21	For after that in the wisdom of God the world by wisdom knew not God, it pleased God by the foolishness of preaching to save them that believe.	For in the wisdom of God, because the world by wisdom knew not God, it pleased God, by the foolishness of preaching, to quicken them who believe.	For because in the wisdom of God, the world by wisdom did not know God, God desired to give life to those who believe by the foolishness of preaching,
22	For the Jews require a sign, and the Greeks seek after wisdom:	Because the Jews ask for signs, and the Gentiles demand wisdom.	because the Judeans ask for signs and the Arameans seek wisdom.
23	But we preach Christ crucified, unto the Jews a stumblingblock, and unto the Greeks foolishness;	But we preach Messiah as crucified; [which is] a stumbling-block to the Jews, and foolishness to the Gentiles;	But we preach Christ crucified, a stumbling block to the Judeans, and to the Arameans, foolishness.

Parallel Translations

	KJV	Murdock	Magiera

I CORINTHIANS Chapter 1

	KJV	Murdock	Magiera
24	But unto them which are called, both Jews and Greeks, Christ the power of God, and the wisdom of God.	but to them who are called, both Jews and Gentiles, Messiah is the energy of God, and the wisdom of God.	But to those who are called, Judeans and Arameans, Christ [is] the power of God and the wisdom of God,
25	Because the foolishness of God is wiser than men; and the weakness of God is stronger than men.	Because the foolishness of God, is wiser than men; and the feebleness of God, is stronger than men.	because the foolishness of God is wiser than men and the weakness of God is stronger than men.
26	For ye see your calling, brethren, how that not many wise men after the flesh, not many mighty, not many noble, are called:	For look also at your calling, my Brethren; that not many among you are wise, according to the flesh; and not many among you are mighty, and not many among you are of high birth.	For consider also your calling, my brothers, that not many among you [are] wise in the flesh and not many among you [are] mighty and not many among you [are] of noble birth.
27	But God hath chosen the foolish things of the world to confound the wise; and God hath chosen the weak things of the world to confound the things which are mighty;	But God hath chosen the foolish ones of the world, to shame the wise; and he hath chosen the feeble ones of the world, to shame the mighty;	But God chose the foolish [ones] of the world to shame the wise and he chose the weak [ones] of the world to shame the strong,
28	And base things of the world, and things which are despised, hath God chosen, yea, and things which are not, to bring to nought things that are:	and he hath chosen those of humble birth in the world, and the despised, and them who are nothing, to bring to naught them who are something:	and he chose those in the world whose birth was inferior and despised [ones] and those who are nothing to make of none effect those who are [something],
29	That no flesh should glory in his presence.	so that no flesh might glory before him.	so that no flesh should boast before him.
30	But of him are ye in Christ Jesus, who of God is made unto us wisdom, and righteousness, and sanctification, and redemption:	And ye, moreover, are of him in Jesus Messiah; who hath become to us wisdom from God, and righteousness and sanctification, and redemption:	But you also are in Jesus Christ, by whom we have wisdom from God and justification and sanctification and redemption,
31	That, according as it is written, He that glorieth, let him glory in the Lord.	according to that which is written: He that glorieth, let him glory in the Lord.	as it is written: HE WHO BOASTS SHOULD BOAST IN THE LORD.

Chapter 2

	KJV	Murdock	Magiera
1	And I, brethren, when I came to you, came not with excellency of speech or of wisdom, declaring unto you the testimony of God.	And I, my Brethren, when I came to you, did not preach to you the mystery of God in magnificent speech, nor in wisdom.	And my brothers, when I came to you, I declared to you the mystery of God, not with excellent speech nor with wisdom.
2	For I determined not to know any thing among you, save Jesus Christ, and him crucified.	And I did not govern myself among you, as if I knew any thing, except only Jesus Messiah; and him also as crucified.	And I did not judge myself among you as though I knew anything, except Jesus Christ and him crucified.
3	And I was with you in weakness, and in fear, and in much trembling.	And in much fear and much trembling, was I with you.	And I was with you in much fear and in trembling.

Parallel Translations

I CORINTHIANS *Chapter 2*

	KJV	Murdock	Magiera
4	And my speech and my preaching was not with enticing words of man's wisdom, but in demonstration of the Spirit and of power:	And my speech and my preaching were not with the persuasiveness of the discourses of wisdom; but with the demonstration of the Spirit, and with power:	And my speech and my preaching were not by persuasion of words of wisdom, but by demonstration of the Spirit and of power,
5	That your faith should not stand in the wisdom of men, but in the power of God.	that your faith might not arise from the wisdom of men, but from the power of God.	so that your faith would not be by the wisdom of men, but by the power of God.
6	Howbeit we speak wisdom among them that are perfect: yet not the wisdom of this world, nor of the princes of this world, that come to nought:	Yet we do speak wisdom, among the perfect; the wisdom not of this world, nor of the potentates of this world, who will come to naught.	Now we speak wisdom among the mature [ones], not the wisdom of this world, nor of the authorities of this world who come to nothing,
7	But we speak the wisdom of God in a mystery, even the hidden wisdom, which God ordained before the world unto our glory:	But we speak the wisdom of God, in a mystery; the wisdom which was hidden, and which God predetermined before the world was, for our glory:	but we speak the wisdom of God in a mystery, which was hidden and [which] God determined beforehand, from before the ages, for our glory.
8	Which none of the princes of this world knew: for had they known it, they would not have crucified the Lord of glory.	which no one of the potentates of this world knew; for had they known it, they would not have crucified the Lord of glory.	Not one of the authorities of this world knew, for if they had known it, they would not have crucified the Lord of glory.
9	But as it is written, Eye hath not seen, nor ear heard, neither have entered into the heart of man, the things which God hath prepared for them that love him.	But, as it is written: The eye hath not seen, nor hath the ear heard, nor hath it entered into the heart of man, that which God hath prepared for those who love him.	But as it is written: THE EYE HAS NOT SEEN AND THE EAR HAS NOT HEARD AND INTO THE HEART OF MAN HAS NOT ENTERED WHAT GOD HAS PREPARED FOR THOSE WHO LOVE HIM.
10	But God hath revealed them unto us by his Spirit: for the Spirit searcheth all things, yea, the deep things of God.	But God hath revealed it to us, by his Spirit; for the Spirit exploreth all things, even the profound things of God.	But God has revealed [it] to us by his Spirit, for the Spirit searches everything, even the deep [things] of God.
11	For what man knoweth the things of a man, save the spirit of man which is in him? even so the things of God knoweth no man, but the Spirit of God.	For what man is there, who knoweth that which is in a man, except it be the spirit of the man, which is in him? So also, that which is in God, no one knoweth, except the Spirit of God.	For who is the man who knows what is in a man, except the spirit of the man that [is] in him? So also, no man knows what is in God, except the Spirit of God.
12	Now we have received, not the spirit of the world, but the spirit which is of God; that we might know the things that are freely given to us of God.	Now we have received, not the spirit of the world, but the Spirit which is from God; that we might know the free gifts, which are given to us by God.	Now we have not received the spirit of the world, but the Spirit that is from God, so that we would know the gifts that were given to us from God,
13	Which things also we speak, not in the words which man's wisdom teacheth, but which the Holy Ghost teacheth; comparing spiritual things with spiritual.	Which things we also speak; not in the teaching of the words of man's wisdom, but in the teaching of the spirit; and we compare spirituals with spirituals.	which also we speak, not in the teaching of the words of the wisdom of men, but in the teaching of the Spirit and to spiritual men, we compare spiritual [things].

Parallel Translations

I CORINTHIANS *Chapter 2*

	KJV	Murdock	Magiera
14	But the natural man receiveth not the things of the Spirit of God: for they are foolishness unto him: neither can he know them, because they are spiritually discerned.	For a man in his natural self, receiveth not spirituals; for they are foolishness to him. Neither can he know them; for they are discerned by the Spirit.	For a man who is natural does not receive spiritual [things], for they are foolishness to him, and he is not able to know that which is judged spiritually.
15	But he that is spiritual judgeth all things, yet he himself is judged of no man.	But he that is spiritual, judgeth of all things: and he is judged of by no one.	Now the spiritual man judges everything and is judged by no one.
16	For who hath known the mind of the Lord, that he may instruct him? But we have the mind of Christ.	For who hath known the mind of the Lord, that he should instruct him? But we have the mind of Messiah.	FOR WHO KNOWS THE MIND OF THE LORD TO TEACH HIM? But we have the mind of Christ.

Chapter 3

	KJV	Murdock	Magiera
1	And I, brethren, could not speak unto you as unto spiritual, but as unto carnal, even as unto babes in Christ.	And I, my Brethren, could not talk with you, as with spiritual [persons], but as with the carnal, as with babes in Messiah.	And my brothers, I was not able to speak with you as with spiritual men, but as with carnal [ones] and as to babies in Christ.
2	I have fed you with milk, and not with meat: for hitherto ye were not able to bear it, neither yet now are ye able.	I gave you milk, and did not give you solid food: for ye were not then able to receive it; and even now, ye are not able.	I gave you milk to drink and I did not give you food, for you were not yet able [to eat]. But not even now are you able,
3	For ye are yet carnal: for whereas there is among you envying, and strife, and divisions, are ye not carnal, and walk as men?	For ye are still in the flesh. For, as there are among you envying, and contention, and parties, are ye not carnal, and walking in the flesh?	for you are yet in the flesh. For where there is among you envy and contention and divisions, behold, are you not carnal [ones] and are you walking in the flesh?
4	For while one saith, I am of Paul; and another, I am of Apollos; are ye not carnal?	For, while one of you saith, I am of Paul; and another saith, I am of Apollos; are ye not carnal?	For when each one of you says, "I am of Paul," and another says, "I am of Apollos," behold, are you not carnal [ones]?
5	Who then is Paul, and who is Apollos, but ministers by whom ye believed, even as the Lord gave to every man?	For, who is Paul, or who is Apollos, but the ministers by whom ye believed, each one as the Lord gave to him?	For who is Paul or who is Apollos, but the ministers by whose hands you believed and each one as the LORD gave to him?
6	I have planted, Apollos watered; but God gave the increase.	I planted, and Apollos watered; but God produced the growth.	I planted and Apollos watered, but God caused increase.
7	So then neither is he that planteth any thing, neither he that watereth; but God that giveth the increase.	Not therefore he that planted, is to be accounted of, nor he that watered, but God who produced the growth.	Therefore, he who plants is nothing, nor he who waters, but God who causes increase.
8	Now he that planteth and he that watereth are one: and every man shall receive his own reward according to his own labour.	And he that planted, and he that watered are on a par; each receiveth his reward, according to his labor.	Now he who plants and he who waters are one and each receives his wage according to his labor.
9	For we are labourers together with God: ye are God's husbandry, ye are God's building.	For we labor with God: and ye are God's husbandry, and God's edifice.	For we work with God and you are the work of God and the building of God.

Parallel Translations

I CORINTHIANS *Chapter 3*

	KJV	Murdock	Magiera
10	According to the grace of God which is given unto me, as a wise masterbuilder, I have laid the foundation, and another buildeth thereon. But let every man take heed how he buildeth thereupon.	According to the grace of God which was given me, I laid the foundation like a wise architect; and another buildeth on it. But let each one see, how he buildeth on it.	And according to the grace of God that was given to me, I laid the foundation as a wise master-builder, but another builds on it. Now everyone should consider how he will build on it.
11	For other foundation can no man lay than that is laid, which is Jesus Christ.	For any other foundation can no man lay, different from that which is laid, which is Jesus Messiah.	For no one is able to lay another foundation other than this that is laid, which is Jesus Christ.
12	Now if any man build upon this foundation gold, silver, precious stones, wood, hay, stubble;	And if any one buildeth on this foundation, either gold, or silver, or precious stones, or wood, or hay, or stubble;	Now if anyone builds on this foundation, gold or silver or precious stones or pieces of wood or grass or straw,
13	Every man's work shall be made manifest: for the day shall declare it, because it shall be revealed by fire; and the fire shall try every man's work of what sort it is.	the work of each will be exposed to view; for the day will expose it; because it is to be tested by fire; and the fire will disclose the work of each, of what sort it is.	the work of everyone is revealed. For that day will reveal it, because it is revealed by fire. And the fire will distinguish the work of everyone, according to what it is.
14	If any man's work abide which he hath built thereupon, he shall receive a reward.	And that builder whose work shall endure, will receive his reward.	And he who builds, whose work will endure, will receive his reward.
15	If any man's work shall be burned, he shall suffer loss: but he himself shall be saved; yet so as by fire.	And he, whose work shall burn up, will suffer loss; yet himself will escape; but it will be, as from the fire.	And he whose work will burn will suffer loss. Now he will escape, but so as from fire.
16	Know ye not that ye are the temple of God, and that the Spirit of God dwelleth in you?	Know ye not, that ye are the temple of God? and that the Spirit of God dwelleth in you?	Do you not know that you are the temple of God and [that] the Spirit of God lives in you?
17	If any man defile the temple of God, him shall God destroy; for the temple of God is holy, which temple ye are.	Whoever shall mar the temple of God, God will mar him: for the temple of God is holy, which [temple] ye are.	And he who corrupts the temple of God, God will corrupt, for the temple of God is holy, because you are [holy].
18	Let no man deceive himself. If any man among you seemeth to be wise in this world, let him become a fool, that he may be wise.	Let no one deceive himself. Whoever among you thinketh that he is wise in this world, let him become a fool, that he may be wise.	No one should delude himself. He among you who thinks that he is wise in this world, should be foolish, so that he may become wise.
19	For the wisdom of this world is foolishness with God. For it is written, He taketh the wise in their own craftiness.	For the wisdom of this world is fatuity with God: for it is written, He catcheth the wise in their own craftiness.	For the wisdom of this world is foolishness with God, for it is written: HE APPREHENDS THE WISE IN THEIR CRAFTINESS.
20	And again, The Lord knoweth the thoughts of the wise, that they are vain.	And again: The Lord knoweth the devices of the wise, that they are vain.	And again [he says]: THE LORD KNOWS THE REASONINGS OF THE WISE THAT THEY ARE FRUITLESS.
21	Therefore let no man glory in men. For all things are yours;	Wherefore, let no one glory in men: for all things are yours;	Because of this, no one should boast in men, for everything is your own,

I CORINTHIANS *Chapter 3*

	KJV	*Murdock*	*Magiera*
22	Whether Paul, or Apollos, or Cephas, or the world, or life, or death, or things present, or things to come; all are yours;	whether Paul, or Apollos, or Cephas, or the world, or life, or death, or things present, or things to come; all things are yours:	whether Paul or Apollos or Peter or the world, whether life or death, whether present [things] or future [things], everything is your own.
23	And ye are Christ's; and Christ is God's.	and ye are Messiah's, and Messiah is God's.	And you are of Christ and Christ [is] of God.

Chapter 4

	KJV	*Murdock*	*Magiera*
1	Let a man so account of us, as of the ministers of Christ, and stewards of the mysteries of God.	Let us be so accounted of by you, as the servants of Messiah, and the stewards of the mysteries of God.	So we should be regarded by you as ministers of Christ and stewards of the mysteries of God.
2	Moreover it is required in stewards, that a man be found faithful.	Now it is required of stewards, that each be found faithful.	Now then it is required in stewards that a man should be found faithful.
3	But with me it is a very small thing that I should be judged of you, or of man's judgment: yea, I judge not mine own self.	But to me, it is a light matter to be judged of by you, or by any man whatever; nay, I am no judge of myself.	Now this is a little matter to me that I should be judged by you or by any man, since I do not even judge myself.
4	For I know nothing by myself; yet am I not hereby justified: but he that judgeth me is the Lord.	(For I am not conscious in myself of any thing [flagrant]; yet I am not by this justified; for the Lord is my judge.)	For I am guilty of nothing in myself, but I am not justified by this, for the LORD is my judge.
5	Therefore judge nothing before the time, until the Lord come, who both will bring to light the hidden things of darkness, and will make manifest the counsels of the hearts: and then shall every man have praise of God.	Therefore pronounce not judgments before the time, [or] until the Lord come, who will pour light upon the hidden things of darkness, and will make manifest the thoughts of [men's] hearts: and then will each one have [due] praise from God.	Because of this, do not judge before the time until the LORD comes, who will bring to light the hidden [things] of darkness and reveal the reasonings of the hearts. And then there will be praise to each one from God.
6	And these things, brethren, I have in a figure transferred to myself and to Apollos for your sakes; that ye might learn in us not to think of men above that which is written, that no one of you be puffed up for one against another.	These things, my Brethren, I have stated concerning the person of myself and of Apollos, for your sakes; that, in us, ye might learn not to think [of men], above what is written; and that no one might exalt himself in comparison with his fellow, on account of any person.	Now these [things], my brothers, because of you I have decided concerning my own person and that of Apollos, so that by us you should learn not to think more than what is written and [that] no one should be elevated above his neighbor because of anyone.
7	For who maketh thee to differ from another? and what hast thou that thou didst not receive? now if thou didst receive it, why dost thou glory, as if thou hadst not received it?	For who exploreth thee? Or what hast thou, which thou didst not receive? And if thou receivedst it, why gloriest thou, as if thou didst not receive it?	For who has examined you or what do you have that you did not receive? And if you received, why are you boasting as one who did not receive?
8	Now ye are full, now ye are rich, ye have reigned as kings without us: and I would to God ye did reign, that we also might reign with you.	Now ye are yourselves full, and enriched; and, without us, are on thrones! And I wish ye were enthroned; that we also might reign with you.	Already you have been satisfied and you have grown rich and without us you have reigned. Oh that you had reigned, so that we would also reign with you!

I CORINTHIANS *Chapter 4*

	KJV	*Murdock*	*Magiera*
9	For I think that God hath set forth us the apostles last, as it were appointed to death: for we are made a spectacle unto the world, and to angels, and to men.	But I suppose, that God hath placed us legates the last, as for death; since we have become a spectacle to the world, to angels and to men.	For I think that God has placed the apostles last, as though for death, since we have become a spectacle to the world and to angels and to men.
10	We are fools for Christ's sake, but ye are wise in Christ; we are weak, but ye are strong; ye are honourable, but we are despised.	We are fools, on account of Messiah; but ye are wise in Messiah! We are feeble; but ye are strong! Ye are lauded, we are contemned.	We are fools on account of Christ, but you are wise in Christ. We are weak and you are strong. You are glorified and we are despised.
11	Even unto this present hour we both hunger, and thirst, and are naked, and are buffeted, and have no certain dwellingplace;	Unto this hour, we hunger, and thirst, and are naked, and are buffeted, and have no permanent home:	Until this time, we are hungry and thirsty and are naked and are mistreated and we have no stable dwelling
12	And labour, working with our own hands: being reviled, we bless; being persecuted, we suffer it:	and we toil, working with our own hands: they defame us, and we bless: they persecute us, and we endure it:	and we labor, working with our hands. They despise us and we bless. They persecute us and we endure.
13	Being defamed, we intreat: we are made as the filth of the world, and are the offscouring of all things unto this day.	they revile us, and we entreat them: we are as the filth of the world, and the expiation for all men, up to this time.	They revile us and we entreat them. We have become as the filth of the world and the refuse of all men until now.
14	I write not these things to shame you, but as my beloved sons I warn you.	I write these things, not to shame you; but I instruct you, as dear children.	I do not write these [things] to shame you, but as beloved sons, I am warning [you].
15	For though ye have ten thousand instructors in Christ, yet have ye not many fathers: for in Christ Jesus I have begotten you through the gospel.	For though ye have a myriad of teachers in Messiah, yet not many fathers; for in Jesus Messiah, I have begotten you by preaching.	For even if you have a large number of instructors in Christ, surely not many fathers, for in Jesus Christ I have fathered you by the gospel.
16	Wherefore I beseech you, be ye followers of me.	I beseech you, therefore, that ye be like me.	Therefore, I beg you to be like me.
17	For this cause have I sent unto you Timotheus, who is my beloved son, and faithful in the Lord, who shall bring you into remembrance of my ways which be in Christ, as I teach every where in every church.	For this cause have I sent to you Timothy, who is my beloved son, and faithful in the Lord, that he might bring to your recollection my ways in Messiah, agreeably to what I teach in all the churches.	Because of this, I sent you Timothy, who is my beloved son and faithful in the LORD, that he would remind you of my ways that are in Christ, according to what I teach in all the churches.
18	Now some are puffed up, as though I would not come to you.	Now some of you are inflated, as though I would not [dare] come to you.	Now some of you are puffed up, as though I am not coming to you.
19	But I will come to you shortly, if the Lord will, and will know, not the speech of them which are puffed up, but the power.	But I will come to you speedily, if God be willing: and I will know, not the speech of them who exalt themselves, but their power:	But if the LORD wills, I will come quickly to you, and I will know, not the word of those who elevate themselves, but their power.
20	For the kingdom of God is not in word, but in power.	for the kingdom of God is not in word, but in power.	For the kingdom of God is not in word, but in power.
21	What will ye? shall I come unto you with a rod, or in love, and in the spirit of meekness?	What will ye? Shall I come to you with the rod, or with love and a gentle spirit?	In what manner do you want [me to come]? Should I come to you with a rod or in love and with a humble spirit?

Parallel Translations

I CORINTHIANS *Chapter 5*

	KJV	*Murdock*	*Magiera*
1	It is reported commonly that there is fornication among you, and such fornication as is not so much as named among the Gentiles, that one should have his father's wife.	In short, it is reported, there is whoredom among you; and such whoredom as is not even named among the heathen, that a son should even take the wife of his father.	Actually, fornication has been reported among you and such fornication as this which is not even named among the heathen, insomuch that a son would take the wife of his father.
2	And ye are puffed up, and have not rather mourned, that he that hath done this deed might be taken away from among you.	And ye are inflated, and have not rather sitten down in grief, that he who hath done this deed might be separated from you.	And you are puffed up and you did not rather sit in grief, that he who did this deed should be cut off from among you.
3	For I verily, as absent in body, but present in spirit, have judged already, as though I were present, concerning him that hath so done this deed,	And I, while distant from you in body but present with you in spirit, have already, as if present, judged him who perpetrateth this deed;	For while I am distant from you in body, yet I am spiritually near to you. I have already, as though present, judged him who did this,
4	In the name of our Lord Jesus Christ, when ye are gathered together, and my spirit, with the power of our Lord Jesus Christ,	that ye all assemble together, in the name of our Lord Jesus Messiah, and I with you in spirit, together with the energy of our Lord Jesus Messiah;	that all of you should be gathered in the name of our Lord Jesus Christ and I with you spiritually with the power of our Lord Jesus Christ,
5	To deliver such an one unto Satan for the destruction of the flesh, that the spirit may be saved in the day of the Lord Jesus.	and that ye deliver him over to Satan, for the destruction of the flesh, that in spirit he may have life, in the day of our Lord Jesus Messiah.	and [that] you should deliver this [one] to Satan for the ruin of his body, so that he will live spiritually in the day of our Lord Jesus Christ.
6	Your glorying is not good. Know ye not that a little leaven leaveneth the whole lump?	Your glorying is not praiseworthy. Know ye not, that a little leaven leaveneth the whole mass?	Your boasting is not pleasing. Do you not know that a little leaven leavens the whole mass?
7	Purge out therefore the old leaven, that ye may be a new lump, as ye are unleavened. For even Christ our passover is sacrificed for us:	Purge out from you the old leaven, that ye may be a new mass, as ye are unleavened. For our passover is the Messiah, who was slain for us.	Purge from you the old leaven, so that you will be a new mass [of] unleavened bread. For our Passover is Christ, who was sacrificed on our behalf.
8	Therefore let us keep the feast, not with old leaven, neither with the leaven of malice and wickedness; but with the unleavened bread of sincerity and truth.	Therefore let us celebrate the festival, not with the old leaven, nor with the leaven of wickedness and bitterness, but with the leaven of purity and sanctity.	Because of this, we should celebrate the feast, not with old leaven and not with the leaven of wickedness and of bitterness, but with the leaven of purity and of holiness.
9	I wrote unto you in an epistle not to company with fornicators:	I wrote to you by letter, not to commingle with whoremongers.	I wrote to you in a letter that you should not associate with fornicators.
10	Yet not altogether with the fornicators of this world, or with the covetous, or extortioners, or with idolaters; for then must ye needs go out of the world.	But I say not, with the whoremongers who are in the world, nor [speak I] of the avaricious, or of the rapacious, or of the idol-worshippers, otherwise ye would be obliged to go out of the world.	Now I was not speaking about fornicators who are in this world or about wrong-doers or about extortioners or about idol worshipers, otherwise you would be required indeed to go out of the world.

	KJV	Murdock	Magiera
	I CORINTHIANS *Chapter 5*		
11	But now I have written unto you not to keep company, if any man that is called a brother be a fornicator, or covetous, or an idolater, or a railer, or a drunkard, or an extortioner; with such an one no not to eat.	But this is what I wrote to you, that ye commingle not, if any one is called a brother, and is a whoremonger, or avaricious, or an idol-worshipper, or a railer, or a drunkard, or rapacious, with him who is such, not even to eat bread.	But this [is] what I wrote to you, that if there is one who is called a brother and he is a fornicator or a wrong-doer or an idol worshiper or a reviler or a drunkard or an extortioner, you should not associate with one who is so, not even to eat bread.
12	For what have I to do to judge them also that are without? do not ye judge them that are within?	For what business have I to judge them who are without? But those within the body, judge ye,	For what [is it] to me to judge ones outside? You judge those who are within,
13	But them that are without God judgeth. Therefore put away from among yourselves that wicked person.	and those without, God judgeth; and remove ye the wickedness from among you.	but God judges the ones outside. YOU SHOULD CUT OFF THE WICKED [ONE] FROM AMONG YOU.
	Chapter 6		
1	Dare any of you, having a matter against another, go to law before the unjust, and not before the saints?	Dare any of you, when he hath a controversy with his brother, litigate before the iniquitous, and not before the sanctified?	Does anyone among you dare, when he has a dispute with his brother, to go to trial before the unrighteous and not before the holy [ones]?
2	Do ye not know that the saints shall judge the world? and if the world shall be judged by you, are ye unworthy to judge the smallest matters?	Or know ye not, that the sanctified will judge the world? And if the world will be judged by you, are ye unfit to decide trivial causes?	Or do you not know that the holy [ones] will judge the world? And if the world is being judged by you, are you not worthy to judge judgments of small [things]?
3	Know ye not that we shall judge angels? how much more things that pertain to this life?	Know ye not, that we shall judge angels? How much more things that are of the world?	Do you not know that you will judge angels? How much more these [things] that are of this world?
4	If then ye have judgments of things pertaining to this life, set them to judge who are least esteemed in the church.	But if ye have a controversy about a worldly matter, seat ye on the bench for you those who are contemned in the church!	But if you have a dispute about a worldly issue, you should cause those who are despised in the church to sit in judgment for you.
5	I speak to your shame. Is it so, that there is not a wise man among you? no, not one that shall be able to judge between his brethren?	For shame to you I say [it]. So, there is not even one wise man among you, who is competent to do equity between a brother and his brother:	Now I say [this] for a reproach to you. So do you not have even one wise [person] who is able to cause agreement between a brother and his brother?
6	But brother goeth to law with brother, and that before the unbelievers.	but a brother litigateth with his brother, and also before them that believe not!	But a brother is judged against his brother, and moreover, before those who do not believe!
7	Now therefore there is utterly a fault among you, because ye go to law one with another. Why do ye not rather take wrong? why do ye not rather suffer yourselves to be defrauded?	Now therefore ye condemn yourselves, in that ye have litigation one with another. For why do ye not rather suffer wrong? why not rather be defrauded?	Already therefore, you have condemned yourselves, because you have a dispute with one another. For why should you not be taken advantage of? And why should you not be defrauded?

Parallel Translations

I CORINTHIANS *Chapter 6*

	KJV	*Murdock*	*Magiera*
8	Nay, ye do wrong, and defraud, and that your brethren.	But ye yourselves commit wrong, and ye defraud even your brethren.	But you take advantage of and you defraud even your brothers.
9	Know ye not that the unrighteous shall not inherit the kingdom of God? Be not deceived: neither fornicators, nor idolaters, nor adulterers, nor effeminate, nor abusers of themselves with mankind,	Or do ye not know, that the unrighteous will not inherit the kingdom of God? Do not mistake; neither whoremongers, nor idol-worshippers, nor adulterers, nor debauchers, nor liers with males,	Or do you not know that wicked [ones] will not inherit the kingdom of God? Do not err. Neither fornicators nor idolaters nor adulterers nor corrupt [ones] nor homosexuals
10	Nor thieves, nor covetous, nor drunkards, nor revilers, nor extortioners, shall inherit the kingdom of God.	nor the avaricious, nor thieves, nor drunkards, nor railers, nor extortioners, will inherit the kingdom of God.	nor wrong-doers nor thieves nor drunkards nor revilers nor extortioners, these will not inherit the kingdom of God.
11	And such were some of you: but ye are washed, but ye are sanctified, but ye are justified in the name of the Lord Jesus, and by the Spirit of our God.	And these things have been in some of you: but ye are washed, and are sanctified, and made righteous, in the name of our Lord Jesus the Messiah, and by the Spirit of our God.	And these [things] have been in some of you, but you are washed and you are made holy and you are justified in the name of our Lord Jesus Christ and by the Spirit of our God.
12	All things are lawful unto me, but all things are not expedient: all things are lawful for me, but I will not be brought under the power of any.	Every thing is in my power: but every thing is not profitable to me. Every thing is in my power; but none [of them] shall have dominion over me.	Everything is lawful to me, but everything is not profitable to me. Everything is lawful to me, but no one will have authority over me.
13	Meats for the belly, and the belly for meats: but God shall destroy both it and them. Now the body is not for fornication, but for the Lord; and the Lord for the body.	Food is for the belly; and the belly is for food; but God will bring them both to naught. But the body is not for whoredom, but for our Lord; and our Lord for the body.	Food [is] for the stomach and the stomach [is] for food, but God makes both void. Now the body [is] not for fornication, but for our Lord and our Lord for the body.
14	And God hath both raised up the Lord, and will also raise up us by his own power.	And God hath raised up our Lord; and he will raise us up, by his power.	Now God raised our Lord and raises us by his power.
15	Know ye not that your bodies are the members of Christ? shall I then take the members of Christ, and make them the members of an harlot? God forbid.	Know ye not, that your bodies are the members of the Messiah? Shall one take a member of the Messiah, and make it the member of a harlot? Far be it.	Do you not know that your bodies are members of Christ? Should one take a member of Christ [and] make it a member of a prostitute? Let it not be so!
16	What? know ye not that he which is joined to an harlot is one body? for two, saith he, shall be one flesh.	Or know ye not, that whoever joineth himself to a harlot, is one body [with her]? For it is said, They twain shall be one body.	Or do you not know that he who joins to a prostitute is one body? For it is said: THE TWO OF THEM WILL BE ONE FLESH.
17	But he that is joined unto the Lord is one spirit.	But he that joineth himself to our Lord, is with him one spirit.	Now he who joins to our Lord becomes one spirit with him.
18	Flee fornication. Every sin that a man doeth is without the body; but he that committeth fornication sinneth against his own body.	Flee whoredom. For every [other] sin which a man committeth, is external to his body; but he that committeth whoredom, sinneth against his own body.	Flee from fornication. Every sin that a man may do is outside of his body. But he who commits fornication sins in his body.

Parallel Translations

I CORINTHIANS *Chapter 6*

	KJV	*Murdock*	*Magiera*
19	What? know ye not that your body is the temple of the Holy Ghost which is in you, which ye have of God, and ye are not your own?	Or know ye not, that your body is the temple of the Holy Spirit who abideth in you, whom ye have received from God? And ye are not your own.	Or do you not know that your body is the temple of the Holy Spirit that lives in you that you received from God and [that] you are not your own?
20	For ye are bought with a price: therefore glorify God in your body, and in your spirit, which are God's.	For ye are bought with a price. Therefore, glorify ye God, with your body, and with your spirit, which are God's.	For you are bought with a price. Therefore, glorify God in your body and in your spirit, which are of God.

Chapter 7

	KJV	*Murdock*	*Magiera*
1	Now concerning the things whereof ye wrote unto me: It is good for a man not to touch a woman.	And concerning the things of which ye wrote to me, it is praiseworthy for a man not to approach a woman.	Now about those [things] that you wrote to me, it is good for a man not to touch a woman.
2	Nevertheless, to avoid fornication, let every man have his own wife, and let every woman have her own husband.	But, on account of whoredom, let each have his own wife and let a woman have her own husband.	But because of fornication, a man should hold fast to his [own] wife and a woman should hold fast to her [own] husband.
3	Let the husband render unto the wife due benevolence: and likewise also the wife unto the husband.	And let the man render to his wife the kindness which is due; and so also the woman to her husband.	A husband should pay to his wife the love that is owed. So also, the wife to her husband.
4	The wife hath not power of her own body, but the husband: and likewise also the husband hath not power of his own body, but the wife.	The woman is not the sovereign over her body, but her husband: so also the man is not the sovereign over his body, but the wife.	The wife [has] no authority over her body, but her husband. So also, the man [has] no authority over his body, but his wife.
5	Defraud ye not one the other, except it be with consent for a time, that ye may give yourselves to fasting and prayer; and come together again, that Satan tempt you not for your incontinency.	Therefore, deprive not one another, except when ye both consent, at the time ye devote yourselves to fasting and prayer; and return again to the same disposition, that Satan tempt you not because of the concupiscence of your body.	Therefore, do not deprive one another, except when both of you consent for a time to be devoted to fasting and to prayer and return again to the same arrangement, so that Satan will not tempt you because of the desire of your body.
6	But I speak this by permission, and not of commandment.	But this I say, as to weak persons, not of positive precept.	But this I say as though to weak [ones], not by commandment.
7	For I would that all men were even as I myself. But every man hath his proper gift of God, one after this manner, and another after that.	For I would that all men might be like me in purity. But every man is endowed with his gift of God; one thus, and another so.	For I want all men to be like me in purity. But everyone is given a gift from God, some in one manner and some in another.
8	I say therefore to the unmarried and widows, It is good for them if they abide even as I.	And I say to them who have no wives, and to widows, that it is advantageous to them to remain as I am.	But I speak to those who do not have wives and to widows, that it is profitable to them if they would remain like me.
9	But if they cannot contain, let them marry: for it is better to marry than to burn.	But if they cannot endure [it], let them marry: for it is more profitable to take a wife, than to burn with concupiscence.	But if they are not enduring, they should marry, for it is more profitable to take a wife than to burn with desire.

I CORINTHIANS Chapter 7

	KJV	Murdock	Magiera
10	And unto the married I command, yet not I, but the Lord, Let not the wife depart from her husband:	And on them who have wives, I enjoin,—not I, but my Lord,—that the woman separate not from her husband.	But to those who have wives, I command, not I, but my Lord, that a wife should not separate from her husband.
11	But and if she depart, let her remain unmarried, or be reconciled to her husband: and let not the husband put away his wife.	And if she separate, let her remain without a husband, or be reconciled to her husband; and let not the man put away his wife.	And if she separates, she should remain without a man or she should be reconciled to her husband. And a man should not leave his wife.
12	But to the rest speak I, not the Lord: If any brother hath a wife that believeth not, and she be pleased to dwell with him, let him not put her away.	And to the rest, say I,— I, not my Lord,—that if there be a brother, who hath a wife that believeth not, and she is disposed to dwell with him, let him not put her away.	But to the rest I say, I, not my Lord, if there is a brother who has a wife who is not a believer, yet she wants to live with him, he should not leave her.
13	And the woman which hath an husband that believeth not, and if he be pleased to dwell with her, let her not leave him.	And that woman, who hath a husband that believeth not, and he is disposed to dwell with her let her not forsake her husband.	And a woman who has a husband that does not believe, yet he wants to live with her, should not leave her husband.
14	For the unbelieving husband is sanctified by the wife, and the unbelieving wife is sanctified by the husband: else were your children unclean; but now are they holy.	For the husband who believeth not, is sanctified by the wife that believeth; and the wife who believeth not, is sanctified by the husband that believeth: otherwise their children would be impure; but now are they pure.	For the husband who does not believe is made holy by the wife who is a believer, and the wife who is not a believer is made holy by the husband who believes. Otherwise, their children are impure, but now they are pure.
15	But if the unbelieving depart, let him depart. A brother or a sister is not under bondage in such cases: but God hath called us to peace.	But if the unbeliever separateth, let him separate: A brother or sister is not in bondage in such cases: it is to peace, God hath called us.	Now if one who does not believe separates, let him separate. A brother or sister is not bound in these [things]. God has called us to peace.
16	For what knowest thou, O wife, whether thou shalt save thy husband? or how knowest thou, O man, whether thou shalt save thy wife?	For how knowest thou, O wife, whether thou wilt procure life to thy husband? Or, thou husband, knowest thou, whether thou wilt procure life to thy wife?	For how do you know, wife, if you may give life to your husband? Or you, husband, [how] do you know if you may give life to your wife?
17	But as God hath distributed to every man, as the Lord hath called every one, so let him walk. And so ordain I in all churches.	Every one, however, as the Lord hath distributed to him, and every one as God hath called him, so let him walk. And also thus I enjoin upon all the churches.	But each one as the LORD has distributed to him and each as God has called him, so he should walk. And so also, I am commanding all the churches.
18	Is any man called being circumcised? let him not become uncircumcised. Is any called in uncircumcision? let him not be circumcised.	Is a circumcised person called, let him not revert to uncircumcision: and if one uncircumcised be called, let him not become circumcised.	If a man was called while circumcised, he should not return to uncircumcision. And if he was called in uncircumcision, he should not be circumcised.
19	Circumcision is nothing, and uncircumcision is nothing, but the keeping of the commandments of God.	For circumcision is nothing, neither is uncircumcision; but the keeping of God's commands.	For circumcision is not anything, neither uncircumcision, but the observances of the commandments of God.

	KJV	Murdock	Magiera
	I CORINTHIANS *Chapter 7*		
20	Let every man abide in the same calling wherein he was called.	Let every one continue in the vocation, in which he was called.	Everyone should remain in the calling in which he was called.
21	Art thou called being a servant? care not for it: but if thou mayest be made free, use it rather.	If thou wert called, being a servant; let it not trouble thee. But if thou canst be made free, choose it rather than to serve.	If you were called [being] a servant, it should not concern you. But even if you are able to be freed, choose to work.
22	For he that is called in the Lord, being a servant, is the Lord's freeman: likewise also he that is called, being free, is Christ's servant.	For he that is called by our Lord, being a servant, is God's freedman: likewise, he that is called, being a free man, is the Messiah's servant.	For he who was called in our Lord [being] a servant is a freeman of God. So also, he who was called a free man is a servant of Christ.
23	Ye are bought with a price; be not ye the servants of men.	Ye are bought with a price; become not the servants of men.	You were bought with a price. You should not become servants of men.
24	Brethren, let every man, wherein he is called, therein abide with God.	Let every one, my Brethren, continue with God, in whatever [state] he was called.	Everyone, my brothers, should remain with God in that [calling] in which he was called.
25	Now concerning virgins I have no commandment of the Lord: yet I give my judgment, as one that hath obtained mercy of the Lord to be faithful.	And concerning virginity, I have no precept from God; but I give counsels as a man who hath obtained mercy from God to be a believer.	Now concerning virginity, I do not hold fast to a commandment from God, but I give counsel as a man who has obtained mercy from God to be faithful.
26	I suppose therefore that this is good for the present distress, I say, that it is good for a man so to be.	And I think this is suitable, on account of the necessity of the times; it is advantageous for a man to remain as he is.	And I think that this is good, because of the urgency of time. [I think] that it is better for a man to be like this.
27	Art thou bound unto a wife? seek not to be loosed. Art thou loosed from a wife? seek not a wife.	Art thou bound to a wife? Seek not a release. Art thou free from a wife? Seek not a wife.	Are you bound with a wife? Do not seek a divorce. Are you divorced from a wife? Do not seek a wife.
28	But and if thou marry, thou hast not sinned; and if a virgin marry, she hath not sinned. Nevertheless such shall have trouble in the flesh: but I spare you.	But if thou takest a wife, thou sinnest not. And if a maiden is given to a husband, she sinneth not. But they who are such, will have trouble in the body: but I am forbearing to you.	Yet if you take a wife, you are not sinning. And if an unmarried woman gets married, she does not sin. Now those who are so will have trouble in the body, but I [want to] spare you.
29	But this I say, brethren, the time is short: it remaineth, that both they that have wives be as though they had none;	And this I say, my Brethren, that the time to come is short; so that they who have wives, should be as if they had none;	And this I say, my brothers, that the time is now shortened, so that those who have wives should be as though they do not have [any],
30	And they that weep, as though they wept not; and they that rejoice, as though they rejoiced not; and they that buy, as though they possessed not;	and they who weep, as if they wept not; and they who rejoice, as if they rejoiced not; and they who buy, as if they acquired not;	and those who weep, as not weeping, and those who rejoice, as not rejoicing, and those who buy, as not acquiring,
31	And they that use this world, as not abusing it: for the fashion of this world passeth away.	and those occupied with this world, not going beyond the just using: for the fashion of this world is passing away.	and those who are occupied with this world, not outside of what is just for use, for the fashion of this world passes away.

Parallel Translations

	KJV	Murdock	Magiera

I CORINTHIANS *Chapter 7*

	KJV	Murdock	Magiera
32	But I would have you without carefulness. He that is unmarried careth for the things that belong to the Lord, how he may please the Lord:	And therefore I wish you to be without solicitude. For he who hath not a wife, considereth the thing of his Lord, how he may please his Lord.	Because of this, I desire for you to be without anxiety, for he who does not have a wife is concerned with the one who is his Lord, how he should please his Lord.
33	But he that is married careth for the things that are of the world, how he may please his wife.	And he who hath a wife, is anxious about the world, how he may please his wife.	And he who has a wife, cares about the world, how he should please his wife.
34	There is difference also between a wife and a virgin. The unmarried woman careth for the things of the Lord, that she may be holy both in body and in spirit: but she that is married careth for the things of the world, how she may please her husband.	There is a difference also between a wife and a maiden. She who is without a husband, thinketh of things pertaining to her Lord, that she may be holy in her body and in her spirit. But she who hath a husband, thinketh of things pertaining to the world, how she may please her husband.	Now there is also a difference between a wife and an unmarried woman. She who is not married is concerned with her Lord, so that she will be holy in her body and in her spirit. And she who has a husband is concerned with the world, how she should please her husband.
35	And this I speak for your own profit; not that I may cast a snare upon you, but for that which is comely, and that ye may attend upon the Lord without distraction.	And this I say for your advantage; I am not laying a snare for you; but that ye may be faithful towards your Lord, in a suitable manner, while not minding worldly things.	Now I say this for your own advantage. I am not laying a snare for you, but rather that you may be faithful toward your Lord in a pleasing manner, while not being concerned with the world.
36	But if any man think that he behaveth himself uncomely toward his virgin, if she pass the flower of her age, and need so require, let him do what he will, he sinneth not: let them marry.	But if any one thinketh that there is reproach, on account of his maiden [daughter], because she hath passed her time, and he hath not presented her to a husband, [and] it be fitting that he present her; let him do what he desireth, he sinneth not; let her be married.	But if a man thinks that he is mocked by his unmarried [daughter] who is past her time and he has not given her to a man and it is fitting that he should give her, he should do as he desires. He does not sin [if] she would be married.
37	Nevertheless he that standeth stedfast in his heart, having no necessity, but hath power over his own will, and hath so decreed in his heart that he will keep his virgin, doeth well.	But he who hath firmly determined in his own mind, and nothing compelleth him, and he can act his own pleasure, and he so judgeth in his heart, that he keep his maiden [daughter], he doeth commendably.	But he who has firmly decided in his mind and is not compelled by the matter and has power over his will and so judges in his heart to keep his unmarried [daughter], he does well.
38	So then he that giveth her in marriage doeth well; but he that giveth her not in marriage doeth better.	And therefore, he who presenteth his maiden [daughter], doeth commendably; and he who presenteth not his maiden [daughter], doeth very commendably.	And therefore, he who gives his unmarried [daughter] does well. And he who does not give his unmarried [daughter] does very well.
39	The wife is bound by the law as long as her husband liveth; but if her husband be dead, she is at liberty to be married to whom she will; only in the Lord.	A woman, while her husband liveth, is bound by the law; but if her husband sleepeth [in death], she is free to marry whom she pleaseth, [yet] only in the Lord.	A wife, while her husband lives, is bound by the law. But if her husband should sleep, she is free to be [married] to whom she wants, only in our Lord.

Parallel Translations

	KJV	*Murdock*	*Magiera*
	I CORINTHIANS *Chapter 7*		
40	But she is happier if she so abide, after my judgment: and I think also that I have the Spirit of God.	But she is happier, in my opinion, if she remain so: and I think also, that I have the Spirit of God.	But she is blessed if she should remain so, according to my own mind. And I am also convinced that the Spirit of God is in me.
	Chapter 8		
1	Now as touching things offered unto idols, we know that we all have knowledge. Knowledge puffeth up, but charity edifieth.	And concerning sacrifices to idols, we know, that in all of us there is knowledge; and knowledge inflateth, but love edifieth.	Now concerning the sacrifices of idols, we know that in all of us there is knowledge and knowledge makes [one] proud, but love builds.
2	And if any man think that he knoweth any thing, he knoweth nothing yet as he ought to know.	And if any one thinketh that he knoweth any thing he knoweth nothing yet, as he ought to know [it].	Now if anyone thinks that he knows anything, he does not know anything yet, as he ought to know it.
3	But if any man love God, the same is known of him.	But if any one loveth God, that man is known of him.	But if anyone loves God, this [one] is known by him.
4	As concerning therefore the eating of those things that are offered in sacrifice unto idols, we know that an idol is nothing in the world, and that there is none other God but one.	As to the eating of the sacrifices of idols, therefore, we know that an idol is nothing in the world; and that there is no other God, but one.	Therefore, concerning the food of the sacrifices of idols, we know that an idol is nothing in the world and that there is no other God, except one.
5	For though there be that are called gods, whether in heaven or in earth, (as there be gods many, and lords many,)	For although there are what are called gods, whether in heaven, or on earth, (as there are gods many, and lords many,)	For although there are [those] who are called gods, either in heaven or on earth, as there are many gods and many lordships,
6	But to us there is but one God, the Father, of whom are all things, and we in him; and one Lord Jesus Christ, by whom are all things, and we by him.	yet to us, on our part, there is one God, the Father, from whom are all things, and we in him; and one Lord, Jesus the Messiah, by whom are all things, and we also by him.	but to us ourselves, [there] is one God, the Father, from whom [are] all [things] and by whom we are, and one LORD, Jesus Christ, by way of him [are] all [things] and we are also by way of him.
7	Howbeit there is not in every man that knowledge: for some with conscience of the idol unto this hour eat it as a thing offered unto an idol; and their conscience being weak is defiled.	But there is not [this] knowledge in every man; for there are some, who, to the present time, in their conscience, eat [it] as an offering to idols; and because their conscience is weak, it is defiled.	But not everyone has [this] knowledge, for there are some who in their conscience until now eat that which is sacrificed to idols. And because their conscience is weak, it is defiled.
8	But meat commendeth us not to God: for neither, if we eat, are we the better; neither, if we eat not, are we the worse.	But food doth not bring us near to God; for if we eat, we do not abound; and if we eat not, we are not in want.	Now food does not bring us near to God, for if we eat, we do not grow, and if we do not eat, we do not lack.
9	But take heed lest by any means this liberty of yours become a stumblingblock to them that are weak.	See to it, however, lest this your authority become a stumbling-block to the weak.	But watch, so that this authority of yours should not become a stumbling block to the weak.

I CORINTHIANS *Chapter 8*

	KJV	Murdock	Magiera
10	For if any man see thee which hast knowledge sit at meat in the idol's temple, shall not the conscience of him which is weak be emboldened to eat those things which are offered to idols;	For if one should see thee in whom there is knowledge, reclining in the temple of idols, will not his conscience, seeing he is a weak person, be encouraged to eat what is sacrificed?	For if someone sees you in whom there is knowledge, that you are sitting to eat [in] the temple of idols, behold, is not his conscience, because he is weak, encouraged to eat what is sacrificed?
11	And through thy knowledge shall the weak brother perish, for whom Christ died?	And by thy knowledge, he who is feeble, and on account of whom the Messiah died, will perish.	And he who is feeble, on account of whom Christ died, will be hurt by your knowledge.
12	But when ye sin so against the brethren, and wound their weak conscience, ye sin against Christ.	And if ye thus sin against your brethren, and wound the consciences of the feeble, ye sin against the Messiah.	And if you are injuring your brothers in this manner and you are wounding the consciences [of] the feeble, you are injuring Christ.
13	Wherefore, if meat make my brother to offend, I will eat no flesh while the world standeth, lest I make my brother to offend.	Wherefore, if food is a stumbling-block to my brother, I will for ever eat no flesh, lest I should be a stumbling-block to my brother.	Because of this, if food causes offense to my brother, I will not eat flesh forever, so that I should not cause offense to my brother.

Chapter 9

	KJV	Murdock	Magiera
1	Am I not an apostle? am I not free? have I not seen Jesus Christ our Lord? are not ye my work in the Lord?	Am I not a free man? Or, am I not a legate? Or, have I not seen Jesus Messiah our Lord? Or, have ye not been my work in my Lord?	Am I not a free man? Or am I not an apostle? Or have I not seen Jesus Christ our Lord? Or are you not my work in my Lord?
2	If I be not an apostle unto others, yet doubtless I am to you: for the seal of mine apostleship are ye in the Lord.	And if I have not been a legate to others, yet I have been so to you; and ye are the seal of my legateship.	And if I am not an apostle to others, yet I am to you and you are the seal of my apostleship.
3	Mine answer to them that do examine me is this,	And [my] apology to my judgers, is this:	And my defense to those who judge me is this:
4	Have we not power to eat and to drink?	Have we not authority, to eat and to drink?	Is it not lawful for us to eat and to drink?
5	Have we not power to lead about a sister, a wife, as well as other apostles, and as the brethren of the Lord, and Cephas?	Or have we not authority to carry about with us a sister as a wife; just as the other legates, and the brothers of our Lord, and as Cephas?	And is it not lawful for us to lead a sister with us, a wife, as the rest of the apostles and as the brothers of our Lord and as Peter?
6	Or I only and Barnabas, have not we power to forbear working?	Or I only, and Barnabas, have we no right to forbear labor?	Or I only and Barnabas, do we not have the authority not to work?
7	Who goeth a warfare any time at his own charges? who planteth a vineyard, and eateth not of the fruit thereof? or who feedeth a flock, and eateth not of the milk of the flock?	Who, that serveth in war, [doth so] at his own expense? Or who, that planteth a vineyard, eateth not of its fruits? Or who, that tendeth sheep, eateth not of the milk of his flocks?	Who is he who does military service at his own expense? Or who is he who plants a vineyard and does not eat from his fruit? Or who is he who tends the flock and does not eat from the milk of his flock?
8	Say I these things as a man? or saith not the law the same also?	Is it as a man, I say these things? Behold, the law also saith them.	Am I saying these [things] as a man? Behold, the law also says these [things].

Parallel Translations

	KJV	Murdock	Magiera
I CORINTHIANS *Chapter 9*			
9	For it is written in the law of Moses, Thou shalt not muzzle the mouth of the ox that treadeth out the corn. Doth God take care for oxen?	For it is written in the law of Moses, Thou shalt not muzzle the ox that thresheth. Hath God regard for oxen?	For it is written in the law of Moses: YOU SHOULD NOT MUZZLE THE OX THAT THRESHES. Is it a concern to God about oxen?
10	Or saith he it altogether for our sakes? For our sakes, no doubt, this is written: that he that ploweth should plow in hope; and that he that thresheth in hope should be partaker of his hope.	But manifest it is, for whose sake he said it. And indeed, for our sakes it was written: because the plougher ought to plough in hope, and the thresher in hope of fruit.	On the contrary, it is known that because of us he said [it] and because of us it was written, because the plowman ought to plow for hope and he who threshes for the hope of harvest.
11	If we have sown unto you spiritual things, is it a great thing if we shall reap your carnal things?	If we have sowed among you the things of the Spirit, is it a great matter, if we reap from you the things of the body?	If we have sown [things] of the Spirit among you, is it a great [thing] if we reap [things] of the body from you?
12	If others be partakers of this power over you, are not we rather? Nevertheless we have not used this power; but suffer all things, lest we should hinder the gospel of Christ.	And if others have this prerogative over you, doth it not belong still more to us? Yet we have not used this prerogative; but we have endured every thing, that we might in nothing impede the announcement of the Messiah.	And if others have authority over you, ought we not [to have] more? Yet we have not used this authority, but we have endured everything, so that we would not hinder the gospel of Christ in anything.
13	Do ye not know that they which minister about holy things live of the things of the temple? and they which wait at the altar are partakers with the altar?	Know ye not, that they who serve in a temple, are fed from the temple? And they who serve at the altar, participate with the altar?	Do you not know that those who serve in the sanctuary are sustained from the sanctuary and those who serve at the altar have a portion of the altar?
14	Even so hath the Lord ordained that they which preach the gospel should live of the gospel.	Thus also hath our Lord commanded, that they who proclaim his gospel, should live by his gospel.	So also, our Lord commanded that those who are preaching his gospel should live from his gospel.
15	But I have used none of these things: neither have I written these things, that it should be so done unto me: for it were better for me to die, than that any man should make my glorying void.	But I have used none of these things: and I write not, that it may be so done to me; for it would be better for me to actually die, than that any one should make void my glorying.	But I have not used one of these [things] and I have not written because of this, that it would be so [done] to me, for it is better for me that I should indeed die, than that anyone should make my boasting void.
16	For though I preach the gospel, I have nothing to glory of: for necessity is laid upon me; yea, woe is unto me, if I preach not the gospel!	For while I preach, I have no [ground of] glorying; because necessity is laid upon me, and woe to me, if I preach not.	For although I preach, I have no boasting, for necessity is laid on me and woe to me if I do not preach!
17	For if I do this thing willingly, I have a reward: but if against my will, a dispensation of the gospel is committed unto me.	For if I do this voluntarily, there is a reward for me: but if involuntarily, a stewardship is intrusted to me.	For if I do this willingly, I have a reward, but if not willingly, I am entrusted with a stewardship.
18	What is my reward then? Verily that, when I preach the gospel, I may make the gospel of Christ without charge, that I abuse not my power in the gospel.	What then is my reward? [It is,] that when I preach, I make the announcement of the Messiah without cost, and use not the prerogative given me in the gospel.	What then is my reward? [It is] that when I am preaching, I make the gospel of Christ without cost and I do not use the authority that he gave me in the gospel.

Parallel Translations

I CORINTHIANS *Chapter 9*

	KJV	*Murdock*	*Magiera*
19	For though I be free from all men, yet have I made myself servant unto all, that I might gain the more.	Being free from them all, I have made myself servant to every man; that I might gain many:	For although I am free from all [things], I have subjected myself to everyone, that I may gain many.
20	And unto the Jews I became as a Jew, that I might gain the Jews; to them that are under the law, as under the law, that I might gain them that are under the law;	and with the Jews, I was as a Jew, that I might gain the Jews; and with those under the law, I was as under the law, that I might gain them who are under the law;	And with the Judeans I was as a Judean, that I would gain Judeans, and with those who are under the law, I was as those under the law, so that I would gain those that are under the law.
21	To them that are without law, as without law, (being not without law to God, but under the law to Christ,) that I might gain them that are without law.	and to those who have not the law, I was as without the law, (although I am not without law to God, but under the law of the Messiah,) that I might gain them that are without the law.	And to those who have no law, I was as without the law (although I am not without the law to God, but in the law of Christ), so that I would also gain those who are without the law.
22	To the weak became I as weak, that I might gain the weak: I am made all things to all men, that I might by all means save some.	I was with the weak, as weak, that I might gain the weak: I was all things to all men, that I might vivify every one.	I was with the weak [ones] as weak, so that I would gain the weak. I am all [things] to everyone, so that I may give life to everyone.
23	And this I do for the gospel's sake, that I might be partaker thereof with you.	And this I do, that I may participate in the announcement.	And I am doing this in order to be a participant of the gospel.
24	Know ye not that they which run in a race run all, but one receiveth the prize? So run, that ye may obtain.	Know ye not that they who run in the stadium, run all of them; yet it is one who gaineth the victory. Run ye, so as to attain.	Do you not know that those who run in a contest all run, but one receives the victory? So, run that you may obtain.
25	And every man that striveth for the mastery is temperate in all things. Now they do it to obtain a corruptible crown; but we an incorruptible.	For every one who engageth in the contest, restraineth his desires in every thing. And they run, to obtain a crown that perisheth; but we, one that perisheth not.	Now everyone who participates in a contest controls his mind in every way. And those are running to receive a crown that is corruptible, but we, one that is incorruptible.
26	I therefore so run, not as uncertainly; so fight I, not as one that beateth the air:	I therefore so run, not as for something unknown; and I so struggle, not as struggling against air;	Therefore, I so run, not as for something unknown, and I so fight, not as one who beats the air,
27	But I keep under my body, and bring it into subjection: lest that by any means, when I have preached to others, I myself should be a castaway.	but I subdue my body, and reduce it to servitude; lest, when I have preached to others, I myself should be a reprobate.	but I subdue my body and I subject [it], so that when I have preached to others, I myself will not be rejected.

Chapter 10

	KJV	*Murdock*	*Magiera*
1	Moreover, brethren, I would not that ye should be ignorant, how that all our fathers were under the cloud, and all passed through the sea;	And, my Brethren, I would have you know, that our fathers were all of them under the cloud, and they all passed through the sea;	But I want you to know, my brothers, that our fathers were all under the cloud and all passed through the sea
2	And were all baptized unto Moses in the cloud and in the sea;	and they were all baptized by Moses, in the cloud and in the sea;	and all were baptized by way of Moses in the cloud and in the sea

Parallel Translations

	KJV	*Murdock*	*Magiera*

I CORINTHIANS *Chapter 10*

	KJV	Murdock	Magiera
3	And did all eat the same spiritual meat;	and they all ate the same spiritual food;	and all ate of the same food of the Spirit
4	And did all drink the same spiritual drink: for they drank of that spiritual Rock that followed them: and that Rock was Christ.	and they all drank the same spiritual drink; for they drank from the spiritual rock that attended them, and that rock was the Messiah.	and all drank of the same drink of the Spirit, for they were drinking from the rock of the Spirit that came with them and that rock was Christ.
5	But with many of them God was not well pleased: for they were overthrown in the wilderness.	But with a multitude of them, God was not pleased; for they fell in the wilderness.	But with many of them God was not well pleased, for they fell in the wilderness.
6	Now these things were our examples, to the intent we should not lust after evil things, as they also lusted.	Now these things were an example for us, that we should not hanker after evil things as they hankered.	Now these [things] were an example for us, so that we should not lust after evil [things] as those lusted.
7	Neither be ye idolaters, as were some of them; as it is written, The people sat down to eat and drink, and rose up to play.	Neither should we serve idols, as some of them served; as it is written, The people sat down to eat and to drink, and rose up to sport.	And neither should we be worshipping idols, as some of them also worshipped, as it is written: THE PEOPLE SAT TO EAT AND TO DRINK AND THEY ROSE UP TO PLAY.
8	Neither let us commit fornication, as some of them committed, and fell in one day three and twenty thousand.	Neither let us commit whoredom, as some of them committed; and there fell in one day twenty and three thousand.	Neither should we commit fornication, as some of them committed fornication, and they fell in one day, twenty-three thousand.
9	Neither let us tempt Christ, as some of them also tempted, and were destroyed of serpents.	Neither let us tempt the Messiah, as some of them tempted; and serpents destroyed them.	And we should not tempt Christ, as some of them tempted, and serpents destroyed them.
10	Neither murmur ye, as some of them also murmured, and were destroyed of the destroyer.	Neither murmur ye, as some of them murmured; and they perished by the destroyer.	Neither should you murmur, as some of them murmured, and were destroyed by the hands of the Violator.
11	Now all these things happened unto them for ensamples: and they are written for our admonition, upon whom the ends of the world are come.	All these things which befell them, were for an example to us; and they are written for our instruction, on whom the end of the world hath come.	Now all these [things] that happened to them were for our example and it was written for our instruction, on whom the end of the ages has come.
12	Wherefore let him that thinketh he standeth take heed lest he fall.	Wherefore, let him who thinketh he standeth, beware lest he fall.	Therefore, he who thinks that he stands should watch, so that he does not fall.
13	There hath no temptation taken you but such as is common to man: but God is faithful, who will not suffer you to be tempted above that ye are able; but will with the temptation also make a way to escape, that ye may be able to bear it.	No trial cometh on you, but what pertaineth to men: and God is faithful, who will not permit you to be tried beyond your ability, but will make an issue to your trial, that ye may be able to sustain it.	No temptation has come on you, except of men, but God is faithful, who will not allow you to be tempted more than what you are able, but will make a way out for your temptation, so that you will be able to endure [it].
14	Wherefore, my dearly beloved, flee from idolatry.	Wherefore, my Beloved, flee from idolatry.	Because of this, my beloved [ones], flee from the worship of idols.
15	I speak as to wise men; judge ye what I say.	I speak as to the wise; judge ye what I say.	I am speaking as to the wise. You judge what I am saying.

	KJV	*Murdock*	*Magiera*

I CORINTHIANS *Chapter 10*

Verse	KJV	Murdock	Magiera
16	The cup of blessing which we bless, is it not the communion of the blood of Christ? The bread which we break, is it not the communion of the body of Christ?	The cup of thanksgiving which we bless, is it not the communion of the blood of the Messiah? And the bread which we break, is it not the communion of the body of the Messiah?	That cup of thanksgiving that we bless, is it not the fellowship of the blood of Christ? And that bread that we break, is it not the fellowship of the body of Christ?
17	For we being many are one bread, and one body: for we are all partakers of that one bread.	As therefore that bread is one, so we are all one body; for we all take to ourselves from that one bread.	As that bread is one, so all of us are one body, for all of us have taken from that one bread.
18	Behold Israel after the flesh: are not they which eat of the sacrifices partakers of the altar?	Behold the Israel who are in the flesh; are not they who eat the victims, participators of the altar?	Look at Israel who are in the flesh. Do not those who eat the sacrifices become participants of the altar?
19	What say I then? that the idol is any thing, or that which is offered in sacrifice to idols is any thing?	What then do I say? That an idol is any thing? Or, that an idol's sacrifice is any thing? No.	Therefore, what am I saying? That an idol is anything or a sacrifice of an idol is anything? No.
20	But I say, that the things which the Gentiles sacrifice, they sacrifice to devils, and not to God: and I would not that ye should have fellowship with devils.	But that what the Gentiles sacrifice, they sacrifice to demons, and not to God. And I would not, that ye should be associates of demons.	But what the heathen sacrifice, they sacrifice to demons and not to God. And I do not want you to be participants with demons.
21	Ye cannot drink the cup of the Lord, and the cup of devils: ye cannot be partakers of the Lord's table, and of the table of devils.	Ye cannot drink the cup of our Lord, and the cup of demons; and ye cannot be partakers at the table of our Lord, and at the table of demons.	You are not able to drink the cup of our Lord and the cup of demons and you are not able to participate with the table of our Lord and with the table of demons.
22	Do we provoke the Lord to jealousy? are we stronger than he?	Or, would we sedulously provoke our Lord's jealousy? Are we stronger than he?	Or are we especially provoking our Lord to jealousy? Are we stronger than him?
23	All things are lawful for me, but all things are not expedient: all things are lawful for me, but all things edify not.	Every thing is in my power; but every thing is not profitable. Every thing is in my power; but every thing doth not edify.	Everything is lawful to me, but not everything is profitable. Everything is lawful for me, but not everything builds up.
24	Let no man seek his own, but every man another's wealth.	Let no one seek his own things, but also the things of his fellow-man.	No one should seek his own [things], but everyone also [should seek] the [things] of his neighbor.
25	Whatsoever is sold in the shambles, that eat, asking no question for conscience sake:	Whatever is sold in the flesh-market, eat ye, without an inquiry on account of conscience:	Everything that is sold in the marketplace, eat without a question on account of conscience,
26	For the earth is the Lord's, and the fulness thereof.	for the earth is the Lord's, in its fullness.	FOR THE EARTH IS OF THE LORD IN ITS FULLNESS.
27	If any of them that believe not bid you to a feast, and ye be disposed to go; whatsoever is set before you, eat, asking no question for conscience sake.	And if one of the Gentiles invite you, and ye are disposed to go, eat ye whatever is set before you, without an inquiry on account of conscience.	But if one of the heathen invites you and you want to go, eat everything that is set before you without a question on account of conscience.

I CORINTHIANS *Chapter 10*

	KJV	*Murdock*	*Magiera*
28	But if any man say unto you, This is offered in sacrifice unto idols, eat not for his sake that shewed it, and for conscience sake: for the earth is the Lord's, and the fulness thereof:	But if any one shall say to you, This pertaineth to a sacrifice; eat not, for the sake of him who told you, and for conscience's sake.	But if anyone should say to you that this is that which is sacrificed, you should not eat, because of him who told you and on account of conscience.
29	Conscience, I say, not thine own, but of the other: for why is my liberty judged of another man's conscience?	The conscience I speak of, is not your own, but his who told you. But why is my liberty judged of, by the conscience of others?	Now the conscience I speak [of] is not your own, but his who told [you]. For why is my liberty judged by the conscience of others?
30	For if I by grace be a partaker, why am I evil spoken of for that for which I give thanks?	If I by grace partake, why am I reproached for that, for which I give thanks?	If I apply grace, why am I reproached for what I give thanks?
31	Whether therefore ye eat, or drink, or whatsoever ye do, do all to the glory of God.	If therefore ye eat, or if ye drink, or if ye do any thing, do all things for the glory of God.	Therefore, whether you eat or drink or do anything, do everything to the glory of God.
32	Give none offence, neither to the Jews, nor to the Gentiles, nor to the church of God:	Be ye without offence to the Jews, and to the Gentiles, and to the church of God:	Be without offense to Judeans and to Gentiles and to the church of God,
33	Even as I please all men in all things, not seeking mine own profit, but the profit of many, that they may be saved.	even as I also, in every thing, please every man; and do not seek what is profitable to me, but what is profitable to many; that they may live.	even as I please everyone in everything and I do not seek what is profitable to me, but what is profitable to many, that they may have life.

Chapter 11

	KJV	*Murdock*	*Magiera*
1	Be ye followers of me, even as I also am of Christ.	Be ye imitators of me, as I am of the Messiah.	Be like me, as also I am in Christ.
2	Now I praise you, brethren, that ye remember me in all things, and keep the ordinances, as I delivered them to you.	Moreover I commend you, my Brethren, that in all things ye are mindful of me, and that ye hold fast the precepts as I delivered them to you.	Now I commend you, my brothers, that in everything you are mindful of me and you hold fast the commandments, even as I delivered [them] to you.
3	But I would have you know, that the head of every man is Christ; and the head of the woman is the man; and the head of Christ is God.	And I would have you know, that the head of every man is the Messiah, and the head of the woman is the man, and the head of the Messiah is God.	Now I want you to know that the head of every man is Christ and the head of the woman is the man and the head of Christ is God.
4	Every man praying or prophesying, having his head covered, dishonoureth his head.	Every man, who prayeth or prophesieth with his head covered, dishonoreth his head.	Every man who prays or prophesies while his head is covered dishonors his head.
5	But every woman that prayeth or prophesieth with her head uncovered dishonoureth her head: for that is even all one as if she were shaven.	And every woman, who prayeth or prophesieth with her head uncovered, dishonoreth her head; for she is on a level with her whose head is shaven.	And every woman who prays or prophesies while her head is uncovered dishonors her head, for she is on a level with her whose head is shaven.
6	For if the woman be not covered, let her also be shorn: but if it be a shame for a woman to be shorn or shaven, let her be covered.	For if a woman be not covered, let her also be shorn; but if it be shameful for a woman to be shorn or shaven, let her be covered.	For if a woman is not covered, she should also be shorn. But if it is disgraceful for a woman to be shorn or to be shaven, she should be covered.

Parallel Translations

I CORINTHIANS *Chapter 11*

	KJV	*Murdock*	*Magiera*
7	For a man indeed ought not to cover his head, forasmuch as he is the image and glory of God: but the woman is the glory of the man.	The man, indeed, ought not to cover his head, because he is the likeness and glory of God: but the woman is the glory of the man.	For a man ought not to cover his head, because he is the likeness and glory of God, but the woman is the glory of the man.
8	For the man is not of the woman; but the woman of the man.	For the man was not from the woman, but the woman from the man.	For a man is not from the woman, but the woman from the man,
9	Neither was the man created for the woman; but the woman for the man.	Neither was the man created for the woman's sake, but the woman for the man's sake.	for neither was the man made for the woman, but the woman for the man.
10	For this cause ought the woman to have power on her head because of the angels.	For this cause ought the woman to have on her head [the mark of] authority, because of the angels.	Because of this, the woman is obliged to have authority on her head, because of the angels.
11	Nevertheless neither is the man without the woman, neither the woman without the man, in the Lord.	Nevertheless, the man is not without the woman, nor the woman without the man, in our Lord.	Nevertheless, the man [is] not outside of the woman, nor the woman outside of the man in our Lord.
12	For as the woman is of the man, even so is the man also by the woman; but all things of God.	For as the woman [was] from the man, so the man is by the woman; and every thing is from God.	For as the woman [was] from the man, so also the man [was] by way of the woman and everything is from God.
13	Judge in yourselves: is it comely that a woman pray unto God uncovered?	Judge for yourselves, among yourselves; is it becoming, that a woman pray to God with her head uncovered?	Judge among yourselves, for yourselves. Is it proper for a woman to pray to God while her head is uncovered?
14	Doth not even nature itself teach you, that, if a man have long hair, it is a shame unto him?	Doth not nature teach you, that in a man, if his hair groweth long, it is a reproach to him?	Does not even nature teach you that it is a shame for a man when his hair grows long?
15	But if a woman have long hair, it is a glory to her: for her hair is given her for a covering.	But for a woman, if her hair is abundant, it is a glory to her; for her hair is given to her for a covering.	And [for] a woman, it is a glory to her when her hair is abundant, because her hair is given to her for a covering.
16	But if any man seem to be contentious, we have no such custom, neither the churches of God.	But if any one is contentious about these things, we on our part have no such custom, nor hath the church of God.	But if anyone contends about these [things], we have no custom as this and not for the church of God.
17	Now in this that I declare unto you I praise you not, that ye come together not for the better, but for the worse.	This which I now enjoin, is not as praising you; for ye have not made progress, but have deteriorated.	Now this which I command [is] not as though I am praising you, because you have not progressed, but rather you have fallen behind.
18	For first of all, when ye come together in the church, I hear that there be divisions among you; and I partly believe it.	Because, first; when ye assemble in the church, there are, I hear, divisions among you; and I partly believe it.	For in the first place, when you are gathered in the church, I hear that there are divisions among you and I believe some [of these things].
19	For there must be also heresies among you, that they which are approved may be made manifest among you.	For there are to be contentions among you, that the approved among you may be known.	For there are also going to be contentions among you, that those who are approved among you may be known.
20	When ye come together therefore into one place, this is not to eat the Lord's supper.	When therefore ye come together, ye eat and drink, not as is becoming on the day of our Lord.	Then when you are gathered, you do not eat and drink as is proper for the day of our Lord.

Parallel Translations

	KJV	Murdock	Magiera
	I CORINTHIANS *Chapter 11*		
21	For in eating every one taketh before other his own supper: and one is hungry, and another is drunken.	But, one and another proceedeth to eat his own supper; and one is hungry, and another is drunken.	But each man eats his meal beforehand and it happens [that] one is hungry and one is drunk.
22	What? have ye not houses to eat and to drink in? or despise ye the church of God, and shame them that have not? What shall I say to you? shall I praise you in this? I praise you not.	What! have ye no houses in which ye can eat and drink? Or, despise ye the church of God, and shame them who have nothing? What shall I say to you? Shall I praise you? In this I praise you not.	Do you not have houses [in] which you may eat and drink? Or do you despise the church of God and shame those who do not have? What can I say to you? Should I praise you in this? I do not praise [you].
23	For I have received of the Lord that which also I delivered unto you, That the Lord Jesus the same night in which he was betrayed took bread:	For I have received from our Lord, that which I imparted to you; that our Lord Jesus, on the night he was betrayed, took bread,	For I have received from our Lord what I committed to you, that our Lord Jesus in that night [in] which he was betrayed took bread
24	And when he had given thanks, he brake it, and said, Take, eat: this is my body, which is broken for you: this do in remembrance of me.	and blessed, and brake [it], and said: "Take, eat; this is my body, which is broken for your sakes: thus do ye, in remembrance of me."	and blessed [it] and broke [it] and said, "Take, eat, this is my body, that is broken on your behalf. Do so for my memorial."
25	After the same manner also he took the cup, when he had supped, saying, This cup is the new testament in my blood: this do ye, as oft as ye drink it, in remembrance of me.	So, after they had supped, he gave also the cup, and said: "This cup is the new testament in my blood: thus do ye, as often as ye drink [it], in remembrance of me."	Likewise, after they had eaten, he also gave the cup and said, "This cup is the new covenant in my blood. Do so, whenever you drink, for my memorial."
26	For as often as ye eat this bread, and drink this cup, ye do shew the Lord's death till he come.	For as often as ye eat this bread, and drink this cup, ye commemorate the death of our Lord, until his advent.	For whenever you eat this bread and drink this cup, you call to remembrance the death of our Lord until his coming.
27	Wherefore whosoever shall eat this bread, and drink this cup of the Lord, unworthily, shall be guilty of the body and blood of the Lord.	He therefore, who eateth of the bread of the Lord, and drinketh of his cup, and is not worthy of it, is guilty of the blood of the Lord, and of his body.	Therefore, whoever eats of the bread of the LORD and drinks from his cup and is not worthy, he is indebted to the blood of the LORD and to his body.
28	But let a man examine himself, and so let him eat of that bread, and drink of that cup.	For this reason, a man should examine himself, and then eat of this bread, and drink of this cup:	Because of this, a man should examine himself and then eat from this bread and drink from this cup,
29	For he that eateth and drinketh unworthily, eateth and drinketh damnation to himself, not discerning the Lord's body.	for, whoever eateth and drinketh of it, while he is unworthy, eateth and drinketh condemnation on himself, by not discerning the body of the Lord.	for he who eats and drinks from it, being unworthy, eats and drinks condemnation to himself, because he has not discerned the body of the LORD.
30	For this cause many are weak and sickly among you, and many sleep.	For this cause, many among you are diseased and sickly, and many sleep.	Because of this, many among you [are] sick and weak and many are asleep.
31	For if we would judge ourselves, we should not be judged.	For if we would judge ourselves, we should not be judged.	For if we judge ourselves, we are not judged.
32	But when we are judged, we are chastened of the Lord, that we should not be condemned with the world.	But when we are judged by our Lord, we are really chastised, that we may not be condemned with the world.	But when we are judged by our Lord, we are indeed instructed, so that we should not be condemned with the world.

	KJV	Murdock	Magiera

I CORINTHIANS *Chapter 11*

	KJV	Murdock	Magiera
33	Wherefore, my brethren, when ye come together to eat, tarry one for another.	Wherefore, my Brethren, when ye assemble to eat, wait ye one for another.	From now on, my brothers, when you are gathered to eat, wait for one another.
34	And if any man hunger, let him eat at home; that ye come not together unto condemnation. And the rest will I set in order when I come.	And let him who is hungry, eat at home; that ye may assemble, not for condemnation. And as to other things, I will give you directions when I come.	And he who is hungry should eat in his house, so that you will not be gathering together to condemnation. Now concerning the rest, I will charge you when I come.

Chapter 12

	KJV	Murdock	Magiera
1	Now concerning spiritual gifts, brethren, I would not have you ignorant.	And concerning spirituals, my brethren, I would have you know,	Now about spiritual [things], my brothers, I want you to know
2	Ye know that ye were Gentiles, carried away unto these dumb idols, even as ye were led.	that ye have been pagans; and have been, without distinction, led away after idols, in which there is no speech.	that you were heathens and were led to idols that have no distinct voice.
3	Wherefore I give you to understand, that no man speaking by the Spirit of God calleth Jesus accursed: and that no man can say that Jesus is the Lord, but by the Holy Ghost.	I therefore inform you, that there is no man, that speaketh by the Spirit of God, who saith that Jesus is accursed: neither can a man say that Jesus is the Lord, except by the Holy Spirit.	Because of this, I make known to you that there is no one who speaks by the Spirit of God and says that Jesus is cursed. And neither is anyone able to say that Jesus is LORD, except by the Holy Spirit.
4	Now there are diversities of gifts, but the same Spirit.	Now there are diversities of gifts; but the Spirit is one.	And there are distributions of gifts, but the Spirit is one.
5	And there are differences of administrations, but the same Lord.	And there are diversities of ministrations; but the Lord is one.	And there are distributions of services, but the LORD is one.
6	And there are diversities of operations, but it is the same God which worketh all in all.	And there are diversities of energies; but God, who worketh all in all men, is one.	And there are distributions of powers, but God is the one who works all in everyone.
7	But the manifestation of the Spirit is given to every man to profit withal.	And to each man, there is given a manifestation of the Spirit, that it may aid him.	Now the manifestation of the Spirit is given to each one as it is profitable for him.
8	For to one is given by the Spirit the word of wisdom; to another the word of knowledge by the same Spirit;	To one, by the Spirit, there is given a word of wisdom; and to another, by the same Spirit, there is given a word of knowledge:	There is a word of wisdom that is given to him by the Spirit, now for another, a word of knowledge by the same Spirit,
9	To another faith by the same Spirit; to another the gifts of healing by the same Spirit;	to another, by the same Spirit, faith: to another, by the same Spirit, gifts of healing:	for another, faith by the same Spirit, for another, gifts of healing by the same Spirit,
10	To another the working of miracles; to another prophecy; to another discerning of spirits; to another divers kinds of tongues; to another the interpretation of tongues:	and to another, miracles: and to another, prophecy: and to another, the discerning of spirits: and to another, [divers] kinds of tongues: and to another, the interpretation of tongues.	now for another, miracles, now for another, prophecy, now for another, discerning of spirits, now for another, kinds of tongues, now for another, the interpretation of tongues.
11	But all these worketh that one and the selfsame Spirit, dividing to every man severally as he will.	But all these, worketh that one Spirit; and he distributeth to every one as he pleaseth.	Now all these [things] the one Spirit works and distributes to everyone as he wills.

Parallel Translations

I CORINTHIANS *Chapter 12*

	KJV	*Murdock*	*Magiera*
12	For as the body is one, and hath many members, and all the members of that one body, being many, are one body: so also is Christ.	For as the body is one, and in it are many members; and all those members of the body, though many, are one body; so also is the Messiah.	For as the body is one and there are many members in it and all the members of the body, although they are many, are one body, so also [is] Christ.
13	For by one Spirit are we all baptized into one body, whether we be Jews or Gentiles, whether we be bond or free; and have been all made to drink into one Spirit.	For all of us, likewise, by one Spirit, have been baptized into one body, whether Jews or Gentiles, whether slaves or free; and all of us have drinked in one Spirit.	For all of us also are baptized in one spirit into one body, whether Judean or Gentile, whether slave or free men. And all of us drink of one Spirit.
14	For the body is not one member, but many.	For a body also, is not one member, but many.	For also the body is not one member, but many.
15	If the foot shall say, Because I am not the hand, I am not of the body; is it therefore not of the body?	For if the foot should say, Because I am not the hand, I am not of the body; is it, on that account, not of the body?	For if the foot should say, "Because I am not the hand, I am not a part of the body," because of this, is it not a part of the body?
16	And if the ear shall say, Because I am not the eye, I am not of the body; is it therefore not of the body?	Or if the ear should say, Because I am not the eye, I am not of the body; is it, on that account, not of the body?	And if the ear should say, "Because I am not the eye, I am not a part of the body," because of this, is it not a part of the body?
17	If the whole body were an eye, where were the hearing? If the whole were hearing, where were the smelling?	And if the whole body were an eye, where would be the hearing? Or if it were all hearing, where would be the smelling?	For if all the body were eyes, where would the hearing be? And if all of it were hearing, where would the smelling be?
18	But now hath God set the members every one of them in the body, as it hath pleased him.	But now hath God placed every one of the members in the body, according to his pleasure.	But now God has placed every one of the members in the body, as he willed.
19	And if they were all one member, where were the body?	And if they were all one member, where would be the body?	Now if they were all one member, where would the body be?
20	But now are they many members, yet but one body.	But now they are many members, yet but one body.	But now, there are many members, but it is one body.
21	And the eye cannot say unto the hand, I have no need of thee: nor again the head to the feet, I have no need of you.	The eye cannot say to the hand, Thou art not needful to me: nor can the head say to the feet, Ye are not needful to me.	The eye is not able to say to the hand, "You are not necessary to me." Nor is the head able to say to the feet, "You are not necessary to me."
22	Nay, much more those members of the body, which seem to be more feeble, are necessary:	But rather, those members which are accounted feeble, are indispensable.	But more, there is a necessity for those members that are thought to be weak.
23	And those members of the body, which we think to be less honourable, upon these we bestow more abundant honour; and our uncomely parts have more abundant comeliness.	And those which we think dishonorable in the body, on them we heap more honor; and those that are uncomely, on them we put the more decoration.	And to those that we think are despised in the body, we give more honor. And for those that are modest, we make more decoration.

Parallel Translations

I CORINTHIANS Chapter 12

	KJV	Murdock	Magiera
24	For our comely parts have no need: but God hath tempered the body together, having given more abundant honour to that part which lacked:	For the honorable members in us, have no need of honor: for God hath tempered the body, and given more honor to the member which is inferior;	Now those members that we have that are honored do not require honor. For God has joined together the body and he has given more honor to the member who is least,
25	That there should be no schism in the body; but that the members should have the same care one for another.	that there might be no disunion in the body, but that all the members, equally, might care for one another;	so that there would not be division in the body, but rather [that] all the members would care for one another equally,
26	And whether one member suffer, all the members suffer with it; or one member be honoured, all the members rejoice with it.	so that, when one member is in pain, they will all sympathize; and if one member is exalted, all the members will be exalted.	so that when one member was hurt, all of them would suffer, and if one member was praised, all the members would be praised.
27	Now ye are the body of Christ, and members in particular.	Now ye are the body of Messiah, and members in your place.	Now you are the body of Christ and members in your place.
28	And God hath set some in the church, first apostles, secondarily prophets, thirdly teachers, after that miracles, then gifts of healings, helps, governments, diversities of tongues.	For God hath placed in his church, first, legates; after them, prophets; after them, teachers; after them, workers of miracles; after them, the gifts of healing, and helpers, and leaders, and [various] kinds of tongues.	For God set in his church, first apostles, after them, prophets, after them, teachers, after them, workers of miracles, after them, gifts of healing and helpers and leaders and kinds of tongues.
29	Are all apostles? are all prophets? are all teachers? are all workers of miracles?	Are they all legates? Are they all prophets? Are they all teachers? Are they all workers of miracles?	[Are] all of them apostles? [Are] all of them prophets? [Are] all of them teachers? [Are] all of them doers of miracles?
30	Have all the gifts of healing? do all speak with tongues? do all interpret?	Have all of them the gifts of healing? Do they all speak with tongues? Or do they all interpret?	Do all of them have gifts of healing? Do all of them speak in tongues? Or do all of them interpret?
31	But covet earnestly the best gifts: and yet shew I unto you a more excellent way.	And if ye are emulous of the superior gifts, on the other hand, I show to you a better way.	Now if you are zealous about the best gifts, I will also show you a way that is of more value.

Chapter 13

	KJV	Murdock	Magiera
1	Though I speak with the tongues of men and of angels, and have not charity, I am become as sounding brass, or a tinkling cymbal.	If I could speak in every tongue of men, and in that of angels, and there should be no love in me, I should be like brass that resoundeth, or the cymbal that maketh a noise.	If I should speak in every tongue of men and with [tongues] of angels and not have love, I would be brass that sounds or a cymbal that gives out noise.
2	And though I have the gift of prophecy, and understand all mysteries, and all knowledge; and though I have all faith, so that I could remove mountains, and have not charity, I am nothing.	And if there should be in me [the gift of] prophecy, and I should understand all the mysteries, and every science; and if there should be in me all faith, so that I could move mountains, and love should not be in me, I should be nothing.	And if I would have prophecy and I would know all mysteries and all knowledge and if I would have all faith so that I could move a mountain and I do not have love, I am nothing.

I CORINTHIANS *Chapter 13*

	KJV	Murdock	Magiera
3	And though I bestow all my goods to feed the poor, and though I give my body to be burned, and have not charity, it profiteth me nothing.	And if I should feed out to the destitute all I possess; and if I should give my body to be burned; and there should be no love in me, I gain nothing.	And if I would feed the poor all that I have and if I would deliver my body to be burned and I do not have love, I am not profiting anything.
4	Charity suffereth long, and is kind; charity envieth not; charity vaunteth not itself, is not puffed up,	Love is long-suffering, and is kind; love is not envious; love is not boisterous; and is not inflated;	Love is long-suffering and kind. Love does not envy. Love is not ruffled and is not puffed up
5	Doth not behave itself unseemly, seeketh not her own, is not easily provoked, thinketh no evil;	and doth nothing that causeth shame; and seeketh not her own; is not passionate; and thinketh no evil;	and does not do that which is shameful and does not seek its own and is not enraged and does not think what is evil,
6	Rejoiceth not in iniquity, but rejoiceth in the truth;	rejoiceth not in iniquity, but rejoiceth in the truth;	does not rejoice in wickedness, but rejoices with truthfulness.
7	Beareth all things, believeth all things, hopeth all things, endureth all things.	beareth all things, believeth all things, hopeth all, and endureth all.	[Love] endures everything, believes everything, hopes all, bears all.
8	Charity never faileth: but whether there be prophecies, they shall fail; whether there be tongues, they shall cease; whether there be knowledge, it shall vanish away.	Love will never cease. But prophesyings will end; and tongues will be silent; and knowledge will vanish.	Love never fails. For prophecies will be made void and tongues will be silent and knowledge will be made void.
9	For we know in part, and we prophesy in part.	For we know but partially; and we prophesy but partially.	For we know in part and we prophesy in part.
10	But when that which is perfect is come, then that which is in part shall be done away.	But when completeness shall come, then that which is partial will vanish away.	Now when what is completed comes, then what is partial will be made void.
11	When I was a child, I spake as a child, I understood as a child, I thought as a child: but when I became a man, I put away childish things.	When I was a child, I talked as a child, and I reasoned as a child, and I thought as a child: but when I became a man, I laid aside the things of childhood.	When I was a child, I spoke as a child and I thought as a child and I reasoned as a child. But when I became a man, I stopped these [things] of youth.
12	For now we see through a glass, darkly; but then face to face: now I know in part; but then shall I know even as also I am known.	And now we see, as by a mirror, in similitude; but then face to face: now I know partially; but then shall I know, just as I am known.	Now as in a mirror, we see in an illustration, but then face to face. Now I know in part, but then I will know as I am known.
13	And now abideth faith, hope, charity, these three; but the greatest of these is charity.	For these three things are abiding, faith, and hope, and love; but the greatest of these is love.	For there are these three that remain, faith and hope and love, but the greatest of these is love.

Chapter 14

	KJV	Murdock	Magiera
1	Follow after charity, and desire spiritual gifts, but rather that ye may prophesy.	Follow after love; and be emulous of the gifts of the Spirit, and especially, that ye may prophesy.	Pursue love and be zealous about the gifts of the Spirit, but especially to prophesy.
2	For he that speaketh in an unknown tongue speaketh not unto men, but unto God: for no man understandeth him; howbeit in the spirit he speaketh mysteries.	For he that speaketh in a tongue, speaketh not unto men, but unto God; for no one understandeth what is said; yet in the spirit, he speaketh a mystery.	For he who speaks in a tongue does not speak to men, but to God, for no one understands anything that he speaks, but spiritually he speaks a mystery.

Parallel Translations

	KJV	Murdock	Magiera
	I CORINTHIANS *Chapter 14*		
3	But he that prophesieth speaketh unto men to edification, and exhortation, and comfort.	But he that prophesieth, speaketh unto men, for edification, and exhortation, and consolation.	Now he who prophesies speaks to men edification and encouragement and comfort.
4	He that speaketh in an unknown tongue edifieth himself; but he that prophesieth edifieth the church.	He that speaketh in a tongue, edifieth himself: and he that prophesieth, edifieth the church.	He who speaks in a tongue builds himself up and he who prophesies builds up the church.
5	I would that ye all spake with tongues, but rather that ye prophesied: for greater is he that prophesieth than he that speaketh with tongues, except he interpret, that the church may receive edifying.	Now I would that ye all spoke with tongues, but rather that ye prophesied; for greater is he that prophesieth, than he that speaketh in a tongue, unless he interpret; and if he interpret, he edifieth the church.	Now I am desiring that all of you would speak in tongues and especially that you would prophesy. For greater is he who prophesies than he who speaks in a tongue, unless he interprets. Now if he interprets, he edifies the church.
6	Now, brethren, if I come unto you speaking with tongues, what shall I profit you, except I shall speak to you either by revelation, or by knowledge, or by prophesying, or by doctrine?	And now, my brethren, if I should come among you, and speak to you in tongues, what should I profit you; unless I should speak to you either by revelation, or by knowledge, or by prophecy, or by doctrine?	And now, my brothers, if I come to you and speak with you in tongues, what am I profiting you, unless I speak with you either by revelation or by knowledge or by prophecy or by teaching?
7	And even things without life giving sound, whether pipe or harp, except they give a distinction in the sounds, how shall it be known what is piped or harped?	For even inanimate things that emit sound, whether pipe or harp, if they make no distinction between one sound and another, how will it be known, what is sung or what is harped?	For even those things that have no life and give out sound, whether flute or harp, if they do not make a distinction between one tone and the other, how is what is sung or what is played known?
8	For if the trumpet give an uncertain sound, who shall prepare himself to the battle?	And if the trumpet shall give an uncertain sound, who will prepare himself for the battle?	And if the trumpet should sound a sound that is not distinct, who will prepare for the battle?
9	So likewise ye, except ye utter by the tongue words easy to be understood, how shall it be known what is spoken? for ye shall speak into the air.	So likewise if ye utter a discourse in a tongue, and there is no interpretation given, how will it be known what ye have said? Ye will have been as if ye spoke into the air.	Likewise also, if you speak a message in a tongue and it will not be interpreted, how is what you spoke known? You will be as if you are speaking to the air.
10	There are, it may be, so many kinds of voices in the world, and none of them is without signification.	For lo, there are many kinds of tongues in the world; and there is not one of them without meaning.	For behold, there are many kinds of tongues in the world and there is not one of them without meaning.
11	Therefore if I know not the meaning of the voice, I shall be unto him that speaketh a barbarian, and he that speaketh shall be a barbarian unto me.	But if I do not know the import of the sound, I shall be a barbarian to him that speaketh, and the speaker will be a barbarian to me.	But if I do not know the significance of the sound, I will be a barbarian to him who speaks, and also he who speaks will be a barbarian to me.
12	Even so ye, forasmuch as ye are zealous of spiritual gifts, seek that ye may excel to the edifying of the church.	So also ye, since ye are emulous of the gifts of the Spirit for the edification of the church, seek ye to excel.	Likewise also, because you are zealous of the gifts of the Spirit, seek to excel for the building up of the church.
13	Wherefore let him that speaketh in an unknown tongue pray that he may interpret.	And let him that speaketh in a tongue, pray that he may interpret.	And he who speaks in a tongue should seek to interpret [it].

Parallel Translations

I CORINTHIANS *Chapter 14*

	KJV	*Murdock*	*Magiera*
14	For if I pray in an unknown tongue, my spirit prayeth, but my understanding is unfruitful.	For if I should pray in a tongue, my spirit prayeth, but my understanding is without fruits.	For if I was to pray in a tongue, my spirit prays, but my understanding is without fruit.
15	What is it then? I will pray with the spirit, and I will pray with the understanding also: I will sing with the spirit, and I will sing with the understanding also.	What then shall I do? I will pray with my spirit, and will pray with my understanding; and I will sing with my spirit, and will sing with my understanding.	What then should I do? I will pray in my spirit and I will pray also with my understanding. And I will sing in my spirit and I will sing with my understanding also.
16	Else when thou shalt bless with the spirit, how shall he that occupieth the room of the unlearned say Amen at thy giving of thanks, seeing he understandeth not what thou sayest?	Otherwise, if thou blessest in the spirit, how shall he that filleth the place of one unlearned, say Amen, on thy giving thanks; for he knoweth not what thou sayest?	Otherwise, if you bless spiritually, how will he who fills the place of the unlearned say "Amen" at your thanksgiving, because he does not know what you said?
17	For thou verily givest thanks well, but the other is not edified.	Thou blessest, indeed, very well; but thy neighbor is not edified.	For you are blessing well, but your associate is not built up.
18	I thank my God, I speak with tongues more than ye all:	I thank God, that I speak with tongues more than all of you.	I thank God that I speak in tongues more than all of you.
19	Yet in the church I had rather speak five words with my understanding, that by my voice I might teach others also, than ten thousand words in an unknown tongue.	But in the church, I would rather speak five words with my understanding, that I might instruct others, than a myriad of words in a tongue.	But in the church I desire to speak five words with my understanding, so that I would also teach others, rather than a great number of words in a tongue.
20	Brethren, be not children in understanding: howbeit in malice be ye children, but in understanding be men.	My brethren, be ye not children in your thoughts; but to evil things be ye infants; and in your thoughts be men.	My brothers, do not be children in your minds. But rather, be babies to evil [things] and be mature in your minds.
21	In the law it is written, With men of other tongues and other lips will I speak unto this people; and yet for all that will they not hear me, saith the Lord.	In the law it is written, With a foreign speech, and in another tongue, will I speak with this people; and even so also they will not hearken to me, saith the Lord.	In the law it is written: WITH A STRANGE SPEECH AND WITH ANOTHER TONGUE I WILL SPEAK WITH THIS PEOPLE. EVEN SO, THEY WILL NOT HEAR ME, says the LORD.
22	Wherefore tongues are for a sign, not to them that believe, but to them that believe not: but prophesying serveth not for them that believe not, but for them which believe.	Wherefore, tongues are established for a sign, not to the believers, but to them that believe not. But prophesyings are not for those who believe not, but for them that believe.	Then tongues are placed for a sign, not to believers, but to those who do not believe. And prophecies are not to those who do not believe, but to those who believe.
23	If therefore the whole church be come together into one place, and all speak with tongues, and there come in those that are unlearned, or unbelievers, will they not say that ye are mad?	If therefore the whole church assemble, and they all speak with tongues, and there come in unlearned persons, or such as believe not, will they not say: These people are crazy?	If therefore all the church is gathered and all would speak in tongues and unlearned [ones] or those who do not believe should enter, will they not say, "These [people] are crazy"?
24	But if all prophesy, and there come in one that believeth not, or one unlearned, he is convinced of all, he is judged of all:	But if ye should be all prophesying, and one unlearned or an unbeliever should come among you, he is explored by you all, and rebuked by you all;	And if all of you would prophesy and an unlearned [one] or one who does not believe enters, he is examined by all of you and reproved by all of you

Parallel Translations

	KJV	Murdock	Magiera

I CORINTHIANS *Chapter 14*

	KJV	Murdock	Magiera
25	And thus are the secrets of his heart made manifest; and so falling down on his face he will worship God, and report that God is in you of a truth.	and the secrets of his heart are laid open [to him]: and so he will fall upon his face, and will worship God, and say: Verily, God is in you.	and the hidden [things] of his heart are revealed. And then he will fall on his face and will worship God and will say, "Truly God is with you."
26	How is it then, brethren? when ye come together, every one of you hath a psalm, hath a doctrine, hath a tongue, hath a revelation, hath an interpretation. Let all things be done unto edifying.	I therefore say [to you] my brethren, that when ye assemble, whoever of you hath a psalm, let him speak; and whoever hath a doctrine, and whoever hath a revelation, and whoever hath a tongue, and whoever hath an interpretation. Let them all be for edification.	Therefore, my brothers, I say that when you are gathered, whoever of you has a psalm should speak. And he who has a teaching and he who has a revelation and he who has a tongue and he who has an interpretation, all of them should be for building up.
27	If any man speak in an unknown tongue, let it be by two, or at the most by three, and that by course; and let one interpret.	And if any speak in a tongue, let two speak or at most, three; and let them speak one by one; and let [some] one interpret.	And if someone speaks in a tongue, two should speak and at the most three. And they should speak one by one and [that] one should interpret.
28	But if there be no interpreter, let him keep silence in the church; and let him speak to himself, and to God.	And if there is none to interpret, let him that speaketh in a tongue, be silent in the church; and let him speak to himself and to God.	And if there is not one to interpret, he who speaks in a tongue should keep silent in the church and should speak to himself and to God.
29	Let the prophets speak two or three, and let the other judge.	And as to prophets, let two or three speak, and let the rest judge.	And the prophets should speak, two or three, and the rest should discern.
30	If any thing be revealed to another that sitteth by, let the first hold his peace.	And if to another sitting by, there should be a revelation, let the first stop speaking.	And if [something] is revealed to another while he sits, the first should be silent.
31	For ye may all prophesy one by one, that all may learn, and all may be comforted.	For ye can all prophesy, one by one; so that every one may learn, and every one be comforted.	For all of you can prophesy one by one, so that everyone may learn and everyone may be comforted.
32	And the spirits of the prophets are subject to the prophets.	For the spirit of the prophets is subject to the prophets.	For the spirit of the prophets is subject to the prophets,
33	For God is not the author of confusion, but of peace, as in all churches of the saints.	Because, God is not [the author] of tumult, but of peace, as in all churches of the saints.	because God is not [one] of confusion, but of peace, as in all the churches of the holy [ones].
34	Let your women keep silence in the churches: for it is not permitted unto them to speak; but they are commanded to be under obedience, as also saith the law.	Let your women be silent in the church: for it is not permitted them to speak, but to be in subjection, as also the law saith.	Your wives should be silent in the church, for they are not allowed to speak, but they are to be subject, as the law also says.
35	And if they will learn any thing, let them ask their husbands at home: for it is a shame for women to speak in the church.	And if they wish to be informed on any subject, let them ask their husbands at home: for it is unbecoming for women to speak in the church.	And if they want to learn anything, they should ask their husbands at home, for it is a shame that wives should speak in the church.
36	What? came the word of God out from you? or came it unto you only?	What! was it from you that the word of God came forth? Or did it reach only to you?	Did the word of God go out from you? Or did it only arrive to you?

	KJV	Murdock	Magiera

I CORINTHIANS Chapter 14

	KJV	Murdock	Magiera
37	If any man think himself to be a prophet, or spiritual, let him acknowledge that the things that I write unto you are the commandments of the Lord.	And if any one among you thinketh that he is a prophet, or that he is spiritual, let him recognize the things which I write to you, as being the precepts of our Lord.	Now if one of you thinks that he is a prophet or that he is [prophesying] of the Spirit, he should acknowledge that these [things] that I write to you are the commandments of our Lord.
38	But if any man be ignorant, let him be ignorant.	But if any one be ignorant, let him be ignorant.	Now if someone does not know, he will not know.
39	Wherefore, brethren, covet to prophesy, and forbid not to speak with tongues.	Wherefore, my brethren, be emulous of prophesying: and to speak with tongues, prohibit not.	Therefore, my brothers, earnestly desire to prophesy and to speak in tongues. Do not hold back.
40	Let all things be done decently and in order.	But let every thing be done with decency and regularity.	Now everything should be [done] with decency and order.

Chapter 15

	KJV	Murdock	Magiera
1	Moreover, brethren, I declare unto you the gospel which I preached unto you, which also ye have received, and wherein ye stand;	And I make known to you, my brethren, the gospel which I preached to you, and which ye received, and in which ye stand,	Now I make known to you, my brothers, the gospel that I preached to you and [that] you received and in which you stand
2	By which also ye are saved, if ye keep in memory what I preached unto you, unless ye have believed in vain.	and by which ye have life. In what terms I preached to you, ye remember; unless ye have believed in vain.	and by which you have life. With what word I preached to you, you remember, unless you have believed fruitlessly.
3	For I delivered unto you first of all that which I also received, how that Christ died for our sins according to the scriptures;	For I delivered to you from the first, as I had received it; that the Messiah died on account of our sins, as it is written:	For I committed to you from the first according to what I received, that Christ died for our sins, as it is written,
4	And that he was buried, and that he rose again the third day according to the scriptures:	and that he was buried and arose on the third day, as it is written:	and that he was buried and rose after three days, as it is written.
5	And that he was seen of Cephas, then of the twelve:	and that he was seen by Cephas; and after him, by the twelve:	And he appeared to Peter and after him, to the twelve.
6	After that, he was seen of above five hundred brethren at once; of whom the greater part remain unto this present, but some are fallen asleep.	and after that, he was seen by more than five hundred brethren at once; many of whom survive at the present time, and some of them sleep.	And after that, he appeared to more than five hundred brothers together, many of whom remain until now, yet some of them sleep.
7	After that, he was seen of James; then of all the apostles.	And subsequently to this, he was seen by James; and after him, by all the legates.	And after these, he appeared to James and after him, to all the apostles.
8	And last of all he was seen of me also, as of one born out of due time.	And last of them all, he was seen by me, as it were by an abortion.	And last of all, he appeared to me also, as one of an untimely birth.
9	For I am the least of the apostles, that am not meet to be called an apostle, because I persecuted the church of God.	I am the least of the legates; and am not worthy to be called a legate; because I persecuted the church of God.	For I am the least of the apostles and am not worthy to be called an apostle, because I persecuted the church of God.

Parallel Translations

I CORINTHIANS *Chapter 15*

	KJV	Murdock	Magiera
10	But by the grace of God I am what I am: and his grace which was bestowed upon me was not in vain; but I laboured more abundantly than they all: yet not I, but the grace of God which was with me.	But by the grace of God, I am what I am: and his grace, that was in me, was not in vain; but I labored more than they all:—not I, but his grace that was with me.	But by the grace of God, I am what I am. And his grace that is in me was not fruitless. But I worked more than all of them, not I, but his grace that is with me.
11	Therefore whether it were I or they, so we preach, and so ye believed.	Whether I, therefore, or whether they, so we preached; and so ye believed.	Whether I, therefore, or they, so we preach and so you have believed.
12	Now if Christ be preached that he rose from the dead, how say some among you that there is no resurrection of the dead?	And if the Messiah is proclaimed, as rising from the dead; how is it that there are some among you, who say, There is no reviviscence of the dead?	And if Christ is preached that he rose from the dead, how are there some among you who say [that] there is no resurrection of the dead?
13	But if there be no resurrection of the dead, then is Christ not risen:	And if there is no reviviscence of the dead, the Messiah also hath not risen.	And if there is no resurrection of the dead, not even Christ has been raised.
14	And if Christ be not risen, then is our preaching vain, and your faith is also vain.	And if the Messiah hath not risen, our preaching is vain, and your faith also vain.	And if Christ did not rise, our preaching is fruitless. Your faith [is] also fruitless.
15	Yea, and we are found false witnesses of God; because we have testified of God that he raised up Christ: whom he raised not up, if so be that the dead rise not.	And we too are found false witnesses of God; for we have testified concerning God, that he raised up the Messiah, when he did not raise him up.	And we are also found [to be] false witnesses of God, because we have witnessed about God that he raised Christ, when he did not raise [him] up.
16	For if the dead rise not, then is not Christ raised:	For, if the dead will not arise, the Messiah also hath not risen.	For if the dead do not rise, not even Christ has been raised.
17	And if Christ be not raised, your faith is vain; ye are yet in your sins.	And if the Messiah rose not, your faith is inane; and ye are yet in your sins:	And if Christ did not rise, your faith is void and you are still in your sins
18	Then they also which are fallen asleep in Christ are perished.	and also, doubtless, they who have fallen asleep in the Messiah, have perished.	and doubtless also, those who sleep in Christ have perished.
19	If in this life only we have hope in Christ, we are of all men most miserable.	And if, in this life only, we have hope in the Messiah, we are the most miserable of all men.	And if in this life only we hope in Christ, we are most miserable of all men.
20	But now is Christ risen from the dead, and become the firstfruits of them that slept.	But now the Messiah hath risen from the dead, and become the first-fruits of them that slept.	But now Christ has risen from the dead and has become the first of those asleep.
21	For since by man came death, by man came also the resurrection of the dead.	And as by a man came death, so also by a man came the reviviscence of the dead.	And as by way of a man came death, so also by way of a man came the resurrection of the dead.
22	For as in Adam all die, even so in Christ shall all be made alive.	For as it was by Adam, that all men die, so also by the Messiah they all live:	For as in Adam all men die, so also in Christ all live,
23	But every man in his own order: Christ the firstfruits; afterward they that are Christ's at his coming.	every one in his order; the Messiah was the first-fruits; afterwards, they that are the Messiah's, at his coming.	each in his order. Christ was the first [and] after that, those who are of Christ at his coming.

Parallel Translations

I CORINTHIANS *Chapter 15*

	KJV	Murdock	Magiera
24	Then cometh the end, when he shall have delivered up the kingdom to God, even the Father; when he shall have put down all rule and all authority and power.	And then will be the end, when he shall have delivered up the kingdom to God the Father; when every prince, and every sovereign, and all powers shall have come to naught.	And then will be the end, when he delivers the kingdom to God the Father, when every ruler and every authority and all powers cease.
25	For he must reign, till he hath put all enemies under his feet.	For he is to reign, until he shall put all his enemies under his feet.	For he is going to reign, until he places all his enemies under his feet.
26	The last enemy that shall be destroyed is death.	And the last enemy, death, will be abolished.	And the last enemy, death, will be abolished.
27	For he hath put all things under his feet. But when he saith all things are put under him, it is manifest that he is excepted, which did put all things under him.	For he hath subjected all under his feet. But when he said, that every thing is subjected to him, it is manifest that he is excepted, who subjected all to him.	FOR HE HAS SUBJECTED ALL UNDER HIS FEET. But when he says that everything has been made subject to him, it is evident that it is apart from him who subjected all to him.
28	And when all things shall be subdued unto him, then shall the Son also himself be subject unto him that put all things under him, that God may be all in all.	And when all shall be subjected to him, then the Son himself will be subject to him who subjected all to him, so that God will be all in all.	And when everything is subjected to him, then the Son will be made subject to the one who subjected all to him, so that God will be all in all.
29	Else what shall they do which are baptized for the dead, if the dead rise not at all? why are they then baptized for the dead?	Otherwise, what shall they do who are baptized for the dead, if the dead rise not? Why are they baptized for the dead?	And if not, what will those who are baptized do for the dead, if the dead do not rise? Why are they baptized? For the dead?
30	And why stand we in jeopardy every hour?	And why also do we stand every hour in peril?	And why do we also stand in danger in every hour?
31	I protest by your rejoicing which I have in Christ Jesus our Lord, I die daily.	I protest, my brethren, by your exultation, which is mine in our Lord Jesus the Messiah, that I die daily.	I swear by your boasting that I have in our Lord Jesus Christ, my brothers, that I am dying daily.
32	If after the manner of men I have fought with beasts at Ephesus, what advantageth it me, if the dead rise not? let us eat and drink; for to morrow we die.	If, as amongst men, I was cast to wild beasts at Ephesus, what did it profit me, if the dead rise not? "Let us eat and drink; for to-morrow we die."	If as among men I was thrown to the beasts in Ephesus, what did I gain, if the dead do not rise? LET US EAT AND DRINK, FOR TOMORROW WE WILL DIE.
33	Be not deceived: evil communications corrupt good manners.	Be not deceived; "Evil stories corrupt well-disposed minds."	Do not err. Evil conversations corrupt good minds.
34	Awake to righteousness, and sin not; for some have not the knowledge of God: I speak this to your shame.	Let your hearts be righteously excited, and sin not: for there are some, in whom is not the love of God: it is to your shame, I say it.	Stir up your heart justly and do not sin, for there are some who do not have the knowledge of God. I am speaking to your shame.
35	But some man will say, How are the dead raised up? and with what body do they come?	But some one of you may say: How will the dead arise? and with what body will they come forth?	One of you will say, "How do the dead rise? And in what body will they come?"
36	Thou fool, that which thou sowest is not quickened, except it die:	Foolish man! The seed which thou sowest, is not quickened, unless it die.	Fool! The seed that you sow does not live unless it dies.

Parallel Translations

	KJV	*Murdock*	*Magiera*
	I CORINTHIANS *Chapter 15*		
37	And that which thou sowest, thou sowest not that body that shall be, but bare grain, it may chance of wheat, or of some other grain:	And that which thou sowest, thou sowest not the body that is to be, but the naked kernel of wheat or barley, or of the other grains:	And what you sow, you are not sowing that body that it is going to be, but the naked kernel of wheat or of barley or of the rest of the grains.
38	But God giveth it a body as it hath pleased him, and to every seed his own body.	and God giveth it a body, as he pleaseth; and to each of the grains its natural body.	Now God gave it a body as he willed and to each one of the grains its natural body.
39	All flesh is not the same flesh: but there is one kind of flesh of men, another flesh of beasts, another of fishes, and another of birds.	And every body is not alike; for the body of a man is one thing, and that of a beast is another, and that of a bird is another, and that of a fish is another.	Now every body is not the same, for the body of a man is one [kind] and another of a beast and another of a bird and another of a fish.
40	There are also celestial bodies, and bodies terrestrial: but the glory of the celestial is one, and the glory of the terrestrial is another.	And there are bodies celestial, and bodies terrestrial; but the glory of the celestial [bodies] is one, and that of the terrestrial is another.	And there are heavenly bodies and there are earthly bodies, but the glory of the heavenly is one [kind] and another of the earthly.
41	There is one glory of the sun, and another glory of the moon, and another glory of the stars: for one star differeth from another star in glory.	And the glory of the sun is one thing, and the glory of the moon is another, and the glory of the stars is another; and one star exceedeth another star in glory.	And the glory of the sun is one [kind] and the glory of the moon [is] another and the glory of the stars another and [one] star is greater than [another] star in glory.
42	So also is the resurrection of the dead. It is sown in corruption; it is raised in incorruption:	So also in the reviviscence of the dead. They are sown in corruption, they arise without corruption:	So also [is] the resurrection of the dead. They are sown in corruption. They are raised without corruption.
43	It is sown in dishonour; it is raised in glory: it is sown in weakness; it is raised in power:	they are sown in dishonor, they arise in glory: they are sown in weakness, they arise in power:	They are sown in disgrace. They are raised in glory. They are sown in weakness. They are raised in power.
44	It is sown a natural body; it is raised a spiritual body. There is a natural body, and there is a spiritual body.	it is sown an animal body, it ariseth a spiritual body. For there is a body of the animal life, and there is a body of the spirit.	It is sown a natural body. It rises a spiritual body. For there is a physical body and there is a spiritual body.
45	And so it is written, The first man Adam was made a living soul; the last Adam was made a quickening spirit.	So also is it written: "Adam, the first man, became a living soul;" the second Adam [became] a quickening spirit.	So also it is written: ADAM, THE FIRST MAN, BECAME A LIVING SOUL. And the last Adam [became] a life-giving spirit.
46	Howbeit that was not first which is spiritual, but that which is natural; and afterward that which is spiritual.	And the spiritual was not first; but the animal, and then the spiritual.	But the spiritual was not first, but the natural and then the spiritual.
47	The first man is of the earth, earthy: the second man is the Lord from heaven.	The first man was of dust from the earth; the second man was the Lord from heaven.	The first man [was] dust from the earth. The second man [was] the LORD from heaven.
48	As is the earthy, such are they also that are earthy: and as is the heavenly, such are they also that are heavenly.	As he was of the dust, so also those who are of the dust; and as was he who was from heaven, so also are the heavenly.	As he was [of] dust, so also [are those of] dust. And as he who was from heaven, so also [are] the heavenly [ones].

Parallel Translations

	KJV	Murdock	Magiera

I CORINTHIANS Chapter 15

	KJV	Murdock	Magiera
49	And as we have borne the image of the earthy, we shall also bear the image of the heavenly.	And as we have worn the likeness of him from the dust, so shall we wear the likeness of him from heaven.	And as we have worn the likeness of him who is from dust, so we will wear the likeness of him who is from heaven.
50	Now this I say, brethren, that flesh and blood cannot inherit the kingdom of God; neither doth corruption inherit incorruption.	But this I say, my brethren that flesh and blood cannot inherit the kingdom of heaven: neither doth corruption inherit incorruption.	And I am saying this, my brothers, that flesh and blood cannot inherit the kingdom of heaven, nor [can] corruption inherit incorruption.
51	Behold, I shew you a mystery; We shall not all sleep, but we shall all be changed,	Lo, I tell you a mystery; we shall not all sleep, but we shall all be changed,	Behold, I am telling you a mystery. Not all of us will sleep, but all of us will be changed,
52	In a moment, in the twinkling of an eye, at the last trump: for the trumpet shall sound, and the dead shall be raised incorruptible, and we shall be changed.	suddenly, as in the twinkling of an eye, at the last trumpet, when it shall sound; and the dead will arise, without corruption; and we shall be changed.	suddenly, as the twinkling of an eye, at the last trumpet sounding, and the dead will rise without corruption and we will be changed.
53	For this corruptible must put on incorruption, and this mortal must put on immortality.	For this which is corruptible, is to put on incorruption; and that which dieth, will put on immortality.	For this [one] that was going to be corrupted will put on incorruption. And this [one] that [was going to] die will put on immortality.
54	So when this corruptible shall have put on incorruption, and this mortal shall have put on immortality, then shall be brought to pass the saying that is written, Death is swallowed up in victory.	And when this that is corruptible, shall put on incorruption, and this that dieth, immortality; then will take place the word that is written, "Death is absorbed in victory."	Now when this [one] that is corrupted puts on incorruption, and this [one] that dies, immortality, then the saying will happen that is written: DEATH IS SWALLOWED IN VICTORY.
55	O death, where is thy sting? O grave, where is thy victory?	Where is thy sting, O death? And where is thy victory, O grave?	WHERE IS YOUR STING, DEATH? OR WHERE IS YOUR VICTORY, GRAVE?
56	The sting of death is sin; and the strength of sin is the law.	Now the sting of death is sin; and the strength of sin is the law.	Now the sting of death is sin and the power of sin is the law.
57	But thanks be to God, which giveth us the victory through our Lord Jesus Christ.	But thanks be to God, that giveth us the victory, through our Lord Jesus the Messiah.	But blessed [be] God who gives us the victory by way of our Lord Jesus Christ.
58	Therefore, my beloved brethren, be ye stedfast, unmoveable, always abounding in the work of the Lord, forasmuch as ye know that your labour is not in vain in the Lord.	Wherefore, my brethren and my beloved, be ye steadfast, and be not vacillating; but be ye at all times abundant in the work of the Lord; seeing ye know, that your labor is not in vain in the Lord.	Therefore, my brothers and my beloved [ones], be steadfast and do not be moved, but excel always in the work of the LORD, knowing that your labor is not fruitless in the LORD.

Chapter 16

	KJV	Murdock	Magiera
1	Now concerning the collection for the saints, as I have given order to the churches of Galatia, even so do ye.	And as to the collection for the saints, as I directed the churches of the Galatians, so do ye.	Now concerning that which is gathered for the holy [ones], as I commanded to the churches of the Galatians, so you should do also.

Parallel Translations

	KJV	Murdock	Magiera
	I CORINTHIANS *Chapter 16*		
2	Upon the first day of the week let every one of you lay by him in store, as God hath prospered him, that there be no gatherings when I come.	On each first day of the week, let every one of you lay aside and preserve at home, what he is able; that there may be no collections when I come.	On every first of the week, each of you in his home should lay aside and keep what he has prepared [to give], so that when I come, then collections will not occur.
3	And when I come, whomsoever ye shall approve by your letters, them will I send to bring your liberality unto Jerusalem.	And when I come, those whom ye shall select, I will send with a letter, to carry your bounty to Jerusalem.	And when I come, I will send those whom you choose with a letter to carry your grace to Jerusalem.
4	And if it be meet that I go also, they shall go with me.	And if it should be suitable that I also go, they shall go with me.	And if the situation is proper for me to also go, they may go with me.
5	Now I will come unto you, when I shall pass through Macedonia: for I do pass through Macedonia.	And I will come to you, when I pass from Macedonia; for I am about to pass through Macedonia.	Now I will come to you when I have crossed over from the Macedonians, for I will cross over Macedonia.
6	And it may be that I will abide, yea, and winter with you, that ye may bring me on my journey whithersoever I go.	And perhaps I shall remain with you, or winter with you; that ye may accompany me whither I go.	And perhaps also I will remain with you or winter with you, so that you may escort me to wherever I may go.
7	For I will not see you now by the way; but I trust to tarry a while with you, if the Lord permit.	For I am not disposed to see you now, as I pass along; because I hope to spend some time with you, if my Lord permit me.	For I do not want to see you now as I pass by the road. For I am trusting to remain a time with you, if my Lord allows me.
8	But I will tarry at Ephesus until Pentecost.	For I shall continue at Ephesus until Pentecost:	Now I will remain in Ephesus until Pentecost,
9	For a great door and effectual is opened unto me, and there are many adversaries.	because a great door is opened to me, which is full of occupations; and the opposers are numerous.	for a great door has opened to me that is full of opportunities and the adversaries are many.
10	Now if Timotheus come, see that he may be with you without fear: for he worketh the work of the Lord, as I also do.	And if Timothy come to you, see that he may be without fear among you; for he doeth the work of the Lord, as I do.	Now if Timothy should come to you, see that he may be with you without fear, for he does the work of the LORD as I [do].
11	Let no man therefore despise him: but conduct him forth in peace, that he may come unto me: for I look for him with the brethren.	Therefore, let no one despise him; but conduct him on in peace, that he may come to me; for I wait for him with the brethren.	Therefore, no one should despise him, but should accompany him in peace, so that he may come to me, for I am waiting for him with the brothers.
12	As touching our brother Apollos, I greatly desired him to come unto you with the brethren: but his will was not at all to come at this time; but he will come when he shall have convenient time.	As for Apollos, my brethren, I entreated him much to go with the brethren to you; but his inclination was not to go to you now; but when he shall have opportunity, he will go to you.	Now about Apollos, my brothers, I begged him much to come to you with the brothers and it may be [his] desire was not to come to you, but when he will have an opportunity, he will come to you.
13	Watch ye, stand fast in the faith, quit you like men, be strong.	Watch ye, stand firm in the faith, act like men, be valiant.	Watch and stand in the faith. Act mature. Be strong.
14	Let all your things be done with charity.	Let all your affairs be conducted with love.	And all your affairs should be [done] with love.

Parallel Translations

	KJV	*Murdock*	*Magiera*

I CORINTHIANS *Chapter 16*

	KJV	Murdock	Magiera
15	I beseech you, brethren, (ye know the house of Stephanas, that it is the firstfruits of Achaia, and that they have addicted themselves to the ministry of the saints,)	I beseech you, my brethren, concerning the household of Stephanas; (for ye know, that they were the first-fruits of Achaia, and that they have devoted themselves to ministering to the saints;)	Now I beg you, my brothers, concerning the house of Stephanas, because you know that they are the first[fruit] of Achaia and have committed themselves to the service of the holy [ones],
16	That ye submit yourselves unto such, and to every one that helpeth with us, and laboureth.	that ye also give ear to them who are such; and to every one, that laboreth with us and aideth.	that you should also listen to those who are so and to everyone who works hard with us and helps.
17	I am glad of the coming of Stephanas and Fortunatus and Achaicus: for that which was lacking on your part they have supplied.	And I rejoice at the arrival of Stephanas and Fortunatus and Achaicus: for they have supplied that wherein ye were deficient towards me.	Now I am rejoicing at the arrival of Stephanas and of Fortunatus and of Achaicus, because what you have neglected regarding me, they have filled,
18	For they have refreshed my spirit and yours: therefore acknowledge ye them that are such.	And they have refreshed my spirit, and yours: therefore acknowledge ye them who are such.	for they have refreshed my spirit and yours. Therefore, acknowledge those who are likewise.
19	The churches of Asia salute you. Aquila and Priscilla salute you much in the Lord, with the church that is in their house.	All the churches that are in Asia, salute you. Aquila and Priscilla, with the church in their house, salute you much in the Lord.	All the churches that are in Asia greet you. Aquila and Priscilla greet you much in our Lord with the church that is in their house.
20	All the brethren greet you. Greet ye one another with an holy kiss.	All the brethren salute you. Salute ye one another with a holy kiss.	All the brothers greet you. Greet one another with a holy kiss.
21	The salutation of me Paul with mine own hand.	The salutation in the handwriting of myself, Paul.	[This] greeting [is] in the handwriting of my own hand, Paul.
22	If any man love not the Lord Jesus Christ, let him be Anathema Maranatha.	Whoever loveth not our Lord Jesus the Messiah, let him be accursed: our Lord cometh.	Whoever does not love our Lord Jesus Christ will be cursed. Our Lord comes.
23	The grace of our Lord Jesus Christ be with you.	The grace of our Lord Jesus the Messiah be with you.	The grace of our Lord Jesus Christ [be] with you.
24	My love be with you all in Christ Jesus. Amen.	And my love be with you all, in the Messiah, Jesus. Amen.	And my love [be] with all of you in Christ Jesus.

Parallel Translations

II CORINTHIANS *Chapter 1*

	KJV	*Murdock*	*Magiera*
1	Paul, an apostle of Jesus Christ by the will of God, and Timothy our brother, unto the church of God which is at Corinth, with all the saints which are in all Achaia:	Paul a legate of Jesus the Messiah, by the good pleasure of God; and Timothy a brother; to the church of God that is at Corinth, and to all the saints that are in all Achaia.	Paul, an apostle of Jesus Christ by the will of God, and Timothy, a brother, to the church of God that is in Corinth and to all the holy [ones] that are in all Achaia:
2	Grace be to you and peace from God our Father, and from the Lord Jesus Christ.	Grace be with you, and peace, from God our Father, and from our Lord Jesus the Messiah.	Grace [be] with you and peace from God our Father and from our Lord Jesus Christ.
3	Blessed be God, even the Father of our Lord Jesus Christ, the Father of mercies, and the God of all comfort;	Blessed be God, the Father of our Lord Jesus the Messiah, the Father of mercies, and the God of all consolation;	Blessed be God, the Father of our Lord Jesus Christ, the Father of mercies and the God of all comfort,
4	Who comforteth us in all our tribulation, that we may be able to comfort them which are in any trouble, by the comfort wherewith we ourselves are comforted of God.	who comforteth us in all our afflictions, that we also might be able to comfort those who are in all afflictions, with the consolation wherewith we are comforted by God.	he who comforts us in all our pressures, so that we would also be able to comfort those who are in all pressures with that comfort [with] which we are comforted by God.
5	For as the sufferings of Christ abound in us, so our consolation also aboundeth by Christ.	For, as the sufferings of the Messiah abound in us, so also our consolation aboundeth by the Messiah.	For as the sufferings of Christ are increased in us, so also by way of Christ our comfort also is increased.
6	And whether we be afflicted, it is for your consolation and salvation, which is effectual in the enduring of the same sufferings which we also suffer: or whether we be comforted, it is for your consolation and salvation.	And whether we be afflicted, it is for your consolation and for your life that we are afflicted; or whether we be comforted, it is, that ye may be comforted; and that there may be in you an eagerness, wherewith ye may endure those sufferings which we also suffer.	Now even if we are pressured, it is for your comfort and [if] we are pressured, [it is] for your life and if we are comforted, [it is] on account of you. You should be comforted and have an earnest care to endure the sufferings that we also suffer.
7	And our hope of you is stedfast, knowing, that as ye are partakers of the sufferings, so shall ye be also of the consolation.	And our hope concerning you is steadfast: for we know, that if ye partake of the sufferings, ye will also partake of the consolation.	And our hope for you is steadfast, for we know that if you are participants in the sufferings, you are also participants in the comfort.
8	For we would not, brethren, have you ignorant of our trouble which came to us in Asia, that we were pressed out of measure, above strength, insomuch that we despaired even of life:	But, my brethren, we wish you to know, respecting the affliction that was upon us in Asia, that we were afflicted exceedingly, beyond our strength, insomuch that our life was ready to terminate.	Now we want you to know, our brothers, about the pressure that we had in Asia. We were greatly pressured beyond our strength, to the point that our lives were about to end.
9	But we had the sentence of death in ourselves, that we should not trust in ourselves, but in God which raiseth the dead:	And we passed a sentence of death upon ourselves, that our confidence might not be in ourselves, but in God, who raiseth up the dead;	And we resigned ourselves to death, that we should not have confidence in ourselves, but in God who raises the dead [and it was]
10	Who delivered us from so great a death, and doth deliver: in whom we trust that he will yet deliver us;	who rescued us from imminent death: and we hope that he will again rescue us,	he who rescued us from violent deaths. And we trust that he will rescue us again

Parallel Translations

II CORINTHIANS *Chapter 1*

	KJV	Murdock	Magiera
11	Ye also helping together by prayer for us, that for the gift bestowed upon us by the means of many persons thanks may be given by many on our behalf.	by the aid of your prayers in our behalf; so that his gift to us may be a favor done for the sake of many, and many may praise him on our account.	with the aid of your prayer for us, that his gift toward us may be a blessing that is done on behalf of many and many will give thanks to him for us.
12	For our rejoicing is this, the testimony of our conscience, that in simplicity and godly sincerity, not with fleshly wisdom, but by the grace of God, we have had our conversation in the world, and more abundantly to you-ward.	For our rejoicing is this, the testimony of our conscience, that in simplicity and purity, and by the grace of God, and not in the wisdom of the flesh, we have conducted ourselves in the world, and especially towards you.	For our boasting is this, the testimony of our mind, that we have conducted ourselves in the world in simplicity and in purity and in the grace of God and not in the wisdom of the flesh and especially toward you yourselves.
13	For we write none other things unto you, than what ye read or acknowledge; and I trust ye shall acknowledge even to the end;	We write no other things unto you, than those which ye know and acknowledge. And I trust, ye will acknowledge them to the end:	We do not write anything else to you, but these [things] that you know [and] also acknowledge. And I trust that you will acknowledge [them] to the end,
14	As also ye have acknowledged us in part, that we are your rejoicing, even as ye also are ours in the day of the Lord Jesus.	as ye have also partially acknowledged that we are your rejoicing, as ye also are ours, in the day of our Lord Jesus the Messiah.	as even you have acknowledged in part that we are your boasting, as also you are ours in the day of our Lord Jesus Christ.
15	And in this confidence I was minded to come unto you before, that ye might have a second benefit;	And in this confidence, I was before disposed to come to you, that ye might receive the grace doubly;	And in this confidence I wanted to come to you before, so that you would doubly receive grace,
16	And to pass by you into Macedonia, and to come again out of Macedonia unto you, and of you to be brought on my way toward Judaea.	and to pass by you into Macedonia, and again to come to you from Macedonia, and [so] ye would accompany me to Judaea.	and [I wanted] to pass by you [on the way] to the Macedonians and to come to you again from Macedonia and [so that] you would accompany me to Judea.
17	When I therefore was thus minded, did I use lightness? or the things that I purpose, do I purpose according to the flesh, that with me there should be yea yea, and nay nay?	When therefore I thus purposed, did I purpose as one inconsiderate? Or, were the things I purposed, things of the flesh; so that there should be in them Yes, yes, and No, no?	This [thing] therefore that I had determined, did I determine [it] hastily? Or perhaps are these [things] that I decided of the flesh? Because it is proper that there should be yes, yes, and no, no.
18	But as God is true, our word toward you was not yea and nay.	God is the witness, that our word to you was not Yes and No.	God is faithful, so that our word to you was not yes and no.
19	For the Son of God, Jesus Christ, who was preached among you by us, even by me and Silvanus and Timotheus, was not yea and nay, but in him was yea.	For the Son of God, Jesus the Messiah, who was preached to you by us, [namely,] by me, by Sylvanus, and by Timotheus, was not Yes and No; but it was Yes in him.	For the Son of God, Jesus Christ, who was preached to you by way of us, by me and by Silvanus and by Timothy, was not yes and no, but was yes in him.
20	For all the promises of God in him are yea, and in him Amen, unto the glory of God by us.	For all the promises of God in him, the Messiah, are Yes; for which cause, we through him give [our] Amen, to the glory of God.	For all the promises of God in him, in Christ, are yes. Because of this by way of him, we give an "Amen" to the glory of God.

Parallel Translations

	KJV	Murdock	Magiera

II CORINTHIANS Chapter 1

	KJV	Murdock	Magiera
21	Now he which stablisheth us with you in Christ, and hath anointed us, is God;	Now it is God who establisheth us, with you, in the Messiah, and hath anointed us,	Now God establishes us with you in Christ, who anointed us
22	Who hath also sealed us, and given the earnest of the Spirit in our hearts.	and hath sealed us, and hath given the earnest of his Spirit in our hearts.	and has sealed us and has placed the downpayment of his Spirit in our hearts.
23	Moreover I call God for a record upon my soul, that to spare you I came not as yet unto Corinth.	Moreover, I call God for a witness on my soul, that it was in order to spare you, that I came not to Corinth.	And I give testimony before God concerning myself that I did not come to Corinth in order to spare you,
24	Not for that we have dominion over your faith, but are helpers of your joy: for by faith ye stand.	Not that we are lords over your faith, but we are helpers of your joy; for it is by faith ye stand.	not because we are lords of your faith, but we are helpers of your joy, for you stand by faith.

Chapter 2

	KJV	Murdock	Magiera
1	But I determined this with myself, that I would not come again to you in heaviness.	And I determined this with myself, that I would not again come to you in sadness.	And I determined this in myself, that I would not come to you again with sadness.
2	For if I make you sorry, who is he then that maketh me glad, but the same which is made sorry by me?	For if I should make you sad, who would make me joyful, unless he whom I had made sad?	For if I cause you sadness, who will make me rejoice, but he whom I made sad?
3	And I wrote this same unto you, lest, when I came, I should have sorrow from them of whom I ought to rejoice; having confidence in you all, that my joy is the joy of you all.	And I wrote that very thing to you, lest when I came, those persons whom I ought to make joyful, should make me sad. For I have confidence concerning you, that my joy is the joy of you all.	And [I determined] that I would write to you this, so that when I come, you will not make me sad, those who ought to make me rejoice. And I am confident about all of you, that my joy is [the joy] of all of you.
4	For out of much affliction and anguish of heart I wrote unto you with many tears; not that ye should be grieved, but that ye might know the love which I have more abundantly unto you.	And in much affliction, and in anguish of heart, I wrote those things to you, with many tears; not that ye might have sorrow, but that ye might know the exceeding love I have for you.	And from great distress and from anguish of heart I wrote to you these [things] with many tears, not that you should be sad, but that you would know the abundant love that I have for you.
5	But if any have caused grief, he hath not grieved me, but in part: that I may not overcharge you all.	And if one hath caused grief, he hath not grieved me [only], but,—that the declaration may not bear too hard on you—in a measure, all of you.	And if anyone has caused sorrow, he has not caused sorrow to me [only], but almost to all of you, lest the word should be heavy for you.
6	Sufficient to such a man is this punishment, which was inflicted of many.	And sufficient for him, is this rebuke proceeding from many:	And this reproof from many is sufficient for him.
7	So that contrariwise ye ought rather to forgive him, and comfort him, lest perhaps such a one should be swallowed up with overmuch sorrow.	so that, on the other hand, ye ought to forgive him and console him; lest he who is such a man, should be swallowed up with excessive grief.	And from now on the contrary, you ought to forgive him and to comfort him, so that he who is such should not be swallowed up in excessive sorrow.
8	Wherefore I beseech you that ye would confirm your love toward him.	I therefore beseech you, that ye confirm to him your love.	Because of this, I am begging you to confirm your love with him.

Parallel Translations

II CORINTHIANS *Chapter 2*

	KJV	Murdock	Magiera
9	For to this end also did I write, that I might know the proof of you, whether ye be obedient in all things.	For it was for this also that I wrote [to you], that I might learn by a trial, whether ye would be obedient in every thing.	For because of this, I have also written [you], so that I would know with proof if you are being obedient in everything.
10	To whom ye forgive any thing, I forgive also: for if I forgave any thing, to whom I forgave it, for your sakes forgave I it in the person of Christ;	And whom ye forgive, I also [forgive]: for that which I forgave to any one, for your sakes I forgave it, in the presence of the Messiah;	Now whom you forgive, I also [forgive]. For also what I forgave whom I forgave because of you, I forgave in the presence of Christ,
11	Lest Satan should get an advantage of us: for we are not ignorant of his devices.	lest Satan should overreach us; for we know his devices.	so that Satan should not take advantage of us, for we know his devices.
12	Furthermore, when I came to Troas to preach Christ's gospel, and a door was opened unto me of the Lord,	Moreover, when I came to Troas in announcing the Messiah, and a door was opened to me by the Lord,	Now when I came to Troas with the gospel of Christ and a door was opened to me by the LORD,
13	I had no rest in my spirit, because I found not Titus my brother: but taking my leave of them, I went from thence into Macedonia.	there was no quietude in my spirit, because I found not Titus my brother: and I took leave of them, and went into Macedonia.	I had no rest in my spirit, because I did not find Titus, my brother. So I left them and went to the Macedonians.
14	Now thanks be unto God, which always causeth us to triumph in Christ, and maketh manifest the savour of his knowledge by us in every place.	But thanks be to God, who always procureth us a triumph in the Messiah, and manifesteth by us the odor of the knowledge of him in every place.	Now thanks be to God who always brings to pass triumph for us in Christ and by us makes evident the fragrance of the knowledge of him in every place.
15	For we are unto God a sweet savour of Christ, in them that are saved, and in them that perish:	For, through the Messiah, we are unto God a sweet odor, in them that live and in them that perish:	For we are a sweet fragrance in Christ to God with those who live and with those who are lost.
16	To the one we are the savour of death unto death; and to the other the savour of life unto life. And who is sufficient for these things?	to these, an odor of death unto death; and to those, an odor of life unto life. And who is adequate to these things!	To those [who are lost], [we are] a fragrance of death to death, and to them [who live], a fragrance of life to life. And who is equal to these [things]?
17	For we are not as many, which corrupt the word of God: but as of sincerity, but as of God, in the sight of God speak we in Christ.	For we are not like others, who dilute the words of God; but as of the truth, and as of God, we speak in the Messiah before God.	For we are not like the rest who dilute the words of God, but as in truth and as from God, we speak before God in Christ.

Chapter 3

	KJV	Murdock	Magiera
1	Do we begin again to commend ourselves? or need we, as some others, epistles of commendation to you, or letters of commendation from you?	Do we begin again to show you who we are? Or do we, like others, need that letters recommendatory of us should be written to you? Or, that ye should write recommendations of us?	Are we starting again from the beginning to show you who we are? Or do you, as others, need letters of recommendations to be written to you concerning us? Or [do we need] you to write [and] recommend us?
2	Ye are our epistle written in our hearts, known and read of all men:	Ye are our epistle, written on our hearts, and known and read by every man.	Now you are our own letter that is written on our heart[s] and known and read aloud by everyone.

Parallel Translations

II CORINTHIANS *Chapter 3*

	KJV	*Murdock*	*Magiera*
3	Forasmuch as ye are manifestly declared to be the epistle of Christ ministered by us, written not with ink, but with the Spirit of the living God; not in tables of stone, but in fleshy tables of the heart.	For ye know that ye are an epistle of the Messiah, ministered by us; not written with ink, but by the Spirit of the living God; not on tables of stone, but on the tablets of the heart of flesh.	For you know that you are a letter of Christ that was ministered by us, written not with ink, but by the Spirit of the living God, not on tablets of stone, but on tablets of the heart of flesh.
4	And such trust have we through Christ to God-ward:	And such confidence have we in the Messiah towards God.	And we have such confidence in Christ toward God,
5	Not that we are sufficient of ourselves to think any thing as of ourselves; but our sufficiency is of God;	Not that we are sufficient to think any thing as of ourselves; but our efficiency is from God:	not that we are sufficient to think anything as though from ourselves, but our power is from God,
6	Who also hath made us able ministers of the new testament; not of the letter, but of the spirit: for the letter killeth, but the spirit giveth life.	who hath fitted us to be ministers of the new Testament, not in the letter, but in the Spirit; for the letter killeth, but the Spirit giveth life.	who made us worthy to be ministers of the new covenant, not by writing, but by the Spirit, for writing kills, but the Spirit gives life.
7	But if the ministration of death, written and engraven in stones, was glorious, so that the children of Israel could not stedfastly behold the face of Moses for the glory of his countenance; which glory was to be done away:	Now if the ministration of death was engraved upon stones in writing, and was so glorious that the children of Israel could not look on the face of Moses, on account of the glory upon his face which vanished away;	Now if the ministering of death was engraved in writing on stones (and was so magnificent that the sons of Israel were not able to look on the face of Moses because of the glory of his face) which ended,
8	How shall not the ministration of the spirit be rather glorious?	how then shall not the ministration of the Spirit be still more glorious?	how then will not the ministering of the Spirit be more glorious?
9	For if the ministration of condemnation be glory, much more doth the ministration of righteousness exceed in glory.	For if there was glory in the ministration of condemnation, how much more shall the ministration of justification excel in glory?	For if the ministering of condemnation had glory, how much more will the ministering of justification be increased in glory?
10	For even that which was made glorious had no glory in this respect, by reason of the glory that excelleth.	For that which was glorious, was as if not glorious, in comparison with this which excelleth in glory.	For that which was glorified [was] as if not worthy of glory, in comparison to this surpassing glory.
11	For if that which is done away was glorious, much more that which remaineth is glorious.	For if that which is abolished was glorious, much more must that which abideth be glorious.	For if what has ended was glorious, that which remains will be increasingly glorious.
12	Seeing then that we have such hope, we use great plainness of speech:	Seeing therefore we have this hope, we the more speak with boldness;	Therefore, because we have this hope, we conduct ourselves more boldly,
13	And not as Moses, which put a vail over his face, that the children of Israel could not stedfastly look to the end of that which is abolished:	and are not like Moses, who threw a vail over his face, that the children of Israel might not behold the termination of that which was abolished.	and [we are] not as Moses, who put a veil over his face so that the sons of Israel would not look at the fullness of that which was abolished.
14	But their minds were blinded: for until this day remaineth the same vail untaken away in the reading of the old testament; which vail is done away in Christ.	But they were blinded in their understanding; for until this day, when the old Testament is read, the same vail resteth upon them; nor is it manifest [to them], that it is abolished by the Messiah.	But they were blinded in their understanding, for until this day when the Old Covenant is read, that veil rests on them and it is not known that it is abolished by Christ.

II CORINTHIANS *Chapter 3*

	KJV	Murdock	Magiera
15	But even unto this day, when Moses is read, the vail is upon their heart.	And unto this day, when Moses is read, a vail is thrown upon their hearts.	And until this day when Moses is read, a veil is lying over their heart[s],
16	Nevertheless when it shall turn to the Lord, the vail shall be taken away.	But when any of them is turned unto the Lord, the vail is taken from him.	yet when one of them turns to the LORD, the veil is lifted from him.
17	Now the Lord is that Spirit: and where the Spirit of the Lord is, there is liberty.	Now the Lord himself is the Spirit. And where the Spirit of the Lord is, there is freedom.	Now the LORD is the Spirit and where the Spirit of the LORD [is], there is freedom.
18	But we all, with open face beholding as in a glass the glory of the Lord, are changed into the same image from glory to glory, even as by the Spirit of the Lord.	And we all, with uncovered faces, behold as in a mirror the glory of the Lord; and are transformed into the same likeness, from glory to glory, as by the Lord the Spirit.	But all of us, with open faces, see the magnificence of the LORD as in a mirror and we are being changed into that likeness from glory to glory, as by the LORD, the Spirit.

Chapter 4

	KJV	Murdock	Magiera
1	Therefore seeing we have this ministry, as we have received mercy, we faint not;	Therefore, we are not weary in this ministry which we have received, according to the mercies that have been upon us:	Because of this, we are not weary in this ministry that we are holding, according to the mercies that are on us.
2	But have renounced the hidden things of dishonesty, not walking in craftiness, nor handling the word of God deceitfully; but by manifestation of the truth commending ourselves to every man's conscience in the sight of God.	But we have renounced the concealments of dishonor, and we walk not in craftiness, nor do we treat the word of God deceitfully; but by the manifestation of the truth, we exhibit ourselves to all the consciences of men before God.	But we have rejected the hidden [things] of shame and we do not walk with cunning, nor are we deceitful with the word of God, but we show ourselves by the evidence of the truth to all the minds of men before God.
3	But if our gospel be hid, it is hid to them that are lost:	And if our gospel is vailed, it is vailed to them that perish;	Now if our gospel is hidden, it is hidden to those who are lost,
4	In whom the god of this world hath blinded the minds of them which believe not, lest the light of the glorious gospel of Christ, who is the image of God, should shine unto them.	to them whose minds the God of this world hath blinded, in order that they might not believe, lest the light of the gospel of the glory of the Messiah (who is the likeness of God) should dawn upon them.	those whose minds the god of this age has blinded so that they would not believe, in order that the light of the gospel of the glory of Christ, who is the likeness of God, should not dawn on them.
5	For we preach not ourselves, but Christ Jesus the Lord; and ourselves your servants for Jesus' sake.	For it is not ourselves that we preach, but the Messiah, Jesus our Lord; and, as to ourselves, that we are your servants for Jesus' sake.	For we do not preach ourselves, but Christ Jesus our Lord, and [we preach] of ourselves that we are your servants because of Jesus,
6	For God, who commanded the light to shine out of darkness, hath shined in our hearts, to give the light of the knowledge of the glory of God in the face of Jesus Christ.	Because God, who commanded the light to arise from darkness, hath himself shined in our hearts, that we might be illuminated with the knowledge of the glory of God on the face of Jesus the Messiah.	because God, who said: FROM DARKNESS LIGHT SHOULD SHINE, has shined in our hearts, so that we would be enlightened with the knowledge of the glory of God in the presence of Jesus Christ.
7	But we have this treasure in earthen vessels, that the excellency of the power may be of God, and not of us.	But we have this treasure in an earthen vessel, that the excellency of the power might be from God, and not from us.	Now we have this treasure in a utensil of earth that the greatness of the power would be from God and not from us.

II CORINTHIANS Chapter 4

	KJV	Murdock	Magiera
8	We are troubled on every side, yet not distressed; we are perplexed, but not in despair;	And in every thing we are oppressed, but not suffocated; we are corrected, but not condemned;	For in everything, we are pressured, but are not overwhelmed. We are harassed, but are not overcome.
9	Persecuted, but not forsaken; cast down, but not destroyed;	we are persecuted, but not forsaken; we are prostrated, but perish not.	We are persecuted, but are not left alone. We are thrown down, but are not destroyed.
10	Always bearing about in the body the dying of the Lord Jesus, that the life also of Jesus might be made manifest in our body.	For we bear in our body, at all times, the dying of Jesus; that the life also of Jesus might be manifested in our body.	We always bear the death of Jesus in our bodies, so that the life of Jesus may also be revealed in our bodies.
11	For we which live are alway delivered unto death for Jesus' sake, that the life also of Jesus might be made manifest in our mortal flesh.	For if we are delivered over alive unto death, for Jesus' sake, even so also will the life of Jesus be manifested in this our mortal body.	For if we are alive, we are delivered to death because of Jesus, so that the life of Jesus may also be revealed in this mortal body.
12	So then death worketh in us, but life in you.	Now therefore, in us death is active, but in you, life.	Now death works in us, yet life in you.
13	We having the same spirit of faith, according as it is written, I believed, and therefore have I spoken; we also believe, and therefore speak;	Having therefore the same spirit of faith, (as it is written, I believed, therefore also have I spoken,) we also believe, and therefore speak;	Even we, therefore, have one Spirit of faith, as it is written: I BELIEVED. BECAUSE OF THIS, I ALSO SPOKE. We believe. Because of this, we also speak.
14	Knowing that he which raised up the Lord Jesus shall raise up us also by Jesus, and shall present us with you.	knowing that he, who resuscitated our Lord Jesus, will also resuscitate us by Jesus, and will receive us, with you, to himself.	And we know that he who raised our Lord Jesus will also raise us by way of Jesus and will bring us with you to him.
15	For all things are for your sakes, that the abundant grace might through the thanksgiving of many redound to the glory of God.	For all things are for your sakes, that while grace aboundeth by means of many, thanksgiving may abound to the glory of God.	For everything is on account of you, so that as grace increases by way of many, thanksgiving would multiply to the glory of God.
16	For which cause we faint not; but though our outward man perish, yet the inward man is renewed day by day.	For this cause we faint not; for though our outward man perish, yet the inner [man] is renovated day by day.	Because of this, we are not weary, for even if our outer man is corrupted, yet that which [is] inside is renewed day by day.
17	For our light affliction, which is but for a moment, worketh for us a far more exceeding and eternal weight of glory;	For the affliction of the present time, though very small and light, prepareth for us great glory, without end, for ever and ever;	For the adversity of this time, being very small and little, prepares for us a great glory, without end forever,
18	While we look not at the things which are seen, but at the things which are not seen: for the things which are seen are temporal; but the things which are not seen are eternal.	while we look not at these seen things, but at those not seen; for these seen things are temporary, but those not seen are eternal.	because we do not rejoice in these [things] that are seen, but in these that are not seen. For [the things] that are seen are for a time, but [the things] that are not seen are eternal.

Parallel Translations

II CORINTHIANS *Chapter* 5

	KJV	*Murdock*	*Magiera*
1	For we know that if our earthly house of this tabernacle were dissolved, we have a building of God, an house not made with hands, eternal in the heavens.	For we know that, if our house on earth—this of the body, were dissolved, yet we have a building of God, a house not made with hands, eternal in heaven.	For we know that if our house that is on earth, this of the body, should be broken down, yet we have a building that is from God, a house that is not by the work of hands, eternal in heaven.
2	For in this we groan, earnestly desiring to be clothed upon with our house which is from heaven:	And on this account also, we groan, and wish to be clothed with our house from heaven:	For also because of this, we groan and long to be clothed with our house that is from heaven,
3	If so be that being clothed we shall not be found naked.	if indeed, when clothed, we shall not be found naked.	since indeed when we are clothed, we will [not] be found naked.
4	For we that are in this tabernacle do groan, being burdened: not for that we would be unclothed, but clothed upon, that mortality might be swallowed up of life.	For while we are here in this house, we groan under its burden; yet ye desire, not to throw it off; but to be clothed over it, so that its mortality may be absorbed in life.	For while we are now in this house, we groan from its burden and we do not desire to put it off, unless we should be clothed over it, so that its mortality would be swallowed by life.
5	Now he that hath wrought us for the selfsame thing is God, who also hath given unto us the earnest of the Spirit.	And he that prepareth us for this thing, is God: who hath given us the earnest of his Spirit.	And he who prepares us for this is God, who has given us the downpayment of his Spirit.
6	Therefore we are always confident, knowing that, whilst we are at home in the body, we are absent from the Lord:	Therefore, because we know and are persuaded, that while we lodge in the body we sojourn away from our Lord;	Therefore, because we know and are persuaded that while we live in the body, we are absent from our Lord
7	(For we walk by faith, not by sight:)	(for we walk by faith, and not by sight;)	(for we walk by faith and not by sight).
8	We are confident, I say, and willing rather to be absent from the body, and to be present with the Lord.	therefore we are confident, and desirous to be away from the body, and to be with our Lord.	Because of this, we are confident and we long to be absent from the body and to be with our Lord.
9	Wherefore we labour, that, whether present or absent, we may be accepted of him.	We are assiduous, that whether we are absent, or whether at home, we may please him.	And we are diligent that whether we are absent [ones] or dwellers [in our body], we would please him.
10	For we must all appear before the judgment seat of Christ; that every one may receive the things done in his body, according to that he hath done, whether it be good or bad.	For we are all to stand before the judgment-seat of the Messiah, that each may receive retribution in the body, [for] what he hath done in it, whether of good, or whether of evil.	For all of us are going to stand before the judgment seat of Christ that each one may be rewarded [for] what was done by him in his body, whether of good or of evil.
11	Knowing therefore the terror of the Lord, we persuade men; but we are made manifest unto God; and I trust also are made manifest in your consciences.	Therefore because we know the fear of our Lord we persuade men; and we are made manifest unto God; and I hope also, we are made manifest to your minds.	Therefore, because we know the fear of our Lord, we persuade men and we are revealed to God and I think that also we are revealed to your own minds.

II CORINTHIANS *Chapter 5*

	KJV	Murdock	Magiera
12	For we commend not ourselves again unto you, but give you occasion to glory on our behalf, that ye may have somewhat to answer them which glory in appearance, and not in heart.	We do not again laud ourselves to you; but we give you occasion to glory in us, to them who glory in appearance and not in heart.	We do not praise ourselves again to you, but we give you cause to be boasting about us to those who are boasting in appearances and not in heart.
13	For whether we be beside ourselves, it is to God: or whether we be sober, it is for your cause.	For if we are extravagant, it is for God: and if we are discreet, it is for you.	For if we are foolish, [it is] for God. And if we are ordained, [it is] for you.
14	For the love of Christ constraineth us; because we thus judge, that if one died for all, then were all dead:	For the love of the Messiah constraineth us to reason thus: One died for all; therefore are all dead.	For the love of Christ compels us to determine this, that one died on behalf of everyone, so then everyone is dead in him.
15	And that he died for all, that they which live should not henceforth live unto themselves, but unto him which died for them, and rose again.	And he died for all, that they who live should not live to themselves, but to him who died for them and rose again.	And he died on behalf of everyone, so that those who live should not live for themselves, but for him who died and rose for them.
16	Wherefore henceforth know we no man after the flesh: yea, though we have known Christ after the flesh, yet now henceforth know we him no more.	And therefore, we know no person after the flesh: and if we have known the Messiah after the flesh, yet henceforth we know [him] no more.	And from now on, we do not know anyone in the flesh. And even if we have known Christ in the flesh, yet now we do not know [him].
17	Therefore if any man be in Christ, he is a new creature: old things are passed away; behold, all things are become new.	Whoever therefore is in the Messiah, is a new creature: old things have passed away;	Everyone who is in Christ is therefore a new creation. Old [things] have passed away
18	And all things are of God, who hath reconciled us to himself by Jesus Christ, and hath given to us the ministry of reconciliation;	and all things are made new, by God; who hath reconciled us to himself by the Messiah, and hath given to us the ministry of reconciliation.	and everything has become new from God, who reconciled us to himself in Christ and has given us the ministry of reconciliation.
19	To wit, that God was in Christ, reconciling the world unto himself, not imputing their trespasses unto them; and hath committed unto us the word of reconciliation.	For God was in the Messiah, who hath reconciled the world with his majesty, and did not reckon to them their sins; and who hath placed in us the word of reconciliation.	For God was in Christ, the one who reconciled the world with his majesty and did not count to them their sins. And he placed in us the word of reconciliation.
20	Now then we are ambassadors for Christ, as though God did beseech you by us: we pray you in Christ's stead, be ye reconciled to God.	We are therefore ambassadors for the Messiah, and it is as if God was beseeching you by us. In behalf of the Messiah, therefore, we beseech [you], be ye reconciled to God.	Therefore, we are ambassadors on behalf of Christ and [it is] as if God were begging you by way of us on behalf of Christ. Therefore, we beg [you], "Be reconciled to God."
21	For he hath made him to be sin for us, who knew no sin; that we might be made the righteousness of God in him.	For, on your account, he hath made him who knew no sin to be sin, that we might by him become the righteousness of God.	For that one who had not known sin, he has made [to be] sin on your account, that we would become the justification of God in him.

Chapter 6

	KJV	Murdock	Magiera
1	We then, as workers together with him, beseech you also that ye receive not the grace of God in vain.	And as aiders we entreat of you, that the grace of God which ye have received, may not be ineffectual in you.	And as helpers, we beg you, that the grace of God that you received should not be fruitless in you.

Parallel Translations

II CORINTHIANS *Chapter 6*

	KJV	*Murdock*	*Magiera*
2	(For he saith, I have heard thee in a time accepted, and in the day of salvation have I succoured thee: behold, now is the accepted time; behold, now is the day of salvation.)	For he hath said, In an acceptable time have I heard thee, and in the day of life I have aided thee. Behold, now is the acceptable time! and behold, now is the day of life!	For he has said: IN AN ACCEPTABLE TIME, I HAVE ANSWERED YOU AND IN THE DAY OF SALVATION, I HAVE HELPED YOU. Behold, now [is] an acceptable time and behold, now [is] the day of salvation.
3	Giving no offence in any thing, that the ministry be not blamed:	Give ye no occasion of offence to any one in any thing, that there may be no reproach on our ministry.	Give no one a cause for stumbling in anything, so that there will be no blemish in our ministering.
4	But in all things approving ourselves as the ministers of God, in much patience, in afflictions, in necessities, in distresses,	But we, in all things, would show ourselves to be the ministers of God, in much endurance, in afflictions, in necessity, in distresses,	But in everything we should show ourselves that we are ministers of God with much endurance, in trials, in necessities, in difficulties,
5	In stripes, in imprisonments, in tumults, in labours, in watchings, in fastings;	in scourgings, in imprisonments, in tumults, in toil, in watching, in fasting;	in beatings, in imprisonments, in riots, in labor, in watching, in fasting,
6	By pureness, by knowledge, by longsuffering, by kindness, by the Holy Ghost, by love unfeigned,	by purity, by knowledge, by long suffering, by benignity, by the Holy Spirit, by love unfeigned,	by purity, by knowledge, by long-suffering, by kindness, by the Holy Spirit, by love without deceit,
7	By the word of truth, by the power of God, by the armour of righteousness on the right hand and on the left,	by the speaking of truth, by the energy of God, by the armor of righteousness on the right hand and on the left;	by the truthful word, by the power of God, by the armor of justification that is on the right hand and on the left,
8	By honour and dishonour, by evil report and good report: as deceivers, and yet true;	amid honor and dishonor, amid praise and contumely; as deceivers, and yet true;	in honor and in disgrace, in good report and in a struggle, as [between] deceivers and true.
9	As unknown, and yet well known; as dying, and, behold, we live; as chastened, and not killed;	as not known, and yet we are well known; as dying, and behold, we live; as chastised, yet not killed;	As though unknown, yet we are known, as though dying, yet behold, we are living, as chastised, yet we are not dying,
10	As sorrowful, yet alway rejoicing; as poor, yet making many rich; as having nothing, and yet possessing all things.	as sorrowful, yet always rejoicing; as indigent, yet enriching many; as possessing nothing, yet having all things.	as though having sorrow, yet we are rejoicing always, as though poor, yet we are causing many to increase, as though not having anything, yet we are holding everything.
11	O ye Corinthians, our mouth is open unto you, our heart is enlarged.	O ye Corinthians, our mouth is opened towards you, and our heart expanded.	Our mouth is opened to you, [oh] Corinthians, and our heart is enlarged.
12	Ye are not straitened in us, but ye are straitened in your own bowels.	Ye are not straitened in us, but ye are straitened in your own bowels.	You are not pressured by us, but you are pressured by your bowels.
13	Now for a recompence in the same, (I speak as unto my children,) be ye also enlarged.	I speak as to [my] children, Pay me the debt which ye owe, and expand your love towards me.	Now I speak as to children, pay me my debt that is for you. Expand your love to me.

II CORINTHIANS *Chapter 6*

	KJV	Murdock	Magiera
14	Be ye not unequally yoked together with unbelievers: for what fellowship hath righteousness with unrighteousness? and what communion hath light with darkness?	And be ye not yoke-fellows with them that believe not: for what fellowship hath righteousness with iniquity? or what communion hath light with darkness?	And you should be not yoke-fellows to those who do not believe. For what fellowship has justification with wickedness or what communion has light with darkness?
15	And what concord hath Christ with Belial? or what part hath he that believeth with an infidel?	or what concord hath the Messiah with Satan? or what part hath a believer with an unbeliever?	Or what agreement has Christ with Satan? Or what part has he who believes with him who does not believe?
16	And what agreement hath the temple of God with idols? for ye are the temple of the living God; as God hath said, I will dwell in them, and walk in them; and I will be their God, and they shall be my people.	or what agreement hath the temple of God with that of demons? For ye are the temple of the living God; as it is said, I will dwell among them, and walk among them, and will be their God, and they shall be my people.	And what alliance has the temple of God with demons? But you are the temple of the living God, as it is said: I WILL LIVE WITH THEM AND I WILL WALK WITH THEM AND I WILL BE THEIR GOD AND THEY WILL BE MY PEOPLE.
17	Wherefore come out from among them, and be ye separate, saith the Lord, and touch not the unclean thing; and I will receive you,	Wherefore, come ye out from among them, and be ye separate from them, saith the Lord; and come not near the unclean thing, and I will receive you;	Because of this, GO OUT FROM AMONG THEM AND BE SEPARATED FROM THEM, says the LORD. AND DO NOT COME NEAR UNCLEAN [THINGS] AND I WILL RECEIVE YOU,
18	And will be a Father unto you, and ye shall be my sons and daughters, saith the Lord Almighty.	and will be to you a Father, and ye shall be sons and daughters to me, saith the Lord Almighty.	AND I WILL BE A FATHER TO YOU AND YOU WILL BE SONS AND DAUGHTERS TO ME, says the LORD, the Almighty.

Chapter 7

	KJV	Murdock	Magiera
1	Having therefore these promises, dearly beloved, let us cleanse ourselves from all filthiness of the flesh and spirit, perfecting holiness in the fear of God.	Seeing, therefore, we have these promises, my beloved, let us cleanse ourselves from all defilement of the flesh and of the spirit; and let us work righteousness, in the fear of God.	Therefore, because we have these promises, my beloved [ones], we should purify ourselves from all defilement of the flesh and of the spirit and we should serve with holiness with reverence for God.
2	Receive us; we have wronged no man, we have corrupted no man, we have defrauded no man.	Bear with us, my brethren; we have done evil to no one; we have corrupted no one; we have wronged no one.	Bear [with us], our brothers, we have caused no one harm, we have corrupted no one, we have wronged no one.
3	I speak not this to condemn you: for I have said before, that ye are in our hearts to die and live with you.	I speak [thus], not to condemn you; for I have said before, that ye are treasured in our hearts, to die and to live together.	I am not speaking to make you guilty, for I have said before that you are in our heart, to die and to live together.
4	Great is my boldness of speech toward you, great is my glorying of you: I am filled with comfort, I am exceeding joyful in all our tribulation.	I have great assurance before you, and have much glorying in you; and I am full of comfort. And joy greatly aboundeth to me, in all my afflictions.	I have great boldness to you and I have great boasting in you and I am full of comfort and a great amount of joy abounds in me, in all my trials.

Parallel Translations

II CORINTHIANS *Chapter 7*

	KJV	*Murdock*	*Magiera*
5	For, when we were come into Macedonia, our flesh had no rest, but we were troubled on every side; without were fightings, within were fears.	For, after we came to Macedonia, there was no rest for our body, but we were distressed in every thing; without was conflict, and within was fear.	For even after we came to the Macedonians, we had no rest for our body, but we were pressured in everything, from without, conflict, and from within, fear.
6	Nevertheless God, that comforteth those that are cast down, comforted us by the coming of Titus;	But God who comforteth the depressed, comforted us by the arrival of Titus.	But God, who comforts the meek, comforted us by the coming of Titus,
7	And not by his coming only, but by the consolation wherewith he was comforted in you, when he told us your earnest desire, your mourning, your fervent mind toward me; so that I rejoiced the more.	And not merely by his arrival, but also by the refreshing with which he was refreshed by you. For he told us of your love towards us, and of your grief, and of your zeal in our behalf: and when I heard it, my joy was great.	and not only by his coming, but also by the rest [with] which he was refreshed by you. For he told us about your love to us and about your grief and your zeal for us. And when I heard it, my joy was great.
8	For though I made you sorry with a letter, I do not repent, though I did repent: for I perceive that the same epistle hath made you sorry, though it were but for a season.	And although I made you sad by the epistle, I do not regret it, though I did regret it; for I see that that epistle, though for a time it made you sad,	For although I made you sad by a letter, I am not sorry, even though I was sorry. For I see that the letter, even if it made you sad for a time,
9	Now I rejoice, not that ye were made sorry, but that ye sorrowed to repentance: for ye were made sorry after a godly manner, that ye might receive damage by us in nothing.	yet it procured me joy, not because ye had sorrow, but because your sorrow brought you to repentance; for ye sorrowed in godly sorrow; so that ye received no detriment from us.	yet produced great joy for me, not because it made you sad, but because your sorrow brought you to repentance. For you had godly sorrow, so that you should lack in nothing from us.
10	For godly sorrow worketh repentance to salvation not to be repented of: but the sorrow of the world worketh death.	For, sorrowing on account of God, worketh a conversion of the soul which is not reversed, and a turning unto life: but the sorrowing of the world worketh death.	For sorrow because of God produces repentance of the soul that is not reversed and turns to life, but the sorrow of the world produces death.
11	For behold this selfsame thing, that ye sorrowed after a godly sort, what carefulness it wrought in you, yea, what clearing of yourselves, yea, what indignation, yea, what fear, yea, what vehement desire, yea, what zeal, yea, what revenge! In all things ye have approved yourselves to be clear in this matter.	For behold this same thing, that ye were distressed on account of God, what solicitude it wrought in you, and apologizing and indignation, and fear, and love, and zeal, and revenge? And in all things ye have shown, that ye are [now] pure in that matter.	For behold this, that you were distressed because of God. How much did it produce in you? Diligence and defense and anger and fear and love and zeal and vindication. And in everything you have shown that you are being pure in the matter.
12	Wherefore, though I wrote unto you, I did it not for his cause that had done the wrong, nor for his cause that suffered wrong, but that our care for you in the sight of God might appear unto you.	And it will be [seen] that I wrote to you, not for the sake of him who did the wrong, nor for the sake of him who received the wrong, [only,] but that your solicitude in respect to us might be known before God.	Now let this be [so]. For I wrote to you, not because of the wrong-doer, not even because of that one who was wronged, but so that your diligence because of us would be known before God.

Parallel Translations

II CORINTHIANS *Chapter 7*

	KJV	Murdock	Magiera
13	Therefore we were comforted in your comfort: yea, and exceedingly the more joyed we for the joy of Titus, because his spirit was refreshed by you all.	Wherefore we were comforted; and with our consolation, we were the more joyful for the joy of Titus, because his spirit was refreshed by you all:	Because of this, we were comforted and with our comfort, we rejoiced greatly in the joy of Titus, for his spirit was refreshed with all of you,
14	For if I have boasted any thing to him of you, I am not ashamed; but as we spake all things to you in truth, even so our boasting, which I made before Titus, is found a truth.	so that I was not ashamed of that in which I had gloried to him, respecting you; but as in every thing we spoke the truth to you, so also our glorying before Titus, is found to be in truth:	so that I was not ashamed of what I boasted to him about you. But as we spoke everything [with] truthfulness with you, so also our boasting to Titus was found [to be] with truthfulness.
15	And his inward affection is more abundant toward you, whilst he remembereth the obedience of you all, how with fear and trembling ye received him.	and also his bowels are the more enlarged towards you, while he remembereth the submission of you all, and how ye received him with fear and trembling.	His compassion has also increased greatly concerning you, when he recalls the obedience of all of you [and] that you received him with reverence and with trembling.
16	I rejoice therefore that I have confidence in you in all things.	I rejoice, that in every thing I have full confidence in you.	I rejoice that in everything I am confident about you.

Chapter 8

	KJV	Murdock	Magiera
1	Moreover, brethren, we do you to wit of the grace of God bestowed on the churches of Macedonia;	And, my brethren, we make known to you the grace of God which was conferred on the churches of the Macedonians;	But we make known to you, our brothers, the grace of God that was given by the churches of the Macedonians,
2	How that in a great trial of affliction the abundance of their joy and their deep poverty abounded unto the riches of their liberality.	that in the great trial of their affliction, there was an abounding to their joy, and the depth of their poverty was exuberant in the riches of their liberality.	that in the great trial of their adversity, there was an increase to their joy and the depth of their poverty was increased by the riches of their simplicity.
3	For to their power, I bear record, yea, and beyond their power they were willing of themselves;	For I testify that, according to their ability, and beyond their ability, in the spontaneity of their mind,	For I testify that, according to their ability and greater than their ability, voluntarily [in] themselves,
4	Praying us with much intreaty that we would receive the gift, and take upon us the fellowship of the ministering to the saints.	they besought us, with much entreaty, that they might participate in the beneficence of the ministration to the saints.	they begged us with much begging to take part in the grace of the service of the holy [ones].
5	And this they did, not as we hoped, but first gave their own selves to the Lord, and unto us by the will of God.	And not [only] as we had expected, but they first gave themselves unto the Lord, and to us by the will of God.	And not as we had expected, but they gave themselves first to our Lord and also to us by the will of God,
6	Insomuch that we desired Titus, that as he had begun, so he would also finish in you the same grace also.	So that we requested Titus, that as he had begun, so he would perfect in you also the same beneficence.	so that we requested Titus, that as he had begun, so he would complete this grace with you also.
7	Therefore, as ye abound in every thing, in faith, and utterance, and knowledge, and in all diligence, and in your love to us, see that ye abound in this grace also.	And as ye are enriched in every thing, in faith, and speech, and knowledge, and in all diligence, and in our love towards you, so abound ye in this beneficence also.	But according as you increase in everything, in faith and in word and in knowledge and in all diligence and in our love to you, so you should increase in this grace also.

	KJV	*Murdock*	*Magiera*

II CORINTHIANS *Chapter 8*

Verse	KJV	Murdock	Magiera
8	I speak not by commandment, but by occasion of the forwardness of others, and to prove the sincerity of your love.	I do not actually command you, but by the promptitude of your fellow [disciples], I would test the sincerity of your love.	I do not actually command you, but by the exhortation of your fellow [believers], I am testing the genuineness of your love.
9	For ye know the grace of our Lord Jesus Christ, that, though he was rich, yet for your sakes he became poor, that ye through his poverty might be rich.	For ye know the goodness of our Lord Jesus the Messiah, who when he was rich, for your sakes became poor, that by his poverty ye might be made rich.	For you know the grace of our Lord Jesus Christ, who on account of you became poor when he was rich, so that you by his poverty would be made rich.
10	And herein I give my advice: for this is expedient for you, who have begun before, not only to do, but also to be forward a year ago.	And I urgently recommend to you, that which is for your advantage; inasmuch as ye began, a year ago, not only to purpose, but also to perform.	Now I highly recommend to you this that is profitable to you, because a year ago, you began not only to will, but also to do.
11	Now therefore perform the doing of it; that as there was a readiness to will, so there may be a performance also out of that which ye have.	And now complete ye by action, what ye purposed; that as ye had a promptitude in your purposing, so ye may fulfill [it] in action, according to your ability.	But now, complete with action what you willed, that as you have an eagerness to will, so you would fulfill [it] in action out of what you have.
12	For if there be first a willing mind, it is accepted according to that a man hath, and not according to that he hath not.	For if there is a willingness, a person is accepted according to what he hath, and not according to what he hath not.	For if there is a willingness, so he is accepted according to what he has, not according to what he does not have.
13	For I mean not that other men be eased, and ye burdened:	For it is not, that others may have easement, and you pressure;	For it is not that others should have relief and you [should have] pressure,
14	But by an equality, that now at this time your abundance may be a supply for their want, that their abundance also may be a supply for your want: that there may be equality:	but that ye may be on equality at the present time; and that your abundance may be [a supply] to their want; that their abundance likewise may be [a supply] to your want; that there may be equality.	but [that] you should be in balance at this time, that your abundance may be for their need, so that also their abundance may be for your need, so that there will be a balance.
15	As it is written, He that had gathered much had nothing over; and he that had gathered little had no lack.	As it is written, He who gathered much, had nothing over; and he that gathered little, was not deficient.	As it is written: HE WHO RECEIVED MUCH DID NOT HAVE EXCESS AND HE WHO RECEIVED LITTLE DID NOT LACK.
16	But thanks be to God, which put the same earnest care into the heart of Titus for you.	But thanks be to God, who put into the heart of Titus this solicitude for you.	But thanks be to God who put this care for you in the heart of Titus.
17	For indeed he accepted the exhortation; but being more forward, of his own accord he went unto you.	For he received our exhortation; and, because he was very anxious, he cheerfully set out to visit you.	For he received our exhortation and because he was very concerned, he went out to you willingly.
18	And we have sent with him the brother, whose praise is in the gospel throughout all the churches;	And we also sent with him that our brother, whose praise in the gospel is in all the churches;	And we sent with him our brother, him whose praise in the gospel [is] in all the churches.
19	And not that only, but who was also chosen of the churches to travel with us with this grace, which is administered by us to the glory of the same Lord, and declaration of your ready mind:	inasmuch as he likewise had been expressly chosen by the churches, to accompany me with this beneficence which is ministered by us to the glory of God and to our cordiality.	So also, he was especially chosen by the churches to go out with us with this grace that is ministered by us for the glory of God and for our own encouragement.

Parallel Translations

	KJV	*Murdock*	*Magiera*

II CORINTHIANS *Chapter 8*

	KJV	Murdock	Magiera
20	Avoiding this, that no man should blame us in this abundance which is administered by us:	And we hereby guarded, that no one should cast censure on us, in [respect to] this abundance which is ministered by us.	And by this we were avoiding [a situation] that no one should put a blemish on us regarding this high position that is ministered by us.
21	Providing for honest things, not only in the sight of the Lord, but also in the sight of men.	For we are attentive to things commendable, not only before God, but also before men.	For we were careful [to do] the right things, not before God only, but also before men.
22	And we have sent with them our brother, whom we have oftentimes proved diligent in many things, but now much more diligent, upon the great confidence which I have in you.	And we also sent with them that brother of ours, who hath often, and in many things, been proved diligent by us; and is now particularly diligent, from the great confidence [he hath] in you.	And we also sent with them our brother who by us has always in many [things] been proven that he is diligent, but now he is especially diligent with the great confidence that [he has] about you.
23	Whether any do enquire of Titus, he is my partner and fellowhelper concerning you: or our brethren be enquired of, they are the messengers of the churches, and the glory of Christ.	And therefore, if Titus [be inquired about], he is my associate and assistant among you: or if our other brethren, they are the legates of the churches of the Messiah's glory.	Therefore, if Titus [is asked about], he is my companion and assistant among you, or if our other brothers, they are sent [ones] of the churches of the glory of Christ.
24	Wherefore shew ye to them, and before the churches, the proof of your love, and of our boasting on your behalf.	Therefore exhibit ye to them, in the presence of all the churches, a demonstration of your love and of our glorying respecting you.	From now on, in the presence of all the churches, show them a demonstration of your love and our boasting about you.

Chapter 9

	KJV	Murdock	Magiera
1	For as touching the ministering to the saints, it is superfluous for me to write to you:	And concerning the ministration by the saints, it would be superfluous for me to write to you:	Now concerning the service of the holy [ones], it would be excessive if I wrote to you.
2	For I know the forwardness of your mind, for which I boast of you to them of Macedonia, that Achaia was ready a year ago; and your zeal hath provoked very many.	for I know the goodness of your mind; and therefore I gloried of you before the Macedonians, that Achaia was ready a year ago; and your zeal hath excited many.	For I know the goodness of your mind and because of this, I boasted of you to the Macedonians that Achaia was ready a year ago and your zeal has excited many.
3	Yet have I sent the brethren, lest our boasting of you should be in vain in this behalf; that, as I said, ye may be ready:	Yet I sent the brethren, lest the glorying with which we have gloried in you in regard to this matter, should prove vain; and that ye, as I said, may be ready;	Now I sent the brothers, so that our boasting that we boasted of you would not be empty about this matter, that as I said, you would be prepared,
4	Lest haply if they of Macedonia come with me, and find you unprepared, we (that we say not, ye) should be ashamed in this same confident boasting.	so that, if the Macedonians should come with me, and should find you unprepared, we—not to say, ye—should be put to shame for that glorying in which we gloried.	that the Macedonians would not come with me and find you not ready and we should be embarrassed (should we not say that you would be embarrassed) by the boasting that we boasted.

Parallel Translations

II CORINTHIANS *Chapter 9*

	KJV	Murdock	Magiera
5	Therefore I thought it necessary to exhort the brethren, that they would go before unto you, and make up beforehand your bounty, whereof ye had notice before, that the same might be ready, as a matter of bounty, and not as of covetousness.	Therefore I was careful to request these my brethren, to go before me unto you, that they might make up this benefaction, of which ye were advised long before to have it ready, as being a benefaction, and not a matter of cupidity.	Because of this, I was concerned to request these my brothers, that they should come before me to you and prepare the bounty that you were previously advised to have prepared, so it is as a bounty, not as greediness.
6	But this I say, He which soweth sparingly shall reap also sparingly; and he which soweth bountifully shall reap also bountifully.	And this [I say]: He that soweth sparingly, shall also reap sparingly; and he that soweth bountifully, shall also reap bountifully.	Now this [I say], "He who sows sparingly will also reap sparingly and he who sows bountifully will reap bountifully,
7	Every man according as he purposeth in his heart, so let him give; not grudgingly, or of necessity: for God loveth a cheerful giver.	Every man, according to his own views, not with sadness, not by constraint: for the Lord loveth a joyous giver.	everyone according to what is in his mind, not from sadness or from constraint, for GOD LOVES A JOYOUS GIVER."
8	And God is able to make all grace abound toward you; that ye, always having all sufficiency in all things, may abound to every good work:	For it is in the power of God, to make all good abound to you, so that ye may have, at all times, and in every thing, what is sufficient for you; and may abound in every good work.	Now all grace comes by the hands of God who causes [it] to increase in you, so that always, in everything, you will have what is sufficient for you and will increase in every good work.
9	(As it is written, He hath dispersed abroad; he hath given to the poor: his righteousness remaineth for ever.	As it is written, He hath dispersed and given to the poor; and his righteousness is established for ever.	As it is written: HE HAS DISTRIBUTED AND GIVEN TO THE POOR AND HIS JUSTIFICATION IS VALID FOREVER.
10	Now he that ministereth seed to the sower both minister bread for your food, and multiply your seed sown, and increase the fruits of your righteousness;)	Now he that giveth seed to the sower, and bread for food, may he give and multiply your seed, and increase the fruits of your righteousness:	Now he who gives seed to the sower and bread for food will give and will multiply your seed and will increase the fruit of your justification,
11	Being enriched in every thing to all bountifulness, which causeth through us thanksgiving to God.	so that in every thing, ye may be enriched unto all liberality, to the completion of our thanksgiving to God.	so that you may be enriched in everything in all simplicity, so that thanksgiving to God is completed by way of us,
12	For the administration of this service not only supplieth the want of the saints, but is abundant also by many thanksgivings unto God;	For the performance of this ministration, not only supplieth the want of the saints, but is also rich in many thanksgivings to God.	because the work of this service not only supplies the needs of the holy [ones], but also increases with much thanksgiving to God.
13	Whiles by the experiment of this ministration they glorify God for your professed subjection unto the gospel of Christ, and for your liberal distribution unto them, and unto all men;	For on account of the test of this ministration, we glorify God, that ye do subject yourselves to the profession of the gospel of the Messiah, and that in your liberality, ye communicate with them and with all men:	For on account of the trial of this service, we glorify God that you have subjected yourselves to the acknowledgment of the gospel of Christ and [that] you have shared fully in your simplicity with them and with everyone.
14	And by their prayer for you, which long after you for the exceeding grace of God in you.	and they put up prayer for you, with much love, because of the abundance of the grace of God that is upon you.	And they offer prayer for you with great love, because of the abundance of the grace of God that is concerning you.

Parallel Translations

	KJV	*Murdock*	*Magiera*
II CORINTHIANS	***Chapter 9***		
15	Thanks be unto God for his unspeakable gift.	Thanks be to God for his unspeakable gift.	Now thanks be to God for his unspeakable gift.
Chapter 10			
1	Now I Paul myself beseech you by the meekness and gentleness of Christ, who in presence am base among you, but being absent am bold toward you:	Now I, Paul, beseech you, by the mildness and gentleness of the Messiah, although I am mild towards you when present, but bold towards you when absent!	Now I, Paul, beg you by the quietness and by the meekness of Christ, that although in presence, I am meek toward you, yet being absent, I am confident about you.
2	But I beseech you, that I may not be bold when I am present with that confidence, wherewith I think to be bold against some, which think of us as if we walked according to the flesh.	yet I beseech of you that, when I come, I may not be compelled by the boldness that is in me to be daring, as I estimate it, towards the persons who think we walk according to the flesh.	Now I beg you, that when I come I may not be compelled by the confidence that I have to be bold (as I consider [it]) to those who think that we are walking according to the flesh.
3	For though we walk in the flesh, we do not war after the flesh:	For, although we walk in the flesh, our warfare is not after the flesh.	For although we walk in the flesh, we do not serve of the flesh.
4	(For the weapons of our warfare are not carnal, but mighty through God to the pulling down of strong holds;)	For the arms of our warfare are not those of the flesh, but those of the power of God; by which we subdue rebellious castles.	For the equipment of our service is not of the flesh, but of the power of God and by it, we overcome rebellious strongholds.
5	Casting down imaginations, and every high thing that exalteth itself against the knowledge of God, and bringing into captivity every thought to the obedience of Christ;	And we demolish imaginations, and every lofty thing that exalteth itself against the knowledge of God, and subjugate all reasonings to obedience to the Messiah.	And we pull down reasonings and all pride that elevates [itself] against the knowledge of God and we lead captive all thoughts to the obedience of Christ.
6	And having in a readiness to revenge all disobedience, when your obedience is fulfilled.	And we are prepared, when your obedience shall be complete, to execute judgment on all the disobeying.	And we are prepared to execute justice on those who are disobedient, when your obedience is finished.
7	Do ye look on things after the outward appearance? If any man trust to himself that he is Christ's, let him of himself think this again, that, as he is Christ's, even so are we Christ's.	Do ye look on outward appearances? If any one is confident in himself that he is of the Messiah, let him know, from himself, that as he is of the Messiah, so also are we.	Are you looking on appearances? If anyone is confident of himself that he is of Christ, let him know of himself that as he is of Christ, so also are we.
8	For though I should boast somewhat more of our authority, which the Lord hath given us for edification, and not for your destruction, I should not be ashamed:	For if I should glory somewhat more, in the authority which our Lord hath given me, I should not be ashamed; for he gave it to us for your edification, and not for your destruction.	For if I also boast more about the authority that our Lord gave to me, I am not ashamed, because he gave [it] to us for your building up and not for your tearing down.
9	That I may not seem as if I would terrify you by letters.	But I forbear, lest I should be thought to terrify you terribly, by my epistles.	Now I hold back, so that I should not be considered that I especially terrified you by my letters,
10	For his letters, say they, are weighty and powerful; but his bodily presence is weak, and his speech contemptible.	For there are some who say, [His] epistles are weighty and forcible, but his bodily presence is weak, and his speech contemptible.	because there are some who say, "The letters are weighty and very hard, but his bodily presence is weak and his speech, worthless."

Parallel Translations

	KJV	*Murdock*	*Magiera*

II CORINTHIANS *Chapter 10*

	KJV	Murdock	Magiera
11	Let such an one think this, that, such as we are in word by letters when we are absent, such will we be also in deed when we are present.	But let him who saith so, consider this, that such as we are in our epistolary discourse, when absent, such also are we in action, when present.	But he who speaks so should consider this, that as we are in the word of our letter while we are absent, so also we are in action when we are present.
12	For we dare not make ourselves of the number, or compare ourselves with some that commend themselves: but they measuring themselves by themselves, and comparing themselves among themselves, are not wise.	For we dare not value, or compare ourselves, with those who vaunt: but they, because they compare themselves with themselves, are not wise.	For we dare not value or compare ourselves with those who are boasting in themselves, but because those are comparing themselves with themselves, they do not understand.
13	But we will not boast of things without our measure, but according to the measure of the rule which God hath distributed to us, a measure to reach even unto you.	But we will not glory beyond our measure, but within the measure of the limits which God hath imparted to us, that we should reach as far as you.	But we will not boast more than our measure, but according to the measure of the boundary that God distributed to us, so that we should also reach all the way to you.
14	For we stretch not ourselves beyond our measure, as though we reached not unto you: for we are come as far as to you also in preaching the gospel of Christ:	For we do not stretch ourselves, as if not reaching to you; for we do reach as far as you in the annunciation of the Messiah.	For we are not stretching ourselves as if we were not reaching you, for we reach all the way to you with the gospel of Christ.
15	Not boasting of things without our measure, that is, of other men's labours; but having hope, when your faith is increased, that we shall be enlarged by you according to our rule abundantly,	And we do not glory beyond our measure, in the toil of others: but we have the hope, that when your faith shall mature, we shall be magnified by you, as [being within] our measure;	And we are not boasting beyond our measure about the labor of others, but we have the hope that when your faith is grown, we will be magnified by you as our measure and [that] it would be increased
16	To preach the gospel in the regions beyond you, and not to boast in another man's line of things made ready to our hand.	and that we shall so abound also, as to make announcements beyond you. It is not in the measure of others, [and] in things ready prepared, that we will glory.	also to preach far beyond you. Not in the measure of others do we boast about things that are prepared.
17	But he that glorieth, let him glory in the Lord.	But let him that will glory, glory in the Lord.	BUT HE WHO BOASTS, LET HIM BOAST IN THE LORD,
18	For not he that commendeth himself is approved, but whom the Lord commendeth.	For not he who praiseth himself, is approved; but he whom the Lord praiseth.	for he who praises himself, that [one] is not approved, but he whom the LORD will praise.

Chapter 11

	KJV	Murdock	Magiera
1	Would to God ye could bear with me a little in my folly: and indeed bear with me.	I would that ye could bear with me a little, that I might talk foolishly: and indeed, bear ye with me.	Oh that you would bear with me a little that I may speak foolishly, only indeed bear with me!
2	For I am jealous over you with godly jealousy: for I have espoused you to one husband, that I may present you as a chaste virgin to Christ.	For I am jealous over you, with a godly jealousy: for I have espoused you to a husband as a chaste virgin, whom I would present to the Messiah.	For I am jealous of you with the jealousy of God, for I have espoused you to a husband, a pure young woman, whom I present to Christ.

II CORINTHIANS *Chapter 11*

	KJV	Murdock	Magiera
3	But I fear, lest by any means, as the serpent beguiled Eve through his subtilty, so your minds should be corrupted from the simplicity that is in Christ.	But I fear, lest, as the serpent beguiled Eve by his craftiness, so your minds should be corrupted from simplicity towards the Messiah.	But I fear, that even as the serpent lead Eve astray by his deceit, so your minds will be corrupted from the simplicity that is to Christ.
4	For if he that cometh preacheth another Jesus, whom we have not preached, or if ye receive another spirit, which ye have not received, or another gospel, which ye have not accepted, ye might well bear with him.	For if he that cometh to you, had proclaimed to you another Jesus, whom we have not proclaimed; or if ye had received another Spirit, which ye have not received; or another gospel, which ye have not accepted; ye might well have given assent.	For if he who came to you had preached to you another Jesus whom we had not preached or you had received another spirit that you had not received or another gospel that you had not accepted, you would have been persuaded well.
5	For I suppose I was not a whit behind the very chiefest apostles.	For, I suppose, I came not short of those legates who most excel.	For I think that I am no less than those apostles who most excel.
6	But though I be rude in speech, yet not in knowledge; but we have been throughly made manifest among you in all things.	For, though I be rude in speech, yet not in knowledge; but in all things we have been manifest among you.	For although I am unskilled in my speech, yet not in my knowledge, but in everything we are being made evident to you.
7	Have I committed an offence in abasing myself that ye might be exalted, because I have preached to you the gospel of God freely?	Did I indeed commit an offence, by humbling myself that ye might be exalted? and by proclaiming the gospel of God to you gratis?	Or did I actually cause offense when I humbled myself so that you would be elevated and [when I] freely preached to you the gospel of God?
8	I robbed other churches, taking wages of them, to do you service.	And I robbed other churches, and I took pay [of them] for ministering to you.	And I robbed other churches and received payments for your service.
9	And when I was present with you, and wanted, I was chargeable to no man: for that which was lacking to me the brethren which came from Macedonia supplied: and in all things I have kept myself from being burdensome unto you, and so will I keep myself.	And when I came among you and was needy, I was burdensome to none of you; for the brethren who came from Macedonia, supplied my wants: and in all things I kept myself, and I will keep myself, from being burdensome to you.	And when I came among you and had lack, I was not burdensome to any of you, for the brothers who came from Macedonia supplied my need and in everything I kept myself and I keep [myself], so that I would not burden you.
10	As the truth of Christ is in me, no man shall stop me of this boasting in the regions of Achaia.	As the truth of the Messiah is in me, this glorying shall not be made vain as to me in the regions of Achaia.	The truth of Christ is in me, that this boasting will not be stopped by me in the regions of Achaia.
11	Wherefore? because I love you not? God knoweth.	Why? Because I do not love you? God knoweth.	Why? Because I do not love you? God knows.
12	But what I do, that I will do, that I may cut off occasion from them which desire occasion; that wherein they glory, they may be found even as we.	But what I do, that also I will do; that I may cut off occasion, from them who seek occasion: so that in the thing wherein they glory, they may be found even as we.	But this that I am doing, I will also do, so that I may cut off the occasion of those who seek an occasion, so that they who are boasting in this may be found as we [are].
13	For such are false apostles, deceitful workers, transforming themselves into the apostles of Christ.	For they are false legates, crafty workers, and feign themselves to be legates of the Messiah.	For these are false apostles and crafty workers and they liken themselves to apostles of Christ

Parallel Translations

	KJV	Murdock	Magiera

II CORINTHIANS *Chapter 11*

	KJV	Murdock	Magiera
14	And no marvel; for Satan himself is transformed into an angel of light.	And in this there is nothing strange. For if Satan feigneth himself an angel of light,	and there is not [anything] to marvel at in this. For if Satan became an imitator of an angel of light,
15	Therefore it is no great thing if his ministers also be transformed as the ministers of righteousness; whose end shall be according to their works.	it is no great thing if his ministers feign themselves ministers of righteousness; whose end shall be according to their works.	it is not a great thing, if his ministers also become imitators of ministers of justification, whose end will be according to their works.
16	I say again, Let no man think me a fool; if otherwise, yet as a fool receive me, that I may boast myself a little.	Again I say, let no one think of me, as being a fool: or if otherwise, receive me as a fool, that I may glory a little.	But again I speak. Should anyone think of me as though I am a fool and if otherwise, receive me as a fool, that also, I may boast a little?
17	That which I speak, I speak it not after the Lord, but as it were foolishly, in this confidence of boasting.	What I am [now] saying, I say not in our Lord, but as in folly, in this matter of glorying.	What I am speaking, I do not speak in our Lord, but as in folly, in this matter of boasting.
18	Seeing that many glory after the flesh, I will glory also.	Because many glory after the flesh, I also will glory.	Because many boast in the flesh, I will also boast,
19	For ye suffer fools gladly, seeing ye yourselves are wise.	For ye hear with indulgence them who lack reason, seeing ye are wise.	for you are content to hear fools, since you are wise.
20	For ye suffer, if a man bring you into bondage, if a man devour you, if a man take of you, if a man exalt himself, if a man smite you on the face.	And ye give ear to him, who putteth you in bondage; and to him, who devoureth you; and to him, who taketh from you; and to him, who exalteth himself over you; and to him, who smiteth you in the face.	And you adhere to him who enslaves you and to him who devours you and to him who takes from you and to him who elevates himself over you and to him who strikes you on your face.
21	I speak as concerning reproach, as though we had been weak. Howbeit whereinsoever any is bold, (I speak foolishly,) I am bold also.	I speak as if under contempt: I speak as if we were impotent, through deficiency of understanding; that in whatever thing any one is presuming, I also am presuming.	I am speaking as if in shame. I am speaking as if we were weak through foolishness, for in everything [in] which anyone is bold, I am also bold.
22	Are they Hebrews? so am I. Are they Israelites? so am I. Are they the seed of Abraham? so am I.	If they are Hebrews, so I also: or if they are Israelites, I also. If they are the seed of Abraham, I also.	If they are Hebrews, I am also. If they are Israelites, I am also. If they are the seed of Abraham, I am also.
23	Are they ministers of Christ? (I speak as a fool) I am more; in labours more abundant, in stripes above measure, in prisons more frequent, in deaths oft.	If they are ministers of the Messiah, (in defect of understanding, I say it,) I am superior to them: in toils more than they, in stripes more than they, in bonds more than they, in deaths many times.	If they are ministers of Christ (I am speaking foolishly), I am greater than them, in labor more than them, in beatings more than them, in prisons more than them, in deaths, many times.
24	Of the Jews five times received I forty stripes save one.	By the Jews, five times was I scourged, each time with forty stripes save one.	Of the Judeans, five times I was beaten, each time forty [lashes] lacking one.
25	Thrice was I beaten with rods, once was I stoned, thrice I suffered shipwreck, a night and a day I have been in the deep;	Three times was I beaten with rods: at one time I was stoned: three times I was in shipwreck, by day and by night; I have been in the sea, without a ship.	Three times I was beaten with rods, one time I was stoned, three times I was shipwrecked, a day and a night I was without a ship in the sea,

Parallel Translations

	KJV	*Murdock*	*Magiera*

II CORINTHIANS *Chapter 11*

	KJV	Murdock	Magiera
26	In journeyings often, in perils of waters, in perils of robbers, in perils by mine own countrymen, in perils by the heathen, in perils in the city, in perils in the wilderness, in perils in the sea, in perils among false brethren;	In journeyings many, in peril by rivers, in peril by robbers, in peril from my kindred, in peril from Gentiles: I have been in peril in cities; I have been in peril in the desert, in peril in the sea, in peril from false brethren.	in many journeys, in danger of rivers, in danger of robbers, in danger from my relatives, in danger from the Gentiles. I was in danger in the cities, I was in danger in the wilderness, in danger in the sea, in danger from false brothers,
27	In weariness and painfulness, in watchings often, in hunger and thirst, in fastings often, in cold and nakedness.	In toil and weariness, in much watching, in hunger and thirst, in much fasting, in cold and nakedness:	in toil and in weariness, in much watching, in hunger and in thirst, in much fasting, in cold and in nakedness,
28	Beside those things that are without, that which cometh upon me daily, the care of all the churches.	besides many other things, and the thronging around me every day, and my anxiety for all the churches.	besides familiar [things] and the crowd that is around me daily and my care on behalf of all the churches.
29	Who is weak, and I am not weak? who is offended, and I burn not?	Who becometh weak, and I become not weak? Who is stumbled, and I burn not?	Who was weakened and I was not weakened? Who was offended and I did not burn?
30	If I must needs glory, I will glory of the things which concern mine infirmities.	If I must glory, I will glory in my infirmities.	If it is necessary to boast, I will boast in my weaknesses.
31	The God and Father of our Lord Jesus Christ, which is blessed for evermore, knoweth that I lie not.	God, the Father of our Lord Jesus the Messiah, blessed for ever and ever, he knoweth that I lie not.	God, the Father of our Lord Jesus Christ, blessed forever, knows that I do not lie.
32	In Damascus the governor under Aretas the king kept the city of the Damascenes with a garrison, desirous to apprehend me:	At Damascus, the commander of the army of Aretas the king, guarded the city of the Damascenes, to seize me.	In Damascus, the commander of the army of Aretas, the king, was guarding the city of the Damascenes to arrest me.
33	And through a window in a basket was I let down by the wall, and escaped his hands.	And from a window, in a basket, they let me down from the wall, and I escaped from his hands.	And they let me down from the wall from a window in a basket and I escaped from his hands.

Chapter 12

	KJV	Murdock	Magiera
1	It is not expedient for me doubtless to glory. I will come to visions and revelations of the Lord.	Glorying must be, but it is not profitable: so I proceed to visions and revelations of our Lord.	To boast is necessary, but not profitable, for I will come to visions and to revelations of our Lord.
2	I knew a man in Christ above fourteen years ago, (whether in the body, I cannot tell; or whether out of the body, I cannot tell: God knoweth;) such an one caught up to the third heaven.	I knew a man in the Messiah fourteen years ago, (but whether in a body, or whether out of a body, I know not; God knoweth:) who was caught up to the third [region] of heaven.	I knew a man in Christ fourteen years ago (but whether with a body or without a body I do not know, God knows) who was caught up to the third heaven.
3	And I knew such a man, (whether in the body, or out of the body, I cannot tell: God knoweth;)	And I knew this same man; (but whether in a body, or out of a body, I know not; God knoweth;)	And I knew this man (but whether with a body or without a body I do not know, God knows)
4	How that he was caught up into paradise, and heard unspeakable words, which it is not lawful for a man to utter.	and he was caught up to Paradise, and heard ineffable words, which it is not permitted a man to utter.	who was caught up to paradise and heard unspeakable words that are unlawful for a man to speak.

	KJV	*Murdock*	*Magiera*

II CORINTHIANS *Chapter 12*

	KJV	Murdock	Magiera
5	Of such an one will I glory: yet of myself I will not glory, but in mine infirmities.	Of him I will glory: but of myself I will not glory, except in my infirmities.	About this I will boast, but I will not boast about myself, except in weaknesses.
6	For though I would desire to glory, I shall not be a fool; for I will say the truth: but now I forbear, lest any man should think of me above that which he seeth me to be, or that he heareth of me.	Yet if I were disposed to glory, I should not be without reason; for I declare the truth. But I refrain, lest any one should think of me, beyond what he seeth in me and heareth from me.	For if I desired to boast, I would not be crazy, for I am speaking the truth. But I refrain, so that no one should think of me more than what he sees in me and what he hears from me.
7	And lest I should be exalted above measure through the abundance of the revelations, there was given to me a thorn in the flesh, the messenger of Satan to buffet me, lest I should be exalted above measure.	And, that I might not be uplifted by the excellency of the revelations, there was imparted to me a thorn in my flesh, the angel of Satan, to buffet me, that I might not be uplifted.	And so that I should not be elevated by the abundance of the revelations, a thorn to my flesh was delivered to me, a messenger of Satan, to buffet me, so that I should not be elevated.
8	For this thing I besought the Lord thrice, that it might depart from me.	Respecting this, I thrice besought my Lord, that it might depart from me.	And concerning this, three times I requested from my Lord that it would go away from me.
9	And he said unto me, My grace is sufficient for thee: for my strength is made perfect in weakness. Most gladly therefore will I rather glory in my infirmities, that the power of Christ may rest upon me.	And he said to me, My grace is sufficient for thee; for my power is perfected in weakness. Gladly, therefore, will I glory in my infirmities, that the power of the Messiah may rest upon me.	And he said to me, "My grace is sufficient for you, for my power is perfected in weakness." Therefore, I will gladly boast in my weaknesses, so that the power of Christ will rest on me.
10	Therefore I take pleasure in infirmities, in reproaches, in necessities, in persecutions, in distresses for Christ's sake: for when I am weak, then am I strong.	Therefore I have pleasure in infirmities, in reproach, in afflictions, in persecutions, in distresses, which are for the Messiah's sake: for when I am weak, then am I strong.	Because of this, I have pleasure in weaknesses, in reproaches, in adversities, in persecutions, in distresses that are on behalf of Christ, for at what time I am weak, then I am strong.
11	I am become a fool in glorying; ye have compelled me: for I ought to have been commended of you: for in nothing am I behind the very chiefest apostles, though I be nothing.	Behold, I have become foolish in my glorying, for ye compelled me. For ye ought to bear witness for me; because I was inferior in nothing to those legates who most excel, although I was nothing.	Behold, I became a fool in my boasting, because you pressured me. For you ought to give testimony about me, because I am no less than the apostles who most excel, even though I was nothing.
12	Truly the signs of an apostle were wrought among you in all patience, in signs, and wonders, and mighty deeds.	I wrought among you the signs of the legates, with all patience; and in prodigies, and in wonders, and in mighty deeds.	I performed the signs of the apostles among you with all patience and with exploits and with wonders and with mighty works.
13	For what is it wherein ye were inferior to other churches, except it be that I myself was not burdensome to you? forgive me this wrong.	For in what fell ye short of the other churches; except in this, that I was not burdensome to you? Forgive me this fault.	For in what were you made less than other churches, except in this, that I did not burden you? Forgive me this fault.

II CORINTHIANS *Chapter 12*

	KJV	Murdock	Magiera
14	Behold, the third time I am ready to come to you; and I will not be burdensome to you: for I seek not yours, but you: for the children ought not to lay up for the parents, but the parents for the children.	Behold, this third time I am ready to come to you, and I will not burden you; for I seek not yours, but you: for children ought not to lay up treasures for the parents, but the parents for their children.	Behold, this is the third time that I am ready to come to you, and I will not burden you, because I do not seek yours, but you, for children ought not to lay up treasures for parents, but parents for their children.
15	And I will very gladly spend and be spent for you; though the more abundantly I love you, the less I be loved.	And cheerfully will I both pay [my] expenses, and also give myself for your souls; although the more I love you, the less ye love me.	And I will both cheerfully pay the expenses and also give myself for you, although the more I love you, the less you love me.
16	But be it so, I did not burden you: nevertheless, being crafty, I caught you with guile.	But perhaps, though I was not burdensome to you, yet, like a cunning man, I filched from you by craftiness!	And perhaps I did not burden you, but like a cunning man, I robbed you by trickery.
17	Did I make a gain of you by any of them whom I sent unto you?	Was it by the hand of some other person whom I sent to you, that I pilfered from you?	Why? [Was it] by way of another man that I sent to you [and] was greedy of [the things] concerning you?
18	I desired Titus, and with him I sent a brother. Did Titus make a gain of you? walked we not in the same spirit? walked we not in the same steps?	I requested Titus, and with him I sent the brethren: did Titus pilfer any thing from you? Did we not walk in one spirit, and in the same steps?	I begged Titus [to go to you] and I sent the brothers with him. Was Titus greedy of anything belonging to you? Did we not walk in one spirit and in the same footsteps?
19	Again, think ye that we excuse ourselves unto you? we speak before God in Christ: but we do all things, dearly beloved, for your edifying.	Do ye again suppose, that we would apologize to you? Before God, in the Messiah we speak: and all these things, my beloved, [are] for the sake of your edification.	Do you again suppose that we should make a defense to you? Before God, we speak in Christ, and all these [things], my beloved, [are] for your building up.
20	For I fear, lest, when I come, I shall not find you such as I would, and that I shall be found unto you such as ye would not: lest there be debates, envyings, wraths, strifes, backbitings, whisperings, swellings, tumults:	For I fear, lest I should come to you and not find you such as I would wish; and lest I also should be found by you, such as ye would not wish; lest [there should be] contention, and envying, and anger, and obstinacy, and slandering, and murmuring, and insolence, and commotion;	For I fear, will I come to you and not find you as I desire and be found by you even as you do not desire? [Will there be] contention and envying and anger and obstinacy and slandering and murmuring and pride and confusion?
21	And lest, when I come again, my God will humble me among you, and that I shall bewail many which have sinned already, and have not repented of the uncleanness and fornication and lasciviousness which they have committed.	lest, when I come to you, my God should humble me; and I should mourn over many, who have sinned, and have not repented of the impurity, the whoredom, and the lasciviousness, which they have committed.	When I come to you, will my God humble me and will I mourn over many who have sinned and have not repented from the uncleanness and from the fornication and from the wantonness that they committed?

Chapter 13

	KJV	Murdock	Magiera
1	This is the third time I am coming to you. In the mouth of two or three witnesses shall every word be established.	This is the third time that I have prepare to come to you; that, by the mouth of two or three witnesses, every word may be established.	This is the third time that I will come to you: BY THE MOUTH OF TWO OR THREE WITNESSES, EVERY WORD WILL BE ESTABLISHED.

	KJV	Murdock	Magiera

II CORINTHIANS *Chapter 13*

	KJV	Murdock	Magiera
2	I told you before, and foretell you, as if I were present, the second time; and being absent now I write to them which heretofore have sinned, and to all other, that, if I come again, I will not spare:	I have before said to you, and again I say to you beforehand, (as also I said to you a second time, while I was with you; and now also, while absent, I write to those who have sinned and to the others,) that if I come again, I will not spare:	I have told you previously and again I tell you beforehand (as if I was with you the second time, I tell you and now also while I am absent, I write to those who have sinned and to the others) that if I come again, I will not refrain,
3	Since ye seek a proof of Christ speaking in me, which to you-ward is not weak, but is mighty in you.	because ye demand proof, that it is the Messiah that speaketh by me, who hath not been powerless among you, but powerful among you.	because you seek proof that it is Christ who speaks by me, who has not been weak among you, but powerful among you.
4	For though he was crucified through weakness, yet he liveth by the power of God. For we also are weak in him, but we shall live with him by the power of God toward you.	For, though he was crucified in weakness, yet he liveth with the power of God. We also are weak with him; yet we are alive with him, by that power of God which is among you.	For although he was crucified in weakness, yet he is alive by the power of God. And if we are weak with him, yet we are alive with him by the power of God that is in you.
5	Examine yourselves, whether ye be in the faith; prove your own selves. Know ye not your own selves, how that Jesus Christ is in you, except ye be reprobates?	Examine yourselves, whether ye stand in the faith: prove yourselves. Do ye not acknowledge that Jesus the Messiah is in you? And if [he is] not, ye are reprobates.	Examine yourselves, whether you stand fast in the faith. Prove yourselves. Or do you not acknowledge that Jesus Christ is in you? And if [you do] not, you are rejected.
6	But I trust that ye shall know that we are not reprobates.	But, I trust, ye will know that we are not reprobates.	But I am trusting that you will know that we are not rejecting [you].
7	Now I pray to God that ye do no evil; not that we should appear approved, but that ye should do that which is honest, though we be as reprobates.	And I beseech God, that there may be no evil in you, so that the proof of us may appear: and yet, that ye may be doers of good things, though we be as reprobates.	But I beg God that there may be no evil in you, so that our proof may be seen, nevertheless, that you may do good [things] and [that] we may be as rejected.
8	For we can do nothing against the truth, but for the truth.	For we can do nothing against the truth, but [only] for the truth.	For we are not able to do anything contrary to truthfulness, but for truthfulness.
9	For we are glad, when we are weak, and ye are strong: and this also we wish, even your perfection.	And we rejoice, when we are weak and ye are strong. And this also we pray for, that ye may be perfected.	Now we rejoice when we are weak and you are strong. For this we also pray, that you would be mature.
10	Therefore I write these things being absent, lest being present I should use sharpness, according to the power which the Lord hath given me to edification, and not to destruction.	Therefore, while absent, I write these things; lest when I come, I should act with rigor, according to the authority which my Lord hath given me for your edification, and not for your destruction.	Because of this, when I am absent I write these [things], so that when I come, I should not act severely according to the authority that my Lord gave me for your building up and not for your tearing down.
11	Finally, brethren, farewell. Be perfect, be of good comfort, be of one mind, live in peace; and the God of love and peace shall be with you.	Finally, my brethren, rejoice, and be perfected, and be comforted: and may harmony and quietness be among you; and the God of love and of peace will be with you.	From now on, my brothers, rejoice and be mature and be comforted and there will be agreement and harmony among you and the God of love and of peace will be with you.

Parallel Translations

	KJV	*Murdock*	*Magiera*

II CORINTHIANS *Chapter 13*

	KJV	Murdock	Magiera
12	Greet one another with an holy kiss.	Salute ye one another, with a holy kiss.	Greet one another with a holy kiss.
13	All the saints salute you.	All the saints salute you.	All the holy [ones] greet you.
14	The grace of the Lord Jesus Christ, and the love of God, and the communion of the Holy Ghost, be with you all. Amen.	The peace of our Lord Jesus the Messiah, and the love of God, and the communion of the Holy Spirit be with you all. Amen.	The peace of our Lord Jesus Christ and the love of God and the fellowship of the Holy Spirit [be] with all of you. Amen.

Parallel Translations

GALATIANS *Chapter 1*

	KJV	*Murdock*	*Magiera*
1	Paul, an apostle, (not of men, neither by man, but by Jesus Christ, and God the Father, who raised him from the dead;)	Paul, a legate, not from men, nor by man, but by Jesus the Messiah, and God his Father, who raised him from the dead;	Paul an apostle, not from men and not by way of man, but by way of Jesus Christ and God his Father, who raised him from the dead,
2	And all the brethren which are with me, unto the churches of Galatia:	and all the brethren who are with me; unto the churches which are in Galatia.	and all the brothers who are with me to the churches that are in Galatia:
3	Grace be to you and peace from God the Father, and from our Lord Jesus Christ,	Grace be with you, and peace, from God the Father, and from our Lord Jesus the Messiah;	Grace and peace [be] with you from God the Father and from our Lord Jesus Christ,
4	Who gave himself for our sins, that he might deliver us from this present evil world, according to the will of God and our Father:	who gave himself for our sins, that he might deliver us from this evil world, agreeably to the pleasure of God our Father:	who gave himself for our sins to deliver us from this evil world, according to the will of God our Father,
5	To whom be glory for ever and ever. Amen.	to whom be glory for ever and ever. Amen.	to whom [be] glory forever and ever. Amen.
6	I marvel that ye are so soon removed from him that called you into the grace of Christ unto another gospel:	I admire, how soon ye have turned from the Messiah, who called you by his grace, unto another gospel;	I am amazed at how quickly you are being turned from Christ, who called you by his grace, to another gospel
7	Which is not another; but there be some that trouble you, and would pervert the gospel of Christ.	which doth not exist, except as there are some who would disquiet you, and are disposed to pervert the gospel of the Messiah.	that is not [a true gospel]. But there are some who are troubling you and want to pervert the gospel of Christ.
8	But though we, or an angel from heaven, preach any other gospel unto you than that which we have preached unto you, let him be accursed.	But if we, or an angel from heaven, should announce to you differently from what we have announced to you, let him be accursed.	Now even if we or an angel from heaven should declare to you [anything] outside of what we have declared to you, he will be cursed.
9	As we said before, so say I now again, If any man preach any other gospel unto you than that ye have received, let him be accursed.	As I have just said, and now I again say it, that if any one announce to you differently from what ye received, let him be accursed.	As I said before and now I am saying again, "If anyone declares to you [anything] outside of what you have received, he will be cursed."
10	For do I now persuade men, or God? or do I seek to please men? for if I yet pleased men, I should not be the servant of Christ.	For do I now persuade men, or God? Or do I seek to please men? For if I had till now pleased men, I should not have been a servant of the Messiah.	For now do I persuade men, or God? Or do I seek to please men? For up to now, if I had pleased men, I would not have been a servant of Christ.
11	But I certify you, brethren, that the gospel which was preached of me is not after man.	But I make known to you, my brethren, that the gospel announced by me, was not from man.	But I make known to you, my brothers, that the gospel that was declared by me was not from man.
12	For I neither received it of man, neither was I taught it, but by the revelation of Jesus Christ.	For I did not receive it and learn it from man, but [I had it] by revelation from Jesus the Messiah.	For also I did not receive it and learn it from man, but [I received it] by the revelation of Jesus Christ.
13	For ye have heard of my conversation in time past in the Jews' religion, how that beyond measure I persecuted the church of God, and wasted it:	For ye have heard of my former course of life in Judaism, that I persecuted the church of God exceedingly, and destroyed it:	For you have heard of my previous way of life that was in Judaism, that I had greatly persecuted the church of God and ruined it.

Parallel Translations

	KJV	*Murdock*	*Magiera*
	GALATIANS *Chapter 1*		
14	And profited in the Jews' religion above many my equals in mine own nation, being more exceedingly zealous of the traditions of my fathers.	and that I went much farther in Judaism than many of my contemporaries who were of my nation, and was peculiarly zealous for the doctrine of my fathers.	And I excelled in Judaism more than many [of] my contemporaries who were my countrymen. And I was very zealous in the teaching of my fathers.
15	But when it pleased God, who separated me from my mother's womb, and called me by his grace,	But when it pleased him, who separated me from my mother's womb, and called me by his grace,	Now when it pleased him, who had set me apart from the womb of my mother and called me by his grace,
16	To reveal his Son in me, that I might preach him among the heathen; immediately I conferred not with flesh and blood:	to reveal his Son by me, that I should proclaim him among the Gentiles; forthwith, I did not open it to flesh and blood;	to reveal his Son in me, that I should declare him among the Gentiles, I did not immediately reveal [this] to flesh and blood
17	Neither went I up to Jerusalem to them which were apostles before me; but I went into Arabia, and returned again unto Damascus.	nor did I go to Jerusalem, to them who were legates before me; but I went into Arabia, and returned again to Damascus:	and I did not go to Jerusalem to the apostles who were before me. But I went to Arabia and returned again to Damascus.
18	Then after three years I went up to Jerusalem to see Peter, and abode with him fifteen days.	and after three years, I went to Jerusalem to see Cephas; and I remained with him fifteen days.	And after three years, I went to Jerusalem to see Peter and remained with him [for] fifteen days.
19	But other of the apostles saw I none, save James the Lord's brother.	But others of the legates I saw not, except James, our Lord's brother.	But I did not see the rest of the apostles, except James, the brother of our Lord.
20	Now the things which I write unto you, behold, before God, I lie not.	In the things which I am writing to you, behold, before God! I lie not.	Now these [things] that I write to you, behold, before God, I am not lying!
21	Afterwards I came into the regions of Syria and Cilicia;	And after that, I went to the regions of Syria and Cilicia.	After these [places], I came to the regions of Syria and of Cilicia.
22	And was unknown by face unto the churches of Judaea which were in Christ:	And the churches in Judaea which were in the Messiah; did not know me personally:	And the churches in Judea that were in Christ did not know me personally.
23	But they had heard only, That he which persecuted us in times past now preacheth the faith which once he destroyed.	but this only had they heard, that he who before persecuted us, now preacheth that faith which in time preceding he subverted:	But they had heard this only, "He who previously was persecuting us, behold, now is preaching the faith that he was overthrowing in a previous time."
24	And they glorified God in me.	and they glorified God in me.	And they were glorifying God on account of me.
	Chapter 2		
1	Then fourteen years after I went up again to Jerusalem with Barnabas, and took Titus with me also.	And again, after fourteen years, I went up to Jerusalem with Barnabas; and I took with me Titus.	Now after fourteen years, I went up again to Jerusalem with Barnabas and took Titus with me.

Parallel Translations

	KJV	*Murdock*	*Magiera*
	GALATIANS *Chapter 2*		
2	And I went up by revelation, and communicated unto them that gospel which I preach among the Gentiles, but privately to them which were of reputation, lest by any means I should run, or had run, in vain.	And I went up by revelation: and I explained to them the gospel which I announce among the Gentiles; and I stated it to them who were esteemed prominent, between myself and them: lest I should have run, or might run in vain.	Now I went up by revelation and I made known to them the gospel that I was preaching among the Gentiles. And I showed it to those who were considered to be something privately, lest somehow I had run or would run in vain.
3	But neither Titus, who was with me, being a Greek, was compelled to be circumcised:	Also Titus, who was with me, and was a Gentile, was not compelled to be circumcised.	Even Titus, who was an Aramean with me, was not compelled to be circumcised.
4	And that because of false brethren unawares brought in, who came in privily to spy out our liberty which we have in Christ Jesus, that they might bring us into bondage:	And in regard to the false brethren, who had crept in to spy out the liberty we have in Jesus the Messiah, in order to bring me under subjection;	Now because of false brothers who had entered among us to spy on the freedom that we have in Jesus Christ in order to enslave us,
5	To whom we gave place by subjection, no, not for an hour; that the truth of the gospel might continue with you.	not for the space of an hour, did we throw ourselves into subjection to them; so that the truth of the gospel might remain with you.	not even for a minute did we submit to their oppression, so that the truth of the gospel would remain with you.
6	But of these who seemed to be somewhat, (whatsoever they were, it maketh no matter to me: God accepteth no man's person:) for they who seemed to be somewhat in conference added nothing to me:	And they who were esteemed prominent, (what they were, I care not; for God regardeth not the persons of men,)—even these persons added nothing to me.	Now those who were considered to be something (now what they were did not concern me, for God does not have respect of persons) now these did not add anything to me.
7	But contrariwise, when they saw that the gospel of the uncircumcision was committed unto me, as the gospel of the circumcision was unto Peter;	But, otherwise; for they saw, that the gospel of the uncircumcision was intrusted to me, as to Cephas was intrusted that of the circumcision.	But [it was] otherwise, for they saw that I had been entrusted with the gospel of the uncircumcision, as Peter had been entrusted with the circumcision.
8	(For he that wrought effectually in Peter to the apostleship of the circumcision, the same was mighty in me toward the Gentiles:)	For he that was operative with Cephas in the legateship of the circumcision, was also operative with me in the legateship of the Gentiles.	For he who worked in Peter in the apostleship of the circumcision also worked in me in the apostleship of the Gentiles.
9	And when James, Cephas, and John, who seemed to be pillars, perceived the grace that was given unto me, they gave to me and Barnabas the right hands of fellowship; that we should go unto the heathen, and they unto the circumcision.	And James, Cephas, and John, who were accounted pillars, when they perceived the grace that was given to me, gave to me and Barnabas the right hand of fellowship; that we [should labor] among the Gentiles, and they among the circumcision.	And when they knew of the grace that was given to me, James and Peter and John, those who were considered to be pillars, gave to me and to Barnabas the right hand of fellowship that we [should work] among the Gentiles and they among the circumcision.
10	Only they would that we should remember the poor; the same which I also was forward to do.	Only [they desired] that we would be mindful of the needy; and I was solicitous to do the same.	[They asked] only that we should remember the poor and I was concerned to do this.
11	But when Peter was come to Antioch, I withstood him to the face, because he was to be blamed.	But when Cephas was come to Antioch, I rebuked him to his face; because they were stumbled by him.	But when Peter came to Antioch, I reproved him to his face, because they were offended by him.

Parallel Translations

	KJV	*Murdock*	*Magiera*

GALATIANS *Chapter 2*

Verse	KJV	Murdock	Magiera
12	For before that certain came from James, he did eat with the Gentiles: but when they were come, he withdrew and separated himself, fearing them which were of the circumcision.	For before certain ones came from James, he ate with the Gentiles: but when they came, he withdrew himself, and separated; because he was afraid of them of the circumcision.	Before some men came from James, he ate with the Gentiles, but after they came, he withdrew and separated himself, because he was afraid of those who were from the circumcision.
13	And the other Jews dissembled likewise with him; insomuch that Barnabas also was carried away with their dissimulation.	And the rest of the Jews also were with him in this thing; insomuch that even Barnabas was induced to regard persons.	And the rest of the Judeans also submitted to this with him, so that even Barnabas was led to respect persons.
14	But when I saw that they walked not uprightly according to the truth of the gospel, I said unto Peter before them all, If thou, being a Jew, livest after the manner of Gentiles, and not as do the Jews, why compellest thou the Gentiles to live as do the Jews?	And when I saw, that they did not walk correctly, in the truth of the gospel, I said to Cephas, before them all: If thou art a Jew, and livest in the Gentile way, and not in the Jewish, why dost thou compel the Gentiles to live in the Jewish way?	And when I saw that they were not walking correctly in the truth of the gospel, I said to Peter in front of all of them, "If you who are a Judean live as a heathen and not as a Judean, how can you compel the Gentiles to live as a Judean?"
15	We who are Jews by nature, and not sinners of the Gentiles,	For if we, who are Jews by nature, and are not sinners of the Gentiles,	For we, who by nature are Judeans and are not sinners of the Gentiles,
16	Knowing that a man is not justified by the works of the law, but by the faith of Jesus Christ, even we have believed in Jesus Christ, that we might be justified by the faith of Christ, and not by the works of the law: for by the works of the law shall no flesh be justified.	because we know that a man is not made just by the works of the law, but by faith in Jesus the Messiah; even we have believed in Jesus the Messiah, in order to be made just by faith in the Messiah, and not by the works of the law: for, by the deeds of the law, no flesh is made just.	because we know that a man is not justified by the works of the law, but by the faith of Jesus Christ, we also believe in Jesus Christ, so that we may be justified by the faith of Christ and not by the works of the law, because by the works of the law, NO FLESH IS JUSTIFIED.
17	But if, while we seek to be justified by Christ, we ourselves also are found sinners, is therefore Christ the minister of sin? God forbid.	And if, while we seek to become just by the Messiah, we are found to be ourselves sinners, is Jesus the Messiah therefore the minister of sin? Far be it!	But if while we are seeking to be justified by Christ, we are also found [that] we are sinners, then is Jesus Christ the minister of sin? Let it not be so!
18	For if I build again the things which I destroyed, I make myself a transgressor.	For if I should build up again the things I had demolished, I should show myself to be a transgressor of the precept.	For if I build up again those [things] that I have broken down, I show about myself that I am a transgressor of the commandment.
19	For I through the law am dead to the law, that I might live unto God.	For I, by the law, have become dead to the law, that I might live to God; and I am crucified with the Messiah.	For by the law I died to the law that I would live for God
20	I am crucified with Christ: nevertheless I live; yet not I, but Christ liveth in me: and the life which I now live in the flesh I live by the faith of the Son of God, who loved me, and gave himself for me.	And henceforth it is no more I who live, but the Messiah liveth in me: and the life I now live in the flesh, I live by faith in the Son of God, who loved me and gave himself for me.	and I am crucified with Christ. And from now on, I am not living, but Christ lives in me, and this [life] that I am now living in the flesh, I am living by the faith of the Son of God, who loved us and gave himself for us.

	KJV	Murdock	Magiera
	GALATIANS *Chapter 2*		
21	I do not frustrate the grace of God: for if righteousness come by the law, then Christ is dead in vain.	I do not spurn the grace of God. For if righteousness is by means of the law, the Messiah died in vain.	I am not denying the grace of God. For if justification is by way of the law, Christ died without cause.
	Chapter 3		
1	O foolish Galatians, who hath bewitched you, that ye should not obey the truth, before whose eyes Jesus Christ hath been evidently set forth, crucified among you?	O ye Galatians, deficient in understanding! Who hath fascinated you? For lo, Jesus the Messiah hath been portrayed as in a picture, crucified before your eyes.	Oh stupid Galatians! Who has made you envious? For behold, as a portrait, Jesus Christ being crucified was portrayed before your eyes.
2	This only would I learn of you, Received ye the Spirit by the works of the law, or by the hearing of faith?	This only would I learn from you, Was it by works of the law, that ye received the Spirit? or by the hearing of faith?	I want to know this only from you. Did you receive the Spirit by the works of the law or by the hearing of faith?
3	Are ye so foolish? having begun in the Spirit, are ye now made perfect by the flesh?	Are ye so foolish, that having begun in the Spirit, ye now would consummate in the flesh?	Are you so foolish that you began by the Spirit, yet now you are finishing in the flesh?
4	Have ye suffered so many things in vain? if it be yet in vain.	And have ye borne all these things in vain? And I would, it were in vain!	Have you endured all these [things] without result? But oh that [it were] without result!
5	He therefore that ministereth to you the Spirit, and worketh miracles among you, doeth he it by the works of the law, or by the hearing of faith?	He therefore who giveth the Spirit in you, and who worketh miracles among you, [doth he these things] by the deeds of the law? or by the hearing of faith?	Therefore, he who imparts the Spirit in you and works miracles among you [does he do these] by the works of the law or by the hearing of faith?
6	Even as Abraham believed God, and it was accounted to him for righteousness.	In like manner Abraham believed God, and it was accounted to him for righteousness.	In like manner, ABRAHAM BELIEVED GOD AND IT WAS COUNTED TO HIM FOR JUSTIFICATION.
7	Know ye therefore that they which are of faith, the same are the children of Abraham.	Know ye, therefore, that those who are of faith, they are the children of Abraham.	Therefore, know that those who are of faith are the sons of Abraham.
8	And the scripture, foreseeing that God would justify the heathen through faith, preached before the gospel unto Abraham, saying, In thee shall all nations be blessed.	For, because God knew beforehand that the Gentiles would be made just by faith, he preannounced it to Abraham; as saith the holy scripture, In thee shall all nations be blessed.	For because God knew beforehand that the Gentiles would be justified by faith, he foretold [it] to Abraham, as the holy scripture says: ALL THE GENTILES WILL BE BLESSED IN YOU.
9	So then they which be of faith are blessed with faithful Abraham.	Believers, therefore, it is, who are blessed with believing Abraham.	So then, believers are blessed with Abraham, the believer.
10	For as many as are of the works of the law are under the curse: for it is written, Cursed is every one that continueth not in all things which are written in the book of the law to do them.	For they who are of the deeds of the law, are under the curse: for it is written, Cursed is every one who shall not do every thing written in this law.	For those who are of the works of the law are under the curse, for it is written: CURSED IS EVERYONE WHO WILL NOT DO ALL THAT IS WRITTEN IN THIS LAW.
11	But that no man is justified by the law in the sight of God, it is evident: for, The just shall live by faith.	And that no one becometh just before God, by the law, is manifest: because it is written, The just by faith, shall live.	Now that a man is not justified to God by the law is evident, because it is written: THE JUST [ONE] WILL LIVE BY FAITH.

Parallel Translations

	KJV	*Murdock*	*Magiera*
	GALATIANS *Chapter 3*		
12	And the law is not of faith: but, The man that doeth them shall live in them.	Now the law is not of faith; but, whoever shall do the things written in it, shall live by them.	Now the law was not of faith. But whoever will do those [things] that are written in it will live by them.
13	Christ hath redeemed us from the curse of the law, being made a curse for us: for it is written, Cursed is every one that hangeth on a tree:	But the Messiah hath redeemed us from the curse of the law, and hath been a curse for us; (for it is written, Cursed is everyone that is hanged on a tree;)	And Christ redeemed us from the curse of the law and became a curse for us, for it is written: CURSED IS EVERYONE WHO IS HUNG ON A TREE
14	That the blessing of Abraham might come on the Gentiles through Jesus Christ; that we might receive the promise of the Spirit through faith.	that the blessing of Abraham might be on the Gentiles, through Jesus the Messiah; that we might receive the promise of the Spirit by faith.	that the blessing of Abraham would be on the Gentiles by Jesus Christ and [that] we would receive the promise of the Spirit by faith.
15	Brethren, I speak after the manner of men; Though it be but a man's covenant, yet if it be confirmed, no man disannulleth, or addeth thereto.	My brethren, I speak as among men; a man's covenant which is confirmed, no one setteth aside, or changeth any thing in it.	My brothers, I speak as among men, because a covenant of man that is established, no man sets aside or changes anything in it.
16	Now to Abraham and his seed were the promises made. He saith not, And to seeds, as of many; but as of one, And to thy seed, which is Christ.	Now to Abraham was the promise made, and to his seed. And it said to him, not, to thy seeds, as being many; but to thy seed, as being one, which is the Messiah.	Now the promise was promised to Abraham and to his seed. And he did not say to him, "To your seeds" as to many, but TO YOUR SEED as to one, who is the Messiah.
17	And this I say, that the covenant, that was confirmed before of God in Christ, the law, which was four hundred and thirty years after, cannot disannul, that it should make the promise of none effect.	And this I say: That the covenant which was previously confirmed by God in the Messiah, the law which was four hundred and thirty years after, cannot set it aside, and nullify the promise.	And this I say, that the covenant, which was previously established by God in Christ, the law, which was four hundred and thirty years after, is not able to set it aside and make the promise void.
18	For if the inheritance be of the law, it is no more of promise: but God gave it to Abraham by promise.	And if the inheritance were by the law, it would not be by promise: but God gave it to Abraham by promise.	Now if the inheritance was by the law, then it was not by promise. But God gave it to Abraham by promise.
19	Wherefore then serveth the law? It was added because of transgressions, till the seed should come to whom the promise was made; and it was ordained by angels in the hand of a mediator.	What then is the law? It was added on account of transgression, until that seed should come, to whom belonged the promise: and the law was given by angels through a mediator.	Why then [was] the law? It was added because of transgression until that seed should come to whom was the promise. And the law was given by way of angels, by the hand of a mediator.
20	Now a mediator is not a mediator of one, but God is one.	Now a mediator is not of one; but God is one.	Now a mediator is not of one, but God is one.
21	Is the law then against the promises of God? God forbid: for if there had been a law given which could have given life, verily righteousness should have been by the law.	Is the law then opposed to the promise of God? Far be it. For if a law had been given, which could make alive, certainly, righteousness would have been by the law.	Therefore, is the law opposite to the promise of God? Let it not be so! For if a law had been given that was able to give life, truly justification would have been from the law.
22	But the scripture hath concluded all under sin, that the promise by faith of Jesus Christ might be given to them that believe.	But the scripture hath inclosed all under sin, that the promise by faith in Jesus the Messiah might be given to them that believe.	But the scripture has confined everything under sin, so that the promise by the faith of Jesus Christ would be given to those who believe.

Parallel Translations

GALATIANS *Chapter 3*

	KJV	*Murdock*	*Magiera*
23	But before faith came, we were kept under the law, shut up unto the faith which should afterwards be revealed.	But before the faith came, the law kept us shut up unto the faith that was to be revealed.	Now until faith came, the law was guarding us, while we were confined from the faith that was going to be revealed.
24	Wherefore the law was our schoolmaster to bring us unto Christ, that we might be justified by faith.	The law, therefore, was a monitor for us unto the Messiah, that we might become just by faith.	Therefore, the law was a tutor for us for Christ, that we would be justified by faith.
25	But after that faith is come, we are no longer under a schoolmaster.	But the faith having come, we are not under the monitor.	Now when faith came, we were not under tutors.
26	For ye are all the children of God by faith in Christ Jesus.	For ye are all the children of God, by faith in Jesus the Messiah.	For all of you are sons of God by the faith of Jesus Christ.
27	For as many of you as have been baptized into Christ have put on Christ.	For they who have been baptized into the Messiah, have put on the Messiah.	For those who were baptized in Christ have put on Christ.
28	There is neither Jew nor Greek, there is neither bond nor free, there is neither male nor female: for ye are all one in Christ Jesus.	There is neither Jew nor Gentile, neither slave nor free-born, neither male nor female; for ye are all one in Jesus the Messiah.	There is neither Judean nor heathen, there is neither servant nor free man, there is neither male nor female, for all of you are one in Jesus Christ.
29	And if ye be Christ's, then are ye Abraham's seed, and heirs according to the promise.	And if ye are the Messiah's, then are ye the seed of Abraham, and heirs by the promise.	And if you are of Christ, then you are the seed of Abraham and heirs in the promise.

Chapter 4

	KJV	*Murdock*	*Magiera*
1	Now I say, That the heir, as long as he is a child, differeth nothing from a servant, though he be lord of all;	But I say, that the heir, so long as he is a child, differeth not from a servant, although he is lord of all;	Now I am saying that as long as the heir [is] a child, he is no different from the servants, although he is lord of all.
2	But is under tutors and governors until the time appointed of the father.	but he is under supervisors and stewards, until the time established by his father.	But he is under guardians and stewards until the time that his father sets.
3	Even so we, when we were children, were in bondage under the elements of the world:	So also we, while we were children, were in subordination under the elements of the world.	So also, while we were babies, we were made subject to the elements of the world.
4	But when the fulness of the time was come, God sent forth his Son, made of a woman, made under the law,	But when the consummation of the time arrived, God sent forth his Son; and he was from a woman, and was under the law;	But when the fulfillment of the time came, God sent his Son. And he was from a woman and was under the law,
5	To redeem them that were under the law, that we might receive the adoption of sons.	that he might redeem them that were under the law; and that we might receive the adoption of sons.	so that he would redeem those who are under the law and [that] we would receive adoption.
6	And because ye are sons, God hath sent forth the Spirit of his Son into your hearts, crying, Abba, Father.	And, because ye are sons, God hath sent forth the Spirit of his Son into your hearts, who crieth, Father, our Father.	And now that you are sons, God sent into your hearts the Spirit of his Son that calls, "Father, our Father."
7	Wherefore thou art no more a servant, but a son; and if a son, then an heir of God through Christ.	Wherefore, ye are no longer servants, but sons; and if sons, then heirs of God through Jesus the Messiah.	From now on, you are not servants, but sons, and if sons, [you are] also heirs of God by way of Jesus Christ.

Parallel Translations

GALATIANS *Chapter 4*

	KJV	Murdock	Magiera
8	Howbeit then, when ye knew not God, ye did service unto them which by nature are no gods.	For then, when ye knew not God, ye served them who in their nature are not gods.	For then, when you did not know God, you served those that by their nature are not gods.
9	But now, after that ye have known God, or rather are known of God, how turn ye again to the weak and beggarly elements, whereunto ye desire again to be in bondage?	But now, since ye have known God, or rather, have been known by God, ye turn yourselves again to the weak and beggarly elements, and wish again to be under them!	But now that you know God, or rather that you are known by God, you have returned again to those weak and poor elements and desire to be made subject to them again.
10	Ye observe days, and months, and times, and years.	Ye observe days and moons, and set times, and years!	You observe days and months and times and years.
11	I am afraid of you, lest I have bestowed upon you labour in vain.	I am afraid, lest I have labored among you in vain.	I am afraid that I have labored among you without result.
12	Brethren, I beseech you, be as I am; for I am as ye are: ye have not injured me at all.	Be ye like me; because I have been like you. My brethren, I beseech you. Ye have not injured me at all.	Become like me, because I have also been like you. My brothers, I am begging you. You have not offended me [in] anything.
13	Ye know how through infirmity of the flesh I preached the gospel unto you at the first.	For ye know, that under the infirmity of my flesh, I at first announced the gospel to you;	For you know that in the weakness of my flesh, I declared the gospel to you at the first
14	And my temptation which was in my flesh ye despised not, nor rejected; but received me as an angel of God, even as Christ Jesus.	and the trial in my flesh, ye did not despise nor nauseate: but ye received me as an angel of God, and as Jesus the Messiah.	and you did not despise or reject the temptation of my flesh, but you received me as a messenger of God and as Jesus Christ.
15	Where is then the blessedness ye spake of? for I bear you record, that, if it had been possible, ye would have plucked out your own eyes, and have given them to me.	Where then is your blessedness? For I testify of you, that if it had been possible, ye would have plucked out your eyes, and have given them to me.	Therefore, where is your happiness? For I testify concerning you that if it had been possible, you would have picked out your eyes and given [them] to me.
16	Am I therefore become your enemy, because I tell you the truth?	Have I become an enemy to you, by preaching to you the truth?	Have I become an enemy to you, because I preached to you the truth?
17	They zealously affect you, but not well; yea, they would exclude you, that ye might affect them.	They are zealous towards you, yet not for good; but they wish to shut you up, that ye may be zealous towards them.	They are not zealous of you for good, but they desire to confine you, so that you would be zealous of them.
18	But it is good to be zealously affected always in a good thing, and not only when I am present with you.	And it is a good thing to be zealous at all times in good things; and not merely when I am present with you.	Now it is good that you should be zealous in good [things] at all times and not only when I am with you.
19	My little children, of whom I travail in birth again until Christ be formed in you,	[Ye are] my children, of whom I travail in birth again, till the Messiah be formed in you.	[You are] my sons, those for whom I labor in birth again until Christ is formed in you.
20	I desire to be present with you now, and to change my voice; for I stand in doubt of you.	And I could wish to be now with you, and to change the tone of my voice; because I am astonished at you.	And I wanted to be with you now and to change my report, because I am astonished at you.
21	Tell me, ye that desire to be under the law, do ye not hear the law?	Tell me, ye who desire to be under the law, do ye not hear the law?	Say to me, you who desire to be under the law, do you not hear the law?

	KJV	Murdock	Magiera

GALATIANS Chapter 4

	KJV	Murdock	Magiera
22	For it is written, that Abraham had two sons, the one by a bondmaid, the other by a freewoman.	For it is written, that Abraham had two sons, one by the bondmaid, and one by the free woman.	For it is written, "Abraham had two sons, one from the bond woman and one from the free [woman]."
23	But he who was of the bondwoman was born after the flesh; but he of the freewoman was by promise.	But he that was by the bondmaid, was born after the flesh; and he that was by the free woman, was by the promise.	But the one from the bond woman was born according to the flesh and the one from the free [woman] was [born] according to the promise.
24	Which things are an allegory: for these are the two covenants; the one from the mount Sinai, which gendereth to bondage, which is Agar.	And these are allegorical of the two covenants; the one from mount Sinai, which bringeth forth for bondage, is Hagar.	Now these [women] are illustrations of the two covenants. The one that is from Mount Sinai gives birth to bondage, which is Hagar.
25	For this Agar is mount Sinai in Arabia, and answereth to Jerusalem which now is, and is in bondage with her children.	For Hagar is the mount Sinai in Arabia, and correspondeth with the present Jerusalem, and is serving in bondage, she and her children.	For Hagar is the mountain of Sinai that is in Arabia and corresponds to this Jerusalem and serves [in] bondage, she and her sons.
26	But Jerusalem which is above is free, which is the mother of us all.	But the Jerusalem above, is the free woman, who is the mother of us.	But that Jerusalem above is the free [woman], who is our mother.
27	For it is written, Rejoice, thou barren that bearest not; break forth and cry, thou that travailest not: for the desolate hath many more children than she which hath an husband.	For it is written, Be joyful, thou barren, who bearest not: exult and shout, thou who hast not travailed: for more numerous are the children of the desolate than the children of the married woman.	For it is written: TAKE DELIGHT, BARREN [WOMAN] WHO BEARS NOT. AND REJOICE AND SHOUT [YOU] WHO HAVE NOT LABORED IN BIRTH, BECAUSE THE SONS OF THE DESOLATE [WOMAN] ARE MANY MORE THAN THE SONS OF THE MARRIED WOMAN.
28	Now we, brethren, as Isaac was, are the children of promise.	Now we, my brethren, like Isaac, are the children of the promise.	Now we, my brothers, like Isaac, are the sons of the promise.
29	But as then he that was born after the flesh persecuted him that was born after the Spirit, even so it is now.	And as then, he that was born after the flesh, persecuted him [who was born] of the Spirit; so also [is it] now.	And as then, he who was born by the flesh persecuted the one who [was born] by the Spirit, so also now.
30	Nevertheless what saith the scripture? Cast out the bondwoman and her son: for the son of the bondwoman shall not be heir with the son of the freewoman.	But what saith the scripture? Cast out the bondmaid, and her son; because the son of the bondmaid shall not inherit with the son of the free woman.	But what does the scripture say? THROW OUT THE BOND WOMAN AND HER SON, BECAUSE THE SON OF THE BOND WOMAN WILL NOT SHARE AN INHERITANCE WITH THE SON OF THE FREE [WOMAN].
31	So then, brethren, we are not children of the bondwoman, but of the free.	So then, my brethren, we are not sons of the bondwoman, but sons of the free woman.	Therefore, my brothers, we are not sons of the bond woman, but sons of the free [woman].

Chapter 5

	KJV	Murdock	Magiera
1	Stand fast therefore in the liberty wherewith Christ hath made us free, and be not entangled again with the yoke of bondage.	Stand fast, therefore, in the liberty with which the Messiah hath made us free; and be not subjected again to the yoke of bondage.	Stand fast, therefore, in the freedom [for] which Christ freed us and do not be subjected again with the yoke of bondage.

Parallel Translations

GALATIANS *Chapter 5*

	KJV	*Murdock*	*Magiera*
2	Behold, I Paul say unto you, that if ye be circumcised, Christ shall profit you nothing.	Behold, I Paul say to you, That if ye become circumcised, the Messiah is of no advantage to you.	Behold, I, Paul, say to you, that if you should be circumcised, Christ does not profit you anything.
3	For I testify again to every man that is circumcised, that he is a debtor to do the whole law.	And again, I testify to every one who becometh circumcised, that he is bound to fulfill the whole law.	Now I testify again to everyone who is circumcised that he is a debtor to do the whole law.
4	Christ is become of no effect unto you, whosoever of you are justified by the law; ye are fallen from grace.	Ye have renounced the Messiah, ye who seek justification by the law: and ye have apostatized from grace.	You have made Christ ineffectual, those who would be justified by the law and you have fallen from grace.
5	For we through the Spirit wait for the hope of righteousness by faith.	For we, through the Spirit, which is from faith, are waiting for the hope of righteousness.	For we, by the Spirit that is from faith, wait for the hope of justification.
6	For in Jesus Christ neither circumcision availeth any thing, nor uncircumcision; but faith which worketh by love.	For, in the Messiah Jesus, circumcision is nothing, neither is uncircumcision, but the faith that is perfected by love.	For in Christ Jesus neither is circumcision anything nor uncircumcision, but faith that is matured by love.
7	Ye did run well; who did hinder you that ye should not obey the truth?	Ye did run well: who hath interrupted you, that ye acquiesce not in the truth?	You were running well. Who disturbed you to not be persuaded by the truth?
8	This persuasion cometh not of him that calleth you.	The bias of your mind is not from him who called you.	Your persuasion is not from the one who called you.
9	A little leaven leaveneth the whole lump.	A little leaven leaveneth the whole mass.	A little leaven leavens the whole lump.
10	I have confidence in you through the Lord, that ye will be none otherwise minded: but he that troubleth you shall bear his judgment, whosoever he be.	I confide in you through our Lord, that ye will entertain no other thoughts. And he that disquieteth you, shall bear his judgment, whoever he may be.	I am confident in you in our Lord that you will not think other things and [that] the one who troubled you will bear his judgment, whoever he is.
11	And I, brethren, if I yet preach circumcision, why do I yet suffer persecution? then is the offence of the cross ceased.	And I, my brethren, if I still preached circumcision, why should I suffer persecution? Hath the offensiveness of the cross ceased?	Now, my brothers, if I was still preaching circumcision, why am I persecuted? Has the offense of the cross ceased?
12	I would they were even cut off which trouble you.	But I would, that they who disquiet you, were actually cut off.	Oh that those who are troubling you would also be actually cut off!
13	For, brethren, ye have been called unto liberty; only use not liberty for an occasion to the flesh, but by love serve one another.	And ye, my brethren, have been called into liberty: only let not your liberty be an occasion to the flesh; but, by love, be ye servants to each other.	Now you were called to freedom, my brothers. Only your freedom should not be an occasion for the flesh, but you should be serving one another in love.
14	For all the law is fulfilled in one word, even in this; Thou shalt love thy neighbour as thyself.	For the whole law is fulfilled in one sentence; in this, Thou shalt love thy neighbor as thyself.	For the whole law is fulfilled in one word, in this: YOU SHOULD LOVE YOUR NEIGHBOR AS YOURSELF.
15	But if ye bite and devour one another, take heed that ye be not consumed one of another.	But if ye bite and devour one another, beware, lest ye be consumed one by another.	Now if you bite and devour one another, be careful that you are not devoured by one another.
16	This I say then, Walk in the Spirit, and ye shall not fulfil the lust of the flesh.	And I say: Walk ye in the Spirit; and never follow the cravings of the flesh.	But I say, "Walk by the Spirit and never serve the desire of the flesh."

Parallel Translations

GALATIANS *Chapter 5*

	KJV	Murdock	Magiera
17	For the flesh lusteth against the Spirit, and the Spirit against the flesh: and these are contrary the one to the other: so that ye cannot do the things that ye would.	For the flesh craveth that which is repugnant to the Spirit; and the Spirit craveth that which is repugnant to the flesh: and the two are the opposites of each other, so that ye do not that which ye desire.	For the flesh desires what is opposed to the Spirit and the Spirit desires what is opposed to the flesh, and the two of them are opposites to each other, so that you are not doing what you want.
18	But if ye be led of the Spirit, ye are not under the law.	But if ye are guided by the Spirit, ye are not under the law.	Now if you are led by the Spirit, you are not under the law.
19	Now the works of the flesh are manifest, which are these; Adultery, fornication, uncleanness, lasciviousness,	For the works of the flesh are known, which are whoredom, impurity, lasciviousness,	For the works of the flesh are known, which are fornication, uncleanness, filthiness,
20	Idolatry, witchcraft, hatred, variance, emulations, wrath, strife, seditions, heresies,	idol-worship, magic, malice, contention, rivalry, wrath, strife, divisions, discords,	the worship of idols, magic, animosity, contention, jealousy, anger, insolence, divisions, discords,
21	Envyings, murders, drunkenness, revellings, and such like: of the which I tell you before, as I have also told you in time past, that they which do such things shall not inherit the kingdom of God.	envy, murder, drunkenness, revelling, and all the like things. And they who perpetrate these things, as I have before told you, and also now tell you, do not inherit the kingdom of God.	envy, murder, drunkenness, rioting and all that are similar to these. And those who do these [things], as I told you before, even now I say that they will not inherit the kingdom of God.
22	But the fruit of the Spirit is love, joy, peace, longsuffering, gentleness, goodness, faith,	But the fruits of the Spirit are, love, joy, peace, long suffering, suavity, kindness, fidelity, modesty, patience.	But the fruit of the Spirit is love, joy, peace, long-suffering, kindness, goodness, faith,
23	Meekness, temperance: against such there is no law.	Against these there standeth no law.	meekness, patience, concerning which the law was not established.
24	And they that are Christ's have crucified the flesh with the affections and lusts.	And they who are of the Messiah, have crucified their flesh, with all its passions and its cravings.	Now those who are of Christ have crucified their flesh with all its passions and its desires.
25	If we live in the Spirit, let us also walk in the Spirit.	Let us therefore live in the Spirit; and let us press on after the Spirit.	Therefore, we should live by the Spirit and we should follow the Spirit.
26	Let us not be desirous of vain glory, provoking one another, envying one another.	And let us not be vain-glorious, despising one another, and envying one another.	And we should not be [seeking] empty glory, so that we ridicule one another and are jealous of one another.

Chapter 6

	KJV	Murdock	Magiera
1	Brethren, if a man be overtaken in a fault, ye which are spiritual, restore such an one in the spirit of meekness; considering thyself, lest thou also be tempted.	My brethren, if one of you should be overtaken in a fault, do ye who are of the Spirit recover him, in a spirit of meekness: and be ye cautious, lest ye also be tempted.	My brothers, if one of you should be overtaken in an offense, you who are spiritual should correct him with a humble spirit and you should be watchful so that you are not tempted also.
2	Bear ye one another's burdens, and so fulfil the law of Christ.	And bear ye one another's burdens, that so ye may fulfill the law of the Messiah.	And bear the burden of one another, so that you may complete the law of Christ.

	KJV	Murdock	Magiera
	GALATIANS *Chapter 6*		
3	For if a man think himself to be something, when he is nothing, he deceiveth himself.	For if any one thinketh himself to be something, when he is not, he deceiveth himself.	For if anyone thinks that he is something when he is not, he deceives himself.
4	But let every man prove his own work, and then shall he have rejoicing in himself alone, and not in another.	But let a man examine his own conduct; and then his glorying will be within himself, and not in others.	But a man should examine his work and then his boasting will be privately to himself and not with others,
5	For every man shall bear his own burden.	For every man must take up his own load.	for everyone should carry his own load.
6	Let him that is taught in the word communicate unto him that teacheth in all good things.	And let him that heareth the word, communicate to him who instructeth him, in all good things.	Now he who has heard the word should communicate to him who instructs him in all good [things].
7	Be not deceived; God is not mocked: for whatsoever a man soweth, that shall he also reap.	Do not mistake; God is not deceived; for what a man soweth, that also will he reap.	Do not err. God is not mocked, for what a man sows, that he reaps.
8	For he that soweth to his flesh shall of the flesh reap corruption; but he that soweth to the Spirit shall of the Spirit reap life everlasting.	He who soweth in the flesh, reapeth from the flesh corruption: and he who soweth in the Spirit, will from the Spirit reap life everlasting.	He who sows in the flesh reaps decay from the flesh and he who sows spiritually will reap eternal life from the Spirit.
9	And let us not be weary in well doing: for in due season we shall reap, if we faint not.	And while we do what is good, let it not be wearisome to us; for the time will come when we shall reap, and it will not be tedious to us.	And when we do that which is good, we should not be weary. For the time will come when we will reap and we will not be weary.
10	As we have therefore opportunity, let us do good unto all men, especially unto them who are of the household of faith.	Now, therefore, while we have the opportunity, let us practice good works towards all men, and especially towards them of the household of faith.	Now therefore, while we have time, we should do good to everyone, especially to the household of faith.
11	Ye see how large a letter I have written unto you with mine own hand.	Behold, this epistle have I written to you with my own hand.	See, I have written these writings to you with my hands.
12	As many as desire to make a fair shew in the flesh, they constrain you to be circumcised; only lest they should suffer persecution for the cross of Christ.	They who are disposed to glory in the flesh, they urge you to become circumcised, only that they may not be persecuted on account of the cross of the Messiah.	Those who want to boast in the flesh are compelling you to be circumcised, only so that they would not be persecuted for the cross of Christ.
13	For neither they themselves who are circumcised keep the law; but desire to have you circumcised, that they may glory in your flesh.	For not even they themselves, who are circumcised, keep the law: but they wish you to become circumcised, that they may glory in your flesh.	For not even those who are circumcised keep the law, but rather they want you to be circumcised, so that they may boast in your flesh.
14	But God forbid that I should glory, save in the cross of our Lord Jesus Christ, by whom the world is crucified unto me, and I unto the world.	But as for me, let me not glory, except in the cross of our Lord Jesus the Messiah; by whom the world is crucified to me, and I am crucified to the world.	But [as] for me, I will have nothing to boast about except the cross of our Lord Jesus Christ, by whom the world is crucified to me and I am crucified to the world.
15	For in Christ Jesus neither circumcision availeth any thing, nor uncircumcision, but a new creature.	For circumcision is nothing; neither is uncircumcision; but a new creation.	For neither circumcision is anything, nor uncircumcision, but a new creation.

	KJV	Murdock	Magiera
	GALATIANS *Chapter 6*		
16	And as many as walk according to this rule, peace be on them, and mercy, and upon the Israel of God.	And they who press forward in this path, peace be on them, and mercy; and on the Israel of God.	And those who follow this path, peace and mercies will be on them and on the Israel of God.
17	From henceforth let no man trouble me: for I bear in my body the marks of the Lord Jesus.	Henceforth let no one put trouble upon me; for I bear in my body the marks of our Lord Jesus the Messiah.	So then, no one should pour trouble on me, for I bear the marks of our Lord Jesus in my body.
18	Brethren, the grace of our Lord Jesus Christ be with your spirit. Amen.	My brethren, the grace of our Lord Jesus the Messiah, be with your spirit. Amen.	The grace of our Lord Jesus Christ [be] with your spirit, my brothers. Amen.

Parallel Translations

EPHESIANS *Chapter 1*

	KJV	*Murdock*	*Magiera*
1	Paul, an apostle of Jesus Christ by the will of God, to the saints which are at Ephesus, and to the faithful in Christ Jesus:	Paul, a legate of Jesus the Messiah by the pleasure of God, to them who are at Ephesus, sanctified, and believing in Jesus the Messiah:	Paul, an apostle of Jesus Christ, by the will of God, to those who are in Ephesus, holy [ones] and faithful [ones] in Jesus Christ:
2	Grace be to you, and peace, from God our Father, and from the Lord Jesus Christ.	Peace be with you, and grace from God our Father, and from our Lord Jesus the Messiah.	Peace [be] with you and grace from God our Father and from our Lord Jesus Christ.
3	Blessed be the God and Father of our Lord Jesus Christ, who hath blessed us with all spiritual blessings in heavenly places in Christ:	Blessed be God, the Father of our Lord Jesus the Messiah, who hath blessed us with all blessings of the Spirit in heaven, by the Messiah:	Blessed be God, the Father of our Lord Jesus Christ, who has blessed us with all spiritual blessings in heaven in Christ,
4	According as he hath chosen us in him before the foundation of the world, that we should be holy and without blame before him in love:	according as he had previously chosen us in him, before the foundation of the world, that we might be holy and without blame before him; and, in love, predestinated us for himself;	even as he chose us beforehand in him, from before the foundations of the world, that we should be holy [ones] and without blemish before him. And in love, he marked us out beforehand for himself
5	Having predestinated us unto the adoption of children by Jesus Christ to himself, according to the good pleasure of his will,	and adopted us for sons, in Jesus the Messiah, as was agreeable to his pleasure:	and he adopted us in Jesus Christ, as was pleasing to his will,
6	To the praise of the glory of his grace, wherein he hath made us accepted in the beloved.	that the glory of his grace might be glorified, which he poured upon us by his Beloved One;	that the glory of his grace would be glorified, which he has poured on us by way of his beloved [one],
7	In whom we have redemption through his blood, the forgiveness of sins, according to the riches of his grace;	by whom we have redemption, and the forgiveness of sins by his blood, according to the riches of his grace,	in whom we have redemption and remission of sins by his blood, according to the wealth of his grace,
8	Wherein he hath abounded toward us in all wisdom and prudence;	which hath abounded in us, in all wisdom and all spiritual understanding.	which he caused to abound in us with all wisdom and with all understanding.
9	Having made known unto us the mystery of his will, according to his good pleasure which he hath purposed in himself:	And he hath made us know the mystery of his pleasure, which he had before determined in himself to accomplish,	And he made known to us the mystery of his will that he had determined beforehand to accomplish in him,
10	That in the dispensation of the fulness of times he might gather together in one all things in Christ, both which are in heaven, and which are on earth; even in him:	in the dispensation of the fullness of times; that all things might again be made new in the Messiah, things in heaven and [things] on earth.	in the administration of the fullness of times, that everything that is in heaven and in earth should be made new again in Christ.
11	In whom also we have obtained an inheritance, being predestinated according to the purpose of him who worketh all things after the counsel of his own will:	And in him we are elected, according as he predestined us and willed, who worketh all things according to the counsel of his pleasure;	And we were chosen in him, even as he marked us out beforehand and he desired, he who performs everything according to the purpose of his will,
12	That we should be to the praise of his glory, who first trusted in Christ.	that we should be they who first hoped in the Messiah, to the honor of his glory.	that we, those who first trusted in Christ, should be for the esteem of his magnificence.

Parallel Translations

EPHESIANS *Chapter 1*

	KJV	*Murdock*	*Magiera*
13	In whom ye also trusted, after that ye heard the word of truth, the gospel of your salvation: in whom also after that ye believed, ye were sealed with that holy Spirit of promise,	In whom, ye also have heard the word of truth, which is the gospel of your life, and have believed in him; and have been sealed with the Holy Spirit, who was promised,	In him also, you heard the word of truthfulness, which is the gospel of your life, and in him, you believed and you were sealed with the Holy Spirit that was promised,
14	Which is the earnest of our inheritance until the redemption of the purchased possession, unto the praise of his glory.	who is the earnest of our inheritance, until the redemption of them that are alive, and for the praise of his glory.	which is the guarantee of our inheritance to the redemption of those who have life and to the glory of his honor.
15	Wherefore I also, after I heard of your faith in the Lord Jesus, and love unto all the saints,	Therefore, lo I also, since I heard of your faith in our Lord Jesus the Messiah, and of your love towards all the saints,	Because of this, behold, I also, since I heard of your faith that is in our Lord Jesus Christ and your love that is toward the holy [ones],
16	Cease not to give thanks for you, making mention of you in my prayers;	cease not to give thanks on your account, and to remember you in my prayers;	have not ceased to give thanks for you and to remember you in my prayers,
17	That the God of our Lord Jesus Christ, the Father of glory, may give unto you the spirit of wisdom and revelation in the knowledge of him:	that the God of our Lord Jesus the Messiah, the Father of glory, may give to you the Spirit of wisdom and of revelation, in the recognition of him;	that the God of our Lord Jesus Christ, the Father of glory, would give you the Spirit of wisdom and of revelation in his knowledge
18	The eyes of your understanding being enlightened; that ye may know what is the hope of his calling, and what the riches of the glory of his inheritance in the saints,	and that the eyes of your hearts may be enlightened, so that ye may know what is the hope of his calling, and what the riches of the glory of his inheritance in the saints;	and [that] the eyes of your hearts would be enlightened, so that you would know what is the hope of his calling and what is the wealth of the glory of his inheritance in the holy [ones]
19	And what is the exceeding greatness of his power to us-ward who believe, according to the working of his mighty power,	and what is the excellence of the majesty of his power in us who believe; according to the efficiency of the strength of his power,	and what is the abundance of the greatness of his power in us, in those who believe, according to the working of the might of his power.
20	Which he wrought in Christ, when he raised him from the dead, and set him at his own right hand in the heavenly places,	which he put forth in the Messiah, and raised him from the dead, and seated him at his right hand in heaven,	[This is] he who worked in Christ and raised him from the dead and seated him at his right hand in heaven,
21	Far above all principality, and power, and might, and dominion, and every name that is named, not only in this world, but also in that which is to come:	high above all principalities, and authorities, and powers, and lordships, and above every name that is named, not only in this world but also in that to come:	higher than all rulers and authorities and powers and lordships and higher than every name that is named, not only in this world, but in the coming [one] also.
22	And hath put all things under his feet, and gave him to be the head over all things to the church,	and he hath subjected all things under his feet; and hath given him who is high over all, to be the head of the church;	And HE SUBJECTED EVERYTHING UNDER HIS FEET and he gave him who is higher than all [to be] the head of the church,
23	Which is his body, the fulness of him that filleth all in all.	which is his body, and the fullness of him who filleth all in all:	which is his body and the fullness of him who is filling all in all.

Parallel Translations

EPHESIANS *Chapter 2*

	KJV	*Murdock*	*Magiera*
1	And you hath he quickened, who were dead in trespasses and sins;	and also you, [he filleth,] who were dead in your sins, and in your offences,	And [God is filling] even you who were dead in your sins and in your transgressions,
2	Wherein in time past ye walked according to the course of this world, according to the prince of the power of the air, the spirit that now worketh in the children of disobedience:	in the which ye before walked, according to the worldliness of this world, and according to the pleasure of the prince potentate of the air, that spirit which is active in the children of disobedience:	in which you had walked previously, according to the worldliness of this world and according to the will of the chief authority of the air and of that spirit that operates in the sons of disobedience.
3	Among whom also we all had our conversation in times past in the lusts of our flesh, fulfilling the desires of the flesh and of the mind; and were by nature the children of wrath, even as others.	in which deeds we also, formerly, were conversant, in the cravings of our flesh; and we did the pleasure of our flesh, and of our mind, and were altogether the children of wrath, like the rest.	We also were occupied in those deeds previously, in the desires of our flesh, and we were doing the will of our flesh and of our mind and we were the sons of wrath [as] fully as the rest.
4	But God, who is rich in mercy, for his great love wherewith he loved us,	But God who is rich in his mercies, because of the great love with which he loved us,	But God, who is rich in his mercies, because of his great love [with] which he loved us,
5	Even when we were dead in sins, hath quickened us together with Christ, (by grace ye are saved;)	when we were dead in our sins, quickened us with the Messiah, and rescued us by his grace;	while we were dead in our sins, gave us life with Christ and, by his grace, redeemed us
6	And hath raised us up together, and made us sit together in heavenly places in Christ Jesus:	and resuscitated us with him, and seated us with him in heaven, in Jesus the Messiah:	and raised us with him and seated us with him in heaven in Jesus Christ,
7	That in the ages to come he might shew the exceeding riches of his grace in his kindness toward us through Christ Jesus.	that he might show to the coming ages the magnitude of the riches of his grace, and his benignity towards us in Jesus the Messiah.	so that he could show to the ages that are coming the greatness of the wealth of his grace and his goodness that is to us in Jesus Christ.
8	For by grace are ye saved through faith; and that not of yourselves: it is the gift of God:	For it is by his grace we are rescued, through faith; and this is not of yourselves, but it is the gift of God:	For by his grace we were redeemed by faith and this was not from yourselves, but is the gift of God,
9	Not of works, lest any man should boast.	not of works, lest any one glory.	not from works, so that no one would boast.
10	For we are his workmanship, created in Christ Jesus unto good works, which God hath before ordained that we should walk in them.	For we are his creation; who are created in Jesus the Messiah, for good works, which God hath before prepared for us to walk in.	For we [are] his own creation, who are created in Jesus Christ for good works, those [works] which God prepared previously that we should walk in.
11	Wherefore remember, that ye being in time past Gentiles in the flesh, who are called Uncircumcision by that which is called the Circumcision in the flesh made by hands;	Wherefore be mindful, that ye formerly were carnal Gentiles; and ye were called the uncircumcision, by that which is called the circumcision, and which is the work of the hands in the flesh.	Because of this, remember that you were previously Gentiles in the flesh and you were called the uncircumcision by that which is called the circumcision and is the work of the hands in the flesh.

Parallel Translations

	KJV	Murdock	Magiera
	EPHESIANS *Chapter 2*		
12	That at that time ye were without Christ, being aliens from the commonwealth of Israel, and strangers from the covenants of promise, having no hope, and without God in the world:	And ye were, at that time, without the Messiah; and were aliens from the regulations of Israel; and strangers to the covenant of the promise; and were without hope, and without God, in the world.	And at that time, you were without Christ and you were aliens from the customs of Israel and you were strangers to the covenant of the promise and you were without hope and without God in the world.
13	But now in Christ Jesus ye who sometimes were far off are made nigh by the blood of Christ.	But now, by Jesus the Messiah, ye who before were afar off, have been brought near by the blood of the Messiah.	But now, in Jesus Christ, you who previously were far have become near by the blood of Christ.
14	For he is our peace, who hath made both one, and hath broken down the middle wall of partition between us;	For he is himself our peace, who hath made the two [become] one, and hath demolished the wall which stood in the midst, and the enmity, by his flesh;	For he was our peace treaty, who made the two of them one and has broken down the wall that stood in the middle
15	Having abolished in his flesh the enmity, even the law of commandments contained in ordinances; for to make in himself of twain one new man, so making peace;	and by his prescriptions he hath abolished the law of ordinances; that, in himself, he might make the two to be one new man; and he hath made peace,	and the conflict, by his flesh. And he brought to an end the law of commandments with its commandments, so that [from] the two of them he would create in himself one new man, and he made a peace treaty.
16	And that he might reconcile both unto God in one body by the cross, having slain the enmity thereby:	and hath reconciled both with God, in one body, and hath slain the enmity by his cross.	And he reconciled the two of them with God in one body and, by his cross, he destroyed the conflict.
17	And came and preached peace to you which were afar off, and to them that were nigh.	And he came, and proclaimed peace to you afar off, and to those near:	And he came [and] HE DECLARED PEACE TO YOU, [BOTH] THE FAR AND THE NEAR,
18	For through him we both have access by one Spirit unto the Father.	because, by him there is access for us both, by one Spirit, unto the Father.	because in him we both have access in one spirit to the Father.
19	Now therefore ye are no more strangers and foreigners, but fellowcitizens with the saints, and of the household of God;	Wherefore, ye are not strangers, nor sojourners, but ye are fellow-citizens with the saints, and of the household of God.	From now on, you are neither strangers nor foreigners, but citizens who are holy [ones] and [of] the household of God.
20	And are built upon the foundation of the apostles and prophets, Jesus Christ himself being the chief corner stone;	And ye are built upon the foundations of the legates and the prophets; and Jesus the Messiah hath become the head of the corner in the edifice.	And you are built on the foundation of the apostles and of the prophets and Jesus Christ is the head of the corner of the building.
21	In whom all the building fitly framed together groweth unto an holy temple in the Lord:	And in him all the edifice is framed together, and groweth into a holy temple in the Lord;	And in him the whole building is fit together and is growing into a holy temple in the LORD,
22	In whom ye also are builded together for an habitation of God through the Spirit.	while ye also are builded in him, for a habitation of God through the Spirit.	while you also are built in him for a dwelling of God spiritually.

Parallel Translations

EPHESIANS *Chapter 3*

	KJV	*Murdock*	*Magiera*
1	For this cause I Paul, the prisoner of Jesus Christ for you Gentiles,	On this account, I Paul am a prisoner of Jesus the Messiah, for the sake of you Gentiles:	Because of this, I, Paul, am a prisoner of Jesus Christ for you Gentiles,
2	If ye have heard of the dispensation of the grace of God which is given me to you-ward:	if so be, ye have heard of the dispensation of the grace of God, which was given to me among you:	even as you have heard of the administration of the grace of God that was given to me among you,
3	How that by revelation he made known unto me the mystery; (as I wrote afore in few words,	that by revelation there was made known to me the mystery, (as I have [now] written to you in brief,	that by revelation the mystery was made known to me (as I have written to you in few [words],
4	Whereby, when ye read, ye may understand my knowledge in the mystery of Christ)	so that while ye read, ye might be able to understand my knowledge of the mystery of the Messiah,)	so that you may be able, while you are reading, to understand my knowledge that is in the mystery of Christ),
5	Which in other ages was not made known unto the sons of men, as it is now revealed unto his holy apostles and prophets by the Spirit;	which in other generations was not made known to the sons of men, as it is now revealed to his holy legates and to his prophets, by the Spirit;	which in other generations was not made known to men, as that which now has been revealed to his holy apostles and to his prophets spiritually,
6	That the Gentiles should be fellowheirs, and of the same body, and partakers of his promise in Christ by the gospel:	that the Gentiles should be sharers. of his inheritance, and partakers of his body, and of the promise which is given in him by the gospel;	that the Gentiles should be his heirs and participants of his body and of the promise that was given in him, by way of the gospel,
7	Whereof I was made a minister, according to the gift of the grace of God given unto me by the effectual working of his power.	of which I have been a minister, according to the gift of the goodness of God, which was imparted to me by the operation of his power:	of which I became a minister according to the gift of the grace of God that was given to me by the working of his power.
8	Unto me, who am less than the least of all saints, is this grace given, that I should preach among the Gentiles the unsearchable riches of Christ;	to me, who am the least of all the saints, hath this grace been given, that I should announce among the Gentiles the unsearchable riches of the Messiah,	To me, who am the least of all the holy [ones], this grace was given, that I should declare among the Gentiles the wealth of Christ that is untraceable
9	And to make all men see what is the fellowship of the mystery, which from the beginning of the world hath been hid in God, who created all things by Jesus Christ:	and should show to all men what is the dispensation of the mystery, which for ages was hid up in God the Creator of all [things]:	and [that] I should bring light to everyone what is the administration of the mystery that was hidden from the ages in God, who created all [things],
10	To the intent that now unto the principalities and powers in heavenly places might be known by the church the manifold wisdom of God,	so that, by means of the church, the manifold wisdom of God might become known to the principalities and powers that are in heaven:	so that by way of the church, the extraordinary wisdom of God would be made known to the rulers and to the authorities that are in heaven,
11	According to the eternal purpose which he purposed in Christ Jesus our Lord:	which [wisdom] he arranged ages before, and he hath executed it by Jesus the Messiah our Lord;	which [wisdom] he had prepared from the ages and has performed in Jesus Christ our Lord,
12	In whom we have boldness and access with confidence by the faith of him.	through whom we have boldness and access, in the confidence of his faith.	in whom we have boldness and access in the confidence of his faith.

EPHESIANS *Chapter 3*

	KJV	*Murdock*	*Magiera*
13	Wherefore I desire that ye faint not at my tribulations for you, which is your glory.	Therefore I pray, that I may not be discouraged by my afflictions, which are for your sakes; for this is your glory.	Because of this, I am petitioning that I will not be weary in my trials that are for you, because this is your glory,
14	For this cause I bow my knees unto the Father of our Lord Jesus Christ,	And I bow my knees to the Father of our Lord Jesus the Messiah,	and I bow my knees to the Father of our Lord Jesus Christ,
15	Of whom the whole family in heaven and earth is named,	from whom the whole family in heaven and on earth is named;	from whom all the family which is in heaven and on earth is named,
16	That he would grant you, according to the riches of his glory, to be strengthened with might by his Spirit in the inner man;	that he would grant you, according to the riches of his glory, to be strengthened with might by his Spirit; that in your inner man	that he would allow you, according to the wealth of his glory, to be strengthened with power by his Spirit, that in your inner man
17	That Christ may dwell in your hearts by faith; that ye, being rooted and grounded in love,	the Messiah may dwell by faith, and in your hearts by love, while your root and your foundation waxeth strong;	Christ would dwell in faith and in your hearts in love, as your root and your foundation becomes strong,
18	May be able to comprehend with all saints what is the breadth, and length, and depth, and height;	and that ye may be able to explore, with all the saints, what is the height and depth, and length and breadth,	that you would be able to understand with all the holy [ones] what is the height and depth and length and breadth
19	And to know the love of Christ, which passeth knowledge, that ye might be filled with all the fulness of God.	and may know the greatness of the Messiah's love; and [that] ye may be filled with all the fullness of God.	and would know the greatness of the knowledge of the love of Christ and would be filled with all the fullness of God.
20	Now unto him that is able to do exceeding abundantly above all that we ask or think, according to the power that worketh in us,	Now to him who is able, by his almighty power, to do for us even more than we ask or think, according to his power that worketh in us;	Now to him who is able, by surpassing power, to do even more for us than what we ask and think, according to his power that is performed in us,
21	Unto him be glory in the church by Christ Jesus throughout all ages, world without end. Amen.	to him be glory, in his church, by Jesus the Messiah, in all generations, for ever and ever. Amen.	to him [be] glory in his church by Jesus Christ in all generations, forever and ever. Amen.

Chapter 4

	KJV	*Murdock*	*Magiera*
1	I therefore, the prisoner of the Lord, beseech you that ye walk worthy of the vocation wherewith ye are called,	I therefore, a prisoner in our Lord, beseech of you, that ye walk, (as it becometh the calling wherewith ye are called,)	I, therefore, a prisoner in our Lord, beg you that you should walk as is proper for the calling that you were called,
2	With all lowliness and meekness, with longsuffering, forbearing one another in love;	with all lowliness of mind, and quietness, and long suffering; and that ye be forbearing one towards another, in love.	with all humbleness of mind and quietness and long-suffering. And hold up one another in love
3	Endeavouring to keep the unity of the Spirit in the bond of peace.	And be ye solicitous to keep the unity of the Spirit, in a bond of peace;	and be diligent to keep the alliance of the Spirit with the girdle of peace,
4	There is one body, and one Spirit, even as ye are called in one hope of your calling;	so that ye may become one body, and one Spirit; even as ye are called unto one hope of your calling.	so that you will be in one body and by one Spirit, even as you are called in one hope of your calling.
5	One Lord, one faith, one baptism,	For, the Lord is one, and the faith one, and the baptism one;	For [there] is one LORD and one faith and one baptism

EPHESIANS Chapter 4

	KJV	*Murdock*	*Magiera*
6	One God and Father of all, who is above all, and through all, and in you all.	and one God is the Father of all, and over all, and by all, and in us all.	and one God, the Father of all and above all and by all and in us all.
7	But unto every one of us is given grace according to the measure of the gift of Christ.	And to each of us grace is given, according to the measure of the gift of the Messiah.	Now to each one of us is given grace according to the measure of the gift of Christ.
8	Wherefore he saith, When he ascended up on high, he led captivity captive, and gave gifts unto men.	Wherefore it is said: He ascended on high, and carried captivity captive, and gave gifts to men.	Because of this, it is said, HE ASCENDED TO THE HEIGHT AND CAPTURED CAPTIVITY AND GAVE GIFTS TO MEN.
9	(Now that he ascended, what is it but that he also descended first into the lower parts of the earth?	Now that he ascended, what is it but that he also previously descended to the interior [regions] of the earth?	(Now what is it that he ascended, unless he had also first descended to the depths of the earth?
10	He that descended is the same also that ascended up far above all heavens, that he might fill all things.)	He who descended, is also the same that ascended up, high above all the heavens, that he might fulfill all things.	He who descended is he who also ascended higher than all the heaven, that he would complete all.)
11	And he gave some, apostles; and some, prophets; and some, evangelists; and some, pastors and teachers;	And he gave some, legates; and some, prophets; and some, evangelists; and some, pastors and teachers:	And he gave some apostles and some prophets and some evangelists and some pastors and some teachers,
12	For the perfecting of the saints, for the work of the ministry, for the edifying of the body of Christ:	for perfecting the saints, for the work of the ministry, for the edification of the body of the Messiah;	for the maturity of the holy [ones], for the work of the ministry, for the building up of the body of Christ,
13	Till we all come in the unity of the faith, and of the knowledge of the Son of God, unto a perfect man, unto the measure of the stature of the fulness of Christ:	until we all become one and the same, in faith and in the knowledge of the Son of God, and one complete man according to the measure of the stature of the fullness of Messiah:	until we all become one in the faith and in the knowledge of the Son of God and one mature man, in the measure of the standing of the fullness of Christ.
14	That we henceforth be no more children, tossed to and fro, and carried about with every wind of doctrine, by the sleight of men, and cunning craftiness, whereby they lie in wait to deceive;	and that we might not be children, agitated and turned about by every wind of the crafty doctrines of men who plot to seduce by their subtilty:	And we should not be babies, who are shaken and blown about by every wind of the deceitful teachings of men, who in their craftiness are plotting to deceive.
15	But speaking the truth in love, may grow up into him in all things, which is the head, even Christ:	but that we might be established in our love; and that every thing in us might progress in the Messiah, who is the head:	But we should be steadfast in our love, so that [in] everything we ourselves may grow up in Christ, who is the head.
16	From whom the whole body fitly joined together and compacted by that which every joint supplieth, according to the effectual working in the measure of every part, maketh increase of the body unto the edifying of itself in love.	and from him [it is], the whole body is framed together and compacted by all the junctures, according to the gift that is imparted by measure to each member, for the growth of the body; that his edifice may be perfected in love.	And from him the whole body is fit together and is knit together in all the joints, according to the gift that is given by measure to each member for the growth of the body, that its building up would be accomplished in love.

Parallel Translations

	KJV	*Murdock*	*Magiera*
	EPHESIANS *Chapter 4*		
17	This I say therefore, and testify in the Lord, that ye henceforth walk not as other Gentiles walk, in the vanity of their mind,	And this I say, and testify in the Lord, that henceforth ye walk not as the other Gentiles, who walk in the vanity of their mind:	Now this I say and I bear witness in the LORD, that from now on you should not walk as the rest of the Gentiles, who walk in the emptiness of their mind[s]
18	Having the understanding darkened, being alienated from the life of God through the ignorance that is in them, because of the blindness of their heart:	and they are dark in their understandings, and are alienated from the life of God, because there is not in them knowledge, and because of the blindness of their heart.	and are dark in their thoughts and are strangers from the life of God, because there is no knowledge in them and because of the blindness of their heart[s],
19	Who being past feeling have given themselves over unto lasciviousness, to work all uncleanness with greediness.	They have cut off their hope, and have given themselves over to lasciviousness, and to the practice of all uncleanness in their greediness.	those who have cut off their hope and have surrendered themselves to perversion and to the work of all uncleanness in their greediness.
20	But ye have not so learned Christ;	But ye have not so learned the Messiah;	But you did not so learn about Christ,
21	If so be that ye have heard him, and have been taught by him, as the truth is in Jesus:	if ye have truly heard him, and by him have learned as the truth is in Jesus.	if truly you have heard him and by him you have learned, as truthfulness is in Jesus.
22	That ye put off concerning the former conversation the old man, which is corrupt according to the deceitful lusts;	But [ye have learned], that ye should lay aside your former practices, the old man that is corrupted with the lusts of error;	But [you have learned] that you should strip off your former ways of life, the old man who was corrupted by the lusts of deceit,
23	And be renewed in the spirit of your mind;	and should be renewed in the spirit of your minds;	and you should be renewed by the Spirit, that is, your minds.
24	And that ye put on the new man, which after God is created in righteousness and true holiness.	and should put on the new man, that is created by God in righteousness and in the holiness of truth.	And you should put on the new man, who was created by God by justification and by the pardoning of truthfulness.
25	Wherefore putting away lying, speak every man truth with his neighbour: for we are members one of another.	Wherefore, put away from you lying, and speak ye the truth each with his neighbor; for we are members one of another.	Because of this, strip off lying and SPEAK [WITH] TRUTHFULNESS, EACH ONE WITH HIS NEIGHBOR, for we are members of one another.
26	Be ye angry, and sin not: let not the sun go down upon your wrath:	Be ye angry, and sin not: and let not the sun go down upon your wrath.	BE ANGRY AND DO NOT SIN and the sun should not go down on your anger.
27	Neither give place to the devil.	And give no place to the Accuser.	And do not give place to the Accuser.
28	Let him that stole steal no more: but rather let him labour, working with his hands the thing which is good, that he may have to give to him that needeth.	And let him that stole, steal no more; but let him labor with his hands, and do good acts; that he may have to give to him who needeth.	And he who was stealing should no longer steal, but he should work with his hands and should do good [things], so that he may have to give to him who has need.
29	Let no corrupt communication proceed out of your mouth, but that which is good to the use of edifying, that it may minister grace unto the hearers.	Let no hateful language come from your mouth, but that which is decorous, and useful for edification, that it may convey grace to those who hear.	No hateful word should come out of your mouth, but that which is pleasing and useful for building up, so that it may give grace to those who hear.

EPHESIANS *Chapter 4*

	KJV	Murdock	Magiera
30	And grieve not the holy Spirit of God, whereby ye are sealed unto the day of redemption.	And grieve not the Holy Spirit of God, whereby ye are sealed for the day of redemption.	And you should not grieve the sanctified Spirit of God, by whom you were sealed until the day of redemption.
31	Let all bitterness, and wrath, and anger, and clamour, and evil speaking, be put away from you, with all malice:	Let all bitterness, and anger, and wrath, and clamoring, and reviling, be taken from you, with all malice:	All bitterness and wrath and anger and contention and reviling should be taken away from you with all wickedness.
32	And be ye kind one to another, tenderhearted, forgiving one another, even as God for Christ's sake hath forgiven you.	and be ye affectionate towards one another, and sympathetic; and forgive ye one another, as God by the Messiah hath forgiven us.	And be kind to one another and merciful and be forgiving to one another, as God in Christ forgave us.

Chapter 5

	KJV	Murdock	Magiera
1	Be ye therefore followers of God, as dear children;	Be ye therefore imitators of God, as dear children:	Therefore, imitate God as beloved sons.
2	And walk in love, as Christ also hath loved us, and hath given himself for us an offering and a sacrifice to God for a sweetsmelling savour.	and walk in love; as the Messiah also hath loved us, and hath given up himself for us, an offering and a sacrifice to God, for a sweet odor.	And walk in love, as Christ also loved us and delivered himself up for us, an offering and a sacrifice to God for a sweet smell.
3	But fornication, and all uncleanness, or covetousness, let it not be once named among you, as becometh saints;	But whoredom, and all impurity, and avarice let them not be at all heard of among you, as it becometh the saints;	But fornication and all uncleanness and greed should also especially not be named among you as is proper to holy [ones],
4	Neither filthiness, nor foolish talking, nor jesting, which are not convenient: but rather giving of thanks.	Neither obscenities, nor words of folly, or of division, or of scurrility, which are not useful; but instead of these, thanksgiving.	and neither obscenities nor words of foolishness or of reproach or of nonsense that are not necessary, but instead of these, [words of] thanksgiving.
5	For this ye know, that no whoremonger, nor unclean person, nor covetous man, who is an idolater, hath any inheritance in the kingdom of Christ and of God.	For this know ye, that every man who is a whoremonger, or impure, or avaricious, or a worshipper of idols, hath no inheritance in the kingdom of the Messiah and of God.	But this you should know, that everyone who is a fornicator or unclean or greedy, who is an idol worshipper, does not have an inheritance in the kingdom of Christ and of God.
6	Let no man deceive you with vain words: for because of these things cometh the wrath of God upon the children of disobedience.	Let no man deceive you with vain words; for it is on account of these things that the wrath of God cometh on the children of disobedience.	[I say this], so that no one deceives you with empty words, for because of these [things] the wrath of God will come on the sons of disobedience.
7	Be not ye therefore partakers with them.	Therefore be ye not like them.	Therefore, do not become partners with them,
8	For ye were sometimes darkness, but now are ye light in the Lord: walk as children of light:	For ye were heretofore darkness, but now are ye light in our Lord: therefore, as the children of light, so walk ye.	for you were first of all [in] darkness, but now you are light in our Lord. Therefore, so walk as sons of light,
9	(For the fruit of the Spirit is in all goodness and righteousness and truth;)	For the fruits of the light are in all goodness, and righteousness, and truth.	for the effects of the light are in all goodness and justification and truthfulness.
10	Proving what is acceptable unto the Lord.	And search out what is pleasing before our Lord:	And determine what is pleasing before our Lord

Parallel Translations

EPHESIANS *Chapter 5*

	KJV	*Murdock*	*Magiera*
11	And have no fellowship with the unfruitful works of darkness, but rather reprove them.	And have no commerce with the works of darkness which are unfruitful, but reprove them.	and do not fellowship with the works of darkness that have no [good] effects, but reprove them,
12	For it is a shame even to speak of those things which are done of them in secret.	For the things they do in secret, it is nauseous even to mention.	for what they do in secret is abominable even to speak,
13	But all things that are reproved are made manifest by the light: for whatsoever doth make manifest is light.	For all things are exposed and made manifest by the light: and whatever maketh manifest, is light.	for everything is exposed and is revealed by the light and everything that reveals is light.
14	Wherefore he saith, Awake thou that sleepest, and arise from the dead, and Christ shall give thee light.	Wherefore it is said: Awake thou that sleepest, and arise from the dead, and the Messiah will illuminate thee.	Because of this, it is said, "Awake, sleeper, and rise up from the dead, and Christ will enlighten you."
15	See then that ye walk circumspectly, not as fools, but as wise,	See therefore, that ye walk circumspectly; not like the simple,	Therefore, see how you should walk accurately, not as fools, but as wise [ones]
16	Redeeming the time, because the days are evil.	but like the wise, who purchase their opportunity; because the days are evil.	who buy their opportunity, because the days are evil.
17	Wherefore be ye not unwise, but understanding what the will of the Lord is.	Therefore, be not lacking in understanding; but understand ye what is the pleasure of God.	Because of this, do not be stupid, but understand what is the will of God.
18	And be not drunk with wine, wherein is excess; but be filled with the Spirit;	And be not drunk with wine, in which is dissoluteness; but be ye filled with the spirit.	And do not be drunk with wine, in which is excess, but be filled with the Spirit,
19	Speaking to yourselves in psalms and hymns and spiritual songs, singing and making melody in your heart to the Lord;	And converse with yourselves in psalms and hymns; and with your hearts sing to the Lord, in spiritual songs.	and speak among yourselves with psalms and with hymns. And sing in your hearts to the LORD with songs of the Spirit.
20	Giving thanks always for all things unto God and the Father in the name of our Lord Jesus Christ;	And give thanks to God the Father, at all times, for all men, in the name of our Lord Jesus the Messiah.	And give thanks always for everyone in the name of our Lord Jesus Christ to God the Father.
21	Submitting yourselves one to another in the fear of God.	And be submissive one to another, in the love of the Messiah.	And be subject to one another in the love of Christ.
22	Wives, submit yourselves unto your own husbands, as unto the Lord.	Wives, be ye submissive to your husbands, as to our Lord.	Wives, be subject to your husbands as to our Lord,
23	For the husband is the head of the wife, even as Christ is the head of the church: and he is the saviour of the body.	Because the husband is the head of the wife, even as the Messiah is the head of the church; and he is the vivifier of the body.	because the man is the head of the wife, as also Christ is the head of the church and he is the life-giver of the body.
24	Therefore as the church is subject unto Christ, so let the wives be to their own husbands in every thing.	And as the church is subject to the Messiah, so also let wives be to their husbands in all things.	But even as the church is subject to Christ, so also wives [should be subject] to their husbands in everything.
25	Husbands, love your wives, even as Christ also loved the church, and gave himself for it;	Husbands, love your wives, even as the Messiah loved his church, and delivered himself up for it;	Men, love your wives as also Christ loved his church and delivered himself up for it,

EPHESIANS *Chapter* 5

	KJV	Murdock	Magiera
26	That he might sanctify and cleanse it with the washing of water by the word,	that he might sanctify it, and cleanse it, by the washing of water, and by the word;	to make it holy and to cleanse it by the washing of water and by the word
27	That he might present it to himself a glorious church, not having spot, or wrinkle, or any such thing; but that it should be holy and without blemish.	and might constitute it a glorious church for himself, in which is no stain, and no wrinkle, and nothing like them; but that it might be holy and without blemish.	and to establish the church for himself, being glorious and having no spot and no wrinkle and nothing like these, but rather to be holy [and] without blemish.
28	So ought men to love their wives as their own bodies. He that loveth his wife loveth himself.	It behooveth men so to love their wives, as [they do] their own bodies. For he that loveth his wife loveth himself.	So it is right for men to love their wives as their [own] bodies, for he who loves his wife loves himself,
29	For no man ever yet hated his own flesh; but nourisheth and cherisheth it, even as the Lord the church:	For no one ever hated his own body; but nourisheth it, and provideth for it, even as the Messiah the church.	for no one ever hates his body, but nourishes it and cares for his own [body]. [It is] even as Christ [nourishes and cares] for his church,
30	For we are members of his body, of his flesh, and of his bones.	For we are members of his body and of his flesh, and of his bones.	because we are members of his body, and we are of his flesh and of his bones.
31	For this cause shall a man leave his father and mother, and shall be joined unto his wife, and they two shall be one flesh.	For this reason, a man should quit his father and his mother, and adhere to his wife; and the two should be one flesh.	Because of this, A MAN SHOULD LEAVE HIS FATHER AND HIS MOTHER AND SHOULD BE JOINED TO HIS WIFE AND THE TWO OF THEM SHOULD BECOME ONE FLESH.
32	This is a great mystery: but I speak concerning Christ and the church.	This is a great mystery; but I am speaking of the Messiah, and of his church.	This mystery is great, but I am speaking about Christ and about his church.
33	Nevertheless let every one of you in particular so love his wife even as himself; and the wife see that she reverence her husband.	Nevertheless, let each of you severally so love his wife, even as himself: and let the wife reverence her husband.	Nevertheless, you also, each and every one of you, should so have compassion for his wife as for himself and the wife should have respect for her husband.

Chapter 6

	KJV	Murdock	Magiera
1	Children, obey your parents in the Lord: for this is right.	Children, obey your parents in our Lord; for this is right.	Children, obey your parents in our Lord, for this [is] upright.
2	Honour thy father and mother; (which is the first commandment with promise;)	And the first commandment with promise, is this: Honor thy father and thy mother;	And this is the first commandment that has a promise: HONOR YOUR FATHER AND YOUR MOTHER,
3	That it may be well with thee, and thou mayest live long on the earth.	that it may be well with thee, and that thy life may be prolonged on the earth.	THAT IT MAY BE WELL FOR YOU AND YOUR LIFE MAY BE LONG ON THE EARTH.
4	And, ye fathers, provoke not your children to wrath: but bring them up in the nurture and admonition of the Lord.	And parents, anger not your children; but train them up in the discipline and doctrine of our Lord.	Parents, do not anger your children, but rear them in the instruction and in the teaching of our Lord.

Parallel Translations

	KJV	Murdock	Magiera
	EPHESIANS *Chapter 6*		
5	Servants, be obedient to them that are your masters according to the flesh, with fear and trembling, in singleness of your heart, as unto Christ;	Servants, be obedient to your masters after the flesh, with fear, and with trepidation, and with simplicity of heart, as unto the Messiah.	Servants, be obedient to your masters that are in the flesh, with reverence and with trembling and with simplicity of heart, as to Christ,
6	Not with eyeservice, as menpleasers; but as the servants of Christ, doing the will of God from the heart;	Not in the sight of the eye, as if ye were pleasing men; but as the servants of the Messiah, who are doing the will of God.	not with what is seen by the eye as if you were pleasing men, but as servants of Christ, who are doing the will of God.
7	With good will doing service, as to the Lord, and not to men:	And serve them with your whole heart, in love, as if serving our Lord and not men;	And minister to them from your whole life in love, as to our Lord, and not as to men,
8	Knowing that whatsoever good thing any man doeth, the same shall he receive of the Lord, whether he be bond or free.	knowing that whatever good thing a man may do, the same will be recompensed to him by our Lord, whether he be a servant or a free man.	knowing that what someone does that is good will be rewarded from our Lord, whether he is a servant or a free man.
9	And, ye masters, do the same things unto them, forbearing threatening: knowing that your Master also is in heaven; neither is there respect of persons with him.	Also ye masters, do ye so to your servants. Forgive them a fault; because ye know, that ye have a master in heaven; and there is no respect of persons with him.	Also, you masters, so serve your servants. Forgive them an error, because you also know that your own Master is in heaven and there is no respect of persons with him.
10	Finally, my brethren, be strong in the Lord, and in the power of his might.	Finally, my brethren, be strong in our Lord, and; in the energy of his power:	From now on, my brothers, be strong in our Lord and in the immensity of his power
11	Put on the whole armour of God, that ye may be able to stand against the wiles of the devil.	And put ye on; the whole armor of God, so that ye may be able to stand against the wiles of the Accuser.	and put on the whole armor of God, so that you may be able to stand against the tactics of the Accuser,
12	For we wrestle not against flesh and blood, but against principalities, against powers, against the rulers of the darkness of this world, against spiritual wickedness in high places.	For our conflict is not with flesh and blood, but with principalities, and with those in authority, and with the possessors of this dark world, and with the evil spirits that are beneath heaven.	because your struggle is not with flesh and blood, but with rulers and with authorities and with the possessors of this dark world and with the evil spirits that are under heaven.
13	Wherefore take unto you the whole armour of God, that ye may be able to withstand in the evil day, and having done all, to stand.	Therefore put ye on the whole armor of God, that ye may be able to meet the evil [one]; and, being in all respects prepared, may stand firm.	Because of this, put on the whole armor of God, so that you will be able to engage the Evil [one] and, being prepared in everything, you will stand firm.
14	Stand therefore, having your loins girt about with truth, and having on the breastplate of righteousness;	Stand up therefore, and gird your loins with truth; and put on the breastplate of righteousness;	Therefore, stand and GIRD UP YOUR WAIST WITH TRUTHFULNESS and PUT ON THE BREASTPLATE OF JUSTIFICATION
15	And your feet shod with the preparation of the gospel of peace;	and defend your feet with the preparation of the gospel of peace.	and BIND [AS A SANDAL] ON YOUR FEET THE GOODNESS OF THE GOSPEL OF PEACE.

	KJV	Murdock	Magiera
	EPHESIANS *Chapter 6*		
16	Above all, taking the shield of faith, wherewith ye shall be able to quench all the fiery darts of the wicked.	And herewith take to you the confidence of faith, by which ye will have power to quench all the fiery darts of the evil [one].	And with these, take to you the shield of faith, by which you will be empowered with strength to quench all the fiery arrows of the Evil [one].
17	And take the helmet of salvation, and the sword of the Spirit, which is the word of God:	And put on the helmet of rescue; and take hold of the sword of the Spirit, which is the word of God.	And SET ON [YOUR HEAD] THE HELMET OF REDEMPTION and take hold of the sword of the Spirit, which is the word of God.
18	Praying always with all prayer and supplication in the Spirit, and watching thereunto with all perseverance and supplication for all saints;	And pray ye, with all prayers and supplications, in spirit, at all times: and in prayer be watchful, at all seasons, praying constantly, and interceding for all the saints:	And with all prayers and with all petitions, pray at all times spiritually, and in prayer, be watchful in every season, praying continually and interceding for all the holy [ones],
19	And for me, that utterance may be given unto me, that I may open my mouth boldly, to make known the mystery of the gospel,	and also for me; that language may be given me, in the opening of my mouth; so that I may boldly proclaim the mystery of the gospel,	[and] also for me, that the word may be given to me in the opening of my mouth, that I would boldly preach the mystery of the gospel,
20	For which I am an ambassador in bonds: that therein I may speak boldly, as I ought to speak.	of which I am a messenger in chains; that I may utter it boldly, as I ought to utter it.	for which I am its ambassador in chains, that with frankness I may speak, as I ought to speak it.
21	But that ye also may know my affairs, and how I do, Tychicus, a beloved brother and faithful minister in the Lord, shall make known to you all things:	And that ye also may know my affairs, and what I am doing, lo, Tychicus, a beloved brother, and a faithful minister in our Lord, will acquaint you;	Now that you also may know about me and what I am doing, behold, Tychicus, a beloved brother and faithful minister in our Lord, will make known [these things] to you,
22	Whom I have sent unto you for the same purpose, that ye might know our affairs, and that he might comfort your hearts.	whom I have sent to you for this purpose, that ye might know what is [going on] with me, and that your hearts may be comforted.	whom I sent to you especially for this, that you would know how [it is] with me and [that] he would comfort your hearts.
23	Peace be to the brethren, and love with faith, from God the Father and the Lord Jesus Christ.	Peace be with the brethren, and love with faith, from God the Father, and from our Lord Jesus the Messiah.	Peace [be] with our brothers and love with faith, from God the Father and from our Lord Jesus Christ.
24	Grace be with all them that love our Lord Jesus Christ in sincerity. Amen.	Grace be with all them who love our Lord Jesus the Messiah without corruptness. Amen.	Grace [be] with all those who love our Lord Jesus Christ without corruption. Amen.

Parallel Translations

	KJV	Murdock	Magiera
	PHILIPPIANS *Chapter 1*		
1	Paul and Timotheus, the servants of Jesus Christ, to all the saints in Christ Jesus which are at Philippi, with the bishops and deacons:	Paul and Timothy, servants of Jesus the Messiah, to all the saints that are in Jesus the Messiah at Philippi, with the elders and deacons.	Paul and Timothy, servants of Jesus Christ, to all the holy [ones] who are in Jesus Christ, who are at Philippi, with the elders and ministers:
2	Grace be unto you, and peace, from God our Father, and from the Lord Jesus Christ.	Grace be with you, and peace from God our Father, and from our Lord Jesus the Messiah.	Grace [be] with you and peace from God our Father and from our Lord Jesus Christ.
3	I thank my God upon every remembrance of you,	I thank my God at the constant recollection of you,	I thank my God for constant remembrance of you,
4	Always in every prayer of mine for you all making request with joy,	in all my prayers respecting you; and while I rejoice, I adore;	because in all my petitions that are for you and as I rejoice, I make intercession
5	For your fellowship in the gospel from the first day until now;	on account of your fellowship in the gospel, from the first day until now.	for your fellowship that is in the gospel from the first day until now,
6	Being confident of this very thing, that he which hath begun a good work in you will perform it until the day of Jesus Christ:	Because I am confident of this, that he who hath begun the good works in you, will accomplish them until the day of our Lord Jesus the Messiah.	because I am confident about this, that he who has begun good works in you will complete [them] until the day of our Lord Jesus Christ.
7	Even as it is meet for me to think this of you all, because I have you in my heart; inasmuch as both in my bonds, and in the defence and confirmation of the gospel, ye all are partakers of my grace.	For thus it is right for me to think of you all, because ye are permanently in my heart, and because, both in my bonds and in the vindication of the truth of the gospel, ye are my associates in grace.	For so it is right for me to think about all of you, because you are established in my heart. And in my bonds and in my defense that is concerning the truth of the gospel, you are my partners in grace.
8	For God is my record, how greatly I long after you all in the bowels of Jesus Christ.	For God is my witness, how I love you in the bowels of Jesus the Messiah.	For God is my witness, how I love you with the compassion of Jesus Christ.
9	And this I pray, that your love may abound yet more and more in knowledge and in all judgment;	And this I pray for, that your love may still increase and abound, in knowledge, and In all spiritual understanding:	And this I pray, that again your love may increase and grow in knowledge and in all spiritual understanding,
10	That ye may approve things that are excellent; that ye may be sincere and without offence till the day of Christ;	so that ye may discern the things that are suitable; and may be pure and without offence, in the day of the Messiah,	so that you may distinguish those [things] that are profitable and [that] you may be pure, without offense in the day of Christ,
11	Being filled with the fruits of righteousness, which are by Jesus Christ, unto the glory and praise of God.	and be full of the fruits of righteousness which are by Jesus the Messiah, to the praise and glory of God.	and [that] you may be full of the fruit of justification that is by Jesus Christ, to the glory and to the honor of God.
12	But I would ye should understand, brethren, that the things which happened unto me have fallen out rather unto the furtherance of the gospel;	And I would that ye might know, my brethren, that the transaction in regard to me, hath eventuated rather for the furtherance of the gospel;	Now I want you to know, my brothers, that my circumstance has increasingly led to advancement in the gospel,
13	So that my bonds in Christ are manifest in all the palace, and in all other places;	so that my bonds, on account of the Messiah, are matter of notoriety in all the court, and to all others.	so that even my bonds in Christ are publicized in all the Praetorium and to everyone else.

Parallel Translations

	KJV	*Murdock*	*Magiera*
	PHILIPPIANS	***Chapter 1***	
14	And many of the brethren in the Lord, waxing confident by my bonds, are much more bold to speak the word without fear.	And many of the brethren in our Lord have become confident, on account of my bonds, and are more bold to speak the word of God without fear.	And many of the brothers who are in our Lord have become confident on account of my bonds and are increasingly bold to speak the word of God without fear.
15	Some indeed preach Christ even of envy and strife; and some also of good will:	And they herald [it], some from envy and contention; but others with good will, and with love for the Messiah;	And some are preaching Christ out of envy and controversy, but others with good will and in love,
16	The one preach Christ of contention, not sincerely, supposing to add affliction to my bonds:	because they know that I am appointed for the vindication of the gospel.	because they know that I am appointed for the defense of the gospel.
17	But the other of love, knowing that I am set for the defence of the gospel.	And they who herald the Messiah in contention, do it not sincerely; but they hope to add pressure to my bonds.	Now those who are preaching Christ with controversy are not [doing it] purely, but they hope to add pressure to my bonds.
18	What then? notwithstanding, every way, whether in pretence, or in truth, Christ is preached; and I therein do rejoice, yea, and will rejoice.	And in this I have rejoiced, and do rejoice, that in every form, whether in pretence or in truth, the Messiah is heralded.	And in this I rejoiced and am rejoicing, that in every way, whether in pretext or with truthfulness, Christ is preached.
19	For I know that this shall turn to my salvation through your prayer, and the supply of the Spirit of Jesus Christ,	For I know, that these things will be found [conducive] to my life, through your prayers and the gift of the Spirit of Jesus the Messiah.	For I know that these [things] will be found for life to me by your prayer and by the gift of the Spirit of Jesus Christ,
20	According to my earnest expectation and my hope, that in nothing I shall be ashamed, but that with all boldness, as always, so now also Christ shall be magnified in my body, whether it be by life, or by death.	So that I hope and expect, that I shall in nothing be put to shame; but with uncovered face, as at all times, so now, the Messiah will be magnified in my body, whether by life or by death.	since I am hoping and expecting that I will not be ashamed in anything, but with boldness (as at all times even so now), Christ will be magnified in my body, whether in life or in death,
21	For to me to live is Christ, and to die is gain.	For my life is, the Messiah; and if I die, it is gain to me.	for my life is Christ and if I die, I have gain.
22	But if I live in the flesh, this is the fruit of my labour: yet what I shall choose I wot not.	But if I have fruits of my labors in this life of the flesh, I know not what I shall choose.	Now if in this life of the flesh I also have the fruit of my works, I do not know what to choose.
23	For I am in a strait betwixt two, having a desire to depart, and to be with Christ; which is far better:	For the two press upon me: I desire to be liberated, that I may be with the Messiah; and this would be very advantageous to me.	For the two [choices] press closely on me. I desire to depart, so that I may be with Christ, and this would be very profitable for me.
24	Nevertheless to abide in the flesh is more needful for you.	But also the business in regard to you, urges upon me to remain in the body.	But also, the matter concerning you urges me to remain in my body.
25	And having this confidence, I know that I shall abide and continue with you all for your furtherance and joy of faith;	And this I confidently know, that I shall continue and remain, for your joy, and for the furtherance of your faith;	And this I confidently know, that I will wait and will remain for your joy and for the growth of your faith,
26	That your rejoicing may be more abundant in Jesus Christ for me by my coming to you again.	so that when I come again to you, your glorying, which is in Jesus the Messiah only, will abound through me.	so that when I come again to you, your boasting that is in Jesus Christ alone will increase with me.

	KJV	Murdock	Magiera

PHILIPPIANS Chapter 1

	KJV	Murdock	Magiera
27	Only let your conversation be as it becometh the gospel of Christ: that whether I come and see you, or else be absent, I may hear of your affairs, that ye stand fast in one spirit, with one mind striving together for the faith of the gospel;	Let your conduct be as becometh the gospel of the Messiah; so that if I come I may see you, and if absent I may hear of you, that ye stand fast in one spirit and in one soul, and that ye strive together in the faith of the gospel.	Conduct yourselves as is becoming to the gospel of Christ, so that if I come, I may see you and if I am distant, I may hear about you, that you are standing in one spirit and in one soul and [that] you are conquering together in the faith of the gospel.
28	And in nothing terrified by your adversaries: which is to them an evident token of perdition, but to you of salvation, and that of God.	And in nothing be ye startled, by those who rise up against us; [which is] an indication of their destruction, and of life for you.	And do not be shaken by anything from those who stand against us, [which is] the evidence of their loss and of your life.
29	For unto you it is given in the behalf of Christ, not only to believe on him, but also to suffer for his sake;	And this is given to you by God, that ye not only really believe in the Messiah, but also that ye suffer on his account;	And this is given to you by God, that you would not only indeed believe in Christ, but also that you would suffer for him
30	Having the same conflict which ye saw in me, and now hear to be in me.	and that ye endure conflict, as ye have seen in me, and now hear concerning me.	and [that] you would endure the contest as you saw in me and now hear concerning me.

Chapter 2

	KJV	Murdock	Magiera
1	If there be therefore any consolation in Christ, if any comfort of love, if any fellowship of the Spirit, if any bowels and mercies,	If, therefore, ye have consolation in the Messiah, or if a commingling of hearts in love, or if a fellowship of the Spirit, or if compassions and sympathies;	Therefore, if you have encouragement in Christ or if [you have] consolation in love or if [you have] fellowship of the Spirit or if [you have] loving-kindness and mercies,
2	Fulfil ye my joy, that ye be likeminded, having the same love, being of one accord, of one mind.	complete ye my joy, by having one apprehension, and one love, and one soul, and one mind.	complete my joy, so that you will have one mind and one love and one soul and one purpose.
3	Let nothing be done through strife or vainglory; but in lowliness of mind let each esteem other better than themselves.	And do nothing in strife, or in vain glory; but, with lowliness of mind, let each esteem his neighbor as better than himself.	And do not do anything with controversy or with empty boasting, but with humbleness of mind. Everyone should count his associate as better than himself.
4	Look not every man on his own things, but every man also on the things of others.	And let not each be solicitous [only] for himself, but every one also for his neighbor.	And a man should not be concerned for himself [only], but each one [should] also [be concerned] for his associate.
5	Let this mind be in you, which was also in Christ Jesus:	And think ye so in yourselves, as Jesus the Messiah also thought;	And think this in yourselves which Jesus Christ also [thought],
6	Who, being in the form of God, thought it not robbery to be equal with God:	who, as he was in the likeness of God, deemed it no trespass to be the coequal of God;	who, as he was in the likeness of God, did not consider it extortion to be the equal of God.
7	But made himself of no reputation, and took upon him the form of a servant, and was made in the likeness of men:	yet divested himself, and assumed the likeness of a servant, and was in the likeness of men, and was found in fashion as a man;	But he emptied himself and took on the likeness of a servant and was in the likeness of men and was found in fashion as a man.

	KJV	Murdock	Magiera
	PHILIPPIANS Chapter 2		
8	And being found in fashion as a man, he humbled himself, and became obedient unto death, even the death of the cross.	and he humbled himself, and became obedient unto death, even the death of the cross.	And he humbled himself and became obedient until death, even the death of the cross.
9	Wherefore God also hath highly exalted him, and given him a name which is above every name:	Wherefore, also, God hath highly exalted him, and given him a name which is more excellent than all names;	Because of this, God also elevated him highly and gave him a name that is greater than all names,
10	That at the name of Jesus every knee should bow, of things in heaven, and things in earth, and things under the earth;	that at the name of Jesus every knee should bow, of [beings] in heaven, and on earth, and under the earth;	that at the name of Jesus every knee should bow that is in heaven and on earth and that is under the earth,
11	And that every tongue should confess that Jesus Christ is Lord, to the glory of God the Father.	and that every tongue should confess that Jesus the Messiah is the Lord, to the glory of God his Father.	and every tongue should confess that Jesus Christ is the LORD, to the glory of God his Father.
12	Wherefore, my beloved, as ye have always obeyed, not as in my presence only, but now much more in my absence, work out your own salvation with fear and trembling.	Therefore, my beloved, as ye have at all times obeyed, not only when I was near to you, but now when I am far from you, prosecute the work of your life, more abundantly, with fear and with trembling.	From now on, my beloved [ones], as you have been obedient at all times, not only when I was near to you, but [also] now that I am far from you, increasingly work the work of your life with reverence and with trembling.
13	For it is God which worketh in you both to will and to do of his good pleasure.	For God is operating in you, both to purpose, and also to perform that which ye desire.	For God energizes you to will as well as to perform what you desire.
14	Do all things without murmurings and disputings:	Do all things without murmuring, and without altercation;	Do everything without murmuring and without division,
15	That ye may be blameless and harmless, the sons of God, without rebuke, in the midst of a crooked and perverse nation, among whom ye shine as lights in the world;	that ye may be perfect and without blemish, as the sincere children of God, who are resident in a perverse and crooked generation; and that ye may appear among them as luminaries in the world;	so that you will be innocent and without blemish, as pure sons of God who are living in a perverted and crooked generation. And be seen among them as lights in the world,
16	Holding forth the word of life; that I may rejoice in the day of Christ, that I have not run in vain, neither laboured in vain.	so that ye may be to them in place of life; for my glory in the day of the Messiah, that I may not have run in vain or toiled for naught.	so that you will be to them in place of life, for my glory in the day of Christ, so that I have not run at random nor worked hard fruitlessly.
17	Yea, and if I be offered upon the sacrifice and service of your faith, I joy, and rejoice with you all.	And if I should be made a libation upon the sacrifice and service of your faith, I rejoice and exult with you all.	But if I am offered for the sacrifice and the service of your faith, I am rejoicing and I am glad with all of you.
18	For the same cause also do ye joy, and rejoice with me.	And so also do ye rejoice and exult with me.	So also, rejoice and be glad with me.
19	But I trust in the Lord Jesus to send Timotheus shortly unto you, that I also may be of good comfort, when I know your state.	But I hope in our Lord Jesus, that I shall shortly send Timothy unto you, so that I also may have composure, when informed concerning you.	Now I expect in our Lord Jesus to send Timothy to you shortly, so that I may also have rest when I learn about you.
20	For I have no man likeminded, who will naturally care for your state.	For I have no other one here, who, like my self, will sincerely care for your welfare.	For I have no others here who are like myself, who earnestly care for your [affairs].

Parallel Translations

	KJV	Murdock	Magiera
	PHILIPPIANS *Chapter 2*		
21	For all seek their own, not the things which are Jesus Christ's.	For they all seek their own, not the [things] of Jesus the Messiah.	For all seek themselves and not Jesus Christ.
22	But ye know the proof of him, that, as a son with the father, he hath served with me in the gospel.	But ye know the proof of him, that as a son with his father, so he labored with me in the gospel.	But you know the proof of him, that as a son with his father, so he has served with me in the gospel.
23	Him therefore I hope to send presently, so soon as I shall see how it will go with me.	Him I hope shortly to send to you, when I shall have seen how [things result] with me.	I expect to send him to you shortly, when I see how [it is] with me.
24	But I trust in the Lord that I also myself shall come shortly.	And I trust in my Lord, that I shall shortly come myself to you.	And I trust in my Lord that I will also come to you shortly.
25	Yet I supposed it necessary to send to you Epaphroditus, my brother, and companion in labour, and fellowsoldier, but your messenger, and he that ministered to my wants.	But now, a circumstance urged me to send to you Epaphroditus, the brother who is an assistant and laborer with me, but is your legate and minister to my wants.	But now, a matter urges me to send Epaphroditus to you, a brother who is a helper and worker with me, but your own apostle and a minister for my need,
26	For he longed after you all, and was full of heaviness, because that ye had heard that he had been sick.	For he longed to see you all, and was anxious, because he knew ye had heard, that he was sick.	because he was longing to see all of you and was distressed, for he knew that you had heard that he was sick.
27	For indeed he was sick nigh unto death: but God had mercy on him; and not on him only, but on me also, lest I should have sorrow upon sorrow.	And indeed he was sick, nigh unto death: but God had mercy on him: nor was it on him only, but also on me, that I might not have trouble upon trouble.	For he was indeed sick almost to death, but God had mercy on him and not on him only, but also on me, so that I would not have distress on distress.
28	I sent him therefore the more carefully, that, when ye see him again, ye may rejoice, and that I may be the less sorrowful.	Promptly, therefore, have I sent him to you; so that when ye see him, ye may again be joyful, and I may have a little breathing.	Therefore, I have sent him to you promptly, so that when you see him again, you would rejoice and [that] I would have a little refreshment.
29	Receive him therefore in the Lord with all gladness; and hold such in reputation:	Receive him then in the Lord, with all joy; and hold in honor those who are such.	Therefore, receive him in the LORD with all joy and hold those who are so in honor.
30	Because for the work of Christ he was nigh unto death, not regarding his life, to supply your lack of service toward me.	For, because of the Messiah's work, he came near to death, and little regarded his life, that he might fulfill what you lacked in the ministration to me.	For because of the work of Christ, he came near to death and despised danger regarding himself, so that he could supply what you had neglected in service to me.
	Chapter 3		
1	Finally, my brethren, rejoice in the Lord. To write the same things to you, to me indeed is not grievous, but for you it is safe.	Finally, my brethren, rejoice in our Lord. To write these [things] again and again to you, is not irksome to me, because they make you cautious.	From now on, my brothers, rejoice in our Lord. That I should write these [things] to you is not wearisome to me, because they caution you.
2	Beware of dogs, beware of evil workers, beware of the concision.	Beware of dogs; beware of evil doers; beware of the clipped in flesh.	Beware of dogs, beware of evil doers, beware of the cutting of flesh.
3	For we are the circumcision, which worship God in the spirit, and rejoice in Christ Jesus, and have no confidence in the flesh.	For we are the [real] circumcision, who worship God in spirit, and glory in Jesus the Messiah, and place no reliance on the flesh.	For we are the circumcision, who serve God by the Spirit and boast in Jesus Christ and are not confident about the flesh,

Parallel Translations

PHILIPPIANS *Chapter 3*

	KJV	Murdock	Magiera
4	Though I might also have confidence in the flesh. If any other man thinketh that he hath whereof he might trust in the flesh, I more:	And yet I might place reliance on the flesh. For, if any one thinketh that his reliance should be on the flesh, I might [do so] more than he.	although I did have confidence also about the flesh. For if anyone thinks that his confidence is in the flesh, I [should have confidence] more than he.
5	Circumcised the eighth day, of the stock of Israel, of the tribe of Benjamin, an Hebrew of the Hebrews; as touching the law, a Pharisee;	Circumcised when eight days old; of the stock of Israel; of the tribe of Benjamin; a Hebrew, descendant of Hebrews; as to the law, a Pharisee;	[I was] circumcised [when] eight days old, from the family of Israel, from the tribe of Benjamin, a Hebrew, the son of Hebrews, in the law, of the Pharisees,
6	Concerning zeal, persecuting the church; touching the righteousness which is in the law, blameless.	as to zeal, a persecutor of the church; and as to the righteousness of the law, I was without fault.	in zeal, a persecutor of the church, and in the justification of the law, I was without blame.
7	But what things were gain to me, those I counted loss for Christ.	But these things, which had been my excellence, I have accounted a detriment, because of the Messiah.	But those [things] that were a gain to me I counted a loss because of Christ.
8	Yea doubtless, and I count all things but loss for the excellency of the knowledge of Christ Jesus my Lord: for whom I have suffered the loss of all things, and do count them but dung, that I may win Christ,	And now also I account them all a detriment, because of the excellency of the knowledge of Jesus the Messiah my Lord; for the sake of whom, I have parted with all things, and have accounted [them] as dung, that I might gain the Messiah,	I also count all of these [things] a loss because of the greatness of the knowledge of Jesus Christ, my Lord, because of whom I have forfeited everything and have counted [it] as dung, so that I would gain Christ
9	And be found in him, not having mine own righteousness, which is of the law, but that which is through the faith of Christ, the righteousness which is of God by faith:	and be found in him; since my righteousness is not [now] that from the law, but that which is from faith in the Messiah, that is, the righteousness which is from God;	and be found in him, not having justification of myself that is from the law, but that which is from the faith of Christ, which is the justification that is from God,
10	That I may know him, and the power of his resurrection, and the fellowship of his sufferings, being made conformable unto his death;	that thereby I might know Jesus, and the efficacy of his resurrection; and might participate in his sufferings, and be assimilated to his death:	so that by it I would know Jesus and the power of his resurrection and would be made a participant in his sufferings and would be conformed to his death,
11	If by any means I might attain unto the resurrection of the dead.	if so be, I may attain to the resurrection from the dead.	that it may be I would be able to arrive at the resurrection that is from the dead.
12	Not as though I had already attained, either were already perfect: but I follow after, if that I may apprehend that for which also I am apprehended of Christ Jesus.	Not as though I had already taken [the prize], or were already complete; but I run [in the race], if so I may take that, for which Jesus the Messiah took me.	I have not yet received [the victory], nor yet been made perfect, but I am running, so that I will attain what Jesus Christ attained [for] me.
13	Brethren, I count not myself to have apprehended: but this one thing I do, forgetting those things which are behind, and reaching forth unto those things which are before,	My brethren, I do not consider myself, as having taken [it]. But one thing I know, that I forget the things behind me, and reach for the things before me;	My brothers, I do not consider myself to have attained. But one [thing] I know, that I am forgetting what is behind me and I am reaching out before me.

	KJV	Murdock	Magiera
	PHILIPPIANS *Chapter 3*		
14	I press toward the mark for the prize of the high calling of God in Christ Jesus.	and I run straight for the goal, that I may obtain the [prize] of victory of the call of God from on high, by Jesus the Messiah.	And I am running toward the goal, so that I would receive the victory of the high calling of God in Jesus Christ.
15	Let us therefore, as many as be perfect, be thus minded: and if in any thing ye be otherwise minded, God shall reveal even this unto you.	Therefore let those who are perfect, have these views; and if ye differently view any thing, God will reveal that also to you.	Therefore, those who are mature should think these [things] and if you think anything otherwise, God will also reveal this to you.
16	Nevertheless, whereto we have already attained, let us walk by the same rule, let us mind the same thing.	Nevertheless, that we may attain to this, let us proceed on in one path, and with one consent.	Nevertheless, to reach this, we should follow in one path and with one agreement.
17	Brethren, be followers together of me, and mark them which walk so as ye have us for an ensample.	Be like me, my brethren; and contemplate them, who walk after the pattern ye have seen in us.	Imitate me, my brothers, and consider those who so walk as an example that you have seen in us.
18	(For many walk, of whom I have told you often, and now tell you even weeping, that they are the enemies of the cross of Christ:	For there are many who walk otherwise; of whom I have often told you, and I now tell you, with weeping, that they are adversaries of the cross of the Messiah;	For there are many who walk otherwise, those whom I have told you about many times, and now weeping, I am saying that they are enemies of the cross of Christ,
19	Whose end is destruction, whose God is their belly, and whose glory is in their shame, who mind earthly things.)	whose end is destruction; whose god is their belly, and their glory their shame; whose thoughts are on things of the earth.	whose end is destruction, whose god [is] their stomach and whose glory [is] their shame, whose thinking is on the earth.
20	For our conversation is in heaven; from whence also we look for the Saviour, the Lord Jesus Christ:	But our concern is with heaven; and from thence we expect our Vivifier, our Lord, Jesus the Messiah;	But our work is in heaven and from there we are expecting the Savior, our Lord Jesus Christ,
21	Who shall change our vile body, that it may be fashioned like unto his glorious body, according to the working whereby he is able even to subdue all things unto himself.	who will change the body of our abasement, that it may have the likeness of the body of his glory, according to his great power, whereby all things are made subject to him.	who will change the body of our humiliation that it would be in the likeness of the body of his glory, according to his great power by which all is made subject to him.
	Chapter 4		
1	Therefore, my brethren dearly beloved and longed for, my joy and crown, so stand fast in the Lord, my dearly beloved.	Wherefore, my beloved and dear brethren, my joy and my crown!---so stand ye fast in our Lord, my beloved!	From now on, my beloved and dear brothers, my joy and my crown, so stand fast in our Lord, my beloved.
2	I beseech Euodias, and beseech Syntyche, that they be of the same mind in the Lord.	I beseech of Euodias and Syntyche, that they be of one mind in our Lord.	I beg Euodias and Syntyche to have one mind in our Lord.
3	And I intreat thee also, true yokefellow, help those women which laboured with me in the gospel, with Clement also, and with other my fellowlabourers, whose names are in the book of life.	I also beseech of thee, my true yokefellow, that thou assist those women who toiled with me in the gospel; together with Clement, and with the rest of my helpers, whose names are written in the book of life.	I beg you also, my true yoke-fellow, that you would help those who are toiling with me in the gospel, with Clement and with the rest of my helpers, whose names are written in the book of life.
4	Rejoice in the Lord alway: and again I say, Rejoice.	Rejoice ye in our Lord, at all times; and again I say, Rejoice.	Rejoice in our Lord at all times, and again I say, "Rejoice."

Parallel Translations

	KJV	Murdock	Magiera

PHILIPPIANS *Chapter 4*

	KJV	Murdock	Magiera
5	Let your moderation be known unto all men. The Lord is at hand.	Let your humility be recognized among all men. Our Lord is near.	And let your meekness be known to everyone. Our Lord is near.
6	Be careful for nothing; but in every thing by prayer and supplication with thanksgiving let your requests be made known unto God.	Be anxious for nothing; but at all times, by prayer and supplication with thanksgiving, make known your requests before God.	Do not be distressed about anything, but at all times, by prayer and by petition and with thanksgiving, your requests should be made known before God.
7	And the peace of God, which passeth all understanding, shall keep your hearts and minds through Christ Jesus.	And the peace of God, which surpasseth all knowledge, will keep your hearts and your minds, through Jesus the Messiah.	And the peace of God that is greater than all knowledge will guard your hearts and your minds in Jesus Christ.
8	Finally, brethren, whatsoever things are true, whatsoever things are honest, whatsoever things are just, whatsoever things are pure, whatsoever things are lovely, whatsoever things are of good report; if there be any virtue, and if there be any praise, think on these things.	Finally, my brethren, what things are true, and what things are decorous, and what things are right, and what things are pure, and what things are lovely, and what things are commendable, and deeds of praise and approbation, on these be your thoughts.	From now on, my brothers, those [things] that are true and those [things] that are modest and those [things] that are upright and those [things] that are pure and those [things] that are lovely and those [things] that are praiseworthy and those works of glory and of commendation, think these [things].
9	Those things, which ye have both learned, and received, and heard, and seen in me, do: and the God of peace shall be with you.	What things ye have learned, and received, and heard, and seen, in me, these do ye: and the God of peace will be with you.	Those [things] that you have learned and received and heard and seen in me, these do and the God of peace will be with you.
10	But I rejoiced in the Lord greatly, that now at the last your care of me hath flourished again; wherein ye were also careful, but ye lacked opportunity.	And I rejoice greatly in our Lord, that ye have [again] commenced caring for me; even as ye had before cared [for me,] but ye had not the opportunity.	Now I rejoice greatly in our Lord that you have begun [again] to care for me, as also you were caring, but you did not have sufficiency.
11	Not that I speak in respect of want: for I have learned, in whatsoever state I am, therewith to be content.	Yet I say this, not because I was in want; for I have learned to make that satisfy me, which I have.	Now I do not say [this] because I am in need, for I have learned that what I have will be sufficient for me.
12	I know both how to be abased, and I know how to abound: every where and in all things I am instructed both to be full and to be hungry, both to abound and to suffer need.	I know how to be depressed, and I also know how to abound in every thing; and in all things am I exercised, both in fullness and in famine, in abundance and in penury.	I know [how] to be humble. I also know [how] to abound in every [situation] and I am disciplined in everything, whether in plenty or in famine, in abundance or in need.
13	I can do all things through Christ which strengtheneth me.	I find strength for every thing, in the Messiah who strengtheneth me.	I find strength for everything in Christ who strengthens me.
14	Notwithstanding ye have well done, that ye did communicate with my affliction.	Yet ye have done well, in that ye communicated to my necessities.	Nevertheless, you have done well to have shared in my difficulties.

	KJV	Murdock	Magiera

PHILIPPIANS *Chapter 4*

	KJV	Murdock	Magiera
15	Now ye Philippians know also, that in the beginning of the gospel, when I departed from Macedonia, no church communicated with me as concerning giving and receiving, but ye only.	And ye know also, Philippians, that in the beginning of the annunciation, when I left Macedonia, not one of the churches communicated with me in respect to receiving and giving, except ye only;	Now you know also, Philippians, that in the beginning of the gospel when I left Macedonia, not even one of the churches shared with me in the accounting of receiving and giving, but you only,
16	For even in Thessalonica ye sent once and again unto my necessity.	that also at Thessalonica, once and again ye sent me relief.	so that even at Thessalonica, once and again, you sent to me for my use.
17	Not because I desire a gift: but I desire fruit that may abound to your account.	Not that I desire a gift; but I wish fruits may multiply unto you.	It is not that I am requesting a gift, but I am requesting that fruit should multiply to you.
18	But I have all, and abound: I am full, having received of Epaphroditus the things which were sent from you, an odour of a sweet smell, a sacrifice acceptable, wellpleasing to God.	I have [now] received all, and I abound, and am full: and I accepted all that ye sent to me by Epaphroditus, a sweet odor, and an acceptable sacrifice that pleaseth God.	I have received everything and I have abundance and I am full. And I have accepted all that you sent to me by way of Epaphroditus, a sweet fragrance and an acceptable sacrifice that is pleasing to God.
19	But my God shall supply all your need according to his riches in glory by Christ Jesus.	And may God supply all your necessity, according to his riches, in the glory of Jesus the Messiah.	And my God will supply all your need according to his riches in the glory of Jesus Christ.
20	Now unto God and our Father be glory for ever and ever. Amen.	And to God our Father, be glory and honor, for ever and ever. Amen.	Now to God our Father [be] glory and honor, forever and ever. Amen.
21	Salute every saint in Christ Jesus. The brethren which are with me greet you.	Salute all the saints who are in Jesus the Messiah. The brethren who are with me, salute you.	Greet all the holy [ones] who are in Jesus Christ. The brothers who are with me greet you.
22	All the saints salute you, chiefly they that are of Caesar's household.	All the saints salute you, especially those of Caesar's household.	All the holy [ones] greet you, especially those who are from the household of Caesar.
23	The grace of our Lord Jesus Christ be with you all. Amen.	The grace of our Lord Jesus the Messiah, be with you all. Amen.	The grace of our Lord Jesus Christ [be] with all of you. Amen.

Parallel Translations

COLOSSIANS *Chapter 1*

	KJV	*Murdock*	*Magiera*
1	Paul, an apostle of Jesus Christ by the will of God, and Timotheus our brother,	Paul, a legate of Jesus the Messiah by the pleasure of God, and Timothy a brother,	Paul, an apostle of Jesus Christ by the will of God, and Timothy, a brother,
2	To the saints and faithful brethren in Christ which are at Colosse: Grace be unto you, and peace, from God our Father and the Lord Jesus Christ.	to them who are at Colosse, the brethren, holy and believing in Jesus the Messiah: peace be with you, and grace from God our Father.	to those who are at Colosse, brothers, holy [ones] and faithful [ones] in Jesus Christ: Peace [be] with you and grace from God, our Father.
3	We give thanks to God and the Father of our Lord Jesus Christ, praying always for you,	We give thanks to God, the Father of our Lord Jesus the Messiah, at all times, and pray for you;	We give thanks at all times to God the Father of our Lord Jesus Christ and we pray for you,
4	Since we heard of your faith in Christ Jesus, and of the love which ye have to all the saints,	lo, ever since we heard of your faith in Jesus the Messiah, and of your love to all the saints;	ever since we heard of your faith that is in Jesus Christ and your love that is toward all the holy [ones]
5	For the hope which is laid up for you in heaven, whereof ye heard before in the word of the truth of the gospel;	because of the hope that is laid up for you in heaven, of which ye heard before in the word of truth of the gospel;	because of the hope that is kept for you in heaven, that which you previously heard in the word of truthfulness of the gospel,
6	Which is come unto you, as it is in all the world; and bringeth forth fruit, as it doth also in you, since the day ye heard of it, and knew the grace of God in truth:	which is announced to you, as also to all the world; and which groweth and yieldeth fruits, as it doth also among you from the day ye heard and knew the grace of God in reality:	that is preached to you as also to all the world. And it grows and yields fruit, as also [it has] in you from the day that you heard and acknowledged the grace of God with truthfulness,
7	As ye also learned of Epaphras our dear fellowservant, who is for you a faithful minister of Christ;	as ye learned from Epaphras, our beloved fellow-servant, who is for you a faithful minister of the Messiah;	as you learned from Epaphras, our beloved fellow-servant, who is for you a faithful minister of Christ
8	Who also declared unto us your love in the Spirit.	and who hath made known to us your love in the Spirit.	and who has made known to us your love that is by the Spirit.
9	For this cause we also, since the day we heard it, do not cease to pray for you, and to desire that ye might be filled with the knowledge of his will in all wisdom and spiritual understanding;	Therefore we also, from the day we heard [of it], have not ceased to pray for you; and to ask that ye may be filled with a knowledge of the good pleasure of God, in all wisdom, and in all spiritual understanding;	Because of this, we also, from the day that we heard, do not cease to pray for you and to ask that you may be filled with knowledge of the will of God with all wisdom and with all spiritual understanding,
10	That ye might walk worthy of the Lord unto all pleasing, being fruitful in every good work, and increasing in the knowledge of God;	that ye may walk as is right, and may please God with all good works, and may yield fruits, and grow in the knowledge of God;	that you may walk as is just and may please God with all good works and may bear fruit and may grow up in the knowledge of God
11	Strengthened with all might, according to his glorious power, unto all patience and longsuffering with joyfulness;	and may be strengthened with all strength, according to the greatness of his glory, in all patience and long suffering;	and may be strengthened with all strength, according to the greatness of his glory. With all patience and long-suffering and with joy,

Parallel Translations

	KJV	Murdock	Magiera

COLOSSIANS *Chapter 1*

	KJV	Murdock	Magiera
12	Giving thanks unto the Father, which hath made us meet to be partakers of the inheritance of the saints in light:	and may, with joy, give thanks to God the Father, who hath fitted us for a portion of the inheritance of the saints in light;	you should give thanks to God the Father, who has made us worthy for a portion of the inheritance of the holy [ones] in light
13	Who hath delivered us from the power of darkness, and hath translated us into the kingdom of his dear Son:	and hath rescued us from the dominion of darkness, and transferred us to the kingdom of his beloved Son;	and has delivered us from the authority of darkness and has transferred us to the kingdom of his beloved Son,
14	In whom we have redemption through his blood, even the forgiveness of sins:	by whom we have redemption and remission of sins:	in whom we have redemption and forgiveness of sins,
15	Who is the image of the invisible God, the firstborn of every creature:	who is the likeness of the invisible God, and the first-born of all creatures:	who is the image of the God who is not seen and the firstborn of all created [ones].
16	For by him were all things created, that are in heaven, and that are in earth, visible and invisible, whether they be thrones, or dominions, or principalities, or powers: all things were created by him, and for him:	and by him was created every thing that is in heaven and on earth, all that is seen and all that is unseen, whether thrones, or dominions, or principalities, or sovereignties; every thing was through him, and was created by him:	And in him everything that is in heaven and on earth was built, all that is seen and all that is not seen, whether thrones or lordships or rulers or authorities, everything [is] by way of him and was built in him.
17	And he is before all things, and by him all things consist.	and he was prior to all, and by him every thing exists.	And he is in front of all and everything stands in him.
18	And he is the head of the body, the church: who is the beginning, the firstborn from the dead; that in all things he might have the preeminence.	And he is the head of the body the church; as he is the head and first-born from among the dead, that he might be the first in all things.	And he is the head of the body, the church, for he is the beginning and the firstborn from the dead in order that he would be the first in all [things].
19	For it pleased the Father that in him should all fulness dwell;	For it pleased [the Father], that in him all fullness should dwell;	For in him, he desired all fullness to live
20	And, having made peace through the blood of his cross, by him to reconcile all things unto himself; by him, I say, whether they be things in earth, or things in heaven.	and by him, to reconcile all things to himself; and through him, he hath pacified, with the blood of his cross, both [those] on earth and those in heaven.	and by way of him to reconcile everything to him. And he made peace by the blood of his cross by his hands, whether in earth or in heaven.
21	And you, that were sometime alienated and enemies in your mind by wicked works, yet now hath he reconciled	And also to you, who were before alienated and enemies in your minds, because of your evil deeds,	For you also, who previously were strangers and enemies in your minds because of your evil works, he has now made peace
22	In the body of his flesh through death, to present you holy and unblameable and unreproveable in his sight:	to you, he hath now given peace, by the body of his flesh, and by his death; that he might establish you in his presence, holy, without blemish, and without offence;	by the body of his flesh and by his death, so that he would establish you before him, holy, without blemish, and without blame.

Parallel Translations

COLOSSIANS *Chapter 1*

	KJV	*Murdock*	*Magiera*
23	If ye continue in the faith grounded and settled, and be not moved away from the hope of the gospel, which ye have heard, and which was preached to every creature which is under heaven; whereof I Paul am made a minister;	provided ye continue in your faith, your foundation being firm, and ye be not removed from the hope of the gospel; of which ye have heard, that it is proclaimed in all the creation beneath heaven; of which [gospel] I Paul am a minister.	Since [this is so], continue in your faith, your foundation being firm, and be not shaken from the hope of the gospel that you heard [and] that was preached in all the creation that is under heaven, of which I, Paul, am a minister.
24	Who now rejoice in my sufferings for you, and fill up that which is behind of the afflictions of Christ in my flesh for his body's sake, which is the church:	And I rejoice in the sufferings which are for your sakes; and, in my flesh, I fill up the deficiency in the afflictions of the Messiah, in behalf of his body, which is the church;	And I rejoice in the sufferings that are for you and I supply the need because of the adversities of Christ in my flesh on behalf of his body, which is the church,
25	Whereof I am made a minister, according to the dispensation of God which is given to me for you, to fulfil the word of God;	of which I am a minister, according to the dispensation of God which is given to me among you, that I should fulfill the word of God,	of which I am a minister, according to the administration of God that was given to me among you, that I should fully supply the word of God,
26	Even the mystery which hath been hid from ages and from generations, but now is made manifest to his saints:	[namely,] that mystery, which was hidden for ages and generations, but is now revealed to his saints;	the mystery that was hidden from ages and from generations, but now is revealed to his holy [ones].
27	To whom God would make known what is the riches of the glory of this mystery among the Gentiles; which is Christ in you, the hope of glory:	to whom God would make known what is the riches of the glory of this mystery among the Gentiles; which [mystery] is the Messiah; who in you is the hope of our glory;	To them, God wanted to make known what is the wealth of the glory of this mystery among the Gentiles, which is the Messiah who is in you, the hope of our glory,
28	Whom we preach, warning every man, and teaching every man in all wisdom; that we may present every man perfect in Christ Jesus:	whom we proclaim, and teach and make known to every man, in all wisdom; that we may present every man perfect in Jesus the Messiah.	[It is] him we preach and teach and make known to every man with all wisdom, so that we may present every man mature in Jesus Christ.
29	Whereunto I also labour, striving according to his working, which worketh in me mightily.	And for this also, I toil and strive, with the aid of the strength that is imparted to me.	For in this also I am working hard and striving with the help of the power that was given to me.

Chapter 2

	KJV	*Murdock*	*Magiera*
1	For I would that ye knew what great conflict I have for you, and for them at Laodicea, and for as many as have not seen my face in the flesh;	And I wish you to know, what a struggle I have for you, and for them of Laodicea, and for the others who have not seen my face in the flesh;	Now I want you to know the kind of struggle I have for you and for them who are in Laodicea and for the rest of those who have not seen my face in the flesh.
2	That their hearts might be comforted, being knit together in love, and unto all riches of the full assurance of understanding, to the acknowledgement of the mystery of God, and of the Father, and of Christ;	that their hearts may be comforted, and that they, by love, may come to all the riches of assurance, and to the understanding of the knowledge of the mystery of God the Father, and of the Messiah,	[The struggle is] that their hearts would be comforted and would be brought near in love to all the wealth of assurance and to the understanding of the knowledge of the mystery of God the Father and of Christ,
3	In whom are hid all the treasures of wisdom and knowledge.	in whom are hid all the treasures of wisdom and of knowledge.	in whom are hidden all the treasures of wisdom and of knowledge.

Parallel Translations

	KJV	*Murdock*	*Magiera*
	COLOSSIANS *Chapter 2*		
4	And this I say, lest any man should beguile you with enticing words.	And this I say, lest any one should mislead you by the persuasiveness of words.	Now I say this, so that no one should deceive you by the persuasiveness of words.
5	For though I be absent in the flesh, yet am I with you in the spirit, joying and beholding your order, and the stedfastness of your faith in Christ.	For though I am separated from you in the flesh, yet I am with you in spirit; and I rejoice at beholding your good order, and the stability of your faith in the Messiah.	For even if I am physically separated from you, nevertheless I am with you spiritually and I rejoice to see your orderliness and the steadfastness of your faith that is in Christ.
6	As ye have therefore received Christ Jesus the Lord, so walk ye in him:	As therefore ye have received Jesus the Messiah our Lord, walk ye in him,	Therefore, as you have received Jesus Christ our Lord, walk in him,
7	Rooted and built up in him, and stablished in the faith, as ye have been taught, abounding therein with thanksgiving.	strengthening your roots and building up yourselves in him, and establishing yourselves in the faith which ye have learned, in which may ye abound in thanksgiving.	your roots being strengthened and built up in him and established in the faith that you have learned, in which you should abound with thanksgiving.
8	Beware lest any man spoil you through philosophy and vain deceit, after the tradition of men, after the rudiments of the world, and not after Christ.	Beware, lest any man make you naked by philosophy, and by vain deception, according to the doctrines of men, according to the rudiments of the world, and not according to the Messiah,	Beware, so that no one will rob you by philosophy and by empty deception, according to the teachings of men and according to the elements of the world and not according to Christ,
9	For in him dwelleth all the fulness of the Godhead bodily.	in whom dwelleth all the fullness of the Divinity corporeally.	in whom all the fullness of divinity lives bodily.
10	And ye are complete in him, which is the head of all principality and power:	And in him ye are also complete, because he is the head of all principalities and authorities.	And in him also you are absolutely completed, him who is the head of all rulers and authorities.
11	In whom also ye are circumcised with the circumcision made without hands, in putting off the body of the sins of the flesh by the circumcision of Christ:	And in him ye have been circumcised with a circumcision without hands, by casting off the flesh of sins, by a circumcision of the Messiah.	And in him you were circumcised with the circumcision that is not by our hands in the putting off of the flesh of sins, [but] by the circumcision of Christ.
12	Buried with him in baptism, wherein also ye are risen with him through the faith of the operation of God, who hath raised him from the dead.	And ye have been buried with him, by baptism; and by it ye have risen with him; while ye believed in the power of God, who raised him from the dead.	And you were buried with him in baptism and in him you have risen with him, for you believed in the power of God who raised him from the dead.
13	And you, being dead in your sins and the uncircumcision of your flesh, hath he quickened together with him, having forgiven you all trespasses;	And you, who were dead in your sins, and by the uncircumcision of your flesh, he hath vivified with him; and he hath forgiven us all our sins:	And you, who were dead in your sins and in the uncircumcision of your flesh, he has made alive with him and he has forgiven us all our sins.
14	Blotting out the handwriting of ordinances that was against us, which was contrary to us, and took it out of the way, nailing it to his cross;	and, by his mandates, he blotted out the handwriting of our debts, which [handwriting] existed against us, and took [it] from the midst, and affixed [it] to his cross.	And he has blotted out, by his commandments, the handwriting of our debts that was against us and he took it from the middle and fastened it to his cross.

Parallel Translations

	KJV	Murdock	Magiera
	COLOSSIANS *Chapter 2*		
15	And having spoiled principalities and powers, he made a shew of them openly, triumphing over them in it.	And, by yielding up his body, he showed contempt for principalities and authorities; and put them to shame, openly, in his own person.	And by the putting off of his body, he exposed rulers and authorities and shamed them openly in his person.
16	Let no man therefore judge you in meat, or in drink, or in respect of an holyday, or of the new moon, or of the sabbath days:	Let no one therefore disquiet you about food and drink, or about the distinctions of festivals, and new moons, and sabbaths;	Therefore, no one should disturb you about food and drink or about the distinctions of feasts and of new moons and of Sabbaths,
17	Which are a shadow of things to come; but the body is of Christ.	which were shadows of the things then future; but the body is the Messiah.	which are shadows of things that are to come. But the body is the Messiah.
18	Let no man beguile you of your reward in a voluntary humility and worshipping of angels, intruding into those things which he hath not seen, vainly puffed up by his fleshly mind,	And let no one wish, by abasing the mind, to bring you under bonds, that ye subject yourselves to the worship of angels; while he is prying into that which he hath not seen, and is vainly inflated in his fleshly mind,	And no one should desire, by [false] humility of mind, to make you guilty, in order to subject you to the worship of angels, by presuming about something that he has not seen. And he is puffed up fruitlessly in the mind of his flesh
19	And not holding the Head, from which all the body by joints and bands having nourishment ministered, and knit together, increaseth with the increase of God.	and holdeth not the head, from which the whole body is framed and constructed, with joints and members, and groweth with the growth [given] of God.	and does not hold the head [in honor], from whom the whole body is fit together and established with joints and with members and grows [with] the growth of God.
20	Wherefore if ye be dead with Christ from the rudiments of the world, why, as though living in the world, are ye subject to ordinances,	For if ye are dead with the Messiah from the rudiments of the world, why are ye judged as if ye were living in the world?	For if you died with Christ to the elements of the world, are you judged as though you live in the world?
21	(Touch not; taste not; handle not;	But, touch thou not, and taste thou not, and handle thou not:	[Those say], "Do not touch and do not taste and do not associate with [these]."
22	Which all are to perish with the using;) after the commandments and doctrines of men?	for these things perish in the using; and they are the commandments and doctrines of men.	For these [things] are a custom that is corrupted and are the commands and teachings of men,
23	Which things have indeed a shew of wisdom in will worship, and humility, and neglecting of the body; not in any honour to the satisfying of the flesh.	And they seem to have a kind of wisdom, in a show of humility, and of the fear of God, and of not sparing the body; not in any thing of excellence, but in things subservient to the body.	and they appear to have a word of wisdom with a face of humility and of the reverence of God and of depriving the body, not about anything of value, but rather about those [things] that are a custom of the flesh.
	Chapter 3		
1	If ye then be risen with Christ, seek those things which are above, where Christ sitteth on the right hand of God.	If then ye have risen with the Messiah, seek the things on high, where the Messiah sitteth on the right hand of God.	Therefore, if you have risen with Christ, seek what is above, where Christ sits at the right hand of God.
2	Set your affection on things above, not on things on the earth.	Think of things on high; not of the things on earth:	Think what is above and not what is on the earth,

Parallel Translations

	KJV	*Murdock*	*Magiera*
	COLOSSIANS *Chapter 3*		
3	For ye are dead, and your life is hid with Christ in God.	for ye are dead; and your life is hidden with the Messiah, in God.	for you are dead and your life is hidden with Christ in God.
4	When Christ, who is our life, shall appear, then shall ye also appear with him in glory.	And when the Messiah, who is our life, shall be manifested, then shall ye also be manifested with him in glory.	And when Christ, who is our life, is revealed, then you also will be revealed with him in glory.
5	Mortify therefore your members which are upon the earth; fornication, uncleanness, inordinate affection, evil concupiscence, and covetousness, which is idolatry:	Mortify therefore your members that are on the earth; whoredom, impurity, and the passions, and evil concupiscence, and avarice which is idolatry.	Therefore, put to death your members that are of the earth, fornication and uncleanness and passions and evil desire and greed, which is the reverence of idols.
6	For which things' sake the wrath of God cometh on the children of disobedience:	For on account of these [things], the wrath of God cometh on the children of disobedience.	For because of these [things] the wrath of God will come on the sons of disobedience.
7	In the which ye also walked some time, when ye lived in them.	And in these [things] ye also formerly walked, when ye lived in them.	And in these [things] also, you were previously walking, when you were occupied with them.
8	But now ye also put off all these; anger, wrath, malice, blasphemy, filthy communication out of your mouth.	But now, put away from you all these, wrath, anger, malice, reviling, filthy talking:	But now, cease all these [things], anger, fury, wickedness, reviling, unclean speech.
9	Lie not one to another, seeing that ye have put off the old man with his deeds;	and lie not one to another; but put off the old man, with all his practices;	And do not lie to one another, but rather strip off the old man with all his practices
10	And have put on the new man, which is renewed in knowledge after the image of him that created him:	and put ye on the new [man], that is renewed in knowledge, after the likeness of his Creator;	and put on the new [man] that is renewed in knowledge in the likeness of his Creator,
11	Where there is neither Greek nor Jew, circumcision nor uncircumcision, Barbarian, Scythian, bond nor free: but Christ is all, and in all.	where there is neither Jew nor Gentile, neither circumcision nor uncircumcision, neither Greek nor barbarian, neither bond nor free; but the Messiah is all, and in all.	where there is not Judean and Aramean, not circumcision and uncircumcision, not Greek and barbarian, not servant and free[men], but Christ is all and in all men.
12	Put on therefore, as the elect of God, holy and beloved, bowels of mercies, kindness, humbleness of mind, meekness, longsuffering;	Therefore, holy and beloved, as the elect of God, put ye on compassions, and tenderness, and suavity, and humbleness of mind, and gentleness, and long suffering.	Therefore, as the chosen [ones] of God, holy and beloved, put on mercies and loving-kindness and gentleness and humbleness of mind and quietness and long-suffering.
13	Forbearing one another, and forgiving one another, if any man have a quarrel against any: even as Christ forgave you, so also do ye.	And be ye indulgent towards one another, and forgiving to one another: and if any one has a complaint against his neighbor, as the Messiah forgave you, so also do ye forgive.	And be forbearing to one another and forgiving to one another. And if someone has a complaint against his associate, as Christ forgave you, so also you forgive.
14	And above all these things put on charity, which is the bond of perfectness.	And with all these, [join] love, which is the girdle of perfection.	And with all these [things], [put on] love, which is the girdle of maturity.

	KJV	Murdock	Magiera

COLOSSIANS Chapter 3

	KJV	Murdock	Magiera
15	And let the peace of God rule in your hearts, to the which also ye are called in one body; and be ye thankful.	And let the peace of the Messiah direct your hearts; for to that ye have been called, in one body; and be ye thankful to the Messiah.	And the peace of Christ will govern your hearts, for to him you were called in one body. And be thankful to Christ,
16	Let the word of Christ dwell in you richly in all wisdom; teaching and admonishing one another in psalms and hymns and spiritual songs, singing with grace in your hearts to the Lord.	And let his word dwell in you richly, in all wisdom. And teach and admonish yourselves, by psalms and hymns and spiritual songs, and with grace in your hearts sing ye unto God.	that his word may live in you richly with all wisdom. And teach and instruct yourselves in psalms and in hymns and in songs of the Spirit and sing with grace in your hearts to God.
17	And whatsoever ye do in word or deed, do all in the name of the Lord Jesus, giving thanks to God and the Father by him.	And whatever ye do in word or act, do it in the name of our Lord Jesus the Messiah, and give thanksgiving through him to God the Father.	And everything that you do in word and in work, do in the name of our Lord Jesus Christ and give thanks by way of him to God the Father.
18	Wives, submit yourselves unto your own husbands, as it is fit in the Lord.	Wives, be ye subject to your husbands, as is right in the Messiah.	Wives, be subject to your husbands as is right in Christ.
19	Husbands, love your wives, and be not bitter against them.	Husbands, love ye your wives, and be not bitter towards them.	Men, love your wives and do not be bitter against them.
20	Children, obey your parents in all things: for this is well pleasing unto the Lord.	Children, obey your parents in every thing; for this is pleasing before our Lord.	Children, be obedient to your parents in everything, for so it is pleasing before our Lord.
21	Fathers, provoke not your children to anger, lest they be discouraged.	Parents, anger not your children, lest they be discouraged.	Parents, do not anger your children, so that they will not be discouraged.
22	Servants, obey in all things your masters according to the flesh; not with eyeservice, as menpleasers; but in singleness of heart, fearing God:	Servants, obey in all things your bodily masters; not in the sight of the eye only, as those who please men, but with a simple heart, and in the fear of the Lord.	Servants, be obedient in everything to your masters of the flesh, not with what is seen by the eye as those who please men, but with a generous heart and in the reverence of the LORD.
23	And whatsoever ye do, do it heartily, as to the Lord, and not unto men;	And whatever ye do, do it with your whole soul, as unto our Lord, and not as to men:	And all that you do, do with your whole self as to our Lord and not as to men.
24	Knowing that of the Lord ye shall receive the reward of the inheritance: for ye serve the Lord Christ.	and know ye, that from our Lord ye will receive a recompense as the inheritance; for ye serve the Lord the Messiah.	And know that from our Lord you will receive a reward in the inheritance, for you serve the LORD the Messiah.
25	But he that doeth wrong shall receive for the wrong which he hath done: and there is no respect of persons.	But the delinquent will receive a recompense, according to the delinquency; and there is no respect of persons.	But the evil-doer is rewarded according to what he did wrong and there is no respect of persons.

Chapter 4

	KJV	Murdock	Magiera
1	Masters, give unto your servants that which is just and equal; knowing that ye also have a Master in heaven.	Masters, do equity and justice to your servants; and be conscious that ye also have a master in heaven.	Masters, serve equality and justice to your servants and know that you also have a Master in heaven.
2	Continue in prayer, and watch in the same with thanksgiving;	Persevere in prayer; and be watchful in it, and in giving thanks.	Be steadfast in prayer and be vigilant in it and give thanks.

Parallel Translations

	KJV	Murdock	Magiera

COLOSSIANS *Chapter 4*

	KJV	Murdock	Magiera
3	Withal praying also for us, that God would open unto us a door of utterance, to speak the mystery of Christ, for which I am also in bonds:	And pray also for us, that God would open to us a door of speech, for uttering the mystery of the Messiah, for the sake of which I am in bonds;	And pray also for us that God will open a door of speech for us to speak the mystery of Christ, because of whom I am imprisoned,
4	That I may make it manifest, as I ought to speak.	that I may unfold it, and utter it, as it behooveth me.	that I may reveal him and speak of him, as it is right for me [to do].
5	Walk in wisdom toward them that are without, redeeming the time.	Walk in wisdom towards them without: and redeem your opportunity.	Walk with wisdom toward outsiders and buy out your opportunity.
6	Let your speech be alway with grace, seasoned with salt, that ye may know how ye ought to answer every man.	And let your speech at all times be with grace; as it were, seasoned with salt: and know ye, how ye ought to give answer to every man.	And your speech at all times should be with grace, as though seasoned with salt. And know how you ought to give an answer to every man.
7	All my state shall Tychicus declare unto you, who is a beloved brother, and a faithful minister and fellowservant in the Lord:	And what is [occurrent] with me, will Tychicus make known to you; who is a beloved brother, and a faithful minister, and our fellow-servant in the Lord:	Now what concerns me, Tychicus, a beloved brother and faithful minister and our fellow-servant in the LORD, will make known to you.
8	Whom I have sent unto you for the same purpose, that he might know your estate, and comfort your hearts;	whom I have sent to you for this purpose, that he might know your affairs, and might comfort your hearts;	I have sent him to you for this [reason], that he would know what concerns you and would comfort your hearts,
9	With Onesimus, a faithful and beloved brother, who is one of you. They shall make known unto you all things which are done here.	together with Onesimus, a faithful and beloved brother, who is from among you. These will make known to you what is [occurrent] with us.	with Onesimus, a faithful and beloved brother, who is one of you. They will make known to you what concerns us.
10	Aristarchus my fellowprisoner saluteth you, and Marcus, sister's son to Barnabas, (touching whom ye received commandments: if he come unto you, receive him;)	Aristarchus, my fellow-captive, saluteth you; also Marcus, an uncle's son to Barnabas, of whom ye have received directions, that if he come to you, ye may kindly receive him:	Aristarchus, a captive with me, greets you and Mark, the cousin of Barnabas, concerning whom you received commandment that if he came to you, you should receive him,
11	And Jesus, which is called Justus, who are of the circumcision. These only are my fellowworkers unto the kingdom of God, which have been a comfort unto me.	also Jesus, who is called Justus. These are of the circumcision, and they only have aided me in the kingdom of God; and they have been a comfort to me.	and Jesus who is called Justus. These who are from the circumcision and they only have assisted me in the kingdom of God and they have been a comfort to me.
12	Epaphras, who is one of you, a servant of Christ, saluteth you, always labouring fervently for you in prayers, that ye may stand perfect and complete in all the will of God.	Epaphras saluteth you, who is from among you, a servant of the Messiah, always laboring for you in prayer, that ye may stand perfect and complete in all the good pleasure of God.	Epaphras greets you, who is one of you, a servant of Christ, laboring at all times for you in prayer, that you would stand, mature [ones] and complete [ones] in all the will of God.
13	For I bear him record, that he hath a great zeal for you, and them that are in Laodicea, and them in Hierapolis.	For I testify for him, that he hath great zeal for you, and for them of Laodicea, and for them of Hierapolis.	For I witness about him that he has great zeal for you and for those who are in Laodicea and in Hierapolis.
14	Luke, the beloved physician, and Demas, greet you.	Luke the physician, our beloved, saluteth you; also Demas.	Luke, our beloved physician, greets you and Demas.

Parallel Translations

COLOSSIANS *Chapter 4*

	KJV	*Murdock*	*Magiera*
15	Salute the brethren which are in Laodicea, and Nymphas, and the church which is in his house.	Salute ye the brethren in Laodicea, and Nymphas, and the church in his house.	Greet the brothers who are in Laodicea and Nymphas and the church that is in his house.
16	And when this epistle is read among you, cause that it be read also in the church of the Laodiceans; and that ye likewise read the epistle from Laodicea.	And when this epistle shall have been read among you, cause it to be read also in the church of the Laodiceans; and that which is written from Laodicea, do ye read.	And when this letter is read among you, cause it to be read also in the church of the Laodiceans, and that which is written from Laodicea, read.
17	And say to Archippus, Take heed to the ministry which thou hast received in the Lord, that thou fulfil it.	And say to Archippus: Be attentive to the ministry which thou hast received in our Lord, that thou fulfill it.	And tell Archippus, "Take care of the ministry that you have received in our Lord to fulfill it."
18	The salutation by the hand of me Paul. Remember my bonds. Grace be with you. Amen.	This salutation is by the hand of me Paul. Remember my bonds. Grace be with you. Amen.	This greeting [is] by my own hand, Paul. Remember my bonds. Grace [be] with you. Amen.

Parallel Translations

I THESSALONIANS *Chapter 1*

	KJV	*Murdock*	*Magiera*
1	Paul, and Silvanus, and Timotheus, unto the church of the Thessalonians which is in God the Father and in the Lord Jesus Christ: Grace be unto you, and peace, from God our Father, and the Lord Jesus Christ.	I Paul and Sylvanus and Timothy, to the church of the Thessalonians, which is in God the Father and in our Lord Jesus the Messiah: Grace be with you, and peace.	Paul and Silvanus and Timothy to the church of the Thessalonians, which is in God the Father and in our Lord Jesus Christ: Grace [be] with you and peace.
2	We give thanks to God always for you all, making mention of you in our prayers;	We give thanks to God at all times, on account of you all, and remember you continually in our prayers:	We give thanks to God at all times for all of you and we remember you in our prayers continually.
3	Remembering without ceasing your work of faith, and labour of love, and patience of hope in our Lord Jesus Christ, in the sight of God and our Father;	and we call to mind before God the Father the works of your faith, and the toil of your love, and the patience of your hope in our Lord Jesus the Messiah.	And we recall before God the Father the works of your faith and the labor of your love and the endurance of your hope that is in our Lord Jesus Christ.
4	Knowing, brethren beloved, your election of God.	For we know your election, my brethren, beloved of God.	For we know your calling, my brothers, beloved of God,
5	For our gospel came not unto you in word only, but also in power, and in the Holy Ghost, and in much assurance; as ye know what manner of men we were among you for your sake.	For our preaching among you, was not in words only; but also in power, and in the Holy Spirit, and in genuine persuasion. Ye also know, how we were among you for your sakes.	because our preaching to you was not only in words, but also with power and with the Holy Spirit and with true conviction. Also, you know how we were among you on your account.
6	And ye became followers of us, and of the Lord, having received the word in much affliction, with joy of the Holy Ghost:	And ye became imitators of us, and of our Lord, in that ye received the word in great affliction, and with the joy of the Holy Spirit.	And you became imitators of us and of our Lord, in that you received the word in great trial and in the joy of the Holy Spirit.
7	So that ye were ensamples to all that believe in Macedonia and Achaia.	And ye were a pattern for all the believers who are in Macedonia and in Achaia.	And you were an example to all the believers who are in Macedonia and in Achaia.
8	For from you sounded out the word of the Lord not only in Macedonia and Achaia, but also in every place your faith to God-ward is spread abroad; so that we need not to speak any thing.	For from you the word of our Lord sounded forth; [and] not only in Macedonia and Achaia, but in every place, your faith in God is heard of; so that we have no need to say any thing concerning you.	For from you the word of our Lord was heard, not only in Macedonia and in Achaia, but in every place your faith that is in God was heard, so that it was not necessary to say anything about you.
9	For they themselves shew of us what manner of entering in we had unto you, and how ye turned to God from idols to serve the living and true God;	For they declare, what an ingress we had to you, and how ye turned from the worship of idols unto God, that ye might worship the living and true God;	For they report what kind of entrance we had to you and how you turned to God from reverence of idols to serve the living and true God,
10	And to wait for his Son from heaven, whom he raised from the dead, even Jesus, which delivered us from the wrath to come.	while ye wait for his Son from heaven, that Jesus whom he raised from the dead, who delivereth us from the wrath to come.	while you wait for his Son from heaven, Jesus, whom he raised from the dead, who has delivered us from the wrath that is coming.

Parallel Translations

I THESSALONIANS *Chapter 2*

	KJV	Murdock	Magiera
1	For yourselves, brethren, know our entrance in unto you, that it was not in vain:	And ye yourselves, my brethren, know our entrance among you, that it was not in vain:	And you know, my brothers, that our entrance to you was not fruitless,
2	But even after that we had suffered before, and were shamefully entreated, as ye know, at Philippi, we were bold in our God to speak unto you the gospel of God with much contention.	but we first suffered and were treated with indignity, as ye know, at Philippi; and then, in a great agony, with confidence in our God, we addressed to you the gospel of the Messiah.	but first we suffered and were dishonored in Philippi, as you know, and then with a great struggle, with the boldness of our God we spoke to you the gospel of Christ.
3	For our exhortation was not of deceit, nor of uncleanness, nor in guile:	For our exhortation proceeded not from deceit, nor from impurity, nor in guile:	For our exhortation was not from deception, nor from uncleanness, nor with treachery.
4	But as we were allowed of God to be put in trust with the gospel, even so we speak; not as pleasing men, but God, which trieth our hearts.	but as we had been approved of God to be intrusted with the gospel, so we speak, not as pleasing men, but God who searcheth our hearts.	But as we were approved of God to be entrusted with his gospel, so we speak, not to please men, but [to please] God, who searches our hearts.
5	For neither at any time used we flattering words, as ye know, nor a cloke of covetousness; God is witness:	For at no time have we used flattering speech; as ye know; nor a cloak of cupidity, God is witness.	For we never used flattering speech, as you know, nor with a plan of greediness. God [is] witness.
6	Nor of men sought we glory, neither of you, nor yet of others, when we might have been burdensome, as the apostles of Christ.	Neither have we sought glory from men, either from you or from others, when we might have been chargeable as legates of the Messiah.	And we did not seek praise from men, nor from you, nor from others, although we could have been honored [ones] as the apostles of Christ.
7	But we were gentle among you, even as a nurse cherisheth her children:	But we were lowly among you; and like a nurse, who fondleth her children,	But we were meek among you, and as a nurse who loves her children,
8	So being affectionately desirous of you, we were willing to have imparted unto you, not the gospel of God only, but also our own souls, because ye were dear unto us.	so we also fondled [you], and were desirous to impart to you, not the gospel of God merely, but also our own soul, because ye were dear to us.	so also we were loving and were desiring to give to you, not only the gospel of God, but also ourselves, because you were beloved.
9	For ye remember, brethren, our labour and travail: for labouring night and day, because we would not be chargeable unto any of you, we preached unto you the gospel of God.	For ye recollect, brethren, that we labored and toiled, working with our own hands, by night and by day, that we might not be chargeable to any one of you.	For you recall, our brothers, that we were laboring and toiling by the work of our hands, by night and by day, so that we would not burden one of you.
10	Ye are witnesses, and God also, how holily and justly and unblameably we behaved ourselves among you that believe:	Ye are witnesses, and God [also], how we preached to you the gospel of God, purely, and uprightly, and were blameless towards all them that believe:	You and God are witnesses how we preached to you the gospel of God, purely and uprightly, and we were without blame to all the believers.
11	As ye know how we exhorted and comforted and charged every one of you, as a father doth his children,	as yourselves know, we entreated each one of you, as a father his children, and comforted your hearts:	As you know, we were entreating each one of you as a father [entreats] his children and we were comforting your heart and were charging you

Parallel Translations

	KJV	*Murdock*	*Magiera*

I THESSALONIANS *Chapter 2*

	KJV	Murdock	Magiera
12	That ye would walk worthy of God, who hath called you unto his kingdom and glory.	and we charged you, to walk as it becometh God, who hath called you to his kingdom and his glory.	that you should walk as is becoming to God, who called you to his kingdom and to his glory.
13	For this cause also thank we God without ceasing, because, when ye received the word of God which ye heard of us, ye received it not as the word of men, but as it is in truth, the word of God, which effectually worketh also in you that believe.	Therefore also we give thanks unceasingly to God, that the word of God which ye received from us, ye did not receive as the word of men, but as being truly the word of God, which worketh efficiently in you and in them that believe.	Because of this also, we give thanks continually to God that you received the word of God that you received from us, not as the word of men, but as it is truly, the word of God, and is effectively working in you who believe.
14	For ye, brethren, became followers of the churches of God which in Judaea are in Christ Jesus: for ye also have suffered like things of your own countrymen, even as they have of the Jews:	For ye, my brethren, became assimilated to the churches of God in Judaea, the persons who are in Jesus the Messiah; in that ye so suffered, even ye from your own countrymen, as also they from the Jews,	But you, my brothers, became imitators of the churches of God that are in Judea, they that are in Jesus Christ. For so you also suffered from your countrymen, as they also from the Judeans,
15	Who both killed the Lord Jesus, and their own prophets, and have persecuted us; and they please not God, and are contrary to all men:	the persons who slew our Lord Jesus the Messiah, and persecuted their own prophets and us; and they please not God, and are made hostile to all men;	who killed our Lord Jesus Christ and persecuted their own prophets and us and are not pleasing God and are acting contrary to all men.
16	Forbidding us to speak to the Gentiles that they might be saved, to fill up their sins alway: for the wrath is come upon them to the uttermost.	and they forbid us to speak to the Gentiles, that they may have life; to fill up their sins at all times. And wrath cometh on them to the uttermost.	[These are they] who forbid us to speak with the Gentiles that they would have life, concluding their sins at all [other] times. But wrath will come on them to the fullest extent.
17	But we, brethren, being taken from you for a short time in presence, not in heart, endeavoured the more abundantly to see your face with great desire.	But we, my brethren, have been bereaved of you for a short time, (in visible presence, not in our hearts,) and have the more exerted ourselves, to behold your faces, with great affection.	But we, our brothers, have been orphans away from you for a short time, in our presence, yet not in our heart. And we have been especially concerned to see your faces with great love.
18	Wherefore we would have come unto you, even I Paul, once and again; but Satan hindered us.	And we purposed to come to you, I Paul, once and again; but Satan hindered me.	And we wanted to come to you (I, Paul, once and again, yet Satan hindered me).
19	For what is our hope, or joy, or crown of rejoicing? Are not even ye in the presence of our Lord Jesus Christ at his coming?	For what is our hope, and our joy, and the crown of our glorying; unless it be ye, before our Lord Jesus at his coming?	For what is our hope and our joy and the crown of our glory, except you, before our Lord Jesus at his coming?
20	For ye are our glory and joy.	For ye are our glory, and our joy.	For you are our praise and our joy.

Chapter 3

	KJV	Murdock	Magiera
1	Wherefore when we could no longer forbear, we thought it good to be left at Athens alone;	And, because we could no longer endure it, we were willing to be left alone at Athens,	And because we could not hold out against [knowing], we were willing to remain in Athens alone

Parallel Translations

I THESSALONIANS *Chapter 3*

	KJV	*Murdock*	*Magiera*
2	And sent Timotheus, our brother, and minister of God, and our fellowlabourer in the gospel of Christ, to establish you, and to comfort you concerning your faith:	and to send to you Timothy our brother, a servant of God, and our assistant in the announcement of the Messiah; that he might strengthen you, and inquire of you respecting your faith:	and to send to you Timothy, our brother and a minister of God and our helper in the gospel of Christ, so that he would strengthen you and would inquire of you concerning your faith,
3	That no man should be moved by these afflictions: for yourselves know that we are appointed thereunto.	lest any of you should be disheartened by these afflictions; for ye know, that we are appointed thereto.	so that none of you should be disheartened by these trials, for you know that we are appointed to this.
4	For verily, when we were with you, we told you before that we should suffer tribulation; even as it came to pass, and ye know.	For also when we were with you, we forewarned you, that we were to be afflicted; as ye know did occur.	For even while we were with you, we previously said to you that we were going to be tried, as you know happened.
5	For this cause, when I could no longer forbear, I sent to know your faith, lest by some means the tempter have tempted you, and our labour be in vain.	Therefore also I could not be quiet, until I sent to learn your faith; lest the Tempter should have tempted you, and our labor have been in vain.	Because of this also, I could not hold out against [it], until I sent to know of your faith, so that the Tempter would not tempt you and our effort would be fruitless.
6	But now when Timotheus came from you unto us, and brought us good tidings of your faith and charity, and that ye have good remembrance of us always, desiring greatly to see us, as we also to see you:	But now, since Timothy hath come to us from among you, and hath informed us respecting your faith and your love, and that ye have a good remembrance of us at all times, and that ye desire to see us, even as we [to see] you;	But now, from when Timothy came to us from among you and told us about your faith and about your love and that you have a good memory of us continually and [that] you are longing to see us, as also we [long to see] you,
7	Therefore, brethren, we were comforted over you in all our affliction and distress by your faith:	therefore we are comforted in you, my brethren, amid all our straits and afflictions, on account of your faith.	because of this, we were comforted by you, our brothers, concerning all our adversities and our trials, because of your faith.
8	For now we live, if ye stand fast in the Lord.	And now, we live, if ye stand fast in our Lord.	And now we live, if you stand fast in our Lord.
9	For what thanks can we render to God again for you, for all the joy wherewith we joy for your sakes before our God;	For what thanks can we render to God in your behalf, for all the joy with which we are joyful on your account;	For what thanks are we able to repay on behalf of you to God concerning all the joy that we rejoice because of you,
10	Night and day praying exceedingly that we might see your face, and might perfect that which is lacking in your faith?	unless it be, that we the more supplicate before God, by night and by day, that we may see your faces, and may perfect what is lacking in your faith?	but that we petition God earnestly, by night and by day, that we may see your faces and [that] we may make whole what your faith is lacking?
11	Now God himself and our Father, and our Lord Jesus Christ, direct our way unto you.	And may God our Father, and our Lord Jesus the Messiah, direct our way unto you;	Now may God our Father and our Lord Jesus Christ direct our way to you.
12	And the Lord make you to increase and abound in love one toward another, and toward all men, even as we do toward you:	and increase and enlarge your love towards one another, and towards all men, even as we love you;	And may he multiply and increase your love to one another and to everyone, even as we love you.

Parallel Translations

I THESSALONIANS *Chapter 3*

Verse	KJV	Murdock	Magiera
13	To the end he may stablish your hearts unblameable in holiness before God, even our Father, at the coming of our Lord Jesus Christ with all his saints.	and establish your hearts unblamable in holiness, before God our Father; at the advent of our Lord Jesus the Messiah, with all his saints.	And may he establish your hearts without blame in holiness before God our Father at the coming of our Lord Jesus Christ with all his holy [ones].

Chapter 4

Verse	KJV	Murdock	Magiera
1	Furthermore then we beseech you, brethren, and exhort you by the Lord Jesus, that as ye have received of us how ye ought to walk and to please God, so ye would abound more and more.	Wherefore, my brethren, I entreat you, and beseech you by our Lord Jesus, that, as ye have received from us how ye ought to walk, and to please God, so ye would make progress more and more.	Therefore, my brothers, we beg you and we entreat you in our Lord Jesus, that as you received from us how you ought to walk and to please God, that you would increasingly do more.
2	For ye know what commandments we gave you by the Lord Jesus.	For ye know what command we gave you in our Lord Jesus the Messiah.	For you know those commandments we gave to you in our Lord Jesus.
3	For this is the will of God, even your sanctification, that ye should abstain from fornication:	For this is the pleasure of God, your sanctification; and that ye be separated from all whoredom;	For this is the will of God, your holiness, and that you should stay away from all fornication,
4	That every one of you should know how to possess his vessel in sanctification and honour;	and that each one of you might know how to possess his vessel, in sanctity and in honor;	and [that] each one of you would know [how] to possess his vessel in holiness and in honor
5	Not in the lust of concupiscence, even as the Gentiles which know not God:	and not in the concupiscence of lust, like the rest of the Gentiles who know not God:	and not with the passions of desire, as the rest of the Gentiles who do not know God.
6	That no man go beyond and defraud his brother in any matter: because that the Lord is the avenger of all such, as we also have forewarned you and testified.	and that ye dare not to transgress and to overreach any one his brother, in this matter; because our Lord is the avenger of all these, as also we have said and testified to you in time past.	And no one should dare to transgress against and oppress his brother in this matter, because our Lord is the avenger concerning all these [things], even as also we previously said and testified to you.
7	For God hath not called us unto uncleanness, but unto holiness.	For God did not call you unto impurity, but to sanctification.	For God did not call you to uncleanness, but to holiness.
8	He therefore that despiseth, despiseth not man, but God, who hath also given unto us his holy Spirit.	He therefore who spurneth, spurneth not man but God, who hath given his Holy Spirit in you.	So then, he who rejects [this] does not reject man, but God who gave his sanctified Spirit to you.
9	But as touching brotherly love ye need not that I write unto you: for ye yourselves are taught of God to love one another.	Now concerning love to the brethren, ye need not that I should write to you; for ye yourselves are taught of God to love one another.	Now concerning love of the brothers, you do not need me to write to you, for you yourselves are taught of God to love one another.
10	And indeed ye do it toward all the brethren which are in all Macedonia: but we beseech you, brethren, that ye increase more and more;	Ye likewise do so, to all the brethren who are in all Macedonia: but I entreat you, my brethren, to be exuberant:	So also, you are serving all the brothers who are in all of Macedonia. But I beg you, my brothers, that you should increase in [love]

Parallel Translations

I THESSALONIANS *Chapter 4*

	KJV	Murdock	Magiera
11	And that ye study to be quiet, and to do your own business, and to work with your own hands, as we commanded you;	and that ye strive to be quiet, and to attend to your own affairs; and that ye labor with your own hands; as we directed you;	and be diligent to be quiet and to be occupied with your business. And work with your hands as we commanded you,
12	That ye may walk honestly toward them that are without, and that ye may have lack of nothing.	and that ye walk becomingly towards those without; and that ye be dependent on no man.	so that you would walk in a proper manner toward outsiders and you should not be dependent on anyone.
13	But I would not have you to be ignorant, brethren, concerning them which are asleep, that ye sorrow not, even as others which have no hope.	And, I wish you to know, my brethren, that ye should not mourn over them who have fallen asleep, like other people who have no hope.	But I want you to know, my brothers, that you should not have sorrow concerning those who are asleep, even as others who have no hope.
14	For if we believe that Jesus died and rose again, even so them also which sleep in Jesus will God bring with him.	For if we believe that Jesus died and rose again, even so them who sleep, will God, by Jesus, bring with him.	For if we believe that Jesus died and rose, so also God will bring with him, by Jesus, those who are asleep.
15	For this we say unto you by the word of the Lord, that we which are alive and remain unto the coming of the Lord shall not prevent them which are asleep.	And this we say to you, by the word of our Lord, that we who may survive and be alive, at the coming of our Lord, shall not precede them who have slept.	Now this we say to you, by the word of our Lord, that we who remain at the coming of our Lord who are living will not overtake those who are asleep,
16	For the Lord himself shall descend from heaven with a shout, with the voice of the archangel, and with the trump of God: and the dead in Christ shall rise first:	Because our Lord will himself descend from heaven, with the mandate, and with the voice of the chief angel, and with the trump of God; and the dead who are in the Messiah, will first arise;	because our Lord, with a command and with the voice of the archangel and with the trumpet of God, will come down from heaven and the dead who are in Christ will rise up first.
17	Then we which are alive and remain shall be caught up together with them in the clouds, to meet the Lord in the air: and so shall we ever be with the Lord.	and then, we who survive and are alive shall be caught up together with them to the clouds, to meet our Lord in the air; and so shall we be ever with our Lord.	And then we who remain who are living will be caught up with them as one in the clouds for the meeting of our Lord in the air and so we will always be with our Lord.
18	Wherefore comfort one another with these words.	Wherefore, comfort ye one another with these words.	Therefore, comfort one another with these words.

Chapter 5

	KJV	Murdock	Magiera
1	But of the times and the seasons, brethren, ye have no need that I write unto you.	But concerning the times and seasons, my brethren, ye need not that I write to you:	Now concerning the times and the seasons, my brothers, you do not need me to write to you.
2	For yourselves know perfectly that the day of the Lord so cometh as a thief in the night.	for ye know assuredly, that the day of our Lord so cometh, as a thief by night.	For you know truly that the day of our Lord will so come as a thief in the night,
3	For when they shall say, Peace and safety; then sudden destruction cometh upon them, as travail upon a woman with child; and they shall not escape.	While they will be saying, Peace and quietness, then suddenly destruction will burst upon them, as distress upon a child-bearer, and they will not escape.	when they say, "Peace and harmony." And then suddenly, destruction will come on them as birth pains on a pregnant woman and they will not escape.
4	But ye, brethren, are not in darkness, that that day should overtake you as a thief.	But ye, my brethren, are not in darkness, that that day should overtake you as a thief.	But you, my brothers, are not in darkness so that day should overtake you as a thief.

Parallel Translations

	KJV	Murdock	Magiera
I THESSALONIANS *Chapter 5*			
5	Ye are all the children of light, and the children of the day: we are not of the night, nor of darkness.	For ye are all children of the light, and children of the day; and are not children of the night, and children of darkness.	For all of you are sons of light and sons of the day. And you are not sons of the night, nor sons of darkness.
6	Therefore let us not sleep, as do others; but let us watch and be sober.	Let us not therefore sleep, like others; but let us be vigilant and considerate.	We should not sleep, therefore, as others, but we should be watchful and be wise,
7	For they that sleep sleep in the night; and they that be drunken are drunken in the night.	For they who sleep, sleep in the night; and they who are drunken, are drunken in the night.	for those who are asleep are asleep in the night and those who are drunk are drunk in the night.
8	But let us, who are of the day, be sober, putting on the breastplate of faith and love; and for an helmet, the hope of salvation.	But let us who are children of the day, be wakeful in mind, and put on the breastplate of faith and love, and take the helmet of the hope of life.	But we who are sons of the day should be watchful in our mind and be clothed with the breastplate of faith and of love and should put on the helmet of the hope of life,
9	For God hath not appointed us to wrath, but to obtain salvation by our Lord Jesus Christ,	For God hath not appointed us to wrath, but to the acquisition of life, by our Lord Jesus the Messiah:	because God has not appointed us to wrath, but to the possession of life in our Lord Jesus Christ,
10	Who died for us, that, whether we wake or sleep, we should live together with him.	who died for us, that whether we wake or sleep, we might live together with him.	who died for us, that whether we are awake or asleep, we will live together with him.
11	Wherefore comfort yourselves together, and edify one another, even as also ye do.	Therefore comfort one another, and edify one another, as also ye have done.	Because of this, comfort one another and build one another up, as also you have done.
12	And we beseech you, brethren, to know them which labour among you, and are over you in the Lord, and admonish you;	And we entreat you, my brethren, that ye recognize them who labor among you, and who stand before your faces in our Lord, and instruct you:	And we beg you, my brothers, recognize those who toil among you and stand before you in our Lord and teach you,
13	And to esteem them very highly in love for their work's sake. And be at peace among yourselves.	that they may be esteemed by you with abundant love; and, on account of their work, live ye in harmony with them.	that they may be regarded by you with abundant love. And because of their work, come to agreement with them.
14	Now we exhort you, brethren, warn them that are unruly, comfort the feebleminded, support the weak, be patient toward all men.	And we entreat you, my brethren, that ye admonish the faulty, and encourage the faint-hearted, and bear the burdens of the weak, and be long suffering towards all men.	Now we beg you, my brothers, instruct the wrong-doers and encourage the faint-hearted [ones] and bear the burden of weak [ones] and be long-suffering to everyone.
15	See that none render evil for evil unto any man; but ever follow that which is good, both among yourselves, and to all men.	And beware, lest any of you return evil for evil, but always follow good deeds, towards one another, and towards all men.	And beware that none of you should repay evil for evil, but always pursue good [things] to one another and to everyone.
16	Rejoice evermore.	And be joyful always.	Rejoice at all times
17	Pray without ceasing.	And pray without ceasing.	and pray unceasingly.
18	In every thing give thanks: for this is the will of God in Christ Jesus concerning you.	And in every thing be thankful: For this is the pleasure of God in Jesus the Messiah, concerning you.	And in everything give thanks, for this is the will of God in Jesus Christ for you.

Parallel Translations

	KJV	*Murdock*	*Magiera*

I THESSALONIANS *Chapter 5*

	KJV	Murdock	Magiera
19	Quench not the Spirit.	Quench not the Spirit.	Do not extinguish the Spirit.
20	Despise not prophesyings.	Despise not prophesying.	Do not reject prophecies.
21	Prove all things; hold fast that which is good.	Explore every thing, and hold fast the good:	Search everything and hold that which is good
22	Abstain from all appearance of evil.	and fly from every thing evil.	and flee from every evil affair.
23	And the very God of peace sanctify you wholly; and I pray God your whole spirit and soul and body be preserved blameless unto the coming of our Lord Jesus Christ.	And may the God of peace sanctify you all, perfectly, and keep blameless your whole spirit, and your soul, and your body, till the coming of our Lord Jesus the Messiah.	Now may the God of peace make all of you holy completely and may he keep your whole spirit and your life and your body without blame until the coming of our Lord Jesus Christ.
24	Faithful is he that calleth you, who also will do it.	Faithful is he that hath called you, who will do it.	Faithful is he who called you who will do [this].
25	Brethren, pray for us.	My brethren, pray for us.	My brothers, pray for us.
26	Greet all the brethren with an holy kiss.	Salute all our brethren with a holy kiss.	Greet all our brothers with a holy kiss.
27	I charge you by the Lord that this epistle be read unto all the holy brethren.	I conjure you by our Lord, that this epistle be read to all the holy brethren.	I charge you by our Lord that this letter should be read to all the holy brothers.
28	The grace of our Lord Jesus Christ be with you. Amen.	The grace of our Lord Jesus the Messiah be with you. Amen.	The grace of our Lord Jesus Christ [be] with you. Amen.

Parallel Translations

II THESSALONIANS *Chapter 1*

	KJV	*Murdock*	*Magiera*
1	Paul, and Silvanus, and Timotheus, unto the church of the Thessalonians in God our Father and the Lord Jesus Christ:	PAUL and Sylvanus and Timothy, to the church of the Thessalonians, which is in God our Father and our Lord Jesus the Messiah:	Paul and Silvanus and Timothy, to the church of the Thessalonians that is in God, our Father, and our Lord Jesus Christ:
2	Grace unto you, and peace, from God our Father and the Lord Jesus Christ.	Grace be with you, and peace, from God our Father, and from our Lord Jesus the Messiah.	Grace [be] with you and peace from God our Father and from our Lord Jesus Christ.
3	We are bound to thank God always for you, brethren, as it is meet, because that your faith groweth exceedingly, and the charity of every one of you all toward each other aboundeth;	We are bound to give thanks to God always, on your account, my brethren, as it is proper; because your faith groweth exceedingly, and, in you all, the love of each for his fellow increaseth.	We are indebted to give thanks to God always for you, my brothers, as is right, because your faith grows abundantly and the love of each one of you increases for his associate,
4	So that we ourselves glory in you in the churches of God for your patience and faith in all your persecutions and tribulations that ye endure:	Insomuch that we also boast of you in the churches of God, on account of your faith, and your patience in all the persecution and trials that ye endure;	so that we will also be boasting about you among the churches of God concerning your faith and concerning your endurance in all your persecution and your trials that you are enduring.
5	Which is a manifest token of the righteous judgment of God, that ye may be counted worthy of the kingdom of God, for which ye also suffer:	for a demonstration of the righteous judgment of God; that ye may be worthy of his kingdom, on account of which ye suffer.	[This is] the evidence of the upright judgment of God, that you should be worthy of his kingdom, for which you suffer.
6	Seeing it is a righteous thing with God to recompense tribulation to them that trouble you;	And since it is a righteous thing with God, to recompense trouble to them that trouble you:	And surely it is upright before God that he should repay oppression to your oppressors.
7	And to you who are troubled rest with us, when the Lord Jesus shall be revealed from heaven with his mighty angels,	and you, who are the troubled, he will vivify, with us, at the manifestation of our Lord Jesus the Messiah from heaven, with the host of his angels;	And you who are oppressed, he will make alive with us at the appearance of our Lord Jesus Christ, who [will appear] from heaven with the power of his messengers,
8	In flaming fire taking vengeance on them that know not God, and that obey not the gospel of our Lord Jesus Christ:	when he will execute vengeance, with the burning of fire, on them that know not God, and on them that acknowledge not the gospel of our Lord Jesus the Messiah.	when he will execute vengeance with the burning of fire on those who do not know God and on those who do not acknowledge the gospel of our Lord Jesus Christ.
9	Who shall be punished with everlasting destruction from the presence of the Lord, and from the glory of his power;	For these will be recompensed with the judgment of eternal destruction, from the presence of our Lord, and from the glory of his power;	For in the judgment, they will be repaid with eternal destruction from the presence of our Lord and from the glory of his power,
10	When he shall come to be glorified in his saints, and to be admired in all them that believe (because our testimony among you was believed) in that day.	when he shall come to be glorified in his saints, and to display his wonders in his faithful ones; for our testimony concerning you, will be believed, in that day.	after he comes to be glorified with his holy [ones] and shows his wonders in his faithful [ones], because our testimony about you will be believed in that day.

Parallel Translations

II THESSALONIANS *Chapter 1*

	KJV	Murdock	Magiera
11	Wherefore also we pray always for you, that our God would count you worthy of this calling, and fulfil all the good pleasure of his goodness, and the work of faith with power:	Therefore we pray for you, at all times; that God would make you worthy of your calling, and would fill you with all readiness for good deeds, and with the works of faith by power;	Because of this, we pray always for you that God will count you worthy of your calling and will fill you with all desire for good [things] and [for] the works of faith by power,
12	That the name of our Lord Jesus Christ may be glorified in you, and ye in him, according to the grace of our God and the Lord Jesus Christ.	so that the name of our Lord Jesus the Messiah, may be glorified in you, (and) ye also in him; according to the grace of God, and of our Lord Jesus the Messiah.	that in you the name of our Lord Jesus Christ will be glorified [and that] you also [will be glorified] in him, according to the grace of our God and our Lord Jesus Christ.

Chapter 2

	KJV	Murdock	Magiera
1	Now we beseech you, brethren, by the coming of our Lord Jesus Christ, and by our gathering together unto him,	But we entreat of you, my brethren, in regard to the coming of our Lord Jesus the Messiah, and in respect to our being congregated unto him,	Now we beg you, my brothers, concerning the coming of our Lord Jesus Christ and concerning our own gathering to him,
2	That ye be not soon shaken in mind, or be troubled, neither by spirit, nor by word, nor by letter as from us, as that the day of Christ is at hand.	that ye be not soon agitated in your mind, nor be troubled, neither by word, nor by spirit, nor by letter, as coming from us, that lo, the day of our Lord is at hand.	that you should not be quickly shaken in your minds, nor be troubled, not by word, nor by a spirit, nor by a letter, as though from us, [saying] namely, "Behold, the day of our Lord has arrived."
3	Let no man deceive you by any means: for that day shall not come, except there come a falling away first, and that man of sin be revealed, the son of perdition;	Let no one deceive you in any way; because [that day will not come], unless there previously come a defection, and that man of sin be revealed, the son of perdition;	Will anyone deceive you in any way? Because [it will not come] except a rebellion should come first and the man of sin should be revealed, the son of destruction,
4	Who opposeth and exalteth himself above all that is called God, or that is worshipped; so that he as God sitteth in the temple of God, shewing himself that he is God.	who is an opposer, and exalteth himself above all that is called God and Worshipful; so that he also sitteth in the temple of God, as a God, and displayeth himself, as if he were God.	who is an opponent of [God] and elevates himself above all that is called God and that is reverenced, so that he will even sit in the temple of God as God and will portray himself as though he is God.
5	Remember ye not, that, when I was yet with you, I told you these things?	Do ye not remember, that, when I was with you, I told you these things?	Do you not remember that while I was with you I told you these things?
6	And now ye know what withholdeth that he might be revealed in his time.	And now, ye know what hindereth his being manifested in his time.	And now, you know what holds back [this day] that he should be revealed in its time.
7	For the mystery of iniquity doth already work: only he who now letteth will let, until he be taken out of the way.	For the mystery of the evil One already beginneth to be operative: and only, if that which now hindereth shall be taken from the midst;	For the mystery of wickedness has already begun to work, however, [it will work] by itself when that which now holds [it] back is taken away from the middle.

II THESSALONIANS *Chapter 2*

	KJV	*Murdock*	*Magiera*
8	And then shall that Wicked be revealed, whom the Lord shall consume with the spirit of his mouth, and shall destroy with the brightness of his coming:	then at length will that evil One be revealed; whom our Lord Jesus will consume by the breath of his mouth, and will bring to naught by the visibility of his advent.	And then the unjust [one] will be revealed, whom our Lord Jesus will consume by the breath of his mouth, and he will put a stop to him with the manifestation of his coming.
9	Even him, whose coming is after the working of Satan with all power and signs and lying wonders,	For the coming of that [evil One], is the working of Satan, with all power, and signs, and lying wonders,	For the coming of that [one] is by the working of Satan, with all power and signs and lying wonders
10	And with all deceivableness of unrighteousness in them that perish; because they received not the love of the truth, that they might be saved.	and with all the deceptiveness of iniquity, in them that perish; because they did not receive the love of the truth, by which they might have life.	and with all the deception of wickedness that is in the perishing [ones], because they did not receive the love of the truth by which they should have life.
11	And for this cause God shall send them strong delusion, that they should believe a lie:	Therefore God will send upon them the operation of deception, that they may believe a lie;	Because of this, God will send them the working of deception that they should believe the lie
12	That they all might be damned who believed not the truth, but had pleasure in unrighteousness.	and that they all may be condemned, who believe not the truth, but have pleasure in iniquity.	and [that] all of them would be condemned, those who did not believe with truthfulness, but delighted in wickedness.
13	But we are bound to give thanks alway to God for you, brethren beloved of the Lord, because God hath from the beginning chosen you to salvation through sanctification of the Spirit and belief of the truth:	But we are bound to give thanks to God always, on your account, my brethren beloved of our Lord, that God hath from the beginning chosen you unto life, through sanctification of the Spirit, and through faith in the truth.	But we are indebted to give thanks to God always for you, our brothers, beloved of our Lord, because God chose you from the beginning to life by the holiness of the Spirit and by the faith of the truth.
14	Whereunto he called you by our gospel, to the obtaining of the glory of our Lord Jesus Christ.	For unto these it was, that God called you by our preaching; that ye might be the glory to our Lord Jesus the Messiah.	For to these [things] he called you by our preaching to be a glory for our Lord Jesus Christ.
15	Therefore, brethren, stand fast, and hold the traditions which ye have been taught, whether by word, or our epistle.	Therefore, my brethren, be established, and persevere in the precepts which ye have been taught, whether by word or by our epistle.	Therefore, my brothers, stand fast and hold firmly to the commandments that you learned, whether by word or by our letter.
16	Now our Lord Jesus Christ himself, and God, even our Father, which hath loved us, and hath given us everlasting consolation and good hope through grace,	And may our Lord Jesus the Messiah himself, and God our Father, who hath loved us, and given us everlasting consolation and a good hope through his grace,	Now our Lord Jesus Christ and God our Father, who loved us and gave us everlasting comfort and good hope by his grace,
17	Comfort your hearts, and stablish you in every good word and work.	comfort your hearts, and establish [you] in every good word, and in every good work.	comfort your hearts and establish [you] in every word and in every good work.

Chapter 3

	KJV	*Murdock*	*Magiera*
1	Finally, brethren, pray for us, that the word of the Lord may have free course, and be glorified, even as it is with you:	Henceforth, brethren, pray ye for us, that the word of our Lord may, in every place, run and be glorified, as with you;	For now, our brothers, pray for us that the word of our Lord may run [its course] and be glorified in every place as [it is] with you

II THESSALONIANS *Chapter 3*

	KJV	*Murdock*	*Magiera*
2	And that we may be delivered from unreasonable and wicked men: for all men have not faith.	and that we may be delivered from evil and perverse men; for faith is not in all.	and that we may be delivered from evil and dishonest men, for not everyone has faith.
3	But the Lord is faithful, who shall stablish you, and keep you from evil.	And faithful is the Lord, who will keep you and rescue you from the evil One.	But the LORD is faithful, who will keep you and rescue you from the Evil [one].
4	And we have confidence in the Lord touching you, that ye both do and will do the things which we command you.	And we have confidence in you, through our Lord, that what we have inculcated on you, ye both have done, and will do.	And we are confident about you in our Lord that the things that we have commanded you, you have done [and] also, you will do.
5	And the Lord direct your hearts into the love of God, and into the patient waiting for Christ.	And may our Lord direct your hearts to the love of God, and to a patient waiting for the Messiah.	And may our Lord direct your hearts to the love of God and to the endurance of Christ.
6	Now we command you, brethren, in the name of our Lord Jesus Christ, that ye withdraw yourselves from every brother that walketh disorderly, and not after the tradition which he received of us.	And we enjoin upon you, my brethren, in the name of our Lord Jesus the Messiah, that ye withdraw from every brother who walketh wickedly, and not according to the precepts which ye received from us.	And we command you, my brothers, in the name of our Lord Jesus Christ, to stay away from every brother who walks very evilly and not according to the commandments that he received from us.
7	For yourselves know how ye ought to follow us: for we behaved not ourselves disorderly among you;	For ye know how ye ought to imitate us, who did not walk wickedly among you.	For you know how you ought to be imitators of us, for we did not walk very evilly among you.
8	Neither did we eat any man's bread for nought; but wrought with labour and travail night and day, that we might not be chargeable to any of you:	Neither did we eat bread gratuitously from any of you; but, with toil and weariness, we labored by night and by day, that we might not be burdensome to any of you.	But rather, we ate bread without an expense for any of you, but with toil and with labor, by night and by day, we worked, so that we would not burden any of you,
9	Not because we have not power, but to make ourselves an ensample unto you to follow us.	It was not because we have no authority, but that we might give you an example in ourselves, that ye might imitate us.	not because we are without authority, but that we would give you an example, in ourselves so that you would imitate us.
10	For even when we were with you, this we commanded you, that if any would not work, neither should he eat.	And while we were with you, we also gave you this precept, That every one who would not work, should likewise not eat.	For even when we were with you, we commanded you this, that everyone who does not want to work should also not eat.
11	For we hear that there are some which walk among you disorderly, working not at all, but are busybodies.	For we hear, there are some among you who walk wickedly, and do nothing except vain things.	For we hear that there are men among you who walk very evilly and are not doing anything except unprofitable [things].
12	Now them that are such we command and exhort by our Lord Jesus Christ, that with quietness they work, and eat their own bread.	Now such persons, we command and exhort, by our Lord Jesus the Messiah, that in quietness they work, and eat their own bread.	Now to those we command, and we beg them by our Lord Jesus Christ, that they should work in quietness and eat their [own] bread.
13	But ye, brethren, be not weary in well doing.	And my brethren, let it not be wearisome to you, to do what is good.	Now you, my brothers, should not be weary of doing what is good.

II THESSALONIANS *Chapter 3*

	KJV	*Murdock*	*Magiera*
14	And if any man obey not our word by this epistle, note that man, and have no company with him, that he may be ashamed.	And if any one hearkeneth not to these [my] words in this epistle, separate that man from you, and have no intimacy with him, that he may be ashamed.	And if anyone does not obey our words (these that are in this letter), he should be separated from you. And do not associate with him so that he may be ashamed.
15	Yet count him not as an enemy, but admonish him as a brother.	Yet, hold him not as an enemy, but admonish him as a brother.	Yet do not consider him as an enemy, but reprove him as a brother.
16	Now the Lord of peace himself give you peace always by all means. The Lord be with you all.	And may the Lord of peace give you peace, always, in every thing. Our Lord be with you all.	And the Lord of peace give you peace always in everything. Our Lord [be] with all of you.
17	The salutation of Paul with mine own hand, which is the token in every epistle: so I write.	The salutation in the writing of my own hand, I Paul have written it; which is the token in all my epistles, so I write.	The salutation [is] in my handwriting. I, Paul wrote [it], which is the sign that is in all my letters. So I write.
18	The grace of our Lord Jesus Christ be with you all. Amen.	The grace of Jesus the Messiah be with you all, my brethren. Amen.	The grace of our Lord Jesus Christ [be] with all of you. Amen.

Parallel Translations

I TIMOTHY *Chapter 1*

	KJV	*Murdock*	*Magiera*
1	Paul, an apostle of Jesus Christ by the commandment of God our Saviour, and Lord Jesus Christ, which is our hope;	Paul, a legate of Jesus the Messiah, by the command of God our life-giver, and of the Messiah, Jesus our hope;	Paul, an apostle of Jesus Christ by the commandment of God, our Life-giver, and of Christ Jesus our hope,
2	Unto Timothy, my own son in the faith: Grace, mercy, and peace, from God our Father and Jesus Christ our Lord.	to Timothy, [my] true son in the faith: grace and mercy and peace, from God our Father, and the Messiah, Jesus our Lord.	to Timothy, a true son in the faith: Grace and mercy and peace from God our Father and Christ Jesus our Lord.
3	As I besought thee to abide still at Ephesus, when I went into Macedonia, that thou mightest charge some that they teach no other doctrine,	When I was going into Macedonia, I requested thee to remain at Ephesus, and to charge certain persons not to teach different doctrines;	I begged you, when I went to Macedonia, to remain in Ephesus and to charge each one that they should not teach different doctrines
4	Neither give heed to fables and endless genealogies, which minister questions, rather than godly edifying which is in faith: so do.	and not to throw themselves into fables and stories about genealogies, of which there is no end, which produce contention rather than edification in the faith of God.	and [that] they should not pay attention to fables and to accounts of endless genealogies. These [things] increasingly bring about controversies and not edification in the faith of God.
5	Now the end of the commandment is charity out of a pure heart, and of a good conscience, and of faith unfeigned:	Now the end of the command is love, which is from a pure heart, and from a good conscience, and from true faith.	But the end of the commandment is love that is from a pure heart and from a good conscience and from the true faith.
6	From which some having swerved have turned aside unto vain jangling;	But from these some have strayed, and have turned aside to vain words;	And from these [things], some have erred and have turned aside to empty words,
7	Desiring to be teachers of the law; understanding neither what they say, nor whereof they affirm.	because they wished to be teachers of the law, while they understood not what they speak, nor the thing about which they contend.	in that they seek to be teachers of the law, not understanding what they speak, nor about which they dispute.
8	But we know that the law is good, if a man use it lawfully;	Now, we know, that the law is a good thing, if a man conduct himself in it, according to the law,	But we know that the law is good if a man conducts himself in it according to it lawfully,
9	Knowing this, that the law is not made for a righteous man, but for the lawless and disobedient, for the ungodly and for sinners, for unholy and profane, for murderers of fathers and murderers of mothers, for manslayers,	he knowing that the law was not established for the righteous, but for the evil, and the rebellious, and the ungodly, and the sinful, and the perverse and for the impure, and for smiters of their fathers and smiters of their mothers, and for murderers,	knowing that the law was not established for the upright [ones], but for the wicked and for the rebellious and for the ungodly and for the sinners and for the deceitful and for those who are not pure and for those who wound their fathers and for those who wound their mothers and for murderers

Parallel Translations

I TIMOTHY *Chapter 1*

	KJV	Murdock	Magiera
10	For whoremongers, for them that defile themselves with mankind, for menstealers, for liars, for perjured persons, and if there be any other thing that is contrary to sound doctrine;	and for whoremongers, and for copulators with males, and for the stealers of free people, and for liars, and for violators of oaths, and for whatever is contrary to sound doctrine,	and for fornicators and for homosexuals and for kidnappers of free men and for liars and transgressors concerning oaths and for everything that is contrary to sound teaching
11	According to the glorious gospel of the blessed God, which was committed to my trust.	[namely] that of the glorious gospel of the blessed God, with which I am intrusted.	of the gospel of the glory of the blessed God, [with] which I am entrusted.
12	And I thank Christ Jesus our Lord, who hath enabled me, for that he counted me faithful, putting me into the ministry;	And I thank him who strengthened me, [even] our Lord Jesus the Messiah; who accounted me faithful, and appointed me to his ministry;	And I thank him who strengthened me, our Lord Jesus Christ, who counted me a faithful [one] and ordained me to his service,
13	Who was before a blasphemer, and a persecutor, and injurious: but I obtained mercy, because I did it ignorantly in unbelief.	me [I say], who before was a blasphemer, and a persecutor, and a reviler; but I obtained mercy, because I did it while ignorant and without faith.	me who previously was a reviler and a persecutor and a scorner, but I received mercy, because when I was ignorant, I acted without faith.
14	And the grace of our Lord was exceeding abundant with faith and love which is in Christ Jesus.	And in me the grace of our Lord abounded, and faith and love, which is in Jesus the Messiah.	Now the grace of our Lord and the faith and love that are in Jesus Christ abounded in me.
15	This is a faithful saying, and worthy of all acceptation, that Christ Jesus came into the world to save sinners; of whom I am chief.	Faithful is the declaration, and worthy to be received, that Jesus the Messiah came into the world to give life to sinners, of whom I was the primary.	The word is faithful and it is worthy to receive, that Jesus Christ came into the world to give life to sinners, of whom I am chief.
16	Howbeit for this cause I obtained mercy, that in me first Jesus Christ might shew forth all longsuffering, for a pattern to them which should hereafter believe on him to life everlasting.	But for this cause had he mercy on me, that in me first Jesus the Messiah might display all his long suffering, for an example to them who were to believe on him unto life eternal.	But because of this, he had mercy on me, that in me first, Jesus Christ would display all his long-suffering as an example to those who were going to believe in him to eternal life.
17	Now unto the King eternal, immortal, invisible, the only wise God, be honour and glory for ever and ever. Amen.	And to the king eternal, incorruptible, and invisible, the sole God, be honor and glory for ever and ever! Amen.	And to the King of the ages, to him who is incorruptible and invisible, who is one God, [be] honor and glory, forever and ever. Amen.
18	This charge I commit unto thee, son Timothy, according to the prophecies which went before on thee, that thou by them mightest war a good warfare;	This injunction I commit to thee, my son Timothy, according to the former predictions concerning thee, that in them thou mightest war this good warfare,	This commandment I am entrusting to you, my son, Timothy, according to the first prophecies that were about you, that you should work this good work
19	Holding faith, and a good conscience; which some having put away concerning faith have made shipwreck:	in faith and a good conscience; for they who have repudiated this, have become destitute of faith;	in faith and in a good conscience. For those, who have rejected this, are destitute of faith,
20	Of whom is Hymenaeus and Alexander; whom I have delivered unto Satan, that they may learn not to blaspheme.	like Hymeneus and Alexander, whom I have delivered up to Satan, that they may learn not to be blasphemers.	like Hymenaeus and Alexander, those whom I have delivered to Satan to be disciplined, so that they would not be blaspheming.

Parallel Translations

I TIMOTHY *Chapter 2*

	KJV	*Murdock*	*Magiera*
1	I exhort therefore, that, first of all, supplications, prayers, intercessions, and giving of thanks, be made for all men;	I exhort thee, therefore, first of all, that thou present to God supplication, and prayer, and intercession, and thanksgiving, for all men:	I beg you, therefore, that before everything you should offer petition to God and prayer and intercession and thanksgiving on behalf of all men,
2	For kings, and for all that are in authority; that we may lead a quiet and peaceable life in all godliness and honesty.	for kings and magistrates, that we may dwell in a quiet and tranquil habitation, with all reverence for God, and with purity.	on behalf of kings and princes, that we may live a peaceful and restful life with all reverence for God and purity,
3	For this is good and acceptable in the sight of God our Saviour;	For this is good and acceptable before God our life-giver;	for this is good and acceptable before God, our Life-giver,
4	Who will have all men to be saved, and to come unto the knowledge of the truth.	who would have all men live, and be converted to the knowledge of the truth.	who wants all men to have life and to turn to the knowledge of the truth.
5	For there is one God, and one mediator between God and men, the man Christ Jesus;	For God is one; and the mediator between God and men is one, [namely] the man Jesus the Messiah;	For God is one and the mediator of God and of men is one, the man, Jesus Christ,
6	Who gave himself a ransom for all, to be testified in due time.	who gave himself a ransom for every man; a testimony that arrived in due time,	who gave himself [as] a ransom for everyone, a witness that arrived in its time,
7	Whereunto I am ordained a preacher, and an apostle, (I speak the truth in Christ, and lie not;) a teacher of the Gentiles in faith and verity.	of which I am constituted a herald and legate. I speak the truth, and do not lie, for I am the teacher of the Gentiles in the belief of the truth.	[of] which I was ordained its preacher and its apostle. I speak [with] truthfulness and I do not lie, for I became a teacher of the Gentiles in the faith of the truth.
8	I will therefore that men pray every where, lifting up holy hands, without wrath and doubting.	I desire therefore, that men may pray in every place, while they lift up their hands with purity, without wrath, and without disputations.	Therefore, I want men to pray in every place, lifting up their hands purely, without anger and without arguments.
9	In like manner also, that women adorn themselves in modest apparel, with shamefacedness and sobriety; not with broided hair, or gold, or pearls, or costly array;	So also, that women [appear] in a chaste fashion of dress; and that their adorning be with modesty and chastity; not with curls, or with gold, or with pearls, or with splendid robes;	So also, women [should dress] in a moderate style of clothing. Their adornment should be with modesty and with moderation, not with braiding [of the hair] or with gold or with pearls or with beautiful outer garments,
10	But (which becometh women professing godliness) with good works.	but with good works, as becometh women who profess reverence for God.	but with good works, as it is proper for women who profess reverence for God.
11	Let the woman learn in silence with all subjection.	Let a woman learn in silence, with all submission:	A wife should learn in quietness with all submission,
12	But I suffer not a woman to teach, nor to usurp authority over the man, but to be in silence.	for I do not allow a woman to teach, or to be assuming over the man; but let her remain in stillness.	for I do not allow a wife to teach nor to be presumptuous over the husband, but she should be at peace.
13	For Adam was first formed, then Eve.	For Adam was first formed, and then Eve.	For Adam was formed first and then Eve,

Parallel Translations

I TIMOTHY *Chapter 2*

	KJV	*Murdock*	*Magiera*
14	And Adam was not deceived, but the woman being deceived was in the transgression.	And Adam was not seduced, but the woman was seduced and transgressed the command.	and Adam did not err, but the woman erred and transgressed the commandment.
15	Notwithstanding she shall be saved in childbearing, if they continue in faith and charity and holiness with sobriety.	Yet she shall live by means of her children, if they continue in the faith, and in love, and in sanctity, and in chastity.	But she has life by way of her children, if they remain in faith and in love and in holiness and in sobriety.

Chapter 3

	KJV	*Murdock*	*Magiera*
1	This is a true saying, If a man desire the office of a bishop, he desireth a good work.	It is a faithful saying, that if a man desireth the eldership, he desireth a good work.	The word is faithful. For if a man desires the office of an elder, he desires good works.
2	A bishop then must be blameless, the husband of one wife, vigilant, sober, of good behaviour, given to hospitality, apt to teach;	And an elder ought to be such, that no blame can be found in him; and he should be the husband of one wife, with a vigilant mind, and sober and regular [in his habits], and affectionate to strangers, and instructive;	Now it is proper for an elder to be one in whom no blemish is found and is the husband of one woman, who [is] of a watchful mind and sober and orderly and loving of strangers and able to teach
3	Not given to wine, no striker, not greedy of filthy lucre; but patient, not a brawler, not covetous;	and not a transgressor in regard to wine, and whose hand is not swift to strike; but he should be humble, and not contentious, nor a lover of money;	and does not transgress concerning wine and is not swift to strike [with] his hand. But he should be humble and not quarrelsome and not loving of money
4	One that ruleth well his own house, having his children in subjection with all gravity;	and one that guideth well his own house, and holdeth his children in subjection with all purity.	and should lead his house well and keep his children in submission with all purity.
5	(For if a man know not how to rule his own house, how shall he take care of the church of God?)	For if he knoweth not how to guide his own house well, how can he guide the church of God.	For if he does not know how to lead his own house well, how is he able to lead the church of God?
6	Not a novice, lest being lifted up with pride he fall into the condemnation of the devil.	Neither let him be of recent discipleship; lest he be uplifted, and fall into the condemnation of Satan.	And his discipleship should not be recent, so that he should not be lifted up and fall into the judgment of Satan.
7	Moreover he must have a good report of them which are without; lest he fall into reproach and the snare of the devil.	And there ought to be good testimony of him from those without; lest he fall into reproach and the snare of Satan.	And also he ought to have a good testimony from those without, so that he should not fall into reproach and into the snares of Satan.
8	Likewise must the deacons be grave, not doubletongued, not given to much wine, not greedy of filthy lucre;	And so also the deacons should be pure, and not speak double, nor incline to much wine, nor love base gains;	And so also, ministers should be pure and should not be double-tongued and should not be inclined to much wine and should not love corrupt profits,
9	Holding the mystery of the faith in a pure conscience.	but should hold the mystery of the faith with a pure conscience.	but they should adhere to the mystery of the faith with a pure conscience.
10	And let these also first be proved; then let them use the office of a deacon, being found blameless.	And let them be first tried, and then let them serve, if they are without blame.	And these should be proven first and then they may serve, when they are without blame.

Parallel Translations

	KJV	Murdock	Magiera
I TIMOTHY	*Chapter 3*		
11	Even so must their wives be grave, not slanderers, sober, faithful in all things.	So also should the wives be chaste and of vigilant minds; and they should be faithful in all things; and they should not be slanderers.	So also, the women should be sober and should be watchful in their minds and should be faithful in everything and should not be slanderers.
12	Let the deacons be the husbands of one wife, ruling their children and their own houses well.	Let the deacons be such as have each one wife and guide well their children and households.	Ministers should be he who has one wife and leads his children and his house well.
13	For they that have used the office of a deacon well purchase to themselves a good degree, and great boldness in the faith which is in Christ Jesus.	For they who serve well [as deacons], procure for themselves a good degree, and much boldness in the faith of Jesus the Messiah.	For those who have ministered well obtain recognition for themselves and much boldness in the faith of Jesus Christ.
14	These things write I unto thee, hoping to come unto thee shortly:	These things I write to thee, while hoping soon to come to thee;	These [things] I am writing to you, although I am hoping to come to you soon,
15	But if I tarry long, that thou mayest know how thou oughtest to behave thyself in the house of God, which is the church of the living God, the pillar and ground of the truth.	but if I should delay, that thou mayest know how thou oughtest to conduct thyself in the house of God, which is the church of the living God. The pillar and the foundation of the truth,	and even if I should delay, so that you may know how you ought to behave in the house of God, which is the church of the living God. The pillar and foundation of truth
16	And without controversy great is the mystery of godliness: God was manifest in the flesh, justified in the Spirit, seen of angels, preached unto the Gentiles, believed on in the world, received up into glory.	and truly great, is this mystery of righteousness, which was revealed in the flesh, and justified in the spirit, and seen by angels, and proclaimed among the Gentiles, and believed on in the world, and received up into glory.	and truly great is this mystery of uprightness, which was revealed in the flesh and was justified spiritually and was seen by angels and was preached among the Gentiles and was believed in the world and was taken up in glory.
Chapter 4			
1	Now the Spirit speaketh expressly, that in the latter times some shall depart from the faith, giving heed to seducing spirits, and doctrines of devils;	But the Spirit saith explicitly, that in the latter times, some will depart from the faith; and will go after deceptive spirits, and after the doctrine of demons.	Now the Spirit plainly says that in the last times some will depart from the faith and will follow deceiving spirits and doctrines of demons,
2	Speaking lies in hypocrisy; having their conscience seared with a hot iron;	These will seduce, by a false appearance; and will utter a lie, and will be seared in their conscience;	those who deceive by false appearance and are speaking a lie and are seared in their conscience
3	Forbidding to marry, and commanding to abstain from meats, which God hath created to be received with thanksgiving of them which believe and know the truth.	and will forbid to marry; and will require abstinence from meats, which God hath created for use and for thankfulness, by them who believe and know the truth.	and forbid to marry. And they keep away from foods, which God created for use and for thanksgiving for those who believe and know the truth,
4	For every creature of God is good, and nothing to be refused, if it be received with thanksgiving:	Because whatever is created by God is good; and there is nothing which should be rejected if it be received with thankfulness;	because everything that was created by God is good and there is not anything that should be rejected, if it is received with thanksgiving,
5	For it is sanctified by the word of God and prayer.	for it is sanctified by the word of God and by prayer.	for it is made holy by the word of God and by prayer.

Parallel Translations

	KJV	Murdock	Magiera
	I TIMOTHY *Chapter 4*		
6	If thou put the brethren in remembrance of these things, thou shalt be a good minister of Jesus Christ, nourished up in the words of faith and of good doctrine, whereunto thou hast attained.	If thou shalt inculcate these things on thy brethren, thou wilt be a good minister of Jesus the Messiah, being educated in the language of the faith, and in the good doctrine which thou hast been taught.	If you teach these [things] to your brothers, you will be a good minister of Jesus Christ, as you grow up in the words of faith and in the good teaching that you were taught.
7	But refuse profane and old wives' fables, and exercise thyself rather unto godliness.	But the silly tales of old women, shun thou; and occupy thyself with righteousness.	Now withdraw from the foolish tales of old [women] and train yourself in uprightness.
8	For bodily exercise profiteth little: but godliness is profitable unto all things, having promise of the life that now is, and of that which is to come.	For, exercising the body is profitable a little while; but righteousness is every way profitable and hath promise of the life of the present time and of that to come.	For the training of the body profits a little [time], but uprightness profits in everything and has the promise of the life of this time and of the future.
9	This is a faithful saying and worthy of all acceptation.	This is a faithful saying, and worthy of reception.	The word is faithful and it is worthy to receive,
10	For therefore we both labour and suffer reproach, because we trust in the living God, who is the Saviour of all men, specially of those that believe.	For on this account, we toil and suffer reproach; because we trust in the living God, who is the life-giver of all men, especially of the believers.	for because of this, we labor and suffer blame, because we trust in the living God, who is the Life-giver of all men, especially of the believers.
11	These things command and teach.	These things teach thou, and inculcate.	These [things] teach and command.
12	Let no man despise thy youth; but be thou an example of the believers, in word, in conversation, in charity, in spirit, in faith, in purity.	And let no one despise thy youth; but be thou a pattern for the believers, in speech, and in behavior, and in love, and in faith, and in purity.	And no one should despise your youth, but be an example to the believers in word and in conduct and in love and in faith and in purity.
13	Till I come, give attendance to reading, to exhortation, to doctrine.	Until I come, be diligent in reading, and in prayer, and in teaching.	Until I come, be diligent in reading and in petition and in teaching.
14	Neglect not the gift that is in thee, which was given thee by prophecy, with the laying on of the hands of the presbytery.	Despise not the gift that is in thee, which was given thee by prophecy, and by the laying on of the hand of the eldership.	And do not despise the gift that you have that was given to you by prophecy and by the laying on of the hand of the eldership.
15	Meditate upon these things; give thyself wholly to them; that thy profiting may appear to all.	On these things meditate; give thyself wholly to them: that it may be obvious to all that thou makest advances.	Meditate on these [things] and be in them, that it may be known to everyone that you are going forward.
16	Take heed unto thyself, and unto the doctrine; continue in them: for in doing this thou shalt both save thyself, and them that hear thee.	Be attentive to thyself, and to thy teaching; and persevere in them. For in doing this, thou wilt procure life to thyself and to them who hear thee.	And watch yourself and your teaching and persevere in them. For as you do these [things], you will give life to yourself and to those who hear you.
	Chapter 5		
1	Rebuke not an elder, but intreat him as a father; and the younger men as brethren;	Chide not an elder, but entreat him as a father; and the younger men, as thy brothers;	You should not reprove an elder, but should persuade him as a father and those who are younger as your brothers

Parallel Translations

I TIMOTHY *Chapter 5*

	KJV	*Murdock*	*Magiera*
2	The elder women as mothers; the younger as sisters, with all purity.	and the elder women, as mothers; and the younger women, as thy sisters, with all purity.	and the elder women as mothers and those who are younger as your sisters with all purity.
3	Honour widows that are widows indeed.	Honor widows, who are truly widows.	Honor widows, who are truly widows.
4	But if any widow have children or nephews, let them learn first to shew piety at home, and to requite their parents: for that is good and acceptable before God.	But if a widow hath children, or grandchildren, let them first learn to show kindness to their own households, and to repay the obligations to their parents; for this is acceptable before God.	And if there is a widow who has children or grandchildren, they should first learn that they should act rightly in their households and they should repay the obligations to their parents, for this is acceptable before God.
5	Now she that is a widow indeed, and desolate, trusteth in God, and continueth in supplications and prayers night and day.	Now she who is truly a widow, and solitary, her hope is in God; and she persevereth in prayers, and in supplications, by night and by day:	Now she who truly is a widow and alone, her trust is in God and she is faithful in prayers and in petitions by night and by day.
6	But she that liveth in pleasure is dead while she liveth.	But she who followeth pleasure, is dead while she liveth.	But she who serves luxury is dead while alive.
7	And these things give in charge, that they may be blameless.	These things enjoin thou on them, that they may be blameless.	Command them these [things], so that they may be without blame.
8	But if any provide not for his own, and specially for those of his own house, he hath denied the faith, and is worse than an infidel.	But if any one careth not for them who are his own, and especially for them who are of the household of faith, he hath rejected the faith, and is worse than the unbelievers.	For if [there is] a man who does not take care of those who are his own and especially those who are [of] the household of faith, this [one] has denied the faith and is more evil than those who do not believe.
9	Let not a widow be taken into the number under threescore years old, having been the wife of one man,	Therefore elect thou the widow, who is not less than sixty years [old], and who hath been the wife of one man,	Therefore, you should choose a widow [to honor] who is not less than sixty years [old], who was [married] to one man
10	Well reported of for good works; if she have brought up children, if she have lodged strangers, if she have washed the saints' feet, if she have relieved the afflicted, if she have diligently followed every good work.	and hath a reputation for good works; if she have trained up children, if she have entertained strangers, if she have washed the feet of saints, if she have relieved the afflicted, if she have walked in every good work.	and has a reputation of good works, whether she brought up children or received strangers or washed the feet of holy [ones] or relieved troubled [ones] or walked in every good work.
11	But the younger widows refuse: for when they have begun to wax wanton against Christ, they will marry;	But the younger widows do thou reject; for they wax wanton against the Messiah, and desire to be married:	But from those widows who are young, excuse yourself, for they may be wanton against Christ and seek to have husbands.
12	Having damnation, because they have cast off their first faith.	and their condemnation is fixed, because they have cast off their former faith.	And their judgment is established, because they have set aside their former faith.

I TIMOTHY *Chapter 5*

	KJV	Murdock	Magiera
13	And withal they learn to be idle, wandering about from house to house; and not only idle, but tattlers also and busybodies, speaking things which they ought not.	And they also learn idleness, wandering from house to house; and not only idleness, but also to talk much, and to pursue vanities, and to utter what they ought not.	And they also learn laziness while circulating among the houses, and not only laziness, but also to talk too much and to distract themselves with fruitless [things] and to speak what is not proper.
14	I will therefore that the younger women marry, bear children, guide the house, give none occasion to the adversary to speak reproachfully.	I would therefore, that the younger women marry, and bear children, and regulate their houses; and that they give no occasion to the adversary for reproach.	Therefore, I want those who are young to marry and to bear children and to direct their homes and not give to the enemy even one cause for reproach.
15	For some are already turned aside after Satan.	For some have already begun to turn aside after Satan.	For at this time some have begun to turn aside after Satan.
16	If any man or woman that believeth have widows, let them relieve them, and let not the church be charged; that it may relieve them that are widows indeed.	If any believing man or believing woman have widows, let them support them; and let them not be a burden on the church; so that there may be a sufficiency for such as are really widows.	If any believing [man] or believing [woman] have widows, they should support them and they should not be a burden on the church, so that there may be a sufficiency for those who are truly widows.
17	Let the elders that rule well be counted worthy of double honour, especially they who labour in the word and doctrine.	Let the elders who conduct themselves well, be esteemed worthy of double honor; especially they who labor in the word and in doctrine.	Those elders who conduct themselves well should be esteemed worthy of double honor, especially those who work hard in the word and in teaching,
18	For the scripture saith, Thou shalt not muzzle the ox that treadeth out the corn. And, The labourer is worthy of his reward.	For the scripture saith Thou shalt not muzzle the ox in threshing; and, The laborer is worthy of his pay.	for the scripture says: YOU SHOULD NOT MUZZLE THE OX IN THE THRESHING and THE LABORER IS WORTHY OF HIS WAGE.
19	Against an elder receive not an accusation, but before two or three witnesses.	Against an elder, receive not a complaint, except at the mouth of two or three witnesses.	Do not accept an accusation against an elder, except by the mouth of two or three witnesses.
20	Them that sin rebuke before all, that others also may fear.	Those who sin before all rebuke; that the rest of the people may fear.	Reprove those who sin before everyone, so that the rest of the people would also have respect.
21	I charge thee before God, and the Lord Jesus Christ, and the elect angels, that thou observe these things without preferring one before another, doing nothing by partiality.	I charge thee, before God, and our Lord Jesus the Messiah, and his elect angels, that thou observe these things; and let not your mind be preoccupied by any thing: and do nothing with a respect for persons.	I charge you before God and our Lord Jesus Christ and his chosen messengers that you observe these [things]. And your mind should not be preoccupied with anything and do not do anything with respect of persons.
22	Lay hands suddenly on no man, neither be partaker of other men's sins: keep thyself pure.	Lay not the hand hastily on any man; and participate not in the sins of others; keep thyself pure.	Do not lay a hand quickly on anyone and do not participate in strange sins. Guard yourself with purity.

	KJV	*Murdock*	*Magiera*
	I TIMOTHY *Chapter 5*		
23	Drink no longer water, but use a little wine for thy stomach's sake and thine often infirmities.	And hereafter drink not water, but drink a little wine; on account of thy stomach, and thy continuing infirmities.	And from now on, do not drink water, but drink a little wine because of your stomach and because of your continuing infirmities.
24	Some men's sins are open beforehand, going before to judgment; and some men they follow after.	There are persons, whose sins are known, and go before them to the place of judgment; and there are some, whom they follow after.	There are men whose sins are well-known and precede them to the house of judgment and there are [some] whose [sins] follow after them.
25	Likewise also the good works of some are manifest beforehand; and they that are otherwise cannot be hid.	So also good deeds are known: and those which are otherwise cannot be hid.	So also, good works are well-known and those that are otherwise are not able to be hidden.
	Chapter 6		
1	Let as many servants as are under the yoke count their own masters worthy of all honour, that the name of God and his doctrine be not blasphemed.	Let them who are under the yoke of servitude, hold their masters in all honor; lest the name of God and his doctrine be reproached.	Those who are under the yoke of bondage should hold their masters in all honor, so that the name of God and his teaching will not be reviled.
2	And they that have believing masters, let them not despise them, because they are brethren; but rather do them service, because they are faithful and beloved, partakers of the benefit. These things teach and exhort.	And let them who have believing masters, not treat them with disrespect, because they are their brethren; but let them be more obedient, because they are believers and beloved, in whose service they enjoy quietness. These things teach thou, and request of them.	And those who have faithful masters should not despise them, because they are their brothers. But rather, they should especially minister to them, because they are believers and beloved, in whose service they are refreshed. These [things] teach and require from them.
3	If any man teach otherwise, and consent not to wholesome words, even the words of our Lord Jesus Christ, and to the doctrine which is according to godliness;	But if there be any one, who teacheth a different doctrine, and doth not accede to the salutary words of our Lord Jesus the Messiah, and to the doctrine of the fear of God,	But if there is a man who teaches another doctrine and does not apply himself to the sound words of our Lord Jesus Christ and to the doctrine of reverence for God,
4	He is proud, knowing nothing, but doting about questions and strifes of words, whereof cometh envy, strife, railings, evil surmisings,	he is one that exalteth himself, while he knoweth nothing; and he languisheth in the search and inquiry about words, from which come envy, and contention, and railing, and evil surmising,	this [one] is proud, knowing nothing. But [he is] sick with controversy and with questioning about words, from which come envy and contention and reviling and the setting of evil in the mind
5	Perverse disputings of men of corrupt minds, and destitute of the truth, supposing that gain is godliness: from such withdraw thyself.	and the disputation of men, whose minds are corrupt and destitute of the truth, and who suppose that gain is godliness. But from these stand thou aloof.	and the strife of men, those whose mind is corrupted and [who] are deprived of truthfulness. And they suppose that reverence for God is gain. But you, avoid these [things],
6	But godliness with contentment is great gain.	But great is our gain, which is the fear of God, with the use of our competence.	for our own gain is great in the use of our sufficiency, because it is reverence for God.
7	For we brought nothing into this world, and it is certain we can carry nothing out.	For we brought nothing into the world; and we know that we can carry nothing out of it.	For we did not bring anything into the world and it is evident that we also cannot carry [anything] out of it.

I TIMOTHY *Chapter 6*

	KJV	*Murdock*	*Magiera*
8	And having food and raiment let us be therewith content.	Therefore, food and clothing satisfy us.	Because of this, food and clothing are sufficient for us.
9	But they that will be rich fall into temptation and a snare, and into many foolish and hurtful lusts, which drown men in destruction and perdition.	But they who desire to become rich, fall into temptations, and into snares, and into many lusts which are foolish and hurtful, and which drown men in destruction and perdition:	But those who want to grow rich fall into temptations and into snares and into many pleasures, which are foolish and are hurtful and are drowning men in corruption and loss.
10	For the love of money is the root of all evil: which while some coveted after, they have erred from the faith, and pierced themselves through with many sorrows.	for the love of money is the root of all these evils. And there are some who, coveting it, have erred from the faith, and brought themselves into many sorrows.	For the root of all evil [things] is the love of money. And there are some who have longed for it and have erred from the faith and have brought to themselves many miseries.
11	But thou, O man of God, flee these things; and follow after righteousness, godliness, faith, love, patience, meekness.	But thou, O man of God, flee from these things; and follow after righteousness, and rectitude, and faith, and love, and patience, and humility.	But you, oh man of God, flee from these [things] and pursue after justification and after uprightness and after faith and after love and after patience and after meekness.
12	Fight the good fight of faith, lay hold on eternal life, whereunto thou art also called, and hast professed a good profession before many witnesses.	And contend in the good contest of faith; and lay hold of life eternal, to which thou art called, and [of which] thou hast confessed a good confession before many witnesses.	And struggle in the good contest of faith and obtain eternal life, to which you were called and confessed a good confession before many witnesses.
13	I give thee charge in the sight of God, who quickeneth all things, and before Christ Jesus, who before Pontius Pilate witnessed a good confession;	I charge thee, before God, who quickeneth all, and [before] Jesus the Messiah who attested a good testimony before Pontius Pilate,	I am charging you before God, who gives life to all, and Jesus Christ, who testified a good testimony before Pontius Pilate,
14	That thou keep this commandment without spot, unrebukeable, until the appearing of our Lord Jesus Christ:	that thou keep the injunction, without stain, and without blemish, until the manifestation of our Lord Jesus the Messiah;	that you keep the commandment without spot and without blemish until the appearance of our Lord Jesus Christ,
15	Which in his times he shall shew, who is the blessed and only Potentate, the King of kings, and Lord of lords;	which God will, in due time make visible; [God] the blessed and only Potentate, the King of kings, and the Lord of lords;	whom God is going to show in its time, the blessed and only powerful [one], King of kings and Lord of lords,
16	Who only hath immortality, dwelling in the light which no man can approach unto; whom no man hath seen, nor can see: to whom be honour and power everlasting. Amen.	who only is incorruptible, and dwelleth in light to which no one can approach; and whom no man hath seen, or even can see: to him be glory and dominion for ever and ever. Amen.	who alone is incorruptible and lives in light, to whom no one is able to draw near and no one from men has seen, nor is even able to see, to whom [be] honor and authority, forever and ever. Amen.
17	Charge them that are rich in this world, that they be not highminded, nor trust in uncertain riches, but in the living God, who giveth us richly all things to enjoy;	Charge the rich of this world, that they be not uplifted in their minds; and that they confide not in riches, in which is no security; but in the living God, who giveth us all things abundantly for our comfort:	Command the rich of this world that they should not be elevated in their minds and that they should not trust in wealth that is not trustworthy, but rather in the living God, who gave us everything richly for our rest.

Parallel Translations

	KJV	Murdock	Magiera
	I TIMOTHY	*Chapter 6*	
18	That they do good, that they be rich in good works, ready to distribute, willing to communicate;	and that they do good works, and be rich in well-doings; and be ready to give and to communicate:	And [command that] they should do good works and should increase in pleasing occupations and should be ready to give and to fellowship,
19	Laying up in store for themselves a good foundation against the time to come, that they may lay hold on eternal life.	and that they lay up for themselves a good foundation for that which is future; that they may take hold of real life.	and they should lay up for themselves a good foundation for that which is to come, that they may obtain true life.
20	O Timothy, keep that which is committed to thy trust, avoiding profane and vain babblings, and oppositions of science falsely so called:	O Timothy, be careful of that which is committed to thee; and shun vain words, and the oppositions of false science:	Oh Timothy, watch over what was entrusted to you and flee from fruitless reports and from the contrary principles of false knowledge,
21	Which some professing have erred concerning the faith. Grace be with thee. Amen.	for they who profess it, have erred from the faith. Grace be with thee. Amen.	for those who profess it have erred from the faith. Grace [be] with you. Amen.

Parallel Translations

	KJV	*Murdock*	*Magiera*

II TIMOTHY *Chapter 1*

	KJV	Murdock	Magiera
1	Paul, an apostle of Jesus Christ by the will of God, according to the promise of life which is in Christ Jesus,	PAUL, a legate of Jesus the Messiah by the pleasure of God, according to the promise of life which is in Jesus the Messiah;	Paul, an apostle of Jesus Christ, by the will of God and by the promise of life that is in Jesus Christ,
2	To Timothy, my dearly beloved son: Grace, mercy, and peace, from God the Father and Christ Jesus our Lord.	to Timothy a beloved son; grace, and mercy, and peace, from God the Father, and from our Lord Jesus the Messiah.	to Timothy, a beloved son: Grace and mercy and peace from God the Father and from our Lord Jesus Christ.
3	I thank God, whom I serve from my forefathers with pure conscience, that without ceasing I have remembrance of thee in my prayers night and day;	I thank God, whom I serve from my forefathers with a pure conscience, that I continually remember thee in my prayers, by night and by day:	I give thanks to God, whom I serve from my fathers with a pure conscience, that I continually remember you in my prayers by night and by day.
4	Greatly desiring to see thee, being mindful of thy tears, that I may be filled with joy;	and I desire to see thee, and I call to mind thy tears; that I may be filled with joy,	And I long to see you and I recall your tears, that I may be filled with joy
5	When I call to remembrance the unfeigned faith that is in thee, which dwelt first in thy grandmother Lois, and thy mother Eunice; and I am persuaded that in thee also.	by the recollection which I have, by thy genuine faith, which dwelt first in thy grandmother Lois, and in thy mother Eunice, and also, I am persuaded, in thee.	by the remembrance I have about your steadfast faith that lived first in your grandmother, Lois, and in your mother, Eunice, and I am persuaded is also in you.
6	Wherefore I put thee in remembrance that thou stir up the gift of God, which is in thee by the putting on of my hands.	Wherefore I remind thee, that thou excite the gift of God, that is in thee by the imposition of my hands.	Because of this, I remind you to stir up the gift of God that you have by the laying on of my hand.
7	For God hath not given us the spirit of fear; but of power, and of love, and of a sound mind.	For God hath not given us a spirit of fear, but of energy, and of love, and of instruction.	For God has not given us a spirit of fear, but [a Spirit] of power and of love and of instruction.
8	Be not thou therefore ashamed of the testimony of our Lord, nor of me his prisoner: but be thou partaker of the afflictions of the gospel according to the power of God;	Therefore be not thou ashamed of the testimony of our Lord, nor of me his prisoner; but endure evils in connection with the Gospel, through the power of God;	Therefore, do not be ashamed about the testimony of our Lord, nor about me, his prisoner, but endure evil [things] connected with the gospel by the power of God,
9	Who hath saved us, and called us with an holy calling, not according to our works, but according to his own purpose and grace, which was given us in Christ Jesus before the world began,	who hath vivified us, and called us with a holy calling; not according to our works, but according to his good pleasure, and his grace that was given us in Jesus the Messiah from time before the ages,	who gave us life and called us with a holy calling, not according to our works, but according to his will and his grace that was given to us by Jesus Christ from before the time of the ages
10	But is now made manifest by the appearing of our Saviour Jesus Christ, who hath abolished death, and hath brought life and immortality to light through the gospel:	and is now made known by the appearing of our Vivifier, Jesus the Messiah; who hath abolished death, and hath made manifest life and immortality, by the gospel:	and now has been revealed by the appearance of our Life-giver, Jesus Christ, who made death of no effect and made life and incorruptibility evident by the gospel,
11	Whereunto I am appointed a preacher, and an apostle, and a teacher of the Gentiles.	of which I am constituted a herald and a legate, and a teacher of the Gentiles.	of which I was appointed a preacher and an apostle and a teacher of the Gentiles.

II TIMOTHY *Chapter 1*

	KJV	*Murdock*	*Magiera*
12	For the which cause I also suffer these things: nevertheless I am not ashamed: for I know whom I have believed, and am persuaded that he is able to keep that which I have committed unto him against that day.	Therefore I suffer these things: and I am not ashamed; for I know in whom I have believed, and I am persuaded that he is competent to keep for me my deposit against that day.	Because of this, I endure these [things] and I am not ashamed, for I know in whom I have believed and I am persuaded that he is able by his hands to keep my deposit for me until that day.
13	Hold fast the form of sound words, which thou hast heard of me, in faith and love which is in Christ Jesus.	Let the form of sound words, which thou hast heard from me, abide with thee; with faith and love, in Jesus the Messiah.	You should continue the pattern of sound words, which you heard from me in the faith and in the love that is in Jesus Christ.
14	That good thing which was committed unto thee keep by the Holy Ghost which dwelleth in us.	Keep thou the good deposit, by the Holy Spirit who dwelleth in us.	Keep the good deposit by the Holy Spirit that lives in us.
15	This thou knowest, that all they which are in Asia be turned away from me; of whom are Phygellus and Hermogenes.	This thou knowest, that all those in Asia have turned from me; and that among them are Phygellus and Hermogenes.	This you know, that all those who were in Asia have turned from me, among whom are Phygellus and Hermogenes.
16	The Lord give mercy unto the house of Onesiphorus; for he oft refreshed me, and was not ashamed of my chain:	May our Lord bestow mercy on the house of Onesiphorus; for, many times, he refreshed me, and was not ashamed of the chains of my imprisonment.	May our Lord give mercies to the house of Onesiphorus, who refreshed me many times and was not ashamed of the chains of my bonds.
17	But, when he was in Rome, he sought me out very diligently, and found me.	But also, when he came to Rome, he sought for me with diligence, and found me.	But also, when he came to Rome, he searched for me with diligence and found me.
18	The Lord grant unto him that he may find mercy of the Lord in that day: and in how many things he ministered unto me at Ephesus, thou knowest very well.	May our Lord grant him, that he may find mercy with our Lord, in that day. And how he ministered to me at Ephesus, thou very well knowest.	May our Lord allow him to find mercies with our Lord in that day. And you know well how he ministered to me in Ephesus.

Chapter 2

	KJV	*Murdock*	*Magiera*
1	Thou therefore, my son, be strong in the grace that is in Christ Jesus.	Thou therefore, my son, be strong in the grace which is by Jesus the Messiah.	You, therefore, my son, be strong in the grace which is in Jesus Christ.
2	And the things that thou hast heard of me among many witnesses, the same commit thou to faithful men, who shall be able to teach others also.	And the things thou hast heard from me by many witnesses, these commit thou to faithful men, who are competent to teach others also.	And those [things] that you have heard from me by way of many witnesses, these entrust to faithful men, who are able by their hands to teach others also.
3	Thou therefore endure hardness, as a good soldier of Jesus Christ.	And endure evils, as a good soldier of Jesus the Messiah.	And endure evil [things] as a good worker of Jesus Christ.
4	No man that warreth entangleth himself with the affairs of this life; that he may please him who hath chosen him to be a soldier.	No man, on becoming a soldier, entangleth himself with the business of the world; that he may please him who enlisted him.	No man works and is entangled with the matters of the world, so that he may please the one who chose him.
5	And if a man also strive for masteries, yet is he not crowned, except he strive lawfully.	And if one contend [in the games], he is not crowned, unless he contendeth according to the rules.	And if a man competes, he is not crowned, if he does not compete according to the rule.

Parallel Translations

II TIMOTHY *Chapter 2*

	KJV	*Murdock*	*Magiera*
6	The husbandman that laboureth must be first partaker of the fruits.	The husbandman who laboreth, ought first to feed on his fruits.	The husbandman who labors ought to be the first fed from his fruits.
7	Consider what I say; and the Lord give thee understanding in all things.	Consider what I say. Our Lord give thee wisdom in all things.	Consider closely what I say. May our Lord give you wisdom in everything.
8	Remember that Jesus Christ of the seed of David was raised from the dead according to my gospel:	Be mindful of Jesus the Messiah, that he arose from the dead; who was of the seed of David, according to my gospel,	Remember Jesus Christ, who rose from the dead who is from the seed of David, according to my gospel,
9	Wherein I suffer trouble, as an evil doer, even unto bonds; but the word of God is not bound.	in which I suffer evils unto bonds, as if an evil-doer: but the word of God is not in bonds.	in which I am suffering evil [things], even unto bonds, as though [I was] an evil-doer. But the word of God is not bound.
10	Therefore I endure all things for the elect's sakes, that they may also obtain the salvation which is in Christ Jesus with eternal glory.	Therefore I endure every thing, for the elect's sake; that they also may obtain life, in Jesus the Messiah, with eternal glory.	Because of this, I endure everything on account of the chosen [ones], so that they may also find life that is in Jesus Christ, with glory that is forever.
11	It is a faithful saying: For if we be dead with him, we shall also live with him:	Faithful is the saying, For if we shall have died with him, we shall also live with him;	The word is faithful. For if we died with him, we will also live with him.
12	If we suffer, we shall also reign with him: if we deny him, he also will deny us:	and, if we shall have suffered, we shall also reign with him. But if we shall have rejected him, he will reject us.	And if we endure, we will also reign with him. But if we deny him, he will also deny us.
13	If we believe not, yet he abideth faithful: he cannot deny himself.	And if we shall have not believed in him, he abideth in his fidelity; for he cannot reject himself.	And if we do not believe in him, he continues in his faithfulness, for he is not able to deny himself.
14	Of these things put them in remembrance, charging them before the Lord that they strive not about words to no profit, but to the subverting of the hearers.	Of these things admonish thou them . and charge [them,] before our Lord, that they dispute not, with unprofitable words, to the subversion of those who hear them.	Remind them of these [things] and give witness before our Lord, that they should not be disputing about words without profit to the overthrow of those who listen to them.
15	Study to shew thyself approved unto God, a workman that needeth not to be ashamed, rightly dividing the word of truth.	And study to present thyself before God, perfectly, a laborer who is not ashamed, one who correctly announceth the word of truth.	And you should be diligent to present yourself maturely before God, a worker without shame, who is rightly proclaiming the word of truth.
16	But shun profane and vain babblings: for they will increase unto more ungodliness.	Avoid vain discourses, in which there is no profit; for they very much add to the wickedness of those occupied with them.	And avoid empty words that have no usefulness in them, for they add more and more to the irreverence of those who are occupied with them.
17	And their word will eat as doth a canker: of whom is Hymenaeus and Philetus;	And their discourse, like an eating cancer, will lay hold upon many. And one of these is Hymeneus, and another Philetus;	And their word, as gangrene, has spread to many. And one of these is Hymenaeus and another, Philetus,

Parallel Translations

	KJV	*Murdock*	*Magiera*

II TIMOTHY *Chapter 2*

	KJV	Murdock	Magiera
18	Who concerning the truth have erred, saying that the resurrection is past already; and overthrow the faith of some.	who have wandered from the truth, while they say, The resurrection of the dead hath passed: and they subvert the faith of some.	who have erred from the truth, saying that the resurrection of the dead has happened. And they are turning away the faith of some.
19	Nevertheless the foundation of God standeth sure, having this seal, The Lord knoweth them that are his. And, Let every one that nameth the name of Christ depart from iniquity.	But the firm foundation of God standeth; and it hath this seal, The Lord knoweth them who are his: and, Let every one who invoketh the name of our Lord, stand aloof from iniquity.	But the foundation of God stands steadfast and it has this seal: AND THE LORD KNOWS THOSE WHO ARE HIS OWN. And EVERYONE WHO CALLS ON THE NAME OF THE LORD SHOULD WITHDRAW FROM WICKEDNESS.
20	But in a great house there are not only vessels of gold and of silver, but also of wood and of earth; and some to honour, and some to dishonour.	But in a great house, there are not only vessels of gold or silver, but also of wood and of pottery; and some of them for honor, and some for dishonor.	Now in a great house, there are not only vessels of gold or of silver, but there are [vessels] also of wood and of pottery, some for honor and some for dishonor.
21	If a man therefore purge himself from these, he shall be a vessel unto honour, sanctified, and meet for the master's use, and prepared unto every good work.	If therefore any one purge himself from these things, he will be a pure vessel for honor, fit for the use of his Lord, and prepared for every good work.	Therefore, if a man will cleanse himself from these [things], he will be a pure vessel for honor that is profitable for the use of his Lord and prepared for every good work.
22	Flee also youthful lusts: but follow righteousness, faith, charity, peace, with them that call on the Lord out of a pure heart.	Fly from all the lusts of youth; and follow after righteousness, and faith, and love, and peace, with them that invoke our Lord with a pure heart.	Flee from all the desires of youth and pursue uprightness and faith and love and peace, with those who call on our Lord with a pure heart.
23	But foolish and unlearned questions avoid, knowing that they do gender strifes.	Avoid those foolish discussions which afford no instruction; for thou knowest, that they generate contests.	Avoid foolish controversies [with] those who are without instruction, for you know that they generate disputes.
24	And the servant of the Lord must not strive; but be gentle unto all men, apt to teach, patient,	And a servant of our Lord ought not to contend, but to be mild towards every one, and instructive, and patient;	Now a servant of our Lord should not dispute, but he should be meek to everyone and adept at teaching and long-suffering,
25	In meekness instructing those that oppose themselves; if God peradventure will give them repentance to the acknowledging of the truth;	that with mildness he may enlighten those who dispute against him, if perhaps God may give them repentance, and they may acknowledge the truth,	so that he may guide those who argue against him with meekness, so that God will give them repentance and they will know the truth
26	And that they may recover themselves out of the snare of the devil, who are taken captive by him at his will.	and may recollect themselves, and may escape out of the snare of Satan, at whose pleasure they have been held ensnared.	and will recall [the truth] to themselves and will break away from the snare of Satan, by whom they were caught for his desire.

Chapter 3

	KJV	Murdock	Magiera
1	This know also, that in the last days perilous times shall come.	But this know thou, that in the latter days hard times will come:	But know this, that in the last days difficult times will come.

Parallel Translations

	KJV	Murdock	Magiera
	II TIMOTHY *Chapter 3*		
2	For men shall be lovers of their own selves, covetous, boasters, proud, blasphemers, disobedient to parents, unthankful, unholy,	and men will be lovers of themselves, and lovers of money, boasters, proud, censorious, unyielding towards their own people, denyers of grace, wicked,	And men will be lovers of themselves and lovers of money, boastful, proud, revilers, those who are not obedient to their parents, ungrateful, wicked,
3	Without natural affection, trucebreakers, false accusers, incontinent, fierce, despisers of those that are good,	calumniators, addicted to concupiscence, ferocious, haters of the good,	slanderers, slaves to desire, cruel, haters of good [things],
4	Traitors, heady, highminded, lovers of pleasures more than lovers of God;	treacherous, rash, inflated, attached to pleasure more than to the love of God,	traitors, unrestrained, haughty, attached to desires, more than the love of God,
5	Having a form of godliness, but denying the power thereof: from such turn away.	having a form of respect for God, but wide from the power of God. Them who are such, repel from thee.	those who have the form of reverence for God, yet are far removed from his power. Push away from you those who are so.
6	For of this sort are they which creep into houses, and lead captive silly women laden with sins, led away with divers lusts,	For of them are they who creep into this and that house, and captivate the women who are plunged in sins and led away by divers lusts,	For of them are they who creep from house to house and captivate women who are steeped in sins and are led away by various desires,
7	Ever learning, and never able to come to the knowledge of the truth.	who are always learning, and can never come to the knowledge of the truth.	who are always learning and are never able to come to the knowledge of the truth.
8	Now as Jannes and Jambres withstood Moses, so do these also resist the truth: men of corrupt minds, reprobate concerning the faith.	Now as Jannes and Jambres withstood Moses, so also do these withstand the truth: men whose mind is corrupted, and [they] reprobates from the faith.	But as Jannes and Jambres stood against Moses, so they are also standing against the truth, one whose mind is corrupt and [who] rejects the faith.
9	But they shall proceed no further: for their folly shall be manifest unto all men, as theirs also was.	But they will not make progress, for their infatuation will be understood by every one, as theirs also was understood.	But they will not go in front of them, for their folly is made known to everyone, as also theirs was made known.
10	But thou hast fully known my doctrine, manner of life, purpose, faith, longsuffering, charity, patience,	But thou hast followed after my doctrine, and my manner of life, and my aims, and my faith, and my long suffering, and my love, and my patience,	But you have followed after my teaching and after my ways and after my will and after my faith and after my long-suffering and after my love and after my patience
11	Persecutions, afflictions, which came unto me at Antioch, at Iconium, at Lystra; what persecutions I endured: but out of them all the Lord delivered me.	and my persecution, and my sufferings. And thou knowest what I endured at Antioch, and at Iconium, and at Lystra; what persecution I endured: and from all these my Lord delivered me.	and after my persecution and after my sufferings. And you know those [things] I endured in Antioch and in Iconium and in Lystra, what persecution I endured. And from all of these my Lord delivered me.
12	Yea, and all that will live godly in Christ Jesus shall suffer persecution.	And likewise all, who choose to live in the fear of God, in Jesus the Messiah, will be persecuted.	Now all those who desire to live in reverence for God in Jesus Christ will be persecuted.
13	But evil men and seducers shall wax worse and worse, deceiving, and being deceived.	But evil and seducing men will add to their wickedness, while they deceive and are deceived.	But evil and deceiving men will add to their evil, while deceiving and being deceived.

Parallel Translations

	KJV	Murdock	Magiera
	II TIMOTHY Chapter 3		
14	But continue thou in the things which thou hast learned and hast been assured of, knowing of whom thou hast learned them;	But continue thou in the things thou hast learned and been assured of; for thou knowest from whom thou learnedst;	Now you remain in those [things] that you learned and were assured of, for you know from whom you learned [them],
15	And that from a child thou hast known the holy scriptures, which are able to make thee wise unto salvation through faith which is in Christ Jesus.	because from thy childhood, thou wast taught the holy books, which can make thee wise unto life, by faith in Jesus the Messiah.	and that from your youth you were taught the holy writings, which are able to make you wise for life by the faith of Jesus Christ.
16	All scripture is given by inspiration of God, and is profitable for doctrine, for reproof, for correction, for instruction in righteousness:	All scripture that was written by the Spirit, is profitable for instruction, and for confutation, and for correction, and for erudition in righteousness;	Every writing that was written by the Spirit is profitable for teaching and for reproof and for correction and for instruction that is about uprightness,
17	That the man of God may be perfect, throughly furnished unto all good works.	that the man of God may become perfect, and complete for every good work.	so that the man of God may be mature and complete for every good work.
	Chapter 4		
1	I charge thee therefore before God, and the Lord Jesus Christ, who shall judge the quick and the dead at his appearing and his kingdom;	I charge thee, before God, and our Lord Jesus the Messiah, who is to judge the living and the dead, at the manifestation of his kingdom,	I charge you before God and our Lord Jesus Christ, who is ready to judge the dead and the living at the appearing of his kingdom.
2	Preach the word; be instant in season, out of season; reprove, rebuke, exhort with all longsuffering and doctrine.	Proclaim the word; and persist [in it] with diligence, in time and out of time; admonish, and rebuke, with all patience and instructiveness.	Proclaim the word and stand with diligence in season and out of season. Admonish and reprove with all long-suffering and teaching,
3	For the time will come when they will not endure sound doctrine; but after their own lusts shall they heap to themselves teachers, having itching ears;	For the time will come, when they will not give ear to sound teaching; but, according to their lusts, will multiply to themselves teachers, in the itching of their hearing;	for the time will come when they will not hear sound teaching, but according to their desires, they will multiply teachers to themselves in the itching of their hearing
4	And they shall turn away their ears from the truth, and shall be turned unto fables.	and will turn away their ears from the truth, and incline after fables.	and they will turn their ear[s] away from the truth and they will turn aside to fables.
5	But watch thou in all things, endure afflictions, do the work of an evangelist, make full proof of thy ministry.	But be thou vigilant in all things; and endure evils, and do the work of an evangelist, and fulfill thy ministry.	But you, be vigilant in everything and endure evil [things] and do the work of an evangelist and complete your ministry.
6	For I am now ready to be offered, and the time of my departure is at hand.	But I am soon to be immolated; and the time of my dissolution hath come.	For from now on, I am being poured out [as a drink offering] and the time that I should depart is coming.
7	I have fought a good fight, I have finished my course, I have kept the faith:	I have fought a good combat, I have completed my race, I have preserved my fidelity;	I have fought a good contest and I have completed my course and I have kept my faith.

Parallel Translations

	KJV	Murdock	Magiera

II TIMOTHY *Chapter 4*

Verse	KJV	Murdock	Magiera
8	Henceforth there is laid up for me a crown of righteousness, which the Lord, the righteous judge, shall give me at that day: and not to me only, but unto all them also that love his appearing.	and henceforth there is preserved for me a crown of righteousness, with which my Lord, the righteous Judge, will recompense me in that day; and not me only, but them also who love his manifestation.	And now a crown of uprightness is reserved for me that my Lord, who is the upright judge, will reward me in that day, and not only me, but also those who love his appearing.
9	Do thy diligence to come shortly unto me:	Exert thyself to come to me quickly.	Be diligent to come to me quickly.
10	For Demas hath forsaken me, having loved this present world, and is departed unto Thessalonica; Crescens to Galatia, Titus unto Dalmatia.	For Demas hath left me; and hath loved this world and gone away to Thessalonica; Crispus to Galatia, Titus to Dalmatia.	For Demas has left me and loved this world and gone to Thessalonica, Crescens to Galatia and Titus to Dalmatia.
11	Only Luke is with me. Take Mark, and bring him with thee: for he is profitable to me for the ministry.	Luke only is with me. Take Mark, and bring him with thee; for he is suitable for me, for ministration.	Only Luke is with me. Take Mark and bring him with you, for he is profitable to me for the ministry.
12	And Tychicus have I sent to Ephesus.	And Tychicus I have sent to Ephesus.	And I have sent Tychicus to Ephesus.
13	The cloke that I left at Troas with Carpus, when thou comest, bring with thee, and the books, but especially the parchments.	And when thou comest, bring the bookcase, which I left at Troas with Carpus, and the books, but especially the roll of parchments.	And when you come, bring the book-carrier that I left in Troas with Carpus and the books, especially the rolls of parchments.
14	Alexander the coppersmith did me much evil: the Lord reward him according to his works:	Alexander the coppersmith showed me many ills: our Lord will reward him according to his doings.	Alexander, the silversmith, showed me many evil [things]. Our Lord will reward him according to his works.
15	Of whom be thou ware also; for he hath greatly withstood our words.	And do thou also beware of him; for he is very insolent against our words.	Now also, you beware of him, for he is very puffed up against our words.
16	At my first answer no man stood with me, but all men forsook me: I pray God that it may not be laid to their charge.	At my first defence, no one was with me, but they all forsook me. Let not this be reckoned to them.	In my first defense, no man was with me, but all of them left me. Do not count this to them.
17	Notwithstanding the Lord stood with me, and strengthened me; that by me the preaching might be fully known, and that all the Gentiles might hear: and I was delivered out of the mouth of the lion.	But my Lord stood by me, and strengthened me; that by me the preaching might be fulfilled; and [that] all the Gentiles might hear: and I was rescued from the mouth of the lion.	But my Lord stood by me and strengthened me, that by me, the preaching would be completed and all the Gentiles would hear that I was rescued from the mouth of the lion.
18	And the Lord shall deliver me from every evil work, and will preserve me unto his heavenly kingdom: to whom be glory for ever and ever. Amen.	And my Lord will rescue me from every evil work; and will give me life in his heavenly kingdom. To him be glory, for ever and ever. Amen.	And my Lord will rescue me from every evil work and will give me life in his kingdom that is in heaven. To him [be] glory, forever and ever. Amen.
19	Salute Prisca and Aquila, and the household of Onesiphorus.	Present a salutation to Priscilla and Aquila, and to the household of Onesiphorus.	Greet Priscilla and Aquila and the house of Onesiphorus.
20	Erastus abode at Corinth: but Trophimus have I left at Miletum sick.	Erastus hath stopped at Corinth; and Trophimus I left sick at the city of Miletus.	Erastus stayed in Corinth and I left Trophimus sick in the city of Miletus.

Parallel Translations

	KJV	Murdock	Magiera
	II TIMOTHY	*Chapter 4*	
21	Do thy diligence to come before winter. Eubulus greeteth thee, and Pudens, and Linus, and Claudia, and all the brethren.	Exert thyself to come before winter. Eubulus saluteth thee, and Pudens, and Linus, and Claudia, and all the brethren.	Be diligent to come before winter. Eubulus greets you and Pudens and Linus and Claudia and all the brothers.
22	The Lord Jesus Christ be with thy spirit. Grace be with you. Amen.	Our Lord Jesus the Messiah be with thy spirit. Grace be with thee. Amen.	Our Lord Jesus Christ [be] with your spirit. Grace [be] with you. Amen.

Parallel Translations

	KJV	*Murdock*	*Magiera*
	TITUS *Chapter 1*		
1	Paul, a servant of God, and an apostle of Jesus Christ, according to the faith of God's elect, and the acknowledging of the truth which is after godliness;	Paul, a servant of God, and a legate of Jesus the Messiah; according to the faith of the elect of God, and the knowledge of the truth which is in the fear of God,	Paul, a servant of God and an apostle of Jesus Christ, according to the faith of the chosen [ones] of God and the knowledge of the truth that is by reverence for God,
2	In hope of eternal life, which God, that cannot lie, promised before the world began;	concerning the hope of eternal life, which the veracious God promised before the times of the world;	concerning the hope of eternal life, which the true God promised before the times of the age
3	But hath in due times manifested his word through preaching, which is committed unto me according to the commandment of God our Saviour;	and in due time he hath manifested his word, by means of our announcement, which was confided to me by the command of God our Life-giver;	and manifested his word in its time by way of our preaching, [with] which I was entrusted by the commandment of God our Life-giver,
4	To Titus, mine own son after the common faith: Grace, mercy, and peace, from God the Father and the Lord Jesus Christ our Saviour.	to Titus, a real son after the common faith: Grace and peace from God our Father, and from our Lord Jesus the Messiah, our Life-giver.	to Titus, a true son in the common faith: Grace and peace from God the Father and from our Lord Jesus Christ, our Life-giver.
5	For this cause left I thee in Crete, that thou shouldest set in order the things that are wanting, and ordain elders in every city, as I had appointed thee:	For this cause left I thee in Crete, that thou mightest regulate the things deficient, and establish elders in every city, as I directed thee:	Because of this, I had left you in Crete, that you would set in order those [things] that were lacking and [that] you would ordain elders in every city as I commanded you.
6	If any be blameless, the husband of one wife, having faithful children not accused of riot or unruly.	him who is blameless, who is the husband of one wife, and hath believing children, who are no revellers, nor ungovernable in sensuality.	[He should be] one who is without blame and is the husband of one wife and has faithful children, who are not speaking evil and are not unruly with intemperance.
7	For a bishop must be blameless, as the steward of God; not selfwilled, not soon angry, not given to wine, no striker, not given to filthy lucre;	For an elder ought to be blameless, as the steward of God; and not be self-willed, nor irascible, nor excessive in wine, nor with hands swift to strike, nor a lover of base gains.	For it is required that an elder should be without blame as a steward of God and should not be led by his own mind and should not be full of rage and should not be a transgressor concerning wine and should not be swift to strike [with] his hand and should not be a lover of corrupt profits.
8	But a lover of hospitality, a lover of good men, sober, just, holy, temperate;	But he should be a lover of strangers, and a lover of good [deeds], and be sober, upright, kind-hearted, and restraining himself from evil passions;	But he should be a lover of strangers and he should be a lover of good [things] and he should be sober and he should be upright and he should be pure and keeping himself from passions

Parallel Translations

TITUS Chapter 1

	KJV	Murdock	Magiera
9	Holding fast the faithful word as he hath been taught, that he may be able by sound doctrine both to exhort and to convince the gainsayers.	and studious of the doctrine of the word of faith, that he may be able by his wholesome teaching both to console, and to rebuke them that are contentious.	and being diligent concerning the teaching of the word of faith, so that he may also be able to encourage by his sound teaching and to reprove those who are quarrelsome.
10	For there are many unruly and vain talkers and deceivers, specially they of the circumcision:	For many are unsubmissive, and their discourses vain; and they mislead the minds of people, especially such as are of the circumcision.	For there are many who are not submissive and their words are empty and they are deceiving the minds of men, especially those who are from the circumcision.
11	Whose mouths must be stopped, who subvert whole houses, teaching things which they ought not, for filthy lucre's sake.	The mouth of these ought to be stopped: they corrupt many families; and they teach what they ought not, for the sake of base gains.	Their mouth[s] ought to be shut closely, for they are corrupting many families and are teaching what is not right because of corrupt profits.
12	One of themselves, even a prophet of their own, said, The Cretians are alway liars, evil beasts, slow bellies.	One of them, a prophet of their own, said, The Cretans are always mendacious, evil beasts, idle bellies.	One of them, their own prophet, said, "The Cretans are always liars, evil beasts and idle gluttons,"
13	This witness is true. Wherefore rebuke them sharply, that they may be sound in the faith;	And this testimony is true. Therefore chide them sharply; that they may be sound in the faith,	and this testimony is truthful. Because of this, reprove them sharply that they should be sound in the faith
14	Not giving heed to Jewish fables, and commandments of men, that turn from the truth.	and may not throw themselves into Jewish fables, and into the precepts of men who hate the truth.	and [that] they should not yield to the fables of the Judeans and the commandments of men who hate the truth.
15	Unto the pure all things are pure: but unto them that are defiled and unbelieving is nothing pure; but even their mind and conscience is defiled.	For to the pure, every thing is pure; but to them who are defiled and unbelieving, nothing is pure; but their understanding is defiled, and their conscience.	For everything is pure to the pure, but those who are corrupted and unbelieving do not have what is pure, but their mind is corrupted and their conscience.
16	They profess that they know God; but in works they deny him, being abominable, and disobedient, and unto every good work reprobate.	And they profess that they know God, but in their works they deny him; and they are odious, and disobedient, and to every good work reprobates.	And they profess to know God, but by their works they deny him and they are detestable and disobedient and rejecters of every good work.

Chapter 2

	KJV	Murdock	Magiera
1	But speak thou the things which become sound doctrine:	But speak thou the things that belong to wholesome doctrine.	But you, speak what is suitable to sound teaching.
2	That the aged men be sober, grave, temperate, sound in faith, in charity, in patience.	And teach the older men to be watchful in their minds, and to be sober, and to be pure, and to be sound in the faith, and in love and in patience.	And teach the elders that they should be watchful in their minds and should be sober and should be pure and should be sound in faith and in love and in patience.

Parallel Translations

	KJV	*Murdock*	*Magiera*

TITUS *Chapter 2*

	KJV	Murdock	Magiera
3	The aged women likewise, that they be in behaviour as becometh holiness, not false accusers, not given to much wine, teachers of good things;	And so also the elder women, that they be in behavior as becometh the fear of God; and not to be slanderers; and not to be addicted to much wine; and to be inculcators of good things,	And also [teach] the elder women likewise that they should be in behavior as is suitable for reverence to God and should not be slanderers and should not be enslaved to much wine and [that] they should be teachers of good [things]
4	That they may teach the young women to be sober, to love their husbands, to love their children,	making the younger women to be modest, to love their husbands and their children,	and moderating those who are younger [women], so that they love their husbands and their children
5	To be discreet, chaste, keepers at home, good, obedient to their own husbands, that the word of God be not blasphemed.	to be chaste and holy, and to take good care of their households, and to be obedient to their husbands; so that no one may reproach the word of God.	and they should be moderate and holy and should be good caretakers of their houses and should be subject to their husbands, so that no one will profane the word of God.
6	Young men likewise exhort to be sober minded.	And likewise exhort young men to be sober.	And likewise, request those who are young [men] to be sober.
7	In all things shewing thyself a pattern of good works: in doctrine shewing uncorruptness, gravity, sincerity,	And in every thing show thyself a pattern, as to all good works: and in thy teaching, let thy discourse be healthful,	Now in everything, show yourself as an example in all good works. And in your teaching, you should have sound speech
8	Sound speech, that cannot be condemned; that he that is of the contrary part may be ashamed, having no evil thing to say of you.	such as is sober and uncorrupt; and let no one despise it: so that he who riseth up against us, may be ashamed, seeing he can say nothing odious against us.	that is moderate and not corrupt. And [let] no one despise it, so that he who stands against us will be ashamed, not being able to say anything hateful against us.
9	Exhort servants to be obedient unto their own masters, and to please them well in all things; not answering again;	Let servants obey their masters in every thing, and strive to please them, and not contradict, nor pilfer;	Servants should serve their masters in everything and should be pleasing and not be disputing
10	Not purloining, but shewing all good fidelity; that they may adorn the doctrine of God our Saviour in all things.	but let them manifest that their fidelity, in all respects, is good: so that they may adorn the doctrine of God our Life-giver, in all things.	and not stealing. But they should demonstrate their integrity in everything, so that in everything they may adorn the teaching of God, our Life-giver.
11	For the grace of God that bringeth salvation hath appeared to all men,	For the all-vivifying grace of God, is revealed to all men;	For the grace of God, the Life-giver of all, is revealed to all men
12	Teaching us that, denying ungodliness and worldly lusts, we should live soberly, righteously, and godly, in this present world;	and it teacheth us, to deny ungodliness and worldly lusts, and to live in this world in sobriety, and in uprightness, and in the fear of God,	and instructs us to deny irreverence and the passions of the world and to live in this world with moderation and with justice and with reverence for God,
13	Looking for that blessed hope, and the glorious appearing of the great God and our Saviour Jesus Christ;	looking for the blessed hope, and the manifestation of the glory of the great God, and our Life-giver, Jesus the Messiah;	looking for the blessed hope and for the manifestation of the glory of the great God and our Life-giver, Jesus Christ,

Parallel Translations

TITUS Chapter 2

	KJV	Murdock	Magiera
14	Who gave himself for us, that he might redeem us from all iniquity, and purify unto himself a peculiar people, zealous of good works.	who gave himself for us, that he might recover us from all iniquity, and purify for himself a new people, who are zealous in good works.	who gave himself for us, so that he could deliver us from all wickedness and would purify for himself a new people who are zealous in good works.
15	These things speak, and exhort, and rebuke with all authority. Let no man despise thee.	These things speak thou, and exhort, and inculcate, with all authority; and let no one despise thee.	Speak these [things] and entreat and reprove with all authority and let no one despise you.

Chapter 3

	KJV	Murdock	Magiera
1	Put them in mind to be subject to principalities and powers, to obey magistrates, to be ready to every good work,	And admonish them to be submissive and obedient to princes and potentates; and that they be ready for every good work;	And remind them that they should obey and should be subject to rulers and to authorities and that they should be prepared for every good work
2	To speak evil of no man, to be no brawlers, but gentle, shewing all meekness unto all men.	and that they speak ill of no man; that they be not contentious, but mild; and that in every thing they manifest benignity towards all men.	and they should not revile anyone and should not be contentious, but rather they should be humble and they should demonstrate their kindness to all men in everything.
3	For we ourselves also were sometimes foolish, disobedient, deceived, serving divers lusts and pleasures, living in malice and envy, hateful, and hating one another.	For we also were formerly reckless, and disobedient, and erring, and serving divers lusts, and living in malice and envy, and were hateful and also hating one another.	For we were also previously without sense and we were disobedient and we were erring and we were serving various passions and we were occupied with wickedness and with envy and we were being hateful. We were even hating one another.
4	But after that the kindness and love of God our Saviour toward man appeared,	But when the kindness and compassion of God our Life-giver was revealed,	But when the kindness and compassion of God, our Life-giver, was revealed,
5	Not by works of righteousness which we have done, but according to his mercy he saved us, by the washing of regeneration, and renewing of the Holy Ghost;	not by works of righteousness which we had done, but according to his mercy, he vivified us, by the washing of the new birth, and by the renovation of the Holy Spirit,	not by works of justification that we did, but by his own mercies, he gave us life by the washing of the birth from above and by the renewing of the Holy Spirit,
6	Which he shed on us abundantly through Jesus Christ our Saviour;	which he shed on us abundantly, by Jesus the Messiah our Life-giver:	which he poured out on us abundantly by way of Jesus Christ, our Life-giver,
7	That being justified by his grace, we should be made heirs according to the hope of eternal life.	that we might be justified by his grace, and become heirs in the hope of eternal life.	that we would be justified by his grace and would be heirs in the hope of eternal life.
8	This is a faithful saying, and these things I will that thou affirm constantly, that they which have believed in God might be careful to maintain good works. These things are good and profitable unto men.	Faithful is the word: and in these things, I would have thee also establish them; so that they, who have believed in God, may be careful to cultivate good works: these are the things, which are good, and profitable to men.	The word is faithful. And these [things] I want you also to affirm to them, so that those who have believed in God may be diligent to perform good works. These [things] are good and profitable for men.

	KJV	Murdock	Magiera
	TITUS	*Chapter 3*	
9	But avoid foolish questions, and genealogies, and contentions, and strivings about the law; for they are unprofitable and vain.	But foolish questions, and stories of genealogies, and the disputes and contests of the scribes, avoid: for there is no profit in them, and they are vain.	But withdraw from foolish questioning and from accounts of genealogies and from contentions and from disputes of the scribes. For there is no profit in them and they are fruitless.
10	A man that is an heretick after the first and second admonition reject;	An heretical man, after thou hast instructed him once and again, avoid:	Withdraw from a heretical man after you have instructed him once and again.
11	Knowing that he that is such is subverted, and sinneth, being condemned of himself.	and know thou, that such a man is perverse, and sinful, and self-condemned.	And know that he who is so is perverse and sinful and he has condemned himself.
12	When I shall send Artemas unto thee, or Tychicus, be diligent to come unto me to Nicopolis: for I have determined there to winter.	When I shall send Artemas to thee, or Tychicus, strive thou to come to me at Nicopolis; for I have purposed to winter there.	When I send to you Artemas or Tychicus, be diligent to come to me at Nicopolis, for I have decided to winter there.
13	Bring Zenas the lawyer and Apollos on their journey diligently, that nothing be wanting unto them.	As for Zenas the scribe, and Apollos, endeavor to help them well on their way, that they may want nothing.	But concerning Zenas, the scribe, and concerning Apollos, be diligent to escort them well [on their journey], so that they should lack nothing.
14	And let ours also learn to maintain good works for necessary uses, that they be not unfruitful.	And let our people learn also to perform good works, on occasions of emergency, that they may not be unfruitful.	And those who are our own should also learn to perform good works in matters that are pressing, so that they will not be without fruit.
15	All that are with me salute thee. Greet them that love us in the faith. Grace be with you all. Amen.	All they that are with me salute thee. Salute all them who love us in the faith. Grace be with you all. Amen.	All those who are with me greet you. Greet all those who love us in the faith. Grace [be] with all of you. Amen.

Parallel Translations

PHILEMON

	KJV	Murdock	Magiera
1	Paul, a prisoner of Jesus Christ, and Timothy our brother, unto Philemon our dearly beloved, and fellowlabourer,	PAUL, a prisoner of Jesus the Messiah, and Timothy a brother;--- to the beloved Philemon, a laborer with us,	Paul, the prisoner of Jesus Christ, and Timothy, a brother, to Philemon, beloved and a worker who is with us,
2	And to our beloved Apphia, and Archippus our fellowsoldier, and to the church in thy house:	and to our beloved Apphia, and to Archippus a laborer with us, and to the church in thy house.	and to our beloved Apphia, and to Archippus, a worker who is with us, and to the church that is in your house:
3	Grace to you, and peace, from God our Father and the Lord Jesus Christ.	Grace be with you, and peace from God our father, and from our Lord Jesus the Messiah.	Grace [be] with you and peace from God our Father and from our Lord Jesus Christ.
4	I thank my God, making mention of thee always in my prayers,	I thank my God always, and remember thee in my prayers,	I thank my God always and I remember you in my prayers,
5	Hearing of thy love and faith, which thou hast toward the Lord Jesus, and toward all saints;	lo, from the time that I heard of thy faith, and of the love thou hast towards our Lord Jesus, and towards all the saints;	since I heard of your faith and the love that you have toward our Lord Jesus and toward all the holy [ones],
6	That the communication of thy faith may become effectual by the acknowledging of every good thing which is in you in Christ Jesus.	that there may be a fellowship of thy faith, yielding fruits in works, and in the knowledge of all the good things ye possess in Jesus the Messiah.	that the fellowship of your faith may yield fruit in works and in the knowledge of all the good [things] that you have in Jesus Christ.
7	For we have great joy and consolation in thy love, because the bowels of the saints are refreshed by thee, brother.	For we have great joy and consolation, because the bowels of the saints are refreshed by thy love.	For we have great joy and comfort, because by your love the bowels of the holy [ones] are refreshed.
8	Wherefore, though I might be much bold in Christ to enjoin thee that which is convenient,	Therefore I might have great freedom in the Messiah, to enjoin upon thee the things that are right.	Because of this, I have great boldness in Christ to command you [to do] those [things] which are just.
9	Yet for love's sake I rather beseech thee, being such an one as Paul the aged, and now also a prisoner of Jesus Christ.	But for love's sake, I earnestly beseech thee---even I, Paul, who am aged, as thou knowest, and now also a prisoner for Jesus the Messiah.	But because of love, I earnestly beg you, I, Paul, who am old, as you know, and now also am a prisoner of Jesus Christ.
10	I beseech thee for my son Onesimus, whom I have begotten in my bonds:	I beseech thee for my son, whom I had begotten in my bonds---for Onesimus;	And I am begging you concerning my son, whom I have born in my bonds, Onesimus,
11	Which in time past was to thee unprofitable, but now profitable to thee and to me:	from whom formerly thou hadst no profit, but now very profitable will he be both to thee and to me; and whom I have sent to thee.	in whom at one time you had no profit, but now is very profitable both to you and also to me.
12	Whom I have sent again: thou therefore receive him, that is, mine own bowels:	And receive thou him, as one begotten by me.	And I have sent him to you. So now, receive him as one born by me.
13	Whom I would have retained with me, that in thy stead he might have ministered unto me in the bonds of the gospel:	For I was desirous to retain him with me, that he might minister to me in thy stead, in these bonds for the gospel.	For I wanted to keep him with me that he should minister to me instead of you during [my] bonds for the gospel.

Parallel Translations

	KJV	*Murdock*	*Magiera*
	PHILEMON		
14	But without thy mind would I do nothing; that thy benefit should not be as it were of necessity, but willingly.	But I would do nothing without consulting thee; lest thy benefit should be as if by compulsion, and not with thy pleasure.	But I did not want to do anything without your counsel, so that your goodness would not be with compulsion, but by your [free] will.
15	For perhaps he therefore departed for a season, that thou shouldest receive him for ever;	And, perhaps, also, he therefore departed from thee for a season, that thou mightest retain him for ever;	Now perhaps, even because of this, he went away for a time, so that you may keep him forever,
16	Not now as a servant, but above a servant, a brother beloved, specially to me, but how much more unto thee, both in the flesh, and in the Lord?	henceforth, not as a servant, but more than a servant, a brother dear to me, and much more to thee, both in the flesh and in our Lord?	from now on, not as a servant, but [as] more than a servant, my own beloved brother, how much more your own, both in the flesh and in our Lord.
17	If thou count me therefore a partner, receive him as myself.	If therefore thou art in fellowship with me, receive him as one of mine.	Therefore, if you are a partner with me, receive him as [you would] me.
18	If he hath wronged thee, or oweth thee ought, put that on mine account;	And if he hath wronged thee, or oweth thee aught, place it to my account.	And if he has harmed you or he owes [you] anything, count this to me.
19	I Paul have written it with mine own hand, I will repay it: albeit I do not say to thee how thou owest unto me even thine own self besides.	I, Paul, have written [it] with my own hand, I will repay:---not to say to thee, that to me thou owest thy ownself.	I, Paul, have written with my hands [that] I will repay. I will not say to you that you also owe your life to me.
20	Yea, brother, let me have joy of thee in the Lord: refresh my bowels in the Lord.	Yes, my brother, let me be refreshed by thee in our Lord: refresh thou my bowels in the Messiah.	Yes, my brother, I [want] to be refreshed by you in our Lord. Refresh my bowels in Christ.
21	Having confidence in thy obedience I wrote unto thee, knowing that thou wilt also do more than I say.	Being confident that thou wilt hearken to me, I have written to thee: and I know that thou wilt do more than I say.	Because I am confident that you will obey me, I have written to you and I know that you will do more than I say.
22	But withal prepare me also a lodging: for I trust that through your prayers I shall be given unto you.	And herewith, prepare also a house for me to lodge in; for I hope that, by your prayers, I shall be given to you.	And one [more thing] also, prepare for me a guest house, for I hope that by your prayers I will be given to you.
23	There salute thee Epaphras, my fellowprisoner in Christ Jesus;	Epaphras, a fellow-captive with me in Jesus the Messiah, saluteth thee;	Epaphras, a captive who is with me in Jesus Christ, greets you,
24	Marcus, Aristarchus, Demas, Lucas, my fellowlabourers.	and Mark, and Aristarchus, and Demas, and Luke, my coadjutors.	and Mark and Aristarchus and Demas and Luke, my helpers.
25	The grace of our Lord Jesus Christ be with your spirit. Amen.	The grace of our Lord Jesus the Messiah be with your spirit, my brethren.---Amen.	The grace of our Lord Jesus Christ [be] with your spirit. Amen.

Parallel Translations

	KJV	*Murdock*	*Magiera*
	HEBREWS	*Chapter 1*	
1	God, who at sundry times and in divers manners spake in time past unto the fathers by the prophets,	In many ways, and many forms, God anciently conversed with our fathers, by the prophets:	In all ways and in all forms, God spoke previously with our fathers by the prophets.
2	Hath in these last days spoken unto us by his Son, whom he hath appointed heir of all things, by whom also he made the worlds;	But in these latter days, he hath conversed with us, by his Son; whom he hath constituted heir of all things, and by whom he made the worlds;	And in these last days, he has spoken to us by his Son, whom he appointed heir of everything and by whom he made the ages,
3	Who being the brightness of his glory, and the express image of his person, and upholding all things by the word of his power, when he had by himself purged our sins, sat down on the right hand of the Majesty on high;	who is the splendor of his glory, and the image of himself, and upholdeth all by the energy of his word; and by himself he made a purgation of sins, and sat down on the right hand of the Majesty on high.	who is the radiance of his glory and the image of his being and almighty by the power of his word. And in his person, he accomplished the cleansing of our sins and sat down at the right hand of majesty in the high places.
4	Being made so much better than the angels, as he hath by inheritance obtained a more excellent name than they.	And he is altogether superior to the angels, as he hath also inherited a name which excelleth theirs.	And this [one] is greater than the angels in every way, even as the name that he inherited is greater than theirs.
5	For unto which of the angels said he at any time, Thou art my Son, this day have I begotten thee? And again, I will be to him a Father, and he shall be to me a Son?	For to which of the angels did God ever say, Thou art my SON, this day have I begotten thee? And again, I will be to him a Father, and he shall be to me a Son?	For to which of the angels did God ever say: YOU ARE MY SON, THIS DAY I HAVE FATHERED YOU, and again, I WILL BE A FATHER TO HIM AND HE WILL BE A SON TO ME?
6	And again, when he bringeth in the firstbegotten into the world, he saith, And let all the angels of God worship him.	And again, when bringing the first begotten into the world, he said: Let all the angels of God worship him.	And again, when he brought the firstborn into the world, he said: LET ALL THE ANGELS OF GOD WORSHIP HIM.
7	And of the angels he saith, Who maketh his angels spirits, and his ministers a flame of fire.	But of the angels he thus said: Who made his angels a wind, and his ministers a flaming fire.	But about the angels he spoke so: HE MADE HIS ANGELS A WIND AND HIS MINISTERS A FLAMING FIRE.
8	But unto the Son he saith, Thy throne, O God, is for ever and ever: a sceptre of righteousness is the sceptre of thy kingdom.	But of the Son he said: Thy throne, O God, is for ever and ever; a righteous sceptre is the sceptre of thy kingdom.	But concerning the Son he said: YOUR THRONE, GOD, [IS] FOREVER. AN UPRIGHT SCEPTER [IS] THE SCEPTER OF YOUR KINGDOM.
9	Thou hast loved righteousness, and hated iniquity; therefore God, even thy God, hath anointed thee with the oil of gladness above thy fellows.	Thou hast loved rectitude, and hated iniquity; therefore God, thy God, hath anointed thee with the oil of gladness more than thy associates.	YOU LOVE UPRIGHTNESS AND HATE WICKEDNESS. BECAUSE OF THIS, GOD, YOUR GOD, HAS ANOINTED YOU WITH THE OIL OF GLADNESS MORE THAN YOUR COMPANIONS.
10	And, Thou, Lord, in the beginning hast laid the foundation of the earth; and the heavens are the works of thine hands:	And again, Thou hast from the beginning laid the foundations of the earth, and the heavens are the work of thy hands:	And again: FROM THE BEGINNING YOU HAVE LAID THE FOUNDATIONS OF THE EARTH AND HEAVEN, [WHICH] ARE THE WORK OF YOUR HANDS.

Parallel Translations

	KJV	*Murdock*	*Magiera*

HEBREWS *Chapter 1*

	KJV	Murdock	Magiera
11	They shall perish; but thou remainest; and they all shall wax old as doth a garment;	they will pass away, but thou endurest; and they all, like a robe, wax old;	THEY WILL PASS AWAY, YET YOU WILL ENDURE, AND ALL OF THEM WILL GROW OLD AS A GARMENT
12	And as a vesture shalt thou fold them up, and they shall be changed: but thou art the same, and thy years shall not fail.	and like a cloak, thou wilt fold them up. They will be changed; but thou wilt be as thou art, and thy years will not be finished.	AND AS AN OVERCOAT YOU WILL ROLL THEM UP. THEY WILL BE CHANGED, YET YOU WILL BE AS YOU ARE AND YOUR YEARS WILL NOT END.
13	But to which of the angels said he at any time, Sit on my right hand, until I make thine enemies thy footstool?	And to which of the angels did he ever say: Sit thou at my right hand, until I shall place thy enemies a footstool under thy feet?	And to which of the angels did he ever say: SIT AT MY RIGHT HAND UNTIL I PLACE YOUR ENEMIES [AS] A FOOTSTOOL UNDER YOUR FEET?
14	Are they not all ministering spirits, sent forth to minister for them who shall be heirs of salvation?	Are they not all spirits of ministration, who are sent to minister on account of them that are to inherit life?	Behold, are they not all spirits of service who are sent in service on account of those who are about to inherit life?

Chapter 2

	KJV	Murdock	Magiera
1	Therefore we ought to give the more earnest heed to the things which we have heard, lest at any time we should let them slip.	Therefore we ought to be exceedingly cautious, in regard to what we have heard, lest we fall away.	Because of this, we ought to be especially cautious in what we have heard, so that we will not fall.
2	For if the word spoken by angels was stedfast, and every transgression and disobedience received a just recompence of reward;	For if the word uttered by the medium of angels was confirmed, and every one who heard it, and transgressed it, received a just retribution;	For if the word that was spoken by way of angels was confirmed and all who heard it and transgressed against it received a reward with uprightness,
3	How shall we escape, if we neglect so great salvation; which at the first began to be spoken by the Lord, and was confirmed unto us by them that heard him;	how shall we escape, if we despise the things which are our life, things which began to be spoken by our Lord, and were confirmed to us by them who heard from him,	how will we escape, if we despise those [things] that are our life, those that began to be spoken by our Lord and were confirmed in us by those who heard,
4	God also bearing them witness, both with signs and wonders, and with divers miracles, and gifts of the Holy Ghost, according to his own will?	while God gave testimony concerning them, by signs and wonders, and by various miracles and distributions of the Holy Spirit, which were given according to his pleasure?	God being a witness about them with signs and with wonders and with various miracles and with distributions of the Holy Spirit that were given according to his will?
5	For unto the angels hath he not put in subjection the world to come, whereof we speak.	For to the angels he hath not subjected the world to come, of which we speak.	For he did not subject the age that is to come, about which we speak, to angels.
6	But one in a certain place testified, saying, What is man, that thou art mindful of him? or the son of man, that thou visitest him?	But as the scripture testifieth, and saith: What is man, that thou art mindful of him? and the son of man, that thou attendest to him?	But as the scripture witnesses and says: WHAT IS MAN THAT YOU REMEMBER HIM AND THE SON OF MAN THAT YOU VISIT HIM?

Parallel Translations

	KJV	*Murdock*	*Magiera*
	HEBREWS	*Chapter 2*	
7	Thou madest him a little lower than the angels; thou crownedst him with glory and honour, and didst set him over the works of thy hands:	Thou hast depressed him somewhat lower than the angels: glory and honor hast thou put on his head; and thou hast invested him with authority over the work of thy hand.	YOU HUMBLED HIM LOWER THAN THE ANGELS. YOU PLACED ON HIS HEAD GLORY AND HONOR AND GAVE HIM AUTHORITY OVER THE WORK OF YOUR HANDS
8	Thou hast put all things in subjection under his feet. For in that he put all in subjection under him, he left nothing that is not put under him. But now we see not yet all things put under him.	And all things hast thou subjected under his feet. And in this subjecting of all things to him, he omitted nothing, which he did not subject. But now, we do not yet see all things subjected to him.	AND YOU SUBJECTED EVERYTHING UNDER HIS FEET. Now in that he subjected everything to him, he did not leave out anything that was not subjected. But now, we do not yet see that everything is subjected to him.
9	But we see Jesus, who was made a little lower than the angels for the suffering of death, crowned with glory and honour; that he by the grace of God should taste death for every man.	But we see him, who was depressed somewhat lower than the angels, to be this Jesus, because of the passion of his death; and glory and honor are placed on his head; for God himself, in his grace, tasted death for all men.	But we see him, who was humbled lower than the angels, to be [this] Jesus, because of the suffering of his death. And glory and honor are placed on his head, for by the grace of God, he tasted death in place of everyone.
10	For it became him, for whom are all things, and by whom are all things, in bringing many sons unto glory, to make the captain of their salvation perfect through sufferings.	For it became him, by whom are all things, and on account of whom are all things, and [who] bringeth many sons unto his glory, to perfect the prince of their life by suffering.	For it was proper for him, by whose hand everything [was] and for whose sake everything [was] and [who] brought many sons into glory, that he should perfect the prince of their life by his suffering.
11	For both he that sanctifieth and they who are sanctified are all of one: for which cause he is not ashamed to call them brethren,	For he that sanctifieth, and they who are sanctified, are all of one [nature]. Therefore he is not ashamed to call them brethren;	For he who makes holy and those who are made holy are all of one. Because of this, he is not ashamed to call them his brothers,
12	Saying, I will declare thy name unto my brethren, in the midst of the church will I sing praise unto thee.	as he saith, I will announce thy name to my brethren; in the midst of the assembly, I will praise thee.	saying: I WILL ANNOUNCE YOUR NAME TO MY BROTHERS AND I WILL PRAISE YOU WITHIN THE CHURCH.
13	And again, I will put my trust in him. And again, Behold I and the children which God hath given me.	And again, I will confide in him. And again, Behold me, and the children whom thou, God, hast given to me.	And again: I WILL BE CONFIDENT ABOUT HIM, and again, BEHOLD, I AND THE CHILDREN THAT GOD HAS GIVEN ME.
14	Forasmuch then as the children are partakers of flesh and blood, he also himself likewise took part of the same; that through death he might destroy him that had the power of death, that is, the devil;	For because the children participated in flesh and blood, he also, in like manner, took part in the same; that, by his death, he might bring to naught him who held the dominion of death, namely Satan;	For because the sons share in flesh and blood, he also in the same manner shared of the same, that by his death he would put a stop to him who held the authority of death, who is Satan,
15	And deliver them who through fear of death were all their lifetime subject to bondage.	and might release them, who, through fear of death, are all their lives subject to bondage.	and would release those who by fear of death were subjected to bondage all their lives.

Parallel Translations

	KJV	*Murdock*	*Magiera*

HEBREWS *Chapter 2*

	KJV	Murdock	Magiera
16	For verily he took not on him the nature of angels; but he took on him the seed of Abraham.	For he did not assume [a nature] from angels, but he assumed [a nature] from the seed of Abraham.	For he did not assume [a nature] from the angels, but he assumed death from the seed of Abraham.
17	Wherefore in all things it behoved him to be made like unto his brethren, that he might be a merciful and faithful high priest in things pertaining to God, to make reconciliation for the sins of the people.	Wherefore it was right, that he should be in all respects like his brethren; that he might be merciful, and a high priest faithful in the things of God, and might make expiation for the sins of the people.	Because of this, it is right that he should be made like his brothers in everything, so that he would be a merciful and faithful high priest in the things of God and would make atonement for the sins of the people.
18	For in that he himself hath suffered being tempted, he is able to succour them that are tempted.	For, in that he himself hath suffered, and been tempted, he is able to succor them who are tempted.	For in that which he [himself] suffered and was tempted, he is able to help those who are tempted.

Chapter 3

	KJV	Murdock	Magiera
1	Wherefore, holy brethren, partakers of the heavenly calling, consider the Apostle and High Priest of our profession, Christ Jesus;	Wherefore, my holy brethren, who are called with a calling that is from heaven, consider this Legate and High Priest of our profession, Jesus the Messiah:	Therefore, my holy brothers, who are called with a calling that is from heaven, consider this apostle and high priest of our confession, Jesus Christ,
2	Who was faithful to him that appointed him, as also Moses was faithful in all his house.	who was faithful to him that made him, as was Moses in all his house.	who was faithful to him who made him, as [was] Moses with all his house.
3	For this man was counted worthy of more glory than Moses, inasmuch as he who hath builded the house hath more honour than the house.	For much greater is the glory of this man, than that of Moses; just as the glory of the builder of a house, is greater than that of the edifice.	For the glory of this [man] is much greater than that of Moses, just as the honor of the builder of the house [is] much greater than [that of] his building.
4	For every house is builded by some man; but he that built all things is God.	For every house is built by some man; but he who buildeth all things is God.	For every house is built by someone, but he who builds all is God.
5	And Moses verily was faithful in all his house, as a servant, for a testimony of those things which were to be spoken after;	And Moses, as a servant, was faithful in all the house, for an attestation to those things that were to be spoken by him:	And Moses, as a servant, was faithful in all his house, for a witness of those [things] that were going to be, [that] were spoken by way of him.
6	But Christ as a son over his own house; whose house are we, if we hold fast the confidence and the rejoicing of the hope firm unto the end.	but the Messiah as the SON, [is] over his own house; and we are his house, if we retain unto the end assurance, and the triumph of hope in him.	Now Christ, as the Son, [is] over his house. And we are his house, if we hold fast the boldness and the boasting of his hope to the end.
7	Wherefore (as the Holy Ghost saith, To day if ye will hear his voice,	Because the Holy Spirit hath said: To-day, if ye will hear his voice,	Because the Holy Spirit said, TODAY IF YOU WILL HEAR HIS VOICE,
8	Harden not your hearts, as in the provocation, in the day of temptation in the wilderness:	harden not your hearts to anger him, like the provocators, and as in the day of temptation in the wilderness,	DO NOT HARDEN YOUR HEARTS TO ANGER HIM AS THE REBELS AND AS [IN] THE DAY OF TEMPTATION IN THE WILDERNESS,

Parallel Translations

	KJV	*Murdock*	*Magiera*
HEBREWS *Chapter 3*			
9	When your fathers tempted me, proved me, and saw my works forty years.	when your fathers tempted me, and proved, [and] saw my works forty years.	WHEN YOUR FATHERS TEMPTED AND TESTED ME [AND] SAW MY WORKS [FOR] FORTY YEARS.
10	Wherefore I was grieved with that generation, and said, They do alway err in their heart; and they have not known my ways.	Therefore I was disgusted with that generation, and said: This is a people, whose heart wandereth, and they have not known my ways:	BECAUSE OF THIS, I WAS WEARIED WITH THAT GENERATION AND I SAID, "[THIS] IS A PEOPLE WHOSE HEART WANDERS AND THEY DO NOT KNOW MY WAYS,"
11	So I sware in my wrath, They shall not enter into my rest.)	so that I swore in my wrath, that they should not enter into my rest.	SO THAT I SWORE IN MY ANGER THAT THEY WOULD NOT ENTER INTO MY REST.
12	Take heed, brethren, lest there be in any of you an evil heart of unbelief, in departing from the living God.	Beware, therefore, my brethren, lest there be in any of you an evil heart that believeth not, and ye depart from the living God.	Watch, therefore, my brothers, so that an evil heart that does not believe will not be in any of you and you should go away from the living God.
13	But exhort one another daily, while it is called To day; lest any of you be hardened through the deceitfulness of sin.	But examine yourselves all the days, during the day which is called to-day; and let none of you be hardened, through the deceitfulness of sin.	But examine yourselves all days until the day that is called, "The day," so that none of you will be hardened by the deception of sin.
14	For we are made partakers of Christ, if we hold the beginning of our confidence stedfast unto the end;	For we have part with the Messiah, if we persevere in this firm confidence, from the beginning to the end:	For we take part with Christ, if we persist from the beginning even to the end in this true covenant,
15	While it is said, To day if ye will hear his voice, harden not your hearts, as in the provocation.	as it is said, To-day, if ye will hear his voice, harden not your hearts, to anger him.	as it is said: TODAY IF YOU WILL HEAR HIS REPORT, DO NOT HARDEN YOUR HEARTS TO ANGER HIM.
16	For some, when they had heard, did provoke: howbeit not all that came out of Egypt by Moses.	But who were they that heard, and angered him? It was not all they, who came out of Egypt under Moses.	For who were those who heard and angered him? Not all those who came out of Egypt by way of Moses [angered him].
17	But with whom was he grieved forty years? was it not with them that had sinned, whose carcases fell in the wilderness?	And with whom was he disgusted forty years, but with those who sinned, and whose carcasses fell in the wilderness?	And with whom was he wearied [for] forty years, but with those who sinned and whose bones fell in the wilderness?
18	And to whom sware he that they should not enter into his rest, but to them that believed not?	and of whom swore he, that they should not enter into his rest, but of those who believed not?	And about whom did he swear that they would not enter into his rest, but about those who were not persuaded?
19	So we see that they could not enter in because of unbelief.	So we see that they could not enter, because they believed not.	We see that they were not able to enter, because they did not believe.
Chapter 4			
1	Let us therefore fear, lest, a promise being left us of entering into his rest, any of you should seem to come short of it.	Let us fear, therefore, lest while there is a firm promise of entering into his rest, any among you should be found coming short of entering.	Therefore, we should fear, so that while the promise of an entrance into his rest is firm, none of you will be found to fall short when [it is time] to enter.

Parallel Translations

	KJV	*Murdock*	*Magiera*
	HEBREWS *Chapter 4*		
2	For unto us was the gospel preached, as well as unto them: but the word preached did not profit them, not being mixed with faith in them that heard it.	For to us also is the announcement, as well as to them: but the word they heard did not profit them, because it was not mingled with the faith of those who heard it.	For we also were brought the gospel, as they were, but the word did not profit those who heard, because it was not mixed with faith by those who heard it.
3	For we which have believed do enter into rest, as he said, As I have sworn in my wrath, if they shall enter into my rest: although the works were finished from the foundation of the world.	But we, who have believed, do enter into rest. But as he said, As I have sworn in my wrath, that they shall not enter into my rest: for lo, the works of God existed from the foundation of the world.	But we who believe are entering into rest. But as he said: AS I SWORE IN MY ANGER, "THEY WILL NOT ENTER INTO MY REST." For behold, the works of God were from the beginning of the world.
4	For he spake in a certain place of the seventh day on this wise, And God did rest the seventh day from all his works.	As he said of the sabbath, God rested on the seventh day from all his works.	As he said about the Sabbath: GOD RESTED ON THE SEVENTH DAY FROM ALL HIS WORKS.
5	And in this place again, If they shall enter into my rest.	And here again, he said, They shall not enter into my rest.	And here again, he said: THEY WILL NOT ENTER INTO MY REST.
6	Seeing therefore it remaineth that some must enter therein, and they to whom it was first preached entered not in because of unbelief:	Therefore, because there was a place, whither one and another might enter; and those earlier persons, to whom the announcement was made, entered not, because they believed not:	Therefore, because there was a place that each one should enter and those first [ones] who were brought the gospel did not enter since they were not persuaded,
7	Again, he limiteth a certain day, saying in David, To day, after so long a time; as it is said, To day if ye will hear his voice, harden not your hearts.	again he established another day, a long time afterwards; as above written, that David said, Today, if ye will hear his voice, harden not your hearts.	again he set another day after a long time, as it was written above, for David said: TODAY IF YOU WILL HEAR HIS VOICE, DO NOT HARDEN YOUR HEARTS.
8	For if Jesus had given them rest, then would he not afterward have spoken of another day.	For if Joshua, the son of Nun, had given them rest, he would not have spoken afterwards of another day.	For if Joshua, the son of Nun, had given them rest, he would not have spoken afterwards about another day.
9	There remaineth therefore a rest to the people of God.	Therefore it is established, that the people of God are to have a sabbath.	Therefore, it is established for the people of God to be given a rest.
10	For he that is entered into his rest, he also hath ceased from his own works, as God did from his.	For he who had entered into his rest, hath also rested from his works, as God did from his.	For he who enters into his rest has also rested from his works, as God [rested] from his.
11	Let us labour therefore to enter into that rest, lest any man fall after the same example of unbelief.	Let us, therefore, strive to enter into that rest; lest we fall short, after the manner of them who believed not.	Therefore, we should be diligent to enter into that rest, so that we will not fall in the likeness of those who were not persuaded.

Parallel Translations

HEBREWS *Chapter 4*

	KJV	*Murdock*	*Magiera*
12	For the word of God is quick, and powerful, and sharper than any twoedged sword, piercing even to the dividing asunder of soul and spirit, and of the joints and marrow, and is a discerner of the thoughts and intents of the heart.	For the word of God is living, and all-efficient, and sharper than a two-edged sword, and entereth even to the severance of the soul and the spirit, and of the joints and the marrow and the bones, and judgeth the thoughts and reasonings of the heart:	For the word of God is living and completely effective and sharper than a two-edged sword and enters all the way to the separation of soul and of spirit, and of the joints and of the marrow and of the bones, and judges the reasonings and the thoughts of the heart.
13	Neither is there any creature that is not manifest in his sight: but all things are naked and opened unto the eyes of him with whom we have to do.	neither is there any creature, which is concealed from before him; but every thing is naked and manifest before his eyes, to whom we are to give account.	And there is no created [thing] that is hidden before him, but everything is naked and evident before of the eyes of him to whom we give an account.
14	Seeing then that we have a great high priest, that is passed into the heavens, Jesus the Son of God, let us hold fast our profession.	Seeing then that we have a great High Priest, Jesus the Messiah, the son of God, who hath ascended to heaven; let us persevere in professing him.	Therefore, because we have a great high priest, Jesus Christ, the Son of God, who went up to heaven, we should persist in confession of him.
15	For we have not an high priest which cannot be touched with the feeling of our infirmities; but was in all points tempted like as we are, yet without sin.	For we have not a high priest, who cannot sympathize with our infirmity; but [one] who was tempted in all respects like us, aside from sin.	For we do not have a high priest who is not able to feel our weakness, but one who was tempted in everything like us, [yet] without sin.
16	Let us therefore come boldly unto the throne of grace, that we may obtain mercy, and find grace to help in time of need.	Let us, therefore, approach with assurance to the throne of his grace, that we may obtain mercy, and may find grace for assistance in the time of affliction.	Therefore, we should boldly come near the throne of his grace to receive mercies and to find grace for help in time of adversity.

Chapter 5

	KJV	*Murdock*	*Magiera*
1	For every high priest taken from among men is ordained for men in things pertaining to God, that he may offer both gifts and sacrifices for sins:	For every high priest, who is from among men, is established over the things of God, in behalf of men, that he may present the offering and the sacrifices for sin:	For every high priest who is ordained of men for men, concerning those [things] that are of God, to offer offerings and sacrifices for sins,
2	Who can have compassion on the ignorant, and on them that are out of the way; for that he himself also is compassed with infirmity.	and he can humble himself, and sympathize with the ignorant and the erring, because he also is clothed with infirmity.	he who is able to humble himself and to feel with those who do not know and [who] err, because he also is clothed with weakness.
3	And by reason hereof he ought, as for the people, so also for himself, to offer for sins.	And, therefore, he is obliged as for the people, so also for himself, to present an offering for his sins.	And because of this, it is necessary for the people, so also for himself, that he should offer [an offering] for his sins.
4	And no man taketh this honour unto himself, but he that is called of God, as was Aaron.	And no one taketh this honor on himself, but he who is called of God, as Aaron [was].	And no man takes the honor for himself, except he who was called by God, as [was] Aaron.
5	So also Christ glorified not himself to be made an high priest; but he that said unto him, Thou art my Son, to day have I begotten thee.	So also the Messiah did not exalt himself to become a High Priest; but He [appointed him] who said to him, Thou art my Son; this day have I begotten thee.	So also, Christ did not glorify himself to become the high priest, but he who said to him: YOU ARE MY SON. TODAY I HAVE FATHERED YOU.

Parallel Translations

HEBREWS *Chapter 5*

	KJV	Murdock	Magiera
6	As he saith also in another place, Thou art a priest for ever after the order of Melchisedec.	As he said also in another place: Thou art a priest for ever, after the likeness of Melchisedec.	As he said also in another place: YOU ARE A PRIEST FOREVER IN THE LIKENESS OF MELCHISEDEC.
7	Who in the days of his flesh, when he had offered up prayers and supplications with strong crying and tears unto him that was able to save him from death, and was heard in that he feared;	Likewise, when he was clothed in flesh, he presented supplication and entreaty with intense invocation, and with tears, to him who was able to resuscitate him from death; and he was heard.	Also, while he was clothed with flesh, he offered petition and intercession with strong crying and with tears to him who was able to make him alive from death and he was heard.
8	Though he were a Son, yet learned he obedience by the things which he suffered;	And though he was a son, yet, from the fear and the sufferings he endured, he learned obedience.	And although he was a Son, from the fear and the sufferings that he bore, he learned obedience.
9	And being made perfect, he became the author of eternal salvation unto all them that obey him;	And thus he was perfected and became the cause of eternal life to all them who obey him.	And so he was matured and became for all those who obey him the cause of eternal life.
10	Called of God an high priest after the order of Melchisedec.	And he was named of God, the High Priest after the likeness of Melchisedec.	And he was named of God, the high priest in the likeness of Melchisedec.
11	Of whom we have many things to say, and hard to be uttered, seeing ye are dull of hearing.	Now, concerning this person, Melchisedec, we have much discourse, which we might utter; but it is difficult to explain it, because ye are infirm in your hearing.	Now concerning this Melchisedec, we have a great speech to say, yet it is difficult to explain it, because you are weak in your hearing.
12	For when for the time ye ought to be teachers, ye have need that one teach you again which be the first principles of the oracles of God; and are become such as have need of milk, and not of strong meat.	For ye ought to be teachers, seeing ye have been long in the doctrine. But now ye need to learn again the first lines of the commencement of the oracles of God: and ye have need of milk, and not of strong food.	For you ought to be teachers because of the time you have had in teaching, but now again you are needing to learn what are the first principles of the beginning of the words of God. And you have need for milk and not for solid food.
13	For every one that useth milk is unskilful in the word of righteousness: for he is a babe.	For every one whose food is milk, is unversed in the language of righteousness, because he is a child.	But everyone whose food is milk is not persuaded in the word of uprightness, because he is a baby.
14	But strong meat belongeth to them that are of full age, even those who by reason of use have their senses exercised to discern both good and evil.	But strong food belongeth to the mature who, being investigators, have trained their faculties to discriminate good and evil.	But solid food belongs to the mature, those who, because they are trained, have exercised their senses to distinguish good and evil.

Chapter 6

	KJV	Murdock	Magiera
1	Therefore leaving the principles of the doctrine of Christ, let us go on unto perfection; not laying again the foundation of repentance from dead works, and of faith toward God,	Therefore let us leave the commencement of the word of the Messiah, and let us proceed to the completion. Or will ye again lay another foundation for the repentance which is from dead works, and for the faith in God,	Because of this, we should leave the starting point of the word of Christ and we should come to maturity. Or will you again lay another foundation for repentance from dead works and for the faith that is in God

Parallel Translations

	KJV	*Murdock*	*Magiera*
	HEBREWS	*Chapter 6*	
2	Of the doctrine of baptisms, and of laying on of hands, and of resurrection of the dead, and of eternal judgment.	and for the doctrine of baptism, and for the laying on of a hand, and for the resurrection from the dead, and for the eternal judgment?	and for the doctrine of baptism and of the laying on of a hand and for the resurrection from the dead and for eternal judgment?
3	And this will we do, if God permit.	We will do this, if the Lord permit.	If the LORD permits, we will do this.
4	For it is impossible for those who were once enlightened, and have tasted of the heavenly gift, and were made partakers of the Holy Ghost,	But they who have once descended to baptism, and have tasted the gift from heaven, and have received the Holy Spirit,	But they are not able, those who once have gone down into baptism and have tasted the gift that is from heaven and have received the Holy Spirit
5	And have tasted the good word of God, and the powers of the world to come,	and have tasted the good word of God, and the power of the world to come,	and have tasted the good word of God and the power of the age that is to come,
6	If they shall fall away, to renew them again unto repentance; seeing they crucify to themselves the Son of God afresh, and put him to an open shame.	cannot again sin, and a second time be renewed to repentance; or a second time crucify and insult the Son of God.	to sin again and to be renewed to repentance from the beginning and to crucify and to disparage the Son of God from the beginning.
7	For the earth which drinketh in the rain that cometh oft upon it, and bringeth forth herbs meet for them by whom it is dressed, receiveth blessing from God:	For the earth that drinketh the rain which cometh often upon it, and produceth the herb that is of use to those for whom it is cultivated, receiveth a blessing from God.	For the earth, which drinks the rain that comes to it many times and produces the green herb that is useful to those because of whom it was cultivated, receives a blessing from God.
8	But that which beareth thorns and briers is rejected, and is nigh unto cursing; whose end is to be burned.	But if it should put forth thorns and briers, it would have reprobation, and be not far from a curse, and its end would be a burning.	But if it produces thorns and thistles, it is rejected and is not far away from a curse, but rather its end is a fire.
9	But, beloved, we are persuaded better things of you, and things that accompany salvation, though we thus speak.	But, in regard to you, my brethren, we are persuaded better things, and things pertaining to life, although we thus speak.	Now concerning you, my brothers, we are persuaded of those [things] that are proper and [that] are approaching life, even though we speak so.
10	For God is not unrighteous to forget your work and labour of love, which ye have shewed toward his name, in that ye have ministered to the saints, and do minister.	For God is not unrighteous, to forget your works, and your charity which ye have shown in his name, in that ye have ministered and do minister to the saints.	For God is not wicked, that he forgets your works and your love that you have shown in his name, for you have ministered and do minister to the holy [ones].
11	And we desire that every one of you do shew the same diligence to the full assurance of hope unto the end:	And we desire, that each one of you may show this same activity, for the completion of your hope, even to the end:	But we want each one of you to show this diligence to the completion of your hope up to the end
12	That ye be not slothful, but followers of them who through faith and patience inherit the promises.	and that ye faint not; but that ye be emulators of them who by faith and patience have become heirs of the promise.	and to not be discouraged, but to be imitators of those who by faith and long-suffering have become heirs of the promise.
13	For when God made promise to Abraham, because he could swear by no greater, he sware by himself,	For when God made the promise to Abraham, because there was none greater than himself by whom he could swear, he swore by himself;	For when God promised Abraham, because he had no one who was greater than himself by whom he could swear, he swore by himself

	KJV	Murdock	Magiera
	HEBREWS *Chapter 6*		
14	Saying, Surely blessing I will bless thee, and multiplying I will multiply thee.	and said: Blessing, I will bless thee, and multiplying I will multiply thee.	and said: I WILL CERTAINLY BLESS YOU AND I WILL GREATLY MULTIPLY YOU.
15	And so, after he had patiently endured, he obtained the promise.	And so he was patient, and obtained the promise.	And so he was long-suffering and received the promise.
16	For men verily swear by the greater: and an oath for confirmation is to them an end of all strife.	For men swear by one greater than themselves: and in every controversy that occurs among them, the sure termination of it is by an oath.	For men swear by that which is greater than them and concerning every controversy that happens among them, the certain end of it is by oaths.
17	Wherein God, willing more abundantly to shew unto the heirs of promise the immutability of his counsel, confirmed it by an oath:	Therefore, God, being abundantly willing to show to the heirs of the promise, that his promising was irreversible, bound it up in an oath;	Because of this, God especially wanted to show to the heirs of the promise that his promise would not change, so he bound it with oaths,
18	That by two immutable things, in which it was impossible for God to lie, we might have a strong consolation, who have fled for refuge to lay hold upon the hope set before us:	so that, by two things which change not, and in which God cannot lie, we, who have sought refuge in him, might have great consolation, and might hold fast the hope promised to us;	that by two things that are unchangeable in which God is not able to lie, we who have sought refuge in him may have great comfort and may hold fast to the hope that was promised to us,
19	Which hope we have as an anchor of the soul, both sure and stedfast, and which entereth into that within the veil;	which is to us as an anchor, that retaineth our soul, so that it swerveth not; and it entereth into that within the veil,	which we have as an anchor that holds our soul, so that it is not shaken and it enters within the veil,
20	Whither the forerunner is for us entered, even Jesus, made an high priest for ever after the order of Melchisedec.	whither Jesus hath previously entered for us, and hath become a priest for ever, after the likeness of Melchisedec.	where Jesus previously entered for us and became a priest forever in the likeness of Melchisedec.
	Chapter 7		
1	For this Melchisedec, king of Salem, priest of the most high God, who met Abraham returning from the slaughter of the kings, and blessed him;	Now this Melchisedec was king of Salem, a priest of the most high God: and he met Abraham, when returning from the slaughter of the kings; and blessed him.	Now this Melchisedec was king of Salem, a priest of the Most High God. And he met Abraham returning from the slaughter of the kings and blessed him.
2	To whom also Abraham gave a tenth part of all; first being by interpretation King of righteousness, and after that also King of Salem, which is, King of peace;	And to him Abraham imparted tithes of all that he had with him. Moreover his name is interpreted king of righteousness; and again [he is called] King of Salem, that is King of Peace.	And Abraham separated out to him tithes of everything that was with him. Now his name is interpreted, "king of uprightness," and again, "king of Salem," that is, "king of peace,"
3	Without father, without mother, without descent, having neither beginning of days, nor end of life; but made like unto the Son of God; abideth a priest continually.	Of whom neither his father nor his mother are written in the genealogies; nor the commencement of his days, nor the end of his life; but, after the likeness of the Son of God, his priesthood remaineth for ever.	whose father and mother are not written in the genealogies, nor the beginning of his days, nor the completion of his life. But in the likeness of the Son of God, his priesthood remains forever.
4	Now consider how great this man was, unto whom even the patriarch Abraham gave the tenth of the spoils.	And consider ye, how great he was; to whom the patriarch Abraham gave tithes and first-fruits.	Now consider how great this [man was], to whom Abraham the patriarch gave tithes of the first [things].

Parallel Translations

	KJV	Murdock	Magiera
5	And verily they that are of the sons of Levi, who receive the office of the priesthood, have a commandment to take tithes of the people according to the law, that is, of their brethren, though they come out of the loins of Abraham:	For they of the sons of Levi who received the priesthood, had a statute of the law, that they should take tithes from the people; they from their brethren, because they also are of the seed of Abraham.	For those of the sons of Levi who received the priesthood have the commandment of the law, that they should receive tithes from the people, from their brothers, when they also came from the loin[s] of Abraham.
6	But he whose descent is not counted from them received tithes of Abraham, and blessed him that had the promises.	But this man, who is not enrolled in their genealogies, took tithes from Abraham; and blessed him who had received the promise.	But this [man], who is not written in their genealogies, took tithes from Abraham and blessed him who had received the promise.
7	And without all contradiction the less is blessed of the better.	But it is beyond controversy, that the inferior is blessed by his superior.	And without controversy, he who is less is blessed by him who is greater than him.
8	And here men that die receive tithes; but there he receiveth them, of whom it is witnessed that he liveth.	And here, men who die, receive the tithes; but there he of whom the scripture testifieth that he liveth.	And here men who die receive tithes. But there he [is] about whom the scripture testifies that he is alive.
9	And as I may so say, Levi also, who receiveth tithes, payed tithes in Abraham.	And through Abraham, as one may say, even Levi who receiveth tithes, was himself tithed.	And as one may say, by way of Abraham, even Levi who received the tithes also paid tithes.
10	For he was yet in the loins of his father, when Melchisedec met him.	For he was yet in the loins of his father, when he met Melchisedec.	For he was yet in the loin[s] of his father when he met Melchisedec.
11	If therefore perfection were by the Levitical priesthood, (for under it the people received the law,) what further need was there that another priest should rise after the order of Melchisedec, and not be called after the order of Aaron?	If, therefore, perfection had been by means of the priesthood of the Levites, in which the law was enjoined on the people; why was another priest required, who should stand up after the likeness of Melchisedec? For it should have said, He shall be after t	Therefore, if perfection is by way of the priesthood of Levi, by which the law was established for the people, why was it necessary that another priest should be raised up in the likeness of Melchisedec? Then he [would have] said, "He will be in the likeness of Aaron."
12	For the priesthood being changed, there is made of necessity a change also of the law.	But as there is a change in the priesthood, so also is there a change in the law.	But in the same way as a change took place in the priesthood, so a change also took place in the law.
13	For he of whom these things are spoken pertaineth to another tribe, of which no man gave attendance at the altar.	For he of whom these things were spoken, was born of another tribe, of which no one ever ministered at the altar.	For he about whom these [things] were spoken was born of another tribe, from which no man ever ministered at the altar.
14	For it is evident that our Lord sprang out of Juda; of which tribe Moses spake nothing concerning priesthood.	For it is manifest that our Lord arose from Judah, from a tribe of which Moses said nothing concerning a priesthood.	For it is revealed that our Lord rose up from Judah, from a tribe about which Moses did not say anything concerning the priesthood.
15	And it is yet far more evident: for that after the similitude of Melchisedec there ariseth another priest,	And moreover this is further manifest, from his saying that another priest will stand up, after the likeness of Melchisedec,	And yet it is further known in that he said that another priest will rise up in the likeness of Melchisedec,

Parallel Translations

	KJV	*Murdock*	*Magiera*

HEBREWS *Chapter 7*

	KJV	Murdock	Magiera
16	Who is made, not after the law of a carnal commandment, but after the power of an endless life.	who was not according to the law of corporeal injunctions, but according to the energy of an indissoluble life.	who was not according to the law of fleshly commandments, but was according to the power of life that is endless.
17	For he testifieth, Thou art a priest for ever after the order of Melchisedec.	For he testified of him: Thou art a priest for ever, after the likeness of Melchisedec.	For he testified about him: YOU ARE A PRIEST FOREVER IN THE LIKENESS OF MELCHISEDEC.
18	For there is verily a disannulling of the commandment going before for the weakness and unprofitableness thereof.	And the change which was made in the first statute, was on account of its impotency, and because their was no utility in it.	Now the change that happened to the first commandment [was] because of its lack of power and it had no profit.
19	For the law made nothing perfect, but the bringing in of a better hope did; by the which we draw nigh unto God.	For the law perfected nothing; but in the place of it there came in a hope, which is better than it, and by which we draw near to God.	For the law did not perfect anything. But a hope that is greater than it entered in its place, by which we are drawn near to God.
20	And inasmuch as not without an oath he was made priest:	And he confirmed it to us by an oath.	And he confirmed it to us with oaths.
21	(For those priests were made without an oath; but this with an oath by him that said unto him, The Lord sware and will not repent, Thou art a priest for ever after the order of Melchisedec:)	For they became priests without an oath; but this man by an oath. As he said to him by David: The Lord hath sworn, and will not lie, Thou art a priest for ever, after the likeness of Melchisedec.	For they became priests without oaths, but this [one] with oaths, as he said to him by way of David: THE LORD HAS SWORN AND WILL NOT LIE, THAT YOU ARE A PRIEST FOREVER IN THE LIKENESS OF MELCHISEDEC.
22	By so much was Jesus made a surety of a better testament.	By all this, is that a better covenant of which Jesus is the sponsor.	[In] all of this is this covenant better, for Jesus was the security in it.
23	And they truly were many priests, because they were not suffered to continue by reason of death:	And they as priests were numerous, because they were mortal, and were not permitted to continue:	And those priests were many, because they died and were not allowed to continue.
24	But this man, because he continueth ever, hath an unchangeable priesthood.	but this man, because he standeth up for ever, his priesthood doth not pass away:	But this [one], because he remains forever, his priesthood does not pass away.
25	Wherefore he is able also to save them to the uttermost that come unto God by him, seeing he ever liveth to make intercession for them.	and he is able to vivify for ever, them who come to God by him; for he always liveth, and sendeth up prayers for them.	And he is able to give life forever to those who come near to God by way of him, for he is always alive and sends up prayer for them.
26	For such an high priest became us, who is holy, harmless, undefiled, separate from sinners, and made higher than the heavens;	For, a priest like to him, was also suitable for us; one pure, and without evil and without stain; one separated from sins, and exalted higher than heaven;	For a priest like this [one] is also right for us, [one who is] pure, without evil and without impurity, one who is separated from sins and elevated higher than heaven
27	Who needeth not daily, as those high priests, to offer up sacrifice, first for his own sins, and then for the people's: for this he did once, when he offered up himself.	and who is not obliged, every day, like the [Aaronic] high priest, to first offer sacrifices for his own sins, and then for the people; for this he did once, by offering up himself.	and has no need daily, like the high priests, to first offer sacrifices for his sins and then for the people, for this he did one time, in that he offered himself.

Parallel Translations

	KJV	*Murdock*	*Magiera*
	HEBREWS *Chapter 7*		
28	For the law maketh men high priests which have infirmity; but the word of the oath, which was since the law, maketh the Son, who is consecrated for evermore.	For the law constituted feeble men priests; but the word of the oath, which was subsequent to the law [constituted] the Son perfect for ever.	For the law established weak men [as] priests, but the word of the oaths that was after the law [established] the Son [as] perfect forever.
	Chapter 8		
1	Now of the things which we have spoken this is the sum: We have such an high priest, who is set on the right hand of the throne of the Majesty in the heavens;	Now the sum of the whole is this, we have a High Priest, who is seated on the right hand of the throne of the Majesty in heaven:	Now the first [point] of all these [things is that] we have a high priest who is seated on the right hand of the throne of the majesty in heaven.
2	A minister of the sanctuary, and of the true tabernacle, which the Lord pitched, and not man.	And he is the minister of the sanctuary, and of the true tabernacle, which God hath pitched, and not man.	And he is a minister of the sanctuary and of the tabernacle of truth that God pitched and not man.
3	For every high priest is ordained to offer gifts and sacrifices: wherefore it is of necessity that this man have somewhat also to offer.	For every high priest is established, to offer oblations and sacrifices; and therefore, it was proper that this one should also have something to offer.	For every high priest is ordained to offer offerings and sacrifices. Because of this, it was right for this [one] to have something to offer also.
4	For if he were on earth, he should not be a priest, seeing that there are priests that offer gifts according to the law:	And if he were on earth, he would not be a priest; because there are priests [there], who offer oblations agreeably to the law:	And if he were on earth, he would not even be a priest, because there are priests who offer offerings as in the law,
5	Who serve unto the example and shadow of heavenly things, as Moses was admonished of God when he was about to make the tabernacle: for, See, saith he, that thou make all things according to the pattern shewed to thee in the mount.	[namely] they, who minister in the emblem and shadow of the things in heaven: as it was said to Moses, when he was about to build the tabernacle, See, and make every thing according to the pattern which was showed thee in the mount.	those who minister for a type and for shadows of those [things] that are in heaven, as was said to Moses while he was making the tabernacle: SEE AND MAKE EVERYTHING ACCORDING TO THE TYPE THAT WAS SHOWN TO YOU IN THE MOUNTAIN.
6	But now hath he obtained a more excellent ministry, by how much also he is the mediator of a better covenant, which was established upon better promises.	But now, Jesus the Messiah hath received a ministry which is better than that: as also the covenant, of which he is made the Mediator, is better, and is given with better promises than the former.	And now, Jesus Christ has received a ministry that is more excellent than that, as also that covenant in which he was made the mediator is more excellent. So [it is] with the promises that are more excellent than what was given.
7	For if that first covenant had been faultless, then should no place have been sought for the second.	For, if the first [covenant] had been faultless, there would have been no place for this second [one].	For if the first [covenant] was without fault, there would be no place for this second.
8	For finding fault with them, he saith, Behold, the days come, saith the Lord, when I will make a new covenant with the house of Israel and with the house of Judah:	For he chideth them and saith: Behold, the days come, saith the Lord, when I will complete with the family of the house of Israel, and with the family of the house of Judah, a new covenant;	For he found fault with them and said: BEHOLD, THE DAYS COME, says the LORD, WHEN I WILL COMPLETE FOR THE HOUSEHOLD OF ISRAEL AND FOR THE HOUSEHOLD OF JUDAH, A NEW COVENANT,

HEBREWS *Chapter 8*

	KJV	Murdock	Magiera
9	Not according to the covenant that I made with their fathers in the day when I took them by the hand to lead them out of the land of Egypt; because they continued not in my covenant, and I regarded them not, saith the Lord.	not like the covenant which I gave to their fathers, in the day when I took them by the hand, and brought them out of the land of Egypt; [and] because they continued not in my covenant, I also rejected them, saith the Lord.	NOT LIKE THAT COVENANT THAT I GAVE TO THEIR FATHERS IN THE DAY THAT I HELD [THEM] BY THEIR HAND AND BROUGHT THEM OUT OF THE LAND OF EGYPT. BECAUSE THEY DID NOT REMAIN IN MY COVENANT, I ALSO REJECTED THEM, says the LORD.
10	For this is the covenant that I will make with the house of Israel after those days, saith the Lord; I will put my laws into their mind, and write them in their hearts: and I will be to them a God, and they shall be to me a people:	But this is the covenant which I will give to the family of the house of Israel after those days, saith the Lord: I will put my law in their minds, and inscribe it on their hearts; and I will be to them a God, and they shall be to me a people.	AND THIS [IS] THE COVENANT THAT I WILL GIVE TO THE HOUSEHOLD OF ISRAEL AFTER THOSE DAYS, says the LORD. I WILL PUT MY LAW IN THEIR MINDS AND I WILL WRITE IT ON THEIR HEARTS AND I WILL BE GOD TO THEM AND THEY WILL BE A PEOPLE TO ME.
11	And they shall not teach every man his neighbour, and every man his brother, saying, Know the Lord: for all shall know me, from the least to the greatest.	And one shall not teach his fellow-citizen, nor his brother, nor say: Know thou the Lord: because they shall all know me, from the youngest of them to the oldest.	AND A MAN WILL NOT TEACH HIS FELLOW-CITIZEN OR EVEN HIS BROTHER AND SAY, 'KNOW THE LORD,' BECAUSE ALL WILL KNOW ME, FROM THE YOUNGEST OF THEM UP TO THE OLDEST.
12	For I will be merciful to their unrighteousness, and their sins and their iniquities will I remember no more.	And I will forgive them their iniquity; and their sins will I remember no more.	AND I WILL FREE THEM FROM THEIR WICKEDNESS AND I WILL NOT REMEMBER THEIR SINS AGAIN.
13	In that he saith, A new covenant, he hath made the first old. Now that which decayeth and waxeth old is ready to vanish away.	In that he said a New [Covenant], he made the first old; and that which is old and decaying, is near to dissolution.	By that which he called new, he made the first old, and that which is outdated and old is near to corruption.

Chapter 9

	KJV	Murdock	Magiera
1	Then verily the first covenant had also ordinances of divine service, and a worldly sanctuary.	Now, under the first [covenant], there were ordinances of ministration, and a worldly sanctuary.	Now in the first [covenant] there were ordinances of service and an earthly sanctuary.
2	For there was a tabernacle made; the first, wherein was the candlestick, and the table, and the shewbread; which is called the sanctuary.	For in the first tabernacle which was erected, there was the candlestick, and the table and the bread of the presence; and this was called the Sanctuary.	For the first tabernacle that was made had a candlestick and a table and show-bread, and it was called the sanctuary.
3	And after the second veil, the tabernacle which is called the Holiest of all;	But the inner tabernacle, which was within the second veil, was called the Holy of Holies.	And the inner tabernacle that was behind the second veil was called the holy of holies.

Parallel Translations

HEBREWS *Chapter 9*

	KJV	*Murdock*	*Magiera*
4	Which had the golden censer, and the ark of the covenant overlaid round about with gold, wherein was the golden pot that had manna, and Aaron's rod that budded, and the tables of the covenant;	And there were in it the golden censer and the ark of the covenant, which was all over laid with gold; and in it were the golden urn which contained the manna and the rod of Aaron which sprouted, and the tables of the covenant;	And in it there was the censer of gold and the ark of the covenant that was completely overlaid with gold and it had a pot of gold that had the manna and the rod of Aaron that sprouted and the tablets of the covenant,
5	And over it the cherubims of glory shadowing the mercyseat; of which we cannot now speak particularly.	and over it were the cherubim of glory, which overshadowed the mercy seat. But there is not time to speak particularly of each of the things which were so arranged.	and on top of it, cherubim of glory that were overshadowing the mercy seat. But there is not time to speak about each one of these [things] that were so arranged.
6	Now when these things were thus ordained, the priests went always into the first tabernacle, accomplishing the service of God.	And into the outer tabernacle the priests, at all times, entered, and performed their ministration.	And into the outer tabernacle the priests were always entering and performing their service.
7	But into the second went the high priest alone once every year, not without blood, which he offered for himself, and for the errors of the people:	But into the interior tabernacle, once a year only, the high priest entered, with the blood which he offered for himself and for the sins of the people.	But into the inner tabernacle once a year the high priest entered alone with the blood that he offered for himself and for the wrong-doing of the people.
8	The Holy Ghost this signifying, that the way into the holiest of all was not yet made manifest, while as the first tabernacle was yet standing:	And by this the Holy Spirit indicated, that the way to the holy [places] was not yet manifested, so long as the first tabernacle was standing:	Now by this, the Holy Spirit was making known that the way to the holy [things] was not yet revealed, as long as the first tabernacle was standing.
9	Which was a figure for the time then present, in which were offered both gifts and sacrifices, that could not make him that did the service perfect, as pertaining to the conscience;	and it was a symbol, for that time, during which oblation and sacrifices were offered that could not make perfect the conscience of him who offered them:	This was a symbol for that time, in which offerings and sacrifices were offered that were not able to perfect the conscience of him who offered them,
10	Which stood only in meats and drinks, and divers washings, and carnal ordinances, imposed on them until the time of reformation.	but [they consisted] only in food and drink, and in the ablutions of divers things; which were carnal ordinances, and were set up until the time of a reformation.	but [were] only in food and drink and in washings of various kinds that are commandments of the flesh that were established until the time of a reformation.
11	But Christ being come an high priest of good things to come, by a greater and more perfect tabernacle, not made with hands, that is to say, not of this building;	But the Messiah who came, was a High Priest of the good things which he wrought: and he entered into the great and perfect tabernacle, which was not made with hands and was not of these created things.	Now Christ who has come [was] a high priest of the good [things] that he did. And he entered the great and perfect tabernacle that was not made by hands and was not of these created [things].
12	Neither by the blood of goats and calves, but by his own blood he entered in once into the holy place, having obtained eternal redemption for us.	And he did not enter with the blood of goats and calves; but with the blood of himself, he entered once into the sanctuary, and obtained eternal redemption.	And he did not enter with the blood of goats or of calves, but with his own blood, he entered the sanctuary one time and obtained redemption forever.

Parallel Translations

HEBREWS *Chapter 9*

	KJV	*Murdock*	*Magiera*
13	For if the blood of bulls and of goats, and the ashes of an heifer sprinkling the unclean, sanctifieth to the purifying of the flesh:	For if the blood of goats and calves, with the ashes of a heifer, was sprinkled upon them that were defiled, and sanctified them as to the purification of their flesh;	For if the blood of goats and of calves and the ash of a heifer was sprinkled on those who were defiled and it made them holy to the cleansing of their flesh,
14	How much more shall the blood of Christ, who through the eternal Spirit offered himself without spot to God, purge your conscience from dead works to serve the living God?	then how much more will the blood of the Messiah, who by the eternal Spirit offered himself without blemish to God, purge our conscience from dead works, so that we may serve the living God?	then how much more will the blood of Christ, who by the eternal Spirit offered himself without spot to God, cleanse our conscience from dead works that we may serve the living God?
15	And for this cause he is the mediator of the new testament, that by means of death, for the redemption of the transgressions that were under the first testament, they which are called might receive the promise of eternal inheritance.	And for this reason he became the Mediator of the new covenant, that he might by his death be redemption, to them who had transgressed the first covenant; so that they, who are called to the eternal inheritance, might receive the promise.	Because of this, he became the mediator of the new covenant, so that by his death he would become the deliverance for those who have transgressed against the first covenant, that those who were called to the eternal inheritance should receive the promise.
16	For where a testament is, there must also of necessity be the death of the testator.	For where there is a testament, it indicateth the death of him who made it.	For where there is a covenant, it shows the death of him who made it,
17	For a testament is of force after men are dead: otherwise it is of no strength at all while the testator liveth.	For it is valid, only of a deceased [person]; because it hath no use, so long as the maker of it liveth.	but it is established only concerning a dead [person], because as long as he who made it is alive, there is no usefulness in it.
18	Whereupon neither the first testament was dedicated without blood.	Therefore also the first [covenant] was not confirmed without blood.	Because of this, neither was the first [covenant] established without blood.
19	For when Moses had spoken every precept to all the people according to the law, he took the blood of calves and of goats, with water, and scarlet wool, and hyssop, and sprinkled both the book, and all the people,	For when the whole ordinance had been propounded by Moses to all the people, according to the law; Moses took the blood of a heifer, and water, with scarlet wool and hyssop, and sprinkled upon the books and upon all the people;	For when the whole commandment had been commanded by Moses to all the people according to the law, Moses took the blood of a heifer and water, with wool of scarlet and hyssop, and he sprinkled [it] over the scrolls and over all the people
20	Saying, This is the blood of the testament which God hath enjoined unto you.	and said to them, This is the blood of the covenant which is enjoined by God.	and said to them: THIS IS THE BLOOD OF THAT COVENANT THAT IS COMMANDED TO YOU BY GOD.
21	Moreover he sprinkled with blood both the tabernacle, and all the vessels of the ministry.	With that blood he also sprinkled upon the tabernacle, and upon all the vessels of ministration:	He also sprinkled part of the blood over the tabernacle and over all the vessels of the service,
22	And almost all things are by the law purged with blood; and without shedding of blood is no remission.	because every thing, according to the law, is purified with blood: and without the shedding of blood, there is no remission.	because everything is cleansed by blood in the law, and without the shedding of blood there is no forgiveness.

HEBREWS *Chapter 9*

	KJV	*Murdock*	*Magiera*
23	It was therefore necessary that the patterns of things in the heavens should be purified with these; but the heavenly things themselves with better sacrifices than these.	For it was necessary that these, the emblems of heavenly things, should be purified, with those things; but the heavenly things themselves, with sacrifices superior to them.	For it was necessary that these that are a type of the heavenly [things] should be purified with those [things], and these heavenly [things] by sacrifices that are more excellent than those.
24	For Christ is not entered into the holy places made with hands, which are the figures of the true; but into heaven itself, now to appear in the presence of God for us:	For the Messiah entered not into the sanctuary made with hands, which is the emblem of the true [sanctuary]: but he entered into heaven itself to appear in the presence of God for us.	For Christ did not enter the sanctuary that was made by hands that was a type of that true [one], but he entered into heaven to appear before the presence of God for us.
25	Nor yet that he should offer himself often, as the high priest entereth into the holy place every year with blood of others;	Neither [was it necessary], that he should offer himself many times, as the high priest entered every year into the sanctuary, with blood not his own:	Neither [was it necessary] to offer himself many times, as the high priest did when he entered the sanctuary every year with blood that [was] not his own.
26	For then must he often have suffered since the foundation of the world: but now once in the end of the world hath he appeared to put away sin by the sacrifice of himself.	otherwise, he must have suffered many times, since the commencement of the world; but now in the end of the world, he hath once offered himself in a self-sacrifice, to abolish sin.	Otherwise, it would be required that he should suffer many times since the beginning of the age. But now in the end of the age, he has offered himself one time by his sacrificing to abolish sin.
27	And as it is appointed unto men once to die, but after this the judgment:	And, as it is appointed to men, that they must once die, and after their death is the judgment;	And as it is appointed to men that they should die one time, and after their death [is] the judgment,
28	So Christ was once offered to bear the sins of many; and unto them that look for him shall he appear the second time without sin unto salvation.	so also the Messiah was once offered; and, by himself, he immolated the sins of many: and a second time, without sins, will he appear for the life of them who expect him.	so also Christ was offered one time. And in his person he sacrificed [for] the sins of many and he will appear a second time without sins for the life of those who wait for him.

Chapter 10

	KJV	*Murdock*	*Magiera*
1	For the law having a shadow of good things to come, and not the very image of the things, can never with those sacrifices which they offered year by year continually make the comers thereunto perfect.	For in the law there was a shadow of the good things to come; not the substance of the things themselves. Therefore, although the same sacrifices were every year offered, they could never perfect those who offered them.	For the law had a shadow of good [things] to come, not the substance of the things themselves. Because of this, although these same sacrifices were offered every year, they were never able to perfect those who offered them.
2	For then would they not have ceased to be offered? because that the worshippers once purged should have had no more conscience of sins.	For, if they had perfected them, they would long ago have desisted from their offerings; because their conscience could no more disquiet them, who were once purified, on account of their sins.	For if they had perfected [them], then doubtless they would have stopped their offerings, because their conscience would no longer trouble them with sins once they have been cleansed.
3	But in those sacrifices there is a remembrance again made of sins every year.	But in those sacrifices, they every year recognized their sins.	But by the sacrifices, they brought their sins to remembrance every year,

HEBREWS Chapter 10

	KJV	Murdock	Magiera
4	For it is not possible that the blood of bulls and of goats should take away sins.	For the blood of bulls and of goats cannot purge away sins.	for the blood of bulls and of goats is not able to cleanse sins.
5	Wherefore when he cometh into the world, he saith, Sacrifice and offering thou wouldest not, but a body hast thou prepared me:	Therefore, when entering the world, he said: In sacrifices and oblations, thou hast not had pleasure; but thou hast clothed me with a body.	Because of this, when he entered the world he said, "You are not pleased with sacrifices and offerings, but you have clothed me with a body.
6	In burnt offerings and sacrifices for sin thou hast had no pleasure.	And holocausts on account of sins, thou hast not asked.	And you have not asked for burnt offerings that are for sins."
7	Then said I, Lo, I come (in the volume of the book it is written of me,) to do thy will, O God.	Then I said: Behold I come, as it is written of me in the beginning of the books, to do thy pleasure, O God.	Then I said: BEHOLD, I COME. FOR IN THE BEGINNING OF THE WRITINGS IT IS WRITTEN ABOUT ME, I WILL DO YOUR WILL, [OH] GOD.
8	Above when he said, Sacrifice and offering and burnt offerings and offering for sin thou wouldest not, neither hadst pleasure therein; which are offered by the law;	He first said: Sacrifices and oblations and holocausts for sins, which were offered according to the law, thou desiredst not;	Above he said: YOU DO NOT DESIRE SACRIFICES AND OFFERINGS AND BURNT OFFERINGS THAT ARE FOR SINS, THOSE THAT ARE OFFERED ACCORDING TO THE LAW.
9	Then said he, Lo, I come to do thy will, O God. He taketh away the first, that he may establish the second.	and afterwards he said: Behold I come to do thy pleasure, O God: hereby, he abolished the former, that he might establish the latter.	And after that he said: BEHOLD, I HAVE COME TO DO YOUR WILL, [OH] GOD. By this he annulled the first, so that he would establish the second.
10	By the which will we are sanctified through the offering of the body of Jesus Christ once for all.	For by this his pleasure, we are sanctified; through the offering of the body of Jesus the Messiah a single time.	For in this, his will, we are made holy by the offering of the body of Jesus Christ one time.
11	And every priest standeth daily ministering and offering oftentimes the same sacrifices, which can never take away sins:	For every high priest who stood and ministered daily, offered again and again the same sacrifices, which never were sufficient to purge away sins.	For every high priest who stood and served daily offered these same sacrifices that were never able to cleanse sins.
12	But this man, after he had offered one sacrifice for sins for ever, sat down on the right hand of God;	But this [Priest] offered one sacrifice for sins, and for ever sat down at the right hand of God;	But this [one] offered one sacrifice for sins and SAT DOWN AT THE RIGHT HAND OF GOD FOREVER.
13	From henceforth expecting till his enemies be made his footstool.	and thenceforth waited, until his foes should be placed as a footstool under his feet.	And he remains [there] from now on, until his enemies will be placed [as] a footstool under his feet.
14	For by one offering he hath perfected for ever them that are sanctified.	For by one offering, he hath perfected for ever, them who are sanctified by him.	For with one offering he perfected those who were made holy by him forever.
15	Whereof the Holy Ghost also is a witness to us: for after that he had said before,	And the Holy Spirit also testifieth to us, by saying:	Now the Holy Spirit also [is] a witness to us for he said:

Parallel Translations

HEBREWS Chapter 10

	KJV	Murdock	Magiera
16	This is the covenant that I will make with them after those days, saith the Lord, I will put my laws into their hearts, and in their minds will I write them;	This is the covenant which I will give them after those days, saith the Lord; I will put my law into their minds, and inscribe it on their hearts;	THIS IS THE COVENANT THAT I WILL GIVE TO THEM AFTER THOSE DAYS, says the LORD. I WILL PLACE MY LAW IN THEIR MINDS AND I WILL WRITE IT ON THEIR HEARTS,
17	And their sins and iniquities will I remember no more.	and their iniquity and their sins, I will not remember against them.	AND I WILL NOT REMEMBER THEIR WICKEDNESS AND THEIR SINS.
18	Now where remission of these is, there is no more offering for sin.	Now, where there is a remission of sins, there is no offering for sin demanded.	Now where there is forgiveness of sins, an offering for sins is not required.
19	Having therefore, brethren, boldness to enter into the holiest by the blood of Jesus,	We have therefore, my brethren, assurance in entering into the sanctuary, by the blood of Jesus, and by a way of life,	We have, therefore, my brothers, boldness in the entering of the sanctuary by the blood of Jesus
20	By a new and living way, which he hath consecrated for us, through the veil, that is to say, his flesh;	which he hath now consecrated for us, through the veil, that is his flesh.	and a way of life that is now made new for us by the veil that is his flesh.
21	And having an high priest over the house of God;	And we have a high priest over the house of God.	And we have a high priest over the house of God.
22	Let us draw near with a true heart in full assurance of faith, having our hearts sprinkled from an evil conscience, and our bodies washed with pure water.	Let us, therefore draw near, with a true heart, and with the confidence of faith, being sprinkled as to our hearts, and pure from an evil conscience, and our body being washed with pure water.	Therefore, we should come near with a steadfast heart and with the confidence of faith, our hearts being sprinkled and pure from an evil conscience and our body washed with pure water.
23	Let us hold fast the profession of our faith without wavering; (for he is faithful that promised;)	And let us persevere in the profession of our hope, and not waver; for he is faithful who hath made the promise to us.	And we should persist in the confession of our hope and we should not waver, for he is faithful who promised us.
24	And let us consider one another to provoke unto love and to good works:	And let us look on each other, for the excitement of love and good works.	And we should gaze on one another with an encouragement to love and good works.
25	Not forsaking the assembling of ourselves together, as the manner of some is; but exhorting one another: and so much the more, as ye see the day approaching.	And let us not forsake our meetings, as is the custom of some; but entreat ye one another; and the more, as ye see that day draw near.	And we should not forsake our assembly, as is the custom for some, but we should desire [to be with] one another, especially the more you see that day approach.
26	For if we sin wilfully after that we have received the knowledge of the truth, there remaineth no more sacrifice for sins,	For if a man sin, voluntarily, after he hath received a knowledge of the truth, there is no longer a sacrifice which may be offered for sins:	For if by his will a man should sin after he has received knowledge of the truth, there is no longer a sacrifice that may be offered for sins,
27	But a certain fearful looking for of judgment and fiery indignation, which shall devour the adversaries.	but the fearful judgment impendeth, and the zeal of fire that consumeth the adversaries.	but a terrible judgment is prepared and the zeal of fire that will devour the adversaries.

Parallel Translations

HEBREWS *Chapter 10*

	KJV	*Murdock*	*Magiera*
28	He that despised Moses' law died without mercy under two or three witnesses:	For if he, who transgressed the law of Moses, died without mercies, at the mouth of two or three witnesses;	For if he who transgressed against the law of Moses died at the mouth of two or three witnesses without mercy,
29	Of how much sorer punishment, suppose ye, shall he be thought worthy, who hath trodden under foot the Son of God, and hath counted the blood of the covenant, wherewith he was sanctified, an unholy thing, and hath done despite unto the Spirit of grace?	how much more, think ye, will he receive capital punishment, who hath trodden upon the Son of God, and hath accounted the blood of his covenant, by which he is sanctified, as the blood of all men, and hath treated the Spirit of grace with contumely?	how much more do you suppose will he receive capital punishment, who has trampled on the Son of God and has counted the blood of his covenant, by which he was made holy like that of any man, and has despised the Spirit of grace?
30	For we know him that hath said, Vengeance belongeth unto me, I will recompense, saith the Lord. And again, The Lord shall judge his people.	For we know him who hath said, Retribution is mine; and I will repay: and again, The Lord will judge his people.	We know him, who said: VENGEANCE IS MINE AND I WILL REPAY, and again, THE LORD WILL JUDGE HIS PEOPLE.
31	It is a fearful thing to fall into the hands of the living God.	It is very terrible, to fall into the hands of the living God.	There is a great fear to fall into the hands of the living God.
32	But call to remembrance the former days, in which, after ye were illuminated, ye endured a great fight of afflictions;	Therefore, recollect ye the former days, those in which ye received baptism, and endured a great conflict of sufferings, with reproach and affliction;	Remember, therefore, the first days, those in which you received baptism and endured a great contest of sufferings, with reproach and with adversities,
33	Partly, whilst ye were made a gazingstock both by reproaches and afflictions; and partly, whilst ye became companions of them that were so used.	and ye were a gazing stock, and also were the associates of persons who endured these things:	and that you were spectacles and also were associated with men who endured these [things].
34	For ye had compassion of me in my bonds, and took joyfully the spoiling of your goods, knowing in yourselves that ye have in heaven a better and an enduring substance.	and ye were grieved for those who were imprisoned; and ye cheerfully endured the plundering of your goods, because ye knew that ye had a possession in heaven, superior and not transitory.	And you were sorry for those who were imprisoned and you endured the robbery of your possessions with joy, because you knew that you had a possession in heaven that is greater and does not pass away.
35	Cast not away therefore your confidence, which hath great recompence of reward.	Therefore cast not away your assurance which is to have a great reward.	Therefore, do not lose the boldness that you have, for it will have a great reward.
36	For ye have need of patience, that, after ye have done the will of God, ye might receive the promise.	For ye have need of patience; that ye may do the pleasure of God, and may receive the promise.	For endurance is necessary for you to do the will of God and to receive the promise:
37	For yet a little while, and he that shall come will come, and will not tarry.	Because, yet a little,—and it is a very little time,—when he that cometh, will come, and will not delay.	BECAUSE IT IS A LITTLE, EVEN A VERY SHORT TIME, THAT HE WHO COMES WILL COME AND HE WILL NOT DELAY.
38	Now the just shall live by faith: but if any man draw back, my soul shall have no pleasure in him.	Now the just by my faith, will live: but if he draw back, my soul will not have pleasure in him.	NOW THE UPRIGHT WILL LIVE BY MY FAITH AND IF HE SHOULD BE DISCOURAGED, I WILL NOT BE PLEASED WITH HIM.

Parallel Translations

	KJV	*Murdock*	*Magiera*
	HEBREWS *Chapter 10*		
39	But we are not of them who draw back unto perdition; but of them that believe to the saving of the soul.	But we are not of that drawing-back, which leadeth to perdition; but of that faith, which maketh us possess our soul.	But we are not of the drawing back that leads to loss, but of the faith that obtains for us our life.
	Chapter 11		
1	Now faith is the substance of things hoped for, the evidence of things not seen.	Now faith is the persuasion of the things that are in hope, as if they were in act; and [it is] the manifestness of the things not seen.	Now faith is the persuasion concerning those [things] that are in hope, as if they had in fact happened, and the evidence of those [things] that are not seen.
2	For by it the elders obtained a good report.	And for it the ancients are well testified of.	And in this there is a testimony about the ancient [ones].
3	Through faith we understand that the worlds were framed by the word of God, so that things which are seen were not made of things which do appear.	For by faith, we understand that the worlds were framed by the word of God; and that things seen, originated from those that are not seen.	For by faith we understand that the ages were prepared by the word of God and [that] those [things] that are seen were from those [things] that are not seen.
4	By faith Abel offered unto God a more excellent sacrifice than Cain, by which he obtained witness that he was righteous, God testifying of his gifts: and by it he being dead yet speaketh.	By faith, Abel offered to God a better sacrifice than that of Cain; and on account of it, he is testified of that he was righteous, and God bore testimony to his offering; and in consequence thereof, though dead he yet speaketh.	By faith, Abel offered a sacrifice that was more excellent than that of Cain to God, and because of it, there is a testimony about him that he was upright. And God testified to his offering and because of it, although [he is] dead, he speaks.
5	By faith Enoch was translated that he should not see death; and was not found, because God had translated him: for before his translation he had this testimony, that he pleased God.	By faith, Enoch was translated, and did not taste death; and he was not found, because God had translated him: for, before he translated him, there was testimony of him, that he pleased God.	By faith, Enoch was removed and did not taste death. And he was not found, because God had removed him, for before he removed him, there was a testimony about him that he pleased God.
6	But without faith it is impossible to please him: for he that cometh to God must believe that he is, and that he is a rewarder of them that diligently seek him.	But, without faith, a man cannot please God. For he that draweth near to God, must believe his existence, and that he will recompense those who seek him.	Now without faith, no one is able to please God. For he who comes near to God is required to believe that he is and [that] he is a rewarder of those who seek him.
7	By faith Noah, being warned of God of things not seen as yet, moved with fear, prepared an ark to the saving of his house; by the which he condemned the world, and became heir of the righteousness which is by faith.	By faith Noah, when he was told of things not seen, feared; and he made himself an ark, for the life of his household; whereby he condemned the world, and became an heir of the righteousness which is by faith.	By faith, Noah, when it was told to him about those [things] that are not seen, feared and made for himself an ark for the life of his household, by which he condemned the world and became heir of the uprightness that is by faith.
8	By faith Abraham, when he was called to go out into a place which he should after receive for an inheritance, obeyed; and he went out, not knowing whither he went.	By faith Abraham, when he was called, obeyed, and departed to the place which he was to receive for an inheritance: and he departed, while he knew not whither he was going.	By faith, Abraham, when he was called to leave for a place that he was going to receive for an inheritance, obeyed and went out, not knowing where he was going.

	KJV	Murdock	Magiera
	HEBREWS Chapter 11		
9	By faith he sojourned in the land of promise, as in a strange country, dwelling in tabernacles with Isaac and Jacob, the heirs with him of the same promise:	By faith, he became a resident in the land that was promised him, as in a foreign land; and abode in tents, with Isaac and Jacob, the heirs with him of the same promise.	By faith, he was a settler in the land that was promised to him as in a foreign country and he lived in tents with Isaac and Jacob, his fellow-heirs of the promise,
10	For he looked for a city which hath foundations, whose builder and maker is God.	For he looked for the city that hath a foundation, of which the builder and maker is God.	for he was waiting for a city that had a foundation, whose craftsman and maker is God.
11	Through faith also Sara herself received strength to conceive seed, and was delivered of a child when she was past age, because she judged him faithful who had promised.	By faith, Sarah also, who was barren, acquired energy to receive seed; and, out of the time of her years, she brought forth; because she firmly believed, that he was faithful who had promised her.	By faith also, Sarah, who was barren, received strength to receive seed and when her years were past, she gave birth, because she was convinced that he who had promised her was faithful.
12	Therefore sprang there even of one, and him as good as dead, so many as the stars of the sky in multitude, and as the sand which is by the sea shore innumerable.	Therefore, from one man failing through age, numbers were born, like the stars in the heavens, and like the sand on the shore of the sea which is innumerable.	Because of this, from one who was failing in old age, many [people] were born, as the stars in heaven and as the sand on the shore of the sea that has no number.
13	These all died in faith, not having received the promises, but having seen them afar off, and were persuaded of them, and embraced them, and confessed that they were strangers and pilgrims on the earth.	All these died in faith, and received not their promise; but they saw it afar off, and rejoiced in it; and they confessed that they were strangers and pilgrims on the earth.	These all died in faith and did not receive their promise, but they saw it from a distance and rejoiced in it and confessed that they were strangers and settlers on the earth.
14	For they that say such things declare plainly that they seek a country.	Now they who say thus, show that they seek a city.	Now those who say these [things] demonstrate that they seek their city.
15	And truly, if they had been mindful of that country from whence they came out, they might have had opportunity to have returned.	But if they had been seeking that city from which they came out, they had opportunity to return again and go to it.	And if they were seeking that city from which they came out, they had an opportunity to return again [and] to go to it.
16	But now they desire a better country, that is, an heavenly: wherefore God is not ashamed to be called their God: for he hath prepared for them a city.	But now it is manifest that they longed for a better [city] than that, [namely,] for that which is in heaven. Therefore God did not refuse to be called their God; for he prepared for them the city.	But now it is evident that they were longing for a better [city] than that, for the [one] that is in heaven. Because of this, God was not ashamed to be called their God, for he has prepared a city for them.
17	By faith Abraham, when he was tried, offered up Isaac: and he that had received the promises offered up his only begotten son,	By faith Abraham, in his trial, offered up Isaac; and he laid on the altar his only son, whom he had received by promise.	By faith, Abraham in his trial offered Isaac and lifted up his only [son] on the altar, whom he had received by promise,
18	Of whom it was said, That in Isaac shall thy seed be called:	For it had been said to him, In Isaac shall thy seed be called.	for it was said to him: IN ISAAC YOUR SEED WILL BE CALLED.
19	Accounting that God was able to raise him up, even from the dead; from whence also he received him in a figure.	And he reasoned with himself, that God was able even to raise [him] from the dead: and therefore, in the similitude [of a resurrection], he was restored to him.	And he reasoned in himself that God was able even to raise [him] from the dead, and because of this, he was given back to him [as] in a parable.

Parallel Translations

	KJV	*Murdock*	*Magiera*
	HEBREWS	*Chapter 11*	
20	By faith Isaac blessed Jacob and Esau concerning things to come.	By faith in what was to be, Isaac blessed Jacob and Esau.	By faith regarding what was going to be, Isaac blessed Jacob and Esau.
21	By faith Jacob, when he was a dying, blessed both the sons of Joseph; and worshipped, leaning upon the top of his staff.	By faith Jacob, when dying, blessed each of the sons of Joseph, and bowed himself on the top of his staff.	By faith, when he was dying, Jacob blessed each one of the sons of Joseph and worshipped [leaning] on the top of his staff.
22	By faith Joseph, when he died, made mention of the departing of the children of Israel; and gave commandment concerning his bones.	By faith Joseph, when dying, was mindful of the departure of the children of Israel, and gave direction concerning his bones.	By faith, Joseph, when he was dying, remembered the departure of the sons of Israel and directed [them] concerning his bones.
23	By faith Moses, when he was born, was hid three months of his parents, because they saw he was a proper child; and they were not afraid of the king's commandment.	By faith the parents of Moses, after he was born, hid him three months; because they saw he was a goodly child; and they were not deterred by the command of the king.	By faith, the parents of Moses hid him after he was born [for] three months, because they saw that he was a special child and they were not afraid of the commandment of the king.
24	By faith Moses, when he was come to years, refused to be called the son of Pharaoh's daughter;	By faith Moses, when be became a man, refused to be called the son of Pharaoh's daughter.	By faith, Moses, when he was a man, insisted that he should not be called a son of the daughter of Pharaoh.
25	Choosing rather to suffer affliction with the people of God, than to enjoy the pleasures of sin for a season;	And he chose to be in affliction with the people of God, and not to live luxuriously in sin for a short season:	And he chose to be in adversity with the people of God and, not even for a short time, to be merry in sin.
26	Esteeming the reproach of Christ greater riches than the treasures in Egypt: for he had respect unto the recompence of the reward.	and he esteemed the reproach of the Messiah a greater treasure than the hoarded riches of Egypt; for he looked upon the recompense of reward.	And he considered that the wealth of the reproach of Christ was more excellent than the treasures of Egypt, for he looked at the payment of the reward.
27	By faith he forsook Egypt, not fearing the wrath of the king: for he endured, as seeing him who is invisible.	By faith, he left Egypt, and was not terrified by the wrath of the king; and he continued to hope, just as if he saw the invisible God.	By faith, he left Egypt and was not afraid of the fury of the king. And he endured as one who has seen God, who is not visible.
28	Through faith he kept the passover, and the sprinkling of blood, lest he that destroyed the firstborn should touch them.	By faith, they kept the passover, and the sprinkling of blood, that he who destroyed the first-born might not approach them.	By faith, he kept the Feast of Passover and the sprinkling of blood, so that he who destroyed the firstborn should not approach them.
29	By faith they passed through the Red sea as by dry land: which the Egyptians assaying to do were drowned.	By faith, they passed the Red Sea, as on dry land; and in it the Egyptians were swallowed up, when they dared to enter it.	By faith, they crossed over the Red Sea, as on dry ground, in which the Egyptians were drowned when they dared to enter it.
30	By faith the walls of Jericho fell down, after they were compassed about seven days.	By faith, the walls of Jericho fell down, when they had been encompassed seven days.	By faith, the walls of Jericho fell after they had been surrounded [for] seven days.
31	By faith the harlot Rahab perished not with them that believed not, when she had received the spies with peace.	By faith Rahab, the harlot, perished not with them who believed not, when she received the spies in peace.	By faith, Rahab, the harlot, was not destroyed with those who did not obey, because she received the spies in peace.

Parallel Translations

HEBREWS *Chapter 11*

	KJV	*Murdock*	*Magiera*
32	And what shall I more say? for the time would fail me to tell of Gedeon, and of Barak, and of Samson, and of Jephthae; of David also, and Samuel, and of the prophets:	What more shall I say? For I have little time to tell of Gideon, and of Barak, and of Sampson, and of Jephtha, and of David, and of Samuel, and of the other prophets:	And what more can I say? For the time is [too] short for me to tell about Gideon and about Barak and about Samson and about Jephthah and about David and about Samuel and about the rest of the prophets,
33	Who through faith subdued kingdoms, wrought righteousness, obtained promises, stopped the mouths of lions,	who, by faith, subdued kingdoms, and wrought righteousness, and received promises, and shut the mouths of lions,	those who by faith overcame kingdoms and worked [with] uprightness and received the promises and shut the mouth[s] of lions
34	Quenched the violence of fire, escaped the edge of the sword, out of weakness were made strong, waxed valiant in fight, turned to flight the armies of the aliens.	and quenched the force of fire, and were rescued from the edge of the sword, and were healed of diseases, and became strong in battle, and routed the camps of enemies,	and quenched the power of fire and were delivered from the edge of the sword and were strengthened of weaknesses and became mighty in battle and routed the armies of the enemies
35	Women received their dead raised to life again: and others were tortured, not accepting deliverance; that they might obtain a better resurrection:	and restored to women their children, by a resurrection from the dead. And some died under tortures, and did not hope to escape, that there might be for them a better resurrection;	and gave [back] to women their children by raising of the dead. And others died in tortures and did not expect to escape, so that they would have the better resurrection.
36	And others had trial of cruel mockings and scourgings, yea, moreover of bonds and imprisonment:	and others endured mockings and, scourgings; others were delivered up to bonds and prisons;	Now others entered into jeering and beatings, others were delivered to prisons and to captivities,
37	They were stoned, they were sawn asunder, were tempted, were slain with the sword: they wandered about in sheepskins and goatskins; being destitute, afflicted, tormented;	others were stoned; others were sawed; others died by the edge of the sword; others roamed about clothed in sheep skins and goat skins, and were needy, and afflicted, and agitated;	others were stoned, others were sawed apart, others died by the edge of the sword, others wandered about clothed with the skins of lambs and of goats and were needy and troubled and wearied,
38	(Of whom the world was not worthy:) they wandered in deserts, and in mountains, and in dens and caves of the earth.	persons of whom the world was not worthy, and yet they were as wanderers in the desert, and in mountains, and in caves, and in caverns of the earth.	men of whom the world was not worthy. And they were as forgotten [ones] in the wilderness and in the mountains and in the caves and in the holes of the earth.
39	And these all, having obtained a good report through faith, received not the promise:	And all these, of whose faith there is testimony, received not the promise:	And all these, about whom there is a testimony by their faith, did not receive the promise,
40	God having provided some better thing for us, that they without us should not be made perfect.	because God had provided the aid for us; so that without us they should not be perfected.	because God had considered beforehand our benefit, that they should not be perfected without us.

Parallel Translations

	KJV	*Murdock*	*Magiera*

HEBREWS *Chapter 12*

Verse	KJV	Murdock	Magiera
1	Wherefore seeing we also are compassed about with so great a cloud of witnesses, let us lay aside every weight, and the sin which doth so easily beset us, and let us run with patience the race that is set before us,	Therefore let us also, who have all these witnesses surrounding us like clouds, cast from us all encumbrances, and sin, which is always prepared for us; and let us run with patience the race that is appointed for us.	Because of this also, we, who have all these witnesses that surround us like a cloud, should unfasten all our burdens from us, even the sin that is always prepared for us, and we should run with patience this race that is set for us.
2	Looking unto Jesus the author and finisher of our faith; who for the joy that was set before him endured the cross, despising the shame, and is set down at the right hand of the throne of God.	And let us look on Jesus, who hath become the commencement and the completion of our faith; who, on account of the joy there was for him, endured the cross, and surrendered himself to opprobrium; and is seated on the right hand of the throne of God.	And we should look at Jesus, who was the initiator and finisher of our faith, who for the joy there was for him endured the cross and discounted the shame and sat down at the right hand of the throne of God.
3	For consider him that endured such contradiction of sinners against himself, lest ye be wearied and faint in your minds.	Behold, therefore, how much he suffered from sinners, from them who are adversaries of their own soul, that ye may not be discouraged, nor your soul become remiss.	See, therefore, how much he endured from sinners who are contrary to themselves, so that you should not be weary or your soul become faint.
4	Ye have not yet resisted unto blood, striving against sin.	Ye have not yet come unto blood, in the contest against sin.	You have not yet come to [shedding of] blood in the contest that is against sin.
5	And ye have forgotten the exhortation which speaketh unto you as unto children, My son, despise not thou the chastening of the Lord, nor faint when thou art rebuked of him:	And ye have forgotten the monition, which saith to you, as to children, My son, disregard not the chastening of the Lord; nor let thy soul faint, when thou art rebuked by him.	And you have forgotten the instruction, which says to you as to children: MY SON, DO NOT DISREGARD THE DISCIPLINE OF THE LORD, NOR LET YOUR SOUL FAINT WHEN YOU ARE REPROVED BY HIM.
6	For whom the Lord loveth he chasteneth, and scourgeth every son whom he receiveth.	For, whom the Lord loveth, he chasteneth; and he scourgeth those sons, for whom he hath kind regards.	FOR THE LORD DISCIPLINES HIM WHOM HE LOVES AND SCOURGES THE SONS WITH WHOM HE IS PLEASED.
7	If ye endure chastening, God dealeth with you as with sons; for what son is he whom the father chasteneth not?	Therefore endure ye the chastisement; because God is dealing with you as with sons. For what son is there, whom his father chasteneth not?	Therefore, endure discipline, because God is dealing with you as with sons. For what son is there whom his father does not discipline?
8	But if ye be without chastisement, whereof all are partakers, then are ye bastards, and not sons.	But if ye are without that chastisement, with which every one is chastened, ye are become strangers and not sons.	And if you are without the discipline with which everyone is disciplined, you have become strangers and not sons.

HEBREWS *Chapter 12*

	KJV	*Murdock*	*Magiera*
9	Furthermore we have had fathers of our flesh which corrected us, and we gave them reverence: shall we not much rather be in subjection unto the Father of spirits, and live?	And if our fathers of the flesh chastened us, and we revered them, how much more ought we to be submissive to our spiritual fathers, and live?	And if our fathers of the flesh disciplined us and we respect them, how much more then ought we to obey our spiritual Father and live?
10	For they verily for a few days chastened us after their own pleasure; but he for our profit, that we might be partakers of his holiness.	For they chastened us for a short time, according to their pleasure; but God, for our advantage, that we may become partakers of his holiness.	For those for a short time disciplined us according to what they wanted, but God [disciplines us] for our benefit, so that we will share in his holiness.
11	Now no chastening for the present seemeth to be joyous, but grievous: nevertheless afterward it yieldeth the peaceable fruit of righteousness unto them which are exercised thereby.	Now all chastisement, in the time of it, is not accounted a matter of joy, but of grief: yet, afterwards, it yieldeth the fruits of peace and righteousness to them who are exercised by it.	Now at the time, no discipline is thought to be [a matter] of joy, but of sorrow. But in the end it bears the fruit of peace and of justification to those who are trained by it.
12	Wherefore lift up the hands which hang down, and the feeble knees;	Wherefore, strengthen ye your relaxed hands, and your tottering knees:	Because of this, strengthen your weak hands and your trembling knees
13	And make straight paths for your feet, lest that which is lame be turned out of the way; but let it rather be healed.	and make straight paths for your feet, that the limb which is lame may not be wrenched, but may be healed.	and make straight paths for your feet, so that the leg that is limping will not stumble, but be healed.
14	Follow peace with all men, and holiness, without which no man shall see the Lord:	Follow after peace with every man; and after holiness, without which a man will not see our Lord.	Run after peace with everyone and after holiness, without which a man does not see our Lord.
15	Looking diligently lest any man fail of the grace of God; lest any root of bitterness springing up trouble you, and thereby many be defiled;	And be careful, lest any be found among you destitute of the grace of God; or lest some root of bitterness shoot forth germs, and trouble you; and thereby many be defiled:	And be watchful, so that no one will be found among you who lacks the grace of God, or so that a root of bitterness will not produce a flower and harm you and by it, many should be corrupted,
16	Lest there be any fornicator, or profane person, as Esau, who for one morsel of meat sold his birthright.	or lest any one be found among you a fornicator; or a heedless one like Esau, who for one mess of food, sold his primogeniture.	or [so that] no one will be found among you who is a fornicator and a careless [one], such as Esau, who sold his birthright for one meal.
17	For ye know how that afterward, when he would have inherited the blessing, he was rejected: for he found no place of repentance, though he sought it carefully with tears.	For ye know that, afterwards when he wished to inherit the blessing, he was rejected; for he found not a place for repentance, although he sought it with tears.	For you know that also afterwards he wanted to inherit the blessing, but was rejected, for he did not find a place of repentance, although he begged for it with tears.
18	For ye are not come unto the mount that might be touched, and that burned with fire, nor unto blackness, and darkness, and tempest,	For ye have not come to the fire that burned, and the tangible [mount]; nor to the darkness and obscurity and tempest;	For you have not come near to the fire [of the mountain] that burned and was tangible, nor even to the darkness and mist and storm,

Parallel Translations

	KJV	Murdock	Magiera

HEBREWS Chapter 12

	KJV	Murdock	Magiera
19	And the sound of a trumpet, and the voice of words; which voice they that heard intreated that the word should not be spoken to them any more:	nor to the sound of the trumpet, and the voice of words, which they who heard, entreated that it might no more be spoken to them;	nor to the sound of the trumpet and the voice of words, which those who heard asked that it should not continue to be spoken to them.
20	(For they could not endure that which was commanded, And if so much as a beast touch the mountain, it shall be stoned, or thrust through with a dart:	for they could not endure what was commanded. And even a beast, if it approached the mountain, was to be stoned.	For they were not able to bear what they were commanded: IF EVEN AN ANIMAL SHOULD COME NEAR TO THE MOUNTAIN, IT SHOULD BE STONED.
21	And so terrible was the sight, that Moses said, I exceedingly fear and quake:)	And so terrible was the sight, that Moses said, I fear and tremble.	And the sight was so terrible that Moses said: I AM AFRAID AND I AM TREMBLING.
22	But ye are come unto mount Sion, and unto the city of the living God, the heavenly Jerusalem, and to an innumerable company of angels,	But ye have come to Mount Zion, and to the city of the living God, the Jerusalem that is in heaven; and to the assemblies of myriads of angels;	But you have come near to the mountain of Zion and to the city of the living God, to the Jerusalem that is in heaven, and to the multitudes of numbers of angels
23	To the general assembly and church of the firstborn, which are written in heaven, and to God the Judge of all, and to the spirits of just men made perfect,	and to the church of the first-born, who are enrolled in heaven and to God the judge of all; and to the spirits of the just, who are perfected;	and to the church of the firstborn, who are written in heaven, and to God, the judge of all, and to the spiritual [things] of the upright [ones] who are matured,
24	And to Jesus the mediator of the new covenant, and to the blood of sprinkling, that speaketh better things than that of Abel.	and to Jesus, the Mediator of the new covenant; and to the sprinkling, of his blood, which speaketh better than that of Abel.	and to Jesus, the mediator of the new covenant, and to the sprinkling of his blood that speaks more than that of Abel.
25	See that ye refuse not him that speaketh. For if they escaped not who refused him that spake on earth, much more shall not we escape, if we turn away from him that speaketh from heaven:	Beware, therefore, lest ye refuse [to hear] him who speaketh with you. For if they escaped not, who refused [to hear] him who spake with them on the earth, how much more shall we not, if we refuse [to hear] him who speaketh with us from heaven?	Watch, therefore, so that you will not refuse [to hear] him who speaks to you. For if those who refuse him who speaks with them on earth are not delivered, how much more we, if we refuse him who speaks with us from heaven,
26	Whose voice then shook the earth: but now he hath promised, saying, Yet once more I shake not the earth only, but also heaven.	Whose voice [then] shook the earth; but now he hath promised, and said, yet again once more, I will shake not the earth only, but also heaven.	whose voice shook the earth? But now he has promised and said: AGAIN, ONCE MORE, I WILL SHAKE, NOT ONLY THE EARTH, BUT ALSO HEAVEN.
27	And this word, Yet once more, signifieth the removing of those things that are shaken, as of things that are made, that those things which cannot be shaken may remain.	And this his expression, Once more, indicateth the mutation of the things that are shaken, because they are fabricated; that the things which will not be shaken, may remain.	Now this that he said, "Once more," indicates a change of those [things] that are shaken, because they are [things that are] made, so that those that are unshakable may remain.

Parallel Translations

	KJV	Murdock	Magiera
HEBREWS *Chapter 12*			
28	Wherefore we receiving a kingdom which cannot be moved, let us have grace, whereby we may serve God acceptably with reverence and godly fear:	Since, therefore, we have received a kingdom that is unshaken, let us grasp the grace whereby we may serve and please God, with reverence and fear.	Therefore, because we have received a kingdom that is unshakable, we should hold fast to the grace, by which we may serve and may please God, with reverence and with fear.
29	For our God is a consuming fire.	For our God is a consuming fire.	FOR OUR GOD IS A DEVOURING FIRE.
Chapter 13			
1	Let brotherly love continue.	Let love for the brethren dwell among you.	Love of the brothers should continue in you.
2	Be not forgetful to entertain strangers: for thereby some have entertained angels unawares.	And forget not kindness to strangers; for thereby some have been privileged to entertain angels, unawares.	And do not forget [to have] compassion to strangers, for by this some have been worthy to receive angels, being unaware [of it].
3	Remember them that are in bonds, as bound with them; and them which suffer adversity, as being yourselves also in the body.	And remember those in bonds, as if ye were bound with them: and recollect those in affliction, as being yourselves clothed in flesh.	Remember those who are imprisoned, as if you are imprisoned with them. Remember those who are troubled, because you [also] are clothed with flesh as a man.
4	Marriage is honourable in all, and the bed undefiled: but whoremongers and adulterers God will judge.	Marriage is honorable in all; and their bed undefiled: but whoremongers and adulterers, God will judge.	Marriage is honorable in all and their bed is pure, but God will judge fornicators and adulterers.
5	Let your conversation be without covetousness; and be content with such things as ye have: for he hath said, I will never leave thee, nor forsake thee.	Let not your mind love money; but let what ye have, satisfy you. For the Lord himself hath said, I will never leave thee, nor slacken the hand towards thee.	Your mind should not love money, but what you have should be sufficient for you. For the LORD has said: I WILL NOT LEAVE YOU AND I WILL NOT LET GO OF YOU.
6	So that we may boldly say, The Lord is my helper, and I will not fear what man shall do unto me.	And it belongeth to us, to say confidently, My Lord is my aider, I will not fear. What can man do to me?	And we can say confidently: MY LORD IS MY HELPER. I WILL NOT BE AFRAID. WHAT DOES A MAN DO TO ME?
7	Remember them which have the rule over you, who have spoken unto you the word of God: whose faith follow, considering the end of their conversation.	Remember your guides, who have spoken to you godly discourse; examine the issue of their course, and imitate their faith.	Remember your leaders who have spoken the word of God with you. Consider the result of their manners of life and imitate their faith.
8	Jesus Christ the same yesterday, and to day, and for ever.	Jesus the Messiah is the same, yesterday, to-day, and for ever.	Jesus Christ is [the same] yesterday and today and forever.
9	Be not carried about with divers and strange doctrines. For it is a good thing that the heart be established with grace; not with meats, which have not profited them that have been occupied therein.	Be not led away by strange and variable doctrines. For it is a good thing, that we strengthen our hearts with grace, and not with meats; for those have not been benefited, who walked in them.	Do not be led away by strange and diverse teachings, for it is good that we strengthen our hearts with grace and not with things to eat, because those who have walked in them have not been benefited.
10	We have an altar, whereof they have no right to eat which serve the tabernacle.	And we have an altar, of which they who minister in the tabernacle have no right to eat.	And we have an altar from which those who serve in the tabernacle have no right to eat.

Parallel Translations

HEBREWS *Chapter 13*

	KJV	*Murdock*	*Magiera*
11	For the bodies of those beasts, whose blood is brought into the sanctuary by the high priest for sin, are burned without the camp.	For the flesh of those animals, whose blood the high priest brought into the sanctuary for sins, was burned without the camp.	For the animals, those whose blood the high priests brought into the sanctuary for sins, their flesh was burned outside of the camp.
12	Wherefore Jesus also, that he might sanctify the people with his own blood, suffered without the gate.	For this reason, Jesus also, that he might sanctify his people with his blood, suffered without the city.	Because of this also, Jesus, so that he would make holy his people by his blood, suffered outside of the city.
13	Let us go forth therefore unto him without the camp, bearing his reproach.	Therefore, let us also go forth to him, without the camp, clothed with his reproach:	And also we, therefore, should go out to him outside of the camp, bearing his reproach.
14	For here have we no continuing city, but we seek one to come.	(for we have here no abiding city; but we expect one that is future:)	For we have no city that remains here, but we expect one to come.
15	By him therefore let us offer the sacrifice of praise to God continually, that is, the fruit of our lips giving thanks to his name.	and through him, let us at all times offer to God the sacrifices of praise, that is, the fruits of lips which give thanks to his name.	And by way of him, we should always offer up the sacrifices of praise to God, which is the fruit of lips that give thanks to his name.
16	But to do good and to communicate forget not: for with such sacrifices God is well pleased.	And forget not commiseration and communication with the poor; for with such sacrifices a man pleaseth God.	And do not forget lovingkindness and sharing with the poor, for with these sacrifices a man pleases God.
17	Obey them that have the rule over you, and submit yourselves: for they watch for your souls, as they that must give account, that they may do it with joy, and not with grief: for that is unprofitable for you.	Confide in your guides, and hearken to them; for they watch for your souls, as men who must give an account of you, that they may do this with joy and not with anguish; for that would not be profitable to you.	Be convicted by your leaders and obey them, for they watch for your lives as men who give an accounting of you, so that with joy they may do this and not with groanings, because that is not profitable for you.
18	Pray for us: for we trust we have a good conscience, in all things willing to live honestly.	Pray ye for us; for we trust we have a good consciousness, that in all things we desire to conduct ourselves well.	Pray for us, for we trust that we have a good conscience, that in everything we want to conduct ourselves well.
19	But I beseech you the rather to do this, that I may be restored to you the sooner.	Especially do I request you to do this, that I may return to you speedily.	I am begging you to do this especially, that I may be returned to you quickly.
20	Now the God of peace, that brought again from the dead our Lord Jesus, that great shepherd of the sheep, through the blood of the everlasting covenant,	May the God of peace, who brought up from the dead the great Shepherd of the flock, by the blood of the everlasting covenant, namely Jesus the Messiah, our Lord,	Now may the God of peace, who brought up from the dead the great Shepherd of the flock by the blood of the everlasting covenant, who is Jesus Christ our Lord,
21	Make you perfect in every good work to do his will, working in you that which is wellpleasing in his sight, through Jesus Christ; to whom be glory for ever and ever. Amen.	make you perfect in every good work, that ye may do his pleasure; and himself operate in you that which is pleasing In his sight, through Jesus the Messiah; to whom be glory for ever and ever. Amen.	mature you in every good work to do his will and to perform in us what is pleasing before him, by way of Jesus Christ, to whom [be] glory forever and ever. Amen.

Parallel Translations

	KJV	Murdock	Magiera

HEBREWS *Chapter 13*

	KJV	Murdock	Magiera
22	And I beseech you, brethren, suffer the word of exhortation: for I have written a letter unto you in few words.	And I beseech you, my brethren, that ye be patient under this word of exhortation; for it is in few words I have written to you.	And I am begging you, my brothers, to be long-suffering in [this] word of encouragement, because I have written to you in few [words].
23	Know ye that our brother Timothy is set at liberty; with whom, if he come shortly, I will see you.	And know ye, that our brother Timothy is set at liberty: and if he come soon, I, with him, shall see you.	And know that our brother Timothy is set free, and if he comes soon, I will see you with him.
24	Salute all them that have the rule over you, and all the saints. They of Italy salute you.	Salute all your guides, and all the saints. All they of Italy salute you.	Greet all your leaders and all the holy [ones]. All who are from Italy greet you.
25	Grace be with you all. Amen.	Grace be with you all. Amen.	Grace [be] with all of you. Amen.

Parallel Translations

JAMES Chapter 1

	KJV	Murdock	Magiera
1	James, a servant of God and of the Lord Jesus Christ, to the twelve tribes which are scattered abroad, greeting.	James, a servant of God, and of our Lord Jesus the Messiah; to the twelve tribes dispersed among the Gentiles; greeting [peace].	James, a servant of God and of our Lord Jesus Christ, to the twelve tribes that are scattered among the nations: Peace.
2	My brethren, count it all joy when ye fall into divers temptations;	Let it be all joy to you, my brethren, when ye enter into many and various trials.	You should have all joy, my brothers, when you enter into various and numerous trials,
3	Knowing this, that the trying of your faith worketh patience.	For ye know, that the trial of [your] faith, maketh you possess patience.	for you know that the experience of faith causes you to obtain patience.
4	But let patience have her perfect work, that ye may be perfect and entire, wanting nothing.	And let patience have its perfect work, so that ye may be complete and perfect, and may lack nothing.	Now patience should have a full work that you may be mature and complete and not lacking in anything.
5	If any of you lack wisdom, let him ask of God, that giveth to all men liberally, and upbraideth not; and it shall be given him.	And if any of you lacketh wisdom, let him ask [it] of God, who giveth to all freely, and reproacheth not; and it will be given him.	Now if any of you lacks wisdom, he should ask [for it] from God, who gives generously to all and does not reproach and it will be given to him.
6	But let him ask in faith, nothing wavering. For he that wavereth is like a wave of the sea driven with the wind and tossed.	But let him ask in faith, not hesitating: he who hesitateth is like the waves of the sea, which the wind agitateth.	But he should ask in faith, not doubting, for he who doubts is like the waves of the sea that the wind stirs up.
7	For let not that man think that he shall receive any thing of the Lord.	And let not that man expect to receive any thing of the Lord,	And that man should not expect to receive anything from the LORD,
8	A double minded man is unstable in all his ways.	who is hesitating in his mind, and unstable in all his ways.	who doubts in his mind and is troubled in all his ways.
9	Let the brother of low degree rejoice in that he is exalted:	And let the depressed brother rejoice, in his elevation;	And the humble brother should boast in his lifted position
10	But the rich, in that he is made low: because as the flower of the grass he shall pass away.	and the rich, in his depression; because, like the flower of an herb, so he passeth away.	and the rich in his humility, because as the flower of an herb, likewise he passes away.
11	For the sun is no sooner risen with a burning heat, but it withereth the grass, and the flower thereof falleth, and the grace of the fashion of it perisheth: so also shall the rich man fade away in his ways.	For the sun riseth in its heat, and drieth up the herb; and its flower falleth, and the beauty of its appearance perisheth: so also the rich man withereth in his ways.	For the sun will rise with its heat and will dry up the herb and its flower will fall and the beauty of its appearance will be destroyed. So also the rich [man] withers in his ways.
12	Blessed is the man that endureth temptation: for when he is tried, he shall receive the crown of life, which the Lord hath promised to them that love him.	Blessed is the man who endureth temptations; so that when he is proved he may receive a crown of life, which God hath promised to them that love him.	Blessed [is] the man who endures trials, so that when he is examined, he may receive the crown of life that God promised to those who love him.
13	Let no man say when he is tempted, I am tempted of God: for God cannot be tempted with evil, neither tempteth he any man:	Let no one when he is tempted, say, I am tempted of God: for God is not tempted with evils, nor doth he tempt any man.	No one should say when he is tempted, "I am tempted by God," for God is not tempted with evil [things] and does not tempt anyone.

JAMES Chapter 1

	KJV	Murdock	Magiera
14	But every man is tempted, when he is drawn away of his own lust, and enticed.	But every man is tempted by his own lust; and he lusteth, and is drawn away.	But each man is tempted by his [own] desire and he desires and is dragged away
15	Then when lust hath conceived, it bringeth forth sin: and sin, when it is finished, bringeth forth death.	And this [his] lust conceiveth, and bringeth forth sin; and sin, when mature, bringeth forth death.	and this desire conceives and produces sin. And sin, when it is matured, produces death.
16	Do not err, my beloved brethren.	Do not err, my beloved brethren.	Do not err, my beloved brothers.
17	Every good gift and every perfect gift is from above, and cometh down from the Father of lights, with whom is no variableness, neither shadow of turning.	Every good and perfect gift cometh down from above, from the Father of lights, with whom is no mutation, not even the shadow of change.	Every good and complete gift [is] from above, coming down from the Father of lights, with whom there is not any inconstancy, not even a shadow of change.
18	Of his own will begat he us with the word of truth, that we should be a kind of firstfruits of his creatures.	He saw fit, and begat us by the word of truth; that we might be the first-fruits of his creatures.	It is he [who] desired and fathered us by the word of truthfulness that we would be the first[fruit] of his created [ones].
19	Wherefore, my beloved brethren, let every man be swift to hear, slow to speak, slow to wrath:	And be ye, my beloved brethren, every one of you, swift to hear, and slow to speak; and slow to wrath:	And you, my beloved brothers, everyone of you should be quick to hear and slow to speak and slow to be angry.
20	For the wrath of man worketh not the righteousness of God.	for the wrath of man worketh not the righteousness of God.	For the anger of man does not serve the justification of God.
21	Wherefore lay apart all filthiness and superfluity of naughtiness, and receive with meekness the engrafted word, which is able to save your souls.	Wherefore, remove far from you all impurity, and the abundance of wickedness; and, with meekness, receive the word that is implanted in our nature, which is able to vivify these your souls.	Because of this, put away from you all uncleanness and the abundance of wickedness and receive with meekness the word that is implanted in our nature that is able to give life to your souls.
22	But be ye doers of the word, and not hearers only, deceiving your own selves.	But be ye doers of the word, and not hearers only; and do not deceive yourselves.	And be doers of the word and not hearers only and do not deceive yourselves.
23	For if any be a hearer of the word, and not a doer, he is like unto a man beholding his natural face in a glass:	For if any man shall be a hearer of the word, and not a doer of it, he will be like one who seeth his face in a mirror:	For if anyone is a hearer of the word and not a doer of it, this [one] is like him who sees his face in a mirror,
24	For he beholdeth himself, and goeth his way, and straightway forgetteth what manner of man he was.	for he seeth himself, and passeth on, and forgetteth what a man he was.	for he sees himself and passes on and forgets what kind [of man] he was.
25	But whoso looketh into the perfect law of liberty, and continueth therein, he being not a forgetful hearer, but a doer of the work, this man shall be blessed in his deed.	But every one that looketh upon the perfect law of liberty and abideth in it, is not a hearer of something to be forgotten, but a doer of the things; and he will be blessed in his work.	And everyone who looks into the fulfilled law of liberty and remains in it is not a hearer of a report that is forgotten, but a doer of deeds. And this [one] will be blessed in his deed.
26	If any man among you seem to be religious, and bridleth not his tongue, but deceiveth his own heart, this man's religion is vain.	And if any one thinketh that he worshippeth God, and doth not restrain his tongue, but his heart deceiveth him; his worship is vain.	And if a man supposes that he serves God and he does not hold his tongue, but the heart of this [man] deceives him, [then] his service is unprofitable.

Parallel Translations

JAMES — Chapter 1

	KJV	Murdock	Magiera
27	Pure religion and undefiled before God and the Father is this, To visit the fatherless and widows in their affliction, and to keep himself unspotted from the world.	For the worship that is pure and holy before God the Father, is this: to visit the fatherless and the widows in their affliction, and that one keep himself unspotted from the world.	For the service that is pure and holy before God the Father is this, to visit orphans and widows in their troubles and to keep oneself without spot from the world.

Chapter 2

	KJV	Murdock	Magiera
1	My brethren, have not the faith of our Lord Jesus Christ, the Lord of glory, with respect of persons.	My brethren, hold ye not the faith of the glory of our Lord Jesus the Messiah, with a respect to persons.	My brothers, do not hold to the faith of the glory of our Lord Jesus Christ with respect of persons.
2	For if there come unto your assembly a man with a gold ring, in goodly apparel, and there come in also a poor man in vile raiment;	For if there come into your assembly a man with rings of gold or splendid garments, and there come in a poor man in sordid garments;	For if a man should enter your assembly with rings of gold or with beautiful garments and a poor man should enter with filthy garments,
3	And ye have respect to him that weareth the gay clothing, and say unto him, Sit thou here in a good place; and say to the poor, Stand thou there, or sit here under my footstool:	and ye show respect to him who is clothed in splendid garments, and say to him, Seat thyself here, conspicuously; while to the poor man, ye say, Stand thou there, or sit thou here before my footstool;	and you look at that one clothed with beautiful garments and say to him, "Sit here [in] a good [place]," and to the poor man you say, "Stand back or sit here before the footstool,"
4	Are ye not then partial in yourselves, and are become judges of evil thoughts?	are ye not divided among yourselves, and become expositors of evil thoughts?	behold, are you not discriminating among yourselves and have you [not] become expounders of evil reasonings?
5	Hearken, my beloved brethren, Hath not God chosen the poor of this world rich in faith, and heirs of the kingdom which he hath promised to them that love him?	Hear, my beloved brethren; hath not God chosen the poor of the world, but the rich in faith, to be heirs in the kingdom which God hath promised to them that love him?	Hear, my beloved brothers, was it not the poor of the world, but [who are] rich in faith [that] God chose to be heirs in the kingdom that God promised to those who love him?
6	But ye have despised the poor. Do not rich men oppress you, and draw you before the judgment seats?	But ye have despised the poor man. Do not rich men exalt themselves over you, and drag you before the tribunals?	But you have rejected the poor. Behold, do not rich [men] elevate themselves over you and drag you to court?
7	Do not they blaspheme that worthy name by the which ye are called?	Do they not revile that worthy name, which is invoked upon you?	Behold, do they not reproach the good name that was called on you?
8	If ye fulfil the royal law according to the scripture, Thou shalt love thy neighbour as thyself, ye do well:	And if in this ye fulfill the law of God, as it is written, Thou shalt love thy neighbor as thyself, ye will do well:	And if you fulfill the law of God in this, as it is written: YOU SHOULD LOVE YOUR NEIGHBOR AS YOURSELF, you are doing well.
9	But if ye have respect to persons, ye commit sin, and are convinced of the law as transgressors.	but if ye have respect of persons, ye commit sin; and ye are convicted by the law, as transgressors of the law.	But if you are respecting persons, you commit sin and you are reproved by the law as transgressors of the law.
10	For whosoever shall keep the whole law, and yet offend in one point, he is guilty of all.	For he that shall keep the whole law, and yet fail in one [precept], is obnoxious to the whole law.	For he who keeps the whole law and offends in one [thing] is found guilty of the whole law.

JAMES Chapter 2

	KJV	Murdock	Magiera
11	For he that said, Do not commit adultery, said also, Do not kill. Now if thou commit no adultery, yet if thou kill, thou art become a transgressor of the law.	For he who said, Thou shalt not commit adultery, said also, Thou shalt not kill. If then thou commit no adultery, but thou killest, thou hast become a transgressor of the law.	For he who said: DO NOT COMMIT ADULTERY, said, DO NOT KILL. Now if you do not commit adultery, but you kill, you have become a transgressor of the law.
12	So speak ye, and so do, as they that shall be judged by the law of liberty.	So speak ye, and so act, as persons that are to be judged by the law of liberty.	So speak and so act, as people who are going to be judged by the law of liberty.
13	For he shall have judgment without mercy, that hath shewed no mercy; and mercy rejoiceth against judgment.	For judgment without mercy shall be on him, who hath practised no mercy: by mercy, ye will be raised above judgment.	For judgment will be without mercy on that one who has not practiced mercy. By mercy, you will be elevated above judgment.
14	What doth it profit, my brethren, though a man say he hath faith, and have not works? can faith save him?	What is the use, my brethren, if a man say, I have faith; and he hath no works? can his faith vivify him?	What is the profit, my brothers, if someone says, "I have faith," and has no works? Is his faith able to give him life?
15	If a brother or sister be naked, and destitute of daily food,	Or if a brother or sister be naked, and destitute of daily food,	And if a brother or a sister should be naked and lacking food for the day
16	And one of you say unto them, Depart in peace, be ye warmed and filled; notwithstanding ye give them not those things which are needful to the body; what doth it profit?	and one of you say to them, Go in peace, warm yourselves, and be full; and ye give them not the necessaries of the body, what is the use?	and one of you says to them, "Go in peace, be warm and be satisfied," and you do not give them what is necessary for the body, what is the profit?
17	Even so faith, if it hath not works, is dead, being alone.	So also faith alone, without works, is dead.	So also, faith alone without works is dead.
18	Yea, a man may say, Thou hast faith, and I have works: shew me thy faith without thy works, and I will shew thee my faith by my works.	For a man may say, Thou hast faith, and I have works; show to me thy faith that is without works; and I will show to thee, my faith by my works.	For a man will say to you, "You have faith," and to me, " I have works." Show me your faith without works and I will show you my faith by my works.
19	Thou believest that there is one God; thou doest well: the devils also believe, and tremble.	Thou believest that there is one God; thou dost well; the demons also believe, and tremble.	You believe that God is one. You do well! Even the demons believe and tremble.
20	But wilt thou know, O vain man, that faith without works is dead?	Wouldst thou know, O frail man, that faith without works is dead?	Now do you want to understand, oh frail man, that faith without works is dead?
21	Was not Abraham our father justified by works, when he had offered Isaac his son upon the altar?	Abraham our father, was not he justified by works, in offering his son Isaac upon the altar?	Was not our father Abraham justified by works when he offered Isaac his son on the altar?
22	Seest thou how faith wrought with his works, and by works was faith made perfect?	Seest thou, that his faith aided his works; and that by the works his faith was rendered complete?	You see that his faith aided his works and [that] by works, his faith was matured.
23	And the scripture was fulfilled which saith, Abraham believed God, and it was imputed unto him for righteousness: and he was called the Friend of God.	And the scripture was fulfilled, which saith: Abraham believed in God, and it was accounted to him for righteousness, and he was called the Friend of God.	And the scripture was fulfilled that said: ABRAHAM BELIEVED IN GOD AND IT WAS COUNTED TO HIM FOR JUSTIFICATION, and he was called the friend of God.

JAMES *Chapter 2*

	KJV	*Murdock*	*Magiera*
24	Ye see then how that by works a man is justified, and not by faith only.	Thou seest, that by works a man is justified, and not by faith alone.	You see that by works a man is justified and not by faith alone.
25	Likewise also was not Rahab the harlot justified by works, when she had received the messengers, and had sent them out another way?	So also Rahab, the harlot, was not she justified by works, when she entertained the spies, and sent them forth by another way?	So also, was not Rahab the harlot justified by works when she took in the spies and sent them out by another way?
26	For as the body without the spirit is dead, so faith without works is dead also.	As the body without the spirit, is dead; so faith without works, is dead also.	As the body without the spirit is dead, so also faith without works is dead.

Chapter 3

	KJV	*Murdock*	*Magiera*
1	My brethren, be not many masters, knowing that we shall receive the greater condemnation.	Let there not be many teachers among you, my brethren; but know ye, that we are obnoxious to a severer judgment.	You should not have many teachers among you, my brothers, but know that we are liable [to have] a greater judgment.
2	For in many things we offend all. If any man offend not in word, the same is a perfect man, and able also to bridle the whole body.	For we all offend in many things. Whoever offendeth not in discourse, is a perfect man, who can also keep his whole body in subjection.	For we all offend [in] many [things]. Anyone who does not offend in word, this [one] is a mature man who is also able to subject his whole body.
3	Behold, we put bits in the horses' mouths, that they may obey us; and we turn about their whole body.	Behold, we put bridles into the mouth of horses, that they may obey us; and we turn about their whole body.	For behold, we place bits in the mouths of horses, so that they may be tamed by us and we turn their whole body.
4	Behold also the ships, which though they be so great, and are driven of fierce winds, yet are they turned about with a very small helm, whithersoever the governor listeth.	Huge ships also, when strong winds drive them, are turned about by a small timber, to what place the pleasure of the pilot looketh.	Also, the mighty boats, although harsh winds drive them, are turned by a small piece of wood to the place that the pilot wants to see.
5	Even so the tongue is a little member, and boasteth great things. Behold, how great a matter a little fire kindleth!	So likewise the tongue is a small member, and it exalteth itself. Also a little fire inflameth large forests.	So also, the tongue is a small member and it elevates itself. Also, a small fire causes large forests to burn.
6	And the tongue is a fire, a world of iniquity: so is the tongue among our members, that it defileth the whole body, and setteth on fire the course of nature; and it is set on fire of hell.	Now the tongue is a fire, and the world of sin is like a forest. And this tongue, which is one among our members, marreth our whole body; and it inflameth the series of our generations that roll on like a wheel; and it is itself on fire.	And the tongue is a fire and the world of sin is like a forest. And the tongue, although it is [one] among the members, marks our whole body and sets on fire the successions of our generations that roll on as wheels and it also burns with fire.
7	For every kind of beasts, and of birds, and of serpents, and of things in the sea, is tamed, and hath been tamed of mankind:	For all natures of beasts and birds and reptiles, of the sea or land, are subjugated by the nature of man.	For all the natures of animals and of birds and reptiles, of the sea and of dry land, are subjected to the nature of mankind.
8	But the tongue can no man tame; it is an unruly evil, full of deadly poison.	But the tongue hath no one been able to tame: it is an evil thing, not coercible, and full of deadly poison.	But the tongue, no one is able to subdue. This evil, when it is not restrained, is full of the poison of death.

JAMES *Chapter 3*

	KJV	*Murdock*	*Magiera*
9	Therewith bless we God, even the Father; and therewith curse we men, which are made after the similitude of God.	For with it, we bless the Lord and Father; and with it we curse men, who were made in the image of God:	With it we bless the LORD and Father and with it we curse men, who are made in the likeness of God.
10	Out of the same mouth proceedeth blessing and cursing. My brethren, these things ought not so to be.	and from the same mouth, proceed curses and blessings. My brethren, these things ought not to be so.	And from the same mouth proceed blessings and cursings. My brothers, it is not right that these [things] be done so.
11	Doth a fountain send forth at the same place sweet water and bitter?	Can there flow from the same fountain, sweet waters and bitter?	Can sweet and bitter water come out of one fountain?
12	Can the fig tree, my brethren, bear olive berries? either a vine, figs? so can no fountain both yield salt water and fresh.	Or can the fig-tree, my brethren, bear olives? or the vine, figs? So also salt waters cannot be made sweet.	Or can a fig tree, my brothers, produce olives, or a vine, figs? So also, you cannot make salty water sweet.
13	Who is a wise man and endued with knowledge among you? let him shew out of a good conversation his works with meekness of wisdom.	Who is wise and instructed among you? Let him show his works in praiseworthy actions, with modest wisdom.	Who is wise and instructed among you? He should show his works with praiseworthy actions, with humble wisdom.
14	But if ye have bitter envying and strife in your hearts, glory not, and lie not against the truth.	But if bitter envy be in you, or contention in your hearts, exalt not yourselves against the truth, and lie not.	But if you have bitter envy or contention in your hearts, do not elevate yourselves above the truth and lie,
15	This wisdom descendeth not from above, but is earthly, sensual, devilish.	For this wisdom cometh not down from above; but is earthly, and from the devices of the soul, and from demons.	because this wisdom does not come down from above, but is earthly, from the reasonings of the soul and from demons.
16	For where envying and strife is, there is confusion and every evil work.	For where envy and contention are, there also is confusion, and every thing wrong.	For where there is envy and contention, there also [is] confusion and everything that is evil.
17	But the wisdom that is from above is first pure, then peaceable, gentle, and easy to be intreated, full of mercy and good fruits, without partiality, and without hypocrisy.	But the wisdom which is from above, is pure, and full of peace, and mild, and submissive, and full of compassion and of good fruits, and without partiality, and without respect of persons.	Now the wisdom that is from above is pure and full of peace and humble and obedient and full of mercy and good fruits and is without division and does not respect persons.
18	And the fruit of righteousness is sown in peace of them that make peace.	And the fruits of righteousness are sown in stillness, by them who make peace.	And the fruit of justification is sown in quietness by those who serve peace.

Chapter 4

	KJV	*Murdock*	*Magiera*
1	From whence come wars and fightings among you? come they not hence, even of your lusts that war in your members?	Whence is it, that there are among you fightings and broils? Is it not from the lusts, which war in your members?	From where are wars and arguments among you? Is it not from the desires that war in your members?
2	Ye lust, and have not: ye kill, and desire to have, and cannot obtain: ye fight and war, yet ye have not, because ye ask not.	Ye covet, and possess not; and ye kill, and envy, and effect nothing: and ye fight and make attacks; and ye have not, because ye ask not.	You desire and you do not have. And you perish and are zealous, yet it does not come into your hands. And you strive and cause wars, yet you have not, because you have not asked.

Parallel Translations

	KJV	Murdock	Magiera
	JAMES	*Chapter 4*	
3	Ye ask, and receive not, because ye ask amiss, that ye may consume it upon your lusts.	Ye ask, and receive not; because ye ask wickedly, that ye may pamper your lusts.	You ask and do not receive, because you ask wrongly, so that you may nourish your desires.
4	Ye adulterers and adulteresses, know ye not that the friendship of the world is enmity with God? whosoever therefore will be a friend of the world is the enemy of God.	Ye adulterers, know ye not, that the love of the world is hostility towards God? He therefore who chooseth to be a lover of this world, is the enemy of God.	Adulterers, do you not know that the friendship of this world is in opposition to God? Therefore, he who wants to be a friend of this world becomes an opponent of God.
5	Do ye think that the scripture saith in vain, The spirit that dwelleth in us lusteth to envy?	Or think ye, that the scripture hath vainly said: The spirit dwelling in us lusteth with envy?	Or do you think that the scripture fruitlessly said: THE SPIRIT THAT LIVES IN US DESIRES WITH ENVY?
6	But he giveth more grace. Wherefore he saith, God resisteth the proud, but giveth grace unto the humble.	But our Lord hath given us more grace. Therefore he said: The Lord humbleth the lofty, and giveth grace to the lowly.	But our Lord has given abundant grace to us. Because of this, he said: GOD HUMBLES THE PROUD AND GIVES GRACE TO THE HUMBLE.
7	Submit yourselves therefore to God. Resist the devil, and he will flee from you.	Subject yourselves therefore to God; and stand firm against Satan, and he will flee from you.	Therefore, be subject to God and stand against Satan and he will flee from you.
8	Draw nigh to God, and he will draw nigh to you. Cleanse your hands, ye sinners; and purify your hearts, ye double minded.	Draw nigh to God, and he will draw nigh to you. Cleanse your hands, ye sinners: sanctify your hearts, ye divided in mind.	And come near to God and he will come near to you. Cleanse your hands, [you] sinners. Set apart your hearts, doubters of self.
9	Be afflicted, and mourn, and weep: let your laughter be turned to mourning, and your joy to heaviness.	Humble yourselves, and mourn: let your laughter be turned into mourning, and your joy into grief.	Humble yourselves and mourn. And your laughter will be changed to mourning and your joy to sorrow.
10	Humble yourselves in the sight of the Lord, and he shall lift you up.	Humble yourselves before the Lord, and he will exalt you.	Humble yourselves before the LORD and he will elevate you.
11	Speak not evil one of another, brethren. He that speaketh evil of his brother, and judgeth his brother, speaketh evil of the law, and judgeth the law: but if thou judge the law, thou art not a doer of the law, but a judge.	Speak not against each other, my brethren; for he that speaketh against his brother, or judgeth his brother, speaketh against the law, and judgeth the law. And if thou judgest the law, thou art not a doer of the law, but its judge.	Do not speak against one another, my brothers, for he who speaks against his brother or judges his brother, speaks against the law and judges the law. And if you judge the law, you are not a doer of the law, but its judge.
12	There is one lawgiver, who is able to save and to destroy: who art thou that judgest another?	There is one Law-giver and Judge, who can make alive, and [can] destroy: but who art thou, that thou judgest thy neighbor?	There is one lawgiver and judge, who is able to give life and to destroy. But who are you that you are judging your neighbor?
13	Go to now, ye that say, To day or to morrow we will go into such a city, and continue there a year, and buy and sell, and get gain:	But what shall we say of those, who say: To-day or to-morrow we will go to such or such a city, and will abide there a year; and we will traffic, and get gain?	Now what will we also say about those who say, "Today or tomorrow we will go to a certain city and we will work there [for] one year and we will do business and increase?"

	KJV	Murdock	Magiera

JAMES *Chapter 4*

	KJV	Murdock	Magiera
14	Whereas ye know not what shall be on the morrow. For what is your life? It is even a vapour, that appeareth for a little time, and then vanisheth away.	And they know not what will be to-morrow: for what is our life, but an exhalation that is seen a little while, and then vanisheth and is gone?	And they do not know what will happen tomorrow. For what is our life, except a vapor that is seen a little while and [then] vanishes and is gone?
15	For that ye ought to say, If the Lord will, we shall live, and do this, or that.	Whereas they should say: If the Lord please, and we live, we will do this or that.	Instead, they should say, "If the LORD wills and we live, we will do this or that."
16	But now ye rejoice in your boastings: all such rejoicing is evil.	They glory in their vaunting. All such glorying is evil.	They boast in their pride. All boasting like this is evil.
17	Therefore to him that knoweth to do good, and doeth it not, to him it is sin.	He that knoweth the good, and doeth it not, to him is sin.	And he who knows good and does not do it, to him it is sin.

Chapter 5

	KJV	Murdock	Magiera
1	Go to now, ye rich men, weep and howl for your miseries that shall come upon you.	O ye rich ones, wail and weep, on account of the miseries that are coming upon you.	Oh rich [men], wail and weep for the miseries that will come on you,
2	Your riches are corrupted, and your garments are motheaten.	For your wealth is spoiled and putrid; and your garments are moth-eaten:	for your wealth is corrupted and is rotten and your garments have been eaten by a moth.
3	Your gold and silver is cankered; and the rust of them shall be a witness against you, and shall eat your flesh as it were fire. Ye have heaped treasure together for the last days.	and your gold and your silver have contracted rust; and the rust of them will be testimony against you; and it will eat your flesh. Ye have heaped up a fire to you against the latter days.	And your gold and your silver have tarnished and their tarnish will be a witness against you and it is going to eat your flesh. You have gathered a fire for you for the last days.
4	Behold, the hire of the labourers who have reaped down your fields, which is of you kept back by fraud, crieth: and the cries of them which have reaped are entered into the ears of the Lord of sabaoth.	Behold, the wages of the laborers who have reaped your ground, which ye have wrongfully retained, crieth out; and the clamor of the reapers hath entered the ears of the Lord of Sabaoth.	Behold, the wage of the laborers who have reaped your lands, which you have withheld, cries out. And the crying of the reapers has entered the ears of the LORD of Hosts.
5	Ye have lived in pleasure on the earth, and been wanton; ye have nourished your hearts, as in a day of slaughter.	For ye have lived in pleasure on the earth, and revelled, and feasted your bodies as in a day of slaughter.	For you have lived in pleasure on the earth and have been greedy and have nourished your bodies as in the day of slaughter.
6	Ye have condemned and killed the just; and he doth not resist you.	Ye have condemned and slain the just, and none resisted you.	You have condemned and killed the Just [one] and he did not stand against you.
7	Be patient therefore, brethren, unto the coming of the Lord. Behold, the husbandman waiteth for the precious fruit of the earth, and hath long patience for it, until he receive the early and latter rain.	But, my brethren, be ye patient until the advent of the Lord; like the husbandman, who waiteth for the precious fruits of his ground, and is patient as to them, until he receive the early and the latter rain.	But you, my brothers, be long-suffering until the coming of the LORD, as the farmer who waits for the precious fruit of his ground and is long-suffering about it, until he receives the early and latter rain.

Parallel Translations

	KJV	*Murdock*	*Magiera*

JAMES *Chapter 5*

	KJV	Murdock	Magiera
8	Be ye also patient; stablish your hearts: for the coming of the Lord draweth nigh.	So also be ye patient, and fortify your hearts; for the advent of our Lord draweth nigh	So also be long-suffering and establish your hearts, for the coming of our Lord draws close.
9	Grudge not one against another, brethren, lest ye be condemned: behold, the judge standeth before the door.	Be not querulous one against another, my brethren, lest ye be judged: for lo, the judgment, standeth before the door.	Do not murmur against one another, my brothers, so that you should not be judged, for behold, judgment stands before the door.
10	Take, my brethren, the prophets, who have spoken in the name of the Lord, for an example of suffering affliction, and of patience.	For patience in your afflictions, my brethren, take to you the example of the prophets, who spoke in the name of the Lord.	Take the prophets [as] an example, my brothers, for long-suffering with respect to your trials, those who spoke in the name of the LORD.
11	Behold, we count them happy which endure. Ye have heard of the patience of Job, and have seen the end of the Lord; that the Lord is very pitiful, and of tender mercy.	For lo, we ascribe blessedness to them who have borne suffering. Ye have heard of the patience of Job; and ye have seen the result which the Lord wrought for him: for the Lord is merciful and compassionate.	For behold, we give a blessing to those who have endured. You have heard of the endurance of Job and have seen the result that the LORD brought to pass for him, because the LORD is merciful and compassionate.
12	But above all things, my brethren, swear not, neither by heaven, neither by the earth, neither by any other oath: but let your yea be yea; and your nay, nay; lest ye fall into condemnation.	But above all things, my brethren, swear ye not; neither by heaven, nor by the earth, nor by any other oath: but let your language be yes, yes, and no, no, lest ye become obnoxious to judgment.	Now above everything, my brothers, do not swear, neither by heaven, nor by earth, not even by [any] other oath. But rather, your word should be, "Yes, yes, and no, no," so that you should not be condemned under judgment.
13	Is any among you afflicted? let him pray. Is any merry? let him sing psalms.	And if any of you shall be in affliction, let him pray; or if he be joyous, let him sing psalms.	And if one of you should be in a trial, he should pray, and if he is glad, he should sing psalms.
14	Is any sick among you? let him call for the elders of the church; and let them pray over him, anointing him with oil in the name of the Lord:	And if one is sick, let him call for the elders of the church; and let them pray for him, and anoint him with oil in the name of our Lord:	And if one is sick, he should call for the elders of the church and they should pray for him and anoint him [with] oil in the name of our Lord.
15	And the prayer of faith shall save the sick, and the Lord shall raise him up; and if he have committed sins, they shall be forgiven him.	and the prayer of faith will heal him who is sick, and our Lord will raise him up; and if sins have been committed by him, they will be forgiven him.	And the prayer of faith will heal him who is sick and our Lord will raise him, and if [any] sins were committed by him, they will be forgiven.
16	Confess your faults one to another, and pray one for another, that ye may be healed. The effectual fervent prayer of a righteous man availeth much.	And confess ye your faults one to another, and pray ye one for another, that ye may be healed; for great is the efficacy of the prayer which a righteous man prayeth.	Now confess your faults to one another and pray for one another to be healed, for great is the power of prayer that a just man prays.
17	Elias was a man subject to like passions as we are, and he prayed earnestly that it might not rain: and it rained not on the earth by the space of three years and six months.	Elijah also was a man of sensations like us, and he prayed that rain might not descend upon the earth; and it descended not, for three years and six months.	Elijah was also a passionate man like us and he prayed that the rain would not fall on the earth. And it did not fall [for] three years and six months.

	KJV	Murdock	Magiera
	JAMES *Chapter 5*		
18	And he prayed again, and the heaven gave rain, and the earth brought forth her fruit.	And again he prayed, and the heavens gave rain, and the earth gave forth its fruits.	And again he prayed and the heaven gave rain and the earth produced its fruit.
19	Brethren, if any of you do err from the truth, and one convert him;	My brethren, if one of you err from the way of truth, and any one convert him from his error;	My brothers, if one of you errs from the way of truthfulness and someone causes him to repent from his error,
20	Let him know, that he which converteth the sinner from the error of his way shall save a soul from death, and shall hide a multitude of sins.	let him know, that he who turneth the sinner from the error of his way, will resuscitate his soul from death, and will cover the multitude of his sins.	he should know that he who turns back a sinner from the error of his way will give life to his soul from death and will blot out a multitude of his sins.

Parallel Translations

	KJV	Murdock	Magiera
	I PETER *Chapter 1*		
1	Peter, an apostle of Jesus Christ, to the strangers scattered throughout Pontus, Galatia, Cappadocia, Asia, and Bithynia,	Peter, a legate of Jesus the Messiah, to the elect and sojourners, who are dispersed in Pontus and in Galatia, and in Cappadocia, and in Asia, and in Bithynia,	Peter, an apostle of Jesus Christ, to the chosen [ones] and settlers who are scattered in Pontus and in Galatia and in Cappadocia and in Asia and in Bithynia,
2	Elect according to the foreknowledge of God the Father, through sanctification of the Spirit, unto obedience and sprinkling of the blood of Jesus Christ: Grace unto you, and peace, be multiplied.	to them who have been chosen, by the foreknowledge of God the Father, through sanctification of the Spirit, unto the obedience and the sprinkling of the blood of Jesus the Messiah: May grace and peace abound towards you.	those who were chosen by the foreknowledge of God the Father by the holiness of the Spirit to be to the obedience and the purifying by sprinkling of the blood of Jesus Christ: Grace and peace be multiplied to you.
3	Blessed be the God and Father of our Lord Jesus Christ, which according to his abundant mercy hath begotten us again unto a lively hope by the resurrection of Jesus Christ from the dead,	Blessed be God, the Father of our Lord Jesus the Messiah, who in his great mercy hath begotten us anew, by the resurrection of our Lord Jesus the Messiah, to the hope of life,	Blessed be God, the Father of our Lord Jesus Christ, who by his great mercy has fathered us anew to the hope of life by the resurrection of Jesus Christ,
4	To an inheritance incorruptible, and undefiled, and that fadeth not away, reserved in heaven for you,	and to an inheritance incorruptible, undefiled, and unfading, which is prepared for you in heaven;	and to an incorruptible and undefiled and unfailing inheritance that is prepared for you in heaven,
5	Who are kept by the power of God through faith unto salvation ready to be revealed in the last time.	while ye are kept, by the power of God and by faith, for the life that is prepared and will be revealed in the last times;	being kept by the power of God and by faith for the life that is prepared to be revealed in the last times,
6	Wherein ye greatly rejoice, though now for a season, if need be, ye are in heaviness through manifold temptations:	wherein ye will rejoice for ever, notwithstanding ye at the present time are pressed a little, by the various trials that pass over you;	in which you will rejoice forever. Even though in this time you are discouraged a little by the various trials that have happened to you,
7	That the trial of your faith, being much more precious than of gold that perisheth, though it be tried with fire, might be found unto praise and honour and glory at the appearing of Jesus Christ:	so that the proof of your faith may appear more precious than refined gold that is tested by fire, unto glory and honor and praise, at the manifestation of Jesus the Messiah:	[it is] so that the testing of your faith may appear more precious than refined gold that is refined by fire, for the glory and honor and praise at the appearing of Jesus Christ.
8	Whom having not seen, ye love; in whom, though now ye see him not, yet believing, ye rejoice with joy unspeakable and full of glory:	whom having not seen, ye love; and in the faith of whom ye rejoice, with joy that is glorious and ineffable,	You have not seen him, yet love, and by his faith, you rejoice with glorious joy that is unspeakable,
9	Receiving the end of your faith, even the salvation of your souls.	that ye may receive the recompense of your faith, the life of your souls;	that you would receive the reward of your faith, the life of your souls.
10	Of which salvation the prophets have enquired and searched diligently, who prophesied of the grace that should come unto you:	that life [namely], about which the prophets inquired, when they were prophesying of the grace which was to be given to you.	[It is] that life that the prophets investigated when they prophesied about the grace that was to come that has been given to you.

	KJV	*Murdock*	*Magiera*

I PETER *Chapter 1*

	KJV	Murdock	Magiera
11	Searching what, or what manner of time the Spirit of Christ which was in them did signify, when it testified beforehand the sufferings of Christ, and the glory that should follow.	And they searched for the time which the Spirit of the Messiah dwelling in them did show and testify, when the sufferings of the Messiah were to occur, and his subsequent glory.	And they searched for what time [that] the Spirit of Christ that was living in them showed and testified, when the sufferings of Christ and his glory that followed would come to pass.
12	Unto whom it was revealed, that not unto themselves, but unto us they did minister the things, which are now reported unto you by them that have preached the gospel unto you with the Holy Ghost sent down from heaven; which things the angels desire to look into.	And it was revealed to them, [in regard to] all they were searching, that, not for themselves were they inquiring, but for us they were prophesying of those things, which are now manifested to you by means of the things we have announced to you, by the Holy Spirit sent from heaven; which things the angels also desire to look into.	And it was revealed to all who were seeking that they were not seeking for themselves, but they were prophesying these [things] for us that now are revealed to you, by way of those [things] that we announced by the Holy Spirit that was sent from heaven, into which [things] even the angels desired to investigate.
13	Wherefore gird up the loins of your mind, be sober, and hope to the end for the grace that is to be brought unto you at the revelation of Jesus Christ;	Wherefore, gird up the loins of your minds. and be awake perfectly, and wait for the joy, which will come to you at the revelation of our Lord Jesus the Messiah,	Because of this, gird up the loins of your thinking and be completely watchful and hope for the joy that will come to you at the appearing of our Lord Jesus Christ
14	As obedient children, not fashioning yourselves according to the former lusts in your ignorance:	as obedient children: and be ye not conversant again with those former lusts, with which ye lusted when without knowledge.	as obedient children. And do not associate again with your former desires that you ignorantly desired.
15	But as he which hath called you is holy, so be ye holy in all manner of conversation;	But be ye holy in all your conduct, as he is holy who hath called you.	Rather, be holy in all your ways, as he who called you is holy,
16	Because it is written, Be ye holy; for I am holy.	Because it is written: Be ye holy, even as I am holy.	because it is written: BE HOLY, EVEN AS I AM HOLY.
17	And if ye call on the Father, who without respect of persons judgeth according to every man's work, pass the time of your sojourning here in fear:	And if so be ye call on the Father, with whom is no respect of persons, and who judgeth every one according to his deeds, pass the time of your sojournment with fear;	And if you call on the Father, before whom there is no respect of persons and [who] judges everyone according to his works, conduct yourself with reverence during this time of your dwelling in a foreign country,
18	Forasmuch as ye know that ye were not redeemed with corruptible things, as silver and gold, from your vain conversation received by tradition from your fathers;	since ye know, that neither with perishable silver, nor with gold, ye were redeemed from your vain doings, which ye had by tradition from your fathers;	knowing that you were not redeemed with silver that is corruptible, nor with gold, by your empty works that you received from your fathers,
19	But with the precious blood of Christ, as of a lamb without blemish and without spot:	but with the precious blood of that Lamb in which is no spot nor blemish, namely, the Messiah:	but with the precious blood of the lamb, who has no spot or blemish, who is Christ.
20	Who verily was foreordained before the foundation of the world, but was manifest in these last times for you,	who was predestined to this, before the foundation of the world; and was manifested at the termination of the times, for your sakes;	He was previously appointed to this before the foundations of the world and was revealed in the end of times for you,

Parallel Translations

I PETER *Chapter 1*

	KJV	Murdock	Magiera
21	Who by him do believe in God, that raised him up from the dead, and gave him glory; that your faith and hope might be in God.	who, by means of him, have believed in God, who raised him from the dead and conferred glory on him; that your faith and hope might be in God,	who by way of him have believed in God, who raised him from the dead and gave him glory, that your faith and your hope would be in God.
22	Seeing ye have purified your souls in obeying the truth through the Spirit unto unfeigned love of the brethren, see that ye love one another with a pure heart fervently:	while your minds became sanctified, by obedience to the truth; and ye be full of love, without respect of persons, so that ye love one another out of a pure and perfect heart;	Your lives are becoming holy by the obedience of the truth and becoming full of love without respect of persons, so that you may love one another out of a pure and mature heart.
23	Being born again, not of corruptible seed, but of incorruptible, by the word of God, which liveth and abideth for ever.	like persons born again, not of seed that perisheth, but of that which doth not perish, by the living word of God, who abideth for ever.	Like a man, you were born anew, not of seed that is corruptible, but of that which is not corruptible, by the living word of God that stands forever.
24	For all flesh is as grass, and all the glory of man as the flower of grass. The grass withereth, and the flower thereof falleth away:	Because all flesh is as grass, and all its beauty like the flower of the field. The grass drieth up, and the flower withereth away;	Because, ALL FLESH [IS] GRASS AND ALL ITS BEAUTY AS A FLOWER OF THE FIELD. THE GRASS DRIES UP AND THE FLOWER WITHERS,
25	But the word of the Lord endureth for ever. And this is the word which by the gospel is preached unto you.	but the word of our God abideth for ever: and this is the word that is announced to you.	YET THE WORD OF OUR GOD STANDS FOREVER. And this is the word that was preached to you.

Chapter 2

	KJV	Murdock	Magiera
1	Wherefore laying aside all malice, and all guile, and hypocrisies, and envies, and all evil speakings,	Therefore, cease ye from all malice, and all guile, and hypocrisy, and envy, and backbiting.	Therefore, put away from you all wickedness and all deceit and respect of persons and envy and accusation.
2	As newborn babes, desire the sincere milk of the word, that ye may grow thereby:	And be like infant children; and crave the word, as being the pure spiritual milk by which ye are nourished up to life;	And be like young infants and desire the word, as for pure and spiritual milk by which you are nourished to life,
3	If so be ye have tasted that the Lord is gracious.	if ye have tasted and seen that the Lord is good:	since you have tasted and seen that THE LORD IS GOOD.
4	To whom coming, as unto a living stone, disallowed indeed of men, but chosen of God, and precious,	to whom ye have come, because he is a living stone, rejected indeed by men, but with God elect and precious.	The one to whom you are drawn is the living stone that men have rejected, yet with God [is] chosen and honored.
5	Ye also, as lively stones, are built up a spiritual house, an holy priesthood, to offer up spiritual sacrifices, acceptable to God by Jesus Christ.	And ye also, as living stones, are builded and become spiritual temples, and holy priests, for the offering of spiritual sacrifices, acceptable before God, through Jesus the Messiah.	And you also, as living stones, are built up and are spiritual temples and holy priests to offer spiritual sacrifices that are acceptable before God by way of Jesus Christ.

Parallel Translations

	KJV	*Murdock*	*Magiera*
	I PETER *Chapter 2*		
6	Wherefore also it is contained in the scripture, Behold, I lay in Sion a chief corner stone, elect, precious: and he that believeth on him shall not be confounded.	For it is said in the scripture, Behold, in Zion I lay a chosen and precious stone, for the head of the corner; and whoever believeth in him, will not be ashamed.	For it is told in the scripture: BEHOLD, I LAY IN ZION AN APPROVED AND PRECIOUS STONE IN THE HEAD OF THE CORNER AND HE WHO BELIEVES ON HIM WILL NOT BE ASHAMED.
7	Unto you therefore which believe he is precious: but unto them which be disobedient, the stone which the builders disallowed, the same is made the head of the corner,	On you therefore who believe, is this honor conferred: but to them who believe not,	Therefore, this honor is given to you who believe. But to those who are not convinced,
8	And a stone of stumbling, and a rock of offence, even to them which stumble at the word, being disobedient: whereunto also they were appointed.	he is a stone of stumbling and a rock of offence. And they stumble at it, because they believe not the word: whereto they were appointed.	HE IS A STONE OF STUMBLING AND A ROCK OF OFFENSE. And they stumbled at him, in that they were not persuaded by the word to which they were appointed.
9	But ye are a chosen generation, a royal priesthood, an holy nation, a peculiar people; that ye should shew forth the praises of him who hath called you out of darkness into his marvellous light:	But ye are an elect race, officiating as priests of the kingdom; a holy people, a redeemed congregation; that ye should proclaim the praises of him who called you out of darkness to his precious light:	Now you are a chosen generation that serves as a priest for the kingdom, a holy people, a redeemed assembly, to declare the praises of him who called you from darkness to his excellent light,
10	Which in time past were not a people, but are now the people of God: which had not obtained mercy, but now have obtained mercy.	who formerly were not accounted a people, but now are the people of God; and also, there were [once] no mercies on you, but now mercies are poured out upon you.	you who previously were not counted a people, but now [are] the people of God. There were even no mercies on you, but now mercies are poured out on you.
11	Dearly beloved, I beseech you as strangers and pilgrims, abstain from fleshly lusts, which war against the soul;	My beloved, I entreat you as strangers and pilgrims, separate yourselves from all lusts of the body; for they war against the soul.	My beloved [ones], I beg you, as strangers and as settlers, be separate from all the desires of the body, those that wage a war against the soul.
12	Having your conversation honest among the Gentiles: that, whereas they speak against you as evildoers, they may by your good works, which they shall behold, glorify God in the day of visitation.	And let your behavior be decorous before all men; so that they who utter evil speeches against you, may see your good actions, and may praise God in the day of trial.	And your conduct should be proper before all men, [so that] those who speak evil words against you may see your good works and may praise God in the day of testing.
13	Submit yourselves to every ordinance of man for the Lord's sake: whether it be to the king, as supreme;	And be ye submissive to all the sons of men, for God's sake; to kings, on account of their authority;	And be subject to all men because of God, to kings because of their authority
14	Or unto governors, as unto them that are sent by him for the punishment of evildoers, and for the praise of them that do well.	and to judges, because they are sent by him for the punishment of offenders, and for the praise of them that do well.	and to judges because they are sent by him for the punishment of wrong-doers and for the praise of the workers of good [things].

Parallel Translations

	KJV	*Murdock*	*Magiera*
	I PETER	***Chapter 2***	
15	For so is the will of God, that with well doing ye may put to silence the ignorance of foolish men:	For so is the pleasure of God, that by your good deeds ye may stop the mouth of the foolish, who know not God:	For so is the will of God, that by your good works you would shut the mouth of the foolish who do not know God.
16	As free, and not using your liberty for a cloke of maliciousness, but as the servants of God.	as free men, yet not like men who make their freedom a cloak for their wickedness, but as the servants of God.	[You are] as free men, and not as men whose freedom is made a veil to them for their wickedness, but as servants of God.
17	Honour all men. Love the brotherhood. Fear God. Honour the king.	Honor all men; love your brethren; fear God; and honor kings.	Honor everyone. Love your brothers and reverence God and honor kings.
18	Servants, be subject to your masters with all fear; not only to the good and gentle, but also to the froward.	And those among you who are servants, be subject to your masters, with reverence; not only to the good and gentle, but also to the harsh and morose.	And those who are servants among you, be subject to your lords with reverence, not only to the good and to the humble, but also to the hard and difficult,
19	For this is thankworthy, if a man for conscience toward God endure grief, suffering wrongfully.	For there is favor before God for them who, for the sake of a good conscience, endure sorrows that come upon them wrongfully.	for they will have grace before God, who because of a good conscience endure sorrows that come on them wrongfully.
20	For what glory is it, if, when ye be buffeted for your faults, ye shall take it patiently? but if, when ye do well, and suffer for it, ye take it patiently, this is acceptable with God.	But they who endure afflictions on account of their offences, what praise have they? But if, when ye do well, they vex you, and ye endure it; then great is your praise with God.	But what praise will they have who endure pressures because of their transgressions? But when you do what is good and they pressure you and you endure, then your praise is great with God.
21	For even hereunto were ye called: because Christ also suffered for us, leaving us an example, that ye should follow his steps:	For unto this were ye called; because the Messiah also died for us, and left us this pattern, that ye should walk in his steps.	For to this you were called, because even Christ died for us and left us this example that you should walk in his footsteps:
22	Who did no sin, neither was guile found in his mouth:	He did no sin; neither was guile found in his mouth.	HE DID NOT COMMIT SIN, NEITHER WAS DECEIT FOUND IN HIS MOUTH,
23	Who, when he was reviled, reviled not again; when he suffered, he threatened not; but committed himself to him that judgeth righteously:	When he was reviled, he reviled not; and he suffered and threatened not, but committed his cause to the Judge of righteousness.	who was reviled, yet did not revile, and was suffering, yet did not threaten, but delivered his case to the judge of uprightness.
24	Who his own self bare our sins in his own body on the tree, that we, being dead to sins, should live unto righteousness: by whose stripes ye were healed.	And he took away all our sins, and, in his body, lifted them to the cross; that we, when dead to sin, might live by his righteousness: for by his wounds, ye are healed.	And he carried all our sins and lifted them in his body to the cross, so that being dead to sin, we would have life by his justification, for by his wounds you were healed.
25	For ye were as sheep going astray; but are now returned unto the Shepherd and Bishop of your souls.	For ye, [once] went astray, like sheep; but ye have now returned to the Shepherd and Curator of your souls.	For you were wandering like sheep, yet you are now returned to the shepherd and overseer of your souls.

Parallel Translations

	KJV	*Murdock*	*Magiera*
	I PETER	*Chapter 3*	
1	Likewise, ye wives, be in subjection to your own husbands; that, if any obey not the word, they also may without the word be won by the conversation of the wives;	So also ye wives, be ye subject to your husbands; that, by your pleasing behavior, ye may gain over, without difficulty, those who obey not the word,	So also, wives, be subject to your husbands, so that those who are not persuaded by the word will be restored without difficulty by your good behavior,
2	While they behold your chaste conversation coupled with fear.	when they see, that ye conduct yourselves with reverence and chastity.	when they observe that you behave with reverence and with modesty.
3	Whose adorning let it not be that outward adorning of plaiting the hair, and of wearing of gold, or of putting on of apparel;	And adorn not yourselves with the external ornaments of curls of the hair, or of golden trinkets, or of costly garments.	And do not adorn yourselves with outer adornments of the braiding of your hair or of ornaments of gold or of costly clothes.
4	But let it be the hidden man of the heart, in that which is not corruptible, even the ornament of a meek and quiet spirit, which is in the sight of God of great price.	But adorn yourselves in the hidden person of the heart, with a mild and uncorrupted spirit, an ornament that is precious before God.	But adorn yourselves with the hidden man of the heart with a humble spirit, without corruption, an adornment that is costly before God.
5	For after this manner in the old time the holy women also, who trusted in God, adorned themselves, being in subjection unto their own husbands:	For so also the holy women of old, who trusted in God, adorned themselves, and were subject to their husbands:	For so also previously, holy women who trusted in God adorned themselves and were subject to their husbands,
6	Even as Sara obeyed Abraham, calling him lord: whose daughters ye are, as long as ye do well, and are not afraid with any amazement.	just as Sarah was subject to Abraham, and called him, My lord: whose daughters ye are, by good works, while ye are not terrified by any fear.	as Sarah was subject to Abraham and called him, "My lord," whose daughters you are by good works, when you are not troubled by any fear.
7	Likewise, ye husbands, dwell with them according to knowledge, giving honour unto the wife, as unto the weaker vessel, and as being heirs together of the grace of life; that your prayers be not hindered.	And ye husbands, likewise, dwell with your wives according to knowledge, and hold them in honor, as the feebler vessels; because they also will inherit with you the gift of eternal life: and let not your prayers be hindered.	And you men, likewise, live with your wives with knowledge. And hold them with honor as delicate vessels, because they will also inherit the gift of eternal life with you, for you should not be hindered in your prayers.
8	Finally, be ye all of one mind, having compassion one of another, love as brethren, be pitiful, be courteous:	The summing up, is, that ye all be in harmony, that ye be sympathetic with them who suffer, and affectionate one to another, and be merciful and kind.	Now the conclusion [is] that all of you should be in agreement and you should suffer with those who suffer and be compassionate to one another and you should be merciful and humble.
9	Not rendering evil for evil, or railing for railing: but contrariwise blessing; knowing that ye are thereunto called, that ye should inherit a blessing.	And that ye recompense to no one evil for evil, neither railing for railing; but, in contrariety to these, that ye bless: for to this were ye called, that ye might inherit a blessing.	And you should not repay anyone evil for evil, nor abuse for abuse, but in contrast to these [things], bless, for you were called to this, so that you may inherit a blessing.

Parallel Translations

	KJV	Murdock	Magiera
	I PETER	*Chapter 3*	
10	For he that will love life, and see good days, let him refrain his tongue from evil, and his lips that they speak no guile:	Therefore, whoever chooseth life, and desireth to see good days, let him keep his tongue from evil, and his lips that they speak no guile;	THEREFORE, HE WHO DESIRES LIFE AND LOVES TO SEE GOOD DAYS SHOULD KEEP HIS TONGUE FROM EVIL AND HIS LIPS SHOULD SPEAK NO DECEIT.
11	Let him eschew evil, and do good; let him seek peace, and ensue it.	let him turn away from evil, and do good; let him seek peace, and follow after it.	HE SHOULD TURN AWAY FROM EVIL AND DO GOOD AND SHOULD SEEK PEACE AND PURSUE IT,
12	For the eyes of the Lord are over the righteous, and his ears are open unto their prayers: but the face of the Lord is against them that do evil.	Because the eyes of the Lord are upon the righteous, and his ears [ready] to hear them: but the face of the Lord is against the wicked.	BECAUSE THE EYES OF THE LORD [ARE] ON THE JUST [ONES] AND HIS EARS TO HEAR THEM AND THE FACE OF THE LORD [IS] AGAINST EVIL [ONES].
13	And who is he that will harm you, if ye be followers of that which is good?	And who will do you harm, if ye are zealous of good works?	And who is he who can do evil to you, if you are zealous of good [things]?
14	But and if ye suffer for righteousness' sake, happy are ye: and be not afraid of their terror, neither be troubled;	But if it should occur, that ye suffer on account of righteousness, happy are ye. And be not terrified, by those who would terrify you, nor be agitated:	And if you should suffer on account of uprightness, you are blessed. And do not be afraid of those who frighten you and do not be troubled.
15	But sanctify the Lord God in your hearts: and be ready always to give an answer to every man that asketh you a reason of the hope that is in you with meekness and fear:	but sanctify the Lord the Messiah, in your hearts. And be ye ready for a vindication, before every one who demandeth of you an account of the hope of your faith,	But make holy the LORD Christ in your hearts and be ready to make a defense to all who ask you a word concerning the hope of your faith, with meekness and with fear,
16	Having a good conscience; that, whereas they speak evil of you, as of evildoers, they may be ashamed that falsely accuse your good conversation in Christ.	in meekness and respect, as having a good conscience; so that they who speak against you as bad men, may be ashamed, for having calumniated your good conduct in the Messiah.	having a good conscience, so that they who speak about you as about evil men will be ashamed, as men who belittle your good behavior that is in Christ.
17	For it is better, if the will of God be so, that ye suffer for well doing, than for evil doing.	For it is profitable to you, that ye suffer evil while ye do good deeds, if this should be the pleasure of God; and not, while ye do evil deeds.	For it is profitable to you that you suffer evil [things] while you do good works (if therefore it is the will of God) and not while you do evil [things].
18	For Christ also hath once suffered for sins, the just for the unjust, that he might bring us to God, being put to death in the flesh, but quickened by the Spirit:	For the Messiah also once died for our sins, the righteous for sinners; that he might bring you to God. And he died in body, but lived in spirit.	For even Christ died one time for our sins, the just [one] for sinners, that he would bring you to God. And he died bodily, but lives spiritually.
19	By which also he went and preached unto the spirits in prison;	And he preached to those souls, which were detained in Hades,	And he preached to those souls who were held captive in Sheol,

Parallel Translations

I PETER *Chapter 3*

	KJV	Murdock	Magiera
20	Which sometime were disobedient, when once the longsuffering of God waited in the days of Noah, while the ark was a preparing, wherein few, that is, eight souls were saved by water.	which were formerly disobedient, in the days of Noah, when the long suffering of God commanded an ark to be made, in hope of their repentance; and eight souls only entered into it, and were kept alive in the waters.	those who previously were disobedient in the days of Noah, when [in] the long-suffering of God he commanded an ark to be made, in hope of their repentance, yet only eight souls entered it and were kept alive on the water.
21	The like figure whereunto even baptism doth also now save us (not the putting away of the filth of the flesh, but the answer of a good conscience toward God,) by the resurrection of Jesus Christ:	And ye also, by a like figure, are made alive by baptism, (not when ye wash your bodies from filth, but when ye confess God with a pure conscience,) and by the resurrection of Jesus the Messiah;	For you also live in the same type by baptism (not when you wash the body of filth, but when you confess God with a pure conscience) and by the resurrection of Jesus Christ,
22	Who is gone into heaven, and is on the right hand of God; angels and authorities and powers being made subject unto him.	who is taken up to heaven, and is on the right hand of God, and angels, and authorities, and powers, are subject to him.	who was raised up to heaven and is at the right hand of God and angels and authorities and powers are subject to him.

Chapter 4

	KJV	Murdock	Magiera
1	Forasmuch then as Christ hath suffered for us in the flesh, arm yourselves likewise with the same mind: for he that hath suffered in the flesh hath ceased from sin;	If then the Messiah hath suffered for you in the flesh, do ye also arm yourselves with the same mind: for every one that is dead in his body, hath ceased from all sins,	If Christ therefore suffered for you in the flesh, you also should arm yourselves with this mind, for whoever dies in his flesh has ceased from all sins,
2	That he no longer should live the rest of his time in the flesh to the lusts of men, but to the will of God.	that he may no longer be alive to the lusts of men, while he is in the body, but [only] to do the pleasure of God.	so that from now on, he should not live for the desires of men for as long as he is in the body, but for the will of God.
3	For the time past of our life may suffice us to have wrought the will of the Gentiles, when we walked in lasciviousness, lusts, excess of wine, revellings, banquetings, and abominable idolatries:	For the time that is past was enough, when ye wrought the pleasure of the profane, in dissoluteness, and in ebriety, and in lasciviousness, and in revelling, and in the worship of demons.	For the time that has passed by is sufficient when you served in the will of the pagans, in excess and in drunkenness and in filthiness and in revelry and in the service of demons.
4	Wherein they think it strange that ye run not with them to the same excess of riot, speaking evil of you:	And lo, they now wonder, and reproach you, because ye revel not with them in the same former dissoluteness;	And behold, now they marvel and criticize you, in that you do not burn with passion with them in that former excess.
5	Who shall give account to him that is ready to judge the quick and the dead.	who must give account to God, who is to judge the living and the dead.	They will give an account to God, who is going to judge the dead and the living.
6	For this cause was the gospel preached also to them that are dead, that they might be judged according to men in the flesh, but live according to God in the spirit.	For on this account the announcement is made also to the dead, that they may be judged as persons in the flesh, and may live according to God in the spirit.	For because of this, it was announced also to the dead, so that they should be judged as men in the flesh and [that] they should live in God spiritually.
7	But the end of all things is at hand: be ye therefore sober, and watch unto prayer.	But the end of all things approacheth: therefore be sober, and be wakeful for prayer.	But the end of all approaches. Because of this, be sober and be watchful in prayer.

Parallel Translations

I PETER *Chapter 4*

	KJV	*Murdock*	*Magiera*
8	And above all things have fervent charity among yourselves: for charity shall cover the multitude of sins.	And above all things, have fervent love one towards another; for love covereth a multitude of sins.	And before everything, have keen love for one another, for love covers a multitude of sins.
9	Use hospitality one to another without grudging.	And be ye compassionate to strangers, without murmuring.	And be compassionate to strangers without murmuring.
10	As every man hath received the gift, even so minister the same one to another, as good stewards of the manifold grace of God.	And let each of you minister to his associates the gift which he hath received from God; as being good stewards of the manifold grace of God.	And everyone of you should minister the gift that he received from God to his friends, as good stewards of the diverse grace of God.
11	If any man speak, let him speak as the oracles of God; if any man minister, let him do it as of the ability which God giveth: that God in all things may be glorified through Jesus Christ, to whom be praise and dominion for ever and ever. Amen.	Whoever will speak, let him speak as the word of God: and whoever will minister, as of the ability that God hath given him: so that in all ye do, God may be glorified, through Jesus the Messiah; to whom belongeth glory, and honor, for ever and ever. Amen.	All who speak should speak according to the word of God and all who serve [should serve] as from the strength that God has given to him, so that in all you do, God will be glorified by way of Jesus Christ, whose glory and honor is forever and ever. Amen.
12	Beloved, think it not strange concerning the fiery trial which is to try you, as though some strange thing happened unto you:	My beloved, be not dismayed at the trials that befall you, as if some strange thing had come upon you; for these things are for your probation.	My beloved [ones], do not be amazed at the trials that have come to you, as though something strange had happened to you, because they are for your experience.
13	But rejoice, inasmuch as ye are partakers of Christ's sufferings; that, when his glory shall be revealed, ye may be glad also with exceeding joy.	But rejoice, that ye participate in the sufferings of the Messiah, that so ye may also rejoice and exult at the revelation of his glory.	But rejoice because you share in the sufferings of Christ, that so you will also rejoice and be glad at the appearing of his glory.
14	If ye be reproached for the name of Christ, happy are ye; for the spirit of glory and of God resteth upon you: on their part he is evil spoken of, but on your part he is glorified.	And if ye are reproached on account of the name of the Messiah, happy are ye: for the glorious Spirit of God resteth upon you.	And if you are reproached on account of the name of Christ, you are blessed, because the glorious Spirit of God rests on you.
15	But let none of you suffer as a murderer, or as a thief, or as an evildoer, or as a busybody in other men's matters.	Only let none of you suffer, as a murderer, or as a thief, or as an evil-doer.	Only none of you should suffer as a murderer or as a thief or as a worker of evil [things].
16	Yet if any man suffer as a Christian, let him not be ashamed; but let him glorify God on this behalf.	But if he suffer as a Christian, let him not be ashamed; but let him glorify God on account of this name.	But if he suffers as a Christian, he should not be ashamed, but he should glorify God in this name.
17	For the time is come that judgment must begin at the house of God: and if it first begin at us, what shall the end be of them that obey not the gospel of God?	For it is the time when judgment will commence with the house of God: and if it commence with us, what will be the end of those who obey not the gospel of God?	For it is the time when judgment will begin from the house of God and if it begins with us, what is the end of those who are disobedient to the gospel of God?
18	And if the righteous scarcely be saved, where shall the ungodly and the sinner appear?	And if the righteous scarcely liveth, where will the ungodly and the sinner be found!	And IF THE JUST SCARCELY WILL LIVE, WHERE WILL THE WICKED AND THE SINNER BE FOUND?

	KJV	*Murdock*	*Magiera*
	I PETER	*Chapter 4*	
19	Wherefore let them that suffer according to the will of God commit the keeping of their souls to him in well doing, as unto a faithful Creator.	Wherefore, let them who suffer according to the pleasure of God, commend their souls to him in well doing, as to a faithful Creator.	Because of this, those who suffer according to the will of God should commend to him their souls by good works, as to a faithful Creator.
	Chapter 5		
1	The elders which are among you I exhort, who am also an elder, and a witness of the sufferings of Christ, and also a partaker of the glory that shall be revealed:	And I, an Elder, your associate, and a witness of the sufferings of the Messiah, and a participator in his glory which is to be revealed, entreat the Elders who are among you:	Now I ask of the elders who are among you, I, an elder, your friend and a witness of the sufferings of Christ and a participant of his glory that is going to be revealed,
2	Feed the flock of God which is among you, taking the oversight thereof, not by constraint, but willingly; not for filthy lucre, but of a ready mind;	Feed ye the flock of God which is committed to you: have care [for it], spiritually; not from compulsion, but voluntarily; not for base gain, but with all your heart;	feed the flock of God that has been committed to you and perform [it] spiritually, not by necessity, but willingly, not for corrupt profits, but from your whole heart,
3	Neither as being lords over God's heritage, but being ensamples to the flock.	not as lords of the flock, but so as to be a good example for them:	You should not be as lords of the flock, but as a good example for them,
4	And when the chief Shepherd shall appear, ye shall receive a crown of glory that fadeth not away.	that when the chief shepherd shall be revealed, ye may receive from him a crown of glory that fadeth not.	so that when the chief of the shepherds is revealed, you will receive a crown of glory from him that will not fade.
5	Likewise, ye younger, submit yourselves unto the elder. Yea, all of you be subject one to another, and be clothed with humility: for God resisteth the proud, and giveth grace to the humble.	And ye juniors submit yourselves to your seniors; and clothe yourselves, stringently, with lowliness of mind one towards another; because God resisteth them who exalt themselves, and giveth grace to the humble.	And you, young ones, be subject to your elders and be clothed diligently with humbleness of mind toward one another, because GOD IS OPPOSED TO THOSE WHO ELEVATE THEMSELVES, BUT HE GIVES GRACE TO THE HUMBLE.
6	Humble yourselves therefore under the mighty hand of God, that he may exalt you in due time:	Humble yourselves, therefore, under the powerful hand of God: and it will exalt you in due time.	Therefore, humble yourselves under the mighty hand of God, so that he will elevate you in the time that is right.
7	Casting all your care upon him; for he careth for you.	And cast all your solicitude upon God; for he careth for you.	And throw all your care on God, because he is concerned for you.
8	Be sober, be vigilant; because your adversary the devil, as a roaring lion, walketh about, seeking whom he may devour:	Be sober and guarded, because Satan your adversary, like a lion, roareth, and goeth about, and seeketh whom he may devour.	Be watchful and remember, because your enemy, Satan, roars as a lion and walks about and seeks whom he may swallow.
9	Whom resist stedfast in the faith, knowing that the same afflictions are accomplished in your brethren that are in the world.	Therefore resist him, being steadfast in the faith: and know ye, that the same sufferings befall your brethren that are in the world.	Therefore, stand against him, being steadfast in faith and know that these sufferings also happen to your brothers who are in the world.

Parallel Translations

	KJV	Murdock	Magiera
	I PETER	*Chapter 5*	
10	But the God of all grace, who hath called us unto his eternal glory by Christ Jesus, after that ye have suffered a while, make you perfect, stablish, strengthen, settle you.	Now it is the God of grace, who hath called us to his eternal glory by Jesus the Messiah, that hath given us, while we sustain these light afflictions, to be strengthened, and confirmed, and established by him for ever:	Now the God of grace who has called us to his eternal glory by way of Jesus Christ, who has given us, while we endure these few trials, to be strengthened and to be made steadfast and to be established by him forever,
11	To him be glory and dominion for ever and ever. Amen.	to whom be glory, and power, and honor, for ever and ever. Amen.	to him [be] glory and dominion and honor, forever and ever. Amen.
12	By Silvanus, a faithful brother unto you, as I suppose, I have written briefly, exhorting, and testifying that this is the true grace of God wherein ye stand.	These as I account [them] few [things], I have written to you by Sylvanus, a faithful brother. And I would persuade, and would testify, that this is the true grace of God, this in which ye stand.	These few [things], as I think of [them], I wrote to you by way of Silvanus, a faithful brother. And I am persuading and bearing witness that this is the true grace of God in which you stand.
13	The church that is at Babylon, elected together with you, saluteth you; and so doth Marcus my son.	The elect church which is in Babylon, saluteth you; also Mark, my son.	The chosen church that is in Babylon and Mark, my son, greet you.
14	Greet ye one another with a kiss of charity. Peace be with you all that are in Christ Jesus. Amen.	Salute ye one another with a holy kiss. Peace be with you all, who are in the Messiah. Amen.	Greet one another with a holy kiss. Peace [be] with all those who are in Christ. Amen.

Parallel Translations

	KJV	*Murdock*	*Magiera*
	II PETER *Chapter 1*		
1	Simon Peter, a servant and an apostle of Jesus Christ, to them that have obtained like precious faith with us through the righteousness of God and our Saviour Jesus Christ:	Simon Peter, a servant and legate of Jesus the Messiah, to those who have obtained equally precious faith with us, through the righteousness of Our Lord and Redeemer, Jesus the Messiah;	Simon Peter, a servant and apostle of Jesus Christ, to those who have been made worthy of the equally precious faith with us by the justification of our Lord and our Savior, Jesus Christ:
2	Grace and peace be multiplied unto you through the knowledge of God, and of Jesus our Lord,	May grace and peace abound to you through the recognition of our Lord Jesus the Messiah,	Grace and peace be multiplied to you in the acknowledgment of our Lord Jesus Christ.
3	According as his divine power hath given unto us all things that pertain unto life and godliness, through the knowledge of him that hath called us to glory and virtue:	as the giver to us of all things that be of the power of God, unto life and the fear of God, through the recognition of him who hath called us unto his own glory and moral excellence:	[It is] he who has given all these [things] of divine power, for life and the reverence of God, by way of the acknowledgment of him who called us into his glory and excellence.
4	Whereby are given unto us exceeding great and precious promises: that by these ye might be partakers of the divine nature, having escaped the corruption that is in the world through lust.	wherein he hath given you very great and precious promises; that by them ye might become partakers of the nature of God, while ye flee from the corruptions of the lusts that are in the world.	For by him he has given you great and precious promises, that by way of these, you would be sharers of the divine nature, having escaped from the corruption of the desires that are in the world.
5	And beside this, giving all diligence, add to your faith virtue; and to virtue knowledge;	And, while ye apply all diligence in the matter, add to your faith moral excellence; and to moral excellence, knowledge;	Now while you are applying all this diligence, add to your faith, excellence, and to excellence, knowledge,
6	And to knowledge temperance; and to temperance patience; and to patience godliness;	and to knowledge, perseverance; and to perseverance, patience; and to patience, the fear of God;	and to knowledge, self-control, and to self-control, endurance, and to endurance, reverence of God,
7	And to godliness brotherly kindness; and to brotherly kindness charity.	and to the fear of God, sympathy with the brotherhood; and to sympathy with the brotherhood, love.	and to reverence of God, brotherly kindness, and to brotherly kindness, love.
8	For if these things be in you, and abound, they make you that ye shall neither be barren nor unfruitful in the knowledge of our Lord Jesus Christ.	For, while these are found in you, and abounding, they render you not slothful, and not unfruitful, in the recognition of our Lord Jesus the Messiah.	For when these are found in you and increase, they establish you [as] neither worthless, nor without fruit in the acknowledgment of our Lord Jesus Christ.
9	But he that lacketh these things is blind, and cannot see afar off, and hath forgotten that he was purged from his old sins.	For he, in whom these things are not found, is blind and seeth not, and hath forgotten the purgation of his former sins.	For he in whom these [things] are not found is blind so that he does not see, because he has forgotten the cleansing of his former sins.
10	Wherefore the rather, brethren, give diligence to make your calling and election sure: for if ye do these things, ye shall never fall:	And therefore, my brethren, be ye exceedingly diligent to make your calling and election sure, by your good actions: for, by so doing, ye will never fall away.	And concerning that, be especially diligent, my brothers, that by way of your good works, you would make your calling and your approval certain, for when you do these [things], you will never falter.

Parallel Translations

II PETER Chapter 1

	KJV	Murdock	Magiera
11	For so an entrance shall be ministered unto you abundantly into the everlasting kingdom of our Lord and Saviour Jesus Christ.	For thus will entrance be given you abundantly, into the everlasting kingdom of our Lord and Redeemer Jesus the Messiah.	For so an entrance will be readily given to you to the eternal kingdom of our Lord and our Savior, Jesus Christ.
12	Wherefore I will not be negligent to put you always in remembrance of these things, though ye know them, and be established in the present truth.	And for this reason I am not wearied in reminding you continually of these things; although ye know them well, and are established in this truth.	And concerning this, I did not give up reminding you continually about these [things], although you also know [them] well and are settled concerning this truth.
13	Yea, I think it meet, as long as I am in this tabernacle, to stir you up by putting you in remembrance;	And it seemeth right to me, so long as I am in this body, to excite you by monition;	And I think that it is right that as long as I am in this body, I should stir you up by remembrance,
14	Knowing that shortly I must put off this my tabernacle, even as our Lord Jesus Christ hath shewed me.	since I know, that the demise of my body is speedy, as also my Lord Jesus the Messiah hath showed me.	since I know that the absence of my body will be soon, as also our Lord Jesus Christ has made known to me.
15	Moreover I will endeavour that ye may be able after my decease to have these things always in remembrance.	And I am anxious, that, after my departure, ye too may have it always with you to make mention of these things.	And I am concerned that you will also continually have [this care], that even after my departure, you will have remembrance of these [things].
16	For we have not followed cunningly devised fables, when we made known unto you the power and coming of our Lord Jesus Christ, but were eyewitnesses of his majesty.	For we have not gone after fables artfully framed, in making known to you the power and advent of our Lord Jesus the Messiah; but [it was] after we had been spectators of his majesty.	For it was not following after sayings that were formed with skill [that] we made known to you the power and the coming of our Lord Jesus Christ, but after we were spectators of his majesty.
17	For he received from God the Father honour and glory, when there came such a voice to him from the excellent glory, This is my beloved Son, in whom I am well pleased.	For, when he received from God the Father honor and glory, and, after the splendid glory of his majesty, a voice came to him thus: This is my beloved Son, in whom I am well pleased;	For after he received honor and glory from God, the Father, when a voice came to him that [was] like this from glory, splendid in its greatness, "This is my beloved Son, in whom I am pleased,"
18	And this voice which came from heaven we heard, when we were with him in the holy mount.	we also heard this identical voice from heaven, which came to him while we were with him in the holy mount.	we also heard this voice from heaven that came to him, when we were with him on the holy mountain.
19	We have also a more sure word of prophecy; whereunto ye do well that ye take heed, as unto a light that shineth in a dark place, until the day dawn, and the day star arise in your hearts:	And we have moreover a sure word of prophecy; and ye will do well, if ye look to it as to a light that shineth in a dark place, until the day shall dawn, and the sun shall arise in your hearts;	And we also have a word of prophecy that is certain, which you do well when you look at it (as to a lamp that shines in a dark place until the day should dawn and the sun should rise) in your hearts,
20	Knowing this first, that no prophecy of the scripture is of any private interpretation.	ye having the previous knowledge, that no prophecy is an exposition of its own text.	knowing this first, that all prophecy was not a sending out of its own writing.
21	For the prophecy came not in old time by the will of man: but holy men of God spake as they were moved by the Holy Ghost.	For at no time was it by the pleasure of man, that the prophecy came; but holy men of God spoke, as they were moved by the Holy Spirit.	For prophecy never came by the will of man, but as they were being led by the sanctified Spirit, men of God spoke sanctified [words].

Parallel Translations

	KJV	Murdock	Magiera
	II PETER Chapter 2		
1	But there were false prophets also among the people, even as there shall be false teachers among you, who privily shall bring in damnable heresies, even denying the Lord that bought them, and bring upon themselves swift destruction.	But in the world, there have been also false prophets, as there will likewise be false teachers among you, who will bring in destructive heresies, denying the Lord that bought them; thus bringing on themselves swift destruction.	But there were also false prophets among the people, as also false teachers will be among you, who will introduce heresies of destruction and deny the Lord who bought them, bringing on themselves swift destruction.
2	And many shall follow their pernicious ways; by reason of whom the way of truth shall be evil spoken of.	And many will go after their profaneness; on account of whom, the way of truth will be reproached.	And many will follow their uncleanness, because of whom the way of truth will be reproached.
3	And through covetousness shall they with feigned words make merchandise of you: whose judgment now of a long time lingereth not, and their damnation slumbereth not.	And, in the cupidity of raving words, they will make merchandise of you: whose judgment, of a long time, is not idle; and their destruction slumbereth not.	And with fraud and with babbling words they will exploit you, whose previous condemnation has not stopped and whose destruction does not sleep.
4	For if God spared not the angels that sinned, but cast them down to hell, and delivered them into chains of darkness, to be reserved unto judgment;	For, if God spared not the angels that sinned, but cast them down to the infernal regions in chains of darkness, and delivered them up to be kept unto the judgment of torture,	For indeed God did not spare the angels who sinned, but cast them down in chains of darkness into the low [regions] and delivered them to be kept for the judgment of torment.
5	And spared not the old world, but saved Noah the eighth person, a preacher of righteousness, bringing in the flood upon the world of the ungodly;	and spared not the former world, but preserved Noah the eighth person, a preacher of righteousness, when he brought a flood on the world of the wicked;	And he did not spare the former world, but protected Noah, the eighth [person], a preacher of uprightness, when he brought a flood over the world of the wicked.
6	And turning the cities of Sodom and Gomorrha into ashes condemned them with an overthrow, making them an ensample unto those that after should live ungodly;	[and] burned up the cities of Sodom and Gomorrah, and condemned them by an overthrow, making them a demonstration to the wicked who should come after them;	And when he burned the cities of Sodom and of Gomorrah and condemned them by an overthrow, setting an example to the wicked who were to come,
7	And delivered just Lot, vexed with the filthy conversation of the wicked:	and also delivered righteous Lot, who was tormented with the filthy conduct of the lawless;	he also delivered just Lot, who was oppressed by the unclean conduct of those who were lawless,
8	(For that righteous man dwelling among them, in seeing and hearing, vexed his righteous soul from day to day with their unlawful deeds;)	for that upright man dwelling among them, in seeing and hearing from day to day, was distressed in his righteous soul by their lawless deeds;	for as that upright [man] was living among them, in seeing and in hearing day after day, his just soul was tormented by [their] lawless works.
9	The Lord knoweth how to deliver the godly out of temptations, and to reserve the unjust unto the day of judgment to be punished:	the Lord knoweth how to rescue from afflictions those who fear him; and he will reserve the wicked for the day of judgment to be tormented,	The LORD knows how to deliver from trial those who reverence him, but he will keep the unjust for the day of judgment, when they will be tormented,

Parallel Translations

II PETER Chapter 2

	KJV	Murdock	Magiera
10	But chiefly them that walk after the flesh in the lust of uncleanness, and despise government. Presumptuous are they, selfwilled, they are not afraid to speak evil of dignities.	and especially them who go after the flesh in the lusts of pollution, and despise government. Daring and arrogant, they shudder not with awe while they blaspheme;	especially those who follow after the flesh with the desire of defilement and rebel against lordship. [These are] daring [ones] and proud [ones], because they are not troubled when they blaspheme against the glory,
11	Whereas angels, which are greater in power and might, bring not railing accusation against them before the Lord.	whereas angels, greater than they in might and valor, bring not against them a reproachful denunciation.	whereas angels that are greater than them in power and in might do not bring on themselves the judgment of blasphemy from the LORD.
12	But these, as natural brute beasts, made to be taken and destroyed, speak evil of the things that they understand not; and shall utterly perish in their own corruption;	But these, like the dumb beasts that by nature are for slaughter and corruption, while reviling the things they know not, will perish in their own corruption;	But these, as dumb animals [that] are by nature for slaughter and corruption, while blaspheming those [things] they do not know, will be corrupted in their own corruption,
13	And shall receive the reward of unrighteousness, as they that count it pleasure to riot in the day time. Spots they are and blemishes, sporting themselves with their own deceivings while they feast with you;	they being persons with whom iniquity is the reward of iniquity, and by them rioting in the daytime is accounted delightful; defiled and full of spots [are they], indulging themselves at their ease, while they give themselves up to pleasure;	being those who have wickedness [as] the wage of wickedness. To them, making merry that happens in the daytime is considered pleasure. [These are] defiled and full of blemishes, for they indulge themselves, while they are making merry in their idleness,
14	Having eyes full of adultery, and that cannot cease from sin; beguiling unstable souls: an heart they have exercised with covetous practices; cursed children:	having eyes that are full of adultery, and sins that never end; seducing unstable souls; and having a heart exercised in cupidity; children of malediction:	having eyes that are full of adultery and sins that do not come to an end, enticing people that are unstable and having a heart that is practiced in fraud, children of a curse,
15	Which have forsaken the right way, and are gone astray, following the way of Balaam the son of Bosor, who loved the wages of unrighteousness;	and, having left the way of rectitude, they have wandered and gone in the way of Balaam the son of Beor, who loved the wages of iniquity,	who, having left the straight way, have swerved and gone in the way of Balaam, the son of Beor, who loved the wage of wickedness.
16	But was rebuked for his iniquity: the dumb ass speaking with man's voice forbad the madness of the prophet.	and who had for the reprover of his transgression a dumb ass, which, speaking with the speech of men, rebuked the madness of the prophet.	And the reproof that he had for his transgression [was] an ass, without a voice, who spoke with the voice of men [and] restrained the foolishness of the prophet.
17	These are wells without water, clouds that are carried with a tempest; to whom the mist of darkness is reserved for ever.	These are wells without water, clouds driven by a tempest, persons for whom is reserved the blackness of darkness.	These [men] are wells without water, clouds that are driven by a whirlwind, those for whom the blackness of darkness is reserved.

II PETER *Chapter 2*

	KJV	Murdock	Magiera
18	For when they speak great swelling words of vanity, they allure through the lusts of the flesh, through much wantonness, those that were clean escaped from them who live in error.	For, while they utter astonishing vanity, they seduce, with obscene lusts of the flesh, them who have almost abandoned these that walk in error.	For while they speak vehement [words] of emptiness, they entice [again] with unclean desires of the flesh, those who had fled for a short time from these [men] who are living in error.
19	While they promise them liberty, they themselves are the servants of corruption: for of whom a man is overcome, of the same is he brought in bondage.	And they promise them liberty, while they themselves are the slaves of corruption: for, by whatever thing a man is vanquished, to that is he enslaved.	And they promise them liberty, while they are slaves of corruption, for by what a man is overcome, to this he is also enslaved.
20	For if after they have escaped the pollutions of the world through the knowledge of the Lord and Saviour Jesus Christ, they are again entangled therein, and overcome, the latter end is worse with them than the beginning.	For if, when they have escaped the pollutions of the world by the knowledge of our Lord and Redeemer Jesus the Messiah, they become again involved in the same, and are vanquished, their latter state is worse than the former.	For if, after they have fled from the pollutions of the world by the acknowledgment of our Lord Jesus Christ, even our Savior, when they are entangled again in the same [and] are overcome, their end will be worse than the beginning.
21	For it had been better for them not to have known the way of righteousness, than, after they have known it, to turn from the holy commandment delivered unto them.	For it would have been better for them, not to have known the way of righteousness, than after having known [it], to turn back from the holy commandment that was delivered to them.	For it would have been better for them not to have known the way of justification, than having known [it], to turn backwards from the holy commandment that was committed to them.
22	But it is happened unto them according to the true proverb, The dog is turned to his own vomit again; and the sow that was washed to her wallowing in the mire.	But the true proverb hath happened to them: the dog returneth to his vomit and the sow that was washed, to her wallowing in the mire.	But these [sayings] of a true proverb have happened to them, "A dog has returned to his vomit and the sow that was washed to wallowing in mud."

Chapter 3

	KJV	Murdock	Magiera
1	This second epistle, beloved, I now write unto you; in both which I stir up your pure minds by way of remembrance:	This second epistle, my beloved, I now write to you; in [both of] which I stir up your honest mind by admonition:	This second letter, my beloved [ones], I write to you now, in which I stir up by remembrance your proper thinking,
2	That ye may be mindful of the words which were spoken before by the holy prophets, and of the commandment of us the apostles of the Lord and Saviour:	that ye may be mindful of the words which were formerly spoken by the holy prophets, and of the injunction of our Lord and Redeemer by the hand of the legates:	so that you will recall the words that were spoken before by the holy prophets and the commandment of our Lord and our Savior by way of the apostles,
3	Knowing this first, that there shall come in the last days scoffers, walking after their own lusts,	knowing this previously, that there will come in the last days scoffers, who will scoff, walking according to their own lusts;	knowing this first, that at the end of days mockers will come who will mock, walking according to their own desires
4	And saying, Where is the promise of his coming? for since the fathers fell asleep, all things continue as they were from the beginning of the creation.	and saying, Where is the promise of his coming? for, since our fathers fell asleep, every thing remaineth just as from the beginning of the creation.	and saying, "Where is the promise of his coming? For since our fathers have slept, everything continues the same from the beginning of the creation."

Parallel Translations

II PETER *Chapter 3*

	KJV	*Murdock*	*Magiera*
5	For this they willingly are ignorant of, that by the word of God the heavens were of old, and the earth standing out of the water and in the water:	For this they willingly forget, that the heavens were of old; and the earth rose up from the waters, and by means of water, by the word of God.	For this is forgotten by them willingly, that the heaven[s] were from before, and the earth rose up out of the water and by way of water, by the word of God.
6	Whereby the world that then was, being overflowed with water, perished:	[And], by means of these [waters], the world which then was, [being submerged] again perished in the waters.	Then by way of these [waters] the world overflowed with water and was destroyed.
7	But the heavens and the earth, which are now, by the same word are kept in store, reserved unto fire against the day of judgment and perdition of ungodly men.	And the heavens that now are, and the earth, are by his word stored up, being reserved for the fire at the day of judgment and the perdition of wicked men.	But the heaven and the earth that are now are kept in store by his word, being reserved for fire on the day of the judgment and of the destruction of wicked men.
8	But, beloved, be not ignorant of this one thing, that one day is with the Lord as a thousand years, and a thousand years as one day.	And of this one thing, my beloved, be not forgetful, That one day, to the Lord, is as a thousand years; and a thousand years, as one day.	Now this one [thing] do not forget, my beloved [ones], that one day to the LORD is as a thousand years and a thousand years as one day.
9	The Lord is not slack concerning his promise, as some men count slackness; but is longsuffering to us-ward, not willing that any should perish, but that all should come to repentance.	The Lord doth not procrastinate his promises, as some estimate procrastination; but he is long suffering, for your sakes, being not willing that any should perish, but that every one should come to repentance.	The LORD does not delay in his promises as men consider delay, but he is long-suffering because of you, in that he does not want anyone to be destroyed, but rather [that] everyone should come to repentance.
10	But the day of the Lord will come as a thief in the night; in the which the heavens shall pass away with a great noise, and the elements shall melt with fervent heat, the earth also and the works that are therein shall be burned up.	And the day of the Lord will come, like a thief; in which the heavens will suddenly pass away; and the elements, being ignited, will be dissolved; and the earth and the works in it, will not be found.	But the day of the LORD will come as a thief, in which the heaven[s] will suddenly pass away and the elements, while burning, will dissolve and the earth and the works that are in it will [not] be found.
11	Seeing then that all these things shall be dissolved, what manner of persons ought ye to be in all holy conversation and godliness,	As therefore all these things are to be dissolved, what persons ought ye to be, in holy conduct, and in the fear of God,	Since therefore all these [things] will be dissolved, how ought you to be in your conduct? [You should be] holy [ones] and with reverence for God,
12	Looking for and hasting unto the coming of the day of God, wherein the heavens being on fire shall be dissolved, and the elements shall melt with fervent heat?	expecting and desiring the coming of the day of God, in which the heavens being tried by fire will be dissolved, and the elements being ignited will melt?	while you expect and you desire the coming of the day of God, in which the heaven[s], being tried by fire, will be dissolved and the elements, while burning, will melt.
13	Nevertheless we, according to his promise, look for new heavens and a new earth, wherein dwelleth righteousness.	But we, according to his promise, expect new heavens, and a new earth, in which righteousness dwelleth.	But we expect a new heaven and a new earth, according to his promise, in which justification will live.

Parallel Translations

II PETER *Chapter 3*

	KJV	Murdock	Magiera
14	Wherefore, beloved, seeing that ye look for such things, be diligent that ye may be found of him in peace, without spot, and blameless.	Therefore, my beloved, as ye expect these things, strive that ye may be found by him in peace, without spot and without blemish.	Because of this, my beloved [ones], while you expect these [things], be diligent to be found by him without spot and without blemish in peace.
15	And account that the longsuffering of our Lord is salvation; even as our beloved brother Paul also according to the wisdom given unto him hath written unto you;	And account the long suffering of the Lord to be redemption; as also our beloved brother Paul, according to the wisdom conferred on him, wrote to you;	And you should consider the long-suffering of the LORD [as] redemption, even as also our beloved brother Paul wrote to you according to the wisdom that was given to him.
16	As also in all his epistles, speaking in them of these things; in which are some things hard to be understood, which they that are unlearned and unstable wrest, as they do also the other scriptures, unto their own destruction.	as also in all his epistles, speaking in them of these things, in which there is something difficult to be understood; [and] which they who are ignorant and unstable, pervert, as they do also the rest of the scriptures, to their own destruction.	As in all his letters, he speaks in them about these [things] (in which there are some [things] hard to understand) that those who are without instruction and are unstable pervert, as they also [pervert] the writings of the rest to their own loss.
17	Ye therefore, beloved, seeing ye know these things before, beware lest ye also, being led away with the error of the wicked, fall from your own stedfastness.	Ye therefore, my beloved, as ye know [these things] beforehand, guard yourselves, lest, by going after the error of the lawless, ye fall from your steadfastness.	You therefore, my beloved [ones], since you know [these things] beforehand, guard yourselves, so that you should not fall from your commitment, following after the error of those who are lawless.
18	But grow in grace, and in the knowledge of our Lord and Saviour Jesus Christ. To him be glory both now and for ever. Amen.	But be ye growing in grace, and in the knowledge of our Lord and Redeemer Jesus the Messiah, and of God the Father: whose is the glory, now, and always, and to the days of eternity. Amen.	But grow in grace and in the knowledge of our Lord and our redeemer, Jesus Christ, and of God the Father, to whom [be] glory, both now and always, even for the days of eternity. Amen.

Parallel Translations

I JOHN *Chapter 1*

	KJV	*Murdock*	*Magiera*
1	That which was from the beginning, which we have heard, which we have seen with our eyes, which we have looked upon, and our hands have handled, of the Word of life;	We announce to you that, which was from the beginning, which we have heard, and have seen with our eyes, looked upon, and handled with our hands, that which is the word of life.	We preach to you that which was from the beginning, which we have heard and seen with our eyes, sensed and touched with our hands, which is the word of life.
2	(For the life was manifested, and we have seen it, and bear witness, and shew unto you that eternal life, which was with the Father, and was manifested unto us;)	And the life was manifested, and we have seen and do testify and announce to you, the life which is eternal; which was with the Father, and was revealed to us.	And life was revealed and we saw [it] and testify and preach to you the eternal life that was with the Father and was revealed to us.
3	That which we have seen and heard declare we unto you, that ye also may have fellowship with us: and truly our fellowship is with the Father, and with his Son Jesus Christ.	And what we have seen and heard, we make known to you also, that ye may have fellowship with us; and our fellowship is with the Father, and with his Son Jesus the Messiah.	And what we have seen and heard, we also make known to you, so that you would have fellowship with us. And our fellowship is with the Father and with his Son, Jesus Christ.
4	And these things write we unto you, that your joy may be full.	And these things we write to you, that our joy in you may be complete.	And these [things] we write to you, so that our joy that is in you would be full.
5	This then is the message which we have heard of him, and declare unto you, that God is light, and in him is no darkness at all.	And this is the announcement, which we have heard from him and declare to you, that God is light, and no darkness at all is in him.	And this is the gospel that we heard from him and we preach to you, that God is light and there is no darkness in him at all.
6	If we say that we have fellowship with him, and walk in darkness, we lie, and do not the truth:	And if we say that we have fellowship with him, and we walk in the darkness, we are liars, and walk not in the truth.	And if we say that we have fellowship with him and walk in darkness, we are liars and we do not proceed in the truth.
7	But if we walk in the light, as he is in the light, we have fellowship one with another, and the blood of Jesus Christ his Son cleanseth us from all sin.	But if we walk in the light, as he is in the light, we have fellowship with each other and the blood of Jesus his Son cleanseth us from all our sins.	But if we walk in the light as he is in the light, we have fellowship with one another and the blood of Jesus his Son cleanses us from all of our sins.
8	If we say that we have no sin, we deceive ourselves, and the truth is not in us.	And if we say that we have no sin, we deceive ourselves, and the truth is not in us.	And if we say that we have no sin, we deceive ourselves and the truth is not in us.
9	If we confess our sins, he is faithful and just to forgive us our sins, and to cleanse us from all unrighteousness.	But if we confess our sins, he is faithful and righteous, to forgive us our sins, and to cleanse us from all our iniquity.	And if we confess our sins, he is faithful and just to forgive us our sins and to cleanse us from all our wickedness.
10	If we say that we have not sinned, we make him a liar, and his word is not in us.	If we say that we have not sinned, we make him a liar, and his word is not with us.	And if we say that we do not sin, we make him a liar and his word is not with us.

I JOHN *Chapter 2*

	KJV	*Murdock*	*Magiera*
1	My little children, these things write I unto you, that ye sin not. And if any man sin, we have an advocate with the Father, Jesus Christ the righteous:	My children, these things I write to you, that ye sin not. But if any one should sin, we have an Advocate with the Father, Jesus the Messiah, the righteous.	My sons, I am writing these [things] to you so that you do not sin. Yet if someone should sin, we have a defense attorney with the Father, Jesus Christ, the Just [one].
2	And he is the propitiation for our sins: and not for ours only, but also for the sins of the whole world.	For he is himself the propitiation for our sins; and not for ours only, but also for all the world.	For he is the payment for our sins and not on behalf of ours only, but also on behalf of [the sins of] the whole world.
3	And hereby we do know that we know him, if we keep his commandments.	And by this we shall be sensible that we know him, if we keep his commandments.	And by this we perceive that we know him, if we keep his commandments.
4	He that saith, I know him, and keepeth not his commandments, is a liar, and the truth is not in him.	For he that saith, I know him, and doth not keep his commandments, is a liar, and the truth is not in him.	For he who says, "I know him," and does not keep his commandments is a liar and the truth is not in him.
5	But whoso keepeth his word, in him verily is the love of God perfected: hereby know we that we are in him.	But he that keepeth his word, in him is the love of God truly completed: for by this we know that we are in him.	But he who keeps his word, in this [one] truly the love of God is completed, for in this we know that we are in him.
6	He that saith he abideth in him ought himself also so to walk, even as he walked.	He that saith, I am in him, is bound to walk according to his walkings.	He who says, "I am in him," ought to conduct himself according to his own conduct.
7	Brethren, I write no new commandment unto you, but an old commandment which ye had from the beginning. The old commandment is the word which ye have heard from the beginning.	My beloved, I write no new commandment to you, but the old commandment which ye had from the beginning; and the old commandment is the word, which ye have heard.	My beloved [ones], I am not writing a new commandment to you, but an old commandment that you have had from the beginning. And the old commandment is the word that you have heard.
8	Again, a new commandment I write unto you, which thing is true in him and in you: because the darkness is past, and the true light now shineth.	Again, a new commandment I write to you, which is true in him and in you; because the darkness hath passed away, and the true light beginneth to appear.	Again, I am writing a new commandment to you that is true in him and in you, because the darkness has passed and the true light has begun to be seen.
9	He that saith he is in the light, and hateth his brother, is in darkness even until now.	Whoever therefore shall say that he is in the light, and hateth his brother, is in darkness until now.	Therefore, he who says that he is in the light and hates his brother is in darkness until now.
10	He that loveth his brother abideth in the light, and there is none occasion of stumbling in him.	He that loveth his brother, abideth in the light, and in him is no stumbling.	But he who loves his brother remains in the light and there is no stumbling in him.
11	But he that hateth his brother is in darkness, and walketh in darkness, and knoweth not whither he goeth, because that darkness hath blinded his eyes.	But he that hateth his brother, is in darkness, and walketh in darkness; and he knoweth not whither he goeth, because the darkness hath blinded his eyes.	But he who hates his brother is in darkness and walks in darkness and does not know where he is going, because the darkness has blinded his eyes.
12	I write unto you, little children, because your sins are forgiven you for his name's sake.	I write to you, ye children, because your sins are forgiven you for his name's sake.	I am writing to you, sons, because your sins are forgiven on account of his name.

Parallel Translations

I JOHN *Chapter 2*

	KJV	*Murdock*	*Magiera*
13	I write unto you, fathers, because ye have known him that is from the beginning. I write unto you, young men, because ye have overcome the wicked one. I write unto you, little children, because ye have known the Father.	I write to you, ye fathers, because ye have known him who existed from the beginning. I write to you, ye young men, because ye have vanquished the evil one.	I am writing to you, fathers, because you have known him who is from the beginning. I am writing to you, young men, because you have overcome the Evil [one]. I have written to you, young boys, because you have known the Father.
14	I have written unto you, fathers, because ye have known him that is from the beginning. I have written unto you, young men, because ye are strong, and the word of God abideth in you, and ye have overcome the wicked one.	I have written to you, ye little ones, because ye have known the Father. I have written to you, ye fathers, because ye have known him who [was] from the beginning, I have written to you, ye young men, because ye are strong, and the word of God dwelleth in you, and ye have vanquished the evil one.	I have written to you, fathers, because you have known him who was from the beginning. I have written to you, young men, because you are strong and the word of God lives in you and you have overcome the Evil [one].
15	Love not the world, neither the things that are in the world. If any man love the world, the love of the Father is not in him.	Love not the world, nor any thing in it; for whoever loveth the world, hath not the love of the Father in him.	Do not love the world and not anything that is in it, for he who loves the world does not have the love of the Father.
16	For all that is in the world, the lust of the flesh, and the lust of the eyes, and the pride of life, is not of the Father, but is of the world.	For all that is in the world, is, the lust of the body, and the lust of the eyes, and the pride of the world; which are not from the Father, but from the world itself.	For everything that is in the world, the desire of the body and the desire of the eyes and the boasting of the world, is not from the Father, but is from the world itself.
17	And the world passeth away, and the lust thereof: but he that doeth the will of God abideth for ever.	And the world is passing away, [both] it and the lust thereof; but he that doeth the pleasure of God, abideth for ever.	And the world and its desire pass away, but he who does the will of God remains forever.
18	Little children, it is the last time: and as ye have heard that antichrist shall come, even now are there many antichrists; whereby we know that it is the last time.	My children, it is the latter time; and as ye have heard that a false Messiah was to arise, so there are now many false Messiahs; and from this we know that it is the latter time.	My sons, it is the last time and according to what you have heard, a false Messiah will come. Even now there are many false Messiahs and from this we know that it is the last time.
19	They went out from us, but they were not of us; for if they had been of us, they would no doubt have continued with us: but they went out, that they might be made manifest that they were not all of us.	From us they went out, but they were not of us; for if they had been of us, they would have continued with us: but they went out from us, that so it might be known, that they were not of us.	They have gone out from us, but they are not of us, for if they had been of us they would have stayed with us, but they went out from us that it would be known that they were not of us.
20	But ye have an unction from the Holy One, and ye know all things.	But ye have an unction from the Holy [One]; and ye discriminate every person.	And you have an anointing from the holy [one] and are distinguishing between everyone.
21	I have not written unto you because ye know not the truth, but because ye know it, and that no lie is of the truth.	I have not written to you, because ye know not the truth, but because ye know it, and because no falsehood is of the truth.	I have not written to you because you do not know the truth, but because you do know it and because no falsehood is of the truth.

	KJV	Murdock	Magiera

I JOHN Chapter 2

	KJV	Murdock	Magiera
22	Who is a liar but he that denieth that Jesus is the Christ? He is antichrist, that denieth the Father and the Son.	Who is false, but he that denieth that Jesus is the Messiah? And that person is a false Messiah. He that denieth the Father, denieth also the Son.	Who is a liar, except he who denies that Jesus is the Messiah? This one is a false Messiah. He who denies the Father also denies the Son.
23	Whosoever denieth the Son, the same hath not the Father: (but) he that acknowledgeth the Son hath the Father also.	And he that denieth the Son, also believeth not the Father. He that confesseth the Son, confesseth also the Father.	And he who denies the Son, also does not believe in the Father. He who confesses the Son, also confesses the Father.
24	Let that therefore abide in you, which ye have heard from the beginning. If that which ye have heard from the beginning shall remain in you, ye also shall continue in the Son, and in the Father.	And what ye heard from the first, let that remain with you. For if that, which ye heard from the first, remaineth with you, ye also will remain in the Father and in the Son.	And what you have heard previously should remain with you, for if what you have heard previously remains with you, you will also remain in the Father and in the Son.
25	And this is the promise that he hath promised us, even eternal life.	And this is the promise, which he hath promised us, [even] life eternal.	And this is the promise that he has promised to us, eternal life.
26	These things have I written unto you concerning them that seduce you.	And these things I have written to you, on account of those who seduce you.	And these [things] I have written to you on account of those who seduce you.
27	But the anointing which ye have received of him abideth in you, and ye need not that any man teach you: but as the same anointing teacheth you of all things, and is truth, and is no lie, and even as it hath taught you, ye shall abide in him.	And ye also, if the unction which ye have received from him remaineth in you, need not that any one should teach you; but as that unction is from God, it teacheth you all things; and it is true, and no falsehood is in it. And as it hath taught you, remain ye in him.	And you also, if the anointing that you have received from him remains with you, will not need anyone to teach you. But as the anointing is from God, it teaches you about everything and it is the truth and there is no falsehood in it. And as he has taught you, remain in him.
28	And now, little children, abide in him; that, when he shall appear, we may have confidence, and not be ashamed before him at his coming.	And now, my children, remain ye in him; that so, when he shall be manifested, we may not be ashamed before him, but may have an open countenance at his coming.	And now, my sons, remain in him, so that when he is revealed, we will not be ashamed before him, but we will have boldness at his coming.
29	If ye know that he is righteous, ye know that every one that doeth righteousness is born of him.	If ye know that he is righteous, ye also know, that whoever doeth righteousness, is from him.	If you know that he is just, know that also everyone who does a just [thing] is from him.

Chapter 3

	KJV	Murdock	Magiera
1	Behold, what manner of love the Father hath bestowed upon us, that we should be called the sons of God: therefore the world knoweth us not, because it knew him not.	And ye see, how great is the love of the Father towards us, who hath called us sons, and made us [such]. Therefore the world knoweth us not, because it likewise knoweth him not.	And see how great [is] the love of the Father toward us, because he has called us, even made us, sons. Because of this, the world does not know us, because it did not even know him.

Parallel Translations

I JOHN *Chapter 3*

	KJV	Murdock	Magiera
2	Beloved, now are we the sons of God, and it doth not yet appear what we shall be: but we know that, when he shall appear, we shall be like him; for we shall see him as he is.	My beloved, now are we the sons of God; and hitherto, it hath not appeared what we are to be: but we know that, when he shall appear, we shall be in his likeness, and we shall see him as he is.	My beloved [ones], now we are the sons of God and it does not yet appear what we are going to be, but we know that when he is revealed, we will be in his likeness and we will see him as he is.
3	And every man that hath this hope in him purifieth himself, even as he is pure.	And every one that hath this hope from him, purifieth himself, as he is pure.	And everyone who has this hope concerning him purifies himself, as he is pure.
4	Whosoever committeth sin transgresseth also the law: for sin is the transgression of the law.	And every one that practiseth sin, perpetrateth iniquity; for all sin is iniquity.	Now he who commits sin performs wickedness, for all sin is wickedness.
5	And ye know that he was manifested to take away our sins; and in him is no sin.	And ye know, that he was manifested to take away our sins; and in him was no sin.	And you know him who was revealed to take away our sins and there was no sin in him.
6	Whosoever abideth in him sinneth not: whosoever sinneth hath not seen him, neither known him.	And every one that abideth in him, sinneth not: and every one that sinneth, hath not seen him, nor hath known him.	And everyone who remains in him does not sin and everyone who sins has not seen him and does not know him.
7	Little children, let no man deceive you: he that doeth righteousness is righteous, even as he is righteous.	My children, let no one deceive you: he that doeth righteousness, is righteous, as the Messiah also is righteous.	My sons, no man should deceive you. He who does a just [thing] is just, as also Christ is just.
8	He that committeth sin is of the devil; for the devil sinneth from the beginning. For this purpose the Son of God was manifested, that he might destroy the works of the devil.	And he that committeth sin, is of Satan; because Satan was a sinner from the beginning: and for this cause, the Son of God appeared, that he might destroy the works of Satan.	He who performs sin is from Satan, because from the beginning Satan was a sinner. And because of this, the Son of God appeared to destroy the works of Satan.
9	Whosoever is born of God doth not commit sin; for his seed remaineth in him: and he cannot sin, because he is born of God.	Every one that is born of God, doth not practise sin; because his seed is in him, and he cannot sin, because he is born of God.	Everyone who is born of God does not practice sin, because his seed is in him and he is not able to sin, because he is born of God.
10	In this the children of God are manifest, and the children of the devil: whosoever doeth not righteousness is not of God, neither he that loveth not his brother.	By this are the children of God discriminated from the children of Satan. Every one that practiseth not righteousness, and that loveth not his brother, is not of God:	By this the sons of God are separated from the sons of Satan. Everyone who does not do a just [thing] and does not love his brother is not from God.
11	For this is the message that ye heard from the beginning, that we should love one another.	because this is the commandment, which ye heard from the beginning, that ye should love one another.	For this is the commandment that you have heard previously, that you should love one another,
12	Not as Cain, who was of that wicked one, and slew his brother. And wherefore slew he him? Because his own works were evil, and his brother's righteous.	Not like Cain, who was of the evil one, and slew his brother. And why did he slay him, but because his own works were evil, and those of his brother righteous?	not as Cain, who was from the Evil [one] and killed his brother. And because of what did he kill him? Because his works were evil and those of his brother were just.
13	Marvel not, my brethren, if the world hate you.	And wonder not, my brethren, if the world hate you.	And do not wonder, my brothers, if the world hates you.

Parallel Translations

	KJV	*Murdock*	*Magiera*

I JOHN *Chapter 3*

	KJV	Murdock	Magiera
14	We know that we have passed from death unto life, because we love the brethren. He that loveth not his brother abideth in death.	We know that we have turned from death unto life, by this, that we love the brethren. He that loveth not his brother, remaineth in death.	We know that we have moved from death to life in this, that we love our brothers. He who does not love his brother remains in death.
15	Whosoever hateth his brother is a murderer: and ye know that no murderer hath eternal life abiding in him.	For every one that hateth his brother, is a man-slayer; and ye know, that no man-slayer can have eternal life abiding in him.	For everyone who hates his brother is a murderer and you know that everyone who is a murderer is not able to remain in eternal life.
16	Hereby perceive we the love of God, because he laid down his life for us: and we ought to lay down our lives for the brethren.	By this we know his love towards us, because he gave up his life for us: and we also ought to give up our lives for our brethren.	In this we know his love toward us, for he gave himself for us. And it is also right for us to give ourselves for our brothers.
17	But whoso hath this world's good, and seeth his brother have need, and shutteth up his bowels of compassion from him, how dwelleth the love of God in him?	But whoever hath worldly possessions, and seeth his brother in want, and shutteth up his bowels from him, how is the love of God in him?	And whoever has property of the world and sees his brother who has a need and withholds his compassion from him, how is the love of God in him?
18	My little children, let us not love in word, neither in tongue; but in deed and in truth.	My children, let us not love one another in words and in tongue, but in acts and in truth.	My sons, do not love one another with words and with the tongue, but with works and in truth.
19	And hereby we know that we are of the truth, and shall assure our hearts before him.	And by this, we recognize that we are of the truth; and, before he shall come, we make our hearts confident.	And in this we recognize that we are from the truth and we will persuade our heart[s] before he comes.
20	For if our heart condemn us, God is greater than our heart, and knoweth all things.	But if our heart condemneth us, how much greater is God than our heart, and knowing all things?	Because if our heart condemns us, how much greater [is] God than our heart? And he knows everything.
21	Beloved, if our heart condemn us not, then have we confidence toward God.	My beloved, if our heart condemneth us not, we have open countenances before God.	My beloved, if our heart does not condemn us, our faces are open before God,
22	And whatsoever we ask, we receive of him, because we keep his commandments, and do those things that are pleasing in his sight.	And whatever we ask, we receive from him; because we keep his commandments, and do acceptable things before him.	and everything that we ask, we will receive from him, because we keep his commandments and do pleasing [things] before him.
23	And this is his commandment, That we should believe on the name of his Son Jesus Christ, and love one another, as he gave us commandment.	And this is his commandment, that we believe on the name of his Son Jesus the Messiah, and that we love one another as he hath commanded us.	And this is his commandment, that we believe on the name of his Son, Jesus Christ, and love one another as he commanded us.
24	And he that keepeth his commandments dwelleth in him, and he in him. And hereby we know that he abideth in us, by the Spirit which he hath given us.	And he that keepeth his commandments, is kept by him, and he dwelleth in him: and by this we understand that he abideth in us, from his Spirit which he hath given to us.	And he who keeps his commandments is kept by him and he lives in him. And by this we understand that he lives in us, from his Spirit that he gave to us.

Parallel Translations

I JOHN *Chapter 4*

	KJV	*Murdock*	*Magiera*
1	Beloved, believe not every spirit, but try the spirits whether they are of God: because many false prophets are gone out into the world.	My beloved, believe not all spirits; but discriminate among spirits, whether they are of God: for many false prophets have gone out into the world.	My beloved [ones], do not believe all the spirits, but discern whether the spirits are from God, because many false prophets have gone out in the world.
2	Hereby know ye the Spirit of God: Every spirit that confesseth that Jesus Christ is come in the flesh is of God:	By this the Spirit of God is known, every spirit that confesseth that Jesus the Messiah hath come in the flesh, is of God.	By this the Spirit of God is known, [for] every spirit that confesses that Jesus Christ has come in the flesh is from God.
3	And every spirit that confesseth not that Jesus Christ is come in the flesh is not of God: and this is that spirit of antichrist, whereof ye have heard that it should come; and even now already is it in the world.	And every spirit which confesseth not that Jesus the Messiah hath come in the flesh, is not of God; but he is of the false Messiah, of whom ye have heard that he cometh, and now is he already in the world.	And every spirit that does not confess that Jesus has come in the flesh is not from God, but this [spirit] is from the false messiah, about whom you have heard that he would come and is now already in the world.
4	Ye are of God, little children, and have overcome them: because greater is he that is in you, than he that is in the world.	But ye children, are of God; and ye have overcome them, because greater is he who is in you, than he who is in the world.	Now you children, are of God and you have overcome them, because greater [is] he who is in you than he who is in the world.
5	They are of the world: therefore speak they of the world, and the world heareth them.	And they are of the world: therefore they speak from the world, and the world heareth them.	And these are from the world. Because of this, they speak from the world and the world hears them.
6	We are of God: he that knoweth God heareth us; he that is not of God heareth not us. Hereby know we the spirit of truth, and the spirit of error.	But we are of God; and he that knoweth God, heareth us; and he that is not of God, heareth us not. By this, we know the spirit of truth, and the spirit of error.	But we are from God and he who knows God hears us and he who is not from God will not hear us. By this we know the Spirit of truth and the spirit of deception.
7	Beloved, let us love one another: for love is of God; and every one that loveth is born of God, and knoweth God.	My beloved, let us love one another: because love is from God; and whoever loveth, is born of God and knoweth God.	My beloved [ones], we should love one another, because love is from God and everyone who loves is born of God and knows God,
8	He that loveth not knoweth not God; for God is love.	Because God is love; and whoever loveth not, doth not know God.	because God is love. And everyone who does not love, does not know God.
9	In this was manifested the love of God toward us, because that God sent his only begotten Son into the world, that we might live through him.	By this was the love of God towards us made known, because God sent his only-begotten Son into the world, that we by him might live.	By this the love of God toward us is known, because God sent his unique Son into the world that we would have life by him.
10	Herein is love, not that we loved God, but that he loved us, and sent his Son to be the propitiation for our sins.	In this is love; it was not that we loved God, but that God loved us, and sent his Son a propitiation for our sins.	In this is love, not that we loved God, but [that] he loved us and sent his Son [as] a payment for our sins.
11	Beloved, if God so loved us, we ought also to love one another.	My beloved, if God hath so loved us, we also ought to love one another.	My beloved [ones], if God so loved us, we also ought to love one another.

	KJV	*Murdock*	*Magiera*

I JOHN *Chapter 4*

	KJV	Murdock	Magiera
12	No man hath seen God at any time. If we love one another, God dwelleth in us, and his love is perfected in us.	No one hath ever seen God; but if we love one another, God abideth in us, and his love is perfected in us.	No one has ever seen God, but if we love one another, God remains in us and his love is completed in us.
13	Hereby know we that we dwell in him, and he in us, because he hath given us of his Spirit.	And by this we know, that we abide in him and that he abideth in us, because he hath given of his Spirit to us.	And by this we know that we remain in him and he remains in us, because he has given us his Spirit.
14	And we have seen and do testify that the Father sent the Son to be the Saviour of the world.	And we have seen, and do testify, that the Father hath sent his Son, a Redeemer for the world.	And we have seen and testify that the Father sent his Son [as] the Redeemer for the world.
15	Whosoever shall confess that Jesus is the Son of God, God dwelleth in him, and he in God.	Whoever confesseth Jesus to be the Son of God, God abideth in him, and he abideth in God.	Everyone who confesses Jesus, that he is the Son of God, God remains in him and he remains in God.
16	And we have known and believed the love that God hath to us. God is love; and he that dwelleth in love dwelleth in God, and God in him.	And we have believed and known the love, which God hath towards us: for God is love, and whoever abideth in love, abideth in God.	And we believe and we know the love that God has toward us, for God is love, and everyone who remains in love remains in God.
17	Herein is our love made perfect, that we may have boldness in the day of judgment: because as he is, so are we in this world.	And hereby is his love perfected with us; that we may have open countenances in the day of judgment; because as he was, so also are we in this world.	And in this his love is completed with us, so that we would have boldness in the day of judgment, because as he was, so are we in this world.
18	There is no fear in love; but perfect love casteth out fear: because fear hath torment. He that feareth is not made perfect in love.	In love there is no fear; but perfect love casteth out fear; because fear existeth in peril, and he that feareth is not perfected in love.	There is no fear in love, but complete love throws out fear, because fear is dangerous. Now he who fears is not completed in love.
19	We love him, because he first loved us.	Let us, therefore, love God; because he hath first loved us.	Therefore, we should love God, because he first loved us.
20	If a man say, I love God, and hateth his brother, he is a liar: for he that loveth not his brother whom he hath seen, how can he love God whom he hath not seen?	And if any one shall say, I love God, and yet hateth his brother, he is a liar: for he that loveth not his brother who is visible, how can he love God who is invisible?	But if someone should say, "I love God," yet hates his brother, he is a liar. For he who does not love his brother, whom he has seen, how can he love God, whom he has not seen?
21	And this commandment have we from him, That he who loveth God love his brother also.	And this command we have received from him, that whoever loveth God, must love also his brother.	And we have received this commandment from him, that everyone who loves God should also love his brother.

Chapter 5

	KJV	Murdock	Magiera
1	Whosoever believeth that Jesus is the Christ is born of God: and every one that loveth him that begat loveth him also that is begotten of him.	Whoever believeth that Jesus is the Messiah, is born of God. And whoever loveth the begetter, loveth him also that is begotten of him.	Everyone who believes that Jesus is Christ is fathered of God and everyone who loves the one fathering loves also the one who is fathered by him.
2	By this we know that we love the children of God, when we love God, and keep his commandments.	And by this we know, that we love the children of God, when we love God, and follow his commandments.	And by this we know that we love the children of God, when we love God and do his commandments.

Parallel Translations

I JOHN *Chapter 5*

	KJV	*Murdock*	*Magiera*
3	For this is the love of God, that we keep his commandments: and his commandments are not grievous.	For this is the love of God, that we keep his commandments: and his commandments are not burdensome.	For this is the love of God, that we should keep his commandments. And his commandments are not difficult,
4	For whatsoever is born of God overcometh the world: and this is the victory that overcometh the world, even our faith.	Because, whoever is born of God, overcometh the world: and this is the victory that overcometh the world, our faith.	because everyone who is born of God has overcome the world and this is the victory that overcomes the world, our faith.
5	Who is he that overcometh the world, but he that believeth that Jesus is the Son of God?	For who is he that overcometh the world, but he that believeth that Jesus is the Son of God?	For who is he who overcomes the world, but he who believes that Jesus is the Son of God?
6	This is he that came by water and blood, even Jesus Christ; not by water only, but by water and blood. And it is the Spirit that beareth witness, because the Spirit is truth.	This is he who came by the water and the blood. Jesus the Messiah; not by the water only, but by the water and the blood. And the Spirit testifieth; because the Spirit is truth.	This is he who came by way of water and blood, Jesus Christ. He was not by water alone, but by water and blood.
7	For there are three that bear record in heaven, the Father, the Word, and the Holy Ghost: and these three are one.	[For there are three that testify in heaven, the Father, the Word, and the Holy Spirit: and these three are one.]	And the Spirit bears witness, for the Spirit is truth.
8	And there are three that bear witness in earth, the Spirit, and the water, and the blood: and these three agree in one.	And there are three witnesses, the Spirit, and the water, and the blood: and these three are in union.	And there are three witnesses, Spirit and water and blood and the three of them are as one.
9	If we receive the witness of men, the witness of God is greater: for this is the witness of God which he hath testified of his Son.	If we receive the testimony of men, how much greater is the testimony of God? And this is the testimony of God, which he hath testified concerning his Son.	If we receive the testimony of men, how much more the testimony of God that is greater? And this is the testimony of God that he testified concerning his Son.
10	He that believeth on the Son of God hath the witness in himself: he that believeth not God hath made him a liar; because he believeth not the record that God gave of his Son.	Whoever believeth in the Son of God, hath this testimony in himself. And whoever believeth not God, hath made him a liar, by not believing the testimony which God hath testified concerning his Son.	Whoever believes in the Son of God has this testimony in himself. Everyone who does not believe has made God a liar, in that he did not believe the testimony that God testified concerning his Son.
11	And this is the record, that God hath given to us eternal life, and this life is in his Son.	And this is the testimony, that God hath given to us life eternal, and this life is in his Son.	And this is the testimony, that God has given us eternal life and the life is in his Son.
12	He that hath the Son hath life; and he that hath not the Son of God hath not life.	Every one that taketh hold of the Son, taketh hold of life; and every one that taketh not hold of the Son, hath not life.	Everyone who holds fast to the Son also holds fast to life. And everyone who does not hold fast to the Son of God does not have life.
13	These things have I written unto you that believe on the name of the Son of God; that ye may know that ye have eternal life, and that ye may believe on the name of the Son of God.	These things have I written to you, that ye may know that ye have life eternal, ye who believe in the name of the Son of God.	These [things] I have written to you, those who believe in the name of the Son of God, that you would know that you have eternal life.

	KJV	*Murdock*	*Magiera*
	I JOHN *Chapter 5*		
14	And this is the confidence that we have in him, that, if we ask any thing according to his will, he heareth us:	And this is the confidence that we have towards him, that whatever we ask of him, agreeably to his will, he heareth us.	And we have this confidence toward him, for everything that we ask of him according to his will, he hears us.
15	And if we know that he hear us, whatsoever we ask, we know that we have the petitions that we desired of him.	And if we are persuaded that he heareth us respecting what we ask of him, we are confident of receiving presently the petitions which we asked of him.	And if we are persuaded that he hears us concerning what we request of him, we are confident that we have already received our requests that we requested of him.
16	If any man see his brother sin a sin which is not unto death, he shall ask, and he shall give him life for them that sin not unto death. There is a sin unto death: I do not say that he shall pray for it.	If any one shall see his brother sin a sin which doth not deserve death, he shall ask, and life will be given him, to them [I say] who sin not as unto death. For there is a sin of death; and I do not say of this, that a man should pray for it.	If someone should see his brother when he sins a sin that is not guilty of death, he should ask and life will be given to those who do not sin as to death. For there is a sin of death, [but] I do not say that anyone should pray for this [sin].
17	All unrighteousness is sin: and there is a sin not unto death.	For all iniquity is sin; and there is a sin which is not of death.	For all wickedness is sin and there is a sin that is not of death.
18	We know that whosoever is born of God sinneth not; but he that is begotten of God keepeth himself, and that wicked one toucheth him not.	And we know, that every one who is born of God, sinneth not: for he that is born of God keepeth himself, and the evil one toucheth him not.	And we know that everyone who is born of God does not sin, for he who is born of God guards himself and the Evil [one] does not come near him.
19	And we know that we are of God, and the whole world lieth in wickedness.	We know, that we are of God; and all the world is reposing on the evil one.	We know that we are of God and all the world is seated in wickedness.
20	And we know that the Son of God is come, and hath given us an understanding, that we may know him that is true, and we are in him that is true, even in his Son Jesus Christ. This is the true God, and eternal life.	And we know that the Son of God hath come, and hath given us knowledge that we might know the True One; and that we might be in the True One, in his Son Jesus the Messiah. He is the true God, and the life eternal.	And we know that the Son of God has come and has given us knowledge that we would know the true [one] and be in him, in the true [one], in his Son, Jesus Christ. This is the true God and eternal life.
21	Little children, keep yourselves from idols. Amen.	My children, keep yourselves from idolatry.	My sons, keep yourselves from idolatry.

Parallel Translations

	KJV	*Murdock*	*Magiera*
	II JOHN		
1	The elder unto the elect lady and her children, whom I love in the truth; and not I only, but also all they that have known the truth;	The Elder, to Kuria the elect, and to her children: whom I love in the truth, and not I only, but all they who know the truth;	The elder, to the chosen lady and to her children, those whom I love in truth, and not I alone, but all those who know the truth,
2	For the truth's sake, which dwelleth in us, and shall be with us for ever.	for the sake of the truth, which abideth in us and is with us for ever.	because of the truth that remains in us and is with us forever:
3	Grace be with you, mercy, and peace, from God the Father, and from the Lord Jesus Christ, the Son of the Father, in truth and love.	May grace be with you, and mercy, and peace, from God the Father, and from our Lord Jesus the Messiah, the Son of the Father, in truth and love.	Grace be with us and mercy and peace from God the Father and from our Lord Jesus Christ, the Son of the Father, in truth and in love.
4	I rejoiced greatly that I found of thy children walking in truth, as we have received a commandment from the Father.	I have rejoiced greatly, that I found [some] of thy children, who walked in the truth, as we have received commandment from the Father.	I rejoiced greatly that I found some of your children walking in truth, as we received commandment from the Father.
5	And now I beseech thee, lady, not as though I wrote a new commandment unto thee, but that which we had from the beginning, that we love one another.	And now, I beseech thee, Kuria, (I write no new commandment to thee, but that which was with us from the beginning,) that we should love one another.	And now I persuade you, [my] lady, not as though I am writing a new commandment to you, but that which we had from the beginning, that we love one another.
6	And this is love, that we walk after his commandments. This is the commandment, That, as ye have heard from the beginning, ye should walk in it.	And this is love, that we walk according to the commandment. This is the commandment, as ye have heard from the beginning, that we should walk in it.	And this is love, that we should walk according to his commandments. This is the commandment as you heard from the beginning that you should walk in it.
7	For many deceivers are entered into the world, who confess not that Jesus Christ is come in the flesh. This is a deceiver and an antichrist.	Because many seducers have gone forth into the world, who confess not that Jesus the Messiah hath come in the flesh. This is a seducer and Antichrist.	For many deceivers have gone out into the world, those who do not confess that Jesus Christ has come in the flesh. This [one] is a deceiver and an antichrist.
8	Look to yourselves, that we lose not those things which we have wrought, but that we receive a full reward.	Take heed to yourselves, that ye lose not what ye have wrought; but that ye may be recompensed with a full reward.	Be watchful of yourselves, so that you do not lose that for which you worked, but rather [that] you may be paid the full reward.
9	Whosoever transgresseth, and abideth not in the doctrine of Christ, hath not God. He that abideth in the doctrine of Christ, he hath both the Father and the Son.	Every one who transgresseth, and abideth not in the doctrine of the Messiah, God is not in him. And he who abideth in his doctrine, he hath the Father and the Son.	Everyone who transgresses and does not remain in the teaching of Christ does not have God. He who remains in his teaching, this [one] has both the Father and the Son.
10	If there come any unto you, and bring not this doctrine, receive him not into your house, neither bid him God speed:	If any one cometh to you, and bringeth not this doctrine, entertain him not in your house, nor say to him, Joy to thee:	If anyone comes to you and does not bring this teaching, do not receive him in the house and do not say to him, "Joy to you,"

Parallel Translations

II JOHN

	KJV	*Murdock*	*Magiera*
11	For he that biddeth him God speed is partaker of his evil deeds.	for he that saith to him, Joy to thee, is a participator in his evil deeds.	for he who says to him, "Joy to you," is sharing in his evil works.
12	Having many things to write unto you, I would not write with paper and ink: but I trust to come unto you, and speak face to face, that our joy may be full.	Having many things I could write to you, I would not with paper and ink; but I hope to come to you, and to converse mouth to mouth, that our joy may be complete.	Since I have many [things] to write to you, I do not want [to write] with paper and ink, but I am hoping to come to you and to speak mouth to mouth, that our joy may be complete.
13	The children of thy elect sister greet thee. Amen.	The children of thy elect sister salute thee. Grace be with you. Amen.	The children of your sister, a chosen [one], greet you. Grace [be] with you. Amen.

Parallel Translations

	KJV	Murdock	Magiera
	III JOHN		
1	The elder unto the wellbeloved Gaius, whom I love in the truth.	The Elder, to my beloved Gaius, whom I love in the truth.	The elder, to Gaius, a beloved [one], whom I love in truth:
2	Beloved, I wish above all things that thou mayest prosper and be in health, even as thy soul prospereth.	Our beloved; in all things, I pray for thee that thou mayest prosper and be in health, as thy soul doth prosper.	Our beloved [one], in everything I pray for you that you would prosper and would be healthy, even as your life prospers.
3	For I rejoiced greatly, when the brethren came and testified of the truth that is in thee, even as thou walkest in the truth.	For I rejoiced greatly, when the brethren came and testified concerning thy integrity, even as thou walkest in the truth.	For I rejoiced greatly when the brothers came and testified about your integrity, even as you walk in integrity.
4	I have no greater joy than to hear that my children walk in truth.	And I have no greater joy, than to hear that my children walk in the truth.	For I have no greater joy than this, than to hear that my children walk in integrity.
5	Beloved, thou doest faithfully whatsoever thou doest to the brethren, and to strangers;	Our beloved, thou doest in faith, what thou performest towards the brethren; and especially towards strangers,	Our beloved [one], you are doing in faith what you perform toward the brothers and especially those who are strangers,
6	Which have borne witness of thy charity before the church: whom if thou bring forward on their journey after a godly sort, thou shalt do well:	who have borne testimony to thy charity before the whole church, to whom thou doest good, as is pleasing to God.	who have given testimony concerning your love before all the church, to whom you are doing well, because you supply them according to what is proper to God.
7	Because that for his name's sake they went forth, taking nothing of the Gentiles.	For they went forth in behalf of his name, taking nothing of the Gentiles.	For they went out on behalf of his name, taking nothing from the Gentiles.
8	We therefore ought to receive such, that we might be fellowhelpers to the truth.	We therefore ought to receive such persons, that we may be aiders of the truth.	Therefore, we ought to receive those who are like these that we may be helpers for the truth.
9	I wrote unto the church: but Diotrephes, who loveth to have the preeminence among them, receiveth us not.	I was desirous of writing to the church; but he who loveth to be foremost among them, Diotrephes, receiveth us not.	I wanted to write to the church, but he who loves to be first among them, Diotrephes, did not receive us.
10	Wherefore, if I come, I will remember his deeds which he doeth, prating against us with malicious words: and not content therewith, neither doth he himself receive the brethren, and forbiddeth them that would, and casteth them out of the church.	Therefore, if he come, remember those his doings, that he treated us with malignant words; and this not sufficing him, he received not the brethren; and those who would receive [them], he prohibited, and even ejected them from the church.	Because of this, if I come, I will remember his works that he did, that he tore us down with evil words. And when these [things] did not satisfy him, he did not receive the brothers and he hindered and threw out of the church those who were receiving [them].
11	Beloved, follow not that which is evil, but that which is good. He that doeth good is of God: but he that doeth evil hath not seen God.	Our beloved, be not a follower of what is evil, but of what is good. He that doeth good, is of God; but he that doeth evil, hath not seen God.	Our beloved [one], do not imitate evil, but good. He who does good is of God. He who does evil has not seen God.

Parallel Translations

III JOHN

	KJV	Murdock	Magiera
12	Demetrius hath good report of all men, and of the truth itself: yea, and we also bear record; and ye know that our record is true.	Of Demetrius, there is good testimony from every one, and from the church, and from the truth itself: and we also bear [him] testimony, and ye know that our testimony is true.	About Demetrius, there is a testimony from everyone and from the church and from the truth. And also we bear [him] testimony and you know that our testimony is true.
13	I had many things to write, but I will not with ink and pen write unto thee:	I had many things to write to thee; but I will not write [them] to thee with ink and pen.	I have many [things] to write to you, but I do not want to write to you with ink and pen,
14	But I trust I shall shortly see thee, and we shall speak face to face. Peace be to thee. Our friends salute thee. Greet the friends by name.	But I hope soon to see thee, and to converse mouth to mouth.	but I am hoping to see you soon and we will speak mouth to mouth.
15		Peace be with thee. The friends salute thee. Salute the friends, severally, by name.	Peace be with you. The friends greet you. Greet the friends, everyone by his name.

Parallel Translations

	KJV	*Murdock*	*Magiera*
	JUDE		
1	Jude, the servant of Jesus Christ, and brother of James, to them that are sanctified by God the Father, and preserved in Jesus Christ, and called:	Jude, a servant of Jesus the Messiah, and the brother of James, to the called people, the beloved of God the Father, the preserved by Jesus the Messiah:	Jude, a servant of Jesus Christ, and the brother of James, to the called nations, who are loved by God, the Father, and are kept in Jesus Christ:
2	Mercy unto you, and peace, and love, be multiplied.	Mercy and peace in love, be multiplied to you.	Mercy and peace and love be multiplied to you.
3	Beloved, when I gave all diligence to write unto you of the common salvation, it was needful for me to write unto you, and exhort you that ye should earnestly contend for the faith which was once delivered unto the saints.	My beloved, while I take all pains to write to you of our common life, it is needful for me to write to you, exhorting you to maintain a conflict for the faith which was once delivered to the saints.	My beloved [ones], while I am being completely diligent to write to you about our own salvation that is common, there is a need for me to write to you, persuading you to contend in the struggle on behalf of the faith that was once delivered to the holy [ones].
4	For there are certain men crept in unawares, who were before of old ordained to this condemnation, ungodly men, turning the grace of our God into lasciviousness, and denying the only Lord God, and our Lord Jesus Christ.	For some have obtained entrance, who from the beginning were registered beforehand under this condemnation: wicked men, who pervert the grace of God to impurity, and deny him who is the only Lord God and our Lord, Jesus the Messiah.	For men have gained entrance, who from the beginning were previously described in this condemnation, wicked men who turn the grace of our God to uncleanness and deny him who is the only Lord God and our Lord Jesus Christ.
5	I will therefore put you in remembrance, though ye once knew this, how that the Lord, having saved the people out of the land of Egypt, afterward destroyed them that believed not.	And I wish to remind you, though ye all know it, that God, after once rescuing the people from Egypt, again destroyed them who believed not.	And I want to remind you, although you all know [it], that God, having rescued the people from Egypt at one time, at a second [time] destroyed those who did not believe.
6	And the angels which kept not their first estate, but left their own habitation, he hath reserved in everlasting chains under darkness unto the judgment of the great day.	And the angels that kept not their primacy, but left their station, he hath reserved in chains unknown, under darkness, unto the judgment of the great day.	And the angels who did not keep their first estate, but left their own dwelling, he has reserved in chains, unknown, under darkness, for the judgment of the great day.
7	Even as Sodom and Gomorrha, and the cities about them in like manner, giving themselves over to fornication, and going after strange flesh, are set forth for an example, suffering the vengeance of eternal fire.	As Sodom and Gomorrah, and the surrounding cities, which in like manner followed whoredom and went after strange flesh, are placed beneath everlasting fire, being, doomed to judgment.	[It is] as Sodom and Gomorrah and the cities of the surrounding area, which committed fornication in the same manner as these and followed other flesh, [which] are placed under a demonstration of fire that is eternal, being condemned to judgment.
8	Likewise also these filthy dreamers defile the flesh, despise dominion, and speak evil of dignities.	In the same manner, too, these sensual dreamers defile the flesh and despise authority, and revile excellency.	In the same manner also, these who are fantasizing in dreams are indeed polluting the flesh and rejecting lordship and blaspheming against the glory.

Parallel Translations

	KJV	*Murdock*	*Magiera*
	JUDE		
9	Yet Michael the archangel, when contending with the devil he disputed about the body of Moses, durst not bring against him a railing accusation, but said, The Lord rebuke thee.	But Michael the archangel, who, in debate with the Accuser, contended about the body of Moses, did not venture to bring against him a reviling declaration; but said, The Lord will rebuke thee.	Now Michael, the archangel, who, when he was debating with the Accuser, spoke about the body of Moses, did not dare to bring on him the judgment of blasphemy, but said, "The LORD will rebuke you."
10	But these speak evil of those things which they know not: but what they know naturally, as brute beasts, in those things they corrupt themselves.	But these [men] revile things which they do not understand; and in the things of which they have a natural persuasion as animal beings, in these they corrupt themselves.	And these [men] are blaspheming about those [things] that they do not know. And in those [things] that they are familiar with naturally as dumb animals, in these they are corrupted.
11	Woe unto them! for they have gone in the way of Cain, and ran greedily after the error of Balaam for reward, and perished in the gainsaying of Core.	Woe to them; for they have gone in the way of Cain; and, after the error of Balaam, they have lusted for gain; and, in the rebellion of Korah, they have perished.	Woe to them, for they have gone in the way of Cain, and after the error of Balaam they have burned with passion for reward, and by the stubbornness of Core they are destroyed.
12	These are spots in your feasts of charity, when they feast with you, feeding themselves without fear: clouds they are without water, carried about of winds; trees whose fruit withereth, without fruit, twice dead, plucked up by the roots;	These are they who, in their feastings, riot while polluting themselves, feeding themselves without fear; clouds without rain, moved about by the winds; trees whose fruit hath failed, and they are without fruit, twice dead, and uplifted from their root;	They are those who in their idleness feast in excess, as they are defiled, feeding themselves without fear. [They are] clouds without rain that are moved by the winds, trees whose produce has ceased, that are without fruit, that die a second time and are pulled up from their roots,
13	Raging waves of the sea, foaming out their own shame; wandering stars, to whom is reserved the blackness of darkness for ever.	raging waves of the sea, which, by their foam, manifest their confusion; shooting-stars, for which is reserved the blackness of darkness for ever.	raging waves of the sea that by way of their foam demonstrate their shame, wandering stars, for which the blackness of darkness is reserved forever.
14	And Enoch also, the seventh from Adam, prophesied of these, saying, Behold, the Lord cometh with ten thousands of his saints,	And of them also prophesied Enoch, who was the seventh from Adam, when he said: Behold, the Lord cometh, with myriads of his saints;	And Enoch, who was the seventh from Adam, also prophesied of these, saying, "Behold, the LORD will come with multitudes of holy [ones]
15	To execute judgment upon all, and to convince all that are ungodly among them of all their ungodly deeds which they have ungodly committed, and of all their hard speeches which ungodly sinners have spoken against him.	to execute judgment upon all; and to convict all the wicked, because of all the deeds they have wickedly committed; and because of all the hard speeches, which they, ungodly sinners, have uttered.	to execute judgment on all and to reprove all people because of all these works that they have impiously practiced and because of all the hardened words that the impious sinners have spoken."

Parallel Translations

	KJV	*Murdock*	*Magiera*
	JUDE		
16	These are murmurers, complainers, walking after their own lusts; and their mouth speaketh great swelling words, having men's persons in admiration because of advantage.	These are they who murmur and complain of every thing, while they walk according to their lusts; and their mouth speaketh shocking things; and they flatter people, for the sake of gain.	These are they who murmur and complain about all matters, walking according to their own desires. And their mouth speaks shocking [things] and they flatter the appearances of people on account of profits.
17	But, beloved, remember ye the words which were spoken before of the apostles of our Lord Jesus Christ;	But do ye, my beloved, remember the words which were before spoken by the legates of our Lord Jesus the Messiah;	But you, my beloved [ones], remember the words that were spoken before by the apostles of our Lord Jesus Christ,
18	How that they told you there should be mockers in the last time, who should walk after their own ungodly lusts.	because they told you, that in the end of the times there would be scoffers, going after wickedness, according to their lusts.	because they told you that at the end of the times there would be those who were mocking, who would follow wickedness according to their own desires.
19	These be they who separate themselves, sensual, having not the Spirit.	These are they that separate [themselves], sensual persons, not having the Spirit.	They are those who are marked out, natural [men] who do not have the Spirit.
20	But ye, beloved, building up yourselves on your most holy faith, praying in the Holy Ghost,	But, my beloved, be ye built up anew, in your holy faith, through the Holy Spirit, while ye pray.	But you, my beloved [ones], be built up anew in your holy faith by the Spirit, sanctified while [you] pray.
21	Keep yourselves in the love of God, looking for the mercy of our Lord Jesus Christ unto eternal life.	And let us keep ourselves in the love of God, while we wait for the mercy of our Lord Jesus the Messiah unto our eternal life.	And we should keep ourselves in the love of God, looking for the mercy of our Lord Jesus Christ for our life that is eternal.
22	And of some have compassion, making a difference:	And some of them, snatch ye from the fire.	And indeed, snatch some of them out of the fire.
23	And others save with fear, pulling them out of the fire; hating even the garment spotted by the flesh.	And when they repent, have compassion on them, with fear, hating even the tunic that is defiled by the flesh.	And when they repent, have compassion on them with fear, hating even the garment that is spotted by the flesh.
24	Now unto him that is able to keep you from falling, and to present you faultless before the presence of his glory with exceeding joy,	And to him who is able to preserve you faultless, and spotless, and to establish you without a blemish,	Now to him who is able to keep us faultless and without spot and to establish [us] without blemish,
25	To the only wise God our Saviour, be glory and majesty, dominion and power, both now and ever. Amen.	before his majesty, with joy, [namely,] the only God, our Deliverer, by means of Jesus the Messiah our Lord, be praise, and dominion, and honor, and majesty, both now and in all ages. Amen.	the only God, our Redeemer, by way of Jesus Christ our Lord, in the presence of his glory with joy, to him [be] glory and dominion and honor and majesty, both now and in all ages. Amen.

Parallel Translations

	KJV	*Murdock*	*Magiera*
	REVELATION *Chapter 1*		
1	The Revelation of Jesus Christ, which God gave unto him, to shew unto his servants things which must shortly come to pass; and he sent and signified it by his angel unto his servant John:	The Revelation of Jesus the Messiah, which God gave to him, to show to his servants the things that must shortly occur: and he signified [it] by sending, through his angel, to his servant John;	The revelation of Jesus Christ that God gave to him to show to his servants what must happen soon. And he made [this] known when he sent by way of his angel to his servant John,
2	Who bare record of the word of God, and of the testimony of Jesus Christ, and of all things that he saw.	who bore witness to the word of God, and to the testimony of Jesus the Messiah, as to all that he saw.	who gave witness to the word of God and to the witness of Jesus Christ, all that he saw.
3	Blessed is he that readeth, and they that hear the words of this prophecy, and keep those things which are written therein: for the time is at hand.	Blessed is he that readeth, and they who hear the words of this prophecy, and keep the things that are written in it; for the time is near.	Blessed [be] he who reads and those who hear the words of this prophecy and keep those [things] that are written in it, for the time has drawn near.
4	John to the seven churches which are in Asia: Grace be unto you, and peace, from him which is, and which was, and which is to come; and from the seven Spirits which are before his throne;	John to the seven churches which are in Asia: Grace to you and quietude, from him who is, and who was, and who is to come, from the seven Spirits which are before his throne;	John, to the seven churches that [are] in Asia: Grace [be] to you and peace from him who is and was and comes and from the seven spirits that are before his throne
5	And from Jesus Christ, who is the faithful witness, and the first begotten of the dead, and the prince of the kings of the earth. Unto him that loved us, and washed us from our sins in his own blood,	and from Jesus the Messiah, the Witness, the Faithful, the First-born of the dead, and the Prince of the kings of the earth; who hath loved us, and released us from our sins by his blood;	and from Jesus Christ, the faithful witness, the firstborn of the dead and the ruler of the kings of the earth, who loved us and released us from our sins by his blood
6	And hath made us kings and priests unto God and his Father; to him be glory and dominion for ever and ever. Amen.	and hath made us a kingdom sacerdotal to God and his Father: to whom be glory and power, for ever and ever. Amen.	and made us a priestly kingdom to God, even his Father. To him [be] glory and dominion, forever and ever. Amen.
7	Behold, he cometh with clouds; and every eye shall see him, and they also which pierced him: and all kindreds of the earth shall wail because of him. Even so, Amen.	Behold, he cometh with clouds; and all eyes shall see him, and also they who speared him; and all the tribes of the earth shall mourn on account of him. Yes: Amen.	Behold, he comes with clouds and all eyes will see him, even those who pierced him, and all the tribes of the earth will mourn concerning him. Yes and amen.
8	I am Alpha and Omega, the beginning and the ending, saith the Lord, which is, and which was, and which is to come, the Almighty.	I am Alpha, also Omega, saith the Lord God; who is, and was, and is to come, the omnipotent.	"I am Aleph and Tau," says the LORD God, "He who is and was and comes, who is the Almighty."
9	I John, who also am your brother, and companion in tribulation, and in the kingdom and patience of Jesus Christ, was in the isle that is called Patmos, for the word of God, and for the testimony of Jesus Christ.	I John, your brother, and partaker with you in the affliction and suffering that are in Jesus the Messiah, was in the island called Patmos, because of the word of God, and because of the testimony of Jesus the Messiah.	I, John, your brother and companion with you in the trial and in the endurance that is in Jesus, was on the island that is called Patmos because of the word of God and because of the witness of Jesus Christ.

Parallel Translations

REVELATION *Chapter 1*

	KJV	*Murdock*	*Magiera*
10	I was in the Spirit on the Lord's day, and heard behind me a great voice, as of a trumpet,	I was in the Spirit on the Lord's day; and I heard behind me a great voice, as of a trumpet, which said:	And I was [seeing] spiritually on the first day of the week and I heard from behind me a loud voice as a trumpet
11	Saying, I am Alpha and Omega, the first and the last: and, What thou seest, write in a book, and send it unto the seven churches which are in Asia; unto Ephesus, and unto Smyrna, and unto Pergamos, and unto Thyatira, and unto Sardis, and unto Philadelphia, and unto Laodicea.	That which thou seest, write in a book, and send to the seven churches, to Ephesus, and to Smyrna, and to Pergamos, and to Thyatira, and to Sardis, and to Philadelphia, and to Laodicea.	that said, "These [things] that you see, write in a book and send to the seven churches, to Ephesus and to Smyrna and to Pergamos and to Thyatira and to Sardis and to Philadelphia and to Laodicea."
12	And I turned to see the voice that spake with me. And being turned, I saw seven golden candlesticks;	And I turned myself to look at the voice that talked with me; and when I had turned, I saw seven candlesticks of gold;	And I turned to know the voice that spoke with me and when I turned, I saw seven lampstands of gold.
13	And in the midst of the seven candlesticks one like unto the Son of man, clothed with a garment down to the foot, and girt about the paps with a golden girdle.	and, in the midst of the candlesticks, one like the Son of man, clothed to the feet, and girded about his paps with a girdle of gold.	And in the middle of the lampstands [was one] like the form of a man clothed with an ephod and his breasts girded with a girdle of gold.
14	His head and his hairs were white like wool, as white as snow; and his eyes were as a flame of fire;	And his head and his hair were white, like white wool, like snow; and his eyes, like a flame of fire:	Now his head and his hair [were] white like wool and like snow, and his eyes [were] like a flame of fire
15	And his feet like unto fine brass, as if they burned in a furnace; and his voice as the sound of many waters.	and his feet were like fine brass, flaming in a furnace: and his voice, like the sound of many waters.	and his feet [were] in the form of Lebanese brass that is burned in a furnace and his voice [was] like the sound of many waters.
16	And he had in his right hand seven stars: and out of his mouth went a sharp twoedged sword: and his countenance was as the sun shineth in his strength.	And he had in his right hand seven stars; and from his mouth issued a sharp two-edged sword; and his visage was like the sun shining in its strength.	And he had in his right hand seven stars and a sharp spear came out of his mouth and his appearance [was] like the sun showing its power.
17	And when I saw him, I fell at his feet as dead. And he laid his right hand upon me, saying unto me, Fear not; I am the first and the last:	And when I saw him, I fell at his feet like one dead. And he laid his right hand upon me, and said, Fear not: I am the First and the Last;	And when I saw him, I fell at his feet as [one] dead. And he laid his right hand on me, saying, "Fear not. I am the first and the last
18	I am he that liveth, and was dead; and, behold, I am alive for evermore, Amen; and have the keys of hell and of death.	and who liveth and was dead; and behold, I am alive for ever and ever. Amen. And I have the keys of death and of the unseen world.	and he who is alive and was dead. And behold, I am alive forever and ever. Amen. And I have the key of death and of Sheol.
19	Write the things which thou hast seen, and the things which are, and the things which shall be hereafter;	Therefore, write what thou hast seen, and the things that are; and the things that are to be hereafter:	Therefore, write what you saw and these [things] that are and are going to happen after these,

REVELATION Chapter 1

	KJV	Murdock	Magiera
20	The mystery of the seven stars which thou sawest in my right hand, and the seven golden candlesticks. The seven stars are the angels of the seven churches: and the seven candlesticks which thou sawest are the seven churches.	the mystery of these seven stars which thou sawest in my right hand, and the seven candlesticks of gold. Those seven stars are the angels of the seven churches; and the seven candlesticks are the seven churches.	the mystery of the seven stars that you saw in my right [hand] and the seven lampstands. The seven stars are the angels of the seven churches and the seven lampstands of gold that you saw are the seven churches."

Chapter 2

	KJV	Murdock	Magiera
1	Unto the angel of the church of Ephesus write; These things saith he that holdeth the seven stars in his right hand, who walketh in the midst of the seven golden candlesticks;	To the angel of the church which is at Ephesus write: These things saith he who holdeth all things, and the seven stars, in his right hand; he that walketh in the midst of the seven candlesticks of gold;	"And to the angel of the church of Ephesus, write, 'So says he who holds the seven stars in his hand, he who walks among the lampstands of gold.
2	I know thy works, and thy labour, and thy patience, and how thou canst not bear them which are evil: and thou hast tried them which say they are apostles, and are not, and hast found them liars:	I know thy works, and thy toil, and thy patience, and [that] thou canst not endure the wicked; and thou hast tried them who say they are legates, and are not; and thou hast found them liars.	I know your works and your labor and your endurance and that you are not able to bear evil [ones]. And you have tested those who say about themselves that they are apostles and are not and you have found them [to be] liars.
3	And hast borne, and hast patience, and for my name's sake hast laboured, and hast not fainted.	And thou hast had patience, and hast borne the burden, on account of my name, and hast not fainted.	And you have endurance and you bear a burden because of my name and you have not become weary.
4	Nevertheless I have somewhat against thee, because thou hast left thy first love.	Yet I have [a charge] against thee, on account of thy former love, which thou hast left.	But I have [something] against you, because you have left your former love.
5	Remember therefore from whence thou art fallen, and repent, and do the first works; or else I will come unto thee quickly, and will remove thy candlestick out of his place, except thou repent.	Therefore remember whence thou hast fallen; and repent, and do the former works: or if not, I will come to thee quickly, and I will remove thy candlestick from its place, except thou repent.	Remember from where you came and do the former works, but if not, I will come to you and I will remove your lampstand, unless you repent.
6	But this thou hast, that thou hatest the deeds of the Nicolaitans, which I also hate.	But this thou hast, that thou hatest the deeds of the Nicolaitans, which I also [hate].	But this you have, that you hate the works of the Nicolaitans, those that I hate.'
7	He that hath an ear, let him hear what the Spirit saith unto the churches; To him that overcometh will I give to eat of the tree of life, which is in the midst of the paradise of God.	He that hath ears, let him hear what the Spirit saith to the churches. To him who is victorious, will I give to eat of the tree of life which is in the paradise of my God.	He who has ears should hear what the Spirit says to the churches. And to him who overcomes, I will allow [him] to eat of the tree of life which is in the paradise of God."
8	And unto the angel of the church in Smyrna write; These things saith the first and the last, which was dead, and is alive;	And to the angel of the church which is at Smyrna, write: These things saith the First and the Last, he who was dead, and liveth.	"And to the angel of the church of Smyrna, write, 'So says the first and the last, he who was dead and lives.

REVELATION *Chapter 2*

	KJV	*Murdock*	*Magiera*
9	I know thy works, and tribulation, and poverty, (but thou art rich) and I know the blasphemy of them which say they are Jews, and are not, but are the synagogue of Satan.	I know thy works, and the affliction, and the poverty, (yet thou art rich;) and the railing which is from them who say they are Jews, and they are not, but are of the congregation of Satan.	I know your trial and your poverty (but you are rich) and the reproach from those who say of themselves [that they are] Judeans when they are not Judeans, but the assembly of Satan.
10	Fear none of those things which thou shalt suffer: behold, the devil shall cast some of you into prison, that ye may be tried; and ye shall have tribulation ten days: be thou faithful unto death, and I will give thee a crown of life.	Be not terrified at any of the things thou art to suffer. For lo, the Accuser will throw some of you into custody, that ye may be tried; and there will be trouble to you ten days. Be faithful unto death, and I will give thee the crown of life.	Do not be afraid of anything, of those [things] that you are going to suffer. Behold, the Accuser is going to throw some of you into the detention hall, so that you may be tried and you will have torment [for] ten days. Be faithful [ones] until death and I will give to you the crown of life.'
11	He that hath an ear, let him hear what the Spirit saith unto the churches; He that overcometh shall not be hurt of the second death.	He that hath ears, let him hear what the Spirit saith to the churches. He that is victorious, shall not be harmed by the second death.	He who has ears should hear what the Spirit says to the churches. 'He who overcomes will not be hurt by the second death.'"
12	And to the angel of the church in Pergamos write; These things saith he which hath the sharp sword with two edges;	And to the angel of the church at Pergamos, write: Thus saith he who hath the sharp two-edged sword;	"And to the angel that is in the church of Pergamos, write, 'So says he who has the sharp sword of two edges.
13	I know thy works, and where thou dwellest, even where Satan's seat is: and thou holdest fast my name, and hast not denied my faith, even in those days wherein Antipas was my faithful martyr, who was slain among you, where Satan dwelleth.	I know thy works, and where thou dwellest, [even] where the throne of Satan is: and thou holdest fast my name, and hast not denied the faith of me, in those days when my faithful witness, who was slain among you, was made a spectacle where Satan dwelleth.	I know where you live, the place of the throne of Satan. And you hold fast to my name and you have not denied my faith, even in the days [when] you were watched and my faithful witness (because every witness of mine is faithful) was killed among you.
14	But I have a few things against thee, because thou hast there them that hold the doctrine of Balaam, who taught Balac to cast a stumblingblock before the children of Israel, to eat things sacrificed unto idols, and to commit fornication.	Yet I have a small [charge] against thee. Thou hast there them who hold the doctrine of Balaam, who taught Balak to throw a stumbling-block before the children of Israel, that they might eat the sacrifices of idols, and might commit whoredom.	But I have a few [things] against you. You have there those who hold the doctrine of Balaam, who taught Balak to set a stumbling stone before the sons of Israel to eat the sacrifices of idols and to commit fornication.
15	So hast thou also them that hold the doctrine of the Nicolaitans, which thing I hate.	So also thou hast them who hold the doctrine of the Nicolaitans. In like manner, repent thou.	So also you have those who adhere in the same manner to the doctrine of the Nicolaitans.
16	Repent; or else I will come unto thee quickly, and will fight against them with the sword of my mouth.	Or if not, I will come to thee quickly, and I will war upon them with the sword of my mouth.	Repent therefore. And if not, I will come to you immediately and I will wage war with them with the sword of my mouth.'

Parallel Translations

REVELATION *Chapter 2*

	KJV	Murdock	Magiera
17	He that hath an ear, let him hear what the Spirit saith unto the churches; To him that overcometh will I give to eat of the hidden manna, and will give him a white stone, and in the stone a new name written, which no man knoweth saving he that receiveth it.	He that hath ears, let him hear what the Spirit saith to the churches. To him that is victorious, will I give to eat of the hidden manna; and I will give him a white counter, and upon the counter a new name written, which no one knoweth but he that receiveth it.	And he who has ears should hear what the Spirit says to the churches. 'To him who overcomes, I will give from the manna that is hidden and I will give to him a white pebble and on the pebble a new name written that no man knows, except him who receives.'"
18	And unto the angel of the church in Thyatira write; These things saith the Son of God, who hath his eyes like unto a flame of fire, and his feet are like fine brass;	And to the angel of the church at Thyatira, write: These things saith the Son of God, who hath his eyes like a flame of fire, and his feet like fine brass:	"And to the angel that is in the church that is in Thyatira, write, 'So says the Son of God, he who has eye[s] like a flame of fire and his feet like Lebanese brass.
19	I know thy works, and charity, and service, and faith, and thy patience, and thy works; and the last to be more than the first.	I know thy works, and love, and faith, and service, and also thy patience; and that these thy latter works are more than the former.	I know your works and your love and your faith and your service and your endurance and your last works are greater than the former [ones].
20	Notwithstanding I have a few things against thee, because thou sufferest that woman Jezebel, which calleth herself a prophetess, to teach and to seduce my servants to commit fornication, and to eat things sacrificed unto idols.	But I have [a charge] against thee, because thou sufferest thy woman Jezabel, who saith she is a prophetess, and teacheth, and seduceth my servants to whoredom, and to eating of the sacrifices of idols.	But I have much against you, because you allowed your wife, Jezebel, who says concerning herself that she is a prophetess and teaches and deceives my servants, to commit fornication and to eat sacrifices of idols.
21	And I gave her space to repent of her fornication; and she repented not.	And I gave her a season for repentance, and she is not disposed to repent of her whoredom.	And I gave her a time for repentance and she does not desire to repent of her fornication.
22	Behold, I will cast her into a bed, and them that commit adultery with her into great tribulation, except they repent of their deeds.	Behold, I will cast her upon a bed, and them who commit adultery with her into great affliction, unless they repent of their deeds.	Behold, I will cast her on a bed and those who commit adultery with her into great torment, unless they repent of their works.
23	And I will kill her children with death; and all the churches shall know that I am he which searcheth the reins and hearts: and I will give unto every one of you according to your works.	And her children will I slay with death: and all the churches shall know, that I am he who searcheth reins and hearts; and I will render to each of you according to your works.	And I will kill her sons with death and all the churches will know that I am searching the emotions and the heart and I will give to all of you according to your works.'
24	But unto you I say, and unto the rest in Thyatira, as many as have not this doctrine, and which have not known the depths of Satan, as they speak; I will put upon you none other burden.	And I say to you, to the rest that are in Thyatira, to all them who have not received this doctrine, the men who have not known the profound things of Satan, as they say; I lay no other burden upon you:	I say to you, to the rest who are in Thyatira, all those who do not have this teaching, those who have not known the deep [things] of Satan (as they say), 'I will not place another burden on you.
25	But that which ye have already hold fast till I come.	but, what ye have, hold fast until I come.	Therefore, that which you have, hold fast until I come.
26	And he that overcometh, and keepeth my works unto the end, to him will I give power over the nations:	And to him that is victorious, and to him that observeth my works unto the end, to him will I give authority, over the nations;	And he who overcomes and keeps my works, to him I will give authority over the nations

Parallel Translations

REVELATION *Chapter 2*

	KJV	Murdock	Magiera
27	And he shall rule them with a rod of iron; as the vessels of a potter shall they be broken to shivers: even as I received of my Father.	and he shall rule them with a rod of iron; and like vessels of pottery, shall they be broken: as I also have received of my Father.	TO RULE THEM WITH A ROD OF IRON AND AS VESSELS OF A POTTER, THEY WILL BE BROKEN. For thus I received from my Father.
28	And I will give him the morning star.	And I will give him the morning star.	And I will give him the star of the morning.'
29	He that hath an ear, let him hear what the Spirit saith unto the churches.	He that hath ears, let him hear what the Spirit saith to the churches.	He who has ears should hear what the Spirit says to the churches."
Chapter 3			
1	And unto the angel of the church in Sardis write; These things saith he that hath the seven Spirits of God, and the seven stars; I know thy works, that thou hast a name that thou livest, and art dead.	And to the angel of the church which is at Sardis, write: These things saith he who hath the seven Spirits of God, and the seven stars: I know thy works, that thou hast a name that thou livest, and thou art dead.	"And to the angel that is in the church of Sardis, write, 'So says he who has the seven spirits of God and the seven stars. I know your works and the name that you have and that you live and that you are dead.
2	Be watchful, and strengthen the things which remain, that are ready to die: for I have not found thy works perfect before God.	Awake, and preserve the things that remain, which are ready to die; for I have not found thy works complete before my God.	And be watchful and establish the rest of those who are going to die, for I have not found that your works are complete before God.
3	Remember therefore how thou hast received and heard, and hold fast, and repent. If therefore thou shalt not watch, I will come on thee as a thief, and thou shalt not know what hour I will come upon thee.	Remember therefore how thou hast received and heard; and observe [those precepts], and repent. If then thou wilt not wake up, I will come upon thee as a thief; and thou shalt not know at what hour I will come upon thee.	Remember how you heard and you received. Beware and repent. And if you do not watch, I will come to you as a thief and you will not know [in] what hour [he] comes to you.
4	Thou hast a few names even in Sardis which have not defiled their garments; and they shall walk with me in white: for they are worthy.	Yet thou hast a few names in Sardis, who have not defiled their garments; and they shall walk with me in white, for they are worthy.	But I have a few names in Sardis, those who have not defiled their clothes and walk before me in white and are worthy.
5	He that overcometh, the same shall be clothed in white raiment; and I will not blot out his name out of the book of life, but I will confess his name before my Father, and before his angels.	He that is victorious, shall be so clothed in white robes; and I will not blot out their name from the book of life; and I will confess their name before my Father, and before his angels.	He who overcomes will be so dressed with white clothes and I will not blot out his name from the scroll of life and I will confess his name before my Father and before his angels.'
6	He that hath an ear, let him hear what the Spirit saith unto the churches.	He that hath ears, let him hear what the Spirit saith to the churches.	He who has ears should hear what the Spirit says to the churches."
7	And to the angel of the church in Philadelphia write; These things saith he that is holy, he that is true, he that hath the key of David, he that openeth, and no man shutteth; and shutteth, and no man openeth;	And to the angel of the church which is at Philadelphia, write: These things saith he that is holy, he that is true, he that hath the key of David, who openeth and no man shutteth, and shutteth and no man openeth;	"And to the angel of the church of Philadelphia, write, 'So says the holy [one], the true [one], he who has the keys of David, the one who opens and no one shuts and [who] shuts and no one opens.

REVELATION *Chapter 3*

	KJV	*Murdock*	*Magiera*
8	I know thy works: behold, I have set before thee an open door, and no man can shut it: for thou hast a little strength, and hast kept my word, and hast not denied my name.	I know thy works. And lo, I have set before thee an open door, which no man can shut: because thou hast a little strength; and thou hast kept my word, and hast not denied my name.	I know your works and behold, I have set before you an open door that no one is able to shut, because you have little strength and you have kept my word and you have not denied my name.
9	Behold, I will make them of the synagogue of Satan, which say they are Jews, and are not, but do lie; behold, I will make them to come and worship before thy feet, and to know that I have loved thee.	Behold, I will give them of the congregation of Satan, who say they are Jews, and are not, but lie, behold I will make them to come and do obeisance before thy feet; and to know that I have loved thee.	And behold, I will give those from the assembly of Satan, who say concerning themselves that they are Judeans and they are not, but they lie, behold, I will make them to come and to worship before your feet and to know that I have loved you.
10	Because thou hast kept the word of my patience, I also will keep thee from the hour of temptation, which shall come upon all the world, to try them that dwell upon the earth.	Because thou hast kept the word of my patience, I also will keep thee from the hour of temptation, that is to come on all the inhabited world, to try them who dwell on the earth.	Because you have kept the word of my patience, I will keep you from the trial that is going to come on all the earth to try all the inhabitants of the earth.
11	Behold, I come quickly: hold that fast which thou hast, that no man take thy crown.	I come quickly: hold fast what thou hast, so that no one take thy crown.	I am coming quickly. Hold fast what you have, so that no man will take your crown.
12	Him that overcometh will I make a pillar in the temple of my God, and he shall go no more out: and I will write upon him the name of my God, and the name of the city of my God, which is new Jerusalem, which cometh down out of heaven from my God: and I will write upon him my new name.	Him that is victorious, will I make a pillar in the temple of my God; and he shall not again go out: and I will write upon him the name of my God, and of the new Jerusalem which descendeth from heaven from my God, and my own new name.	And I will make him who overcomes a pillar in the temple of God and he will not go outside again and I will write on him the name of my God and the name of the new city, Jerusalem, that comes down from my God, and my own new name.'
13	He that hath an ear, let him hear what the Spirit saith unto the churches.	He that hath ears, let him hear what the Spirit saith to the churches.	And he who has ears should hear what the Spirit says to the churches."
14	And unto the angel of the church of the Laodiceans write; These things saith the Amen, the faithful and true witness, the beginning of the creation of God;	And to the angel of the church which is at Laodicea, write: These things saith the Amen, the witness, the faithful, the true, the Chief of the creation of God:	"And to the angel of the church of Laodicea, write, 'So says the true [one], the faithful and true witness and the first[fruit] of the creation of God.
15	I know thy works, that thou art neither cold nor hot: I would thou wert cold or hot.	I know thy works, that thou art neither hot, nor cold; I would that thou wert cold or hot.	I know your works. You are neither cold nor hot. You ought to be either cold or hot.
16	So then because thou art lukewarm, and neither cold nor hot, I will spue thee out of my mouth.	So, because thou art lukewarm, neither hot nor cold, I am about to vomit thee from my mouth.	And you are lukewarm and neither cold nor hot. I am going to vomit you from my mouth,
17	Because thou sayest, I am rich, and increased with goods, and have need of nothing; and knowest not that thou art wretched, and miserable, and poor, and blind, and naked:	Because thou sayest, I am rich and affluent, and have no want of any thing; and thou knowest not, that thou art impotent, and miserable, and needy, and blind, and naked;	because you have said that you are rich, 'and I have grown rich and I am not in need of anything,' and you do not know that you are weak and miserable and poor and naked.

Parallel Translations

	KJV	Murdock	Magiera

REVELATION *Chapter 3*

	KJV	Murdock	Magiera
18	I counsel thee to buy of me gold tried in the fire, that thou mayest be rich; and white raiment, that thou mayest be clothed, and that the shame of thy nakedness do not appear; and anoint thine eyes with eyesalve, that thou mayest see.	I counsel thee to buy of me gold tried in the fire, that thou mayest become rich; and white raiment, to be clothed, and that the shame of thy nakedness may not be seen; and put eye-salve on thine eyes, that thou mayest see.	I counsel you to buy gold from me that is tried by fire, so that you may become rich, and white garments to clothe yourself, so that the shame of your nakedness should not be revealed. And apply eye salve to the eyelids, so that you may see.
19	As many as I love, I rebuke and chasten: be zealous therefore, and repent.	As many as I love, I rebuke and chasten. Be emulous therefore, and repent.	I reprove and I correct those whom I love. Be zealous, therefore, and repent.
20	Behold, I stand at the door, and knock: if any man hear my voice, and open the door, I will come in to him, and will sup with him, and he with me.	Behold, I have been standing at the door, and I will knock: if any man hear my voice, and open the door, I will come in to him, and will sup with him, and he with me.	Behold, I stand at the door and knock. If anyone hears my voice and will open the door, I will enter and I will eat supper with him and he with me.
21	To him that overcometh will I grant to sit with me in my throne, even as I also overcame, and am set down with my Father in his throne.	And to him that is victorious, to him will I give to sit with me on my throne, even as I was victorious, and sat down with my Father on his throne.	And to him that overcomes, I will allow [him] to sit with me on my throne, even as I overcame and sat with my Father on his throne.'
22	He that hath an ear, let him hear what the Spirit saith unto the churches.	He that hath ears to hear, let him hear what the Spirit saith to the churches.	He who has ears should hear what the Spirit says to the churches."

Chapter 4

	KJV	Murdock	Magiera
1	After this I looked, and, behold, a door was opened in heaven: and the first voice which I heard was as it were of a trumpet talking with me; which said, Come up hither, and I will shew thee things which must be hereafter.	After these things, I looked and lo, a door [was] open in heaven. And the first voice which I heard, was as of a trumpet talking with me. It said, Come up hither; and I will show thee the things that must occur hereafter.	After these [things], I looked and behold, [there was] an open door in heaven. And the voice that I heard [was] like a trumpet speaking with me saying, "Come up here and I will show you what must happen after these [things]."
2	And immediately I was in the spirit: and, behold, a throne was set in heaven, and one sat on the throne.	Instantly, I was in the Spirit: and lo, a throne was placed in heaven; and there was [one] seated on the throne.	And immediately I was [seeing] spiritually. And behold, a throne was placed in heaven and [someone] was sitting on the throne.
3	And he that sat was to look upon like a jasper and a sardine stone: and there was a rainbow round about the throne, in sight like unto an emerald.	And he who sat, was like the appearance of a jasper-stone, and of a sardine [sard], and of a rainbow of the clouds, round about the throne, in form as the appearance of emeralds.	And he who was sitting [was] like the appearance of a stone of jasper and of sardius, and the rainbow around the throne [was] like the appearance of emeralds.
4	And round about the throne were four and twenty seats: and upon the seats I saw four and twenty elders sitting, clothed in white raiment; and they had on their heads crowns of gold.	Around the throne were twenty and four seats; and upon those seats sat twenty and four Elders, who were clothed in white robes, and on whose heads were coronets of gold.	And around the throne [were] twenty-four thrones. And on the thrones, twenty-four elders were sitting, clothed in white garments. And on their heads [were] crowns of gold.

REVELATION *Chapter 4*

	KJV	*Murdock*	*Magiera*
5	And out of the throne proceeded lightnings and thunderings and voices: and there were seven lamps of fire burning before the throne, which are the seven Spirits of God.	And from the throne proceeded lightnings, and the sound of thunders; and seven lamps of fire were burning before his throne, which are the seven Spirits of God.	And thunderings and lightning bolts and shouts came out from the thrones and seven burning lights [were] before the throne that are the seven spirits of God.
6	And before the throne there was a sea of glass like unto crystal: and in the midst of the throne, and round about the throne, were four beasts full of eyes before and behind.	And before the throne, as it were a sea of glass like crystal; and in the midst of the throne, and around it, and before the throne, were four Animals, full of eyes in their front and in their rear.	And before the throne [was] a sea of glass like crystal. And between the throne and around the throne [were] four living creatures full of eyes in front and behind.
7	And the first beast was like a lion, and the second beast like a calf, and the third beast had a face as a man, and the fourth beast was like a flying eagle.	And the first Animal resembled a lion; and the second Animal resembled a calf; and the third Animal had a face like a man; and the fourth Animal resembled an eagle when flying.	The first living creature was like a lion and the second living creature [was] like a calf and the third living creature had a face as a man and the fourth living creature [was] like an eagle that was flying.
8	And the four beasts had each of them six wings about him; and they were full of eyes within: and they rest not day and night, saying, Holy, holy, holy, Lord God Almighty, which was, and is, and is to come.	And these four Animals had, each of them, six wings around it: and within they were full of eyes: and they have no cessation, day or night, from saying: Holy, Holy, Holy, the Lord God, the Omnipotent, who was, and is, and is to come.	Each one of the four living creatures stood and had from its claws and upward, six wings full of eyes around [it] and from within. And they have no rest, day or night, saying, "Holy, holy, holy, LORD God Almighty, he who was and is and comes."
9	And when those beasts give glory and honour and thanks to him that sat on the throne, who liveth for ever and ever,	And when these Animals give glory and honor and praise to him that sitteth on the throne, to him who liveth for ever and ever,	And when the four living creatures give glory and honor and thanksgiving to him who sits on the throne and to him who truly lives forever and ever,
10	The four and twenty elders fall down before him that sat on the throne, and worship him that liveth for ever and ever, and cast their crowns before the throne, saying,	the twenty and four Elders fall down before him who sitteth on the throne, and they worship him who liveth for ever and ever; and they cast their coronets before the throne, saying,	the twenty-four elders would fall down before him who sits on the throne and worship him who truly lives forever and ever. And they would throw their crowns before the throne, saying,
11	Thou art worthy, O Lord, to receive glory and honour and power: for thou hast created all things, and for thy pleasure they are and were created.	Worthy art thou, O Lord our God, the Holy, to receive glory and honor and power; for thou hast created all things, and by thee they exist; and because of thy pleasure they had being and were created.	"Worthy is our Lord and our God to receive glory and honor and power, because you created all, and by way of your will, they came to be and were created."

Chapter 5

	KJV	*Murdock*	*Magiera*
1	And I saw in the right hand of him that sat on the throne a book written within and on the backside, sealed with seven seals.	And I saw, at the right hand of him who sat on the throne, a book, which was written within and on the back side, and which was sealed with seven seals.	And I saw on the right hand of him who sat on the throne a book inscribed from within and from without and sealed with seven seals.

Parallel Translations

REVELATION *Chapter 5*

	KJV	Murdock	Magiera
2	And I saw a strong angel proclaiming with a loud voice, Who is worthy to open the book, and to loose the seals thereof?	And I saw a strong angel, who proclaimed with a loud voice, Who is competent to open the book, and to loose the seals thereof?	And I saw another strong angel who proclaimed with a loud voice, "Who is worthy to open the book and to loosen its seals?"
3	And no man in heaven, nor in earth, neither under the earth, was able to open the book, neither to look thereon.	And no one either in heaven above, or on the earth, or beneath the earth, was able to open the book, or to look thereon.	And there was no one who was able, in heaven or on earth or under the earth, to open the book and to loosen its seals and to see it.
4	And I wept much, because no man was found worthy to open and to read the book, neither to look thereon.	And I wept much, because no one was found, who was competent to open the book, or to look on it.	And I was weeping very much, because there was no one who was found who was worthy to open the book and to loosen its seals.
5	And one of the elders saith unto me, Weep not: behold, the Lion of the tribe of Juda, the Root of David, hath prevailed to open the book, and to loose the seven seals thereof.	And one of the Elders said to me, Weep not; behold, the Lion of the tribe of Judah, the Root of David, hath been victorious: He will open the book, and its seven seals.	And one of the elders said to me, "Do not weep. Behold, the lion from the tribe of Judah, the root of David, has conquered. He will open the book and its seals."
6	And I beheld, and, lo, in the midst of the throne and of the four beasts, and in the midst of the elders, stood a Lamb as it had been slain, having seven horns and seven eyes, which are the seven Spirits of God sent forth into all the earth.	And I looked, and in the midst of the Elders stood a lamb, as if slain; and it had seven horns, and seven eyes, which are the seven Spirits of God that are sent into all the earth.	And I saw in the middle of the throne and of the four living creatures and of the elders a lamb that stood as if it was being sacrificed. And it had seven horns and seven eyes that are the seven spirits of God that are sent to all the earth.
7	And he came and took the book out of the right hand of him that sat upon the throne.	And he came, and took the book from the right hand of him who sat on the throne.	And he came and took the book from the hand of him who sat on the throne.
8	And when he had taken the book, the four beasts and four and twenty elders fell down before the Lamb, having every one of them harps, and golden vials full of odours, which are the prayers of saints.	And when he took the book, the four Animals and the twenty and four Elders fell down before the Lamb, each of them having a harp, and cups of gold full of odors, which are the supplications of the saints.	And when he took the book, the four living creatures and the twenty-four elders fell down before the lamb, each one of them having a harp and a bowl of gold filled with perfumes, which are the prayers of the holy [ones],
9	And they sung a new song, saying, Thou art worthy to take the book, and to open the seals thereof: for thou wast slain, and hast redeemed us to God by thy blood out of every kindred, and tongue, and people, and nation;	And they sung a new anthem, saying: Competent art thou, to take the book, and to open the seals thereof; because thou wast slain, and hast redeemed us to God by thy blood, out of every tribe, and tongue, and people, and nation;	who were praising a new praise-hymn and saying, "You are worthy to take the book and to loosen its seals, because you were sacrificed and you bought us with your blood for God from all the tribes and nations and peoples.
10	And hast made us unto our God kings and priests: and we shall reign on the earth.	and thou hast made them kings and priests to our God; and they reign on the earth.	And you made them a kingdom for our God and priests and kings and they will reign on the earth."

Parallel Translations

REVELATION *Chapter 5*

	KJV	*Murdock*	*Magiera*
11	And I beheld, and I heard the voice of many angels round about the throne and the beasts and the elders: and the number of them was ten thousand times ten thousand, and thousands of thousands;	And I looked, and I heard, as it were the voice of many angels, around the throne, and the Animals and the Elders; and the number of them was a myriad of myriads, and thousand of thousands,	And I saw and I heard [a sound] like the voice of many angels around the throne and of the living creatures and of the elders. And their number was a multitude of multitudes and a thousand of thousands.
12	Saying with a loud voice, Worthy is the Lamb that was slain to receive power, and riches, and wisdom, and strength, and honour, and glory, and blessing.	who said, with a loud voice; Competent is the Lamb that was slain, to receive power, and riches, and wisdom, and strength, and honor, and glory, and blessing;	And they were saying with a loud voice, "Worthy is the sacrificed Lamb to receive power and wealth and wisdom and strength and honor and glory and blessing
13	And every creature which is in heaven, and on the earth, and under the earth, and such as are in the sea, and all that are in them, heard I saying, Blessing, and honour, and glory, and power, be unto him that sitteth upon the throne, and unto the Lamb for ever and ever.	and [to be over] every created thing, that is in heaven, or on earth, or under the earth, or in the sea; and all that are in them. And I heard him who sat on the throne say: Unto the Lamb be given, blessing, and honor, and glory, and power, for ever and ever.	and the whole creation that is in heaven and on the earth and under the earth and is in the sea and all that is in them." And I heard them saying to him who sits on the throne and to the Lamb, "Blessing and honor and praise and dominion, forever and ever."
14	And the four beasts said, Amen. And the four and twenty elders fell down and worshipped him that liveth for ever and ever.	And the four Animals said: Amen. And the Elders fell down, and adored.	And the four living creatures were saying, "Amen." And the elders fell down and worshipped.

Chapter 6

	KJV	*Murdock*	*Magiera*
1	And I saw when the Lamb opened one of the seals, and I heard, as it were the noise of thunder, one of the four beasts saying, Come and see.	And, when the Lamb had opened one of the seven seals, I looked, and I heard one of the four Animals say, as with a voice of thunder, Come, and see.	And I saw when the Lamb opened one of the seven seals and I heard one of the four living creatures that spoke as the sound of thunderings, "Come and see."
2	And I saw, and behold a white horse: and he that sat on him had a bow; and a crown was given unto him: and he went forth conquering, and to conquer.	And I looked, and there was a white horse: and he who sat on it, had a bow; and a coronet was given to him, and he went forth conquering, that he might conquer.	And I heard and I saw and behold, [there was] a white horse and he who sat on it had an archery bow and a crown was given to him and he went out a conqueror, both conquering and to conquer.
3	And when he had opened the second seal, I heard the second beast say, Come and see.	And when he had opened the second seal, I heard the second Animal say, Come.	And when he opened the second seal, I heard the second living creature, saying, "Come."
4	And there went out another horse that was red: and power was given to him that sat thereon to take peace from the earth, and that they should kill one another: and there was given unto him a great sword.	And there went forth another, a red horse; and to him who sat thereon, it was given, to take tranquillity from the earth; and that they should kill one another; and there was given to him a great sword.	And a red horse went out and it was given to him who sat on it to take peace from the earth that they would slaughter one another and there was given to him a large sword.

Parallel Translations

	KJV	Murdock	Magiera

REVELATION *Chapter 6*

	KJV	Murdock	Magiera
5	And when he had opened the third seal, I heard the third beast say, Come and see. And I beheld, and lo a black horse; and he that sat on him had a pair of balances in his hand.	And when he had opened the third seal, I heard the third Animal say, Come, and see. And I looked, and lo, a black horse; and he that sat thereon, had a balance in his hand.	And when the third seal was opened, I heard the third living creature, saying, "Come." And behold, [there was] a black horse and he who sat on it had a balance in his hand.
6	And I heard a voice in the midst of the four beasts say, A measure of wheat for a penny, and three measures of barley for a penny; and see thou hurt not the oil and the wine.	And I heard a voice in the midst of the four Animals, saying: A choenix of wheat for a denarius, and three choenices of barley for a denarius; and hurt not the oil and the wine.	And I heard a voice from among the living creatures, saying, "A measure of wheat for a denarius and three measures of barley for a denarius and do not hurt the wine and the oil."
7	And when he had opened the fourth seal, I heard the voice of the fourth beast say, Come and see.	And when he had opened the fourth seal, I heard the fourth Animal say, Come, and see.	And when he opened the fourth seal, I heard the voice of the living creature, saying, "Come."
8	And I looked, and behold a pale horse: and his name that sat on him was Death, and Hell followed with him. And power was given unto them over the fourth part of the earth, to kill with sword, and with hunger, and with death, and with the beasts of the earth.	And I looked, and lo, a pale horse; and the name of him who sat thereon was Death; and Hades followed after him. And there was given him authority over the fourth part of the earth, to slay with the sword, and by famine, and by death, and by the ravenous beast of the earth.	And I saw a pale horse and the name of him who sat on it [was] Death and Sheol followed him. And authority was given to him over one-fourth of the earth to kill by the sword and by famine and by death and by the wild animal of the earth.
9	And when he had opened the fifth seal, I saw under the altar the souls of them that were slain for the word of God, and for the testimony which they held:	And when he had opened the fifth seal, I saw under the altar the souls of them who were slain on account of the word of God, and on account of the testimony to the Lamb which was with them.	And when he opened the fifth seal, I saw under the altar the people that were killed because of the word of God and because of the testimony of Jesus that they had.
10	And they cried with a loud voice, saying, How long, O Lord, holy and true, dost thou not judge and avenge our blood on them that dwell on the earth?	And they cried with a loud voice, saying: How long, O Lord, thou holy and true, dost thou not judge and avenge our blood on them that dwell on the earth?	And they cried with a loud voice and said, "How long, LORD, holy and true, do you not judge and require our blood of the inhabitants of the earth?"
11	And white robes were given unto every one of them; and it was said unto them, that they should rest yet for a little season, until their fellowservants also and their brethren, that should be killed as they were, should be fulfilled.	And to each one of them was given a white robe; and it was told them, that they must be quiet yet a little while, until the consummation of their fellow-servants and brethren, who were to be killed as they had been.	And there was given to each one of them a white robe and it was said that they should rest for a short period of time until it should be completed, even their fellows and their brothers who were going to be killed, as also they [had been].
12	And I beheld when he had opened the sixth seal, and, lo, there was a great earthquake; and the sun became black as sackcloth of hair, and the moon became as blood;	And I looked, when he had opened the sixth seal, and there was a great earthquake; and the sun became black, like sackcloth of hair; and the whole moon became like blood.	And I saw when he opened the sixth seal and there was a great earthquake. And the sun was as sackcloth of black hair and the whole moon was as blood.

Parallel Translations

	KJV	*Murdock*	*Magiera*
	REVELATION *Chapter 6*		
13	And the stars of heaven fell unto the earth, even as a fig tree casteth her untimely figs, when she is shaken of a mighty wind.	And the stars of heaven fell on the earth, as a fig-tree casteth its unripe figs, when it is shaken by a strong wind.	And the stars of heaven fell on the earth, as a fig tree that casts its unripe figs when it is shaken by a powerful wind.
14	And the heaven departed as a scroll when it is rolled together; and every mountain and island were moved out of their places.	And the heavens separated, as a book is rolled up: and all mountains and islands were removed out of their places.	And heaven was parted, as scrolls that are rolled out, and every mountain and every island were moved out of their place[s].
15	And the kings of the earth, and the great men, and the rich men, and the chief captains, and the mighty men, and every bondman, and every free man, hid themselves in the dens and in the rocks of the mountains;	And the kings of the earth, and the nobles, and the captains of thousands, and the rich men, and the men of valor, and every servant and free man, hid themselves in caves, and in the clefts of the mountains;	And the kings of the earth and the great and the rulers of thousands and the rich and the strong [ones] and all the servants and the free men hid themselves in caves and in the rocks of the mountains.
16	And said to the mountains and rocks, Fall on us, and hide us from the face of him that sitteth on the throne, and from the wrath of the Lamb:	and they said to the mountains and to the clefts, Fall over us, and hide us from the face of him who sitteth on the throne, and from the wrath of the Lamb:	And they were saying to the mountains and the rocks: FALL ON US AND HIDE US FROM THE FACE OF THE LAMB,
17	For the great day of his wrath is come; and who shall be able to stand?	For the great day of their wrath is come; and who is able to stand?	BECAUSE THE GREAT DAY OF THEIR ANGER HAS COME AND WHO IS ABLE TO STAND?
	Chapter 7		
1	And after these things I saw four angels standing on the four corners of the earth, holding the four winds of the earth, that the wind should not blow on the earth, nor on the sea, nor on any tree.	And after these things I saw four angels, who stood on the four corners of the earth; and they held the four winds of the earth, so that the wind blew not on the earth, nor on the sea, nor on the trees.	And after this, I saw four angels standing on the four corners of the earth and holding back the four winds, so that the wind would not blow on the earth, nor on the sea, nor on any tree.
2	And I saw another angel ascending from the east, having the seal of the living God: and he cried with a loud voice to the four angels, to whom it was given to hurt the earth and the sea,	And I saw another angel, and he came up from the rising of the sun; and he had the seal of the living God; and he called out, with a loud voice, to the four angels to whom it was given to hurt the earth and the sea, saying:	And I saw another angel who came up from the rising of the sun and he had the seal of the living God. And he cried out with a loud voice to the four angels to whom it was given to hurt the earth and the sea.
3	Saying, Hurt not the earth, neither the sea, nor the trees, till we have sealed the servants of our God in their foreheads.	Hurt ye not the earth, nor the sea, nor the trees, until we shall have sealed the servants of our God upon their foreheads.	And he said, "Do not hurt the earth nor the sea, not even the trees, until we seal the servants of God on their foreheads."
4	And I heard the number of them which were sealed: and there were sealed an hundred and forty and four thousand of all the tribes of the children of Israel.	And I heard the number of them that were sealed, a hundred and forty and four thousand, sealed from every tribe of Israelites.	And I heard the number of the sealed [ones], one hundred and forty-four thousand from all the tribes of Israel,
5	Of the tribe of Juda were sealed twelve thousand. Of the tribe of Reuben were sealed twelve thousand. Of the tribe of Gad were sealed twelve thousand.	Of the tribe of Judah, twelve thousand were sealed: of the tribe of Reuben, twelve thousand: of the tribe of Gad, twelve thousand:	from the tribe of Judah, twelve thousand, from the tribe of Reuben, twelve thousand, from the tribe of Gad, twelve thousand,

Parallel Translations

REVELATION *Chapter 7*

	KJV	*Murdock*	*Magiera*
6	Of the tribe of Aser were sealed twelve thousand. Of the tribe of Nepthalim were sealed twelve thousand. Of the tribe of Manasses were sealed twelve thousand.	of the tribe of Ashur, twelve thousand: of the tribe of Naphtali, twelve thousand: of the tribe of Manasseh, twelve thousand:	from the tribe of Asher, twelve thousand, from the tribe of Naphtali, twelve thousand, from the tribe of Manasseh, twelve thousand,
7	Of the tribe of Simeon were sealed twelve thousand. Of the tribe of Levi were sealed twelve thousand. Of the tribe of Issachar were sealed twelve thousand.	of the tribe of Simeon, twelve thousand: of the tribe of Levi, twelve thousand: of the tribe of Issachar, twelve thousand:	from the tribe of Simeon, twelve thousand, from the tribe of Issachar, twelve thousand, from the tribe of Levi, twelve thousand,
8	Of the tribe of Zabulon were sealed twelve thousand. Of the tribe of Joseph were sealed twelve thousand. Of the tribe of Benjamin were sealed twelve thousand.	of the tribe of Zebulon, twelve thousand: of the tribe of Joseph, twelve thousand: of the tribe of Benjamin, twelve thousand.	from the tribe of Zebulun, twelve thousand, from the tribe of Joseph, twelve thousand, from the tribe of Benjamin, twelve thousand sealed [ones].
9	After this I beheld, and, lo, a great multitude, which no man could number, of all nations, and kindreds, and people, and tongues, stood before the throne, and before the Lamb, clothed with white robes, and palms in their hands;	And after these things, I looked, and lo, a great multitude, which no one could number, from all kindreds, and nations, and tribes, and tongues; who stood before the throne, and before the Lamb, clothed in white robes, and palms in their hands;	And afterwards, I saw a large crowd, which no one was able to number, from every nation and tribe and peoples and languages, that stood before the throne and before the Lamb and were clothed with white robes and [with] palm branches in their hands.
10	And cried with a loud voice, saying, Salvation to our God which sitteth upon the throne, and unto the Lamb.	and they cried, with a loud voice, saying: Salvation to our God, to him who sitteth on the throne, and to the Lamb.	And they were crying out with a loud voice and saying, "Deliverance to our God and to him who sits on the throne and to the Lamb."
11	And all the angels stood round about the throne, and about the elders and the four beasts, and fell before the throne on their faces, and worshipped God,	And all the angels stood around the throne and the Elders and the four Animals; and they fell upon their faces before his throne, and worshipped God,	And all the angels were standing around the throne and the elders and the four living creatures. And they fell down before the throne on their faces,
12	Saying, Amen: Blessing, and glory, and wisdom, and thanksgiving, and honour, and power, and might, be unto our God for ever and ever. Amen.	saying: Amen. Blessing, and glory, and wisdom, and thanksgiving, and honor, and power, and might, [be] to our God, for ever and ever: Amen.	saying, "Amen. Glory and blessing and wisdom and thanksgiving and honor and power and strength [be] to our God, forever and ever. Amen."
13	And one of the elders answered, saying unto me, What are these which are arrayed in white robes? and whence came they?	And one of the Elders turned, and said to me: These who are clothed in white robes, who are they, and whence came they?	And one of the elders answered and said to me, "Who are those who are clothed with white robes and from where did they come?"
14	And I said unto him, Sir, thou knowest. And he said to me, These are they which came out of great tribulation, and have washed their robes, and made them white in the blood of the Lamb.	And I said to him: My lord, thou knowest. And he said to me: These are they who came from great affliction; and they have washed their robes, and made them white in the blood of the Lamb.	And I said to him, "My lord, you know." And he said to me, "They are those who came from great torment and have washed their robes and whitened them in the blood of the Lamb.

	KJV	Murdock	Magiera
	REVELATION *Chapter 7*		
15	Therefore are they before the throne of God, and serve him day and night in his temple: and he that sitteth on the throne shall dwell among them.	Therefore are they before the throne of God; and they serve him day and night, in his temple; and he who sitteth on the throne, will protect them:	Because of this, they are before the throne of God and serve him day and night in his temple. And he who sits on the throne will dwell with them.
16	They shall hunger no more, neither thirst any more; neither shall the sun light on them, nor any heat.	they will not hunger, nor thirst any more; nor will the sun fall on them, nor any heat.	They will not hunger and not thirst and the sun will not fall on them and not any heat,
17	For the Lamb which is in the midst of the throne shall feed them, and shall lead them unto living fountains of waters: and God shall wipe away all tears from their eyes.	Because the Lamb, which is in the midst of the throne, will feed them; and will lead them to fountains of living water; and God will wipe every tear from their eyes.	because the Lamb who is in the middle of the throne will feed them and will guide them to life and to the fountains of water and will wipe away all the tears from their eyes."
	Chapter 8		
1	And when he had opened the seventh seal, there was silence in heaven about the space of half an hour.	And when he had opened the seventh seal, there was silence in heaven, for about half an hour.	And when he opened the seventh seal, there was silence in heaven for about half an hour.
2	And I saw the seven angels which stood before God; and to them were given seven trumpets.	And I saw the seven angels, who stood before God; and to them were given, seven trumpets.	And I saw seven angels who were standing before God. Seven trumpets were given to them.
3	And another angel came and stood at the altar, having a golden censer; and there was given unto him much incense, that he should offer it with the prayers of all saints upon the golden altar which was before the throne.	And another angel came and stood by the altar; and he held a golden censer: and much incense was given him, so that he might offer, with the prayers of all the saints, upon the golden altar before the throne.	And another angel came and stood by the altar and he had a censer of gold. And much incense was given to him to offer with the prayers of all the holy [ones] on the altar that is before the throne.
4	And the smoke of the incense, which came with the prayers of the saints, ascended up before God out of the angel's hand.	And the smoke of the incense of the prayers of the saints went up before God from the hand of the angel.	And the smoke of the incense went up with the prayers of the holy [ones] from the hand of the angel before God.
5	And the angel took the censer, and filled it with fire of the altar, and cast it into the earth: and there were voices, and thunderings, and lightnings, and an earthquake.	And the angel took the censer, and filled it with fire from the altar, and cast it upon the earth: and there were thunders, and lightnings, and voices, and an earthquake.	And the angel took the censer and filled it from the fire on the altar and threw [it] on the earth and there were thunderings and shouts and lightning bolts and an earthquake.
6	And the seven angels which had the seven trumpets prepared themselves to sound.	And the seven angels, who had the seven trumpets, prepared themselves to sound.	And the seven angels who [had] the seven trumpets on them prepared themselves to sound.
7	The first angel sounded, and there followed hail and fire mingled with blood, and they were cast upon the earth: and the third part of trees was burnt up, and all green grass was burnt up.	And the first sounded; and there was hail, and fire, which were mingled with water: and these were thrown upon the earth; and a third part of the earth was burned up, and a third part of the trees were burned, and all green grass was burned.	And that first [angel] sounded and there was hail and fire mingled with water and [these] were thrown on the earth. And a third of the earth was burned and a third of the trees were burned and all the grass of the earth was burned.

Parallel Translations

	KJV	Murdock	Magiera

REVELATION Chapter 8

	KJV	Murdock	Magiera
8	And the second angel sounded, and as it were a great mountain burning with fire was cast into the sea: and the third part of the sea became blood;	And the second angel sounded, and, as it were a great mountain burning with fire, was cast into the sea; and also a third part of the sea became blood.	And the second [angel] sounded and it was as a huge mountain that was burning. It fell into the sea and a third of the sea became blood.
9	And the third part of the creatures which were in the sea, and had life, died; and the third part of the ships were destroyed.	And a third part of all the creatures in the sea, that had life, died; and a third part of the ships were destroyed.	And a third of all the created [ones] that are in the sea that have life died and a third of the ship[s] were destroyed.
10	And the third angel sounded, and there fell a great star from heaven, burning as it were a lamp, and it fell upon the third part of the rivers, and upon the fountains of waters;	And the third angel sounded, and there fell from heaven a star, burning like a lamp; and it fell upon a third part of the rivers, and upon the fountains of water.	And the third [angel] sounded and a large star fell from heaven that was burning as a flame and it fell on a third of the rivers and on the fountains of waters.
11	And the name of the star is called Wormwood: and the third part of the waters became wormwood; and many men died of the waters, because they were made bitter.	And the name of the star was called Wormwood; and a third part of the waters became wormwood; and many persons died from the waters, because they were bitter.	And the name of the star was called Wormwood and a third of the waters became as wormwood and a great number of men died, because the waters were made bitter.
12	And the fourth angel sounded, and the third part of the sun was smitten, and the third part of the moon, and the third part of the stars; so as the third part of them was darkened, and the day shone not for a third part of it, and the night likewise.	And the fourth angel sounded, and a third part of the sun was smitten, and the third part of the moon, and the third part of the stars; so that the third part of them were dark, and they became dark; and the day did not give light for the third part of it, and the night in like manner.	And the fourth [angel] sounded and a third of the sun was struck and a third of the moon and a third of the stars and a third of them became dark. And the day did not show [for] a third part of it and the night likewise.
13	And I beheld, and heard an angel flying through the midst of heaven, saying with a loud voice, Woe, woe, woe, to the inhabiters of the earth by reason of the other voices of the trumpet of the three angels, which are yet to sound!	And I saw and heard an eagle, which flew in the midst, and it had a tail of blood, while it said, with a loud voice: Woe, woe, to them who dwell on the earth, because of the remaining sounds of the trumpets of the three angels, who are to sound.	And I heard one eagle flying in heaven that said, "Woe, woe, woe, to the inhabitants of the earth, because of the sound of the trumpets of the three angels that are going to sound!"

Chapter 9

	KJV	Murdock	Magiera
1	And the fifth angel sounded, and I saw a star fall from heaven unto the earth: and to him was given the key of the bottomless pit.	And the fifth angel sounded; and I saw a star, which fell from heaven upon the earth. And there was given to him the key of the pit of the abyss.	And the fifth [angel] sounded and I saw a star that fell from heaven on the earth and the key of the pits of the abyss was given to him.
2	And he opened the bottomless pit; and there arose a smoke out of the pit, as the smoke of a great furnace; and the sun and the air were darkened by reason of the smoke of the pit.	And he opened the pit of the abyss; and smoke issued from the pit, like the smoke of a furnace that is in blast; and the sun and the air were darkened by the smoke of the pit.	And smoke went up from the pits, as the smoke of a large furnace that was heated up. And the sun was darkened and the air [also] from the smoke of the pits.
3	And there came out of the smoke locusts upon the earth: and unto them was given power, as the scorpions of the earth have power.	And out of the smoke, came locusts upon the earth: and power was given them, like that which scorpions have on the earth.	And from the smoke, locusts went out on the earth and the authority that belongs to the scorpions of the earth was given to them.

Parallel Translations

	KJV	Murdock	Magiera

REVELATION *Chapter 9*

Verse	KJV	Murdock	Magiera
4	And it was commanded them that they should not hurt the grass of the earth, neither any green thing, neither any tree; but only those men which have not the seal of God in their foreheads.	And it was commanded them, that they should not hurt the grass of the earth, nor any herb, nor any tree; but [only] the persons, who had not the seal of God upon their foreheads.	And it was told to them that they should not harm the grass of the earth or any herb, not even the trees, but only the men who did not have the seal of God on their foreheads.
5	And to them it was given that they should not kill them, but that they should be tormented five months: and their torment was as the torment of a scorpion, when he striketh a man.	And it was given them, that they should not kill them, but should torment them five months: and their torment was like the torment of a scorpion, when it striketh a person.	And it was given to them that they should not kill them, but [that] they should be tormented [for] five months. And their torment [was] like the torment of a scorpion when it falls on a man.
6	And in those days shall men seek death, and shall not find it; and shall desire to die, and death shall flee from them.	And in those days, men will desire death, and will not find it; and they will long to die, and death will fly from them.	And in those days, men will seek death and will not find it. And they will earnestly desire to die and death will flee from them.
7	And the shapes of the locusts were like unto horses prepared unto battle; and on their heads were as it were crowns like gold, and their faces were as the faces of men.	And the appearance of the locusts [was this]; they were like the appearance of horses prepared for battle; and on their heads, was, as it were a coronet, resembling gold; and their faces were like the faces of men.	And the form of the locusts [was] like horses that are prepared for battle. And on their heads [it was] like a crown with the form of gold and their faces [were] like the face of a man.
8	And they had hair as the hair of women, and their teeth were as the teeth of lions.	And they had hair, like the hair of women: and their teeth were like those of lions.	And they had hair like the hair of women and their teeth [were] like [those] of lions.
9	And they had breastplates, as it were breastplates of iron; and the sound of their wings was as the sound of chariots of many horses running to battle.	And they had breastplates, like breastplates of iron: and the sound of their wings, was like the sound of the chariots of many horses rushing into battle.	And they had a breastplate like a breastplate of iron and the sound of their wings [was] like the sound of the chariots of many horses that are running to battle.
10	And they had tails like unto scorpions, and there were stings in their tails: and their power was to hurt men five months.	And they had tails like those of scorpions, and stings; and with their tails they had the power of hurting men five months.	And they had tails like a scorpion and stings in their tails and their authority [was] to hurt men [for] five months.
11	And they had a king over them, which is the angel of the bottomless pit, whose name in the Hebrew tongue is Abaddon, but in the Greek tongue hath his name Apollyon.	And they had a king over them, the angel of the abyss; and his name, in Hebrew, is Abaddon; and in Greek, his name is Apollyon.	And there was a king over them, the angel of the abyss, whose name in Hebrew [is] Abaddon, and in Aramaic, his name is "Breaker."
12	One woe is past; and, behold, there come two woes more hereafter.	One woe is past; lo, there come yet two woes after them.	One woe is past. Behold, there are still two woe[s].
13	And the sixth angel sounded, and I heard a voice from the four horns of the golden altar which is before God,	And the sixth angel sounded; and I heard a voice from the horns of the golden altar which was before God,	After these [things], the sixth angel sounded and I heard one voice from the four horns of the altar of gold that was before God
14	Saying to the sixth angel which had the trumpet, Loose the four angels which are bound in the great river Euphrates.	that said to the sixth angel having a trumpet: Loose the four angels that are bound at the great river Euphrates.	that said to the sixth angel that had the trumpet, "Release the four angels that are bound at the great river Euphrates."

Parallel Translations

REVELATION Chapter 9

	KJV	Murdock	Magiera
15	And the four angels were loosed, which were prepared for an hour, and a day, and a month, and a year, for to slay the third part of men.	And the four angels were loosed; who are prepared, for an hour, and a day, and a month, and a year, to slay the third part of men.	And the four angels were released, who were prepared for an hour and for a day and for a month and for a year to kill a third of mankind.
16	And the number of the army of the horsemen were two hundred thousand thousand: and I heard the number of them.	And the number of the warrior horsemen was two myriads of myriads: and I heard their number.	And the number of the hosts of the cavalry was two thousand thousands. I heard their number.
17	And thus I saw the horses in the vision, and them that sat on them, having breastplates of fire, and of jacinth, and brimstone: and the heads of the horses were as the heads of lions; and out of their mouths issued fire and smoke and brimstone.	And while I looked on the horses in the vision, and on them who sat on them [I saw] that the breastplates were of fire, and of jacinth, and of sulphur. And the heads of the horses were like the heads of lions; and from their mouths issued fire, and smoke, and sulphur.	And so I saw the horses in the vision and those sitting on them had a breastplate of fire and chalcedony and sulfur. And the heads of the horses [were] like the heads of lions and from their mouth[s] came out fire and sulfur and smoke.
18	By these three was the third part of men killed, by the fire, and by the smoke, and by the brimstone, which issued out of their mouths.	And by these three plagues, a third part of the men were slain; [namely,] by the fire, and by the smoke, and by the sulphur, which issued from their mouths.	And by these three plagues, a third of mankind was killed, even by the fire and by the sulfur and by the smoke that came out of their mouth[s],
19	For their power is in their mouth, and in their tails: for their tails were like unto serpents, and had heads, and with them they do hurt.	For the power of the horses was in; their mouth, and in their tails; for their tails were like serpents, having heads to strike with.	because the power of the horses [was] in their mouth[s] and also in their tails.
20	And the rest of the men which were not killed by these plagues yet repented not of the works of their hands, that they should not worship devils, and idols of gold, and silver, and brass, and stone, and of wood: which neither can see, nor hear, nor walk:	And the residue of men who were not slain by these plagues, repented not of the works of their hands, so as not to worship demons, and idols of gold, and of silver, and brass, and stone, and wood, which cannot see, nor hear.	And the rest of the men who were not killed by these plagues did not repent of the work of their hands that they should not worship demons and images of gold and of silver and of brass and of wood and of stone, those that are not able to see, nor to hear or to walk.
21	Neither repented they of their murders, nor of their sorceries, nor of their fornication, nor of their thefts.	And they repented not of their murders, nor of their sorceries, nor of their whoredom, nor of their thefts.	And they did not repent of their murders or of their sorceries or of their fornication.

Chapter 10

	KJV	Murdock	Magiera
1	And I saw another mighty angel come down from heaven, clothed with a cloud: and a rainbow was upon his head, and his face was as it were the sun, and his feet as pillars of fire:	And I saw another mighty angel, that descended from heaven, clothed with a cloud; and a cloud-bow was over his head, and his face was like the sun, and his feet like pillars of fire.	And I saw another angel who came down from heaven and was clothed with a cloud and a rainbow of heaven [was] on his head and his appearance [was] like the sun and his feet [were] like pillars of fire.
2	And he had in his hand a little book open: and he set his right foot upon the sea, and his left foot on the earth,	And he had in his hand an open little book: and he placed his right foot upon the sea, and his left upon the land:	And he had in his hand a little open book and he placed his right foot on the sea and the left on the land.

	KJV	Murdock	Magiera

REVELATION Chapter 10

Verse	KJV	Murdock	Magiera
3	And cried with a loud voice, as when a lion roareth: and when he had cried, seven thunders uttered their voices.	and he cried with a loud voice, as a lion roareth: and when he had cried, the seven thunders uttered their voices.	And he cried out with a loud voice as a roaring lion. And when he had cried out, the seven thunders spoke with their voices.
4	And when the seven thunders had uttered their voices, I was about to write: and I heard a voice from heaven saying unto me, Seal up those things which the seven thunders uttered, and write them not.	And when the seven thunders had spoken, I was about to write. And I heard a voice from heaven, saying: Seal up the things which the seven thunders have uttered, and write them not.	And when the seven thunders spoke, I was preparing to write. And I heard a voice from heaven of the seven, saying, "Seal up what the seven thunders have said and do not write it."
5	And the angel which I saw stand upon the sea and upon the earth lifted up his hand to heaven,	And the angel whom I saw standing upon the sea and the land, raised his right hand to heaven,	And the angel that I saw standing on the sea and on the dry land, who lifted his hand to heaven,
6	And sware by him that liveth for ever and ever, who created heaven, and the things that therein are, and the earth, and the things that therein are, and the sea, and the things which are therein, that there should be time no longer:	and swore, by him who liveth for ever and ever, who created heaven and the things in it, and the earth and the things in it, and the sea and the things in it, that the time should be no longer;	even he swore by him who lives forever and ever, he who created the heaven and that which is in it and the earth and that which is in it, that there should not be any more time.
7	But in the days of the voice of the seventh angel, when he shall begin to sound, the mystery of God should be finished, as he hath declared to his servants the prophets.	but, in the days of the voice of the seventh angel, when he shall sound, and the mystery of God shall be consummated; as he announced to his servants the prophets.	But in the days of the seventh angel, when he is about to sound, the mystery of God will be completed that he announced to his servants, the prophets.
8	And the voice which I heard from heaven spake unto me again, and said, Go and take the little book which is open in the hand of the angel which standeth upon the sea and upon the earth.	And the voice which I heard from heaven, spoke to me again, and said: Go, take the little open book in the hand of the angel that standeth on the sea and on the land.	And I heard a voice from heaven again speaking with me and saying, "Go [and] take the little book that is in the hand of the angel who stands on the land and on the sea."
9	And I went unto the angel, and said unto him, Give me the little book. And he said unto me, Take it, and eat it up; and it shall make thy belly bitter, but it shall be in thy mouth sweet as honey.	And I went to the angel, telling him to give me the little book. And he said to me, Take, and eat it: and it will make thy bowels bitter, but in thy mouth it will be sweet as honey.	And I came near to the angel, telling him to give the little book to me. And he said to me, "Take and eat it and it will be bitter to your stomach, but in your mouth it will be like honey."
10	And I took the little book out of the angel's hand, and ate it up; and it was in my mouth sweet as honey: and as soon as I had eaten it, my belly was bitter.	And I took the little book from the hand of the angel, and ate it: and it was in my mouth sweet like honey: and when I had eaten it, my bowels were bitter.	And I took the little book from the hand of the angel and I ate it. And it was in my mouth sweet as honey. And when I ate it, my stomach became bitter.
11	And he said unto me, Thou must prophesy again before many peoples, and nations, and tongues, and kings.	And be said to me, Thou must again prophesy upon many nations, and peoples, and princes, and kings.	And he said to me, "You must prophesy another time about the nations and peoples and languages and many kings."

Parallel Translations

	KJV	Murdock	Magiera
	REVELATION *Chapter 11*		
1	And there was given me a reed like unto a rod: and the angel stood, saying, Rise, and measure the temple of God, and the altar, and them that worship therein.	And a reed was given to me, like a rod; and the angel stood, saying, Arise, and measure the temple of God, and the altar, and them that worship therein.	And a reed was given to me like a rod and the angel stood and said, "Rise up and measure the temple of God and the altar and those who worship in it,
2	But the court which is without the temple leave out, and measure it not; for it is given unto the Gentiles: and the holy city shall they tread under foot forty and two months.	But the court which is without the temple, leave out, and measure it not; because it is given to the Gentiles; and they will tread down the holy city forty and two months.	and leave out the court within the temple and do not measure it, because it is given to the Gentiles and they will trample down the holy city [for] forty-two months.
3	And I will give power unto my two witnesses, and they shall prophesy a thousand two hundred and threescore days, clothed in sackcloth.	And I will give my two witnesses; and they will prophesy a thousand and two hundred and sixty days, clothed in sackcloth.	And I will give my two witnesses [authority] to prophesy, one thousand, two hundred and sixty days, being clothed with sackcloth.
4	These are the two olive trees, and the two candlesticks standing before the God of the earth.	These are the two olive-trees, and the two candlesticks which stand before the Lord of the earth.	These are two olive [trees] and two lampstands who stand before the Lord of the whole earth.
5	And if any man will hurt them, fire proceedeth out of their mouth, and devoureth their enemies: and if any man will hurt them, he must in this manner be killed.	And if any person will harm them, fire cometh out of their mouth, and consumeth their adversary; and if any one will harm them, thus must he be slain.	And [if] one seeks to harm them, fire comes out of their mouth[s] and consumes their enemies. And [if] anyone wishes to harm them, so they must be killed.
6	These have power to shut heaven, that it rain not in the days of their prophecy: and have power over waters to turn them to blood, and to smite the earth with all plagues, as often as they will.	They have power to shut up heaven, so that the rain shall not fall in those days: and they have power over the waters, to turn them into blood; and to smite the earth with all plagues, as often as they please.	And these have authority to shut heaven, so that rain will not fall in the days of their prophecy. And they have authority to turn the waters to blood and to strike the earth with all plagues, as much as they desire.
7	And when they shall have finished their testimony, the beast that ascendeth out of the bottomless pit shall make war against them, and shall overcome them, and kill them.	And when they shall have completed their testimony, the beast of prey that came up from the abyss, will make war upon them, and will overcome them.	And when they have completed their testimony, the creature who came up from the sea will wage war with them and will conquer them and will kill them.
8	And their dead bodies shall lie in the street of the great city, which spiritually is called Sodom and Egypt, where also our Lord was crucified.	And their dead bodies [will be] in the open street of that great city, which is spiritually called Sodom and Egypt, where also their Lord was crucified.	And their corpses [will be] on the streets of the great city that is spiritually called Sodom and Egypt, where their Lord was crucified.
9	And they of the people and kindreds and tongues and nations shall see their dead bodies three days and an half, and shall not suffer their dead bodies to be put in graves.	And [they] of the nations and tribes and peoples and tongues, will look upon their dead bodies, three days and a half; and will not suffer their dead bodies to be laid in the grave.	And some of the peoples and tribes and languages and nations see their corpses [for] three and a half days and they will not allow their corpses to be placed in graves.

Parallel Translations

	KJV	*Murdock*	*Magiera*

REVELATION *Chapter 11*

	KJV	Murdock	Magiera
10	And they that dwell upon the earth shall rejoice over them, and make merry, and shall send gifts one to another; because these two prophets tormented them that dwelt on the earth.	And they who dwell on the earth will rejoice over them, and will be merry, and will send presents to one another; because those two prophets tormented them who dwell on the earth.	And the inhabitants of the earth will rejoice over them and will be glad and they will send gifts to one another, because of the two prophets who tormented the inhabitants of the earth."
11	And after three days and an half the Spirit of life from God entered into them, and they stood upon their feet; and great fear fell upon them which saw them.	And after these three days and a half, the spirit of life from God entered into them, and they stood upon their feet: and great fear fell on those who saw them.	And after three and a half days, the living Spirit from God entered into them and they rose up on their feet and the Spirit of life fell on them and great fear was on those who saw them.
12	And they heard a great voice from heaven saying unto them, Come up hither. And they ascended up to heaven in a cloud; and their enemies beheld them.	And they heard a great voice from heaven, which said to them: Come up hither. And they ascended to heaven in a cloud; and their enemies saw them.	And they heard a loud voice from heaven that said to them, "Come up here." And they went up to heaven in a cloud and their enemies gazed at them.
13	And the same hour was there a great earthquake, and the tenth part of the city fell, and in the earthquake were slain of men seven thousand: and the remnant were affrighted, and gave glory to the God of heaven.	And in the same hour there was a great earthquake, and the tenth part of the city fell: and the persons killed in the earthquake, were seven thousand names: and they who remained were afraid, and gave glory to God.	And in that hour there was a huge earthquake and one-tenth of the city fell and they were killed in the earthquake. The names of the men [were] seven thousand and the remainder were in fear and gave praise to God who is in heaven.
14	The second woe is past; and, behold, the third woe cometh quickly.	The second woe is passed: behold, the third woe cometh quickly.	Behold, two woe[s] have come and behold, the third woe comes quickly.
15	And the seventh angel sounded; and there were great voices in heaven, saying, The kingdoms of this world are become the kingdoms of our Lord, and of his Christ; and he shall reign for ever and ever.	And the seventh angel sounded; and there were voices and thunders, which said: The kingdom of the world hath become [the kingdom] of our Lord and of his Messiah; and he will reign for ever and ever.	And the seventh angel sounded and there were loud voices in heaven, saying, "The kingdom of the age has become [the kingdom] of our God and of his Messiah and he reigns forever and ever."
16	And the four and twenty elders, which sat before God on their seats, fell upon their faces, and worshipped God,	And the twenty and four Elders, who are before the throne of God, [and] who sit upon their seats, fell upon their faces, and worshipped God,	And the twenty-four elders, who were sitting before God on their thrones, fell on their faces and worshipped God,
17	Saying, We give thee thanks, O Lord God Almighty, which art, and wast, and art to come; because thou hast taken to thee thy great power, and hast reigned.	saying: We praise thee, O Lord God, Omnipotent, who art, and wast; because thou hast assumed thy great power, and hast reigned.	saying, "We praise you, LORD God Almighty, who is and was, because you have taken your great power and you have reigned.

REVELATION *Chapter 11*

	KJV	*Murdock*	*Magiera*
18	And the nations were angry, and thy wrath is come, and the time of the dead, that they should be judged, and that thou shouldest give reward unto thy servants the prophets, and to the saints, and them that fear thy name, small and great; and shouldest destroy them which destroy the earth.	And the nations were angry; and thy anger is come, and the time of the dead, that they should be judged: and that thou shouldst give a reward to thy servants, the prophets, and the saints, and to them that fear thy name, the small and the great; and that thou shouldst destroy them who destroyed the earth.	And the nations were angry, yet your anger has come and the time of the dead that they should be judged. And you will give a reward to your servants, the prophets, and to the holy [ones] and to those who reverence your name, the small with the great. And you will corrupt those who corrupted the earth.
19	And the temple of God was opened in heaven, and there was seen in his temple the ark of his testament: and there were lightnings, and voices, and thunderings, and an earthquake, and great hail.	And the temple of God in heaven was opened; and the ark of his covenant was seen in his temple: and there were lightnings, and thunders, and voices, and an earthquake, and great hail.	And the temple was opened in heaven and the ark of his covenant was seen in the temple. And there were lightning bolts and thunderings and shouts and an earthquake and large hail.

Chapter 12

	KJV	*Murdock*	*Magiera*
1	And there appeared a great wonder in heaven; a woman clothed with the sun, and the moon under her feet, and upon her head a crown of twelve stars:	And a great wonder was seen in heaven; a woman clothed with the sun, and the moon under her feet, and on her head a coronet of twelve stars.	And a great sign was seen in heaven, a woman clothed with the sun and the moon under her feet and a crown of twelve stars on her head,
2	And she being with child cried, travailing in birth, and pained to be delivered.	And, being with child, she cried, and travailed, and had the pangs of bringing forth.	and [she was] pregnant and crying and laboring in childbirth, also being in pain to give birth.
3	And there appeared another wonder in heaven; and behold a great red dragon, having seven heads and ten horns, and seven crowns upon his heads.	And there appeared another wonder in heaven; and lo, a great fiery dragon, which had seven heads and ten horns, and upon his head seven diadems.	And another sign was seen in heaven, and behold, [I saw] a great dragon of fire that had seven heads and ten horns and seven crowns on its heads.
4	And his tail drew the third part of the stars of heaven, and did cast them to the earth: and the dragon stood before the woman which was ready to be delivered, for to devour her child as soon as it was born.	And his tail drew along the third part of the stars of heaven, and cast them on the earth. And the dragon was standing before the woman, who was about to bring forth, so that, when she should bring forth, he might devour her child.	And its tail drew away a third of the stars that were in heaven and threw them on the earth. And the dragon was standing before the woman who was about to give birth, so that when she gave birth, he would devour her son.
5	And she brought forth a man child, who was to rule all nations with a rod of iron: and her child was caught up unto God, and to his throne.	And she brought forth a male child, who was to rule all nations with a rod of iron. And her child was caught up to God and to his throne.	And she gave birth to a male child who was going to rule all the nations with a rod of iron and her son was caught up to God and to his throne.
6	And the woman fled into the wilderness, where she hath a place prepared of God, that they should feed her there a thousand two hundred and threescore days.	And the woman fled into the wilderness, where she had a place which was prepared for her by God; so that they might nourish her there a thousand and two hundred and sixty days.	And the woman fled to the wilderness, where she had a place that was prepared there by God, so that they would nourish her [for] one thousand, two hundred and sixty days.

Parallel Translations

REVELATION *Chapter 12*

	KJV	*Murdock*	*Magiera*
7	And there was war in heaven: Michael and his angels fought against the dragon; and the dragon fought and his angels,	And there was war in heaven: Michael and his angels fought against the dragon, and the dragon and his angels fought,	And there was a war in heaven and Michael and his angels were warring with the dragon, and the dragon and his angels warred.
8	And prevailed not; neither was their place found any more in heaven.	and prevailed not; nor was their place found any more in heaven.	And they did not prevail and no place was found for them in heaven.
9	And the great dragon was cast out, that old serpent, called the Devil, and Satan, which deceiveth the whole world: he was cast out into the earth, and his angels were cast out with him.	And the great dragon was cast out, the old serpent, who is called the Deceiver, and Satan, who seduceth all the inhabited world: he was cast upon the earth, and his angels were cast out with him.	And the great dragon was thrown out, that chief serpent, who is called the Accuser and Satan, who deceived the whole earth. And he was thrown out on the earth and his angels were thrown out with him.
10	And I heard a loud voice saying in heaven, Now is come salvation, and strength, and the kingdom of our God, and the power of his Christ: for the accuser of our brethren is cast down, which accused them before our God day and night.	And I heard a great voice in heaven, which said: Now is there deliverance, and the power and the kingdom of our God, and the dominion of his Messiah: because the Accuser of our brethren is cast out, who accused them day and night before our God.	And I heard a loud voice from heaven saying, "Behold, there is deliverance and power and the kingdom of our God, because the Despiser of our brothers is thrown out, who despised them, night and day, before our God.
11	And they overcame him by the blood of the Lamb, and by the word of their testimony; and they loved not their lives unto the death.	And they overcame him, because of the blood of the Lamb, and because of the word of their testimony: and they loved not their life, even to death.	And they overcame by the blood of the Lamb and by way of the word of his testimony and they did not love their own lives, until death.
12	Therefore rejoice, ye heavens, and ye that dwell in them. Woe to the inhabiters of the earth and of the sea! for the devil is come down unto you, having great wrath, because he knoweth that he hath but a short time.	Therefore, be joyful, O heaven, and ye that dwell there. Woe to the earth, and to the sea; for the Deceiver hath come down to you, being in great wrath since he knoweth that his time is short.	Because of this, rejoice, [oh] heaven and those who live in them! Woe to the earth and to the sea, because the Accuser, who has great fury, has come down to them, knowing he has a short time."
13	And when the dragon saw that he was cast unto the earth, he persecuted the woman which brought forth the man child.	And when the dragon saw that he was cast out upon the earth, he persecuted the woman who brought forth the male child.	And when the dragon saw that he was thrown on the earth, he persecuted the woman who gave birth to the male child.
14	And to the woman were given two wings of a great eagle, that she might fly into the wilderness, into her place, where she is nourished for a time, and times, and half a time, from the face of the serpent.	And to the woman were given the two wings of the great eagle, that she might fly into the wilderness, to her place; where she is nourished a time and times and half a time, from the face of the serpent.	And two wings of a large eagle were given to the woman, so that she would fly to the wilderness to her place to be fed there [for] a time, times, and half of a time, from before the face of the serpent.
15	And the serpent cast out of his mouth water as a flood after the woman, that he might cause her to be carried away of the flood.	And the serpent ejected from his mouth waters like a river, after the woman, that he might cause her to be carried away by the flood.	And the serpent threw water as a river out of his mouth after the woman, so that the water would cause her to be carried away.

Parallel Translations

	KJV	Murdock	Magiera

REVELATION Chapter 12

	KJV	Murdock	Magiera
16	And the earth helped the woman, and the earth opened her mouth, and swallowed up the flood which the dragon cast out of his mouth.	And the earth helped the woman: and the earth opened its mouth, and drank up the flood which the serpent ejected from his mouth.	And the earth helped the woman and the earth opened its mouth and swallowed the river that the dragon threw out of its mouth.
17	And the dragon was wroth with the woman, and went to make war with the remnant of her seed, which keep the commandments of God, and have the testimony of Jesus Christ.	And the dragon was enraged against the woman; and he went to make war upon the residue of her seed, who keep the commandments of God, and have the testimony of Jesus.	And the dragon was furious about the woman and he went to wage war with the rest of her seed, those who keep the commandments of God and have the testimony of Jesus.

Chapter 13

	KJV	Murdock	Magiera
1	And I stood upon the sand of the sea, and saw a beast rise up out of the sea, having seven heads and ten horns, and upon his horns ten crowns, and upon his heads the name of blasphemy.	And he stood on the sand of the sea. And I saw a beast of prey come up from the sea, having ten horns, and seven heads; and upon his horns ten diadems, and upon his heads names of blasphemy.	And I stood on the sand of the sea. And I saw a creature coming up from the sea that had ten horns and seven heads, and on his horns, ten crown headbands, and on his head, the name of blasphemy.
2	And the beast which I saw was like unto a leopard, and his feet were as the feet of a bear, and his mouth as the mouth of a lion: and the dragon gave him his power, and his seat, and great authority.	And the beast of prey which I saw, was like a leopard; and his feet like [those] of a wolf, and his mouth like the mouth of lions: and the dragon gave to him his own power and his throne, and great authority.	And the creature that I saw was like a leopard and his feet [were] like those of a bear and his mouth [was] like that of lions. And the dragon gave him his power and his throne and great authority.
3	And I saw one of his heads as it were wounded to death; and his deadly wound was healed: and all the world wondered after the beast.	And one of his heads was wounded as it were to death; and his deadly wound was healed. And all the earth wondered after the beast of prey.	And one of his heads [was] as wounded to death and the deadly wound was healed and the whole world was amazed at the creature.
4	And they worshipped the dragon which gave power unto the beast: and they worshipped the beast, saying, Who is like unto the beast? who is able to make war with him?	And they worshipped the dragon, because he had given authority to this beast of prey, and [they said], who can make war upon him?	And they worshipped the dragon who gave authority to the creature and they worshipped the creature, saying, "Who is like this creature and who is able to make war with him?"
5	And there was given unto him a mouth speaking great things and blasphemies; and power was given unto him to continue forty and two months.	And there was given to him a mouth speaking great things, and blasphemies: and authority was given him to operate forty and two months.	And a mouth was given to him for speaking great [things] and blasphemy and authority was given to him to act [for] forty-two months.
6	And he opened his mouth in blasphemy against God, to blaspheme his name, and his tabernacle, and them that dwell in heaven.	And he opened his mouth in blasphemy towards God, to blaspheme his name and his tabernacle, and them who dwell in heaven.	And he opened his mouth to blaspheme in the presence of God, to blaspheme the name and the dwelling of those who dwell in heaven.
7	And it was given unto him to make war with the saints, and to overcome them: and power was given him over all kindreds, and tongues, and nations.	And authority was given him over every tribe and people and tongue and nation: and it was given him to wage war with the saints, and to overcome them.	And it was given to him to wage war with the holy [ones] and to conquer them and authority was given to him over all the tribes and peoples and languages and nations.

	KJV	Murdock	Magiera

REVELATION *Chapter 13*

	KJV	Murdock	Magiera
8	And all that dwell upon the earth shall worship him, whose names are not written in the book of life of the Lamb slain from the foundation of the world.	And all that dwell on the earth, whose names are not written in the book of life of the Lamb slain from the foundation of the world, will worship him.	And all the inhabitants of the earth will worship him, those who are not written in the book of life of the slain Lamb before the foundations of the world.
9	If any man have an ear, let him hear.	If any one hath ears, let him hear.	He who has ears should hear.
10	He that leadeth into captivity shall go into captivity: he that killeth with the sword must be killed with the sword. Here is the patience and the faith of the saints.	If [any one] carrieth into captivity, he shall himself go into captivity; and if any one slayeth with the sword, he must be slain with the sword: here is the patience and the faith of the saints.	He who leads into captivity will go into captivity and he who kills with the sword will be killed with the sword. Here is the faith and the patience of the holy [ones].
11	And I beheld another beast coming up out of the earth; and he had two horns like a lamb, and he spake as a dragon.	And I saw another beast of prey, which came out of the earth; and he had two horns like those of a lamb, and he spoke like the dragon.	And I saw another creature coming up from the earth and he had two horns like a lamb and he was speaking as the dragon.
12	And he exerciseth all the power of the first beast before him, and causeth the earth and them which dwell therein to worship the first beast, whose deadly wound was healed.	And before him he exercised all the authority of the first beast of prey, whose deadly wound was healed.	And he will exercise all the authority of the first creature before him and he will cause the earth and those who live in it to worship the first creature, whose deadly wound was healed.
13	And he doeth great wonders, so that he maketh fire come down from heaven on the earth in the sight of men,	And he wrought great signs, even so as to make fire come down from heaven upon the earth, before men.	And he will do great signs, such as, he will make fire to come down from heaven on the earth before men.
14	And deceiveth them that dwell on the earth by the means of those miracles which he had power to do in the sight of the beast; saying to them that dwell on the earth, that they should make an image to the beast, which had the wound by a sword, and did live.	And he seduced them that dwell on the earth, to erect an image to the beast of prey who had the wound from a sword and recovered.	And he will seduce those who are living on the earth by way of the signs that are given to him to do in the presence of the creature, telling those who are living on the earth to make an image for the creature who had the wound of the sword and lived.
15	And he had power to give life unto the image of the beast, that the image of the beast should both speak, and cause that as many as would not worship the image of the beast should be killed.	And it was given him to put life into the image of the beast of prey; and to cause that all they who would not worship the image of the beast of prey, should be slain:	And it was given to him to give breath to the image of the creature and to cause all who would not worship the image of the creature to be killed,
16	And he causeth all, both small and great, rich and poor, free and bond, to receive a mark in their right hand, or in their foreheads:	and to cause that all, great and small, rich and poor, bond and free, should receive a mark on their right hands, or upon their foreheads;	and to cause all, small and great, rich and poor, lords and servants, to be given a mark on their right hands or on their foreheads,
17	And that no man might buy or sell, save he that had the mark, or the name of the beast, or the number of his name.	so that no one might be able to buy or to sell, except those who had the mark of the name of the beast of prey, or the number of his name.	so that no one could buy or sell again, except those who had the mark of the name of the creature or the number of his name.

Parallel Translations

	KJV	Murdock	Magiera
	REVELATION	*Chapter 13*	
18	Here is wisdom. Let him that hath understanding count the number of the beast: for it is the number of a man; and his number is Six hundred threescore and six.	Here is wisdom: let him that hath intelligence, compute the number of the beast of prey; for it is the number of a man: and its number is six hundred and sixty and six.	Here is wisdom. And he who has understanding should count the number of the creature, for it is the number of a man, six hundred and sixty-six.
	Chapter 14		
1	And I looked, and, lo, a Lamb stood on the mount Sion, and with him an hundred forty and four thousand, having his Father's name written in their foreheads.	And I looked, and behold, a Lamb stood on mount Zion; and with him the number of a hundred and forty and four thousand, having his name and the name of his Father written upon their foreheads.	And I saw, and behold, a lamb was standing on the mountain of Zion and with him [were] one hundred and forty-four thousand who had his name and the name of his Father written on their foreheads.
2	And I heard a voice from heaven, as the voice of many waters, and as the voice of a great thunder: and I heard the voice of harpers harping with their harps:	And I heard a sound from heaven, as the sound of many waters, and as the sound of great thunder; and the sound which I heard, was like that of harpers striking on their harps.	And I heard a sound from heaven as the sound of many waters and as the sound of great thunder. The sound that I heard [was] as a harpist who strikes on his harps.
3	And they sung as it were a new song before the throne, and before the four beasts, and the elders: and no man could learn that song but the hundred and forty and four thousand, which were redeemed from the earth.	And they sang a new song before the throne, and before the four Animals and the Elders: and no one was able to learn that song, except the hundred and forty and four thousand who were redeemed from the earth.	And they were praising as a new praise song before the throne and before the four living creatures and before the elders. And no one was able to learn the praise song, except the one hundred and forty-four thousand purchased [ones] from the earth.
4	These are they which were not defiled with women; for they are virgins. These are they which follow the Lamb whithersoever he goeth. These were redeemed from among men, being the firstfruits unto God and to the Lamb.	These are they who have not defiled themselves with women, for they are virgins. These are they who followed the Lamb, whithersoever he went. These have been redeemed by Jesus from among men, the first fruits to God and the Lamb.	These are they who have not defiled themselves with women, for they are virgins, they who followed the Lamb everywhere he would go. These were purchased from mankind, the first[fruit] to God and to the Lamb,
5	And in their mouth was found no guile: for they are without fault before the throne of God.	And in their mouth was found, no falsehood; for they are without faults.	in whose mouth falsehood was not found, for they are without blemish.
6	And I saw another angel fly in the midst of heaven, having the everlasting gospel to preach unto them that dwell on the earth, and to every nation, and kindred, and tongue, and people,	And I saw another angel flying in heaven: and with blood, he had the everlasting gospel, to proclaim to dwellers on the earth, and to every nation and tribe and tongue and people;	And I saw another angel flying in the middle of heaven and he had the everlasting gospel with him to preach to the inhabitants of the earth and to all the people and nations and tribes and language[s],
7	Saying with a loud voice, Fear God, and give glory to him; for the hour of his judgment is come: and worship him that made heaven, and earth, and the sea, and the fountains of waters.	saying with a loud voice, Worship God, and give glory to him; because the hour of his judgment is come; and adore ye Him, who made heaven and earth, and the sea, and the fountains of water.	saying with a loud voice, "Fear God and give him glory, because the hour of his judgment has come, and worship him who made heaven and earth and the sea and the fountains of waters."

Parallel Translations

	KJV	*Murdock*	*Magiera*
REVELATION	*Chapter 14*		
8	And there followed another angel, saying, Babylon is fallen, is fallen, that great city, because she made all nations drink of the wine of the wrath of her fornication.	And another, a second angel followed him, saying: Fallen, fallen is Babylon the great, which made all nations drink of the wine of the rage of her whoredom.	And another, a second [angel], followed him and said, "Babylon, the great, has fallen, has fallen, she who gave all the nations to drink of the fury of her fornication."
9	And the third angel followed them, saying with a loud voice, If any man worship the beast and his image, and receive his mark in his forehead, or in his hand,	And another, a third angel followed them, saying with a loud voice: If any man shall worship the beast of prey and its image, and shall receive its mark upon his forehead or on his hand,	And another, a third angel, followed them, saying with a loud voice, "He who worshipped the creature and his image and took his mark on his forehead
10	The same shall drink of the wine of the wrath of God, which is poured out without mixture into the cup of his indignation; and he shall be tormented with fire and brimstone in the presence of the holy angels, and in the presence of the Lamb:	he also shall drink of the wine of the wrath of God, which is poured undiluted into the cup of his indignation, and shall be tormented with fire and sulphur, before the holy angels, and before the throne.	will also drink of the wine of the fury of the LORD that is poured without mixture into the cup of his anger. And he will be tormented with fire and with sulfur before the holy angels and before the Lamb
11	And the smoke of their torment ascendeth up for ever and ever: and they have no rest day nor night, who worship the beast and his image, and whosoever receiveth the mark of his name.	And the smoke of their torment ascendeth up for ever and ever; and there is no rest, by day or by night, to those that worship the beast of prey and its image.	and the smoke of their torment will rise forever and ever. And they will not have relief, day or night, those who were worshipping the creature and his image and who took the mark of his name."
12	Here is the patience of the saints: here are they that keep the commandments of God, and the faith of Jesus.	Here is the patience of the saints, who keep the commandments of God, and the faith of Jesus.	Here is the patience of the holy [ones], who keep the commandments of God and the faith of Jesus.
13	And I heard a voice from heaven saying unto me, Write, Blessed are the dead which die in the Lord from henceforth: Yea, saith the Spirit, that they may rest from their labours; and their works do follow them.	And I heard a voice from heaven, saying: Write, Blessed are the dead that die in the Lord, henceforth: yes, saith the Spirit, that they may rest from their toils; for their deeds do accompany them.	And I heard a voice from heaven saying, "Write. Blessed [are] the dead who depart in our Lord from now on. 'Yes,' says the Spirit, because they will rest from their labors."
14	And I looked, and behold a white cloud, and upon the cloud one sat like unto the Son of man, having on his head a golden crown, and in his hand a sharp sickle.	And I looked, and lo, a white cloud; and upon the cloud sat one who was like the Son of man; and on his head was a crown of gold, and in his hand a sharp sickle.	And behold, [there was] a white cloud and on the cloud sat [one] like the Son of Man and he had on his head a crown of gold and in his hand [was] a sharp sickle.
15	And another angel came out of the temple, crying with a loud voice to him that sat on the cloud, Thrust in thy sickle, and reap: for the time is come for thee to reap; for the harvest of the earth is ripe.	And another angel came out of the temple, crying with a loud voice, to him that sat on the cloud.	And another angel came out from the temple and cried out with a loud voice to him who sat on the cloud, "Send your sickle and harvest, because the hour to harvest has come."
16	And he that sat on the cloud thrust in his sickle on the earth; and the earth was reaped.	And he thrust his sickle over the earth; and the earth was reaped.	And that [one] who sat on the cloud cast out his sickle on the earth and the earth was harvested.

	KJV	Murdock	Magiera
	REVELATION *Chapter 14*		
17	And another angel came out of the temple which is in heaven, he also having a sharp sickle.	And another angel came out of the temple that is in heaven, having also a sharp sickle.	And another angel came out from the temple that is in heaven and a sharp sickle was on him.
18	And another angel came out from the altar, which had power over fire; and cried with a loud cry to him that had the sharp sickle, saying, Thrust in thy sharp sickle, and gather the clusters of the vine of the earth; for her grapes are fully ripe.	And another angel came out from the altar, having authority over fire. And he cried with a loud voice, to him who had the sharp sickle, saying: Thrust in thy sickle which is sharp, and gather the clusters of the vineyard of the earth, because the grapes of the earth are ripe.	And another angel came out from the altar, who had authority over fire and cried out with a loud voice to him who had the sharp sickle, "Send your sharp sickle and gather the clusters of the vineyard of the earth, because of the ripeness of her grapes."
19	And the angel thrust in his sickle into the earth, and gathered the vine of the earth, and cast it into the great winepress of the wrath of God.	And the angel thrust in his sickle on the earth, and gathered the vintage of the earth, and cast [it] into the wine-press of the wrath of the great God.	And the angel cast out his sickle on the earth and gathered the vineyard of the earth and he cast [it] into the great winepress of the fury of God.
20	And the winepress was trodden without the city, and blood came out of the winepress, even unto the horse bridles, by the space of a thousand and six hundred furlongs.	And the wine-press was trodden, up to the horses' bridles, for a thousand and six hundred furlongs.	And the winepress was trodden outside the city and blood came out from the winepress to the bridles of the horses for one thousand and two hundred furlongs.
	Chapter 15		
1	And I saw another sign in heaven, great and marvellous, seven angels having the seven last plagues; for in them is filled up the wrath of God.	And I saw another prodigy in heaven, great and wonderful; seven angels, having seven plagues, the last in order, because with them the wrath of God is consummated.	And I saw another sign in heaven, great and marvelous, angels who had the seven last injuries, for in them the fury of God is completed.
2	And I saw as it were a sea of glass mingled with fire: and them that had gotten the victory over the beast, and over his image, and over his mark, and over the number of his name, stand on the sea of glass, having the harps of God.	And I saw as it were, a sea of glass mixed with fire: and they, who had been victorious over the beast of prey, and over its image, and over the number of its name, were standing on the sea of glass; and they had the harps of God.	And I saw as a sea of glass mingled with fire and those who had conquered over the creature and over his image and over the number of his name were standing on top of the sea of glass and they had the harps of God.
3	And they sing the song of Moses the servant of God, and the song of the Lamb, saying, Great and marvellous are thy works, Lord God Almighty; just and true are thy ways, thou King of saints.	And they sing the song of Moses the servant of God, and the song of the Lamb, saying: Great and marvellous are thy deeds, Lord God Almighty; just and true are thy ways, O King of worlds.	And they were praising the praise song of Moses, the servant of God, and the praise song of the Lamb and were saying, "Great and wondrous [are] your works, LORD God Almighty, upright and true [are] your works, King of the ages.
4	Who shall not fear thee, O Lord, and glorify thy name? for thou only art holy: for all nations shall come and worship before thee; for thy judgments are made manifest.	Who shall not fear thee, O Lord, and glorify thy name? Because thou only art holy and just: Because all nations shall come and worship before thee, since thy righteousnesses have been revealed.	Who will not fear you, LORD, and glorify your name? Because you alone are innocent, because all the nations will come and will worship before you, because you are right."

Parallel Translations

REVELATION *Chapter 15*

	KJV	*Murdock*	*Magiera*
5	And after that I looked, and, behold, the temple of the tabernacle of the testimony in heaven was opened:	And after this I beheld, and the temple of the tabernacle of the testimony in heaven, was opened.	And after these [things], I looked and the temple of the tabernacle of witness was opened in heaven.
6	And the seven angels came out of the temple, having the seven plagues, clothed in pure and white linen, and having their breasts girded with golden girdles.	And the seven angels who had the seven plagues, went forth from the temple, clothed in clean splendid linen, and girded about their breast with girdles of gold.	And the seven angels came out from the temple, who had the seven injuries, being clothed with pure and shining linen cloth and girded on their breasts [with] a girdle of gold.
7	And one of the four beasts gave unto the seven angels seven golden vials full of the wrath of God, who liveth for ever and ever.	And one of the four Animals gave to those seven angels seven cups of gold, full of the wrath of God who liveth for ever and ever.	And one of the four living creatures gave to the seven angels seven bowls filled with the fury of God, who is alive forever and ever. Amen.
8	And the temple was filled with smoke from the glory of God, and from his power; and no man was able to enter into the temple, till the seven plagues of the seven angels were fulfilled.	And the temple was filled with smoke, from the glory of God and from his power; and no one was able to enter the temple, until the seven plagues of the seven angels were accomplished.	And the temple was filled with the smoke of the glory of God and with his power and there was no one who was able to enter the temple until the seven injuries of the seven angels were completed.

Chapter 16

	KJV	*Murdock*	*Magiera*
1	And I heard a great voice out of the temple saying to the seven angels, Go your ways, and pour out the vials of the wrath of God upon the earth.	And I heard a voice, which said to the seven angels: Go forth, and pour those seven cups of the wrath of God upon the earth.	And I heard a loud voice from the temple that said to the seven angels, "Go and pour the seven bowls of the fury of God on the earth."
2	And the first went, and poured out his vial upon the earth; and there fell a noisome and grievous sore upon the men which had the mark of the beast, and upon them which worshipped his image.	And the first went, and poured his cup upon the earth; and there was a malignant and painful ulcer upon those men who had the mark of the beast of prey, and who worshipped its image.	And the first went and poured his bowl on the earth and an evil and painful ulcer came on the men who had the mark of the creature and [on] those who were worshipping his image.
3	And the second angel poured out his vial upon the sea; and it became as the blood of a dead man: and every living soul died in the sea.	And the second angel poured his cup upon the sea; and it became blood, like that of a dead person; and every living soul of things in the sea, died.	And the second angel poured his bowl into the sea and the sea became as dead and every living creature died in the sea.
4	And the third angel poured out his vial upon the rivers and fountains of waters; and they became blood.	And the third angel poured his cup upon the rivers and the fountains of water; and they became blood.	And the third angel poured his bowl into the rivers and into the fountains of waters and they became blood.
5	And I heard the angel of the waters say, Thou art righteous, O Lord, which art, and wast, and shalt be, because thou hast judged thus.	And I heard the angel of the waters say: Righteous art thou, who art and who wast, and art holy; because thou hast done this judgment.	And I heard the angel of the waters saying, "You are just, who is and was, and innocent, for you have judged these,
6	For they have shed the blood of saints and prophets, and thou hast given them blood to drink; for they are worthy.	For they have shed the blood of saints and prophets; and thou hast given them blood to drink, for they deserve it.	because they have shed the blood of the prophets and the holy [ones]. And you have given them blood to drink, [which] they deserve."

Parallel Translations

	KJV	*Murdock*	*Magiera*
	REVELATION *Chapter 16*		
7	And I heard another out of the altar say, Even so, Lord God Almighty, true and righteous are thy judgments.	And I heard [one from] the altar say: Yes, Lord God Almighty: true and righteous is thy judgment.	And I heard [another] at the altar who said, "Yes, LORD God Almighty, true and just [are] your judgments."
8	And the fourth angel poured out his vial upon the sun; and power was given unto him to scorch men with fire.	And the fourth poured his cup upon the sun: and it was permitted him, to scorch men with fire.	And the fourth angel poured his bowl on the sun and it was given to him to scorch men with fire.
9	And men were scorched with great heat, and blasphemed the name of God, which hath power over these plagues: and they repented not to give him glory.	And men were scorched with great heat; and men blasphemed the name of God, who hath authority over these plagues; and they repented not, to give glory to him.	And men were scorched by the great heat and they reviled the name of God, who has authority over these injuries, and they did not repent, to give him glory.
10	And the fifth angel poured out his vial upon the seat of the beast; and his kingdom was full of darkness; and they gnawed their tongues for pain,	And the fifth poured his cup on the throne of the beast of prey; and his kingdom became darkness; and they gnawed their tongues, from pain;	And the fifth angel poured his bowl on the throne of the creature and his kingdom became dark and they were biting their tongues from pain.
11	And blasphemed the God of heaven because of their pains and their sores, and repented not of their deeds.	and they blasphemed the God of heaven, on account of their pains and their ulcers, and did not repent of their deeds.	And they reviled the name of the God of heaven because of their pains and because of their ulcers and they did not repent of their works.
12	And the sixth angel poured out his vial upon the great river Euphrates; and the water thereof was dried up, that the way of the kings of the east might be prepared.	And the sixth poured his cup upon the great river Euphrates; and its waters dried up, so that a way might be prepared for the kings from the rising of the sun.	And the sixth angel poured his bowl on the great river, Euphrates, and its water dried up to prepare the road for the kings from the east.
13	And I saw three unclean spirits like frogs come out of the mouth of the dragon, and out of the mouth of the beast, and out of the mouth of the false prophet.	And I saw [issuing] from the mouth of the dragon, and from the mouth of the beast of prey, and from the mouth of the false prophet, three unclean spirits like frogs:	And I saw [coming] out of the mouth of the dragon and out of the mouth of the creature and out of the mouth of the false prophet, three unclean spirits, like frogs,
14	For they are the spirits of devils, working miracles, which go forth unto the kings of the earth and of the whole world, to gather them to the battle of that great day of God Almighty.	(for they are the spirits of demons, who work prodigies;) and they go forth to all the kings of all the habitable world, to gather them to the battle of the great day of God Almighty.	for they are the spirits of demons that do signs, that are going against the kings of the inhabited earth to gather them for the battle of that great day of God Almighty.
15	Behold, I come as a thief. Blessed is he that watcheth, and keepeth his garments, lest he walk naked, and they see his shame.	(And lo, I come as a thief. Blessed is he that watcheth, and keepeth his garments; lest he walk naked, and they see his shame.)	Behold, he comes as a thief. Blessed [is] he who watches and keeps his garments, so that he should not walk naked and they should see his shame.
16	And he gathered them together into a place called in the Hebrew tongue Armageddon.	And they collected them together in a place called, in Hebrew, Armageddon.	And he gathered them to a place that is called Megiddo in Hebrew.
17	And the seventh angel poured out his vial into the air; and there came a great voice out of the temple of heaven, from the throne, saying, It is done.	And the seventh poured his cup on the air; and there issued a loud voice from the temple, from the throne, which said: It is done!	And the seventh angel poured his bowl into the air and a loud voice came out of the temple from before the throne that said, "It is [done]."

REVELATION *Chapter 16*

	KJV	*Murdock*	*Magiera*
18	And there were voices, and thunders, and lightnings; and there was a great earthquake, such as was not since men were upon the earth, so mighty an earthquake, and so great.	And there were lightnings, and thunders, and voices; and there was a great earthquake, the like of which there was never, since men were on the earth, such an earthquake, and so great.	And there were lightning bolts and thunderings and there was a huge earthquake, the like of which had not happened since men had been on the earth, for so great was this shaking.
19	And the great city was divided into three parts, and the cities of the nations fell: and great Babylon came in remembrance before God, to give unto her the cup of the wine of the fierceness of his wrath.	And the great city became three parts. And the city of the nations fell; and Babylon the great was remembered before God, to give her the cup of the wine of the heat of his wrath.	And the great city became three parts and the cities of the nations fell, and Babylon the great was remembered before God to give to her the cup of the wine of his fury and of his anger.
20	And every island fled away, and the mountains were not found.	And every island fled away; and the mountains were not found.	And every island fled away and the mountains were not found.
21	And there fell upon men a great hail out of heaven, every stone about the weight of a talent: and men blasphemed God because of the plague of the hail; for the plague thereof was exceeding great.	And a great hail, as it were of a talent weight, fell from heaven upon men: and the men blasphemed God, on account of the plague of hail; for the plague of it was very great.	And large hail, as a talent, came down from heaven on men and the men reviled God because of the injury of the hail, because the injury of it was very great.

Chapter 17

1	And there came one of the seven angels which had the seven vials, and talked with me, saying unto me, Come hither; I will shew unto thee the judgment of the great whore that sitteth upon many waters:	Then came one of the seven angels who have the seven cups, and talked with me, saying: Come, I will show thee the judgment of the great harlot, who sitteth upon many waters;	And one of the seven angels who had the seven bowls came and spoke with me, saying, "Follow me. I will show you the judgment of the harlot who sits on many waters,
2	With whom the kings of the earth have committed fornication, and the inhabitants of the earth have been made drunk with the wine of her fornication.	with whom the kings of the earth have practised whoredom, and the inhabitants of the earth have been inebriated with the wine of her whoredom.	with whom the kings of the earth fornicated and all the inhabitants of the earth became drunk from the wine of her fornication."
3	So he carried me away in the spirit into the wilderness: and I saw a woman sit upon a scarlet coloured beast, full of names of blasphemy, having seven heads and ten horns.	And he led me in spirit into the wilderness: and I saw a woman sitting on a red beast of prey, which was full of names of blasphemy, and had seven heads and ten horns.	And he led me to the wilderness spiritually and I saw a woman who was sitting on the red creature that was full of the names of blasphemy that had seven heads and ten horns.
4	And the woman was arrayed in purple and scarlet colour, and decked with gold and precious stones and pearls, having a golden cup in her hand full of abominations and filthiness of her fornication:	And the woman was clothed in purple and scarlet, and gilded with gold, and precious stones, and pearls; and she had a cup of gold in her hand, which was full of the pollutions and impurity of her whoredoms of the earth.	And the woman was clothed with purple and scarlet [garments] that were gilded with gold and precious stones and pearls and she had a cup of gold in her hand and it was full of the abomination and pollution of her fornication.

Parallel Translations

	KJV	*Murdock*	*Magiera*

REVELATION *Chapter 17*

	KJV	Murdock	Magiera
5	And upon her forehead was a name written, MYSTERY, BABYLON THE GREAT, THE MOTHER OF HARLOTS AND ABOMINATIONS OF THE EARTH.	And upon her forehead was the name written: Mystery: Babylon the great; the Mother of Harlots, and of the contaminations of the Earth.	And on her forehead it was written, "Mystery, Babylon the great, mother of harlots and of pollutions of the earth."
6	And I saw the woman drunken with the blood of the saints, and with the blood of the martyrs of Jesus: and when I saw her, I wondered with great admiration.	And I saw that the woman was intoxicated with the blood of the saints, and with the blood of the witnesses of Jesus. And when I saw her, I wondered with great amazement.	And I saw that the woman was drunk from the blood of the holy [ones] and from the blood of the witnesses of Jesus. And I wondered [with] great wonder when I saw her.
7	And the angel said unto me, Wherefore didst thou marvel? I will tell thee the mystery of the woman, and of the beast that carrieth her, which hath the seven heads and ten horns.	And the Angel said to me, Why dost thou wonder? I will tell thee the mystery of the woman, and of the beast of prey that beareth her, which hath the seven heads and the ten horns.	And the angel said to me, "Why do you wonder? I will tell you the mystery of the woman and of the creature that carries her that has seven heads and ten horns.
8	The beast that thou sawest was, and is not; and shall ascend out of the bottomless pit, and go into perdition: and they that dwell on the earth shall wonder, whose names were not written in the book of life from the foundation of the world, when they behold the beast that was, and is not, and yet is.	The beast of prey which thou sawest, was, and is not; and he will ascend from the abyss and go into perdition: and the dwellers on the earth, whose names are not written in the book of life from the foundation of the world, will wonder when they see the beast of prey, which was, and is not, and approacheth.	The creature that you saw was and is not [and] is going to come up from the sea and go to destruction. And [those] living on the earth will wonder, whose names are not written in the scroll of life from the foundations of the world, when they see the creature that was and is not and approaches.
9	And here is the mind which hath wisdom. The seven heads are seven mountains, on which the woman sitteth.	Here is intelligence, for him who hath wisdom. Those seven heads are the seven mountains, on which the woman sitteth.	Here [is] understanding for him who has wisdom. The seven heads are seven mountains on which the woman sits.
10	And there are seven kings: five are fallen, and one is, and the other is not yet come; and when he cometh, he must continue a short space.	And there are seven kings: of whom five have fallen, one exists, and the other hath not yet come; and when he cometh he must continue for a short time.	And there are seven kings, five have fallen and one is [and] the other has not yet come. And when he comes, he must continue [for] a little while.
11	And the beast that was, and is not, even he is the eighth, and is of the seven, and goeth into perdition.	And the beast of prey, which was and is not, is the eighth, and is from the seven, and is for perdition.	And the dragon and the creature that was and is not, even he is the eighth and is one of the seven and goes to destruction.
12	And the ten horns which thou sawest are ten kings, which have received no kingdom as yet; but receive power as kings one hour with the beast.	And the ten horns which thou sawest, are ten kings. These persons have not yet received royalty; but they receive authority, as if kings, with the beasts of prey, for one hour.	And the ten horns that you saw are ten kings who have not yet received a kingdom, but they take authority as kings [for] one hour with the creature.
13	These have one mind, and shall give their power and strength unto the beast.	They have one mind; and they will give their power and authority unto the beast of prey.	These have one will, and they give their own power and authority to the creature.

REVELATION *Chapter 17*

	KJV	Murdock	Magiera
14	These shall make war with the Lamb, and the Lamb shall overcome them: for he is Lord of lords, and King of kings: and they that are with him are called, and chosen, and faithful.	They will make war upon the Lamb; and the Lamb will vanquish them; because he is Lord of lords, and King of kings, and these with him [are] called and chosen and faithful.	These will make war with the Lamb and the Lamb will conquer them, because he is Lord of lords and King of kings and those with him [are] the called and chosen and faithful [ones]."
15	And he saith unto me, The waters which thou sawest, where the whore sitteth, are peoples, and multitudes, and nations, and tongues.	And he said to me: The waters which thou sawest, where the harlot sitteth, are peoples, and multitudes, and nations, and tongues.	And he said to me, "The waters that you saw, on which the harlot sits, are nations and multitudes and peoples and languages.
16	And the ten horns which thou sawest upon the beast, these shall hate the whore, and shall make her desolate and naked, and shall eat her flesh, and burn her with fire.	And the ten horns which thou sawest, and the beast of prey, will hate the harlot; and they will make her desolate and naked, and will eat her flesh, and burn her with fire.	And the ten horns that you saw of the creature will hate the harlot and they will make her desolate and naked and they will eat her flesh and they will burn her with fire.
17	For God hath put in their hearts to fulfil his will, and to agree, and give their kingdom unto the beast, until the words of God shall be fulfilled.	For God hath put into their hearts, to do his pleasure, and to execute one purpose, and to give their kingdom to the beast of prey, until these words of God shall be fulfilled.	For God has put in their hearts to do his will and they will do their one will and they will give their kingdom to that creature until the words of God are fulfilled.
18	And the woman which thou sawest is that great city, which reigneth over the kings of the earth.	And the woman whom thou sawest, is the great city, which hath dominion over the kings of the earth.	And the woman whom you saw [is] the great city which has dominion over the kings of the earth."

Chapter 18

	KJV	Murdock	Magiera
1	And after these things I saw another angel come down from heaven, having great power; and the earth was lightened with his glory.	After these things, I saw another angel come down from heaven; and he had great authority and the earth was illumined by his glory.	And after these [things], I saw another angel who came down from heaven who had great authority and the earth was shining from his glory.
2	And he cried mightily with a strong voice, saying, Babylon the great is fallen, is fallen, and is become the habitation of devils, and the hold of every foul spirit, and a cage of every unclean and hateful bird.	And he cried with a strong voice, saying: Fallen, fallen is Babylon the great: and hath become a cavern of demons, and the home of every unclean spirit, and the home of every unclean and hateful bird and the home of every unclean and hateful beast of prey.	And he cried out with a loud voice, "Babylon the great has fallen, has fallen, and has become a dwelling for demons and a garrison for all unclean and hateful spirits,
3	For all nations have drunk of the wine of the wrath of her fornication, and the kings of the earth have committed fornication with her, and the merchants of the earth are waxed rich through the abundance of her delicacies.	For all the nations have drunken of the wine of her wrath; and the kings of the earth have practised whoredom with her; and the merchants of the earth have been enriched by the abundance of her luxuries.	because she has mixed the wine of her fornication for all the nations, and the kings of the earth have fornicated with her and the merchants of the earth have grown rich from the power of her madness."

Parallel Translations

REVELATION Chapter 18

	KJV	Murdock	Magiera
4	And I heard another voice from heaven, saying, Come out of her, my people, that ye be not partakers of her sins, and that ye receive not of her plagues.	And I heard another voice from heaven, saying: Come ye out of her, my people; that ye may not participate in her sins, and may not partake of her plagues.	And I heard another voice from heaven, saying, "Come out from within her, my people, so that you do not share in her sins, so that you do not receive of her injuries,
5	For her sins have reached unto heaven, and God hath remembered her iniquities.	For her sins have reached up to heaven; and God hath remembered her iniquities.	because her sins have reached up to heaven and God has remembered her wicked [deeds].
6	Reward her even as she rewarded you, and double unto her double according to her works: in the cup which she hath filled fill to her double.	Recompense ye to her, as she also hath recompensed; and render to her double, according to her deeds; in the cup which she hath mixed, mix ye to her two fold.	Render to her, even as also she has rendered, and double to her double for her works. In the cup that she mixed, mix for her double.
7	How much she hath glorified herself, and lived deliciously, so much torment and sorrow give her: for she saith in her heart, I sit a queen, and am no widow, and shall see no sorrow.	As much as she pleased herself with lasciviousness, so much of anguish and sorrow give ye to her. Because she saith in her heart, I sit a queen, and am no widow, and I shall see no sorrow;	About what she glorified herself and was arrogant, likewise [give her] torment and sorrow, because in her heart, she said, 'I sit [as] a queen and I am not a widow and I will see no sorrow.'
8	Therefore shall her plagues come in one day, death, and mourning, and famine; and she shall be utterly burned with fire: for strong is the Lord God who judgeth her.	therefore, in one day, shall these her plagues come, death, and mourning, and famine; and she shall be burned with fire: for strong is the Lord God who judgeth her.	Because of this, in one day injuries will come on her, death and sorrow and famine, and she will be burned by fire, because the LORD [is] mighty who has judged her.
9	And the kings of the earth, who have committed fornication and lived deliciously with her, shall bewail her, and lament for her, when they shall see the smoke of her burning,	And the kings of the earth who committed whoredom and were lascivious with her, shall weep, and mourn, and bewail her, when they shall see the smoke of her burning,	And the kings of the earth will cry and wail over her, those who fornicated with her and were arrogant, when they see the smoke of her burning,
10	Standing afar off for the fear of her torment, saying, Alas, alas, that great city Babylon, that mighty city! for in one hour is thy judgment come.	standing afar off, from fear of her torment, [and] saying, Alas, alas! that great city Babylon, that powerful city; for in one hour is thy judgment come!	while standing away from [her] out of fear of her torment. And they will say, 'Woe, woe, woe, [to] the great city, Babylon, the powerful city, because in one hour your judgment has come!'
11	And the merchants of the earth shall weep and mourn over her; for no man buyeth their merchandise any more:	And the merchants of the earth will mourn over her, because no one purchaseth their cargo;	And the businessmen of the earth will cry and will mourn over her and there is no one who will buy their merchandise any more,
12	The merchandise of gold, and silver, and precious stones, and of pearls, and fine linen, and purple, and silk, and scarlet, and all thyine wood, and all manner vessels of ivory, and all manner vessels of most precious wood, and of brass, and iron, and marble,	no more, the cargo of gold, and silver, and precious stones, and pearls, and fine linen, and purple, and silk, and scarlet, and every aromatic wood, and all vessels of ivory, and all vessels of very precious wood, and of brass, and of iron, and of marble,	the merchandise of gold and of silver and of precious stones and of pearls and of fine linen and of purple clothing and silk of scarlet and every aromatic wood and every vessel of ivory and every vessel of precious wood and brass and iron and marble

Parallel Translations

	KJV	Murdock	Magiera

REVELATION *Chapter 18*

	KJV	Murdock	Magiera
13	And cinnamon, and odours, and ointments, and frankincense, and wine, and oil, and fine flour, and wheat, and beasts, and sheep, and horses, and chariots, and slaves, and souls of men.	and cinnamon, and amomum, and aromatics, and unguents, and frankincense, and wine, and oil, and fine flour, and wheat, and beasts of burden, and sheep, and horses, and chariots, and the bodies and souls of men.	and cinnamon and perfumes and myrrh and incense and wine and oil and fine flour and sheep and horses and chariots and the bodies and souls of men.
14	And the fruits that thy soul lusted after are departed from thee, and all things which were dainty and goodly are departed from thee, and thou shalt find them no more at all.	And the fruits which thy soul desired, have departed from thee; and all things delicious and splendid have perished from thee; and the traders in them shall obtain them no more.	And your fruit, the desire of your soul, has gone away from you and everything luxurious and celebrated has gone away from you and you will not see them any more,
15	The merchants of these things, which were made rich by her, shall stand afar off for the fear of her torment, weeping and wailing,	And they who were enriched from her, will stand afar off, for fear of her torment; and will weep and mourn,	nor find them. The businessmen of these [things], who were made rich by her, will stand away from [her] out of fear of her torment, crying and wailing
16	And saying, Alas, alas, that great city, that was clothed in fine linen, and purple, and scarlet, and decked with gold, and precious stones, and pearls!	saying: Alas, alas! that great city, which was clothed in fine linen, and purple, and scarlet, and gilded with gold, and precious stones, and pearls; because, in one hour, such riches are laid waste.	and saying, 'Woe, woe, [to] the great city that was clothed with fine linen and purple and scarlet [clothes] that were gilded with gold and precious stones and pearls,
17	For in one hour so great riches is come to nought. And every shipmaster, and all the company in ships, and sailors, and as many as trade by sea, stood afar off,	And every pilot, and every navigator to the place, and the sailors, and all who do business by sea) stood afar off,	because in one hour wealth like this is laid waste!' And all the masters of ships and all those traveling to places in ships and the sailors and all those who do business by sea stood a distance away.
18	And cried when they saw the smoke of her burning, saying, What city is like unto this great city!	and cried, when they saw the smoke of her burning, saying: What [other] is like this great city!	And they cried over it as they were watching the smoke of its burning and saying, 'What [city] is like the great city?'
19	And they cast dust on their heads, and cried, weeping and wailing, saying, Alas, alas, that great city, wherein were made rich all that had ships in the sea by reason of her costliness! for in one hour is she made desolate.	And they cast dust on their heads, and cried, weeping, and mourning, and saying: Alas, alas that great city, in which all that have ships in the sea became rich, by her preciousness; for in one hour she hath become desolate.	And they threw dust on their heads and cried out, crying and wailing and saying, 'Woe, woe, [to] the great city, in which those who had ship[s] in the sea became rich from her greatness, for in one hour she is devastated!'
20	Rejoice over her, thou heaven, and ye holy apostles and prophets; for God hath avenged you on her.	Rejoice over her, O heaven, and ye Angels, and Legates, and Prophets; because God judgeth your cause with her.	Exult over her, [oh] heaven and holy [ones] and apostles and prophets, because God has judged your judgment on her."

REVELATION Chapter 18

	KJV	Murdock	Magiera
21	And a mighty angel took up a stone like a great millstone, and cast it into the sea, saying, Thus with violence shall that great city Babylon be thrown down, and shall be found no more at all.	And an angel took up a stone like a great millstone, and cast it into the sea, saying: So shall Babylon, the great city, be thrown down with violence, and shall no more be found:	And one of the mighty angels took a huge stone like a millstone and threw [it] into the sea and said, "So with violence Babylon, the great city, will be thrown down and you will not find [it] any more.
22	And the voice of harpers, and musicians, and of pipers, and trumpeters, shall be heard no more at all in thee; and no craftsman, of whatsoever craft he be, shall be found any more in thee; and the sound of a millstone shall be heard no more at all in thee;	and the voice of harpers and musicians and pipers and trumpeters, shall no more be heard in thee; and no artificer of any trade, shall be found any more in thee.	And the sound of the harp and of the shofar and of all kinds of music and trumpeters will not be heard in you any more.
23	And the light of a candle shall shine no more at all in thee; and the voice of the bridegroom and of the bride shall be heard no more at all in thee: for thy merchants were the great men of the earth; for by thy sorceries were all nations deceived.	And the light of a candle, shall not be seen in thee; and the voice of a bridegroom and bride, shall no more be heard in thee: for thy merchants were the great men of the earth, because all nations were seduced by thy sorceries.	And the light of the lamp will not be seen in you any more and the voice of the bridegroom and the voice of the bride will not be heard in you any more, because your merchants were the great [ones] of the earth, because you seduced all the nations with your enchantments,
24	And in her was found the blood of prophets, and of saints, and of all that were slain upon the earth.	And in her was found the blood of prophets and saints, and of all those that have been slain on the earth.	and the blood of the prophets and the holy [ones] who were killed on the earth was found in her."

Chapter 19

	KJV	Murdock	Magiera
1	And after these things I heard a great voice of much people in heaven, saying, Alleluia; Salvation, and glory, and honour, and power, unto the Lord our God:	And after these things, I heard a loud voice of a great multitude in heaven, saying: Hallelujah: Deliverance, and strength, and glory, and honor, unto our God:	And after these [things], I heard a loud voice of a large multitude in heaven who were saying, "Hallelujah! Deliverance and glory and power [be] to our God,
2	For true and righteous are his judgments: for he hath judged the great whore, which did corrupt the earth with her fornication, and hath avenged the blood of his servants at her hand.	for, true and righteous are his judgments; for he hath judged that great harlot, who corrupted the earth with her whoredom; and hath avenged the blood of his servants at her hand.	because true and upright [are] his judgments, because he has judged the great harlot who has corrupted the earth with her fornication and has avenged the blood of his servants from her hands."
3	And again they said, Alleluia. And her smoke rose up for ever and ever.	And again they said: Hallelujah: and her smoke ascendeth up for ever and ever.	A second [time] they said, "Hallelujah!" And her smoke went up, forever and ever.
4	And the four and twenty elders and the four beasts fell down and worshipped God that sat on the throne, saying, Amen; Alleluia.	And the twenty-four Elders fell down, and the four Animals, and worshipped God who sitteth on the throne, saying: Amen: Hallelujah!	And the twenty-four elders and the four living creatures fell down and worshipped our God who sat on the throne and said, "Amen. Hallelujah!"

Parallel Translations

	KJV	*Murdock*	*Magiera*

REVELATION *Chapter 19*

	KJV	Murdock	Magiera
5	And a voice came out of the throne, saying, Praise our God, all ye his servants, and ye that fear him, both small and great.	And a voice came forth from the throne, saying: Praise our God, all ye his servants; and such as fear him, small and great.	And a voice [came] from the throne saying, "Praise our God, all his servants and all those who reverence his name, the small with the great."
6	And I heard as it were the voice of a great multitude, and as the voice of many waters, and as the voice of mighty thunderings, saying, Alleluia: for the Lord God omnipotent reigneth.	And I heard, as it were the voice of a great multitude, and as the voice of many waters, and as the voice of heavy thunders, saying: Hallelujah; for our Lord God, Omnipotent, reigneth.	And I heard a voice, as of a large crowd and as the voice of many waters and as the voice of mighty thunderings, saying, "Hallelujah, because the LORD God Almighty reigns!
7	Let us be glad and rejoice, and give honour to him: for the marriage of the Lamb is come, and his wife hath made herself ready.	Let us rejoice and exult, and give glory to him: for the marriage supper of the Lamb hath come, and his bride hath made herself ready.	We are glad and rejoice. We will give him praise, because the marriage feast of the Lamb has come and his wife has made herself ready."
8	And to her was granted that she should be arrayed in fine linen, clean and white: for the fine linen is the righteousness of saints.	And it was granted her to be clothed in fine linen, bright and clean: for fine linen is the righteousnesses of the saints.	And it was given to her to be clothed with fine linen, clean and shining, for the fine linen represents the straight ways of the holy [ones].
9	And he saith unto me, Write, Blessed are they which are called unto the marriage supper of the Lamb. And he saith unto me, These are the true sayings of God.	And he said to me, Write; Blessed are they who are called to the supper of the marriage feast of the Lamb. And he said to me, These my [sayings] are the true words of God.	And they said to me, "Write. Blessed [are] those who are invited [ones] to the supper of the marriage feast of the Lamb." And he said to me, "These are the true words of God."
10	And I fell at his feet to worship him. And he said unto me, See thou do it not: I am thy fellowservant, and of thy brethren that have the testimony of Jesus: worship God: for the testimony of Jesus is the spirit of prophecy.	And I fell at his feet, to worship him. And he said to me, See, [thou do it] not; I am thy fellow-servant, and of those thy brethren who have the testimony of Jesus. Worship ye God: for the testimony of Jesus is the spirit of prophecy.	And I fell at his feet and worshipped him. And he said to me, "No. I am your fellow-servant and one of your brothers, those who have the testimony of Jesus. Worship God abundantly, for the testimony of Jesus is the Spirit of prophecy."
11	And I saw heaven opened, and behold a white horse; and he that sat upon him was called Faithful and True, and in righteousness he doth judge and make war.	And I saw heaven opened: and lo, a white horse; and he that sat on it, is called Faithful and True: and in righteousness he judgeth, and maketh war.	And I saw heaven opened, and behold, [I saw] a white stallion and he who sat on it was called faithful and true and with uprightness he judges and makes war.
12	His eyes were as a flame of fire, and on his head were many crowns; and he had a name written, that no man knew, but he himself.	His eyes [were] like a flame of fire, and on his head [were] many diadems; and he had names inscribed; and the name which was written on him, no one knew, except himself.	And his eyes [were] like a flame of fire and on his head [were] many crown headbands. And he had a name written [on him] that no [one] knew, except he.
13	And he was clothed with a vesture dipped in blood: and his name is called The Word of God.	And he was clothed with a vesture sprinkled with blood; and his name is called, The Word of God.	And he was clothed with a garment dipped in blood and his name was called "The Word of God."

REVELATION *Chapter 19*

	KJV	*Murdock*	*Magiera*
14	And the armies which were in heaven followed him upon white horses, clothed in fine linen, white and clean.	And the soldiery of heaven followed him, on white horses, clad in garments of fine linen, pure [and] white.	And the armies in heaven were following him on white horses and were clothed with fine linen, white and pure.
15	And out of his mouth goeth a sharp sword, that with it he should smite the nations: and he shall rule them with a rod of iron: and he treadeth the winepress of the fierceness and wrath of Almighty God.	And from his mouth issued a sharp two-edged sword, that with it he could smite the nations; and he will rule the nations with a rod of iron; and he will tread the wine-press of the wrath of God Almighty.	And from their mouth[s] a sharp sword came out, with which to kill the nations. And he will rule them with a rod of iron and he will tread the winepress of the anger of God Almighty.
16	And he hath on his vesture and on his thigh a name written, KING OF KINGS, AND LORD OF LORDS.	And he hath upon his vesture and upon his thigh the words written: King of kings, and Lord of lords.	And he had a name written on his garments, on his thighs, "King of kings and Lord of lords."
17	And I saw an angel standing in the sun; and he cried with a loud voice, saying to all the fowls that fly in the midst of heaven, Come and gather yourselves together unto the supper of the great God;	And I saw an angel standing in the sun; and he cried with a loud voice, saying to all the fowls that fly in the midst of heaven: Come ye, assemble unto this great supper of God;	And I saw another angel standing in the sun and he cried out with a loud voice and said to the bird[s] that fly in the middle of heaven, "Come, gather together for the great supper of God,
18	That ye may eat the flesh of kings, and the flesh of captains, and the flesh of mighty men, and the flesh of horses, and of them that sit on them, and the flesh of all men, both free and bond, both small and great.	that ye may eat the flesh of kings, and the flesh of captains of thousands, and the flesh of valiant men, and the flesh of horses and of those who sit on them, and the flesh of all the free-born and of slaves, and of the small and the great.	that you may eat the flesh of the kings and the flesh of the rulers of thousands and the flesh of the powerful [ones] and the flesh of the horses and of those who sit on them and the flesh of the free [men] and of the servants and of the small and of the great."
19	And I saw the beast, and the kings of the earth, and their armies, gathered together to make war against him that sat on the horse, and against his army.	And I saw the beast of prey, and the kings of the earth, and their warriors, that they assembled to wage battle with him who sat on the [white] horse, and with his warriors.	And I saw the creature and his hosts and the kings of the earth and their soldiers gathering to wage war with him who sits on the stallion and with his armies.
20	And the beast was taken, and with him the false prophet that wrought miracles before him, with which he deceived them that had received the mark of the beast, and them that worshipped his image. These both were cast alive into a lake of fire burning with brimstone.	And the beast of prey was captured, and the false prophet that was with him, who did those prodigies before him, whereby he seduced them who had received the mark of the beast of prey and who worshipped his image. And they were both cast alive into the lake of fire, which burneth with sulphur.	And the creature was captured and the false prophet with him, who performed signs before him by which he seduced those who received the mark of the creature and those who worshipped his image. And both of them went down and they were thrown into the lake of burning fire and of sulfur.
21	And the remnant were slain with the sword of him that sat upon the horse, which sword proceeded out of his mouth: and all the fowls were filled with their flesh.	And the rest were slain by the sword of him that sat on the horse, by that [sword] which issueth from his mouth: and all the fowls were satiated with their flesh.	And the rest were killed by the sword of him who sat on the stallion, by that [sword] that came out of his mouth, and every bird of prey was full of their flesh.

Parallel Translations

	KJV	*Murdock*	*Magiera*
	REVELATION *Chapter 20*		
1	And I saw an angel come down from heaven, having the key of the bottomless pit and a great chain in his hand.	And I saw an angel that descended from heaven, having the key of the abyss, and a great chain in his hand.	And I saw another angel that came down from heaven, who had the key of the abyss and a great chain in his hand.
2	And he laid hold on the dragon, that old serpent, which is the Devil, and Satan, and bound him a thousand years,	And he seized the dragon, the old serpent, who is the Deceiver and Satan, who seduced the whole habitable world: and he bound him a thousand years.	And he grabbed the dragon, the ancient serpent, who is the Accuser and Satan, and bound him [for] one thousand years.
3	And cast him into the bottomless pit, and shut him up, and set a seal upon him, that he should deceive the nations no more, till the thousand years should be fulfilled: and after that he must be loosed a little season.	And he cast him into the abyss, and closed and sealed upon him; so that he might deceive the nations no more, until these thousand years shall be completed: but after that, he will be loosed for a little time.	And he threw him into the abyss and closed and sealed the top over him, so that he would not seduce all the nations any more. After these [things], he must release him [for] a short time.
4	And I saw thrones, and they sat upon them, and judgment was given unto them: and I saw the souls of them that were beheaded for the witness of Jesus, and for the word of God, and which had not worshipped the beast, neither his image, neither had received his mark upon their foreheads, or in their hands; and they lived and reigned with Christ a thousand years.	And I saw thrones, and [persons] sat on them, and judgment was given to them, and to the souls that were beheaded for the testimony of Jesus and for the word of God: and these are they who had not worshipped the beast of prey, nor its image, neither had they received the mark upon their forehead or on their hand, and they lived and reigned with their Messiah those thousand years.	And I saw seats and they sat on them and judgment was given to them. And [I saw] the souls, those who were cut off because of the testimony of Jesus and because of the word of God and those who did not worship the creature nor his image, neither received the mark on their foreheads or on their hands, that they lived and reigned with the Messiah [for] one thousand years.
5	But the rest of the dead lived not again until the thousand years were finished. This is the first resurrection.	This is the first resurrection.	And this is the first resurrection.
6	Blessed and holy is he that hath part in the first resurrection: on such the second death hath no power, but they shall be priests of God and of Christ, and shall reign with him a thousand years.	Blessed and holy is he that hath part in this first resurrection: over them the second death hath no dominion; but they shall be, [nay] are, priests of God and of his Messiah; and they will reign with him the thousand years.	Blessed and holy is he who has a part in the first resurrection. And on them the second death has no authority, but they will be priests of God and of Christ and will reign with him [for] one thousand years.
7	And when the thousand years are expired, Satan shall be loosed out of his prison,	And when these thousand years shall be completed, Satan will be released from his prison;	And when one thousand years is completed, Satan will be released from his imprisonment
8	And shall go out to deceive the nations which are in the four quarters of the earth, Gog and Magog, to gather them together to battle: the number of whom is as the sand of the sea.	and will go forth to seduce the nations that are in the four corners of the earth, Gog and Magog; and to assemble them for battle, whose number is as the sand of the sea.	and will go out to seduce all the nations in the four corners of the earth, to Gog and to Magog, and to assemble them for battle, whose number [is] as the sand of the sea.

REVELATION *Chapter 20*

	KJV	Murdock	Magiera
9	And they went up on the breadth of the earth, and compassed the camp of the saints about, and the beloved city: and fire came down from God out of heaven, and devoured them.	And they went up on the breadth of the earth, and encompassed the camp of the saints, and the beloved city. And fire came down from God out of heaven, and consumed them.	And they went up on the space of the land and surrounded the city of the camp of the holy [ones] and the beloved city and fire came down from heaven from God and consumed them.
10	And the devil that deceived them was cast into the lake of fire and brimstone, where the beast and the false prophet are, and shall be tormented day and night for ever and ever.	And the Accuser who seduced them, was cast into the lake of fire and sulphur, where also were the beast of prey and the false prophet: and they shall be tormented, day and night, for ever and ever.	And the Accuser, their seducer, was thrown into the lake of fire and sulfur, where the creature and the false prophet [were]. And they will be tormented, day and night, forever and ever.
11	And I saw a great white throne, and him that sat on it, from whose face the earth and the heaven fled away; and there was found no place for them.	And I saw a great white throne, and Him who sitteth thereon; from whose presence the earth and heaven fled away, and this their place was not found.	And I saw a large white throne and him who sat on top of it, from before whose face the earth and heaven fled away, and a place was not found for them.
12	And I saw the dead, small and great, stand before God; and the books were opened: and another book was opened, which is the book of life: and the dead were judged out of those things which were written in the books, according to their works.	And I saw the dead, great and small standing before the throne; and the books were opened; and another book was opened, which is [the book] of life. And the dead were judged from the things written in the books, according to their deeds.	And I saw the dead, great and small, who stood before the throne, and the scrolls were opened. And another scroll was opened that is [the one] of judgment, and the dead were judged from those [things] that were written in the scroll, according to their works.
13	And the sea gave up the dead which were in it; and death and hell delivered up the dead which were in them: and they were judged every man according to their works.	And the sea gave up the dead in it; and death and the grave gave up the dead in them. And they were judged, each one according to his deeds.	And the sea gave up the dead in it and death and Sheol gave up the dead with them and each one of them was judged according to their works.
14	And death and hell were cast into the lake of fire. This is the second death.	And death and the grave were cast into the lake of fire. This is the second death, [namely,] this lake of fire.	And death and Sheol were thrown into the lake of fire. This is the second death.
15	And whosoever was not found written in the book of life was cast into the lake of fire.	And if any one was not found enrolled in the book of life, he was cast into this lake of fire.	And he who was not found inscribed in the book of life was thrown into the lake of fire.

Chapter 21

	KJV	Murdock	Magiera
1	And I saw a new heaven and a new earth: for the first heaven and the first earth were passed away; and there was no more sea.	And I saw new heavens, and a new earth: for the former heaven and the former earth had passed away: and the sea was no more.	And I saw a new heaven and a new earth, for the former heaven and the former earth had gone away and there was no more sea.
2	And I John saw the holy city, new Jerusalem, coming down from God out of heaven, prepared as a bride adorned for her husband.	And I saw the holy city, the New Jerusalem, descending from God out of heaven, prepared like a bride adorned for her husband.	And I saw the holy city, the new Jerusalem, come down from heaven from God, prepared as a bride adorned for her husband.

REVELATION *Chapter 21*

	KJV	*Murdock*	*Magiera*
3	And I heard a great voice out of heaven saying, Behold, the tabernacle of God is with men, and he will dwell with them, and they shall be his people, and God himself shall be with them, and be their God.	And I heard a great voice from heaven, which said: Behold, the tabernacle of God is with men; and he dwelleth with them: they will be his people; and God will be with them, a God to them.	And I heard a loud voice from heaven that said, "Behold, the dwelling of God [is] with men, and he [will] live with them and they will be his own people and God is with them and will be a God to them.
4	And God shall wipe away all tears from their eyes; and there shall be no more death, neither sorrow, nor crying, neither shall there be any more pain: for the former things are passed away.	And every tear will be wiped from their eyes; and there will no more be death, nor mourning, nor wailing; nor shall pain be any more; because the former things are passed away.	And he will wipe all tears from their eyes and there will no longer be death, neither sorrow, nor crying, nor will there be any more pain on account of him,"
5	And he that sat upon the throne said, Behold, I make all things new. And he said unto me, Write: for these words are true and faithful.	And He who sat on the throne, said: Behold, I make all things new. And he said: Write; because these are the faithful and true words of God.	and it went away. And he who sat on the throne said to me, "Behold, I am making all [things] new." And he said to me, "Write. These words are faithful and true."
6	And he said unto me, It is done. I am Alpha and Omega, the beginning and the end. I will give unto him that is athirst of the fountain of the water of life freely.	And he said to me: I am Alpha and Omega, the Beginning and the Completion: to him who thirsteth, will I give of the fountain of living water, gratis.	And he said to me, "I am Aleph and I am Tau, the beginning and the completion. To the thirsty, I will give from the fountain of living water, freely.
7	He that overcometh shall inherit all things; and I will be his God, and he shall be my son.	He that overcometh, shall inherit these things; and I will be his God, and he shall be my son.	And he who overcomes will inherit these [things] and I will be God to him and he will be a son to me.
8	But the fearful, and unbelieving, and the abominable, and murderers, and whoremongers, and sorcerers, and idolaters, and all liars, shall have their part in the lake which burneth with fire and brimstone: which is the second death.	But to the timid, and the unbelieving, and to the sinful, and polluted, and to manslayers, and whoremongers, and sorcerers, and idolaters, and to all false persons, their portion shall be in the lake that burneth with fire and sulphur, which is the second death.	But for the fearful and the unbelieving and the wicked and the defiled and murderers and sorcerers and fornicators and idolaters and all liars, their portion [will be] in the lake burning with fire and sulfur, which is the second death."
9	And there came unto me one of the seven angels which had the seven vials full of the seven last plagues, and talked with me, saying, Come hither, I will shew thee the bride, the Lamb's wife.	And there came one of those seven angels, who have the seven cups filled with the seven last plagues, and talked with me, saying: Come, I will show thee the bride, the wife of the Lamb.	And one of the seven angels came, who had the seven bowls filled with the seven last injuries, and spoke with me, saying, "Come, I will show you the bride, the wife of the Lamb."
10	And he carried me away in the spirit to a great and high mountain, and shewed me that great city, the holy Jerusalem, descending out of heaven from God,	And he bore me away in the spirit, to a mountain great and high, and he showed me the holy city, Jerusalem, descending out of heaven from God;	And he carried me spiritually to a great and high mountain and showed me the holy city, Jerusalem, coming down out of heaven from God.
11	Having the glory of God: and her light was like unto a stone most precious, even like a jasper stone, clear as crystal;	in which was the glory of God, as a brilliant light, and resembling a very precious gem; like a jasper stone, resembling crystal.	And it had the glory of God and its light [was] like a precious stone such as jasper, like crystal.

Parallel Translations

	KJV	*Murdock*	*Magiera*

REVELATION *Chapter 21*

	KJV	Murdock	Magiera
12	And had a wall great and high, and had twelve gates, and at the gates twelve angels, and names written thereon, which are the names of the twelve tribes of the children of Israel:	And it had a wall great and lofty, which had twelve gates, and names inscribed on them, which are the names of the twelve tribes of the children of Israel.	And it had a great and high wall and it had twelve gates. And on the gates [were] twelve angels and the names written on them were the names of the twelve tribes of Israel.
13	On the east three gates; on the north three gates; on the south three gates; and on the west three gates.	On the east, three gates; on the north, three gates; [on the south, three gates; and on the west, three gates].	On the east [were] three gates and on the north [were] three gates and on the south [were] three gates and on the west [were] three gates.
14	And the wall of the city had twelve foundations, and in them the names of the twelve apostles of the Lamb.	And the wall of the city had twelve foundations, and upon them the twelve names of the twelve legates of the Lamb.	And the wall of the city had twelve foundations and on them [were] the twelve names of the apostles of the Son.
15	And he that talked with me had a golden reed to measure the city, and the gates thereof, and the wall thereof.	And he that talked with me, had a measure, a golden reed; so that he could measure the city, and its gates, and its wall.	And that [one] who was speaking with me had a measuring rod of gold with him to measure the city and its wall.
16	And the city lieth foursquare, and the length is as large as the breadth: and he measured the city with the reed, twelve thousand furlongs. The length and the breadth and the height of it are equal.	And the city stood up four square; and its length was the same as its breadth. And he measured the city with the reed, to twelve furlongs of twelve thousand; and the length and the breadth and the height of it were [all] equal.	And the city was laid out four-square and its length [was] as its width. And he measured the city with the rod, about twelve thousand furlongs. Its length and its width and its height were equal.
17	And he measured the wall thereof, an hundred and forty and four cubits, according to the measure of a man, that is, of the angel.	And he measured its wall, a hundred and forty and four measures of the cubits of a man, that is, of the angel.	And he measured its wall, one hundred and forty-four cubits, by the measure of a man, that is, of the angel.
18	And the building of the wall of it was of jasper: and the city was pure gold, like unto clear glass.	And the structure of its wall [was of] jasper; and the city was of pure gold, like pure glass.	And the structure of its wall [was of] jasper and the city [was] of pure gold with the appearance of pure glass.
19	And the foundations of the wall of the city were garnished with all manner of precious stones. The first foundation was jasper; the second, sapphire; the third, a chalcedony; the fourth, an emerald;	And the foundations of the wall of the city were adorned with every precious stone. The first foundation, a jasper; the second, a sapphire; the third, a chalcedony; the fourth, an emerald;	And the foundations of the wall of the city were adorned with precious stones. And the first foundation [was] jasper and the second, sapphire and the third, chalcedony and the fourth, emerald
20	The fifth, sardonyx; the sixth, sardius; the seventh, chrysolite; the eighth, beryl; the ninth, a topaz; the tenth, a chrysoprasus; the eleventh, a jacinth; the twelfth, an amethyst.	the fifth, a sardonyx; the sixth, a sardius; the seventh, a chrysolite; the eighth, a beryl; the ninth, a topaz; the tenth, a chrysoprasus; the eleventh, a jacinth; the twelfth, an amethyst.	and the fifth, sardius and onyx and the sixth, sardius and the seventh, chrysolite and the eighth, beryl and the ninth, topaz and the tenth, chrysoprasus, the eleventh, jacinth, the twelfth, amethyst.
21	And the twelve gates were twelve pearls; every several gate was of one pearl: and the street of the city was pure gold, as it were transparent glass.	And the twelve gates [were] twelve pearls; each [pearl] one gate, and each [gate] one pearl: and the broad street of the city was pure gold, like brilliant glass.	And the twelve gates and the twelve pearls, one for each and every one of the gates, were from one pearl. And the broad street of the city [was] of pure gold, as though glass were in it.

Parallel Translations

	KJV	Murdock	Magiera
	REVELATION *Chapter 21*		
22	And I saw no temple therein: for the Lord God Almighty and the Lamb are the temple of it.	And I saw no temple in it; for the Lord Almighty is its temple, and the Lamb.	And I saw no temple in it, for the LORD God Almighty was its temple,
23	And the city had no need of the sun, neither of the moon, to shine in it: for the glory of God did lighten it, and the Lamb is the light thereof.	And the city hath no need of the sun or of the moon, to enlighten it; for the glory of God enlighteneth it, and the Lamb is the lamps of it.	and the Lamb. And for the city, neither the sun, nor the moon, was needed to illuminate it, for the glory of God will illuminate it and the lamp of it was the Lamb.
24	And the nations of them which are saved shall walk in the light of it: and the kings of the earth do bring their glory and honour into it.	And the nations that were saved, shall walk by means of its light, and the kings of the earth will bring their glory and the wealth of the nations into it.	And the nations were walking in his light and the kings of the earth were bringing him praise.
25	And the gates of it shall not be shut at all by day: for there shall be no night there.	And its gates shall not be shut by day; for there is no night there.	And its gates will not be shut by day, for there will be no night there.
26	And they shall bring the glory and honour of the nations into it.	And they will bring the glory and honor of the nations into it.	And they will bring the glory and honor of the nations into it.
27	And there shall in no wise enter into it any thing that defileth, neither whatsoever worketh abomination, or maketh a lie: but they which are written in the Lamb's book of life.	And there shall not enter it, any thing polluted, or that practiseth impurity and falsehood; but they who are registered in the Lamb's book of life.	And there will not be there any[one] unclean, nor he who practices corruption and falsehood, but only those who are written in the book of the Lamb.
	Chapter 22		
1	And he shewed me a pure river of water of life, clear as crystal, proceeding out of the throne of God and of the Lamb.	And he showed me a river of living water, transparent [as] crystal, which proceeded from the throne of God and the Lamb.	And he showed me a pure river of living water, also shining as crystal, coming out from the throne of God and of the Lamb.
2	In the midst of the street of it, and on either side of the river, was there the tree of life, which bare twelve manner of fruits, and yielded her fruit every month: and the leaves of the tree were for the healing of the nations.	And in the middle of its broad avenue, and near the river, on this side and on that, [was] the tree of life; which bore twelve [sorts of] fruits yielding one of its fruits each month: and the leaves of the tree [were] for the healing of the nations.	And in the middle of its broad streets, on this side and on that side by the river, was the tree of life that produced twelve fruits and in every month gave its fruits. And its leaves [were] for the healing of the nations.
3	And there shall be no more curse: but the throne of God and of the Lamb shall be in it; and his servants shall serve him:	And there will be no blight any more: and the throne of God and the Lamb will be in it; and his servants will minister to him.	And there will be no devoted [thing] there and the throne of God and of the Lamb will be in it and his servants will minister to him.
4	And they shall see his face; and his name shall be in their foreheads.	And they will see his face, and his name [will be] on their foreheads.	And they will see his face and his name [will be] on their foreheads.
5	And there shall be no night there; and they need no candle, neither light of the sun; for the Lord God giveth them light: and they shall reign for ever and ever.	And there will be no more night; and they have no need of the light of a candle, or of the light of the sun; because the Lord God giveth them light: and they will reign for ever and ever.	And there will be no night there and light will not be needed for them or a lamp or the light of the sun, because the LORD God illuminates them and their king, forever and ever.

Parallel Translations

	KJV	*Murdock*	*Magiera*

REVELATION *Chapter 22*

	KJV	Murdock	Magiera
6	And he said unto me, These sayings are faithful and true: and the Lord God of the holy prophets sent his angel to shew unto his servants the things which must shortly be done.	And he said to me: These words [are] faithful and true. And the Lord God of the spirit of the prophets, hath sent me, his angel, to show unto his servants the things that must soon occur.	And he said to me, "These words [are] faithful and true and the LORD God of the spirits of the holy prophets sent his angel to show his servants what must happen soon.
7	Behold, I come quickly: blessed is he that keepeth the sayings of the prophecy of this book.	And, lo, I come quickly: Blessed is he that keepeth the words of the prophecy of this book.	And behold, I am coming soon. Blessed [is] he who keeps the words of the prophecy of this book."
8	And I John saw these things, and heard them. And when I had heard and seen, I fell down to worship before the feet of the angel which shewed me these things.	And more-over I am John, the hearer and the seer of these things. And when I heard and saw, I fell down to worship at the feet of the angel who showed me these things.	I am John who saw and heard these [things]. And when I saw and heard, I fell down to worship before the feet of the angel who showed me these [things].
9	Then saith he unto me, See thou do it not: for I am thy fellowservant, and of thy brethren the prophets, and of them which keep the sayings of this book: worship God.	And he said to me: See, [thou do it] not: I am thy fellow-servant, and of thy brethren the prophets, and of them that observe the words of this book. Worship God.	And he said to me, "See, [do] not [worship me]. I am your fellow-servant and of your brothers the prophets and of those who keep these words of this book. Worship God."
10	And he saith unto me, Seal not the sayings of the prophecy of this book: for the time is at hand.	And he said to me: Seal not the words of the prophecy of this book; for the time is near.	And he said to me, "Do not seal the words of the prophecy of this book, for the time is near.
11	He that is unjust, let him be unjust still: and he which is filthy, let him be filthy still: and he that is righteous, let him be righteous still: and he that is holy, let him be holy still.	He that doth evil, let him do evil still; and he that is filthy, let him be filthy still; and he that is righteous, let him practise righteousness still; and he that is sanctified, let him be sanctified still.	And he who does evil will do evil again and he who is filthy will be filthy again and the just will practice justification again and the holy will be holy again.
12	And, behold, I come quickly; and my reward is with me, to give every man according as his work shall be.	Behold, I come quickly; and my reward is with me, to recompense every one according to his work.	Behold, I am coming quickly and my reward [is] with me and I will give to everyone according to his work.
13	I am Alpha and Omega, the beginning and the end, the first and the last.	I am Alpha and Omega, the First and the Last, the Commencement and the Completion.	I am Aleph and I am Tau, the first and the last and the starting point and the completion.
14	Blessed are they that do his commandments, that they may have right to the tree of life, and may enter in through the gates into the city.	Blessed are they who do his commandments, that they may have a right to the tree of life, and may enter through the gates into the city.	Blessed [are] they who do his commandments. Their authority will be over the tree of life and they will enter into the city by the gate.
15	For without are dogs, and sorcerers, and whoremongers, and murderers, and idolaters, and whosoever loveth and maketh a lie.	Without [will be] dogs, and sorcerers, and whoremongers, and manslayers, and idolaters, and every one that loveth and doeth falsehood.	And the fornicators and the murderers and the idolaters [will be] outside and the unclean and the sorcerers and all observers and doers of falsehood.

REVELATION *Chapter 22*

	KJV	*Murdock*	*Magiera*
16	I Jesus have sent mine angel to testify unto you these things in the churches. I am the root and the offspring of David, and the bright and morning star.	I Jesus have sent my angel, to testify to you these things before the churches. I am the root and offspring of David: like the splendid star of the morning.	I, Jesus, have sent my angel to testify these [things] with you before the churches. I am [of] the root and the tribe of David and his people and the bright star of the morning.
17	And the Spirit and the bride say, Come. And let him that heareth say, Come. And let him that is athirst come. And whosoever will, let him take the water of life freely.	And the Spirit and the bride say, Come thou. And let him that heareth, say, Come thou. And let him who thirsteth, come; and he that is inclined, let him take the living water gratis.	And the Spirit and the bride say, 'Come.' And he who hears should say, 'Come.' And he who is thirsty should come and take the living water, freely.
18	For I testify unto every man that heareth the words of the prophecy of this book, If any man shall add unto these things, God shall add unto him the plagues that are written in this book:	I testify to every one that heareth the words of the prophecy of this book, that if any one shall add to them, God will add to him the plagues that are written in this book.	I testify to all who hear the word of the prophecy of this book, that whoever will add to them, God will add to him the injuries that are written in this book.
19	And if any man shall take away from the words of the book of this prophecy, God shall take away his part out of the book of life, and out of the holy city, and from the things which are written in this book.	And if any one shall take away from the words of the book of this prophecy, God will take away his portion from the tree of life, and from the holy city, which are described in this book.	And whoever takes away from the words of the book of this prophecy, God will take away his portion of the tree of life and of the holy city [and of] those [things] that are written in this book."
20	He which testifieth these things saith, Surely I come quickly. Amen. Even so, come, Lord Jesus.	He who testifieth these things, saith: Yes, I come quickly. Amen. Come, Lord Jesus!	He said, testifying these [things], "Yes, I am coming soon." Come, LORD Jesus.
21	The grace of our Lord Jesus Christ be with you all. Amen.	The grace of our Lord Jesus the Messiah, [be] with all the saints. Amen.	The grace of our Lord Jesus Christ [be] with all his holy [ones]. Amen.

Appendix 1
Old Testament Quotations and References

Reference	OT Quotation	Other OT Reference
Mat 1:23	Isa 7:14	Isa 8:8, 10
Mat 2:6	Mic 5:2	2Sa 5:2
Mat 2:15	Hos 11:1	Num 24:8
Mat 2:18	Jer 31:15	
Mat 3:3	Isa 40:3	
Mat 4:4	Deu 8:3	
Mat 4:6	Psa 91:11, 12	
Mat 4:7	Deu 6:16	
Mat 4:10	Deu 6:13	
Mat 4:15, 16	Isa 9:1, 2	
Mat 5:21a	Exo 20:13	Deu 5:17
Mat 5:21b	Lev 24:21	Num 35:16
Mat 5:27	Exo 20:14	Deu 5:18
Mat 5:31	Deu 24:1	
Mat 5:33a	Lev 19:12	
Mat 5:33b	Num 30:2	
Mat 5:38	Exo 21:24	Deu 19:21
Mat 5:43	Lev 19:18	Psa 139:21
Mat 7:23	Psa 6:8	
Mat 8:17	Isa 53:4	
Mat 9:13	Hos 6:6	
Mat 10:36	Mic 7:6	
Mat 11:10	Mal 3:1	
Mat 12:7	Hos 6:6	
Mat 12:18-21	Isa 42:1-4	
Mat 12:40	Jon 1:17	
Mat 13:14, 15	Isa 6:9, 10	
Mat 13:35	Psa 78:2	
Mat 15:4a	Exo 20:12	
Mat 15:4b	Exo 21:17	
Mat 15:8, 9	Isa 29:13	
Mat 18:16, 17	Deu 19:15	
Mat 19:4	Gen 1:27	
Mat 19:5	Gen 2:24	
Mat 19:7	Deu 24:1,3	
Mat 19:18, 19a	Exo 20:12-16	Deu 5:16-20
Mat 19:19b	Lev 19:18	
Mat 21:5	Zec 9:9	Isa 62:11
Mat 21:9	Psa 118:25, 26	
Mat 21:13	Isa 56:7	Jer 7:11
Mat 21:16	Psa 8:2	
Mat 21:42	Psa 118:22, 23	
Mat 22:24	Deu 25:5	Gen 38:8
Mat 22:32	Exo 3:6, 15	
Mat 22:37	Deu 6:5	

Appendix 1
Old Testament Quotations and References

Reference	OT Quotation	Other OT Reference
Mat 22:39	Lev 19:18	
Mat 22:44	Psa 110:1	
Mat 23:39	Psa 118:26	
Mat 24:15	Dan 9:27	Dan 11:31; 12:11
Mat 24:30	Dan 7:13	
Mat 26:31	Zec 13:7	
Mat 27:46	Psa 22:1	
Mar 1:2	Isa 40:3	Mal 3:1
Mar 4:12	Isa 6:9, 10	
Mar 7:6, 7	Isa 29:13	
Mar 7:10a	Exo 20:12	
Mar 7:10b	Exo 21:17	
Mar 10:6	Gen 1:27	Gen 5:2
Mar 10:19	Exo 20:13	Deu 5:17
Mar 11:17	Isa 56:7	Jer 7:11
Mar 12:11	Psa 118:23	
Mar 12:19	Deu 25:5	Gen 38:8
Mar 12:26	Exo 3:6, 15	
Mar 12:29-31	Deu 6:4, 5	Lev 19:18
Mar 12:36	Psa 110:1	
Mar 13:14	Dan 9:27	Dan 11:31; 12:11
Mar 13:26	Dan 7:13	
Mar 14:27	Zec 13:7	
Mar 14:62	Dan 7:13	
Mar 15:34	Psa 22:1	
Luk 2:23	Exo 13:2	
Luk 2:24	Lev 12:8	
Luk 3:6	Isa 40:5	
Luk 4:4	Deu 8:3	
Luk 4:8	Deu 6:13	
Luk 4:11	Psa 91:11, 12	
Luk 4:12	Deu 6:16	
Luk 7:27	Mal 3:1	
Luk 8:10	Isa 6:9, 10	
Luk 10:27	Deu 6:4, 5	Lev 19:18
Luk 13:35	Psa 118:26	
Luk 18:20	Exo 20:12-16	Deu 5:16-20
Luk 19:38	Psa 118:26	
Luk 20:17	Psa 118:22	
Luk 20:37	Exo 3:6, 15	
Luk 20:43	Psa 110:1	
Luk 21:27	Dan 7:13	
Luk 22:37	Isa 53:12	
Luk 23:30	Hos 10:8	
Luk 23:46	Psa 31:5	
Joh 1:23	Isa 40:3	
Joh 2:17	Psa 69:9	

Appendix 1
Old Testament Quotations and References

Reference	OT Quotation	Other OT Reference
Joh 6:31	Psa 78:24	
Joh 6:45	Isa 54:13	
Joh 10:34	Psa 82:6	
Joh 12:15	Zec 9:9	Isa 62:11
Joh 12:38	Isa 53:1	
Joh 12:40	Isa 6:9, 10	
Joh 13:18	Psa 41:9	
Joh 15:25	Psa 69:4	Psa 35:19
Joh 19:24	Psa 22:18	
Joh 19:36	Psa 34:20	Num 9:12
Joh 19:37	Zec 12:10	
Act 1:20a	Psa 69:25	
Act 1:20b	Psa 109:8	
Act 2:25-28	Psa 16:8-11	
Act 2:31	Psa 16:10	
Act 2:34, 35	Psa 110:1	
Act 3:22	Deu 18:15, 16	
Act 3:23	Deu 18:19	Lev 23:29
Act 3:25	Gen 22:18	Gen 26:4
Act 4:11	Psa 118:22	
Act 4:25. 26	Psa 2:1, 2	
Act 7:3	Gen 12:1	
Act 7:7	Gen 15:13, 14	Exo 3:12
Act 7:28	Exo 2:14	
Act 7:32	Exo 3:6	
Act 7:34	Exo 3:5-10	
Act 7:40	Exo 32:1, 23	
Act 7:43	Amo 5:25, 27	
Act 7:50	Isa 66:1, 2	
Act 8:33	Isa 53:7, 8	
Act 13:22	1Sa 13:14	Psa 89:20
Act 13:33	Psa 2:7	
Act 13:34	Isa 55:3	
Act 13:35	Psa 16:10	
Act 13:41	Hab 1:5	
Act 13:47	Isa 49:6	
Act 15:16-18	Amo 9:11, 12	
Act 23:5	Exo 22:28	
Act 28:26, 27	Isa 6:9, 10	
Rom 2:24	Isa 52:5	
Rom 3:4	Psa 51:4	
Rom 3:10-12	Psa 14:1-3	Psa 53:1-3
Rom 3:13	Psa 5:9	Psa 140:3
Rom 3:14	Psa 10:7	
Rom 3:17	Isa 59:7, 8	
Rom 3:18	Psa 36:1	
Rom 4:3	Gen 15:6	

Appendix 1
Old Testament Quotations and References

Reference	OT Quotation	Other OT Reference
Rom 4:9	Gen 15:6	
Rom 4:18	Gen 15:5	
Rom 4:22	Gen 15:6	
Rom 7:7	Exo 20:17	
Rom 8:36	Psa 44:22	
Rom 9:7	Gen 21:12	
Rom 9:9	Gen 18:10	
Rom 9:12	Gen 25:23	
Rom 9:13	Mal 1:2, 3	
Rom 9:15	Exo 33:19	
Rom 9:17	Exo 9:16	
Rom 9:25	Hos 2:23	
Rom 9:26	Hos 1:10	
Rom 9:27-28	Isa 10:22, 23	
Rom 9:29	Isa 1:9	
Rom 9:33	Isa 28:16	Isa 8:14
Rom 10:5	Lev 18:5	
Rom 10:7-8	Deu 30:13-14	
Rom 10:11	Isa 28:16	
Rom 10:13	Joe 2:31	
Rom 10:15	Isa 52:7	
Rom 10:16	Isa 53:1	
Rom 10:18	Psa 19:4	
Rom 10:19	Deu 32:21	
Rom 10:20	Isa 65:1	
Rom 10:21	Isa 65:2	
Rom 11:3	1Ki 19:10	
Rom 11:4	1Ki 19:18	
Rom 11:8	Isa 29:10	
Rom 11:9, 10	Psa 69:22, 23	
Rom 11:26, 27	Isa 59:20, 21	
Rom 11:34	Isa 40:13	
Rom 11:35	Job 41:11	Job 35:7
Rom 12:19	Deu 32:35	
Rom 12:20	Pro 25:21, 22	
Rom 13:9a	Exo 20:13-17	Deu 5:17-21
Rom 13:9b	Lev 19:18	
Rom 14:11	Isa 45:23	
Rom 15:3	Psa 69:9	
Rom 15:9	2Sa 22:50	Psa 18:49
Rom 15:10	Deu 32:43	
Rom 15:11	Psa 117:1	
Rom 15:12	Isa 11:10	
Rom 15:21	Isa 52:15	
1Co 1:19	Isa 29:14	
1Co 1:31	Jer 9:24	
1Co 2:9	Isa 64:4	

Appendix 1
Old Testament Quotations and References

Reference	OT Quotation	Other OT Reference
1Co 2:16	Isa 40:13	
1Co 3:19	Job 5:13	
1Co 3:20	Psa 94:11	
1Co 5:13	Deu 17:7	Deu 19:19
1Co 6:16	Gen 2:24	
1Co 9:9	Deu 25:4	
1Co 10:7	Exo 32:6	
1Co 10:26	Psa 24:1	
1Co 14:21	Isa 28:11, 12	
1Co 15:27	Psa 8:6	Psa 110:1
1Co 15:32	Isa 22:13	
1Co 15:45	Gen 2:7	
1Co 15:54	Isa 25:8	
1Co 15:55	Hos 13:14	
2Co 4:13	Psa 116:10	
2Co 6:2	Isa 49:8	
2Co 6:16	Lev 26:12	Eze 37:27
2Co 6:17	Isa 52:11	
2Co 6:18	2Sa 7:8, 14	1Ch 17:13
2Co 8:15	Exo 16:18	
2Co 9:9	Psa 112:9	
2Co 10:17	Jer 9:24	
2Co 13:1	Deu 19:15	
Gal 3:6	Gen 15:6	
Gal 3:8	Gen 12:3	Gen 18:18
Gal 3:10	Deu 27:26	
Gal 3:11	Hab 2:4	
Gal 3:12	Lev 18:5	
Gal 3:13	Deu 21:23	
Gal 3:16	Gen 12:7	
Gal 4:27	Isa 54:1	
Gal 4:30	Gen 21:10	
Gal 5:14	Lev 19:18	
Eph 4:8	Psa 68:18	
Eph 4:25	Zec 8:16	
Eph 4:26	Psa 4:4	
Eph 5:31	Gen 2:24	
Eph 6:3	Deu 5:16	Exo 20:12
1Ti 5:18	Deu 25:4	
2Ti 2:19a	Num 16:5	
2Ti 2:19b	Job 36:10	
Heb 1:5	2Sa 7:14	Psa 2:7
Heb 1:6	Deu 32:43	
Heb 1:7	Psa 104:4	
Heb 1:10-12	Psa 102:25-27	
Heb 1:13	Psa 110:1	
Heb 2:6-8	Psa 8:4-7	

Appendix 1
Old Testament Quotations and References

Reference	OT Quotation	Other OT Reference
Heb 2:12	Psa 22:22	
Heb 2:13	Isa 8:17, 18	
Heb 3:15	Psa 95:7, 8	
Heb 4:3	Psa 95:11	
Heb 4:4	Gen 2:2	
Heb 4:5	Psa 95:11	
Heb 5:5	Psa 2:7	
Heb 5:6	Psa 110:4	
Heb 6:14	Gen 22:16, 17	
Heb 7:17	Psa 110:4	
Heb 8:5	Exo 25:40	
Heb 8:8-12	Jer 31:31-34	
Heb 9:20	Exo 24:8	
Heb 10:5-7	Psa 40:6-8	
Heb 10:16	Jer 31:33	
Heb 10:17	Jer 31:34	
Heb 10:28	Deu 17:6	
Heb 10:30	Deu 32:35, 36	
Heb 10:37, 38	Hab 2:3, 4	
Heb 11:18	Gen 21:12	
Heb 12:6	Pro 3:12	
Heb 12:20	Exo 19:12, 13	
Heb 12:21	Deut 9:19	
Heb 12:29	Deut 4:24	
Heb 13:5	Deut 31:6	
Heb 13:6	Psa 118:6	
Jas 2:8	Lev 19:18	
Jas 2:11a	Lev 24:21	Num 35:16
Jas 2:11b	Exo 20:13, 14	Deu 5:17, 18
Jas 2:23	Gen 15:6	
Jas 4:6	Pro 3:34	
1Pe 1:16	Lev 19:2	
1Pe 1:25	Isa 40:8	
1Pe 2:6	Isa 28:16	
1Pe 2:8	Isa 8:14	
1Pe 2:22	Isa 53:9	
1Pe 3:12	Psa 34:12-16	
1Pe 4:18	Pro 11:31	
1Pe 5:5	Pro 3:34	
2Pe 2:22	Pro 26:11	
Rev 13:7	Dan 7:21	

CPSIA information can be obtained
at www.ICGtesting.com
Printed in the USA
BVOW07*1021190417
481673BV00015BA/32/P